DICTIONARY

OF

MUSIC AND MUSICIANS

GROVE'S
DICTIONARY OF MUSIC AND MUSICIANS

AMERICAN SUPPLEMENT

BEING THE SIXTH VOLUME
OF THE COMPLETE WORK

WALDO SELDEN PRATT
EDITOR

CHARLES N. BOYD
ASSOCIATE EDITOR

THEODORE PRESSER COMPANY
PHILADELPHIA, PA.
1926

Norwood Press
J. S. Cushing Co. — Berwick & Smith Co.
Norwood, Mass., U.S.A.

PREFACE

THE project of this volume, when proposed by The Macmillan Company to the Editor whom they had selected, was finally taken up by him only with great hesitation, not because an American Supplement to the existing five volumes of Grove's famous *Dictionary of Music and Musicians* was not most desirable, but because of the inherent difficulties in the problem of making it satisfactory. After prolonged consultation the working-plan adopted was recognized as not so much a 'counsel of perfection' as a frank adjustment of ideals to what was practical within the limits of time, space and scope proposed.

In view of the fact that a work of this sort is essentially historical, an unusual arrangement of the material was at length devised as useful in this particular case. The volume is laid out in two distinct divisions, the one interlocking more or less with the other. The first division consists of a compact Historical Introduction, surveying the unique environment of music in America and certain peculiarities in its development, combined period by period with a Chronological Register, indicating those workers who seem representative of the spirit and effort of the successive stages of progress. The second division, which is much larger, consists of specific descriptive articles about leading individuals, organizations, institutions and interests, arranged in the customary alphabetical order. In this division, also, a great number of the names mentioned elsewhere are catalogued for ease of reference.

It is believed that this twofold presentation, though involving some duplication, has definite advantages. The Introduction is not in any sense a formal history of American music as such, yet it provides a sketch of the historic framework, of both external circumstances and of internal tendencies, upon which alone such a history can properly be modeled. In connection with this the Register affords opportunity for brief reference to some 1700 persons, representing a variety of interests, some of whom have not often been remembered or even catalogued. The descriptive articles in the main body of the Dictionary then take up about 700 of these persons for more particular treatment, often with extensive lists of their works, and also give a vast amount of information about numerous enterprises of a general or corporate nature. The aim throughout the entire volume is to present as many facts as possible in the clearest manner, so as to make them accessible for reference, but to avoid the expression of critical opinions except in general terms or in quoted form.

The Editor and the Associate Editor wish to express their great obligation to the host of correspondents who have courteously supplied both material and encouragement. They can only regret that certain lines of inquiry, though somewhat earnestly pursued, proved surprisingly fruitless, so that many topics marked for inclusion, at last had to be treated superficially or omitted altogether.

Throughout the volume the words 'America' and 'American' are often used of the United States and Canada taken together. Canadian musicians are here counted with those of the United States, not only because no other course was seemly in an American extension of a work originally published in Great Britain, but also because the cordial fraternity in musical art on this side of the ocean has always disregarded the political frontier that stretches across the continent. To a very limited extent, furthermore, it has been possible to include some representative names from Central and South America. In the Register all who were born outside of the United States and Canada, whether in Europe or in other parts of the Americas, are designated by a special sign.

Inasmuch as the latest edition of Grove's Dictionary was issued ten to fifteen years ago, the publishers desired that this volume should include continuations of those articles that relate to the more conspicuous foreign musicians, as well as notices of some that for any reason were previously omitted. Accordingly, in the Dictionary proper will be found statements regarding more than a hundred musicians who are entirely outside the American field. All these articles are indicated by a special sign.

Every work of this class rests largely upon its predecessors in the same field, as well as upon other literary sources. This particular volume would have been almost impossible to prepare except for the several historical studies that have appeared regarding American music and musicians, and especially without the invaluable material gathered in works like *Who's Who in Music* (1918) and *Baker's Dictionary of Musicians* (3rd edition, 1919). To the authors and editors of all of these the most hearty acknowledgment of constant indebtedness is due.*

* Books that have been specially utilized include Jones, *Handbook of American Music and Musicians* (1886), Mathews, *Hundred Years of Music in America* (1889), Ritter, *Music in America* (3rd ed., 1893), Elson, *History of American Music* (2nd ed., 1915), *The Art of Music*, Vol. iv (1916), *The American History and Encyclopedia of Music*, Vol. on American Music (1910), articles on 'Music' in *The International Year-Book* (1907–19), Hughes, *American Composers* (revised ed., 1915), Sonneck, *Early Concert-Life in America* (1907) and *Early Opera in America* (1915), Krehbiel, *Chapters of Opera* (1911) and *More Chapters of Opera* (1917), Upton, *Musical Memories* (1918), etc.

LIST OF ILLUSTRATIONS

In previous volumes of the Dictionary will be found also portraits of MME. ALBANI, GEORGE W. CHADWICK, CLARA LOUISE KELLOGG, the KNEISEL QUARTET, EDWARD A. MACDOWELL, CHRISTINE NILSSON, JOHN K. PAINE, HORATIO W. PARKER, ANTON SEIDL, MARCELLA SEMBRICH, ALEXANDER W. THAYER, THEODORE THOMAS and CARL ZERRAHN.

HISTORICAL INTRODUCTION

AND

CHRONOLOGICAL REGISTER

INTRODUCTION AND REGISTER

NOTE. The cross-reference 'See art.' indicates that a more extended notice will be found in the body of the Dictionary. The larger cities of the United States and Canada are regularly entered without naming the states in which they lie.

Persons born outside of the United States or Canada are indicated by *.

HISTORICAL INTRODUCTION

WITH

CHRONOLOGICAL REGISTER OF NAMES

The history of music in America is decidedly peculiar in many of its aspects, owing to the unusual way in which civilization and culture have here been established. Although permanent settlements in North America multiplied from about 1600 and the independent existence of the United States is counted from 1776, musical life remained quite immature, or at most provincial, until after 1800. After the middle of the 19th century, however, when an extensive and vital connection with the progressive artistic culture of Europe began to be effected, the rapidity, variety and vigor of the ensuing advance were altogether phenomenal. Developments that have taken centuries were then crowded into decades and elaborate enterprises often took shape without the gradual preparation that might have been expected.

In view of this, a compact statement is here presented of some of the historic conditions within which American musical progress has come to pass and of its more salient features from period to period. With this is combined at each successive stage a REGISTER of the persons who seem to have been representative and influential, taking them in groups by the time when they entered upon professional activity. It is believed that this method of presentation will illuminate the whole evolution and be a guide to placing various matters in due sequence and relation.

THE CENTURY OF SETTLEMENT

After being casually and vaguely known for perhaps five hundred years, America was formally 'discovered' in 1492 by Colombo, a Genoese navigator sent out by the court of Spain. The name 'America' was conferred upon it, as has been picturesquely remarked, 'by an obscure German professor in a French college after another Italian [Amerigo Vespucci] in the service of Portugal.'

'The New World,' as it was generally known — which, by the way, did not originally include North America — was at first simply an object for romantic and greedy exploitation. The incursions and conquests of Spain produced nothing permanent except a nominal domination over Mexico (from 1520) and the Pacific Coast, with a precarious foothold upon the peninsula of Florida, where St. Augustine was founded in 1565. The effective occupation of the coast of North America was the later task of the 17th century, and was wrought out by other nations.

3

In 1607 Jamestown (Va.) was settled by about a hundred adventurers from England, establishing an area of Cavalier sympathies which ultimately acquired the popular name of 'The Old Dominion' under Charles II. At the same time, far to the north, French traders and missionaries began at Quebec (1608) and Montreal (1611) to lay down the long chain of frontier posts that finally stretched westward to the Great Lakes and thence southward down the Mississippi Valley to New Orleans (1718). In 1613 the Dutch located themselves at the mouth of the Hudson River, where New York now is, retaining control of its valley and of some territory east and west of it until ousted by the English in 1664. In 1620 Plymouth (Mass.) was founded by a party of about a hundred English folk (Separatists or Independents), commonly called 'The Pilgrims,' because their migration to America, like their earlier one to Holland, was to escape from the oppressive autocracy of the Church of England. In 1628–30 the much stronger settlements at Salem, Cambridge and Boston (Mass.), not many miles away, were begun by perhaps a thousand Puritans, members of the English Church who desired reform in its practice and spirit, though at first without meaning to leave it. These Massachusetts settlements were consolidated under one government in 1692. In 1632 English Roman Catholics established themselves at Baltimore (Md.). In 1638 a few Swedes were pioneers in the region that later came to be called Delaware. In 1636–38 groups breaking away from Massachusetts effected the settlement first of Providence (R. I.) and then of Hartford and New Haven (Conn.), the last two being consolidated in 1662. In 1670–80 similar branch-colonies from Virginia pushed southward into North and South Carolina. In 1681 came the unique and influential Quaker settlement of Philadelphia (Pa.). It was not till 1733 that the series of primary establishments was completed by the founding of Savannah (Ga.), originally intended to be a refuge for English prisoners for debt or conscience, but early utilized also by refugees from intolerance in southern Germany. To all these centers, with their outlying dependencies, a gradually increasing stream of additional colonists came from year to year.

Out of the several grants, patents or charters from the English Crown with which most of these settlements began were developed the distinct administrations of them as colonies. These were the autonomous units known later as 'The Thirteen Original States' (New Hampshire, Massachusetts, Rhode Island, Connecticut, New York, New Jersey, Pennsylvania, Delaware, Maryland, Virginia, North Carolina, South Carolina, Georgia), the federation of which in 1781–88 constituted the United States.

The pioneer conditions of the whole 17th century were manifestly unconducive to artistic life. Even at its close the total population may not have exceeded 275,000 (including many negro slaves), sparsely distributed over almost a thousand miles of coastland — a distance about equal to that from London to Budapest. Large towns were almost wanting. Even Boston in 1700 had less than 7000 inhabitants. The several colonies were as yet not bound together by much community of interest or sentiment, and their social habits differed greatly.

What records there are of this early period are strikingly deficient in references to music or instruments. In the North there was a tendency to treat the art as 'worldly' and hence objectionable, so that even church-singing became curiously degenerate because unsupported by general knowledge. In the South there was probably much more freedom of thought and practice, though exact data are wanting. It seems that at first none of the colonists possessed any special taste or aptitude in the musical field.

THE COLONIAL CENTURY

During the 18th century the total population grew at the rate of about one-third in every decade, so that in 1750 it amounted to nearly 1,250,000 and in 1800 to over 5,300,000, of which, however, about one-sixth were slaves. More than 90 per cent were farmers. The occupied territory lay close to the Atlantic coast, until late in the century nowhere reaching inland more than 150 miles. Military outposts were planted here and there at more distant points, but, even allowing for these, the total area effectively taken up by the English colonies can hardly have exceeded 250,000 square miles. By 1800 a few cities had attained considerable size, especially Philadelphia (69,400 inhabitants), New York (60,500), Baltimore (26,500), Boston (25,000) and Charleston (20,500), with Salem, New Orleans, Providence, Norfolk, Newport, Newburyport, Richmond, Nantucket (!), Albany, Hartford and Portsmouth completing the list of large towns down to 5000 inhabitants.

In the middle of the century (1754–63) occurred the struggle with the aggressive French interests in Canada, assisted by a strong Indian alliance. The issue of this contest settled the critical point that not only Canada, but the entire basin of the Mississippi, was thenceforth to come under English influence. It also broke the power of the dangerous Indian confederacies. Close upon this followed the controversies with England that culminated in the War of Independence (1775–83), by which for the first time all the colonies were drawn into virtual union as a nation. This war, however, naturally led to a prolonged period of discussion and internal readjustment. Except in the cities and large towns, conditions were still not specially favorable for much cultural advance.

On the whole, social thought and customs were strongly dominated by English influences. The sense of an independent destiny awoke only late in the period, when also appeared a new sensitiveness to ideas from France, due in part to sympathy received in the American Revolution and given in the French Revolution. Although there was as yet no great influx of immigration from Europe and no habit of foreign travel, commerce with England was steady and enterprising, so that not only commodities, but social ideas and practices, were rather promptly communicated, at least to the main ports of entry. In these latter centers wealth and leisure had increased enough to create a demand for something more than small diversions.

It is not strange, therefore, that such musical entertainments as were popular in England — concerts and operas of the ballad or song type — should have become more and more frequent. The performers were almost wholly visiting artists from abroad, at first from England, but after 1790 from France as well. Many of these remained for a series of years and some of them permanently. Not a few represented a high degree of knowledge and taste, as measured by the standards of the day. So far as these artists became known they undoubtedly exerted a positive and stimulating artistic influence. In certain instances we know that they started definite currents of native effort.

Side by side with this exotic influence, especially in New England, ran a movement for the improvement of congregational singing in churches which had some importance and which continued far into the 19th century. The absolute artistic results were slight, but the awakening of social interest through 'singing-schools' under peripatetic leaders and through the multiplication of song-manuals foreshadowed more significant undertakings later. (See article on Tune-Books.)

Musical instruments slowly became noticeable among the articles of importation and sale, implying an increasing interest in them and some ability to use them. This developing interest led also to the first steps in commercial manufacture, giving promise of the remarkable energy that was displayed in the early 19th century in making pianos, organs and some stringed instruments.

Associations for the promotion and practice of music were formed here and there, indicating an instinctive desire to make it a substantial factor in social life.

The only native-born musician of distinction was Francis Hopkinson. But the line of contributors to 'psalmody' was well established before 1800.

In the two sections of the CHRONOLOGICAL REGISTER that are here inserted will be found references to many details, personal and otherwise, which do not lend themselves readily to summary statement. The chief purpose of these lists, it should be remembered, is to record a fairly large number of persons who are known to have had some importance in the total development, to group them according to the time when their professional work seems to have begun, and in each case to indicate in a few words the place and character of their activities. It is fully recognized that such lists must be tentative and provisional.

Our information regarding the 18th century is fragmentary, in spite of Sonneck's invaluable researches. His two books, *Concert-Life* and *Early Opera*, refer by name to nearly 500 musicians of greater or less degree, of whom about one-fourth appeared prior to the Revolution and the remainder in the two decades after it. The majority of them were only visitors and exercised their talents only in those few centers where music had acquired a fashionable vogue. It is not yet clear how deep and lasting was their artistic impress. Their total repertory was extensive, including more than 200 operas and other musical plays, a great variety of popular songs, usually of the English ballad type, and a notable array of instrumental works by the composers who were most admired before the time when Mozart began to be recognized. From the point of view of permanent culture, it is likely that the standards unconsciously established by the instrumentalists, either by public performance or through teaching of pupils, were specially important.

CHRONOLOGICAL REGISTER

1. Before the Revolution, 1700–1775

NOTE. Throughout the Register the persons named are entered under the period when they apparently began professional activity, even though this activity continued and increased later. Those foreign-born are entered according to the dates of arrival in America, and are designated by a * before their names. Such names are often given in their common anglicized form.

All those who are separately treated in the body of the Dictionary are entered briefly in the Register in their proper chronological place, with the cross-reference ' See art.'

For ease of consultation, the dates of birth and death are uniformly printed together, with the place of birth preceding and the place of death following.

*Behrent, John, either a German or a Swede, in 1775 made in Philadelphia what appears to have been the first American piano. See Spillane, *American Pianoforte*, p. 76.

*Beissel, Johann Conrad (Palatinate, 1690–1768, Ephrata, Pa.), was an odd, but gifted, mystic who in 1720 came to Germantown, Pa., and in 1735 founded a communistic fraternity at Ephrata (about 50 miles west of Philadelphia), which flourished till about 1800. He was a well-trained violinist. Some of his poems made up the first German book issued in America (1730, printed by Franklin). This book was followed by a curious series of reprints of German hymn-books and new collections, edited by various hands and published mainly at Germantown or Ephrata (at least 30 *Gesangbücher* and similar works before 1800).

*Biferi, Nicholas, a Neapolitan harpsichordist, in 1775 gave concerts in New York, having opened a school for music and dancing in 1774. Sonneck (*Concert-Life*, p. 175) queries whether he may be the same as Francesco Biferi (b. 1739?), who in 1770 issued an instruction-book at Paris.

Billings, William (Boston, 1746–1800, Boston), was one of the earliest leaders of singing-schools and an ambitious, but crude, tune-composer. See Tune-Books and art.

Brattle, Thomas (d. 1713, Boston), a prominent Boston merchant who imported an organ which he bequeathed to the Brattle Square Church, but which, there refused, went to King's Chapel. In 1756 it was taken to Newburyport, and in 1836 to St. John's in Portsmouth, N. H., where it still is. See Brooks, *Olden-Time Music*, p. 49, Sonneck, *Concert-Life*, p. 9, and ' New Music Review,' May, 1902.

*Bremner, James (d. 1780, Philadelphia), a relative of Robert Bremner, the Edinburgh music-publisher, came to Philadelphia in 1763, opened a music-school, was Hopkinson's teacher, played the organ at Christ Church, and did much to promote good music. See Sonneck, *Concert-Life*, pp. 66–70, and *Hopkinson and Lyon*.

Bromfield, Edward, Jr. (Boston, 1723–1746, Boston), graduated from Harvard in 1742 and is said soon after to have partially constructed an organ. See Brooks, p. 32.

*Dipper, Thomas (d. 1763?, Jamaica), an Englishman who in 1756–62 was organist at King's Chapel, Boston.

*Douglass, David (d. 1786?, Jamaica), a capable English singer, actor and manager, who came to New York in 1758, succeeded Hallam as head of the American Company (marrying his widow), and gave plays and operas North and South till 1775, when he left for Jamaica. See Sonneck, *Early Opera*, pp. 26–52.

*Enstone, Edward, an Englishman, who from 1714 was organist at King's Chapel, Boston, taught music and dancing and sold various instruments.

Flagg, Josiah (Boston, 1738–1794, Boston), issued a tune-book in 1764 (engraved by Paul Revere), gave concerts in 1769–71 and organized a military band. See Sonneck, *Concert-Life*, pp. 261–4, and Tune-Books.

Franklin, Benjamin (Boston, 1706–1790, Philadelphia). See Vol. ii. 103–4, 297–8, and art.

*Gualdo, Giovanni, an Italian who in 1767 came to Philadelphia as wine-dealer and music-teacher, and in 1769–71 gave concerts, including instrumental works of his own (not extant). See Sonneck, *Concert-Life*, pp. 70–4.

*Hallam, a family of English actors and singers who were active in America from 1753, when Lewis Hallam (d. 1755, Jamaica) came as manager of the London Company. His widow married Douglass, who directed the troupe in 1758–74 under the names American Company and Old American Company. Among the singers after 1759 were Lewis Hallam, Jr. (1741–1808) and his sister, both competent artists. The former returned as manager in 1784, and was more or less associated with Henry and Hodgkinson (see sec. 2). See Sonneck, *Early Opera* and *Concert-Life*.

*Harman, Catharine Maria (d. 1773), a granddaughter of Colley Cibber, was a light-opera singer in the American Company from 1759, as was also her husband.

*Harrison, Thomas, an Englishman who was organist of Trinity Church, New York, probably in 1753–64, and also gave concerts in 1769–70.

*Hesselius, Gustavus, a Swedish organ-maker, who made spinets and virginals in Philadelphia as early as 1742 — apparently the first in America.

Hopkinson, Francis (Philadelphia, 1737–1791, Philadelphia), the distinguished lawyer and publicist, who was also the first American composer (from 1759). See art.

*Jacobi, John Owen, an organist brought from England in 1736 by Trinity Church, Newport, R. I., to play the organ given in 1733 by Bishop Berkeley.

Johnston, Thomas (d. 1768?), in 1752 made an organ for Christ Church, Boston, and in 1754 one for St. Peter's, Salem. The latter in 1819 went to St. Michael's, Marblehead, and finally to Hook & Hastings, the organ-builders. See Brooks, pp. 50, 65-6.

*Juhan [Joan], James, a Frenchman who was in Boston in 1768-70 and in Charleston in 1771 as teacher of French, music and dancing, besides tuning, repairing and making instruments. In 1783 he exhibited at Philadelphia his 'great North American Forte Piano.' Alexander Juhan (see sec. 2) was probably his son. See Sonneck, *Concert-Life*, pp. 123-4, 264-5.

*Klemm, Johann Gottlob (Saxony, 1690-1762, Bethlehem, Pa.), an organ-maker who came to Philadelphia in 1736 and worked in New York in 1745-57. About 1740 he made the first American organ for Trinity Church, New York. See Sonneck, *Concert-Life*, p. 169, and references there.

*Knoetchel, John Ernest (d. 1769), was organist of Trinity Church, Newport, R. I., and probably the father of another there in 1774.

Lyon, James (Newark, 1735-1794, Machias, Me.), a contemporary of Hopkinson, wrote a graduation-ode at Princeton in 1759, and issued the tune-book *Urania* in 1761, containing some original pieces. See Sonneck, *Hopkinson and Lyon*, and Tune-Books.

*Morris, Owen (1719-1809), an English actor-singer in Hallam's Company from 1759 and again after the Revolution. In 1792 he and his wife joined Wignell.

*Pachelbel, Charles Theodore, a German in Boston who in 1733 helped erect the organ in Trinity Church, Newport, became organist there, and in 1736-37 gave concerts in New York and Charleston. See Sonneck, *Concert-Life*, pp. 13, 158, 317.

*Pelham, Peter, Jr. (b. England, 1721), the son of an engraver and teacher in Boston and musically trained from boyhood (probably in England), set out as music-teacher in Boston in 1743. In 1768 he was harpsichordist for an operatic troupe in Virginia.

*Propert, David, at first a music-teacher in New York, moved to Boston in 1770 and from 1771 was organist at Trinity Church. He organized concerts in 1773-74 and was still active in 1789.

*Rice, John, an Englishman, from 1744 was organist at Trinity Church, New York, and from 1753 at Trinity Church, Boston. See Sonneck, *Concert-Life*, pp. 159, 169, 254.

*Selby, William (England, 1738-1798, Boston), from 1771 an influential player and composer in Boston. See art.

*Storer, Maria (d. 1795, Philadelphia), a talented English actress and singer, in 1768 came to New York with Hallam and had great popularity till 1794. In 1787 she married the singer and manager **John Henry** (d. 1795). Her sister Fanny was also a favorite. See Sonneck, *Early Opera* and *Concert-Life*.

*Tuckey, William (England, 1708-1781, Philadelphia), from 1753 organist of Trinity Church, New York, and an enterprising promoter of musical interest. See art.

*Valton, Peter, from 1764 organist at St. Philip's, Charleston, and for some years a prominent teacher, concert-giver and dealer in instruments, besides writing a set of harpsichord-sonatas. See Sonneck, *Concert-Life*, pp. 15-6, 21.

*Wainwright, Miss, an excellent English actress-singer (probably a pupil of Dr. Arne) who appeared in Charleston and New York in 1765-69.

*Woolls, Stephen (d. 1799), another fine English stage-singer (also one of Arne's pupils) who appeared frequently before and after the Revolution. See Sonneck, *Early Opera* and *Concert-Life*.

*Yarnold, Benjamin, organist in Charleston, from 1753 at St. Philip's and from 1764 at St. Mary's.

*Zimmerman, Matthias, of Philadelphia, in 1737 bequeathed an organ that he himself had made. This seems to antedate the one made by Klemm (see above), but the record is not quite clear. See Spillane, p. 47.

Sonneck has found presumable references to *plays* in 1703 at Charleston and New York (Tony Aston), in 1718 at Williamsburg, Va., and in 1749 at Philadelphia, besides a possible concert in 1733 at New York. The earliest *musical* entertainments for which definite data are now at hand at various places are as follows:

1731	Boston — at Pelham's Great Room.
1732	Charleston — by John Salter.
1736	New York — by C. T. Pachelbel.
1744	Bethlehem — by the Collegium Musicum.[1]
1750	Philadelphia — by the Kean-Murray Company.
1751	Williamsburg — by the Kean-Murray Company.
1752	Annapolis — by the Kean-Murray Company.
1761	Newport — by the Douglass (Hallam) Company.
1762	Providence — by the Douglass (Hallam) Company.
1766	Savannah — by John Stevens, Jr.
1774	Princeton — by Hoar, of New York.

[1] At the famous Moravian settlement at Bethlehem, Pa., in 1741, under the lead of Count Zinzendorf (1700-1760), singing and instruments were early prominent. In 1744 a society for cultivating music was formed, led by Rev. J. C. Pyrlaeus and later by J. E. Westmann, which was the forerunner of the present Bach Choir. The first spinet was imported in 1744, a small organ set up by Klemm in 1746 and a larger one in 1751, and trombones were introduced in 1754. See Walters, *Bethlehem Bach Choir*, pp. 9 ff.

2. After the Revolution, 1775-1800

Adgate, Andrew (d. 1793, Philadelphia), from 1784 was a promoter of psalmody in Philadelphia and in 1787 founded the Uranian Academy. See art. and Tune-Books.

*Albrecht, Charles, in 1789 a piano-maker in Philadelphia, succeeded in 1825 by Christian F. L. Albrecht (son?), who in 1842 sold out to Blasius & Son.

*Arnold, Mrs., an English singer, prominent in concerts and plays from 1796. She married a Mr. Tubbs in that year.

*Bentley, John, an English harpsichordist, in 1783-85 managed concert-series in Philadelphia, and from 1785 led the orchestra of the Old American Company in New York and elsewhere. In 1785 he ' selected and composed ' music for three pantomimes, including ' The Touchstone.'

*Bergmann, B., a violinist who in 1792 came from England to New York, appearing as soloist and in quartet, and was later heard at Boston and Charleston, where in 1795 he drafted accompaniments for Storace's ' The Doctor and the Apothecary.'

*Berkenhead, John L., a blind organist and pianist, in 1795 gave concerts in Boston and in 1796-1804 was organist at Trinity Church, Newport.

*Boullay, Louis, a French violinist who from 1793 appeared often, especially in New York and Philadelphia.

*Broadhurst, Miss, a brilliant English soprano, from 1794 was a leading artist in the Wignell-Reinagle Company, though then not yet twenty.

*Brown, William, from 1783 a prominent flutist at various places. In Philadelphia he was associated with Reinagle, and in 1785 organized concerts in New York. In 1787 he dedicated three rondos to Hopkinson. See Sonneck, *Concert-Life*, p. 185, etc.

*Capron, Henri, a French 'cellist (pupil of Gaviniés) who had played in Paris since 1768, from 1786 was active in Philadelphia, New York and elsewhere. He figured also as singer, guitarist, teacher and composer. See Sonneck, *Concert-Life*, especially as to his quarrel with Brown.

*Carr, Benjamin (England, 1769-1831, Philadelphia), from 1793 conspicuous in Philadelphia as singer, pianist, organist and composer. See art.

Crehore, Benjamin (d. 1819, Milton, Mass.), became widely known from 1785 as maker of 'cellos and basses at Milton. In 1792 he also made improved harpsichords and towards 1800 pianos as well. He taught Osborn and the Babcocks (see sec. 3). See Spillane, pp. 50-6.

*Darley, William, an English singer, prominent in the Wignell-Reinagle Company from 1793 and in concerts. His wife and son also were singers.

*Demarque, a French 'cellist, and his wife, a singer, were active from 1793. He also

played the violin, compiled pantomimes and wrote for the 'cello.

*D'Hemard, Mme., a French refugee who, though an amateur, was from 1795 a popular harpist.

*Douvillier, M. and Mme., French opera-singers who from 1793 appeared in leading rôles in Boston and Charleston.

*Dubois, a French clarinettist, active from 1795. He also sang in opera and composed.

*Foucard, another French clarinettist, appeared from 1793.

*Francis, William (England, 1763-1827) and his wife from 1794 were useful members of the Wignell-Reinagle Company. They were specially good as dancers and pantomimists.

*Gehot, Jean (b. Belgium, 1756?), a competent violinist, known in Europe since 1780, who in 1792 came to Philadelphia. He was a fertile composer, among his works being an overture in twelve movements 'expressive of a voyage from England to America'! See Sonneck, *Concert-Life*, pp. 191, 230-1, etc.

*Gilfert, George, from 1786 a music-dealer in New York and publisher of a ' Musical Magazine,' besides being in 1789-91 head of the Musical Society and playing the viola somewhat at concerts.

*Gillingham, George, a superior English violinist (in the band at the Handel Commemoration of 1784) who from 1794 for over thirty years was a leading player in Philadelphia and New York. See Sonneck, *Concert-Life*, p. 54, etc., and note concert in Boston in 1836 by three Misses Gillingham, Brooks, p. 176.

*Graupner, Johann Christian Gottlieb (Hanover, 1767-1836, Boston), an experienced oboist, who in 1792 came to America, in 1795 appeared in Charleston and from 1797 was influential in Boston. See art.

*Hewitt, James (England, 1770-1827, New York), in 1792 came to New York, where he was long an important violinist, composer and publisher. See art.

*Hodgkinson, John (England, 1767-1805, Washington), and his wife (née Brett) from 1792 were popular and influential singers in New York. See art.

Holden, Oliver (Shirley, Mass., 1765-1834?, Charlestown, Mass.), a carpenter who by 1792 took up music-teaching and compiling tunes (see Tune-Books) with much success. His organ is in the Old State House at Boston (see cut in Fisher, *Music in Old Boston*, pp. 13-4).

Holyoke, Samuel Adams (Boxford, Mass., 1762-1820, Concord, N. H.[1]), studied at Dartmouth and became a teacher of psalmody (see Tune-Books), from about 1800 living in Salem, where in 1805 he led an Instrumental Club and in 1808-09 gave choral concerts.

*Jackson, George K. (England, 1745-1823, Boston), having been a choir-boy in the Chapel Royal and also teacher and author of harmony text-books, in 1796 came to Norfolk and taught

[1] Dates from Nason, *Gazetteer of Massachusetts,* 1876, p. 120.

successively there and in Alexandria, Baltimore, Philadelphia and New York, settling in 1812 in Boston as organist in turn at Brattle Street, King's, Trinity and St. John's. He promoted choral concerts and published some church-music. See Tune-Books.

*Juhan (Joan), Alexander, a French violinist (perhaps son of James Juhan named in sec. 1) who was an able concert-player in Philadelphia from 1783 or '86.

*Kenna, J., and his wife, English actorsingers who from 1788 gave plays in the South and at Philadelphia with a troupe for a time known as the New Americans.

Law, Andrew (Cheshire, Conn., 1748-1821, Cheshire), one of the pioneers in psalmody and from 1778 indefatigable as teacher and compiler. See Tune-Books.

*Mallet, Francis, a Frenchman who probably came to America in 1777. After varied concertizing he settled in Boston not later than 1793. He was singer, organist, player on other instruments, teacher and publisher. Two daughters became well-known musicians at Salem. See Sonneck, Concert-Life, p. 291, etc., and Brooks, pp. 165-7, 226, 248, etc.

*Marshall, Mr. and Mrs., able and popular English singers and actors who appeared variously from 1793. Marshall returned to England in 1801, and his wife later became Mrs. Wilmoth.

*Moller, John Christopher, presumably a German (works of J. C. Möller are listed by Eitner), from 1790 was active at New York and Philadelphia as pianist, organist, violist and harmonica-player. His daughter was also singer and pianist.

*Oldmixon, Mrs., née George (England, 1768- ?, Philadelphia), a highly gifted soprano who, after brilliant success in England, somewhat in rivalry with Mrs. Billington, came to America in 1793 as the leading artist of the period. She finally settled in Philadelphia, opening a girls' school. Her husband, whom she married about 1790, was Sir John Oldmixon, well known in London smart society.

*Pelissier, Victor, a French hornist who from 1792 was not only popular as player, but skillful in composing and arranging accompaniments or incidental music for at least 18 plays in New York, mostly in 1794-96. See Sonneck, 'Early American Operas,' I. M. G. Sammelbde. 6. 475.

*Petit, a French violinist who from 1793 played much in concert in both the North and the South.

*Phile, Philip, a violinist who from 1784 was often heard in New York and Philadelphia. He may have composed 'The President's March' in 1789 to which in 1798 'Hail, Columbia' was fitted by Joseph Hopkinson (1770-1842). See Sonneck, Reports on 'Hail, Columbia,' 'Yankee Doodle,' etc., and Elson, American Music, pp. 147-53.

*Pownall, Mrs. (d. 1796, Charleston), a superior English actress and singer (earlier known as Mrs. Wrighten — see Vol. v. 570 — and a Vauxhall favorite from about 1770), in 1792 came to Boston and at once became popular there and elsewhere. See Sonneck, Concert-Life, p. 36, etc.

*Priest, William, an English bassoonist and trumpeter who from 1793 was heard in concert and opera. He published Travels in the United States, 1793-97, London, 1802. See Sonneck, Concert-Life, p. 156, etc., and Early Opera, the latter showing him still active in 1799.

*Rausch, Frederick, from 1793 a pianist in New York, and in 1799 vice-president of the St. Cecilia Society.

Read, Daniel (Rehoboth, Mass., 1757-1836, New Haven), by trade a comb-maker or ivoryworker, was from 1785 an industrious contributor to psalmody. See Tune-Books.

*Reinagle, Alexander (England, 1756-1809, Baltimore), from 1786 the leading musician of Philadelphia, as well as prominent in New York. See Vol. iv. 57, and art.

*Saliment, George Edward, a flutist much in evidence in New York concerts in 1791-1800.

*Schaffer [Scheffer], Francis C., from 1796 a clarinettist in Boston. He also claimed to have invented the ' spiccato,' the nature of which is not clear.

*Schetky, George (d. 1831, Philadelphia), a Scot, nephew of Reinagle, who in 1787 came to Philadelphia and, but for short visits to England, remained identified with musical interests there. He was a good 'cellist, singer and arranger. He was intimate with Carr and J. C. Taws, and joined with them in starting the Musical Fund Society in 1820. See Madeira, Music in Philadelphia.

*Stone, a flutist, oboist and clarinettist who flourished in Boston from 1793.

*Sully, Mrs., an English pianist often heard from 1794. She and her husband and daughter were also actor-singers.

Swan, Timothy (Worcester, Mass., 1758-1842, Northfield, Mass.), began teaching psalmody about 1775 and from 1785 published tune-collections (see Tune-Books). Elson, American Music, p. 22, places his birth in 1757 at Suffield, Conn.

*Taws, Charles (d. 1833?, Philadelphia), a Scottish piano-maker who in 1786 came to New York and in 1788 went to Philadelphia, where he began making pianos before 1795, was associated with Reinagle and, with his sons, held in much esteem. See Spillane, pp. 78-80.

*Taylor, Raynor (England, 1747-1825, Philadelphia), a gifted singer, organist and composer, from 1793 influential in Philadelphia. See art.

Thomas, Isaiah (Boston, 1749-1831, Worcester), early noted as printer, editor and publisher, first at Boston and from 1775 at Worcester. In 1785 he advertised music-printing from type (see Fisher, Music in Old Boston, p. 14), and in 1786 issued the successful Worcester Collection (see Tune-Books). From

1770 he was proprietor of ' The Massachusetts Spy ' and other periodicals, a leading publisher and also author of a *History of Printing*, 1810. He founded and endowed the noted American Antiquarian Society of Worcester.

*Tyler, a good English actor and singer, popular from 1793.

*Van Hagen, Peter Albrecht (d. 1800?, New York), a Dutch violinist, pianist and manager who in 1774 came to Charleston and was later in Philadelphia and New York. See art.

*Van Vleck, Jacob, was noted as organist and composer among the Moravians at Bethlehem, Pa., from about 1780. See Walters, p. 12.

*West, J., an actor-singer who, after thirty years' experience in England, from about 1790 was with Bignall in the Virginia Company of Comedians. In 1792 he built a notable theater at Charleston. His wife was also a singer.

*Westray, the Misses (three), versatile English stage-singers who first appeared at the new Haymarket Theater in Boston in 1796.

*Wignell, Thomas (d. 1803), a brilliant English actor and singer who from 1785 was with the Old American Company and from 1792, after much success in New York, joined Reinagle in Philadelphia in starting the famous Chestnut Street Theater (opened in 1794) and in giving plays and concerts there and in New York, Baltimore and Washington. See Sonneck, *Early Opera*.

*Wolff, A., a clarinettist widely known from 1786, especially in concert.

*Young, William, an English flutist who appeared in Philadelphia in 1787.

Continuing the list given in sec. 1, note that the earliest concerts or operas thus far identified in several other places are as follows:

1783 Salem — by the Massachusetts Band.
1783 Portsmouth — by an artillery band.
1785 Albany — by an operatic troupe.
1786 Richmond — by the American Company.
1791 New Orleans — by French comedians from San Domingo.
1791 New London — by Mrs. Solomon's troupe.
1793 Alexandria — by ' an unfortunate emigrant.'
1793 Norfolk — by the West-Bignall troupe.
1794 Hartford — by the American Company.
1795 Petersburg — by Mrs. Sully and Mrs. Pick.

1796 Portland — by Mrs. Tubbs (Arnold).
1797 Newark — by the] West-Bignall troupe.
1798 Trenton and New Brunswick — by D. Salter.

Organizations for promoting or performing music doubtless became somewhat common before 1800, though many were short-lived and of shadowy influence. Below is a list of names and dates, mostly collated from Sonneck, *Concert-Life:*

1744 Collegium Musicum, Bethlehem.
1759 Orpheus Club, Philadelphia.
1762+ St. Coecilia (sic) Society, Charleston.
1772 Orphæus Society, Charleston.
1773–4 Harmonic Society, New York.
1782 Aretinian Society, Boston.
1784+ Uranian Society, Philadelphia.
1785–9? Musical Society, Boston.
1786+ Musical Society, Stoughton, Mass.
1786 Society for Promoting Vocal Music, New York.
1788–94 Musical Society (sacred), New York.
1789 Independent Musical Society, Boston.
1791 Amateur Society, Charleston.
1791–9 St. Cecilia Society, New York.
1793 St. Cæcilia Society, Newport.
?1793–8? Uranian Society, New York.
1794 Harmonic Society, Charleston.
1795–1800? Columbian Anacreontic Society, New York.
1795 Society of the Sons of Apollo, Boston.
1796–9 Harmonical Society, New York.
1797 Essex Musical Association, Newburyport.
1797? Musical Society, Concord, N.H.
1798–9 Polyhymnian Society, New York.
1799+ Philharmonic Society, New York.
1799 Musical Society, Baltimore.
1799 Philharmonic Society, Boston.
1800+ Euterpean Society, New York.

No doubt, many of these were merely transient social clubs, but they are nevertheless signs of the time. Probably there were many more, some of them, like the noted Stoughton Society, growing out of ' singing-schools.'

Ritter (*Music in America*, ch. vii) emphasizes an ' Apollo Society ' as ' foremost ' among early New York societies, but his data are not identifiable.

THE ERA OF NATIONAL EXPANSION

The development of the United States during the first two-thirds of the 19th century is much too complicated to be summarized in a sketch like the present. But among the enormous changes in the body politic, social and intellectual, between 1800 and the Civil War a few major points require mention.

Although the United States assumed the form of a nation at the time of the Revolution, a truly 'national' feeling and spirit were hardly attained until after the second war with England in 1812–14. That a knitting together of the elements of the confederation then took place cannot be denied. And yet the interests of different sections remained so diverse and their views of internal policy so opposed that many of their relations continued difficult. Indeed, the period culminated in the strenuous and exhausting Civil War of 1861–65. Along with these divisive influences, however, ran movements that were constructive in the highest degree.

Until after 1770 the population had been mainly limited to what is now called the Atlantic Division of the country—the section east of the long Appalachian Range. But from thence on settlers began to cross the hills in force into the East Central Division — the section west of the Appalachians and east of the Mississippi. The march of this expansion is registered by the dates at which nine new 'Territories' were successively recognized in this region.[1] All these were admitted to equality with the original thirteen as 'States' before 1848.

Soon after 1800, by the Louisiana Purchase in 1803 and then by cessions from Spain and Mexico, the door was opened wide into the West Central Division — the section west of the Mississippi, but east of the Rocky Mountains. Into this soon poured a veritable flood of migration, which did not pause until presently it had pressed on through the Mountain Division that lay beyond the Great Plains and reached the Pacific Division beyond the mountains. Thus within the space of a few decades the national domain was extended clear across the continent.[2]

The process thus sketched increased the area of the United States at least sixfold, so that it included more than 3,000,000 square miles or nearly as much as the whole of Europe.[3] The penetration of this vast domain by settlers proceeded without much system and very unequally. But the rapidity of occupation and its total bulk, even before the Civil War, are nevertheless extremely impressive. In 1800 the Atlantic Division held not less than 93 per cent of the whole population. In 1860 this Division contained only about 51 per cent, while the East Central had 35 per cent and the West Central over 12 per cent. Yet, since the total had

---

[1] Kentucky, 1792; Tennessee, 1796; Mississippi, 1798; Indiana, 1800; Ohio, 1803; Michigan, 1806; Illinois, 1809; Alabama, 1817; Wisconsin, 1836.

[2] In the West Central Division governments were organized as follows: Louisiana, 1804; Missouri, 1812; Arkansas, 1819; Iowa, 1838; Texas, 1848; Minnesota, 1849; Kansas and Nebraska, 1854; the Dakotas, 1861; Oklahoma (consisting largely of the previous unorganized Indian Territory), 1890.
In the Mountain Division the dates were these: New Mexico and Utah, 1850; Colorado and Nevada, 1861; Arizona and Idaho, 1863; Montana, 1864; Wyoming, 1868.
Owing to various circumstances the enrollment in the Pacific Division somewhat antedated that further east: Oregon, 1848; California, 1850; Washington, 1853.
Meanwhile, the number in the Atlantic Division was increased as follows: Vermont, 1791; Maine, 1820; Florida, 1822; West Virginia, 1862. None of these except Florida represented new territory. Thus before 1870 the Union had come to include 48 actual or potential 'States.'

[3] Roughly stated, the area-proportions of the five great Divisions are as follows: Atlantic, 14%; East Central, 15%; West Central, 32%; Mountain, 28%; Pacific, 11%.

meantime grown to over 31,000,000, the East in 1860 had 16,000,000 inhabitants, more than three times its size in 1800. The large absolute increase and the startling changes in distribution could not fail greatly to affect every aspect of social culture. The entire country suffered from being in a state of flux, though, on the other hand, in every section the period was instinct with energy and prophetic aspiration.

A conspicuous feature of the time was the setting in of a great stream of immigration from abroad, in part occasioned by the political unrest in Europe between 1830 and 1850. The incoming tide of people not only helped to swell the total population, often determining the character of new settlements in the West, but within it were hundreds of educated and able individuals who were destined to be dynamic in the formation of the later national culture. For the first time America began to feel the force of the best qualities of German civilization, not simply as it was transferred hither by incoming immigrants, but also as more and more it was apprehended at its source by outgoing students and visitors.[1]

Another feature of the period that was artistically weighty and potential was the multiplication of cities and their striking advance in relative importance. In 1800 the Census officially recognized only six 'cities,' which contained but 4 per cent of the whole population. In 1860 there were one hundred and forty, containing 16 per cent (or over 5,000,000 in all). At the head of the list in 1860 remained New York (with its neighbors Brooklyn and Newark), Philadelphia (quadrupled in 1854 by taking in many suburbs), Baltimore and Boston. But the shift in the general center of population is shown by the fact that high on the list are many new names, such as Pittsburgh and Cincinnati (from 1820), Buffalo and Louisville (from 1830), St. Louis (from 1840), Chicago and San Francisco (from 1850), with Cleveland, Detroit and Milwaukee soon following. The development of the Mississippi is indicated by the rise of New Orleans (from 1820) to a place among the leaders. For various reasons the big cities from the first were strongholds of foreign settlement, so that the leadership in social and intellectual matters which cities always exercise was in this case particularly affected by the stimulus to artistic knowledge and achievement that was felt from abroad.

It is needless to dilate upon the fact that the period was remarkable for the rapid advance in industrial and commercial enterprise, leading to the accumulation of a striking total of wealth. The drift of population to the West was primarily to open up agricultural resources. But equally significant were the quests for coal and oil in Pennsylvania and for metals and lumber in the Northwest and on the Pacific Slope. The invention and rapid adoption of labor-saving machinery for farming operations wrought a phenomenal economic revolution, since by the end of the period two-fifths of the population had become able to provide food for the remaining three-fifths. This is but a single illustration of a transformation that was taking place in all directions. Water-transportation for inland commerce

---

[1] In the decade 1830–40 the total immigration was about 600,000, in 1840–50 about 1,700,000, in 1850–60 nearly 2,600,000. In 1850 one person in every ten in the United States was foreign-born, and in 1860 one in every eight. In 1860 there were more than 4,000,000 who were foreign-born, and of these 1,278,000 had come from Germany.

assumed large proportions upon the Ohio and Mississippi Rivers, through the Great Lakes and by means of the Erie Canal (opened in 1825). Between 1830 and 1850 some 9000 miles of railroad were opened, and before 1860 not less than 21,600 miles were added. These lines of communication made feasible a wholly new social interchange, quite aside from their bearing upon economic development.

It was in this period that original impetus in the fields of science, letters and several forms of fine art first became notable. Systematic popular education was undertaken with extraordinary zest, not only through a system of public schools supported by local taxation, but more and more through institutions of higher education privately endowed or else founded by religious organizations. Newspapers and magazines multiplied, and both the number and the variety of published books were rapidly extended. Native fiction and poetry, besides literature of an educational or technical character, broke forth with energy and originality. Even painting and sculpture began to be cultivated with strength and independence. The taste for the drama grew more general and more discriminating. In short, this stirring period, especially in the quarter-century before 1860, was marked by a display of manifold mental vigor that was akin to its physical and economic enterprise. Whether or not the immediate products had enduring importance, the field of cultural activity was certainly brought fully into view and its wide appeal to human interest in some part perceived.

It is not strange, therefore, that in this period musical life should have become more abundant and significant. The number of professional musicians, both visiting performers and resident teachers, decidedly increased, the most important influence naturally still being exerted by those coming from abroad. Church-music, concert-undertakings, operatic performances of a kind, ensemble instrumental music — all these lines of public enterprise, though on a small scale as yet, gave promise of future attainment. And any thoughtful examination of accessible lists of musical workers makes plain that the subtle, but powerful, leaven of private instruction was now beginning to work here and there, not as yet producing results that can readily be catalogued, but still undoubtedly raising the standards of popular appreciation, discrimination and aspiration. The time had not come for widespread skill in performance, for familiar acquaintance with the trend of musical affairs in any large sense, or for creative freedom in the upper ranges of composition, except among some of the incoming foreigners. But the basic importance of the period as a whole with reference to the future is obvious.

Until about 1850 individual persons are as a rule not so conspicuous in the history as certain general advances in diffused interest. Two lines of activity were brought over from the preceding period, namely, (a) the cultivation of 'psalmody,' primarily in New England, but soon extending southward and westward, resulting frequently in the stimulus of more advanced choral music, of a craving for discipline in solo-singing, and of interest in class-instruction in the rudiments of composition; and (b) repeated efforts, mostly without continuity or wise planning, to provide ambitious operatic and concert-performances, not seldom making important impressions through the passing vogue of talented vocalists or through the drawing of trained instrumentalists into permanent residence.

A third point in the development from soon after 1800 was the founding in several centers of energetic instrument-manufacture, especially the making of pianos, with a large consequent effect on popular interest through the extensive sale and use of the products. Part of this was simply a phase of the general awakening to mechanical pursuits. But the rapid expansion of trade in pianos — not to mention other instruments — implies that a considerable demand for them existed or was impending, and the display of original ingenuity in novel construction — often preceding similar advances abroad — bespeaks something more than a mere desire for profits. In the single year 1829 it has been estimated that 2500 pianos were made, valued at $750,000. In 1850 there were over 200 establishments at work upon musical instruments, the value of the annual product being nearly $2,600,000.[1] Progress was greatly stimulated by competitive exhibitions held in Philadelphia from 1824 by the Franklin Institute and in New York from 1830 by the Mechanics' Institute.[2]

It is to be noted that, whereas in the later 18th century foreign influences in music came almost wholly from England or France, after perhaps 1810 the impress of Germany began to be notable in certain cities, like Baltimore, Philadelphia and New York. It is said that in New York as late as 1835 there still remained a decided prejudice in piano-making against German workmen, which was overcome only with some difficulty. But ten years later in such trade-circles the German element had become highly respected.[3] A parallel transition was even more evident among executive musicians. After 1840 able German players and leaders began to arrive in increasing numbers, and wherever they settled they became centers of fruitful influence. And from that date American students began to go to Germany for training, especially after the Leipzig Conservatory entered the field. Significant events were the advent of the so-called Germania Orchestra in 1848 and the formation of the Mendelssohn Quintette Club in 1849. Even more significant in its way was the arrival in 1845 of the boy Theodore Thomas.

The most striking organizations of the period were the Handel and Haydn Society of Boston, founded in 1815, the Musical Fund Society of Philadelphia, founded in 1820, and the New York Philharmonic Society, founded in 1842, representing more or less different lines of interest, but all making for substantial progress. From time to time ambitious opera-houses were erected, of which probably the most famous was the Academy of Music in New York, opened in 1854. Almost equally notable was the Boston Music Hall, erected in 1852, in which just at the end of the period (1863) was set up the first elaborate concert-organ in the country (made by Walcker of Ludwigsburg). New Orleans had a series of opera-houses from 1808, the latest and finest being opened in 1859.

[1] See Bishop, *History of the Arts and Industries of the United States*, 1864, pp. 339, 486.

[2] Regarding piano-making in America important books of reference are Spillane, *History of the American Pianoforte*, New York, 1890, and Dolge, *Pianos and their Makers*, 2 vols., Covina, Cal., 1911–13, together with Hipkins, *History of the Pianoforte*, London, 1896, and his article in Vol. iii. 716–32 of this Dictionary.

[3] See Spillane, pp. 186–8.

There is as yet a marked default in detailed information about the individuals and organizations that probably exerted a formative influence in many places during the early decades of the 19th century. Until work like that done by Sonneck for the 18th century has been undertaken the data will remain fragmentary and disconnected. But, happily, it is possible to give some hint of the striking advance of the mechanical and commercial sides of musical life, especially as evidenced by the founding of businesses that were more than transiently important. Accordingly to these considerable attention is here paid, especially in sec. 3. In sec. 4, also, it is possible to emphasize many of the incoming foreigners who were invaluable in awakening artistic thought and ambition. Yet, at best, the time before the Civil War remains relatively defective in presentation, except as imagination and conjecture fill in its manifest gaps of definite fact.

CHRONOLOGICAL REGISTER

3. The Early 19th Century, 1800–1840

Adams, F. W. (Montpelier, Vt., 1787–1859), a violin-maker after about 1805 who made about 140 instruments, marked by much excellence of tone.

Appleton, Thomas, from about 1810 a noted organ-maker in Boston who learned his trade with W. M. Goodrich, from 1813 was partner of Babcock the piano-maker, and from 1820 was successively associated with Ebenezer Goodrich, Corri and the elder Warren (father of S. P. Warren). Among his many organs was one for the Handel and Haydn Society.

*Arquier, Joseph (France, 1763–1816, France), a 'cellist and composer of operas who conducted a French opera-troupe in New Orleans in 1800–04.

*Austin, Mrs., an accomplished English opera-singer who from 1829 did much to make popular certain works of Rossini, Boieldieu and Weber.

Babcock, Alpheus, an ingenious and successful piano-maker, trained by Crehore, who in 1810 opened a shop in Boston with his brother **Lewis Babcock** (d. 1817), was for a time associated with Appleton and the Hayts (firm dissolved in 1815, see Brooks, *Olden-Time Music*, p. 270) and from 1822 with Mackay, who supplied capital. In 1829 he moved to Philadelphia and was associated with Klemm (probably the son of the organ-builder in sec. 2 above). His pianos won prizes repeatedly from 1824. In 1825 he patented a solid metal plate which was the first successful application of the principle later universally adopted. See Spillane, *Hist. of the American Pianoforte*, pp. 85–7, 120–3, etc.

Bacon, George (d. 1856, New York), joined Dubois and Chambers, the Boston piano-makers, in 1836. About 1841 the firm became Bacon & Raven, and in 1856 Francis Bacon took his father's place in Raven & Bacon, continuing the business now carried on by the Bacon Piano Company of New York.

Baker, Benjamin Franklin (Wenham, Mass., 1811–1889, Boston), from 1831 singer, teacher, editor, author and composer, first at Salem and from 1837 in Boston. See art. and Tune-Books.

Beckel, James Cox (b. Philadelphia, 1811), of German parentage, from 1824 assisted his father as organist and from 1829 for more than fifty years held posts in various Philadelphia churches, composing several cantatas, an organ-method, etc.

Blake, George E. (Philadelphia, 1775–1871, Philadelphia), the son of an earlier music-dealer, began music-publishing in 1802 and became a leader in musical affairs. He was an original member of the Musical Fund Society in 1820, and from 1824 active at exhibitions of the Franklin Institute. See Tune-Books.

*Boucher, A., a good 'cellist who came to New York in 1833 with Rivafinoli's opera-troupe and was long prominent. He collaborated with Schlesinger in 1837 and was concerned in the establishment of the Philharmonic Society in 1842.

Bourne, William (d. 1885, Boston), began making pianos in Dayton, O., in 1837, soon moved to Cincinnati and in 1842 to Boston, where in 1846, after being foreman at Chickering's, he established the firm now known as the Wm. Bourne & Son Piano Co., his son Charles E. Bourne coming into it in 1863.

Bradbury, William Batchelder (York, Me., 1816–1868, Montclair, N. J.), from 1834 organist in Boston and soon a teacher under Mason, and from 1840 teacher, editor, composer and also piano-maker in New York. See art. and Tune-Books.

Brainard, Silas (Lempster, N. H., 1814–1871, Cleveland), set up a music-store in Cleveland in 1836 and in 1845 began publishing, thus establishing the firm later known as S. Brainard's Sons (Charles S. and Henry M.)

*Bristow, William Richard (England, 1803–1867, New York), came to New York about 1824 and was long a leading teacher and conductor. See Bristow, George F. (sec. 4).

Brown, Bartholomew, from about 1800 a teacher in Boston, was one of the editors of the significant *Bridgewater Collection* in 1802 (see Tune-Books) and in 1832–38 conductor of the Handel and Haydn Society.

*Caradori-Allan, Maria Caterina (Italy, 1800–1865, England), a gifted and distinguished concert- and opera-singer in England, who from 1837 made a marked success in New York, Philadelphia, etc. See Vol. i. 461–2.

Chickering, Jonas (New Ipswich, N. H., 1798–1853, Boston), came to Boston in 1818 and in 1823 established the piano-making business which speedily became famous. See art.

*Clark, John, came from England about 1830 and joined William Nunns, the piano-maker of New York. See Nunns below.

Cross, Benjamin (Philadelphia, 1786–1857, Philadelphia), a graduate of the University of Pennsylvania and pupil of Carr and Taylor, was one of the founders and conductors of the Musical Fund Society from 1820, and as singer and teacher was highly influential. See Madeira, *Music in Philadelphia.*

*Da Ponte, Lorenzo (Italy, 1749–1838, New York), the librettist of two of Mozart's operas, was from 1805 teacher and promoter of opera in New York. See Vol. iii. 789–90, and art.

*Davis, John, came to New Orleans from San Domingo with an operatic troupe in 1811, and in 1813 built the Théâtre d'Orléans, where opera was regularly given with exceptional artistic perfection for forty years. Pierre Davis succeeded his father as manager.

*De Begnis, Giuseppe (Italy, 1793–1849, New York?), a gifted opera-singer, specially strong in buffo parts, who came to New York in 1838 and appeared with the Seguins. See Vol. i. 277–8.

Ditson, Oliver (Boston, 1811–1888, Boston), the famous music-publisher, became a clerk in a music-store in 1823 and in 1835 began business for himself. See art.

*Dubois, William, was a good piano-maker in New York, from 1821 associated with Stodart and later with Bacon and Warriner. See Spillane, pp. 108, 150, etc.

Dunham, J. B. (New Hampshire, 1799–1873, New York), originally a cabinet-maker in the South, from 1834 worked for Nunns in New York and from 1836 was partner of Adam Stodart in piano-making, succeeding to Osborn's business. From 1849 the firm name was J. B. Dunham & Co., and from 1867 Dunham & Sons. Though not an inventor, he was influential in popularizing the overstrung scale.

*Dyhrenfurth, Julius, a German violinist who came to America after 1830, gave concerts with Joseph Hermanns, a pianist, in the upper Ohio Valley and in New Orleans and the South, in 1841–47 was in Germany and then settled in Chicago. With other German musicians, he formed an orchestra which in 1850 gave eight concerts as the Philharmonic Society. See Upton, *Musical Memories,* pp. 253–9, etc.

*Firth, John (England, 1789–1864, New York), was in 1815 a maker of wood-wind instruments in New York, deriving his skill from Edward Riley (also English, at work in New York by 1812), whose daughter he married. In 1821 or '24 the firm of Firth & Hall was

formed, dealing in both small instruments and music, and from 1830 adding piano-making and music-publishing. S. B. Pond joined the firm in 1832 and W. A. Pond in 1847. Firth parted from them in 1863, and, with his son Thaddeus established the publishing business which in 1867 was bought by Ditson and made the nucleus of his New York branch.

*Garcia, Manuel del Popolo Vicente (Spain, 1775–1832, France), the distinguished singer, composer and conductor, brought an opera-troupe to New York in 1825, introducing Italian opera in a series of 79 performances. Among the singers were his wife, his son Manuel (1805–1906), later the great singing-master, and especially his daughter Maria Felicita (1808–36), later known as Malibran (from the French merchant whom she married in New York in 1826), whose singing made a deep impression. Of his troupe, Crivelli and Angrisani were otherwise the ablest members. See Vols. ii. 143–4, iii. 33–5, Ritter, *Music in America,* chap. x., and Krehbiel, *Chapters of Opera,* pp. 25–30.

*Geib, John and Adam, piano-makers who appeared in New York in 1802, were sons of John Geib, one of the Germans who from 1760 established piano-making in England and the inventor of the ' hopper ' (1786). John probably died before 1809, but Adam and two of John's sons, John, Jr. (from 1815) and William (from 1821), long continued prominent. From about 1830 Geib & Walker were pianomakers, importers and music-publishers of note. [In Brown, *Dict. of Musicians,* is also a reference to a George Geib (New York, 1780–?), piano-teacher in New York and author of an instruction-book in 1819.]

Gilbert, Timothy, with his brother Lemanuel Gilbert, was trained in piano-making by Osborn of Boston before 1820, and began business in 1829, promptly establishing a reputation for ingenious ability, especially in improving the action of uprights (1841) and squares (1847). In 1847 he brought out an ' organ-piano,' based on a patent of Obed Coleman (1844). His brother was less gifted and successful. Both continued active till about 1870.

*Gilles, P., a 'cellist in Philadelphia, prominent in the organization and leadership of the Musical Fund Society from 1820.

Goodrich, William M. (Templeton, Mass., 1777–1833?), was the first important American organ-builder, during almost thirty years from 1805 nearly monopolizing the business in Boston. From about 1822 he also made pianos. He trained Elias Hook. His brother Ebenezer Goodrich succeeded him, though without equal distinction.

Gould, Nathaniel Duren (Chelmsford, Mass., 1781–1864, Boston), from about 1800 an active teacher of singing-schools (also penmanship), claiming to have had 50,000 pupils before 1843. From 1819 his headquarters was Boston. His *Church Music in America,* 1853, has curious interest. See Tune-Books.

C

Hastings, Thomas (Litchfield, Conn., 1787–1872, New York), from 1816 conspicuous as leader, compiler, composer and author in the field of psalmody, from 1823 at Utica and from 1832 in New York. See Tune-Books.

*****Hawkins, John Isaac**, an English civil engineer who, while living in Philadelphia, devised, made and for a short time put upon the market a notable cottage-piano, having many features not practically developed till later. This piano was patented both in America and in England in 1800. See Spillane, pp. 80–3, etc., Hipkins, *Hist. of the Pianoforte*, p. 111, and cut in Dolge, *Pianos and their Makers*, p. 53.

*****Hayter, A. U.** (England, 1799–1873, Boston), having been cathedral-organist at Salisbury and Hereford, came to New York in 1835, was for a short time at Grace Church and from 1838 at Trinity Church, Boston, and in 1838–49 organist of the Handel and Haydn Society.

*****Heinrich, Anton Philipp** (Bohemia, 1781–1861, New York), a singular character in Kentucky who began composing by instinct in 1818, from 1827 was in London, studying and composing, in 1834 visited Germany and Austria, then came to New York, where he was much in evidence as an 'American' composer, but with ephemeral success. See Baker, *Dict. of Musicians*, 1918, pp. 1087–8, and note in 'Musical Quarterly,' April, 1920, p. 249.

Hewitt, Miss S., was organist of the Handel and Haydn Society, Boston, in 1820–29.

Hews, George (1806–1873), from about 1830 was tenor soloist, teacher, organist and piano-maker in Boston. He was prominent in the Handel and Haydn Society.

Hill, Ureli Corelli (New York, 1802?–1875, New York), early active in New York as violinist, from 1831 was conductor of the Sacred Music Society (in that year giving 'The Messiah' with orchestra), from 1836 studied with Spohr at Cassel, in 1842 organized and was the first conductor of the Philharmonic Society, and attempted to start regular chamber-concerts. After 1850 he wandered from place to place, engaging in ill-starred business ventures, and finally committed suicide. Though not a strong musician, he was historically important. See Ritter, *Music in America*, pp. 266–7, and Krehbiel, *Philharmonic Society of New York*.

*****Hiskey** was a good German piano-maker in Baltimore from before 1820 till about 1845. His pianos were widely popular in the South and to the West.

*****Hodges, Edward** (England, 1796–1867, England), came to Toronto as organist in 1838 and to New York in 1839, from 1846 being at Trinity Church, and returned to England in 1863. See Vol. ii. 414, and art.

Holt, Benjamin (1774–1861), besides compiling church music (see Tune-Books), was one of the founders and early conductors of the Handel and Haydn Society from 1815.

Hook, Elias (1805–1881), with his brother **George G. Hook** (1807–1880), the former having been trained by Goodrich, began making organs at Salem in 1827, removed to Boston in 1832 and became recognized as leaders in the industry. From 1855 Francis H. Hastings (1836–1916) was associated with them, the firm name becoming Hook & Hastings in 1865.

*****Horn, Charles Edward** (England, 1786–1849, Boston), from 1809 actor-singer and composer of operettas, came to New York in 1832–33 and brought out English operas until diverted by illness into teaching and music-publishing. After being in England in 1843–47, in 1848 he became conductor of the Handel and Haydn Society in Boston. See Vol. ii. 433–4.

*****Hupfeld, Charles P.**, a competent German violinist, who from about 1815 joined Carr and Taylor in Philadelphia in promoting chamber- and orchestral music. He was one of the founders and early conductors of the Musical Fund Society. See Madeira.

*****Jackson, Samuel P.** (England, 1818–1885, Brooklyn), son of an organ-maker who came to New York in 1825, was from 1830 organist at St. Clement's, from 1842 at St. Bartholomew's and from 1861 at other leading churches. Besides being an excellent teacher, he published much organ-music, anthems, etc., and for nearly thirty years was proof-reader for the publisher Schirmer.

*****Jardine, John**, an English piano-maker in New York from 1832 who made 'overstrung' pianos as early as 1833. His brother **George Jardine** (1801– ?), a highly trained organ-maker, came to New York in 1837 and soon founded the successful firm from 1860 known as Jardine & Son.

*****Jarvis, Charles**, an English pianist and teacher who was prominent in Philadelphia from about 1835. He published a successful instruction-book in 1852.

*****Knabe, William** (Prussia, 1803–1864, Baltimore), a trained piano-maker, came to Baltimore in 1833, worked under the talented Henry Hartye, formed a partnership with Henry Gaehle in 1839 which continued till 1854, and then proceeded alone. Before 1860 he had become known as one of the best makers in the country. After the War the business was finely continued by his two sons, William (d. 1889) and Ernest (d. 1894), and handed on to grandsons. In 1908 it was merged into the American Piano Co. See Dolge, pp. 282–6.

*****Lindeman, William** (Saxony, 1795–1875, New York), came to New York in 1834 and soon developed a notable piano-making business which still continues. Lindeman was instrumental in overcoming the strong prejudice in New York against German workmen. The 'cycloid' piano patented in 1860 by his son Henry Lindeman (b. 1838) presaged the later small or 'baby' grands.

*****Loud, Thomas** (d. 1834, New York), an English piano-maker who patented an upright in 1802, was the head of a notable family of makers. He came to New York about 1816. Meanwhile his son **Thomas Loud, Jr.** had settled in Philadelphia in 1812 as pianist and piano-maker, soon becoming prominent in all musical enterprises. With three brothers he constituted the energetic firm of Loud Brothers in 1824, which was broken up in 1837. **Thomas C. Loud** (b. Philadelphia, 1812), however, upheld the family reputation till about 1855. The Louds, besides being strong inventively, were important promoters of the industry.

Lucas, George W. (b. Glastonbury, Conn., 1800), from 1816 for over thirty years was active as a teacher of singing-schools, in 1820–35 at Northampton, Mass., later at Troy, N. Y., and farther west, and in Canada.

Mackay, John (d. 1841, at sea), a Boston ship-merchant, became in 1822 the financial supporter of Babcock in piano-making and in 1829 of Chickering.

Mason, Lowell (Medfield, Mass., 1792–1872, Orange, N. J.), the distinguished teacher, organizer and tune-composer, was choir-leader in 1808 at Medfield and 1812–27 at Savannah. His Boston activity began in 1827. See Vol. iii. 74, art. and Tune-Books.

*McPhail, A. M. (d. 1902, Omaha), came to Boston from New Brunswick and began piano-making in 1837, after training from Gilbert. He remained in high repute till his retirement in 1891.

Meneely, Andrew (West Troy, N. Y., 1801–1851, West Troy), in 1826 founded a famous bell-founding business in West Troy (now Watervliet), continued by his sons and now by his grandson.

*Meyer, Conrad (d. 1881, Philadelphia), a gifted Hessian piano-maker who came to Baltimore in 1819 and to Philadelphia in 1829. He is noted for making in 1833 one of the earliest pianos with a full iron plate and for general excellence of work, maintained for a half-century.

Mitchell, Nahum (Bridgewater, Mass., 1769–1853, Bridgewater), collaborated with Brown on the *Bridgewater Collection* in 1802. See Tune-Books.

*Montressor, a French opera-singer, brought a good troupe to New York in 1832 and gave thirty-five performances in Italian. With him were the soprano Pedrotti and the bass Fornasari. He was strongly supported by Da Ponte, but the enterprise was financially disastrous. It was useful, however, in bringing several orchestral players to America. See Krehbiel, *Chapters of Opera*, pp. 17–19.

*Nunns, Robert and **William**, English piano-makers, came to New York in 1821 and worked together till 1833, when Robert combined with John Clark as Nunns, Clark & Co., continuing till 1858, and William proceeded, at first alone and in 1839–40 with the Fischers. The Nunns pianos were highly esteemed for about forty years. The brothers were the first in America to use the French ' rocker ' action, the excellent scale of Sackmeister (1827) and Kreter's application of felt to hammers (1851). William Nunns was the teacher of William Steinway.

Oliver, Henry Kemble (Beverly, Mass., 1800–1885, Boston), sang as a boy in Boston,

graduated from Dartmouth in 1818, was active as teacher at Salem, starting choral societies in 1823 and '26, and from 1844 at Lawrence. He was mayor of Lawrence in 1859 and of Salem later, and was State Treasurer in 1861–65. See Tune-Books.

Osborn, John (d. 1835, New York), a pupil of Crehore, was a piano-maker in Boston from 1815, soon becoming known as ' the best in the country,' went to Albany in 1829 and settled in New York in 1830. Erecting a large factory in 1834 led to derangement and suicide. He was the teacher of Chickering. See Spillane, 56–7, 156–7, etc.

Perkins, Orson (Hartland, Vt., 1802–1882, Taftsville, Vt.), from 1822 for about forty years useful as a leader of choirs and singing-schools. He was the father of several sons later active (see sec. 5).

Perry, Emory (b. Holliston, Mass., 1799), from 1821 noted as tenor-singer and teacher at Worcester. He is said to have had 20,000 pupils in his singing-classes.

*Phillips, Thomas (Wales, 1774–1841, England), a fine tenor, visited New York as an opera-singer in 1816 with Incledon (see Vol. ii. 463–4) and again in 1823. He also appeared in concerts and lectured in Boston.

Pond, Sylvanus Billings (near Worcester, Mass., 1792–1871, New York), a piano-maker at Albany before 1820, moved to New York in 1832 and joined the Firth brothers (see above), beginning the business from 1863 known as Wm. A. Pond & Co. He wrote and compiled tune-music, especially for Sunday-schools.

Porter, William S., in 1834 published at Boston a *Musical Cyclopedia* of over 400 pages which was prepared under the supervision of Lowell Mason.

Prescott, Abraham (b. Deerfield, N. H., 1789), was probably the best-known of early makers of 'cellos and basses. He started in 1809 at his birthplace, but in 1833 went to Concord, N. H., where he worked till 1845, engaging in organ-making as well from 1836. Many later workers were trained in his shop. See *Violinist's Guide*, 1916, p. 16.

*Prévost, Eugène Prosper (France, 1809–1872, New Orleans), a popular singing-teacher, opera-conductor and composer at New Orleans from 1838 to 1862. See Vol. iii. 812.

*Rivafinoli, an Italian singer and manager who in 1833–34, with Da Ponte, attempted a season of Italian opera, including sixty-eight performances in New York and fifteen in Philadelphia. His singers were fairly good and the orchestra decidedly so. But the venture was a failure pecuniarily, the deficit being nearly $30,000. The New York series was given in the first opera-house to be erected in the city, built at the instigation of Da Ponte. See Ritter, *Music in America*, chap. x., and Krehbiel, *Chapters of Opera*, pp. 19–22.

*Russell, Henry (England, 1812–1900, England), famous for his descriptive songs, was in Canada from 1833 and then (till 1841) organist at Rochester or traveling. See Vol. iv. 194-5, and Madeira, pp. 131-7.

*Scharfenberg, William (Hesse, 1819-1895, Quogue, N. Y.), pianist (pupil of Hummel) and violinist under Spohr, came to New York in 1838 and was long prominent as teacher and concertist. He was active in the Philharmonic Society and for many years was reader and editor for Schirmer.

*Schlesinger, Daniel (Hamburg, 1799-1838, New York), pupil of Ferdinand Ries and Moscheles in England, came to New York in 1836, taught and gave a few concerts, besides being chosen to lead the Concordia, giving promise of fine influence.

*Schmitz, Adolph, a musician from Düsseldorf, was brought to Philadelphia in 1826 as teacher by the Musical Fund Society. He long continued to be useful artistically.

*Schomacker [Schumacher], Johann Heinrich (Schleswig-Holstein, 1800-1875, Philadelphia), after training as piano-maker in Vienna and activity in Bavaria, in 1837 came to Philadelphia and, after a short partnership with William Bossert, in 1842 started the Schomacker Piano Co., which soon acquired the excellent reputation still maintained. Its later development was largely in the hands of H. W. Gray (b. Ephrata, Pa., 1830) and the founder's son Henry C. Schomacker (b. Philadelphia, 1840).

*Seguin, Arthur Edward Sheldon (England, 1809-1852, New York), and his wife Ann Seguin, née Childe (England, 1814-1888, New York), bass- and soprano-singers of ability, came to New York in 1838 and were active there and elsewhere till after 1850, Mrs. Seguin continuing as a teacher. See Vol. iv. 408.

*Stewart, James, a Scottish piano-maker, came to Baltimore in 1812, moved to Boston in 1820 and, after a short association with Osborn, became Chickering's first partner in 1823. In 1826 he returned to London, and from 1827 for more than thirty-five years was connected with the Collards. Through him many American ideas were conveyed into English practice. See Spillane, pp. 30-1, 42-3, 57-8, etc., and also Vol. iii. 731-2.

*Stodart, Robert, another Scottish piano-maker, probably the grandnephew of the well-known English pioneer of the same name, came to New York in 1819 and in 1820-35? worked with Dubois, building up a fine reputation. In 1836 the firm of Stodart, Worcester & Dunham was formed, in which an Adam Stodart figures (nephew of Robert). From about 1850 for twenty years the firm was highly regarded. On the original Stodart see Vols. iv. 700 and iii. 722-31.

*Taylor, Samuel Priestley (England, 1779-1875?, Brooklyn), from 1806 was organist and teacher in New York and Brooklyn and, except for a sojourn in Boston in 1819-26, continued active there until after the Civil War.

*Timm, Henry Christian (Hamburg, 1811-1892, New York), a competent pianist, came to New York in 1835 and there and elsewhere gave

concerts, served as organist, joined in chamber-music and taught. He was often drawn into operatic work as conductor or chorus-master. In 1847-64 he was president of the Philharmonic Society. He wrote a grand mass, transcriptions for two pianos, part-songs, etc.

*Traetta, Filippo (Italy, 1777-1854, Philadelphia), came to Boston in 1799, soon removed to New York, toured with opera-troupes, lived for a time in Virginia, and settled in Philadelphia in 1822. See art.

*Wainwright, Jonathan Mayhew (England, 1792-1854, New York), coming to America as a boy, graduated at Harvard in 1812 and was tutor there in 1815-17, was Episcopal minister from 1818, chiefly in New York, where from 1837 he was at St. John's and in 1852-54 Bishop of New York. See Tune-Books.

Warren, Samuel Russel (d. 1882, Montreal), born in Rhode Island, was an organ-maker with Appleton in Boston about 1830, went to Montreal in 1837, becoming a leader in the industry in Canada. (See S. P. Warren, sec. 5.)

*Webb, George James (England, 1803-1887, Orange, N. J.), came to Boston in 1830 as organist, singing-teacher and colaborer with Mason. He removed to Orange in 1870 and taught in New York. See art. and Tune-Books.

Webb, Thomas Smith (d. 1819), long prominent in Rhode Island as a Freemason and interested in developing lodge-music, was one of the founders of the Handel and Haydn Society of Boston in 1815 and for two years its conductor.

White, John (Abington, Mass., 1785-1865, Barre, Mass.), was a pioneer American violin-maker, beginning in 1802. In 1806 he removed to Barre. His sons, Ira J. White (Barre, 1813-1895) and Asa Warren White (Barre, 1826-1893), continued the family tradition with success. See Violinist's Guide, 1916, p. 18.

Willard, Benjamin W., originally a maker of clocks, began making 'cellos and basses at Lancaster, Mass., about 1805 and by 1810 had produced about sixty instruments.

Winchester, Amasa, was conductor of the Handel and Haydn Society in Boston in 1819-26.

*Wise, John J., from 1829 till after 1850 a leading piano-maker in Baltimore, instituted several useful features in action, stringing and sound-boards. From about 1860 the business was continued by his sons.

*Wood, Mary Anne, née Paton (Scotland 1802-1864, England), a brilliant and charming soprano, with her husband Joseph Wood, a good tenor, appeared from 1833 in New York and other cities with striking success. See Vol. iii. 653-4.

*Zeuner, Charles (Saxony, 1795-1857, Philadelphia, suicide), came to Boston in 1824, where he was organist at Park Street Church and in 1830-37 for the Handel and Haydn Society, besides being a leader in other artistic enterprises. In 1854 he went to Philadelphia as organist. Besides much church-music, he composed an oratorio, 'The Feast of Tabernacles' (1832). See Tune-Books.

In a survey such as this the decades before and after 1850 cannot well be separated, although combining them makes a period that is somewhat unwieldy.

At this time the attention to 'psalmody,' though absolutely greater in amount, became relatively much less significant. After 1850 it tended to change in character and to divide into two lines of effort, which diverged more and more (see Tune-Books).

The salient note of the time was the increased contact in musical matters between America and Europe. From 1840 American students began to go abroad for training, especially to Germany. And from even before that date, as previously stated, the tide of immigration from Europe, especially from Germany and Austria, began to be impressive.

From about 1850 American audiences had the chance to hear visiting artists of ability and magnetic power, besides several good visiting orchestras. Their concerts in many cases aroused remarkable enthusiasm, tended to spread a knowledge of standard musical works and of executive skill, and did much to stimulate efforts for individual and local improvement.

Although the number of names plainly worthy of mention now becomes considerable, it is certain that the number should be larger. A list like this must confine itself to such data as are now accessible. Further investigation should add to this material.

4. The Middle of the 19th Century — 1840–1860

a **Becket, Thomas** (Philadelphia, 1843–1918, Philadelphia), a pupil of his father and Engelke, appeared as pianist in 1850 and at intervals later, but made a specialty of accompanying leading artists. He became a favorite teacher and for almost half a century taught at Girard College. He was also valued as an editorial adviser.

Adams, Charles R. (Charlestown, Mass., 1834–1900, West Harwich, Mass.), a concert-tenor from 1856, from 1861 also an operatic singer in Europe, and from 1877 conspicuous in Boston. See art.

Aiken, Charles (Goffstown, N. H., 1818–1882, Cincinnati), graduated from Dartmouth in 1838, studied under Lowell Mason and from 1844 was music-director and teacher-trainer in the Cincinnati public schools, producing extraordinary results (as shown in festivals from 1873).

Aiken, Henry M. (b. 1824?), a bass in Boston from about 1842 who continued active in church-music and oratorio for fifteen years.

*__Albrecht, H. F.__ (d. 1875, at sea), a Mecklenburger (with the Germania Orchestra in 1848), noted as collector of a remarkable musical library finally sold to J. W. Drexel of Philadelphia. He was greatly interested in the communistic ideas of Cabet, and about 1850 joined the latter's colony at Nauvoo, Ill., moving to Philadelphia about 1856. See Ritter, *Music in America*, chap. xvii.

Allen, Benjamin Dwight (Sturbridge, Mass., 1831–1914, Wellesley, Mass.), from 1845 was identified with Worcester, Mass., as teacher and organist, from 1894 was professor at Beloit College, in 1902–05 was organist in New York, and then retired. See art.

Allen, George N. (1812–1877, Cincinnati), early a pupil of Lowell Mason and a graduate of Oberlin in 1838, becoming musical instructor there and in 1841–64 professor of sacred music. He organized a chorus and orchestra, and prepared the way for the Oberlin Conservatory in 1865. In 1844 he compiled a hymn-book, including original tunes and even hymns. In 1848–77 he also taught geology.

*__Anschütz, Karl__ (Rhine Prov., 1815–1870, New York), son of a well-known musician of Coblenz, after being head of his father's school there and conductor and teacher in London, came to New York in 1857 as director for Strakosch. In 1862 he made an early and creditable attempt to establish German opera, and in 1860–62 led the Arion Society.

*__Appy, Henri__ (b. Holland, 1828), who had had concert-experience in Holland, came to America in 1851, toured with Mme. Biscaccianti and Jenny Lind, and became a teacher and conductor in Rochester, N. Y.

*__Arbuckle, Matthew__ (Scotland, 1828–1883, New York), came to America in 1853, was long associated with Gilmore and became a well-known cornettist. He wrote a cornet-method.

*__Arditi, Luigi__ (Italy, 1822–1903, England), from before 1840 noted in Italy as violinist, composer and conductor, from 1846 was opera-conductor for Marty in Havana and from 1847 in New York, returning often during the next forty-five years. See Vol. i. 102–3.

*__Balatka, Hans__ (Moravia, 1827–1899, Chicago), well trained in Vienna and choral conductor there, came to Milwaukee in 1849, founded and conducted the Musikverein in 1851–60, when he moved to Chicago to lead the Philharmonic Society and the Musical Union. In subsequent years he directed other organizations in Chicago and Milwaukee, toured in 1870 with Mme. Pappenheim, and composed a cantata, many choruses, some songs and orchestral fantasias, etc.

Barnabee, Henry Clay (Portsmouth, N. H., 1833–1917, Boston), about 1854 became popular as singer and comedian, continuing active for over fifty years. Before 1870 he organized companies to give light opera, from 1879 was with the Boston Ideal Opera Company, and in 1887, with Karl, organized The Bostonians, in all these enterprises being strikingly successful. He published *My Wanderings*, 1913.

Bassford, William Kipp (New York, 1839–1902, New York), from about 1855 was prominent in New York as pianist, teacher and composer. See art.

Battell, Robbins (Norfolk, Conn., 1819–1895, Norfolk), graduated from Yale in 1839 and became prominent in business and civic life. For years (till 1851) he led an enterprising choral society and from 1875 instituted various musical undertakings in or near Norfolk. In 1854–90 he and his brother endowed the professorship of music at Yale — one of many large benefactions. The Litchfield County Choral Union was founded in his memory in 1899 by his son-in-law, Carl Stoeckel.

*Berge, William (d. 1883, New York), came to New York in 1846 and became favorably known as pianist and writer of arrangements and transcriptions.

*Bergmann, Karl (Saxony, 1821–1876, New York), came to America in 1850, joined the Germania Orchestra, was a leading conductor in Boston and from 1855 in New York, and was also a competent 'cellist. See Vol. i. 308–9.

*Bergner, Frederic (Baden, 1827–?, New York), came to New York in 1849, and was leading 'cellist in the Philharmonic Society for over forty years, besides playing in the Eisfeld and Mason-Thomas quartets.

Bethune, Thomas G. [' Blind Tom '] (Columbia, Ga., 1849–1908, Hoboken, N. J.), a negro, blind and half-witted, who yet evinced from 1858 singular gifts as player and improviser on the piano in concerts at many places.

*Biedermann, August Julius (Saxony, 1825–1907, New York), came to America in 1848, settled in Milwaukee as piano-teacher and composer, and from 1859 worked in NewYork.

Biscaccianti, Eliza, née Ostinelli (Boston, 1825–?), daughter of an Italian violinist of Boston, after studying in Italy, appeared there in opera in 1847 and also in America, extending her tours to California in 1853–4. She ultimately settled in Rome.

*Bishop, Anna, née Rivière (England, 1814–1884, New York), the noted soprano, from 1847 appeared in America for some years and at intervals later. See Vol. i. 330–1, 345 (under Bochsa).

Blodgett, Benjamin Colman (b. Boston, 1838), from 1850 was organist in or near Boston, from 1858 studied at Leipzig, and from 1861 was at Park Street Church, Boston.

From 1865 he taught in Pittsfield, Mass., and in 1878–1903 was professor at Smith College, was then organist at Stanford University, and in 1906 retired to Seattle. See art.

*Boudousquié was the projector of the New Orleans Opera House in 1859 and its manager for some years, continuing the high standard previously established by Davis.

*Brandeis, Frederic (Austria, 1835–1899, New York), arriving in New York in 1849, from 1851 became a valued pianist, organist, conductor and composer. See art.

*Brignoli, Pasqualino (d. 1884, New York), an Italian tenor who first appeared in New York in 1855 and was thenceforward extremely popular in opera. Though rather stiff as an actor, his voice and method made him famous. See Upton, *Musical Memories*, pp. 121–5, etc.

*Brinkerhoff, Clara M., née Rolph (England, before 1830–?), came to America as a child, was carefully trained in singing and first appeared in New York about 1845. For more than forty years she was prominent in concert and oratorio and as a teacher. After 1861 she concertized in Europe.

Bristow, George Frederick (Brooklyn, 1825–1898, New York), even before 1840 known as violinist, and later conspicuous as organist, conductor and composer. See art.

*Bull, Ole Bornemann (Norway, 1810–1880, Norway), the celebrated violinist, from.1843 made several visits to America, and in 1852 projected a Norwegian colony in Pennsylvania. See Vol. i. 418–20, and art.

Campbell, Francis Joseph (Winchester, Tenn., 1832–1914, England), educated at the school for the blind in Nashville, became musical instructor there in 1850 and at Perkins Institute in Boston, studied in Germany, and from 1871 developed a notable enterprise in London that became the Royal Normal College for the Blind at Upper Norwood. In 1886 and '88 he made tours with pupils in America. He was knighted in 1909, and was an Officier de l'Académie.

*Cappa, Carlo Alberto (b. Sardinia, 1834), from 1858 was a noted band-master and trombonist in New York.

*Carter, Henry (England, 1837–?) from 1854 was organist at Quebec Cathedral, from 1864 in Boston and Providence and from 1873 at Trinity Church, New York, in 1880–83 taught in Cincinnati and was then again in Brooklyn and New York. See art.

*Castle, William (England, 1836–1909, Chicago), from 1858 till about 1890 was a well-known operatic and concert-tenor, and later teacher in Chicago.

Christy, Edwin T., from about 1844 one of the best-known promoters of negro ' minstrel ' entertainments.

*Clarke, James Peyton (Scotland, 1808–1877, Toronto), previously organist in Edinburgh, came to Canada in 1835, settling in 1840 at Toronto, where from 1845 he was instructor in the University, organist of the

Cathedral and leader of choral societies. Mus. D. of Toronto University in 1856.

Clarke, William Horatio (Newton, Mass., 1840–1913, Reading, Mass.), organist from 1856, after foreign study, went in 1871 to Dayton, O., as public-school supervisor and thence as organist to Indianapolis. In 1878–87 he was organist in Boston. See art.

Coleman, Obed M. (Barnstable, Mass., 1817–1845), a pioneer in improving the accordion, in 1844 patented an ' æolian attachment ' (set of reeds) for pianos, which was first popularized by Gilbert in 1847.

Cornell, John Henry (New York, 1828–1894, New York), from 1848 was an important organist, teacher, theorist and composer in New York. See art.

Cross, Michael Hurley (Philadelphia, 1833–1897, Philadelphia), from 1848 noted as organist and conductor, mostly in Philadelphia. See art.

*****Crouch, Frederick William Nicholls** (England, 1808–1896, Portland, Me.), 'cellist and singer, came to New York in 1849 with Maretzek, and worked in Portland, Philadelphia, Washington, Richmond and Baltimore as singer and teacher. He wrote many popular songs and two operas. See Vol. i. 641–2.

Cutler, Henry Stephen (Boston, 1825–1902, Boston), after training in Germany in 1844–46, from 1852 was organist at the Church of the Advent, Boston, in 1858–65 at Trinity Church, New York, and then in Brooklyn, Providence, Philadelphia and Troy. Mus.D. of Columbia University in 1864.

Danks, Hart Pease (New Haven, 1834–1903, Philadelphia), a church-singer before 1850, especially in Chicago, where he also took up writing hymn-tunes and popular songs. Some of the latter had wide circulation. He also wrote anthems and an operetta.

Davis, George H. (d. 1879, Boston), was partner of the Hallets in Boston from 1843, contributing much to the success of the Hallet & Davis pianos.

Decker, Myron A. (Manchester, N. Y., 1823–1901, New York), early trained as pianomaker in Albany, opened a factory there in 1856, achieved decided success and in 1859 removed to New York. After some vicissitudes, in 1875 the firm of Decker & Son was formed by including Frank C. Decker, who is head of the present business.

Deems, James Monroe (Baltimore, 1818–1901, Baltimore), early showed ability in band-music, from 1839 studied 'cello under Dotzauer in Dresden, taught and played in Baltimore, in 1849–58 was music-instructor at the University of Virginia, went abroad again, from 1861 was in the Civil War (becoming Brigadier-General), and then resumed musical work in Baltimore. He wrote an opera, a comic operetta and the oratorio ' Nebuchadnezzar.' See Mathews, *Hundred Years*, pp. 298–300.

Doane, William Howard (Preston, Conn., 1832–1915, Cincinnati), was all his life engaged in making wood-working machinery, but was also musically active. He studied under B. F. Baker in Boston and other teachers, and from 1862 became one of the best of the many writers of ' Gospel hymns.' He made a considerable collection of instruments. Mus. D. of Denison University in 1875.

*****Dohn, Adolph W.**, a Chicago business-man who in 1858–65 was conductor of the Mendelssohn Society and in 1872–74 the first permanent conductor of the Apollo Club. See Upton, *Musical Memories*.

*****Dresel, Otto** (Rhine Prov., 1826–1890, Beverly, Mass.), came to New York in 1848 as concert-pianist and settled in Boston in 1852. See art.

Dwight, John Sullivan (Boston, 1813–1893, Boston), founder and editor of a notable ' Journal of Music,' 1852–81. See Vol. i. 759, and art.

*****Eberhard, Ernst** (Hanover, 1839–1910?, New York), came to New York before 1860, was organist in various churches, conducted choral societies and orchestral concerts, and in 1876 established the Grand Conservatory. He prepared several instruction-books.

*****Eichberg, Julius** (Rhine Prov., 1824–1893, Boston), came to New York in 1856 and from 1859 was conductor and eminent educator in Boston. See Vol. i. 770, and art.

*****Eisfeld, Theodor** (Brunswick, 1816–1882, Hesse), violinist and conductor, was influential in New York in 1848–66, returning then to Wiesbaden. See art.

Emerick, Albert G. (Philadelphia, 1817–? , Philadelphia), who had been organist since 1832, in 1841 compiled a successful collection of people's songs and later was correspondent for musical papers. From 1850 he managed high-class concert-series in Philadelphia.

Emerson, Luther Orlando (Parsonsfield, Me., 1820–1915, Hyde Park, Mass.), one of the most facile of the later ' psalmody ' composers, active from about 1840 at Salem, Boston and Greenfield, Mass., with various tune-books from 1853 (see Tune-books). He was in request as conductor of ' conventions.' Mus.D. of Findlay College in 1891. See Hall, *Gospel Song and Hymn Writers*, pp. 44–9.

Emmett, Daniel Decatur (Mt. Vernon, O., 1818–1904, Mt. Vernon), from 1843 was foremost in developing ' negro minstrel' troupes, with New York as a center. In 1859, while with Bryant, he wrote the song 'Dixie.' See art.

Everett, L. C. (1818–1867) and **Everett, Asa Brooks** (1828–1875), two Virginians who studied music in Boston (the younger also four years at Leipzig), organized a system of normal instruction at Richmond in the '50s which had results analogous to Mason's in the North. In 1861 they had fifty teachers of singing-schools representing them and using their publications. See Hall, pp. 96–100.

Fairlamb, James Remington (Philadelphia, 1838–1908, New York), from 1852 organist in Philadelphia, in 1859–61 studied at Paris and Florence, then consul at Zurich, continuing musical culture in many ways, in 1865–72 mostly in Washington as organist, and then organist and teacher in New York. He wrote many songs, choral and church works, and the operas ' Valérie ' (privately given in Washington), ' Treasured Tokens ' (Phila.), ' Love's Stratagem ' and ' The Interrupted Marriage.'

*Fischer, John U. (b. Italy, 1816) and **Fischer, Charles S.** (b. Italy, 1818), learned piano-making in Naples from their father and grandfather (of Austrian descent), came to New York in 1839 and in 1840 succeeded to part of the Nunns' business, which they developed into artistic and commercial success. In 1873 John returned to Italy and Charles was then joined by his four sons.

Fischer, William Gustavus (Baltimore, 1835–1912, Philadelphia), a book-binder in Philadelphia, developed capacity as music-teacher and leader of choruses, in 1858–68 was instructor at Girard College (preceding a Becket) about 1868 became a prosperous piano-dealer (retired in 1898), was prominent as leader of Welsh choral societies (Penn Bicentenary, 1881), and as composer of ' Gospel hymns.' See Hall, pp. 130–2.

*Formes, Karl Johann (Rhine Prov., 1816–1889, San Francisco), who had been since 1842 a noted operatic bass in Europe, from 1857 at intervals for twenty years was often heard in America, finally settling as teacher in San Francisco. See Vol. ii. 88, and art.

Foster, Stephen Collins (Pittsburgh, 1826–1864, New York), a spontaneous writer of popular songs in Pittsburgh till 1860, then in New York. See Vol. ii. 90–1, and art.

*Fries, Wulf (Holstein, 1825–1902, Roxbury, Mass.), who had been 'cellist in Norway, came to Boston with his brother **August Fries** (b. 1822) in 1847, long continuing prominent as a player. See art.

Fry, William Henry (Philadelphia, 1813–1864, W. Indies), a journalist in New York and from 1845 composer of operas, orchestral pieces, cantatas and songs. See art.

*Gabler, Ernest (d. 1883, New York), a Silesian piano-maker, came to New York in 1851 and in 1854 established a firm that still continues.

*Gemünder, August Martin Ludwig (Würtemberg, 1814–1895, New York), gifted violin-maker, trained by Vuillaume, came to Springfield, Mass., in 1846, and was joined by his equally able brother, **Georg Gemünder** (1816–1899). Later they worked in Boston and New York, establishing a notable business, still continued by descendants. See art.

*Gilmore, Patrick Sarsfield (Ireland, 1829–1892, St. Louis), a band-master who came to Canada about 1845, went to Salem in 1849 and thence to Boston, organizing a famous band that traveled widely. See Vol. ii. 169, and Upton, *Musical Memories*, pp. 194–206.

*Goldbeck, Robert (Prussia, 1839–1908, St. Louis), early noted as pianist, from 1857 was

in New York, from 1868 in Chicago, from 1873 in St. Louis, from 1880 again in New York, etc., becoming famous as player, teacher, conductor and composer. See art.

Gottschalk, Louis Moreau (New Orleans, 1829–1869, Brazil), the original and talented pianist, trained in Paris, where he made his début in 1844, who from 1853 gave concerts throughout the United States. See Vol. ii. 205, and art.

Guiraud, Ernest (New Orleans, 1837–1892, France), produced his first opera in New Orleans in 1852, but was later wholly identified with Paris, from 1876 as professor in the Conservatoire. See Vol. ii. 259, and art.

*Hagen, Theodor (Hamburg, 1823–1871, New York), came to New York in 1854, edited ' The Musical Gazette,' later called ' The Musical Review and Gazette,' and was a useful journalist and critic. While still in Germany he wrote articles for the ' Neue Zeitschrift,' *Civilisation und Musik*, 1845, and *Musikalische Novellen*, 1848.

*Haines, Napoleon J. (England, 1824–1900, New York), and his brother **Francis W. Haines** (1822–1887, New York), came to New York as boys, from 1839 worked at piano-making under A. H. Gale, in 1851 opened their own factory and rapidly gained a solid reputation. They kept abreast of all improvements and were among the first (about 1870) to foresee the popularity of the upright. N. J. Haines was a foremost financier during the Civil War and afterward. The Haines piano-business is now part of the American Piano Company.

Hamlin, Emmons (d. 1881, Boston), a workman in Prince's melodeon-factory in Buffalo, in 1847 made discoveries in adjusting the reeds then used which greatly improved their tone. In 1854 he joined Henry Mason of Boston in the firm of Mason & Hamlin.

Haynes, John C. (Brighton, Mass., 1830–1907, Boston), became a clerk for Ditson in 1845, was admitted to the firm in 1857, and in 1889, after Ditson's death, was made president.

Hays, William Shakespeare (Louisville, 1837–1907, Louisville), began to write popular songs in 1853 and gradually became widely known. In later life he was on the staff of the Louisville ' Courier-Journal.'

Hazleton, Henry (b. New York, 1816), was an apprentice in Dubois & Stodart's piano-making shop in New York from 1831, began business at Albany in 1838, moved to New York in 1841, and in 1849, with his brothers **Frederick Hazleton** and later **John Hazleton**, established the firm of Hazleton Brothers, whose excellent reputation has been kept up by their descendants.

*Healy, Patrick Joseph (Ireland, 1840–1905, Chicago), brought to Boston as a boy and employed in music-stores, developed such ability that in 1864 Ditson sent him, with George W. Lyon, to Chicago to establish a branch house. Lyon & Healy soon ranked among the leading music-dealers of the country, specializing in the production of instruments of many kinds, including harps, violins, pianos and organs. See Dolge, *Pianos and their Makers*, pp. 350–4.

*Heintzmann, Theodore A. (Prussia, 1817–1899, Toronto), an experienced piano-maker, came to New York in 1850, went to Buffalo in 1853 and in 1860 to Toronto, becoming the pioneer manufacturer in Canada.

*Held, Ernst Carl Eberhardt (Saxony, 1823–1913?, Syracuse), originally a mining-engineer in Prussia, joined in the revolution of 1848 and then migrated to America, and from 1849 was teacher, composer and writer in Syracuse. Mus.D. of Syracuse University in 1903.

*Hoffman, Richard (England, 1831–1909, Mt. Kisco, N. Y.), came to New York in 1847 and became a leading pianist and composer for the piano. See Vol. ii. 414–5, and art.

*Hohnstock, Carl (Brunswick, 1828–1889, Brunswick), from 1848 till 1860 was prominent in Philadelphia as pianist and teacher. His sister **Adelaide Hohnstock** (d. 1856) was associated with him.

*Holmes, Edward (England, 1797–1859, America), author of works on Mozart and Purcell, etc., came to America in 1849 and worked as editor and critic.

Hopkins, Edward Jerome (Burlington, Vt., 1836–1898, Athenia, N. J.), from 1846 a self-taught organist, composer, lecturer and organizer, from 1856 with headquarters at New York. See art.

*Hülskamp, Gustav Heinrich, a German piano-maker who worked in Troy from 1850 and in New York from 1866, introducing many improvements in construction, including striking experiments with ' symmetrical ' grands.

*Huss, George John (Bavaria, 1828–1904, New York), from 1848 was organist and piano-teacher in or near New York, with some compositions.

Jarvis, Charles H. (Philadelphia, 1837–1895, Philadelphia), began as a child-pianist in 1844 and developed into a competent and influential artist. See art.

*Keller, Matthias (Würtemberg, 1813–1875, Boston), a band-master and violinist who came to Philadelphia in 1846, was later conductor in New York and finally went to Boston, where his ' American Hymn ' was brought out in 1869.

Kemp, Robert [' Father Kemp '] (Wellfleet, Mass., 1820–1897, Boston), a shoe-dealer in Boston, started in 1854 giving ' old-folks' concerts' of early American music. See autobiography, 1868.

Kimball, William Wallace (Maine, 1828–1904, Chicago), after clerical and commercial experience in the East, began dealing in pianos and organs at Chicago in 1857, rapidly becoming prominent, took up reed-organ-making in 1881, piano-making in 1887 and organ-making soon after, developing one of the strongest establishments in the country.

*Klauser, Karl (Russia [Swiss parents], 1823–1905, Farmington, Conn.), from 1850 piano-teacher, arranger and editor in New York, and in 1856–83 teacher in Farmington, Conn. He edited *Famous Composers*, 1891 (with Thomas and Paine), and *Half-Hours with the Best Composers*, 1894.

*Kotzschmar, Hermann (Prussia, 1829–1909, Portland, Me.), came to America in 1848 and from 1849 was active in Portland as organist, teacher, conductor and composer. See art.

*Kreissmann, August (Saxony, 1823–1879, Saxony), active in Boston from 1849 to 1876 as singer, teacher and leader of the Orpheus Club.

*Krell, Albert (Germany, 1833–1900, Cincinnati), of a family of instrument-makers, came to America in 1848 and was known at Cincinnati as an expert violin-maker. In 1889, with his sons, he started a piano-factory.

Lang, Benjamin Johnson (Salem, 1837–1909, Boston) from 1852 eminent as organist and conductor in Boston. See Vol. ii. 631–2, and art.

Ludden, William (b. Williamsburg, Mass., 1823), a pupil of Mason and Webb, from 1840 taught in Pittsfield, Mass., from 1842 in Williston Seminary at Easthampton, was organist and conductor in New Haven while at Yale College, in 1853–4 studied singing in Paris, taught at New Haven and from 1862 at Chicago, removing in 1870 to Savannah as music-dealer. He compiled a *Pronouncing Musical Dictionary* (terms), 1875.

Madeira, Louis Cephas, identified from 1843 with the Musical Fund Society of Philadelphia till its dissolution in 1858, first as manager and then as secretary, supplied data for *Annals of Music in Philadelphia and History of the Musical Fund Society, 1820–58*, 1896 (edited by P. H. Goepp).

*Maretzek, Max (Moravia, 1821–1897, Staten Island, N. Y.), an experienced violinist and opera-conductor, brought to New York in 1848 by Fry, from 1849 till 1878 was the indefatigable and usually clever manager of a variety of operatic ventures in New York, Havana and Mexico, introducing many noted singers. He wrote two operas, ' Hamlet ' (1843) and ' Sleepy Hollow ' (1879), orchestral music, etc., besides the autobiographic *Crochets and Quavers*, 1855, and *Sharps and Flats*, 1890.

Mason, Daniel Gregory (Savannah, 1820–1869, Europe), son of Lowell Mason, with his brother Lowell was engaged in music-publishing in Boston from 1853.

Mason, Henry (Boston, 1831–1890, Boston), son of Lowell Mason, in 1854 with Emmons Hamlin founded the Mason & Hamlin firm of reed-organ-makers, to which in 1869 was added his brother Lowell. Before this, in 1861, they had begun making the improved ' cabinet organ.' In 1882 the firm began to make pianos of the highest quality.

Mason, Lowell, Jr. (Westboro, Mass., 1823–1885, Orange, N. J.), son of Lowell Mason, was from 1853 associated with his brother Daniel Gregory in the publishing-firm of Mason

Brothers, but, after the latter's death, joined his other brother in the Mason & Hamlin firm.

Mason, Luther Whiting (Turner, Me., 1828–1896, Buckfield, Me.), from 1853 music-supervisor in Louisville, in 1865 moved to Boston, in 1879–82 was employed by the Japanese government, and later went abroad. See art.

Mason, William (Boston, 1829–1908, New York), son of Lowell Mason, made his début as pianist at Boston in 1846, studied in Germany, appeared in America in 1854 and settled in New York as eminent player and teacher. See Vol. iii. 74, and art.

*****Mathushek, Frederick** (Baden, 1814–1891, New York), highly trained as piano-maker at Worms and with Pape in Paris, came to New York in 1849, was first associated with Dunham, from 1852 alone, from 1857 with Spencer B. Driggs, from 1866 at New Haven as head of the Mathushek Piano Co., and from 1871 in New York again. He is said to have devised a successful ' overstrung ' scale in 1850, and soon after invented a machine for hammer-covering. He had uncommon delicacy of ear and planned small instruments with remarkable breadth of tone. See Dolge, pp. 321–5.

*****Matzka, George** (b. Coburg, 1825), came to New York in 1852 and was long identified with the Philharmonic Society, acting as conductor for a time in 1876. He wrote several overtures, two string-quartets, a violin-sonata, choruses and songs.

*****Merz, Karl** (Hesse, 1836–1890, Wooster, O.), came to Philadelphia in 1854, from 1861 taught at Oxford, O., and in 1882 became professor in Wooster University. See art.

*****Meyer, Julius Eduard** (Altenburg, 1822–1899, Brooklyn), an accomplished singing-teacher, trained at Leipzig, settled in Brooklyn in 1852 and was active there for over forty years, though twice invited back to Leipzig.

Millard, Harrison (Boston, 1830–1895, Boston), a singer from boyhood, studied in Italy in 1851–54, taught in Boston and from 1856 in New York, served as lieutenant in the Civil War, and was employed in the New York Custom House for many years. He wrote an opera, ' Deborah,' a grand mass and other church-music, many adaptations of foreign songs and about 350 original songs.

Miller, Henry F. (Providence, 1825–1884, Wakefield, Mass.), had a good musical education, early became an organist, besides showing mechanical genius and learning the trade of watch-making, in 1850 took up piano-making with Brown & Allen in Boston, in 1858 with Emerson, and in 1863 in his own Company, which soon became famous. At his death the business was continued by five sons.

*****Mills, Sebastian Bach** (England, 1838–1898, Germany), came to New York in 1856 as a visiting pianist, and was so warmly received that he remained as player, teacher and composer. See Vol. iii. 210, and art.

*****Mollenhauer, Eduard** (Saxony, 1827–1914, Owatonna, Minn.), and his brother **Friedrich**

Mollenhauer (1818–1885), expert violinists, came to New York in 1853 with Jullien and remained as valued soloists, orchestral players and teachers. Another brother, **Heinrich Mollenhauer** (1825–1889), 'cellist, followed in 1856 and established a school in Brooklyn, still carried on by his sons.

Moore, John Weeks (Andover, N. H., 1807–1887, Boston), began as printer and editor of country newspapers in Maine, New Hampshire and Vermont, settling finally in Manchester, N. H. From before 1840 he displayed interest in musical subjects, writing or editing a variety of manuals and collections, partly in periodical form. His chief works were The *Musician's Lexicon*, 1845–46, and a *Complete Encyclopædia of Music*, 1854, and Appendix, 1875, an ambitious production for the time.

*****Morgan, George Washbourne** (England, 1822–1892, Tacoma, Wash.), came to New York in 1853 and served as organist in a series of churches. See art.

*****Mosenthal, Joseph** (Hesse, 1834–1896, New York), a gifted violinist, came to New York in 1853 and was long prominent as ensemble-player, organist, conductor and composer. See art.

*****Müller, Carl Christian** (Meiningen, 1831–1914, New York), came to New York in 1854, worked in a piano-factory and led Barnum's orchestra, and from 1879 was harmony-teacher in the College of Music. See art.

*****Neuendorff, Adolf** (Hamburg, 1843–1897, New York), was brought to New York in 1855 and from 1859 was active as pianist, violinist, conductor, manager and composer. See art.

*****Nuno, James** (Spain, 1824–1908, Buffalo), after study in Italy, in 1851 came to Cuba as bandmaster, and went thence to Mexico, touring in the United States from 1856. In 1869 he settled in Buffalo. See art.

Paillard, M. J. (Switzerland, ? –1868, Switzerland), in 1850 started the New York branch of the famous Swiss manufacture of music-boxes, long continued by others of the family.

Palmer, Horatio Richmond (Sherburne, N. Y., 1834–1907, Yonkers, N. Y.), from 1852 active in ' conventions,' popular choruses and school-instruction, from 1881 led the Church Choral Union in New York and from 1887 was dean of the Chautauqua Institution. See art.

Parker, James Cutler Dunn (Boston, 1828–1916, Boston), originally a law-student, studied at Leipzig and in 1854 settled in Boston as organist, conductor, teacher, theorist and composer. See art.

Perkins, Charles Callahan (Boston, 1823–1886, Windsor, Vt.), graduated from Harvard in 1843, went to Italy to study painting, later to Paris, where he became equally interested in music. In 1849–51 and 1854–57 he was in Boston, organizing musical activities and composing, in 1850 being at the head of the Handel and Haydn Society and in 1852 the chief contributor to the erection of the well-known Music Hall. After prolonged residence in Europe,

in 1869 he returned to Boston as critic and
patron of fine art in general.

Phelps, Ellsworth C. (b. Middletown, Conn.,
1827), organist from 1846 at New London,
Syracuse and New York, and from 1857 in
Brooklyn, engaging also in public-school
music and composing two symphonies, four
symphonic poems, concert-overtures, two
comic operas, the cantata ' David,' an extended choral ' Elegie,' Psalm 145, etc.

*****Phillipps, Adelaide** (England, 1833–1882,
Bohemia), was brought up in Boston, from 1842
appeared there as a dancer, but, after training
in Italy, from 1855 became famous as concert-
and operatic contralto. See Vol. iii. 709–10.

Phillips, Philip (near Chautauqua, N. Y.,
1834–1895, Delaware, O.), from 1853 noted as
a leader of singing-schools, from 1860 was a
music-dealer and publisher in Cincinnati,
removing in 1867 to New York, where he published many popular song-books, mostly
sacred. His tenor voice made him famous and
from 1868 he conducted ' song-services ' in all
parts of the world. See Hall, pp. 118–23.

Poole, Henry Ward (Salem, Mass., 1825–
?), brother of William F. Poole, the librarian, while a student at Yale in 1842 became
absorbed in problems of musical acoustics,
especially those of temperament. In 1849 at
Newburyport he made an enharmonic organ,
described in 1850 in the ' American Journal of Science,' thus coming into touch with
foreign investigators, so that his work is repeatedly quoted (as in Ellis' Helmholtz). He
also made studies in the theory of chords.
His business as mining-engineer took him to
Mexico in 1856, where he settled. See
Mathews, *Hundred Years*, pp. 341–6.

*****Pychowski, Jan Nepomucene** (Bohemia,
1818–1900, Hoboken, N. J.), a pianist and
teacher in New York and Hoboken from 1850.
He was a good composer of chamber- and
piano-music.

Richardson, Nathan (Reading, Mass., 1827–
1859, France), pupil of Moscheles, Dreyschock
and others, compiled a piano-method in 1859
which had much vogue for many years.

*****Richings, Caroline**, née Bernard (England,
1827–1882, Richmond, Va.), brought to America as a child, appeared as pianist at Philadelphia in 1847 and in opera in 1852, remaining
a favorite singer till about 1870, and then
taught at Baltimore and Richmond.

*****Ritter, Frédéric Louis** (Alsace, 1834–1891,
Belgium), came to Cincinnati in 1856 as conductor and to New York in 1861, becoming
from 1867 professor at Vassar College and
well known as composer and author. See
Vol. iv. 109, and art.

*****Rivé, Caroline**, née Staub (France, 1822–
1882, New York), pupil of Garcia in singing
and a good pianist, came to New Orleans
about 1850 and taught successfully there and
from 1854 at Cincinnati.

Root, George Frederick (Sheffield, Mass.,
1820–1895, Bailey's Island, Me.), from about

1840 with Mason and Webb at Boston, was
organist and teacher in New York from 1844,
studied a year in Paris, became a music-
publisher in Chicago in 1859 (business sold
in 1871 to the John Church Co., Cincinnati),
and wrote many songs and other vocal music.
See Vol. iv. 138–9, art. and Tune-Books.

*****Rudolphsen, John Frederick** (Hamburg,
1827– ? , Cincinnati), came as violinist with
Gungl in 1849, appeared as opera-singer in
1853, from 1862 taught in Boston and from
1879 in the Cincinnati College of Music.

*****Ryan, Thomas** (Ireland, 1827–1903, New
Bedford, Mass.), came to Boston in 1844, from
1849 for forty years played viola and clarinet
in the Mendelssohn Quintette Club. See his
Recollections of an Old Musician, 1899.

Ryder, Thomas Philander (Cohasset, Mass.,
1836–1887, Somerville, Mass.), from 1856
organist at Hyannis, later at Tremont Temple,
Boston, and a popular teacher, conductor and
composer.

*****Schilling, Gustav** (Hanover, 1803–1881,
Nebraska), who from 1830 had been head of
the Stöpel Music School in Stuttgart and a
prolific writer on theory and æsthetics, came
to New York in 1857, in 1859 went to Canada,
from 1871 was in Burlington, Ia., and thence
moved to Nebraska. For a list of his publications (all in Europe) see Baker, *Dictionary
of Musicians*, p. 826.

*****Schirmer, Gustav** (Saxony, 1829–1893,
Thuringia), came as a boy to New York in
1837, was clerk in a music-store, from 1854 manager for the publisher Breusing, and from 1861
his successor, building up a business of international fame. See Vol. iv. 265–6.

*****Schuberth, Julius** (Saxony, 1804–1875,
Saxony), founder of a publishing-house at
Hamburg in 1826, opened a branch in New
York in 1850, to which later he gave much
personal attention. In 1867 he started the
' New-Yorker Musikzeitung.'

*****Schultze, Wilhelm Heinrich** (Hanover,
1828–1888, Syracuse), came to America in
1848 with the Germania Orchestra, from 1858
was leader of the Mendelssohn Quintette
Club, and from 1877 professor at Syracuse
University. Mus.D. there in 1877.

Sharland, John B. (Halifax, 1837–1909, Boston), was early in Chickering's piano-factory,
but turned to piano-playing and conducting, led
many choral societies in or near Boston, and
from about 1870 was music-supervisor in the
schools. He compiled song-books from 1865.

Southard, Lucien H. (Sharon, Vt., 1827–
1881, Augusta, Ga.), studied in Boston, from
1851 was music-supervisor there, taught in
Norfolk, Va., in 1860–61 was organist at
Hartford, Conn., served in the Civil War, in
1865–68 and 1871–75 taught in Boston, and
in 1868–71 was head of the Peabody Conservatory in Baltimore. See art.

*****Steck, George** (Hesse, 1829–1897, New
York), an expert piano-maker, trained by
Scheel at Paris, came to New York in 1853

and in 1857 established the firm that long continued in high repute (absorbed in 1904 into the Æolian Company). He was especially gifted in scale-designing.

*Steinbrecher, Frederic W. (b. Prussia, 1818), in 1843–44 a pupil of Chopin, came to Cincinnati in 1848 as pianist, teacher and composer.

*Steinert, Morris (Bavaria, 1831–1912, New Haven, Conn.), came to America about 1854, played in orchestras, and about 1865 became a music-dealer in New Haven and a collector of keyboard-instruments. See art.

*Steinway, Henry Engelhardt (Harz, 1797–1871, New York), an established maker of organs and pianos at Seesen since 1820, came to New York in 1851 with three sons (another preceded him in 1849), and in 1853 organized the firm since famous throughout the world. See Vols. iii. 729–32, iv. 691–2.

*Stieff, Charles M. (Würtemberg, 1805–1862, Baltimore), came to Baltimore in 1831, at first as teacher of languages, but from 1842 as importer of pianos. In 1852 he went to Europe to examine methods in piano-making, and then, with two sons and **Jacob Gross** (b. 1819), who had had long experience before coming to America in 1848, inaugurated the business that has had an honorable record in the hands of his descendants.

*Stoeckel, Gustav Jakob (Bavaria, 1819–1907, Norfolk, Conn.), came to America in 1847 and in 1855–96 was instructor and professor of music at Yale College.

*Strakosch, Maurice (Galicia, 1825–1887, France), from 1845 worked in New York as pianist and teacher, and from 1857 as manager, succeeded by his brother **Max Strakosch** (1834–1892). See Vol. iv. 713, and art.

Thayer, Alexander Wheelock (Natick, Mass., 1817–1897, Austria), graduated from Harvard in 1843 and assistant-librarian there, from 1849 was almost continuously in Europe, from 1865 as consul at Trieste, where he produced a monumental biography of Beethoven. See Vol. v. 79–80, and art.

*Thomas, John Rogers (Wales, 1829–1896, New York), in 1849 came to New York, in 1852 sang with the Seguins and other artists, and wrote many popular songs, an operetta, church-music, etc.

*Thomas, Theodore (East Friesland, 1835–1905, Chicago), came to New York as a boy in 1845, soon found employment as violinist, touring from 1851, and from 1864 was conspicuous as a phenomenal organizer and conductor of orchestras, living in Cincinnati in 1878–80 and moving to Chicago in 1891. See Vol. v. 88, and art.

*Torrington, Frederick Herbert (England, 1837–1917, Toronto), came to Montreal in 1856 as organist and violinist, from 1869 was in Boston, and from 1873 was organist, conductor, etc., in Toronto. See art.

Tourjée, Eben (Warwick, R. I., 1834–1891, Boston), from about 1851 teacher at Fall River, in 1859 started a music-school at East Greenwich, R. I., and, after a sojourn in Europe for study of methods, founded larger schools at Providence and in 1867 at Boston. See Vol. v. 134, and art.

Tuckerman, Samuel Parkman (Boston, 1819–1890, Newport, R. I.), organist in Boston in 1840–49 and 1853–56, and from 1864 at Trinity Church, New York. See Vol. v. 173–4, and Tune-Books.

Tufts, John Wheeler (Dover, N. H., 1825–1908, Camden, Me.), from 1846 studied at Frankfort and Leipzig, from 1848 was organist and conductor at Bangor, Me., and later at Portland, and from about 1880 at Boston, where he was efficient in promoting public-school music, besides being for fifteen years organist at King's Chapel.

*Urso, Camilla (France, 1842–1902, New York), a child-prodigy as violinist, appeared in America in 1852–55 and again after 1862, when she acquired world-wide celebrity. She settled in New York in 1895. See art.

Warner, James F., published translations of Gottfried Weber's *Generalbasslehre* and *Theorie der Tonsetzkunst*, 1841–42, and a *Dictionary of Musical Terms*, 1842.

Warren, George William (Albany, 1828–1902, New York), was organist at Albany from 1846, in Brooklyn from 1860, and from 1870 at St. Thomas', New York. See art.

*Watson, Henry C. (England, 1818–1875, New York), musically well-educated, came to New York in 1841 and began a notable editorial career, both as critic for several papers and as founder in 1843 of the 'Musical Chronicle' (in 1847 transformed into 'The American Musical Times'), from 1855 as the first editor of Leslie's 'Illustrated Newspaper,' and in 1863 as founder of 'The American Art Journal.' He helped establish the Philharmonic Society and other organizations, and for thirty years remained conspicuous in promoting musical progress. See Mathews, *Hundred Years*, pp. 377–80, and Dolge, pp. 415–6.

*Weber, Albert (Bavaria, 1828–1879, New York), came to New York in 1845, took up piano-making with Holder and Van Winkle and about 1852 opened his own shop, gradually developing from about 1860 the solid reputation of his instruments. He was a specialist in tone-quality. The Weber business is now part of the Æolian Company.

*Wels, Charles (Bohemia, 1825–1906, New York), pupil of Tomaschek and from 1847 Polish court-musician, came to New York as pianist, organist and teacher in 1849. He wrote an orchestral suite and overture, five masses, a piano-concerto, many facile piano-pieces, part-songs and songs.

White, Edward L., besides other publications of an educational character, made a translation of Friedrich Schneider's *Harmonie und Tonsetzkunst* (about 1850). See also Tune-Books.

White, Henry Kirk (d. 1907, Meriden, Conn.), from 1845 a maker of instruments in

Connecticut, from 1853 at Washington, N. J., and from about 1860 in Philadelphia, was called in 1865 to the Estey factory at Brattleboro, Vt., and in 1877 joined H. C. Wilcox at Meriden, Conn., founding the firm of Wilcox & White, makers of reed-organs. His three sons all distinguished themselves in developing the industry. See Dolge, pp. 367–70.

Whiting, George Elbridge (b. Holliston, Mass., 1842), an organist from 1855, from 1858 was Buck's successor at Hartford, and since 1862 has been mostly identified with churches in Boston, and an eminent teacher. See Vol. v. 517–8, and art.

Whitney, Myron William (Ashby, Mass., 1836–1910, Sandwich, Mass.), after study in England and Italy, in 1858 began a notable career as operatic and concert-bass in Boston. See art.

Willcox, John Henry (Savannah, 1827–1875, Boston), graduated from Trinity College (Hartford) in 1849, settled as organist in Boston and was noted as a talented player and as expert in organ-construction, as well as writer of Catholic church-music.

*Williams, Victor (b. Sweden, 1816), from about 1840 was a well-known teacher in Cincinnati, for more than twenty years in public-school work.

Willis, Richard Storrs (Boston, 1819–1900, Detroit), graduated from Yale in 1841, studied in Germany and settled in New York as a literary worker, editing ' The Musical Times ' and ' The Musical World,' writing and compiling vocal music, especially *Church Chorals*, 1850, and writing also the practical handbook *Our Church Music*, 1855.

Wilson, Henry (Greenfield, Mass., 1828–1878, Hartford, Conn.), studied in Boston and Leipzig, from about 1850 was organist at Greenfield, in Springfield in 1854, and from 1855 at Hartford, becoming widely known as player, choir-master and composer of church-music. See art.

*Wolfsohn, Carl (Hesse, 1834–1907, New Jersey), already known in the Rhine Valley

as pianist, came to Philadelphia in 1854, from 1856 was associated with Thomas in chamber-concerts there and on tour, organized the Beethoven Society in 1869, removed to Chicago in 1873 and organized a similar society there, continued till 1884. See art.

*Wollenhaupt, Hermann Adolf (Saxony, 1827–1863, New York), came to New York in 1845 as concert-pianist and teacher of brilliance and popular power. In 1855 he made a European tour. He composed about 100 piano-pieces in a fluent and clever style.

Wood, David Duffield (Pittsburgh, 1838–1910, Philadelphia), trained in Philadelphia in the Institute for the Blind, was instructor there from 1853 and from 1864 also organist at St. Stephen's, becoming noted as player, teacher and composer. See art.

Woodman, Jonathan Call (Newburyport, Mass., 1813–1894, Brooklyn), about 1840 associated with Mason in Boston and an oratorio-singer, was later in various church positions in New York and Brooklyn, besides teaching after 1880 in Rutgers Institute and Packer Institute.

Work, Henry Clay (Middletown, Conn., 1832–1884, Hartford), a printer by trade and a self-taught song-writer, caught the popular ear before 1855, when he moved to Chicago. He wrote many stirring war-songs after 1861 and temperance-songs later.

*Zerrahn, Carl (Mecklenburg, 1826–1909, Milton, Mass.), came to Boston with the Germania Orchestra in 1848, and from 1854 till 1895 was famous as conductor of the Handel and Haydn Society, besides other similar activities. See Vol. v. 595, and art.

*Zundel, John (Würtemberg, 1815–1882, Würtemberg), trained as violinist under Molique and as organist under Rinck, after being organist at St. Petersburg from 1840, came to New York in 1847 and for thirty years was a well-known organist, in 1850–55, 1858–65 and 1867–78 at Plymouth Church, Brooklyn. He wrote instruction-books, collections of voluntaries, a Te Deum and a *Treatise on Harmony*.

For purposes of reference, a few notes may be added about the establishment of opera-houses in New Orleans and New York before 1860.

During the whole 19th century New Orleans maintained a fairly continuous and often brilliant operatic activity. The first French troupe appeared there in 1791. In 1808 the Théâtre St. Philippe was opened (not used for opera after 1820), in 1813 the Théâtre d'Orléans (burnt in 1817), in 1818 the same rebuilt (burnt again in 1866), and in 1859 the New Orleans Opera House (burnt in 1919). The works given were mostly French, but opera in English occurred

in 1817. After the Civil War New Orleans troupes occasionally visited the North, going especially to Chicago and New York.

The first real opera-house in New York was opened in 1833 (after 1835 the National Theater), Palmo's Italian Opera House in 1844 (from 1848 Burton's Theater), the Astor Place Opera House in 1847 (given up in 1852 and later the Mercantile Library), and the Academy of Music in 1854. From 1849 the New York operatic world was the scene of managerial rivalries between Maretzek, the Strakosch brothers and Ullmann.

THE PERIOD AFTER THE CIVIL WAR

The Civil War was a national event of the first magnitude. While it lasted, and for some years afterward, social life was much disorganized and cultural pursuits suffered a check. The struggle accentuated the differences between North and South that had been previously visible. It was the North that had experienced the more vigorous development of physical resources, the principal influence of copious immigration, and, in consequence, the greater broadening of social and intellectual interests. So, after the War, while for a time the South was prostrated, the North was soon ready to resume powerful advance. By 1890, however, the South had so far recovered that it began to take its due place in progress.

During the half-century between 1860 and 1910 the total population grew from about 31,500,000 to about 92,000,000 — that is, was practically tripled. Of the net gain, the North as a whole secured thirty-five millions, the South eighteen, and the Far West seven and a half. There was a steady shift in balance to the west, so that the percentage of population east of the Mississippi fell from 86 to 70.

During the fifty years not less than 23,000,000 immigrants arrived, the rate rising after 1905 to more than a million per year. In the opening decade of the 20th century immigration supplied more than half of the total increase. For the fifty years it amounted to almost 37 per cent of that increase. Such figures are eloquent as to the factor of transition and instability in social conditions so far as affected by changes in population. The derivation of the newcomers was no longer chiefly English or Teutonic, but for a time Scandinavian, and then Italian, Hungarian, and Slav.

The drift toward the city became more pronounced than ever. Whereas in 1800 only one out of twenty-five was a city-dweller, and in 1850 only one in eight, in 1900 the ratio had become one in three. This increased concentration tended powerfully to intensify the mental life of the nation. In this particular case the city-ward drift had a peculiar relation to the total culture — one but slightly evident earlier, and one not easily matched elsewhere in the world. Because the total area of the country is so great, the large cities are generally far apart and consequently tend to have strong individuality, as well as decided influence over the sections dependent on them. Nothing quite like this is found in any single European country. And with this dissociation by mere distance there is a healthy rivalry between them and between the several states or sections which they represent. Much of the rapidity, variety, and virility of the development in recent decades is due to this geographic peculiarity in the American situation.

No succinct statement of the immense economic activity of the period is here possible. Every phase of agriculture, mining, manufacture, and internal commerce made enormous gains. As to the general economic result it is enough to recall that in 1850 the total 'wealth' of the country (the fair value of real and personal property) was estimated at somewhat over seven billions, but that in 1910 this was estimated at about one hundred and thirty billions — or about $1400 per person. It was during the latter part of the 19th century that the use of inventions like the telephone and the electric railroad became so general as really to transform the practical conditions of life and thought. All these factors of material progress — and many more — had direct bearings upon the artistic progress of the period.

Here is the place to remark that during this period occurred the expansion of the great Dominion of Canada, which was formed in 1867 out of the then existent provinces of Lower Canada or Quebec and Upper Canada or Ontario, with New Brunswick and Nova Scotia. In the next fifteen years this area was augmented by the administrative inclusion of the whole vast territory westward to the Pacific and northward as well. British Columbia, on the west coast, was admitted in 1871, and the great Northwest Territories (Manitoba, Assiniboia, Saskatchewan, Alberta, Keewatin, Athabasca, Mackenzie and Yukon) were systematically developed so that since 1905 they have all been counted as constituent provinces.

The total area of the Dominion is larger than that of the United States proper, so that it is much the largest division of the British Empire. But, owing to the rigorous climate in many parts of it and to the recency of its decided advance, its population is on the whole small — between eight and nine millions. Ontario, however, in the center, has had a commercial, social and artistic unfolding similar to that of the neighboring United States, though, as is natural, emphatically dependent upon England. Since the setting up of the unified Dominion its cultural advance has been quite as remarkable as that of the United States, though the bulk of it is necessarily less.

The population is prevailingly British in origin except in the Province of Quebec and eastern Ontario, where the French have always been numerous; but western Ontario, Manitoba and even the provinces beyond have received many of other nationalities by immigration from near-by portions of the United States.

The large cities are Montreal, Toronto, Winnipeg, Vancouver, Ottawa, Hamilton and Quebec.

Among the forces that explain the extraordinary progress of music after 1865 in both the United States and Canada a large place must be given to the indirect influence of organized education. In the United States the educational purpose of the colonial settlers declared itself early in the founding of 'colleges.' At least thirty of these which still flourish were established before 1800, representing every State from Maine to South Carolina and Tennessee except one. The process of college-founding went on with growing momentum throughout the 19th century, spreading a network of institutions over nearly the whole country, until now they number over 600, of which about 140 are for men, 110 for women and the rest for both sexes. They naturally differ widely in grade and scope. Some are really 'academies' or detached 'high schools.' Others are members of true university systems. Most of them represent types that are more or less peculiar to America.

A closely related movement after 1800 was the development of 'public schools,' distributed according to need and maintained by taxes laid upon the communities served. The total system, although analogous to that of some other countries, has always had strong individuality, especially in its expression of the spirit of democracy. During the 19th century it had a prodigious expansion and gradually acquired somewhat standardized methods of grading and classification, with the addition of the kindergarten and other primary forms at the bottom and of 'high schools' at the top, besides many 'normal schools' and ·'teachers' colleges' for the preparation of the teaching-force. Most of the 'state universities' belong technically to this general class, being free civic establishments, but some of them originated as 'colleges.' They aim to provide specialized opportunities in many distinct fields of knowledge.

Organized education has also become highly developed in many other directions, especially in preparation for various occupations, like law, medicine, theology, engineering, mining, agriculture, etc. Private schools for the youth of both sexes, too, have become increasingly common. Still other lines of effort might be specified.

No exact appraisal is possible of the reaction of this manifold activity upon that form of culture which demands artistic expression. The one normally stands to the other in some relation of cause and effect. All 'education' does not issue in artistic aspiration. But such aspiration does not attain general popular significance except where there is a wide educational basis. In both the 'college' and the 'school' systems of America artistic topics were long almost ignored. And yet every step in the development of these systems helped to prepare the way for the rational pursuit of artistic topics. It was not until after the Civil War that the study and cultivation of music began definitely to show the results of the previous activities in general education. As musical enterprises took shape their educational connections were evident. It was in this period that instructors and professors of music began to become common in colleges and universities, that instruction in music in public schools began to be widely and permanently adopted, that responsible music-schools began to be founded, that the occupation of music-teaching began to be recognized as a 'profession,' that regular concert- and opera-series began to be established, that choral societies and orchestras began to be organized in such a way as to continue, that influential musical periodicals and books began to multiply, and thus that the whole social and intellectual status of musical art began to acquire general significance. With this came, of course, a great unfolding of artistic power in performance, composition and technical appreciation. Certainly any consideration of the sudden outburst of musical interest which is implied, for instance, in the appended lists of musical workers appearing between 1860 and 1900 must take into account its relation to the preceding advance in popular 'education,' even though baffled when it attempts to describe the operation of all the factors with precision.

The important point to be borne in mind is that there has always been a peculiar zeal in America for the development of education democratically — not created by the general government, but locally or corporately sustained, and not for any class, but for the whole people. When at length this zeal began to take hold of the problem of musical education, it moved with surprising celerity and enterprise — not always, perhaps, with the utmost wisdom as neasured by the thought of a half-century later, but at least with striking vigor and practical result.

In seeking to analyze the forces that came into play after the Civil War the first place belongs to the private teachers. At the beginning of the period a majority of the best of these were doubtless of foreign birth. But by 1900, though foreigners were absolutely more numerous, they were relatively much less in evidence. No statistics are available, but it is clear that the total number of American teachers increased prodigiously between 1865 and 1900, and their geographical distribution became extensive. It goes without saying, also, that in this period there was great improvement in their average equipment and artistic outlook. Music-teaching became, as it had not been earlier, a recognized educational occupation, and began to give tokens of the ideality and aspiration that mark a true 'profession.' One sign of awakening self-consciousness was the starting of teachers' associations (from about 1875), both national and local. More and more it was seen that for good teaching good preparation is requisite. Every teacher who was finely equipped tended to create a widening circle of followers. Competition operated to stimulate the able and to eliminate the feeble. Whatever gains there were in general pedagogical practice gradually made their way into the field of musical pedagogy as a specialty. Teaching music certainly became steadily more systematic and rational rather than spasmodic and intuitional. Text-books and 'methods' were published in increasing numbers, and discussion of teaching-praxis grew animated and thoughtful. Gradually about the army of teachers grew up a great clientage of pupils, attracted, no doubt, by a variety of considerations, but more and more subjected to whatever of information, sympathy and inspiration there was in the teaching-body. It is impossible to adduce exact evidence in detail, but no one can compare the musical situation in 1865 and that in 1900 without realizing in some degree that an enormous pervasive force of personal influence had been exerted in transforming the one into the other.

One of the chief means of recruiting the ranks of teachers are music-schools. At the opening of this period such schools were almost unknown. At its end they were scattered rather freely throughout the country. The most influential pioneers were the Oberlin Conservatory and the New England Conservatory in Boston, founded in 1865 and 1867 respectively. The former soon became the forerunner of the institutional or collegiate type (though not technically so at first), as the latter was of the independent or detached type. The former also

D

represented the class of those in small towns where general education is a controlling interest, while the latter represented the class of those in large cities, where many collateral advantages are available.   It was the second type that was first strongly developed.   As instances it is enough to refer to the Cincinnati Conservatory (1867), the Chicago Musical College (1867), the Peabody Conservatory in Baltimore (1868), the Philadelphia Musical Academy (1869), the Cleveland Conservatory (1871), the Detroit Conservatory (1874), the College of Music in Cincinnati (1878), the New York College of Music (1878), the Cleveland School of Music (1884), the National Conservatory in New York (1885), the Chicago Conservatory (1885), the Northwestern Conservatory in Minneapolis (1885), the American Conservatory in Chicago (1886) and the Toronto Conservatory (1886).   No extensive musical work was common in colleges or universities till later.   And yet it is to be remembered that there had been musical instructors at Oberlin College since 1838, at the University of Toronto since 1845, and at both Yale College and the University of Virginia since 1849, and that after 1860 such significant appointments were made as those of J. K. Paine at Harvard College in 1862, F. L. Ritter at Vassar College in 1867, J. C. Fillmore at Ripon College in 1868, M. W. Chase at Hillsdale College in 1869, Thomas a Becket at Girard College in 1870, Max Piutti at Wells College in 1874, H. A. Clarke at the University of Pennsylvania, F. A. Parker at the University of Wisconsin and Willard Kimball at Grinnell College in 1875, G. W. Chadwick at Olivet College in 1876, W. H. Schultze at Syracuse University and R. A. Heritage at Valparaiso University in 1877, B. C. Blodgett at Smith College in 1878, C. B. Cady at the University of Michigan and Louis Lisser at Mills College in 1880, W. A. Chalfant at Drury College in 1881, Karl Merz at Wooster University in 1882, J. W. Hill at Wellesley College and J. H. Howe at DePauw University in 1884, W. F. Bentley at Knox College in 1885 and C. H. Farnsworth at the University of Colorado in 1888.   In the large majority of cases the instruction thus initiated led to the formation of strong and flourishing departments or schools of music.   From the first the collegiate and the independent types of institution have been distinct, but each has rendered substantial service to the total progress.

During this period the attitude toward music in the public schools changed from comparative apathy to decided interest and even considerable sustained endeavor.   By 1900 the children in many places were learning something of song as they did of other subjects, and the function of music-supervisor was beginning to assume dignity in pedagogical discussion.   Many manuals of instruction had been published, and there was almost amusing contention over methods.

These powerful influences were greatly stimulated and broadened by those of another class, equally educational in real value, but operating through the avenue of public performance rather than that of personal instruction.

One of these was the steady formation of choral societies of varying degrees of importance, working out somewhat freely into clubs for the study of secular as well as sacred music, of glees and part-songs as well as oratorios.   There is no roster of these associations available.   Some lasted but a few years, like many of their predecessors. Some grew into established institutions, especially in the large cities and in connection with some colleges, exerting a cumulative cultural influence upon singers and communities — indirectly, also, providing fields for the artistic ability of vocal soloists and presently of orchestras. In the one year 1873 the Oratorio Society in New York, the Apollo Club in Chicago and the Cincinnati Festival Association were founded — three diverse enterprises, each highly influential in its way. A score of other societies might be named that were started before 1890 in different places and that have continued effective.

Another potent force was the formation of orchestras and of ensemble-groups. Here the virile ardor of Theodore Thomas was a leading factor. In 1864 he organized Symphony Soirées in New York and in 1869 made his first concert-tour — a practice continued till 1878. As examples of other significant efforts may be named the Philharmonic Society of Chicago (1860–68), the orchestra of the Harvard Musical Association (1865–82), which prepared the way for the Boston Symphony Orchestra (1881), and the Symphony Society of New York (1878). Although ensemble-groups kept springing up from time to time, none can be said to have exerted a truly national influence until the formation in 1886 of the Kneisel Quartet. It is plain that the stimulus supplied by the steadily increasing number of concerts in various places from 1870 onward by bands of highly-trained artists was of utmost importance in lifting the level of knowledge, appreciation and desire among a multitude of hearers. Such concerts, with those by competent soloists, whether resident or visiting, effected a vast amount of education by demonstration.

The analogous influence of operatic performances is necessarily more fitful and irregular, except when nucleated by the erection of permanent buildings intended for them. From 1870 onward, just as at intervals for a century before, American audiences had varied chances to hear opera of different kinds given by visiting troupes. But the establishment of opera as a fixed element of popular culture was specially promoted by the existence of such buildings as the Théâtre d'Orléans in New Orleans (1813–66) and the Academy of Music in New York (erected in 1854 and used for opera till 1886), which prepared the way for the Metropolitan Opera House in 1883, and also by the opening in Chicago of the Crosby Opera House in 1865, which, though destroyed in the great fire of 1871, in the same way prepared for the Auditorium in 1889. Even where such buildings were not at hand various opera-companies appeared as visiting troupes in theaters with more and more regularity, so that before 1900 a long list of works had been brought before an extensive clientage of hearers.

The holding of 'festivals' was also a feature of the period. To a slight degree these recall the 'conventions' of an earlier time, but their artistic level was much higher. The so-called 'Peace Jubilees' at Boston in 1869 and 1872, organized under Gilmore, were monster affairs, too big to be satisfactory, and yet not without a considerable stimulating value upon popular interest. Much more important were the choral festivals at intervals arranged by permanent organizations. The first of these was inaugurated in 1865 by the Handel and Haydn

Society of Boston in celebration of its fiftieth anniversary and continued triennially thereafter. About the same time began the annual festivals at the neighboring city of Worcester. In Cincinnati, growing out of interest aroused by gatherings held for many years by German singing-clubs, a festival was held in 1873 under Thomas, followed by the formation of a Festival Association to maintain a biennial series. In 1881 Damrosch organized a festival in New York with the Oratorio and Symphony Societies as the nucleus of the forces. In 1882 and 1884 Thomas held festivals in Chicago. The musical features of the Columbian Exposition at Chicago in 1893, of which Thomas was general director, amounted to a prolonged festival, lasting over three months. These conspicuous illustrations of the festival idea led to many less ambitious undertakings, so that by 1900 clusters of choral and instrumental concerts, usually held once a year, had become fairly numerous. As a rule, all these enterprises have proved decidedly effective as educational forces, though there is an obvious difficulty in holding them to any consistent artistic policy.

Among smaller factors in the development after the Civil War reference should be made to church-music. This type of musical effort has always presented much more variety in America than in other countries, since there is no state church and no one communion holds the primacy. The differences between different parts of the country also affect usages, as do those between urban and rural communities. Yet the very number of distinct 'denominations,' many of them large and finely organized, and even their marked differences of liturgical tendency, have on the whole broadened the field of musical opportunity. It is striking how many of the musicians just after the Civil War were organists or church-singers. In this period in the older parts of the country the ideals of sacred music underwent a marked change from those of the 'psalmody' period. Choir-music was more emphasized than congregational singing, and organ-playing for accompaniment or alone became more conspicuous. Whatever may have been the result devotionally, the practical effect on popular interest in music was useful. In studying the total progress of the time this factor cannot be ignored.

Place must also be made for the rise of musical literature in the hands of critics, editors and authors, and of collections of musical books. Musical periodicals were by no means new to America in 1865 — Dwight's 'Journal of Music,' which began in 1852, went on till 1881, not to speak of many less or earlier undertakings — but they now began to grow more numerous and to exert more influence. The daily newspapers were quick to magnify the criticism — or, better, the reporting — of important concerts and operas, at least in the larger centers. It is significant that Hassard joined the staff of the New York 'Tribune' in 1866, setting a pattern that several others imitated or bettered soon afterward. By about 1880 the issue of books upon musical subjects had begun to make some show in the total annual output. Data concerning private libraries are not accessible, but it is worth noting that the New York Public Library contains the Drexel Collection, presented in 1888 to the Lenox Library, but catalogued in 1869–71; that the Newberry Library in Chicago began systematic acquisitions in 1888; that in 1894 the Boston Public Library received the Brown Collection; and that the Music Division of the Library of Congress in Washington was definitely constituted in 1897. In this connection, also, it should be recalled that the nucleus of the Brown Collection of Instruments, now in the Metropolitan Museum of Art in New York, was formed in 1884–89. All these undertakings imply an advancement of intellectual interest in music of which there were only rare and small indications prior to the Civil War.

It is instructive to observe how the decades after 1860 gradually bring into view musicians of American birth who presently gained real and permanent distinction as either performers, composers or conductors. That these represent on the whole a much higher standard and spirit than those of earlier periods is obvious. Most of them secured extended discipline abroad, usually in Germany. Their number, the variety of their interests and the scope of their professional influence rapidly increases, so that even before 1900 the phrase 'the American school' became perhaps prematurely frequent. Of those first appearing after 1860 the most conspicuous were Buck and Paine; of those after 1870, Chadwick, Foote, Gilchrist, and Gleason; of those after 1880, Mrs. Beach, Kelley, MacDowell and Parker; and of those after 1890, Converse, Gilbert, Hadley and Oldberg. Six of them have now died, but none of them before 1900. Much of the most creative work of all these dates from after that time. It is not therefore the bulk or the absolutely original quality of American composition before 1900 that arrests attention — except the remarkable work of MacDowell — but the fresh, ambitious, thoughtful and confident spirit that animates it. It all gives token of that striking animation and expansion in musical art which is the impressive characteristic of the period as a whole.

With reference to this and other features of the time a survey of the four chronological groups of names below is full of suggestion.

CHRONOLOGICAL REGISTER

5. The Civil War Decade, 1860–1870

*Agramonte, Emilio (Cuba, 1844– ?), trained in Spain (first as a lawyer) and France (pupil of Marmontel), came to New York in 1869, and was a skillful choral conductor and teacher of singing. He sought to extend the range of choral répertoire, to promote interest in American composers, and to advance the giving of opera in English. He composed somewhat, but without publishing.

Albani [Marie Emma Lajeunesse] (b. near Montreal, 1852) began singing in Albany in 1864, studied in Paris and Milan, made her début in opera in 1870, and continued active till 1906. See Vol. i. 59, and art.

Allen, Heman (St. Alban's, Vt., 1836– ?), finely educated in Philadelphia (from 1845 his father was professor in the University) and at Leipzig, was from 1862 a noted violinist, pianist and teacher in Philadelphia and from 1867 in Chicago, where till 1881 he was organist at the R. C. Cathedral. He was specially interested in Gregorian music. See Mathews, *Hundred Years*, pp. 300–2.

Allen, William Francis (Northboro, Mass., 1830–1889), in 1867–89 professor of ancient languages at the University of Wisconsin, was the compiler (with Charles P. Ware and Lucy McK. Garrison) of the first and largest book upon Negro music, *Slave-Songs of the United States*, 1867.

*Andres, Henry George (France, 1838– ?), after fine training at Paris, came to Cincinnati in 1860 and became a leader in developing musical taste by recitals and teaching. After about 1880 he was head of the piano-department at the College of Music.

*Arnold, Richard (Prussia, 1845–1918, New York), lived in New York as a boy, but studied in Leipzig, returning as superior violinist in 1867. See art.

Arthur, Alfred (Pittsburgh, 1844–1918, Lakewood, O.), educated at Boston, settled in 1871 at Cleveland as teacher, conductor and founder in 1885 of the Cleveland School of Music. See art.

Auerbach, Nannette, née Falk, a superior German pianist, in 1868–81 was teacher and concert-player in Baltimore, from 1871 at the Peabody Conservatory. See art.

Baker, Theodore (b. New York, 1851), about 1865 was organist at Concord, Mass., lived in Germany in 1874–90, and has since worked in New York as editor, translator and author. See art.

Bartlett, Homer Newton (b. Olive, N. Y., 1846–1920, Hoboken, N. J.), from about 1860 an important organist and composer in New York. See art.

Bartlett, Maro Loomis (b. Brownhelm, O., 1847), trained at Oberlin, conducted choral societies at Meadville, Pa., and Newark, N. J., engaged in public-school work in Newark and New York, with some concert-singing, and in 1880 moved to Chicago and thence to Des Moines, becoming head of the Musical College. Mus.D. of Drake University in 1889.

*Baur, Clara (Würtemberg, ? –1912, Cincinnati), founded the Cincinnati Conservatory in 1867.

Biddle, Horace Peters (Logan, O., 1811–1900), by profession a lawyer (finally in the Supreme Court of Indiana), published a book on *The Musical Scale*, Cincinnati, 1860, besides other essays on musical topics.

Bliss, Philip Paul (Clearfield Co., Pa., 1838–1876, Ashtabula, O., killed in accident), early a ' singing-school ' teacher, from about 1864 was employed by Root in Chicago and before 1870 became an evangelistic singer, in 1874 joining Maj. D. W. Whittle and traveling widely in the Central States. He was a pioneer in the ' Gospel hymn ' movement, a fertile composer of both hymns and tunes, and (with Sankey) edited Nos. 1–2 of the *Gospel Hymn* series, 1875–6. He had a remarkable voice and great magnetism, and hearing him led Moody to use solo-singing in his meetings.

*Boekelman, Bernardus (b. Holland, 1838), since 1866 has been prominent in New York as pianist, teacher and editor. See art.

Boise, Otis Bardwell (Oberlin, O., 1844–1912, Baltimore), after study at Leipzig and Berlin, from 1865 taught in Cleveland, from 1878 in New York, from 1888 in Berlin and from 1901 at the Peabody Conservatory, Baltimore. See art.

*Bonawitz, Johann Heinrich (Rhine Prov., 1839–1917, England), studied at Liège and New York (1852–61), toured as pianist and taught at Wiesbaden, Paris and London, in 1872–76 gave concerts and operas in New York and Philadelphia, then going to London. See art.

Bowman, Edward Morris (Barnard, Vt., 1848–1913, Brooklyn), from 1867 organist at St. Louis, with intervals abroad, from 1887 in Newark, from 1891 at Vassar College, and from 1895 in Brooklyn and New York. See art.

Buck, Dudley (Hartford, Conn., 1839–1909, Orange, N. J.), after study in Germany and France, was from 1862 organist at Hartford, from 1867 in Chicago, from 1872 in Boston, and from 1875 in Brooklyn. See Vol. i. 413–4, and art.

Candidus, William (Philadelphia, 1845– ?), originally a piano-maker with the Steinways, became an opera-tenor in New York, went abroad for study and became well known in Germany and England, after 1880 making several visits to America to sing at festivals.

*Carreño, Maria Teresa (Venezuela, 1853–1917, New York), began as a child-pianist in New York in 1862, was mostly abroad until 1875, and was then identified with New York. See Vol. i. 474, and art.

Cary, Annie Louise (b. Wayne, Me., 1842), a church-singer in Boston from about 1860, spent several years in Europe, where she appeared in opera from 1867, came to New York in 1870 and for about fifteen years was a favorite alto, there and abroad, especially in concert. In 1882 she married Charles C. M. Raymond, a New York banker, and lives at Norwalk, Conn. See Vol. i. 476.

Chase, Melville Warren (b. Minot, Me., 1842), graduated from Bates College and trained in Boston, since 1869 has been professor in Hillsdale College, Mich.

*Christiani, Adolf Friedrich (Hesse, 1836–1885, Elizabeth, N. J.), after a few years in London, came to America in the Civil War period and taught in Poughkeepsie, Pittsburgh, Cincinnati, New York and (from 1880) Elizabeth, where he conducted a school. He is known by his *Principles of Expression in Pianoforte-Playing*, 1886 (also in German).

Clarke, Hugh Archibald (b. near Toronto, 1839), pupil of his father, James P. Clarke (see sec. 4), came to Philadelphia about 1860, became an honored organist and conductor, and since 1875 has been professor in the University of Pennsylvania. See art.

Cole, Belle (Chautauqua, N. Y., 1845–1905, England), from about 1865 active as concert-contralto, living from 1888 in England, but making extensive tours throughout the world.

Colson, William Brewster (b. Rochester, 1846), has been organist and teacher for more than fifty years, since 1878 in Cleveland, giving many recitals there and elsewhere.

Converse, Charles Crozat (Warren, Mass., 1832–1918, Highwood, N. J.), after study at Leipzig and also preparing for the legal profession, practiced law in Erie, Pa., for some years, but engaged more and more in musical work. See art.

*Dolge, Alfred (b. Saxony, 1848), came to New York in 1866, worked in a piano-factory, in 1871 started a hammer-felting shop in Brooklyn, in 1874 removed to Dolgeville,

N. Y., adding the making of soundboards, inventing many new processes and machines and winning international recognition, and since 1903 has been located at Covina, Cal. (near Los Angeles). He has published *Pianos and their Makers*, 2 vols., 1911–13, giving invaluable data about American piano-making.

Emery, Stephen Albert (Paris, Me., 1841–1891, Boston), after study in Leipzig and Dresden, from 1864 taught in Portland and from 1867 in Boston. See art.

*Errani, Achille (Italy, 1823–1897, New York), pupil of Vaccai and for fifteen years a noted operatic tenor in Europe, came to America in 1860, sang in the United States, Cuba and Mexico, and settled in 1864 in New York as a leading teacher of singing.

Estey, Jacob (Hinsdale, N. H., 1814–1890, Brattleboro, Vt.), by trade a plumber, from 1850 invested his savings in a melodeon-making shop at Brattleboro, losing all by fire in 1857. In 1858 he took up the business himself, in 1860 secured Levi K. Fuller (1841–1896) as helper, and, with him and his own son Julius Estey (1845–1902), formed the Estey Organ Company, which had remarkable success, becoming the parent of many later concerns. In 1885 the Company added piano-making and in 1901 the making of pipe-organs. See Dolge, *Pianos and their Makers*, pp. 364–6.

*Falk, Louis (b. Germany, 1848), brought up in Pittsburgh and Rochester, where he was already organist in 1859, went to Chicago in 1861 as organist. In 1865–69 he studied at Homburg and Leipzig, returning to be a noted church- and concert-player and chief organ-teacher in the Chicago Musical College.

Fillmore, John Comfort (Franklin, Conn., 1843–1898, Franklin), graduated from Oberlin College, studied at Leipzig, in 1867–68 was head of the Oberlin Conservatory, in 1868–78 at Ripon College, from 1878 at Milwaukee, and from 1895 at Pomona College, becoming significant as theorist from 1883. See art.

*Florio, Caryl [William James Robjohn] (b. England, 1843), came to New York in youth, from before 1865 became known as singer and organist, and later as conductor, composer and critic at many different places. See art.

Franko, Sam (b. New Orleans, 1857), a precocious violinist, studying at Breslau and Berlin, and appearing there in 1867 and in New York in 1869. Since then, except for sojourns abroad, he has been active in concerts and teaching, mainly in New York. See art.

*Gilbert, Walter Bond (England, 1829–1910, England), after extensive and distinguished service in England as organist and composer, in 1869–99 was organist of Trinity Chapel, New York. See art.

*Glover, William Henry (England, 1819–1875, New York), long known in England as violinist, singer and composer of operas, orchestral and piano-pieces, songs, etc., and also as critic, lived from 1863 in New York. See Vol. i. 183.

*Gomes, Antonio Carlos (Brazil, 1839–1896, Brazil), after study in Milan, from 1861 became increasingly famous as an opera-writer, producing ten or more works in Italy and Brazil. In 1876 he contributed a hymn, 'Il Saluto del Brasile,' for the Centennial Exposition, and in 1892 a cantata, ' Colombo,' for the Columbus Festival. See Vol. ii. 200.

Gottschalk, L. Gaston (New Orleans, 1847–?), brother of the noted pianist (see sec. 4), after study at Paris, was concert-singer throughout the United States, studied further in Italy, and for many years was active in opera in many European capitals, visiting America occasionally. From 1886 for a few years he taught in the Chicago Musical College.

Hahn, Jacob H. (Philadelphia, 1847–1902, Detroit), was early trained in Chicago, where he became organist, teacher and concert-manager from before 1865. After study at Leipzig, from 1872 he taught in Detroit, founding the Detroit Conservatory in 1874 and soon bringing it to striking success.

Hassard, John Rose Green (New York, 1836–1888, New York), graduated from St. John's College, Fordham, developed into an expert journalist in New York, and from 1866 was on the staff of the ' Tribune,' serving as its chief musical critic and evincing ability and force as a writer, especially in advocacy of Wagner. He was Krehbiel's predecessor.

Hauk, Minnie (b. New York, 1852), pupil of Errani, began her career as operatic soprano in 1866 in Brooklyn, appearing often in America for thirty years. See Vol. ii. 341–2, and art.

*Hess, Willy (b. Baden, 1859), the distinguished violinist, now remembered as concertmaster of the Boston Symphony Orchestra in 1904–10, lived in America as a boy, appearing with the Thomas Orchestra in 1868–72. See Vol. ii. 390, and art.

Hill, Junius Welch (b. Hingham, Mass., 1840), after studying at Leipzig, from 1863 was organist in Boston, in 1884–97 at Wellesley College, then organist in Boston, and has lived lately in Los Angeles. See art.

*Hodges, Faustina Hasse (d. 1896, New York), and Hodges, John Sebastian Bach (England, 1830–1915, Baltimore), children of Edward Hodges (see sec. 3), both became active as organists and composers in the Civil War period. See Vol. ii. 414, and art.

Howard, George Henry (Norton, Mass., 1843–1917, Boston), studied in Boston and began teaching there in 1864, in 1869–70 studied in Leipzig and Berlin, and then taught again in Boston, London, Olivet, Mich., and from 1882 Boston again, where in 1891 he started a school for teachers.

Howe, Elias (Framingham, Mass.. 1820–1895, Boston), was founder in 1865 of a well-known firm in Boston dealing in fine violins, etc. He was one of the earliest (from 1871) to make collections of rare instruments.

Hutchings, George S. (Salem, Mass., 1835–1913, Boston), trained in Boston as an organ-maker in the Hooks' factory, in 1869 started a separate business with Willcox and others (becoming sole owner in 1884) and was in partnership with Votey in 1901–08. He was the inventor or first successful user of many mechanical features, such as improved electric action, movable console, etc.

*Inten, Ferdinand von (Saxony, 1848–1918, New York), after study at Leipzig, came to New York in 1868 as concert-pianist and ensemble-player. In chamber-concerts he was associated with Thomas and Damrosch, exerting a significant influence. He was also a fine teacher.

*Jehin-Prume, François (Belgium, 1839–1899, Montreal), highly trained as a violinist at Liège and Brussels, began European tours in 1855 and from 1863 appeared frequently not only in the United States and Canada, but in Cuba and Mexico. In 1887–96 he was teacher and organizer of chamber-music in Montreal. He wrote two violin-concertos, violin-pieces and songs. Ysaÿe was at one time his pupil.

Kellogg, Clara Louise (Sumterville, S. C., 1842–1916, New Hartford, Conn.), the brilliant operatic and concert-soprano, was educated in New York, made her début there in 1861 and in London in 1867, continuing active in England and America for about twenty-five years. See Vol. ii. 563, and art.

*Kunkel, Charles (Palatinate, 1840– ?), and ⫶Kunkel, Jacob (1846–1882, St. Louis), were brought to America in 1848, studied with their father, Thalberg and Gottschalk, and excelled in duet-playing. From 1868 they were publishers and dealers in St. Louis.

Lavallée, Calixa (Verchères, Que., 1842–1891, Boston), a precocious pianist and composer, was educated in Paris, where he remained many years, started a conservatory in Quebec, and about 1880 removed to Boston. See art.

Leavitt, W. J. D. (Boston, 1841– ?) after European study, from 1865 taught at Oneida, N. Y., and from 1870 taught in Boston, becoming organist at the Music Hall in 1875 and giving many recitals. He wrote the opera 'Mercedes,' several operettas, an organ-sonata and organ-pieces, etc.

*Leckner, Max (b. Prussia, 1842), well trained as a musician, came to America in 1860 and finally settled in Indianapolis, where for more than a half-century he has been a notable artistic force.

*Levy, Jules (b. 1840), appeared in England in 1860 as solo cornettist, came to New York in 1864, 1868 and 1875, joining Gilmore.

*Liebling, Emil (Silesia, 1851–1914, Chicago), educated at Berlin, came to America in 1867, teaching first in Kentucky, but, after study abroad in 1871–72, at Chicago, where he was honored as pianist, composer, and writer. See art. His brother Max Liebling (b. Silesia, 1845), also a noted concert-pianist, settled in New York.

*Listemann, Bernhard (Thuringia, 1841–1917, Chicago), having won distinction as

violinist in Germany, came to America in 1867 as a superior teacher, virtuoso and conductor at Boston, New York and Chicago. See art. His brother Fritz Listemann (Thuringia, 1839–1909, Boston), came with him and was almost equally prominent.

Main, Hubert Platt (b. Ridgefield, Conn., 1839), early interested in church-music and a tune-writer from 1855, after some years of clerical and editorial work in New York, in 1867 entered the employ of Bradbury, continued with his successors, Biglow & Main (his father, Sylvester Main, being the junior partner), and has since been identified with that firm. He has written much vocal music, secular and sacred, has edited many hymn-books, and is an expert on hymnody. See Hall, Gospel Song and Hymn Writers, pp. 140–6.

Marston, George W. (Sandwich, Mass., 1840–1901, Sandwich), pupil of Tufts, with some foreign study, was from 1860 organist in Portland, Me., becoming noted for his choir and as composer of sacred music, including the cantata ' David,' songs and part-songs.

*Marzo, Eduardo (b. Italy, 1852), came to New York as accompanist for various artists in 1867, was pianist in concert-companies, organist and fertile composer of church-music, songs, part-songs, operettas, etc., and editor of many works. See art.

Mathews, William Smith Babcock (New London, N. H., 1837–1912, Denver), began teaching in 1860 in the South, but in 1867 removed to Chicago, where he was active as teacher, editor and author. See art.

*Maylath, Heinrich (Austria, 1827–1883, New York), concert-pianist, came to New York in 1867 and made a fine reputation as player, teacher and composer for the piano.

*Messiter, Arthur Henry (England, 1834–1916, New York), in 1866–97 was organist of Trinity Church, New York, and historian in 1907 of its music.

*Mischka, Joseph (b. Bohemia, 1846), brought up in Buffalo, has long been active there as organist and choral conductor.

Mollenhauer, Emil (b. Brooklyn, 1855), now the honored conductor of the Handel and Haydn Society of Boston, appeared as a boy-violinist in 1864 and played with Thomas and Damrosch from 1872. See art.

Morgan, John Paul (Oberlin, O., 1841–1879, Oakland, Cal.), an organist before 1860 in Mt. Vernon, O., studied in New York and at Leipzig, in 1865 established the Oberlin Conservatory, in 1866–73 was organist and choral conductor in New York, but was forced to give up activity by ill-health, which, however, did not prevent further work in Oakland and San Francisco. Besides being a fine player he composed with ability.

*Napoleão, Arthur (b. Portugal, 1843), a precocious pianist from 1849, appearing at Lisbon, London, Berlin and Paris, in 1857–61 visited South America, the West Indies and the United States, and, after further concertizing in Europe, became in 1868 a music-dealer in Rio de Janeiro, publishing some piano-pieces and occasionally serving as conductor.

*Orth, John (b. Bavaria, 1850), brought as a child to America, was organist in early youth, studied in Boston and abroad, resumed teaching in Boston in 1875, becoming known as pianist, lecturer, composer and author. See art.

Paine, John Knowles (Portland, Me., 1839–1906, Cambridge, Mass.), having studied with Kotzschmar and at Berlin, from 1862 was instructor and from 1875 professor at Harvard and eminent as organist and versatile composer. See Vol. iii. 596–7, and art.

Parker, Fletcher Andrew (b. Lodi, O., 1842), trained at Boston and later at Stuttgart, in 1868–73 taught in Bloomington, Ill., in 1874 in London, and since 1875 has been identified with the University of Wisconsin as instructor and professor (emeritus since 1907), besides conducting the Madison Choral Union in 1890–1905. He has exercised a wide and fruitful influence throughout Wisconsin.

⋈ Pattison, John Nelson (Niagara Falls, N. Y., 1845–1905, New York), having studied at Berlin in 1859–61 and with Henselt in 1862, became favorably known as a pianist in Berlin, Paris, etc., and toured with Thalberg in Italy, from about 1870 traveled extensively in America with various artists, gave a striking series of recitals at the Centennial Exposition in 1876, and made his home in New York. He wrote a symphony, ' Niagara', for orchestra and band, a concert-overture, a piano-concerto or fantasia, and many piano-pieces.

*Pearce, Stephen Austen (England, 1836–1900, Jersey City), visited America in 1864 and from 1872 was teacher, organist and critic in New York. See art.

Pease, Alfred Humphries (Cleveland, 1838–1882, St. Louis), though without musical opportunities in youth, after six years' study in Germany from about 1865 was active throughout the United States as a popular pianist. He wrote a piano-concerto (1875) and some other works for orchestra, many transcriptions for four hands, and many songs.

Penfield, Smith Newell (Oberlin, O., 1837–1920, New York), after study at New York, Leipzig and Paris, from about 1869 taught in Rochester, then in Savannah, and from 1882 in New York. See art.

*Perabo, Johann Ernst (b. Hesse, 1845), brought to America in childhood, taught by his father and at Leipzig later, from 1865, after a year of concertizing, settled as concert-pianist and teacher in Boston. See art.

Perkins, Henry Southwick (Stockbridge, Vt., 1833–1914, Chicago), son of Orson Perkins (see sec. 3), trained in Boston, from 1861 taught in Chicago, often conducting ' conventions ' in various places, from 1867 was in Iowa City, in the State University two years, and director of the Academy of Music five years, from 1870 at Leavenworth, Kan., for five years conducting a summer-school, and

after 1872 made his home in Chicago, where in 1891 he established the National College of Music, continuing at its head till his death. He was one of the organizers of the Music Teachers' National Association in 1876, and energetically active in its affairs. He compiled about thirty song-books.

Perkins, Julius Edson (Stockbridge, Vt., 1845–1875, England), brother of the above, studied in Boston, Paris and Italy, appeared as operatic bass in 1868 in Italy and in 1874 in England, and in that year, with his wife, née Marie Roze, made a visit to America. Though but thirty at death, he had already gained high repute in opera and oratorio.

Perkins, William Oscar (Stockbridge, Vt., 1831–1902, Boston), elder brother of the two preceding, after study in London and Milan, settled in Boston as teacher and leader of ' conventions.' He was editor of some forty song-books, sacred and secular.

Petersilea, Carlyle (Boston, 1844–1903, near Los Angeles), was carefully instructed by his father and at Leipzig. After touring in Germany as pianist, from 1866 he taught in Boston, establishing in 1871 his own Academy, joined the New England Conservatory in 1886 and removed to California in 1892. He was gifted as performer and teacher.

Presser, Theodore (b. Pittsburgh, 1848), began teaching in Ohio in 1869, later spending two years in foreign study. In 1883 he started publishing ' The Etude ' at Lynch-burg, Va., which he transferred in 1884 to Philadelphia, rapidly building up there an extensive publishing business. See art.

*Remmertz, Franz (Rhine Prov., 1845 – ?) came to New York in 1869 and for many years was much in request as a concert-bass of the ' robust ' order.

Rice, Fenelon B. (Greensburg, O., 1841–1901, Oberlin), studied in Boston and Leipzig, in 1863–67 was music-director at Hillsdale College in Michigan, and from 1871 was head of the Oberlin Conservatory. See art.

*Ronconi, Giorgio (Italy, 1810–1890, Spain), son of Domenico Ronconi of Milan and Munich, came to New York in 1867 and for several years was a respected singing-teacher.

Root, Frederick Woodman (Boston, 1846–1916, Chicago), was organist in Chicago from 1863, and, after foreign study in 1869–70, became a leading teacher of singing there. See Vol. iv. 139, and art.

*Rosewald, Julie, née Eichberg (b. Hesse, 1850), came to America in 1866, married I. H. Rosewald, a violinist and conductor, and appeared successfully in concert, then studied at Frankfort, returning to America with Abt. In 1875–84 she sang in opera both here and abroad, and then removed to San Francisco.

*Schmidt, Arthur P. (b. Schleswig, 1846), came to Boston in 1866 as clerk for Russell & Co., and since 1876 has been a prominent music-publisher, issuing a large number of works by American composers.

*Seiler, Emma (Bavaria, 1821– ?) pupil of Wieck and Helmholtz and an experienced investigator of the voice, came to Philadelphia in 1866 as vocal teacher. She published *Altes und Neues über die Ausbildung des Gesangorgans*, 1861, *The Voice in Singing*, 1869, and *The Voice in Speaking*, 1875. Her observations gave her wide reputation among scientists.

Seward, Theodore Frelinghuysen (Florida, N. Y., 1835–1902, Orange, N. J.), self-educated except for courses in the Mason-Root Normal Institute, was an organist and teacher in New London, Conn., and in Rochester before 1860, went to New York in 1862, which remained his headquarters for editorial and literary work, though from about 1870 he was music-supervisor at Orange, N. J., and also director for the ' Jubilee Singers ' of Fisk University in tours at home and abroad. While visiting England in 1869 he was impressed with the Tonic Sol-Fa system of teaching and became its advocate and representative in America. He published many song-books for schools and from 1864 edited ' The Musical Pioneer ', from 1867 ' The Musical Gazette,' from 1881 ' The Tonic Sol-Fa Advocate,' and from 1886 ' Musical Reform.'

Shepard, Thomas Griffin (Madison, Conn., 1848–1905, Brooklyn), pupil of G. W. and J. P. Morgan, was organist in New Haven from 1865 and for different periods conductor of choral societies, besides critical writing. He published the comic opera ' Pennikeese,' a Christmas cantata, and much choir-music.

*Singer, Otto (Saxony, 1833–1894, New York), after teaching in Leipzig and Dresden, from 1867 was pianist and teacher in New York, removing in 1873 to Cincinnati. See art.

Smith, Dexter (Peabody, Mass., 1839–1909, Boston), from 1865 was editor in Boston of several musical periodicals, chief of which was Ditson's ' Monthly Musical Record,' started in 1878. He was also a facile writer of verse.

Squier, J. B. (Ohio, 1838–1912, Boston), after the Civil War noted as one of the best American violin-makers, with headquarters at Boston. See *Violinist's Guide* (1916), p. 39.

Stanley, Albert Augustus (b. Manville, R. I., 1851), studied at Providence and Leipzig, from 1876 was organist at Providence, and since 1888 has been professor and conductor at the University of Michigan. See art.

Sterling, Antoinette (Sterlingville, N. Y., 1850–1904, England), appeared in concert in 1868, studied in Germany and England, becoming an eminent contralto. She lived mainly in England. See Vol. iv. 693–4.

Thayer, Whitney Eugene (Mendon, Mass., 1838–1889, Burlington, Vt.), from 1862 was organist in Boston, studied in Germany in 1865–6, and was then engaged in touring, conducting and editing. From 1881 he was organist in New York. See art.

Thoms, William M. (New York, 1852–1913, New York), was connected with Watson's ' American Art Journal ' from 1867, becoming editor in 1875. In 1870–71 he edited a musical daily, ' The Journal of the Day,' and in 1873–74 ' The Musical Monthly,' and published an extensive work, *The World of Art*, 1877–78, largely concerned with musicians. He was constantly active as musical critic.

Tracy, James Madison (b. Bath, N. H., 1839), after study at Leipzig and Weimar, from 1861 taught in Rochester, from 1866 in Boston, for many years in the New England Conservatory, then at Des Moines, and is now at Denver, where he founded the Liszt School of Music. He has published a book on Harmony, *Three Years of Student-Life in Germany*, and two musical novels.

Tremaine, William B. (1868–1907, New York), took up piano-making in 1868, became from 1878 one of the leading promoters of automatic organs and pianos, forming companies that led to the present Æolian Company, of which H. B. Tremaine (b. Brooklyn, 1866), is president. See Dolge, pp. 327–33.

Upton, George Putnam (Roxbury, Mass., 1835–1919, Chicago), graduated from Brown University in 1854, entered editorial work in 1855, and from 1861 was in Chicago, becoming a conspicuous critic and author. See art.

Veazie, George Augustus (Boston, 1835–1915, Chelsea, Mass.), in 1869–1903 was music-supervisor in the Chelsea schools, promoting improved methods, besides in 1888–1902 teaching in the New England Conservatory.

Walter, George William (New York, 1851–1911, Washington), a precocious organist, studied with Paine and S. P. Warren, and moved from New York to Washington in 1869, where he established a reputation for unusual skill in improvisation, registration, etc., besides gathering an exceptional library. Mus.D. of Columbian University in 1892.

Warren, Samuel Prowse (Montreal, 1841–1915, New York), son of S. R. Warren (see sec. 3), after study in Germany, was from 1866 a distinguished organist in New York, in 1868–94 at Grace Church, and from 1895 at East Orange, N. J. See art.

Weil, Oscar (b. Columbia Co., N. Y., 1840), after study at Leipzig and Paris, served gallantly in the Civil War, removed to San Francisco in 1868 and has been largely occupied with composition and criticism. Besides piano-pieces and songs, he wrote the operas ' Suzette ' and ' The War-Time Wedding ' and three operettas.

*Welte, Emil (b. Baden, 1841), son of Michael Welte, maker of automatic organs at Voehrenbach, came to New York in 1865 to set up a branch of the business. He invented improvements in the use of paper-rolls.

Wheeler, Lyman Warren (Swampscott, Mass., 1837–1900, Columbus), after experience as leader of ' conventions,' studied extensively in England and Italy, appearing as concert and operatic tenor, and from 1863 was in Boston as soloist and teacher, from 1870 in the New England Conservatory.

Whitney, Samuel Brenton (Woodstock, Vt., 1842–1914, Brattleboro, Vt.), began organ-playing in 1855, studied with Paine, after short engagements elsewhere, was from 1871 at the Church of the Advent, Boston, celebrated as player and choir-trainer. See art.

Wilkins, Herve D. (Italy, N. Y., 1848–1913, Rochester), organist at Auburn, N. Y., from 1866, graduated at the University of Rochester, studied in Berlin, and was then well known in Rochester as church- and concert-organist.

*Woolf, Benjamin Edward (England, 1836–1901, Boston), brought to America as a child, studied in New York, served as theater-conductor in Boston, Philadelphia and New Orleans, and from 1870 was musical critic for various Boston papers. He wrote several comic operas, such as ' Westward, Ho!' (1894), an overture to ' A Comedy of Errors,' and considerable orchestral and chamber-music.

*Zeckwer, Richard (b. Prussia, 1850), trained as pianist at Leipzig, came to Philadel-phia in 1869 as organist and teacher in the Musical Academy, becoming head of the latter in 1876. See art.

*Ziegfeld, Florenz (b. Oldenburg, 1841), came first to New York in 1856, moving in 1863 to Chicago, where in 1867 he opened the first of the series of schools of which the present Musical College is the successor. Of this he is now president-emeritus.

*Ziehn, Bernhard (Thuringia, 1845–1912, Chicago), came to Chicago in 1868 as teacher in the Lutheran Seminary, and after 1871 turned to general instruction, becoming emi-nent as a theorist. See art.

*Zielinski, Jaroslaw de (b. Galicia, 1847), came to America in 1864, served in the Civil War, from 1865 was concert-pianist and teacher in New York, later in Grand Rapids, Mich., and Detroit, from 1888 in Buffalo, and since 1910 in Los Angeles, where he founded a Trio Club and is head of a music-school. Besides being an accomplished player, he has composed effectively for the piano and written articles on Russian and Polish music.

6. The Decade after the Civil War — 1870-1880

Abbott, Emma (Chicago, 1850–1891, Salt Lake City), at first self-trained, but from 1870 studying in New York, Milan and Paris, became known as an effective soprano in con-cert and opera. See art.

*Adamowski, Timothée (b. Poland, 1858), came to America in 1879, at first as traveling violinist, but from 1884 located at Boston. See art.

Aiken, Walter H. (b. Cincinnati, 1856), son of Charles Aiken (see sec. 4), followed his father in 1879 in the Cincinnati schools, becoming superintendent in 1900.

Alden, John Carver (b. Boston, 1852), studied in Boston and Leipzig, and has taught in the New England Conservatory, in South Carolina and lately near Boston. See art.

*Allen, Charles N. (England, 1837–1903, Boston), in 1871 came to Boston as violinist in ensemble-groups and teacher. See art.

Allen, Nathan Hale (b. Marion, Mass., 1848), after study at Berlin, from 1870 organist at Hartford, Conn., and in 1906–11 at Wor-cester, is now teaching in Hartford. See art.

Andrews, George Whitfield (b. Wayne, O., 1861), trained at Oberlin, Leipzig, Munich and Paris, began as organist in 1877 and since 1882 has been identified with Oberlin as emi-nent player, conductor and teacher. See art.

Andrews, J. Warren (b. Lynn, Mass., 1860), an organist since 1872, located from 1879 at Newport, then at Cambridge and Minne-apolis, and since 1898 in New York. See art.

Apthorp, William Foster (Boston, 1848–1913, Switzerland), graduated from Harvard in 1869, taught for years in Boston, but was best known as critic and author. See art.

Aronson, Rudolph (New York, 1856–1919, New York), studied in Berlin and Paris, re-turning to New York as promoter of popular concerts after the model of Johann Strauss. He projected the Metropolitan Concert Hall and the Casino, and composed considerable orchestral music. He published Theatrical and Musical Memoirs, 1913.

Baldwin, Samuel Atkinson (b. Lake City, Minn., 1862), organist from 1877, studied extensively abroad, was in Chicago from 1885, in St. Paul and Minneapolis from 1889, and has been an eminent recitalist in New York since 1895. See art.

Bartlett, James Carroll (b. Harmony, Me., 1850), trained as tenor in Boston and London, in 1875–76 toured with Camilla Urso, later with the actors Booth and Barrett, and has been organist, teacher and song-composer in Boston and Worcester.

Batchelder, John C. (b. Topsham, Vt., 1852), after four years' study at Berlin, has been an able organist in Detroit, teacher in the Detroit Conservatory and recitalist elsewhere.

Beel, Sigmund (b. California, 1863), a boy-violinist at Oakland in 1872, studied in Berlin and Brussels, toured extensively in England and on the Continent, and recently has been concertmaster of the Los Angeles Orchestra, but lives now in San Francisco.

Benbow, William (b. Columbus, O., 1865), graduated from Ohio State University, after study in Philadelphia and England, has served as organist at various places, chiefly Colum-bus, Reading, Pa., and (since 1913) Buffalo.

*Benson, Harry (b. England, 1848), came to America in youth and was partly trained in Boston, where he has taught in the New Eng-land Conservatory and since 1891 in the Train-ing School for Music. He has also been or-ganist, choral conductor and a Tonic Sol-Fa advocate.

*Bidez, L. Aloys (b. Belgium, 1847), taught in America from 1876 till 1904, when he re-turned to Belgium. He has composed an operetta, a piano-concerto, an orchestral monody, etc., and is the author of *The Art of Fingering* (1877).

Biedermann, Edward Julius (b. Milwaukee, 1849), son of A. J. Biedermann (see sec. 4), after study in Germany, since 1864 has been organist in New York, chiefly at St. Mary's. He has composed masses and other vocal music. Mus.D. of Beaver College in 1906.

Bird, Arthur (b. Cambridge, Mass., 1856), studied in Berlin, from 1877 was organist and teacher in Nova Scotia and since 1881 has lived in Berlin as composer. See Vol. i. 328-9, and art.

Bischoff, John W. (Chicago, 1850-1909, Washington), trained at the Wisconsin Institute for the Blind and in London, from 1875 was organist, singing-teacher and song-writer at Washington.

*Blumenschein, William Leonard (Germany, 1849-1916, Dayton, O.), brought to Pittsburgh in childhood, studied at Leipzig, from 1876 was choral conductor in Portsmouth, O., from 1881 of the Dayton Philharmonic Society and organist, and in 1891-96 chorus-master of the Cincinnati Festivals. He published over 100 effective works for piano and voice.

Boott, Francis (Boston, 1813-1904, Boston), graduated from Harvard in 1831, lived in Italy until about 1875, then returning to Cambridge. Though nominally an amateur, he composed a Grand Mass, a Te Deum, a Miserere a cappella, a cantata, 'The Song of Zechariah,' anthems, sacred and secular songs, and several string-quartets. He left $10,000 to establish a prize at Harvard for the best 4-part vocal work written by a Harvard man.

*Brandt, Hermann (Hamburg, 1842- ?), a pupil of David and from 1868 concert-master in Prague, came to New York in 1873 as concertmaster in the Thomas Orchestra and later in the Philharmonic Society.

*Bretherick, Henry (b. England, 1849), came to America in youth, receiving part of his training here, and has been organist from 1872 in Jacksonville, Ill., from 1885 in Quincy, Ill., and since 1895 in San Francisco.

Brewer, John Hyatt (b. Brooklyn, 1856), since 1871 has been active and successful in Brooklyn as organist and conductor. See art.

Cady, Calvin Brainerd (b. Barry, Ill., 1851), educated at Oberlin and Leipzig, from 1874 taught at Oberlin, from 1880 at the University of Michigan, moving thence to Chicago, Boston, New York and Portland, Ore. See art.

*Campanini, Italo (Italy, 1846-1896, Italy), operatic tenor, came to America first in 1873 and from about 1880 lived in New York, with frequent sojourns elsewhere. For a time his popularity was supreme. See Vol. i. 450, and Krehbiel, *Chapters of Opera*, pp. 81-2, etc.

*Capoul, Joseph Amédée Victor (b. France, 1839), already an established opera-tenor, made the first of several visits to America in 1873. In 1892-97 he taught at the National Conservatory in New York. See Vol. i. 460-1, and art.

Chadwick, George Whitefield (b. Lowell, Mass., 1854), studied at Boston, Leipzig and Munich, in 1876-77 taught at Olivet College and since 1880 has been identified with Boston as organist, teacher and from 1897 director of the New England Conservatory, and eminent composer. See Vol. i. 494-5, and art.

Chaffin, Lucien Gates (b. Worcester, 1846), graduated from Brown University in 1867, for a time gave himself to educational work in Southboro, Mass., Buffalo and Hobart College, but also qualified as a concert-organist and critic. Since 1884 he has been in New York, furthering the Manuscript Society, the People's Symphony Concerts, etc. His compositions include Psalm 23, a cantata, 'Holy Night,' anthems, many organ-pieces, songs, etc.

Chapman, William Rogers (b. Hanover, Mass., 1855), has been choral conductor since 1876, founding the Apollo and Rubinstein Clubs in New York and since 1903 having charge of the annual Maine Festivals at Portland and Bangor.

Chittenden, Kate Sara (b. Hamilton, Ont., 1856), began teaching before 1880 at Hellmuth College, London, Ont., coming thence to New York to be organist and director of large music-schools. See art.

Clark, Melville (b. Oneida Co., N. Y., ?), began as an organ-maker at Oakland, Cal., in 1875, removing in 1880 to Chicago, where from 1894 he turned to making pianos. He was one of the first (1901) to develop the player-piano, the extended paper-roll and devices for recording actual performance, holding numerous important patents.

Cogswell, Hamlin Elisha (b. Silverlake, Pa., 1852), began as band-leader and choirmaster at Scranton in 1876 and later at Elmira. Since 1890 he has been prominent in public-school music, especially in Pennsylvania State Normal Schools and since 1915 at Washington.

Cole, Samuel Winkley (b. Meriden, N. H., 1848), began teaching at Portsmouth, N. H., in 1877, since 1882 has been influential in public-school music in Boston, teaching in the New England Conservatory, conducting the People's Choral Union, and publishing several text-books on sight-singing.

*Conried, Heinrich (Austria, 1855-1909, Austria), in 1877-1908 director or manager of operatic and theatrical enterprises, mostly in New York, the last five years at the Metropolitan Opera House. See art.

Corey, Newton John (b. Hillsdale, Mich., 1861), began organ-playing before 1880, studied at Boston, and since 1891 has been organist at Detroit, with much lecturing upon music with varied illustration and writing for musical papers. He has been manager of the Detroit Orchestral Association. Mus.D. of Hillsdale College in 1910.

Crane, Julia Ettie (b. Potsdam, N. Y., 1855), since 1877 prominent in public-school music, first at Shippensburg, Pa., and since 1884 at Potsdam, N. Y., where her Normal Institute has become notable for training teachers and supervisors. She is the author of a *Manual for Teachers of School Music.*

*Damrosch, Leopold** (Prussian Poland, 1832–1885, New York), the distinguished violinist, conductor and composer, came to New York in 1871 as leader of the Arion Society, later of the Oratorio and Symphony Societies, and finally of German opera. See Vol. i. 656, and art.

Dana, William Henry (Warren, O., 1846–1916, Warren), after study at Berlin, established a Musical Institute at Warren, O., which has remained successful ever since. He was the author of text-books on Harmony (1873, '84), Orchestration and Band-Instrumentation (1875, '76).

Dannreuther, Gustav (b. Cincinnati, 1853), was trained in Berlin and worked first at London, returned to America in 1877 and has been prominent at Boston, Buffalo and New York as violinist and teacher. He is the brother of Edward George Dannreuther (1844–1905), for whom see Vol. i. 661–2. See art.

Davis, Jessie, née Bartlett (b. Morris, Ill., 1860–1905, Crown Point, Ind.), after study in Chicago and New York, from 1879 was contralto in light opera and from 1888 with the Bostonians.

Dickinson, Edward (b. West Springfield, Mass., 1853), graduated from Amherst College in 1876, studied at Boston and Berlin, from 1872 was organist at Springfield, Mass., from 1879 at Elmira, N. Y., and since 1893 has been professor at the Oberlin Conservatory and distinguished as an author. See art.

*Doenhoff, Helene von,** née Spuller (b. Hungary, 1861), came to America in 1874 and developed into a favorite operatic contralto, associated with many strong companies and in 1893 organizing her own. Recently she has taught in New York.

Doerner, Armin W. (b. Marietta, O., 1851), after study at Berlin, Stuttgart and Paris, appeared as pianist at Cincinnati in 1877, in 1878–97 was teacher in the College of Music there and later head of his own school, and in 1905 established a school at Denver.

Dressler, Louis Raphael (b. New York, 1861), has been an organist in New York since 1877, for many years at All Souls', besides being choral conductor, accompanist and on the editorial staff of C. H. Ditson & Co.

*Dulcken, Ferdinand Quentin** (England, 1837–1902, New York), son of Luise Dulcken (see Vol. i. 740), was developed as a pianist at Leipzig, then professor at the Warsaw Conservatory and for a time at Paris, besides touring widely. In 1876 he came to America, touring with eminent artists, and settled in New York, where he taught in the National Conservatory. His works included the opera ' Wieslav,' a mass, cantatas, piano-pieces, etc.

Dunham, Henry Morton (b. Brockton, Mass., 1853), trained in Boston, has been organist since 1873, first at Brockton and from

1883 in Boston, besides since 1878 teaching in the New England Conservatory. See art.

Eddy, Hiram Clarence (b. Greenfield, Mass., 1851), after study at home and in Berlin, from 1874 was church- and concert-organist in Chicago, with extensive tours in America and abroad. See Vol. i. 768, and art.

Eddy, Sara, née Hershey (b. Lancaster Co., Pa., 1852), after study at Berlin, Milan and London, was singer and teacher in New York from 1871, then in Pittsburgh and from 1875 in Chicago, where, with Mathews, she established a strong school, a leading teacher being Clarence Eddy, whom she married in 1879.

Elson, Louis Charles (Boston, 1848–1920, Boston), trained in Boston and Leipzig, was prominent in Boston from 1876 as critic, editor, lecturer and author, besides teaching from 1881 in the New England Conservatory. See art.

*Ende, Amelia von,** née Kremper (b. Poland, 1856), came in youth to America, studied in Milwaukee, Chicago and also Warsaw, has been a pianist and teacher since 1874, first at Milwaukee, from 1879 in Chicago, and from 1897 in New York. She has been correspondent of musical papers in America and Europe, has written a monograph on New York (Berlin, 1909), and has composed songs and piano-pieces. In 1876 she married Heinrich von Ende.

*Fanciulli, Francesco** (Italy, 1853–1915, New York), trained at Florence and opera-conductor there, came to New York as organist and teacher in 1876, in 1893 followed Sousa as leader of the Marine Band in Washington, and from 1898 was leader of bands in New York. He wrote the operas ' Gabriele de Montgomery,' ' Priscilla ' and ' Melinche,' and two comic operettas.

Farnsworth, Charles Hubert (b. Turkey, 1859, of American parents), studied mostly at Worcester, from 1876 was organist and teacher there, from 1888 professor in the University of Colorado, and since 1901 at Teachers College in New York. See art.

Fay, Amy (b. Bayou Goula, Miss., 1844), after extended study in Berlin and Weimar, appeared as concert-pianist in 1876 in New York and toured widely for a time, and settled in New York as lecturer and recitalist, specializing as teacher of the Deppe method of instruction. She is best known as the author of *Music-Study in Germany,* 1881 (20th ed., 1912, and also in French and German).

Fisher, Edward (Jamaica, Vt., 1848–1913, Toronto), trained in Boston, from 1875 taught in Ottawa and from 1879 in Toronto, where in 1886 he established the Toronto Conservatory, which he developed as director with remarkable success. See art.

Flagler, Isaac Van Vleck (Albany, 1848–1909, Auburn, N. Y.), trained as organist at Albany and Paris, after brief service at Poughkeepsie and Albany, was eight years in Chicago, removing before 1880 to Auburn. In 1879–84 he was instructor at Syracuse University, later at Cornell University and at the Utica Conservatory. For twenty years he gave recitals and lectures at Chautauqua. He edited collections of organ-music, choir-music and hymns, and wrote some organ-pieces.

*Floersheim, Otto (Rhine Prov., 1853–1917, Switzerland), came to New York in 1875 and in 1880–94 was editor of ' The Musical Courier,' returning then to Berlin.

Foerster, Adolph Martin (b. Pittsburgh, 1854), after training at Leipzig, since 1876 has been a teacher of singing and piano at Pittsburgh and a fertile composer. See art.

Foote, Arthur William (b. Salem, Mass., 1853), graduated from Harvard in 1874, was trained in Boston, and has been an eminent piano-teacher there since 1876, organist of the First Unitarian Church in 1878–1910, and a noted pianist and composer. See Vol. ii. 71, and art.

Franko, Nahan (b. New Orleans, 1861), educated in Berlin, as boy-violinist toured with Patti in 1869, came to New York about 1875 to play in the Metropolitan Orchestra, becoming concertmaster in 1883 and conductor in 1905–07, and then organized his own orchestra for private occasions.

*Franosch, Adolph (Rhine Prov., 1830–1880, New York), an opera-bass of experience, came to New York in 1870 and sang there and on tour for ten years.

Furlong, Atherton Bernard (b. Greenwood, Me., 1849), after study in Boston and abroad, from 1870 was concert-tenor in Boston, from 1872 in Brooklyn, from 1880 in England, France and Germany with oratorio societies, and since 1888 has been head of the College of Vocal Art, Toronto. He has composed songs, published a novel and poems, and exhibited animal and landscape paintings.

*Fursch-Madi, Emmy (France, 1847–1894, Warrenville, N. J.), well known in Europe as a notable operatic soprano, first came to New York in 1874 and for twenty years was frequently heard there as well as abroad. She was a broad and conscientious artist, exerting a strong and inspiring influence.

*Gantvoort, Arnold Johann (b. Holland, 1857), came to America in 1876, taught in various colleges in Kentucky and Ohio, and from 1894 was head of public-school work in the Cincinnati College of Music, becoming its manager in 1901–19. He has published *Familiar Talks on the History of Music*, 1913, and a series of readers for public-school use.

Gilchrist, William Wallace (Jersey City, 1846–1916, Easton, Pa.), after a year at Cincinnati, was from 1873 identified with Philadelphia as organist, conductor and gifted composer. See art.

Gleason, Frederick Grant (Middletown, Conn., 1848–1903, Chicago), trained chiefly at Leipzig, Berlin and London, was organist from 1875 at Hartford, Conn., removing in 1877 to Chicago and becoming prominent as teacher, composer and critic. See Vol. ii. 177,

and art. His wife, Grace Gleason, née Hiltz (b. 1854?), was a superior soprano.

*Goepfart, Christian Heinrich (Saxony, 1835–1890, Baltimore), previously organist at Weimar, was from 1873 active in Baltimore as organist and conductor of choral societies.

Goetschius, Percy (b. Paterson, N. J., 1853), was trained at Stuttgart, where from 1876 he was teacher and critic, from 1890 was professor at Syracuse University, from 1892 organist and teacher in Boston, and since 1905 has taught at the Institute of Musical Art, New York. See art.

Goodrich, Alfred John (Chilo, O., 1847–1920, France), began teaching harmony about 1870 in New York, from 1876 at Fort Wayne, Ind., Chicago, Abingdon, Va., and St. Louis, besides living in 1909–15 in Paris. See art.

*Grau, Maurice (Moravia, 1849–1907, France), brought up as a child in New York, in 1872–1903 was a foremost manager of concerts and opera. See art.

Grout, Charles Henry (b. Worcester, 1854), trained in Boston and Berlin, has been organist in Worcester since 1873, both in Central Church and for the annual Festivals.

Hale, Philip (b. Norwich, Vt., 1854), graduated from Yale in 1876 (also qualified as lawyer), was from 1879 organist in Albany, Troy and Roxbury, Mass., with study at Berlin, Munich and Paris, and since 1889 has been a distinguished critic in Boston. See art.

*Hamerik, Asger (b. Denmark, 1843), a gifted composer, was in 1871–1898 director of the Peabody Conservatory in Baltimore and conductor of the Peabody Orchestra, returning then to Copenhagen. See Vol. ii. 277–8, and art.

Hanchett, Henry Granger (Syracuse, 1853–1918, Siasconset, Mass.), trained as both pianist and physician, made his début in concert in 1879 in New York, where he was long active as teacher and lecturer, from 1907 in Washington and from 1913 at Brenau College in Georgia. See art.

Hastreiter, Hélène (b. Louisville, 1858), began as choir-singer in 1870 at Chicago, and after careful study developed into a competent operatic contralto, reappearing in Chicago in 1883. She was then prominent in Italy and at Paris. See Vol. ii. 341, and art.

Hattstaedt, John James (b. Monroe, Mich., 1851), after study in Boston and in Germany, began teaching in 1872 at Detroit and St. Louis, was from 1875 in the Chicago Musical College, and in 1886 founded the American Conservatory.

Hawley, Charles Beach (Brookfield, Mass., 1858–1915, Redbank, N. J.), was trained in New York, where from 1876 he was favorably known as bass-soloist, organist and song-composer. In 1885 he joined Herbert W. Greene in establishing the Metropolitan Conservatory.

Heath, Wilbur F. (Corinth, Vt., 1843–1915, Danville, Ill.), a band-master in the Civil War, studied in Boston, from about 1870 entered public-school work in Iowa, from 1873 was music-supervisor at Fort Wayne, Ind., Osh-kosh, Wis., and Ottawa, Ill. He was active in the Music Teachers' National Association.

Heckscher, Céleste DuLongpré, née Massey (b. Philadephia, 1860), began composing when only a child, studied in Philadelphia and mar-ried there. See art.

*Heinrich, Max (Saxony, 1853–1916, New York), came to Philadelphia in 1873 as singer and teacher, from 1876 taught in Alabama, from 1882 in New York, from 1888 in London, from 1894 in Chicago, from 1903 in Boston, and from 1910 again in New York, everywhere noted as a baritone of fine ability. See art.

*Hennig, Rudolph (Germany, 1845– ? , a graduate at Leipzig, was in 1872–79 leading 'cellist in the Thomas Orchestra and later in the Mendelssohn Quintette Club. In 1869 he was one of the founders of the Philadelphia Musical Academy.

Henschel, Lillian June, née Bailey (Colum-bus, O., 1860–1901, England), trained in Bos-ton, made her début as soprano in 1876, then studied further in Paris and London, married Georg Henschel in 1881 and was much associated with him in concerts.

Hensel, Octavia [Mrs. G. A. Fonda] (1837–1897), published *The Life and Letters of L. M. Gottschalk,* Boston, 1870, and other books.

Heritage, Richard Abraham (b. Mont-pelier, O., 1853), studied in Chicago, from 1877 was dean of the music-school of Valparaiso University, from 1895 at Willamette Uni-versity in Oregon, and since 1905 head of the Musical College at Spokane, Wash. He is known as bass-soloist and choral conductor.

*Herman, Reinhold Ludwig (b. Prussia, 1849), singer, pianist and composer, in 1871–78 worked in New York, and, after being head of the Stern Conservatory in Berlin, from 1881 was again in New York, where from 1884 he conducted the Liedertafel and from 1887 was instructor in music at Union Theological Seminary, removing in 1898 to Boston as leader of the Handel and Haydn Society, and in 1900 returning to Berlin. For list of works, see Baker, *Dict. of Musicians,* p. 389.

Heyman, Henry (b. Oakland, Cal., 1855), studied at Leipzig, from 1877 was violinist in San Francisco, with tours on the Pacific Coast and to Hawaii, and has been influential in promoting orchestral and chamber-con-certs. See art.

*Hille, Gustav (b. Saxony, 1851), a good violinist, came to America in 1879 to join the Mendelssohn Quintette Club, from 1880 taught at the Philadelphia Musical Academy, in 1899, with Leefson, established a separate school, and in 1910 returned to Germany. For works, see Baker, *Dict. of Musicians,* p. 400.

*Hinrichs, Gustav (b. Mecklenburg, 1850), was from 1870 teacher and conductor in San Francisco, in 1885–86 assistant of Thomas in the American Opera Company, for ten years manager and conductor of his own organiza-tion, with headquarters at Philadelphia, in

1899–1906 conductor at Columbia University, and in 1903–08 at the Metropolitan Opera House. He directed the first American per-formance of ' Cavalleria ' (1891), ' I Pagliacci ' (1893) and ' Manon Lescaut ' (1894). He composed two operas, ' Die vierjährige Posten ' (1877) and ' Onti-Ora ' (1891), a symphonic suite, and some vocal works.

Holden, Albert James (Boston, 1841–1916, Longmeadow, Mass.), from about 1870 was organist in prominent New York churches, composer of much church-music, and compiler of collections of choral music.

*Holst, Edvard (Denmark, 1843–1899, New York), came to New York about 1874, chiefly as dancer and play-writer, but also brought out much comedy-music, including the operetta ' Our Flats ' (1897), band-music, songs, etc.

*Horsley, Charles Edward (England, 1822–1876, New York), the competent English organist, composer and critic, spent his last years in New York. See Vol. ii. 435–6.

*Jacobsohn, Simon E. (Russia, 1839–1902, Chicago), having studied at Riga and Leipzig and served as concertmaster at Bremen from 1860, took the same post under Thomas in 1872, from 1878 was violin-teacher in the Cincinnati College of Music and later in the Chicago Musical College.

Jordan, Jules (b. Willimantic, Conn., 1850), trained as concert-tenor in Boston, London and Paris, has worked since 1870 in Providence, where he is eminent as teacher, conductor and vocal composer. See art.

*Joseffy, Raphael (Hungary, 1852–1915, New York), already noted as a remarkable pianist, came to New York in 1879, immedi-ately becoming a foremost figure. See Vol. ii. 545–6, and art.

*Jung, J. B. (b. Switzerland, 1848), a Roman Catholic priest, trained at Coire, came to America in 1870, settling first in Ohio, and was active in the American branch of the Cäcilien-verein, started in 1873 by Singenberger.

*Karl, Tom (Ireland, 1846–1916, Roches-ter), a favorite operatic tenor, came to Amer-ica in 1871 with Parepa-Rosa, turned soon to light opera, from 1887 joined Barnabee in the Bostonians, contributing much to their success, and retired in 1896, teaching for some years in New York, later in Rochester.

Kimball, Willard (b. Columbus, O., 1854), studied at Oberlin and Leipzig, in 1875 estab-lished what is now the School of Music at Grinnell College in Iowa, remaining its direc-tor till 1894, when he founded the University School of Music at Lincoln, Neb., of which he is still the head. He has also been organist, conductor and lecturer, and in 1898 was Director of Music at the Omaha Exposition.

Klauser, Julius (New York, 1854–1907, Milwaukee), son of Karl Klauser (see sec. 4) and trained by him and at Leipzig, from 1874 was a teacher at Milwaukee. He published an able treatise on Harmony, *The Septonate,* 1890, and *The Nature of Music,* 1909.

*Klein, Bruno Oscar (Hanover, 1858–1911, New York), trained by his father and at Munich, came to America in 1878 as concert-pianist, and from 1884 was teacher, organist and composer in New York. See art.

*Koelling, Adolph (Hamburg, 1840– ?), brother and pupil of Karl W. P. Koelling and otherwise trained at Hamburg, came to America in 1872, and, after teaching at Poughkeepsie, became head of the theory-department of the Chicago Musical College.

*Kofler, Leo (Tyrol, 1837–1908, New Orleans), from 1877 was organist of St. Paul's Chapel in New York and vocal teacher. He published *The Art of Breathing*, 1889 (also in German, 1897) — a thoughtful handbook.

*Korbay, Francis Alexander (Hungary, 1846–1913, England), operatic tenor and concert-pianist, came to America in 1871, touring as player and then teaching in New York until 1894, when he removed to London. See Vol. ii. 595, and art.

Krehbiel, Henry Edward (b. Ann Arbor, Mich., 1854), after studying law at Cincinnati, was musical critic there from 1874, removing in 1880 to New York, where he is distinguished as critic, lecturer, author and editor. See Vol. ii. 599, and art.

Lanier, Sidney (Macon, Ga., 1842–1881, Lynn, N. C.), the gifted Southern poet, from 1873 was flutist in the Peabody Orchestra, Baltimore, and lecturer at Johns Hopkins University. See art.

Levett, David Maurice (New York, 1844–1914, New York), trained at Leipzig, from 1876 taught in New Brunswick, N. J., Jacksonville, Ill., and Chicago, settling in New York in 1885, after 1900 teaching in the College of Music. In 1898–1900 he was in the faculty of the Stern Conservatory in Berlin. He composed the symphonic poems ' Harlequinade ' and ' Memories,' a Romance and Serenade for violin and piano, etc.

Lichtenberg, Leopold (b. San Francisco, 1861), a precocious violinist, touring with Wieniawski in 1873, then studied at Brussels with him, toured in America and abroad, was in the Boston Symphony Orchestra and from 1899 head of the violin-department of the National Conservatory in New York. Since 1904 he has played in the Margulies Trio. See art.

*Lisser, Louis (b. Pomerania, 1850), after study at Berlin and tours in Prussia as pianist, came to San Francisco in 1879, and since 1880 has been Dean of Music in Mills College, Oakland (now emeritus). He has been active in many musical organizations.

Lorenz, Edmund Simon (b. Stark Co., O., 1854), graduated from Otterbein University and Yale Divinity School and continued theological study at Leipzig, from 1885 was pastor in Dayton, O., and in 1887–88 president of Lebanon Valley College in Pennsylvania, but in 1890 turned to publishing and established his now extensive business at Dayton. Since 1875 he has edited many books for choirs, congregations and Sunday-schools, and a manual on *Practical Church Music*, 1909. See Hall, *Gospel Song and Hymn Writers*, pp. 318–22.

Lutkin, Peter Christian (b. Thompsonville, Wis., 1858), trained in Chicago, Berlin, Paris and Vienna, organist and teacher in Chicago from 1872, and since 1891 at Northwestern University, Evanston (dean from 1897), choral conductor, composer and author. See art.

Macdougall, Hamilton Crawford (b. Warwick, R. I., 1858), studied in Boston and London, from 1874 was organist in Providence and later in Boston, and since 1900 has been professor at Wellesley College. See art.

*Manoly, Ludwig Emanuel (b. Hungary, 1855), came to America in 1876 as double-bassist in the Thomas Orchestra and has since been a noted player and teacher in New York.

*Mapleson, James Henry (England, 1829–1901, England), a versatile impresario, conducted opera seasons in New York at the Academy of Music in 1878–86 and again in 1896–97, introducing many important singers, but maintaining no consistent artistic standard. See Vol. iii. 44.

*Maurel, Victor (b. France, 1848), the distinguished operatic baritone, visited America in 1874, and again in 1894–95, and in 1909–10 was a teacher in New York. See Vol. iii. 94, and Baker, *Dict. of Musicians*, p. 592.

McCoy, William J. (b. Crestline, O., 1848), studied in New York and Leipzig, began producing orchestral works in 1872 in Germany, and settled in San Francisco as composer and author. See art.

Mees, Arthur (b. Columbus, O., 1850), trained at Berlin, began teaching in the Cincinnati College of Music, and since 1880 has been a versatile and accomplished conductor as well as a forceful critic and writer. See art.

Morgan, Maud (b. New York, 1864), daughter and pupil of George W. Morgan (see sec. 4), appeared as harpist in 1875, and, after study in London, became a favorite concert-performer in New York.

Morse, Charles Henry (b. Bradford, Mass., 1853), trained in Boston, from 1873 taught there and at Wellesley College, in 1885 established the Northwestern Conservatory at Minneapolis, from 1891 was organist in Brooklyn, and since 1901 has been professor at Dartmouth College. See art. His brother, Frank Eugene Morse (b. 1856), has long been a prominent teacher of singing in Wellesley and Boston.

Myer, Edmund John (b. York Springs, Pa., 1846), eminent as vocal teacher and expert since 1877, chiefly at New York. See art.

*Nicholl, Horace Wadham (b. England, 1848), came to Pittsburgh in 1871 as organist, removing in 1878 to New York, where he has been notable as player, teacher, composer and writer. See Vol. iii. 372, and art.

*Nilsson, Christine (b. Sweden, 1843), the great operatic soprano, first appeared in

America in 1870 and was heard at intervals thereafter till her retirement in 1891. See Vol. iii. 380–1, and art.

Nordica, Lillian [Lillian Norton] (Farmington, Me., 1859–1914, Java), made her début as soprano at Boston in 1876, opening a career of brilliant success in America and abroad which continued till her death. See Vol. iii. 389–90, and art.

Osgood, Emma Aline (Boston, 1849–1911, Philadelphia), appeared as soprano in Boston in 1873, studied later in London and became a favorite in concert and oratorio there and from 1878 in America. See art.

Osgood, George Laurie (b. Chelsea, Mass., 1844), graduated from Harvard in 1866, studied in Germany and Italy, from 1872 was famous in Boston as singer, teacher, conductor, composer and author, and since 1903 has lived abroad. See art.

Otis, Philo Adams (b. Berlin Heights, O., 1846), graduated from Western Reserve College in 1868, though occupied in business, has long been musically prominent in Chicago, and has composed considerable church music. See Baker, *Dict. of Musicians*, p. 669.

Paine, Richmond Peck (b. New Bedford, Mass., 1858), organist from 1872 at New Bedford, from 1878 in Hartford, Meriden and New Britain, Conn., becoming also notable as choral leader, and in 1905–15 conducted the Litchfield County Choral Union. See art.

Parsons, Albert Ross (b. Sandusky, 'O., 1847), studied in New York, Leipzig and Berlin, and since 1872 has been a leading teacher of piano in New York, with considerable literary work. See art.

Patton, Willard (b. Milford, Me., 1853), trained as tenor in Boston, began concert-singing in 1877, and since 1883 has been identified with Minneapolis as teacher, conductor, composer and organizer. In 1886–89 he taught at Hamline University, and in 1890 started the Philharmonic Club, conducting it till 1894. His works include the operettas ‘ The Gallant Garroter ’ (1882) and ‘ La Fianza ’ (1889), the oratorio ‘ Isaiah,’ the opera ‘Pocahontas ’ (1911), a symphonic fantasy, ‘The Spirit of ’61 ’ (1915), and other patriotic works, such as ‘ The Star of Empire ’ (1900), ‘ Footstones of a Nation ’ (1906), and ‘ Usona ’ (1918).

*Piutti, Max (Saxony, 1852–1885, Jackson, Mich.), came to America in 1874, and till 1883 was instructor at Wells College. He left unfinished a work on *The Folk-Songs of the Nations.*

Pratt, Silas Gamaliel (Addison, Vt., 1846–1916, Pittsburgh), trained in Chicago and Berlin, founded the Apollo Club in Chicago in 1872 and till 1888 was active as teacher, pianist and composer there, in 1888–1902 was in New York, and from 1906 in Pittsburgh. See art.

Pratt, Waldo Selden (b. Philadelphia, 1857), organist from about 1875, since 1882 has been professor in the Hartford Theological Seminary

E

and in 1905–20 lecturer at the Institute of Musical Art in New York. See Baker, *Dict. of Musicians*, pp. 721–2.

Ritter, Fanny, née Raymond (Philadelphia, 1840–1890, Poughkeepsie), wife of Frédéric L. Ritter (see sec. 4), published *Woman as a Musician*, 1877, and *Some Famous Songs*, 1878, and translated Ehlert's *Briefe über Musik*, 1877, and Schumann's *Gesammelte Schriften*, 2 vols., 1878–80.

Rivé-King, Julie (b. Cincinnati, 1857), daughter of Caroline Rivé (see sec. 4), after study in New York and Germany, began her career as concert-pianist in 1874–75 in Leipzig and New York, becoming a favorite in the Middle West and Canada. She is now teaching at the Bush Conservatory, Chicago. See art.

Robyn, Alfred George (b. St. Louis, 1860), has been known as organist and pianist since 1876. He has written a symphony, the symphonic poem ‘ Pompeii,’ a piano-concerto and other chamber-music, a mass, three sacred cantatas, and many light operas.

*Rogers, Clara Kathleen, née Barnett (b. England, 1844), studied at Leipzig, Berlin and Milan, made her début as operatic soprano at Turin in 1863, came to America in 1871 with Parepa-Rosa, and since 1873 has lived in Boston (marrying Henry M. Rogers in 1878), since 1902 on the staff of the New England Conservatory. She has published many songs, some piano-pieces, a violin-sonata, *The Philosophy of Singing*, 1893, *My Voice and I*, 1910, *English Diction in Song and Speech*, 1912, *The Voice in Speech*, 1915, and *Memories of a Musical Career*, 1920. Her stage-name was ‘ Clara Doria.’

Roosevelt, Hilbourne Lewis (New York, 1848–1885, New York), from 1872 was a gifted and original organ-maker in New York, a pioneer in novel voicing and electric action. Till 1893 the business was finely maintained by his brother, Frank H. Roosevelt (1861–93). See art.

*Rosenbecker, Adolph (Hesse, 1851–1919, San Francisco), well-trained as a violinist, came to New York late in 1869, till 1877 played under Thomas, and then settled in Chicago as teacher and conductor.

*Rudersdorff, Hermine (Russia, 1822–1882, Boston), the noted operatic soprano, after a long career in Europe, in 1870 came to Boston as concert-singer and effective teacher. See Vol. iv. 189.

Russell, Louis Arthur (b. Newark, N. J., 1854), trained in New York and London, since 1878 has been organist, teacher, conductor and composer in Newark. He has been active in promoting popular interest, especially in organizing and conducting the Schubert (Oratorio) Society since 1878 and the Symphony Orchestra since 1894. He has written for piano and voice, the cantata ‘ A Pastoral Rhapsody,’ and church-music, besides many pedagogical works, especially upon singing. See *Who's Who in Music*, 1918, p. 545.

Salter, Mary Elizabeth, née Turner (b. Peoria, Ill., 1856), studied in Burlington, Ia., Boston and New York, was from 1874 for twenty years church- and concert-soprano in New York and has since been active as song-composer. See art.

Salter, Sumner (b. Burlington, Ia., 1856), graduated from Amherst College in 1877, was trained in Boston, and since 1878 has been a teacher and organist in Boston, New York and elsewhere, since 1905 at Williams College. He has published songs and church-music, besides work as editor and writer. See art.

Sanford, Samuel Simons (Bridgeport, Conn., 1849–1910, New York), trained in New York, under Rubinstein and in Paris, became a remarkable pianist and occasionally appeared in concert, though not widely known until 1894, when he joined the Yale School of Music.

Sankey, Ira David (Edinburg, Pa., 1840–1908, Brooklyn), though known as singer before 1860, did not take up evangelistic singing till 1871, when he joined D. L. Moody, until 1899 touring with him throughout the United States and Great Britain. He wrote many hymn-tunes and songs of popular character, published in Sacred Songs and Solos, 1873, Gospel Hymns, Nos. 1–6, 1875–91, Winnowed Songs, 1890, etc. He wrote My Life and the Story of the Gospel Hymns, 1906.

*Scharwenka, Franz Xaver (b. Prussian Poland, 1850), the brilliant pianist and pedagogue, toured in America in 1874–80, conducted a conservatory in New York in 1891–98, and came again in 1910–14. Otherwise he has been associated with Berlin. See Vol. iv. 249 and art.

*Schnecker, Peter August (Hesse-Darmstadt, 1850–1903, New York), arrived in New York in 1865, studied there and later at Leipzig, and from 1872 was organist of the West Presbyterian Church. He composed much church-music and edited collections of organ-pieces.

Schoenefeld, Henry (b. Milwaukee, 1857), began orchestral playing in 1873, was trained as concert-pianist at Leipzig and Weimar, from 1879 was teacher and conductor at Chicago, and since 1904 has been conductor and composer at Los Angeles. See art.

Shelley, Harry Rowe (b. New Haven, Conn., 1858), studied first at New Haven, where he began as organist in 1872, later removing to Brooklyn and New York, and becoming noted as player, composer and editor. See art.

Sherwood, William Hall (Lyons, N. Y., 1854–1911, Chicago), studied in New York and Germany, from 1876 appeared as fine concert-pianist, settling successively in Boston, New York and (from 1889) Chicago, where in 1897 he founded the Sherwood Piano School. See art.

*Singenberger, Johannes B. (b. Switzerland, 1848), highly trained in Jesuit colleges and at Munich, came to America in 1873 to teach in St. Francis' Academy, Milwaukee, and to represent the Gregorian revival promoted since 1865 by F. X. Witt of Landshut (1834–1888). In 1874 he organized a branch of the Cäcilienverein and started the periodical 'Cecilia.' He has written 20 masses and other ritual-music.

Smith, Gerrit (Hagerstown, Md., 1859–1912, Darien, Conn.), a graduate of Hobart College, studied in New York, Stuttgart and Berlin, was organist in college, at Buffalo and Albany and from 1885 in New York, where from 1898 he was professor in Union Theological Seminary. See art.

Sousa, John Philip (b. Washington, 1854), began leading theater-orchestras about 1870, was violinist under Offenbach in 1876, in 1880–92 led the U. S. Marine Band, and since has won international fame with his own band. See Vol. iv. 628, and art.

Strong, George Templeton (b. New York, 1856), early an oboist, from 1879 studied and lived in Germany, in 1891–92 taught in Boston, and has since lived in Switzerland as composer. See Vol. iv. 728–9, and art.

*Tamaro, Josef (Spain, 1824–1902, New York), a pupil of Lamperti, from 1876 was a singing-teacher in New York.

Thayer, Arthur Wilder (b. Dedham, Mass., 1857), trained in Boston, was choral conductor from before 1880 and in 1882–88 music-supervisor at Dedham and Milton, and since 1888 has been organist at Newton, Mass., composing church-music, songs and piano-pieces.

Thursby, Emma Cecelia (b. Brooklyn, 1854), trained as soprano in New York, Boston and Milan, sang in America in 1875 and frequently after 1879, besides tours all over the world. See Vol. v. 99, and art.

Toedt, Theodore J. (b. New York, 1853), studied in New York, from about 1873 became known as an artistic concert-tenor, and since 1895, becoming blind, has been a teacher in New York. His wife, Ella A. Toedt, née Earle, is an accomplished soprano and teacher.

*Tomlins, William Lawrence (b. England, 1844), came to New York in 1870, from 1875 till 1910 was located at Chicago as conductor and director of public-school music. See art.

Trowbridge, John Eliot (b. Newton, Mass., 1845–1912, Newton), studied at Northampton and Wellesley, Mass., and about 1870 became organist and composer in Boston and from 1881 at Newton. He wrote the oratorio 'Emmanuel,' a mass and other church-music, the cantata 'The Heroes of '76,' part-songs and songs.

Tubbs, Frank Herbert (b. Brighton, Mass., 1853), trained in Boston, London and Milan, became choir-master and vocal teacher in New York, founding the Vocal Institute and writing upon the voice. For some years he has been engaged in business.

Tucker, Hiram G. (b. Cambridge, Mass., 1851), studied at Boston, becoming a concert-pianist and organist there, later conductor of choral and chamber-concerts. Since 1878 he has taught at Wheaton College, Norton, Mass.

Turner, Alfred Dudley (St. Albans, Vt., 1854–1888, St. Albans), trained at the New England Conservatory in Boston, where he became a valued piano-teacher. His published works include chamber-music, piano-pieces and a Method of Octave-Playing.

Valleria, Alwina [Mrs. R. H. P. Hutchinson] (b. Baltimore, 1848), studied in England, becoming a striking operatic soprano from 1871. Though living in England and active in Europe, in 1879–86 she appeared often in America. See Vol. v. 211–2.

Van Cleve, John Smith (b. Maysville, Ky., 1851), studied in Columbus, Boston and Cincinnati, from 1872 taught at the Institute for the Blind in Columbus, from 1875 at Janesville, Wis., in 1879–97 was teacher, lecturer and critic at Cincinnati, removed thence to Chicago, later to Troy, and in 1913 to New York. See art.

Van Zandt, Marie (New York, 1861–1919, France), trained as opera-soprano in Milan, made her début at Turin in 1879, sang in Paris, London, and throughout Europe, in 1891–92 was at the Metropolitan Opera House, in 1896 returned to Paris, and retired in 1898. See Vol. v. 585–6, and art.

*Vogrich, Max Wilhelm Karl (Transylvania, 1852–1916, New York), already noted as pianist and composer, came first to New York in 1878, returned in 1886–1902, and again from 1914. See art.

Webb, Frank Rush (b. Covington, Ind., 1851), studied in Boston and Indianapolis,

becoming organist in 1873, from 1876 at Lima, O., from 1883 at Staunton, Va., where he was music-director in the school now known as Stuart Hall, and since 1910 has been critic in Baltimore. He has written band-music, piano-pieces, and vocal music.

*Weiss, Carl Thomas (b. Bavaria, 1844), trained in Munich, since 1870 has been organist in Roman Catholic churches in New Orleans, besides conducting singing-societies and teaching in convent-schools. He has written articles connected with the Cäcilia movement.

*Werrenrath, George (Denmark, 1838–1898, Brooklyn), an experienced operatic tenor, came to New York in 1876, becoming widely recognized as an accomplished singer, especially in concert. He was one of the first to give series of song-recitals.

Wild, Harrison Major (b. Hoboken, N. J., 1861), trained at Leipzig and Chicago, since 1876 has been organist in Chicago and since 1895 distinguished choral conductor. See art.

Woodman, Raymond Huntington (b. Brooklyn, 1861), son of J. C. Woodman (see sec. 4), trained in Brooklyn and Paris, has been organist since 1875, from 1880 at the First Presbyterian Church, Brooklyn, and since 1894 professor at Packer Institute. See art.

*Zeisler, Fannie, née Bloomfield (b. Austrian Silesia, 1863), came to Chicago as a child, was first trained there, appearing as pianist in 1876, then studied in Vienna, and since 1883 has been famous on both sides of the Atlantic. See Vol. i. 341, and art.

No one who studies the details of musical activity in America — as suggested, for example, in the lists of persons here given, or as otherwise brought together — can miss the fact that from 1880 onward there was a noteworthy awakening of artistic interest and effort in all directions. The number of significant foreign musicians who now become residents is at least twice that in any preceding decade, and the number of those native-born increases in almost the same proportion. Part of this merely statistical appearance may be due to the lack before about 1880 of systematic effort to make record of the lives and work of musicians. But the fact remains impressive after all allowances.

Certain events, already mentioned, were specially important. One was the founding in 1881 of the Boston Symphony Orchestra, destined to become an educational force felt throughout the country. Another was the fruitage of the many years of faithful planting of taste and aptitude on the part of the veteran Theodore Thomas. Another was the establishment in New York in 1884–85 of German opera under Leopold Damrosch on a scale and with a popular appeal that were unprecedented. Another was the extension of series of classical concerts in many places, gradually opening the minds of widening circles of hearers to the wealth of sterling musical literature. Another was the coming to bear of the influence of the earlier conservatories through their graduates, who now begin to become centers of stimulus as private teachers. In connection with all these, as in arousing proper interest in the ability of native composers and performers, the increase of rational criticism and discussion in periodicals and books played no small part.

Quite apart from these specific factors in progress, it may be that much of the sudden access of momentum musically was due to diffused influences permeating the whole social fabric.   The strain of the Civil War time was passing away, and a new era of consolidated advance in things economic, political and educational was setting in.   The observer of musical progress notes the reaction of all this in his own field.   Doubtless observers in other fields would note it similarly in theirs.

Here is an appropriate point to refer to the influence of national and international expositions.   Those held in Europe prior to 1880 had no relation to the advance of music in America except as they stimulated makers of instruments — chiefly pianos — to compete for recognition.   But those held in the United States from 1876 onward not only gave a similar industrial impetus, but usually exalted elaborate musical features into prominence and thus contributed positively to popular education.

The first of the larger American expositions was the Centennial, held at Philadelphia in 1876.   Aside from some general exercises and frequent piano- and organ-recitals, its main importance to music was in the display and competition of instruments.   The second was the Columbian, held at Chicago in 1893.   Here the musical provisions were extraordinarily profuse and generally superior, largely due to the imagination, energy and authority of Theodore Thomas, and the impress upon popular thought was correspondingly significant.   The third was the Louisiana Purchase, held at St. Louis in 1904, at which the effort was made to emulate the musical elaboration of its Chicago predecessor, though without achieving quite the same practical success.   Meanwhile a host of lesser expositions were brought to pass — among them the California Mid-Winter at San Francisco in 1894, the Trans-Mississippi at Omaha in 1898, and the Pan-American at Buffalo in 1901 — all taking pains to magnify music in a greater or less degree.   To these may be added — though outside the period here under review — those at Jamestown in 1907, at Portland and Seattle in 1905 and 1909, and, still more important, the Panama celebrations at San Diego and San Francisco in 1915–16.

The cultural reaction of these numerous and often immense undertakings is beyond question.   In the domain of the fine arts they tended to arouse interest and elevate taste in regard to architecture, painting, sculpture and music by means of manifold demonstrations of a more or 'less monumental kind.

In analyzing the lists of names that follow, attention should be given not only to the wider range from which both the foreign-born and the native-born come, but also to the wider range geographically and occupationally to which they go.   If the facts could be depicted graphically, it would appear that both derivations and destinations now begin to spread out like the unfolding leaves of a fan.

CHRONOLOGICAL REGISTER

7. The Decade of Artistic Awakening — 1880–1890

Abbey, Henry Eugene (Akron, O., 1846–1896, New York), who had been a jeweler and later owner and manager of theaters, in 1883–84 leased the Metropolitan Opera House in New York at its opening, provided a brilliant troupe and a fair Italian repertory, but with a net loss of perhaps $500,000. Recouping himself at Chicago in 1889–91, with Schoeffel and Grau in 1891–92 and 1894–97 he undertook the Metropolitan again, this time with more success, but died in the effort.

*Adamowski, Joseph (b. Poland, 1862), an expert 'cellist, joined the Boston Symphony Orchestra in 1889, and since 1903 has taught at the New England Conservatory. See art.

Adams, Mrs. Crosby, née Juliette Graves (b. Niagara Falls, N. Y., 1858), from about 1880 organist and teacher in Leroy, N. Y., Buffalo and Kansas City, from 1892 in Chicago, and since 1913 at Montreat, N. C. She has specialized in teaching children and training teachers, has composed and edited pedagogical music, and has written *Chapters from a Musical Life*, 1903, and *What the Piano Writings of MacDowell Mean to the Piano-Student*, 1913.

Aldrich, Perley Dunn (b. Blackstone, Mass., 1863), studied at Boston, London and Paris, in 1885–87 taught at the University of Kansas, from 1889 at the Utica Conservatory, from 1891 at Rochester, and since 1903 in Philadelphia. See art.

Ambrose, Paul (b. Hamilton, Ont., 1868), trained mostly in New York, was organist there in 1886–1917, and since 1904 has been music-director in the State Normal School at Trenton, N. J. See art.

*Archer, Frederick (England, 1838–1901, Pittsburgh), who had been organist and conductor in London, in 1881 came as organist to Brooklyn and New York, from 1885 editing 'The Keynote,' from 1887 conducted the Boston Oratorio Society, and in 1896–98 led the Pittsburgh Orchestra. See Vol. i. 101–2, and art.

*Arens, Franz Xavier (b. Rhine Prov., 1856), brought up in Milwaukee, but trained mostly in Germany, from 1885 was conductor in Cleveland, in 1890–92 concertized in Europe, and since 1900 has given high-class popular concerts in New York. See art.

*Ashmall, William E. (b. England, 1860), for many years organist in New York, Brooklyn and (since 1912) Newark, N. J., and head of a music-school in Arlington, N. J., has played much in concert and edited ' The Organist's Journal ' and many organ-collections.

*Austin, John Turnell (b. England, 1869), came to Detroit in 1889 as organ-maker, soon became noted as the inventor of 'the universal wind-chest,' and in 1899 organized the Austin

Organ Company at Hartford, Conn., of which he is president, ably assisted by his brother, **Basil George Austin** (b. 1874), who joined him in 1893.

Ayres, Eugene Edmond (Russellville, Ky., 1859–1920, Philadelphia), instructor in Greek from 1879 in various colleges and from 1903 professor at Crozer Theological Seminary (Chester, Pa.), was expert in music from youth. He published a brief *Handbook of Musical History*, 1882, and *Counterpoint and Canon*, 1886, was on the staff of ' The Etude ' in 1888–93, and was musical editor of the notable Baptist hymnal *Sursum Corda*, 1898.

*Baermann, Carl, Jr. (Bavaria, 1839–1913, Newton, Mass.), pianist and composer, came to Boston in 1881, becoming at once a leading artist and teacher. See Vol. i. 162, and art.

Baier, Victor (b. New York, 1861), has been organist at Trinity Church, New York, since 1884 (assistant till 1897), and active in the A. G. O. (warden in 1920).

Bassett, Franklin (Wheeling, W. Va., 1852–1915, Pasadena, Cal.), finely trained at Leipzig, from 1877 was pianist in Cleveland, and from 1882, with Heydler (see below), directed the Cleveland Conservatory. See art.

Beach, Amy Marcy, née Cheney [Mrs. H. H. A.] (b. Henniker, N. H., 1867), trained in Boston, from 1883 appeared as concert-pianist, and soon became eminent in composition. See Vol. i. 210, and art.

Beck, Johann Heinrich (b. Cleveland, 1856), trained at Leipzig, settled in 1882 in Cleveland as violinist, founded the Schubert Quartet, from 1886 conducted his own works in many cities, and in 1901–12 led the Cleveland Symphony Orchestra and other organizations. See art.

Bendix, Max (b. Detroit, 1866), studied in New York, Cincinnati and Berlin, was concert-master at the Metropolitan Opera House in 1886 and 1905, also under Thomas in 1886–96, and since 1906 has been conductor in New York, Chicago, London, etc. See art.

*Bendix, Otto (Denmark, 1845–1904, San Francisco), who had been piano-teacher and oboist in Copenhagen, came in 1880 to Boston as teacher in the New England Conservatory, and from 1895 directed a school in San Francisco.

Benham, Victor (b. Brooklyn, 1871), a boy-pianist from 1880, first in New York, in 1882 in London and in 1885 in Paris, and then toured the Continent. Except in 1890–1900 and 1904–12, he has lived abroad as virtuoso, teacher and writer. See art.

Bentley, William Frederick (b. Lenox, O., 1859), graduated from Oberlin College in 1883, studied at Chicago, Leipzig, Berlin, Paris and London, taught at New Lyme, O., and since 1885 has been head of the Knox Conservatory,

Galesburg, Ill., and since 1899 conductor of the Musical Union. See art.

Berger, Wilhelm (Boston, 1861–1911, Saxony), brought up in Germany, became a strong piano-teacher, conductor and composer, and spent his whole life abroad. See Vol. i. 308, and art.

Binder, Fritz (b. Baltimore, 1873), brought up in Germany and appearing widely as a prodigy from 1880, studied at Cologne, developing as pianist and choral leader, from 1896 was conductor at Solingen (near Cologne), and since 1901 has been head of the Singakademie at Danzig.

*Blanck, Hubert de (b. Holland, 1856), in 1880 toured South America as pianist, in 1881–82 taught in New York, and in 1883 went to Havana, establishing in 1885 what is now the Conservatorio Nacional. See art.

*Bonvin, Ludwig (b. Switzerland, 1850), trained as a Jesuit priest, came to Canisius College, Buffalo, in 1887 as music-director, and has been much engaged upon historical studies and composition. See art.

*Bott, Jean Joseph (Hesse, 1826–1895, New York), well known as violinist and composer at Meiningen and Hanover, from 1885 lived in New York.

Brooks, Henry Mason, of Salem, Mass., from 1886 published a series of studies of old New England life, chiefly gathered from newspapers, including *Olden-Time Music*, 1888.

*Browne, John Lewis (b. England, 1866), finished training as organist in New York, from 1888 played in Chicago, from 1892 at San Francisco, also leading symphony-concerts, from 1899 at Atlanta, in 1908–10 at Philadelphia, and since 1912 at Chicago. See art.

*Bruenner, Leopold (b. Bavaria, 1869), finished his education in Minneapolis, where from 1886 he taught, in 1889 became organist and teacher in St. Paul, and in 1910 organized the Choral Art Society, largely devoted to a cappella music. He has composed a grand mass (1895), songs, etc.

*Brune, Adolf Gerhard (b. Hanover, 1870), in 1889 came to Peoria, Ill., as organist, from 1894 studied at Chicago, in 1898 becoming a useful teacher at the Musical College, with much composition. See art.

Bryant, Gilmore Ward (b. Bethel, Vt., 1859), trained in Boston and New York, has taught since 1885 in various schools in the South, especially the Southern Conservatory, Durham, N. C., which he founded in 1898 and has since directed.

Burdett, George Albert (b. Boston, 1856), graduated from Harvard in 1881, studied in Boston, Hanover and Berlin, settled in Boston as church-organist, chiefly at the New Old South Church. Besides being a gifted player and choir-director, he has composed church-music, songs and piano-pieces, and written for periodicals.

Burleigh, Henry Thacker (b. Erie, Pa., 1866), was a church-singer before 1890, in 1892 won a scholarship and studied in the National Conservatory, New York, taught there two years, since 1894 has been baritone at St. George's and since 1899 also at Temple Emanu-El, and has sung in concert both in America and Europe. He has written striking songs, has arranged Negro religious melodies, and in 1917 received a prize for conspicuous achievement as representing the Negro race.

*Burmeister, Richard (b. Hamburg, 1860), was director of the Peabody Conservatory, Baltimore, in 1885–97, and of the Scharwenka Conservatory, New York, in 1897–99. Since 1903 he has worked at Dresden and Berlin. See art.

Burr, Willard, Jr. (b. Ravenna, O., 1852), trained at Oberlin and Berlin, since about 1880 has been an industrious composer in Boston, his works including string-quartets, piano-trios, a violin-sonata, many piano-pieces, songs and considerable church-music.

Burton, Frederick Russell (Jonesville, Mich., 1861–1909, Lake Hopatcong, N. J.), graduated from Harvard in 1882, went into journalism and also became a leading exponent of the music of the Indians, making extensive investigations, publishing articles and books, and composing upon Indian themes. See art.

Busch, Carl (b. Denmark, 1862), in 1887 came to Kansas City, where he has been increasingly active as conductor and composer, since 1912 leading the Symphony Orchestra. See art.

Camp, John Spencer (b. Middletown, Conn., 1858), graduated from Wesleyan University in 1878, studied in New York, since 1882 has been prominent in Hartford, Conn., as organist in leading churches, in 1902–11 conductor of the Philharmonic Orchestra, and a composer in several forms. See art.

*Campanari, Giuseppe (b. Italy, 1858), in 1884 joined the Boston Symphony Orchestra as 'cellist, but since 1893 has been a noted operatic baritone, mostly in New York. See art.

*Campanari, Leandro (b. Italy, 1857), appeared in Boston as violinist in 1881, becoming teacher in the New England Conservatory and organizing a Quartet, in 1887–90 was in Europe, from 1890 taught at the Cincinnati Conservatory, in 1897–1905 was director at La Scala, Milan, in 1906–07 was substitute-conductor at the Metropolitan Opera House and of the Philadelphia Symphony Orchestra, and since 1907 has taught in San Francisco. He has published instruction-books and songs.

*Campanini, Cleofonte (Italy, 1860–1919, Chicago), appeared in 1883 as assistant-conductor at the Metropolitan Opera House, again in 1887, from 1906 at the Manhattan Opera House, and from 1910 with the Chicago Opera Company. See art. His wife, **Eva Campanini**, née Tetrazzini (b. Italy, 1864), noted as stage-soprano since 1883, is a singer in the Chicago Company.

Carl, William Crane (b. Bloomfield, N. J., 1865), studied in New York and Paris, from

1882 was organist at Newark, and since 1892 at the First Presbyterian Church, New York, and also since 1899 director of the Guilmant Organ School, which he founded. See art.

*Carnegie, Andrew (Scotland, 1837–1919, Lenox, Mass.), the iron-manufacturer and philanthropist, began his extensive gifts to musical enterprises before 1890. See art.

Cawley, Edgar Moore (b. Pyrmont, O., 1871), trained at Cincinnati and later at Leipzig, from 1887 taught at the Cincinnati Conservatory, and in 1897 established the Indianapolis Conservatory, of which he is now manager.

Chace, Frank Wilbur (b. Providence, R. I., 1868), studied in Boston and New York, began as organist in 1883, holding positions in Mobile, Nashville and Seattle, appearing also as recitalist and conductor, and since about 1910 has been music-director at Willamette University, Salem, Ore.

Champlin, John Denison (Stonington, Conn., 1834–1915, New York), was from 1873 to 1912 editor of many books of reference, including a *Cyclopedia of Music and Musicians*, 3 vols., 1888–90 (with W. F. Apthorp), carefully executed along its chosen lines.

*Chapek, Joseph Horymir (b. Bohemia, 1860), came in 1883 to Milwaukee as violinist, organized a Quintet Club and a Quartet Club in 1885, was concertmaster in the Bach Symphony Orchestra in 1885–88, and since 1888 has worked at Chicago, teaching in various schools, playing in the Thomas Orchestra, and since 1910 directing his own Music School. He represents the method of his teacher Sevčik.

Chase, Mary Wood (b. Brooklyn, 1868), trained as pianist at Boston and Berlin, began public appearances in 1886 in Boston, in 1894–96 assisted Raif at Berlin, concertized extensively for some years, and since 1906 has been head of her own school for advanced piano-playing in Chicago. See art.

*Claassen, Arthur (Prussia, 1859–1920, San Francisco), already known as conductor and composer, came in 1884 as leader of the Arion Society in Brooklyn, later of the New York Liederkranz and of various festivals, and from 1910 was conductor and organizer of many enterprises at San Antonio, Tex. For list of works, see Baker, *Dict. of Musicians*, p. 161.

Clarke, Herbert Lincoln (b. Woburn, Mass., 1867), son of Wm. H. Clarke (see sec. 4), developed early as cornettist, first at Toronto, then under Gilmore, Herbert, and Sousa (till 1918 the latter's assistant), and has toured the world.

Clippinger, David A. (b. Ohio, 1860), studied at Fort Wayne, Ind., Boston, Chicago, Berlin and London, from 1885 taught at Fort Wayne, and since 1887 has been a leading teacher of singing in Chicago. See art.

Clough-Leighter, Henry (b. Washington, 1874), trained at Toronto, in 1888 became organist at Washington, from 1899 at Provi-dence, and since 1901 at Boston, with much editorial work. See art.

Combs, Gilbert Raynolds (b. Philadelphia, 1863), began musical activity in Philadelphia before 1880. In 1885 he established the Broad Street Conservatory, of which he is director. See art.

Commery, Stephen (b. Cleveland, 1862), trained at Cincinnati, has been a piano-teacher in Cleveland since 1885, founding the West Side Musical College in 1901 and directing it since.

Coppet, Edward J. de (New York, 1855–1916, New York), a New York banker and broker who from 1886, besides assisting individual artists, maintained choice chamber-music at his residence, and in 1902 established the famous Flonzaley Quartet. See art.

Cottlow, Augusta (b. Shelbyville, Ill., 1878), gave a piano-recital as early as 1885, studied in Chicago, and appeared often from 1888, but since 1896 has mostly lived abroad. See art.

Curtis, Henry Holbrook (New York, 1856–1920, New York), from 1880 specialist in laryngology and vocal hygiene, and author of *Voice-Building and Tone-Placing*, 1894.

Cutter, Benjamin (Woburn, Mass., 1857–1910, Boston), trained in Boston and Stuttgart, was from 1882 teacher at the New England Conservatory, violinist, composer and author. See art.

*Damrosch, Frank Heino (b. Silesia, 1859), son of Leopold Damrosch (see sec. 6), studied in New York, from 1882 was conductor and supervisor in Denver, from 1885 chorus-master at the Metropolitan Opera House, New York, also head of important choral enterprises, and since 1905 director of the Institute of Musical Art. See Vol. i. 656–7, and art.

*Damrosch, Walter Johannes (b. Silesia, 1862), brother of the foregoing, trained in New York and Germany, in 1885 succeeded his father in New York as conductor, in 1894–1900 directed the Damrosch Opera Company, in 1900–02 was conductor at the Metropolitan Opera House, etc., besides much composition. See Vol. i. 657, and art.

Dann, Hollis Ellsworth (b. Canton, Pa., 1861), has taught in Ithaca, N. Y., since 1887, at first in the public schools and since 1906 as professor in Cornell University. See art.

*Davis, David (b. Wales, 1855), since 1880 has been prominent at Cincinnati as church-singer, choral conductor and promoter of Welsh singing-societies.

Davis, John Herbert (b. Lexington, Mass., 1860), after extended study in Boston and London, was organist at Phillips Academy, Andover, Mass., in 1884–86 teacher at the Illinois Woman's College in Jacksonville, in 1886–99 director of the Illinois Conservatory there, and since 1899 music-director at Randolph-Macon Woman's College, Lynchburg, Va.

Dayas, William Humphries (New York, 1864–1903, England), studied in New York, was organist there for some years, went to Germany, becoming concert-pianist, and

toured with Senkrah in 1888. After 1890 he
lived mostly abroad, at Helsingfors, Düsseldorf,
Wiesbaden, Cologne, and from 1896 at Manchester, England. See art.

De Koven, Henry Louis Reginald (Middletown, Conn., 1859–1920, Chicago), brought
up in England, studied there and on the
Continent, from 1887 was highly successful
as composer of light opera, from 1889 also
music-critic, mostly in New York, and a
prolific song-composer. See art.

Dennée, Charles Frederick (b. Oswego,
N. Y., 1863), educated at the New England
Conservatory in Boston, since 1883 has been
a leading piano-teacher in that institution,
and until 1897, when disabled by accident, also
a successful concert-player. See art.

Dickinson, Clarence (b. La Fayette, Ind.,
1873), trained at Chicago, Berlin and Paris,
appeared in concert in 1885 as pianist, and
has been organist and conductor since 1890,
chiefly in Chicago and New York. See art.

Donley, William Henry (b. New Haven,
Conn., 1863), after study at Boston and London, began his long career as concert-organist
in 1882, becoming also an expert on organ-
construction. Lately he has been conductor
in Seattle. See art.

Douglas, Charles Winfred (b. Oswego, N.
Y., 1867), trained at Syracuse and Denver,
from 1889 was organist at Syracuse and singing-teacher in Syracuse University one year,
from 1894 at Denver, from 1907 canon preceptor at the Fond du Lac Cathedral, and
since 1910 living at Peekskill, N. Y. See art.

*Douillet, Pierre** (b. Russia, 1861), came to
America as pianist before 1890, taught in
New York, from 1897 at the College of the
Pacific, San José, Cal., and since 1913 in his
own school in San Francisco. He has pub-
lished piano-pieces and a piano-concerto.

Douty, Nicholas (b. Philadelphia, 1870),
trained in Philadelphia, London and Paris,
from 1887 was organist in Philadelphia, and
since about 1895 has been eminent as concert-
tenor throughout the country, specializing
in the music of Bach. See art.

Eames, Emma Hayden (b. China, 1865, of
American parents), studied in Boston and
Paris, made her début at Paris in 1889 and
at New York in 1891, and continued famous
as an operatic soprano for twenty years. See
Vol. i. 761, and art.

*Edwards, Julian** (England, 1855–1910,
Yonkers, N. Y.), from 1888 lived at Yonkers,
mainly occupied with composition. Of his
operas, the more serious are ' Corinne ' (1880),
' Victorian ' (1883), ' Elfinella,' ' King René's
Daughter ' (1893), ' The Patriot ' (1907),
and the lighter, ' Jupiter ' (1892), ' Friend
Fritz ' (1893), ' Brian Boru ' (1893), ' Goddess
of Truth ' (1896), ' Madeleine ' (1902), ' Dolly
Varden ' (1902); also the cantatas ' The
Redeemer,' ' Lazarus,' ' Mary Magdalen,'
' The Lord of Light and Love,' and the song-
collection *Sunlight and Shadow.*

Egbert, William Grant (b. Danby, N. Y.,
1869), a precocious violinist, appearing first
in 1877, studied at Syracuse and Prague,
where for three years he was concertmaster
of the Sevčik String Orchestra, in 1892 founded
the Ithaca Conservatory, of which he has been
director in 1892–1903 and since 1917.

Epstein, Marcus Isaac (b. Mobile, Ala.,
1855) and **Epstein, Abraham Isaac** (b. Mobile,
1857), brothers, educated at Leipzig, early
made a reputation for two-piano playing, and
since 1902 have conducted the Beethoven
Conservatory at St. Louis.

*Faelten, Carl** (b. Thuringia, 1846), an
experienced piano-teacher, came to the Peabody Conservatory, Baltimore, in 1882, removed to the New England Conservatory,
Boston, in 1885, becoming its head in 1890,
and since 1897 has directed his own Pianoforte
School with much success. See art. His
brother, **Reinhold Faelten** (b. 1856), has been
associated with him in all these undertakings.

Fairclough, George Herbert (b. Hamilton,
Ont., 1869), educated at Toronto and Berlin,
has been organist since 1882, from 1900 at St.
Paul, where he has also been teacher of piano
in Macalester Conservatory since 1904.

Fairclough, William Erving (b. near Barrie,
Ont., 1859), brother of the foregoing, trained
in London, from 1885 was organist in England,
from 1887 in Montreal, and since 1890 in
Toronto, where he also teaches in the College
of Music and is examiner for the University.

*Federlein, Gottlieb Heinrich** (b. Bavaria,
1835), from about 1880 organist and vocal
teacher in New York, now living at the Presser
Home in Philadelphia. He has published
a vocal method and essays on Wagner's ' Ring.'

Finck, Henry Theophilus (b. Bethel, Mo.,
1854), graduated from Harvard in 1876,
studied there and in Munich, has been since
1881 musical critic for the ' Evening Post ' in
New York and a voluminous author. See art.

*Fiqué, Karl** (b. near Bremen, 1867), since
1887 has been organist, pianist, conductor and
lecturer in Brooklyn. He has composed the
comic operas ' Papa Priesewitz ' (1898) and
' Der falsche Mufti ' (1901), a string-quartet,
some choral works, etc.

*Fischer, Emil** (Brunswick, 1838–1914,
Hamburg), the distinguished operatic bass,
sang at the Metropolitan Opera House in 1885–
91, and in 1895 and '97. He decided to remain permanently as singing-teacher. See art.

Fisher, William Arms (b. San Francisco,
1861), studied in Oakland, New York and
London, taught at the National Conservatory,
New York, and since 1897 has been editor for
the Ditson Company in Boston. See art.

*Foley, Allan James** [Signor Foli] (Ireland,
1835–1899, England), a notable operatic bass,
was widely known in America from about 1880.
See Vol. ii. 70.

*Fremstad, Olive Nayan** (b. Sweden c.
1870), was brought as a child to Minneapolis,
from about 1886 was a church-singer, from

1890 taught the piano in New York, studied in Berlin, from 1896 was a leading stage-soprano in Germany, and since 1903 has been even more famous in America. See art.

*Freund, John Christian** (b. England, 1848), since 1871 in editorial work in New York, about 1885 turned to music-journalism, largely on the side of the music-trades, and since 1898 has published ' Musical America.' See art.

Gale, Walter C. (b. Cambridge, Mass., 1871), graduated from the College of the City of New York in 1891, began as organist in New York in 1887 and has been continuously in service since, from 1905 at the Broadway Tabernacle. See art.

*Gariel, Edoardo** (b. Monterey, Mex., 1860), trained in Paris, since 1887 has been in government employ, from 1887 at Saltillo, and since 1900 in Mexico City. See art.

*Geibel, Adam** (b. Baden, 1855), brought to America as a child, studied in Philadelphia, and since 1885 has been active as organist, conductor and publisher (from 1897). He has written sacred cantatas, etc. He is one of the striking examples of a blind musician.

*Gericke, Wilhelm** (b. Styria, 1845), coming from Vienna, in 1884–89 and 1898–1906 was conductor of the Boston Symphony Orchestra, since then in retirement at Vienna. See Vol. ii. 159, and art.

*Godowsky, Leopold** (b. Russian Poland, 1870), the distinguished pianist, visited America in 1884–85 and again in 1890–91, from 1892 taught in Philadelphia and from 1894 in Chicago, leaving for Berlin in 1900, and since 1914 has made his headquarters at New York or in the West. See Vol. ii. 194, and art.

*Gomes de Aranjo, João** (b. Brazil, 1849), trained as dramatic composer at Rio de Janeiro and in Italy, produced the opera ' Carmosina ' in 1887 at Milan, followed by several others, and has also written symphonies and other orchestral works. Since 1905 he has taught in the Conservatory at São Paulo.

Goodrich, John Wallace (b. Newton, Mass., 1871), studied in Boston and later in Munich and Paris, was organist in Newton from 1886, and since 1897 has been teacher and from 1907 dean at the New England Conservatory in Boston, as well as organist in prominent churches and with the Boston Symphony Orchestra, and choral conductor. See art.

*Gorno, Albino** (b. Italy, ?), after acting as Patti's accompanist in 1881–82, joined the faculty of the Cincinnati College of Music, where he still is. See art.

Gow, George Coleman (b. Ayer, Mass., 1860), graduated from Brown University in 1884, studied at Pittsfield and Worcester, Mass., later also at Berlin, from 1889 taught at Smith College, and since 1895 has been professor at Vassar College. See art.

Greene, Herbert Wilber (b. Holyoke, Mass., 1851), trained in New York, London and Paris, in 1885, with Charles B. Hawley (see sec. 6), founded the Metropolitan College of

Music in New York, and in 1900 started the Summer School of Singing at Brookfield Center, Conn., which he still directs. Besides his gifts as a singing-teacher, he has shown much ability as an organizer, and has been president of the Clef Club in New York in 1895–6, of the Music Teachers' National Association in 1897–8, and of the National Association of Teachers of Singing in 1909–10. He has also been on the staff of ' The Etude ' and ' The Musician,' and edited *The Standard Graded Course of Singing*, 4 vols. His wife, *Caia Greene**, née Aarup (b. Denmark, 1864), a fine pianist, educated at Copenhagen and Paris, came to America about 1887.

Griswold, Gertrude (New York, 1861–1912, England), studied in Paris, made a brilliant début as operatic soprano there in 1881 and later was further successful in England, in 1887 singing with Patti in New York.

*Hackh, Otto Christoph** (Würtemberg, 1852–1917, Brooklyn), an able concert-pianist, in 1880–89 taught in the Grand Conservatory, New York, in 1891–95 lived abroad, and from 1895 was again teacher and composer in New York. His piano-works and songs are numerous, effective and popular.

*Hahn, Reynaldo** (b. Venezuela, 1874), was taken as a child to Paris, where he was educated and has remained as an opera-composer. For list of works see Baker, *Dict. of Musicians*, p. 353 ; also see Vol. ii. 271.

Hale, Edward Danforth (b. Aquebogue, N. Y., 1859), graduated from Williams College in 1880, studied at the New England Conservatory, taught there from 1885, and since 1905 has been dean of the School of Music in Colorado College.

Hall, Jay Rollin (b. Brighton, O., 1860), trained at Oberlin, Leipzig, and later Berlin, from 1884 was head of the music-school in the Illinois Wesleyan University, from 1892 teacher in the Oberlin Conservatory, and since 1898 has been organist at Cleveland.

*Hall, Walter Henry** (b. England, 1862), arriving in 1883, from 1884 was organist in Germantown, Pa., from 1890 in Albany, and in 1896–1913 at St. James', New York, being also from 1889 conductor of choral societies in Brooklyn and New York, and since 1909 professor in Columbia University. See art.

Hamilton, Clarence Grant (b. Providence, 1865), graduated from Brown University in 1888, studied in Boston and London, from 1889 was organist in Providence, and since 1904 has been professor at Wellesley College, as well as organist and author. See art.

*Hammerstein, Oscar** (Prussia, 1847–1919, New York), came to New York as a cigar-maker, from 1888 was noted as a daring promoter of theatrical and operatic enterprises, among which was the Manhattan Opera House, opened in 1906, and the Philadelphia Opera House, opened in 1908. See art.

Hammond, William Churchill (b. Rockville, Conn., 1860), studied in Hartford and New

York, was organist in Connecticut, and since 1885 has been at Holyoke, Mass., becoming widely known as a superior concert-player. From 1890 he also taught at Smith College, and since 1900 has been professor at Mount Holyoke College. See art.

*Harris, Charles L. M. (b. England, 1863), educated at Toronto, from about 1886 was identified with Hamilton, Ont., as organist, conductor and teacher, and is now organist at Port Huron, Mich.

Harris, William Victor (b. New York, 1869), studied in New York and since 1889 has been organist, conductor and composer there, from 1902 leading the St. Cecilia Club. See art.

*Harriss, Charles Albert Edwin (b. England, 1862), since 1883 has been organist, conductor and composer at Montreal, recently returning to England. See art.

*Hartmann, Arthur Martinus (b. Hungary, 1881), was taken as a child to Philadelphia, studied there and in Boston, appeared as early as 1887 as child-violinist, developing into a finished virtuoso. See art.

Hayden, Philip Cady (b. Brantford, Ont., 1854), educated at Oberlin, has been music-supervisor at Quincy, Ill., in 1888–1900, and also at Keokuk, Ia., since 1892. Since 1900 he has edited ' School Music,' devoted to the interests of public-school workers, and has been prominent in various teachers' associations.

Hedden, Warren Rosecrans (b. New York, 1861), trained in New York, has been church- and concert-organist there and elsewhere, besides activity in the A. G. O. See art.

Henderson, William James (b. Newark, N. J., 1855), in journalistic work since 1883, since 1887 has been a leading musical critic in New York, first on ' The Times ' and later on ' The Sun,' and also a brilliant lecturer and author. See art.

Henry, Hugh Thomas (b. Philadelphia, 1862), a highly trained Roman Catholic priest, has since 1889 been professor in Overbrook Seminary in Philadelphia, emphasizing the subject of church-music. In 1905–09 he edited ' Church-Music,' and has written for other journals, including ' The Musical Quarterly.'

*Henschel, Isidor Georg (b. Silesia, 1850), the eminent baritone, was in 1881–84 conductor of the Boston Symphony Orchestra, having previously toured as singer. In 1905–08 he taught in New York. See Vol. ii. 381–2, and art.

*Herbert, Victor (b. Ireland, 1859), the well-known 'cellist, came to New York in 1886 as leading player in several orchestras, conductor and composer, remaining there except in 1898–1904, when he led the Pittsburgh Orchestra. See Vol. ii. 384, and art. His wife, **Therese Herbert**, née Förster, earlier an opera-singer in Vienna, appeared in New York from 1887.

*Herrmann, Eduard (b. Germany, 1850), since 1871 concert-violinist, came to New York in 1881, organized a Quartet and later a Trio of importance, and has been a useful

teacher. He has written much violin- and chamber-music, including a concerto, quartet, quintet and sextet, a violin-method, songs, etc.

Heydler, Charles (b. Cleveland, 1861), has been known as 'cellist in chamber-ensembles in Detroit, Buffalo and Cleveland for many years, and since 1885 has been head of the Cleveland Conservatory.

Higginson, Henry Lee (New York, 1834–1919, Boston), a wealthy Boston banker, in 1881 founded the famous Boston Symphony Orchestra, which he continued to control until 1918. See art.

*Hofmann, Josef Casimir (b. Galicia, 1876), gave over fifty concerts in America in 1887–88, and since 1898 has been immensely popular, spending much time in residence. See Vol. ii. 417, and art.

Holman-Black, Charles (b. Philadelphia, ?), trained in New York and Paris, since about 1880 has been widely known as an operatic singer, appearing in America from 1888 for some years, but mostly in England and France. He lives in Paris.

Hood, Helen (b. Chelsea, Mass., 1863), studied in Boston and Berlin, and is notable in the Boston circle as a gifted composer of songs. See art.

*Hopekirk, Helen (b. Scotland, 1856), already a successful pianist, toured in America in 1883–85 and in 1891–92, and since 1897 has lived in Boston as player, teacher and composer. See art.

*Houseley, Henry (b. England, 1851), having been organist in England, came to America in 1888, and settled in Denver as cathedral-organist, choral conductor and composer. See art.

Howell, William (b. Worcester, Mass., 1871), studied in New York and London, in 1889 began to be favorably known as a concert- and operatic bass, from 1895 was active in New York, Worcester and Boston, from 1900 taught in the University of Michigan, and since 1914 has taught in Detroit.

Humiston, William Henry (b. Marietta, O., 1869), studied in Chicago and New York, from 1889 was organist in or near Chicago, from 1896 at East Orange, N. J., and in 1906–09 at Rye, N. Y. In 1909–12 he conducted operatic troupes, and since 1912 has been connected with the New York Philharmonic Society, from 1916 as assistant-conductor. See art.

Huneker, James Gibbons (b. Philadelphia, 1860), after study in Philadelphia, New York and Paris, from 1881 taught at the National Conservatory in New York, and since 1891 has become conspicuous as a brilliant critic and author. See art.

Huss, Henry Holden (b. Newark, N. J., 1862), son of George J. Huss (see sec. 4), trained in New York and Munich, has been since 1885 a leading pianist, teacher and composer in New York. See art.

*Hyllested, August (b. Sweden, 1858, of Danish parents), after notable early tours as pianist abroad, in 1885 toured in America, from 1886 was assistant-director of the Chicago Musical College, from 1891 taught in the Gottschalk Lyric School, in 1894–97 concertized in Europe, and then returned to Chicago. See art.

*Januschowsky, Georgine von [Frau Adolf Neuendorff] (Austria, 1859?–1914, New York), a gifted operatic soprano, sang successfully in New York in 1880–91 and in 1893–95 in Vienna.

Johns, Clayton (b. Newcastle, Del., 1857), at first educated as an architect, studied music at Boston and Berlin, and since 1884 has made his headquarters at Boston as concert-pianist, teacher, composer and author. See art.

*Johnstone, Arthur Edward (b. England, 1860), brought to New York as a boy and educated there, has devoted himself to systematizing piano-methods and manuals for public-school music, especially as editor for the American Book Company. See art.

Johnstone-Bishop, Mrs. Genevra (b. Van Wert, O., 1864), trained as a dramatic soprano at Oberlin, London and Paris, made her début in 1889, toured extensively in England and America, and has lately taught in Chicago.

Jones, F. O., in 1886 published a notable Handbook of American Music and Musicians, compiled with care and intelligence.

Juch, Emma Antonia Joanna (b. Austria, 1865, of American parents), trained in New York, appeared there in concert in 1882 and in opera in 1883, and until her retirement about 1895 was a favorite soprano. See art.

*Kaun, Hugo (b. Prussia, 1863), the distinguished composer, was teacher and conductor at Milwaukee in 1887–1902. See art.

Kelley, Edgar Stillman (b. Sparta, Wis., 1857), studied at Chicago and Stuttgart, from 1880 was organist in Oakland and San Francisco, from 1886 lectured in New York, from 1902 taught in Berlin, and since 1910 has been theory-teacher, composer and author at Cincinnati. See Vol. ii. 562–3, and art.

Kelly, Thomas James (b. Ireland, 1870), in 1889–1916 was organist at Omaha, singing-teacher, conductor and critic, having charge of the music at the Exposition there in 1898, conducting festivals in 1911–15 and leading the Mendelssohn Choir. Since 1916 he has taught in Chicago, specializing in recitals of Irish music and community-singing.

Kelso, Hugh Alexander, Jr. (b. Charleston, Ill., 1862), trained at Chicago, from 1885 concert-pianist at New York, has been since 1893 head of the School of Musical and Dramatic Art in Chicago. See art.

*Kneisel, Franz (b. Rumania, 1865, of German parents), came to the Boston Symphony Orchestra as concertmaster in 1885, remaining till 1903, and since 1905 has taught at the Institute of Musical Art, New York. In 1886 he founded the famous Kneisel Quartet (dissolved in 1917). See Vol. ii. 589, and art.

Kobbé, Gustav (New York, 1857–1918, Bay Shore, N. Y.), trained at Wiesbaden and New York, a graduate of Columbia (arts, 1877, law, 1879), was for over thirty years a facile writer on musical subjects. See art.

*Kreisler, Fritz (b. Austria, 1875), the gifted violinist, first toured in America in 1889, came again in 1900, and often since. See Vol. ii. 599–600, and art.

Kroeger, Ernest Richard (b. St. Louis, 1862), studied at St. Louis, and since 1883 has been active there as organist, pianist, teacher, conductor and composer, also as concert-pianist and lecturer elsewhere. See art.

*Kronold, Hans (b. Poland, 1872), appeared in New York as 'cellist in 1886, played with the Symphony Society in 1893–97, and has taught many years at the New York College of Music. See art.

*Küzdö, Victor (b. Hungary, 1869), visited America as concert-violinist in 1884, and, after study in London, returned in 1887, settling as player and teacher in New York. He has published several works for violin.

Lachmund, Carl Valentine (b. Booneville, Mo., 1857), trained at Wiesbaden and Berlin and under Liszt, appeared as pianist in America in 1880 and '87, from 1891 has taught in New York, and in 1896–1908 conducted the Women's String Orchestra, which he organized. See art.

*Lahee, Henry Charles (b. England, 1856), came to Boston about 1883, in 1891–99 was secretary of the New England Conservatory, and since then has conducted a musicians' agency. He has published a series of popular historical handbooks — singers, 1898, violinists, 1899, pianists, 1900, the opera in America, 1901, organists, 1902, opera-singers, 1912.

L'Allemand, Pauline, née Ellhasser (b. Syracuse, 1862?), educated at Dresden and Paris, appeared with the American Opera Company in New York in 1886 as a brilliant operatic soprano.

*Lambert, Alexander (b. Poland, 1862), came to New York in 1880 as a visiting pianist, returned in 1884, in 1887–1905 was director of the College of Music, and has continued since as teacher. See art.

*Lankow, Anna (Rhine Prov., 1850–1908, Rhine Prov.), since 1870 a noted singer, came to New York in 1885, first as concert-singer, later as teacher. She published Die Wissenschaft des Kunstgesangs, 1899, 4th ed., 1905.

*Leefson, Maurits (b. Holland, 1861), came as concert-pianist in 1887 to Philadelphia, where he taught some years in the Musical Academy, and in 1899 joined Gustav Hille (see sec. 6) in the Leefson-Hille Conservatory, which he still conducts.

Lehmann, George (b. New York, 1865), trained at Leipzig and Berlin, since 1883 has been violinist, teacher, conductor and writer, from 1886 at Cleveland, from 1889 abroad, from 1893 in New York, from 1907 in Berlin, and since 1916 again in New York. See art.

*Lehmann, Lilli (b. Bavaria, 1848), a famous stage-soprano since 1865, came to America in

1885–89, returning in 1891–92. See Vol. ii. 667.

*Lewing, Adele (b. Hanover, 1866), a Leipzig graduate in 1885, taught in Chicago and Boston and became known as concert-pianist, in 1893–96 studied in Vienna, and since 1897 has been player and composer in New York. See art.

Lilienthal, Abraham Wolf (b. New York, 1859), studied in New York, from about 1880 was violinist under Damrosch and Thomas, in 1891–93 played viola in the New York String Quartet, and has taught composition as well as string-instruments. He has written a violin-sonata (1911), a trio, two quartets, a quintet, a sextet, dances and transcriptions for orchestra, and songs.

Listemann, Paul (b. Boston, 1871), son of Bernhard Listemann (see sec. 5), highly trained as a violinist, from 1888 toured with his father and uncle, in 1890–95 studied at Leipzig and Berlin, in 1895–97 was concertmaster at Pittsburgh and New York, then toured with the Redpath Concert Company, and since 1903 has taught in New York and played at the Metropolitan Opera House.

Locke, Flora Elbertine, née Huie (b. Wilson, N. Y., 1866), studied at Boston, New York and Leipzig, has taught in Buffalo since before 1890, from 1904 devoting herself to perfecting methods for teaching children, and publishing *The Foundation of Music in Rhymes and Songs*, 1908, '16.

*Loeffler, Charles Martin Tornov (b. Alsace, 1861), came as an experienced violinist to the Boston Symphony Orchestra in 1883, and after twenty years' service devoted himself to composition. See Vol. ii. 763, and art.

*Lorenz, Julius (b. Hanover, 1862), came as a visiting pianist in 1887–88 with Senkrah, in 1895–1911 was conductor of the Arion Society, New York, and other societies, and then returned to Glogau, Silesia. For works, see Baker, *Dict. of Musicians*, p. 550.

Lucas, Clarence (b. Niagara, Ont., 1866), trained at Montreal and Paris, from 1889 taught theory at Toronto and was conductor also at Hamilton, from 1891 was in the Utica Conservatory, and since 1893 has lived in London as composer, editor and critic, also in New York. See Vol. ii. 776, and art.

Luckstone, Isidore (b. Baltimore, 1861), early associated as musician with Jefferson the actor, in 1883–84 was accompanist for Urso, in 1884–91 for Remenyi on his world-tour, then with other artists till 1897, when he settled in New York.

*Lund, John Reinhold (b. Hamburg, 1859), in 1884 came as assistant-conductor to Damrosch, continuing with the German Opera Company, from 1887 led the Buffalo Orchestra and Orpheus Society, from 1903 toured as conductor of Herbert's operas, and since 1914 has been in Buffalo again. See art.

Lussan, Zélie de [Mme. Fronani] (b. New York, 1863), trained as an operatic soprano by her mother, was heard in concert in 1879, from 1885 was with the Boston Ideal Opera Company, from 1889 with the Carl Rosa Company, in 1894–95 at the Metropolitan Opera House (also in 1900–01), from 1895 was popular at London, Paris and Madrid, but retired after her marriage in 1907.

Lynes, Frank (Cambridge, Mass., 1858–1913), trained in Boston and Leipzig, from 1885 was organist in Boston. He composed chamber-music, piano-pieces, part-songs and songs.

*Maas, Louis Philipp Otto (Hesse, 1852–1889, Boston), having taught since 1875 at the Leipzig Conservatory, from 1880 was pianist, teacher and composer in Boston. See art.

MacDowell, Edward Alexander (New York, 1861–1908, New York), studied in New York, Paris, Wiesbaden and Frankfort, from 1882 taught at Wiesbaden, from 1888 lived in Boston as concert-pianist and gifted composer, from 1896 was professor at Columbia University, after 1902 suffered from ill-health, retiring in 1904. See Vol. iii. 4–6, and art.

*Macfarlane, William Charles (b. England, 1870), trained in New York, from 1885 was organist there, in 1912–19 municipal organist at Portland, and now in New York. See art.

*Mahr, Emil (Hesse, 1851–1914, Boston), who had been violinist at Bayreuth and under Richter and Henschel in London, from 1887 was a valued instructor at the New England Conservatory in Boston.

Manchester, Arthur Livingston (b. Bass River, N. J., 1862), educated in Philadelphia, began organ-playing in 1875, from 1882 taught in schools at Beaver, Pa., Clarion, Pa., and from 1886 in Abingdon, Va., from 1893 was editor of 'The Etude' and from 1896 of 'The Musician,' from 1904 dean of music at Converse College in South Carolina, from 1913 at Southwestern University in Texas, and since 1918 at Hardin College in Missouri. See art.

*Mannes, David (b. New York, 1866), trained in New York, Berlin and Brussels, early played in New York in theater-orchestras, from 1891 was in the Symphony Society, becoming concertmaster in 1898, and since 1902 has led the Symphony Club and taught in the Music School Settlement and other schools. See art. His wife, Clara Mannes, née Damrosch (b. Silesia, 1869), daughter of Leopold Damrosch (see sec. 6), is an accomplished pianist, has taught since 1889, and has joined him since 1898 in recitals.

Marcosson, Sol (b. Louisville, 1869), trained mostly in Berlin, appeared as boy-violinist in 1877, toured extensively abroad and in America, from 1892 was first violin in the Mendelssohn Quintette Club of Boston, from 1893 in the Philharmonic Club of New York, from 1895 concertmaster in the Cleveland Symphony Orchestra, from 1896 in the Chicago Orchestra, has taught much at Chautauqua and Lake Erie College, and now conducts a music-school in Cleveland.

*Margulies, Adele (b. Austria, 1863), made her début as pianist in 1881 at New York, since 1887 has been teacher at the National Conservatory, in 1890–92 started a Trio, which was reorganized in 1904 and has become famous. See art.

Mason, Henry Lowell (b. Boston, 1864), son of Henry Mason (see sec. 4), entered the employ of Mason & Hamlin, Boston, in 1888, becoming head of the firm in 1906. Since 1915 he has been president of the Cecilia Society. He has written *The Modern Artistic Pianoforte*, 1901, *The History and Development of the American Cabinet Organ*, 1901, and *Opera-Stories*, 1911, and is preparing an authoritative biography of his grandfather, Lowell Mason.

*Mattioli, Lino (b. Italy, 1853), came to New York in 1884 as 'cellist, and since 1885 has been singing-teacher at the Cincinnati College of Music. He has written for piano, 'cello and voice.

Maxson, Frederick (b. Beverly, N. J., 1862), trained in Philadelphia and Paris, since 1884 has been organist in Philadelphia, teaching since 1906 at the Leefson-Hille Conservatory and also appearing in recital. See art.

*Meltzer, Charles Henry (b. England, 1852), since 1888 has been critic, librettist and translator of opera-texts in New York. See art.

Miller, Dayton Clarence (b. Strongsville, O., 1866), since 1890 professor of physics at the Case School of Applied Science, Cleveland, has published *Boehm on the Flute and Flute-Playing*, 1908, and *The Science of Musical Sounds*, 1916, besides many articles. He has much extended the science of musical acoustics.

Miller, Frank E. (b. Hartford, Conn., 1859), graduated from Trinity College in 1881 and was trained as a physician, becoming known as a specialist in laryngology. See art.

*Mohr, Hermann (near Hamburg, 1830–1896, Philadelphia), who had taught in Berlin since 1850, from 1886 was in the Philadelphia Musical Academy. He wrote the cantata ' Bergmannsgruss,' male choruses and songs.

Mollenhauer, Louis (b. Brooklyn, 1863), son of Heinrich Mollenhauer (see sec. 4), was trained as violinist by his uncle, toured for some years in quintet-parties, in 1889 succeeded his father in his Brooklyn school, and since 1891 has been head of his own school.

*Monestel, Alexander (b. Costa Rica, 1865), studied at Brussels, from 1884 was organist at the Costa Rica Cathedral and professor in the Seminary, from 1902 organist in Brussels, and since 1909 organist in Brooklyn. He has written fourteen masses, an oratorio, ' The Seven Last Words,' and instrumental music.

Moore, Homer, from 1887 was a singer in opera and oratorio in New York. In recent years he has been singer, teacher and critic for the ' Republic ' in St. Louis, where his opera ' Louis XIV ' was given in 1917. Other operas are ' The Fall of Rome ' and the trilogy (text and music) ' The New World,' ' The Pilgrims,' ' The Puritans.'

*Morgan, Tali Esen (b. Wales, 1858), came to Scranton, Pa., in 1876 and was engaged for some years in journalism, from 1887 took up festival-work with Walter Damrosch and Seidl, first in New York and soon at Ocean Grove, N. J., where he has conducted summer gatherings of singers and organists.

Morrison, Charles Walthall (b. Covington, Ky., 1856), trained at Oberlin, Leipzig and Berlin, since 1880 has been in the faculty of the Oberlin Conservatory, in 1902 becoming its efficient director.

Morse, George Francis (b. Brooklyn, ?), educated in Brooklyn and New York, from 1887 was organist at Nyack, N. Y., and in 1890–1915 in Brooklyn. He has written ensemble-works for organ and other instruments.

Morsell, Herndon (b. Alexandria, Va., 1858), trained in Washington, Milan and Florence, early appeared as concert- and operatic tenor, and for many years has been singer and choral conductor in Washington.

*Musin, Ovide (b. Belgium, 1854), notable as violinist since 1870, came to New York in 1883 and toured extensively until 1892, from 1897 was located at Liège, but visited New York steadily until 1908, when he established a school there. See Vol. iii. 342, and art. His wife, née Annie Louise Hodges (b. 1856), a competent soprano, has joined him in tours.

*Neupert, Edmund (Norway, 1842–1888, New York), well known as pianist and teacher at Berlin, Copenhagen and Moscow, from 1882 was prominent in New York. See art.

Nevada, Emma [real name Wixom] (b. near Nevada City, Cal., 1862), studied for the stage in Vienna, from 1880 won European fame as a soprano, appeared in New York from 1884, and after some years settled in Paris. See Vol. iii. 365, and art.

Nevin, Ethelbert Woodbridge (Edgeworth, Pa., 1862–1901, New Haven, Conn.), studied at Pittsburgh, New York, Boston, Dresden and Berlin, spent a short life at various places, devoting himself to composing songs of unusual poetic quality. See Vol. iii. 366, and art. His older relative, George Balch Nevin (b. Shippensburg, Pa., 1859), is also a song-composer.

*Nikisch, Artur (b. Hungary, 1855), famous as violinist and conductor, in 1889–93 was leader of the Boston Symphony Orchestra, and in 1912 returned with the London Symphony Orchestra. See Vol. iii. 379–80, and art.

Nikita [Louisa Margaret Nicholson] (b. Philadelphia, 1872), after early training in Washington, sang in a traveling opera-troupe, became a facile coloratura-soprano, studied in Paris, won renown in Germany, and in 1894 became a leading singer at the Opéra at Paris.

Norris, Homer Albert (Wayne, Me., 1860–1920, New York), studied at Boston and Paris, from before 1890 was organist at Lewiston and Portland, Me., from 1892 at Boston, and in 1904–13 at St. George's, New York, becoming known as composer and author. See art.

Noyes, Edward Hibbard (b. London, Ont., 1867), studied as pianist in Chicago, Berlin and Vienna, in 1885–87 was organist in and near Boston, in 1890–95 toured in Europe, and since 1895 has been an efficient teacher in Boston and Hartford, with some ensemble-playing. See art.

O'Brion, Mary Eliza (b. Limerick, Me., 1859), highly trained as a pianist in Portland, Florence, Frankfort and Vienna, from 1883 for several years appeared in Boston and elsewhere with success, but finally devoted herself to teaching.

Oesterle, Otto (St. Louis, 1861–1894, Darien, Conn.), from about 1880 was an accomplished flutist in leading New York orchestras, also teaching in the National Conservatory.

Orth, Lizette E., née Blood (d. 1913, Boston), from 1883 wife of John Orth (see art.), wrote piano-pieces, songs, operettas, etc., for children.

O'Shea, John Augustine (b. Milford, Mass., 1864), trained in Boston, since about 1887 has been concert-organist there and lately also supervisor in the public schools. See art.

Page, Nathaniel Clifford (b. San Francisco, 1866), brought out his first opera in 1889, and, besides much composition, since 1905 has been in editorial work in Boston and New York. See art.

Parker, George Albert (b. Kewanee, Ill., 1856), studied at Chicago, Stuttgart, Berlin and Paris, since 1882 has taught in the School of Music at Syracuse University, becoming its head in 1888 and Dean of Fine Arts in 1906. He is an accomplished pianist and organist. Mus.D. of Syracuse University in 1893.

Parker, Horatio William (b. Auburndale, Mass., 1863–1919, Cedarhurst, N. Y.), trained in Boston and Munich, from 1885 taught at Garden City, N. Y., from 1888 was organist at New York, in 1893–1901 at Trinity Church, Boston, and from 1894 was head of the Yale School of Music. See Vol. iii. 622–3, and art.

Parkhurst, Howard Elmore (Ashland, Mass., 1848–1916, Lavallette, N. J.), for many years organist in New York, published a *System of Harmony*, 1908, an organ-method, 1911, *The Church Organist*, 1913, *The Beginnings of the World's Music*, 1914, and *Rambles in Music-Land*, 1914, besides books on birds and plants. He also composed somewhat in large forms.

Pasmore, Henry Bickford (b. Jackson, Wis., 1857), studied in San Francisco, Leipzig and London, since 1885 has been organist, teacher and composer in San Francisco. See art.

Perry, Edward Baxter (b. Haverhill, Mass., 1855), blind from infancy, studied in Boston and in Germany, in 1881–83 taught in the Oberlin Conservatory, and since then has devoted himself mostly to giving piano-recitals in all parts of the country. See art.

Porter, Frank Addison (b. Dixmont, Me., 1859), trained at Boston and Leipzig, since 1884 has been piano-teacher at the New England Conservatory and since 1892 also director of normal work in piano. He has published

instruction-books and composed a sonata and other piano-music.

Powell, Maud [Mrs. H. Godfrey Turner] (Peru, Ill., 1868–1920, Uniontown, Pa.), having studied at Chicago, Leipzig, Berlin and Paris, from 1885 was universally known as a violinist of the first rank. See Vol. iii. 802, and art.

Pratt, John Harraden (b. Freeport, Me., 1848), trained in Portland, Oakland and Leipzig, has been organist, teacher and composer in or about San Francisco since about 1885. See art.

*Preyer, Carl Adolph (b. Baden, 1863), came to America in 1884, in 1889–91 taught at Baker University in Kansas, and since 1893 has been professor at the University of Kansas, becoming in 1915 associate dean of the School of Fine Arts. See art.

*Protheroe, Daniel (b. Wales, 1866), from 1886 conducted a Welsh choral society at Scranton, Pa., from 1894 was in Milwaukee as baritone and teacher, and since 1904 has also been conductor in Chicago. See art.

Randolph, Harold (b. Richmond, Va., 1861), studied at Baltimore, from 1885 became prominent there as organist and notable concert-pianist, and since 1898 has been head of the Peabody Conservatory. See art.

Reuss, Eduard (New York, 1851–1911, Saxony), studied at Göttingen, Weimar and Paris, from 1880 taught at Karlsruhe, from 1896 at Wiesbaden (head of the Conservatory from 1899), and from 1902 was professor at the Dresden Conservatory. He visited America in 1902–03 with his wife, who is a noted operatic singer. He published a notable biography of Liszt in 1898 and a work on Liszt's songs in 1906, besides many articles.

Rivarde, Serge Achille (b. New York, 1865), studied at New York and Paris, in 1881–84 appeared as violinist in New York, in 1886–91 was concertmaster under Lamoureux at Paris, and since 1899 has taught in the London Royal College. See Vol. iv. 110.

Rogers, James Hotchkiss (b. Fair Haven, Conn., 1857), studied in Chicago, Berlin and Paris, began teaching in 1882 at Burlington, Ia., and since 1883 has been organist and composer at Cleveland. See art.

*Rosenfeld, Maurice Bernard (b. Austria, 1867), came to America as a boy, studied at Chicago, from 1888 taught piano there, since 1907 has been critic and editor, and since 1916 head of his own school. See art.

*Rotoli, Augusto (Italy, 1847–1904, Boston), from 1885 taught at the New England Conservatory, Boston. While maestro in Italy he wrote a mass and a psalm for the funeral of Victor Emmanuel in 1878.

*Ruifrok, Henri Willem Johan (b. Holland, 1862), from 1889 was music-director at Valparaiso University in Indiana, from 1892 at the Gottschalk Lyric School, Chicago, from 1895 at the Musical College, Des Moines, from 1904 head of his own school there, and since 1915 professor at Drake University.

Russell, Ella [Countess di Rhigini] (b. Cleveland, 1864), studied at Paris and Milan, and since 1882 has been a celebrated operatic soprano on the Continent and especially in England. See art.

Russell, Lillian [Helen Louise Leonard, now Mrs. Alexander P. Moore] (b. Clinton, Ia., 1861), educated in Chicago, from about 1880 was long a favorite stage-soprano in light opera and vaudeville.

Saenger, Gustav (b. New York, 1865), from about 1885 violinist and theater-conductor, has since 1897 been editor for Carl Fischer. See art.

Saenger, Oscar (b. Brooklyn, 1868) trained in New York, has taught singing there since 1889, and was for a time also an effective stage-baritone. See art.

Sanderson, Sibyl (Sacramento, Cal., 1865–1903, France), trained as an operatic soprano at San Francisco and Paris, was from 1888 noted at Paris, chiefly in connection with Massenet's works, appearing in America in 1895 and '98. See art.

*****Santelmann, William Henry** (b. Hanover, 1863), trained at Leipzig, from 1887 played in the U. S. Marine Band, from 1895 conducted a theater-orchestra, and since 1898 has led the Marine Band. See art.

*****Sapio, Romualdo** (b. Sicily, 1858), from before 1890 was concert-conductor for Patti, Albani and Nordica, from 1892 taught singing at the National Conservatory, New York, and has been otherwise active.

*****Scheve, Edward Benjamin** (b. Westphalia, 1865), from 1888 organist and teacher at Rochester, from 1892 was concert-organist and head of his own school at Chicago, and since 1906 professor at Grinnell College in Iowa. See art.

*****Schiller, Madeline** [Mrs. Marcus E. Bennett] (England, 1850?–1911, New York), after success as concert-pianist in England and Australia, lived for some years in Boston, then toured abroad, and after 1895 was a prominent teacher in New York.

Schirmer, Gustave (New York, 1864–1907, Boston), and **Schirmer, Rudolph Ernest** (New York, 1859–1919, Santa Barbara, Cal.), sons of Gustav Schirmer (see sec. 4), became partners in their father's publishing-business in New York in 1885, making it one of the great music-houses of the world. See art.

*****Schlesinger, Sebastian Benson** (Hamburg, 1837–1917, France), studied in Boston, where later for years he was German Consul, and, though assuming to be but an amateur, composed many graceful songs and piano-pieces.

*****Schneider, Hans** (b. Posen, 1863), came to Providence in 1887 as choral and orchestral conductor, establishing a piano-school in 1904, which he still conducts. He has specialized in the psychology of piano-playing, writing many articles for periodicals.

Schoen, Isaac Leopold (b. St. Louis, 1858), trained at St. Louis, New York and Berlin, since 1887 has been prominent as violinist at St.

Louis, in orchestral and chamber-organizations, and now teaches in the Kroeger School of Music.

*****Schradieck, Henry** (Hamburg, 1846–1918, New York), in 1883–89 was violin-teacher at the Cincinnati College of Music, from 1898 taught in Philadelphia at the Broad Street Conservatory, and from 1912 was at the Institute of Applied Music in New York. See Vol. iv. 274, and art.

*****Schuëcker, Heinrich** (Austria, 1867–1913, Boston), in 1885 came as harpist in the Boston Symphony Orchestra and teacher at the New England Conservatory. In 1893 he formed a Trio (violin, 'cello and harp) with Jacques Hoffmann and Karl Barth.

*****Schulz, Leo** (b. Posen, 1865), a superior 'cellist, from 1889 in the Boston Symphony Orchestra and the New England Conservatory, since 1890 has been in the New York Philharmonic Society, and in 1904–15 in the Margulies Trio. See art.

Sealy, Frank Linwood (b. Madison, N. J., 1858), organist and conductor for many years at Newark, N. J., has also been efficient as organist for the New York Oratorio Society.

*****Seeboeck, William Charles Ernest** (Austria, 1859–1907, Chicago), trained as pianist at Vienna and Petrograd, from 1881 was player, teacher and composer in Chicago. See art.

*****Seidl, Anton** (Hungary, 1850–1898, New York), the eminent Wagner interpreter, in 1885–91 and from 1895 was conductor at the Metropolitan Opera House in New York, from 1891 also conductor of the Philharmonic Society. See Vol. iv. 408, and art.

*****Sembrich, Marcella** [Praxede Marcelline Kochanska] (b. Galicia, 1858), an operatic and concert-singer of the first rank, appeared in New York in 1883–84, and in 1898–1909 sang at the Metropolitan Opera House. See Vol. iv. 409–10, and art.

Senkrah [Arma Leoretta Hoffmann, née Harkness] (New York, 1864–1900, Saxony), educated at Leipzig, Brussels and Paris, from 1882 became celebrated as a violinist on the Continent.

Shackley, Frederick Newell (b. Laconia, N. H., 1868), trained in Boston, from 1885 was organist at Lewiston, Me., and since 1892 in Boston. He has written valuable church-music and organ-pieces and transcriptions.

Shepard, Frank Hartson (Bethel, Conn., 1863–1913, Orange, N. J.), trained in Boston, from 1881 was organist at various places, in 1886–90 was in Leipzig studying, and from 1888 organist at the English Chapel, and in 1891, with his wife **Annie Agnes Shepard**, née Boll (b. New York, 1859), established a piano-school at Orange, N. J., which she continues. They have published several instruction-books, of which the most noted is *Harmony Simplified* (many editions).

Sinsheimer, Bernard (b. New York, 1870), trained as violinist at Paris and Berlin, from 1886 appeared as soloist in New York, and since 1902 has led his own Quartet with notable enterprise.

Smith, Ella May, née Dunning (b. Uhrichsville, O., 1860), since about 1880 has been active as teacher, organist and critic, chiefly in Columbus, and prominent in music-club enterprises.

Smith, Wilson George (b. Elyria, O., 1855), studied at Cincinnati and Berlin, and since 1882 has been a prominent teacher and composer at Cleveland. See art.

Spalding, Walter Raymond (b. Northampton, Mass., 1865), graduated at Harvard in 1887, in 1887–91 was instructor in languages at St. Mark's School, Southboro, Mass., from 1891 studied in Paris and Munich, and since 1895 has been in the music-faculty of Harvard University. See art.

*Spicker, Max (Prussia, 1858–1912, New York), from 1882 conducted the Beethoven Männerchor in New York, from 1888 was head of the Brooklyn Conservatory, and from 1895 taught at the National Conservatory and was reader for the Schirmer firm. See art.

Stair, Patty (b. Cleveland, 1869), trained in Cleveland, since 1889 has taught in the Cleveland Conservatory, besides able work as organist and composer. See art.

Stanton, Edmund C., is notable as the effective manager of German opera at the Metropolitan Opera House, New York, in 1885–91, succeeding Leopold Damrosch.

Sterling, Winthrop Smith (b. Cincinnati, 1859), was educated at Cincinnati, Leipzig and London, began as organist in London, later in Cincinnati, from 1887 taught in the College of Music there, and in 1903 founded the Metropolitan College. See art.

*Sternberg, Constantin Ivanovitch, Edler von (b. Russia, 1852), an experienced pianist, conductor and composer, from 1880 concertized in America, from 1886 taught in Atlanta, and since 1890 has been head of his own school in Philadelphia. See art.

Stevenson, Edward Irenæus Prime (b. Madison, N. J., 1868), from 1881 a frequent writer on musical subjects in ' The Independent ' and from 1895 also in ' Harper's Weekly.' Among his numerous books on many subjects are *Some Men, and Women, and Music,* and two musical novels.

*Stevenson, Frederick (b. England, 1845), for many years singing-teacher in London, in 1883 was organist and conductor at Denver, and since 1894 has been organist, conductor and composer in California. See art.

*Stewart, Humphrey John (b. England, 1856), from 1886 was organist in San Francisco, in 1901–02 at Boston, from 1903 again at San Francisco, and since 1915 at San Diego. See art.

Stocker, Stella, née Prince (b. Jacksonville, Ill., 1858), graduated from the University of Michigan in 1880, was trained at Jacksonville and abroad, after teaching in the Middle West, has devoted herself to Indian music, upon which she has lectured widely, and to composition. See art.

*Stoeving, Carl Heinrich Paul (b. Saxony, 1861), toured in America as concert-violinist in 1884 and 1892, from 1898 was professor at the Guildhall School in London, and since 1914 has taught in New York and New Haven. See art.

Surette, Thomas Whitney (b. Concord, Mass., 1862), trained in Boston, from 1883 was organist at Concord, in 1893–94 taught at Pottstown, Pa., in 1895–96 was organist in Baltimore, and since 1895 has been lecturer on musical subjects, as well as composer and author. See art.

*Sutro, Florence Edith, née Clinton [Mrs. Theodore Sutro] (England, 1865–1906, New York), from 1888 known as pianist and song-composer, from 1898 was founder of the National Federation of Musical Clubs. She published *Women in Music,* 1899.

*Svečenski, Louis (b. Croatia, 1862), was in 1885–1903 violinist in the Boston Symphony Orchestra, in 1885–1917 violist in the Kneisel Quartet, and is now teaching in New York. He has published viola-studies.

Tapper, Thomas (b. Canton, Mass., 1864), after study at home and abroad, since before 1890 has been a forceful teacher and writer upon music-pedagogy, from 1905 at the Institute of Musical Art in New York. See art. His wife, ***Bertha Tapper,** née Feiring (Norway, 1859–1915, New York), studied at Leipzig and Vienna, came to America in 1881, from 1889 was piano-teacher at the New England Conservatory in Boston, and from 1905 at the Institute of Musical Art in New York. She published piano-pieces and songs and edited many of Grieg's piano-works.

Thunder, Henry Gordon (b. Philadelphia, 1865), trained in Philadelphia, since 1881 has been a prominent organist there, also since 1897 conductor of the Choral Society and in 1897–1900 of his own Symphony Orchestra. He has written several cantatas, a mass, and is at work upon an opera.

Thurber, Jeannette, née Meyer, wife of a prominent New York merchant, in 1885 founded the National Conservatory there, which has had a notable history under eminent directors. In 1885 she was also the promoter of the American Opera Company.

*Tirindelli, Pier Adolfo (b. Italy, 1858), since about 1885 has been violin-teacher at the Cincinnati Conservatory and for thirty years conductor of the Conservatory Orchestra. He has written a violin-concerto and other violin-works, the operas ' Athénaïde ' and ' Blanc et Noir,' cantatas, etc.

*Tonning, Gerard (b. Norway, 1860), from 1887 was conductor at Duluth, Minn., and since 1905 has lived at Seattle as composer. He has written the opera ' Leif Erikson ' (1910), two operettas and a musical pantomime, a piano-trio, chamber-music, piano-pieces and songs.

Truette, Everett Ellsworth (b. Rockland, Mass., 1861), graduated from Boston University in 1883, studied in Berlin, Paris and England, since 1885 has been a notable organist in Boston and vicinity, from 1897 at the Eliot Church, Newton, besides giving recitals elsewhere. See art.

*Van Broekhoven, John A. (b. Holland, 1856), in 1889–99 was teacher at the Cincinnati College of Music and conductor of symphony-concerts, played viola under Thomas at various occasions, and since 1905 has lived in New York as teacher. He has written the short opera ' A Colonial Wedding' (1905), the opera ' Camaralzaman,' a ' Creole Suite,' the ' Columbia' overture, a string-quartet, etc., besides *The Tone-Producing Functions of the Vocal Organs*, 1905, *The True Method of Tone-Production*, 1908, a book on Harmony, etc.

Van der Stucken, Frank Valentin (b. Fredericksburg, Tex., 1858), trained at Antwerp and Leipzig, after travels, work at Breslau and further study, from 1884 was conductor in New York, from 1895 at Cincinnati, continuing at intervals though residing abroad in 1908–17. See Vol. v. 217, and art.

*Venth, Carl (b. Rhine Prov., 1860), in 1880 came as violinist to New York, from 1884 playing at the Metropolitan Opera House, from 1888 directed a school in Brooklyn and from 1889 led the Brooklyn Symphony Orchestra, from 1907 was conductor of the St. Paul Orchestra, going thence in 1908 to similar positions in Dallas and later Fort Worth, Tex. See art.

*Vere, Clémentine Duchêne de [Mme. Sapio] (b. France, ?), from about 1880 for nearly twenty years was a favorite operatic and concert-soprano in New York. See art.

Vilim, Joseph Alois (b. Chicago, 1861), studied at Prague, since 1884 has been violinist and teacher in Chicago, first in the Musical College, from 1887 in the American Conservatory, and since 1899 as head of his own school. He has also been active in establishing ensemble-groups. See art.

Vogt, Augustus Stephen (b. Washington, Ont., 1861), trained at Boston and Leipzig, from 1888 taught at the Toronto College of Music, and from 1892 at the Toronto Conservatory, becoming its head in 1913. From 1888 he was also organist and in 1894 founded the famous Mendelssohn Choir, which he conducted until 1917. See art.

Warren, Richard Henry (b. Albany, 1859), son of George W. Warren (see sec. 4) and trained by him, has been an organist in New York since 1880, and the founder in 1886 of the Church Choral Society, which he led till 1895 and in 1903–07.

Weld, Arthur Cyril Gordon (b. Jamaica Plain, Mass., 1862), trained in Dresden, Berlin and Munich, became known as orchestral composer from 1885, from 1890 was critic for the Boston ' Post.' See Champlin and Apthorp, *Cyclopedia of Music*, iii. 623, and art.

Whelpley, Benjamin Lincoln (b. Eastport,

Me., 1864), studied in Boston and Paris, since 1886 has been known in Boston as pianist and organist. He has written an orchestral Intermezzo, Preludes for violin, 'cello and organ, songs, piano-pieces, choruses, etc.

White, John (West Springfield, Mass., 1855–1902, Hesse), studied at Hartford and Berlin, from 1880 was organist in New York, studied in Munich, in 1887–96 was again in New York, and then removed to Munich. See art.

Whiting, Arthur Battelle (b. Cambridge, Mass., 1861), studied in Boston and Munich, was concert-pianist in Boston from 1880 and in New York since 1895, devoting himself much to lecturing and to bringing out 18th-century keyboard-music. See art.

*Williams, Alberto (b. Argentina, 1862), trained at Buenos Aires and Paris, since 1889 has been conductor of symphony-concerts at Buenos Aires, established and now directs the Conservatorio there, since 1903 with numerous branches in all parts of the Republic. He has composed several symphonies and other orchestral music, many piano-pieces, etc., and has written on theory. See art.

Wilson, George H., of Boston, from 1883 for ten years issued a useful *Musical Year-Book of the United States*, in 1893–94 with C. B. Cady.

Wiske, C. Mortimer (b. Bennington, Vt., 1853), after study at Troy and early work as organist, in 1882 became Thomas' assistant as chorus-conductor at New York, was later leader of the Chorus Society there, and since 1902 has had charge of festivals at Paterson and Newark, N. J.

*Wodell, Frederick William (b. England, 1859), since before 1890 has been prominent, first at Rochester, of recent years at Boston, as baritone, choral conductor and composer. He has written a light opera, the cantata ' The American Flag' (1915), part-songs and anthems, *Choir and Chorus Conducting*, 1908, and *How to Sing by Note*, 1915. See art.

Wolle, John Frederick (b. Bethlehem, Pa., 1863), studied at Philadelphia and Munich, from 1881 was organist in Philadelphia, from 1885 organist at Bethlehem, from 1905 professor at the University of California, and since 1911 has been at Bethlehem again, conducting the festivals of the Bach Choir. See art.

Wood, Mary, née Knight [now Mrs. Alfred B. Mason] (Easthampton, Mass., 1859), educated in Boston and New York, has long been a song-composer of distinction.

*Wrightson, Sydney Lloyd (b. England, 1869), came to America in 1889, in 1904 founded the College of Music in Washington, remaining its head till 1914, and has been choral conductor there. As singer he has appeared with many orchestras.

*Zach, Max Wilhelm (b. Galicia, 1864), in 1886–1907 was violist in the Boston Symphony Orchestra, in 1887–97 member of the Adamowski Quartet, and since 1907 has conducted the St. Louis Symphony Orchestra.

F

Zech, Frederick (b. Philadelphia, 1858), studied in San Francisco and Berlin, taught at Berlin from 1880, and since 1882 has been piano-teacher and conductor at San Francisco, and a prolific composer.

***Ziegler, Anna Elizabeth**, née Koelling (b. Hamburg, 1867), was educated in New York, early became known as pianist and singer, was director of the Berlin Conservatory there and now is head of the Ziegler Institute of Normal Singing.

Zoellner, Joseph (b. Brooklyn, 1862), trained mostly in New York and Dresden, from 1882 was violinist and teacher in Brooklyn, from 1903 in Stockton, Cal., in 1907–12 played and taught in Brussels, there forming with two sons and a daughter the Zoellner Quartet, which since 1912 has toured the United States. In this he plays viola.

8. The Closing Decade of the 19th Century

Abott, Bessie Pickens (Riverdale, N. Y., 1878–1919, New York), studied in New York and later in Paris, from 1894 appeared as soprano in light opera, and from 1901 in grand opera, until 1906 in Paris and then in the United States, besides concert-tours in many countries. In 1912 she married T. W. Story.

Adams, Suzanne (b. Cambridge, Mass., 1873), was trained as soprano in Paris, from 1894 appearing in opera there, from 1897 at Nice and since 1898 at London. She sang in New York in 1899 and was at the Metropolitan Opera House in 1902. See art.

Aldrich, Richard (b. Providence, 1863), graduated from Harvard in 1885, entered journalistic work, first in Providence, from 1889 in Washington, where he began musical criticism. Since 1891 he has been critic in New York, till 1902 on the ' Tribune ' and then on the ' Times.' See art.

Aller, George Henry (b. Shiremanstown, Pa., 1871), trained as singer at Doane College in Nebraska, Chicago, Berlin and Paris, since 1893 has taught in Nebraska, from 1914 as music-director at Doane College, developing notable interest in vocal music.

***Anger, Joseph Humphrey** (England, 1862–1913, Toronto), after experience in England, was from 1893 theory-professor at the Toronto Conservatory, notable also as organist, conductor and author. See art.

Armstrong, William Dawson (b. Alton, Ill., 1868), trained in St. Louis and Chicago, from 1890 was organist at Alton and in 1896–1908 at St. Louis, and since 1908 has been head of his own school in Alton. He has written the opera ' The Spectre Bridegroom ' (1899), an orchestral suite and an overture, vocal and instrumental pieces, etc. See biography by W. F. Norton, 1916.

Arnold [-Strothotte], Maurice (b. St. Louis, 1865), studied at Cincinnati, Berlin, Cologne and Breslau, taught in St. Louis, from 1894

was instructor in composition in the National Conservatory in New York, where he still lives. He has twice gone abroad as conductor or performer. For list of works, see Baker, *Dict. of Musicians*, p. 28, and Hughes, *Contemporary American Composers*, pp. 135–9.

Ashton, Joseph Nickerson (b. Salem, Mass., 1868), graduated from Brown University in 1891, taught there from 1895 and also in Boston, in 1898–1904 being associate-professor in the University. Since 1905 he has been organist at Brookline. See art.

Atherton, Percy Lee (b. Boston, 1871), graduated from Harvard in 1893, studied in Munich, Berlin, Rome and Paris, has been known as composer since 1890, at first of comic operas, later of orchestral and vocal works. See art.

Avery, Stanley R. (b. Yonkers, N. Y., 1879), trained in New York and Berlin as organist, from 1896 worked at Yonkers and since 1910 at Minneapolis. See art.

Baldwin, Ralph Lyman (b. Easthampton, Mass., 1872), musically educated in Boston, from about 1895 was organist in Easthampton and Northampton, and since 1904 in Hartford, Conn., where he is also supervisor and choral conductor. See art.

Baltzell, Winton James (b. Shiremanstown, Pa., 1864), graduated from Lebanon Valley College in 1884, studied in Philadelphia, Boston and London, taught in Reading, Pa., in 1897–99 and 1900–07 edited ' The Etude,' in 1907–18 ' The Musician,' and has since been in literary work in New York. See art.

Barbour, Florence, née Newell (b. Providence, 1867), gained her training in America, and has won success as concert-pianist and composer, chiefly of piano-works and songs. See art.

***Barford, Vernon West** (b. England, 1876), came as organist in 1895 to Qu'Appelle, Que., and since 1900 has been organist and conductor at Edmonton, Alberta.

Bartholomew, Edward Fry (b. Sunbury, Pa., 1846), trained as a Lutheran minister, professor at Augustana College since 1888, has published *The Relation of Psychology to Music*, 1899, 1903, *Rational Musical Pedagogy*, 1905, and many magazine articles, and edited *The Musical Profession*, 1905.

Beach, John Parsons (b. Gloversville, N. Y., 1877), studied in Boston and Minneapolis, taught in both cities and from 1904 in New Orleans, went abroad in 1910 and has lived in Paris and Italy as composer. See art.

Beaton, Isabella (b. Grinnell, Ia., 1870), after study at Grinnell, Berlin and Paris, since 1899 has worked at Cleveland as pianist, composer and teacher, first at the Cleveland School of Music and from 1910 in her own school. See art.

Benson, Louis FitzGerald (b. Philadelphia, 1855), both lawyer and clergyman by profession, since 1894 has been hymnal-editor for the Presbyterian Church and has become a foremost hymnologist. His chief publication as editor is *The Hymnal*, 1895, 1911, and as author *The English Hymn*, 1915. For full list, see *Who's Who in America*.

Bergquist, John Victor (b. St. Peter, Minn., 1877), studied at St. Peter, Minneapolis, Berlin and Paris, from 1895 was organist in Lutheran churches in Minnesota, with recitals in Minneapolis in 1903–12 and elsewhere, in 1905–08 taught at Gustavus Adolphus College, and since 1912 has been music-director at Augustana College, Rock Island, Ill. He has written the oratorio 'Golgotha' (1906), a Christmas cantata, a Reformation cantata (1917), three organ-sonatas, etc.

*Berwald, William Henry (b. Mecklenburg, 1864), since 1892 has been professor at Syracuse University and active as conductor and fertile composer. See art.

Bispham, David Scull (b. Philadelphia, 1857), a singer from youth, took up careful study in Milan and London in 1886, appearing as operatic baritone from 1891 in London and from 1896 in America. Latterly he has been heard chiefly in concert. See Vol. **i**. 333, and art.

Blass, Robert (b. New York, 1867), studied in New York, Leipzig and Frankfort, made his début as operatic bass at Weimar in 1895, sang in Germany, and since 1900 mostly at the Metropolitan Opera House in New York.

Blauvelt, Lillian Evans (b. Brooklyn, 1874), was trained as operatic soprano at New York and Paris, making her début at Brussels in 1893. She has appeared widely in both America and Europe. See Vol. i. 338–9, and art.

*Bochau, Charles Henry (b. Holstein, 1870), brought to America as a boy, studied in Baltimore, and since 1897 has taught singing in the Peabody Conservatory, besides work as conductor and composer. See art.

*Boeppler, William (b. Germany, 1863), came to Milwaukee in 1894, started the Wisconsin Conservatory in 1899 and the Symphony Orchestra in 1902, and since 1904 has also been active in Chicago. See art.

Bogert, Walter Lawrence (b. Flushing, N. Y., 1864), graduated from Columbia in 1888 and trained as a lawyer, was also broadly educated in music in New York, where since 1898 he has been teacher, lecturer, conductor and writer, especially on vocal art.

Bollinger, Samuel (b. Fort Smith, Ark., 1871) trained mostly at Leipzig, taught in the Conservatory there in 1893–95 and was organist of the American Church, from 1896 was at Fort Smith, from 1898 in San Francisco, and since 1907 in St. Louis, directing his own school. See art.

*Borowski, Felix (b. England, 1872), son of a Polish musician, studied extensively in London and Cologne, from 1892 taught in Aberdeen and London, in 1897 came to the Chicago Musical College as teacher of composition, and since 1916 has been president there. He is distinguished as composer and critic as well. See art.

Bowen, George Oscar (b. Castle Creek, N. Y., 1873), from about 1895 was prominent as music-supervisor at Stamford, Conn., Northampton, Mass., Homer and Yonkers, N. Y., and in 1917–20 was Municipal Director of Music in Flint, Mich., conducting various enterprises for popular musical culture, going thence to the University of Michigan.

Boyd, Charles N. (b. Pleasant Unity, Pa., 1875), since 1894 has been organist in Pittsburgh, from 1903 also instructor at the Western Theological Seminary, and from 1915 a director of the Pittsburgh Musical Institute. See Baker, *Dict. of Musicians*, p. 1078.

Breil, Joseph Carl (b. Pittsburgh, 1870), studied in Leipzig and Milan, in 1891–92 was tenor in the Juch Opera Company, from 1892 singer at St. Paul's, Pittsburgh, from 1897 theater-conductor there and on tour, and since 1909 has written much for plays and especially photo-plays, besides comic operas. His 'The Legend' was produced in 1919 at the Metropolitan Opera House.

Brockway, Howard A. (b. Brooklyn, 1870), trained at Berlin, from 1895 taught in New York, from 1903 in Baltimore, and since 1910 again in New York. Besides much composition, he has made important studies of Kentucky folk-tunes. See art.

*Broome, William Edward (b. England, 1868), in 1893 came to America as conductor of a visiting Welsh chorus, from 1894 was organist in Montreal, and since 1905 in Toronto, where he is also conductor of the Oratorio Society. See art.

*Bruening, Hans (b. Prussia, 1868), after extended tours in Europe as concert-pianist, in 1899 founded the Wisconsin College of Music at Milwaukee, of which he is director.

Buck, Dudley, Jr. (b. Hartford, Conn., 1869), son of the organist (see sec. 5), studied singing at Florence, Frankfort, Paris and London, appearing in opera and concert from 1895 in England and from 1899 in America. Since 1902 he has taught in New York.

Bullard, Frederick Field (Boston, 1864–1904, Boston), after study at Munich, from 1892 was teacher and popular vocal composer in Boston. See art.

Burrowes, Katharine (b. Kingston, Ont., ?), trained in Detroit and Berlin, since 1895 has taught in Detroit, at the Conservatory and since 1903 in her own Piano School, specializing in work for children. See art.

Butler, Harold Lancaster (b. Silver City, Ida., 1874), studied in Chicago and Paris, from 1895 taught singing at Valparaiso University and from 1900 was director of the music-department there, from 1904 at Syracuse University, and since 1915 has been dean of Fine Arts in the University of Kansas.

*Cadek, Joseph Ottokar (b. Bohemia, 1868), from about 1890 appeared as violinist in the United States, and since 1895 has taught in Chattanooga, Tenn., where he established a school in 1904.

Carter, Ernest Trow (b. Orange, N. J., 1866), trained in New York and Berlin, from 1892 taught in Nordhoff, Cal., in 1897–98 was organist of the American Church in Berlin, in 1899–1901 was organist and lecturer at Princeton University, and has since been conductor and composer in New York. He has written the opéra comique ' The Blonde Donna,' a symphonic suite, a string-quartet, and many songs and anthems.

*Caruso, Enrico (b. Italy, 1873), the great operatic tenor, appeared in South America in 1899–1903, and in New York since 1903. See Vol. v. 622, and art.

Clark, Charles William (b. Van Wert, O., 1865), trained as concert-baritone in Chicago and London, since 1897 has been widely heard in America and Europe, besides teaching in the Bush Conservatory, Chicago.

*Clemens, Charles Edwin (b. England, 1858), came to Cleveland in 1896 as organist, and since 1899 has been lecturer or professor at Western Reserve University. See art.

Coerne, Louis Adolphe (b. Newark, 1870), studied at Harvard and in Boston and Munich, from 1894 was conductor in Buffalo, from 1897 in Columbus, in 1899–02 and again in 1905–07 lived in Europe, in 1903–04 was professor at Smith College, in 1907–09 music-director in Troy, N. Y., from 1900 professor at Olivet College in Michigan, from 1910 at the University of Wisconsin, and since 1915 at Connecticut College. See art.

Cole, Rossetter Gleason (b. Clyde, Mich., 1866), graduated from the University of Michigan in 1888, studied there and in Berlin, from 1892 was professor at Ripon College, from 1894 at Grinnell College, from 1907 at the University of Wisconsin, and since 1909 is teacher and composer in Chicago. See art.

Converse, Frederick Shepherd (b. Newton, Mass., 1871), graduated from Harvard in 1893, was trained in Boston and Munich, from 1899 taught at the New England Conservatory and at Harvard until 1907, since then being engaged upon composition. See art.

Cooke, James Francis (b. Bay City, Mich., 1875), studied in New York and Würzburg, began teaching before 1890 in New York and was organist and choral conductor in Brooklyn, engaged in much literary work, and since 1907 has been editor of ' The Etude ' in Philadelphia, from 1917 also president of the Presser Foundation. See art.

Coombs, Charles Whitney (b. Bucksport, Me., 1859), after study in Stuttgart, Dresden and England, being in 1887–91 organist of the American Church at Dresden, since 1892 has been organist in New York. See art.

Copp, Evelyn Ashton, née Fletcher (b. Woodstock, Ont., 1872), after study in Canada, England, Berlin and Paris, began teaching in 1894 in Canada, evolved special methods of kindergarten and primary instruction, and since 1897 has taught in Boston, at first in the New England Conservatory.

Dana, Lynn Boardman (b. Middleport, N. Y., 1875), son of William H. Dana (see sec. 6), since 1916 has been head of Dana's Musical Institute in Warren, O. Since 1904 he has also taught at Chautauqua and directed the annual festivals at Lockport, N. Y. See art.

DeLamarter, Eric (b. Lansing, Mich., 1880), studied in Chicago and Paris, from about 1898 was organist in Chicago, in 1904–05 taught at Olivet College, in 1909–10 at the Chicago Musical College, since 1906 has been organist in Chicago, since 1908 music-critic, and since 1911 choral and orchestral conductor. See art.

Demarest, Clifford (b. Tenafly, N. J., 1874), trained in or near New York, from about 1895 was organist at Tenafly, and since 1900 in New York. See art.

*Déthier, Gaston Marie (b. Belgium, 1875), in 1894 came to New York as organist at St. Francis Xavier's, and since 1907 has taught at the Institute of Musical Art, besides concert-playing. See art.

*Dippel, Johann Andreas (b. Hesse, 1866), the operatic tenor and impresario, first appeared in New York in 1890–91, toured in 1892, from 1898 was at the Metropolitan Opera House, becoming in 1908 its executive head, from 1910 managed the Chicago-Philadelphia Opera Company, and since 1913 has directed his own company in light opera. See art.

Doenhoff, Albert von (b. Louisville, 1880), son of Helene von Doenhoff (see sec. 6), studied at Cincinnati and New York, in 1899–1907 taught at the National Conservatory in New York, and since 1905 has been frequently heard as concert-pianist there and elsewhere.

Drake, Earl R. (Aurora, Ill., 1865–1916, Chicago), trained as violinist at Chicago, Cincinnati and Berlin, in 1893–97 taught in the Gottschalk Lyric School, Chicago, directed his own Quartet, making many concert-tours, and from 1900 conducted his own school. He wrote the operas ' The Blind Girl of Castel-Cuillé ' (1914) and ' The Mite and the Mighty ' (1915), several orchestral and many violin-pieces, etc.

*Dunkley, Ferdinand Luis (b. England, 1869), came to Albany, N. Y., in 1893 as teacher, from 1899 was in Asheville, N. C., as teacher and conductor, from 1901 was organist in New Orleans, from 1909 in Vancouver, and since 1912 in Seattle. See art.

*Dvořák, Antonin (Bohemia, 1841–1904, Bohemia), the distinguished composer, spent the years 1892–95 as artistic director of the National Conservatory in New York. See Vol. i. 755–9, and art.

Dykema, Peter William (b. Grand Rapids, Mich., 1873), graduated (in law) from the University of Michigan in 1895, combined musical study with public-school teaching in Aurora, Ill., Indianapolis and New York (from 1901), and since 1913 has been professor at the University of Wisconsin. See art.

Eames, Henry Purmort (b. Chicago, 1872), graduated from Cornell College (Iowa), studied in Chicago, from 1894 traveled as accompanist and pianist in America and abroad, from 1898 taught in Lincoln, Neb., in 1911–12 in Omaha, and since 1912 at the Cosmopolitan School in Chicago. See art.

Earhart, Will (b. Franklin, O., 1871), after working in public-school music at Franklin and Greenville, O., from 1900 was supervisor at Richmond, Ind., and since 1912 has been music-superintendent in Pittsburgh. See art.

*Ebann, William Benedict (b. Bremen, 1873), came to America in youth, studied at Cincinnati and Berlin, from 1896 appeared as 'cellist and composer, in 1897–98 taught at the Cincinnati College of Music, and since 1898 in New York, from 1907 at the German Conservatory. For list of works, see *Who's Who in Music.*

*Elsenheimer, Nicholas J. (b. Hesse, 1866), in 1890 came to Cincinnati as teacher in the College of Music, organist and concert-pianist, and since 1907 has taught in the Granberry Piano School. For list of works, see Baker, *Dict. of Musicians,* pp. 237–8.

Elson, Arthur B. (b. Boston, 1873), son of Louis C. Elson (see sec. 6), graduated from Harvard in 1895, trained there and in Boston, besides teaching and some composition, since 1901 has written various useful books. See art.

Ende, Herwegh von (Milwaukee, 1877–1919, New York), son of Amelia von Ende (see sec. 6), studied in Chicago and Berlin, began teaching in Chicago in 1893, appeared widely as violinist, from 1903 taught at the American Institute of Applied Music in New York, and from 1910 directed his own school there. He organized the Von Ende Quartet in 1907 (with Modest Altschuler), and was one of a Trio with Rybner and Altschuler. He married the daughter of Remenyi, the Hungarian violinist.

*Enna, Emil (b. Denmark, 1877), nephew of the composer August Enna, came to America in 1897, has toured as concert-pianist, and now lives in Portland, Ore. He has made a specialty of Scandinavian music. He has composed the opera ' The Dawn of the West ' (1915), a piano-sonata, the song-cycle ' Legends of Seaside ' (1916), etc.

Erb, John Lawrence (b. near Reading, Pa., 1877), began as organist in 1892–94 at Pottstown, Pa., studied in New York, where he was organist and teacher, in 1905 became director at Wooster University in Ohio, and since 1914 has been at the University of Illinois. See art.

Farwell, Arthur (b. St. Paul, 1872), graduated from the Institute of Technology, Boston, studied music there and in Paris, from 1899 taught at Cornell University, from 1901 carried on the Wa-Wan Press, made studies of Indian music in the Far West, and since 1909 has worked in New York. See art.

Fay, Charles Norman (b. Burlington, Vt., 1848), from 1877 banker and capitalist in Chicago, in 1890 secured the guaranty of $ 50,000 by which the Chicago Orchestral Association attracted Theodore Thomas to remove from New York to Chicago.

*Ferrata, Giuseppe (b. Italy, 1865), after experience in Italy as concert-pianist, in 1892 came to America, teaching first at Beaver College, Beaver, Pa., and since about 1910 at Newcomb College, New Orleans. See art.

Fischer, Carlo (b. Washington, 1872), studied in Washington and Frankfort, was 'cellist in European orchestras, appeared from 1899 in America and joined the Pittsburgh Orchestra, from 1903 was with the Cincinnati Orchestra, and since 1906 has been with the Minneapolis Orchestra as player, assistant-manager and program-editor. In 1906 he organized the Minneapolis String Quartet.

Fletcher, Alice Cunningham (b. Boston, 1845), whose life has been given to anthropological study, especially as concerns the North American Indians, began publishing upon Indian music in 1893. See art.

Forsyth, Wesley Octavius (b. near Toronto, 1863), trained in Toronto, Leipzig and Vienna, since 1892 has been teacher and pianist in Toronto, part of the time as director of the Metropolitan School of Music. See art.

Foster, Fay (b. Leavenworth, Kan., ?), trained in Chicago and later abroad, besides early work as teacher, pianist and organist, since 1911 has been known as composer of songs and choruses in New York. See art.

*Fox, Félix (b. Silesia, 1876), brought to America when a child, studied in Boston, New York, Leipzig and Paris, and since 1897 has been pianist and teacher in Boston, in 1898 founding the Fox-Buonamici School. See art.

Freer, Eleanor, née Everest (b. Philadelphia, 1864), trained in Philadelphia and Paris, has devoted herself chiefly to song-writing, publishing from 1902, but known earlier. See art.

*Frey, Adolph (b. Bavaria, 1865), has been piano-teacher at Syracuse University since 1893, in 1905–06 acting-dean of the College of Fine Arts. He has written vocal and instrumental pieces, and the music for the Latin play ' Trinummus,' 1895. Mus.D. of Syracuse University in 1914.

*Friedheim, Arthur (b. Russia, 1859, of German parents), the eminent pianist and conductor, toured in America in 1891–95, taught in Chicago in 1900–01, from 1910 was often heard in America, and since 1914 has lived in New York. See Vol. ii. 110, and art.

Fry, Henry S. (b. Pottstown, Pa., 1875), since before 1900 has been organist in or near Philadelphia, becoming noted as recitalist and church-composer. See art.

Fullerton, Charles Alexander (b. Manchester, N. H., 1861), trained chiefly in Chicago, from 1890 was superintendent of schools in Iowa, and since 1897 has been teacher and conductor at the Iowa State Teachers College at Cedar Falls. He is a prominent authority upon public-school music.

*Gadski, Johanna Emilia Agnes (b. Pomerania, 1872), the famous Wagnerian soprano, from 1895 till 1917 was constantly engaged in America. See art.

*Gale, Clement Rowland (b. England, 1862), an experienced organist, since 1890 has been organist in New York, for many years also teaching in the General Theological Seminary and the Guilmant Organ School. See art.

Gales, Weston (b. Elizabeth, N. J., 1877), graduated from Yale in 1898, studied there and in New York, from 1899 was organist in or near New York, from 1908 in Boston, in 1913 conducted orchestral concerts in Europe, and in 1914–18 was the first conductor of the Detroit Symphony Orchestra. See art.

*Gallico, Paolo (b. Trieste, 1868), since 1892 has been concert-pianist and teacher in New York. See art.

*Gandell, Shirley Mark Kerr (b. England, 1866), since 1895 has taught in America, from 1897 in Chicago, with the Balatka School from 1899, the Sherwood School from 1901, and the Cosmopolitan School since 1908.

Gaul, Harvey Bartlett (b. New York, 1881), studied first in New York, later in England and Paris, from 1898 was organist in New York, in Paris, in Cleveland, and since in Pittsburgh. See art.

Gaynor, Jessie Lovel, née Smith (b. St. Louis, 1863), after study in Boston and Chicago, devoted herself to developing methods of teaching children. She has taught in Chicago, Nashville and St. Joseph, Mo., and for some years in St. Louis. See art.

*Genss, Hermann (b. East Prussia, 1856), in 1899 came as teacher to the Irving Institute, San Francisco, and since 1905 has been director there. He has written the opera 'Hunold der Spielmann' (1914), orchestral and chamber-music, songs, etc.

Gilbert, Henry Franklin Belknap (b. Somerville, Mass., 1868), studied in Boston, from 1893 was variously employed there and in Paris, in 1901 joined Farwell in founding the Wa-Wan Press, and is living at Cambridge as composer. See art.

Gilman, Benjamin Ives (b. New York, 1852), who since 1893 has been secretary of the Boston Museum of Fine Arts, has made original investigations in the music of the American Indians, publishing Zuñi Melodies, 1891, and Hopi Melodies, 1908.

*Giorza, Paolo (Italy, 1838–1914, Seattle), known in Italy since 1853 as composer of ballets, from about 1890 taught in New York and lived later in London, San Francisco and Seattle (from 1906). For list of works, see Baker, Dict. of Musicians, p. 311.

*Glasson, T. Bath (b. England, ?), educated in New York, from 1892 taught at Pratt Institute, Brooklyn, from 1895 in Michigan, and since 1900 has been organist and conductor in Brooklyn, publishing pedagogical works and some vocal music.

Glen, Irving Mackey (b. Brooklyn, 1871), graduated from the University of Oregon in 1894 and then student of English at Johns Hopkins, from 1896 was professor of languages in Oregon, but also kept up musical studies, in 1901 becoming dean of music in the University of Oregon and since 1911 professor in the University of Washington (dean of Fine Arts since 1915). He is a concert-baritone, and since 1903 has conducted various festivals.

Goepp, Philip Henry (b. New York, 1864), graduated from Harvard in 1884 (also trained as a lawyer), studied music in college, New York and Philadelphia, and since 1891 has been organist, teacher, composer and author in Philadelphia. See art.

Gogorza, Emilio Edoardo de (b. Brooklyn, 1874), was educated in Spain, France, England and finally New York, where since 1897 he has been a popular concert-baritone. In 1911 he married the soprano Emma Eames (see sec. 7).

Goldmark, Rubin (b. New York, 1872), nephew of the composer Karl Goldmark, studied in New York and Vienna, from 1891 taught at the National Conservatory in New York, from 1894 was director at Colorado College, and since 1902 has been teacher, composer and recitalist in New York. See art.

Grant-Schaefer, George Alfred (b. Williamstown, Ont., 1872), studied in Montreal, Chicago and London, from 1896 was organist in Chicago, and since 1908 has been vocal teacher at Northwestern University, composing songs and piano-pieces.

*Gray, Herbert Willard (b. England, 1868), since 1894 has been American representative of Novello, and from 1906 head of the H. W. Gray Co. in New York, publishers of ' The New Music Review ' and of high-class musical literature.

Grimm, Carl William (b. Dayton, 1863), studied in Chicago and Leipzig, and since 1893 has been teacher in Cincinnati and author of many instruction-books. See art.

*Gruenberg, Eugene (b. Galicia, 1854), after long experience as violinist at Leipzig, in 1891 joined the Boston Symphony Orchestra, in 1893–96 also taught at the Boston Conservatory, and since 1899 at the New England Conservatory. He has composed a symphony, the ballet ' Tanzbilder ' (both given at Leipzig), a violin-sonata, a ' Suite im antiken Stil ' and other violin-works, and published works on violin-playing (1897, 1901).

Gunn, Glenn Dillard (b. Topeka, Kan., 1874), studied in Topeka and Leipzig, from 1896 was concert-pianist in Germany, and since 1900 has been teacher, pianist, critic and conductor in Chicago. See art.

Hackett, Karleton Spalding (b. Brookline, Mass., 1867), graduated from Harvard in 1891, studied in Florence, Munich and London, has worked in Chicago since 1893 as concert-singer, teacher at Northwestern University and the American Conservatory, lecturer and critic. See art.

Hadley, Henry Kimball (b. Somerville, Mass., 1871), trained in Boston and Vienna, appeared as composer in 1895, from that year taught at Garden City, N. Y., in 1904–09 conducted and composed in Germany, led the Seattle Orchestra from 1909 and the San Francisco Orchestra from 1911, and since 1915 has lived in New York. See art.

Haesche, William Edwin (b. New Haven, Conn., 1867), trained in Boston and New Haven, since 1897 has been violinist and from 1902 conductor in New Haven. See art.

Hahn, Carl (b. Indianapolis, 1874), studied in Cincinnati, from about 1895 was 'cellist there, from 1900 orchestral and choral conductor in San Antonio, and since 1913 conductor in New York of the Arion (till 1918) and Mozart Societies and in Brooklyn.

*Hall, William John (b. England, 1867), came to America as tenor in the Boston Lyric Opera Company, taught in Rock Island, Ill., and Cedar Rapids, Ia., was conductor at St. Paul and organist at Davenport, Ia., and latterly has been located at St. Louis. See art.

*Ham, Albert (b. England, 1858), since 1897 has been a prominent organist, conductor and composer in Toronto. See art.

*Hambourg, Mark (b. Russia, 1879), the noted pianist, has made American tours in 1899–1900, 1902–03, 1907–08 and 1915–16.

Hamlin, George John (b. Elgin, Ill., 1868), a concert-tenor since about 1895, in 1904–06 sang in Europe, and since 1911 has been active in opera and concert in America. See art.

*Hein, Karl (b. Schleswig, 1864), having been a 'cellist in Hamburg, from 1891 taught in the German Conservatory, New York, and since 1900, with August Fraemcke, has been its director. Since 1906 they have also conducted the New York College of Music. He has published vocal text-books.

Heinroth, Charles (b. New York, 1874), studied in New York and Munich, from 1893 was organist in Brooklyn and New York, teaching also at the National Conservatory, and since 1907 has been organist at the Carnegie Institute, Pittsburgh. See art.

*Herzog, Sigmund (b. Hungary, 1868), trained as pianist at Vienna, in 1890–94 taught at the German Conservatory in New York, and has since been teacher and ensemble-player. He has edited useful instruction-books and been active in musicians' associations.

*Hesselberg, Edouard Gregory (b. Russia, 1870), came to America in 1892, from 1895 taught at Ithaca, N. Y., from 1896 at Denver, from 1900 at Macon, Ga., from 1905 at Nashville, Tenn., and since 1912 at Toronto. He has written two orchestral suites, piano- and violin-pieces, etc., and was a contributor to *The Art of Music*, 1916.

Heyman, Katherine Ruth Willoughby (b. Sacramento, Cal., ?), trained as concert-pianist in both America and Europe, from 1899 toured in the United States, from 1905 was widely heard in Europe, and in 1916 returned to America again. See art.

Hill, Edward Burlingame (b. Cambridge, Mass., 1872), graduated from Harvard in 1894, studied there and in Boston, and since 1908 has taught at Harvard, with fine critical work and able composition. See art.

Hinckley, Allen Carter (b. Gloucester, Mass., 1877), graduate of the University of Pennsylvania, trained in Philadelphia and New York, after some teaching and conducting, sang from 1901 with the Bostonians, from 1903 in opera in Germany and England, and since 1908 has been prominent in America in opera and concert.

Hinshaw, William Wade (b. Union, Ia., 1867), graduated from Valparaiso University in 1888, studied there and in Chicago, began teaching in 1891, from 1895 was dean at Valparaiso, and since 1899 has been active in the operatic field. See art.

Hissem-DeMoss, Mary (b. California, Ky., 1871), having studied at Cincinnati and New York, since 1899 has been a favorite church- and oratorio singer in New York.

*Holmberg, Gustaf Fredrik (b. Sweden, 1872), came to America in 1891, graduated in 1899 from Bethany College in Kansas, becoming teacher of violin. Since 1903 he has taught at the University of Oklahoma, in 1909 becoming dean of Fine Arts. See art.

*Holmes, Henry (England, 1839–1905, San Francisco), the violinist and composer, from 1894 lived in California. See Vol. ii. 421–2.

Homer, Louise Dilworth, née Beatty (b. Pittsburgh, 1872?), trained as contralto in Philadelphia, Boston and Paris, in 1894 a church-singer in Boston, went to Paris in 1896 with her husband (see below), from 1898 appeared in opera in France and England, from 1900 in New York, and has since been eminent in opera and concert. See art.

Homer, Sidney (b. Boston, 1864), studied in Boston, Leipzig and Munich, from 1890 taught in Boston, in 1895 married Louise Beatty (see above), and since 1900 has lived in New York, chiefly as song-composer. See art.

Hopkins, Harry Patterson (b. Baltimore, 1873), trained at Baltimore and Prague, since 1899 has been organist in Baltimore and teacher in Washington. He has written two overtures, two suites, the orchestral fantasy 'The Dreamer,' the chorus 'A Tragedy,' a piano-quintet, piano-pieces and many songs.

Hughes, Rupert (b. Lancaster, Mo., 1872), graduated from Adelbert College in 1892, has published songs since 1892, and has been a notable author and critic since 1898, including much outside the field of music. See art.

Hugo, John Adam (b. Bridgeport, Conn., 1873), trained at Stuttgart, from 1899 taught in Baltimore, and since 1906 in Bridgeport. He has written the operas 'The Hero of Byzanz' and 'The Temple Dancer,' a symphony, two piano-concertos, a piano-trio, etc.

Hyde, Arthur Sewall (Bath, Me., 1875–1920, New York), graduated at Harvard in 1896, was then organist at Immanuel Church in Boston, and from 1905 at St. Bartholomew's in New York, becoming noted as player and choir-trainer. He was captain in the war and died from after-effects of being gassed at Cantigny.

Jackson, Leonora (b. Boston, 1879), studied in Berlin, appeared as concert-violinist in Germany and other European countries, receiving many distinctions, and from 1900 was for a time active in the United States.

Jepson, Harry Benjamin (b. New Haven, Conn., 1870), trained at New Haven and Paris, since 1895 has been instructor in the Yale School of Music and university-organist, as well as concert-organist elsewhere. See art.

*Jonás, Alberto (b. Spain, 1868), from 1894 chief piano-teacher at the University of Michigan, from 1898 was head of a school in Detroit, besides making tours as player, in 1904–14 worked in Berlin, and since 1914 has taught in New York. See art.

*Jordan, Mary (b. Wales, 1879), early brought to America, studied in Seattle, San Francisco and New York, was a church-singer from about 1892 in Brooklyn and New York and soon in concert as well. In 1911–14 she was contralto in the Boston Opera Company. In 1919 she married C. C. Cresson.

Kaufmann, Maurice (b. New York, 1876), studied violin in Newark, Frankfort and Brussels, early became a concert-player, was concertmaster in the Russian and Volpe Orchestras in New York, now in the People's Orchestra, and member of various ensemble-groups, including since 1907 his own Quartet.

Keller, Walter (b. Chicago, 1873), trained in Chicago and Leipzig, from 1899 taught at Northwestern University, from 1906 at the Sherwood School in Chicago, of which he became director in 1911, and in 1903–18 was organist at St. Vincent's. See art.

*Kinder, Ralph (b. England, 1876), came to America when a boy, studied in Providence and England, from 1898 was organist in Providence, and since 1899 in Philadelphia. He has played extensively elsewhere, conducts three choral societies, directs his own organ-school, and has written many effective organ-pieces, choruses, anthems, songs, etc.

Kinkeldey, Otto (b. New York, 1878), graduated from the College of the City of New York in 1898, studied there and in Berlin, from 1898 was organist in New York, from 1903 at the American Church in Berlin, in 1909–14 professor at the University of Breslau, and since 1915 head of the music-division in the New York Public Library. See art.

*Klee, Eugen (b. Bavaria, 1869), in 1894 came to Philadelphia as organist and conductor of the Sängerbund and other German singing-societies, from 1914 was leader of the Brooklyn Arion, and since 1917 of the New York Liederkranz.

*Klengel, Paul K. (b. Saxony, 1854), conductor and since 1908 professor at Leipzig, in 1898–1902 was leader of the Liederkranz in New York.

*Koemmenich, Louis (b. Rhine Prov., 1866), came to Brooklyn in 1890 to lead the Sänger-bund, and since then has directed important choral societies in New York and Philadelphia. See art.

Kohler, Franz (Clinton, Ia., 1877–1918, Erie, Pa.), trained as violinist at Weimar and Berlin, from 1898 was in the Pittsburgh Orchestra and the Mendelssohn Trio, from 1911 taught at Oberlin Conservatory, and since 1913 has been conductor of the Symphony Orchestra at Erie, Pa.

*Korn, Clara Anna, née Gerlach (b. Prussia, 1866), brought to America as a child, studied in New York, in 1893–98 taught in the National Conservatory there, and since then in other schools and privately. See art.

Kraft, Edwin Arthur (b. New Haven, Conn., 1883), trained at New Haven and Paris, from 1898 was organist in New Haven, in 1901–03 in Brooklyn, from 1905 at Wheeling, W. Va., from 1907 at Trinity Cathedral, Cleveland, from 1914 city-organist at Atlanta, and since 1916 again at Cleveland. See art.

Kraft, William Jacob (b. New Haven, Conn., 1872), brother of the above, studied at New Haven, where from 1891 he was organist, from 1909 was in public-school work in New York, and since 1912 has been associate professor at Teachers College there. See art.

*Krauss, Arnold (b. Rumania, 1866), concert-violinist, since 1897 has lived in Los Angeles as player and teacher, lately being concertmaster of the Symphony Orchestra.

*Kunits, Luigi von (b. Austria, 1870), from 1893 taught in Chicago, from 1896 was concert-master of the Pittsburgh Orchestra, in 1910–12 taught in Vienna, and since 1912 has been on the staff of the Canadian Academy of Music in Toronto. See art.

Kürsteiner, Jean Paul (b. Catskill, N. Y., 1864), since 1893 has been instructor at the Ogontz School in Philadelphia and in 1896–1906 also at the Baldwin School, Bryn Mawr. Since 1906 he has also taught in New York, publishing *Essays on Expert Aid to Artistic Piano-Playing*.

La Flesche, Francis (b. Omaha Reservation, Neb., 1860?), while employed in the Bureau of Indian Affairs in Washington, collaborated with Alice C. Fletcher (see above) in *A Study of Omaha Music*, 1893, besides writing often for scientific journals.

Lang, Henry Albert (b. New Orleans, 1854), after study at Stuttgart and Karlsruhe and much experience as pianist, returned to America in 1890, and since 1891 has been a noted teacher and composer in Philadelphia. See art.

Lang, Margaret Ruthven (b. Boston, 1867), daughter of B. J. Lang (see sec. 4), was trained in Boston and Munich, and since about 1890 has been mainly occupied with composition in Boston. See Vol. ii. 632, and art.

Lehmann, Friedrich J. (b. Cleveland, 1866), studied at Oberlin and Leipzig, since 1902 has been professor of theory in the Oberlin Conservatory. He has published handbooks on harmony and counterpoint.

*Le Sueur, Peter (b. Isle of Jersey, 1871), from 1895 organist, teacher and conductor at St. John's, N. F., since 1905 has held similar positions at Erie, Pa., from 1913 at the head of the Erie Conservatory.

Lewis, Leo Rich (b. South Woodstock, Vt., 1865), graduated from Tufts College in 1887, studied in Munich, and since 1892 has been instructor at Tufts, at first in French, since 1895 in music. See art.

Lichtenstein, Victor (b. St. Louis, 1872), trained as violinist at Leipzig and Brussels, has played in concert since 1895, long conducting the Young People's String Orchestra in St. Louis, leading the Lichtenstein Quartet, teaching and acting as lecturer and critic.

Liebling, Leonard (b. New York, 1874), nephew of Emil Liebling (see sec. 5), graduated from the College of the City of New York, studied at Berlin, since 1899 has been critic and librettist in New York, with ' The Musical Courier ' from 1902 and its editor from 1914. See art.

Limbert, Frank L. (b. New York, 1866), has lived in Germany since boyhood, studying at Frankfort, Munich, Berlin and Strassburg, and becoming teacher and conductor at Frankfort, Düsseldorf and (since 1906) Hanau. For list of works, see Who's Who in Music.

Listemann, Franz (b. New York, 1873), son of Bernhard Listemann (see sec. 5), trained as 'cellist at Boston, Leipzig and Berlin, in 1896–97 played in the Pittsburgh Orchestra, and then went to New York as teacher, soloist and member of chamber-music groups.

Lockwood, Albert Lewis (b. Troy, N. Y., 1871), studied the piano at Albany, Leipzig, Vienna and Florence, appeared in concert in 1895–96 in Paris and London and in 1896 in New York, toured extensively at home and abroad, and since 1900 has been influential as professor at the University of Michigan.

*Longy, Georges (b. France, 1868), after many years' experience as oboist at Paris, in 1898 joined the Boston Symphony Orchestra. In 1900 he founded the Longy Club. See art.

Loomis, Harvey Worthington (b. Brooklyn, 1865), after study in New York, since about 1895 has been engaged upon composition, largely in the field of light opera. See art.

Loud, John Hermann (b. Weymouth, Mass., 1873), trained in Boston, Berlin, Paris and England, has been concert-organist since 1895, also at churches in Springfield, Mass., from 1896, in or near Boston since 1900. He has written organ-music, piano-pieces, anthems, etc.

Lovewell, Samuel Harrison (b. Wellesley, Mass., 1865), studied in Boston, from 1891 was organist at Easton, Pa., from 1893 at Georgetown, Ky., from 1896 at Columbia, S. C., from 1898 director at Whitman College, Walla Walla, Wash., from 1906 director of the Quincy (Ill.) Conservatory, in 1911–12 organist at Jenkintown, Pa., and since 1917 at Taunton, Mass. He has long been editor for C. W. Thompson & Co., Boston. See art.

*Malcherek, Karl August (b. Hesse, 1873), from 1899 violinist in the Thomas Orchestra in Chicago, since 1902 has been player and teacher in Pittsburgh, till 1910 in the Pittsburgh Orchestra and since 1913 in the faculty of the Carnegie Institute of Technology.

Manney, Charles Fonteyn (b. Brooklyn, 1872), trained in Boston, since 1898 has been on the editorial staff of the Ditson Company, conductor and composer, chiefly of vocal music. See art.

Manning, Edward Betts (b. St. John, N. B., 1874), after studying law in St. John, took up music in New York, later also in Berlin and Paris, from 1897 taught in New York, from 1905 at Oberlin College, from 1908 was music-supervisor in New York, and since 1915 has been instructor in Columbia University. He has written a piano-trio and some other works.

Marshall, John Patton (b. Rockport, Mass., 1877), trained in Boston, from 1896 was organist there, and since 1902 has been professor in Boston University. See art.

Matlack, Henry William (b. Steubenville, O., 1875), studied at Oberlin, from 1897 was instructor there, in 1901–03 and since 1908 has been teacher of organ and theory at Grinnell College, besides engagements as organist in Ohio and Iowa.

*Mattfeld, Marie, a German operatic mezzo-soprano, since 1896 almost steadily engaged with American opera-troupes, from 1905 at the Metropolitan Opera House, New York.

*Matthews, Harry Alexander (b. England, 1879), since 1899 organist and composer in Philadelphia, is best known for several cantatas, sacred and secular. See art.

*Matthews, John Sebastian (b. England, 1870), brother of the preceding, from 1891 organist in Philadelphia, from 1901 at Morristown, N. J., and since 1916 at Providence. He also has written cantatas, etc. See art.

McClellan, John Jasper (b. Payson, Utah, 1874), studied mostly at the University of Michigan, where from 1893 he was organist and conductor, from 1896 taught at Salt Lake City and Provo, Utah, and since 1901 has been professor at the University of Utah and organist at the Tabernacle in Salt Lake City. In 1908 he started the Salt Lake Symphony Orchestra and in 1911 the Utah Conservatory.

McConathy, Osbourne (b. Pittspoint, Ky., 1875), trained in Louisville and Boston, since about 1895 has been successful in public-school work, first at Louisville, then at Chelsea, Mass., and latterly on the staff of Northwestern University, Evanston, Ill. He has also served as choral conductor and edited many text-books for school-singing.

McCutchan, Robert Guy (b. Mountayr, Ia., 1877), graduated from Park College in Missouri in 1898, began teaching in 1899, from 1904 taught at Baker University in Kansas, in 1910–11 studied in Europe, and since 1911 has been dean of music at DePauw University in Indiana. See art.

McWhood, Leonard Beecher (b. Brooklyn, 1870), graduated from Columbia in 1893, took graduate courses in music and other subjects, in 1897-1910 taught there, also at Vassar College in 1902-07, in 1907-1916 at Drew Theological Seminary, also at Washington in 1910-13 and in the Newark High School in 1913-18, and since 1918 has been music-director at Dartmouth College. See art.

Mead, Olive (b. Cambridge, Mass., 1874), trained as violinist in Boston, has appeared in concert from 1898 and in 1904 formed a well-known Quartet. See art.

*Middelschulte, Wilhelm (b. Westphalia, 1863), after having been organist in Berlin, came to Chicago in 1891, where he has been eminent as player and composer. See art.

*Miersch, Karl Alexander Johannes (Saxony, 1865-1916, Cincinnati), an expert violinist, joined the Boston Symphony Orchestra in 1892, in 1894-1902 was teaching in Athens or touring, returned to America and from 1910 was professor in the Cincinnati College of Music.

*Miersch, Paul Friedrich Theodor (b. Saxony, 1868), brother of the preceding and a fine 'cellist, came to New York in 1892, from 1893 playing in the Symphony Society and since 1898 at the Metropolitan Opera House. He has written 'cello-concertos, an ' Indian Rhapsody ' for orchestra, chamber-music and songs.

Miller, Russell King (b. Philadelphia, 1871), trained in Philadelphia and New York, since about 1895 has been noted as organist, teacher and composer in Philadelphia. See art.

*Mills, Charles Henry (b. England, 1873), in 1892-93 toured in America as pianist, in 1907-08 taught theory at Syracuse University, from 1908 was professor at the University of Illinois, and since 1914 has been professor at the University of Wisconsin. See art.

Mueller, Frederick William (b. Sandusky, O., 1863), studied at Oberlin and Leipzig, from 1891 taught at Knox College, from 1902 was director of the Tarkio Conservatory in Missouri, from 1913 vice-president of Tarkio College, in 1915-16 head of the Northwestern Conservatory, Minneapolis, and since 1916 is director of the Twin City Conservatory there.

Neidlinger, William Harold (b. Brooklyn, 1863), trained in New York and London, from 1890 was organist and conductor in Brooklyn, from 1896 taught in London and Paris, from 1898 was an effective singing-teacher in Chicago, specialized in child-psychology and songs for children, and established a school for subnormal children at East Orange, N. J. Besides the comic operas ' Ulysses ' (1901) and ' Sweet Anne Page ' (1903), and the cantata ' Prayer, Promise and Praise,' he has written many songs, including (from 1900) several favorite sets for children.

*Nepomuceno, Alberto (b. Ceará, Brazil, 1864), for many years has been head of the Instituto Nacional de Música in Rio de Janeiro. He is a composer of importance

and collector of Brazilian folk-songs. See Who's Who in Music, 1918.

Nevin, Arthur Finley (b. Edgeworth, Pa., 1871), brother of Ethelbert W. Nevin (see sec. 7), studied in Boston and Berlin, from 1897 taught in Pittsburgh, in 1903-04 traveled much in the West to study Indian music and legends, in 1910-11 went abroad, then lived at Charlottesville, Va., composing and in 1914-15 conducted at Peterboro, N. H. Since 1915 he has been professor at the University of Kansas. See art.

Nielsen, Alice (b. Nashville, Tenn., 1876), trained as operatic soprano in San Francisco, from 1893 sang in light opera, in 1896-98 was with the Bostonians, from 1901 studied in Rome and from 1903 appeared in grand opera as well, since 1906 being connected with various companies in America. In 1892 she married Benjamin Nentwig, organist in Kansas City.

*Nováček, Ottokar Eugen (Hungary, 1866-1900, New York), an accomplished violinist and composer, joined the Boston Symphony Orchestra in 1891 and in 1892-99 played in New York. See Vol. iii. 410, and art.

Noyes, Edith Rowena (b. Cambridge, Mass., 1875), studied in Boston and since 1895 has been pianist and teacher there, with European tours in 1899 and 1909, besides considerable composition. See art.

*Oberhoffer, Emil (b. Bavaria, 1867), came to America about 1895, from 1897 was conductor in St. Paul, and since 1901 in Minneapolis, where since 1903 he has led the Minneapolis Symphony Orchestra. See art.

Oetting, William H. (b. Pittsburgh, 1875), trained at Pittsburgh and Berlin, has been a prominent organist and teacher in Pittsburgh since 1897. See art.

Oldberg, Arne (b. Youngstown, O., 1874), studied at Chicago, Vienna and Munich, and since 1899 has been professor at Northwestern University and a notable composer. See art.

Orem, Preston Ware (b. Philadelphia, ?), trained in Philadelphia, has been teacher and organist there, and since 1900 editor for the Presser Company. See art.

O'Sullivan, Denis (San Francisco, 1868-1908, Columbus, O.), trained in San Francisco, Florence, London, and Paris, from 1895 was a popular concert- and opera-bass in England and from 1897 in America. See Vol. iii. 571-2.

*Otterström, Thorvald (b. Denmark, 1868), since 1892 has worked as a thoughtful composer in Chicago. See art.

*Owst, Wilberfoss George (b. England, 1861), since 1893 has been organist in Baltimore, and since 1903 also teacher at the College of Music in Washington, and in 1897-1910 at the Maryland College of Music. He has written the cantata ' The Message of the Winds,' the melodrama ' The White Ship,' church-music and other vocal music.

*Pache, Joseph (b. Silesia, 1861), came to America in 1891, for a time was conductor in or near New York, and since 1894 has conducted the Oratorio Society in Baltimore and other societies. See art.

Padelford, Frederick Morgan (b. Haverhill, Mass., 1875), since 1901 professor of English in the University of Washington, while fellow at Yale University published *Old English Musical Terms*, Bonn, 1899, an exhaustive study from Anglo-Saxon sources, with glossary.

*Paderewski, Ignace Jan (b. Russian Poland, 1860), the great pianist, was a frequent visitor in America from 1891 till 1915, when he forsook the concert-stage for the leadership of the new Polish Republic. See Vol. iii. 587-8, and art.

Palliser, Esther (b. Philadelphia, 1872), trained as operatic soprano in Paris, from 1890 appeared in France and England and from about 1895 also in America. She lives in London.

*Panizza, Ettore (b. Argentina, 1875), studied at Milan, began operatic conducting at Rome in 1899, in 1907-13 was engaged for Italian operas in London, and since 1916 has been conductor at La Scala, Milan. He has written the operas ' Il Fidanzato del Mare ' (1897), ' Medio Evo Latino ' (1900) and ' Aurora' (1908), and edited a translation of Berlioz' *Instrumentation*, 3 vols., 1913.

*Pasternack, Josef Alexander (b. Poland, 1881), came to America in 1895, from 1900 played viola at the Metropolitan Opera House, from 1910 conducted Sunday concerts there, in 1913-14 was conductor for the Century Opera Co., and since 1914 has directed summer opera at Ravinia Park, Chicago.

*Paur, Emil (b. Bukovina, 1855), the distinguished violinist and conductor, in 1893-98 was conductor of the Boston Symphony Orchestra, in 1898-1902 of the New York Philharmonic Society and in 1899-1900 at the Metropolitan Opera House as well, in 1904-10 led the Pittsburgh Symphony Orchestra, and then returned to Berlin. In 1899-1902 he directed the National Conservatory in New York. See Vol. iii. 658, and art.

Penny, George Barlow (b. Haverstraw, N. Y., 1861), trained in New York and Chicago, from 1890 was dean of Fine Arts in the University of Kansas, from 1903 dean at Washburn College, Topeka, also in 1903-07 city-organist, in 1905-09 director of the Fine Arts Institute and leader of the Oratorio Society, and since 1911 has been in Rochester as head of the Rochester Conservatory, organist and professor at Rochester University and Theological Seminary.

Perkins, David Walton (b. Rome, N. Y., 1847), studied in New York and Berlin, established the Sherwood School in Chicago in 1897, continuing as its head till 1901, and since 1907 has been president of the Musical College there, besides work as critic. He has published *Piano-Technique*, piano-pieces and songs, and edited vocal collections.

*Peters, Richard Harry (b. England, 1867), was organist and conductor in Canada from about 1890, for ten years led festivals at Spartanburg, S. C., which he first organized, and since about 1910 has been organist in Baltimore, besides conducting a choral society in York, Pa. He has written pieces for organ, piano and voice, the cantata ' St. Cecilia's Day ' and the oratorio ' Elisha.' Mus.D. of Toronto University in 1892.

Quarles, James Thomas (b. St. Louis, 1877), studied in St. Louis, becoming organist there in 1893, soon establishing himself as an accomplished concert-player and conductor. Since 1913 he has been organist at Cornell University. See art.

Rains, Leon (b. New York, 1870), trained at New York and Paris, has been well known as operatic bass since 1897, from 1899 chiefly in connection with the Dresden Court Opera.

Ralston, Fanny Marion (b. St. Louis, 1875), trained in St. Louis and Boston, has been teacher and composer since 1896 at St. Louis, in girls' schools in Virginia and Missouri, from 1908 music-director at Rockford College in Illinois, and recently at Wellesley College. She has written for the piano with ability.

Raymond, George Lansing (b. Chicago, 1839), in 1893-1905 professor of æsthetics at Princeton University, has published a striking series of books upon the nature and relations of the fine arts, including *Rhythm and Harmony in Poetry and Music*, 1895, which, with parts of other writings, displays an original and profound grasp of musical philosophy.

Read, Angelo McCallum (b. near St. Catherine's, Ont., 1854), trained at Leipzig and Vienna, since 1894 has been teacher, conductor and composer at Buffalo. See art.

Redman, Harry Newton (b. Mt. Carmel, Ill., 1869), studied in Boston, and since 1897 has been harmony-teacher at the New England Conservatory. He has written two string-quartets, two violin-sonatas, piano-pieces, songs, etc.

Reed, Frank LeFevre (b. Richmond, Ind., 1871), trained at Ithaca, Cincinnati and New York, after teaching at Fremont, Neb., and at Ithaca, from 1906 was at the Pennsylvania College of Music, Meadville, Pa., and since 1913 has been professor at the University of Texas, also conducting the municipal chorus and orchestra of Austin. He has written orchestral pieces for pageants held at Austin, Tex., and Auburn, N. Y., respectively.

*Remy, Alfred (b. Rhine Prov., 1870), came to New York in youth, graduated from the College of the City of New York in 1890, later pursuing musical studies, from 1895 was teacher and critic, and since 1901 has done much editorial work of superior quality. See art.

Renwick, Llewellyn Laraway (b. Ann Arbor, Mich., 1876), studied at Ann Arbor and Paris, from 1898 was organist and teacher at Ann Arbor, from 1903 organist of the American Church in Paris, and since 1906 has taught at the Detroit Conservatory.

Reynolds, Walter Guernsey (b. Tioga, Pa., 1873), studied at Mansfield, Pa., and in Paris, began teaching in 1890, from 1893 was organist at St. Paul, in 1897–99 at Chippewa Falls, Wis., from 1901 director at Doane College in Nebraska, from 1905 organist at Tacoma, also from 1906 professor at Whitworth College and choral conductor, and since 1912 has been organist in Seattle. He has written vocal and organ-music.

Riemenschneider, Albert (b. Berea, O., 1878), trained at Vienna and Paris, since 1898 has been head of the music-department of Baldwin-Wallace College in Berea and also organist and conductor in Cleveland, besides touring as concert-organist.

Robinson, Franklin Whitman (b. New York, 1875), graduated from the College of the City of New York, studied music in New York and became organist there. Since 1908 he has taught at the Institute of Musical Art, developing a novel system of ear-training, besides in 1904–17 being organist in Philadelphia. See art.

*****Roeder, Martin** (Prussia, 1851–1895, Boston), the noted conductor and composer, from 1892 taught singing at the New England Conservatory in Boston. See Baker, *Dict. of Musicians*, p. 776.

Rogers, Francis (b. Roxbury, Mass., 1870), graduated from Harvard in 1891, studied in Boston, New York, Florence and Paris, and since 1898 has been a popular concert-baritone, occasionally appearing in opera. He has published *Some Famous Singers of the 19th Century*, 1915. He lives in New York.

Royer, Clarence DeVaux (b. Lancaster, Pa., 1874–1919, Lancaster), trained as violinist in Philadelphia, Berlin and Brussels, in 1897 made his début in Paris, toured extensively on the Continent and then in the United States, has taught in Canada, at Raleigh, N. C., Ithaca, N. Y., and since 1910 at the New York School of Music and Art. See art.

*****Saar, Louis Victor Franz** (b. Holland, 1868), from 1894 was accompanist at the Metropolitan Opera House in New York, from 1896 theory-teacher at the National Conservatory, from 1898 at the College of Music, besides much work as critic and composer, from 1906 at the Cincinnati College of Music, and since 1917 at the Chicago Musical College. See art.

*****Sabin, Wallace Arthur** (b. England, 1869), after much experience as organist in England, since 1894 has been a prominent player at San Francisco. See art.

Salmon, Alvah Glover (Southold, N. Y., 1868–1917, Boston), trained as pianist in Boston, New York, Germany and Russia, from about 1895 toured in the United States, specializing in Russian music.

Sanderson, Lillian (b. Sheboygan, Wis., 1867), studied mainly at Frankfort, from 1890 appeared as concert-soprano throughout Europe, in 1899 married the painter Richard Müller in Dresden and has since lived there.

*****Sansone, Errico** (b. Italy, 1859), after long experience in Italy as violinist, conductor and composer, about 1890 came to Chicago, taught at the Chicago Conservatory and the Balatka Academy, was for a time concert-master of the St. Paul Orchestra, and has played much in chamber-ensembles. See art.

*****Saslavsky, Alexander** (b. Russia, 1876), in 1893 toured in Canada as violinist, joined the New York Symphony Orchestra, becoming concertmaster in 1903, was active in 1904 in the formation of the Russian Symphony Orchestra, since 1907 has led his own Quartet, and has toured extensively. See art.

Savage, Henry Wilson (b. Boston, 1860?), a successful real-estate dealer in Boston, since about 1895 has been notable as the efficient promoter of enterprises for giving opera in English throughout the United States. See art.

*****Scharwenka, Ludwig Philipp** (Posen, 1847–1918, Prussia), the distinguished composer, in 1891–92 was associated with his brother (see sec. 6) in the latter's Conservatory in New York. See Vol. iv. 248–9, and art.

*****Scheel, Fritz** (Lübeck, 1852–1907, Philadelphia), from 1869 conductor in Germany, in 1893–94 was orchestral conductor in Chicago, in 1895–98 in San Francisco, and then in Philadelphia, after 1900 being leader of the Philadelphia Orchestra. See art.

Schenuit, Alfons William (b. Pittsburgh, 1864), studied in Baltimore and Philadelphia, and since 1892 has been organist of the Baltimore Cathedral and from 1897 founder and director of the Maryland College of Music.

*****Schoettle, Gustav** (b. Würtemberg, 1877), from 1894 taught in Kansas City and directed choral societies, from 1910 was professor at the State University of Iowa, in 1914–16 organized and led the Des Moines Orchestra, in 1916–17 taught at Mitchell, S. D., and since 1917 has been director of the Northwestern Conservatory at Minneapolis.

Schofield, Robert LeRoy (b. Northfield, Minn., 1876), trained at Minneapolis, Philadelphia, New York and Paris, from 1891 taught in Minnesota, from 1901 at the Stetson University in Florida, from 1903 in Philadelphia, from 1906 at Whitman College, and since 1911 has been organist and director at Seattle and Tacoma.

*****Schroeder, Alwin** (b. Saxony, 1855), the eminent 'cellist, joined the Boston Symphony Orchestra and the Kneisel Quartet in 1891, in 1907–08 was in Frankfort, in 1910–12 in the Hess-Schroeder Quartet, and since 1915 in the Margulies Trio and the Boston String Quartet. See art.

*****Schuëcker, Edmund** (Austria, 1860–1911, Rhine Prov.), the superior harpist, brother of Heinrich Schuëcker (see sec. 7), in 1891–1900 played in the Thomas Orchestra in Chicago, in 1903–04 in the Pittsburgh Orchestra, in 1904–09 in the Philadelphia Orchestra, and in 1909–10 at the Metropolitan Opera House. See Baker, *Dict. of Musicians*, pp. 846–7.

*Schumann-Heink, Ernestine, née Rössler (b. Bohemia, 1861), the famous operatic soprano, since 1898 has been almost continuously active on the stage and in concert in America. See Vol. iv. 383–4, and art.

Schwartz, George Foss (b. Cincinnati, 1872), graduated from Wooster University in 1895, studied at Cincinnati, Boston and Leipzig, from 1895 taught in New York, California and Ohio, and since 1902 has been at the University of Illinois. He has written church-music and instruction-books in harmony.

*Scotti, Antonio (b. Italy, 1866), the eminent opera-baritone, since 1899 has sung regularly at the Metropolitan Opera House. From 1890 he had previously been heard in South America. See Vol. v. 666, and art.

*Seashore, Carl Emil (b. Sweden, 1866), graduated from Gustavus Adolphus College in 1891, took graduate study at Yale University (from 1895 assistant in the psychological laboratory), and since 1897 has been at the State University of Iowa, becoming dean of the Graduate College in 1908. See art.

Semmann, Liborius (b. Grafton, Wis., 1873), studied in Milwaukee, and since 1896 has taught there, from 1899 in the Wisconsin Conservatory and since 1911 in Marquette University, where he is dean of music. He has been active in music-teachers' associations and in 1915 founded an association of presidents of such bodies.

*Severn, Edmund (b. England, 1862), brought to America as a child, trained in Boston and Berlin, from 1890 was violinist in Hartford, Conn., and Springfield, Mass., also conductor of choral societies in Westfield and Warren, Mass., and since 1897 has been teacher and composer in New York. See art.

Sewall, Maud Gilchrist (b. Urbana, O., 1872), trained as violinist abroad, self-taught in organ and theory, since 1896 has been organist in Washington, giving many lecture-recitals.

Shapleigh, Bertram (b. Boston, 1871), studied in Boston, not confining himself to music, in 1898–1915 lived in England, engaged in composition and critical work, and now lives in New York. See art.

Shepherd, Arthur (b. Paris, Ida., 1880), studied in Boston, from 1897 was teacher and conductor in Salt Lake City, and since 1908 has been in the faculty of the New England Conservatory in Boston. See art.

Singleton, Esther (b. Baltimore, ?), has published a variety of popular handbooks in many fields, including A Guide to the Opera, 1899, 1909, The Orchestra and its Instruments, 1917, translations from Lavignac under the titles The Music-Dramas of Richard Wagner, 1898, and Musical Education, 1903, and wrote on American music for Lavignac's Encyclopédie de la Musique, 1915.

Skilton, Charles Sanford (b. Northampton, Mass., 1868), graduated from Yale in 1889, studied in New York and Berlin, from 1893 was teacher and conductor at Salem, N. C.,

from 1897 at the State Normal School, Trenton, N. J., and since 1903 has been professor at the University of Kansas, until 1915 being dean of the School of Fine Arts. See art.

Sleeper, Henry Dike (b. Patten, Me., 1865), studied mainly in Boston, from 1891 taught at Beloit College, in 1894–95 at Georgetown, Ky., from 1895 at the University of Wisconsin, and since 1898 has been professor at Smith College (director from 1904). See art.

Sohn, Joseph (b. New York, 1867), graduated from the College of the City of New York, studied at Berlin, has been long a writer on musical subjects in New York and piano-teacher at the Metropolitan College of Music. He has published Robert Schumann, 1896, Lessons of the Opera, 1903, Music in America and Abroad, 1904, Joseph Joachim, 1904, Opera in New York, 1907, The Mission of Richard Wagner, 1910, besides many articles.

Sonneck, Oscar George Theodore (b. Jersey City, 1873), received his whole education in Germany, studying music at Munich and Frankfort, began research-work in Germany and Italy, from 1902 was head of the Music Division of the Library of Congress, becoming famous as a musicologist, and since 1917 has been with the Schirmer publishing-house in New York, editing 'The Musical Quarterly' from 1915. See art.

Spargur, John Mitchell (b. Cincinnati, 1879), a violinist from boyhood, from 1894 was conductor for the Ben Greet Players, from 1901 played in the New York Philharmonic and Russian Orchestras, and in 1911 founded the Philharmonic Orchestra at Seattle.

Speaks, Oley (b. Canal Winchester, O., 1876), trained in New York, since 1898 has been known there as a church- and concert-baritone and composer of effective songs.

Spencer, Allen Hervey (b. Fairhaven, Vt., 1870), studied in Rochester and Chicago and since 1892 has taught at the American Conservatory in Chicago, appearing extensively as concert-pianist. See art.

*Spielter, Hermann (b. Bremen, 1860) from 1894 was conductor of the Beethoven Männerchor in New York, in 1897–1911 theory-teacher at the College of Music, and since 1915 at the Von Ende School. He has written the operetta Die Rajahsbraut (1910), many cantatas and choruses, instrumental works, etc. For list, see Baker, Dict. of Musicians, p. 894.

Spiering, Theodore (b. St. Louis, 1871), trained as violinist in St. Louis, Cincinnati and Berlin, in 1892–96 played in the Thomas Orchestra in Chicago, in 1893–1905 toured with his own Quartet, in 1898–1905 taught at the Chicago Conservatory, his own school and the Chicago Musical College, in 1906–09 and 1911–14 was teaching and touring in Europe, in 1909–11 was concertmaster of the New York Philharmonic Society and its conductor in 1911 (taking Mahler's place), and since 1914 has taught in New York. See art.

Spross, Charles Gilbert (b. Poughkeepsie, N. Y., 1874), studied at Poughkeepsie and New York, has been organist since 1891 in Poughkeepsie, Paterson, N. J., and New York, and is an eminent accompanist. See art.

Spry, Walter (b. Chicago, 1868), trained at Chicago, Vienna, Berlin and Paris, from 1897 was director of the Quincy (Ill.) Conservatory, from 1900 editor of Summy's ' Music Review,' in 1905–17 head of his own school in Chicago, and is now teacher in the Columbia School there. See art.

*****Stahlberg, Frederick** (b. Prussia, 1877), the violinist, in 1899 joined the Pittsburgh Orchestra, and since 1908 has been in the New York Philharmonic Society, from 1912 assistant-conductor. He has written an opera, two symphonies, several orchestral suites, etc.

*****Stasny, Karl Richard** (b. Hesse, 1855), after much experience as pianist and teacher, since 1891 has been on the staff of the New England Conservatory in Boston.

Stebbins, George Waring (b. East Carlton, N. Y., 1869), trained in Brooklyn, New York, Paris and London, since 1893 has been organist, conductor and teacher in Brooklyn. See art.

*****Steindel, Bruno** (b. Saxony, 1866), having been 'cellist in Berlin, in 1892–1918 was first 'cellist in the Chicago Orchestra.

*****Stock, Frederick A.** [Friedrich Wilhelm August] (b. Rhine Prov., 1872), since 1895 has been in the Chicago Orchestra, first as violinist, from 1901 as assistant to Thomas, and since 1905 his successor as conductor. See Vol. iv. 698, and art.

Stoeckel, Carl (b. New Haven, Conn., 1858), son of G. J. Stoeckel (see sec. 4), since 1899 has been patron of the festivals at Norfolk, Conn., of the Litchfield County Choral Union.

Strong, Susan (b. Brooklyn, 1875?), trained as opera-soprano in New York and London, in 1895–96 appeared abroad, from 1896 in New York, and since 1900 has sung in London.

*****Strube, Gustav** (b. Anhalt, 1867), in 1890 joined the Boston Symphony Orchestra as violinist, acting also as conductor there and in Worcester, and since 1913 has taught composition at the Peabody Conservatory in Baltimore and since 1916 has conducted the Baltimore Orchestra. See art.

Sutro, Rose Laura (b. Baltimore, 1870) and **Sutro, Ottilie** (b. Baltimore 1872), trained as pianists in Baltimore and Berlin, since 1893 have been noted for two-piano performances, first in Germany and England, from 1894 in America, and in 1910–15 in Europe again. See Baker, *Dict. of Musicians*, p. 929.

Swift, Samuel (Newark, N. J., 1873–1914, New York), graduated from the University of Pennsylvania in 1894, from 1891 was organist in Wilmington, Del., and from 1894 critic and editor in New York. See art.

*****Szumowska, Antoinette** (b. Poland, 1868), the concert-pianist, first appeared in Boston and New York in 1895, in 1896 married Josef

Adamowski (see sec. 7) and with him and his brother (see sec. 6) formed the Adamowski Trio, with headquarters in Boston. See art.

Talbot, Howard [last name originally Munkittrick] (b. Yonkers, N. Y., 1865), has lived in England since childhood, developing from 1894 into a successful composer of comic operettas. For list see Baker, *Dict. of Musicians*, p. 931.

*****Theodorini, Helena** (b. Rumania, 1862), the operatic soprano, was visiting artist in Buenos Aires and Rio de Janeiro before 1900, about 1910 settled in the former as teacher, and since 1916 has lived in New York.

Thompson, John Winter (b. Leland, Mich., 1867), trained at Oberlin and Leipzig, since 1890 has been teacher of organ and theory at Knox College, Galesburg, Ill. He has published anthems and organ-pieces. Mus. D. of Knox College in 1909.

*****Towers, John** (b. England, 1836), from 1890 was organist and teacher in Indianapolis, from 1892 at the Utica Conservatory, from about 1895 in New York, from 1904 at the Forest Park University and the Kroeger School in St. Louis, and since 1915 has been in Philadelphia. He has published a catalogue of 28,000 operas (1910).

*****Troostwyk, Isidore** (b. Holland, 1862), an expert violinist, came to America in 1890, and since 1895 has taught in the Yale School of Music, becoming concertmaster of the New Haven Orchestra and in 1907 founder of the New Haven String Orchestra. See art.

Turner, Arthur Henry (b. Meriden, Conn., 1873), trained as baritone and organist in New York and Paris, has been organist in Meriden and from 1900 in Springfield, Mass., also conducting choral clubs, giving recitals and composing songs.

Tyler, Abram Ray (b. Brooklyn, 1868), trained in New York, from about 1895 was organist there and in Brooklyn, from 1902 was professor at Beloit College in Wisconsin, and since 1911 has been organist at Detroit. He has played often in recital and has written a piano-trio, a violin-sonata, anthems and other choral music.

*****Valle Riestra, José** (b. Peru, 1859), trained mainly in London and Paris, has become notable as a composer seeking to preserve themes from Aztec music. Since 1909 he has been professor in the Academia Nacional de Música in Lima. He has written the operas ' Ollanta ' (1901), ' Atahualpa,' ' Las Rosas de Jamaica,' a requiem, pieces for orchestra, choruses and songs.

Van Dresser, Marcia (b. Memphis, Tenn., 1880), studied in Chicago and later in Munich and Paris, from 1898 sang in light opera and in minor parts in grand opera, from 1904 studied abroad, from 1907 appeared as soprano in many German cities, and since 1914 has been active again in America.

Van Hoose, Ellison (b. Murfreesboro, Tenn., 1869), trained as operatic tenor at New York,

Paris, Rome and London, has appeared widely in America and Europe since 1897. See art.

Virgil, Almon Kincaid, of New York, in 1892 first patented his Practice Clavier, which was widely adopted in America and England as a means of manual training. See Vol. ii. 266.

*Volpe, Arnold (b. Russia, 1869), came to New York in 1898, where in 1902 he organized the Young Men's Symphony Orchestra, and since 1910 has led other valuable organizations. See art.

Walker, Edyth (b. Hopewell, N. Y., 1870), studied mostly at Dresden, first appeared as operatic contralto in 1895 at Vienna, singing at the Hofoper for several years, from 1903 was at the Metropolitan Opera House in New York, from 1906 sang chiefly at Berlin and Hamburg, and since 1912 at Munich.

Ward, Frank Edwin (b. Wysox, Pa., 1872), studied in Washington and New York, from 1891 was organist at Washington, in 1900-05 at Rye, N. Y., in 1902-13 at Columbia University, and since 1906 at Holy Trinity, New York. See art.

Watt, Charles E. (b. Lima, O., ?), studied in Chicago, in 1894 founded the Chicago Piano College and in 1908 the periodical ' Music News,' of which he is proprietor and editor.

*Weidig, Adolf (b. Hamburg, 1867), in 1892 came as violinist in the Chicago Symphony Orchestra and viola in the Spiering Quartet. Since 1898 he has been one of the managers of the American Conservatory and a fertile composer. See art.

*Weisbach, Harry (b. Russia, 1886), brought to New York as a child, played in public in 1896, studied in New York, Brussels and Berlin, toured in Europe and America, and since 1912 has been concertmaster of the Chicago Symphony Orchestra.

*Wetzler, Hermann Hans (b. Hesse, 1870), came to New York in 1892, from 1897 was organist of Trinity Church, from 1902 gave orchestral concerts, and since 1905 has been conductor and composer in Germany. See art.

Whitmer, Thomas Carl (b. Altoona, Pa., 1873), studied in Philadelphia and New York, in 1898-99 was organist at Harrisburg, from 1899 taught at Stephens College in Missouri, from 1909 at the College for Women in Pittsburgh, from 1916 at the Pittsburgh Musical Institute, and since 1919 privately. See art.

Whittlesey, Walter R. (b. Hartford, Conn., 1861), from the opening of the new building of the Library of Congress in 1897 had charge of organizing the Music Division, after 1902 was Sonneck's assistant, and since 1917 has been acting as his successor. They collaborated on *The First Editions of Stephen C. Foster*, 1915, and he has also written *Music in the South, 1860-69*, and *Negro Music*, not yet published.

Williams, Harry Evan (Mineral Ridge, O., 1867-1918, Akron, O.), studied in Cleveland, from 1891 appeared as concert-tenor, and speedily became famous. See art.

Witherspoon, Herbert (b. Buffalo, 1873), graduated from Yale in 1895, studied there and later in New York, Paris, London and Berlin, has been noted since 1897 as a concert-bass and since 1898 also in opera, in 1908-16 at the Metropolitan Opera House.

*Wrightson, Herbert James (b. England, 1869), came to Chicago in 1897 as teacher and critic, in 1908-09 taught at the Philadelphia Musical Academy, and in 1911-14 at the Sherwood Music School in Chicago. He has written four organ-sonatas, an organ-concerto, a violin-sonata, piano-pieces, songs, etc.

York, Francis Lodowick (b. Ontonagon, Mich., 1861), graduated from the University of Michigan in 1882, studied music there, at Detroit and in Paris, from 1892 taught at the University of Michigan, from 1896 at the State Normal School, Ypsilanti, and since 1902 has been head of the Detroit Conservatory and organist. See art.

Zahm, John Augustine (b. New Lexington, O., 1851), a member of the Order of the Holy Cross (designated to scientific studies), while professor of physics at the University of Notre Dame published *Sound and Music*, 1892, a notably clear and comprehensive handbook of musical acoustics. For other works, see *Who's Who in America.*

Zay, William Henri (b. Findlay, O., 1869), studied at Cleveland and later at London, from 1890 taught singing at Cleveland, from 1895 was in London as voice-specialist, and since 1917 has been in New York. He has published *The Practical Psychology of Voice and of Life*, 1918, and has written many songs.

Zeckwer, Camille (b. Philadelphia, 1875), son of Richard Zeckwer (see sec. 6), studied in Philadelphia, New York and Berlin, and since before 1900 has been a noted pianist, teacher and composer in Philadelphia. See art.

THE OPENING OF THE TWENTIETH CENTURY

It may seem that there is no evident reason for breaking into two parts the half-century between the end of the Civil War in 1865 and the outbreak of the World War in 1914. During this half-century the United States and Canada moved forward continuously along lines of development that did not essentially change except in momentum and acceleration. Because of this apparent continuity certain statements in earlier paragraphs were allowed to range across the hypothetical line dividing the 19th from the 20th century.

But, on the other hand, especially as concerns the United States, the two recent decades are distinct as a historical period. The date 1900 stands out as a convenient landmark for a significant alteration in the world-relations of both the United States and Canada — an alteration that brought with it important shifts of internal life and consciousness. From the Civil War onward was a time of *national* consolidation on an unexampled scale in both countries. After 1900 this became transformed into a time of *international* outlook and adjustment, also unexampled and as yet of somewhat unpredictable results. Regarding this a few illustrative points may well be cited.

On the commercial side it is enough to note that in 1900 for the first time the annual foreign trade of the United States crossed the two-billion mark. In 1910 it was over three billions, in 1913 over four, and in 1919 over ten. The average volume of exports in the twenty years since 1900 has been more than seven times what it was in the twenty years before 1900. Not only has the volume thus expanded, but the character of this vast international commerce has become infinitely diversified and its geographical scope has been extended into all corners of the earth. Thus America has recently become linked by the cords of trade, as never before, with all lands and peoples.

On the diplomatic side, also, the years just before and after 1900 set the United States into relations with other nations that were unprecedented. In 1898 occurred the brief, but momentous, contest with Spain, leading to the acquisition of the Philippines and Porto Rico and indirectly to that of the Hawaiian Islands. In 1896 had begun the spectacular exploitation of Alaska, and in 1904 the cutting of the Panama Canal was undertaken in earnest (opened to trade in 1914). In 1900–01 came the Boxer Uprising in China and in 1904–05 the Russo-Japanese War, in the progress and settlement of both of which the United States was forced to bear a part. These events, with their political involutions, though mostly located in the region of the Pacific Ocean, really served to push the United States into intimate and vital connection with world-politics and world-tendencies — a connection that rapidly became closer until crowned in 1917 by its impassioned union with the Allies in their struggle against German imperialism. Thus the opening decades of the 20th century widened the horizon and altered the perspective of America's thought and sentiment beyond anything previously experienced. That all this is to have profound reactions upon its future culture cannot be doubted.

Another aspect of international relationship is suggested by the statistics of immigration. In 1900 the United States proper had a population of about 79 millions, in 1910 about 92 millions, and in 1920 presumably about 105 millions — an increase per decade of about 15 per cent. Of this increase immigration supplied a larger proportion than ever before. In 1903–14 the inflow was at the rate of almost a million per year. Seven-eighths of the 14½ millions of aliens received in 1900–19 came from eight countries — Italy and Austria-Hungary, each nearly 22 per cent; Russia, 18 per cent; Great Britain, over 9 per cent; Canada, about 5½ per cent; Scandinavia, 5 per cent; Germany, 3½ per cent; and Greece, about 2½ per cent. The balance of derivation is thus in sharp contrast with all earlier records, the proportion from Italy, Austria and Russia being unexampled. This fact — with many lesser points that cannot here be enumerated — indicates that America's internationalization since 1900 was not only in external relations, but in internal elements. Its foreign-born population was larger than ever, and the derivation of that population was indefinitely more diversified. It is true that this portentous fact has seemed to many depressing, especially since they feel that just when American society was gaining a wider and nobler vision over the world at large its lower strata were being made heavy and inert, if nothing worse, by the influx of multitudes who were ignorant and clannish, uninspired by anything but greed. In the 19th century it is known that the United States was greatly enriched by the flood of immigration, but this has seemed to some not to be the case with the new flood with which the 20th century began. Acknowledging all the difficulties of assimilation that now exist, however, it is a fair question whether in the long run America is not to be infinitely enriched again by the fresh racial elements that are being poured into its composite life. Particularly is this likely on the side of its imaginative and artistic culture, since the new strains of sentiment and tradition are undoubtedly intensely strong and eager. There are already signs that this recent impulse is to have musical consequences.

Here is the appropriate place to remark upon an intricate problem in all American history, particularly in its cultural history, namely, the part played by those who are Americans only by migration and adoption. In the field of music it is evident that since about 1840 all progress has been affected — often dominated — by the influence of those who were foreigners by birth and training. This factor in the historic equation is in America much greater than in any other musical country. It has always been natural for America to welcome the foreigner, whether visitor or settler. When native musicians were few and inexperienced, the coming of seasoned artists from abroad was in every way fruitful. So many of them proved teachers and leaders of power that a tradition formed itself that the places of most distinction, the ranks of organizations like orchestras and opera-companies, and, of course, the items upon standard programs for performance, should all be given to them. Inspection of the lists given in the middle sections of the Chronological Register accompanying this Introduction suggests ample reason why this tradition should have become established. Later sections of the Register indicate how the proportion and importance of native musicians have

G

steadily increased. In view of this advance the persistence of the old tradition in favor of music and musicians from overseas has since 1900 become increasingly unfortunate.

It needs to be remembered, however, that alien-born musicians are not all of one class. Some of them, no doubt, are mere visitors — even when they prolong their stay for several years — transient exploiters of this among many fields of professional éclat and profit. Again, some settle permanently, and even acquire technical citizenship, without really losing their exotic quality — especially in the larger cities — so that, though they are in America, they are not properly of it. But the larger number in their transplanting become so firmly rooted and acclimated that they are not essentially diverse from many native-born musicians who have had training abroad. They must be counted as in a sense true Americans, just as the settlers of the 18th century were. Many of them at the time of their coming are either older than their immediate American associates or have had experience of more breadth and intensity. Hence, so far as they are artists of a 'picked' class, it is not strange that they step into prominence. In every period the inclusion of such forces in the totality of American musical life is all to the good, even though they add to the complexity of its cosmopolitan character.

Since before 1850 American students have tended to seek much of their professional training in Europe. Thus the American response to the opening of the Leipzig Conservatory was notably hearty, as later to the beckoning of other German schools. Still later Paris, London, Vienna and certain Italian cities were also sought. Thus grew up a tradition of the necessity of foreign study if one were to be a master. The force of this has now been much diminished, owing to the obvious excellence of educational advantages at home. At least, it no longer works hardship. But while it lasted, like the other tradition about the superiority of foreign-born artists, it played its part in keeping the standards and trend of music in America singularly cosmopolitan — not strictly indigenous, but compiled from many sources.

Here comes in a question that has been more urgent since 1900 than before — the question as to an American 'type' or 'school' of composition. The question is by no means new, but its serious discussion is comparatively recent. The claim has been pressed that here, as in many other countries, a 'national' type should rest upon something in the nature of folk-music. Among several possible illustrations of such music two have been specially considered.

On the one hand, the songs of the Negroes of the South have been emphasized. Thoughtful attention to these began at the time of the Civil War and especially about 1870, when the original 'Jubilee Singers' were heard at home and abroad. Of course, the picturesque sentiment in such melodies had been felt long before and artistically used, as, for example, by Foster as early as 1845. But in 1885 Negro themes were put to orchestral use by Chadwick and in 1894 more ostentatiously by Dvořák. Since then the latent richness of this vein of melodic and rhythmic ore has been diligently searched out by many composers, with results most interesting and often impressive.

On the other hand, the songs of the Indians of the West have also been emphasized. Attention to these was first called by the original study of Theodore Baker in 1882 — a study which in part inspired the drafting of MacDowell's 'Indian Suite' some ten years later. Since 1901 the value of this source has been valiantly upheld by a circle of enthusiasts led by Arthur Farwell. The result is that this vein, too, has been worked with great ability and increasing tangible results. It has the obvious advantage of bringing into view not only tonal patterns, but the literary or dramatic quality inherent in Indian fantasy and legend.

Highly characteristic and fascinating as both of these sources undoubtedly are, neither of them is fully expressive of America as a whole, of its cosmopolitan derivation, its kaleidoscopic history, or its essentially unique national spirit. Hence there has been more and more an instinctive search for musical means to embody impressions from the physical environment of American life, from the reaction upon the imagination of its historic epochs, from reflections over the motives and traits of its characteristic spiritual nature. It is not unlikely that this last holds special promise for the future.

The notes in earlier parts of this Introduction about the growth of cities should now be extended to the time after 1900. Final data from the census of 1920 are not yet available, but the salient facts are clear from the preliminary reports that have been made. In 1900 there were in the United States 36 cities with 100,000 inhabitants or more; in 1910 there were 50 such; and in 1920 there were about 70, with a total estimated population of about 30 millions. It will be useful to name about fifty of them, arranged by sections and with their estimated size in 1920 stated in round thousands:

EASTERN STATES
Boston, Mass. 748 (000)
Providence, R. I. . . . 238
Worcester, Mass. . . . 180
New Haven, Conn. . . 163
Bridgeport, Conn. . . 143
Hartford, Conn. . . . 138
Springfield, Mass. . . 129

MIDDLE STATES
New York, N. Y. . . . 5621
Philadelphia, Pa. . . . 1823
Baltimore, Md. . . . 734
Pittsburgh, Pa. . . . 588
Buffalo, N. Y. 507
Washington, D. C. . . 438
Newark, N. J. 414
Jersey City, N. J. . . 298
Rochester, N. Y. . . . 296
Syracuse, N. Y. . . . 172
Scranton, Pa. 138
Paterson, N. J. . . . 136

SOUTHERN STATES
New Orleans, La. . . . 387
Louisville, Ky. . . . 235
Atlanta, Ga. . . . 201
Birmingham, Ala. . . 178
Richmond, Va. . . . 172
Memphis, Tenn. . . . 162

CENTRAL STATES
Chicago, Ill. 2701 (000)
Detroit, Mich. 994
Cleveland, O. 797
St. Louis, Mo. 773
Milwaukee, Wis. . . . 457
Cincinnati, O. 401
Minneapolis, Minn. . . 380
Kansas City, Mo. . . . 324
Indianapolis, Ind. . . . 314
Toledo, O. 243
Columbus, O. 237
St. Paul, Minn. . . . 235
Akron, O. 208
Dayton, O. 153
Grand Rapids, Mich. . . 138
Youngstown, O. . . . 132

WESTERN STATES
Denver, Colo. 256
Omaha, Neb. 192
San Antonio, Tex. . . . 161
Dallas, Tex. 159
Houston, Tex. 140
Salt Lake City, Utah . . 130

PACIFIC STATES
Los Angeles, Cal. . . . 577
San Francisco, Cal. . . 508
Seattle, Wash. . . . 316
Portland, Ore. 258
Oakland, Cal. 216

It is not practicable to go into detail as to the ways in which most of these cities are serving as musical centers. Perhaps half of them have more or less permanent orchestras and at least three-quarters of them somewhat competent choral societies. Though but a few as yet have operatic performances, a large majority enjoy regular concert-seasons of some significance. Nearly all boast one or more strong music-schools, and all doubtless contain some or many superior teachers. Comparatively few of them fail to provide in their public libraries for the demands of those who would cultivate themselves in musical knowledge through books.

The opening of the 20th century brought a striking quickening of effort in the presentation of opera. The Metropolitan Opera House in New York remained the conspicuous center, with the Auditorium in Chicago a good second. From 1900 several efforts were made to establish opera in English through traveling troupes — the chief being those of Savage and of the Aborns — efforts that have since been continued at intervals and in different forms, though constantly tending to veer off into the more lucrative field of light opera. Much more important was the spectacular undertaking of Hammerstein in 1906 at his Manhattan Opera House in New York (with branch-efforts in Philadelphia, leading to his Philadelphia Opera House in 1908) to dispute the leadership of the Metropolitan. This competition led in 1908 to the transfer of the Metropolitan to the capable hands of Gatti-Casazza, its present manager, to the erection of the Boston Opera House in 1909 and a determined effort to link New York and Boston operatically, and in 1910 to the restriction of the Hammerstein interest by the Metropolitan. This last step was immediately followed by the formation of the strong and enterprising Chicago Opera Association, which has ever since been foremost as a friendly competitor with the Metropolitan. In 1913–15 an energetic effort was made in New York to set up a fresh center at the Century Opera House.

The number of permanent orchestras was rapidly increased. The dates in some cases are not easy to fix precisely, since tentative experiments often preceded positive establishment, but it may be noted that Archer and Herbert began as conductors at Pittsburgh even before 1900, that Scheel was at Philadelphia from 1900, Oberhoffer at Minneapolis from 1903, Altschuler and his Russian Symphony Orchestra at New York from 1904, Zach at St. Louis from 1907, Rothwell at St. Paul from 1908, Stokowski at Cincinnati in 1909 (reorganization), Hadley at Seattle in 1909 and at San Francisco in 1911, Busch at Kansas City from 1910, Gales at Detroit in 1914, Gunn and the American Orchestra at Chicago from 1915, Strube at Baltimore from 1916, etc. These are but varied samples of a movement that now reaches more or less over the whole country. In 1911 the cause of orchestral music was furthered by a princely bequest to the Philharmonic Society of New York, in 1914 by an analogous gift to the New York Symphony Society and in 1915 by another to the Cincinnati Symphony Orchestra — these endowments following the example already set in Boston and Chicago. The larger orchestras now usually make extended tours each season, so that their influence is spread over a wide area. Most of them also engage, in whole or in part, in a multiplicity of 'festival' undertakings.

The cultivation of chamber-music has grown apace since the Kneisel Quartet led the way in 1886.   Among its early successors was the Spiering Quartet of Chicago (1893–1905).   In 1900 was organized the Longy Club of Boston (wind-instruments), to which was added in 1910 the parallel Barrère Ensemble of New York.   In 1903 it was an American banker who joined the list of great patrons by founding the Flonzaley Quartet, which forthwith became internationally significant.   Among many other organizations of the period may be named the Olive Mead Quartet and the Margulies Trio, both launched in New York in 1904. Among recent additions are the Philharmonic Ensemble of New York (1913), the Kortschak Quartet of Chicago (1915, transformed in 1916 into the Berkshire), the Letz Quartet of New York (1917), etc.

In the choral field there has been a steady, though not rapid, multiplication of societies.   Perhaps the most striking are those devoted to the production of comparatively unusual works.   The Musical Art Society of New York, which was founded as early as 1893, initiated an interest in historical programs, especially in a cappella form, that has spread to several other cities.   Somewhat akin is the Schola Cantorum of New York, which followed in 1908.   Two Canadian societies, the Mendelssohn Choir of Toronto (from 1894) and the Elgar Choir of Hamilton (from 1904), have acquired much more than a local reputation through tours in the United States.   German, Scandinavian, Welsh and other national choruses have aroused enthusiasm in various parts of the country.   To the list of annual festivals there are two striking additions, though very dissimilar in character, namely, that of the Bach Choir at Bethlehem, Pa. (since 1898) and that of the Litchfield County Choral Union at Norfolk, Conn. (since 1902).   The Worcester (Mass.) festivals have maintained their position of importance.   Among others those at Ann Arbor, Mich., and Evanston, Ill., may be named as representative of many that are associated with large educational institutions.   Those at Peterboro, N. H., and at Lockport, N. Y., may be cited as specimens of still other classes.

After 1900, even more than during the decade before, the influx of visiting artists of every kind from abroad was notable for amount and quality.   After 1910, and especially as the cloud of impending war arose, this influx increased, bringing many who probably will remain permanently.   In a single year the number of immigrants who are classed as 'musicians' has risen as high as 350.   Thus the factor of internationality in American music is at present on the increase.

No proper summary can here be made of the advance of technical music-education.   The recent period has seen the steady strengthening of the older institutions and the addition of many new ones.   Many of those that are comparatively unpretentious serve a useful purpose for their own circle and region. Some command a clientage from the whole country — and even from foreign countries.   The Institute of Musical Art in New York, founded in 1905, is perhaps unique in the size of its initial endowment and its policy of administration.   In most of the leading conservatories great changes of scope and method have taken place.   Almost all of them now provide extensively for the pursuit of dramatic music, for experience in ensemble-playing, for discipline in applied pedagogy, and for other branches not easily accessible in private instruction. All maintain ample demonstrative courses of concerts and recitals.

To this recent period belongs the advance of the music-departments in colleges and universities into marked importance. The origin of many of them was far back in an earlier time, but their development on broad lines has mostly come since 1900. The state universities as a class, with the colleges for women, have become notable for their attention to music as an element in or adjunct to general education. They, like the music-schools generally, have also magnified the pursuit of music as an occupational preparation. In the public schools music-instruction has not only become much more customary in cities and larger towns, but has been greatly improved in quality, scope and status. Its administration by highly trained supervisors has made it more professional in character. In many cases school-choruses and school-orchestras have reached a remarkable pitch of artistic excellence. Urgent efforts are being put forth to link up private musical study by pupils with their school program and standing by means of some system of credits. The importance of all this is shown by the attention to it given by bodies like the National Education Association and a governmental department like the Bureau of Education.

Musical periodicals have not so much increased in number as gained in dignity, circulation and influence. A capital event in this field was the founding in 1915 of 'The Musical Quarterly,' which is plainly on a much higher level than anything previously attempted in America.

In the field of church-music the most influential organization is the American Guild of Organists, founded in 1896, which works through a system of examinations to measure and attest the ability of players, and by means of local chapters and frequent services aims to develop and guide enthusiasm. There is also an energetic National Association of Organists, founded in 1908.

A singular feature of the period is the prodigious expansion of mechanical appliances for reproducing music. Experiments in this direction were originally made in Europe and somewhat in America long before 1900, but the exploitation of such appliances on a large scale is mostly confined to the last twenty-five years. It is in America that they have been best perfected and most extensively adopted. Their popularity has aroused much discussion. On one hand it is naturally said that they do not usually represent musical effects accurately or adequately, especially in correct intonation, delicacy of nuance and the subtle personal magnetism of the living performer. Yet, on the other hand, it is evident that for many users, especially those of limited opportunity or of uncritical habit of listening, they supply a real means of entrance into the world of musical literature. They have proved of value as adjuncts to technical music-teaching in some forms and stages. The balance between their good and bad possibilities must be struck according to circumstances. It is true that the eagerness for large sales has led many manufacturers of records, like some publishers of printed music, to flood the market with inferior and even obnoxious material and to stimulate its purchase. Yet remarkably fine records of important works, vocal and instrumental, have been prepared and their number increases. For those who are minded to use mechanical means with discretion and educational design an extensive repertory is available and for its actual presentation all kinds of reproducers are now obtainable in remarkable perfection. This commercial evolution, then, with its hold upon popular attention, must be counted as an important factor in the present situation.

Slightly related to this is the extraordinary development of music as an adjunct to moving-picture theaters. In the larger of these organs of both power and delicacy are now common, and the use of them is becoming a specialty among organ-players. In a few cases there is also an orchestra of superior quality. It is not yet clear how great an influence this rather sudden development is to have, or along what lines.

It is mostly since 1900 that the American-born composer, along with the American-born concert-performer, may be said to have begun to come into his heritage. In recent years works by both the older and the younger groups of composers have begun to be given as never before by orchestras, choral societies, chamber-ensembles, vocal and instrumental soloists, and even the great opera-companies. Recitalists and teachers are giving far more attention to American works, and several publishers are specializing in them. Thus at length the musical public is becoming aware of much that lies ready at its hand. In all this progress the adopted American, also, is receiving his share of recognition. Almost the only direct result of the World War as regards musical matters has been the access of emphasis upon that which represents America and American sentiment. At the same time, however, it must be confessed that the social conditions issuing from the war period are so complicated that it is harder than ever to say precisely what is distinctively 'American.' With every succeeding decade compact generalizations as to the national qualities, tendencies and destinies become more difficult and hazardous.

Among the younger composers a few names begin to stand out in succession to those named at an earlier point, names like D. G. Mason, Carpenter, Schelling, Campbell-Tipton, D. S. Smith, Fairchild, Cadman, Powell, Clapp and Sowerby. But whether or not these are typical is a question for time and critical judgment to answer. The purpose of this Introduction is not to describe the history of American composition or appraise the works or style of even its chief representatives, but simply to indicate the conditions surrounding that evolution and some of the social connections of musical effort. Almost every page of this volume offers data as to the variety and abundance of production, especially during the last half-century. The critical sifting of these data it is perhaps not yet time to attempt.

There seems not to be any book that devotes itself to the topics that have been here emphasized — the material and social setting or environment of musical and other artistic progress. Yet in the larger histories and in many similar discussions passages or chapters might perhaps be cited to some advantage. Instead of attempting this, however, the following brief list of compact manuals of the history as a whole may be set down: *Epochs of American History*, 3 vols.; Farrand, *The Development of the United States*, 1918; Elson, *Sidelights on American History*, 2 vols., 1899–1900; Sparks, *The Men who Made the Nation*, 1900; Muzzey, *American History*, 1911.

CHRONOLOGICAL REGISTER

9. The Opening of the 20th Century — 1900–1910

Aborn, Milton (b. Marysville, Cal., 1864), and his brother **Sargent Aborn** (b. Boston, 1866), active since 1885 as theatrical players or managers, from 1902 managed the Aborn Opera Company, giving opera in English at low prices, and in 1913–15 made a decided success with the Century Opera House in New York.

*Alda, Frances [Frances Davis] (b. New Zealand, 1883), having appeared from 1904 as operatic soprano in Europe and South America, since 1908 has been a favorite at the Metropolitan Opera House in New York. In 1910 she married the manager Gatti-Casazza. See art.

Aldrich, Mariska (b. Boston, 1881), studied in Paris and London, made her début as dramatic soprano in 1908 in New York, and since 1909 has been (except in 1914 at Berlin) at the Metropolitan Opera House. Since 1917 she has been Mrs. W. E. S. Davis.

*Altschuler, Modest (b. Russia, 1873), an expert 'cellist, in 1903 organized the Russian Symphony Orchestra, of which he has since been conductor. See art.

*Amato, Pasquale (b. Italy, 1878), the well-known operatic baritone, since 1908 has been at the Metropolitan Opera House. See art.

Anderson, Arthur Olaf (b. Newport, R. I., 1880), trained in Boston, Paris, Berlin and Rome, in 1905 began theory-teaching in Berlin, and since 1908 has taught at the American Conservatory in Chicago. See art.

*Ara, Ugo (b. Italy, 1876), from 1903 was violist in the Flonzaley Quartet until recalled to Italy by the World War in 1917, his place being taken by Louis Bailly.

*d'Archambeau, Ivan (b. Belgium, 1879), since 1903 has been 'cellist in the Flonzaley Quartet.

*Arimondi, Vittorio (b. Italy, ?), the operatic bass, from 1906 sang at the Manhattan Opera House in New York, and since 1910 has been with the Chicago Opera Company.

*Audsley, George Ashdown (b. Scotland, 1838), since 1892 an architect in New York, from 1905 has published sumptuous treatises on organ-building. See art.

Ayres, Frederic (b. Binghamton, N. Y., 1876), studied in New York and Boston, and since 1901, with some teaching and lecturing, has been engaged on composition, living in Colorado Springs. See art.

Barnes, Edward Shippen (b. Seabright, N. J., 1887), studied at the Yale School of Music, from 1909 was assistant University organist, and, after study in Paris, from 1911 was organist in New York, joining the Naval Reserve in 1918–19. See art.

Barnhart, Harry Horner (b. 1874), trained as baritone and choral leader in London and Florence, has been successful in organizing and leading large enterprises in community-singing, notably at Rochester and New York.

*Barrère, Georges (b. France, 1876), from 1895 a well-known flutist in Paris, since 1905 has been in the New York Symphony Society and teaching at the Institute of Musical Art, besides founding ensemble-groups. See art.

*Bauer, Harold (b. England, 1873), from 1893 a distinguished concert-pianist in Europe, since 1900 has been repeatedly and enthusiastically heard in America. See art.

*Becker, René Louis (b. Alsace, 1882), from 1904 was teacher and from 1908 organist in St. Louis, from 1912 in Belleville, Ill., and since 1915 in Alton, Ill. See art.

*Beebe, Carolyn (b. Westfield, N. J., ?), studied piano and ensemble-playing in New York and abroad, made her début in Berlin in 1903, in 1905–19 taught at the Institute of Musical Art in New York, and since 1914 has been head of the New York Chamber Music Society.

Bellamann, Heinrich Hauer (b. Fulton, Mo., 1882), studied in Paris, and since 1907 has taught at Chicora College for Women, Columbia, S. C., becoming dean of the music-department. See art.

*Benedictis, Savino di (b. Brazil, 1883), theorist and composer, has for several years been professor in the Conservatory at São Paulo. See art.

*Berger, Rudolf (Moravia, 1874–1915, New York), having sung for ten years in Germany as dramatic baritone, in 1907–08 studied in New York, his voice changing to tenor, and in 1914–15 sang at the Metropolitan Opera House. In 1913 he married the soprano Marie Rappold (see below).

Bergh, Arthur (b. St. Paul, 1882), from 1903 was violinist in the Symphony Society in New York and at the Metropolitan Opera House, and in 1911–14 conducted municipal concerts. See art.

*Betti, Adolfo (b. Italy, 1875), since 1903 has been first violin in the Flonzaley Quartet.

Biggs, Richard Keys (b. Glendale, O., 1886), trained in Cincinnati and London, since 1908 has been organist in Cincinnati, Detroit, Cleveland and Brooklyn, with much recital-playing.

Bingham, Walter Van Dyke (b. Swan Lake, Ia., 1880), graduated from Beloit College in 1901, from 1908 was instructor in psychology in Columbia University, from 1910 professor at Dartmouth College, and since 1915 has been at the Carnegie Institute of Technology, Pittsburgh. He has written articles (' Psychological Review ') upon physiological psychology in relation to music, and *Studies in Melody*, 1910.

Birge, Edward Bailey (b. Florence, Mass., 1868), graduated from Brown University in 1891, studied music in Providence and New

Haven, since 1901 has been director of music in the Indianapolis public schools, since 1908 also superintendent of the American Institute of Normal Methods and since 1910 conductor of the People's Chorus. He has written a concert-overture (1904), a children's cantata, and much school-music.

Bliss, Philip Paul (b. Chicago, 1872), son of P. P. Bliss (see sec. 5), graduated from Princeton in 1894, was trained as organist in Philadelphia and Paris, from 1900 taught at Owego, N. Y., and since 1904 has been in editorial work in Cincinnati. See art.

*Blum, Elias (b. Hungary, 1881), came to Boston as a boy, studied there and at Weimar, from 1905 was organist and tenor in Boston, from 1909 music-director at Whitman College, Walla Walla, Wash., and since 1917 has taught at Grinnell College in Iowa. See art.

Bond, Carrie, née Jacobs (b. Janesville, Wis., 1862), since 1903 has been noted as poet-composer in Chicago of many very popular songs, published at the Bond Shop (Carrie Jacobs-Bond & Son).

Bornschein, Franz Carl (b. Baltimore, 1879), studied in Baltimore, and since 1905 has been teacher and conductor in the Peabody Conservatory there and also leader of choral societies elsewhere. See art.

Braham, Herbert J. (b. Brooklyn, 1885), trained in London and Leipzig, from 1905 was with the Savage Opera Company, and since 1907 has been conductor of the Brooklyn Symphony Orchestra, the Brooklyn Orchestral Society and other organizations. He has written two light operas.

Branscombe, Gena (b. Picton, Ont., 1881), studied at Chicago and later at Berlin, from 1900 taught at the Chicago Musical College, in 1907–09 at Whitman College in Walla Walla, and since 1910 (as Mrs. John F. Tenney) has lived in New York as composer. See art.

*Bressler-Gianoli, Clotilde (Switzerland, 1875–1912, Switzerland), a brilliant stage-soprano, sang with the San Carlo Opera Company in New Orleans and New York from 1906, at the Metropolitan Opera House in 1909–10, and with the Philadelphia-Chicago Opera Company from 1910.

Brosky, Frank J. (b. Pittsburgh, 1883), studied at Leipzig and Prague, appeared as concert-violinist at Prague in 1904, played in orchestras there, in Leipzig and Pittsburgh, and since 1910 has had a school in Pittsburgh.

*Brounoff, Platon G. (b. Russia, 1863), since 1892 has been lecturer (mainly on Russian music) and conductor in New York. See art.

*Buchhalter, Simon (b. Russia, 1881), since 1905 has made tours as pianist in America, in 1907 taught at the Wichita College of Music, and since 1913 has lived at Chicago. He has written the opera ' A Lovers' Knot ' (1916), the oratorio ' A Drama of Exile,' a setting of Psalm 142, a symphonic overture, piano-pieces and songs.

*Buehrer, Geoffrey Carl (b. Switzerland, 1878) trained at Paris and New York, from 1900 was organist and teacher at San José, Cal., from 1906 organist at Stanford University, from 1913 in New York, and since 1916 in Baltimore, where he is head of the Association School of Music. He arranged and conducted a musical Passion-Play at Santa Clara three seasons, led the first festival at Stanford University, and has written a string-quartet on the Flight into Egypt, the cantata ' As it Began to Dawn,' etc.

Buhlig, Richard (b. Chicago, 1880), studied in Chicago and Vienna, from 1901 toured in Europe as concert-pianist, visiting America in 1907–08, in 1916 came to New York, and since 1918 has taught at the Institute of Musical Art.

Buhrman, Thomas Scott Godfrey (b. Waynesboro, Pa., 1887), studied in New York, and since 1909 has been known as an expert concert-organist, specializing in the works of Bach, and as writer on organ-subjects.

*Buonamici, Carlo (b. Italy, 1875), besides appearing as concert-pianist, since 1908 has been associated with Félix Fox in the Fox-Buonamici School in Boston.

Burleigh, Cecil (b. Wyoming, N. Y., 1885), studied mainly in Berlin and Chicago, from 1907 toured as violinist, from 1909 taught in Denver, from 1911 at Morningside College in Sioux City, and in 1914–19 at the University of Montana. See art.

Burlin, Natalie, née Curtis (b. New York, ?), studied in New York and several European cities, and since 1905 has published important collections of Indian and Negro songs. See art.

Burnham, Thuel (b. Vinton, Ia., 1884), appeared as a child-pianist from 1890, studied in New York and Vienna, from 1900 toured in England and from 1904 on the Continent, and since 1915 in the United States.

*Butcher, Frank Charles (b. England, 1882), from 1898 organist in England, from 1908 taught at the Hoosac School, Hoosick, N. Y., and since 1916 has been organist at St. Stephen's, Pittsfield, Mass. He has written church-music and songs.

Cadman, Charles Wakefield (b. Johnstown, Pa., 1881), studied in Pittsburgh, where he was critic, organist and conductor, and since 1906 has specialized in the study of Indian music and its use in highly original composition, from 1910 living in Los Angeles. See art.

Calzin, Alfred Lucien (b. Marine City, Mich., 1885), studied in Brussels and Berlin, in 1907–08 toured in Europe as pianist, from 1908 in America, from 1912 taught in Chicago, and since 1916 has been at the Northwestern Conservatory, Minneapolis. He has written and edited music for the piano.

Campbell-Tipton, Louis (b. Chicago, 1877), studied mainly in Leipzig, in 1900–01 taught in Chicago, and has since lived in Paris as teacher and composer. See art.

*Cantu, Agostinho (b. Italy, 1879), for several years has been piano-teacher in the Conservatory of the Capital at São Paulo, Brazil. He has written for string-ensemble, besides piano-pieces and songs.

Carey, Bruce Anderson (b. Hamilton, Ont., 1877), trained at Hamilton, London, Florence and Munich, since 1904 has been conductor of the famous Elgar Choir of Hamilton.

Carpenter, John Alden (b. Park Ridge, Ill., 1876), graduated from Harvard in 1897, studied music there and later in Chicago, where he has been active in commercial life, but also fertile in composition. See art.

*Carrillo, Julián (b. Mexico, 1875), trained in Mexico City, Leipzig and Ghent, in 1906–07 toured in Mexico as pianist, and from 1907 was connected with the Conservatorio Nacional in Mexico City, becoming its head in 1913, but removing in 1915 to New York. He has composed the operas 'Mathilda' and 'Ossian,' two symphonies, two orchestral suites, a piano-quintet, a string-quartet and sextet, two masses and a Requiem, and published *Discursos sobre la Música*, 1913, and *Tratado Sintético de Harmonia*, 1913, '15, besides other theoretical works in manuscript.

*Casals, Pablo (b. Spain, 1876), the eminent 'cellist, since 1901 has made successful tours in the United States and South America. In 1914 he married the singer Susan Metcalfe. See art.

Case, Anna (b. Clinton, N. J., 1889), trained in New York, made her début as operatic soprano there in 1909, till 1916 sang at the Metropolitan Opera House, turning then to concert-work. See art.

*Cavalieri, Lina (b. Italy, 1874), the dramatic soprano, in 1906–07 sang at the Metropolitan Opera House, in 1907–08 at the Manhattan Opera House, and in 1915–16 with the Chicago Opera Company. In 1913 she married the tenor Lucien Muratore (see sec. 10). See art.

*Charlier, Marcel (b. Belgium, ?), having been opera-conductor in London, from 1906 was assistant-conductor (for French operas) at the Manhattan Opera House, and since 1910 has held a similar position with the Chicago Opera Company.

Cheatham, Kitty [Katharine Smiley C.] (b. Nashville, Tenn., ?), a mezzo-soprano, now living in New York, who has specialized in Negro folk-songs and songs of childhood, giving many recitals in America and abroad. She has published two song-collections.

Cisneros, Eleonora de, née Broadfoot (b. New York, 1880), studied in New York and later in Paris, first appeared as opera-soprano in New York in 1900, in 1901–06 sang in European capitals, and since 1906 has been mainly engaged in America, from 1910 with the Chicago Opera Company. See art.

Clapp, Philip Greeley (b. Boston, 1888), graduated from Harvard in 1908, studied there and in Stuttgart, from 1911 taught at Harvard and near Boston, from 1915 was

music-director at Dartmouth College, and since 1919 has been professor at the State University of Iowa. See art.

Class, Franklin Morris (b. New York, 1881), graduated from Harvard in 1903 and from 1907 a practicing physician, since 1903 has been known as composer and writer. See art.

Clemens, Clara (b. Elmira, N. Y., 1871?), daughter of 'Mark Twain,' studied in Hartford, Conn., Berlin and Vienna, and since 1906 has appeared in Europe and America as concert-contralto. In 1909 she married the pianist and conductor Gabrilovitch. See art.

*Clément, Edmond (b. France, 1867), the noted opera-tenor of the Opéra-Comique, in 1909–10 sang at the Metropolitan Opera House in New York, and in 1911–13 with the Boston Opera Company.

Colburn, George (b. Colton, N. Y., 1878), trained in Chicago, from 1902 taught in the American Conservatory there, besides some conducting after 1913, and since 1915 has been municipal music-director at Winona, Minn. He has composed incidental orchestral music and 'masques,' the symphonic poem 'Spring's Conquest' (1913), a piano-trio (1909), and a piano-quartet (1915).

*Courboin, Charles Marie (b. Belgium, 1886), already noted as a gifted organist, since 1904 has been organist at Oswego, N. Y., and at Syracuse, with stated work also at Springfield, Mass., and in Philadelphia, and many recitals elsewhere. See art.

Cowles, Walter Ruel (b. New Haven, Conn., 1881), graduated from Yale in 1906, was trained there and later in Paris, from 1907 taught in Newport, R. I., and since 1911 has been piano-instructor in the Yale School of Music and church-organist. He has written a piano-concerto (1907), a piano-trio (1916), a violin-sonata (1914), music for the Yale Pageant of 1916, etc.

Craft, Marcella (b. Indianapolis, 1880), studied in Boston and Milan, from 1902 appeared as operatic soprano at Morbegno and other Italian cities, from 1907 sang at Mainz, Kiel and Munich, and since 1914 in America. See art.

Cunningham, Claude (b. Manchester, Va., 1880), studied in New York and Paris, made his début as concert-baritone in 1903 with Patti on her last American tour, and has since sung with success in oratorio and concert throughout the United States and also in Germany (1908). He has published *The World-Spirit and Other Essays*, 1916.

Curry, Arthur Mansfield (b. Chelsea, Mass., 1866), a pupil of Kneisel and MacDowell, became known as composer about 1900, in 1914 taught in Berlin and later at the New England Conservatory in Boston. See art.

*Dalmorès, Charles (b. France, 1871), an experienced stage-tenor, in 1906–10 sang at the Manhattan Opera House in New York, and since 1910 has been with the Chicago Opera Company. See art.

*Destinn, Emmy [original name Kittl] (b. Bohemia, 1878), the brilliant operatic soprano, since 1908 has been in the Metropolitan Opera House forces, though retaining her home in Prague. Besides being a gifted actress and singer, she is also novelist and poet. See Baker, *Dict. of Musicians*, p. 205.

*Déthier, Édouard (b. Belgium, 1885), brother of Gaston M. Déthier (see sec. 8), since 1906 has toured extensively in America as concert-violinist and has also taught at the Institute of Musical Art in New York.

Dett, R. Nathaniel (b. Drummondville, Que., 1882), trained at Oberlin and New York, first appeared as pianist in 1908, from 1909 was music-director at Lane College in Tennessee, from 1912 at Lincoln Institute in Missouri, and since 1913 at Hampton Institute in Virginia. See art.

*Diggle, Roland (b. England, 1885), from 1908 was organist in Canada, from 1911 in Quincy, Ill., and since 1914 in Los Angeles, with concert-tours. He has written string-quartets, organ-sonatas, an orchestral ‘Fairy Suite,’ church-music, piano-pieces and songs.

*Dolmetsch, Arnold (b. France, 1858), the expert upon old instruments and their music, in 1902–09 lived in the United States as recitalist, lecturer, and maker of spinets, etc., at the Chickering factory in Boston.

Donalda, Pauline [original name Lightstone] (b. Montreal, 1884), trained in Montreal and Paris, in 1904 made her début as operatic soprano at Nice, appeared at Brussels and London, in 1906–07 sang at the Manhattan Opera House, and has since been mainly engaged at the Opéra-Comique in Paris. In 1906 she married the French tenor Seveilhac.

Downes, Edwin Olin (b. Evanston, Ill., 1886), studied in Boston, and since 1907 has been music-critic on the ‘Post’ there, with much lecturing and literary work, and also teaching at Chautauqua in 1913–14. See art.

*Drangosch, Ernesto (b. Argentina, 1882), studied at Berlin, toured as pianist, and since 1905 has been head of the Conservatorio in Buenos Aires.

*Dufranne, Hector (b. France, ?), well known in France and England as an opera-tenor, from 1908 sang at the Manhattan Opera House in New York, and since 1910 has been with the Chicago Opera Company, but retains his residence in France.

Dunn, James Philip (b. New York, 1884), graduated from the College of the City of New York in 1903, studied music at Columbia University, and has been organist in New York and Jersey City. See art.

Durst, Sidney C. (b. Hamilton, O., 1870), trained at Cincinnati and Munich, since about 1903 has taught in Cincinnati, at first at the College of Music, later at the Metropolitan College, besides serving more or less as accompanist and organist at the May Festivals. He has composed an orchestral suite, cantatas and other vocal music.

Edvina, Marie Louise Lucienne, née Martin (b. Montreal, ?), studied in Paris, made her début as operatic soprano in 1908 in London, where she has since sung regularly, and in 1911–13 was with the Boston Opera Company, and since 1915 with the Chicago Opera Company. In 1901 she married Hon. Cecil Edwards (whence her stage-name).

Edwards, John Harrington (Acton, Mass., 1834–1918?, Seattle), a retired Presbyterian clergyman, then of Brooklyn, published *God and Music*, 1903, arguing that the being and nature of God are especially exhibited in the facts of tone and the tonal art — a novel application of the argument from design.

Egg, Arthur Henry (b. Montreal, 1891), studied in Montreal and later in London, in 1909–10 was organist in Montreal, from 1910 in a suburb of London, and since 1913 at Christ Church Cathedral, Montreal. See art.

*Elman, Mischa (b. Russia, 1892), the eminent violinist, since 1908 has made frequent tours in the United States with striking success. See Vol. v. 634, and art.

*Evans, Edwin (b. Wales, 1876), educated in Philadelphia, since 1907 has been an effective concert-baritone in oratorio and song-recital, besides teaching in Philadelphia.

Evans, Frederick Vance (b. Des Moines, Ia., 1883), trained in Iowa and Wisconsin, from about 1905 concert-bass and teacher in Des Moines music-schools, and since 1913 has been dean of music at Lawrence College, Appleton, Wis.

*Ezerman, D. Hendrik (b. Holland, 1880), since 1901 has been concert-pianist in Philadelphia, and for some years head of the Philadelphia Conservatory.

*Fabri, Ludwig Schmitt (b. Bavaria, 1874), after experience in Germany as opera-tenor and conductor, for several years has been active in Philadelphia, conducting his own Opera School.

Fairchild, Blair (b. Belmont, Mass., 1877), studied at Harvard and in Florence, from 1901 was in diplomatic service at Constantinople and Teheran, and since 1905 has lived in Paris, occupied with composition. See art.

Farnam, W. Lynnwood (b. Sutton, Que., 1885), trained mostly in London, from 1904 was organist in Montreal, after 1908 at Christ Church Cathedral, in 1913–18 at Emmanuel Church, Boston, and from 1919 in New York. See art.

Farrar, Geraldine (b. Melrose, Mass., 1882), studied in Boston, New York, Washington and Paris, was heard in concert in 1895, but made her début as opera-soprano in 1901 at Berlin, resulting in immediate engagements there and elsewhere. Since 1906 she has been at the Metropolitan Opera House. See art.

Fay, Maude (b. San Francisco, 1883), trained at San Francisco and Dresden, in 1906–15 was soprano at the Hofoper in Munich, besides appearing often elsewhere. Her home is in San Francisco.

Federlein, Gottfried Heinrich (b. New York, 1883), son of Gottlieb H. Federlein (see sec. 7), studied in New York, and since 1907 has been organist there, giving recitals elsewhere. He has written considerable church-music.

*****Fiedler, August Max** (b. Saxony, 1859), the distinguished pianist and conductor, in 1908–12 was conductor of the Boston Symphony Orchestra, returning then to Berlin.

*****Flodin, Karl** (b. Finland, 1858, of German parents), since 1907 has lived as composer and author at Buenos Aires, giving special attention to Finnish music. See art.

*****Floridia, Pietro** (b. Sicily, 1860), came to America in 1904, in 1906–08 taught at the Cincinnati College of Music, and since then has lived in New York as composer and from 1913 conductor of the Italian Symphony Orchestra. See art.

Fornia-Labey, Rita, née Newman (b. San Francisco, 1878), studied in San Francisco and Paris, appeared first as opera-soprano in Germany, from 1906 sang with the Savage Opera Company, and since 1908 has been at the Metropolitan Opera House. See art.

Fradkin, Fredric (b. Troy, N. Y., 1892), studied violin in New York and Paris, from 1909 was concertmaster at Bordeaux and Monte Carlo, in 1911 appeared in New York, was then again abroad, from 1914 was concertmaster in New York, and in 1918–19 with the Boston Symphony Orchestra. See art.

*****Fraemcke, August** (b. Hamburg, 1870), since 1900 has been associated with Karl Hein (see sec. 8) in the management of the German Conservatory in New York and also since 1906 of the New York College of Music.

*****Friml, Charles Rudolf** (b. Bohemia, 1881), accompanied the violinist Kubelik on his American tour in 1901 and again in 1906, since then living in New York as composer. See art.

Frysinger, J. Frank (b. Hanover, Pa., 1878), studied in Baltimore, New York, Philadelphia and London, began organ-playing when a boy, from 1909 was organist at York, Pa., and also music-director at Hood College, Frederick, Md., from 1911 organist in Lincoln, Neb., and teacher at the University School of Music, and since 1918 has taught at Augustana College in Illinois. See art.

Fullerton, Robert (b. Dundalk, Ont., 1867), brother of C. A. Fullerton (see sec. 8), trained at Cedar Falls, Ia., Oberlin, New York, Boston and Florence, in 1901–05 and 1907–11 was vocal teacher at the State Teachers College, Cedar Falls, and since 1914 has been in Minneapolis, from 1916 as head of the Twin City Conservatory.

*****Gabrilovitch, Ossip Salomonovitch** (b. Russia, 1878), an eminent pianist since 1896, from 1900 made repeated tours in the United States, in 1917–18 conducted orchestral concerts in New York, and since 1918 has been conductor of the Detroit Orchestra. See art.

*****Ganz, Rudolph** (b. Switzerland, 1877), the noted pianist, from 1900 taught in the Chicago Musical College, and since 1905 has toured extensively in America and Europe. See art.

*****Garden, Mary** (b. Scotland, 1877), spent her childhood and early youth in the United States, studied for the opera-stage in Paris, making her début in 1900, returned to sing at the Manhattan Opera House in New York in 1907, and since 1910 has been with the Chicago Opera Company. See art.

*****Gatti-Casazza, Giulio** (b. Italy, 1869), after much experience as impresario in Italy, since 1908 has been the able manager of the Metropolitan Opera House in New York. See art.

*****Gay, Maria** (b. Spain, 1879), the operatic contralto, came to the Metropolitan Opera House in New York in 1908, from 1910 was with the Boston Opera Company, and in 1913–14 was also in the Chicago Opera Company. See art.

*****Gebhard, Heinrich** (b. Rhine Prov., 1878), brought to Boston as a boy, studied there and in Vienna, appeared as concert-pianist in 1900, and has since lived in Boston as a favorite player and teacher. See art.

Geer, E. Harold (b. Tabor, Ia., 1886), graduated from Doane College in 1906, studied at Tabor, Oberlin and later Paris, from 1907 taught at Lake Erie College in Ohio, and was also organist in Cleveland, from 1909 was at Albion College in Michigan, in 1911–13 in Paris, from 1913 organist at Fall River, Mass., and since 1916 has been assistant-professor at Vassar College. See art.

Gehrkens, Karl Wilson (b. Kelleys Island, O., 1882), graduated from Oberlin College in 1905, studied music there, from 1905 was supervisor in the local high school, and since 1907 has been professor in the Conservatory, specializing in public-school music. See art.

*****Gerville-Réache, Jeanne** (France, 1882–1915, New York), from 1907 was contralto at the Manhattan Opera House, in 1911–12 with the Chicago Opera Company, and in 1913–14 with the (Canadian) National Grand Opera Company. She also appeared in song-recitals. In 1908 she married G. Gibier-Rabeaud.

Gideon, Henry (b. Louisville, Ky., 1877), studied at Harvard and in Paris, and since 1908 has been organist and conductor at Boston, with lecturing, writing and composition. See art.

*****Gilibert, Charles** (France, 1866–1910, New York), a noted opera-baritone at Brussels for many years, won much favor at the Metropolitan Opera House in 1900–03 and at the Manhattan Opera House in 1906–10. He was also gifted as song-interpreter.

Gilman, Lawrence (b. Flushing, N. Y., 1878), in journalistic work since 1896, from 1901 was music-critic for 'Harper's Weekly,' and since 1913 has written for 'The North American Review,' besides publishing many valuable books. See art.

*****Gluck, Alma** (b. Rumania, 1886), brought to New York as a child, studied there and later in Berlin, in 1909–12 was highly successful as soprano at the Metropolitan Opera House, and since then has been engaged in concert-work. In 1914 she married the violinist Zimbalist (see sec. 10). See art.

*Goldblatt, Maurice Henry** (b. Russia, 1883), came to America when a boy, studied in St. Louis, Milwaukee and Chicago, since 1909 has taught violin at the Chicago Musical College, besides being concertmaster of the Philharmonic Orchestra, etc. He has written for the violin, 'cello and orchestra.

*Goodrich, Frederick William** (b. England, 1867), after much experience in England, since 1904 has been prominent as organist in Portland, Ore., from 1907 at St. Mary's Cathedral. He has written church-music, edited the *Oregon Catholic Hymnal*, 1912, a *List of Approved Church Music*, 1912, and articles on Catholic music.

*Goritz, Otto** (b. Prussia, 1873), the opera-baritone, from 1903 made a fine impression in Wagnerian rôles at the Metropolitan Opera House, but in 1917 became involved in hostile political activity. See Baker, *Dict. of Musicians*, pp. 324–5.

Grasse, Edwin (b. New York, 1884), studied in New York and Brussels, appeared as violinist in Berlin in 1902 and since 1903 has been much heard in concert in New York and elsewhere. See art.

Griffes, Charles Tomlinson (b. Elmira, N. Y., 1884–1920, New York), studied in Elmira and Berlin, taught for a time in Berlin, and from 1907 was teacher and composer in New York. See art.

Grimm, Carl Hugo (b. Zanesville, O., 1890), son of Carl W. Grimm (see sec. 8), trained in Cincinnati, has since 1905 been teacher and organist there. See art.

Griswold, Putnam (Minneapolis, 1875–1914, New York), after study at London, Paris, Frankfort and Berlin, made his début as opera-bass in London in 1901, in 1904–05 was with the Savage Opera Company, from 1906 sang in Berlin, and from 1911 was at the Metropolitan Opera House in New York, especially excelling in Wagner's works. See art.

*Guttman-Rice, Melanie** (b. Austria, 1873), in 1904–07 taught in the Metropolitan School of Opera in New York, and since 1905 at the Master School of Music, Brooklyn, becoming its head in 1913.

*Hagemann, Richard** (b. Holland, 1882), having been conductor at Amsterdam, in 1906–07 toured in America with Yvette Guilbert and Macmillen, and since 1907 has been one of the conductors at the Metropolitan Opera House, as well as since 1916 in the summer at Ravinia Park, Chicago, and in 1918 for the Society of American Singers.

*Haile, Eugen** (b. Würtemberg, 1873), the violinist and composer, in 1903–05 conducted the Scranton Männerchor, and since 1907 has lived mostly in New York, much hampered after 1912 by ill-health. He has written the opera 'Viola d'Amore' (1912), music for

'The Happy Ending' (1916), and over a hundred fine songs.

*Hammer, Heinrich Albert Eduard** (b. Thuringia, 1862), for many years conductor in Europe, since 1908 has been active in Washington, founding and conducting the Washington Symphony Orchestra and choral societies. He has written an opera, the oratorio 'St. George,' a symphony, three 'Indian Rhapsodies' for orchestra, the ode 'Columbia Triumphant in Peace' (1915), etc.

*Harker, F. Flaxington** (b. Scotland, 1876), in 1901–04 and 1907–14 was organist at Biltmore, N. C., in 1904–07 in New York, and since 1914 in Richmond, where he is also choral conductor. See art.

Harris, George, Jr. (b. Andover, Mass., 1884), graduated from Amherst College in 1906, studied in Boston and Paris, and since 1909 has been active as concert-tenor, from 1916 also teaching in the Mannes School in New York.

Henry, Harold (b. Neodesha, Kan., 1884), trained at Lawrence, Kan., Berlin and Paris, appeared as pianist in Berlin in 1904, and since 1906 has toured the United States and Canada with notable success. His home is in Chicago.

Hering, John Norris (b. Baltimore, 1886), studied in Baltimore, and since 1901 has been organist there, except in 1909–10, when he was in New Orleans. He has appeared often in recitals, has taught in several institutions and is on the staff of the daily 'Star.' See art.

*Hertz, Alfred** (b. Hesse, 1872), in 1902–15 was distinguished conductor at the Metropolitan Opera House in New York, especially of Wagner's works, and since 1915 has led the San Francisco Orchestra. See art.

*Hope-Jones, Robert** (England, 1859–1914, Rochester), an expert electrician and organ-maker, from 1903 worked with the Austins at Hartford, Conn., from 1905 with Skinner at Boston, and from 1907 in his own company at Elmira and later North Tonawanda, N. Y. See art.

*Horner, Ralph Joseph** (b. England, 1848), after long English experience, from 1906 toured the United States as conductor of light opera, and since 1909 has been at Winnipeg as director of the Academy of Music and (till 1912) conductor of the Oratorio Society. See art.

Howard, Kathleen (b. Clifton, Ont., ?), after study in New York and Paris, from 1907 sang as stage-contralto in Metz, Darmstadt and elsewhere, in 1913–15 was with the Century Opera Company in New York and since 1916 at the Metropolitan Opera House. See art.

*Huberdeau, Gustave** (b. France, 1878?), from 1908 was a favorite bass at the Manhattan Opera House, and since 1910 has been with the Chicago Opera Company.

Hughes, Edwin (b. Washington, 1884), trained in New York and Vienna, in 1909 was Leschetizky's assistant, in 1910–12 appeared in America as concert-pianist, in 1912–16

lived in Munich, with much concert-work, and since 1916 has been in New York, from 1918 teaching at the Institute of Musical Art. See art.

*Hutcheson, Ernest (b. Australia, 1871), well known as concert-pianist since 1890, from 1900 taught at the Peabody Conservatory in Baltimore, in 1912-14 was teaching and touring in Europe, and since 1914 has lived in New York. See art.

Ide, Chester Edward (b. Springfield, Ill., 1878), trained in London, for many years worked at Springfield, and since 1916 has taught at the Music School Settlement in New York. See art.

*Jacchia, Agide (b. Italy, 1875), in 1902 visited the United States as conductor with Mascagni, and since 1907 has been conductor of various operatic enterprises in different parts of America. See art.

James, Philip (b. New York, 1890), studied in New York, from about 1905 was organist there and in Jersey City, in 1908 gave recitals in London and Paris, and has since been occupied with conducting and composition. See art.

Jordan, Eben Dyer (Boston, 1857-1916, Boston), from 1880 in the firm of Jordan, Marsh & Co., in Boston, in 1902 was a large donor to the New England Conservatory's new buildings, including the auditorium ' Jordan Hall,' and in 1909 was a leading promoter of the Boston Opera House.

*Jörn, Karl (b. Russia, 1876), the operatic tenor, has sung at the Metropolitan Opera House in New York since 1908 and also at Buenos Aires since 1913.

*Kahn, Otto Hermann (b. Baden, 1867), engaged in banking in New York since 1893 (from 1897 in Kuhn, Loeb & Co.), since about 1900 has been eminent as patron and promoter of important musical interests. See art.

*Kéfer, Paul (b. France, 1875), an excellent 'cellist, in 1908-13 was leading player in the New York Symphony Society, in 1913, with Barrère and Salzedo, formed the Trio de Lutèce, and has played much in concert as well as teaching.

*Kelbe, Theodore (b. Brunswick, 1862), a violinist of experience in Germany, from 1901 was concertmaster of the Milwaukee Symphony Orchestra, and since 1904 has conducted the Sängerbund des Nordwestens, giving large festivals at various centers, and since 1910 has taught at the Schenuit Conservatory in Milwaukee.

*Klein, Hermann (b. England, 1856), who had been music-critic in England from 1877, publishing annual *Musical Notes*, 1886-89, was vocal teacher in New York in 1901-09, then returning to London, publishing *Thirty Years of Musical Life in London*, 1903, and *Unmusical New York*, 1909.

Klein, Karl (b. New York, 1884), son of B. O. Klein (see sec. 6), studied in New York, Leipzig, Brussels and London, from 1905

was concert-violinist in Europe, from 1907 toured in America, and in 1911-12 was concert-master of the Russian Symphony Orchestra.

*Kolar, Victor (b. Hungary, 1888, of Bohemian parents), came to America in 1904 as concert-violinist, from 1905 played in the Pittsburgh Orchestra, and since 1907 in the New York Symphony Society, becoming assistant-conductor in 1915. See art.

Kraus, Adrienne, née Osborne [Eisbein] (b. Buffalo, 1873), trained in Germany as operatic contralto, in 1899 married the eminent Wagnerian tenor Felix von Kraus, and, after wide tours, settled in Munich, singing Wagnerian rôles exclusively.

*Kriens, Christiaan Pieter Wilhelm (b. Holland, 1881), favorably known as violinist since 1895, in 1906-07 conducted the French Opera Company in New Orleans, in 1907 came to New York, where in 1911 he formed a Quartet and in 1912 a Symphony Club. See art.

LaForge, Frank (b. Rockford, Ill., 1879), studied in Chicago and Vienna, and since 1904 has been eminent as accompanist and composer of songs and piano-pieces. See art.

Lambord, Benjamin (Portland, Me., 1879-1915, Lake Hopatcong, N. Y.), studied in Boston, New York and abroad, from 1904 was organist at Kingsbridge, N. Y., and in 1912 organized a choral society which in 1914 became the Modern Music Society. See art.

*Langenus, Gustav (b. Belgium, 1883), for about ten years has been leading clarinettist in the New York Symphony Society and instructor at the Institute of Musical Art. In 1915, with Carolyn Beebe, he organized the Chamber Music Society and was its conductor one season, and in 1916 conducted municipal band-concerts. He has written instruction-books for the clarinet.

Lanham, McCall (b. Weatherford, Tex., 1877), trained in New York and Paris, since 1901 has appeared widely as concert-baritone, especially as song-interpreter, and since 1902 has taught at the American Institute of Applied Music in New York.

LaRoss, Earle Douglass (b. Easton, Pa., 1887), studied in New York, from 1906 appeared as concert-pianist, and since 1914 has conducted the Easton Symphony Orchestra.

*Laucella, Nicola (b. Italy, 1882), came to New York in boyhood and studied there, from 1903 was flutist in the Pittsburgh Orchestra, and since 1906 in the New York Philharmonic Society. He has written a string-quartet, several orchestral poems or sketches, and the opera ' Mochanà.'

*Lemare, Edwin Henry (b. England, 1865), the distinguished organist, in 1902-05 was organist at the Carnegie Institute in Pittsburgh, in 1915 gave many recitals at the Panama Exposition in San Francisco, and since 1917 has been city organist there. See Vol. ii. 673, and art.

Lemont, Cedric Wilmot (b. Fredericton, N. B., 1879), studied in Boston, from 1904 was organist and teacher in Fredericton, and since 1906 has been teacher and a director in the Chicago Institute of Music, composing for piano and violin, church-music and songs.

*Lerner, Tina (b. Russia, 1890), a gifted pianist, toured in the United States in 1908–10 and repeatedly since 1912. In 1915 she married the violinist Vladimir Shavitch in San Francisco. See art.

*Letz, Hans (b. Baden, 1887), from 1908 appeared often as concert-violinist, from 1911 was concertmaster of the Chicago Symphony Orchestra, from 1914 second violin in the Kneisel Quartet, and since 1917 has been head of his own Quartet.

Lévy, Heniot (b. Poland, 1879), since 1905 has been concert-pianist in Chicago, teaching also in the American Conservatory. See art.

Locke, Arthur Ware (b. Cambridge, Mass., 1883), graduated from Harvard in 1905, studied in Boston, in 1909–10 was instructor in Brown University, in 1910–11 piano-teacher at Washburn College in Kansas, from 1911 assistant-professor at the University of Wisconsin, and since 1915 at Smith College.

Lockwood, Samuel Pierson (b. Troy, N. Y., 1879), brother of A. L. Lockwood (see sec. 8), graduated from Columbia in 1902, and since 1907 has been violin-teacher at the University of Michigan and conductor of the Symphony Orchestra there.

Loeb, James (b. New York, 1867), for a time a member of the New York banking firm of Kuhn, Loeb & Co., in 1905 gave $ 500,000 for the establishment of the Institute of Musical Art, and later was chief donor of the Musical Building at Harvard University.

Loring, Harold Amasa (b. Portland, Me., 1879), trained in Boston and New York, since about 1905 has been a student of and lecturer upon Indian music, having spent seven years on reservations collecting data. He is also director of music at Olivet College in Michigan. He has transcribed Indian melodies.

Loth, Louis Leslie (b. Richmond, Va., 1888), studied in New York and Berlin, since 1908 has appeared as concert-pianist, chiefly in Germany, where he was assistant-teacher to Jonás prior to 1914, when he returned to Richmond. He has written two symphonies, much chamber-music, piano-pieces and songs.

*Maclennan, Florence Gertrude, née Easton (b. England, 1884), came as a child to Toronto, studied in London, Paris and Berlin, made her début as operatic soprano in London in 1903, married the tenor Francis Maclennan in 1904, and has since appeared extensively with him in America and Europe. See art.

Maclennan, Francis (b. Bay City, Mich., 1879), trained in New York, London and Berlin, appeared as operatic tenor in London in 1902, from 1904 was with the Savage Opera Company, from 1907 sang at the Royal Opera, Berlin, from 1913 at Hamburg, and in 1915–17 with the Chicago Opera Company. He married Florence Easton (see above). See art.

Macmillen, Francis (b. Marietta, O., 1885), trained in Chicago, Brussels and Petrograd, made a brilliant début as violinist at Brussels in 1903, at London the same year and in New York in 1906, and has since made repeated tours in America and Europe. See art.

*Mahler, Gustav (Bohemia, 1860–1911, Austria), the eminent composer and conductor, from 1907 was conductor at the Metropolitan Opera House, and from 1909 of the Philharmonic Society, resigning for ill-health in 1911. See Vol. iii. 27–8, and art.

Maitland, Rollo Francis (b. near Liberty,. Pa., 1884), trained in Philadelphia, since 1901 has been organist there, lately giving much attention to music for photoplays, with critical work and composition.

Marcel, Lucille [name originally Wasself] (b. New York, 1887?), trained as operatic soprano in New York, Berlin and Paris, appeared first at Vienna in 1908, married the conductor and composer Felix Weingartner in 1913, and has since sung under his direction. In 1912 she visited America.

*Marks, James Christopher (b. Ireland, 1863), from 1902 was organist in Pittsburgh, and since 1904 has been at the Church of the Heavenly Rest in New York. He has written the cantata 'Victory Divine' and many anthems and services. Mus. D. of the Grand Conseratory, New York, in 1908.

Martens, Frederick Herman (b. New York, 1874), studied in New York, and since 1907 has been librettist and author there. See art.

Martin, Riccardo [originally Hugh Whitfield Martin] (b. Hopkinsville, Ky., 1881), trained at New York and Paris, appeared as operatic tenor in 1904 at Nantes, in 1905 at Verona and in 1906 at New Orleans, from 1907 sang at the Metropolitan Opera House, with engagements also in Europe, and in 1916–17 was with the Boston Opera Company. See art.

Maryott, Harold Burnham (b. Lonsdale, R. I., 1878), graduated from Brown University in 1900, studied in Chicago, and since 1902 has been head of public-school work at the Chicago Musical College. He has published the text-book *Musical Essentials*, 1907.

Mason, Daniel Gregory (b. Brookline, Mass., 1873), son of Henry Mason (see sec. 4), graduated from Harvard in 1895, studied in Boston and Paris, and since 1902 has been a prominent author, lecturer and composer in New York, latterly also professor at Columbia University. See art.

*Maubourg[-Goffaux], Jeanne (b. Belgium, 1875), from 1909 was one of the sopranos at the Metropolitan Opera House, and since 1914 has taught in New York.

Maxwell, Leon Ryder (b. Medford, Mass., 1883), graduated from Tufts College in 1904, studied there and in Boston, from 1905 was supervisor in schools near Boston, studied abroad, and since 1909 has been professor and from 1910 head of the music-department in Newcomb College in New Orleans. See art.

*McCormack, John (b. Ireland, 1884), the eminent tenor, in 1909–10 sang at the Manhattan Opera House, in 1910–11 with the Boston Opera Company, in 1912–13 with the Chicago Opera Company, and has since been heard in concert. See Vol. v. 652, and art.

*Melis, Carmen (b. Sardinia, 1885), was from 1909 a soprano at the Manhattan Opera House, from 1911 with the Boston Opera Company, and since 1913 at the Paris Opéra or the Metropolitan Opera House.

*Meyer, Max Friedrich (b. Prussia, 1873), since 1900 professor of psychology at the University of Missouri, has been specially interested in problems of musical theory, and has written articles upon musical acoustics, instruments, etc.

Michalek, Bohumil (b. Chicago, 1885), studied mainly in Brussels and Prague, from 1906 was concertmaster at the Prague Opera and also assistant to Sevčik, and since 1908 has been head of his own Master School for Violinists in Chicago.

Middleton, Arthur D. (b. Logan, Ia., 1880), studied at Simpson College in Iowa, beginning vocal teaching and concert-work as baritone while still a student, in 1905–06 taught at the Des Moines Musical College, in 1906–11 at the Chicago Musical College, and since 1914 has sung at the Metropolitan Opera House.

Miessner, W. Otto (b. Huntingburg, Ind., 1880), trained in Cincinnati, from 1900 was music-supervisor at Booneville, Ind., from 1904 at Connersville, Ind., from 1910 at Oak Park, Ill., and since 1914 has been music-director at the State Normal School in Milwaukee. See art.

Miller, Horace Alden (b. Rockford, Ill., 1872), graduated from Cornell College in Iowa in 1896, studied at Oberlin and later in Munich and Berlin, since 1905 has been instructor at Cornell College, besides making special studies of Indian music and composing on Indian themes. See art.

Montani, Nicola Aloysius (b. Utica, N.Y., 1880), studied in Rome and with Mocquereau (Isle of Wight), and since 1907 has been organist in Philadelphia. In 1914 he organized the Society of St. Gregory to promote Gregorian music in the Roman Catholic Church, and a Catholic Choral Club, besides editing ' The Catholic Choir-master.' He has written two masses, a Stabat Mater, motets, etc.

Moog, Wilson Townsend (b. Baltimore, 1881), graduated from St. Lawrence University in 1902, studied at New Haven and Boston, from 1904 was organist in Boston, in 1907–08 taught at Westminster College in Pennsylvania, and since 1906 has been professor at Smith College. He has composed an overture (1916), and works for organ, piano and voice.

Moore, Mary, née Carr, in 1912 produced at Seattle the grand opera ' Narcissa ' with success. She has also written songs.

Morse, Charles Frederic (b. Mishawaka, Ind., 1881), trained at Ann Arbor, Detroit and Paris, from 1902 was music-director at the State Normal School, California, Pa., from 1907 organist in Pittsburgh, and since 1909 at Detroit, where he teaches in the Institute of Musical Art and conducts the Orpheus and Madrigal Clubs.

*Muck, Karl (b. Hesse, 1859), the celebrated conductor, was conductor of the Boston Symphony Orchestra in 1906–08 and in 1912–18, when he was interned as an enemy alien, and in 1919 returned to Germany. See Vol. iii. 314, and art.

*Mukle, May Henrietta (b. England, 1880), since 1900 has toured as concert-'cellist in the United States and Canada, and joined with Maud Powell and her own sister in the Maud Powell Trio. See art.

*Narodny, Ivan (b. Russia, 1874), since about 1905 has written upon Russian music in New York and also upon dancing. He published *Echoes of Myself*, 1909, and contributed to *The Art of Music*, 1914–17. His wife, **Maria Narodny**, née Mieler (b. Russia, 1888), is a concert-soprano, specializing in Russian and Finnish music.

Newcomb, Ethel (b. Whitney Point, N.Y., 1879), trained at Vienna, making her début there as concert-pianist in 1903 and in London in 1904, from 1904 assisted Leschetizky, and since 1908 has appeared in America and Germany as an effective soloist and ensemble-player.

*Noack, Sylvain (b. Holland, 1881), in 1908 joined the Boston Symphony Orchestra as second concertmaster, in 1915 formed the Boston Quartet, and since 1919 has been concertmaster of the Los Angeles Philharmonic Orchestra. See art.

Norden, N. Lindsay (b. Philadelphia, 1887), graduated from Columbia in 1909, from 1905 was choirmaster in Brooklyn and from 1909 organist there, and since 1917 has been organist and conductor in Philadelphia. He is active in promoting Russian church music. See art.

Osborn-Hannah, Jane (b. Chicago, 1880?), studied at Cincinnati and Berlin, made her début as operatic soprano at Leipzig in 1904, continued singing in Germany and England, both in opera and in concert, in 1910 appeared at the Metropolitan Opera House, and has since been with the Chicago Opera Company.

Parker, Henry Taylor (b. Boston, 1867), from 1892 was in active journalistic work, and since 1905 has been musical and dramatic critic of the Boston ' Transcript,' besides writing somewhat for magazines.

Parkinson, Elizabeth [' Parkina '] (b. Missouri, 1882), studied in Kansas City and Paris, from 1902 was soprano at the Opéra-Comique in Paris, in 1904–07 in London, with a striking tour in Australia in 1905, and has since been a favorite concert-singer in England.

Parlow, Kathleen (b. Calgary, Alberta, 1890), studied violin in San Francisco, London and Petrograd, and from 1905 appeared in Europe and since 1910 also in America. See art.

*Pedrell, Carlos (b. Uruguay, 1878), studied in Montevideo, Madrid and Paris, since 1906 has been teacher, composer and organizer at Buenos Aires. See art.

*Perrin, Harry Crane (b. England, 1865), after many years' experience as organist in England, since 1908 has been professor in McGill University in Montreal. See art.

Persinger, Louis (b. Rochester, Ill., 1887), studied as violinist at Leipzig, and later at Brussels and Paris, appeared first in 1904 abroad and in America, in 1908 was concertmaster at La Monnaie, Brussels, in 1914–15 of the Berlin Philharmonic, and in 1915–17 of the San Francisco Symphony Orchestra, and has made many tours throughout the United States and Europe.

*Phillips, Harold Dockray (b. England, ?), from 1903 was organist in Toronto, and since 1906 has taught organ and history in the Peabody Conservatory in Baltimore, besides activity as organist and critic. See art.

Pilzer, Maximilian (b. New York, 1890), studied violin in Berlin and appeared there in 1904. From 1904 he was concertmaster of the Russian Symphony and People's Orchestras in New York, in 1914–17 of the Philharmonic Society, and has since been in concert-work.

*Pirani, Eugenio di (b. Italy, 1852), known in Europe from 1870 as pianist, teacher and critic, in 1904–14 was associated with Mrs. A. W. Powell (see below) in directing the Musical Institute in Brooklyn. See art.

*Pochon, Alfred (b. Switzerland, 1878), since 1903 has been second violin in the Flonzaley Quartet.

*Polacco, Giorgio (b. Italy, 1875), an eminent conductor, in 1906 visited Mexico and San Francisco, in 1911–12 was with the Savage Opera Company, and since 1912 has been with the Metropolitan Opera House in New York and also at Covent Garden in London. See art.

Powell, Alma Webster, née Hall (b. Chicago, 1874), studied in New York and Berlin, appeared as operatic soprano at Berlin in 1901, in 1904 joined E. di Pirani (see above) in managing the Musical Institute in Brooklyn. See art.

Powell, John (b. Richmond, Va., 1882), graduated from the University of Virginia in 1901, studied in Vienna, appeared there as concert-pianist in 1907, and since 1912 has been heard in America. As composer he is specially interested in Negro and American themes. See art.

*Rachmaninov, Sergei Vassilievitch (b. Russia, 1873), the distinguished pianist and composer, came to America in 1909–10, and since the war has lived much in New York. See art.

Rappold, Marie, née Winterroth (b. Brooklyn, 1880?), studied in New York, and since 1905 has been with the Metropolitan Opera House as a leading soprano. See art.

Rich, Thaddeus (b. Indianapolis, 1885), graduated at the Leipzig Conservatory in 1900, with

further study at Berlin, was violinist in the Gewandhaus Orchestra and later concertmaster at the Opera des Westens, Berlin, and returned to America in 1905. Since 1906 he has been concertmaster of the Philadelphia Orchestra. He is also music-director at Temple University. See art.

*Richardson, Alfred Madeley (b. England, 1868), who since 1897 had been a prominent organist in London, from 1909 was organist in Baltimore, and since 1912 has been theory-teacher at the Institute of Musical Art, New York. See art.

Rider-Kelsey, Corinne (b. near Buffalo, 1879), trained at Oberlin, Chicago and New York, appeared in oratorio in 1904 and (in London) in opera in 1908, and has since been a popular concert-soprano. She has given notable duet-recitals with Cunningham, the baritone (see above).

Rio, Anita (b. Alameda, Cal., 1880), studied in San Francisco and New York, made her début as soprano in oratorio in 1901 and in opera in 1909 (in London), sang and studied in Italy, and since 1914 has been successful in America, especially in concert. She married J. Armour Galloway of New York.

*Rittmeister, Heinrich (b. Bremen, 1881), has been successively concertmaster of the Minneapolis Symphony Orchestra, the Russian Symphony Orchestra in New York, and now of the Kansas City Symphony Orchestra.

Robeson, Lila P. (b. Cleveland, 1880), graduated from Western Reserve University in 1902, studied in Cleveland and New York, was at first contralto in church and concert, and since 1911 also in opera, with the Aborn Opera Company and from 1912 at the Metropolitan Opera House.

*Rothwell, Walter Henry (b. England, 1872), an experienced conductor, from 1904 was with the Savage Opera Company, from 1908 led the St. Paul Symphony Orchestra, from 1915 was teacher and municipal conductor in New York, and since 1919 has led the Los Angeles Philharmonic Orchestra. See art.

*Rybner, Peter Martin Cornelius (b. Denmark, 1855), noted as pianist and conductor, in 1904–19 was professor at Columbia University. See art.

*Saerchinger, César (b. Rhine Prov., 1884), studied partly in New York, where since 1906 he has been an industrious editor and valuable writer on musical subjects. See art.

*Safonov, Vassily Ilyitch (Caucasus, 1852–1918, Caucasus), well known as pianist, teacher and conductor since 1880, in 1904–09 conducted the New York Philharmonic Society and was head of the National Conservatory, then returning to Petrograd. See Vol. v. 626, and art.

Saltzman-Stevens, Minnie (b. Bloomington, Ill., 1885?), first sang in Chicago churches, studied in Paris, made her début as operatic soprano in 1909 in London, sang in various European capitals, and in 1911–14 was with the

H

Chicago Opera Company. In 1905 she married A. N. Stevens of Bloomington. See art.

Samaroff, Olga, née Hickenlooper (b. San Antonio, Tex., 1882), studied at Philadelphia, Baltimore, Paris and Berlin, from 1905 began to tour the United States as concert-pianist, appearing also in Europe in 1908–09, in 1912–14 was interrupted by ill-health, but then resumed activity. In 1911 she married the conductor Stokowski (see below). See art.

*Sampaix, Léon** (b. Belgium, 1878), from 1900 was piano-teacher at the Peabody Conservatory in Baltimore, from 1904 at the Liège Conservatory, from 1910 in his own school in Indianapolis, then at Ithaca, N. Y., and is now head of the Toledo Conservatory.

Schelling, Ernest Henry (b. Belvidere, N. J., 1876), studied extensively in Europe, from 1903 appeared as concert-pianist there, in South America and from 1905 in the United States, making his home until 1914 in Switzerland. See art.

*Schindler, Kurt** (b. Prussia, 1882), from 1905 was assistant-conductor at the Metropolitan Opera House in New York, and since 1907 has been reader for Schirmer and since 1908 also conductor of the Schola Cantorum (originally the MacDowell Chorus). See art.

Schnabel-Tollefsen, Augusta (b. Boisé, Ida., 1885), studied in Europe, where she was known as a child-prodigy, toured in the United States in 1900–01, studied further in New York, and since 1906 has been prominent as pianist, especially in the Tollefsen Trio, led by her husband, Carl Tollefsen (see below).

Schneider, Edward Faber (b. Omaha, Neb., 1872), studied at San José, San Francisco, New York and Berlin, and since about 1900 has been teacher and composer in San Francisco and dean of music at Mills College. He has written for the Bohemian Club the dramas 'The Triumph of Bohemia' (1907) and 'Apollo' (1915), the symphony 'In Autumn Time' (1913), and effective shorter works.

*Schuëcker, Joseph E.** (b. Saxony, 1886), son of Edmund Schuëcker (see sec. 8), in 1904–05 and 1908–09 harpist in the Pittsburgh Orchestra, from 1909 was in the Philadelphia Orchestra, from 1911 with the Savage Opera Company, and since 1914 has taught at the Carnegie Institute of Technology, Pittsburgh.

Schwab, Charles M. (b. Williamsburg, Pa., 1862), the head of the Bethlehem (Pa.) Steel Works, in 1905 became guarantor of the Lehigh Valley Symphony Orchestra, and since 1911 has been the munificent supporter of the Bethlehem Bach Choir.

Scott, Henri Guest (b. Coatesville, Pa., 1876), trained in Philadelphia and New York, from about 1900 appeared as concert-bass, in 1909–10 sang at the Manhattan Opera House, in 1910–11 in Rome, from 1911 with the Chicago Opera Company, and since 1915 at the Metropolitan again. See art.

Shattuck, Arthur (b. Neenah, Wis., 1881), studied at Vienna, from 1902 became known as a striking pianist, making extended tours from Paris as center and visited the United States in 1911–12 and since 1915. See art.

Silber, Sidney (b. Waupun, Wis., 1881), trained in Berlin and Vienna, since 1905 has been concert-pianist both in Europe and America, and latterly has taught in the University School of Music, Lincoln, Neb. He has lectured and written many articles on musical subjects.

Simpson, George Elliott (b. Orange, N. J., 1876), studied in New York, Kansas City and Leipzig, from 1903 taught in Kansas City, from 1907 at Baylor Female College, Belton, Tex., from 1912 at the Polytechnic College in Fort Worth and later in the Texas Christian University there. He has written two symphonies, four overtures, three suites, etc.

*Skovgaard, Axel** (b. Denmark, 1875), after tours in Scandinavian countries, since 1903 has been an industrious concert-violinist in the United States and Canada.

Smith, David Stanley (b. Toledo, O., 1877), graduated from Yale in 1900, studied music there and in Munich and Paris, since 1903 has been at the Yale School of Music, and from 1920 its dean, with work also as organist, conductor and lecturer elsewhere. See art.

Smith, Thomas Max (b. New York, 1874), graduated from Yale in 1898 and from Columbia Law School in 1901, studied in New York, New Haven and Dresden, from 1903 was music-critic of the New York 'Press,' and since 1916 of the 'American.' He was on the advisory board of *The Art of Music*, 1914–17.

Spalding, Albert (b. Chicago, 1888), trained as violinist in Florence and Paris, from 1905 was eminent as soloist in Europe and since 1908 has been equally so in America. See art.

*Spencer, Vernon** (b. England, 1875), from 1903 taught piano at the Nebraska Wesleyan University, from 1908 in Berlin, and since 1911 has been teacher, concert-pianist and lecturer in Los Angeles. Besides other literary work, he edits 'The Music-Student.'

Stockhoff, Walter William (b. St. Louis, 1887), self-taught, has been teacher and composer in St. Louis since 1904. See art.

*Stojowski, Sigismund Denis Antoine** (b. Poland, 1870), well known in Paris as pianist and composer since about 1890, from 1905 taught at the Institute of Musical Art in New York, with concert-work elsewhere and some trips to Europe, from 1911 at the Von Ende School, and since 1917 privately. See art.

*Stokowski, Leopold Anton Stanislaw** (b. England, 1882, of Polish parents), from 1905 was organist in New York, in 1908 conducted orchestral concerts in London, from 1909 was conductor of the Cincinnati Orchestra, and since 1912 of the Philadelphia Orchestra. In 1911 he married the pianist Olga Samaroff (see above). See art.

Strickland, Lily Teresa (b. Anderson, S. C., 1887), studied at Converse College in South

Carolina and in New York, in 1907–10 was organist at Anderson, and since 1911, when she married Courtney Anderson, has lived in New York. She has written three operas, a symphonic suite on Negro themes, and published about 75 songs.

*Sturani, Giuseppe (b. Italy, ?), from about 1905 was operatic conductor in Buenos Aires and Rio de Janeiro, from 1908 at the Manhattan Opera House, from 1910 at the Metropolitan Opera House, and since 1912 with the Chicago Opera Company.

Swarthout, Max van Lewen (b. Pawpaw, Ill., 1880), studied at Chicago and Leipzig, from 1905 was music-director at the Oxford College for Women in Ohio, from 1911 taught at the Illinois Woman's College in Jacksonville, and since 1914 has been music-director at the James Millikin University.

Taylor, David Clark (New York, 1871–1918, New York), graduated from the College of the City of New York, studied there, and from 1908 published several valuable works on singing. See art.

*Tetrazzini, Luisa (b. Italy, 1874), the celebrated operatic soprano, having been heard in South America and Mexico, in 1904 appeared at San Francisco, in 1905–06 was again in South America, in 1908–10 was at the Manhattan Opera House, in New York, then toured extensively, in 1913–14 was with the Chicago Opera Company. See art.

Thatcher, Howard Rutledge (b. Baltimore, 1878), studied in Baltimore, and since 1902 has been organist there, also teaching at the Peabody Conservatory and the Maryland College for Women at Lutherville. He has written a concert-overture (1906), a string-quartet, synagogue-music, etc.

*Thibaud, Jacques (b. France, 1880), the eminent violinist, since 1903 has made several tours of the United States. See Vol. v. 83, and art.

*Tollefsen, Carl Henry (b. England, 1882), came to America in boyhood, studied in New York, in 1908–10 was violinist in the Symphony Society, in 1909 organized the Tollefsen Trio, has taught in the National Conservatory, and now teaches in Brooklyn. In 1907 he married Augusta Schnabel (see above). See art.

*Toscanini, Arturo (b. Italy, 1867), the noted operatic conductor, in 1908–15 was famous as conductor at the Metropolitan Opera House in New York, then returning to Italy. See art.

Tramonti, Enrico (b. Sicily, 1876), since 1902 has been leading harpist of the Chicago Symphony Orchestra.

*Unschuld, Marie von (b. Moravia, 1881), since 1904 has been head of her own school in Washington, besides lecturing elsewhere. See art.

Van Vechten, Carl (b. Cedar Rapids, Ia., 1880), graduated from the University of Chicago in 1903, and has since been critic and author in New York. See art.

*Vigna, Arturo (b. Italy, ?), was conductor at the Metropolitan Opera House in New York in 1903–07.

Waller, Frank Laird (b. St. Paul, ?), a graduate of the University of Wisconsin, began as teacher and opera-singer in 1908, and in 1909–15 was coach and accompanist with the Boston Opera Company and in 1917–18 with the Chicago Opera Company.

Ware, Harriet (b. Waupun, Wis., 1877), having studied in New York, Paris and Berlin, from 1906 lived in New York as composer, and lately has made her home at Garden City. In 1913 she married · H. M. Krumbhaar of New Orleans. See art.

*Warnke, Heinrich (b. Holstein, 1871), an experienced 'cellist, since 1905 has played in the Boston Symphony Orchestra, and in 1905–07 was a member of the Boston Symphony Quartet.

Wead, Charles Kasson (b. Malone, N. Y., 1848), since 1892 an examiner in the Patent Office in Washington, has been a diligent student of musical acoustics, publishing Contributions to the History of Musical Scales, 1900 (U. S. Nat. Museum Report), which embodies original investigations upon instruments, besides many articles in scientific journals.

Wells, Howard (b. Rockford, Ill.), studied in Chicago, from about 1900 appeared there as concert-pianist, from 1907 studied in Vienna and from 1908 was one of Leschetizky's assistants, part of the time living in Berlin and also touring, and since 1914 has taught in Chicago. See art.

Werrenrath, Reinald (b. Brooklyn, 1883), son of George Werrenrath (see sec. 6), graduated from New York University in 1905, from 1907 has been a favorite concert-baritone, and since 1919 has also sung at the Metropolitan Opera House. See art.

Weyman, Wesley (b. Boston, 1877), graduated from Harvard in 1898, studied there and in New York, from 1901 appeared as concert-pianist, in 1905–08 taught at the Institute of Musical Art, in 1909–14 studied and toured in Europe, and has since taught in New York and Boston, with much literary work. See art.

*Wheeldon, Herbert Arthur (b. England, 1864), from 1882 organist in England, in 1907–13 was organist of the Metropolitan Church in Toronto, and in 1908–15 examiner in music at Toronto University. See art.

White, Carolina (b. Boston, 1886), studied in Boston and Naples, made her début as operatic soprano in 1908, sang in Italy, in 1910–14 was with the Chicago Opera Company, and has since been heard in concert or light opera. See art.

Whitehill, Clarence Eugene (b. Marengo, Ia., 1871), studied mainly at Paris, appeared as operatic baritone in 1899 in Brussels, and since 1900 has sung in American and European opera-houses, in 1911–15 with the Chicago Opera Company and in 1909–11 and since 1916 at the Metropolitan Opera House. See art.

Whithorne [Whittern], Emerson (b. Cleveland, 1884), trained in Cleveland, Vienna and Berlin, from 1907 was teacher and writer in London, and since 1915 has been executive editor for the Art Publication Society of St. Louis. His compositions include a ' Japanese Suite ' for orchestra, two symphonic poems, two string-quartets (' Three Greek Impressions,' 1914) and a ' Quartettino Orientale ' (1916), a song-cycle for quartet, ' Songs of Sappho ' (1913), with piano-works and songs.

Wickham, Florence (b. Beaver, Pa., 1882), trained in Philadelphia and Berlin, has appeared widely as operatic contralto since 1902, at first in Europe, in 1904–05 and 1909–12 in the United States. In 1911 she married Eberhard L. Lueder of New York. See art.

*Willeke, Willem (b. Holland, 1878), from 1896 solo 'cellist at Riga, Düsseldorf, London and Vienna, in 1907–17 was Schroeder's successor as 'cellist in the Kneisel Quartet, and has since taught and concertized in New York.

Wilson, Mortimer (b. Chariton, Ia., 1876), studied in Chicago, from 1901 taught at the University of Nebraska, in 1907–10 studied and taught in Leipzig, in 1911–15 was conductor of the Atlanta Symphony Orchestra, and in 1916–18 taught at Brenau College in Georgia. See art.

Wood, Carl Paige (b. Taunton, Mass., 1885), graduated from Harvard in 1906, studied there and in Boston, Berlin and Paris, from 1906 was music-director at Denison University in Ohio, in 1915–16 organist at Vassar College, and since 1916 music-director at Carleton College in Minnesota. He has written choral works and songs, and won the Boott Prize at Harvard in 1915.

*Wrangell, Ludvig Heinrich (b. Norway, 1872), after some years as concert-violinist and teacher in Norway, from 1908 taught in the Wisconsin Conservatory in Milwaukee, and since 1913 has had his own school there. He has written violin-pieces, a violin-method, etc.

*Yon, Pietro Alessandro (b. Italy, 1886), since 1907 has been organist at St. Francis Xavier's in New York, and is eminent as recitalist and composer. See art.

Zeuch, William Edward (b. Chicago, 1878), a graduate of Northwestern University, studied music there and in Paris, where he was organist of the English Church. For some years he has lived in Boston as concert-organist, member of the Skinner Organ Co., and from 1917 organist at the South Church (Unitarian).

Zucca [Zukermann], Mana (b. New York, 1891), appeared in 1899 as a precocious pianist, studied in New York, London, Berlin and Paris, toured throughout Europe as pianist, and since 1914 has sung much in light opera, in both America and Europe. She has written the ' fugato humoresque ' ' Nerves,' for orchestra (Russian Symphony and Philharmonic Orchestras), many songs and instrumental pieces.

10. The Decade of the World War

Althouse, Paul Shearer (b. Reading, Pa., 1889), studied in New York, and since 1913, when he appeared as tenor at the Metropolitan Opera House, has been prominent in both opera and concert. He assisted at the first performances of ' Boris Godunov,' ' Madeleine ' and ' Madame Sans-Gêne.'

*Ariani, Adriano (b. Italy, 1877), a pianist, conductor and composer of Italian reputation, has lately lived in New York. See *Who's Who in Music*, 1918, p. 1.

*Auer, Leopold (b. Hungary, 1845), the great violinist and teacher, came to America early in 1918 and settled in New York. See Vol. i. 130, and art.

*Bachmann, Alberto Abraham (b. Switzerland, 1875), an experienced violinist and writer on violin-topics, made a tour of the United States in 1916, and has since lived in New York.

*Baklanov, George (b. Russia, 1882), who had been baritone at the Imperial Opera in Petrograd, sang for a time with the Boston Opera Company, and from 1917 with the Chicago Opera Company.

Ballantine, Edward (b. Oberlin, O., 1886), studied in Boston and Berlin, from 1912 was teacher of theory at Harvard University, and from 1918 was an enlisted musician in the Army. See art.

*Barraja, Enrico (b. Italy, 1885), has been pianist and teacher in Boston since 1911. He has written an opera, two chamber-suites, many songs and short instrumental pieces.

*Barrientos, Maria (b. Spain, 1885), from 1899 widely known in Europe and also South America as a brilliant coloratura-soprano, since 1916 has sung at the Metropolitan Opera House, especially in Italian works. See art.

Barstow, Vera (b. Celina, O., 1893), studied at Pittsburgh and Vienna, and since 1912 has been recognized as a superior concert-violinist.

*Bimboni, Alberto (b. Italy, 1882), in 1911–12 was conductor for the Savage Opera Company, in 1913–14 for the Century Opera Company, and in 1915 at the Havana Opera House.

*Bloch, Ernest (b. Switzerland, 1880), the eminent Jewish composer, came to America in 1916, at first associated with Maud Allan, the dancer, taught for two years at the Mannes School of Music in New York, and has had marked success as composer. See art.

*Bodanzky, Artur (b. Austria, 1877), the famous operatic conductor, came to the Metropolitan Opera House in 1915, and since 1919 has also been leader of the New Symphony Orchestra. See art.

*Bori, Lucrezia (b. Spain, 1888), after visiting Argentina as operatic soprano, since 1913 has sung at the Metropolitan Opera House.

*Bosetti, Joseph (b. Italy, 1886), priest and doctor in the Roman Catholic Church and a trained organist, since 1913 has been choir-master in the Denver Cathedral, where he has not only developed liturgical music, but organized forces for giving operas and oratorios.

*Botta, Luca (Italy, 1882–1917, New York), the opera-tenor, from 1912 sang with the Pacific Coast Opera Company, and from 1914 at the Metropolitan Opera House, as well as in South America. His répertoire included most of the later Italian works.

*Boyle, George Frederick (b. Australia, 1886), having toured as concert-pianist since about 1900 in Australia and Europe, since 1910 has taught at the Peabody Conservatory in Baltimore. See art.

Braslau, Sophie (b. New York, ?), studied in New York, and since 1913 has been contralto at the Metropolitan Opera House, besides singing much in concert elsewhere.

Brown, Eddy (b. Chicago, 1895), trained as violinist in Chicago, Budapest and Petrograd, from 1910 concertized in Europe, and since 1916 has been heard in America. See art.

Chalmers, Thomas Hardie (b. New York, 1884), studied in New York and Florence, appeared as operatic baritone in 1911 in Italy, in 1911–12 sang with the Savage Opera Company, from 1913 with the Century Opera Company, from 1915 with the Boston Opera Company, and since 1917 at the Metropolitan Opera House.

*Cherniavsky, Jan (b. Russia, 1892), Leo (b. 1890) and Michael (b. 1893), brothers, are respectively pianist, violinist and 'cellist in the Cherniavsky Trio, which from 1916–17 made many successful appearances in the United States and Canada.

Clark, Melville Antone (b. Syracuse, 1883), nephew of Melville Clark (see sec. 6), since 1910 has made improvements in harps and harp-playing, perfecting a small, portable harp of considerable artistic value.

*Claussen, Julia, née Ohlson (b. Sweden, 1879), known in Sweden since 1903 as an able operatic mezzo-soprano, from 1913 sang with the Chicago Opera Company, and since 1917 at the Metropolitan Opera House, besides extensive concert-tours.

Clifton, Chalmers (b. Jackson, Miss., 1889), graduated from Harvard in 1912, studied there and in Paris, and since 1914 has been known as conductor, composer and critic, mostly in or near Boston. See art.

Crist, Bainbridge (b. Lawrenceburg, Ind., 1883), brought up in Washington, became a practicing lawyer, then studied music in London and Berlin, and since 1914 has been teacher and composer in Boston. See art.

Curtis, Vera (b. Stratford, Conn., 1880), studied in Boston and New York, from about 1910 was church-soprano in New York, and since 1912 has sung at the Metropolitan Opera House. In 1912 she toured with the Russian Symphony Orchestra.

*Dambois, Maurice Félix (b. Belgium, 1889), noted as a superior 'cellist since 1901, in 1917

came to America with Ysaÿe, making his head-quarters in New York.

*Darby, W. Dermot (b. Ireland, 1885), trained in England and New York, secretary of the Modern Music Society in 1916, was one of the editors of *The Art of Music*, 1914–17.

*DeLuca, Giuseppe (b. Italy, 1876), for twenty years a leading operatic baritone in Italy, appeared at the Metropolitan Opera House from 1915, participating in the initial performance of ' Goyescas ' in 1916.

Dow, Martha Cora (d. 1915, Cincinnati), bequeathed $ 700,000 as an endowment for the Cincinnati Symphony Orchestra.

*Dufau, Jenny (b. Alsace, ?), since 1911 has been lyric soprano in the Chicago Opera Company. In that year she sang in the première of ' Cendrillon.'

*Dworzak, Zdenko von (b. Moravia, 1875), educated as physician, now practicing in Denver, is also a trained musician. He has written a symphonic poem, an overture, two suites, two string-quartets, songs, etc., besides medical essays upon the voice.

Eastman, George (b. Waterville, N. Y., 1854), of the Eastman Kodak Co., in 1919 gave $ 3,500,000 for the establishment in Rochester of the Eastman Music School, adding $ 1,000,000 more in 1920. See art.

*Epstein, Richard (Austria, 1869–1919, New York), after having taught in the Vienna Conservatory and for ten years in London, came to New York in 1914, making a fine impression as pianist, especially as accompanist and ensemble-player.

*Ferrari-Fontana, Edoardo (b. Italy, 1878), after a phenomenal leap into prominence as operatic tenor in 1910, appeared in Buenos Aires in 1912, joined the Boston Opera Company in 1913, and since 1914 has sung at the Metropolitan Opera House. In 1912 he married the soprano Margarete Matzenauer.

Flagler, Harry Harkness (b. Cleveland, 1870), a wealthy New York capitalist, in 1914 became the liberal patron and guarantor of the Symphony Society.

*Forsyth, Cecil (b. England, 1870), known in England as conductor of light opera, composer and author, since 1914 has lived in New York. See art.

*Frederiksen, Frederik Christian (b. Norway, 1869), an experienced violinist, conductor and teacher, in 1915 organized the Scandinavian Orchestra in Chicago. He is violin-teacher in several conservatories in Chicago and Milwaukee.

*Fricker, Herbert Austin (b. England, 1868), from 1884 organist in England and from 1900 conductor at Leeds, since 1917 has been conductor of the Mendelssohn Choir in Toronto and organist at the Metropolitan Church. He has published considerable church-music.

*Friedberg, Carl Rudolf Hermann (b. Hesse, 1872), noted as pianist in Germany since 1892, toured in America in 1914, and in 1916–17 taught at the Institute of Musical Art in New York.

*Galli-Curci, Amelita (b. Italy, 1889), the coloratura-soprano, since 1916 has been conspicuous in the Chicago Opera Company and also a successful concert-singer. See art.

Garrison, Mabel (b. Baltimore, ?), trained in Baltimore and New York, from 1912 was lyric soprano in the Aborn Opera Company, and since 1914 has sung at the Metropolitan Opera House.

Gillette, James Robert (b. Roseboom, N. Y., 1886), studied at Syracuse University, and since 1914 has been concert-organist and teacher in Macon, Ga. He has written the cantata ' The Light Everlasting ' and several organ-pieces.

*Giorni, Aurelio (b. Italy, 1895), since 1915 has made effective tours in the United States as concert-pianist.

Gittelson, Frank (b. Philadelphia, 1896), studied in Philadelphia, New York and Berlin, made his début as violinist at Berlin in 1913, toured in Germany and England, since 1914 has been heard extensively in America, from 1919 teaching at the Peabody Conservatory in Baltimore. See art.

*Grainger, Percy Aldridge (b. Australia, 1882), the highly original pianist and composer, has been repeatedly heard in America since 1915. See Vol. v. 643, and art.

*Grassi, Antonio de' (b. Italy, 1880), after prominent appearances as violinist in Europe from 1905, since 1915 has taught in Berkeley, Cal., organizing a Trio with Vladimir Shavitch and Stanislaus Bern as pianist and 'cellist.

*Grolle, Johan Hendrik (b. Holland, ?), a well-trained violinist, since about 1910 has been active in promoting popular education through schools like the Philadelphia Settlement Music School, of which he is director.

*Gulli, Luigi (b. Italy, 1859), from 1896 pianist in the famous Società del Quintetto in Rome, since 1916 has been soloist and teacher in Chicago.

Hagan, Helen Eugenia (b. New Haven, Conn., 1893), studied in New Haven and Paris, and since 1912 has been organist and concert-pianist in New Haven. She has written considerable music for piano.

Hall, Leland (b. Malden, Mass., 1883), studied at Harvard and in Paris, from 1910 taught music-history at the University of Wisconsin, in 1913-14 lectured at Columbia University and wrote program-notes for the Symphony Society, and was one of the editors of *The Art of Music*, 1914-17.

*Hambourg, Boris (b. Russia, 1884), the distinguished 'cellist, brother of Mark Hambourg (see sec. 8), since 1910 has toured in America, in 1911-16, with his father and brother (see below), directed the Hambourg Conservatory in Toronto, and since 1916 has lived in New York. See art.

*Hambourg, Jan (b. Russia, 1882), brother of the foregoing and a striking violinist,

collaborated with him in Toronto, and since 1916 has also lived in New York.

*Hambourg, Michael (Russia, 1856-1916, Toronto), father of the above and a good piano-teacher, from 1911 was associated with his sons in their Toronto school.

Hanson, Howard Harold (b. Wahoo, Neb., 1896), trained at Luther College in Nebraska, New York and Evanston, Ill., in 1913 was critic and coach in Kansas City, in 1915-16 taught at Northwestern University, and since 1916 has been theory-teacher at the College of the Pacific, San José, becoming dean in 1919. He has written two symphonic poems, a Symphonic Rhapsody, a piano-concerto, a piano-quintet, a piano-sonata and pieces, and songs, besides articles on musical science.

*Harmati, Sandor (b. Hungary, 1892), who had been violinist and conductor in Budapest, came to New York in 1914, and since 1917 has been second violin in the Letz Quartet.

*Heifetz, Jascha (b. Russia, 1901), the precocious violinist, having been heard from 1910 in Europe, since 1917 has toured in the United States. See art.

*Heinecke, Paul (b. Saxony, 1885), since 1910 has been head of the New York branch of Breitkopf & Härtel in Leipzig, and of the independent corporation formed in 1917 to take over the American business.

*Hempel, Frieda (b. Saxony, 1885), the distinguished operatic soprano, since 1912 has sung at the Metropolitan Opera House with brilliant success. In 1918 she married William B. Kahn. See art.

*Herbst, Gottfried (b. Thuringia, 1887), from 1902 violinist and conductor in central Germany, since 1912 has been violin-teacher and concert-player at the State College, Pullman, Wash.

*Holy, Alfred (b. Portugal, 1866), the famous harpist, since 1913 has been a member of the Boston Symphony Orchestra. See art.

Horvath, Cecile, née Ayres (b. Boston, 1889), daughter of Eugene E. Ayres (see sec. 7), studied in Philadelphia, New York and Berlin, and since 1910 has been concert-pianist both abroad and in America. Her husband, **Zoltan de Horvath** (b. Chicago, 1886), is pianist and teacher in Philadelphia.

*Ingram, Frances (b. England, 1888), was educated in Brooklyn and New York, first appeared as operatic contralto at Philadelphia in 1911, and has since sung with the Chicago Opera Company, except in 1913-14 with the Montreal Opera Company and in 1914-15 on concert-tours. In 1913 she married Karl G. MacVitty of Chicago.

Kernochan, Marshall Rutgers (b. New York, 1880), studied in New York and Frankfort, since 1910 has worked in or near New York as composer.

*Kihl, Viggo Richard (b. Denmark, 1882), concert-pianist since 1901 in Copenhagen and London, since 1913 has been in the faculty of the Toronto Conservatory.

*Kilenyi, Edward (b. Hungary, 1884), studied at Columbia, and since about 1912 has been a frequent writer upon musical subjects, with some composition. See art.

*Kindler, Hans (b. Holland, 1892), since 1914 has been 'cellist in the Philadelphia Orchestra.

*Knoch, Ernst (b. Baden, 1876), having had wide experience since 1898 in operatic conducting, especially of Wagner's works, in 1914 joined the Century Opera Company, and in 1916 was conductor at Ravinia Park, Chicago, and then of the Interstate Opera Company, Cleveland.

Kramer, Arthur Walter (b. New York, 1890), graduated from the College of the City of New York in 1910, and has since then been on the staff of 'Musical America' and a prolific composer and writer. See art.

*Kreiner, Edward (b. Poland, 1890), after playing for some time in the New York Symphony Society, since 1917 has been violist in the Letz Quartet.

*Kunwald, Ernst (b. Austria, 1868), who had been eminent as conductor in Europe from 1895, in 1912–17 directed the Cincinnati Symphony Orchestra, resigning for political reasons.

*Kurt, Melanie (b. Austria, 1880), who had been concert-pianist from 1897 and eminent operatic soprano from 1902, in 1915–17 was a leading artist at the Metropolitan Opera House. In 1910 she married Prof. Deri in Berlin.

Lamont, Forrest (b. Springfield, Mass., 1889), after study at home and abroad, made his début as operatic tenor in Rome, toured in Italy, the West Indies and South America, and since 1917 has sung with the Chicago Opera Company.

Langdon, William Chauncy (b. Italy, 1871, of American parents), a New York lawyer, since about 1910 has been the arranger and librettist of many 'pageants' and similar musico-dramatic undertakings — Thetford, Vt., 1911, St. Johnsbury, Vt., 1912, Meriden, N. H., 1913, Darien, Conn., 1913, Cape Cod, Mass., 1914, Austin, Tex., 1915, Bloomington, Indianapolis and Corydon, Ind., 1916, Amherst, Mass., 1917, University of Illinois, 1918, etc.

*Lange, Daniel de (Holland, 1841–1918, Point Loma, Cal.), from 1895 director of the Amsterdam Conservatory, resigned in 1913 and came to America. See Vol. ii. 633.

*Lester, Thomas William (b. England, 1889), was brought to America in boyhood, studied in Chicago, from 1911 was active as critic and writer, and since 1912 has also been organist and concert-accompanist. He has written chamber-, piano- and organ-suites, a string-quartet, a violin-sonata, several cantatas, etc.

*Levitzki, Mischa (b. Russia, 1898), came to New York as a boy, continued there and in Berlin studies begun in Warsaw, made his début as concert-pianist in 1912, toured in Europe and since 1916 has been active in New York.

Lindquest, Albert Charles (b. Chicago, 1892), studied at Chicago, Ann Arbor and New York, since 1914 has been a successful concert-tenor with many orchestras and choral societies, living in New York.

*Lorenzo, Leonardo de (b. Italy, 1875), known in Europe since 1897 as a superior flutist, from 1910 played with the New York Philharmonic Society, from 1912 with the Symphony Society, and since 1914 with the Minneapolis Orchestra. He has written a flute-method and many studies.

*Maas, Gerald Christopher (b. Baden, 1888), an expert 'cellist since 1908, first appeared as soloist in America in 1916, and since 1917 has been in the Letz Quartet.

Maas, Marguerite Wilson (b. Baltimore, 1888), studied in Baltimore and Berlin, appeared as concert-pianist in Berlin in 1914, then in Baltimore and vicinity, in 1915–16 taught at the Skidmore School, Saratoga Springs, N. Y., and now lives near Baltimore. She has written a piano-sonata and other pieces, several songs, etc.

Macbeth, Florence (b. Mankato, Minn., 1891), trained in St. Paul, Pittsburgh and abroad, made her début as operatic soprano in 1913 at Darmstadt, with other European appearances, and since 1914 has sung with the Chicago Opera Company.

*Maguenat, Alfred (b. France, ? , of Swiss parents), a baritone known in Italy, France and England from 1907, since 1916 has sung with the Chicago Opera Company.

*Maitland, Robert Gillies (b. England, 1875), from 1896 prominent in England, Germany and the Low Countries as concert-baritone and expert in lyric interpretation, since 1914 has taught in New York and concertized more or less.

*Mansfield, Orlando Augustine (b. England, 1863), from 1885 an experienced organist in England, from 1912 taught at Wilson College in Pennsylvania, and since 1918 at Brenau College in Georgia. See art.

*Marcoux, Vanni (b. Italy, 1879), an operatic baritone favorably known in France and England since 1899, joined the Chicago Opera Company in 1912.

*Martinelli, Giovanni (b. Italy, 1885), the able dramatic tenor, since 1913 has been with the Metropolitan Opera Company, besides singing regularly in London and in 1916 in Buenos Aires.

*Martucci, Paolo (b. Italy, 1885), son of the notable pianist, conductor and composer Giuseppe Martucci, from 1911 taught piano at the Cincinnati Conservatory, and since 1913 has been concert-player and teacher in New York.

Mason, Edith Barnes (b. St. Louis, 1892), trained as stage-soprano in New York, Boston, Philadelphia and Paris, in 1912 sang with the Boston Opera Company, in 1913–15 at Nice, Marseilles and Paris, and since 1915 at the Metropolitan Opera House.

*Matzenauer, Margarete (b. Hungary, 1881), the celebrated operatic singer, originally a contralto, but since 1911, when she came to the Metropolitan Opera House, turning to soprano parts. In 1902–11 she was the wife of Ernst Preuse of Munich and in 1912–17 of the tenor Ferrari-Fontana (see above). See Baker, *Dict. of Musicians*, p. 591.

*Megerlin, Alfred (b. Belgium, 1880), from 1894 an able violinist in Belgium, came to America in 1914 and since 1917 has been concertmaster of the New York Philharmonic Society.

Milligan, Harold Vincent (b. Astoria, Ore., 1888), studied in New York, where since about 1910 he has been organist, besides tours as concert-player. See art.

Moderwell, Hiram Kelly (b. Fort Wayne, Ind., 1888), graduated from Harvard in 1912, and since 1913 has been critic and author in New York. He contributed to *The Art of Music*, 1914–17, and wrote *The Theatre of To-Day*, 1914.

*Monteux, Pierre (b. France, 1875), the distinguished conductor, in 1916 conducted the Russian Ballet in New York, in 1917 led municipal concerts there, from 1917 was engaged at the Metropolitan Opera House, and since 1919 has led the Boston Symphony Orchestra. See art.

*Muratore, Lucien (b. France, 1878), the operatic tenor, since 1913 has been with the Chicago Opera Company, in 1917 also singing at Buenos Aires. In 1913 he married the soprano Lina Cavalieri (see sec. 9). See art.

*Muzio, Claudia (b. Italy, 1892), known in Italy as dramatic soprano from 1912, and having also sung in Paris, London, Cuba and South America, since 1916 has been at the Metropolitan Opera House.

*Nachez, Tivadar (b. Hungary, 1859), for thirty years a noted concert-violinist and composer, from 1889 working in London, since 1916 has lived at Santa Barbara, Cal. For works, see Baker, *Dict. of Musicians*, p. 639.

*Noble, Thomas Tertius (b. England, 1867), the celebrated organist, since 1913 has been at St. Thomas' in New York, besides concert-tours elsewhere. See Vol. v. 655, and art.

*Novaës, Guiomar (b. Brazil, 1895), studied at São Paulo and Paris, from 1911 became known in Europe and South America as a highly gifted pianist, and since 1915 has been widely heard in the United States. See art.

*Ober, Margarete (b. Prussia, 1885), the eminent mezzo-soprano, since 1913 has been a leading singer at the Metropolitan Opera House, until 1916 also singing at Berlin. In 1910 she married Arthur Arndt. See art.

*Ornstein, Leo (b. Russia, 1895), studied in Petrograd and New York, made his début as pianist in 1911 in the latter city, and has lived there as player and unusual composer. See art.

*Perini, Flora (b. Italy, 1887), since 1910 has been a noted operatic mezzo-soprano at the chief South American capitals, and also since 1915 at the Metropolitan Opera House. She is the wife of Amleto Polattri.

*Pfitzner, Walther (b. Saxony, 1882), since 1896 concert-pianist in Germany, from 1915 has been teacher at Bethany College, Lindsborg., Kan., choral conductor and concert-accompanist.

*Pulitzer, Joseph (Hungary, 1847–1911, Charleston, S. C.), the eminent journalist, from 1883 proprietor of the New York 'World,' by his will left $500,000 to the New York Philharmonic Society. See art.

*Rabaud, Henri Benjamin (b. France, 1873), the distinguished conductor and composer, in 1918–19 was conductor of the Boston Symphony Orchestra, returning to become director of the Paris Conservatory.

*Raisa, Rosa (b. Poland, 1893), since 1914 has been one of the foremost sopranos in the Chicago Opera Company, besides many appearances in South America.

Rice, William Gorham (b. Albany, N. Y., 1856), who has held various offices in Albany in politics and business, has published *The Carillons of Belgium and Holland*, 1914, *The Carillon in Literature*, 1915, and various articles upon campanology.

*Riley, Herbert (b. Brazil, 1888), educated in Germany and appearing there as 'cellist from 1909, in 1911–12 toured in the West of the United States and settled in San Francisco as soloist, ensemble-player and teacher. He has been associated with Saslavsky (see sec. 8) in annual quartet-concerts.

*Roentgen, Engelbert (b. Holland, 1886), a skillful 'cellist, son of Julius Roentgen (see Vol. iv. 119), since 1916 has played in the New York Symphony Society and also taught at the Mannes Music School.

*Rosen, Max (b. Rumania, 1900), was brought to New York in infancy, studied there and (as protégé of Coppet) in Europe, made his début as violinist at Dresden in 1915, with tours in Germany and Scandinavia, and since 1918 has appeared with success in America.

*Rothier, Léon (b. France, 1874), whose record as dramatic bass began in 1899, came to the Metropolitan Opera House in 1910. Since 1916 he has also taught at the Volpe Institute of Music.

*Rybner, Dagmar de Corval (b. Baden, 1890), daughter of Cornelius Rybner (see sec. 9), studied in Baden, Switzerland and New York, and since 1912 has been concert-pianist and composer in New York. See art.

*Sainton, Joseph (b. England, 1878), who from 1908 had been in charge of municipal concerts at Brighton, from 1912 was conductor for the Aborn Opera Company, and since 1915 has led municipal concerts in Minneapolis.

*Salzédo, Carlos (b. France, 1885), an able harpist, since 1913 has been with the Trio de Lutèce, with Barrère and Kéfer (see sec. 9 for both). He has written for the harp and for other instruments, and a treatise upon the harp.

*Sandby, Herman (b. Denmark, 1881), from 1900 a notable 'cellist in Europe, from 1912 played in the Philadelphia Orchestra and taught in the Broad Street Conservatory, and since 1916 has concertized from New York as headquarters. See art.

Schminke, Oscar Eberhard (b. New York, 1881), after having been a practicing dentist in New York for some years, from about 1911 has devoted himself to composition. See art.

Search, Frederick Preston (b. Pueblo, Colo., 1889), trained in Boston, Cincinnati and Leipzig, from 1912 has been concert-'cellist, in 1915–16 with the American Symphony Orchestra in Chicago, in 1916–17 with the Chicago Opera Company, and has since directed summer plays in California. See art.

Seeger, Charles Louis, Jr. (b. Mexico City, 1886), graduated from Harvard in 1908, in 1910–11 was assistant-conductor of opera at Cologne, and since 1912 has been professor in the University of California. See art.

Seydel, Irma (b. Boston, 1896), daughter and pupil of a player in the Boston Symphony Orchestra, since 1913 has been concert-violinist in America and Germany. See art.

*Smith, Leo (b. England, 1881), an experienced 'cellist, since 1911 has taught at the Toronto Conservatory, besides writing articles for periodicals.

*Sorrentino, Umberto (b. Italy, 1889), since 1910 has toured as concert-tenor or operatic star in the West Indies, Mexico, the United States and Canada.

Sowerby, Leo (b. Grand Rapids, Mich., 1895), studied in Chicago, and since 1913 has been composer there, besides teaching in the American Conservatory and some work as critic. See art.

Spaeth, Sigmund (b. Philadelphia, 1885), graduated from Haverford College in 1906, from 1910 taught in Asheville, N. C., and since 1912 has been engaged in editorial or critical work in New York. See art.

Spelman, Timothy Mather (b. Brooklyn, 1891), graduated from Harvard in 1913, studied there and in New York and Munich, and since 1914 has been composer in New York, his works including an opera, an orchestral suite, a melodrama and a pantomime, besides songs, etc.

Spencer, Eleanor (b. Chicago, 1890), studied in Chicago, New York, Paris and Vienna, from 1910 appeared in England, Germany and Holland as concert-pianist, and since 1913 has been regularly heard in America. See art.

*Stefano, Salvatore di (b. Sardinia, 1887), since 1913 has toured in the United States as concert-harpist.

Stoessel, Albert Frederic (b. St. Louis, 1894), studied in St. Louis and Berlin, where he made his début as violinist and was a member of the Hess Quartet, and since 1915 has toured in America. See art.

*Stransky, Josef (b. Bohemia, 1874), the distinguished conductor, since 1911 has led the New York Philharmonic Society. See art.

*Talbot, Thomas R. (b. Ireland, 1884), since 1913 has been organist in Minneapolis, interested in promoting improvement in Roman Catholic music along strict lines. He has organized a Cecilian Society for this purpose.

Taylor, Joseph Deems (b. New York, 1885), graduated at New York University in 1906, and has since been in editorial work, from 1910 also composing various choral and orchestral works, etc. See art.

*Teyte [Tate], Maggie (b. England, 1889), since 1911 has sung regularly in America as both concert- and opera-soprano, in 1911–14 with the Chicago Opera Company, in 1914–17 with the Boston Opera Company. See art.

*Thalberg, Marcian (b. Russia, 1877), from 1902 a prominent concert-pianist at Paris and elsewhere in Europe, since 1913 has been teacher of advanced pupils at the Cincinnati Conservatory.

*Tourret, André (b. France, 1882), noted as violinist in Paris from 1896, both in the Colonne Orchestra and in ensemble-playing, from 1913 lived in New York, with some tours, returning lately to Belgium.

*Treharne, Bryceson (b. Wales, 1879), after ten years of teaching in Australia and further experience in Europe, since 1916 has been composer in New York. See art.

*Trunk, Richard (b. Baden, 1879), conductor and teacher in Germany from 1896, since 1912 has led the Arion Society in New York and since 1913 also the Arion Society in Newark.

Uhe, Arthur Emil (b. Chicago, 1892), studied at Chicago and Brussels, first appeared as violinist at Brussels in 1912, toured in Norway, Switzerland and England, and since 1914 has been teacher and orchestral conductor at Bethany College in Kansas. He has written a violin-concerto and other works for violin and piano.

Van Gordon, Cyrena [name originally Pocock] (b. Camden, O., 1893), trained at Cincinnati, where she appeared as contralto in a pageant in 1912, since 1913 has been prominent in the Chicago Opera Company, besides some concert-singing. In 1912 she married Dr. Shirley B. Munns of Chicago.

*Van Vliet, Cornelius (b. Holland, 1886), noted 'cellist in European orchestras from about 1900, came to Chicago in 1911, from 1912 played with the Minneapolis Orchestra, and since 1919 has concertized from New York as center. See art.

*Vecsei, Desider Josef (b. Hungary, 1882), concert-pianist in Europe from 1907, since 1915 has toured in the United States.

*Vigneti, Georges (b. France, 1882), who had appeared widely as violinist in France and on a world-tour, since 1911 has taught in New York and played in trio with Arthur Whiting and Georges Barrère.

*Vix, Geneviève (b. France, 1887), from 1910 lyric soprano at Madrid and Buenos Aires, in 1917–18 appeared with the Chicago Opera Company. In 1918 she married the Russian banker Cyril Narishkin in New York.

*Volavy, Marguerite (b. Moravia, 1886), from 1902 known as concert-pianist throughout Europe and America. At her New York début in 1915 with the Russian Symphony Orchestra she introduced a new concerto by Bortkiewicz.

Ware, Helen (b. Woodbury, N. J., 1887), studied at Philadelphia, Vienna and Budapest, and since 1912 has toured Europe and America as concert-violinist, specializing in Hungarian and Slav music. See art.

*Warnery, Edmond (b. France, 1876, of Swiss parents), originally a baritone, now a tenor, since 1910 has sung with the Chicago Opera Company with sustained success.

*Weil, Hermann (b. Germany, 1878), the Wagnerian baritone, since 1911 has appeared at the Metropolitan Opera House and in concert. He has published songs.

*Witek, Anton (b. Bohemia, 1872), long eminent as concertmaster and ensemble-player in Berlin, in 1910–18 was concertmaster of the Boston Symphony Orchestra, besides continuing, with his wife, *Vita Witek, née Friese (b. Denmark, 1868), and Joseph Malkin, the Witek-Malkin Trio (formed in 1902 at Berlin) and teaching in New York. See art.

*Ysaÿe, Eugène (b. Belgium, 1858), since 1880 famous as a great violinist and also able conductor, since 1918 has been conductor of the Cincinnati Festivals and Symphony Orchestra. See Vol. v. 580–2, and art.

*Zbinden, Theodore (b. Alsace, 1877), graduated from the University of Michigan in 1899, with degrees later in both music and medicine, from 1912 taught in Toledo, but since 1918 has been a practicing physician. He has written a violin-sonata, the cantata ' The Chambered Nautilus,' etc.

*Zimbalist, Efrem (b. Russia, 1889), the distinguished violinist, settled in America in 1911 and has played extensively and with great success. In 1914 he married the soprano Alma Gluck (see sec. 9). See Vol. v. 596, and art.

The several sections of the REGISTER refer to about 1700 persons, of whom over 900 are native-born and nearly 800 are foreign-born. It is interesting to observe how the derivation of these classes changes from period to period.

For convenience, those native-born may be grouped in six regions, namely, *a.* New England; *b.* Middle States; *c.* Southern States (Va. to Tex.); *d.* Central States (Ohio to Kan.); *e.* Western States; *f.* Canada, West Indies, Mexico and South America. Still more roughly, those foreign-born may be grouped in four classes, namely, *a.* Great Britain, Holland and Scandinavia; *b.* Germany, Bohemia and Austria; *c.* Latin Countries (including Belgium and Switzerland); *d.* Slavic and Other Countries.

The statistics work out (as far as birthplaces are known or probable) as follows:

	NATIVE-BORN							FOREIGN-BORN				
	NAMES	a.	b.	c.	d.	e.	f.	NAMES	a.	b.	c.	d.
18th cent.	15	80%	20%	—	—	—	—	100	70%	15%	15%	—
1800–40 .	50	75	21	2%	—	—	2%	50	54	24	22	—
1840–60 .	80	60	23	12	3%	—	2	95	24	67	9	—
1860–70 .	70	44	30	4	12	—	10	45	22	64	14	—
1870–80 .	120	36	28	4	29	2%	1	60	25	46	15	14%
1880–90 .	175	28	38	5	20	2	7	115	33	48	10	9
1890–1900	195	21	38	4	29	3	5	95	32	49	10	9
1900–10 .	150	15	32	6	34	4	9	115	27	22	37	14
1910–20 .	50	10	38	2	38	6	6	105	27	18	36	19
	905	32%	32%	5%	23%	3%	5%	780	35%	37%	20%	8%

If existing dictionaries be collated, it will be found that the trend of percentages does not vary much from the above, although the total number of names included is much larger — about 2700 native-born and about 1000 foreign-born.

PERSONAL AND DESCRIPTIVE ARTICLES

AND

ALPHABETICAL INDEX

NOTE. The few abbreviations used are mostly self-explanatory. Marks like '[R.7]' at the end of biographies indicate where the names are entered in the Chronological Register. Several Associations are often referred to by initials, as 'M. T. N. A.' for Music Teachers' National Association, 'A. G. O.' for American Guild of Organists, 'N. A. O.' for National Association of Organists, 'R. A. M.' for Royal Academy of Music, 'R. C. M.' for Royal College of Music, 'R. C. O.' for Royal College of Organists, and 'I. M. G.' for Internationale Musik-Gesellschaft. In some cross-references 'C.' stands for College and 'U.' for University.

Articles relating to those who are outside the American field are marked by ‡.

A

ABBEY, HENRY EUGENE (1846–1896). See Register, 7.

ABBOTT, EMMA (Dec. 9, 1850, Chicago : Jan. 5, 1891, Salt Lake City), attained success as a stage-soprano by hard work and pertinacity. During her youth in Peoria, Ill., she had few advantages, and her voice was neither large nor sympathetic. In 1870, however, aided by Miss Kellogg, she became a leading church-singer in New York and had lessons from Errani. Her advance was so marked that in 1872 friends enabled her to study at Milan under Sangiovanni and then at Paris under Mme. Marchesi, Wartel and Delle Sedie. Her operatic début at Covent Garden in 1876 and in New York in 1877 in 'La Fille du Régiment' was followed by a tour in Great Britain under Mapleson's direction. From 1878 she pursued an active career in America, mostly as the head of her own operatic troupe, which was managed by Eugene Wetherell of New York, whom she married in 1878. She appeared in standard Italian works and English operettas, but in Chicago she is credited with bringing out such works as Gounod's 'Mireille' and Massé's 'Paul et Virginie.' For a time she almost rivaled Miss Kellogg in popularity, and she and her husband (who died in 1888) became wealthy. [R.6]

A BECKET, THOMAS (1843–1918). See Register, 4.

ABORN, MILTON (b. 1864) and SARGENT (b. 1866). See Register, 9.

ABORN OPERA COMPANY, THE, was an operatic troupe organized in 1902 by the brothers Aborn for producing lighter operas in English, which continued for several years in different parts of the country with considerable success.

ABOTT, BESSIE PICKENS (1878–1919). See Register, 8.

ACADEMY OF MUSIC, THE, of Boston, was an association, formed in 1833 under the lead of Lowell Mason, which established a music-school, promoted the recognition of music in the public schools and the holding of 'conventions' in many places, organized a chorus and an orchestra, and arranged public lectures on musical topics. After 1847 its functions were taken over by other agencies. In 1838 the Academy chorus of about 200 gave Romberg's 'Song of the Bell,' Neukomm's 'David' and Zeuner's 'Feast of Tabernacles,' the latter perhaps the first American oratorio. In 1840–41 Beethoven's 1st and 5th Symphonies were played by the orchestra. See L. C. Elson, *History of American Music*, pp. 52, 78–80, and Ritter, *Music in America*, chap. xii.

ACADEMY OF MUSIC, THE, of New York. See Vol. i. 12, Krehbiel, *Chapters of Opera*, and article by Saerchinger in 'The Musical Quarterly,' January, 1920, pp. 84–5. As an operatic headquarters it ceased to be important in 1897.

ACADEMY OF MUSIC, THE, of Philadelphia, was a theater and opera-house, erected in 1857, which long served as a center for opera-performances and concerts, like its New York predecessor.

ADAMOWSKA, Mme. See Szumowska.

ADAMOWSKI, JOSEPH (July 4, 1862, Warsaw, Poland), in 1871–77 was a 'cello-student with Kontski and Goebelt at the Warsaw Conservatory. He then went to the Moscow Conservatory and studied 'cello with Fitzenhagen, composition with Tchaikovsky and piano with Pabst. Meanwhile he also entered the University and graduated. In 1883 he began concert-tours in Poland and Germany, and in 1885–87 was professor of 'cello and ensemble-playing at the Conservatory of Cracow. Coming to America in 1889, he played in the Boston Symphony Orchestra till 1907, and also in the Adamowski Quartet and Adamowski Trio. He has been professor in the New England Conservatory since 1903. He is one of the founders and directors of the Boston Symphony Orchestra pension-fund. In 1896 he married the pianist Antoinette Szumowska. [R.7]

ADAMOWSKI, TIMOTHÉE (Mar. 24, 1858, Warsaw, Poland), having studied at the Warsaw Conservatory with Kontski and Roguski and in Paris with Massart, came to the United States in 1879 as a violin-virtuoso. He toured with Clara Louise Kellogg, Emma Thursby and Max Strakosch, and finally with a company of his own. In 1884–1908 he was a member of the Boston Symphony Orchestra, resigning to become teacher of the advanced violin-classes at the New England Conservatory. In 1890–94 he conducted popular concerts in the summer. As soloist he has appeared in Paris with the Colonne Orchestra, in London with the Philharmonic Society under Nikisch, and in Warsaw with the opera orchestra. He has composed, for violin and piano, 'Novelette,' 'Air de Ballet,' 'Barcarolle,' 'Mouvement de Valse' and 'Berceuse.' [R.6]

ADAMOWSKI QUARTET, THE, was formed at Boston in 1888 with Timothée Adamowski as leader, E. Fiedler as second, D. Kuntz as violist and Giuseppe Campanari as 'cellist. In 1890 it was reconstituted with A. Moldauer, Max Zach and Joseph Adamowski in the place of the last three.

ADAMOWSKI TRIO, THE, was formed at Boston in 1896 with Mme. Adamowska as pianist, Timothée and Joseph Adamowski as violinist and 'cellist.

ADAMS, CHARLES R. (1834, Charlestown, Mass. : July 3, 1900, West Harwich, Mass.), had for early teachers Edwin Bruce and Mme. Arnault. In 1856 he was the tenor in 'The Creation' with the Handel and Haydn Society, and for the next five years sang in concert and oratorio. In 1861, with his teacher Mulder and Mme. Febbri-Mulder, he appeared in concert and opera in the West Indies and in Holland. Called to Vienna, he learned his part in 'La Sonnambula' in three days, with successful result. After a tour in Russia he was engaged for three years at Budapest, but cut this short to accept a similar offer from the Royal Opera in Berlin. With an interim of one year, he was principal tenor at the Imperial Opera at Vienna in 1867–76. He sang also at Madrid, London, and Milan. Early in 1877 he returned to America, and sang in German opera in 1877–78, including the first American performances of 'Rienzi.' From 1879 he lived in Boston, where he was extremely successful as a teacher. His most effective rôles were Lohengrin, Tannhäuser, Raoul, Masaniello, Rienzi, Manrico, Vasco da Gama and Don José. J. S. Dwight in 1877 said that 'his was the robust kind of tenor, of large compass, evenly developed, under complete control and intrinsically very sweet in quality. He sang superbly, in a large, frank, masterly, dramatic style, each tone fraught with meaning and intention.' [R.4]

ADAMS, MRS. CROSBY, née Graves (b. 1858). See Register, 7.

ADAMS, F. W, (1787–1859). See Register, 3.

ADAMS, SUZANNE (1873, Cambridge, Mass.), early went abroad for study, becoming a pupil of Bouhy in Paris. In 1894 her début was made as Juliette at the Paris Opéra where she sang for three years, followed by one season at Nice. In 1898 she was engaged by Grau at Covent Garden, and appeared there each year until 1906. In 1898 she made her American début in Chicago, and at the Metropolitan Opera House in 1899. She married the English 'cellist Leo Stern in 1898, toured the United States with him in 1902–03 and on his death in 1904 retired from the stage for a year. She has been a favorite singer at Buckingham Palace and has frequently appeared in oratorio in England, where she has made her home since 1903. Her favorite operatic rôles are Juliette, Marguerite, Euridice, Gilda, Micaela, Zerlina, Cherubino and Donna Elvira. [R.8]

ADDINGTON, STEPHEN. See TUNE-BOOKS, 1807.

ADES, LUCIUS. See COLLEGES, 3 (Friends U., Kan.).

ADGATE, ANDREW (d. 1793, Philadelphia), in 1784 founded in Philadelphia an Institution for the Encouragement of Church Music, and the next year established a Free School for Spreading the Knowledge of Vocal Music, which developed in 1787 into the Uranian Academy. Among the managers of the latter were many prominent citizens, like Hopkinson and Dr. Rush. From before 1785 Adgate promoted choral concerts at intervals, with programs including not only music by Billings, Lyon, Tuckey and others, but also the 'Hallelujah' from 'The Messiah.' On May 4, 1786, he gave a concert at the Reformed German Church with a chorus of 230 and an orchestra of 50. His programs and plans (often excellent) are detailed in Sonneck, *Early Concert-Life in America*, pp. 103–20. He died in the epidemic of yellow fever in 1793, but the Uranian Academy seems to have continued till after 1800. For his publications, see TUNE-BOOKS, 1785. [R.2]

ÆOLIAN CHOIR, THE, of Brooklyn, N. Y., is a select chorus of forty-five voices organized in 1912 by N. Lindsay Norden for the cultivation and promotion of Russian a cappella church-music. He prepared for it English adaptations of over ninety Russian compositions that were previously inaccessible, including many that are extended and elaborate, sometimes in eight-part and even ten-part form. The publication of these works, illustrated by the recitals which the Choir gave in or about New York, aroused a widespread interest in the Russian style. See articles by Norden in the *M. T. N. A. Proceedings*, 1915, and 'The Musical Quarterly,' April, 1918.

ÆOLIAN COMPANY, THE, of New York, has long been famous for making automatic instruments like the Æolian and the Pianola. It is part of the complex corporation known as the Æolian, Weber Piano and Pianola Co. (capital, $10,000,000), which also has absorbed the Weber Piano Co., Steck & Co., the Wheelock Piano Co., the Stroud Piano Co., the Vocalion Organ Co., the Votey Organ Co., the Orchestrelle Co. of Great Britain, the Choralion Co. of Germany and Austria, etc. This combination of interests is one of the largest instrument-makers in the world. The central office is at 29–33 West 42nd St., and in its building is Æolian Hall, which is one of the fine concert-halls in New York. The president of the Company is H. B. Tremaine.

AGRAMONTE, EMILIO (1844– ?). See Register, 5.

AIKEN, CHARLES (1818–1882). See Register, 4.

AIKEN, HENRY M. (1824?– ?). See Register, 4.

AIKEN, WALTER H. (b. 1856). See Register, 6.

AIKIN, J. B. See Tune-Books, 1847.

AITKEN, JOHN. See Tune-Books, 1787.

AKER, J. HARRY. See Colleges, 3 (Central C., Ark.).

ALBANI, EMMA. See article in Vol. i. 59. The correct birth-year is 1852. She retired from active work in 1906 and in 1911 made her farewell appearance at a concert in Albert Hall, London. See her autobiography, *Emma Albani, Forty Years of Song*, 1911, and H. S. Edwards, *The Prima Donna*, 1888. [R.5]

ALBEE, AMOS (1772– ?). See Tune-Books, 1805.

ALBRECHT, CHARLES. See Register, 2.

ALBRECHT, H. F. (d. 1875). See Register, 4.

ALDA, FRANCES [name originally Davis] (May 31, 1883, Christchurch, New Zealand), received her general education in Melbourne, Australia. She studied singing in Paris with Mme. Marchesi, and in 1904 made her début at the Opéra-Comique as Manon. She then sang at Brussels, London, Milan, Warsaw and Buenos Aires. In 1908 she made her first appearance at the Metropolitan Opera House as Gilda in 'Rigoletto,' and has since sung there regularly. In 1910 she married Giulio Gatti-Casazza, the manager of the Metropolitan. She has created soprano rôles in Gilson's 'Princesse Rayon de Soleil,' Messager's 'Madame Chrysanthème,' Puccini's 'Le Villi,' Damrosch's 'Cyrano de Bergerac' and Herbert's 'Madeleine,' and in American productions of Borodin's 'Prince Igor,' Zandonai's 'Francesca da Rimini' and Rabaud's 'Mârouf.' In addition to these works her répertoire includes the rôles of Mimi, Desdemona, Marguerite (in 'Faust'), Juliette, Traviata, Aida, Manon Lescaut (Puccini) and Margherita (in 'Mefistofele'). She is also an esteemed concert-singer. [R.9]

ALDEN, JOHN CARVER (Sept. 11, 1852, Boston), studied piano with Faelten in Boston and in Leipzig was a pupil of Paul, Plaidy and Papperitz. In 1880 he began teaching in Boston as an associate of Faelten in the New England Conservatory. He taught for a period in New York, then for some years at Converse College, Spartanburg, S. C., and more recently at the Quincy Mansion School, Wollaston, Mass. Besides being highly esteemed as a piano-teacher, he has composed a piano-concerto in G minor, piano-pieces and technical studies, songs like 'Du bist wie eine Blume,' and anthems. [R.6]

ALDRICH, A. See Tune-Books, 1859.

ALDRICH, MARISKA (b. 1883). See Register, 9.

ALDRICH, PERLEY DUNN (Nov. 6, 1863, Blackstone, Mass.), was trained at the New England Conservatory in Boston, studying in 1883–86 with Emery, Maas and Whiting. In 1892 he went to London for three years of vocal study with Shakespeare and then proceeded to Paris for lessons with Trabadello. He taught at the University of Kansas in 1885–87, at the Tremont School of Music, Boston, in 1888, at the Utica Conservatory in 1889–91, privately at Rochester in 1891–1903, and since 1903 in Philadelphia. During the summers of 1903, '04 and '08 he was assistant to Sbriglia in Paris. He has given many song-recitals with unique programs, and has composed the cantatas 'La Belle Dame sans Merci,' for male voices (1895) and 'The Sleeping Wood-Nymph' (1896), and about 25 songs. He is the author of *Vocal Economy*, 1895, and has been a frequent contributor to musical magazines. [R.7]

ALDRICH, RICHARD (July 31, 1863, Providence, R. I.), was educated at the Providence High School and Harvard College, where he graduated in 1885. He studied music with Paine, but upon graduation engaged in newspaper-work on the Providence 'Journal.' In 1888–89 he studied in Germany, giving much attention to music. In 1889–91 he was in Washington as private secretary to Senator Dixon, with some critical work on the 'Evening Star.' In 1891–1902 he held various positions on the New York 'Tribune,' such as assistant literary editor and Sunday editor, besides helping with musical criticism under Krehbiel. In October, 1902, he became music-editor of the New York 'Times,' continuing until December, 1917, when he resigned to enter military work in Washington. He was commissioned captain in the National Army (as it was then) and later became captain in the United States Army, attached to the Intelligence Division of the General Staff. In 1919 he returned to his place on the 'Times.' His writings on musical subjects, in newspapers and books, are highly valued for their sanity and clarity. He has published a *Guide to Parsifal*, 1904, a *Guide to the Ring of the Nibelung*, 1905, and a translation of Lilli Lehmann's *Meine Gesangskunst* or *How to sing*, 1902, '14. He joined with Krehbiel in contributing American articles to the revised edition of this Dictionary in 1904–10. [R.8]

ALEXANDER, LLOYD L. See Colleges, 3 (Hanover C., Ind.).

ALLEN, BENJAMIN DWIGHT (Feb. 16, 1831, Sturbridge, Mass. : Mar. 4, 1914, Wellesley, Mass.), was educated in Worcester, where he lived almost sixty years. From 1845 he was teacher and organist there, from 1857 for thirty-seven years at the Union Congregational Church. In 1858 he was one of the founders of the association which later established the Worcester Festivals, and was always active in it as accompanist, organist, associate-conductor and on the directorate. In 1871–76 he also taught at the New England Conservatory in Boston, and gave some lectures at Boston University. After 1876 he often lectured elsewhere. From 1894 he was head of the music-department of Beloit College in Wisconsin, and in 1902–05 was organist in New York both at the Manhattan Congregational Church and at Teachers College, retiring in 1905 to Wellesley, Mass., to busy himself with composition. About a score of his songs and anthems have been published, but many others remain in manuscript. He was a thorough and scrupulous teacher, and counted among his pupils the heads of music-departments in at least six colleges. He was a member of the Harvard Musical Association and a founder of the A. G. O. [R.4]

ALLEN, CHARLES N. (1837, York, England : Apr. 7, 1903, Boston), gained his mastery of the violin under Saenger at Paris, and for some years was in the orchestra at the Opéra. In 1871 he came to Boston, where for thirty years he was a foremost player and teacher. In 1873 he organized the Beethoven Quintette Club, in 1877 joined the Mendelssohn Quintette Club, and later was a member of the Boston Symphony Orchestra. Among his pupils was Henry K. Hadley. Besides being a superior musician, he was a man of great culture and charm. [R.6]

ALLEN, EDWIN L. See COLLEGES, 3 (Mt. Union C., Ohio).

ALLEN, FRANCIS D. See TUNE-BOOKS, 1818.

ALLEN, GEORGE N. (1812–1877). See Register, 4.

ALLEN, HEMAN (1836– ?). See Register, 5.

ALLEN, NATHAN HALE (Apr. 14, 1848, Marion, Mass.), after schooling in Providence and at Phillips (Andover) Academy, in 1868 went to Germany. In Berlin he was a pupil of Grell in singing and of Haupt in organ-playing, and later studied instrumentation with Van der Stucken in New York. From about 1870 he was organist in Hartford, Conn., in 1883–1906 at the Center Congregational Church. Five years were then spent at Piedmont Church in Worcester, and in 1915 he returned to Hartford. He has taught many prominent organists and has been active as concert-organist and chorus-conductor. He has composed many songs, part-songs, organ- and piano-pieces, a collection of 40 liturgical responses and two sacred cantatas. Many of his fifty published anthems have been widely used. Among the compositions as yet unpublished are a number of organ-pieces, including a 'Pièce Symphonique' and a 'Symphonic Fantasia'; a 'Concertante' for organ

and piano ; 'In Memoriam' for organ, piano and strings ; pieces for piano, violin and 'cello ; and numerous vocal compositions, including the cantata 'The Apotheosis of St. Dorothy.' He has several printed addresses on musical subjects, and has devoted much time to investigating the musical history of New England. He is one of the founders of the A. G. O., an original member of the New York Manuscript Society, and has repeatedly served as associate-conductor of the Litchfield Festival Chorus. With Leonard W. Bacon he edited *The Hymns of Martin Luther*, 1883. [R.6]

ALLEN, WARREN DWIGHT (b. 1885). See COLLEGES, 3 (C. of the Pacific, Cal.).

ALLEN, WILLIAM FRANCIS (1830–1889). See Register, 5.

ALLER, GEORGE HENRY (b. 1871). See Register, 8.

ALTHOUSE, PAUL SHEARER (b. 1889). See Register, 10.

ALTSCHULER, MODEST (Feb. 15, 1873, Mogilev, Russia), was at first a violin-student, but soon changed to the 'cello, which he studied in 1884–86 with Gobelt at the Warsaw Conservatory. His first public appearance, at thirteen, was with the conservatory orchestra under the direction of Zarzycki. Graduating with honors, he won a scholarship at the Moscow Conservatory, where he studied 'cello with Fitzenhagen and Von Glen and composition with Arensky, Tanieiev and Safonov. On graduating in 1890 he was awarded a silver medal. He toured Europe with the Moscow Trio, and finally came to New York as 'cellist and teacher. In 1903 he organized the Russian Symphony Orchestra, of which he has since been conductor. Its first concert was on Jan. 7, 1904, in New York. Since that time the Orchestra has visited most of the cities in the United States, making three trans-continental tours before 1914. He has orchestrated several modern Russian works, including the Tchaikovsky piano-trio. [R.9]

AMATO, PASQUALE (Mar. 21, 1878, Naples, Italy), after graduating from the Instituto Tecnico Domenico, studied at the Naples Conservatory in 1896–99 and made his début as Germont in 'La Traviata' at the Teatro Bellini in 1900. He then made the round of the leading theaters of Italy, and sang in Prague, Munich, Dresden, Leipzig, Berlin, Budapest, Vienna, Brussels and Paris. In 1908 he came to the Metropolitan Opera House in New York, continuing to the present. He has sung two seasons in London and six in Buenos Aires, and is regarded as one of the leading operatic baritones of the day. His favorite rôles are in 'I Pagliacci,' 'Il Trovatore,' 'Un Ballo in Maschera,' 'Prince Igor,' Napoleon in 'Madame Sans-Gêne,' Amfortas in 'Parsifal' and the Toreador in 'Carmen.'

He has created the parts of King Hadraot (in 'Armida'), Carlo Worms (in 'Germania'), Jack Rance (in 'The Girl of the Golden West') and Golaud (in 'Pelléas et Mélisande'). Equally popular as a concert-singer, he has appeared with the Boston, Philadelphia and Chicago Symphony Orchestras and the New York Philharmonic Society. He is a popular 'festival-artist' and has made many concert-tours. [R.9]

AMBROSE, PAUL (Oct. 11, 1868, Hamilton, Ont.), was the son of the composer Robert S. Ambrose. His general education was in the public schools of Hamilton and at the Collegiate Institute. He studied piano there with his father, and in New York with Parsons and Miss Chittenden, composition with Klein and orchestration with Buck. He was organist at the Madison Avenue (M. E.) Church in 1886–1890, organist at St. James' (M. E.) Church in 1890–1917, and since 1917 at the First Presbyterian Church in Trenton, N. J. He has taught and lectured on music-history at several schools, including the Institute of Applied Music in New York, and since 1904 has been director of music at the State Normal School at Trenton. He has composed songs, choruses, piano- and organ-pieces. [R.7]

'AMERICA' is the title usually applied either to the patriotic hymn beginning 'My country, 'tis of thee' or to the tune associated with it. The hymn is by Rev. Samuel Francis Smith, D. D. (1808–1895), a distinguished Baptist clergyman, professor, editor and hymnist. The tune is the same as that of the English 'God save the King,' which has also been adopted into German and Danish use. Dr. Smith wrote the verses early in 1832, while still a theological student at Andover Seminary, to fit the music as found in a German song-book referred to him by Lowell Mason. They were probably first sung publicly under Mason's direction at a children's celebration at Park Street Church in Boston on July 4, 1832, and they soon became popular and were included in standard hymn-books from Smith and Stow's *Psalmist* (1843) onwards. See Burrage, *Baptist Hymn-Writers*, pp. 329–34, Julian, *Dict. of Hymnology*, under 'Smith' and 'God save the King,' and many other books on hymnody, and also Vol. ii. 188–91, of this Dictionary, Sonneck, *Report on 'The Star Spangled Banner*,' etc., pp. 73–8, 158–60, and many books on popular and national airs.

'AMERICAN ART JOURNAL, THE,' established in New York in 1863, for many years gave much attention to musical subjects. See Watson, H. C., in Register, 4, and Thoms, W. M., in Register, 5.

AMERICAN COLLEGE OF MUSICIANS, THE, was organized in 1884 by Edward M. Bowman under the general auspices of the Music Teachers' National Association. It was modeled upon the College of Organists in England, and was intended to be exclusively an agency for examination and certification as to professional proficiency. The branches included were piano, organ, voice, violin, theory and, later, public-school teaching, and grades of attainment were marked by granting the use of the terms 'associate,' 'fellow' or 'master.' About 1895 the Board of Regents of the State of New York empowered the College to grant the degrees of Mus.B. and Mus.D. The organization began with about 140 charter-members, including a fine representation of foremost musicians. The president from 1884 was Mr. Bowman, who was succeeded in 1893 by A. R. Parsons. For ten years or more the system of examinations was maintained upon a high plane, and the total number of candidates was about 235, of whom about half were approved, mostly as 'associates.' But after 1895, apparently for mechanical and financial reasons, the organization became inoperative. In 1910 Mr. Bowman urged the revival of its work, but without practical result. See Mathews, *Hundred Years of Music*, pp. 539–41, and a paper by Bowman in *M. T. N. A. Proceedings*, 1912, pp. 145–56.

AMERICAN CONSERVATORY OF MUSIC, THE, of Chicago, was organized in 1886 and incorporated in 1887. The founder was John J. Hattstaedt, who has remained its director since 1894, assisted by Karleton Hackett and Adolf Weidig. Its aim is 'to offer the best instruction in all branches of music and dramatic art by teachers of broad education thoroughly in sympathy with American life and its needs.' The number of teachers is about 100, and the number of students over 2200 annually. There are over 1400 graduates, of whom about 275 received the degree of Mus.B. In addition to all the lines of usual instruction fine opportunities are given for choral and orchestral experience, for operatic and dramatic training, for musical pedagogy in all its applications, etc.

AMERICAN FEDERATION OF MUSICIANS, THE, founded in 1895, aims to promote the interests of musicians employed in orchestras, bands and the like. It has about 750 local unions in the United States and Canada, with a total membership of about 85,000, the president being J. N. Weber, 110–112 W. 40th St., New York.

AMERICAN GUILD OF ORGANISTS, THE, See Vol. i. 77, and add that in 1919 the Guild had over 23 chapters in the United States and Canada, and a total membership of 1925, of whom 150 now rank as 'fellows.' The honorary presidents have been from 1896

Dudley Buck, from 1899 Gerrit Smith, from 1902 S. P. Warren, from 1906 H. W. Parker, and in 1909–12 Arthur Foote; in 1912 the office was discontinued. The wardens have been successively Gerrit Smith, Sumner Salter, W. H. Hall, R. H. Woodman, S. A. Baldwin, J. H. Brewer, W. R. Hedden, Frank Wright, J. W. Andrews, Clifford Demarest and Victor Baier. The Clemson anthem-prize has been won by W. C. Macfarlane, S. N. Penfield, H. J. Stewart, J. S. Ford, W. Y. Webbe, Mark Andrews, Herbert Sanders and William Berwald. The general office is at 29 Vesey Street, New York.

AMERICAN INSTITUTE OF APPLIED MUSIC, THE, in New York, was incorporated in 1900 to continue the work of the Metropolitan College of Music and other schools. Kate S. Chittenden, founder of the Synthetic Piano School in 1887 and on the staff of the College from 1892, has been the efficient dean from the first. In its regular curriculum the Institute aims at systematic thoroughness, with much emphasis upon pedagogical method, largely with reference to those expecting to teach. The enrolment averages about 350 per year. More than 1000 teachers have received certificates. The Institute is located at 212 West 59th Street.

AMERICAN OPERA COMPANY, THE, was an enterprise organized in 1885 under the lead of Mrs. Jeannette Thurber of New York for the giving of opera in English with extreme artistic perfection and, so far as practicable, with American artists, not only in New York, but in several other cities. Theodore Thomas was secured as musical director, and no pains were spared in recruiting the orchestra, the staff of soloists and the chorus. The Academy of Music was tastefully renovated for the New York season, which opened on Jan. 4, 1886, and ran to sixty-six performances, with a later tour to Boston, Philadelphia, Baltimore, Washington, Chicago, etc. The répertoire included 'Orpheus,' 'The Magic Flute,' 'Martha,' 'The Merry Wives,' 'The Flying Dutchman,' 'Lohengrin,' Massé's 'The Marriage of Jeannette,' 'The Taming of the Shrew' and 'Lakmé.' The venture proved overambitious and its financial foundation insufficient, and in 1887 it was abandoned and was succeeded by a new organization, called the National Opera Company. See Mrs. Thomas, *Memoirs of Theodore Thomas*, pp. 279–96, and Krehbiel, *Chapters of Opera*, pp. 139–44.

AMERICAN ORGAN. The English name for the type of reed-organ developed in the United States from about 1850–60. See Vol. i. 77–8, and pamphlet by Henry L. Mason, *The History and Development of the American Cabinet Organ*, n. d.

AMERICAN PIANO COMPANY, THE, of New York, was formed in 1908, with a capital of $12,000,000, to unite the interests of Chickering & Sons, Knabe & Co., Haines Brothers, Marshall & Wendell and several other firms. It has not only carried forward the established business of all of these, but developed with marked success the player-pianos and similar devices connected with them. The name 'Ampico' is applied to the most perfect of these latter, which has exceptional facility in recording and reproducing tone-colors and nuances. Its inventor was Charles D. Stoddard, and it was first publicly shown in 1916.

'AMERICAN SYMPHONY.' A name often given to Dvořák's Symphony No. 5, in E minor, 'From the New World,' produced in New York in 1893.

AMERICAN SYMPHONY ORCHESTRA, THE, of Chicago, was founded in 1915 by Glenn Dillard Gunn, who has remained its conductor. Its object is to present American compositions exclusively. Among the important works thus far brought forward are the following:

H. K. Hadley: Dramatic Overture, 'Herod.'
Eric DeLamarter: 'Alice in Wonderland' Suite; 'Overture to a Comedy.'
J. A. Carpenter: 'Gitangili,' songs for soprano and orchestra (texts by Tagore).
Leo Sowerby: 'Homage to English Country-Folk.' settings of three folk-songs; Symphonic Poem, 'The Sorrows of Midath'; Concerto for violin and orchestra; 'Marching-Song,' for strings and piano.
Clarence Loomis: Concerto for piano and orchestra; Fantasy for piano and orchestra.
R. G. Cole: Symphonic Prelude, 'King Robert of Sicily.'
Arthur Dunham: Overture, 'In Autumn.'
George Colburn: 'Montezuma' Suite; 'The Song of the Drum,' for chorus and orchestra.
Clarence Burley: Concerto for violin and orchestra.
C. W. Cadman: 'Indian' Suite.
Roland Leach: Overture, 'Legend.'
Herbert Butler: Ballade.

ANDERSON, ARTHUR OLAF (Jan. 30, 1880, Newport, R. I.), was a pupil of Norris in Boston, of Guilmant, Guiraud and d'Indy in Paris, of Dura in Berlin, and of Sgambati in Rome. In 1905–08 he taught theory in Berlin. In 1908 he came to Chicago and joined the faculty of the American Conservatory, with which he is still connected. He has composed an orchestral suite, 'The Brook'; other music for large and small orchestra; suites for piano, organ and violin; two sonatas for piano; twelve fugues; an 'Ave Maria,' for soprano and orchestra; two song-cycles, 'Pilgrimage to Kevlaar' and 'The Child's Garden of Verses'; fifty songs and various choruses. [R.9]

ANDERSON, JOHANNA. See COLLEGES, 3 (U. of Omaha, Neb.).

ANDERSON, O. WALDEMAR. See COLLEGES, 3 (Gustavus Adolphus C., Minn.).

ANDERSON, STYLES R. See COLLEGES, 3 (Simmons C., Tex.).

ANDRES, HENRY GEORGE (1838- ?). See Register, 5.

ANDREWS. See TUNE-BOOKS, 1800.

ANDREWS, GEORGE WHITFIELD (Jan. 19, 1861, Wayne, O.), has been associated with Oberlin, O., for almost his entire life. He began the study of piano there at six, organ at nine (with F. B. Rice) and at twelve made his first public appearance, playing a Bach Prelude and Fugue. For a time before 1879 he was organist of the First Church of Oberlin, and then played and taught two years at Meadville, Pa., and one year at Toledo. In 1882 he became organist of the Second Church in Oberlin, a position he still holds. Since 1882, also, he has been connected with the Musical Union, first as organist and since 1900 as conductor. In 1886 he began teaching at the Conservatory, and since 1892 has been professor of organ, composition and orchestration. He graduated from the Conservatory in 1879 in organ, piano, violin and theory, and studied in Leipzig with Papperitz (organ) and Jadassohn (theory, composition and piano), in Munich with Rheinberger (organ, composition and orchestration, 1885-6), and in Paris with Guilmant (organ and composition) and d'Indy (composition and orchestration, 1898-99). He was made Mus.D. by Oberlin College in 1903. His interest has centered in the duties connected with his work as teacher and conductor, and he has been highly successful in both fields, besides appearing as organ-recitalist in all parts of the country, including the great Expositions. He was a founder of the A. G. O. and is now dean of the Northern Ohio Chapter. His published organ-compositions are a March in C Minor and 'Poco Agitato' (Schirmer), Serenade No. 1 and 'Aria' (Ashmall), Serenade No. 2 and 'Con Grazia' (J. Fischer & Bro.), and Fugue in A minor (Leduc, Paris). The Church Co. publishes three sacred songs for baritone. Still in manuscript are a Suite in C for orchestra (played at Oberlin by the Chicago Symphony Orchestra), six organ-sonatas, four suites for organ, a Theme and Variations, many separate pieces for organ, a piano-trio, 'Morning' for piano, a Magnificat for soprano and piano, and a Processional and Recessional for chorus. [R.6]

ANDREWS, J. WARREN (Apr. 6, 1860, Lynn, Mass.), was organist at Swampscott, Mass., when but twelve. At sixteen he went to the First Baptist Church of Lynn, Mass., and also played at the Boston Street Methodist Church. In 1879 he was engaged by Old Trinity Church at Newport, R. I., where he remained nine years. Then followed a three-year sojourn at the Pilgrim Church in Cambridge and seven years at the Plymouth Church in Minneapolis. In 1898 he removed to the Church of the Divine Paternity in New York, where he still remains. He was a founder of the A. G. O., its warden in 1913-16 and a member of the council for many years. He has also held official positions in the N. A. O. In 1895 he established a school for organists and singers in Minneapolis, and has continued as teacher in New York. Many well-known church-musicians have been among his pupils. His published works are few, but he has organ-pieces, anthems, Te Deums and Canticles that may sometime be published. [R.6]

ANGER, JOSEPH HUMPHREY (June 3, 1862, Berkshire, England : June 11, 1913, Toronto), had his first appointment as organist at Frenchay, near Bristol, and while there (1888) he won the gold medal offered by the Bath Philharmonic Society for a setting of Psalm 96 for voices and orchestra. Later he matriculated at Oxford, proceeding as Mus.B. in 1889. He became assistant-master of Surrey County School, Cranleigh, and then organist at Ludlow. In 1893 he was appointed professor of harmony and theory at the Toronto Conservatory, a position he retained until his death. He was also examiner in music at the University of Toronto, president of the Clef Club, conductor of the Philharmonic Society, dean of the Ontario chapter of the A. G. O., and organist at St. Andrew's Presbyterian Church and later at the Central Methodist Church. He received the degree of Mus.D. from the University in 1902 in appreciation of his services toward the advancement of musical education in Canada, particularly in Toronto. He was the author of a text-book on harmony, *Form in Music*, and a pamphlet on *The Modern Enharmonic Scale*, 1907, which have had wide use. His madrigal 'Bonnie Belle' won the London Madrigal Society's prize in 1890. [R.8]

ANSCHÜTZ, KARL (1815-1870). See Register, 4.

'ANTONIO.' A lyric opera by Silas G. Pratt, written about 1870 while studying at Munich and Berlin. Selections were performed at Chicago in 1874 under Balatka, and in March, 1887, a rewritten version under the title 'Lucille' was given entire at the Columbian Theatre there.

'APOLLO.' No. 13 of the 'Grove-Plays' of the San Francisco Bohemian Club, produced in 1915. The text is by Frank Pixley and the music by Edward F. Schneider.

APOLLO CLUB, THE, of Boston, was founded in 1871 and incorporated in 1873, its nucleus being the earlier Chickering Club. It has had a singularly unbroken history along the lines originally planned. It aims to maintain a male chorus of superior singers for the study and performance of part-songs and concerted works for an audience limited to singers and subscribers. The active members now number about 80, and the associate members 500. From 1871 till his resignation in 1901 the conductor was B. J. Lang, who made the Club famous. He was followed by Emil Mollenhauer, who has continued the same brilliant record. The Club Rooms are at 3 Joy Street. Four concerts are given annually, the total number being about 250, with eminent soloists, vocal and instrumental, and often a full orchestra as well. In the list of works with orchestra given in Boston for the first time have been Mendelssohn's 'Antigone' and 'Œdipus in Colonos,' Hiller's 'Easter Morning,' Brambach's 'Columbus,' Bruch's 'Roman Song of Triumph,' Paine's 'Œdipus Tyrannus' and 'Summons to Love,' Brahms' 'Rinaldo,' Whiting's 'March of the Monks of Bangor,' 'Free Lances' and 'Henry of Navarre,' Foote's 'Farewell of Hiawatha,' and Nicodé's 'The Sea' — several of these having been written for the Club. Many part-songs by American composers have been prominent on the programs. See Vol. i. 369, and article in 'The New England Magazine,' April, 1910, by Ethel Syford.

APOLLO CLUB, THE, of Brooklyn. See Vol. iii. 367.

APOLLO CLUB, THE, of Cincinnati, was organized in 1882 and under the leadership of B. W. Foley attained a position of marked importance.

APOLLO CLUB, THE, of St. Louis, was founded in 1893. Its conductor till 1910 was Alfred G. Robyn and since that time Charles Galloway. It is a male chorus, limited to eighty voices. As a rule, three concerts are given annually to subscribers and guests.

APOLLO MALE CHORUS, THE, of Pittsburgh, was organized in 1904 by Rinehart Mayer, who has been its conductor since then.

APOLLO MUSICAL CLUB, THE, of Chicago, was organized in 1872 — the year after the Great Fire — through the efforts of Silas G. Pratt and George P. Upton, and its first concert was given in January, 1873. Originally planned as a male chorus after the model of the Apollo Club of Boston, in 1875 it was expanded into a mixed chorus, so as to undertake works of the largest dimensions. Its early conductors were A. W. Dohn (1872–74) and Karl Bergstein (1874–75), but the establishment of the Club as a highly significant artistic force was due to the leadership of

William L. Tomlins (1875–98) and since 1898 that of Harrison M. Wild, who has brought the standard of quality, balance and interpretation to the highest point. The chorus now numbers about 250 singers. The usual number of concerts annually is five, and the total number since the beginning is over 200.

The Club's répertoire includes all the standard oratorios and similar large works. 'The Messiah' has been given more than fifty times. In the list are Bach's St. Matthew Passion, Mass in B minor and Magnificat, Handel's 'Judas Maccabæus,' Mozart's Requiem Mass, Schumann's Missa Sacra, Berlioz' Requiem and Te Deum, Verdi's Requiem, Brahms' Requiem, Bruch's 'Frithjof,' Dvořák's Stabat Mater, Massenet's 'Mary Magdalene' and 'Eve,' Grieg's 'Olaf Trygvason,' Elgar's 'Light of Life,' 'Apostles' and 'Caractacus,' Pierné's 'Children's Crusade,' Parker's 'St. Christopher' and 'Hora Novissima,' Georg Schumann's 'Ruth,' Schmitt's 49th Psalm, Wolf-Ferrari's 'New Life,' etc. First performances in America include Elgar's 'Dream of Gerontius' (1903), Busch's 'King Olaf' (1903), Woyrsch's 'Dance of Death' (1911), and Cowen's 'The Veil' (1915).

APPLETON, THOMAS. See Register, 3.

APPY, HENRI (1828– ?). See Register, 4.

APTHORP, WILLIAM FOSTER (Oct. 24, 1848, Boston : Feb. 19, 1913, Vevey, Switzerland), was long the most influential critic in Boston. In 1856–60 he attended schools in Dresden, Berlin and Rome. He graduated from Harvard in 1869. Six years earlier he had begun piano, harmony and counterpoint with Paine and piano-study was continued under Lang. During his last year at Harvard he was conductor of the Pierian Sodality. He taught piano and harmony at the National College of Music in Boston in 1872–73, and for thirteen years was with the New England Conservatory, teaching piano and various branches of theory. In 1872 Howells, then editor of 'The Atlantic Monthly,' engaged him as musical editor. In 1876 he undertook musical criticism for the 'Sunday Courier' and two years later both musical and dramatic criticism for the 'Traveller.' In 1881 he became music-critic on the 'Evening Transcript,' soon assuming also the dramatic work. Both positions he held until 1903, when he gave up actual work. His remaining years were spent chiefly in Switzerland. In addition to his critical writing, which included many contributions to magazine and periodical literature, he taught æsthetics and musical history for some years in the College of Music of Boston University, and gave courses of lectures at the Lowell Institute in Boston and at the Peabody Institute in Baltimore. From 1892 to 1901 he edited the program-books for the Boston Symphony Orchestra concerts. His published volumes are *Musicians and Music-Lovers*, 1894, *By the Way*, 2 vols., 1898, *The Opera, Past and Present*, 1901, and these translations: *Hector Berlioz — Selections from his Letters and Writings*, 1879, *Jacques Damour, etc.*, from Zola, 1895. He was also critical editor (with Champlin) of Scribner's *Cyclopedia of Music and Musicians*, 3 vols., 1888–90. [R.6]

ARA, UGO (b. 1876). See Register, 9.

ARBUCKLE, MATTHEW (1828–1883). See Register, 4.

ARCHAMBEAU, IVAN D' (b. 1879). See Register, 9.

ARCHER, FREDERICK (June 16, 1838, Oxford, England : Oct. 22, 1901, Pittsburgh). See article in Vol. i. 101. His work in Pittsburgh began with the opening of the Carnegie Library and Music Hall on Nov. 7, 1895, when the first free organ-recital was given. The series of Pittsburgh Orchestra concerts began on Feb. 27, 1896, and his engagement as conductor expired on Jan. 28, 1898. The Saturday evening and Sunday afternoon free organ-recitals were continued till his death. He was also organist at the Church of the Ascension in Pittsburgh and musical examiner for the University of Toronto. [R.7]

'ARCHERS, THE,' An opera by Benjamin Carr, first given in April, 1796, at the John Street Theater in New York, there at least twice repeated, and in Boston in 1797. The libretto was by William Dunlap (1766–1839), the painter and play-writer, and is based on the story of William Tell. Of the music the only fragments known are a Rondo from the overture and the song 'Why, huntress, why?' See Sonneck, 'Early American Operas,' in *I. M. G. Sammelbde.* 6. 465–73, and *Early Opera in America*, pp. 98–100.

ARDITI, LUIGI (1822–1903). See Vol. i. 102–3, and Register, 4.

ARENS, FRANZ XAVIER (Oct. 28, 1856, Neef, Germany), came to America when a child, and was educated at the Normal College at St. Francis, Wis. He studied music with his father, Clemens Arens, with John Singenberger in Milwaukee, and in Germany with Rheinberger, Abel, Wüllner, Janssen and Hey. He has been professor in Canisius College at Buffalo, conductor of the Cleveland Philharmonic Society and Gesangverein (1885–88), and president of the Metropolitan School of Music in Indianapolis. In 1890–92 he gave concerts of music by Americans in Vienna and the principal cities of Germany. Since 1896 he has been located in New York as vocal teacher and from 1900 as founder and musical director of the People's Symphony Concerts, the object of which is to provide good music at low prices. He has composed a Symphonic Fantasia for orchestra, a canon and

fugue for organ, choral works with orchestra, and many songs and choruses. [R.7]

‡ARENSKY, ANTON STEPANOVITCH (July 31, 1861, Novgorod, Russia : Feb. 26, 1906, Tarioki, Finland). See article in Vol. i. 103, and add to the list of compositions the ballades 'The Diver,' op. 61, for solo, chorus and orchestra, and 'The Wolves,' op. 59, for bass with orchestra, a violin-concerto in A minor, op. 54, a fourth suite, op. 62, for piano duet, and numerous smaller instrumental pieces.

ARIANI, ADRIANO (b. 1877). See Register, 10.

ARIMONDI, VITTORIO. See Register, 9.

ARION CLUB, THE, of Providence, a mixed chorus of about 200 voices, has a high reputation for artistic excellence. Started in 1880, it has given three or four concerts annually since that time, the conductor from the first being Jules Jordan. Besides giving standard oratorios regularly and modern works like Elgar's 'Gerontius,' 'Caractacus,' 'King Olaf,' Pierné's 'Children's Crusade,' Parker's 'Hora Novissima' and Chadwick's 'Phœnix Expirans,' the club has given a number of operas in concert-form, such as 'Faust,' 'Roméo et Juliette,' 'Aida,' 'Tannhäuser' and 'Lohengrin,' all first times thus in America.

ARION MUSICAL CLUB, THE, of Milwaukee, has long been foremost in the production of choral works of large dimensions. Its most famous conductors have been William L. Tomlins in 1879–88 and Daniel Protheroe since 1899.

ARION SOCIETY, THE, of New York, was founded in 1854 as a rival male chorus to the older Liederkranz. Its conductors have been Bergmann in 1859–60 and 1867–71, Anschütz in 1860–62, Ritter in 1862–67, Leopold Damrosch in 1871–84, Van der Stucken in 1884–94 (tour to Europe with the Society in 1892), Lorenz in 1895–1913, and Carl Hahn in 1913–18. See Vol. iii. 369–70.

ARMSTRONG, JOHN. See TUNE-BOOKS, 1816.

ARMSTRONG, WILLIAM DAWSON (b. 1868). See Register, 8.

ARNOLD, MR., MRS. and MISS. See Register, 2.

ARNOLD [–STROTHOTTE], MAURICE (b. 1865). See Register, 8.

ARNOLD, RICHARD (Jan. 10, 1845, Eilenburg, Prussia : June 21, 1918, New York), was brought to America in 1853 and attended schools in Buffalo, Memphis and Columbus. By his twelfth year he had conducted theater-orchestras in Memphis and Columbus. From 1864 he was a pupil of Ferdinand David at Leipzig, where he remained three years. Returning to New York, he played in the orchestra at Niblo's Garden for a time, and then became a first violinist under Thomas in

1869–76. In 1878–91 he was solo violinist in the New York Philharmonic Club. In 1877 he entered the New York Philharmonic Society, and in 1880–1909 was its concert-master, playing under a long list of celebrated conductors. In 1897 he organized the Richard Arnold String Sextet. The last years of his life were spent in New York as teacher and player. [R.5]

ARONSON, RUDOLPH (1856–1919). See Register, 6.

ARQUIER, JOSEPH (1763–1816). See Register, 3.

ARTHUR, ALFRED (Oct. 8, 1844, Pittsburgh : Nov. 20, 1918, Lakewood, O.), had his early schooling in Ashland, O., then studied in Boston with Baker, Howard and Arbuckle, and graduated at the Boston Music School in 1869. He also studied harmony and composition with Eichberg at the New England Conservatory. In 1869–71 he was tenor at the Church of the Advent in Boston, and then moved to Cleveland, where he remained until his death. In 1871–78 he was tenor-soloist at the Second Baptist Church, in 1878–90 conductor of the Sacred Music Society of the Pilgrim Church, in 1878–90 conductor of the Bach Society of the Woodland Avenue Church, in 1873–1902 conductor of the Cleveland Vocal Society. From 1885 he was founder and director of the Cleveland School of Music, and his last years were given entirely to it. He composed three operas (MS.), 'The Water-Carrier' (1875), 'The Roundheads and Cavaliers' (1878) and 'Adaline' (1879) ; songs and church-music. He published Progressive Vocal Studies, 1887, Album of Vocal Studies, 1888, Technical Exercises for Soprano or Tenor (Schmidt), 74 Lessons in Voice-Training (Presser), 40 Vocal Art-Studies for Soprano and Elementary Theory of Music (not yet out). [R.5]

ASHMALL, WILLIAM E. (b. 1860). See Register, 7.

ASHTON, JOSEPH NICKERSON (Sept. 7, 1868, Salem, Mass.), secured his A.B. from Brown University in 1891 and his A.M. from Harvard in 1893. He began to teach in Boston in 1895 and the same year became instructor in musical theory and history at Brown University and in 1898–1904 was associate-professor there. In 1907–08 he was acting-professor of music at Wellesley College. Since 1907 he has been music-director at Abbot Academy, Andover, Mass., and in 1908–12 was also director and organist at Phillips Academy there. In 1905 he succeeded Goetschius as organist of the First Parish Church in Brookline, Mass. He has devoted much time and attention to music as a college-study and to church-music. He edited a Hymn Book for Schools and Colleges, 1913,

and has published The History of the Salem Athenæum, Salem, Mass., 1810–1910. He is a trustee of this latter institution. [R.8]

ASPLUND, JOHN (d. 1807). See TUNE-BOOKS, 1793.

ASSOCIATION OF PRESIDENTS AND PAST PRESIDENTS OF STATE AND NATIONAL MUSIC TEACHERS' ASSOCIATIONS, THE, was organized in 1916 under the lead of Liborius Semmann of Milwaukee. Its object is to promote united action to standardize instruction, to publish a joint periodical for the several associations, to advocate music as a major subject in public schools, with credit for outside work in praxis, to work for a National School of Music, etc. It has published five annual reports, in the third of which are requirements for certificates as 'licentiate,' 'associate' and 'fellow.' The president for 1919–20 is David A. Clippinger of Chicago, and the secretary Arthur L. Manchester of Mexico, Mo.

ASTOR PLACE OPERA HOUSE, THE, erected in 1847, was the first suitable opera-house in New York. In 1847–48 it was managed by Sanquirico and Salvatore Patti (father of the singer), in 1848–49 by Edward R. Fry (brother of W. H. Fry, the composer), and after 1848 by Maretzek. It was supported by a subscription for five years, but competition was so strong that in 1852 it was given up. The building became the Mercantile Library. See Krehbiel, Chapters of Opera, pp. 14–5, 45ff., and article by Saerchinger in 'The Musical Quarterly,' January, 1920, pp. 88–9.

ATHERTON, PERCY LEE (Sept. 25, 1871, Boston), was graduated from Harvard in 1893 with honors in music, and then proceeded to the Munich Conservatory, where he spent two years under Rheinberger and Thuille. In 1896 he studied with Boise in Berlin, in 1900 with Sgambati in Rome and later with Widor in Paris. He has composed the comic opera 'The Heir Apparent,' text by Alfred Raymond (1888–90) ; 'The Maharaja,' an Oriental opéra comique, text by Raymond (1897–1900) ; a comic opera as yet unnrmed (1918–19) ; the symphonic poem 'Noon in the Forest' and several orchestral sketches ; two sonatas, a suite, and smaller pieces for violin and piano ; a suite for flute and piano ; many piano-pieces ; choruses, part-songs, song-cycles and about 100 solo songs. [R.8]

'ATONEMENT OF PAN, THE.' No. 10 of [the 'Grove-Plays' of the San Francisco Bohemian Club, produced in 1912. The text is by Joseph D. Redding and the music by Henry K. Hadley. The title-rôle was taken by Bispham.

ATWELL, THOMAS H. See TUNE-BOOKS, 1794.

AUDITORIUM, THE, in Chicago, is a complex building, including an opera-house, a hotel and numerous offices. Its erection was due to an association formed in 1886, of which Ferdinand W. Peck, a public-spirited man of wealth, was president. The building was dedicated on Dec. 9, 1889, with ceremonies that included Dubois' 'Fantaisie Triomphale,' La Tombelle's 'Fantaisie de Concert,' Gleason's 'Festival Ode,' several oratorio choruses and songs by Patti. The opera-house is one of the largest (over 4000 seats) and best-equipped in the world. From the first, especially under the efficient management of Milward Adams (till 1910), it has been famous as the headquarters not only for opera-seasons, but for every variety of superior concert.

AUDITORIUM, THE, in Milwaukee, is an extensive building for exhibition and concert purposes, erected in 1909. The main hall has a seating capacity of 10,000, and there are six other halls. The Auditorium Orchestra of 45–50 players was organized in 1909 to give popular symphony concerts on Sunday afternoons. Until 1913 there were various conductors and the enterprise was supported by popular subscription. Since 1913 the conductor has been Hermann A. Zeitz, and the city has appropriated about $4000 annually to cover deficits in receipts. The average number of concerts is sixteen each season.

AUDSLEY, GEORGE ASHDOWN (Sept. 6, 1838, Elgin, Scotland), was educated as an architect and followed that profession in Elgin until 1856. He then moved to Liverpool and became noted by designing many important public and private buildings. Since 1892 he has worked in the United States, adding to his reputation as architect, decorator and author. As early as 1865 he became interested in organs and organ-construction, the first result being the construction, by himself, of a house-organ of his own. This instrument, unique in specification and arrangement, earned the approval of Saint-Saëns, Hollins and others, and recitals were given upon it by distinguished players. In 1886–88 he published a series of articles on organ-making in 'The English Mechanic and World of Science,' and later gave a course of lectures, advocating flexibility and expression in all the divisions, manual or pedal, of the instrument. His large work is *The Art of Organ-Building*, 2 vols., 1905, and he has added *The Organ of the Twentieth Century*, 1919, a manual of 'the science and art of tonal-appointment and divisional-apportionment with compound expression, and a treatise on *Organ Stops*, 1920. The scheme of the large organ at the Louisiana Purchase Exposition at St. Louis, 1904, was made by him. He is author

and joint-author of over twenty works on architecture, art and industry. [R.9]

AUER, LEOPOLD (June 7, 1845, Veszprém, Hungary). See article in Vol. i. 130. In May, 1917, he went to Norway for a vacation, but could not return to Petrograd because of chaotic political and social conditions. He decided to visit America, and reached New York in February, 1918. After giving recitals in New York, Boston, Philadelphia and Chicago, he located in New York, where he has since taught privately. He has lately revised and edited many old and new violin-works, composed new cadenzas to numerous concertos and made many transcriptions (being published by Carl Fischer). Among his many successful pupils may be named Elman, Zimbalist, Kathleen Parlow, Eddy Brown, Heifetz, Seidel and Rosen. [R.10]

AUERBACH, NANNETTE, née Falk (about 1838, Danzig, Germany), came with her husband to Baltimore in 1867 and on Jan. 18, 1868, appeared as pianist at a Peabody Concert. Her striking ability led to her engagement as teacher at the Peabody Conservatory in 1871, where she continued until 1881, highly regarded by her pupils (among whom was Harold Randolph, the present head of the Conservatory) and frequently heard in public. As indicating the solidity of her equipment, it is said that she had at instant command not only all the Beethoven Sonatas, but the whole of the 'Well-Tempered Clavichord,' the latter in any key. It is said that she was still living in 1917. [R.5]

'AURORA.' An opera by Ettore Panizza, produced in 1908 at Buenos Aires.

AUSTIN, Mrs. See Register, 3.

AUSTIN, JOHN TURNELL (b. 1869) and **BASIL GEORGE** (b. 1874). See below and Register, 7.

AUSTIN, T. MERRILL. See COLLEGES, 3 (Monmouth C., Ill.).

AUSTIN ORGAN COMPANY, THE, of Hartford, Conn., was organized in 1899 to make instruments under the patents of John T. Austin and Basil G. Austin. Chief among these is the 'Universal Wind-Chest,' which is described in Vol. iii. 553–4 (and see i. 291), but to this have been added many other novel and ingenious mechanical devices. The Company has an extensive factory, equipped with the most modern appliances. They have made about 900 organs, including one five-manual (Medinah Temple, Chicago) and over 60 four-manual.

AUTOMATIC APPLIANCES. The reference in Vol. i. 135–6, to the development of mechanical music-making would need to be greatly extended if completeness of statement were here possible. The number of devices that have been worked out by American inventors is not only large, but constantly growing. Some general points about the tendency of invention are set down under PLAYER-PIANO and PHONOGRAPH.

AUTOPIANO COMPANY, THE, of New York, began business in 1904 and was incorporated in 1905 (capital, $1,000,000). It was one of the first firms to devise and put upon the market a successful player-piano (as distinct from a piano-player), and its business has increased so that it now claims to have the largest factory in the world solely devoted to making player-pianos. This building is on the Hudson River between 51st and 52d Streets. The firm has made over 70,000 instruments and ten million rolls.

AVERY, STANLEY R. (Dec. 14, 1879, Yonkers, N. Y.), studied organ in New York with Heinroth and Macfarlane, composition and orchestration with MacDowell and choir-training with Stubbs, and in Berlin he continued organ with Grunicke and composition with Pfitzner. In 1896–1910 he was organist at St. Andrew's in Yonkers, and has since been at St. Mark's in Minneapolis, where the vesper services are musically important. He has regularly given cantatas and oratorios, and plans are being made for annual festivals by the combined choirs of the city. He is president of the Civic Music League, director of music at the Northrop Collegiate School, organist for the Sunday evening services at the Auditorium and conductor of civic pageants. His published works include a Te Deum in E-flat (congregational) (Summy), an Evening Service in D-flat, 'Shout the Glad Tidings' (Schirmer), 'In Loud, Exalted Strain,' 'How Sweet the Name' (Presser) and other anthems, carols and choruses; many songs, such as 'Song of the Timber-Trail' (Ditson), 'Two Love-Songs' (Schirmer), 'I love thee still' (Presser), etc.; the operetta 'The Merry Mexican' (Schirmer); a Scherzo in G for organ (Summy); a Scherzo in G minor for violin (Ditson); and several piano-pieces. He has also the one-act opera 'The Quartet,' the comic opera 'Katrina,' incidental music to Josephine Peabody's 'The Piper,' two musical comedies, the overture 'The Taming of the Shrew,' the orchestral scherzo 'A Joyous Prelude,' and one or two chamber-works. [R.8]

AYRES, CECILE. See HORVATH.

AYRES, EUGENE EDMOND (1859–1920). See Register, 7.

AYRES, FREDERIC (Mar. 17, 1876, Binghamton, N. Y.), had his general education in Binghamton and at Cornell University. In 1897–1901 he studied composition with Kelley, but spent part of 1899 with Foote in Boston. For some years he has made his home in Colorado Springs, and has taught theory and composition, lectured and written articles on musical subjects. His compositions include the overture 'From the Plains,' op. 14; a string-quartet, op. 16; a sonata for violin and piano, op. 15; two trios for piano, violin and 'cello, opp. 13 (Stahl) and 17; two piano-fugues, op. 9 (Stahl), 'The Open Road,' op. 11, 'The Voice of the City,' op. 12, and 'Moonlight,' op. 12, all for piano; the song-cycle 'The Seeonee Wolves,' op. 10 (Schirmer); a 'Book of Mother Goose Melodies,' op. 7; and songs, opp. 2–6 (Stahl, Schirmer). [R.9]

'AZARA.' An opera in three acts by John K. Paine, completed about 1900, but not performed except in concert-form (1906). The libretto, by the composer, is based on the old French romance of Aucassin and Nicolette. It was published in Germany in 1906 with German translation by Carl Pflueger.

'AZORA, DAUGHTER OF MONTE-ZUMA.' A three-act opera by Henry K. Hadley, produced by the Chicago Opera Company on Dec. 26, 1917, under the direction of the composer.

B

BABCOCK, ALPHEUS and LEWIS (d. 1817). See Register, 3.

BABCOCK, S. See TUNE-BOOKS, 1795.

BACHMANN, ALBERTO ABRAHAM (b. 1875). See Register, 10.

BACON, GEORGE (d. 1856). See Register, 3.

BACON PIANO COMPANY, THE, of New York, makers of uprights, grands and player-pianos, have had a long history. In 1789 John Jacob Astor, dealer in furs, began importing pianos from England, simply to make his trading reciprocal. In 1802 this importing business passed to John and Michael Paff and then to William Dubois. In 1821 the later was joined by Robert Stodard (see Register, 3), and they began manufacturing. In 1836 the firm was reorganized as Dubois, Bacon & Chambers, George Bacon having come in. In 1841 it became Bacon & Raven, and in 1856 Raven & Bacon, including Francis Bacon, who was George Bacon's son. The present president is W. P. H. Bacon, who represents still another generation.

BAERMANN, CARL, JR. (July 9, 1839, Munich, Germany : Jan. 17, 1913, Newton, Mass.). See article in Vol. i. 162. He held the title of Royal Professor from the king of Bavaria. His work in Boston from 1881 earned him the greatest esteem. Among his best-known pupils are Mrs. Beach and F. S. Converse. A series of twelve piano-studies are published by André of Offenbach; other piano-pieces, including a suite, are in manuscript. A festival-march for orchestra has been played in Munich. See Elson, *Hist. of American Music*, pp. 287–9. [R.7]

BAIER, VICTOR (b. 1861). See Register, 7.

BAILEY, ARCHIBOLD A. See STATE UNIVERSITIES (Iowa State C.).

BAILEY, DANIEL (1725?–1799). See TUNE-BOOKS, 1764.

BAILEY, HERBERT MEAD (b. 1886). See COLLEGES, 3 (Huron C., S. D.).

BAIRD, T. D. See TUNE-BOOKS, 1816.

BAKER, BENJAMIN FRANKLIN (July 16, 1811, Wenham, Mass. : March 11, 1889, Boston), succeeded Mason as teacher of music in the Boston public schools in 1841–47, having been for ten years a singer or director in church-choirs in Salem and Boston. He was also active in 'convention' work. He was vice-president of the Handel and Haydn Society in 1841–47, and soloist at numerous concerts. In 1851 he founded the Boston Music School, becoming principal and head of the vocal department. At the dissolution of this school in 1868 he retired from active musical work. He wrote three cantatas, 'The Storm King,' 'The Burning Ship' and 'Camillus, the Roman Conqueror,' and other vocal compositions. He compiled several volumes of glees and anthems, was author of *Thorough-Bass and Harmony*, 1870, and edited the 'Boston Musical Journal.' See TUNE-BOOKS, 1842. [R.3]

BAKER, E. H. See TUNE-BOOKS, 1846.

BAKER, THEODORE (June 3, 1851, New York), was educated in New York and in or near Boston, early serving as organist in Concord, Mass. After a short business experience, in 1871–2 he journeyed across the continent to Olympia, Wash., looking for a suitable opening for a career. Not finding this, in 1874 he went to Germany for study, first under Oscar Paul at Leipzig and from 1878 at the University there, receiving the degree of Ph.D. in 1881. His thesis (title below) was based upon investigations made in 1880 among the Seneca Indians of New York State, when he was initiated into the tribe and given remarkable facilities for observing tribal songs and dances, supplemented by further researches at the Indian Training School at Carlisle, Pa., and extended reading in the literature of early exploration and settlement. This thesis was the first thoroughgoing study of Indian music and marked an epoch in both matter and method. Shown by Gilbert to MacDowell after 1890, it provided the latter with suggestions for his 'Indian Suite.' Baker lived in Germany until 1890. Since 1892 he has been with the firm of G. Schirmer in New York as literary editor. Besides putting the stamp of his culture upon thousands of its publications, he has translated many works of importance and edited two masterly dictionaries.

His works include *Ueber die Musik der nordamerikanischen Wilden*, 1882, *Dictionary of Musical Terms*, 1895 (18th ed., 1918), *Pronouncing Pocket-Manual of Musical Terms*, 1905, *Biographical Dictionary of Musicians*, 1900, supplement, 1905 (3rd ed. 1919), *The Musician's Calendar and Birthday-Book*, 1915–17. Translations: O. Paul, *Manual of Harmony*, 1885, L. Bussler, *Elements of Notation and Harmony*, 1890, *Elementary Harmony*, 1891, J. C. Lobe, *Catechism of Composition*, 1891, A. Kullak, *The Æsthetics of Pianoforte-Playing*, 1892, S. Jadassohn, *Manual of Harmony*, 1893, C. F. Weitzmann, *History of Pianoforte-Playing*, 1893, F. Kullak, *Beethoven's Piano-Playing*, 1901, M. Brée, *The Groundwork of the Leschetizky Method*, 1902, S. Jadassohn, *Manual of Single, Double and Quadruple Counterpoint*, 1902, G. B. Lamperti, *The Technics of Bel Canto*, 1905, M. Loewengard, *Harmony Modernized*, 1910, F. Busoni, *A New Æsthetic of Music*, 1911, E. F. Richter, *Manual of Harmony*, 1912, V. d'Indy, *Beethoven*, 1913, P. Bona, *Complete Method for Rhythmical Articulation*, O. Klauwell, *On Musical Execution*. With two exceptions all the above were published by Schirmer. Among translated articles, mention should be made of many prepared for 'The Musical Quarterly.' [R.5]

BAKLANOV, GEORGE (b. 1882). See Register, 10.

‡BALAKIREV, MILY ALEXEIEVITCH (Jan. 2, 1837, Nishni Novgorod, Russia : May 28, 1910, Petrograd). Add to article in Vol. i. 168–9, that his last works include a second symphony, in D minor (1909), and a piano-concerto. See Montagu-Nathan, *Hist. of Russian Music*, pp. 63–73, and other works on Russian music.

BALATKA, HANS (1827–1899). See Register, 4.

BALDWIN, RALPH LYMAN (Mar. 27, 1872, Easthampton, Mass.), although first preparing as organist and composer, has also become a leader in public-school music, active in promoting higher standards of teaching and musical material and in obtaining credit for music-work in high schools. He graduated from Williston Seminary in 1890 and studied in Boston with Chadwick, Emery, Heindl and Elson. After being organist in Easthampton and Northampton, Mass., in 1904 he became musical director at the Fourth Congregational Church in Hartford and in 1917 moved to the Immanuel Congregational Church there. He was music-supervisor in Northampton in 1899–1904 and has since held a similar position in Hartford. He directed the Vocal Club of Northampton in 1894–1904, and since 1906 the Choral Club of Hartford. Since 1900 he has been one of the proprietors of the Institute of Music Pedagogy at Northampton (summer-school), where he has trained a great number of supervisors. His organ-sonata, op. 10 (Schirmer) and his 'Burlesca e Melodia' (Schmidt) are popular on recital-programs, and he has published anthems and songs (Schmidt, Boston Music Co.) The light opera 'Wanita' has had amateur performances. Choruses for men's voices are still in manuscript. For school use he has published *Progressive Melodies*, *Progressive Songs*, and a series of ten pamphlets of *Standard Song Classics* (Ginn). [R.8]

BALDWIN, SAMUEL ATKINSON (Jan. 25, 1862, Lake City, Minn.), at fifteen was organist of the House of Hope Presbyterian Church in St. Paul. In 1884 he graduated from the Dresden Conservatory, where his teachers were Merkel for organ, Wüllner for composition and directing, Rieschbieter for harmony and counterpoint and Nicodé for piano. In 1886–89 he was organist at Plymouth Church in Chicago. He was then in St. Paul and Minneapolis as organist and conductor, founding choral societies in both cities. Coming to New York in 1895, he was organist at the Chapel of the Intercession till 1902 and then at Holy Trinity in Brooklyn till 1911. In 1907 he was appointed to the new chair of music at the College of the City of New York.

Here he instituted the Sunday and Wednesday afternoon organ-recitals which have become notable. About 700 of these recitals have been given, including toward 1000 different works of every school of organ-composition. The annual attendance has averaged about 70,000. He is a founder and fellow of the A. G. O. and was one of the ten Americans to play at the Columbian Exposition in Chicago in 1893. He also gave recitals at the St. Louis Exposition in 1904 and at San Francisco in 1915. His published compositions are songs, anthems and church-services. His unpublished works are mostly in larger forms, including a string-quartet; a piano-trio; the 18th Psalm and 'The Triumph of Love' for solo voices, chorus and orchestra; two concert-overtures, 'A Journey in Norway' and 'Frithjof and Ingeborg'; a symphony in C minor; and an orchestral suite, 'A Summer Idyl.' [R.6]

BALDWIN COMPANY, THE, of Cincinnati, organized in 1862, is the corporation that controls the Baldwin, Ellington, Howard, Hamilton and Monarch pianos. The Baldwin piano was awarded the Grand Prix at the Paris Exposition of 1900 and a similar prize at the St. Louis Exposition in 1904. The Baldwin type of player-piano is known as the 'Manualo.'

BALLANTINE, EDWARD (Aug. 8, 1886, Oberlin, O.), secured his general education at Springfield, Mass., and at Harvard, where he was a special student in 1903–07. Meanwhile he studied piano with Mary Regal, Edward Noyes and Mme. Hopekirk, and composition with Spalding and Converse. In 1907–09 he continued piano with Schnabel and Ganz in Berlin and composition with Rüfer. From 1912 he was instructor in theory at Harvard. In 1918 he enlisted as musician and was assigned as saxophone-player to the 1st Regt. Band at Vancouver Barracks, Wash., with the rank of sergeant. His song 'Retrospect' came out in the 'Harvard Musical Review,' April, 1913, and his piano-piece 'Morning' in December, 1913. His Prelude to 'The Delectable Forest' (Hagedorn) was first performed at the MacDowell Festival, Peterboro, N. H., in 1914; the Boston Symphony Orchestra played his symphonic poem 'The Eve of Saint Agnes' in January, 1917. These works are still in manuscript, as are more incidental pieces for Hagedorn's fairy-play for small orchestra and chorus of women's voices; the tone-poem 'The Awakening of the Woods'; an 'Overture to the Piper'; songs; and pieces for piano, violin and piano, and 'cello and piano. [R.10]

BALTIMORE SYMPHONY ORCHESTRA, THE, was established in 1916 by the municipality and is carried on by it. Its conductor is Gustav Strube. The number of players is 65, and seven concerts are usually given each year. Its repertory includes all standard symphonies and similar high-class orchestral works.

BALTZELL, WINTON JAMES (Dec. 18, 1864, Shiremanstown, Pa.), was the son of Rev. Isaiah Baltzell (1832–93), who from 1859 edited many collections of evangelistic and Sunday-school hymns and tunes. He was educated in Harrisburg, Pa., and at Lebanon Valley College at Annville, Pa., graduating in 1884. His early training in music, including elementary harmony, was largely self-directed. In 1886–88 he was proof-reader in the United Brethren Publishing House at Dayton, O., and studied with local teachers. In 1888–89, at the New England Conservatory, he came under Emery (harmony), Elson (theory), Mahr (violin) and Arthur Thayer (singing). He taught singing and harmony at Fredericksburg College (Pa.), harmony at Lebanon Valley College, and in 1889 privately at Lebanon, Pa. In 1890 he was in London, where Packer and Shakespeare were his teachers in singing, Bridge in composition and Lowden in organ. For three years he taught privately at Reading, Pa., and at Albright College, Myerstown, Pa., and pursued composition with Clarke at the University of Pennsylvania, where he was made Mus.B. in 1896. He was assistant-editor of 'The Etude' in 1897–99, teacher of history and theory at the Ohio Wesleyan University, Delaware, O., in 1899–1900; editor of 'The Etude' in 1900–07, editor of 'The Musician' in 1907–18, and since 1919 secretary of the National Academy of Music in New York, and associate-editor of the University Course of Music-Study. He is author of *A Complete History of Music*, 1905, and a *Biographical Dictionary of Musicians*, 1910, supplement, 1914. His published compositions include songs, part-songs and anthems. In manuscript are works in large form for orchestra, for chamber-ensemble and for chorus. [R.8]

BANJO. See Vol. i. 179–180, and add references to Stanley, *Catalogue of the Stearns Collection*, p. 166–7, and note in *The Art of Music*, iv. 296.

‡BANTOCK, GRANVILLE (Aug. 7, 1868, London, England). See article in Vol. i. 181. To the list of works add the tone-poems 'The Pierrot of the Minute' (1908), 'Dante and Beatrice' (1911) and 'The Hebridean Symphony' (1916); the choral symphony 'Atalanta in Calydon' (1912) and 'The Vanity of Vanities' (1914), a choral symphony a cappella; 'Omar Khayyám' (1906–07); 'Sea-Wanderers' (1907); 'Overture to a Greek Tragedy' (1911); the ballet 'The Enchanted Garden' (1916); the choral suite 'A Pageant of Human Life'; 'Ferishtah's Fancies,' thirteen lyrics for tenor and orchestra; music to 'Elektra'; many

choruses for men's, women's and mixed voices; three 'Dramatic Dances' for orchestra; and 'Scenes from the Scottish Highlands' for orchestra. He is engaged upon a 'Celtic Folk-Opera' (with Mrs. Kennedy Fraser), an opera, a 'Pagan Symphony' and a Ballet. In an article in 'The Musical Quarterly,' July, 1918, Antcliffe calls him 'the arch-experimentalist among British composers,' and claims that he 'has introduced the world of art, and particularly of British art, to new phases and new inspirations over which he has planted the British flag of his own music and that of his disciples.' Since 1908, in addition to his other duties, he has been professor of music at the University of Birmingham. See Anderton, *Granville Bantock*, London, 1915.

BARBOUR, FLORENCE, née Newell (Aug. 4, 1867, Providence, R. I.), pursued her study of piano and composition entirely in America. She has made frequent appearances as solo-pianist and in ensemble. She has written the words as well as the music of many of her songs, and personally draws and designs the cover-pages. Among her published compositions for piano are two suites, 'Venice' and 'A Day in Arcady,' seven 'Forest-Sketches,' five 'Nature-Pieces,' six 'Melodic Études,' and numerous detached pieces. Her songs make a long list. There are also anthems, choruses for women's voices and a 'Reverie' for strings and piano. 'Child-Land in Song and Rhythm' is published in two books. Her most recent works are 'Three Rossetti Lyrics,' a piano-suite, 'All in a Garden Fair,' a set of piano-studies, and new groups of songs. [R.8]

BARFORD, VERNON WEST (b. 1876). See Register, 8.

BARNABEE, HENRY CLAY (1833–1917). See Register, 4.

BARNES, EDWARD SHIPPEN (Sept. 14, 1887, Seabright, N. J.), began organ-study with Van Dyck at the Lawrenceville School, then studied composition at the Yale School of Music with Parker and organ with Jepson. After graduating at Yale in 1910 he continued his studies under d'Indy, Decaux and Vierne at the Schola Cantorum in Paris. Since 1911 he has been organist in New York, at first at the Chapel of the Incarnation and from 1912 at the Rutgers Presbyterian Church. In 1918–19 he was in the Naval Reserve. He has composed and published much for the organ, piano, and voice, with two church-cantatas and many anthems. His chief works include an organ 'Symphonie,' op. 18; two organ-suites, opp. 23 and 26; a 'Fantasia' for organ and chorus, op. 27; and the sacred cantatas 'The Comforter' and 'Remember now thy Creator.' He is author of *Bach for Beginners* (Boston Music Co.) and *A Method of Organ-Playing* (in press). [R.9]

BARNHART, HARRY HORNER (b. 1874). See Register, 9.

BARRAJA, ENRICO (b. 1885). See Register, 10.

BARRÈRE, GEORGES (Oct. 31, 1876, Bordeaux, France), studied flute in 1889–95 at the Paris Conservatory with Altès and Taffanel, harmony with Schwarz, Pugno and Grandjany, winning a first prize in flute-playing. From 1897 he was solo flutist at the Colonne Concerts and the Opéra. He also taught at the Schola Cantorum, and in 1895 founded La Société Moderne d'Instruments à Vent, which brought out over 100 new compositions. Coming to America in 1905, he joined the New York Symphony Society and became teacher at the Institute of Musical Art. In 1910 he founded the Barrère Ensemble (wind-instruments), in 1913 the Trio de Lutèce (flute, harp and 'cello) and in 1914 the Little Symphony (ordinarily three violins, viola, 'cello, bass, flute, oboe, clarinet, horn, bassoon and tympani). As soloist and director he has become well known throughout the country and has introduced many interesting works. He is an Officer of the French Academy. He has written a 'Nocturne' for flute and piano and the song 'Chanson d'Automne' (both Schirmer) and has edited an Arioso by Bach for flute and piano and Altès' 26 Études for flute. [R.9]

BARRÈRE ENSEMBLE, THE. See preceding article.

BARRIENTOS, MARIA (Mar. 10, 1885, Barcelona, Spain), graduated from the Barcelona Conservatory at twelve, having studied piano, violin and composition. She won medals for violin-playing when only eleven, and composed and conducted a symphony at twelve. At fourteen, after lessons with Bennet, she made her début as soprano at the Teatro de las Novedades in 'L'Africaine.' Within a year she also appeared in Milan as Lakmé. She was engaged at La Scala, and sang at principal theaters in Italy, Russia, France, England, Germany, Austria and South America till 1913. She then retired for three years, but was engaged for the Metropolitan Opera House in New York, making her first appearance as Lucia in 1916, and has since sung there. Her répertoire includes 'I Puritani,' 'La Sonnambula,' 'Il Barbiere di Siviglia,' 'Lucia,' 'Don Pasquale,' 'L'Elisir d'Amore,' 'La Traviata,' 'Rigoletto,' 'Les Pêcheurs de Perles,' 'Linda,' 'Dinorah,' 'Lakmé,' 'Mignon,' 'Hamlet' and 'Martha.' [R.10]

BARROWS, FRANK ELIOT. See COLLEGES, 3 (Simpson C., Iowa).

BARSTOW, VERA (b. 1893). See Register, 10.

BARTHOLOMEW, EDWARD FRY (b. 1846). See Register, 8.

BARTLETT, HOMER NEWTON (Dec. 28, 1846, Olive, N. Y. : Apr. 3, 1920, Hoboken, N. J.), was descended from Josiah Bartlett, a signer of the Declaration of Independence and the first governor of New Hampshire. After general training at the Ellenville Academy and under tutors in New York, from 1861 he studied piano with S. B. Mills and Emil Guyon, organ and composition with Max Braun and O. F. Jacobsen. As early as 1855 he played in public and in 1856 began to compose. From about 1860 he was organist in New York, his longest service being in the Madison Avenue Baptist Church, where he remained nearly thirty-five years. He was a founder of the A. G. O. and served terms as president of the N. A. O. and vice-president of the New York Manuscript Society, besides other posts of honor. Not long ago the Fraternity of American Musicians celebrated the fiftieth anniversary of his wedding with a banquet, and in 1918, when the Hunt Memorial Hall was dedicated in Ellenville, N. Y., a Bartlett program was given, with his violin-concerto as the chief item, played by Miss Gunn and the composer. From the long list of his compositions — nearly 250 in number — may be mentioned the 3-act opera 'La Vallière' (1887) and the operetta 'Magic Hours'; the symphonic poem 'Apollo,' based upon the Iliad, the Concerto in G and Ballade for violin and orchestra, the 'Légende' for orchestra; 'Khamsin,' a concert-aria for tenor and orchestra (rewritten in 1908); Toccata in E, Suite in C, 'Festival Hymn,' 'De Profundis,' and 'Méditation Sérieuse,' all for organ; three piano-ballades, 'Gavotte Concertante,' 'Barcarolle' and some études; besides many anthems, songs, etc. Several of his piano-pieces are based on Japanese themes. See Hughes, Contemporary American Composers, pp. 317–23, and The Art of Music, 4. 383–4. [R.5]

BARTLETT, JAMES CARROLL (b. 1850). See Register, 6.

BARTLETT, MARO LOOMIS (1847–1919). See Register, 5.

BASSETT, FRANKLIN (Apr. 7, 1852, Wheeling, W. Va. : Mar. 7, 1915, Pasadena, Cal.), studied at Leipzig under Reinecke, Plaidy and Jadassohn. While there an attack of pianist's neuritis destroyed his hopes of a concert career and set him searching for a technical system less dangerous to the hand than those in use. In 1877 he established himself in Cleveland and from 1882 was one of the directors of the Cleveland Conservatory and organist of the First Methodist Church. His mode of instruction aroused general interest and he soon had many brilliant piano-pupils whose devotion to his personality and principles was a remarkable tribute. He was considered the first exponent in Ohio of a modern system of piano-technique. His physical misfortune restricted his concert-work as pianist to chamber-music. Here also he proved a pioneer and, with the aid of local string-players, gave first performances in Cleveland of the quartets and quintets of Schumann, Brahms and others. He was a founder of the A. G. O., and, besides his first position, 'was organist at the Plymouth Congregational and St. Paul's Episcopal Churches. He was the first to give series of organ-recitals in Cleveland. [R.7]

BASSFORD, WILLIAM KIPP (April 23, 1839, New York : Dec. 22, 1902, New York), having studied under Samuel Jackson, was a successful pianist at an early age and for a time made extensive concert-tours. Dislike of travel caused him to settle in New York as organist and teacher of many noted pupils. His last organ-position was at Calvary Church, East Orange, N. J. His compositions include the two-act opera 'Cassilda', a mass in E-flat, church-music, many songs and piano-pieces of the salon type. He was engaged by Mme. Wallace to complete Wallace's unfinished opera 'Estrella' (see Vol. v. 425). [R.4]

BATCHELDER, JOHN C. (b. 1852). See Register, 6.

‡BATH, HUBERT (Nov. 6, 1883, Barnstaple, England). See article in Vol. v. 611. He conducted opera for the Thomas Quinlan Company on its world-tour in 1912–13, and has since conducted in London, where he has charge of the opera-class at the Guildhall School of Music and is musical adviser to the London County Council. To the list of works add 'Two Sea-Sketches' (1909) and an 'African Suite' for orchestra (1915); the cantatas 'The Jackdaw of Rheims' (1911), 'Look at the Clock' (1911) and 'The Wake of O'Connor' (1914); and numerous songs and instrumental pieces.

BATTELL, ROBBINS (1819–1895). See Register, 4, and LITCHFIELD COUNTY CHORAL UNION.

'BATTLE-HYMN OF THE REPUBLIC, THE.' The title of a poem by Julia Ward Howe (1819–1910), beginning 'Mine eyes have seen the glory of the coming of the Lord,' written in 1861 in Washington in order to supply better words for a march-song popular among the Union troops. The music is supposed to have originated in South Carolina — possibly a Negro melody. The original words began 'Say, brothers, will you meet us.' See Elson, Hist. of American Music, pp. 156–61.

BAUER, A. O. See COLLEGES, 2 (Winthrop C., S. C.).

BAUER, HAROLD (Apr. 28, 1873, New Malden, near London, England), began his career as a violinist. He studied with Pollitzer, at nine played in public, and for several years gave concerts with his two sisters. In 1892

he gave up the violin for the piano. He had some lessons from Paderewski, but is largely self-taught. He made his début as pianist in Paris in 1893 and a tour of Russia followed. He has given recitals and played with orchestras in the leading cities of Europe, including Spain and Sweden, and in South America, and has made many tours in the United States. His first appearance in the latter was with the Boston Symphony Orchestra on Dec. 1, 1900, playing Brahms' Concerto in D minor. He is distinguished as an ensemble-player, and has participated with the leading organizations and soloists in innumerable performances of classic and modern music. As soloist his répertoire is almost unlimited. His unhackneyed programs present the entire range of piano-music, and he plays works for the harpsichord with the same enjoyment and success as works by the most modern composers. He has been especially active in the presentation of Brahms, Schumann and Franck. Some of his views on piano-playing and music are set forth in the Introduction he contributed to The Art of Music, Vol. vii. As teacher he has influenced many players of the younger generation, and in recent years he has edited and revised some valuable piano-music. He was the prime mover in organizing the Beethoven Association, which began its performances of rarely-given chamber-music by Beethoven in the fall of 1919 at Æolian Hall in New York. The distinguished artists who assist in these programs contribute their services, and the proceeds are to be devoted at first to the publishing of Krehbiel's translation of Thayer's Beethoven and later to the relief of needy musicians. [R.9]

BAUR, CLARA (d. 1912). See Register, 5.

‡BAX, ARNOLD E. TREVOR (Nov. 8, 1883, London, England.) See article in Vol. v. 612. To the list of works add the symphonic poems 'Into the Twilight' (1908), 'In the Fairy Hills' (1909) and 'Christmas Eve on the Mountains' (1911); 'Three Pieces' for orchestra (1912); the choruses with orchestra 'Fatherland' (1907) and 'The Enchanted Summer' (1909); the two-act ballet 'King Kojata' (1911); the 'Festival Overture' (1909); two string-quartets, a piano-trio and a sonata for violin and piano; piano-pieces and songs.

'BAY PSALM-BOOK, THE.' The common name for the metrical version of the Psalms prepared by Revs. Mather, Weld and Eliot for the churches of the colony of Massachusetts Bay and published in 1640, being the first book (in the proper sense) printed in the colonies. It had extensive use not only in America, but in England, and passed through numerous editions (27th in 1762). Of the first edition only eight copies are known, but it has been reprinted in facsimile

(1862). Not until the 9th edition, 1698, was music added and then only 12–14 tunes. See TUNE-BOOKS and numerous books upon the history of hymnody. Elson, *Hist. of American Music*, pp. 6–7, gives three pages in facsimile, and Fisher, *Old Music in Boston*, p. 4, reproduces two tunes.

BEACH, AMY MARCY, née Cheney (Sept. 5, 1867, Henniker, N. H.). See article in Vol. i. 210. She has been an active concert-pianist since 1885, appearing with the Boston Symphony Orchestra and other orchestras, as well as with the Kneisel Quartet and similar organizations. In 1888, playing with the Boston Orchestra, she added an original cadenza to Beethoven's C minor Concerto. Her first compositions were a group of songs in 1884. Her first work in large form was the Mass in E-flat, given by the Handel and Haydn Society in 1892. Her Scena and Aria from Schiller's 'Maria Stuart' was first sung by Mrs. Alvès with the New York Symphony Society in 1892. In 1893 she was asked to provide a Festival Jubilate for the opening of the Columbian Exposition at Chicago; in 1898 also a 'Song of Welcome' for the Trans-Mississippi Exposition at Omaha; and in 1915 a 'Panama Hymn' for the Panama-Pacific Exposition at San Francisco. Her 'Gaelic' Symphony was first given from manuscript by the Boston Orchestra in 1896, and has become frequent on the programs of other orchestras. Her Concerto in C-sharp minor she brought out in 1900 with the Boston Orchestra, and she has since played it often both in America and abroad. After the death of her husband in 1910 she spent four years in Europe, where she was heard in many cities, notably Rome, Munich, Dresden, Hamburg, Leipzig and Berlin. Her 'Gaelic' Symphony was performed in Hamburg and Leipzig, and her piano-quintet and violin-sonata also won recognition. In recent years her songs, church-music and piano-works have received favorable attention. The full list of her works is as follows:

Piano —
op. 3 Cadenza for Beethoven's C minor Concerto.
   4 Valse-Caprice.
   6 Ballade in D-flat.
  15 Four Sketches — 'In Autumn,' 'Phantoms,' 'Dreaming,' 'Fireflies.'
  22 Bal Masque; Waltz.
  25 Children's Carnival — 'Promenade,' 'Columbine,' 'Pantalon,' 'Pierrot and Pierrette,' 'Secrets,' 'Harlequin.'
  28 'Barcarolle,' 'Menuet Italien,' 'Danse des Fleurs.'
  36 Children's Album — Minuet, Gavotte, Waltz, March, Polka.
  — Transcription of Richard Strauss' 'Serenade.'
  54 'Scottish Legend,' 'Gavotte Fantastique.'
  60 Variations on Balkan Themes.

op. 64 Eskimo Pieces—'Arctic Night,' 'Returning Winter,' 'Exiles,' 'With Dog-Teams.'
  65 Suite Française, 'Les Rêves de Columbine' — 'La Fée de la Fontaine,' 'Le Prince Gracieux,' 'Valse Amoureuse, 'Sous les Étoiles,' 'Danse d'Arlequin.' '
  81 Prelude and Fugue.
  47 Six Duets, 'Summer Dreams.'
  45 Concerto in C-sharp minor, with orchestra.
  67 Quintet in F-sharp minor, with string-quartet.

Violin —
op. 23 Romance.
  34 Sonata in A minor.
  40 'La Captive' (G-string), 'Berceuse,' 'Mazurka.'
  55 Invocation.

Orchestra —
op. 23 'Gaelic' Symphony in E minor.

Songs —
op. 1 'With Violets,' 'The Four Brothers,' 'Jeune Fille et Jeune Fleur,' 'Ariette.'
  2 'Twilight,' 'When Far from Her,' 'Empress of Night.'
  11 'Dark is the Night,' 'The Western Wind,' 'The Blackbird.'
  12 'Wilt thou be my dearie?' 'Ye banks and braes of bonnie Doon,' 'My luve is like a red, red rose.'
  13 'A Hymn of Trust.'
  14 'The Summer Wind,' 'The Secret,' 'Sweetheart, sigh no more,' 'The Thrush.'
  18 Scena and Aria, 'Wandering Clouds,' from Schiller's 'Maria Stuart.'
  19 'For me the jasmine-buds unfold,' 'Ecstasy,' 'Golden Gates.'
  20 Villanelle, 'Across the World.'
  21 'Chanson d'Amour,' 'Exstase,' 'Elle et Moi.'
  26 'My Star,' 'Just for This,' 'Spring,' 'Wouldn't that be queer?'
  29 'Within my Heart,' 'The Wandering Knight,' 'Sleep, Little Darling,' 'Haste, O Beloved.'
  35 'Night,' 'Alone,' 'With Thee,' 'Forget-me-not.'
  37 Shakespeare Songs — 'O Mistress Mine,' 'Take, O take those lips away,' 'Fairy Lullaby.'
  41 'Anita,' 'Thy Beauty,' 'Forgotten.'
  43 Burns Songs — 'Dearie,' 'Scottish Cradle-Song,' 'O were my love yon lilac fair,' 'Far Awa',' 'My Lassie.'
  44 Browning Songs — 'The year's at the spring,' 'Ah, love, but a day,' 'I send my heart up to thee.'
  48 'Come, ah, come,' 'Good-Morning,' 'Good-Night,' 'Canzonetta.'
  51 'Silent Love,' 'We Three,' 'June,' 'For my Love.'
  53 Aria, 'Jephtha's Daughter.'
  56 'Autumn-Song,' 'Go not too far,' 'I know not how to find the spring,' 'Shena Van.'
  62 'When soul is joined to soul.'
  68 'After.'
  69 Mother-Songs — 'Baby,' 'Hush, baby dear.'
  71 'A Prelude,' 'O Sweet Content,' 'An Old Love-Story.'
  72 'An Old Prayer,' 'Flowers and Fate.'
  73 'With Granny,' 'The Children's Thanks,' 'Separation,' 'The Lotos-Isles.'

MRS. H. H. A. BEACH

op. 75 Children's Songs — 'The Candy-Lion,'
       'A Thanksgiving Fable,' 'Dolladine,'
       'The Prayer of a Tired Child.'
  77 'I,' 'Wind o' the Westland.'
  79 'Meadow-Larks,' 'A Night-Song at
       Amalfi,' 'In Blossom-Time.'
  10 Duets — 'A Canadian Boat-Song,' 'The
       Night Sea,' 'Sea-Songs.'
  61 Duet, 'Give me not love.'

Part-Songs —
Men's voices:
  op. 19 'Ecstasy.'
Women's Voices:
  op. 9 'Little Brown Bee.'
    31 Flower-Songs — 'Over hill, over dale,'
       'Come unto these yellow sands,'
       'Through the house give glimmering
       light.'
    57 'Only a Song,' 'One Summer Day.'
    — 'An Indian Lullaby.'
    82 'Dusk in June.'
Mixed Voices:
  op. 42 'A Song of Welcome.'
    49 'A Song of Liberty.'
    52 'A Hymn of Freedom' ('My country,
       'tis of thee').
    74 'Panama Hymn.'

Anthems —
op. 7 ' Praise the Lord, all ye nations.'
   8 'Nunc Dimittis,' ' Peace I leave with you,'
       'With Prayer and Supplication.'
  24 'Bethlehem' (Christmas).
  27 'Alleluia ! Christ is risen ' (Easter).
  33 'Teach me Thy way.'
  38 'Peace on Earth' (Christmas).
  50 Motet a cappella, 'Help us, O God.'
  63 Service in A.
  74 'All hail the power of Jesus' name '
       (Panama Hymn arranged).
  76 'Thou knowest, Lord.'
  78 Four Canticles.

Concerted Works —
op. 5 Mass in E-flat.
  16 'The Minstrel and the King' (men's
       voices).
  17 Festival Jubilate.
  30 'The Rose of Avontown' (women's
       voices).
  46 Wedding Cantata, 'Sylvania.'
  59 'The Sea-Fairies' (women's voices).
  66 'The Chambered Nautilus' (women's
       voices).

In Manuscript —
op. 70 Suite for two pianos, 'Iverniana.'
  80 Variations for flute with string-quartet.
  — Tyrolean Valse-Fantaisie.

See Goetschius, *Mrs. H. H. A. Beach*, 1906,
Hughes, *Contemporary American Composers*,
pp. 425–32, and Elson, *Hist. of American
Music*, pp. 294–305. [R.7]

BEACH, JOHN PARSONS (Oct. 11, 1877,
Gloversville, N. Y.), is a graduate of the New
England Conservatory in Boston and a pupil
of Johns, Chadwick, and Loeffler. He went
to the Northwestern Conservatory in Minneapolis in 1900 as teacher of piano, and also taught
in the University of Minnesota. In 1904–07
he was teaching in New Orleans, and then
returned to Boston for three years. In 1910
he went to Paris, studying composition with
Gédalge and piano with Bauer. For several

years he has spent the summers at Asolo, Italy,
and during the war was engaged in activities
on the Italian front. His published works
include, for piano, an Intermezzo, a Rhapsody,
'New Orleans Miniatures,' 'A Garden Fancy'
and ' Monologue' ; and the songs, 'A Woman's
Last Word,' 'Autumn Song,' ''Twas in a world
of living leaves,' 'A Song of the Lilac,' 'The
Kings,' 'In a Gondola,' 'Take, O take those
lips away,' etc. Unpublished are 'The
Asolani,' three pieces for string-quartet, wood-
quartet and harp ; 'Naïve Landscapes,' four
pieces for piano, flute, oboe and clarinet ; and
'Pippa's Holiday,' a theater-scene for soprano
and orchestra, from the Introduction to
Browning's 'Pippa Passes' (1915–16, Théâtre
Réjane, Paris) and ' Jornida and Jornidel,' a
short opera in two scenes from Grimm's fairy-
tale. [R.8]

BEALE, FREDERIC FLEMING (b. 1876).
See STATE UNIVERSITIES (Ida., Wash.).

BEATON, ISABELLA (May 20, 1870,
Grinnell, Ia.), having graduated from the Iowa
Conservatory at Grinnell in 1890, in 1894–99
was in Berlin, studying piano and composition
with Moszkowski and composition with Boise.
In 1898 she won a teacher's certificate in
singing, declamation and Italian from the
Ziska School of Opera and Oratorio in Paris.
In 1899–1910 she taught piano, history and
composition in the Cleveland School of Music,
meanwhile taking courses in languages,
history and acoustics at Western Reserve
University, leading to the degrees of Ph.B.
and M.A. In 1910 she established the Beaton
School of Music, and for five seasons played
a recital-course of twenty programs. Her
compositions include a Scherzo for orchestra
(Schneeklüd, Paris), played under Paur, Van
der Stucken and others ; a string-quartet in
A minor (Schneeklüd) ; a string-quartet in
C ; ten fugues for piano ; a setting of Keats'
'Eve of St. Agnes ' ; an Ave Maria for contralto and orchestra ; a piano-sonata in G
minor ; piano-pieces and songs. [R.8]

BECK, JOHANN HEINRICH (Sept. 12,
1856, Cleveland, O.), after a general education
in Cleveland, studied in Leipzig in 1879–82
under Schradieck and Hermann (violin), A.
Richter (theory), Paul (history), Reinecke and
Jadassohn (composition). His début as violinist was at the Gewandhaus in May, 1882.
On his return to Cleveland he organized the
Schubert String Quartet. In 1889–90 he was
conductor of the Detroit Symphony Orchestra,
and in 1901–1912 directed orchestral concerts
in Cleveland. He has also conducted the
Pilgrim Orchestral Club (1904–10), the
Elyria Orchestra (1905–07), and has made
many appearances as guest-conductor of his
own compositions. The latter include the
overtures to 'Romeo and Juliet,' 'Lara'

(1886, Boston Symphony Orchestra) and 'Skirnismal' (1887, Thomas Orchestra, Chicago); a string-sextet (1888, Indianapolis); a 'Moorish Serenade' for orchestra (1889, Philadelphia); a Scherzo in A (1890, Thomas Orchestra, Detroit); 'A Kiss of Joy' (1900, Cleveland Orchestra, and 1904, St. Louis Exposition); 'Aus meinem Leben,' a tone-poem for orchestra; 'The Sea at Evening' and 'Wie schön bist du,' for voice and orchestra; the cantata 'Deukalion'; a Scherzo in F (1896, Thomas Orchestra, Cleveland); a string-sextet in D minor; and a string-quartet in C minor. See Hughes, *Contemporary American Composers*, pp. 406–11. [R.7]

BECKEL, JAMES COX (1811– ?). See Register, 3.

BECKER, RENÉ LOUIS (Nov. 7, 1882, Bischheim, Alsace), studied organ with Adolph Gessner, piano with Fritz Blumer and composition with Carl Somborn. He came to America in 1904 and settled in St. Louis, where he soon won distinction in recital-work and composition, and as organist. He is now organist at St. Peter and St. Paul's Cathedral in Alton, Ill. His organ-sonatas, especially op. 40, and the Cantilène in E-flat, rank high and are frequently heard at recitals, while some of his choral pieces have place on important church-music programs. His principal published works include the following:

Piano —
op. 15 Five Miniatures.
  19 Valse in A-flat.
  22 Gavotte and Toccatella.
      10 Melodious Studies and 'Scenes from Childhood.'
  24 'Carnival Sketches.'
      'A String of Merry Strains.'
      Six Children's Dances.

Organ —
op. 1 'Marche Nuptiale,' 'Marche Pontificale,' 'Marche Triomphale,' 'Chant des Seraphim.'
      'Lullaby,' 'Summer Idyll,' 'Réverie,' 'Méditation,' 'Canzonetta.'
  31 Toccata in D.
  40, 42, 43 Three Sonatas.
  41 Cantilena.
      'Légende,' 'Chanson Matinale,' 'Chanson du Soir,' 'Cantilène' in E-flat.
      'Chanson sans Paroles.'

Church-Music —
  Mass in honor of St. Barbara.
  Mass 'Salvator Noster.'
  Mass in honor of St. Catherine (women's voices).
  'Terra Tremuit' (Easter offertory).
  'Lætentur Coeli' (Christmas offertory).
  'Tui sunt Coeli' (Christmas offertory).

In Manuscript —
  Organ-Suite in B-flat.
  Organ-Sonatas in E-flat and B minor.
  Organ-Variations in C minor.
  Several Masses and other church-music. [R.9]

BEEBE, CAROLYN. See Register, 9.

‡BEECHAM, THOMAS (April 29, 1879, Liverpool, England), was educated at Rossall

School, Fleetwood, where he had lessons in harmony from Sweeting, followed by some study with Roberts at Oxford. In 1899 he organized an amateur orchestra at Huyton, a suburb of Liverpool, and soon displayed talent as conductor. In 1902 he was conductor with Kelson Truman's traveling opera-company, and the next year worked upon three operas (unpublished). His first important appearance as conductor in London was in 1905. The next year he founded the New Symphony Orchestra, from which he resigned in 1908 and organized the Beecham Symphony Orchestra. In 1910 he leased Covent Garden, and began a series of operatic performances which rapidly gained in popularity. Delius' 'Romeo and Juliet in the Village,' Smythe's 'The Wreckers' and Strauss' 'Elektra' were early presented. Stanford's 'Shamus O'Brien' and 'The Critic,' Holbrooke's 'Dylan,' Liza Lehmann's 'Everyman,' and many other novelties were produced later. In 1915 he became conductor of the Philharmonic Society. His success in conducting both opera and symphony has made him conspicuous in English music. He was knighted in 1916. See 'Musical Times,' October, 1910.

BEEL, SIGMUND (b. 1863). See Register, 6.

BEETHOVEN CONSERVATORY, THE, St. Louis, was founded in 1871 by a group of public-spirited citizens. In 1872 it passed into the control of August Waldauer, the violinist, and Hermann Lavitsky (d. 1874). The former long remained at its head and developed it into efficiency. Since 1902 the directors have been the brothers Epstein.

BEETHOVEN QUARTET (or QUINTET) CLUB, THE, of Boston, was organized in 1873 by Charles N. Allen, the violinist, and Wulf Fries, the 'cellist, at first with Gustave Dannreuther and H. Heindl. For more than twenty years it continued under some similar name and with changing personnel, exemplifying a worthy standard of ensemble-playing.

BEETHOVEN SOCIETY, THE, of Chicago, organized in 1873, was the first important choral society (mixed voices) in that city after the Apollo Club (male voices). Its conductor was Carl Wolfsohn, the pianist, who was drawn from Philadelphia for the purpose. Among the works introduced were Beethoven's Mass in C and Choral Fantasia, Bruch's 'Odysseus,' Hofmann's 'Fair Melusina,' etc. In 1884 it ceased to exist, being overshadowed by later enterprises.

BEHNING PIANO COMPANY, THE, of New York, was founded in 1861 by Henry Behning, a German piano-maker who had had fine training, and since his death has been carried on successfully by his two sons. Its total output has been over 50,000 instruments.

BEHR BROTHERS PIANO COMPANY, THE, of New York, was founded in 1881 by Henry and Edward Behr. William J. Behr, the son of the former, is now its president. Their pianos have won high awards at the Expositions at New Orleans in 1885, at Melbourne in 1889 and at Chicago in 1893. The total number made is over 50,000.

BEHRENT, JOHN. See Register, 1.

BEISSEL, JOHANN CONRAD (1690–1768). See Register, 1.

BELCHER, SUPPLY (1751–1836). See TUNE-BOOKS, 1794.

BELKNAP, DANIEL (1771–1815). See TUNE-BOOKS, 1797.

‡ BELL, WILLIAM HENRY (Aug. 20, 1873, St. Alban's, England). See article in Vol. v. 612–63. Since 1912 he has been principal of the South African College of Music in Cape Town. His recent larger works are a set of Symphonic Variations in G (1917, Cape Town Orchestra), a 2nd Symphony, in A (1918, ibid.), and a 3rd Symphony, in F, written in 1918–19. See 'Musical Times,' May–July, 1920.

BELLAMANN, HEINRICH HAUER (Apr. 28, 1882, Fulton, Mo.), secured his general education at Westminster College in Missouri and the University of Denver. He then went to Paris, studying piano with Philipp and organ and composition with Widor. Since 1907 he has been director of the School of Fine Arts in Chicora College for Women at Columbia, S. C. He has interested himself in the advancement of modern French music in the South, and has presented for the first time in America many of the more important works by d'Indy, Widor, Debussy, Magnard, Labey, Roussel, de Sévérac, de Bréville, Chausson and others. He is an authorized representative of Philipp's method. His compositions include a piano-concerto, a violin-sonata, a piano-sonata, a piano-quintet and choral works. He has also written numerous magazine articles. In 1907 he was made Mus.D. by Grayson College (Tex.). His wife is an accomplished singer and since 1907 has also taught at Chicora College. He comes of a distinguished line of German musicians. [R.9]

BELTZ, OLIVER S. See COLLEGES, 3 (Union C., Neb.)

BENBOW, WILLIAM (b. 1865). See Register, 6.

BENDIX, MAX (Mar. 28, 1866, Detroit, Mich.), having appeared in public as violinist at eight, before he was twenty gained orchestral experience under conductors like Thomas, Van der Stucken and Seidl. His training as soloist was chiefly with Jacobsohn. In 1886 he was concertmaster at the Metropolitan Opera House and also concertmaster and assistant-conductor of the Thomas Or-

chestra, remaining with the latter ten years, during which he was assistant and successor to Thomas at the Columbian Exposition at Chicago in 1893. Concertizing alone or with the Bendix Quartet occupied the years 1897–1903. He conducted the orchestra at the World's Fair at St. Louis in 1904. The next season he was concertmaster for the Wagnerian performances at the Metropolitan Opera House in New York. He was concertmaster and conductor at the Manhattan Opera House there in 1906; concertized in this country and in Europe for two years; and conducted again at the Metropolitan in 1909–10. Then came four years as conductor of light opera. In 1915 he was conductor of the Exposition Orchestra at the Panama-Pacific Exposition at San Francisco. Since then he has devoted himself to teaching in New York. His compositions include a violin-concerto; 'Pavlowa,' a valse-caprice for orchestra; a theme and variations for 'cello and orchestra; 'The Sisters,' a ballad for soprano and orchestra; music for the play 'Experience'; and a number of songs. [R.7]

BENDIX, OTTO (1845–1904). See Register, 7.

BENEDICTIS, SAVINO DI (Jan. 20, 1883, São Paulo, Brazil), having been for some years a specialist in theory, is now professor of harmony and composition in the Conservatorio Drammatico e Músical at Sao Paulo. His compositions include a four-movement suite for orchestra, 'Mariage de Pierrot et Pierrette'; 'Tramonto,' an 'essai lyrique'; and a number of graceful pieces for piano. He has written a Traité d'Harmonie, 2 vols., and a Théorie Musicale. [R.9]

BENHAM, ASAHEL. See TUNE-BOOKS, 1790.

BENHAM, VICTOR (Apr. 12, 1871, Brooklyn, N. Y.), in 1877 appeared in public as singer and in 1880 as pianist with the Thomas Orchestra in New York. He toured as a child-pianist with Patti, Gerster, Wilhelmj and other artists. In 1882 he was first heard in London, playing at the Crystal Palace concerts under Manns and on Monday Popular Concert programs with Joachim, Piatti and others. By this time he had composed in various forms. In 1885 he played a Fantaisie for piano and orchestra at the Lamoureux Concerts in Paris. There he studied at the Conservatory under Marmontel, receiving a first prize in 1886. After European tours he returned to America, where he spent the years 1890–1900. During 1900–04 he was again in London, and then for eight years in Detroit, teaching, composing and lecturing on various art-subjects. In 1912 he returned to Europe, playing in Germany, Austria, Hungary, Italy, France and England. Since 1914 he has lived

K

in England, active as teacher and critic. His compositions include two symphonies, two piano-concertos, a violin-concerto, five string-quartets, a piano-quintet, many piano-pieces and songs. [R.7]

BENJAMIN, JONATHAN. See TUNE-BOOKS, 1799.

BENSON, HARRY (b. 1848). See Register, 6.

BENSON, LOUIS FITZGERALD (b. 1855). See Register, 8.

BENTLEY, JOHN. See Register, 2.

BENTLEY, WILLIAM FREDERICK (Sept. 12, 1859, Lenox, O.), has been largely identified with Knox College in Illinois. Graduating from Oberlin Conservatory in 1883, he studied piano with Sherwood and Perry in America and with Zwintscher and Kullak in Germany, and voice with Delle Sedie and Escalais in Paris and Randegger in London. In 1883–85 he was music-director in the Institute at South New Lyme, O. Since 1885 he has been director of the Knox Conservatory in Galesburg, Ill., teacher of voice there since 1898 and conductor of the Galesburg Musical Union since 1899. He is also conductor of the Choral Union at Kewanee, Ill. Two of his songs are published and about twenty-five others are in manuscript. [R.7]

BERGE, WILLIAM (d. 1883). See Register, 4.

BERGER, RUDOLF (1874–1915). See Register, 9.

BERGER, WILHELM (Aug. 9, 1861, Boston : Jan. 16, 1911, Meiningen, Germany). See article in Vol. i. 308. He taught piano at the Klindworth-Scharwenka Conservatory in Berlin in 1888–1903 and then succeeded Fritz Steinbach as director of the Meiningen Orchestra. He was Royal Prussian Professor and member of the Royal Academy of Arts. To the list of works add a Symphony in B minor, op. 80; Variations and Fugue for orchestra, op. 97; three Ballades for baritone and orchestra; 'Der Totentanz,' op. 86, for mixed chorus and large orchestra; many songs, choruses, and piano-pieces. [R.7]

BERGH, ARTHUR (Mar. 24, 1882, St. Paul), began violin-study at five, and received his entire training in America. In 1903 he came to New York, for five years was violinist in the New York Symphony Society, and then was in the orchestra of the Metropolitan Opera House. He taught violin, harmony and composition at the New York Institute of Music and conducted the Municipal Concerts in 1911–14. He has lectured on American music and is secretary of the American Music Society. His melodramatic music to Poe's 'Raven,' op. 20, was first produced in 1909, with orchestra under his direction and with Bispham as reader. A second melodrama, also with orchestra, is on Browning's 'Pied Piper of Hamelin,' op. 23. He has also a symphonic choral for orchestra and chorus, 'The Unnamed City'; a romantic opera, 'Niorada'; two overtures; a Festival March for orchestra; 'The Night Rider,' a song with orchestra; piano- and violin-pieces and some thirty songs. [R.9]

BERGMANN, B. See Register, 2.

BERGMANN, KARL (1821–1876). See Vol. i. 308–9, and Register, 4.

BERGNER, FREDERIC (1827– ?). See Register, 4.

BERGQUIST, JOHN VICTOR (b. 1877). See Register, 8.

BERKENHEAD, JOHN L. See Register, 2.

BERKSHIRE FESTIVALS OF CHAMBER MUSIC, THE, held at Pittsfield, Mass., were established in 1918 by Mrs. Frederick S. Coolidge of New York, whose summer-home at Pittsfield provides an ideal place for them. The first Festival occurred on Sept. 16–18, 1918, the participants being the Berkshire String Quartet, the Elshuco Trio, the Longy Club and the Letz Quartet. The five programs included Loeillet's Sonata for flute, oboe and piano, Mozart's Quartet in G (Köchel, 387), Quintet (Köchel, 516) and Quintet for piano and wood-wind, Beethoven's Quartets in E-flat, opp. 74 and 127, Schubert's Trio in B-flat, op. 99, no. 1, Brahms' Sextet in B-flat, op. 18, and Trio in C minor, op. 101. Thuille's Quintet, op. 20, Reiser's Quartet in E minor, Tanieiev's Quartet in B-flat, op. 19, Iarecki's Quartet (prize composition), Ravel's Trio in A minor, d'Indy's 'Chanson et Danses,' op. 50, Pierné's 'Pastorale Variée,' op. 30, and Caplet's 'Suite Persane.' The second Festival occurred on Sept. 25–27, 1919, the participants being the Berkshire String Quartet, the Flonzaley Quartet, and many individual artists, including Harold Bauer, the pianist, Gustav Langenus and Ugo Savolini from the New York Chamber Music Society, and several singers. The five programs included Mozart's Quartet in B-flat (Köchel, 458), Beethoven's Quartets in A minor and F, opp. 132 and 135, and Septet in E-flat, op. 20, Brahms' Trio in D, op. 40, Saint-Saëns' Quartet in G, op. 153 (first time in America), Dvořák's Quartet in E-flat, op. 51, Elgar's Quartet in E minor, op. 83 (first time in America), Mason's Pastorale in D, op. 8, Sowerby's Trio in E minor (first time), Bloch's Suite for viola and piano (prize composition), Rebecca Clarke's Sonata for viola and piano, and a variety of vocal selections for soli or quartet with chamber-accompaniment. A prize of $1000 is offered annually for the best chamber-work submitted, the winners being Tadeusz Iarecki in 1918, Ernest Bloch in 1919 and Francesco Malipiero in 1920.

BERKSHIRE STRING QUARTET, THE, is the name adopted for the Kortschak Quartet of Chicago as reorganized in 1917 under the patronage of Mrs. Frederick S. Coolidge of New York in connection with the Berkshire Festivals (see above). It consists of Hugo Kortschak and Sergei Kotlarsky, violins, Clarence Evans, viola (in place of George Dasch), and Emmeran Stoeber, 'cello. It is understood that after the Festival of 1920 the Quartet is to be discontinued.

‡BERNERS, Lord [Gerald Hugh Tyrwhitt] (Sept. 18, 1883, London, England), received his musical training in Dresden and London, entered the British diplomatic service in 1909 and since 1912 has been attached to the British Embassy at Rome. He succeeded as Baron Berners in 1918. His first published works were three funeral-marches for piano, the first for a statesman, the second for a canary, the third for a rich aunt. Then followed 'Fragments Psychologiques' and the miniature tone-poem 'Le Poisson d'Or' and 'Valses Bourgeoises,' all for piano. For orchestra are two sets of three pieces each, the first including 'Chinoiserie,' 'Valse Sentimentale' and 'Kasatchok'; the second, a 'Fantaisie Espagnole,' including a Prelude, Fandango and March. The latter set was played at the London Promenade Concerts in 1919. Lord Berners' work is said to be influenced by his association with his friends Casella and Stravinsky.

BERWALD, WILLIAM HENRY (Dec. 26, 1864, Schwerin, Germany), studied composition in 1883–87 with Rheinberger in Munich and in 1887–88 with Faiszt in Stuttgart. In 1889 he became director of the Philharmonic Society in Libau, Russia, and in 1892 came to America as professor of composition and piano in the College of Fine Arts of Syracuse University, succeeding Goetschius. He is director of the Ladies' Chorus of the College and choir-director at the Fourth Presbyterian Church. The degrees of Mus.M. and Mus.D. were conferred upon him by the University in 1903 and 1912. He won the prize offered by the Philadelphia Manuscript Society for a quintet for piano and strings, a gold medal in the Clemson anthem-competition for 1912 and first prize for a part-song for mixed voices in the 'Etude' competition. His works for orchestra have been performed abroad as well as here. Tertius Noble, at St. Thomas' Church in New York, gave the initial performance of his cantata 'The Seven Last Words of Christ.' His violin-sonata in F received special recognition from Joachim, and his piano-compositions were valued by William Mason. He has been a most industrious composer, long lists of his works being found in the catalogues of leading publishers. They

include 73 piano-pieces, 36 songs, 7 vocal duets, 13 part-songs and 11 anthems for women's voices, 106 anthems for mixed voices, 19 anthems for men's voices, 10 cantatas, 3 secular part-songs for mixed voices, two sonatas for violin and piano and two Romances for 'cello and piano. His unpublished compositions are the prize piano-quintet, a piano-trio, a dramatic overture (played by the Court Opera Orchestra in Schwerin, and by the New York Symphony Society in Pittsburgh, Chicago and Syracuse) and an overture, 'Walthari' (played at the Syracuse Festival by the New York Symphony Society and by the American Symphony Orchestra in Chicago). [R.8]

BETHANY COLLEGE, Lindsborg, Kan., has become a notable center for the musical enthusiasm of Swedish Lutherans. Its first class was graduated in 1891, and from that time music has been a conspicuous element in its entire life. Besides elaborate opportunities for individual instruction, including many instruments, there are two large choruses, two orchestras, two bands and several glee-clubs. For nearly thirty years a May Festival of several days has been held that has become famous. The director is Hagbard Brase, with 14 other instructors.

BETHLEHEM BACH CHOIR, THE, of Bethlehem, Pa., was organized in its present form in 1900 through the efforts of Mrs. Ruth Porter Doster and under the inspiration of J. Fred Wolle, at that time organist of the Moravian Church. After 1905 it was suspended, owing to Dr. Wolle's removal to California, but resumed in 1912, this time with generous assistance from Charles M. Schwab. Dr. Wolle has been conductor throughout. Up to 1920 fifteen Bach Festivals have been held, those before 1905 in the Moravian Church and those since 1912 at Lehigh University in South Bethlehem. The Festivals now regularly occupy two days, but in the past they have once covered six and once were distributed in three groups of three each. The programs have varied much in part, but the B minor Mass has been sung at every Festival. The St. Matthew Passion has been given three times, the St. John Passion twice, the Christmas Oratorio (complete) four times and the Magnificat four times. Some forty cantatas have been produced, about one-quarter of them more than once, and many detached chorales. The Second and Third Brandenburg Concertos and the Suites in B minor and D have been played. In the early years the chorus was small, even under 100, but has lately been increased to about 250. Originally the orchestra was made up of local players, many of them amateurs, but since 1912 members of the Philadelphia Orchestra have been utilized. Altogether about 700 of the people of Bethlehem and vicinity have been members of the chorus. The audiences have been phenomenal not simply for size, but for their representative quality, including professional musicians from all over the country and many others. In more than one respect, therefore, these Festivals are unique and extraordinary. They have been carried on with infinite industry and devotion, and their artistic quality has been universally acknowledged.

Back of the present Bach Choir lies much history. One of the first acts of the founders of the Moravian settlement at Bethlehem in 1742 was to hold a *Singstunde*, and from 1744 a Collegium Musicum was steadily maintained, credited with very early performances of parts of several oratorios. In 1820 this was replaced by the Philharmonic Society, which was an oratorio society of more constant character. In 1882 the young Wolle organized the Bethlehem Choral Union, which lasted ten years and gave the St. Matthew Passion in 1892. See Walters, *The Bethlehem Bach Choir*, 1918.

BETHUNE, THOMAS G. (1849?–1908). See Register, 4.

BETTI, ADOLFO (b. 1875). See Register, 9.

BEUTEL, CARL. See COLLEGES, 3 (Nebraska Wesleyan U.).

'BIANCA.' An opera by Henry K. Hadley, awarded the $1000 prize offered by W. W. Hinshaw in 1917, was first produced on Oct. 18, 1918, by the Society of American Singers in New York under the composer's direction.

BIDDLE, HORACE PETERS (1811–1900). See Register, 5.

BIDEZ, L. ALOYS (b. 1847). See Register, 6.

BIEDERMANN, AUGUST JULIUS (1825–1907). See Register, 4.

BIEDERMANN, EDWARD JULIUS (b. 1849). See Register, 6.

BIFERI, NICHOLAS. See Register, 1.

BIGELOW, WILLIAM PINGRY (b. 1867). See COLLEGES, 1 (Amherst C., Mass.).

BIGGS, RICHARD KEYS (b. 1886). See Register, 9.

BIGLOW & MAIN, of New York, is the publishing-firm organized in 1868 by Lucius H. Biglow (1833–1907) and Sylvester Main (1817–73), primarily to take over the publication of W. B. Bradbury's books. Almost immediately they began the issue of the series known as the 'Gospel Hymns' of Moody and Sankey. From that time they became the chief publishers of popular hymns and tunes of this class by a great variety of editors. Hubert P. Main (see Register, 5), the well-known hymnologist, has been connected with the firm since its foundation and is now its treasurer. As a hint of the magnitude of the business it is enough to recall that in 1886 no

less than 18,000,000 copies of popular hymn-books had been sold. When interest in Tonic Sol-Fa arose Biglow & Main became its principal representatives in America. They have issued some English choir-music of high quality.

BILES, ETHEL. See COLLEGES, 3 (Cotner C., Neb.).

BILLINGS, WILLIAM (Oct. 7, 1746, Boston : Sept. 29, 1800, Boston), often erroneously called 'the first American composer,' was an uneducated man of humble origin, by trade a tanner, who had an irrepressible enthusiasm for developing popular singing. He was somewhat grotesque in personal appearance, unconventional in expression and far from technically expert in music. But his zeal was contagious and the freshness of his tunes caught popular attention. His first efforts came when the New England churches were beginning to use hymns by Watts and others in addition to the traditional versified Psalms, and the rhythmical swing and curious 'fuguing' effects of his tunes corresponded to the independent feeling of the time.[1] His later work, after the Revolutionary War, often gave voice to the patriotic fervor of that period. His name appears in 1764 in connection with the sale of concert-tickets. His series of six books began in 1770 (see list under TUNE-BOOKS), continuing till 1794. In 1774 he seems to have conducted a singing-class at Stoughton, which became the germ of the Stoughton Musical Society in 1786. It is probable that he taught many similar classes. Selections from his works, mostly 'anthems,' have been noted in concert-programs in Boston in 1782, '87 and '96, and in Philadelphia in 1786–88. A few of his tunes, such as 'Chester' (for which he provided patriotic words), continued in use for some time, though steadily replaced by the better productions of later writers. It is supposed that he first introduced, or at least made popular, the use of the pitch-pipe and also of the 'cello or double-bass for accompaniment. See Ritter, *Music in America*, chap. iii (needlessly caustic), Mathews, *Hundred Years of Music*, pp. 25–9, Elson, *Hist. of American Music*, pp. 12–9, etc. [R.1]

BIMBONI, ALBERTO (b. 1882). See Register, 10.

BINDER, FRITZ (b. 1873). See Register, 7.

BINGHAM, WALTER VAN DYKE (b. 1880). See Register, 9.

BINTLIFF, ELIZABETH, née Battle. See COLLEGES, 3 (Ripon C., Wis., Olivet C., Mich.).

BIRD, ARTHUR (July 23, 1856, Cambridge, Mass.). To the works listed in Vol. i. 328–9 may be added a set of 'Oriental Scenes'

[1] There are interesting analogies between this outbreak of popular tunes in America in 1770 and the rise of Methodist singing in England about 1740.

for organ. The comic opera 'Daphne' was given in New York in 1897. [R.6]

BIRGE, EDWARD BAILEY (b. 1868). See Register, 9.

BIRMINGHAM CONSERVATORY, THE, Birmingham, Ala., was founded in 1895 by Benjamin Guckenberger, who remained in charge till 1902, when he was succeeded by Edna Gockel and (from 1903) her husband, William Gussen. The institution is affiliated with the chain of schools of the Sherwood Music School in Chicago.

BISCACCIANTI, ELIZA, née Ostinelli (1825– ?). See Register, 4.

BISCHOFF, JOHN W. (1850–1909). See Register, 6.

BISHOP, ANNA (1814–1884). See Vol. i. 330–1, and Register, 4.

BISPHAM, DAVID SCULL (Jan. 5, 1857, Philadelphia). See article in Vol. i. 333. Add to the list of works which he has introduced in America and England the following: Liza Lehmann's 'Persian Garden' and her romantic opera 'The Vicar of Wakefield' (London, Nov. 12, 1906); Schilling's 'Witch's Song,' Cole's 'King Robert of Sicily,' Bergh's setting of 'The Raven' and many other pieces for recitation. He has constantly championed the use of English versions wherever practicable, and has made a specialty of song-cycles in English, such as Beethoven's 'To a Distant Beloved,' Schubert's 'Songs of the Mill' and 'Winter Journey,' and Schumann's 'The Poet's Love.' He has been foremost in reviving the art of declamation to music, and is noted for his performance of Sophocles' 'Antigone' with Mendelssohn's music and of Byron's 'Manfred' with Schumann's music. His operatic repertory includes over fifty parts, and he has sung in more than a hundred oratorios and cantatas — his Elijah being particularly famous. Of songs of all schools he has sung at least 1500. His powers as an actor are universally recognized, but it is as a singer in opera and concert that he is most widely known. He has edited two volumes of songs under the title of *Bispham's Albums*, and has published *A Quaker Singer's Recollections*, 1920. [R.8]

BISSELL, T. See TUNE-BOOKS, 1846.

BLACK, LOUIS. See STATE UNIVERSITIES (W. Va.).

BLAKE, GEORGE E. (1775–1871). See Register, 3, and TUNE-BOOKS, 1810.

BLAKESLEE, SAMUEL H. See COLLEGES, 3 (Ohio Wesleyan U.).

BLANCHARD, AMOS. See TUNE-BOOKS, 1807.

BLANCK, HUBERT DE (June 11, 1856, Utrecht, Holland), was a pupil of Dupuy in composition at the Liège Conservatory, and of Ledent in piano, and won a scholarship from the Belgian government. At seventeen he toured Russia, Sweden and Germany as pianist, and then conducted at the El Dorado Theater in Warsaw. In 1880 he visited South America with the violinist Dengremont, in 1881 taught piano at the New York College of Music and in 1883 settled in Havana. Two years later he established the first conservatory there. He was imprisoned for revolutionary activity in 1896 and banished by order of General Weyler. On the establishment of order he returned and reopened the school as the Conservatorio Nacional. It is now a large institution, with branches in the leading cities of Cuba. He has composed piano-pieces and songs. [R.7]

BLASS, ROBERT (b. 1867). See Register, 8.

BLAUVELT, LILLIAN EVANS (Mar. 16, 1874, Brooklyn, N. Y.). See article in Vol. i. 338–9. Until 1914 she made annual tours in Europe and America. In 1902 she sang the Coronation Ode by special command at Albert Hall in London and received a medal from Edward VII. In 1905 she sang in Russia and made a tour of Europe in 1908–09. In 1906–07 she starred in the comic opera 'The Rose of Alhambra.' She received the Order of St. Cecilia at Rome in 1901. [R.8]

'BLIND GIRL OF CASTEL-CUILLÉ, THE.' A three-act opera, with ballet, by Earl R. Drake, produced in 1914 in Chicago.

'BLIND TOM.' See BETHUNE, THOMAS G.

BLISS, CHARLES MERIT (b. 1866). See COLLEGES, 3 (Phillips U., Okla.).

BLISS, PHILIP PAUL (1838–1876). See Register, 5.

BLISS, PHILIP PAUL, JR. (Nov. 25, 1872, Chicago), was the son of the noted writer of 'Gospel hymns' and was educated for the ministry. He graduated from Princeton in 1894. His musical education was under Clarke and Zeckwer in Philadelphia, and in Paris in 1896–98 he studied organ with Guilmant and composition with Massenet. In 1900–04 he was organist, director and teacher of public-school music at Owego, N. Y. In 1904 he went to Cincinnati, as musical editor for the John Church Co., and in 1911 took a similar position with the Willis Music Co., where he is still engaged. He has composed about 200 instructive piano-pieces, many operettas (both words and music), sacred and secular cantatas, choruses, about 100 songs, duets and five song-cycles (two published), a piano-suite, a book on pedal-study, a graded course for piano, 4 vols., solos for organ, violin and 'cello, a comic opera (unpublished), etc. He has also increased the répertoire of four-, six- and eight-hand music for one and two pianos and for two violins and piano, and of musical recitations with piano. [R.9]

BLOCH, ERNEST (July 24, 1880, Geneva, Switzerland), was a pupil at Geneva of Jaques-Dalcroze in 1894–96, at Brussels of Ysaÿe and Rasse in 1896–99, and at Frankfort of Ivan Knorr in 1899–1900. He spent time in Paris and Munich before returning to Geneva in 1904. He conducted concerts in Lausanne and Neuchâtel in 1909–10, and occasionally acted as guest-conductor of his own works. In 1911–15 he lectured at the Geneva Conservatory. Since 1916 he has lived in the United States, for two years teaching composition at the Mannes School of Music in New York. His compositions are the symphonic poem 'Vivre et Aimer' (1900) ; Symphony in C-sharp minor (1901–03) ; 'Hiver-Printemps' (1904–05, Schirmer) ; 'Poèmes d'Automne' (1906, Schirmer) ; 'Macbeth,' drame lyrique (1904–10), given at the Opéra-Comique in 1910–11 (Astruc-Enoch), and 'Historiettes au Crépuscule' (Demets). Works inspired by Jewish themes are '3 Poëmes Juifs' (1913, Schirmer) ; Psalms 137, 114 and 22 for voice and orchestra (1911–14, Schirmer) ; 'Schelomo,' a rhapsody for 'cello and orchestra (1916, Schirmer). 'Israël,' a symphony for orchestra and voices, was begun in 1914 ; the Jewish opera 'Jézabel,' piano-pieces and other works are still in an incomplete stage. The string-quartet in B has been played in America by the Flonzaley Quartet. A suite for viola and orchestra (or piano) is in MS. He has conducted performances of his orchestral works in Boston, New York, Philadelphia and Chicago, and they have also been given in Minneapolis, St. Paul, St. Louis and San Francisco. The symphony in C-sharp minor has been pronounced by Romain Rolland ' one of the most important works of the modern school.' In 1919 he won the prize in the Coolidge (Berkshire) competition for his Suite for viola and piano. [R.10]

BLODGETT, BENJAMIN COLMAN (Boston, Mar. 12, 1838), from 1847 studied piano with James Hooton of Boston and organ with W. R. Babcock. He became organist of the Essex Street Church in 1850 and in 1853 went to the Eliot Church in Newton, where he remained five years. Then followed a period of three years at Leipzig. In 1861 he returned to Boston and was active as teacher, concert-pianist and organist of the Park Street Church. He became music-master at the Maplewood Institute in Pittsfield, Mass., in 1865, and this led to the establishment in 1870 of a separate music-school under his direction. In 1878 he became professor of music at Smith College in Northampton, and there soon established the Smith College School of Music, of which he was principal until 1903. A year later he became organist and choir-director at Leland Stanford University in California. Here he gave many organ-recitals until the destruction of the chapel by the earthquake of April, 1906. Illness in his family caused his retirement from public life in 1914, and he has since lived in Seattle. He has made numerous trips to Europe, appearing as pianist several times in London and Leipzig, and making the acquaintance of many distinguished musicians (Liszt at Weimar in 1860, Wagner at Bayreuth in 1876 and 1882). As a musical educator he exercised influence for almost half a century. Comparatively little of his attention has been given to composition, but he has published a set of Études for advanced piano-students, op. 20, a cantata, 'The Prodigal Son,' op. 31 (1895), piano-pieces and church-music. Unpublished works in larger form are the oratorio 'Job' (Smith College Commencement, 1889, revised 1890), an overture, concert-pieces for orchestra and a string-quartet. [R.4]

BLUM, ELIAS (Feb. 22, 1881, Isaacfalln, Hungary), was brought to Boston in 1891, and there received his general education, studying piano with Kelterborn and composition with Goetschius. After four years' study at the Grand-Ducal School in Weimar (organ, piano, voice, composition and conducting) he returned to Boston and was active for a time as singer and organist. In 1909 he went to Walla Walla, Wash., as music-director at Whitman College. In 1917 he removed to Grinnell College in Iowa. His published compositions are a Passacaglia and Scherzo for organ, a Capriccio for piano, songs, choruses and anthems. A number of works are still in manuscript, among them a piano-trio in G minor. [R.9]

BLUMENSCHEIN, WILLIAM LEONARD (1849–1916). See Register, 6.

BOCHAU, CHARLES HENRY (July 7, 1870, Holstein, Germany), was brought to America as a boy. He had no opportunity for serious musical study until 1892, when he entered the Peabody Conservatory in Baltimore, studying harmony and composition with Hamerik, Kahmer and Boise, and piano with Burmeister. After graduation in 1899 he also studied voice with Heimendahl. In 1897 he was appointed on the staff of the Conservatory, where he is now in the vocal department. Since 1905 he has also had charge of music at the Maryland School for the Blind. The Kimball Prize of the Chicago Madrigal Club was awarded to him in 1908. In 1910–14 he was choir-master of the Madison Avenue Synagogue and devoted much time to the arrangement and development of Jewish music. He became director of the Arion Singing Society in 1913, succeeding David Melamet, and has recently been appointed conductor of the new Johns Hopkins University Orchestra (60 players), consisting of

members of the student-body and faculty
and the best amateurs of the community.
The first concert was given in May, 1919, and
inaugurated a new musical activity in the
institution. His published compositions are
the prize-chorus 'I know the way of the wild
blush-rose,' for mixed voices; the anthems
'Hark the sound of holy voices' (Summy),
'As it began to dawn' (Novello), 'There were
shepherds' (Schirmer), Easter and Christmas
Carols (Schirmer, Ditson), 'Sing, O daughter
of Zion,' for voice and piano (Summy), and
several violin-pieces (Ditson, and Carl Fischer).
Still in MS. are a Concert-Overture and Fantaisie for large orchestra, a String-Quartet in
G, a Serenade for strings and flute, a Nocturne
for 'cello and piano, and a Fugue for two
choirs on 'Ein' feste Burg,' Hebraic music for
chorus and organ, detached choruses, and
further pieces for violin and piano. [R.8]

BODANZKY, ARTUR (Dec. 16, 1877,
Vienna, Austria), was a pupil of Grün,
Grädener and J. N. Fuchs at the Vienna Conservatory. He became a violinist in the
orchestra of the Imperial Opera in 1896. His
first engagement as conductor was in 1900 at
Budweis in Bohemia, going thence to the
Carl-Theater in Vienna. He conducted a
season of light opera in Petrograd in 1901.
In 1902 he returned to the Vienna Opera as
assistant to Mahler. Two years later he was
in Paris conducting the first French performance of 'Fledermaus' ('La Chauve-Souri').
Returning to Vienna, he became conductor at
the Theater an der Wien. For nearly three
seasons from 1906 he was director at the Royal
Opera in Prague and also conductor of the
Philharmonic Concerts there. In 1909 he
became director of the Grand-Ducal Theater at
Mannheim, where he also conducted the Philharmonic and Oratorio Society concerts.
At the same time he made frequent visits as
guest-conductor to London, Milan, Rome,
Petrograd, Moscow, Brussels, Cologne, Vienna,
Munich and other prominent centers. In
1914 he conducted the first performance of
'Parsifal' in England. In 1915 he came to
the Metropolitan Opera House in New York.
His most conspicuous single achievement there
is his new version of Weber's 'Oberon,' the
score and orchestral parts of which he reëdited.
In the spring of 1919 he made his début in
New York as a symphonic conductor, leading
the New Symphony Orchestra. He has continued in this post through the courtesy of
the management of the Opera. [R.10]

BOEKELMAN, BERNARDUS (June 9,
1838, Utrecht, Holland), had his first musical
studies with his father, Anton J. Boekelman,
who was a chorus-director and organist. He
studied at the Leipzig Conservatory in 1857-
60 under Moscheles, Richter and Hauptmann,
and in 1862–64 was a private pupil of von
Bülow, Kiel and Weitzmann. He migrated
to Mexico during Maximilian's régime, but in
1866 settled in New York. The same year he
toured with Carl Formes and Jehin-Prume
under the management of Strakosch. With
R. Richter, violinist, and E. Schenck, 'cellist,
he founded the New York Trio Club, and
played at the first performance in New York
of Tchaikovsky's Trio, op. 50, Scharwenka's
Concerto in B minor and Liszt's 'Danse Macabre.' In 1883–97 he was music-director
at Miss Porter's School in Farmington, Conn.,
and since 1897 has been in the same position
at Mrs. Dow's School at Briarcliff, N. Y., as
well as teaching privately in New York. His
published works include a Festival March,
op. 1, for piano, four hands (also for band,
string-orchestra and two pianos); a Romance,
op. 2, for violin or 'cello and piano; a 'Balla-
bile,' op. 3, for piano or string-orchestra; a
Concert Polonaise, op. 4, for piano (also for
two pianos, eight hands, string-orchestra
military band); 'Valse de la Reine,' op. 5, fo
piano; 'À Cheval,' op. 6, for piano; 'In der
Einsamkeit,' op. 7, for string-orchestra;
'Sehnsucht,' op. 8, for piano; three songs
for high voice, op. 9; 'Gondoliera,' op. 10,
for violin and piano; 'Romance,' op. 11, for
piano; six thumb-studies, op. 12, for piano;
'Tête-à-Tête,' op. 13, a piano-waltz; and
three octave-studies for piano, op. 14. His
analytical editions of sixteen fugues from
Bach's 'Well-Tempered Clavichord' and 'Inventions' have had a wide circulation. In
these the themes are printed in colors and
rhombic notes, to facilitate the study of contrapuntal style. The fundamental harmony
is printed separately for a second piano or the
organ. [R.5]

BOEPPLER, WILLIAM (Feb. 21, 1863,
Pferdsfeld, Germany), secured his university
education at Leipzig and Bonn. In music he
was trained by Gisbert Enzian in Kreuznach,
Reinecke, Fiedler and Langer in Leipzig, and
Arnold Mendelssohn in Bonn. His first
teaching in America was at Milwaukee in
1894. In 1895 he organized there the A
Cappella Chorus, in 1899 the Wisconsin Conservatory, and in 1902 the Milwaukee Symphony Orchestra. In 1895 he was musical
editor of the Milwaukee 'Herald', in 1896–97
of the 'Germania.' Since 1904 he has also
been active in Chicago, conducting the Sing-
verein, the Germania Club, the Turner-Män-
nerchor, and the male chorus of the First
National Bank. Among his pupils are numerous singers of prominence. [R.8]

BOGERT, WALTER LAWRENCE (b.
1864). See Register, 8.

BOHANAN, GEORGE SMILEY (b. 1869).
See COLLEGES, 3 (West Virginia Wesleyan C.).

BOHEMIAN CLUB, THE, of San Francisco, has become famous for maintaining unique open-air performances for its members and their guests in which literary, dramatic and musical elements are mingled in varying proportions. The initial experiment was made in 1878, leading to a series of 'Midsummer High Jinks' that continued from 1879 to 1901. The programs for these were at first miscellaneous, but tended after 1890 to become unified upon some plan proposed by the leader or 'sire' for the year, resulting often in a continuous play or drama. From 1880 the exercises regularly culminated in a symbolic ceremony called 'The Cremation of Care,' and until about 1910 the thought underlying this dominated other exercises. Of late years, however, this ceremony has been transferred to the opening of the celebration. Since 1902 the principal event has been the presentation of a 'Grove-Play,' which has become increasingly significant artistically. In these 'plays,' as in the earlier 'Jinks,' music has figured largely, either in melodrama or in fairly complete operatic form, enlisting the genius of many composers and interpreters. From almost the first the 'revels' have been held in the impressive redwood forests of Sonoma County to the northwest of San Francisco. They are now domiciled at 'The Grove,' a tract of over 800 acres on the Russian River near Guerneville. Here the Club holds a two weeks' encampment in August. The theater or arena at its center now has (1920) a 3-manual open-air organ resembling that successfully installed at San Diego in 1915.

Among the earlier productions which approximated the later musico-dramatic type were 'The Sermon of the Myriad Leaves' (1892), 'The Sacrifice in the Forest' (1893) and 'The Enigma of Life' (1901). The list of 'Grove-Plays' is as follows:

1902 'The Man in the Forest,' text by C. K. Field, music by Joseph D. Redding.
1903 'Montezuma,' text by L. A. Robertson, music by Humphrey J. Stewart.
1904 'The Hamadryads,' text by Will Irwin, music by W. J. McCoy.
1905 'The Quest of the Gorgon,' text by N. J. Tharp, music by Theodor J. Vogt.
1906 'The Owl and Care,' text by C. K. Field, music by H. J. Stewart. Not strictly a Grove-Play.
1907 'The Triumph of Bohemia,' text by George Sterling, music by Edward F. Schneider.
1908 'The Sons of Baldur,' text by Herman Scheffauer, music by Arthur Weiss.
1909 'St. Patrick of Tara,' text by H. M. Stephens, music by Wallace A. Sabin.
1910 'The Cave-Man,' text by C. K. Field, music by W. J. McCoy.
1911 'The Green Knight,' text by Porter Garnett, music by Edward G. Stricklen.
1912 'The Atonement of Pan,' text by J. D. Redding, music by Henry K. Hadley.

1913 'The Fall of Ug,' text by Rufus Steele, music by Herman Perlet.
1914 'Nec-Natoma,' text by J. W. Shiels, music by Uda Waldrop.
1915 'Apollo,' text by Frank Pixley, music by Edward F. Schneider.
1916 'Gold,' text by F. S. Myrtle, music by Humphrey J. Stewart.
1917 'The Land of Happiness,' text by C. T. Crocker, music by Joseph D. Redding.
1918 'The Twilight of the Kings,' text by R. M. Hotaling, music by Wallace A. Sabin.
1919 'Life,' text by H. L. Wilson, music by Domenico Brescia.
1920 'The Ilya of Muron,' text by C. C. Dobie, music by Ulderico Marcelli.

In 1918 there were published in a limited edition three volumes of *Grove-Plays of the Bohemian Club*, with a thoughtful Introduction by the editor, Porter Garnett, the well-known dramatic critic and author. Many of the plays are preceded by special introductions by the authors of the words, and in most cases notes are given of the principal themes employed in the musical settings. Articles upon the work of the Club have been written by Jesse L. Williams in 'Collier's Magazine' (Sept. 7, 1907), by Arthur Farwell in 'Musical America' (Oct. 16, 1909) and by Percy Mackaye in *The Civic Theatre* (1912). See also an appreciative notice in *The Art of Music*, iv. 396–9.[1]

BOHEMIANS, THE, of New York, is a fraternal union of musicians, started in 1907, of which Rubin Goldmark was president in 1907–10 and Franz Kneisel since 1910.

BOISE, OTIS BARDWELL (Aug. 13, 1844, Oberlin, O. : Dec. 2, 1912, Baltimore), while attending school in Cleveland began to play the organ in church when but fourteen. In 1861 he went to Leipzig, studying with Hauptmann, Richter and Moscheles for three years and then continued at Berlin with Kullak. In 1865 he returned to Cleveland and for five years was teacher and organist there. Then followed six years in New York, teaching composition in the New York Conservatory and serving as organist at the Fifth Avenue Presbyterian Church. In 1877 he went to Europe again as student and composer and enjoyed the advice and assistance of Liszt. In 1878–88 he was in New York, for three years in music and for seven years in other business. Then for thirteen years he was in Berlin, gaining a fine reputation as teacher of theory. He returned to America in 1901, becoming teacher of theory and composition at the Peabody Conservatory in Baltimore and music-critic of the 'News,' holding both positions until his death. Among his well-known pupils are Huss, Brockway, Hutcheson, Arthur Nevin and Atherton. His

[1] The data for the above summary were supplied by the courtesy of Mr. Henry Bretherick of San Francisco.

compositions included both orchestral and
other works. His *Harmony Made Practical*,
1900, has had wide acceptance and he also
wrote *Music and its Masters*, 1901. [R.5]

‡BOITO, ARRIGO (Feb. 24, 1842, Padua,
Italy : June 10, 1918, Milan). See article in
Vol. i. 353–8. To the last he was busy over
his opera 'Nero,' whispering 'Nerone é finito'
just before his death. In March, 1912, he
was made Senator of the Kingdom.

BOLLINGER, SAMUEL (Sept. 22, 1871,
Fort Smith, Ark.), was the son of a musician
and early played the piano in his father's trio.
His first piano-lessons were with Emil Winkler;
later he studied at Leipzig with Reinecke,
Zwintscher, Schreck and Quasdorf. He won
a scholarship at the Conservatory, taught
there, and was organist of the American Church
in 1893–5. In 1896 he founded the Bollinger
Conservatory at Fort Smith, Ark., but two
years later removed to San Francisco. Eight
years were spent there and one in Chicago
before starting the Bollinger Piano School in
St. Louis in 1907. He has performed programs of his own compositions, besides lecturing on symphonies. His works include

'The Sphinx,' a fantaisie-suite for orchestra in five
scenes — 'Slumber-Song,' 'The Awakening,' 'The
Riddle,' 'Theban Festival,' 'Death-Song of the
Sphinx' (prize from the St. Louis Art League, 1916),
op. 18.
'Pompilia and Caponsacchi,' a dramatic overture,
based on Browning's 'Ring and the Book,' op. 3.
Waltzes for orchestra, op. 9.
Petite Sonate, for violin, op. 2.
Sonate quasi une Fantaisie, for violin, op. 9.
Romanza, for violin, op. 6 (Breitkopf).
Caprice, for violin, op. 11.
Songs: 'Fancy' and 'Wilt thou weep?' op. 16
(Schirmer); 'Youth and Love' and 'A Confession,'
op. 12.
Piano-pieces: Scherzo, Mazurka and Romanza
Lamentosa, op. 1 (Grude, Leipzig); 'Danse Mélan-
colique' (F. A. Mills, New York); 'Chopinesques':
op. 4, including Prélude ('At Sea'), Nocturne and
Impromptu (Schirmer); op. 5, including Idylle,
Barcarolle and Humoresque (Breitkopf), and op.
7, including 'Danse Caprice' and 'Danse Humor-
istique' (Breitkopf); 'Lament,' op. 8, no. 1 (Breit-
kopf); Tone-Poem, op. 8, no. 2 (Schirmer);
'Élégie' and 'Impromptu Fantastique,' op. 15
(Shattiger, St. Louis); Symphonic Prelude, a concert-
study, op. 10; op. 20, including 'Trudging' and Romance; op. 21, 'American Dance.'
Fantaisie Romantique, for organ, op. 17. [R.8]

BONAWITZ, JOHANN HEINRICH (Dec.
4, 1839, Dürkheim, Germany : Aug. 15, 1917,
London), was of Polish origin. He studied
at the Liège Conservatory, and was brought
to America in 1852. At twenty-two he returned to Europe and made several concert-
tours as pianist with Joachim. He also taught
in Wiesbaden, Paris and London. In 1872–73
he organized popular symphony-concerts in
New York, but these failed from lack of popular
appreciation. His piano-recitals on a tour in
1873 were more successful. In Philadelphia

he produced two operas, 'The Bride of
Messina' (1874) and 'Ostrolenka' (1875). In
1876 he removed to Vienna, and his last thirty
years were spent in London. Here he founded
the Mozart Society, which gave annual series
of concerts largely devoted to Mozart's
music. Excerpts from his opera 'Napoleon'
were given in concert-form in London in 1911.
His works included the above operas and also
'Diogenes' (1870) and 'Irma' (1885, London),
a Requiem, a Stabat Mater, a piano-quintet,
a string-quartet, a trio, many piano-pieces
and songs. [R.5]

BOND, CARRIE, née Jacobs (b. 1862).
See Register, 9.

BONVIN, LUDWIG (Feb. 17, 1850, Siders,
Switzerland), after completing his college
course in Sion in 1870, studied medicine in
Vienna and law in Sion, but entered the Jesuit
Order in 1874 in Holland. There and in
England for several years he held positions
as organist. He was ordained priest in
Liverpool in 1885. Since 1887 he has been at
Canisius College in Buffalo, as head of the
college music-department till 1907, director
of the choir in 1887–95 and 1897–1905, and
of the orchestra in 1888–1907. As a musician
he is chiefly self-taught. Though once engaged about equally in secular and ecclesiastical music, he has lately worked to improve
the music and text of Catholic English hymnology and to restore the original rhythmic
values in Gregorian chant. He has published
several hymn-books, among which 'Hosanna'
is most notable. Taking up the work of A.
Dechevreus and Gietmann, he has also published many historical, scientific and controver-
sial essays in various languages and issued
several practical rhythmizations of the Vatican
melodies. His compositions are as follows:

'A Christmas-Night Dream,' op. 10, for string-
orchestra (Siegel) — also, as op. 8a, for violin, 'cello
and reed-organ (Coppenroth).
Three 'Tone-Pictures,' op. 12, for orchestra (Breitkopf).
Ballade, op. 25, for orchestra (Breitkopf) — also
for violin, 'cello and piano.
'Festival Procession,' op. 25, for orchestra (Breit-
kopf) — also in chamber-arrangements.
'Reminiscences,' op. 31, for orchestra (Breitkopf),
also for violin, 'cello and piano, or violin and piano.
Symphony in G minor, op. 67 (Breitkopf).
Two Symphonic Movements, op. 71 (Breitkopf).
'Suppressed Sadness at the Joyous Feast,' op. 12a,
for 2 violins, 'cello, reed-organ and piano (Coppen-
roth).
Andante Cantabile, op. 77, for violin, 'cello, reed-
organ and piano (Coppenroth) — also for organ
(Leuckart).
Romanza, op. 19, for violin with orchestra or piano
(Breitkopf).
Melody, op. 56, for violin and piano (Breitkopf), or
for string-quartet (Leuckart).
Three 'Tone-Poems,' op. 8, for organ (Leuckart).
Accompaniments for the Kyriale Parvum, the
hymnals 'Hosanna' and 'Cantemus Domino,' and

three Gregorian Masses (Coppenroth, Herder and Breitkopf respectively).

'O World, Full of Sunny Delight,' op. 20, for chorus, soli and orchestra (Breitkopf).

'Wittekind,' op. 28, ballad for men's chorus, soli and orchestra (Breitkopf).

'In the Summer Night,' op. 39, for chorus, baritone and orchestra (Breitkopf).

'Faring Minstrels,' op. 43, for men's chorus (Siegel) — also in German version.

'Song of the Spinning-Wheel,' op. 48, for women's chorus and piano (Hug).

'Morn on the Northern Coast,' op. 50, for chorus, baritone and orchestra (Breitkopf).

'Brittany,' op. 60, for chorus, baritone and orchestra (Breitkopf).

'Springtime,' op. 73, for soprano and alto with orchestra (Breitkopf).

Masses : Cordis Jesu, op. 6, three arrangements (Capra, J. Fischer).

St. Canisius, op. 26 (Boessnecker).

Mariæ Virginis, op. 49 (Schwann).

St. Cæcilia, op. 63 (Breitkopf).

'Te Christe Supplices,' op. 83 (Capra).

St. Ignatius, op. 84 (Coppenroth).

Gregoriana, op. 88 (Feuchtinger).

Immaculate Conception, op. 114 (in 'Cæcilia,' 1915).

Gregorian (eight), including Requiem (Breitkopf, Coppenroth).

Psalm 103, op. 68, for chorus, soprano and orchestra, German and English text (Breitkopf).

Many other works for the Catholic service, including Vespers, Litanies, Offertories, Hymns, etc.

Many songs, sacred and secular.

He has been a frequent contributor to musical journals in Europe and America, especially upon liturgical music. [R.7]

BOOTT, FRANCIS (1813–1904). See Register, 6.

‡ BORDES, CHARLES (May 12, 1863, Vouvray-sur-Loire, France : Nov. 8, 1909, near Toulon). See article in Vol. i. 362. In 1905 he was compelled by a nervous breakdown to leave the Schola Cantorum, but in the same year founded the Schola de Montpellier. His opera 'Les Trois Vagues' was not quite complete at his death. For orchestra he composed the overture 'Errege Juan' and 'Danses Béarnaises,' for piano and orchestra a 'Rhapsodie Basque,' for trumpet and orchestra, a 'Divertissement,' for flute and string-quartet, and a 'Suite Basque.' To these should be added pieces for piano and organ and choruses. He collaborated with Saint-Saëns on the new French edition of Rameau's works. See article in *Musiciens Français d'Aujourd'hui*, 2nd ed., 1911.

BORI, LUCREZIA (b. 1888). See Register, 10.

BORNSCHEIN, FRANZ CARL (Feb. 10, 1879, Baltimore), had his first musical instruction from his father, Theodore W. Bornschein, and then entered the Peabody Conservatory in 1896 as violin-student under Van Husteyn and of theory and composition under Hamerik, Kahmer and Boise. He

gained a prize for his String-Quartet in D in 1900 and received his diploma in 1902, giving a program of original works which included the prize string-quartet, groups of songs and a concerto in G minor for violin, played by himself. In 1905 he became violin-instructor and conductor of student-orchestras at the Conservatory. In 1906 his setting of Cunningham's 'A Wet Sheet and a Flowing Sea' was awarded the prize offered by Kimball through the Chicago Madrigal Club. In 1912, in the competition of the Mendelssohn Club of Cleveland, he won part of the divided first prize for a setting of Hugo's 'The Djinns' for orchestra, mixed chorus and baritone solo. In 1915 his cantata 'Onowa,' for mixed voices, soprano and orchestra, was awarded the first prize ($500) by the Tri-City Music Festival Association of New Jersey. His published works include a violin-concerto, groups of violin-compositions, choruses, cantatas with orchestra, piano-pieces and songs. His material in manuscript includes orchestral works in large forms, like the symphonic suite 'The Phantom Canoe,' the symphonic ballad 'Louisiana,' the symphonic poems 'The Rime of the Ancient Mariner' and 'A Hero's Espousal.' Other works are a Sextet for flute and strings, a Quintet in B minor for piano and strings, pieces for violin, songs and numerous choral works. He was music-critic on the Baltimore 'Evening Sun' for several years. In 1913 he became correspondent for 'Musical America.' He has contributed to leading periodicals, made editorial revisions and enlargements of standard violin-works, and supplied pedagogical material for his instrument in the Ditson Edition. In 1915 he became director of the orchestras at the Baltimore Music School Settlement and in 1916 organized a choral society at Smithsburg, Md. In 1918 he took charge of the Women's Chorus of the Myrtle Club in Baltimore, and was also appointed choir-director at the First Unitarian Church. [R.9]

BOROWSKI, FELIX (Mar. 10, 1872, Burton, England), came of distinguished Polish stock. His father gave him his early instruction on the piano and the violin. His mother was English, a pupil of Sterndale Bennett. She too had a large part in his training. During his school-days at London and at Tunbridge Wells he studied the violin with Jacques Rosenthal, a pupil of Léonard. He gained much from the constant practice of chamber-music at home. In 1887 he went to the Cologne Conservatory, taking violin with Japha, piano with Ernst Heuser and composition with Gustav Jensen. In London from 1889 he had violin-lessons from Pollitzer and counterpoint with Pearce. In 1892 he became violin-teacher at a school in Aberdeen, but the school soon failed and he returned to

London. In 1896 he produced his 'Russian Sonata,' which won strong commendation from Grieg, as also from Leschetizky, Sauer, Rosenthal and others. Its success led to a call to join the faculty of the Chicago Musical College as teacher of composition, beginning in August, 1897. Here he also taught the violin and lectured on music-history. Recently (April, 1916) he has succeeded to the presidency of the College. In 1905 he also was Chicago correspondent of the 'Musical Courier,' from 1906 critic for the Chicago 'Evening Post,' and in 1909–18 for the 'Record-Herald.' Since 1908 he has been the maker of the program-books for the Chicago Symphony Orchestra. His chief compositions are

'Marche Triomphale,' in D minor, for orchestra (1899, Chicago).
Concerto for piano and orchestra (1914, Chicago).
'Eugène Onégin,' symphonic poem.
'Crépuscule' and 'Sérénade,' for string-orchestra (1914, Ravinia Park).
'Allegro de Concert,' for organ and orchestra (1915, Chicago).
'Valse Pathétique,' for orchestra (1915, Chicago).
'Elégie Symphonique,' for orchestra (1917, Chicago).
'Trois Peintures' — 'Portrait d'une Jeune Fille,' 'Le Jardin de Nuit,' 'La Fête' (1918, Chicago).
String-Quartet in A minor, dedicated to Grieg.
'Boudour,' a pantomime-ballet (1920, Chicago).
Two Organ-Sonatas, in A minor and C.
Suite in E minor, for organ.
Many piano-pieces, largely, in small forms (over 60 published), but including the 'Russian Sonata' and a set of Seven Preludes.
Many shorter violin-pieces, of which the best-known is 'Adoration.'
Motet for 6-part chorus, organ and 'cello.
About 20 songs.   [R.8]

BOSETTI, JOSEPH (b. 1886). See Register, 10.

‡**BOSSI, MARCO ENRICO** (Apr. 25, 1861, Salò, Italy). See article in Vol. i. 366–7. In 1912 he resigned from the directorship of the Liceo Musicale at Bologna and has since lived at Como. Among his later works are a Suite for orchestra, op. 126, 'Intermezzi Goldoniani,' for string-orchestra, op. 127, and 'Giovanna d'Arco,' for soli, chorus and orchestra. See list of works in Baker, *Dict. of Musicians*, pp. 105–6.

BOSTON ACADEMY OF MUSIC. See ACADEMY OF MUSIC, Boston.

BOSTON CONSERVATORY OF MUSIC, THE, was founded in 1867 by Julius Eichberg, the eminent violinist, who continued at its head till his death in 1893. For many years it was one of the leading schools of the country, and before 1886 is said to have educated some 15,000 pupils. In violin-instruction it was especially eminent. As with its competitor, the New England Conservatory (also founded in 1867), much teaching was for a long time done in small groups instead of individually.

After Eichberg's death the Conservatory was for a time continued with success by Herman P. Chelius.

BOSTON IDEAL OPERA COMPANY, THE, was the name used from 1879 by a troupe of light-opera singers, the best of whom later (1887) formed the more famous company known as 'The Bostonians.' 'The Ideals' were first assembled by Miss Ober for the production of 'Pinafore.' Leading singers were Barnabee and Karl.

BOSTON MUSIC CO., THE, was started in 1885 by Gustave Schirmer, the son of the founder of the Schirmer house in New York, and conducted by him till 1891, when he returned to New York to succeed his father and the Boston house became a branch of that in New York. The Company has always maintained a considerable amount of independent publishing and has put forth much music by American composers.

BOSTON MUSIC SCHOOL, THE, was one of the early attempts to establish an institution in several departments. Preparation for it was begun by Benjamin F. Baker in 1847, when the Academy of Music, started by Mason in 1833, came to an end. The School was incorporated in 1851 and opened with a considerable faculty. Baker remained at its head until 1868, when the enterprise was given up.

BOSTON OPERA COMPANY, THE, was organized in 1908 on lines similar to those of the Metropolitan in New York and in such affiliation with it as to admit of more or less exchange of artists, especially for German works. A superb new opera-house was built and in November, 1909, the first season opened with 'La Gioconda.' To increase the supply of singers, the Boston Opera School was started, with an arrangement for 'débutante-nights' at intervals for the appearance of promising aspirants. In 1910 first American performances were given of Debussy's 'L'Enfant Prodigue,' Laparra's 'Habanera' and Rachmaninov's 'The Miser-Knight,' in 1911 of Converse's 'The Sacrifice,' and in 1913 of Bizet's 'Djamileh,' Aubert's 'La Forêt Bleue' and Février's 'Monna Vanna.' The number of performances each season was about 90. The outbreak of the war in 1914 led to the canceling of the next season, and in May, 1915, the enterprise went into bankruptcy. Many of its singers and most of its property were secured by Max Rabinoff, who for two years longer made tours with what was called the Boston National Opera Company, at first with remarkable success, especially in the fine presentation of ballets. But in 1917 this, too, became bankrupt.

BOSTON SINGERS' SOCIETY, THE. See BOYLSTON CLUB.

BOSTON SINGING CLUB, THE. See Vol. i. 369.

BOSTON STRING QUARTET, THE, was a chamber-group maintained in 1915–19 by players in the Boston Symphony Orchestra. It consisted of Sylvain Noack and Otto Rath, violins, Emil Ferir, viola, and Alwin Schroeder, 'cello.

BOSTON SYMPHONY ORCHESTRA, THE. See Vol. iv. 800–1. The supreme excellence of the Orchestra has been steadily maintained and its commanding influence widened and intensified. The character of the programs and of their interpretation has naturally varied somewhat with changing conductors, but the liberal and catholic policy of attention to the whole range of orchestral literature has been constant. Dr. Muck's first incumbency as conductor, on leave from Berlin, covered the seasons of 1906–08. From 1908 to 1912 he was followed by Max Fiedler. In 1912 Muck returned as permanent conductor, but in March, 1918, he was arrested as an enemy alien and in 1919 was sent out of the country. The conductor for 1918–19 was the French composer Henri Rabaud, and since 1919 Pierre Monteux (who had also led some performances in 1918 before Rabaud's arrival). In 1918 Witek resigned as concertmaster and was followed for one season by Fredric Fradkin, whose appointment was notable in view of his American birth. The stress connected with the removal of Muck in 1918 led to a reorganization of the management of the Orchestra, Major Higginson retiring from active direction, though without ceasing his hearty support, and the control passed into the hands of a strong Board of Directors. In 1919 Major Higginson died. It is commonly understood that his endowment of the Orchestra amounts to about $1,000,000. Since 1901 the program-books of the concerts have been prepared by Philip Hale. They form an extraordinary library of historical and critical information, set forth with force and much literary dexterity. See Howe, *The Boston Symphony Orchestra*, 1914.

BOSTONIANS, THE, were a troupe formed in 1887 for the giving of light opera. Its leaders were Henry C. Barnabee, Tom Karl and W. H. Macdonald, and the company derived many of its members and its initial prestige from the previous Boston Ideal Opera Company. The latter troupe had set a fine standard for artistic finish and the new company carried it still higher. The organization continued for about twenty-five years with remarkable success, bringing out a long list of graceful or comic works and introducing a notable succession of effective singers. See Barnabee, *My Wanderings*, and also the résumé of works and singers in *The Art of Music*, iv. 175–7.

BOTT, JEAN JOSEPH (1826–1895). See Register, 7.

BOTTA, LUCA (1882–1917). See Register, 10.

BOUCHER, A. See Register, 3.

BOUSDOUSQUIÉ. See Register, 4.

‡BOUGHTON, RUTLAND (1878, England), was a pupil of Stanford at the Royal College of Music, where he studied in 1900–01. In 1904–11 he taught singing at the Birmingham School of Music. When the World War broke out he tried to enlist, but was declined at first for physical reasons. In the belief that artistic effort had value for quickening national spirit, he started in August, 1914, a series of musico-dramatic festivals at Glastonbury in Somerset, aiming at first only to bring out a cycle of music-dramas on Arthurian subjects by the late Reginald R. Buckley and himself. In spite of some checks and interruptions, the enterprise has gone on and expanded until now it has enthusiastic support from a large circle of musical and literary people and there is prospect of the erection of a special theater for the plays. Up to 1919 there had been 79 performances, of which 47 were operatic. Five were premières of dramas by English composers. Boughton's compositions include the following:

Stage-works —
'The Immortal Hour,' choral drama, libretto by Fiona MacLeod.
'The Birth of Arthur,' choral drama, libretto by Buckley; and 'The Round Table,' choral drama, libretto by Buckley — these forming the cycle 'Arthur of Britain.'
'Bethlehem,' based on the Coventry Nativity-Play.
'The Death of Columbine,' opera-ballet in one act, text by Bostock.
'Dawn at Agincourt,' dramatic scene, text from Shakespeare.
'The Moon-Maiden,' choral ballet.
'The Death-Dance of Graine,' ballet.
'Snow-White,' ballet, scenario by Margaret Morris.
Choral works with orchestra —
'Sir Galahad,' choral march, text from Tennyson.
'The Skeleton in Armor,' symphonic poem, text from Longfellow.
'The Invincible Armada,' symphonic poem, text from Schiller-Lytton.
'Midnight,' symphonic poem, text by Edward Carpenter.
'A Song of Liberty,' text by Helen Bantock.
Choral works unaccompanied —
Five sets of Choral Variations on English Folk-Songs (Reeves).
'The City,' motet, text by Henry Bryan Binns.
Chamber and orchestral works —
'The Chapel of Lyonesse,' for piano, string-quartet and three solo voices, text by William Morris.
'A Celtic Prelude,' for piano, violin and 'cello.
'March of the British,' for orchestra (Reeves).
Three Folk-Dances for strings (Curwen).
Also several smaller choral works.

See article by Herbert Antcliffe in 'The Musical Quarterly,' January, 1918.

BOULLAY, LOUIS. See Register, 2.

BOURNE, WILLIAM (d. 1885). See Register, 3.

BOWEN, GEORGE OSCAR (b. 1873). See Register, 8.

‡ BOWEN, YORK (Feb. 22, 1884, London). See article in Vol. v. 618-9. Further works are :

Two Symphonies (the latter produced by the New Orchestra in London, Feb. 1, 1912).
'Tasso,' symphonic poem.
Concert-Overture.
Suite in D minor, for violin and piano.
Two viola-sonatas, in C minor and F (Cobbett Prize).
Phantasy-Trio, for violin, 'cello and piano.
Quartet, for four violas.
Phantasy-Septet, for clarinet, horn, string-quartet and piano (one movement).
String-Quartet in D minor, op. 41 (two movements).
'Poem,' for solo viola, harp and organ.
Three Suites and 'Suite Mignonne,' for piano.

BOWMAN, EDWARD MORRIS (July 18, 1848, Barnard, Vt. : Aug. 27, 1913, Brooklyn), was a graduate of St. Lawrence University, Canton, N. Y. He came to New York in 1866 for a year's study with William Mason (piano) and J. P. Morgan (organ and theory). In 1867 he went to St. Louis, where for three years he was organist at the Union Methodist Church and for two at the Second Presbyterian Church. In 1872-74 he was in Berlin under Bendel in piano, Haupt and Rohde in organ and Weitzmann in composition, twice going to Paris in summer for organ-lessons with Batiste. Returning to St. Louis, he resumed his place at the Second Presbyterian Church, taught piano and organ, and in 1877 published an English version of Weitzmann's *Manual of Musical Theory*, which was based on his own notes of Weitzmann's teaching (from this a German version was made). For a time in 1881 he was with Guilmant in Paris and also worked in London with Macfarren, J. F. Bridge and Turpin. He was the first American to become an associate of the Royal College of Organists. Save for this year abroad he was organist at the Second Baptist Church in St. Louis from 1877 to 1887. In 1883 he was president of the M. T. N. A. (also in '84, '93, '94 and 1905). In 1884 he was the organizer and till 1893 president of the American College of Musicians, which did much to raise standards of teaching. In 1887-94 he was organist at the Peddie Memorial Baptist Church in Newark, in 1895-1906 at the Baptist Temple in Brooklyn (with a noted choir of 200) and from 1906 at Calvary Baptist Church in New York (also with large choir and orchestra). While at Newark (1891-95) he also served as music-professor at Vassar College in Poughkeepsie,

following Ritter. In 1896 he was a founder of the A. G. O. He was not only a superior organist, but had marked ability as a teacher. His forceful personality impressed itself upon music-education in many ways. [R.5]

BOYD, CHARLES N. (b. 1875). See Register, 8.

BOYLE, GEORGE FREDERICK (June 29, 1886, Sydney, Australia), was the son of music-teachers, began piano-lessons at five and made his first public appearance in Sydney at seven. He undertook concert-tours as pianist at fourteen, continuing thus in Australia, Tasmania and New Zealand for five years. He then went to Berlin and studied for a time with Busoni. His first recital-program in Berlin (March, 1908) included MacDowell's 'Keltic' Sonata (first time there). He concertized in Holland from October, 1906, and in London from June, 1908, being associated in Holland with Emma Nevada and in Great Britain with Pauline Donalda and Maud Allan. In 1908 he played at the reception to the King and Queen of Spain, and in 1910 appeared with the Queen's Hall Orchestra under Wood. In 1910 he came to America as teacher of piano at the Peabody Conservatory in Baltimore. While thus busy with teaching he has found opportunity to give recitals not only in Baltimore, but in New York, Boston and other cities. He has made several tours in the South. His compositions include

Concerto in D minor, for piano and orchestra (Schirmer), given at the Worcester Festival of 1911, in New York in 1912 and elsewhere, with Hutcheson as pianist, as well as in England and Australia.
Symphonic Fantasie, for orchestra, given by St. Louis Orchestra in 1916 and New York Symphony Society in 1918.
Concerto for 'cello and orchestra, given by Philadelphia Orchestra in 1918 with Kindler as 'cellist.
Sonata for 'cello and piano, given in London in 1909 with Jacques Renard as 'cellist.
Sonata in B, for piano, given in Baltimore in 1916 by composer.
'The Pied Piper of Hamelin,' cantata for tenor, baritone, contralto, chorus and orchestra (Chappell).
'Don Ramiro,' dramatic cantata (text from Heine) for soprano, tenor, bass, chorus and orchestra.
'Slumber-Song,' for orchestra, given by American Orchestra, Chicago, in 1915.
'Aubade,' for orchestra, given by St. Louis Orchestra in 1916.
Andante Lamentoso for string-quartet.
Many shorter piano-pieces and songs, some published by Schirmer, Novello, Carl Fischer, etc.
[R.10]

BOYLSTON CLUB, THE, of Boston, was organized in 1873 as a choral society of about 200 voices. In 1875-93 it was led by George L. Osgood and speedily achieved a fine reputation for artistic efficiency in interpreting secular works. After 1890 it was known as the Boston Singers' Society.

BRADBURY, WILLIAM BATCHELDER
(Oct. 6, 1816, York, Me. : Jan. 7, 1868,
Montclair, N. J.), from 1830 had lessons on
the piano and organ in Boston from Sumner
Hill and Lowell Mason and attended the
latter's singing-classes. From 1834 he served
as church-organist. In 1836 Mason sent
him to Machias, Me., to lead a class and later
to St. John's, N. B. In 1840 he was organist
in Brooklyn, and from 1841 at the Baptist
Tabernacle in New York, where and in other
churches he organized popular singing-classes.
These latter led to annual 'festivals,' held at
the Broadway Tabernacle, and hastened the
recognition of music in the public schools.
In 1841 he published his first book, *The Young
Choir*, assisted by Hastings, with whom in
1844–51 he collaborated upon four others of
more importance. In 1847–49 he was in England and Germany, studying at Leipzig with
Hauptmann, Moscheles, Ernst Wenzel and
Böhme, besides investigating methods of
popular instruction. After his return to New
York he was active in classes and 'conventions'
and in editing song-books, sacred and secular.
In 1854, with his brother E. G. Bradbury,
he went into the business of piano-making
with success. Altogether, he was author or
editor of about sixty collections of popular music.
Among these, *The Jubilee* (1858) had a sale
of over 200,000 copies, and *Fresh Laurels* and
the 'Golden' series had even greater popularity. Of his two Sunday-school cantatas,
'Daniel' (1853) and 'Esther' (1856), the latter for many years had an enormous vogue.
Many of his simple, but melodious tunes are
still in wide use. See TUNE-BOOKS, 1841, and
under Hastings; also Hall, *Gospel Song and
Hymn Writers*, pp. 23–7. [R.3]

BRADBURY PIANO CO., THE, of New
York, is the present name of the business
established in 1854 by E. G. and W. B. Bradbury. Its development on modern lines was
due to the skill and enterprise of F. G. Smith,
who in 1861 helped perfect the 'Bradbury'
piano and in 1867 became W. B. Bradbury's
successor as head of the firm. It has been
continued under F. G. Smith, 2nd, and F. G.
Smith, 3rd. Since 1917 William Knabe, 3rd
(b. 1872), has been general manager.

BRADFORD, SAMUEL F. See TUNE-
BOOKS, 1830.

BRAHAM, HERBERT J. (b. 1885). See
Register, 9.

BRAINARD, SILAS (1814–1871). See Register, 3.

BRAINARD'S SONS & CO., of Cleveland,
is the publishing-house founded in 1836 by
Silas Brainard and taken over in 1871 by his
sons Charles S. and Henry M. Brainard. In
1876 the firm erected a large building of its
own. They also have a house in Chicago.

BRANDEIS, FREDERIC (July 5, 1835,
Vienna, Austria : May 14, 1899, New York),
was early a pupil of Czerny and Fischhof
(piano) and of Rufinatscha (composition).
He was brought to America at fourteen and
studied with Meyerhofer in New York, making
his début as pianist in New York in 1851.
He toured with concert-companies, like that
of Wallace, but finally settled in New York
as teacher and composer. He was organist
of the (R. C.) Cathedral in Brooklyn and of
one of the large New York synagogues. His
larger works, though performed, are unpublished (see list in Baker, *Dict. of Musicians*,
p. 113). [R.4]

BRANDT, HERMANN (b. 1842). See
Register, 6.

BRANSCOMBE, GENA (Nov. 4, 1881,
Picton, Ont.), is descended from a family that
settled in New York in 1640. She was a
pupil at the Chicago Musical College in 1897,
studying piano with Ziegfeld and Friedheim
and composition with Borowski. On graduating in 1899 she won a medal for composition.
A further year of piano-study with Hans von
Schiller brought another medal and appointment in the faculty of the College, which she
held for seven years. In 1904 she studied
piano with Ganz, and in 1905 composition,
especially song-writing, with Von Fielitz.
In 1907–09 she was piano-teacher at the
Whitman Conservatory in Walla Walla, Wash.
Going to Berlin in 1909 she resumed work
under Ganz, with composition under Humperdinck. In 1910 she married John Ferguson
Tenney of New York and has since lived there.
Her songs have been widely sung. About
seventy are published (Schirmer, Ditson,
Schmidt), and the following have won special
favor : 'The Morning Wind,' 'I bring you
heartsease,' 'Krishna,' 'Hail, ye tyme of
holie-dayes,' 'Dear little hut by the rice-
fields,' 'There's a woman like a dewdrop,'
'Three Mystic Ships,' 'Boot and Saddle,'
'Dear is my inlaid sword,' and 'Just in the
hush.' She has also four cycles for solo
voice, many part-songs for women's or mixed
voices and piano- and violin-pieces. A 'Festival Prelude' for orchestra was composed for
the MacDowell Festival at Peterboro, N. H.,
in 1914. [R.9]

BRASE, HAGBARD (b. 1877). See COL-
LEGES, 3 (Bethany C., Kan.).

BRASLAU, SOPHIE. See Register, 10.

BRATTLE, THOMAS (d. 1713). See Register, 1.

BREIL, JOSEPH CARL (b. 1870). See
Register, 8.

BREMNER, JAMES (d. 1780). See Register, 1.

BRESSLER–GIANOLI, CLOTILDE (1875–
1912). See Register, 9.

BRETHERICK, HENRY (b. 1849). See
Register, 6.

BREWER, JOHN HYATT (Jan. 18, 1856,
Brooklyn), for seven years from 1864 was boy-
soprano in various Brooklyn and New York
churches, meanwhile taking lessons on the
piano and the organ. From 1871 he was
organist for two years at the City Park Chapel
in Brooklyn, for four at the Church of the
Messiah (P. E.), for four at the Clinton Avenue
Church (Congregational), and finally, since
1881, at the Lafayette Avenue Church (Presbyterian). Besides general teaching and some
recital-work, he has been active as conductor,
having been leader of the Cecilia Society,
the Flatbush Glee Club, the Hoadley Amateur
Orchestra, and especially the Apollo Club
(all in Brooklyn). He was one of the original
members of the Apollo Club in 1877 and
during the twenty-five years of Buck's
leadership its only accompanist. When Buck
retired in 1903 he became his successor, continuing ever since. He was a charter-member
of the music-section of the Brooklyn Institute,
its secretary from the first and since 1906 one
of its fellows. He was a founder of the A. G.
O., fellow since 1902 and in 1905-08 warden.
In 1914 he was made Mus.D. by New York
University. In his youth he was for ten
years (1878-88) a pupil of Buck in composition. The influence of his teacher may doubtless be seen in the following list of works :

String-Quartet in D minor.
Suite in G minor, for orchestra — Prelude, Bar-
    carolle, Intermezzo, Peasants' Dance and Finale
    (1891).
'April Winds,' a fantasie for orchestra.
'Valse Caprice' and 'Romanza,' for string-quintet
    and flute.
'A Springtime Sketch,' a scherzo for string-quartet.
'An April Song,' a cantilena for string-
    quartet.
'Rêverie,' for organ, harp, 'cello and violin (Gray).
'Forest Song' and 'Dance of the Gnomes,' sketches
    for 'cello and piano.
'The Lady of the Lake,' for organ, piano and 'cello
    (1891, Mason & Hamlin prize).
'Up with the Flag !' (1894, Brooklyn City prize).
'Lord of the Dunderberg,' cantata for men's
    voices and orchestra (1905, Schubert Glee Club
    prize).
'Bedouin Love-Song,' a cappella chorus for mixed
    voices (Chicago Madrigal Club prize, 1906).

The total number of his compositions is
about 200. [R.6]

'BRIDE OF MESSINA, THE.' An opera
by J. H. Bonawitz, brought out at Philadelphia in 1874.

‡BRIDGE, FRANK (Feb. 26, 1879,
Brighton, England). See article in Vol. v.
619. In 1910-11 he conducted the Brema
opera-season at the Savoy Theatre and in
1913 the Beecham season at Covent Garden.
Additional works are a 'Dance-Rhapsody'
for orchestra (1909, Liverpool Festival), the
orchestral suite 'The Sea' (1912), a 'Dance

Poem' for orchestra (1914, Philharmonic) and
notable extensions of his chamber-music list.

BRIGNOLI, PASQUALINO (d. 1884).
See Register, 4.

BRINKERHOFF, CLARA M., née Rolph.
See Register, 4.

BRISTOW, GEORGE FREDERICK (Dec.
19, 1825, Brooklyn : Dec. 13, 1898, New
York), at eleven was playing the violin at the
Olympic Theatre in New York. From 1842
for over thirty years he was a first violinist in
the New York Philharmonic Society. He
was conductor of the Harmonic Society in
1851-62, a church-organist and from 1854
until his death a visiting-teacher in the New
York public schools. W. J. Henderson has
described him as 'a most earnest man, filled
with a real love for his art, and self-sacrificing
in labor for its benefit' and as 'one of the
earliest of the long-suffering band of American
composers, who will be remembered always as
one who strove to push American music into
artistic prominence.' His chief work was the
opera 'Rip Van Winkle,' performed in New
York on Sept. 27, 1850, and again in 1870. An
overture was played by the Philharmonic
Society on Jan. 9, 1847, his second symphony
on Mar. 1, 1856, his third symphony on Mar.
26, 1859, and his 'Arcadian' symphony on
Feb. 14, 1874. He also wrote two oratorios,
'Praise to God' (1860) and 'Daniel' (1867) ;
two cantatas, 'The Great Republic' (1880)
and 'Niagara'; an unfinished opera, 'Columbus'; two symphonies besides those noted
above ; two string-quartets; and many smaller
works. [R.4]

BRISTOW, WILLIAM RICHARD (1803-
1867). See Register, 3.

BROADHURST, MISS (1775?- ?). See
Register, 2.

BROCKWAY, HOWARD A. (Nov. 22,
1870, Brooklyn), after beginning the piano
with Kortheuer, from 1890 spent five years
at Berlin with Barth (piano) and Boise (composition). In February, 1895, he gave a
concert there which included, besides piano-
solos, his Symphony in D and his violin-
sonata, making the impression of unusual
maturity. From 1895 he worked in New York
as pianist and teacher and in 1903-10 was in
the faculty of the Peabody Conservatory in
Baltimore, then returning to New York. In
1910 he was the judge of the Earl Grey Competition at Toronto. Later he joined Lorraine
Wyman in collecting the folk-songs of the
Kentucky highlands, published as *Lonesome
Tunes*, 1916 (Gray). His works include the
following :

Symphony in D, op. 12 (1895), given by Boston
    Symphony Orchestra in 1907.
Ballade in G minor, op. 11, for orchestra (1895).
Scherzino for orchestra.

'Sylvan Suite,' op. 19, for orchestra — 'Midsummer Idyl,' 'Will o' the Wisps,' 'Dance of the Sylphs,' 'Evening Song,' 'Midnight,' 'At Daybreak,' given by Boston Symphony Orchestra in 1903.

Sonata in G minor, op. 9, for violin and piano (1895).

Cavatina and Romanza, for violin and orchestra (1895).

Suite in E minor, for 'cello and orchestra (or piano).

Variations on an original theme, for piano.

'Charakterstücke,' 'Phantasiestücke,' 'Moods,' 'Serenade' and many sets of pieces for piano.

'Sir Oluf,' cantata for mixed chorus and orchestra.

'Des Sängers Fluch' and two others, for 8-part chorus a cappella.

Suite for 'cello and piano, op. 35.

Quintet for strings and piano, op. 36.

Concerto for piano, op. 37.

See appreciations in Hughes, *Contemporary American Composers*, pp. 298–304, and *The Art of Music*, iv. 382–3. [R.8]

BROMFIELD, EDWARD, Jr. (1723–1746). See Register, 1.

BROOKFIELD SUMMER SCHOOL OF SINGING, THE, Brookfield Center, Conn., was founded in 1900 by Herbert W. Greene, who has continued at its head ever since. The enterprise has developed into a significant colony of musical workers and students.

BROOKLYN ORATORIO SOCIETY, THE, was organized in 1893 by Walter Henry Hall, who has remained its conductor to the present time. Adopting a high standard from the first, it speedily secured recognition. During the first twenty years two concerts were given annually in the Academy of Music, the only adequate concert-hall in the city. When this was burnt, for the season of 1904–05 the concerts were transferred to Carnegie Hall in New York, but later resumed in the superior new Academy of Music in Brooklyn. The Society in its early days was much aided by the interest of Howard W. Connelly, who had been secretary of Thomas' Brooklyn choral society, and by the adoption of its concerts into the system of entertainments under the Brooklyn Institute of Arts and Sciences. In 1912 Mr. Hall became professor at Columbia, and the Society was made one of the two sections in the University Chorus, assisting there on festival occasions, but with entire freedom for its own local concerts. Besides the more usual oratorios, the Society has to its credit Handel's 'Samson' and 'Acis and Galatea,' Bach's St. Matthew Passion, Liszt's 'St. Elizabeth,' the second performance in America of Henschel's Requiem (Metropolitan Opera House), Elgar's 'Black Knight' and 'Banner of St. George,' and the first performances in America of Elgar's 'King Olaf,' 'The Music-Makers,' 'Spirit of England' and Harty's 'Mystic Trumpeter.' Two Brooklyn composers have also been represented, Buck by 'The Light of Asia' and

'The Golden Legend,' and Shelley by his 'Vexilla Regis.'

BROOKLYN PHILHARMONIC SOCIETY, THE. See Vol. iv. 801.

BROOKS, HENRY MASON. See Register, 7.

BROOME, WILLIAM EDWARD (1868, Manchester, England), had his early training from Roland Rogers of Bangor Cathedral; in theory he is largely self-taught. He was assistant-organist of Bangor Cathedral and of St. Mary's at Bangor in 1883–90. He conducted the Penrhyn Male Chorus, which visited the Chicago Eisteddfod in 1893, and gave many organ-recitals in the United States and Canada. He located first in Brockville, Ont., moved to Montreal in 1894, and in 1905 to Toronto, where in 1907 he succeeded Vogt at the Jarvis Baptist Church. In 1910 he organized the Toronto Oratorio Society, which has given important works with the assistance of the New York Philharmonic, Russian Symphony and Toronto Symphony Orchestras. He holds the degree of Mus.D. (by examination) from Toronto University. He has officiated as judge in the choral contests at the Chicago, Buffalo and St. Louis Expositions and in many other cities. He has published about 100 works (chiefly Schirmer, Ditson, Boston Music Co., Schmidt). These include the short cantata 'A Hymn of Trust,' for tenor solo, chorus and orchestra (Schirmer); the dramatic chorus 'Sea-Song,' with orchestra (Ditson); many anthems and a series of Opening Sentences from the Psalms. He was the recipient in Wales of eight national prizes for composition, the most important being for the opera 'The Siege of Cardiff Castle,' when Bridge, Parry and Mackenzie were the judges. [R.8]

BROSKY, FRANK J. (b. 1883). See Register, 9.

BROUNOFF, PLATON G. (May, 1863, Elizabethgrad, Russia), had his musical education at the Musical Institute in Warsaw and the Imperial Conservatory at Petrograd, Rubinstein and Rimsky-Korsakov being among his teachers. In 1891 he came to America and in 1892 settled in New York as teacher, singer and lecturer. He has lectured on Russian music and kindred topics for the Board of Education in New York and many other cities, taught operatic classes at the Institute of Musical Art and been lecturer on art and supervisor at the Modern Arts Forum. He has written the Indian opera, 'Ramona'; the oratorio 'The Glory of God'; a music-drama, 'Xilona'; four symphonies — 'Russian Revolution,' 'Return of the Jews to Palestine,' 'Carnival in Rome' and 'Titanic'; four suites for piano and two for violin; the overture 'Russia'; and numerous songs. He is the author of *The Ten Commandments of Piano-Practice.* [R.9]

BROWN, ALLING. See TUNE-BOOKS, 1823.

BROWN, BARTHOLOMEW. See Register, 3, and TUNE-BOOKS, 1802.

BROWN, EDDY (July 15, 1895, Chicago), whose father was an Austrian Pole and his mother a Russian, began violin-study at an early age and continued with Hubay in Budapest, receiving the artists' diploma from the Royal Conservatory when only twelve. He then went to Petrograd and studied with Auer. In 1910 he made a sensational début in Berlin, and appearances with many European orchestras followed, under conductors like Nikisch, Mengelberg, Safonov and Steinbach. Since 1916 he has toured in America, playing with all the large orchestras and appearing in every important city. He has composed much for violin and piano, besides many songs, and has made numerous arrangements for violin. A musical comedy, finished in 1919, is promised an early New York production. [R.10]

BROWN, WILLIAM. See Register, 2.

BROWN COLLECTION OF MUSICAL INSTRUMENTS, THE, at the Metropolitan Museum of Art in New York, one of the largest in the world, was gathered mainly by Mary E. (Adams) Brown (d. 1917), wife of John Crosby Brown, who for many years was at the head of the banking-firm of Brown Brothers. In 1884 Mrs. Brown, having procured a few Italian instruments for decorative purposes, became interested in their historic and scientific value and became a zealous collector. In 1889 she offered the 275 specimens that she then had to the Metropolitan Museum, retaining the right to increase and supervise the Collection during her lifetime. This offer was accepted, and a small but interesting group of instruments, mostly given by Joseph Drexel, was combined with her donation. The growth of the Collection from that time was rapid and so wisely directed that it soon became one of the remarkable features in the Museum. In 1893 adequate rooms for its display were assigned in the new north wing, the number of items then being about 700. In 1899 this number had increased to over 2000, in 1906 to over 3500, and is now about 3700.

In its present arrangement, the Collection offers opportunity for study in three ways: (*a*) ethnographically, by countries or races; (*b*) historically, by periods or stages; (*c*) systematically or analytically, by classes and types. In each series, where actual specimens of importance are not available, they are represented by reproductions or photographs. Great pains is taken to facilitate intelligent study by explanatory labels, diagrams and other illustrations, collateral information and

book-references. A notable extension of the Collection is the series of engraved, etched or lithographed portraits of composers, performers and writers — numbering nearly 1000 specimens — which has developed from initial gifts by Thatcher M. Adams in 1899 and Mrs. Charles B. Foote soon after. The manufacture of many leading modern instruments is illustrated by analytic models of parts in process of formation. Because of its comprehensiveness and system the Collection is not only valuable for musical history, but also significant for the ethnologist, the student of social manners and implements, and inquirers about matters so diverse as the arts of decoration and the science of acoustics. Because of its size, and especially because displayed with unparalleled clearness and convenience, it has but one or two rivals anywhere.

Though exceedingly rich in other directions, the Collection is noted for its rare specimens of keyboard-instruments. Chief among these is the Cristofori piano of 1720, the earliest of the two known examples of his own handiwork. The elegant double spinet of Grovellus (1600) is one of but three known instances of this peculiar type. Of harpsichords there are two fine specimens with two banks, from the 17th and the 18th centuries respectively, and one with three banks, made by Sodi in 1779. Curious and historic is the claviorganum (harpsichord and organ combined), originally made in 1712 for the Elector of Hanover, but its harpsichord division remodeled into a piano, which was once in Carl Engel's famous collection. In 1911 the Museum received from Bernardus Boekelman a Ruckers virginal of 1622 and a Pasquino Querci spinet.

BROWN MUSICAL LIBRARY, THE ALLEN A., in the Boston Public Library, was presented in 1894 by Allen A. Brown, a Boston business-man. It then contained about 7000 volumes. By further gifts from Mr. Brown and others and by purchases it was increased to about 11,000 in 1910, and is now reckoned at about 15,000. It is rich in many different directions — in scores of every sort, instrumental and vocal, in standard critical editions of the complete works of great composers, in historical, theoretical and critical works about music, in unique collections of programs, etc. The collection is located in a separate section of the Library, and is for reference only. See Vol. ii. 717, and paper by H. G. Wadlin, the librarian, in *M. T. N. A. Proceedings*, 1910, pp. 192–200.

BROWNE, JOHN LEWIS (May 18, 1866, London), the son of an English organist, was brought to America in 1873 and studied with S. P. Warren and Archer. In 1888–92 he was organist of the Holy Name Cathedral in Chicago, in 1892–98 at San Francisco, in 1899–

L

1907 at Atlanta, in 1908–10 at Wanamaker's in Philadelphia, and since 1912 at St. Patrick's Church in Chicago and also theory-teacher at the Metropolitan Conservatory. In 1901 he was soloist at the Royal Academy of St. Cecilia in Rome, and appeared at the World's Fairs at St. Louis in 1904 and at Jamestown in 1907. In Philadelphia he gave over 500 concerts and has been heard in recital in most of the larger cities. He designed the great organ in the Medinah Temple in Chicago, at its opening playing Borowski's 'Allegro de Concert' for organ and orchestra for the first time, the composer conducting. At Atlanta he conducted the Symphony Orchestra and the Atlanta Festival for three years. In 1914 he was elected to the Royal Philharmonic Academy in Rome, and in 1916–19 was dean of the Illinois Chapter of the A. G. O. He has written the opera 'La Corsicana' (New York, 1903), a Missa Solemnis (1913), the motet 'Ecce Sacerdos Magnus' (Paulist Choristers at the Vatican, 1912), and more than sixty lesser pieces, vocal and instrumental. In manuscript are a suite for orchestra, a 'Romanza' for orchestra and an organ-sonata. He was made Mus.D. by the Grand Conservatory, New York, in 1902. [R.7]

BROWNLEE, CORNELIA. See COLLEGES, 3 (Shurtleff C., Ill.).

BROWNSON, OLIVER. See TUNE-BOOKS, 1783.

‡BRUCH, MAX (Jan. 6, 1838, Cologne, Germany). See article in Vol. i. 407–8.[1] He retired from active participation in musical affairs in 1910. His later compositions include

'Szene der Marfa,' op. 80, for mezzo-soprano and orchestra, text from Schiller.
Osterkantate, op. 81, for soprano, chorus, orchestra and organ.
'Das Wessobrunner Gebet,' op. 82 (arranged from op. 19), for mixed chorus, orchestra and organ.
Eight Trios, op. 83, for piano, violin and 'cello (or three clarinets).
Konzertstück, op. 84, for violin and orchestra (Norfolk Festival, 1911).
Romanza in F, op. 85, for violin and orchestra.
Six songs, op. 86, for mixed chorus.
'Die Macht des Gesanges,' op. 87, for baritone, chorus, orchestra and organ, text from Schiller.
Concerto, op. 88, for two pianos and orchestra.
'Heldenfeier,' op. 89, for chorus and orchestra.
Also male-chorus arrangements of Welsh and Scotch folk-songs, and the male choruses 'Dem Kaiser' and 'Vom Rhein.'

BRUENING, HANS (b. 1868). See Register, 8.

BRUENNER, LEOPOLD (b. 1869). See Register, 7.

BRUNDAGE, RUTH. See COLLEGES, 3 (Wilmington C., Ohio).

[1] The statement in Vol. v. 620, that 'he died in Vienna, Sept. 17, 1907,' should have been entered under the name of *Ignaz Brüll.*

BRUNE, ADOLF GERHARD (June 21, 1870, Baccum, Germany), first studied with his father. From 1887 he took the regular course at the Teachers' Seminary in Osnabrück, and in addition kept up studies in piano, violin and clarinet. In 1889–94 he was organist at Peoria, Ill. Since 1894 he has been in Chicago, from 1898 to 1917 as teacher of piano and theory at the Chicago Musical College. At the start of his Chicago career he worked with Liebling and he also had advice from Ziehn in composition. Concert-playing was given up in favor of teaching and composing. His list of compositions now extends to op. 76. The Ballade in E minor for piano, op. 2, and the Ballade in F, op. 11, are published by Leuckart, while Schott & Sons have published the Sonata in D minor for piano and violin, which has been praised for harmonic richness and contrapuntal skill. The string-quartet, op. 5, has been played by the Spiering, Philadelphia and Flonzaley Quartets, and movements from the string-quartets, opp. 26 and 38, by the Chicago and Kneisel Quartets. The 'Lied des Singschwans,' a symphonic poem for large orchestra, has been given by the Chicago Orchestra under Stock; 'Ein Dämmerungsbild' was introduced by Kunwald and the Cincinnati Orchestra in 1917; and the 'Overture to a Drama' was brought forward by Stock. Many of his songs, organ-pieces and choral works have been heard in public, though not yet published. A fuller list of works is given in Baker, *Dict. of Musicians*, p. 124. [R.7]

BRUNER, MINNIE C., née Brown (b. 1864). See COLLEGES, 3 (Franklin C., Ind.).

BRYANT, ANNA G. See COLLEGES, 3 (Lombard C., Ill.).

BRYANT, GILMORE WARD (b. 1859). See Register, 7.

BUCHHALTER, SIMON (b. 1881). See Register, 9.

BUCK, DUDLEY (Mar. 10, 1839, Hartford, Conn. : Oct. 6, 1909, Orange, N. J.). See article in Vol. i. 413–4. Buck's career, becoming established just when and as it did, exerted an important formative impression on American development. He had solid musicianship as organist and composer, combined with the wisdom and tact required to win and hold popular appreciation. Much of his early work as organ-recitalist was educational in much the same way as that of Thomas when on his early orchestral tours. For a long time he exerted a profound influence upon choir-music, especially as the American exaltation of the quartet-choir fell in with his own predilections. In this field what he set out to do was extraordinarily well done. Regarding his choral works it is fair to point out his fine sympathy

DUDLEY BUCK.

with his texts and the versatility with which he secured expression. He was the direct inspiration of many pupils, but he was also an indirect educator of the public taste. [R.5]

BUCK, DUDLEY, JR. (b. 1869). See Register, 8.

‡BUCK, PERCY CARTER (Mar. 25, 1871, West Ham, England). See article in Vol. v. 620. Besides the positions at Harrow and Dublin there mentioned, which he still holds, he has been president of the Royal College of Organists and of the Union of Graduates in Music. He has published *Ten Years of University Music at Oxford*, 1894 (with Mee and Woods), *Unfigured Harmony*, 1911, *The Organ: a Complete Method*, other instruction-books and *The Oxford Song Book*.

BUEHRER, GEOFFREY CARL (b. 1878). See Register, 9.

BUHLIG, RICHARD (b. 1880). See Register, 9.

BUHRMANN, THOMAS SCOTT GODFREY (b. 1887). See Register, 9.

BULL, OLE BORNEMANN (Feb. 5, 1810, Bergen, Norway : Aug. 17, 1880, Lysöen, near Bergen). See article in Vol. i. 418–9. His first concert in America was on Nov. 23, 1843. The first tour included Havana as well as the eastern United States. It lasted nearly two years, the concerts numbered over 200 and the receipts were about $400,000. His second trip was in 1852, and it was then that he made the ill-fated purchase of the tract in Pennsylvania which he named Oleana, hoping 'to found a New Norway, consecrated to freedom, baptized in independence, and protected by the mighty flag of the Union.' On this trip he went to California, via Panama, and his fellow-travelers were Adelina Patti and Maurice Strakosch. For about two months early in 1855 he was lessee of the Academy of Music in New York, and offered a prize of $1000 for 'a grand opera by an American composer on an American subject.' After the collapse of the colony-scheme and the ensuing litigation he returned to Bergen in the autumn of 1857. In 1867 came his third trip, in which the first concert was in Chicago. In 1868 he married Sara Chapman Thorp in Wisconsin. [She wrote his biography, *Ole Bull — A Memoir*, 1883, and died on Jan. 18, 1911, at Cambridge, Mass.] After spending the summer of 1872 in Norway, in the autumn he returned for the fourth time. This trip was but one year in duration. His last tour was in 1879–80, with Emma Thursby. See biography by Vik, Bergen, 1890. [R.4]

BULL, WILLIAM (1762–1842). See TUNE-BOOKS, 1813.

BULLARD, FREDERICK FIELD (Sept. 21, 1864, Boston : June 24, 1904, Boston), was first a student of chemistry at the Massachusetts Institute of Technology, but left to study music with Rheinberger at Munich in 1888–92. Returning to Boston, he lived there as teacher of harmony and counterpoint and composer. Of his forty published songs the best-known are 'In the Greenwood,' 'A June Lullaby,' 'From Dreams of Thee,' 'At Daybreak,' 'Hymn of Pan,' 'On the Way,' 'The Sword of Ferrara,' 'The Singer,' 'The Hermit' and 'The Stein Song.' He also published church-music, choruses for men's voices and edited song-collections. See Hughes, *Contemporary American Composers*, pp. 351–7. [R.8]

BULLOCK, ARTEMAS ERWIN. See COLLEGES, 3 (Ellsworth C., Iowa).

BULLOCK, WILLIAM. See TUNE-BOOKS, 1854.

BUONAMICI, CARLO (b. 1875). See Register, 9.

BURDETT, GEORGE ALBERT (b. 1856). See Register, 7.

BUREAU OF EDUCATION, THE, which is a division of the Interior Department of the National Government, has shown its interest in the promotion of music in public institutions by the issue of Bulletins on 'The Study of Music in Public Schools,' 1886, 'Music-Education in the United States,' by Arthur L. Manchester, 1908, and 'Music in the Public Schools,' by Will Earhart, 1914. Another, on the Music-Libraries of the country, is almost ready.

BURLEIGH, CECIL (Apr. 17, 1885, Wyoming, N. Y.), after preliminary violin-study with L. E. Hersey in Bloomington, Ill., in 1903–05 was in Berlin, studying violin with Witek and composition with Leichtentritt. Two years were then spent in Chicago, where his teachers were Sauret and Herrmann for violin and Borowski for composition. Then came two years of concert-work and two of violin-teaching at the Western Institute of Music and Dramatic Art in Denver. He taught violin and theory at Morningside College in Sioux City, Ia., in 1911–14, and at the State University at Missoula, Mont., in 1914–19. In the summer of 1919 he was with Auer and in the autumn located in New York as player and teacher. His interest in composition began about 1901, but was not specially manifest until about 1910. Since then he has been diligent and his works have met with unusual success. His violin-concerto in E minor (prize for a violin-concerto by an American, Chicago, 1916) he played with the American Symphony Orchestra in Chicago on Mar. 2, 1916, and later with the Minneapolis, Milwaukee and other Orchestras, besides being brought forward by Maud Powell. The 'Song of the Brook' has been much used by

Galli-Curci, and 'What does little Birdie say' by McCormack. The 'Ascension' sonata has been played by David and Clara Mannes and others. His list of works is as follows:

Two Fancies, op. 5, for piano (Summy).
Eight Characteristic Pieces, op. 6, for violin and piano (Wood).
'The Letter,' a song, op. 8 (Pond).
'Coasting,' op. 9, for piano (Presser).
'Childhood Fancies,' op. 10, for piano (Schirmer).
Four Rocky Mountain Sketches, op. 11(Schirmer).
'Scherzando Fantastique', op. 12 (Carl Fischer).
Four Prairie Sketches, op. 13 (Schirmer).
Five Sketches, op. 14 (Schirmer).
'Snow-Bound,' a Winter Idyl, op. 15, after Whittier (Schirmer).
Six Winter-Evening Tales, op. 16 (Schirmer).
Five Tone-Poems, op. 17 (Schirmer).
Twelve Short Poems, op. 18 (Ditson).
Eight Concert-Studies, op. 19, for violin and piano.
'Skeleton Dance,' op. 20, for violin and piano (Schirmer).
Four Small Concert-Pieces, op. 21 (Schirmer).
Sonata, 'The Ascension,' op. 22, for violin and piano (Schirmer).
Six 'Nature Studies,' op. 23, for violin and piano (Fischer).
Five Characteristic Pieces, op. 24 (Ditson).
Concerto in E minor, op. 25, for violin and orchestra (Summy).
Three Pieces, op. 26, for piano (Ditson).
'Sonnets of Autumn,' op. 27, seven piano-pieces (Ditson).
'Fairyland Cycle,' op. 28, five songs.
Sonata, on the Life of St. Paul, op. 29, for violin and piano (Schirmer).
Six Pictures, op. 30 (Fischer).
Six Fancies, op. 31, for violin and piano (Boston Music Co.).
Five Songs, op. 32 (Ditson).
Seven Songs, op. 33 (Fischer).
Fantastic Suite, 'Jack and the Bean-stalk,' op. 35, for violin and piano.
Plantation Sketches, op. 36, for violin and piano (Fischer).
'To a River,' op. 37, song (Schirmer).
Four Fancies, op. 38 (Schirmer).
'Evangeline,' op. 41, a tone-poem for full orchestra, after Longfellow.
Three Mountain Pictures, op. 42, for full orchestra.
Second Concerto, op. 43, for violin and orchestra or piano (Fischer).
'Nature's Voices,' op. 44, four pieces for violin and piano.
Two Songs, op. 45, from Lowell (Schirmer).
Two Songs, op. 46 (Church).
Three Songs, op. 47 (Ditson).
'Songs of Nature,' op. 49 (Church).
Seven Idyls in Song, op. 50.   [R.9]

BURLEIGH, HENRY THACKER (b. 1866). See Register, 7.

BURLIN, NATALIE, née Curtis, is a niece of George William Curtis. She was born in New York and studied in the National Conservatory there with Friedheim, as well as in Berlin, Paris, Bonn and Bayreuth. She has made extensive original studies of the music, lore and pictorial art of the American Indians, and of music among the Negroes of America and among the Ndaus and Zulus in Africa. She has published *Songs of Ancient America*, 1905, *The Indian's Book* (200 songs from 18 tribes), 1907, *Negro Folk-Songs*, 4 vols., 1918, and *African Folk-Songs*. She has also lectured often and written many articles for magazines. In 1917 she married the painter Paul Burlin. [R.9]

BURMEISTER, RICHARD (Dec. 7, 1860, Hamburg, Germany), had the privilege of study and association with Liszt in 1880–83 at Weimar, Rome and Budapest. Till 1885 he traveled in Europe as pianist, and then came to America as chief piano-instructor in the Peabody Conservatory in Baltimore. His twelve years' work there was broken in 1893 by a concert-tour in Europe. In 1897 he became director of the Scharwenka Conservatory in New York. Since 1903 he has taught abroad, till 1906 in the Dresden Conservatory and since 1907 in the Klindworth-Scharwenka Conservatory in Berlin. His compositions are a piano-concerto in D minor, op. 1; a symphonic fantasy, 'Die Jagd nach dem Glück,' op. 2; Cadenza to Chopin's F minor Concerto, op. 3; three songs, op. 4; Capriccio for piano, op. 5; a setting of Tennyson's 'The Sisters,' for alto with orchestra; a Romanza for violin and orchestra; and piano-transcriptions of songs. He has rescored Chopin's Concerto in F minor and arranged an orchestral accompaniment for Liszt's 'Pathetic' Concerto. [R.7]

BURNHAM, THUEL (b. 1884). See Register, 9.

BURR, WILLARD, JR. (b. 1852). See Register, 7.

BURROWES, KATHARINE (Kingston, Ont.), has devoted herself to improving teaching-methods for children. In her first teaching in Detroit she made a specialty of the primary grades. After six years' study with Batchelder, in 1895 she entered the faculty of the Detroit Conservatory. Later she studied for a time with Klindworth in Berlin. In 1903 she founded the Burrowes Piano School. Her copyrighted *Course of Music-Study* involves the use of songs, stories, games, charts and mechanical devices, besides printed music and the piano. It has been gradually developed to produce an all-round musical education for children. She has provided many other aids for teaching primary music and has composed much music for children. She has published *The Burrowes Course of Music-Study for Beginners* (kindergarten and primary), 1895, *Manual for Teachers*, 1901, *The Note-Gatherers*, 1903, *Musical Puzzle-Stories*, 1905, *New Manual for Teachers* 1910, *Tales of the Great Composers*, 1911, *New Musical Note-Gatherers*, 1915, and *The New Success Music-Method*, 1917. She has also contributed to musical magazines. [R.8]

BURTON, FREDERICK RUSSELL (Feb. 23, 1861, Jonesville, Mich. : Sept. 30, 1909, Lake Hopatcong, N. J.), was graduated from Harvard in 1882 *summa cum laude* and with highest honors in music. While there he wrote music for 'Hiawatha,' a favorite legend with him from childhood. This setting, notable as one of the first attempts to use Indian themes, was sung at a glee-club concert in 1882, completed as a dramatic cantata and published in 1898. He undertook an intimate study of Indian music in Canada and the United States, spending much of his time and means, and living among the Indians for long periods. In 1903 he published *Songs of the Ojibway Indians*, later expanded into the masterly treatise *American Primitive Music* (containing 28 Ojibway songs) and published in 1909, just after his death. In 1896 he organized and conducted a choral society at Yonkers, N. Y. For some years he wrote musical criticisms for the New York 'Sun.' Other compositions are 'The Legend of Sleepy Hollow' (1900), an 'Inauguration Ode' (1901) for the second inauguration of President McKinley, and various songs and choruses. He also wrote the novels *The Song and the Singer, Her Wedding Interlude, Shifting Sands,* and *Strongheart.* [R.7]

BUSCH, CARL (Mar. 29, 1862, Bjerre, Denmark), first entered the University of Copenhagen as a law-student, but the appeal of music soon led to study with Olavesen, Krugel and Langgaard and then to taking violin with Tofte at the Conservatory, piano with Bondesen and theory with Hartmann and Gade. During a three years' course he played under Gade in the Musical Society, Svendsen in the Philharmonic and Dahl in the Tivoli Orchestra. By way of Brussels, in 1886 he went to Paris, playing and studying under Godard. In 1887 he came to Kansas City, where for over thirty years he has conferred prestige upon the city by many useful undertakings. He formed the Orchestral Society and conducted it for five years, and its successor, the Philharmonic, which emphasized Scandinavian works in a long series of Sunday concerts. Several festivals were

under his direction. Since 1912 he has led the Symphony Orchestra, and is active in choral and church-music. As guest-conductor he has given his own works with various American orchestras, and also in Leipzig, Dresden and Copenhagen. He is a naturalized citizen here, but was knighted in 1912 by the Danish government in recognition of his services to Scandinavian music. As composer he has become widely known. His list of works includes

'The Passing of Arthur,' a symphonic prologue after Tennyson (Breitkopf).
'Minnehaha's Vision,' a symphonic poem (Ditson).
'Elegy,' for string-orchestra (Breitkopf).
Cantatas:
  'The League of the Alps' (Ditson).
  'King Olaf' (Ditson).
  'Paul Revere's Ride' (Ditson).
  'A Song of Spring' (Ditson).
  'The Four Winds' (Gray) — prize at Philadelphia.
  'The American Flag' (Gray).
  'May,' for children's voices and orchestra (Gray) — prize at Evanston Festival.
  'The Brown Heather,' for men's chorus and orchestra (Gray).
  'The Voice of Spring' (Luckhardt & Belder).
  'America' (Boston Music Co.) — prize at New Jersey Tri-City Festival.
  'Quivera' — prize at Topeka Festival.
  'The Song of a Star' — prize from Brooklyn Arion.
  'Alexander's Feast,' for men's chorus — prize at Pittsburgh.
  'Ode to Breckinridge' — prize at Lexington, Ky.
  'Denmark's Day.'
  'The Fourth of July.'
  'Ode to France.'
About 20 choruses and anthems, and over 40 songs and many violin-pieces (above publishers).
Symphony in C.
String-Quartet.
Two Suites for orchestra.
'When the Heart is Young' and 'The Day is Done' — prizes from the Chicago Madrigal Club.

Busch is a Longfellow enthusiast and has set many of his poems. He has also delved much into Negro and Indian music, as shown by themes in his suites, songs and other works. [R.7]

BUSHNELL, J. See TUNE-BOOKS, 1807.

BUTCHER, FRANK CHARLES (b.1882). See Register, 9.

BUTLER, HAROLD LANCASTER (b. 1874). See Register, 8.

C

CABLE COMPANY, THE, of Chicago, includes the piano-making enterprises previously carried on under the names Cable, Conover, Kingsbury and Wellington. Its capital is over $6,000,000, and it occupies its own building on Wabash Avenue and Jackson Boulevard. Its special automatic device is known as the 'Carola Inner-Player.'

CADEK, JOSEPH OTTOKAR (b. 1868). See Register, 8.

CADMAN, CHARLES WAKEFIELD (Dec. 24, 1881, Johnstown, Pa.), acquired his musical education entirely in Pittsburgh, with Edwin Walker, Leo Oehmler, W. K. Steiner and Luigi von Kunits. In 1904–10 Paur gave him valuable assistance. Aside from composition, he was engaged in piano-teaching, writing criticisms for the 'Dispatch' and as organist at the East Liberty Presbyterian Church till 1910, when he removed to Los Angeles, where he has been busy with composing and lecture-recitals. His well-known interest in the music of the American Indians dates from 1906, when he first came to know the ethnological studies of Miss Fletcher and La Flesche. The results of his early experiments were embodied in four 'American Indian Songs,' op. 45 (1908), of which 'The Land of the Sky-blue Water' was made popular by Nordica. He spent the summer of 1909 on the Omaha and Winnebago Reservations with La Flesche, gathering material by phonograph-records and otherwise. An immediate result was the 'American Indian Music-Talk,' which he has given often in America, as well as in Paris and London in 1910. In recent years the Indian mezzo-soprano Princess Tsianina Redfeather has acted as his vocal illustrator. The culmination of his use of Indian themes is found in the three-act opera 'The Land of Misty Water' (or 'Daoma'), begun in Pittsburgh in 1909 and finished in Colorado in 1912, libretto by La Flesche and Mrs. Eberhart; the opera 'Shanewis' (or 'The Robin-Woman'), libretto by Mrs. Eberhart; and the 'Thunderbird' orchestral suite, based on Blackfeet Indian melodies. The last has been played by the Russian, Kansas City and Los Angeles Orchestras, and is to be published by Boosey. His first opera has not yet been performed, but 'Shanewis' was given five times at the Metropolitan Opera House in 1918 and three times in 1919. Of it Finck said in the 'Evening Post,' 'At last the Metropolitan has a novelty of American origin which is worth preserving for future seasons'; Henderson in the 'Sun,' 'He has shown greater command in the technic of opera than any of his pre-decessors at this opera-house'; and Chase in the 'Times,' 'A more concise, telling series of incidents has not been seen nor heard in grand opera.' His theories about using Indian themes are thus stated in an article in 'The Musical Quarterly,' July, 1915:

'Only one-fifth of all Indian thematic material is valuable in the hands of a composer — is suitable for harmonic investment. It becomes necessary to choose an Indian song or chant that is attractive in its simplicity, one that will stand alone by virtue of its inherent melodic line, and is fairly good in symmetry; otherwise the idealizer is confronted with a formidable problem. When found, these themes are pure gold. And they exist, certain critics to the contrary notwithstanding.'

The catalogue of his published compositions and arrangements (1919) forms a 30-page booklet. It lists 77 secular and 6 sacred songs; the song-cycles 'Four American Indian Songs,' op. 45, 'From Wigwam and Tepee,' op. 57, four songs on tribal melodies, and 'Idyls of the South Sea,' op. 55; the Japanese Romance 'Sayonara,' op. 49; 'Three Songs to Odysseus,' op. 50; the song-cycle 'The Morning of the Year,' op. 46, for four solo voices; the cantata for male voices, 'The Vision of Sir Launfal'; and many part-songs for men's, women's or mixed voices. There is a long list of piano-pieces; several cycles for piano, including the 'Idealized Indian Themes,' op. 54; and many original compositions and arrangements for organ, violin and piano, etc. The outstanding instrumental compositions are the Sonata in A, op. 58, for piano, and the Trio in D, op. 56, for violin, 'cello and piano (both White-Smith). Of the latter *The Art of Music* says: 'The leading characteristics are melodic spontaneity and freshness of musical impulse. Everywhere are buoyancy, directness of expression, motion, but little of thematic involution or harmonic or formal sophistication. It is the trio of a lyrist; from the standpoint of modern chamber-music it might be called naïve, but the strength, sincerity and beauty of its melodies claim, and sometimes compel, one's attention.' In manuscript (1919) is the one-act opera 'The Garden of Mystery,' libretto by Mrs. Eberhart, based on Hawthorne's story of 'Rappaccini's Daughter.' [R.9]

CADY, CALVIN BRAINERD (June 21, 1851, Barry, Ill.), had his first training at Oberlin, where he also taught in the public schools in 1871–72. In 1872–74 he was at the Leipzig Conservatory, where his teachers were Richter, Papperitz and Paul. Returning to Oberlin, he taught harmony and piano at the Conservatory in 1874–79. His ambition was to see music given recognition in college

150

CHARLES WAKEFIELD CADMAN

education. So in 1880 he gladly accepted
a call to the University of Michigan, where,
perhaps for the first time, music became
eligible as a major subject for the A.B. and
A.M. degrees. To lead up to such courses,
music was also made a major in the Ann
Arbor high school, then a special preparatory
school for the University, and thus this high
school was about twenty-five years in advance
of the present widespread movement. A
careful study of the work done by his students
convinced him that it raised problems about
the primal education of the child. This led
to his present work, carried on under the name
'Music-Education,' with the motto from
D'Israeli, 'Music teaches most exquisitely
the art of development.' The Music-Education School in Portland, Ore., was founded
in 1913, and has steadily grown in numbers
and influence. In it music is only one of the
subjects, of equal value with, but no more than
any other subject. In 1888–94 he taught in
the Chicago Conservatory, and in 1892–94 was
editor of 'The Music Review.' In 1901–07 he
was in Boston as private teacher; in 1907–10
he lectured in the music-extension department
of Teachers College (Columbia University) in
New York; in 1908–13 he was lecturer on
pedagogy in the Institute of Musical Art there.
For many years he has conducted summer normal courses in the larger cities of the country.
He is author of *Music Education*, 3 vols.,
1902–07, and articles in the *Encyclopedia of
Education* and magazines. [R.6]

CAHOON, HELEN FOUTS. See Colleges, 3 (Texas Christian U.).

CAIN, LLEWELLYN B. (b. 1867). See
Colleges, 3 (Whitman C., Wash.).

CALZIN, ALFRED LUCIEN (b. 1885).
See Register, 9.

CAMP, JOHN SPENCER (Jan. 30, 1858,
Middletown, Conn.), graduated from Wesleyan
University in 1878 and took a post-graduate
year in Latin, besides some law-study. His
training in piano and harmony was with E. A.
Parsons in New Haven, in organ with Shelley,
Buck and S. P. Warren, and in theory and
composition with Buck and Dvořák. His chief
engagements as organist have been in 1882–
1906 at the Park Congregational Church in
Hartford and at the First (Congregational)
Church there in 1906–18. In 1902–11 he
was conductor of the Hartford Philharmonic
Orchestra (50 players), bringing out both
standard and new works of importance, and
retiring because of ill-health. He was one
of the founders of the A. G. O. in 1896 and
served for several years on its Council. He
has given many organ-recitals and musical
lectures. From 1890 he was active in the
Connecticut Music Teachers' Association
and was its president in 1898. For many

years he has been treasurer of the Austin
Organ Company in Hartford. He has published the cantatas 'The Morning Star'
(Christmas), 'The Prince of Peace' (Christmas) and 'The Prince of Life' (Easter);
'The Song of the Winds,' for soli, chorus and
orchestra; 'God is our Refuge' (Psalm 46),
for soli, chorus and orchestra; anthems,
songs and piano-pieces. He has also an
overture, 'Der Zeitgeist'; a 'Pilgrim' Suite
for orchestra, in three movements, based
on Bunyan's allegory; a string-quartet in G;
'Chant d'Amour' and 'Spring-Song' for orchestra; a Romanza and Serenade for violin,
'cello and piano; a Romanza-Fantasia for 'cello
and small orchestra; and a small suite for
violin and piano. [R.7]

CAMPANARI, GIUSEPPE (Nov. 17, 1858,
Venice, Italy), having been first trained as
a 'cellist, was for some years in the orchestra
at La Scala in Milan. His first engagement
in America in 1884 was as 'cellist in the Boston
Symphony Orchestra. In 1888–90 he also
played in the Adamowski Quartet. He had
been studying singing meanwhile, and in 1893
made his début as leading baritone of Hinrichs'
Opera Company in New York. He sang Tonio
in the first American performance of 'I Pagliacci' during his first season, and proved equally
successful in both opera and concert. From
1895 for three seasons he was engaged at the
Metropolitan Opera House. Since then he
has devoted himself largely to concert-work
and teaching. [R.7]

CAMPANARI, LEANDRO (b. 1857).
See Register, 7.

CAMPANINI, CLEOFONTE (Sept. 1.
1860, Parma, Italy : Dec. 19, 1919, Chicago),
in 1870–78 studied violin with Ferrarini in
Parma and later with Bazzini in Milan. In
1883 he made his début at Parma as conductor
in 'Carmen,' and the same year was assistant-
conductor to Vianesi at the Metropolitan
Opera House in New York. In 1887 he
returned to the Metropolitan to conduct the
first American performance of 'Otello.' He
conducted at Covent Garden in London in
1900–12, at La Scala in Milan in 1903–06, and
at San Carlo in Naples for one year. He also
made extensive tours in Spain, Portugal and
South America. In 1906 he was engaged by
Hammerstein as conductor and artistic director of the Manhattan Opera House in New
York, where he remained until differences of
opinion led to his resignation in 1909. At
that time De Koven, writing in the New
York 'World' of his popularity and influence,
said, 'Campanini is one of the best operatic
conductors that we have ever had in New
York. His authority, his wide artistic sympathies, his untiring energy and faithful care
in the study and rehearsal and rare interpre-

tative grasp of a composer's meaning, as well
as his absolute control of his orchestra in all
the varying shades of orchestral expression
stamp him as a conductor of the very first
rank.' In 1910, when the Chicago Opera
Company was organized, he became principal
conductor and in 1913 general director, a
position held till his death. He produced the
following works for the first time in America:
Massenet's 'Thaïs,' 'Le Jongleur de Nôtre-
Dame,' 'Grisélidis,' 'Sapho,' 'Hérodiade,'
'Cendrillon,' 'Cléopâtre' and 'Marie Made-
leine'; Debussy's 'Pelléas et Mélisande';
Charpentier's 'Louise'; Wolf-Ferrari's 'I
Giojelli della Madonna' and 'Il Segreto di
Suzanna'; Parelli's 'I Dispettosi Amanti';
Goldmark's 'The Cricket on the Hearth';
Camille Erlanger's 'Aphrodite'; Frédéric
d'Erlanger's 'Noël'; Kienzl's 'Ranz des
Vaches'; Franchetti's 'Cristoforo Colombo';
Gnecchi's 'Cassandra'; Nouguès' 'Quo
Vadis?'; Herbert's 'Natoma'; Blockx'
'Princesse d'Auberge'; Saint-Saëns' 'Déjanire';
Buchhalter's 'A Lovers' Knot'; and Guns-
bourg's 'Le Vieil Aigle.' His sudden death was
due to pneumonia. His wife, Eva (b. 1864),
the sister of Louisa Tetrazzini, was a favorite
operatic soprano, but has not been active in
recent years. [R.7]

CAMPANINI, ITALO (1846–1896). See
Vol. i. 450, and Register, 6.

CAMPBELL, CHARLES DIVEN (b.1877).
See STATE UNIVERSITIES (Ind.).

CAMPBELL, FRANCIS JOSEPH (1834–
1914). See Register, 4.

CAMPBELL, WILLIAM WILSON (b.
1871). See COLLEGES, 3 (Westminster C., Pa.,
Trinity U., Tex.).

CAMPBELL–TIPTON, LOUIS (Nov. 21,
1877, Chicago), began music spontaneously as
a child, and at fifteen was already publishing
simple songs. In 1896 he entered the Leipzig
Conservatory, where he studied theory with
Schreck and had help from Reinecke — the
latter finding him rather an intractable and
independent pupil. After three years he returned to America and remained two years.
Since 1901 he has resided in Paris, where his
piano-works and songs have been frequently
heard. Though he has specialized in these
directions, he has in manuscript two operas,
orchestral works, etc., of which the titles are
not yet available. He thinks that 'the prospect is not so hopeless as formerly of getting
a production for American works of this
calibre,' and adds that he has 'never been fond
enough of work to be ready to sacrifice time
and energy for the completion of a large work,
where I have seen no hope of its ever being
made known.' His published works include,
for violin and piano, a 'Suite Pastorale'
(Leuckart), a 'Romanza Appassionata' (Con-

solidated Music Co.), and a 'Lament' (Schir-
mer) ; for piano, a 'Sonata Heroic' (Schirmer),
the suite 'The Four Seasons' (Leuckart), two
'Legends' (Schirmer), two Preludes, two
Bagatelles, a 'Nocturnale' and a 'Matinale'
(Leuckart) ; and about thirty songs, including
'Three Shadows,' 'A Spirit-Flower,' 'Four
Sea-Lyrics,' 'A Fool's Soliloquy,' 'Love's Jes-
ter,' 'Rhapsodie,' 'Invocation,' 'All the words
that I gather,' 'The Opium-Smoker,' 'Mem-
ory,' 'Love's Logic,' 'Homeward' (Schirmer) ;
'Elegy,' 'At the Tomb' (Boston Music Co.) ;
'Hymn to the Night' (Gray) ; Seven Tone-
Poems, 'Thou art my All,' 'Serenade,' 'If I
were a King' (Consolidated Music Co.).
[R.9]

CANADIAN ACADEMY OF MUSIC,
THE, of Toronto, was established in 1911.
With it in 1918 was amalgamated the Toronto
College of Music, which since 1888 had been
under the leadership of the late F. H. Torrington. Thus was formed an institution of excellent quality, which not only serves a large
clientèle in Toronto, but has examination-cen-
ters throughout the Dominion.

CANADIAN GUILD OF ORGANISTS,
THE, founded in 1909, is an organization
upon the same lines as the American Guild of
Organists. The president since the beginning
has been Albert Ham of Toronto.

CANDIDUS, WILLIAM (b. 1845). See
Register, 5.

'CANTERBURY PILGRIMS, THE.' An
opera by Reginald De Koven, first given at the
Metropolitan Opera House on Mar. 8, 1917,
under Bodanzky's direction. The libretto
is by Percy Mackaye. It was five times
repeated in 1917.

CANTU, AGOSTINHO (b. 1879). See
Register, 9.

CAPEN, SAMUEL. See TUNE-BOOKS, 1805.

CAPOUL, JOSEPH AMÉDÉE VICTOR
(Feb. 27, 1839, Toulouse, France). See article in Vol. i. 460. He first came to America
in 1873 as a member of the Strakosch troupe
which included Nilsson, Miss Cary, Campanini and Maurel. In 1879–80 he toured the
country with the French Opéra Bouffe Company. In 1892 he was engaged as professor
of operatic singing at the National Conservatory in New York. In 1897 he became
stage-manager at the Opéra in Paris. Since
his retirement from this post he has lived near
Toulouse and is reported to be writing his
memoirs. [R.6]

CAPPA, CARLO ALBERTO (b. 1834).
See Register, 4.

CAPRON, HENRI. See Register, 2.

CARADORI–ALLAN, MARIA CATE-
RINA (1800–1865). See Register, 3.

CARDEN, ALLEN D. See TUNE-BOOKS,
1827.

CAREY, BRUCE ANDERSON (b. 1877). See Register, 9.

CARL, WILLIAM CRANE (Mar. 2, 1865, Bloomfield, N. J.), was first trained on the piano by his sister and by Madeline Schiller. His study of organ and theory was under S. P. Warren in New York and Guilmant in Paris. In 1882–90 he was organist of the First Presbyterian Church in Newark, and since 1892 has been organist at the First Presbyterian Church in New York. Here he has produced many important oratorios and has given over 150 recitals, the programs being devoted mostly to French, English, Italian and American works. Many compositions have been specially written for these recitals by leading composers. In 1899 he founded the Guilmant Organ School, where he is still director and chief organ-teacher. This school has a roll of over 100 full graduates, many holding prominent positions. He was one of the founders of the A. G. O. and has always been prominent in its affairs. New York University made him Mus.D. in 1911. The French Government in 1909 had already given him the title of Officier de l'Instruction Publique. He was largely influential in arranging the American tours of Guilmant and Bonnet. He himself has toured extensively and inaugurated many important organs. The record includes recitals in both Europe and America and as soloist with the leading orchestras, solo engagements at the World's Expositions for several years, and even a series in the Klondike, Alaska. Among the works which he has edited are *Master-Pieces for the Organ*, *Thirty Postludes*, *Novelties for the Organ*, 2 vols., *Ecclesiæ Organum*, *Festival Music*, 5 vols., *Master-Studies for the Organ*, and a *Historical Album of Organ Music*. [R.7]

CARNAL, JAMES EDWARD (b. 1870). See COLLEGES, 3 (Kansas Wesleyan U.).

CARNEGIE, ANDREW (Nov. 25, 1837, Dunfermline, Scotland : Aug. 11, 1919, Lenox, Mass.). Among the many interests of this remarkable man music was not the least. He had unusually quick and delicate hearing, as is shown by his being one of the first to take telegraphic messages by ear. This led to his promotion while yet a boy to be assistant to Thomas A. Scott, the head of the Western Division of the Pennsylvania Railroad. He always delighted in 'the concord of sweet sounds,' and often quoted the oriental exclamation, 'O music, sacred tongue of God, I hear thee calling, and I come.' To him listening to an organ as played by a master was a devotional experience, and hence he found pleasure in helping congregations to acquire instruments that might enrich their worship. One of the first gifts he made in early manhood, when his prosperity began,

was an organ for the little church in Allegheny where his relatives and friends attended. The total number of churches thus aided was 7689, of which 4092 were in the United States (1351 in Pennsylvania alone), 2119 in England, 1005 in Scotland, 219 in Ireland, 32 in Wales and the remainder in the British Colonies all over the world. The aggregate expended by him in this way was about $6,250,000. He was also responsible for the installation of concert-organs in many places, among the earliest being those in the assembly-halls of the libraries which he built in Pittsburgh and adjoining towns. He provided for the perennial giving of recitals twice a week in Pittsburgh, both at the Library on the North Side (formerly Allegheny) and at the Carnegie Institute, making them 'free to the people.' This unique provision took effect in Allegheny in 1889 and in Pittsburgh in 1895.

He became a member of the Oratorio Society of New York in 1885 and was its president for thirty years (1888–1918). He was also a member and president of the Philharmonic Society there in 1901–09. His interest in the Oratorio Society resulted in 1891 in the erection of Carnegie Music Hall at Seventh Avenue and Fifty-Sixth Street, which became at once a chief center of musical art in the metropolis. He was the friend of many musicians, and in quiet and unostentatious ways aided some of them to secure recognition and success. His home in New York and his country-houses in Scotland and the United States were all provided with noble organs, and he employed the most capable organists to play on them.

The Trust which he created for the United Kingdom, having its seat at Dunfermline, has displayed sedulous care for musical education, and in 1916 announced a plan under which it agrees to publish important new musical works, at the same time guaranteeing the copyright to the composer. This has already resulted in the publication of a number of musical compositions of merit.[1] [R.7]

CARNEGIE INSTITUTE, THE, of Pittsburgh, erected by Andrew Carnegie in 1895, besides being the center for many other educational facilities and undertakings, includes a large concert-hall where free organ-recitals are given twice a week. The official organists have been Frederick Archer (1895–1901), Edwin H. Lemare (1902–05) and Charles Heinroth (since 1907). The organ, built by the Skinner Company in 1918, has four manuals and 115 stops.

CARPENTER, JOHN ALDEN (Feb. 28, 1876, Park Ridge, Ill.), has won a notable

[1] For the data for this article special thanks are due to Dr. William J. Holland, Director of the Carnegie Institute in Pittsburgh.

place among American composers through his fortunate, straightforward and untrammeled faculty of musical expression, prompted by technical fluency and skill and marked by unusual charm and refinement. His mother, a distinguished amateur singer, gave him his first lessons, and Miss Fay and Seeboeck were his next teachers. In 1897 he graduated from Harvard University, having taken all the musical courses available. For a short time he studied with Elgar, and in 1908–12 was under Ziehn in Chicago. Despite all this musical activity, since 1897 he has primarily engaged in the mill, railway and vessel supply-business of George B. Carpenter & Co., and since 1909 has been its vice-president. His first published work in larger form was the sonata for violin and piano (1913). An orchestral suite, 'Adventures in a Perambulator' (1915), has been played by the Chicago and New York Symphony Orchestras. The Concertino for piano and orchestra, written in 1915, was published in 1919. His Symphony No. 1, written in 1916–17 and played at the Norfolk Festival of 1917, has not yet been published. Among his songs, made familiar by leading singers, are the song-cycles 'Gitanjali' (poems by Tagore), 'Improving Songs for Anxious Children' (poems, music and pictures by John and Rue Carpenter), 'Water-colors,' four Chinese tone-poems, as well as twenty-four detached songs. From the latter may be singled for special mention 'Go, Lovely Rose,' 'A Cradle-Song,' 'The Green River,' 'Les Silhouettes' and 'Chanson d'Automne.' Only four piano-compositions have yet appeared in print. [R.9]

CARR, BENJAMIN (1769, England : May 24, 1831, Philadelphia), came to America in 1793. He had had excellent advantages, among them experience in the enterprise known as 'The Antient Concerts' under Joah Bates. He established the first music-store in Philadelphia, with a branch in New York from 1794 (later sold to James Hewitt), and from 1794 for more than thirty years was noted as a ballad-and opera-singer, pianist, organist, conductor and composer, chiefly in Philadelphia. In 1820 he was a leader in the organization of the Musical Fund Society there and was one of its early conductors. The Society erected a tablet to his memory in St. Peter's Church and his portrait, by Darley, was the first of its collection (reproduced in Sonneck, *Early Opera*, p. 102). Besides many other works, all marked by taste and facility, in 1796 he brought out in New York the opera 'The Archers,' libretto by William Dunlap, which was repeated at least twice there and also in Boston. Of this work only two fragments are known (see Sonneck, *Early Opera*, pp. 98–100). About 1800 he edited a 'Musical

Journal,' and from 1805 published several collections of sacred music (see TUNE-BOOKS), as well as theoretical text-books. His sound musicianship and his practical versatility made him highly influential. See note in *I. M. S. Sammelbde.* 6. 466, many references in Sonneck, *Concert-Life* and *Early Opera*, Madeira, *Music in Philadelphia*, etc. [R.2]

CARREÑO, MARIA TERESA (Dec. 22, 1853, Caracas, Venezuela : June 12, 1917, New York). See article in Vol. i. 474. Her début as pianist occurred at the instance of Gottschalk at Irving Hall in New York on Nov. 7, 1862, leading to a series of six concerts from Nov. 25 to Dec. 22, the last in the Academy of Music before an audience of 4000. A longer series followed in Boston, where she played with orchestra. She toured England and the Continent in 1865–74, and it was at Edinburgh on May 24, 1872, that she sang the part of the Queen in 'Les Huguenots.' On her return to America in 1875 she studied singing with Mme. Rudersdorff in Boston, and began an operatic career which lasted until 1882. During the winter of 1875–76 she gave occasional piano-lessons to MacDowell, prior to his departure for Paris. His second piano-concerto is dedicated to her, and she, the first other than himself to play his works in public, was an ardent propagandist for his music. After 1882 she appeared widely as concert-pianist, but her greatest fame dates from her European trip of 1889–90. She was four times married — in 1872 to the violinist Sauret, in 1875(?) to the baritone Giovanni Tagliapietra, in 1892 to the pianist d'Albert, and in 1902 to Arturo Tagliapietra. Two children by the second marriage have become musically noted. Her last recital was in Havana on Mar. 21, 1917. Her compositions were written in early life. The best known is the waltz 'Mi Teresita.' There are also études and concert-pieces for the piano, a string-quartet, and a 'Petite Danse Tsigane' for orchestra — about 40 in all. The Venezuelan Hymn she composed is not the national anthem, but a festival hymn for the centenary of Bolivar (1883). [R.5]

CARRILLO, JULIÁN (b. 1875). See Register, 9.

CARROLL, JAMES P. See TUNE-BOOKS, 1820.

‡ CARSE, ADAM [formerly A. von Ahn] (May 19, 1878, Newcastle-on-Tyne, England). See article in Vol. v. 622. Add to the list of compositions Symphony No. 2, in G minor (1909, Newcastle Festival) ; Variations in A, for orchestra (1911, London, Queen's Hall) ; 'Norwegian Fantasia,' for violin and orchestra (Williams) ; 'Fritiof,' grand opera in three acts (1915) ; Miniature Suite, for string-orchestra (Augener) ; Miniature Suite for

orchestra (1917, France); Sonata for violin and piano, in C minor (1919, Augener); and Variations on a theme in A minor for piano-duet (1919, Williams). He has also written a *Summary of the Elements of Music* and *Practical Hints on Orchestration* (both Augener). The list of his published piano- and violin-pieces, songs, and educational works makes a considerable catalogue. He was in active service in France as a private in the infantry in 1917–19.

CARTER, ERNEST TROW (b. 1866). See Register, 8.

CARTER, HENRY (Mar. 6, 1837, London, England : ?), of a family of organists, had early training from his father, Pauer, Goss and Steggall in England and from Haupt, Kiel and Hiller in Germany. He began church-playing at nine and at seventeen went to Canada, where from 1854 he was organist at the Quebec (English) Cathedral and founded the first Canadian oratorio society. In 1864 he removed to Boston to become one of the regular players on the new organ in Music Hall, as well as organist at the Church of the Advent and later at St. Stephen's in Providence. In 1873–80 he was organist at Trinity Church in New York, where he gave weekly recitals. In 1880–83 he taught in the College of Music in Cincinnati, but in 1883 returned to be organist at Plymouth Church in Brooklyn and later at the Collegiate Church (48th Street) in New York. He became widely known as an effective recitalist. His works included two string-quartets, an anthem for soli, chorus and orchestra, other church-music, part-songs and songs. His brother, William Carter (b. 1838), well-known in England as player and choral conductor, exchanged work with him at Quebec in 1859 and then led the largest Handel festival that had been held in Canada. Another brother, George Carter (b. 1835), in 1861–70 was organist at the Montreal Cathedral and in 1865–67 gave many organ-recitals in the United States, returning to London later. [R.4]

CARUSO, ENRICO (Feb. 25, 1873, Naples, Italy). See article in Vol. v. 622. He first appeared in 1894 at the Teatro Nuovo in Naples in 'L'Amico Francesco.' A year later he sang at the Fondo there in 'La Traviata,' 'La Favorita' and 'La Gioconda.' In 1898 he made a sensation at the Teatro Lirico in Milan as Marcello in Leoncavallo's 'La Bohème,' and engagements at Genoa, Petrograd and Buenos Aires quickly followed. His first appearance at La Scala was in 1901, and his fame as one of the greatest tenors of this generation was then established. His New York début was at the Metropolitan Opera House on Nov. 23, 1903, in 'Rigoletto,' as in London the year before. Since then he has been regularly at the Metropolitan,

and on Mar. 21, 1919, celebrated his twenty-fifth anniversary as an opera-singer there with a gala performance, illuminated addresses and many gifts from associates and admirers. He had then sung 549 times in New York. He has created the leading tenor-rôles in 'Fedora' (1898), 'Le Maschere' (1901), 'Adriana Lecouvreur,' 'Germania,' 'Madama Butterfly' (1904) and 'La Fanciulla del West' (1910). His répertoire of over fifty operas includes, besides those mentioned, (in Italian) 'Aida,' 'L'Africaine,' 'La Sonnambula,' 'Les Huguenots,' 'Cavalleria Rusticana,' 'I Pagliacci,' 'L'Amore dei Tre Rè,' 'Un Ballo in Maschera,' 'Lodoletta,' 'Marta,' 'L'Elisir d'Amore,' 'Manon Lescaut,' 'Lucia di Lammermoor,' 'Il Trovatore,' 'Don Giovanni,' 'Iris,' 'Lucrezia Borgia,' 'Tosca' and 'La Forza del Destino'; (in French) 'Les Pêcheurs de Perles,' 'Armide,' 'Faust,' 'Julien,' 'Le Prophète,' 'Carmen,' 'Samson et Dalila' and 'Manon.'   [R.8]

CARY, ANNIE LOUISE [Mrs. Charles M. Raymond] (b. 1842). See Vol. i. 476, and Register, 5.

CASALS, PABLO (Dec. 30, 1876, Vendrell, Spain), was first taught by his father, an organist, on the piano, the flute and the violin. At twelve he took up the 'cello with José Garcia, and after two years won a first prize at the Barcelona Conservatory. Meanwhile he had studied composition with Rodereda. Under the Queen's patronage in 1894–96 he was a pupil of Tomás Bretón in composition at Madrid, and also assisted in the chamber-music class of Jésus de Monasterio. He was solo 'cellist at the Paris Opéra in 1895–98 and made concert-tours of Western Europe. His professional début was at the Concerts Lamoureux in 1898, and he first appeared in London the same year. Since 1901 he has made repeated trips to America and his success, both as soloist and in ensemble, has been phenomenal. He married the American singer Susan Metcalfe in 1914. He is a Chevalier of the Légion d'Honneur, and received a gold medal from the Royal Philharmonic Society of London in 1912. His compositions are a symphonic poem, 'La Vision de Fray Martin,' for orchestra, organ, soli and chorus; a symphonic poem for orchestra (1902); a Miserere; pieces for orchestra, 'cello and piano, violin and piano, etc.   [R.9]

CASAVANT FRÈRES, organ-makers at St. Hyacinthe, Que., started in business in 1879. The two partners, J. C. Casavant (b. 1855) and Samuel Casavant (b. 1850), were sons of Joseph Casavant, who worked as organ-maker at St. Hyacinthe in 1845–66, but was forced to stop by ill-health. The older son had had training under the Abbeys at Versailles. In 1882 they began using the adjustable combination-pedal invented by

Duval of Montreal, which was also employed by Roosevelt in New York after 1889. From 1885 they added a crescendo-pedal moving the stop-knobs. This novelty Archer called 'a triumph of ingenuity.' From 1891 they developed the form of electric action which they still use. They have built about 825 organs, including 175 with three manuals and about 70 with four — notable examples being at Notre Dame, Montreal, St. Paul's and the University, Toronto, Emmanuel, Boston, First Baptist, Syracuse, and Sinai Temple, Chicago.

CASE, ANNA (Oct. 29, 1889, Clinton, N. J.), was educated entirely in the United States, having but one teacher, Mme. Ohrstrom-Renard of New York. Her début in 1909 was at the New Theatre in New York as the Dutch Boy in 'Werther.' In 1909–16 she was a member of the Metropolitan Opera Company. In first American performances she created the rôles of Sophie in 'Der Rosenkavalier' (1913) and Feodor in 'Boris Godunov' (1912), singing also Olympia in 'Tales of Hoffmann,' Mimi in 'La Bohème' and Micaëla in 'Carmen.' Since 1916 she has devoted her entire time to concerts and recitals throughout the United States and Canada, and has gained a reputation as a foremost recital-singer. She has composed the songs 'Our America' (Church) and 'The Robin's Song' (Flammer). [R.9]

CASTLE, WILLIAM (1836–1909). See Register, 4.

CASTLE SQUARE OPERA COMPANY, THE, organized in Boston about 1895 by Henry W. Savage, took its name from the Castle Square Theatre, which he owned. The primary object was to give light opera in English, but it essayed some larger works, and its success led in 1900 to more ambitious undertakings under the name of the Henry W. Savage Opera Company.

CAVALIERI, LINA (Dec. 25, 1874, Rome, Italy), is said to have risen into fame as an operatic soprano from singing at café-concerts. She studied with Mme. Mariani-Masi in Paris, and made her début as Nedda in 'I Pagliacci' at Lisbon in December, 1900. She sang in Naples, Palermo, Florence, Milan, Paris, Warsaw, Petrograd and Moscow. In 1906–07 she was at the Metropolitan Opera House in New York, in 1908–09 at the Manhattan Opera House, and in 1915–16 with the Chicago Opera Company. She has appeared in 'Faust,' 'La Bohème,' 'La Traviata,' 'Manon,' 'Fedora,' 'Rigoletto,' 'Manon Lescaut' and 'Adriana Lecouvreur.' She married the tenor Lucien Muratore in 1913. [R.9]

'CAVE–MAN, THE.' The eighth of the 'Grove-Plays' of the Bohemian Club of San Francisco, produced in 1910. The text was written by Charles K. Field, the scenes being laid in a sequoia forest 'about 50,000 years ago,' and the music was composed by William J. McCoy.

CAWLEY, EDGAR MOORE (b. 1871). See Register, 7.

CECILIA SOCIETY, THE, of Boston. See note in Vol. i. 369. B. J. Lang resigned in 1907, having been conductor for thirty years and given the Society an enviable reputation for breadth of policy and efficiency of performance. The succeeding conductors have been Wallace Goodrich in 1907–10, Max Fiedler in 1910–11, Arthur Mees and Henry Gideon in 1911–15, Chalmers Clifton in 1915–17 and Arthur Shepherd since 1917. As a rule, the Society gives three concerts annually, which are now open to the public as well as to subscribers, and during the period 1891–1910 the series was repeated at low prices for wage-earners. Its relation to the Boston Symphony Orchestra has always been close, and in 1910–11 the two arranged a season in conjunction. It has often had the assistance of other choral organizations, and has served on numerous civic and other occasions of importance, as, for example, at the final concert in the old Music Hall and the dedication of Symphony Hall in 1900. Among guest-conductors have been Bruch in 1882, Parker in 1889, Dvořák in 1892, Henschel in 1902 and Colonne in 1904. The list of distinguished soloists is long and varied.

Though originally formed to cultivate a cappella singing, especially of smaller secular works, the repertory has included many works of the first magnitude, like Beethoven's Missa Solennis (1897), Bach's Mass in B minor (1901), Tinel's 'St. Francis' (1893), Elgar's 'The Dream of Gerontius' (1904) and Wolf-Ferrari's 'La Vita Nuova' (1909). Nearly 150 works, large and small, have been sung for the first time in Boston. Among the absolute premières are Mendelssohn's 'Athalie' with the Racine text (1887), Chadwick's 'The Pilgrim's Hymn' (1891), Henschel's Requiem (1902) and Paine's 'Azara' in concert-form (1907). First times in America include Foote's 'The Wreck of the Hesperus' (1888), Berlioz' 'The Fifth of May' (1891), Perosi's 'The Transfiguration' (1899), Coleridge-Taylor's 'Hiawatha's Departure' (1900), Massenet's 'The Promised Land' (1902), Charpentier's 'The Poet's Life' (1905), d'Indy's 'St. Mary Magdalene' (1906) and 'The Song of the Bell' (1916) and Florent Schmitt's Psalm 46 (1913). Second times in America include Berlioz' Requiem (1882), Dvořák's Requiem (1892), Bantock's 'Omar Khayyám' (1910) and Elgar's 'The Music-Makers' (1913), besides the works of Tinel, Bach and Wolf-Ferrari named above.

See W. C. Hill, *History of the Cecilia Society*, 1874–1917.

CECILIA SOCIETY, THE, of Charleston, S. C., appears to have been the earliest musical organization in America. It was founded in 1762 as an exclusive social club, and was so maintained until after 1800. Its 'Rules,' as adopted in 1773, were published in 1774 (reprinted in Sonneck, *Concert-Life*, pp. 16–18). They provide for four meetings annually, the chief being on Nov. 22, St. Cecilia's Day. The programs included vocal and instrumental numbers either by members of the Society or by visiting artists — the latter ultimately sometimes drawn from a distance, as from Boston. From the first the Society proved a constant stimulus artistically and was the principal reason for the notable musical activity of Charleston before and after 1800. [Until about 1790 the name was written 'Cœcilia.']

CECILIA SOCIETY, THE, of Cincinnati, was organized in 1856 by Frédéric L. Ritter and conducted by him till 1861. Starting as a choral society, it soon undertook orchestral work as well, and thus exercised a valuable influence in promoting musical interest. See Ritter, *Music in America*, chap. xxi.

CECILIENVEREIN, DER ALLGEMIE-NE DEUTSCHE, founded by Franz X. Witt of Ratisbon in 1867, is represented in America by the St. Cecilia Society, organized in 1873 by John B. Singenberger of Milwaukee, who since 1874 has conducted its journal 'Cecilia.'

CENTURY OPERA COMPANY, THE, was organized in 1913 at the instigation of the City Club of New York, with a guaranty from a group of public-spirited men, largely those also interested in the Metropolitan Opera House, the leader being Otto H. Kahn. Its design was to give performances at popular prices and in English as far as possible. The managers were the brothers Aborn, and the Century Theater was secured and enlarged. The conductors in 1913–14 were Alfred Szendrei and Carlo Nicosia, in 1914–15 Agide Jacchia and Ernst Knoch. In spite of much enthusiasm at first and worthy effort throughout, the enterprise had to be abandoned early in 1915, after an unsuccessful series of performances in Chicago. See *The Art of Music*, 4. 155–7.

CHACE, FRANK WILBUR (b. 1868). See Register, 7.

CHADWICK, GEORGE M. See STATE UNIVERSITIES (Colo.).

CHADWICK, GEORGE WHITEFIELD (Nov. 13, 1854, Lowell, Mass.). See article in Vol. i. 494–5. His organ-playing began at fifteen. Attempts at composition followed soon, while he was still at school. Despite this attention to music he finished his course at the Lawrence Academy and seemed likely to go into business. But in 1872 he took up theory with Buck and organ with Whiting at the New England Conservatory. This preceded his study with Eugene Thayer. By this time he had written two overtures for small orchestra and some piano-trios.

While at Leipzig in 1877–79 he had two string-quartets performed, as well as the 'Rip van Winkle' overture. The latter was given also in Dresden and three times in Boston in 1879–80. After settling in Boston in 1880 he was often in request as conductor for choral and orchestral organizations. Notable engagements were for the Springfield Festivals in 1889–99 and the Worcester Festivals in 1897–1901. He has also served as guest-conductor with all the larger orchestras throughout the country. At the New England Conservatory, where he has been director since 1897, besides raising the standards in other departments, he has impressed himself especially upon the work in composition and in ensemble-playing. From his orchestra of 80 many players have gone into orchestras elsewhere, some of them becoming conductors. He was made A.M. by Yale in 1897 and LL.D. by Tufts College in 1905.

In the list of compositions note that the Symphony in C, No. 1, was first given by the Harvard Musical Association on Feb. 23, 1882, and that the Symphony in F, No. 3, was played by the Boston Symphony Orchestra on Oct. 20, 1894. The Quartet in C, No. 2, dates from 1879, not 1897. The Sinfonietta was first given in Jordan Hall, Boston, by an orchestra of players from the Symphony Orchestra, under the composer's direction, on Nov. 21, 1904, and on the same program were the 'Symphonic Sketches' (1896), the 3rd Symphony, the ballad 'Lochinvar,' for baritone and orchestra (1897), and several songs. 'Judith,' his most ambitious choral work, was produced at Worcester on Sept. 28, 1901. The symphonic poem 'Cleopatra' was played by the Chicago Orchestra in 1905. The symphonic poem 'Aphrodite' was written for the Norfolk Festival in June, 1912. The symphonic poem 'Angel of Death,' based on the famous group by the sculptor Daniel C. French, was given by the Symphony Society of New York at the memorial concert for Theodore Roosevelt in 1919. His 'Suite Symphonic' in E-flat received the first prize from the American Federation of Musical Clubs and was performed by the Philadelphia Orchestra in March, 1917. From 1917 dates the symphonic ballade 'Tam o' Shanter.' 'Noël,' a Christmas pastoral for chorus, soli and orchestra, was written for the Norfolk Festival in June, 1908. Other vocal works are 'Aghadoe,' a ballade for contralto and orchestra, 'Love's Sacrifice,' a pastoral opera in one act (1915), 'Land of our Hearts,' a patriotic hymn for chorus and orchestra (given by the Boston Symphony Orchestra in September, 1918), and incidental music to 'Everywoman,' the play by Walter Brown, produced in New York on Feb. 21,

1911. In manuscript there is a tragic opera, 'The Padrone,' in two parts.

Concerning his work Edward Burlingame Hill has said: "His chief attributes are fluency and beauty of melodic inventiveness, mastery of part-writing, a logical and coherent grasp of form. His harmonic structure is solid, yet he always manages to obtain effects that are romantic, poetic or dramatic in color without resorting to the devices of ultra-modern eccentricity. His instrumentation is brilliant and resourceful without employing either a gigantic orchestra or semi-obsolete instruments; he does not disregard the natural limitations of the orchestral player's technique in order to invent new combinations. His contrapuntal dexterity is remarkable in an age that delights in contrapuntal *tours de force*. His command of the sonata and symphonic forms and his spontaneity of expression in them is striking, yet he has shown most convincingly in the overture 'Melpomene' that he can depart from the strict letter of the poem and justify the result. His most salient characteristics as an artist are the sincerity and depth of his artistic purposes, an uncompromising honesty which will permit nothing vague or inconsistent to stand, and a sense of balance and wholesome moderation. He invariably lays a firm constructive foundation in his composition in larger forms, in order that he may be free to elaborate detail as he pleases." [R. 6]

CHAFFEE, EDMUND WALTER (b. 1862). See COLLEGES, 3 (Valparaiso U., Ind.).

CHAFFIN, LUCIEN GATES (b. 1846). See Register, 6.

CHALFANT, WILLIAM ADDISON (b. 1854). See Register, 6.

CHALMERS, THOMAS HARDIE (b. 1884). See Register, 10.

CHAMBER MUSIC. Much of the instrumental music performed in various places during the late 18th century and the early 19th was virtually of the 'chamber' class, though usually with chance combinations of instruments and players. Doubtless in some cases this led to rather more definite groups, such as that of the Hupfelds, Gilles and Schetky in Philadelphia about 1815. In New York, when German musicians began to multiply after 1840, sundry ensemble-groups were formed, as by Pirsson about 1848, under the lead of Saroni's 'Musical Times' in 1849, and, more fruitfully, by Eisfeld from 1851 and by William Mason and Thomas in 1855–66. In Boston the famous Mendelssohn Quintette Club was founded in 1849 by the Fries brothers, and for many years continued by its extensive travels and its popularity to foster interest in instrumental part-music. Similar pioneer work

was done in Chicago in 1860–61 by the Briggs House Concerts, followed in 1863–64 by Balatka's Classical Chamber Concerts.

CHAMPLIN, JOHN DENISON (1834–1915). See Register, 7.

CHAPEK, JOSEPH HORYMIR (b. 1860). See Register, 7.

CHAPIN, NATHAN. See TUNE-BOOKS, 1810.

CHAPMAN, FRANK THOMAS. See COLLEGES, 3 (Pacific U., Ore.).

CHAPMAN, JAMES W. See STATE UNIVERSITIES (Fla.).

CHAPMAN, WILLIAM ROGERS (b. 1855). See Register, 6.

CHAPPELL, W. L. See TUNE-BOOKS, 1831.

CHARACTER-NOTES. From the beginning of pedagogical effort in America on behalf of popular singing, experiments were made in devising novel ways of printing what was to be sung. The chief of these were based upon the principle, now exemplified in the Tonic Sol-fa system, that what is presented to the eye shall recall some tone-conception with which the ear is familiar, and do this by something more than merely relative position on a staff. Tufts' experiment in the early 18th century was short-lived, and that of Law about 1800 was equally transient, though made known to many more users. But Law's idea of varying the shape of the note-heads so as to indicate tone-relations has had considerable influence. From about 1825–30 collections of tunes began to be frequent, especially in Ohio and Virginia, in which the music is printed on a staff exactly as in ordinary notation, but with a system of note-heads that indicates the scale-degree intended — do, △, re, ▽, mi, ◇, fa, ▷, sol, ◯, la, ▢, ti, ▽. Many popular teachers and leaders evidently believed that the use of these 'character-notes' or 'shaped notes' facilitated practical singing. Thousands of books in this notation have been put into circulation, and the types required to print them are recognized by first-class music-typographers. But the system has never made its way generally, and is now dying out.

* Change of key.

CHARLIER, MARCEL. See Register, 9.

CHASE, MARY WOOD (Jan. 21, 1868, Brooklyn), was the daughter of a professor in Cornell University, a mining engineer and later a banker. From her mother, who had a fine soprano voice, she had her first instruction. After a year with George B. Penny, at sixteen she entered the New England Conservatory in Boston, taking piano and harmony with Sarah E. Newman, voice with F. E. Morse and O'Neill, and theory with Apthorp. Her début in 1886 was at Music Hall. After four years of study with Raif in Berlin (becoming his assistant), she returned to America and made several tours as pianist. She appeared with the Thomas Orchestra in Chicago in 1902, giving the Sinding concerto its first performance in America. In recent years she has devoted herself mostly to the development of teaching-methods. To this end she founded at Chicago in 1906 the Mary Wood Chase School of Musical Arts (incorporated 1912), with a faculty especially trained to teach her methods. In 1912 a summer-school was added at Epworth, Mich. She has the reputation of having trained many fine pianists and successful teachers. In 1910 was published her *Natural Laws in Piano-Technic* (Ditson). She has in preparation works on the philosophy of interpretation and on modern educational methods. She has contributed articles to 'Music,' 'The Etude,' and 'The Musician,' and has written many compositions in smaller forms which remain unpublished. [R.7]

CHASE, MELVILLE WARREN (b. 1842). See Register, 5.

CHASE COMPANY, THE A. B., of Norwalk, O., was incorporated in 1875, originally for the making of reed-organs of high grade. In 1885 piano-making was added, and speedily attained significant success, as attested, for example, by high awards at the Columbian Exposition in 1893. The Chase pianos are distinguished for excellence of tone and for beauty of external form. The player-device used in them is known as the 'Artistano.'

CHAUTAUQUA INSTITUTION, THE, is the extensive organization that has been developed from the Sunday School Assembly first held at Chautauqua Lake in western New York in 1874. The popularity of the initial efforts led to rapid extensions, both in the direction of summer-school courses and in reading- and correspondence-courses, covering many kinds of subjects. Among these has been special provision for musical instruction and leadership. The musical directors have been William F. Sherwin in 1874, Charles C. Case in 1875–86, Horatio R. Palmer in 1887–1901, Alfred Hallam in 1902–19 and William C. Bridgman from 1920. The advantages include many courses of instruction by well-known teachers, classes in singing and orchestral playing, and numerous recitals and concerts. In 1912 a Music Studio was erected in memory of the pianist William H. Sherwood.

CHEATHAM, KATHARINE SMILEY [Kitty Cheatham]. See Register, 9.

CHERNIAVSKY, JAN (b. 1892), LEO (b. 1890), and MISCHEL (b. 1893). See Register, 10.

CHICAGO CONSERVATORY OF DRAMATIC AND MUSICAL ART, THE, was founded in 1885 by Samuel Kayzer, who had previously been dramatic instructor in the Hershey School. Since 1907 the president has been Walton Perkins.

CHICAGO MADRIGAL CLUB, THE, was organized in 1900 by D. A. Clippinger, who has been its only conductor. It is composed of 60 singers, all chosen by examination as soloists. Two regular concerts are given each season, with several extras usually, so that the total number up to the present is about 150. The Club is supported wholly by its sale of season-tickets. In 1903 the W. W. Kimball Co. established an endowment yielding $100 annually, to be used as a prize for the best madrigal submitted for competition. Nearly 900 compositions have been thus submitted, including many notable works as prize-winners. About 50 compositions have also been written for the Club by various American composers.

CHICAGO MUSICAL COLLEGE, THE, was founded in 1867 by Florenz Ziegfeld, becoming incorporated in 1877. He remained its active head for nearly fifty years, and is now president emeritus. With him since 1905–06 have been associated Felix Borowski and Carl D. Kinsey, who are now president and vice-president respectively. The teaching-staff numbers over 100 and the annual enrolment over 4000. During its history more than 90,000 students have pursued courses, of whom nearly 3500 have graduated. The degree of Mus.B. has been given to about 150, that of Mus.M. to about 100, and that of Mus.D. to 12. The College occupies its own building at 624 South Michigan Avenue, where it has extraordinary conveniences. Its faculty has always been notable for ability, and from time to time it has been augmented by a system of guest-instructors.

CHICAGO MUSICAL UNION, THE, though not the first choral society in Chicago, was one of the first to exercise a positive influence. It was organized in 1857 and continued in efficient operation till 1865. Its first conductor was C. M. Cady, later associated with George F. Root in the firm of Root & Cady. He was followed in 1860 by A. L. Coe and in 1863 by Hans Balatka. The Union undertook both sacred and secular works. It gave 'The Creation' in 1857 and 'Elijah' in 1860, some of its oratorio concerts being made memorable by the assistance of Charles R. Adams and Christine Nilsson.

In 1864 it bought out Lortzing's 'Czar und Zimmermann' in English, arranged by Balatka, which had five performances. See Upton, *Musical Memories*, pp. 130, 271–4.

CHICAGO NORTH SHORE FESTIVAL ASSOCIATION, THE, of Evanston, Ill., organized in 1908, consolidates work previously undertaken by the Musical Clubs of Evanston and Ravenswood, Ill., and the School of Music in Northwestern University. Its object is to present annually a series of superior concerts. usually five in number, of which three are given to choral music. At present the Festival chorus numbers about 600 voices, but at times is augmented to 1100. There is also a children's chorus of 1500, drawn from the public schools. The concerts are given in the Gymnasium of Northwestern University, which seats 5000. Their artistic excellence has attracted wide attention and brought fame to the conductor, Dean P. C. Lutkin, to the University and to Evanston. Among the novelties brought forward have been Bantock's 'Omar Khayyám,' Harty's 'The Mystic Trumpeter,' Pierné's 'St. Francis of Assisi' and Smith's 'Rhapsody of St. Bernard' (1918). In addition, works by Elgar, Coleridge-Taylor, Bath and Clutsam that are comparatively unknown have been brought out. See notice in 'The New Music Review,' July, 1910.

CHICAGO ORCHESTRAL ASSOCIATION, THE, organized in 1891, is the corporate name of the trustees of the Chicago (formerly Thomas) Symphony Orchestra and the owners of Orchestra Hall on Michigan Avenue, built in 1904. See Vol. iv. 801–3.

CHICAGO-PHILADELPHIA OPERA COMPANY, THE, or the Chicago Opera Association, was formed in 1910 chiefly from the forces previously drawn together by Hammerstein for his ventures in New York and Philadelphia. Its manager in 1910–13 was Andreas Dippel, with Cleofonte Campanini as chief conductor. After 1913 the latter was manager till 1915, when, the original organization having become bankrupt, a new one was formed with the same name, Campanini remaining as artistic director, with Bernhard Ulrich as business manager. Until his death in 1919 Campanini was the most influential factor in the enterprise, which he brought to a high pitch of artistic perfection. In 1920 he was succeeded as artistic director by Gino Marinuzzi. Except for a break in 1914–15 due to the World War, regular seasons have been presented in both Chicago and Philadelphia, and since 1918 in New York as well. The Company has also given performances after the regular season in other places. The list of novelties includes, in 1911, Herbert's 'Natoma,' Wolf-Ferrari's 'Il Segreto di Susanna,' Nouguès' 'Quo Vadis?' and

Massenet's 'Cendrillon'; in 1912, Wolf-Ferrari's 'I Giojelli della Madonna,' Parelli's 'A Lovers' Quarrel' and Goldmark's 'The Cricket on the Hearth'; in 1913, d'Erlanger's 'Noël,' Zandonai's 'Conchita,' Kienzl's 'Der Kuhreigen,' Massenet's 'Don Quichotte' and Franchetti's 'Cristoforo Colombo'; in 1914, Gnecchi's 'Cassandra'; in 1916, Massenet's 'Cléopâtre' and Buchhalter's 'A Lovers' Knot'; in 1917, Mascagni's 'Isabeau' and Hadley's 'Azora'; in 1918, Nevin's 'A Daughter of the Forest' and Lazzari's 'Le Sauteriot'; and in 1919, Février's 'Gismonda,' Catalani's 'Loreley,' Leroux' 'Le Chemineau' and Montemezzi's 'La Nave,' besides Borowski's 'Boudour' and Carpenter's 'The Birthday of the Infanta' (ballets).

CHICAGO SYMPHONY ORCHESTRA, THE. For the early history, see Vols. iv. 801–3 and v. 88. After the death of Theodore Thomas in 1905 the conductorship passed to Frederick A. Stock, who had been his assistant. Though at that time a young man for so responsible a position, the new conductor speedily established himself with both players and public. The personnel and discipline have been steadily improved and the répertoire kept fully abreast of the times. In recent years the Orchestra has toured extensively. About 75 concerts are given annually in Chicago and about 25 elsewhere. The usual number of players is about 90. Since 1912 the concertmaster has been Harry Weisbach. In 1915 Mrs. Elizabeth Sprague Coolidge gave $100,000 as a pension-fund. In 1916 she gave a like amount (later increased by other gifts to $237,500) to constitute the Albert and Nancy Sprague Memorial Fund. In 1918–19, when Mr. Stock's leadership was temporarily intermitted (because he had not then acquired full American citizenship), the concerts were directed by Eric DeLamarter and various visiting conductors.

From the excellent program-books prepared by Felix Borowski it appears that the total répertoire of the Orchestra since 1891 comprises works by over 300 composers and covering the entire field of symphonic and concerted literature. In this list are the names of about fifty composers who are Americans or associated with America, represented by about 150 works, including the following: Paine's 2nd Symphony and 'The Tempest'; Gleason's 'Edris' and 'Song of Life'; Vogrich's Violin Concerto; Foote's Tema con Variazioni, 'Cello-Concerto and Suites, opp. 36 and 63; Chadwick's 3rd Symphony, Overtures 'Melpomene' and 'Euterpe,' Suite Symphonique, 'Cleopatra,' 'Aphrodite' and 'Tam O'Shanter'; Foerster's Suite, 'Cyrano de Bergerac'; Schoenfeld's Pastoral Symphony; Shelley's 'Francesca da Rimini'; Van der Stucken's 'William Ratcliff,' 'Pax Triumphans' and Suite, 'The Tempest'; Herbert's 2nd 'Cello-Concerto; Paderewski's 1st Symphony; Seeboeck's Piano-Concerto; Loeffler's 'Mort de Tintagiles,' 'Villanelle du Diable' and 'A Pagan Poem'; MacDowell's 1st and 2nd Piano-Concertos, 'Lancelot and Elaine' and 1st and 2nd Suites; Arthur Whiting's Fantasy, op. 11;

JONAS CHICKERING

Kaun's three Symphonies, 'Minnehaha,' 'Hiawatha'; etc.; Middelschulte's Organ-Concerto and Passacaglia; Parker's Overture, 'Count Robert of Paris,' 'Northern Ballad' and Organ-Concerto; Cole's Symphonic Prelude; Lucas' Overture, 'Macbeth'; Mrs. Beach's 'Gaelic' Symphony and Piano-Concerto; Strube's Comedy Overture, 'Puck'; Weidig's 'Semiramis' and Symphonic Suite; Otterstroem's 'Negro' Suites; Skilton's 'Two Indian Dances'; Converse's 'Festival of Pan,' 'Endymion's Narrative,' 'Mystic Trumpeter' and 'Ormazd'; Hadley's 2nd, 3rd and 4th Symphonies, 'Salome' and 'Culprit Fay'; Rubin Goldmark's 'Samson'; Borowski's 'Élégie Symphonique' and 'Peintures'; Stock's Symphony in C minor, Symphonic Variations, 'Eines Menschenleben,' Overture, 'Life's Springtide,' etc.; Oldberg's 2nd Symphony, Festival and Dramatic Overtures, Symphonic Organ-Variations, etc.; Carpenter's 1st Symphony and 'Perambulator' Suite; Schelling's Symphonic Legend and Fantastic Suite; D. S. Smith's Symphony and Overture, 'Prince Hal'; DeLamarter's Symphony; John Powell's Violin-Concerto; Ballantine's 'Eve of St. Agnes'; and Boyle's Piano-Concerto.

CHICKERING, JONAS (Apr. 5, 1798, New Ipswich, N. H. : Dec. 8, 1853, Boston), was trained as a cabinet-maker. In 1818 he became an apprentice of John Osborn, the able Boston piano-maker, who had been a pupil of Benjamin Crehore of Milton. In 1823 James Stewart, a Scotchman who had come from Baltimore in 1820 to work with Osborn, induced Chickering to join him in the new firm of Stewart & Chickering. Stewart went back to England in 1826. In 1829 John Mackay, who had gained wealth as a ship-captain and who had been the financial backer of Alpheus Babcock, the inventor, joined Chickering, the firm name being Chickering & Mackay. This partnership was highly successful, since Mackay brought considerable capital and was a vigorous promoter on the commercial side, while Chickering devoted himself to technical improvement. They were pioneers in developing the upright type of instrument. In 1837 Chickering applied for a patent for a full metal plate for squares, but the application was held up on a technicality till 1840. In 1843 his full metal plate for grands was patented, together with a device for casting the agraffes in the plate. In 1853, at the time of his death, he was working upon a metal plate that should provide for overstringing. After 1841, when Mackay died, Chickering proceeded alone until he could take his three sons into the business. Besides becoming famous for his inventions and for the notable excellence of his instruments, he was active in various musical undertakings in Boston. He sang in the choir of the Park Street Church and in the chorus of the Handel and Haydn Society, of which from 1834 he was vice-president.[1] For

[1] A humorous compliment to his personal qualities was embodied on one occasion in the toast, 'Jonas Chickering — grand, square, and upright!'

M

various points about his inventive work, see Vols. i. 514 and iii. 728–32. [R.3]

CHICKERING & SONS, of Boston, is the name of the piano-making firm founded in 1823 by Jonas Chickering and enlarged by the admission of his sons Thomas E. Chickering (1824–1871), Charles Frank Chickering (1827–1891) and George H. Chickering (1830–1896). Of these the second, C. Frank Chickering, especially inherited his father's genius as inventor and designer, in token of which he received the decoration of the Légion d'Honneur in 1867, at the same time that the firm won first prize at the Paris Exposition. In 1852 the firm's entire stock in trade was destroyed by fire, the loss being estimated at a quarter-million. Despite this calamity, the business quickly recovered its leading position. Since 1908 it has been absorbed into the American Piano Company.

CHILD, EBENEZER. See TUNE-BOOKS, 1804.

CHITTENDEN, KATE SARA (April 17, 1856, Hamilton, Ont.), is descended from an old Connecticut family. She early began piano-study with an aunt, continuing with Jules Fossier and Lucy H. Clinton. She was educated at Hellmuth College, London, Ont., receiving the Dufferin medal for art in 1873, and began to teach there at seventeen. In 1876 she came to New York, where she has since been constantly engaged as a teacher. In 1879 she became organist at Calvary Baptist Church, where she remained for twenty-seven years. In 1890 she was elected head of the piano-department at the Catherine Aiken School in Stamford, Conn., retaining the position until the school was given up in 1914. In 1892 she was the first woman to lecture under the New York Board of Education, giving, with the assistance of C. Judson Bushnell, baritone, the first lectures on music, and this work has been continued until recently. Her connection with Vassar College dates from 1898. In 1899 she became head of the piano-department, and since practical music was recognized as an elective in 1918 she has been assistant-professor. In 1890 she became associated with Albert Ross Parsons in the preparation of *The Synthetic Method.* The first part only was issued, as subsequently it was deemed advisable that the material belonging to each party be published separately, in sheet form. She joined the staff of the (then) Metropolitan Conservatory in 1892. This was later reorganized as The American Institute of Applied Music. In the Institute she is now vice-president and dean of the faculty as well as president of the trustees of the Metropolitan College. She has taught over 3000 piano-pupils, and has specialized in the training of teachers. Technical works for the piano and some tunes for children represent her compositions. She has written for musical magazines and is active in state and national music-teachers' organizations. [R. 6]

'CHOIR AND CHORAL MAGAZINE, THE.' See Vol. iii. 689.

'CHOIR JOURNAL, THE.' See Vol. iii. 689.

CHORAL ART CHOIR, THE, of New Haven, Conn., was organized in 1918 by George C. Stock. It is a mixed chorus of 60 selected voices for the performance of the best part-songs and cantatas. The conductor is David Stanley Smith. Two concerts are given annually.

CHORAL ART SOCIETY, THE, of Boston. See Vol. i. 369. Wallace Goodrich continued as conductor till 1907, when he became leader of the Cecilia.

CHORAL CLUB, THE, of Hartford, Conn., a superior male chorus of 70–80 voices, was founded in 1907. It gives two concerts each year, besides occasional performances in nearby cities. Its conductor from the beginning has been Ralph L. Baldwin. In addition to a large number of part-songs, about twenty-five longer works in cantata-form have been given. American compositions have always been numerous and conspicuous, among them Foote's 'The Farewell of Minnehaha,' Parker's 'The Norseman's Raid' and 'The Leap of Roushan Beg,' Protheroe's 'The Nun of Nidaros,' Strube's 'Hymn to Eros,' Baldwin's 'Hymn before Action,' Cadman's 'The Vision of Sir Launfal' and Harling's 'The Death of Minnehaha' (first time, conducted by the composer).

CHORAL SOCIETIES. The first impetus in the direction of choral music in America was given by the 'singing-schools' that sprang up in New England from the middle of the 18th century. From one of these 'schools' came in 1786 the Musical Society of Stoughton, Mass., which though apparently not the first of its kind, was the only one that has endured (see list at end of Register, 2). The organization in 1815 of the Handel and Haydn Society of Boston marked the solid beginning of permanent societies. To this followed in 1820 the Musical Fund Society of Philadelphia and in 1823 the Sacred Music Society of New York. Various influences combined to foster numerous experiments of the same general sort during the next half-century, especially in the East. After 1850 interest in choral undertakings began to manifest itself in Cincinnati, Chicago and Milwaukee, often stimulated by the large proportion of Germans in the population. After about 1870 the multiplication of choral societies of dignified ambition and persistent

energy set in with notable results. They have now become so numerous that no adequate catalogue of them is practicable.[1]

'CHOROPHONE' is the trade-name of a small pipe-organ devised by the Austin Organ Company of Hartford, Conn., to supply the needs of churches that cannot afford expensive instruments. By ingenious extensions and duplexing of a few stops much variety, flexibility and sonority are obtained. There are two manuals and pedal, controlled from a standard console.

CHRISTIANI, ADOLF FRIEDRICH (1836–1885). See Register, 5.

CHRISTIANSEN, F. MELIUS. See COLLEGES, 3 (St. Olaf C., Minn.).

CHRISTY, EDWIN T. See Register, 4.

CHURCH COMPANY, THE JOHN, of Cincinnati, was founded in 1854 by John Church as a music-publishing business, to which was added dealing in all kinds of musical merchandise. After the Chicago fire of 1871 this Company acquired the business formerly carried on in Chicago by Root & Cady. From about 1875 it shared with Biglow & Main of New York the publication of the 'Gospel Hymns' series. It has also given much attention to music for both instrumental and vocal instruction, and of late years has put forth many works of still higher class. Since about 1908 piano-making has been added, and the Company is now the owner of the Everett and Harvard pianos as well.

CHURCH CHORAL SOCIETY, THE, of New York. See Vol. iii. 367–8, and add that Mr. Warren continued as leader till 1907. [A society of the same name was formed in 1852 by Edward Hodges, the organist of Trinity Church, and under its auspices choral services were first held in that church.]

'CHURCH MUSIC.' See Vol. iii. 688, and add that Rev. Hugh T. Henry continued as editor till 1909.

CHURCH MUSIC ASSOCIATION, THE, of New York, was formed in 1868 through the efforts of George T. Strong, with Dr. James Pech, then organist of St. John's Chapel, as conductor, succeeded soon by Charles E. Horsley. Although an exclusive, social enterprise and by no means limited to sacred music, it perhaps prepared for the foundation in 1873 of the Oratorio Society.

‡ CILÈA, FRANCESCO (July 23, 1866, Palmi, Italy). See article in Vol. v. 624. His 'Poema Sinfonico,' for solo, chorus and orchestra, was given at Genoa in 1913. In

[1] In Who's Who in Music, 1918, a list of over 400 is given, which, however, is far from complete. It is interesting to note that in this imperfect list there are over 100 societies more or less of the 'oratorio' class, located in over 30 States, besides perhaps 15 in Canada.

1908 he was made an Officer of the Order of the Crown of Italy. He was director of the Conservatory at Palermo in 1913–16, and since 1916 has been director of the Conservatory at Naples.

CINCINNATI CONSERVATORY OF MUSIC, THE, was started in 1867 by Clara Baur, who continued in charge till her death in 1912, being then succeeded by her niece Bertha Baur. Its original plan was more or less modeled after that of the Stuttgart Conservatory. Emphasis has always been laid upon general education in connection with special musical training, both by requiring at least high-school preparation from all who seek to graduate, by providing some literary advantages in the Conservatory, and by urging all looking forward to a musical career to take a general college course besides their Conservatory course. Since its beginning the Conservatory has maintained a summer-school, which has contributed much to its success. The instruction is arranged in five grades — Juvenile, Preparatory, Normal, Artist and Master. The faculty numbers about 75. The usual enrollment is from 1200 to 1500. A noteworthy feature is the Student Orchestra, which for more than thirty years has been led by Pier A. Tirindelli. The department of opera is also strongly emphasized. In 1918 a performance of Laparra's 'La Habanera' was given to the satisfaction of the composer, who was present. Since 1902 the institution has occupied spacious grounds on Highland Avenue with four principal buildings finely adapted to its use.

CINCINNATI FESTIVALS. See Vol. i. 537–8. The long-extended leadership of Thomas continued till 1904, when he was followed till 1912 by Frank Van der Stucken, in 1914 and 1916 by Ernst Kunwald, and in 1918 by Eugène Ysaÿe. In 1906 Elgar also conducted four of his own works. The record of principal choral works is as follows:

1904. Bach, Mass in B minor; Elgar, 'The Dream of Gerontius'; Beethoven, Missa Solemnis.
1906. Elgar, 'The Apostles,' 'The Dream of Gerontius'; Brahms, Requiem; Bach, 'Actus Tragicus'; Beethoven's 'Choral' Symphony.
1908. Bach, St. Matthew Passion; Pierné, 'The Children's Crusade.'
1910. Handel, 'Judas Maccabæus'; Beethoven, Missa Solemnis; Berlioz, 'Les Troyens.'
1912. Mendelssohn, 'Elijah'; Berlioz, Requiem; Franck, 'Les Béatitudes'; Wolf-Ferrari, 'La Vita Nuova.'
1914. Bach, Mass in B minor; Beethoven, 'Choral' Symphony; Berlioz, 'The Damnation of Faust'; Verdi, Requiem.
1916. Beethoven, Missa Solemnis; Mendelssohn, 'St. Paul'; Pierné, 'The Children's Crusade.'
1918. Bach, St. Matthew Passion; Haydn, 'The Creation'; Kelley, 'Pilgrim's Progress.'

CINCINNATI SYMPHONY ORCHESTRA, THE. See Vol. iv. 803. In December,

1909, after a two years' interval, the Orchestra was reorganized with a competent force of 70 players under Leopold Stokowski, who rapidly brought it to notable efficiency. On his resignation in 1912 Ernest Kunwald, formerly of the Berlin Philharmonic, succeeded as conductor. In 1913 the players were increased to 85, in 1914 the regular season lengthened from twenty-four to thirty-two concerts, and in 1915 the Orchestra became permanently endowed by the bequest of $700,000 in the will of Martha Cora Dow. In 1917 Kunwald offered to resign in the fall, but was persuaded to go on. In December, however, he was arrested as an enemy alien and his resignation was then accepted. In 1918 various guest-conductors appeared, including Walter Rothwell, Victor Herbert, Henry Hadley, Ossip Gabrilovitch and Eugène Ysaÿe. In May of that year the latter was appointed permanent conductor.

CISNEROS, ELEONORA DE, née Broadfoot (Nov. 1, 1880, New York), made her début as Rossweise in 'Die Walküre' at the Metropolitan Opera House in 1900. She was then a pupil of Mme. Murio-Celli, but had not been abroad. On Édouard de Reszké's advice she now went to Paris and Italy to study with his brother Jean, Maurel, Trabadello and Lombardi. Her success as stage-soprano was immediate, so that since 1902 she has sung, often for successive seasons, in all the leading European opera-houses and in Cuba, Brazil and Australia besides. In 1906–08 she was a principal artist at the Manhattan Opera House in New York, leaving for Milan to create the rôle of Clytemnestra in Strauss' 'Elektra.' In 1909 she took the part of Eboli at the revival of Verdi's 'Don Carlos.' In 1910 she sang in 'Aida' at the inaugural performance of the Chicago Opera Company, with which she has since been identified. Her last European engagement was at the Champs Élysées in Paris in 1914, when she sang 'Tristan und Isolde' in German. In 1915–16 she was with the Havana Opera Company. She has also sung in concert in Honolulu and in Australia and New Zealand. In 1907 she married Count Francesco de Cisneros. [R.9]

CLAASSEN, ARTHUR (1859–1920). See Register, 7.

CLAPP, PHILIP GREELEY (Aug. 4, 1888, Boston), began lessons at six with an aunt, Mrs. Mary C. A. James. Later he studied piano and theory with J. P. Marshall and violin with Jacques Hoffman. He prepared for college at the Roxbury Latin School, and at Harvard completed the course in three years, receiving his A.B. in 1908 *magna cum laude*. A large part of his course consisted of work in composition, orchestration, etc., offered in the musical department, chiefly

under Spalding. He remained for a fourth
year, receiving the degree of A.M. with
highest final honors in music in 1909. He
also won the Boott Prize in 1907 for a concerted vocal composition. For two years he
was conductor of the Pierian Sodality, and was
elected chorister by the class of 1909. In
1909–11 he studied in Europe as Sheldon
Fellow of the University, emphasizing composition in Stuttgart with Schillings and the
æsthetics of music at the British Museum. In
1911 he received the degree of Ph.D. from
Harvard, presenting original compositions
and a thesis on 'Modern Tendencies in Musical
Form.' In 1911–12 he was assistant in music
at Harvard; in 1912–14 instructor in music
at the Middlesex School in Concord, Mass.;
in 1914–15 acting director of the School of
Music in Gloucester, Mass. In 1915–19 he
was director of music at Dartmouth College,
with leave of absence for service as band-
leader with the 73rd Artillery, A. E. F., in
France. In 1919 he became professor of music
at the State University of Iowa in Iowa City.
Since 1909 he has been a frequent contributor
to the Boston 'Evening Transcript' on various
musical subjects. In 1913 he conducted the
Cincinnati Symphony Orchestra for two weeks
in an emergency caused by Kunwald's illness.
His compositions include the tone-poem
'Norge,' for orchestra and piano, written for
the centennial of the Pierian Sodality in 1908
(also Boston Symphony Orchestra, 1909);
a string-quartet in C minor (1909, not yet
performed); the tone-poem 'A Song of
Youth,' for orchestra (privately given in
Stuttgart in 1910 by the Court Orchestra,
the composer conducting); Symphony in
E minor (1911, revised 1913, given in 1914 by
the Boston Symphony Orchestra, the composer conducting); a 'Dramatic Poem,' for
trombone and orchestra (1912, written to
show the capacity of the Sax 7-valve trombone
played by Modest Alloo, given in New York
by M. Alloo and the Pierian Sodality, the
composer conducting); the orchestral prelude 'In Summer' (1913, given in 1914 by the
St. Louis Symphony Orchestra); Symphony
in E-flat (1916, given in 1917 by the Boston
Symphony Orchestra, the composer conducting); stage-music for the Pageant of
the Massachusetts Agricultural College (1917,
given in 1920); Symphony in A (1918–19);
and several songs and part-songs, a few with
orchestral accompaniment. [R.9]

CLARK, CHARLES WILLIAM (b. 1865).
See Register, 8.

CLARK, JOHN. See Register, 3.

CLARK, MELVILLE (d. 1918). See Register, 6.

CLARK, MELVILLE ANTONE (b. 1883).
See Register, 10.

CLARK COMPANY, THE MELVILLE,
of Chicago, was organized in 1900 to utilize the
various patents of Melville Clark. Besides
making pianos, including a small grand of novel
design, the firm specializes in player-pianos, using devices under the trade-name of 'Apollo.'

CLARKE, HERBERT LINCOLN (b.
1867). See Register, 7.

CLARKE, HUGH ARCHIBALD (Aug. 15,
1839, near Toronto, Ont.), was the son of the
Canadian organist James P. Clarke, who was
his only teacher. He came to Philadelphia
in 1859, served as organist in several churches
(till 1897), and for some years conducted the
Abt Male Chorus. In 1875 he became
professor in the University of Pennsylvania,
teaching harmony, counterpoint, orchestration
and musical form, and this position he still
holds. In 1886 the University conferred on
him the degree of Mus.D., after the performance of his overture and choruses for Aristophanes' 'Acharnians.' He has also written
music for Euripides' 'Iphigenia in Tauris,' the
oratorio 'Jerusalem' (Philadelphia, 1891),
a piano-quartet and several sonatas for violin
and piano. Of his many songs a few are published. His treatises on Harmony and
Counterpoint have been largely used. He is
also the author of The Scratch Club, 1888, a
Dictionary of Musical Terms, 1896, Music
and the Comrade Arts, 1899, and Highways
and Byways of Music, 1901. As an educator
and lecturer he has exerted a wide and salutary
influence. The late Dr. Gilchrist was one of
his pupils. [R.5]

CLARKE, JAMES PEYTON (1808–1877).
See Register, 4.

CLARKE, WILLIAM HORATIO (Mar.
8, 1840, Newton, Mass. : Dec. 11, 1913,
Reading, Mass.), at sixteen became organist
at Dedham, Mass., and three years later at
Berkeley Temple in Boston, teaching also
in the Perkins Institute for the Blind. In
1871 he became music-superintendent in the
schools of Dayton, O., later removing to
Indianapolis as organist and organ-builder.
In 1878–87 he was organist at Tremont
Temple in Boston. After retiring in 1887
he was much sought as consulting-expert
in organ-building. In 1890 he erected on his
estate at Reading a music-chapel, 'Clarigold
Hall,' which contained a four-manual organ
of 100 stops. Illness prevented his plan for
establishing there a school for organ-instruc-
tion. He wrote An Outline of the Structure
of the Pipe-Organ, 1877, The Organist's Retrospect, 1896, and Standard Organ-Building,
1913, and besides several non-musical books,
prepared instruction-books for piano, organ
and voice, and composed organ-pieces and
church-music. Three sons took up musical
careers, Herbert L. Clarke (b. 1867) becoming

a widely-known cornet-virtuoso and band-master. [R.4]

CLASS, FRANKLIN MORRIS (May 2, 1881, New York), graduated from Harvard in 1903 (*cum laude* in music) and as M.D. from Columbia in 1907, then becoming an attending physician at Bellevue Hospital in New York. At Harvard he studied under Paine. He has composed three volumes of piano-music; five 'Intermezzi,' op. 6; five 'Vignettes,' op. 7 (Ditson); five 'Pieces for Piano' (Church); and some 30 songs (Schirmer, Ditson, Breitkopf). His operetta 'Hasty Pudding' was performed at Harvard in 1903. Unpublished are a string-quartet, various pieces for piano, violin, 'cello and flute, and some motets. [R.9]

CLAUSSEN, JULIA (b. 1879). See Register, 10.

CLEMENS, CHARLES EDWIN (Mar. 12, 1858, Devonport, England), had his first appointment as organist when only eleven. He studied under local teachers, with occasional lessons from cathedral organists, and became active as pianist, organist and viola-player. Going to London, he entered the Royal College of Music, studying piano with Pauer. On Grove's advice he finally made the organ his chief study, his teachers being Weekes, Martin and Bridge. From 1889 he taught organ and harmony at the Klindworth Conservatory in Berlin and was organist of the Royal Chapel (English). From 1896 he was organist at St. Paul's in Cleveland. In 1899 he began lecturing on music-history at Western Reserve University, and soon was appointed organist and professor. Since 1911 he has been organist at the Euclid Avenue Presbyterian Church. The University made him Mus. D. in 1916. His *Modern Progressive Pedal-Technique*, 2 vols., 1894 (Breitkopf), and *The Modern School for the Organ*, 1903 (Schirmer), are both popular works. A treatise on Harmony is still unpublished, though used in classes at the University. [R.8]

CLEMENS, CLARA (1871?, Elmira, N. Y.), the daughter of 'Mark Twain', spent her childhood in Hartford, Conn. She was allowed to take lessons on the piano when she was six years old. Later she studied with Moszkowski and also Leschetizky. Meantime her voice was discovered and she began to prepare herself for concert-singing, abandoning the piano. In 1904 she made her début in Florence, where her voice was likened to Scalchi's, but her career was then interrupted by several years of illness. In 1909 she married the Russian pianist Gabrilovitch, and in 1912 resumed singing in Germany and appeared often in the principal cities. Since 1914 she has been in America, touring extensively and giving recitals both alone and with her

husband. Her voice is a mezzocontralto, with a range of over two octaves. [R.9]

CLÉMENT, EDMOND (b. 1867). See Register, 9.

'CLEOPATRA'S NIGHT.' A two-act opera by Henry K. Hadley, the libretto by Mrs. Alice Leal Pollock (after Gauthier). It was first given at the Metropolitan Opera House on Jan. 31, 1920.

CLEVELAND CONSERVATORY OF MUSIC, THE, was founded in 1881. Its directors have been Franklin Bassett from 1882 to 1915 and Charles Heydler since 1885. For a time from 1888 it was affiliated with Western Reserve University as a music-department.

CLEVELAND SCHOOL OF MUSIC, THE, was started in 1885 by Alfred Arthur, who remained at its head till his death in 1918.

CLEVELAND SYMPHONY ORCHESTRA, THE, was organized in 1918 under the auspices of the Musical Arts Association, in which Mrs. Adella P. Hughes is the moving spirit. The aim is two-fold, to provide superior concerts for patrons and to serve the whole community through so-called 'popular' performances. Under the skillful leadership of Nikolai Sokoloff both purposes have been strikingly achieved. There are about 15 symphony concerts and at least 45 others, besides many outside of Cleveland. The larger concerts are given in the New Masonic Hall, erected in 1919. The number of players ranges from 75 to 85. From 1920 Arthur Shepherd is to be assistant-conductor. The concertmaster is Louis Edlin. The enterprise is in part supported by a considerable maintenance-fund, secured by annual subscription. As a part of its plan of popular education, some fifteen of the players give instruction on their instruments in the public-school system.

Besides gradually pushing its way into the general symphonic repertory, the Orchestra has already given special attention to American composition, including Beck's Overture to 'Lara,' Griffes' 'Shojo,' Herbert's 'American Fantasy,' Hill's 'Stevensoniana,' Hopekirk's 'Sundown,' two movements from Kelley's 'Aladdin' Suite, Loeffler's 'Pagan Poem,' MacDowell's 'Indian Suite,' Rogers' 'The Name of France,' Skilton's 'Two Indian Dances,' W. G. Smith's 'Autumn Suite' and two pictures of Whithorne's, 'The Night' and 'The Rain.' Several choral works have been given with the Oberlin Musical Union and the Mendelssohn choir of Pittsburgh.

Earlier orchestras in Cleveland were those led by George Lehmann in 1886–89 and by Johann H. Beck from 1899.

CLIFTON, ARTHUR. See TUNE-BOOKS, 1819.

CLIFTON, CHALMERS (Apr. 30, 1889, Jackson, Miss.), studied at the Cincinnati

Conservatory in 1903–08, graduating with distinction in 1907. He then entered Harvard and in 1912 graduated *summa cum laude*, with highest honors in music. He conducted the first MacDowell Festival at Peterboro, N. H., in 1910. As Sheldon Fellow of Harvard in 1912–14 he was a pupil in Paris of d'Indy and Gédalge. A few months spent in Russia in 1913 also made a deep impression upon him. Returning to America in July, 1914, he conducted the first performance of E. B. Hill's pantomime, 'Pan and the Star,' at the MacDowell Festival in Peterboro in August, and other performances in Boston and Cincinnati in 1914–15. He composed and conducted music for the Lexington (Mass.) Pageant in June, 1915, commemorating one hundred and forty years of American Independence. In 1915–17 he followed Mees and Gideon as conductor of the Cecilia Society of Boston, during which time he conducted the first performance in America of d'Indy's 'Chant de la Cloche.' At the outbreak of the war, after several attempts to enter the service, he went to Paris as one of the Harvard representatives in the American University Union, was commissioned 2nd Lieutenant (Infantry) in March and was attached to the Intelligence Section under Col. Cabot Ward. He was promoted 1st Lieutenant in February, 1919, and honorably discharged in May. He conducted a concert of American music with the Société des Concerts at the Conservatoire on May 26, 1919, the program including works by Converse, MacDowell and Gilbert. His compositions are two sonatas for piano; 'The Poppy,' a poem for tenor and orchestra; music for 'A Pageant of Lexington'; and songs. He has written articles for the Boston 'Transcript' and notes on Massenet, Saint-Saëns and 'Solo' in *The Art of Music*. [R.10]

CLIPPINGER, DAVID A. (Sept. 2, 1860, O.), began to teach singing-schools when only a lad of sixteen. He attended the Northwestern Ohio Normal University and the Fort Wayne (Ind.) Conservatory. His vocal study was with Lyman Wheeler in Boston, F. W. Root in Chicago, Hey in Berlin, and Shakespeare and Behnke in London. Later he coached with Randegger, Henschel and Van Bos. He also studied theory with Eugene Thayer in New York and Gleason in Chicago. For two years he taught at Fort Wayne, but in 1887 removed to Chicago, where he has since been a leading teacher of singing, conductor and author. He has written *The Development of the Singing-Voice, Systematic Voice-Training, The Head-Voice and Other Problems, The Elements of Voice-Culture — Studio Notes Nos. 1, 2, and 3*, besides many articles on vocal topics. For four years he

was editor of the 'Western Musical Herald,' and at present he is associate-editor of 'The Musical Monitor.' In 1900 he organized the Chicago Madrigal Club, which has not only won renown by its performances, but stimulated composition by an annual prize of $100 for the most acceptable madrigal. In addition, he conducts the Carson, Pirie, Scott & Co. chorus (175 voices), the Swift & Co. Male Chorus (75 voices), the Swift & Co. Female Chorus (100 voices) and the Berwyn Choral Society. He is active in both State and National Music Teachers' Associations. [R.7]

CLOUGH–LEIGHTER,[1] HENRY (May 13, 1874, Washington), began his general education at the Columbian University in Washington, where he held a scholarship at thirteen, but gave it up for music. He had been chorister at St. John's, and, after taking up the organ with G. W. Walter, from 1888 was organist at various churches in Washington, including Epiphany in 1892–99. Meanwhile he was pursuing theoretical study with Edward Kimball, Henry Zander and Dr. Anger of Toronto. In 1899–1900 he was organist at Grace Church in Providence, in 1900–01 at Christ Church there and also music-supervisor in Westerly, R. I., and teacher at the Howe School in Boston, and since 1901 has been in editorial work in Boston, in 1901–08 with the Ditson Company and from 1908 with the Boston Music Company. Since 1901 he has also been organist at Milton, Mass. His published works include five cantatas with organ or orchestra; a lyric suite, 'The Day of Beauty,' for solo, piano and string-quartet; the symphonic ballad 'Lasca,' for tenor and orchestra; the Victorian ode 'Recessional,' for chorus and orchestra; the symphonic ode 'The Christ of the Andes,' for chorus and orchestra, op. 64; many song-cycles; over 100 songs, and a like number of choral works. He has made many transcriptions for organ, particularly of modern works, and has edited a great number of musical, technical and pedagogical works. He has newly edited and revised Anger's *Treatise on Harmony*. [R.7]

CLOUGH & WARREN COMPANY, THE, of Detroit, started in 1850 as Simmons & Clough and gradually built up a fine reputation as makers of reed-organs, particularly from 1870, when the firm was reorganized under its present name. They applied 'qualifying tubes' in connection with the reeds, securing an unusual fullness of tone. Adding the making of pipe-organs, from 1889 they were interested in developing the Austin 'universal wind-chest.' Since 1900 they have

[1] Also Clough-Leiter. The 'Clough' was added at his birth to perpetuate a family surname.

turned to making pianos, player-pianos and 'Manophone' phonographs.

COERNE, LOUIS ADOLPHE (Feb. 27, 1870, Newark, N. J.), whose father was of Dutch and Swedish derivation, was early educated in Germany and France, graduated from the Boston Latin School in 1888, and attended Harvard University in 1888–90, studying harmony and composition with Paine and violin with Kneisel. From 1890 he attended the Royal Academy at Munich, where he took organ and composition with Rheinberger, violin and conducting with Abel, and graduated with highest honors in 1893. Returning to Boston, he conducted his symphonic poem 'Hiawatha' with the Boston Symphony Orchestra in 1894, and was called to Buffalo, where in 1894–97 he was musical director of the Vocal Society, the Liedertafel and at the Church of the Messiah. In 1897–99 he was in Columbus as musical director at Trinity Church, and of the Arion Club and the Männerchor. In 1899–1902 he was again abroad, composing and publishing; he also completed and edited Rheinberger's posthumous Mass in A minor. Returning in 1902, he had charge of the music-department at Harvard in the summer session of 1903, was associate-professor at Smith College in 1903–04, and in 1904–05 was engaged in research-work in New York and at Harvard, writing *The Evolution of Modern Orchestration* (1908), and receiving for it a Ph.D. from Harvard — the first bestowal of that degree for special work in music. In 1905–07 he again lived and traveled abroad, and was present at five renderings of his opera 'Zenobia' at Bremen under the direction of Pollak, this being the first performance in Europe of a grand opera by a native of the United States. In 1907–09 he was engaged as musical director at Troy, N. Y., and in 1909–10 was director of the conservatory at Olivet College, where he received the degree of Mus.D. He then became professor and director of the School of Music at the University of Wisconsin, being also organist at the Congregational Church and leader of the Männerchor. In 1915 he became professor at the Connecticut College for Women in New London. His compositions number over 500, of which over 300 have been published. They include

Fantasy in A, op. 5, for orchestra.
Concerto-Overture in D, op. 7, for orchestra.
Suite in D minor, op. 10, for strings (1892, Stuttgart).
Concerto in E, op. 12, for organ, strings, horns, and harp (1892, Munich, also Columbian Exposition, 1893, Buffalo, 1895).
Ballet, 'Evadne,' op. 15 (extracts, Boston Symphony Orchestra, 1894).
Symphonic Poem, 'Hiawatha,' op. 18 (1893, Munich and Chicago, also Cambridge, Mass., Boston Symphony Orchestra, 1894).
String-Quartet in C minor, op. 19.

Jubilee March in E-flat, op. 20, for military band (1893, Columbian Exposition and New York, also Buffalo, 1895, Columbus, 1898).
Overture, op. 36, for orchestra.
Tone-Picture, op. 39, for orchestra.
'A Woman of Marblehead,' opera in two acts, op. 40 (extracts, Buffalo Symphony Orchestra, 1897).
'Beloved America,' patriotic hymn, op. 41, for male chorus and orchestra (1896, Buffalo).
Festival Cantata, op. 45, for soli, chorus and orchestra.
Festival Morning and Communion Services in A, opp. 46–47.
Concert-Piece in E, op. 48, for piano (1910, Madison, Wis.).
'Talitha Cumi', sacred cantata, op. 50, or soli, chorus, organ, strings and harp.
'Romantic' Violin-Concerto in G minor, op. 51, with orchestra.
Mass in D minor, op. 53, for six voices a cappella, organ ad libitum (Leuckart).
Tone-Poem, op. 59, for orchestra.
'Swedish' Sonata in A minor, op. 60, for violin and piano (1904, Colorado Springs, also Stuttgart, 1906, Madison, Wis., 1910, New London, 1916) (Hofmeister).
Three Trios in Canon, op. 62, for violin, 'cello and piano (Bosworth).
Concertino in D, op. 63, for violin and piano (Bosworth).
Three Trios, op. 64, for violin, 'cello and piano (André).
'Zenobia,' opera in three acts, op. 66 (1905–06, Bremen, also extracts, Minneapolis Orchestra, 1914, Chicago and St. Louis Orchestras, 1915) (Seemann).
'Sakuntala,' a melodrama, op. 67 (1904, Smith College, also Albany, N. Y., 1914).
'The Maiden Queen,' operetta, op. 69.
Dedication Ode, op. 82, for orchestra (opening of Connecticut College, 1915).
Incidental Music to 'The Trojan Women' of Euripides, op. 113 (1917, Connecticut College).
'Until the Day Break,' sacred cantata, op. 124, for soli, chorus and piano or orchestra (Ditson).
'A Song of Victory,' patriotic cantata, op. 125, for soli, chorus and piano or orchestra (Ditson).
'On Mountain-Crests,' op. 127, for orchestra.
'Skipper Ireson's Ride,' cantata, op. 131, for baritone, chorus and piano or orchestra (Ditson).
'The Landing of the Pilgrims,' cantata, op. 135, for baritone, chorus and piano or orchestra (Ditson).
Trio, op. 139, for flute, 'cello and harp.
'The Man of Galilee,' cantata, op. 141, for soli, chorus and organ (Schirmer).
Many Songs, mostly secular, some in 'cycles,' opp. 1, 4, 13–4, 21, 23, 27–30, 34, 42–3, 49, 55, 57–8, 68, 72–3, 76–81, 84, 91, 94, 96, 98, 104, 106, 108, 110, 112, 116, 119, 123, 128, 130, 140, 148 (Thompson, Ditson, Bosworth, Breitkopf, Grueninger, Schuberth, Summy, Presser, Boston Music Co., Flammer, Schirmer).
Anthems, opp. 6, 25, 33, 38 (tunes), 44, 52, 70, 88, 92, 95, 97, 102, 122, 126, 132 (Thompson, Ditson, Summy, Schirmer, Boston Music Co., Presser).
Choruses and Part-Songs, opp. 9, 11, 22, 31, 35, 56, 71, 83, 100, 118, 133–4, 138 (Breitkopf, Schmidt, Summy, Ditson, Presser).
Piano-Pieces and Studies, opp. 3, 8, 17, 32, 54, 74, 85–7, 89–90, 93, 99, 101, 103, 105, 107, 111, 114, 117, 120–1, 129, 136–7, 142–5, 147 (Thompson, Ditson, Siegel, Summy, Flammer, Schirmer, Boston Music Co., Presser).
Organ-Pieces, opp. 2, 16, 24, 26, 37, 109 (Thompson, Ditson, Millet, Schirmer).
Violin-Pieces, opp. 61, 65, 75, 103*b*, 146 (Siegel, Summy, Schirmer).   [R.8]

COGSWELL, HAMLIN ELISHA (b. 1852). See Register, 6.

COLBURN, GEORGE (b. 1878). See Register, 9.

COLE, BELLE (1845–1905). See Register, 5.

COLE, ISAAC P. See Tune-Books, 1815.

COLE, JOHN (1774–1855). See Tune-Books, 1800.

COLE, ROSSETTER GLEASON (Feb. 5, 1866, Clyde, Mich.), was educated at Ann Arbor, Mich., graduating from the University of Michigan in 1888. While in college he took all the courses in theory under C. B. Cady. At his graduation the University Musical Society performed his lyric cantata 'The Passing of Summer,' composed during his senior year. For two years he taught English and Latin in high-schools. While in Berlin in 1890–92 he won a scholarship in the Königliche Meisterschule under Bruch. Here Van Eycken was also his teacher in counterpoint and composition, Kogel in conducting and Middelschulte in organ. In 1892–94 he was professor at Ripon College in Wisconsin. In 1894–1901 he was at Grinnell College in Iowa, and in 1907–09 at the University of Wisconsin. In 1901–07 and since 1909 he has lived in Chicago as composer, lecturer, teacher of composition and theory, and musical writer. Since 1908 he has been in charge of the music-courses at the summer-session of Columbia University in New York. In 1902 and 1909–10 he was president of the M. T. N. A. and in 1912–14 dean of the Illinois Chapter of the A. G. O. He has given much time to composition. His 'Symphonic Prelude,' op. 28, was played by the Chicago Orchestra in 1915 and has since been repeated several times, and his overture 'Pioneer (1818–1918),' op. 35, was played by the same orchestra on Mar. 14–15, 1919, the composer conducting. 'The Passing of Summer' (1888) was later revised and published as op. 14. A cantata, 'The Broken Troth,' for women's voices, soli and orchestra, was performed by the Chicago Teachers' Chorus in 1917. Three recitations with musical settings are 'Hiawatha's Wooing,' op. 20, (published 1904), 'King Robert of Sicily' (1906) and 'Pierrot Wounded,' op. 33 (1917). 'King Robert' was first given at a Cincinnati Orchestra concert in 1911, and Bispham, to whom it is dedicated, has used it over 500 times. For the tercentenary anniversary in 1920 of the settlement of Plymouth he wrote the cantata 'The Rock of Liberty' (Schmidt). For organ are the 'Fantaisie Symphonique,' op. 28 (1912, arranged from the 'Symphonic Prelude'), 'Rhapsody,' op. 30, 'Marche Céleste,' op. 6 (1896), 'Andante Religioso,' op. 10, 'Meditation,' op. 29 (1914), and the two pieces of op. 34, 'A Song of Con-

solation' and 'A Song of Gratitude' (1919). The Ballad, op. 25, for 'cello and orchestra, was performed by Carlo Fischer and the Minneapolis Orchestra in 1909. For piano there is an effective 'Legend,' op. 31 (1916), and for piano and violin a sonata in D, op. 8. His published compositions number about 85, of which 35 are songs, 15 piano-pieces, 8 organ-pieces and the rest for chorus, violin, 'cello and orchestra. Of the songs the best known are 'If' and 'What can you do?' from a set of eight children's songs, op. 7 (1897); 'Auf Wiedersehen,' 'A Kiss and a Tear' and 'When love is in her eyes,' op. 12 (1898); 'My true love hath my heart' and 'Absence,' op. 17 (1903); 'Unnumbered,' op. 18 (1904); 'When thou art nigh,' op. 23 (1906); and 'Your lad and my lad' (1918). He prepared Vol. vi. of *The Art of Music*, on Church and Choral Music, 1917. [R.8]

COLE, SAMUEL WINKLEY (b. 1848). See Register, 6.

COLEMAN, OBED M. (1817–1845). See Register, 4.

‡COLERIDGE–TAYLOR, SAMUEL (Aug. 15, 1875, London : Sept. 1, 1912, Thorton Heath). See article in Vol. v. 32–3. His last year was spent as a member of the faculty of the Guildhall School of Music in London. In 1904 and 1906 he made visits to America, and conducted concerts of his music in many cities. To the list of works should be added

op. 60 24 Negro Melodies, transcribed for piano.
    62 Music to 'Nero.'
    63 Symphonic Variations on an African Air (1906, Philharmonic Society, London).
    64 Scènes de Ballet, for piano.
    65 'Endymion's Dream,' Rhapsody for soprano and tenor, women's chorus and orchestra.
    66 'Forest Scenes,' for piano.
    67 Three Part-Songs.
    68 'Bon-bon' Suite, for baritone, chorus and orchestra (1909, Brighton Musical Festival).
    69 'Sea-Drift,' Rhapsody for chorus a cappella.
    70 Music to 'Faust.'
    71 Valse Suite, for piano.
    72 'Thelma,' grand opera in three acts.
    73 Ballade in C minor, for violin and piano.
    73a (?) Four Part-Songs for men's voices.
    74 'Scenes from an Imaginary Ballet,' for piano.
    75 'Bamboula,' Rhapsodic Dance for orchestra (1910, Norfolk, Conn., Festival).
    76 'A Tale of Old Japan,' cantata.
    77 'Petite Suite de Concert,' for orchestra.
    78 Three Impromptus, for organ.
    79 Incidental music to 'Othello.'
    80 Concerto in G minor, for violin and orchestra (1911, Norfolk Festival).
    81 'Waiting' and 'Red o' the Dawn,' songs with orchestra (MS).
    82 'Hiawatha,' ballet in five scenes, for orchestra (MS).

Without opus-number.
  Incidental music to 'The Forest of Wild Thyme.'
  Eight Part-Songs.
  Two Impromptus, for piano.
  Slow movement on a Negro Melody, for violin.
  Two accompaniments to the poems 'Clown and Columbine' and 'St. Agnes' Eve.'
  Two Song-Albums.
  Some fifteen songs.

Sir Hubert Parry said of him: 'It was the very simplicity and unconsciousness of his character which caused the racial motives and impulses to be revealed so clearly. He had no occasion to conceal them; and the niche which he made for himself in musical history derives its individuality from the frankness with which he revealed the qualities which were the inevitable outcome of an exceptional and interesting combination of influences.' ('Musical Times,' October, 1912.)

See M. Byron, *A Day with Coleridge-Taylor*, 1912; Anon., *Golden Hours with Coleridge-Taylor*, 1913; and W. C. B. Sayers, *Coleridge-Taylor, His Life and Letters*, 1915.

COLLEGE OF MUSIC OF CINCINNATI, THE, was founded in 1878 through the enthusiasm of George Ward Nichols and developed through the progressive liberality of Reuben R. Springer, to whom it owes its endowment and much of its equipment. Theodore Thomas was director in 1878–80, but resigned because of disagreement with Nichols as to administrative policy. Nichols was succeeded as president in 1885 by Peter Rudolph Neff, who continued till 1894. In 1894–99 Frank Van der Stucken was director, and in 1899–1920 Arnold J. Gantvoort was general manager. From the first the College has had close relations with the Festival Association. The faculty numbers about 25, including many names of national reputation. The total number of students since the beginning has been about 30,000, and the annual enrolment is about 700. There have been about 500 full graduates, besides perhaps 1400 receiving certificates. The College has its own buildings, which contain unusually commodious concert-halls.

COLLEGES, MUSIC IN. The American 'college' was originally an adaptation to colonial conditions of a type of institution for higher education that was prevalent in England. The pioneer settlers were alive to the importance of training intellectual and moral leaders. Of the colleges now existing 2 date from before 1700, about 25 from before 1800, and about 35 from before 1835. Though technically organized in somewhat different forms, these really exemplified a single type. They were for men only, especially of the upper social classes, were designed to prepare for 'the learned professions,' especially the

ministry, and offered a fixed four years' curriculum leading to the degree of A.B.

After about 1835 the number of these institutions increased rapidly, but the original type was either much modified or replaced by new types. Colleges for men gradually altered the balance of the curriculum, so as to make a more democratic appeal and prepare for varied careers, and tended to allow increasing freedom in the choice of studies. The new types included colleges for women only, those for both sexes, the composite 'state universities,' and a variety of special or occupational schools. A few of the earlier colleges had had something of a true 'university' ideal, and others adopted it, though without dropping or minimizing their 'academic' or 'collegiate' departments. In general, except in the case of the 'state universities' and a few others, all colleges are private corporations and with few exceptions are affiliated with some religious denomination, either by origin or by present administration. After about 1835, in consequence of the rapid expansion of the country, great differences of policy and standard became common in different sections. Much of this inequality still persists, though with a tendency toward a degree of uniformity through competition or mutual agreement.

The number of institutions counted in this general class by the United States Bureau of Education is now over 600. Of these, those for men number only about 60 (almost wholly in the East), those for women about 90 (chiefly in the East and South), and those for both men and women at least 350, including the 'state universities' as a class. The balance are special institutions not important for consideration here.

Music as a topic for study had no place in the older curriculum. It did not appear until differentiation set in, and even then for a long time only sporadically. It is still unusual in colleges for men, except where they have expanded into universities. But in almost every divergent type it has been emphasized — in colleges for women, in those for men and women, in state and most other universities, and even in some specializing colleges. The growth of this recognition has become so extensive that some summary statements about it are demanded here, although the amount and intricacy of the data at hand defy satisfactory presentation in any brief form.[1]

In the topics that may be offered for entrance to many colleges, 'music' is often included, but credit is confined to certain lines of theory or information rather than expertness in per-

[1] In preparing this article far more material was collected than it has proved possible to use.

formance. This brings the colleges into relation with those high schools that offer musical courses.

Within college systems two distinct policies are in evidence. The first makes music a 'chair' or 'department' like other subjects, with a professor who is a member of the general faculty. The second sets music apart in a distinct 'school' or 'conservatory,' with its own faculty and curriculum, either directly controlled by the college authorities or bound up with the system by some form of affiliation. In a few cases under this second class music is grouped with drawing, painting, sculpture, architecture or other expressional arts in a 'school of fine art.' Under the first type access to music-courses is usually limited to those fully matriculated in the college, and the courses that are magnified are those that are readily coördinated with other courses in science, history and literature, though there is an increasing tendency to allow credit for courses in musical praxis as well. Credit in music counts (within some limitations) toward the A.B. degree. Under the second type music-courses are usually open to students not otherwise matriculated, so that the institution becomes a public music-school (though usually with requirements for admission equivalent to those in the college proper). To college-credit is given toward an A.B., and in some cases this degree may be taken with music as a 'major.' The topics most universally credited are harmony, appreciation and history, though the exact method of credit varies much. Work in praxis is also being credited more and more, though with much natural restriction. For non-collegiate students full music-courses usually cover at least four years, with latitude as to emphasis upon an instrument or the voice, leading generally to the degree of Mus. B. Less strenuous courses lead to a diploma of graduation, a teacher's certificate (usually for three years' work) or a public-school certificate (usually for two years' work). In all such cases the student is required to follow a somewhat extensive curriculum, including some subjects not musical. But many schools also admit special students for limited courses of their own choosing.

Topics that are taken in class, especially if for college credit, are generally not subject to fees, but individual lessons are as a rule charged for at rates that vary widely in different institutions. The use of rooms and instruments for practice also involves extra expense to the student. This pecuniary factor places much music-study on a different footing from other studies. On the other hand, most institutions that emphasize music take over into their general budget a large portion of the 'overhead' charges of the department or school.

In general, theory-courses include rudimentary training, appreciation (usually with considerable demonstration), harmony (synthetic and analytic), form, composition (often extending to fugue and orchestration), history (usually lectures and demonstration combined), pedagogical methods (especially for public-school work, but also for individual teaching), and sometimes acoustics, æsthetics and the relation of fine art to culture. The praxis-courses usually include piano, organ, violin and voice, and sometimes a variety of other instruments. In most cases there are one or more choruses (often large oratorio-societies), a choir and one or two glee-clubs. Orchestras and bands are becoming increasingly common. Many institutions have at least one large organ. Several have musical libraries of importance. Wherever music is emphasized a separate building is provided, including a large recital-hall, often with an elaborate equipment of practice-rooms, etc. Extended and varied opportunities are quite generally offered in the way of frequent recitals and concerts, either by members of the staff or by visiting artists and organizations. In many cases there is an annual 'festival.' Thus even institutions remote from musical centers are able to supply a certain amount of musical demonstration and experience.

The pedagogical consequences of bringing music-courses into close connection with those in other subjects are obvious. They are forced to become definite and systematic, so as to be stated with precision and be subject to periodic examination. This is evidently bringing to pass a notable degree of standardization. Emphasis is naturally laid upon securing teachers whose training and quality are comparable with that in the rest of the faculty-body. There is a marked tendency to exalt the relation of music as a discipline to general culture rather than to treat it as merely a means for securing a livelihood. Whatever pervasive influence for culture exists in the institution as a whole reacts on all who pursue music, even as special students. Even those who rank as only music-students are often required to take some literary or other studies.

It is impracticable to give details, except in a few conspicuous cases, about the scope, organization and facilities of the music-departments or schools in each institution. But the following register, with its occasional notes, will have some utility. In each case the head of the department is named (the director, dean, professor or chief instructor), with the total number in the music-faculty and the names of previous heads who have had long or notable service. The institutions are given in geographical order by states, but alphabetically by places within the states.

1. COLLEGES FOR MEN

Bowdoin College, Brunswick, Me.
Edward H. Wass.
Dartmouth College, Hanover, N. H.
Leonard B. McWhood (from 1918). Charles H. Morse, 1901–16 and emeritus; Philip G. Clapp, 1916–18.
Amherst College, Amherst, Mass.
William P. Bigelow (from 1894).
Harvard University, Cambridge, Mass.
Walter R. Spalding (from 1903) +4. John K. Paine, 1862–1906.
Williams College, Williamstown, Mass.
Sumner Salter (from 1905).
Yale University, New Haven, Conn.
David Stanley Smith (from 1920) +11. Gustav J. Stoeckel, 1854–96, Horatio Parker, 1894–1919.
Colgate University, Hamilton, N. Y.
William H. Hoerrner (from 1912) +1.
College of the City of New York, New York City.
Samuel A. Baldwin (from 1907).
Princeton University, Princeton, N. J.
George A. Russell (from 1917).
Seton Hall College, South Orange, N. J.
Francis C. Schreiner.
Catholic University of America, Washington, D. C.
Abel L. Gabert.
University of Notre Dame, Notre Dame, Ind.
Charles Marshall +4.
Marquette University, Milwaukee, Wis.
Liborius Semmann (from 1911) +35. See art.
DePaul University, Chicago, Ill.
Walter Keller (from 1912).

2. COLLEGES FOR WOMEN

Girls' schools were occasionally undertaken in New England from about 1810. After 1837 more significant 'seminaries' began to be established, including Mount Holyoke in Massachusetts, many in the South, and some in Ohio and Illinois, but only two or three offering anything like a 'college' curriculum. After the Civil War the number increased and the standard was rapidly raised. There was no music-instruction till about 1860, but it has now become almost universal (with Simmons, Bryn Mawr and Goucher as striking exceptions). As a rule, these music-departments are well organized and decidedly effective.

Radcliffe College, Cambridge, Mass.
Walter R. Spalding (from 1903), with some opportunities at Harvard University.
Smith College, Northampton, Mass.
Henry Dike Sleeper (from 1903) +23. Benjamin C. Blodgett, 1878–1903, Louis A. Coerne, 1903–04.
Wheaton College, Wheaton, Mass.
Hiram G. Tucker (from 1878) +1.
Mount Holyoke College, South Hadley, Mass.
William C. Hammond (from 1900) +10.
Wellesley College, Wellesley, Mass.
Hamilton, C. Macdougall (from 1900)+10. Charles H. Morse, 1875–84, Junius W. Hill, 1884–97.
Connecticut College, New London, Conn.
Louis A. Coerne (from 1915) +3.

Wells College, Aurora, N. Y.
Emil K. Winkler (from 1894) +5.
Elmira College, Elmira, N. Y.
George M. McKnight (from 1894) +7. Max Piutti, 1874–83, Edward Dickinson, 1883–92.
Barnard College, New York City.
Some courses open at both Columbia University and the Institute of Musical Art.
Hunter College, New York City.
Henry T. Fleck +7.
Vassar College, Poughkeepsie, N. Y.
George C. Gow (from 1895) +8. Frédéric L. Ritter, 1867–91, Edward M. Bowman, 1891–95.
Skidmore School of Arts, Saratoga Springs, N. Y.
A. Stanley Osborn (from 1917) +3.
Beaver College, Beaver, Pa.
M. Ellery Reed (from 1918) + 6.
Moravian Seminary, Bethlehem, Pa.
T. Edgar Shields + 3.
Wilson College, Chambersburg, Pa.
Rudolph Wertime (from 1917) +3. Orlando A. Mansfield, 1912–17.
Irving-College, Mechanicsburg, Pa.
Harry C. Harper, 1903–18.
Pennsylvania College for Women, Pittsburgh, Pa.
Walter Wild (till 1920) +4. T. Carl Whitmer, 1909–16.
Hood College, Frederick, Md.
Henry W. Pearson (from 1916) +5.
Maryland College for Women, Lutherville, Md.
Howard R. Thatcher (from 1906) +5.
Sullins College, Bristol, Va.
Carl Fallberg (from 1917) +8.
Hollins College, Hollins, Va.
Erich Rath (from 1907) +6. J. A. E. Winkler, 1852–62, H. L. Pauli, 1873–92.
Randolph-Macon Woman's College, Lynchburg, Va.
John H. Davis (from 1899) +7.
Sweet Briar College, Sweet Briar, Va.
Helen F. Young +5.
Queen's College, Charlotte, N. C.
J. R. Niniss +4.
Greensboro College for Women, Greensboro, N. C.
Conrad Lahser (from 1914) +6.
Meredith College, Raleigh, N. C.
Charlotte Ruegger (from 1915) +9.
Salem College, Winston-Salem, N. C.
H. A. Shirley (from 1896) +13.
Chicora College, Columbia, S. C.
Heinrich H. Bellamann (from 1907) +9.
Coker College, Hartsville, S. C.
Carl J. Tolman (from 1908) +7. Festivals since 1911.
Winthrop College, Rock Hill, S. C.
Henry D. Guelich (from 1914) +12. A. O. Bauer, 1902–14.
Converse College, Spartanburg, S. C.
Edmon Morris (from 1913) +6. Arthur L. Manchester, 1904–13. Festivals since 1895.
Agnes Scott College, Decatur, Ga.
Christian W. Dieckmann (from 1918) +3. Joseph Maclean, 1893–1918.
Bessie Tifft College, Forsyth, Ga.
William P. Twaddell (from 1920) +10.
Brenau College, Gainesville, Ga.
Otto W. G. Pfefferkorn + 11. August Geiger, 1903–10.
Wesleyan College, Macon, Ga.
Joseph Maerz (from 1914) +11.
Florida State College for Women, Tallahassee, Fla.
Ella S. Opperman (from 1911)+7.
Oxford College for Women, Oxford, O.
Clem A. Towner (from 1914) +4. Karl Merz, 1861–82, Max V. Swarthout, 1905–11.

Western College for Women, Oxford, O.
Alice A. Porter (from 1901) +6. Edgar S. Kelley, associated from 1910.
Lake Erie College, Painesville, O.
Henry T. Wade +3.
Milwaukee-Downer College, Milwaukee, Wis.
Claudia W. McPheeters (from 1895) +7. John C. Fillmore, 1878-84.
Illinois Woman's College, Jacksonville, Ill.
Henry V. Stearns +11.
Rockford College, Rockford, Ill.
Laura G. Short (from 1918). F. Marion Ralston, 1909-18.
Hamilton College, Lexington, Ky.
Isabel Mets (from 1914) + 3.
Tennessee College, Murfreesboro, Tenn.
Stanley Levey (from 1918) +4.
Judson College, Marion, Ala.
Edward L. Powers (from 1900) +7.
Woman's College of Alabama, Montgomery, Ala.
Edward B. Perry (from 1917) +5.
Belhaven College, Jackson, Miss.
Mary Wharton +5.
College of St. Catharine, St. Paul, Minn.
S. Scionti +11.
College of St. Teresa, Winona, Minn.
Glenn D. Gunn, Horace G. Seaton, William McPhail, Ancella M. Fox.
Central College, Lexington, Mo.
Delano F. Conrad (from 1897) + 4.
Hardin College, Mexico, Mo.
Arthur L. Manchester (from 1918).
Central College, Conway, Ark.
J. Harry Aker +6.
H. Sophie Newcomb College, New Orleans, La.
Leon R. Maxwell (from 1909) +13.
Baylor Female College, Belton, Tex.
T. S. Lovette +6.
Colorado Woman's College, Denver, Colo.
Josephine S. White (from 1911) +3.
Mills College, Mills College, Cal.
Edward F. Schneider + 10. Louis Lisser, 1880-1900 and emeritus.

3. COLLEGES FOR MEN AND WOMEN

Coeducation in colleges first appeared in 1833 at Oberlin and from 1850 steadily became more common, especially in the State Universities as they were founded and in other institutions in the Interior and the West. (For the State Universities, see article.) As a class, colleges of this order tend to provide musical instruction, often in an extended and impressive way. They are often notably successful in arousing enthusiasm for choral music of different grades. While the cultural ideal is usually emphasized, occupational preparation is also provided for, especially as regards teaching.

Bates College, Lewiston, Me.
Edwin L. Goss.
Colby College, Waterville, Me.
Alice H. White.
Middlebury College, Middlebury, Vt.
Lewis J. Hathaway.
Boston University, Boston, Mass.
John P. Marshall (from 1903) +8 lecturers. After the founding of the New England Conservatory in 1867 Boston University was loosely affiliated with it, offering advanced work in composition.

Tufts College, Tufts College, Mass.
Leo R. Lewis (from 1895).
Brown University, Providence, R. I.
Edwin E. Wilde (from 1914).
Alfred College, Alfred, N. Y.
Ray W. Wingate (from 1912).
Adelphi College, Brooklyn, N. Y.
William A. Thayer +1.
Hobart College, Geneva, N. Y.
William L. Wood.
Cornell University, Ithaca, N. Y.
Hollis E. Dann (from 1906).
Columbia University, New York City.
Daniel Gregory Mason (from 1910) +3. Edward A. MacDowell, 1896-1904, Cornelius Rybner, 1904-19. In Teachers College, Charles H. Farnsworth (from 1900).
New York University, New York.
Thomas Tapper (from 1908) and William L. Wright (from 1914).
Syracuse University, Syracuse, N. Y.
George A. Parker (from 1882) +20.
Upsala College, Kenilworth, N. J.
Oscar M. Magnusson.
Lebanon Valley College, Annville, Pa.
E. Edwin Sheldon +5.
Geneva College, Beaver Falls, Pa.
Frances E. Waddel +4.
Ursinus College, Collegeville, Pa.
John M. Jolls +2.
Thiel College, Greenville, Pa.
Stanley J. Seiple +4.
Grove City College, Grove City, Pa.
Hermann Poehlmann +3.
Juniata College, Huntingdon, Pa.
Edythe M. Ring +2.
Bucknell University, Lewisburg, Pa.
Paul G. Stolz +7.
Westminster College, New Wilmington, Pa.
Per Nielsen +6. William W. Campbell, 1906-19.
Temple University, Philadelphia, Pa.
Thaddeus Rich +13.
University of Pittsburgh, Pittsburgh, Pa.
Will Earhart (from 1919) +2.
Susquehanna University, Selinsgrove, Pa.
Rudolph J. Meyer +2.
Blue Ridge College, New Windsor, Md.
William Z. Fletcher +4.
Western Maryland College, Westminster, Md.
Maude E. Gesner +3.
Bridgewater College, Bridgewater, Va.
Charles W. Roller (from 1905) +3. George B. Holsinger, 1882-98.
Bethany College, Bethany, W. Va.
Jean C. Moos (from 1899) +2.
West Virginia Wesleyan College, Buckhannon, W. Va.
George S. Bohanan (from 1916) +3.
Elon College, Elon, N. C.
Ava L. B. Dodge +4.
Atlantic Christian College, Wilson, N. C.
Ivy M. Smith +3.
Piedmont College, Demorest, Ga.
S. P. Spencer +2.
J. B. Stetson University, DeLand, Fla.
Paul R. Geddes +4.
Rollins College, Winter Park, Fla.
Susan H Dyer +7.
Ohio Northern University, Ada, O.
Frederic T. Killeen (from 1916) +2.
Mount Union College, Alliance, O.
Edwin L. Allen (from 1917) +5.
Ohio University, Athens, O.
Alexander S. Thompson (from 1913) +9.
Baldwin-Wallace College, Berea, O.
Albert Riemenschneider (from 1898) +9.

Bluffton College, Bluffton, O.
Gustav A. Lehmann +8.
Cedarville College, Cedarville, O.
Florence Russell (from 1918) +1.
Western Reserve University, Cleveland, O.
Charles E. Clemens (from 1899) +1.
Defiance College, Defiance, O.
Flossie E. Whitney (from 1916) +3.
Ohio Wesleyan University, Delaware, O.
Horace Whitehouse (from 1918) +8. Samuel H.
Blakeslee, 1884–96, Charles M. Jacobus, 1901–
18. Music-courses since 1854.
Findlay College, Findlay, O.
Royal D. Hughes (from 1916) +3.
Denison University, Granville, O.
Karl H. Eschman (from 1913) +7. Otto Eng-
werson, 1894–1904, Carl P. Wood, 1906–13.
Musical instruction began about 1840. Festi-
vals since 1905.
Hiram College, Hiram, O.
T. Morgan Phillips +2.
Muskingum College, New Concord, O.
Edward H. Freeman (from 1914) +2.
Oberlin College, Oberlin, O.
Charles W. Morrison (from 1902) +35. George
N. Allen, 1837–64, Fenelon B. Rice, 1869–1901.
Rio Grande College, Rio Grande, O.
Edna V. Starr.
Wittenberg College, Springfield, O.
Miriam H. Weaver +4.
Heidelberg University, Tiffin, O.
Frank W. Gilles +6.
Otterbein College, Westerville, O.
Glenn G. Grabill +4.
Wilmington College, Wilmington, O.
Ruth Brundage +1.
College of Wooster, Wooster, O.
Neille O. Rowe (from 1914) +6. Karl Merz,
1882–90, J. Lawrence Erb, 1905–13.
Adrian College, Adrian, Mich.
Harrison D. LeBaron (from 1919) +2.
Albion College, Albion, Mich.
Harlan J. Cozine +4.
Alma College, Alma, Mich.
Clifford F. Royer +3.
Hillsdale College, Hillsdale, Mich.
Melville W. Chase (from 1869) +3.
Hope College, Holland, Mich.
Oscar Cress +2.
Olivet College, Olivet, Mich.
Elsie Duffield (from 1920) +3. Elizabeth B. Bint-
liff, 1893–1909.
Earlham College, Earlham, Ind.
Samuel B. Garton +2.
Franklin College, Franklin, Ind.
Minnie B. Bruner (from 1898) +1.
Goshen College, Goshen, Ind.
Amos S. Ebersole (from 1915) +4.
DePauw University, Greencastle, Ind.
Robert G. McCutchan (from 1911) +11. James
H. Howe, 1884–94, Belle A. Mansfield, 1894–
1911.
Hanover College, Hanover, Ind.
Lloyd L. Alexander.
Indiana Central University, Indianapolis, Ind.
Marged E. Jones +1.
Taylor University, Upland, Ind.
A. Verne Westlake +6.
Valparaiso University, Valparaiso, Ind.
Edmund W. Chaffee (from 1899) +9. Henri W. J.
Ruifrok, 1889–95, William W. Hinshaw, 1895–99.
Vincennes University, Vincennes, Ind.
Joyce H. Hetley +2.
Lawrence College, Appleton, Wis.
Frederick V. Evans +14.

Beloit College, Beloit, Wis.
Max Miranda (from 1919). B. D. Allen, 1894–
1902, Abram R. Tyler, 1902–11.
Ripon College, Ripon, Wis.
Elizabeth B. Bintliff (from 1909) +5. John C.
Fillmore, 1868–77, Rossetter G. Cole, 1892–
94.
Carroll College, Waukesha, Wis.
Clarence E. Shepard +2.
Hedding College, Abingdon, Ill.
Mrs. Henry Lee Gash (from 1919) +3.
Shurtleff College, Alton, Ill.
Cornelia Brownlee (from 1918).
Illinois Wesleyan University, Bloomington, Ill.
Edward Y. Mason (from 1919) +6. Henry P.
Eames, 1913–19.
Carthage College, Carthage, Ill.
Ann Dvorsky (from 1914) +4.
University of Chicago, Chicago, Ill.
Robert W. Stevens (from 1911).
James Millikin University, Decatur, Ill.
Max V. Swarthout (from 1914) +18. Hermann
H. Kaeuper, 1903–14.
Eureka College, Eureka, Ill.
F. J. Sucher (from 1918) +4.
Northwestern University, Evanston, Ill.
Peter C. Lutkin (from 1897) +33.
Knox College, Galesburg, Ill.
William F. Bentley (from 1885) +9. Festivals
since 1900.
Lombard College, Galesburg, Ill.
Anna G. Bryant (from 1912) +4.
Greenville College, Greenville, Ill.
Louwillie Kessler +4.
Illinois College, Jacksonville, Ill.
William E. Kritch +10.
Lake Forest College, Lake Forest, Ill.
Henry P. Eames +5.
Lincoln College, Lincoln, Ill.
Herbert O. Merry +3.
Monmouth College, Monmouth, Ill.
T. Merrill Austin +5.
Northwestern College, Naperville, Ill.
J. Francis Maguire +3.
Augustana College, Rock Island, Ill.
J. Victor Bergquist (from 1912).
Wheaton College, Wheaton, Ill.
Mabel A. Rippe +2.
Berea College, Berea, Ky.
Ralph Rigby (from 1905) +3.
Georgetown College, Georgetown, Ky
Bertram C. Henry +3.
Asbury College, Wilmore, Ky.
Edwin A. Gowen (from 1917) +4.
Kentucky Wesleyan College, Winchester, Ky.
Anna C. Goff +1.
Cumberland University, Lebanon, Tenn.
W. H. A. Moore +1.
Fisk University, Nashville, Tenn.
Jennie A. Robinson +6.
Carleton College, Northfield, Minn.
Edward Strong (from 1912) +5.
St. Olaf College, Northfield, Minn.
F. Melius Christiansen +10.
Hamline University, St. Paul, Minn.
John A. Jaeger +3.
Macalester College, St. Paul, Minn.
Harry Phillips (from 1896) +15.
Gustavus Adolphus College, St. Peter, Minn.
O. Waldemar Anderson +3.
Coe College, Cedar Rapids, Ia.
Earle G. Killeen (from 1910) +7.
Des Moines College, Des Moines, Ia.
Edith M. Usry (from 1912) +2. Maro L. Bartlett,
1885–1919.

Drake University, Des Moines, Ia.
 Holmes Cowper (from 1909) +16.
Parsons College, Fairfield, Ia.
 Charles W. Mountain +4.
Upper Iowa University, Fayette, Ia.
 Charles D. Neff (from 1900) +4.
Grinnell College, Grinnell, Ia.
 George L. Pierce (from 1907) +12. Willard Kimball, 1875–94, Rossetter G. Cole, 1894–1901.
 Festivals since 1912.
Simpson College, Indianola, Ia.
 Frank E. Barrows (from 1895) +5.
Ellsworth College, Iowa Falls, Ia.
 Artemas E. Bullock (from 1894) +4.
Iowa Wesleyan College, Mt. Pleasant, Ia.
 Elmer K. Gannett (from 1918) +2. A. Rommel, 1878–1918.
Cornell College, Mt. Vernon, Ia.
 Frank H. Shaw (from 1915) +6.
Penn College, Oskaloosa, Ia.
 Charles L. Griffith +4.
Morningside College, Sioux Falls, Ia.
 Paul MacCollin +5.
Buena Vista College, Storm Lake, Ia.
 Fred W. Mimberley (from 1914) +1.
Tabor College, Tabor, Ia.
 Ralph W. Soule +2.
Missouri Wesleyan College, Cameron, Mo.
 Joseph E. Layton (from 1907) +3.
Culver-Stockton College, Canton, Mo.
 Robert E. Crossland (from 1919) +1.
Missouri Valley College, Marshall, Mo.
 Claude L. Fichthorn +2. Edgar S. Place, 1890–1912.
Drury College, Springfield, Mo.
 T. Stanley Skinner (from 1917) +2. William A. Chalfant, 1881–1914.
Tarkio College, Tarkio, Mo.
 Claude C. Pinney (from 1913) +3.
Henderson-Brown College, Arkadelphia, Ark.
 Frederick Harwood +5.
Ouachita College, Arkadelphia, Ark.
 Livingston H. Mitchell +4.
Arkansas Cumberland College, Clarksville, Ark.
 Virgia Poynor +3.
Fargo College, Fargo, N. D.
 Albert J. Stephens (from 1908) +10.
Jamestown College, Jamestown, N. D.
 Harry D. Jackson (from 1918) +2.
Huron College, Huron, S. D.
 Herbert M. Bailey (from 1916) +6.
Dakota Wesleyan University, Mitchell, S. D.
 George H. Miller (from 1915) +3.
Yankton College, Yankton, S. D.
 Lee N. Dailey (from 1904) +7.
Cotner College, Bethany, Neb.
 Ethel Biles +7.
Union College, College View, Neb.
 Oliver S. Beltz (from 1915) +3.
Doane College, Crete, Neb.
 George H. Aller (from 1914) +5.
Midland College, Fremont, Neb.
 Charles K. Nicholas (from 1919) +3. William Davies, 1906–19.
Grand Island College, Grand Island, Neb.
 Jane L. Pinder +6.
Hastings College, Hastings, Neb.
 Hayes M. Fuhr (from 1912) +2.
University of Omaha, Neb.
 Johanna Anderson.
Nebraska Wesleyan Univ., University Place, Neb.
 Carl Beutel (from 1917) +7.
Baker University, Baldwin City, Kan.
 Marvin D. Geere (from 1912) +4. Robert G. McCutchan, 1904–10.

College of Emporia, Emporia, Kan.
 Daniel A. Hirschler (from 1914) +2.
Kansas City University, Kansas City, Kan.
 Ada L. Harrington.
Bethany College, Lindsborg, Kan.
 Hagbard Brase +14. Festivals since 1900.
Ottawa University, Ottawa, Kan.
 Paul R. Utt (from 1917) +3.
Kansas Wesleyan University, Salina, Kan.
 Ernest L. Cox (from 1917) +4. James E. Carnal, 1903–13.
Sterling College, Sterling, Kan.
 Clyde E. Matson +2.
Washburn College, Topeka, Kan.
 Horace Whitehouse +7.
Fairmount College, Wichita, Kan.
 Frank A. Power +5.
Friends University, Wichita, Kan.
 Lucius Ades +3.
Southwestern College, Winfield, Kan.
 Elvis C. Marshall (from 1911) +3.
Phillips University, East Enid, Okla.
 Charles M. Bliss +6.
Kingfisher College, Kingfisher, Okla.
 Frederick Drake +3.
Henry Kendall College, Tulsa, Okla.
 John K. Weaver (from 1909) +4.
Simmons College, Abilene, Tex.
 Styles R. Anderson +6.
Howard Payne College, Brownwood, Tex.
 Henry E. Meyer (from 1918) +3.
Southern Methodist University, Dallas, Tex.
 Harold von Mickwitz (from 1916) +6.
Texas Christian University, Fort Worth, Tex.
 Helen F. Cahoon +3.
Southwestern University, Georgetown, Tex.
 Frederick W. Kraft (from 1914) +3.
Baylor University, Waco, Tex.
 Rudolf Hoffmann +8.
Colorado College, Colorado Springs, Colo.
 Edward D. Hale (from 1905) +6. Rubin Goldmark, 1894–1901.
College of Idaho, Caldwell, Ida.
 Frederick F. Beale (from 1912) +2.
Whitworth College, Spokane, Wash.
 Thomas Moss.
College of Puget Sound, Tacoma, Wash.
 Robert L. Schofield (from 1912) +6.
Whitman College, Walla Walla, Wash.
 Llewellyn B. Cain +3. Samuel H. Lovewell, 1898–1906.
Pacific University, Forest Grove, Ore.
 Frank T. Chapman (from 1914) +5.
McMinnville College, McMinnville, Ore.
 Carrie C. Potter (from 1904) +3.
Pacific College, Newberg, Ore.
 Alexander Hull (from 1908) +1.
Willamette University, Salem, Ore.
 John R. Sites (from 1918) +4.
Pomona College, Claremont, Cal.
 Ralph H. Lyman (from 1917) +5.
University of Redlands, Redlands, Cal.
 Charles H. Marsh (from 1919) +4.
Pacific Union College, St. Helena, Cal.
 Noah E. Paulin +2.
College of the Pacific, San José, Cal.
 Howard H. Hanson (from 1919) +12. Pierre Douillet, 1897–1913.
Leland Stanford University, Stanford University, Cal.
 Lewis H. Eaton (from 1913).
Whittier College, University Park, Cal.
 Howard L. Hockett +1.

For much further information, see Rose Yont, *Status and Value of Music in Education*, 1916.

COLLEGE ENTRANCE EXAMINA-TION BOARD, THE, is an association of about 35 colleges in the East for arranging and holding uniform entrance-examinations in various subjects. The system has been so successful that its standards have been widely adopted throughout the country.

The present requirement in music is confined to harmony and the test is wholly in writing. The candidate must show

(1) The ability to harmonize, in four vocal parts, simple melodies of not fewer than eight measures, in soprano or in bass — these melodies will require a knowledge of triads and inversions, in the major and minor modes; and of modulation, transient or complete, to nearly-related keys.

(2) Analytical knowledge of ninth-chords, all non-harmonic tones, and altered chords (including augmented chords).

The student is expected to have a full knowledge of the rudiments of music, scales, intervals, and staff-notation, including the terms and expression-marks in common use.

Credit for passing is counted as 'one unit' towards entrance — a 'unit' representing 'a year's study in a secondary school.' The total number of 'units' required for entrance is usually fifteen.

'COLONIAL WEDDING, A.' A one-act opera by John A. Van Broekhoven, brought out at Cincinnati in 1905.

COLSON, WILLIAM BREWSTER (b. 1846). See Register, 5.

COLUMBIA UNIVERSITY, New York, established a Department of Music in 1896, when a fund for the purpose was given by Mrs. E. Mary Ludlow in memory of her son Robert Center. In 1906 this was transformed into a School of Music, including courses in the University proper and in Teachers College. The purpose is 'to teach music historically and æsthetically as an element of liberal culture, to teach it scientifically and practically with a view to training musicians who shall be competent to teach and to compose, and to provide practical training in orchestral and choral music.' Most of the courses in praxis are given in Teachers College, while the University proper emphasizes history, theory and form, but also maintains a chorus and orchestra. Edward MacDowell was professor in 1896–1904, and Cornelius Rybner in 1904–19. Among the associate professors have been Leonard B. McWhood in 1897–1910, Charles H. Farnsworth since 1900 (Teachers College), Daniel Gregory Mason since 1910 and Walter Henry Hall since 1913. The School has a fine library of scores and books about music. The Mosenthal Fellowship, awarded biennially, and the Cutting Fellowships and the Pulitzer Scholarship, awarded annually, afford opportunity for advanced study.

COLUMBIAN ANACREONTIC SOCIETY, THE, of New York, probably formed in 1795, was modeled after the Anacreontic Society of London (see Vol. i. 79–80), though less aristocratic. It fostered attention to glees and part-songs, and may have been the first in America to attempt melodrama. The president till 1799 was John Hodgkinson. See Sonneck, Concert-Life, pp. 204–7.

COMBS, GILBERT RAYNOLDS (Jan. 5, 1863, Philadelphia), from his fifteenth to his twenty-second year was actively engaged in playing the organ, piano and 'cello, teaching piano and violin, and directing orchestras, operatic companies and choruses. By these early activities he was prepared for his later work as founder, in 1885, of a large conservatory (see article below). For twelve years he was organist at the Immanuel Presbyterian Church, later musical director at the South Broad Street Baptist Church and for six years organist at the Tenth Presbyterian Church. As composer he is best known by his piano-pieces, but he has written in all forms. The 'Erato' for piano, dedicated to Godowsky, the 'Romance,' op. 17, 'Norwegian Dance,' 'Autumn' and 'Wind of Memory' are all well known. His 'Reverie,' op. 7, for violin and piano, was dedicated to and often played by Schradieck. His Scotch and Irish songs, and many instructive pieces for piano and violin, have been much used. His Science of Piano-Playing and Introductory Steps to the Science of Piano-Playing are published in loose-leaf ledger form. His 'Dramatic Symphony' was first performed in 1908. His Ritualistic Music for the 32nd Degree A. A. S. R., for men's voices and organ, was written for the Philadelphia Consistory and first presented in 1917. The orchestral setting for 'Sheherazade,' an oriental drama, was given at the Metropolitan Opera House, Philadelphia, in May, 1918. He is a member of local and national musical organizations, one of the founders and twice president of the Sinfonia, and a member of all Masonic organizations. [R.7]

COMBS BROAD STREET CONSERVATORY OF MUSIC, THE, was founded in 1885 by Gilbert R. Combs, who has remained at its head ever since. Its teaching-force numbers about 80. The number of pupils is over 2300, and the total since foundation about 42,000, including about 200 full graduates. The Conservatory is highly organized for efficiency and offers a wide range of opportunity for instruction from elementary to advanced grades. Its students have certain privileges at the University of Pennsylvania. Two orchestras are maintained, one of 85 members, the other of 60. The Conservatory occupies five buildings on South Broad Street.

COMER, THOMAS. See TUNE-BOOKS, 1841.

COMMERY, STEPHEN (b. 1862). See Register, 7.

COMMONWEALTH SCHOOL OF MUSIC, THE, is the name of a summer-school at Boothbay Harbor, Me., started in 1913 by Clarence G. Hamilton and directed by him, with three other teachers. Courses are offered in piano, violin, harmony, analysis and public-school supervision, with emphasis on teachers' needs. The sessions occupy three weeks.

CONRAD, DELANO FRANZ (b. 1861). See COLLEGES, 2 (Central C., Mo.).

CONRIED, HEINRICH (Sept. 13, 1855, Bielitz, Austria : Apr. 26, 1909, Meran, Tyrol), was first an actor at the Burg-Theater in Vienna and with traveling troupes. In 1877 he directed the Bremen Stadt-Theater, and in 1878 became manager of the Germania Theater in New York. Later he managed the Thalia, and, with Aronson, produced light opera at the Casino. In 1892 he took charge of the Irving Place Theater, making it the leading German theater in the country. After Grau's retirement, in 1903, he became manager of the Metropolitan Opera House and organizer of the Conried Opera Company. Signal events in his régime were the first American production of 'Parsifal' on Dec. 24, 1903, which Frau Wagner tried in vain to prevent by injunction, and the single rendering of Strauss' 'Salome' on Jan. 22, 1907, which was at once withdrawn by the directors. In the San Francisco fire of 1906 his company suffered large losses. During his last two years at the Metropolitan he was broken in health, and in 1908 resigned. [R.6]

CONSERVATORIO NACIONAL DE MÚSICA, EL, of Mexico City, was founded in 1868 and is a constituent part of the Universidad Nacional. The directors have been Agustin Caballero in 1868–76, Antonio Balderas in 1877–82, Alfredo Bablot in 1882–88, José Rivas in 1889–1906, Gustavo E. Campa in 1907–08 and 1909–13, Carlos J. Meneses in 1908–09, Julián Carrillo in 1913–14, Rafael J. Tello in 1914–15, José R. Muñoz in 1915–17, and Eduardo Gariel since 1917. The faculty includes 35 instructors in all theoretical and practical branches, with considerable emphasis on dramatic music. The number of pupils varies from about 400 to over 800, the total since foundation being about 28,000, of whom about half graduated. The institution is supported by a subsidy from Mexico City.

CONVENTIONS, MUSICAL. Gatherings under this name were a natural development of the 'singing-school,' but less narrowly local and capable of more varied expansion. Such occasional assemblies were held in New Hampshire in 1829–31 under the direction of Henry E. Moore. In 1834 the Boston Academy of Music started a normal class for singing-school teachers which in 1836 became a 'convention' by adding discussions by the members and in 1840 adopted the name of 'The National Musical Convention' (later changed to 'American'). At one time this enterprise was split by the adherents of Mason and Webb respectively. These two, with Hastings, Bradbury, Root, Woodbury, Baker and Emerson, were active promoters of the 'convention' idea, not only in New England, but in the West and South, and they were followed by a host of other leaders. The methods naturally varied greatly, but usually combined in some way elementary and normal instruction, with practice in choral singing of a popular sort. The program occupied three or four days, with three sessions per day. Though at first no emphasis was placed upon concertizing — except a closing 'exhibition' — more or less demonstration by teachers in attendance and even recitals by outside artists were not uncommon later. In spite of their brief and casual character, and though often dominated by commercial interests, the many 'conventions' held from about 1845 for twenty-five years or more undoubtedly exerted a beneficial influence. Their effort to provide some rudimentary training for adults probably contributed to the later recognition of such work for public-school children. Their encouragement of voluntary combination or affiliation led directly to the formation (from 1876) of Music Teachers' Associations in many states and of the National Association — most of these bodies still retaining the name 'convention' for their annual meetings. Their pedagogical purpose was presently expanded and made more efficient by what were called 'Normal Institutes,' which were summer-schools lasting three weeks or more, such as Root started in New York in 1852. Thus they promoted interest in the founding of permanent music-schools. From them, also, may have come part of the impulse to the holding of 'festivals' or groups of concerts, either occasionally (as the Peace Jubilees of 1869 and 1872) or regularly (as at Worcester and elsewhere). That the movement as a whole had value and significance is attested both by the number of earnest men who sought careers as 'convention-leaders' and by the fact that many later teachers and performers gained their first musical inspiration from these leaders.

CONVERSE, CHARLES CROZAT (Oct. 7, 1832, Warren, Mass. : Oct. 18, 1918, Highwood, N. J.), was musically trained in Germany, where in 1855–59 he studied theory and composition with Richter, Hauptmann and Plaidy at Leipzig. On his return he entered the Albany Law School, graduating in 1861. From 1875 he was in law practice at Erie, Pa., and also a partner in the Burdette Organ Company. His last years were spent at Highwood, N. J. He composed an 'American Concert Overture' (1869), based on 'Hail, Columbia'; a 'Festouvertüre' (1870); six German songs (Leipzig, 1856); and an American national hymn, 'God for us' (1887). He left in manuscript two symphonies, two oratorios, several overtures, string-quartets and quintets. Of his hymn-tunes, 'What a Friend we have in Jesus' has had wide use. In 1895 he received the degree of LL.D. from Rutherford College. He was an inventor as well as lawyer and musician, and endeavored to establish the use of the pronoun 'thon.' He used the pen-name 'Karl Redan.'   [R.5]

CONVERSE, FREDERICK SHEPHERD (Jan. 5, 1871, Newton, Mass.), graduated from Harvard in 1893 with highest honors in music under Paine, and his Sonata for violin and piano was then performed. For two years he studied piano with Baermann and composition with Chadwick, and then went to Munich for work under Rheinberger at the Royal Academy. On his graduation in 1898 his Symphony in D minor had its first performance. In 1899-1901 he taught harmony at the New England Conservatory in Boston, in 1901-04 was teacher of composition at Harvard, and in 1904-07 was assistant-professor there. Since 1907 he has devoted himself to composition. The list of his works is as follows :

Sonata, op. 1, for violin and piano.
Suite, op. 2, for piano.
Quartet, op. 3, for strings.
Waltzes, op. 4, for piano, 4-hands.
'Walzer Poetici,' op. 5, for piano, 4-hands.
Concert-Overture, 'Youth,' op. 6 (1897, Munich).
Symphony in D minor, op. 7 (1898, Munich).
Festival March, op. 8, for orchestra.
Romance, 'Festival of Pan,' op. 9, for orchestra (1900, Boston Symphony Orchestra).
Romance, 'Endymion's Narrative,' op. 10, for orchestra (1903, Boston Orchestra).
Two Poems, 'Night' and 'Day,' op. 11, for piano and orchestra.
Ballad, 'La belle dame sans merci,' op. 12, for baritone and orchestra (1902).
Concerto, op. 13, for violin and piano.
Three Love-Songs, op. 14.
Concert-Overture, 'Euphrosyne,' op. 15.
Two Songs, op. 16, for soprano.
Quartet, op. 17, for strings (1904, Kneisel Quartet, Brooklyn).
Orchestral Fantasy, 'The Mystic Trumpeter,' op. 19, after poem by Whitman (1905, Philadelphia Orchestra).
Songs, 'Adieu' and 'Silent Noon,' op. 20.
Romantic Opera, 'The Pipe of Desire,' op. 21, in one act (1906, Boston, also 1910, Metropolitan Opera House).
'Laudate Dominum,' op. 22, for men's voices, trombones and organ.
Overture, entr'actes and incidental music for

N

Mackaye's 'Jeanne d'Arc,' op. 23 (1906, Philadelphia).
Dramatic Poem, 'Job,' op. 24, for soli, chorus and orchestra (1907, Worcester Festival, and 1908, Hamburg).
Serenade, op. 25, for soprano, tenor, men's chorus, flute, harp and strings.
'Hagar in the Desert,' op. 26, dramatic narrative for low voice and orchestra (written for Mme. Schumann-Heink and sung by her at Hamburg, 1908).
Symphonic Poem, 'Ormazd' (1912, St. Louis and Boston Orchestras).
'The Sacrifice,' opera in three acts, text by the composer (1911, Boston Opera Company).
Music for the Masque of St. Louis (1914, St. Louis).
'The Peace-Pipe,' cantata (1916).
Symphonic Poem, 'Ave atque Vale' (1917, Boston Orchestra).
[Of the above, opp. 3, 6, 7, 8, 13, 18 are still in manuscript.]

'The Pipe of Desire' has the distinction of being the first work by an American composer to be performed at the Metropolitan Opera House. [R.8]

COOKE, JAMES FRANCIS (Nov. 14, 1875, Bay City, Mich.), was educated in the New York schools and with private teachers. He studied music there with W. H. Hall, Woodman, Eberhard and Medorn, and with Meyer-Olbersleben and Hermann Ritter at the Royal Conservatory in Würzburg. Beginning at thirteen, he continued teaching piano in New York for over twenty years, developing original ideas based upon psychological experiments, some of which have had wide acceptance. He was also for some years organist in Brooklyn churches, conductor of choral clubs and vocal teacher. With his wife, née Betsey Ella Beckwith, as singer, he has given many recitals and lectures on musical history and interpretation. He has written extensively for musical periodicals — for three years was correspondent for the 'Neue Zeitschrift für Musik' and the 'Musikalisches Wochenblatt,' and in 1901-05 published notes of extensive investigations of the conservatory-systems of Europe.   Since 1907 he has been editor of 'The Etude' in Philadelphia. The results of conferences with great living pianists he collected under the title *Great Pianists upon Piano-Playing*, 1913.   He has also published *The Standard History of Music*, 1910, *Mastering the Scales and Arpeggios*, 1913, *Musical Playlets*, 1917, and *Music-Masters Old and New*. Some of his piano-pieces and songs have had large circulation. He has also composed works of more serious character as yet unpublished. He was president of the Philadelphia Music Teachers' Association in 1911-18, of the Writeabout Club in 1915-16, of the Philadelphia Drama League since 1917, and of the Presser Foundation since 1917. He was made Mus.D. by the Ohio Northern University in 1919. He has written plays (four produced professionally), stories, a novel, etc. During the war as a 'Four-Minute Man' he addressed over 300,000 people. [R.8]

COOMBS, CHARLES WHITNEY (Dec. 25, 1859, Bucksport, Me.), from 1878 lived in Stuttgart, studying piano with Speidel, theory and composition with Seifritz, and also modern languages and literature. In 1883 he was in Italy and Switzerland, and in 1884 went to Dresden, where his teachers were Draeseke for composition, Janssen for organ, Hermann John for instrumentation and Lamperti for voice. He made long visits to Paris and London. In 1887–91 he was organist at the American Church in Dresden. In 1892–1908 he was organist at the Church of the Holy Communion in New York, and since 1908 at St. Luke's. His compositions include the following (mostly Schirmer) :

Cantatas — 'The Vision of St. John,' 'The First Christmas,' 'Ancient of Days,' 'The Sorrows of Death.'
Canticles and Anthems — Gloria in Excelsis, Benedictus, Deus Misereatur, 'Bethlehem,' 'The Christ-Child,' 'The Christmas Herald,' 'Under the Silent Stars,' 'Brightest and Best,' 'Joyously Peal,' 'Light of Earth,' three Christmas Carols, 'Christ is Risen,' 'Christ is Risen from the Dead,' 'As it Began to Dawn,' 'Where is He?' 'Let your Light so Shine,' 'The Evening Shadows,' 'A Hymn of Praise,' 'The Heavenly Message,' 'How Lovely upon the Mountains,' 'God shall Wipe away all Tears,' 'Sing, O Daughter of Zion,' 'At the Rising of the Sun,' 'How Goodly are thy Tents,' 'O Lord, Thou art Great' (Schmidt).
About 75 songs (Schirmer, Schmidt, Presser, Church, Boosey). [R.7]

COOPER, WILLIAM. See TUNE-BOOKS, 1803.

COPP, EVELYN ASHTON, née Fletcher (b. 1872). See Register, 8.

COPPET, EDWARD J. DE (May 28, 1855, New York : Apr. 30, 1916, New York), was of Swiss descent. He succeeded his father as a banker and stock-broker in New York. In 1886 he began a series of chamber-music recitals at his residence, and these continued till the afternoon before his death, the last being the 1054th. At first different artists were engaged, but in 1902 the Flonzaley Quartet was organized and became an important factor in the series. The name Flonzaley was that of his summer-home near Vevey, on Lake Geneva. Thanks to his patronage, the Quartet has had the opportunity to become one of the finest chamber-music organizations in the world. Since his death his policies have been continued by his son André. See Mason's article in 'The Musical Quarterly,' October, 1916. [R.7]

COREY, NEWTON JOHN (b. 1861). See Register, 6.

CORNELL, JOHN HENRY (May 8, 1828, New York : Mar. 1, 1894, New York), was educated in New York and in Germany and

England. In 1848 he was organist at St. John's Chapel, in 1868–77 at St. Paul's Chapel (both belonging to Trinity Parish), and in 1877–82 at the Brick (Presbyterian) Church. Besides being a solidly trained composer of church-music, part-songs and songs, he was an erudite and methodical student of theory, and an able author and translator. His books include a *Primer of Modern Musical Tonality*, 1877, *The Practice of Sight-Singing*, *The Theory and Practice of Musical Form* (based on Bussler), 1883, an *Easy Method of Modulation*, 1884, a *Manual of Roman Chant*, *The Introit Psalms*, set to original chants, 1871, and a *Congregational Tune-Book*. Among his translations were Langhans' *Geschichte der Musik*, 1886, and Ambros' *Die Grenzen der Musik und Poesie*, 1893. [R.4]

'CORSICAN BRIDE, THE.' An opera by Eduard Mollenhauer, produced at the Winter Palace in New York in 1861.

'CORSICANA, LA.' An opera by John Lewis Browne, which received honorable mention in the Sonzogno competition at Milan in 1902, was given in New York in 1903, and was published by the Church Co.

COTTLOW, AUGUSTA (Apr. 2, 1878, Shelbyville, Ill.), after early lessons from her mother, gave a piano-recital in Chicago when only seven. She studied there with Wolfsohn (piano) and Gleason (harmony), and made her début with orchestra in 1889. In 1891 she first appeared in New York, playing the Chopin E minor concerto under Seidl. In 1896 at Berlin she studied piano with Busoni and theory with Boise. Concert-tours through Germany, Holland, England and Russia followed, and in 1900 she returned to America, appearing first at the Worcester Festival. She has made repeated tours, has played with the Boston Symphony and other orchestras, and, after a long sojourn in Berlin, is now permanently in the United States. She married Edgar A. Gerst of Berlin in 1912. [R.7]

COURBOIN, CHARLES MARIE (Apr. 2, 1886, Antwerp, Belgium), early evinced musical talent, playing concertos and symphonies by ear at seven. He was taken as piano-pupil by Blockx, then director of the Antwerp Conservatory, continuing five years. He played the organ at Notre Dame College at twelve, writing his first composition, 'Vias Tuas,' for boy-choir, string-quartet and organ. At the solicitation of Mailly, of the Brussels Conservatory, he entered on a four-years course in organ and became his favorite pupil. He took harmony with Gilson and Huberti, counterpoint with Tinel, and won prizes in piano and harmony in 1901, and in counterpoint, fugue, and transposition in 1902, besides the International Competition (against eight contestants). From 1902 he was organist at Antwerp Cathedral, giving recitals also in London, Paris, Rheims, Lille, Boulogne, Lübeck, Hamburg, Louvain, Bruges, Liège, etc. In 1904 he came to Oswego, N. Y., as organist at St. Paul's, going thence to the First Baptist Church in Syracuse, where he has the largest organ in the State outside of New York City. In 1917–18 he was also municipal organist at Springfield, Mass. He has lately undertaken concert-work, playing with success in the East and the Middle West. In 1919–20 he was concert-organist at the Wanamaker Auditoriums in Philadelphia and New York. At Philadelphia in March, 1919, he brought out Widor's Sixth Symphony (dedicated to him) with the Philadelphia Orchestra under Stokowski. He has written several anthems, masses, other choral works, and a 'Toccatina,' op. 13 — all still in manuscript. [R.9]

‡ COWEN, FREDERIC HYMEN (Jan. 29, 1852, Kingston, Jamaica). See article in Vol. i. 630–1. He served as conductor of the Cardiff Festival in 1902, '04. '07, '10, of the Handel Festival at the Crystal Palace in 1903, '06, '09, '12, '20, and of the Liverpool Philharmonic Society till 1914. He received an honorary Mus.D. from Edinburgh University in 1910, and was knighted in 1911. Add to the list of works the cantata 'John Gilpin' (1904), the oratorio 'The Veil' (1910), the pantomime 'Monica's Blue Boy' (1917) and the comedy-ballet 'Cupid's Conspiracy' (1918). He has published *My Art and My Friends*, 1913, and a humorous glossary, *Music as She is Wrote*, 1915.

COWLES, WALTER RUEL (b. 1881). See Register, 9.

COWPER, HOLMES [Harry Mattingly] (b. 1870). See COLLEGES, 3 (Drake U., Ia.).

COX, ERNEST L. See COLLEGES, 3 (Kansas Wesleyan U.).

COZINE, HARLAN J. See COLLEGES, 3 (Albion C., Mich.).

CRAFT, MARCELLA (1880, Indianapolis), had a high-school course at Riverside, Cal. Thence she went to Boston, from 1897 studied with Charles R. Adams, and sang in concert and oratorio throughout New England. In 1901 she went to Europe, studying singing under Guagni and acting under Mottino in Milan. She made her début as Leonora in 'Il Trovatore' at Morbegno in March, 1902, and sang in various Italian theaters for three years. In 1905 began engagements of two years at Mayence, two at Kiel and five at the Royal Opera in Munich, with guest-appearances in many other cities. She had just finished at Munich when the war began, and she sailed for America in August, 1914. Here she has appeared with the Chicago, Cincinnati, St. Louis, Philadelphia and Minneapolis

Orchestras. During 1917–18 she sang as guest with the San Carlo Opera Company and with the Society of American Singers in New York. She has also been heard at the Worcester, Maine, Oberlin and other Festivals, and at four of the remarkable Easter services on Mt. Rubidoux, Cal. She has given many song-recitals in the larger cities. She has taken the leading soprano-rôles in 'Madama Butterfly,' 'La Bohème,' 'La Traviata,' 'Faust,' 'Salome,' 'I Pagliacci,' 'Il Segreto di Susanna,' 'Il Trovatore,' 'Aida,' 'Otello,' 'Martha,' 'Rigoletto,' 'Carmen,' 'Tales of Hoffmann,' 'Tiefland,' 'Lohengrin,' 'Tannhäuser,' 'Die Meistersinger,' 'The Magic Flute,' 'Don Giovanni,' 'Benvenuto Cellini' and 'Le Donne Curiose.' [R.9]

CRANE, JULIA ETTIE (b. 1855). See Register, 6.

CREHORE, BENJAMIN (d. 1819). See Register, 2.

CRESS, OSCAR. See COLLEGES, 3 (Hope C., Mich.).

CRIST, BAINBRIDGE (Feb. 13, 1883, Lawrenceburg, Ind.), spent his youth in Washington, where he graduated from the Law School in 1906. He then practiced in Boston until after six years he abandoned the law for music, which he had pursued since childhood. He then studied in London, Paris and Berlin, taking composition under Juon, and singing under Emerich and Shakespeare. For a time he settled in London, but the outbreak of the war caused him to return to Boston, where he is engaged in composition, vocal teaching and coaching. In 1918 he temporarily abandoned music to put his legal experience into war-work, but resigned shortly after the armistice was signed. His compositions include the following:

For orchestra — the choreographic drama 'Le Pied de la Momie' (1914, England), the symphonic suite 'Egyptian Impressions' (1915, Boston Symphony Orchestra), the vocal poem 'The Parting,' and the coloratura aria 'O come hither' (last three, Carl Fischer).
For string-quartet — 'Japonaise' and 'Clavecin.'
For piano — 'Egyptian Impressions,' 'Retrospections' (both Fischer) and 'Miniatures' (Augener).
For voice — 'Chinese Mother Goose Rhymes,' 'Drolleries from an Oriental Doll's House,' 'Into a ship, dreaming,' 'This is the moon of roses,' 'The Old Soldier,' 'You will not come again,' 'Yesteryear,' 'April Rain,' 'To the Water-Nymphs,' 'Butterflies,' 'C'est mon ami,' 'Tell Me,' 'Girl of the red mouth,' 'Three Balladettes' (Fischer); 'Mistletoe,' 'Some One,' 'To Arcady,' 'If there were dreams to sell,' 'The Little Bird,' 'A Memory,' 'To Columbine,' 'Like April's kissing May,' 'No Limit,' 'Shower of Blossoms,' 'September Eve,' 'The Window,' 'I can't abear,' 'The Little Old Cupid' (Boston Music Co.); 'A Bag of Whistles,' 'The auld Scotch sangs' (Ditson); 'The Lost Path,' 'Roses' (Augener); 'To Folly and Whim' (Schott); 'Au Clair de la Lune' (Homeyer). [R.10]

CROSBY OPERA HOUSE, THE, in Chicago, was built in 1865 by Uranus H. Crosby on Washington Street, between State and Dearborn. It contained by far the best opera-auditorium that Chicago had had, a music-hall, art-gallery and numerous studios for artists and others. It was opened with opera-seasons under Grau and a concert-season under Max Strakosch, and for a time was the arena for much good music. But the investment did not pay, and in January, 1867, the building was put up at lottery, but in some way merely transferred to Albert Crosby, who continued it with curiously diversified undertakings. In the fall of 1871 it was renovated at large expense and the work had just been completed when on Oct. 8, the day before it was to be reopened with a concert by the Thomas Orchestra, it was destroyed in the great fire. See Upton, *Musical Memories*, pp. 236–51.

CROSS, BENJAMIN (1786–1857). See Register, 3.

CROSS, MICHAEL HURLEY (Apr. 13, 1833, Philadelphia : Sept. [26, 1897, Philadelphia), son and pupil of the foregoing, also studied composition with Meignen, violin with Charles Hommann and 'cello with Engelke. From 1848 he was organist, first at St. Patrick's and other churches, from 1862 at the (R. C.) Cathedral and from 1880 at Holy Trinity (P. E.). He directed various local organizations, besides others in New York and Brooklyn, and was a prominent teacher (Huneker was one of his pupils). Like his father, he exerted a powerful influence for good in the musical life of Philadelphia. [R.4]

CROSSLAND, ROBERT EXELBY. See COLLEGES, 3 (Culver-Stockton C., Mo.).

CROUCH, FREDERICK WILLIAM NICHOLLS (1808–1896). See Register, 4.

‡ CUI, CÉSAR ANTONOVITCH (Jan. 18, 1835, Vilna, Russia : Mar. 14, 1918, Petrograd). See article in Vol. i. 643–5, adding that 'Mam'zelle Fifi' was produced in Petrograd in 1903 and that two further operas were 'Matteo Falcone' (1908, Moscow) and 'The Captain's Daughter' (1911, Petrograd). Note also critical sketch by the Comtesse Mercy-Argenteau, Paris, 1888, and Weimarn, *Cui as Song-Writer*, Petrograd, 1897, besides general works on Russian music.

CUNNINGHAM, CLAUDE (b. 1880). See Register, 9.

CURRIER, AARON HEALY. See STATE UNIVERSITIES (Mont. State C.).

CURRY, ARTHUR MANSFIELD (Jan. 27, 1866, Chelsea, Mass.), was a pupil of Kneisel in violin and of MacDowell in composition and orchestration. For some years he was engaged as choral and orchestral conductor. In 1914 he taught in Berlin, but then became teacher of harmony at the New England Conservatory in Boston. His larger works, still in manuscript, are the overture 'Blomidon' (1902, Worcester); an 'Élégie' in the form of an overture; the symphonic poem 'Atala,' after Chateaubriand (1908, given 1911, Boston Symphony Orchestra); and 'The Winning of Amarac,' a Keltic legend for reader, women's chorus and orchestra. He has published choruses for men's, women's or mixed voices, 11 songs, a Barcarolle and other piano-pieces. [R.9]

CURTIS, HENRY HOLBROOK (1856–1920). See Register, 7.

CURTIS, NATALIE. See BURLIN.

CURTIS, VERA (b. 1880). See Register, 10.

CUTLER, HENRY STEPHEN (1825–1902). See Register, 4.

CUTTER, BENJAMIN (Sept. 6, 1857, Woburn, Mass. : May 10, 1910, Boston), was the son of a physician of musical tastes. He studied violin with Eichberg in Boston and with Edmund Singer in Stuttgart, harmony with Emery in Boston and composition with Goetschius and Seifriz in Stuttgart. On his return to Boston he first taught violin, but from 1888 concentrated upon harmony and analysis, becoming professor at the New England Conservatory. In 1882–89 he played in the Boston Symphony Orchestra. He was held in high regard as a superior teacher by a large number of pupils. His larger compositions were a Mass in D, the cantata 'Sir Patrick Spens,' considerable chamber-music, and choral works, sacred and secular. He also wrote *Exercises in Harmony*, 1901, *Harmonic Analysis*, 1902, and *How to Study Kreutzer*, 1903. [R.7]

'CYRANO DE BERGERAC.' An opera in four acts by Walter Damrosch on a libretto made by William J. Henderson after the play by Rostand. It was first given at the Metropolitan Opera House in New York on Feb. 27, 1913, under the direction of Hertz, and four times repeated.

LEOPOLD DAMROSCH

D

DAILEY, LEE N.   See COLLEGES, 3 (Yankton C., S. D.).

‡ DALE, BENJAMIN JAMES (July 17, 1885, London, England). See note in Vol. v. 628. The list of his works in 1919 was

Symphony in A, for orchestra.
Overture, 'The Tempest,' for orchestra (1902).
Fantasia for organ and orchestra (1903).
Concert-Overture in G minor, for orchestra (1904).
Suite for viola and piano (1907) (Novello).
Phantasy for viola and piano (1911) (Schott).
Introduction and Andante for six violas (1913).
English Dance, for violin and piano (1916) (Anglo-French Music Co.).
'Before the paling of the stars,' for chorus and orchestra (1912) (Novello).
Sonata in D minor, for piano (1905) (Novello).
'Night-Fancies,' for piano (1907) (Ricordi).
The songs 'Carpe Diem' and 'A Dirge of Love' (1918) (Shakespeare, Novello).
Three Carols, 'In Bethlehem, that noble place,' 'The Holy Birth,' 'The Shepherds and the Mother' (first two, Novello, third, Stainer & Bell).

His viola-music has received special attention, and, despite its novelty, has been widely performed. From August, 1914, he was long interned at Ruhleben, Germany.

DALMORÈS, CHARLES (Dec. 31, 1871, Nancy, France), was trained at the Nancy Conservatory, where he took prizes for French horn and solfeggio, with 'cello as a secondary study. The city of Nancy provided means for his going on with the horn at the Paris Conservatory. Here he took first prize in 1890 and played two years each in the Colonne and Lamoureux Orchestras. In 1894 he became professor at the Lyons Conservatory. Meanwhile he studied singing with Dauphin, and in 1899 made his début as tenor at the Théâtre des Arts in Rouen. Then followed six years at La Monnaie in Brussels, seven at Covent Garden and four (1906–10) at the Manhattan Opera House in New York. Since 1910 he has been with the Chicago Opera Company. He took the rôle of Lohengrin at Bayreuth in 1908 and in Berlin. He sings in French, Italian and German, and has appeared in 'Thaïs,' 'Louise,' 'Pelléas et Mélisande,' 'Salome,' 'Samson et Dalila,' 'Quo Vadis,' 'Roméo et Juliette,' 'Aida,' 'Siegfried,' 'Die Götterdämmerung,' 'Le Roi Arthus,' 'Carmen' and 'Faust.' [R.9]

DAMBOIS, MAURICE FÉLIX (b. 1889). See Register, 10.

DAMROSCH, FRANK HEINO (June 22, 1859, Breslau, Germany). See article in Vol. i. 656–7. He was educated in the public schools and the College of the City of New York. Among his piano-teachers was Joseffy. In 1879 he went to Denver because he wished to make his own way on his merits. He

organized the Denver Chorus Club in 1882, and was appointed music-director in the public schools in 1884. Among his many engagements as choral conductor in or near New York after 1885 the most important was with the Oratorio Society, which continued till 1912. In 1905 he became director of the Institute of Musical Art, founded and endowed by James Loeb, and still occupies this position. The aim of his life has been to spread the appreciation and culture of good music among all classes. The People's Singing-Classes have initiated thousands of wage-earners into the choral works of the great masters. The Symphony Concerts for Young People are training children and adults to appreciate symphonic music. The Musical Art Society emphasizes the old Flemish and Italian masters, such as Palestrina and Orlando di Lasso, and also the modern schools of a cappella singing, appealing to a highly cultivated taste. The Institute of Musical Art provides for serious and talented students the best obtainable musical education, equal to that of the foremost European conservatories. He has written *Some Essentials in the Teaching of Music*, 1916, and has edited many choral works, particularly for the Musical Art Society. In 1904 he received the degree of Mus.D. from Yale University. [R.7]

DAMROSCH, LEOPOLD (Oct. 22, 1832, Posen, Germany : Feb. 15, 1885, New York). See article in Vol. i. 656. Dr. Damrosch was of commanding presence and strong character. Although his constitution was not robust he had an impressive fund of energy and magnetism. All his life he strove with every fiber of body and spirit for the realization of the highest art-ideals and was able to communicate his zeal to all about him. On his arrival in America he found the old Italian operas esteemed the greatest treat of the musical season. Symphonic music was presented with mechanical precision in execution, but failed to render the spirit of the music. Oratorios were performed in a tedious and perfunctory manner. Against opposition from the established forces, he gradually attracted the coöperation of men and women of true culture with whose help he organized the musical societies mentioned in Vol. i. and gained the opportunity to bring the true genius of the great masters to the consciousness of the musical public. It was often a struggle against ignorance, indifference and ill-will, but by his energy, perseverance and knowledge, by his high artistic perception, and by the charm of his personality, he succeeded in winning the admiration and confidence of the lovers of good music. Indeed, the great advance in the appreciation and culture of music in America during the last forty years dates from the years of his activity in New York and is largely due to his labors. [R.6]

DAMROSCH, WALTER JOHANNES (Jan. 30, 1862, Breslau, Germany). See article in Vol. i. 657. He is still conductor of the New York Symphony Society, which was endowed in 1914 by Harry Harkness Flagler, its president, with an annual income of $100,000. In 1917 he also returned to the conductorship of the New York Oratorio Society. He directed the first American productions of Tchaikovsky's Fifth and Sixth Symphonies, Brahms' Fourth, and Elgar's First and Second; Saint-Saëns' 'Samson and Delilah,' Tchaikovsky's 'Eugene Onegin' and Wagner's 'Parsifal.' His opera 'Cyrano de Bergerac' was performed at the Metropolitan Opera House on Feb. 27, 1913; the comic opera 'The Dove of Peace' (libretto by Wallace Irwin) at Philadelphia and New York in 1912; his incidental music to Euripides' 'Iphigenia in Aulis' in California in 1915; and he has also composed incidental music to Euripides' 'Medea' and Sophocles' 'Electra.' He received the degree of Mus. D. from Columbia University in 1914. The numerous and country-wide tours of the orchestras under his direction have done much for the enlargement of popular acquaintance with standard orchestral works, besides introducing many novelties. In 1920 the Symphony Society, under his leadership, made an extended tour in Europe. At Rome he was made a member of the Order of the Crown of Italy. [R.7]

DANA, LYNN BOARDMAN (Oct. 15, 1875, Middleport, N. Y.), in 1916 succeeded his father, William H. Dana, as head of Dana's Musical Institute at Warren, O. He studied piano with Jacob Schmitt, di Kontski, Sherwood and Goldbeck, and theory with H. Clark Thayer, W. H. Dana and J. D. Cook. For fifteen years he was connected with the Chautauqua Institution, in 1914–16 was president of the Ohio M. T. A., and he was the first secretary of the Association of Present and Past Presidents of State Music Teachers' Associations. He has composed the oratorio 'The Triumph of Faith'; many piano-pieces and songs; a sonata for violin and piano; and a trio for violin, 'cello and piano. He is director of the American Musical Festival held annually at Lockport, N. Y. [R.8]

DANA, WILLIAM HENRY (1849–1916). See Register, 6.

DANKS, HART PEASE (1834–1903). See Register, 4.

DANN, HOLLIS ELLSWORTH (May 1, 1861, Canton, Pa.), after graduating from the Canton High School in 1878, attended the Elmira Business College and the Rochester School of Music, and continued his musical education for several years with private instructors in Boston. He received the degree of [Mus.D. from Alfred University in 1906. In 1887–1903 he had charge of public-school music in Ithaca, N. Y. In 1906 he became the head of the department of music in Cornell University. Under his direction the Cornell Music Festival and the Cornell Glee Club have become renowned. In 1910 he established courses in the University summer-school for training supervisors and teachers of music, which has become a foremost agency of its kind. In 1918–19 he was song-leader at Camp Taylor in Kentucky. In 1919 he was chorus-conductor for the National Music Supervisors' Conference, and was made president of the Conference for 1920. He has contributed much to public-school music, through text-books, pamphlets and papers. Since 1910 he has published *Christmas Carols and Hymns, The School Hymnal, Assembly Songs*, 2 vols., *Standard Anthems*, vol. 1, and *The Hollis Dann Music Course*, in seven grades, with a *Manual for Teachers*. [R.7]

DANNREUTHER, GUSTAV (July 21, 1853, Cincinnati), after preliminary lessons from local teachers, was sent by his brother Edward to study in Berlin, where at the Hochschule in 1871–73 his violin-teachers were Joachim and De Ahna. After six months in Paris he went to London, where he taught and played for four years. In 1877 he returned to America and joined the Mendelssohn Quintette Club, with which he traveled for three years. He then settled in Boston as teacher and player. With C. N. Allen and Wulf Fries he played in the Beethoven String Quartette, and for two years was with the then newly-organized Boston Symphony Orchestra under Henschel. In 1882–84 he directed the Buffalo Philharmonic Society and gave about sixty chamber-concerts. Coming to New York in 1884, he founded the Beethoven String Quartette (from 1894 till 1917 known as the Dannreuther Quartet) which was a leading chamber-music organization. Lately he has devoted himself entirely to teaching. He has published *Elementary Scale- and Chord-Studies for the Violin* (Breitkopf) and has in manuscript an extensive work on violin-technique. [R.6]

'DAPHNE.' A comic opera by Arthur Bird, produced in New York in 1897.

DA PONTE, LORENZO (Mar. 10, 1749, Ceneda [Vittorio], Italy : Aug. 17, 1838,

New York). See article in Vol. iii. 789-90. In New York he not only joined himself to Garcia in 1825-26, but largely through his efforts the French tenor Montressor undertook an opera-season late in 1832 at the Richmond Hill Theater, which failed after thirty-five performances. He then promoted the erection of the Italian Opera House at Church and Leonard Streets, which was opened on Nov. 18, 1833, with a company led by Rivafinoli. Six Rossini operas and one each by Cimarosa, Pacini and Salvioni (conductor of the company) formed the répertoire, and the deficit after eight months was $30,000. His *Memorie*, 4 vols., were published in New York in 1823-27. He was buried in the Catholic Cemetery on East Eleventh Street, but in a grave unmarked. See Krehbiel, *Chapters of Opera*, pp. 30-6. [R.3]

DARBY, W. DERMOT (b. 1885). See Register, 10.

DARLEY, WILLIAM. See Register, 2.

DARLEY, W. H. W. See TUNE-BOOKS, 1844.

'DAUGHTER OF THE FOREST, THE.' An opera by Arthur F. Nevin, produced on Jan. 5, 1918, by the Chicago Opera Company under the composer's direction.

‡ DAVEY, HENRY (Nov. 29, 1853, Brighton, England), as he possessed an exceptional memory, was very successful in his school-days. In his youth he assisted in his father's business. At 20 he went to Leipzig and studied piano, composition and especially harmony for three years. He then lived at Brighton as teacher and writer on musical subjects till he retired in 1903. Literary work, particularly Shakespearean research, has since been his principal occupation. Besides many articles in *The Dictionary of National Biography*, he has written much in various English, German and American musical journals. His principal works are *The Student's Musical History*, 1891 (7th ed., 1919), *History of English Music*, 1895 (revised edition preparing), *Handel*, in *Masterpieces of Music*, 1912, and appreciations in *Kirchenmusikalisches Jahrbuch* (1896), *Monatshefte für Musik-Geschichte* (1896), in Riemann's *Geschichte der Musik seit Beethoven* (1900) and in Soubies' *Histoire de la Musique, Iles Britanniques*. His most important literary work is the *Memoir* in the Stratford Town Edition of Shakespeare. An extensive commentary on Shakespeare's works is well advanced.

‡ DAVIES, HENRY WALFORD (Sept. 6, 1869, Oswestry, England). See articles in Vols. i. 670-1 and v. 628-9. In addition to his duties at the Temple Church, he was conductor of the London Church Choir Association in 1901-13, has been active as an examiner and lecturer on musical subjects, and during the war was a leader in the provision of music for British soldiers. He has recently become professor at the University of Wales. His recent compositions are the cantatas 'Five Sayings of Jesus' (1911) and 'The Song of St. Francis' (1912); the choral suite 'Noble Numbers'; the orchestral suites 'Parthenia' (1911) and 'Wordsworth' (1913); 'Conversations,' a suite for piano and orchestra (1914); and the a cappella 'Short Requiem' (1915).

DAVIES, WILLIAM. See COLLEGES, 3 (Midland C., Neb.).

DAVIS, DAVID (b. 1855). See Register, 7.

DAVIS, GEORGE H. (d. 1879). See Register, 4.

DAVIS, JESSIE, née Bartlett (1860-1905). See Register, 6.

DAVIS, JOHN. See Register, 3.

DAVIS, JOHN HERBERT (b. 1860). See Register, 7.

DAY, H. W. See TUNE-BOOKS, 1842.

'DAWN OF THE WEST, THE.' An opera in four acts by Emil Enna, on a text by Freda Gratke, privately performed at Portland, Ore., on Nov. 7, 1915.

DAYAS, WILLIAM HUMPHRIES (Sept. 12, 1864, New York : May 3, 1903, Manchester, England), having been an organist from an early age, studied piano with S. B. Mills and Joseffy, and organ and counterpoint with S. P. Warren. In Germany (from 1881) he was the pupil of Kullak, Ehrlich, Urban and Haupt, and was one of the last group of those under Liszt. In 1888 he made a concert-tour with Senkrah. In 1890 he succeeded Busoni as principal piano-teacher at the musical college in Helsingfors. Thence he went to Wiesbaden and Cologne, tarried a while in New York, and in 1896 became principal piano-teacher at the Manchester College of Music, succeeding Hallé and holding this position till his death. He composed two sonatas for organ, a string-quartet, a sonata for violin and piano, a sonata for 'cello and piano, four-hand waltzes for piano, a suite for strings (1886, Weimar), songs, and pieces for piano and organ. His daughter, Karin Elin Dayas, appeared as a pianist in Berlin in 1916. [R.7]

DEARBORN, B. See TUNE-BOOKS, 1796.

DEARBORN, E. R. See TUNE-BOOKS, 1841.

DE BEGNIS, GIUSEPPE (1793-1849). See Register, 3.

‡ DEBUSSY, CLAUDE ACHILLE (Aug. 22, 1862, St. Germain-en-Laye, France : Mar. 26, 1918, Paris). See article in Vol. i. 676. Madame de Sivry, pupil of Chopin and mother of Charles de Sivry, was his first teacher. He entered the Paris Conservatory in 1873, studying piano with Marmontel,

harmony with Lavignac and composition with
Guiraud. Beginning with 1874, he won the
solfége medal for three successive years, in
1877 the second prize for piano, in 1882 a
prize for counterpoint and fugue, and two
years later the Prix de Rome. In Italy in
1887 he composed his 'Printemps' for orchestra and chorus, the cantata 'La Demoiselle
Élue' and a 'Fantaisie' for piano and orchestra.
The dates in the appended list indicate the
progress after his return. The 'Prélude à
l'Après-Midi d'un Faune,' first performed
in 1894, and published eight years later, was
his first work to attract general attention.
Ten years were spent on 'Pelléas et Mélisande,'
first performed in 1902. In 'The Musical
Times,' for May, 1918, Jean-Aubry presented
the following complete list of his compositions :

For Orchestra —
Symphonic Poem, 'Almanzor,' after Heine (1886).
Symphonic Suite, 'Printemps,' in two parts, for
  chorus and orchestra (1887, revised and enlarged
  1913).
Fantaisie for piano and orchestra (1889).
'Marche Écossaise sur un Thème Populaire' (1891).
Eglogue, 'Prélude à l'Après-Midi d'un Faune,'
  after Mallarmé (1892, first given in 1894).
Incidental Music to 'King Lear' (1897–99).
'Trois Nocturnes' — 'Nuages,' 'Fétes,' 'Sirènes'
  — for chorus and orchestra (1897).
'Danse Profane' and 'Danse Sacrée,' for harp and
  orchestra or piano and strings (1904).
Symphonic Sketches, 'La Mer' — 'De l'aube à
  midi sur la mer,' 'Jeux de vagues,' 'Dialogue du
  vent et de la mer' — (1903–05).
'Images,' Set 3 — 'Gigues,' 'Iberia,' 'Rondes de
  Printemps' (1909).
Incidental Music to 'Le Martyre de Saint-Sébas-
  tien' (1911).
Ballet, 'Jeux' (1912).
Légende Dansée, 'Khamma' (1912).
Chamber-Music —
String-Quartet, op. 10 (1893).
Rhapsody for clarinet and piano (1910).
Sonata for 'cello and piano (1915).
Sonata for flute, viola and harp (1916).
Sonata for violin and piano (1917).
Piano-Music —
'Arabesque,' nos. 1 and 2 (1888).
'Rêverie'; Ballade; Danse; 'Danse Roman-
  tique'; Nocturne (1890).
'Suite Bergamasque' — Prélude, Menuet, 'Clair
  de Lune,' Passepied (1890), Mazurka (1891).
'Pour le Piano' — Prélude, Sarabande, Toccata
  (1901).
'Estampes' — 'Pagodes,' 'Soirée dans Grenade,'
  'Jardins sous la pluie' (1903).
'D'un Cahier d'Esquisses' (1903) (Schott).
'Masques'; 'L'Isle Joyeuse' (1904).
'Images,' Set 1 — 'Reflets dans l'Eau,' 'Hommage
  à Rameau,' 'Mouvement' (1905).
'Images,' Set 2 — 'Cloches à travers les Feuilles,'
  'Et la Lune descend sur le Temple qui fut,'
  'Poissons d'Or' (1907).
'The Children's Corner,' six pieces (1908).
'Hommage à Haydn' (1909).
Valse, 'La Plus que Lente' (1910).
Twelve Préludes, Sets 1 and 2 (24 in all) (1910).
Children's Ballet, 'La Boite à Joujoux' (1910).
'Berceuse Héroïque,' dedicated to King Albert of
  Belgium (1914).

Twelve Études, dedicated to the memory of
  Chopin (1915).
Petite Suite for four hands — 'En Bateau,' Cor-
  tége, Menuet, Ballet (1904).
Six 'Épigraphes Antiques,' for four hands (1915).
'En Blanc et Noir,' three pieces for two pianos
  (1915).
Lyrical Works —
Cantata, 'L'Enfant Prodigue' (1884).
'La Demoiselle Élue,' for women's voices and
  orchestra (1887).
'Pelléas et Mélisande,' lyric drama in five acts and
  twelve scenes, from Maeterlinck (1892–1902).
Songs —
'Nuit d'Étoiles,' from De Banville (1876)
  (Coutarel).
'Beau Soir,' from Bourget : 'Fleurs des Blés,' from
  Girod (1878) (Girod).
'Mandoline,' from Verlaine (1880).
Three Mélodies — 'Belle au Bois Dormant,'
  'Voici que le Printemps,' 'Paysage Sentimental'
  (1887) (Sociètè Nouvelle).
'Les Cloches' and 'Romance,' from Bourget (1887).
Five Poems from Baudelaire — 'La Balcon,'
  'Harmonie du Soir,' 'Le Jet d'Eau,' 'Recueille-
  ment,' 'La Mort des Amants' (1890) (Librairie
  de l'Art Indépendant).
'Dans le Jardin,' from Gravollet : 'Le Angélus,'
  from Le Roy (1891) (Hamelle).
Three Mélodies from Verlaine — 'Le Mer est plus
  Belle,' 'Le Son du Cor s'Afflige,' 'L'Eschelon-
  ment des Haies' (1891) (Hamelle).
'Fêtes Galantes,' Set 1, from Verlaine — 'En
  Sourdine,' 'Fantoches,' 'Clair de Lune' (1892).
'Proses Lyriques,' text by composer — 'De
  Rêve,' 'De Grève,' 'De Fleurs,' 'De Soir' (1894–
  95).
'Chansons de Bilitis,' from Louys — 'La Flûte de
  Pan,' 'La Clevelure,' 'Le Tombeau des Naïades'
  (1898).
'Airettes Oubliées,' from Verlaine, six pieces (1888–
  1903).
'Fêtes Galantes,' Set 2, from Verlaine — 'Les In-
  génus,' 'Le Faune,' 'Colloque Sentimental' (1904).
'Trois Chansons de France' — Rondel, 'La
  Grotte,' Rondel (1904).
Three Ballades of Villon (1910).
'Le Promenoir des Deux Amants,' from Tristan
  l'Hermite (1910).
'Noël des Enfants qui n'ont plus de Maison,'
  text by composer (1915).
Three Chansons for quartet, from Charles, Duke
  of Orleans (1908).
Transcriptions —
Schumann's 'À la Fontaine,' op. 35, for piano solo.
Gluck's 'Caprice sur les Airs de Ballet de Alceste'
  (Saint-Saëns) for piano, four hands.
Saint-Saëns' 'Introduction et Rondo Capriccioso,'
  for two pianos.
Ballet-Music from Saint-Saëns' 'Étienne Marcel,'
  for two pianos.
Saint-Saëns' 2nd Symphony in A minor, for two
  pianos.
Overture to Wagner's 'The Flying Dutchman,'
  for two pianos.
Schumann's 'Six Studies in Canon,' op. 56, for
  two pianos.
Satie's 'Gymnopédies,' nos. 1 and 3, for orchestra.
In addition, M. Jean-Aubry gives a list of
Debussy's literary works. A bibliography
of works upon Debussy is given in Baker,
Dict. of Musicians, pp. 197, 1082. Gilman's
guide to 'Pelléas et Mélisande' (1907) should
also be mentioned.

DECKER, MYRON A. (1823–1901). See Register, 4.

DECKER & SON is a well-known piano-making business, founded at Albany, N. Y., in 1856 by Myron A. Decker. In 1864 it was removed to New York and took its present name in 1875, when Frank C. Decker was admitted. He is now its president.

DEEMS, JAMES MONROE (1818–1901). See Register, 4.

DEGREES IN MUSIC, ACADEMIC. In the United States the right to confer academic degrees is vested in universities and colleges by the charters which they hold from the States as such, not from the Federal Government. The anomalies and infelicities in American practice about such degrees which are often noted arise both from the excessive freedom with which the right has been granted and with which it has sometimes been exercised. In those subjects in which a gradation of degrees is observed that of 'Bachelor' is given on the completion of a stipulated course of undergraduate study, that of 'Master' either for the completion of a further or post-graduate course or for the execution of some meritorious piece of professional work, but in the United States that of 'Doctor,' except in medicine (and allied subjects) and 'philosophy,' has usually been given *honoris causa* — a practice obviously open to abuse.

It is said that the first instance of the degree of Mus.B. was in 1876 (Boston University). The use of it as marking the completion of a four-years' course in music (somewhat analogous to that leading to A.B.) gradually became established and since 1900 has been widespread. The degree of Mus.M., also resting upon some form of examination, has not become common. There is no definite consensus as to the requirements for either of these degrees, though the standard is evidently being advanced by most institutions. Some institutions give an A.B. 'in music' for college or university work in which music has been a 'major' subject. As a rule, the Canadian universities tend to follow the English practice, giving musical degrees only upon examination or 'exhibition.' Composition figures more largely with them than with institutions in the United States.

For obvious reasons there is nothing in America corresponding to the Union of Graduates in Music in England. Indeed, there is little information accessible as to who have received the degree of Mus.D. For this reason the following list, compiled from such sources as are at hand, may be interesting as a contribution to the curious history of the subject. It is certainly not complete and may not be entirely accurate, but its magnitude is at least surprising.

1849	Henry Dielman (Georgetown [1]).
1855	Lowell Mason (New York).
1856	James P. Clarke (Toronto).
1858	Thomas Hastings (New York).
1864	Henry S. Cutler (Columbia).
	S. Austen Pearce (Oxford, Eng.).
	Gustav J. Stoeckel (Yale).
	John H. Willcox (Georgetown).
1865	John Caulfield (Georgetown).
	William H. Walter (Columbia).
1867	James G. Barnett (Yale).
1869	Eben Tourjée (Wesleyan).
1872	Uzziah C. Burnap (New York).
	William Mason (Yale).
	George F. Root (Chicago [2]).
1874?	W. Eugene Thayer (Oxford, Eng.).
1875	William H. Doane (Denison).
1877	Frédéric L. Ritter (New York).
	William H. Schultze (Syracuse).
1879	Joseph P. Holbrook (Western Reserve C.).
	Fenelon B. Rice (Hillsdale C.).
1880	Leopold Damrosch (Columbia).
	Horatio R. Palmer (Chicago [2]).
	Theodore Thomas (Yale).
1881	John M. Loretz, Jr. (New York).
	Horatio R. Palmer (Alfred).
1882	J. Max Mueller (Georgetown).
	George W. Walter (Columbian).
1883	Smith N. Penfield (New York).
1886	Hugh A. Clarke (Pennsylvania).
	Walter B. Gilbert (Toronto).
	Frank L. Humphreys (St. Stephen's C.).
	John R. Sweney (Pa. Milit. Acad.).
1887	Reginald De Koven (Racine C.).
	J. Albert Jeffrey (St. Stephen's C.).
	Arthur H. Messiter (St. Stephen's C.).
1888	Walter B. Gilbert (Oxford, Eng.).
1889	Maro L. Bartlett (Drake).
	Anton Gloetzner (Georgetown).
	Henry C. Sherman (Georgetown).
1890	Orlando A. Mansfield (Toronto).
	John K. Paine (Yale).
1891	Luther O. Emerson (Findlay C.).
	Gerrit Smith (Hobart C.).
1892	Élysée Aviragnet (Bucknell).
	Percy Goetschius (Syracuse).
1893	La Frone Merriman (Alfred).
	George A. Parker (Syracuse).
1894	Albert Ham (Dublin, Ire.).
	Horatio W. Parker (Yale).
1895	Jules Jordan (Brown).
	Wilson F. Morse (Syracuse).
1896	William W. Gilchrist (Pennsylvania).
	Edward A. MacDowell (Princeton).
	Alfred M. Richardson (Oxford, Eng.).
	James B. Tipton (St. Stephen's C.).
1897	Louis R. Dressler (Hope C.).
1898	Edward Fisher (Toronto).
	Charles L. M. Harriss (Toronto).
	Richard A. Heritage (Willamette).
	Ralph J. Horner (Durham, Eng.).
	Felix J. Kelly (Scharw. Cons., Berlin).
	Waldo S. Pratt (Syracuse).
	Humphrey J. Stewart (Pacific).
1900	Peter C. Lutkin (Syracuse).
	William Rhys-Herbert (Toronto).
	D. Brink Towner (Tennessee).
1901	Charles R. Fisher (Toronto).
	Hamilton C. Macdougall (Brown).
	Arthur Mees (Alfred).
	Harry C. Perrin (Dublin, Ire.).

[1] With the name of the institution 'University' is to be understood, unless 'C.' for 'College' is added.

[2] Not the present University of Chicago, but the earlier Chicago University, discontinued in 1886.

1902 J. Humfrey Anger (Toronto).
      J. Lewis Browne (Grand Cons., N. Y.).
      Edward A. MacDowell (Pennsylvania).
      Horatio W. Parker (Cambridge, Eng.).
1903 George W. Andrews (Oberlin C.).
      George C. Gow (Brown).
      Ernst C. E. Held (Syracuse).
      Eva C. Taylor [Mrs. O. J. Nurse] (Toronto).
1904 Will G. Butler (Grand Cons., N. Y.).
      Frank H. Damrosch (Yale).
      Hermann Poehlmann (Grove City C.).
      J. Fred Wolle (Moravian C.).
1905 Orlando A. Mansfield (Toronto).
1906 Edward J. Biedermann (Beaver C.).
      Hollis E. Dann (Alfred).
      Henry P. Eames (Cornell C.).
      Albert Ham (Toronto).
      Augustus S. Vogt (Toronto).
1907 Heinrich H. Bellamann (Grayson C.).
      Hyland E. Slatre-Wilson (Grand Cons., N. Y.).
      Alle D. Zuidema (Detroit Cons.).
1908 William E. Broome (Toronto).
      J. Christopher Marks (Grand Cons., N. Y.).
      William H. Santelmann (Geo. Washington).
      Alfred Wooler (Grand Cons., N. Y.).
1909 William F. Bentley (Knox C.).
      John J. Landsbury (Simpson C.).
      John W. Thompson (Knox C.).
1910 Victor Baier (St. Stephen's C.).
      Louis A. Coerne (Olivet C.).
      Newton J. Corey (Hillsdale C.).
      Frank Nagel (Highland Park C.).
      James H. Pearce (Toronto).
      Frank L. Rogers (St. Stephen's C.).
      Percy C. Starnes (St. Stephen's C.).
1911 George S. Bohanan (Rio Grande C.).
      William C. Carl (New York).
      Adam Geibel (Temple).
      Franz Kneisel (Yale).
      Henry A. Lang (Philadelphia Cons.).
      Edward Y. Mason (Ohio Northern).
      Charles H. Mills (McGill).
1912 William H. Berwald (Syracuse).
      Adolf Frey (Syracuse).
      J. E. Hodgson (McGill).
      Tali Esen Morgan (Temple).
      Herbert Sanders (McGill).
      Edward B. Scheve (Grinnell C.).
1913 A. L. Gabert (Pontifical Sch., Rome).
      Thaddeus Rich (Temple).
      Robert L. Schofield (Puget Sound C.).
      Alexander S. Thompson (Des Moines C.).
1914 Walter J. Damrosch (Columbia).
1915 Franz Kneisel (Princeton).
      Henry F. Perrin (Oskaloosa C.).
1916 John H. Brewer (New York).
      Charles E. Clemens (Western Reserve).
      James P. Dodd (St. Stephen's C.).
      Miles Farrow (Pittsburgh).
      Walter Keller (DePaul).
      Albert A. Stanley (Northwestern).
1917 Clarence Dickinson (Northwestern).
      John McCormack (Holy Cross C.).
      Ignaz J. Paderewski (Yale).
      Leopold Stokowski (Pennsylvania).
1918 John W. Holland (Potomac).
      William C. Macfarlane (Bates C.).
      David S. Smith (Northwestern).
1919 James F. Cooke (Ohio Northern).
      John T. Erickson (Potomac).
      Arthur Foote (Trinity C.).
      Philip H. Goepp (Temple).
      Victor Liska (Potomac).
      Donald C. MacGregor (Potomac).

1919 Jean C. Moos (Bethany C.).
      Frederick C. Thomas (Potomac).
      J. Fred Wolle (Pennsylvania).
1920 Will Earhart (Pittsburgh).
      H. Alexander Matthews (Muhlenberg C.).

The following are Ph.D. :

1881 Theodore Baker (Leipzig, Ger.).
1892 John S. VanCleve (Twin Valley C.).
1894 John C. Griggs (Leipzig, Ger.).
1905 Charles D. Campbell (Strassburg, Alsace).
      Louis A. Coerne (Harvard).
1908 Archibald T. Davison (Harvard).
1909 Otto Kinkeldey (Berlin, Ger.).
1910 Sigmund Spaeth (Princeton).
1911 Philip G. Clapp (Harvard).
1914 Alma W. Powell (Columbia).

The following are Litt.D. :

1911 Edward Dickinson (Oberlin C.).
1916 Edgar S. Kelley (Miami).
1920 Clarence Dickinson (Miami).

The following are LL.D. :

1895 C. Crozat Converse (Rutherford C.).
1905 George W. Chadwick (Tufts C.).
1914 David Bispham (Haverford C.).
1917 Edgar S. Kelley (Cincinnati).
1920 Ignace J. Paderewski (Oxford, Eng.).

DE KOVEN, HENRY LOUIS REGINALD
(Apr. 3, 1859, Middletown, Conn. : Jan.
16, 1920, Chicago), was the son of a clergyman who removed to England in 1872. He
graduated from St. John's College, Oxford,
in 1879. At Stuttgart he studied piano with
Speidel and Lebert and harmony with Pruckner,
at Frankfort composition with Hauff, at
Florence singing with Vannuccini, at Vienna
and Paris composition with Genée and Delibes.
In 1889-90 he was music-critic for the Chicago
'Evening Post,' in 1891-97 for the New York
'World,' in 1898-1900 for the 'Journal,' in
1907-12 for the 'World' again, and in 1895-97
also for 'Harper's Weekly.' In 1902-05 he
conducted the Philharmonic Orchestra in
Washington, which he organized. He became
from 1887 one of the most successful American
composers of light opera, the list of works
including

'The Begum' (1887, Philadelphia, McCaull Opera Company).
'Don Quixote' (1889, Boston, The Bostonians).
'Robin Hood' (1890, Chicago, 1891, London, as 'Maid Marian').
'The Fencing-Master' (1892, Boston).
'The Knickerbockers' (1893, Boston).
'The Algerian' (1893, Philadelphia).
'Rob Roy' (1894, Detroit).
'The Tzigane' (1895, New York).
'The Mandarin' (1896, Cleveland).
'The Paris Doll' (1897, Hartford).
'The Highwayman' (1897, New Haven).
'The Three Dragoons' (1899, New York).
'Red Feather' (1903, New York).
'Happyland' (1905, New York).
'Student King' (1906, New York).
'The Golden Butterfly' (1907, New York).
'The Beauty-Spot' (1909, New York).
'The Wedding-Trip' (1911, New York).
'Her Little Highness' (1913, New York).

His grand operas were 'The Canterbury Pilgrims,' produced in New York at the Metropolitan Opera House in March, 1917, and 'Rip van Winkle,' produced in Chicago and New York in January, 1920 — the librettos in both cases being by Percy Mackaye. In addition, he wrote upwards of 400 songs — many very popular — piano-pieces, a piano-sonata (unpublished), an orchestral suite and several ballets. His melodic fertility and facile scoring gave him a unique place, somewhat analogous to that of Arthur Sullivan. [R. 7]

DE LAMARTER, ERIC (Feb. 18, 1880, Lansing, Mich.), early began organ-study with G. H. Fairclough and at fifteen was choir-director in Kalamazoo, Mich. After a year in Albion College, he began to study piano with Mary Wood Chase in Chicago and organ with Middelschulte. While still in his teens he became organist at the New England Congregational Church there. The year 1901–02 he spent in Paris with Guilmant and Widor. In 1904–05 he taught at Olivet College in Michigan. In 1911 he succeeded Stock as director of the Musical Art Society of Chicago. The next year he became organist of the First Church of Christ, Scientist, and since 1914 has been organist of the Fourth Presbyterian Church, where his frequent recitals present notable programs, especially of modern works. He was music-critic for the Chicago 'Record-Herald' in 1908–09, for the 'Tribune' in 1909–10, and for the 'Inter-Ocean' since 1910. In 1918–19 he acted as director of the Chicago Symphony Orchestra in Stock's absence. His overture to a fantastic comedy, 'The Faun,' was played by the Chicago Orchestra in 1915. He has also composed chamber-music, songs, piano- and organ-pieces, and incidental music for plays. [R.8]

‡ DELIUS, FREDERICK (Jan. 29, 1863, Bradford, England). See article in Vol. v. 629–31. A dated list of his compositions is published in 'The Musical Times,' March, 1915, and includes, in addition to those mentioned in the above article:

Five Songs (1888); Seven Songs (1889); Three Songs by Shelley (1890).
'Irmelin,' a lyric drama in three acts (1890).
'The Magic Fountain,' a lyric drama in three acts (1894).
Five Songs from the Danish (1897).
Part-Songs — 'Midsummer Songs,' 'On Craig Dhu,' both for mixed voices, 'Wanderer's Song,' for men's voices.
'Songs of Sunset,' for baritone, soprano, chorus and orchestra (1906).
'Dance Rhapsody,' for full orchestra (1909).
Three Songs from Verlaine (1893–1910).
'Fennimore and Gerda,' lyric drama, from Jacobsen's 'Niels Lynne' (1910–12).
'The Song of the High Hills,' for orchestra and chorus (1911–12).
'An Arabesk,' for baritone, chorus and orchestra (1912).

Two Tone-Poems for small orchestra — 'On Hearing the First Cuckoo in Spring,' 'Summer-night on the River' (1912–12).
'North-Country Sketches' (1913–14).
Songs — 'Chanson d'Automne,' from Verlaine, 'The nightingale has a lyre of gold,' from Henley, 'Black Roses,' from the Swedish of Josefson, 'I Brasil,' from Fiona McLeod.
Requiem, for soli, choir and orchestra (1914).
Sonata for violin and pianoforte (1905, revised 1915).

Later compositions mentioned in the musical press are a violin-concerto, a double concerto for violin and 'cello, and a ballade for orchestra. His orchestral works have had numerous performances in America, and Grainger has played the piano-concerto in C minor.

DE LUCA, GIUSEPPE (b. 1876). See Register, 10.

DEMAREST, CLIFFORD (Aug. 12, 1874, Tenafly, N. J.), had his first organ-lessons from his mother and became her substitute and later her successor. For five years he studied with Woodman in Brooklyn. At present he is organist of the Church of the Messiah (Unitarian) in New York. He is a fellow of the A. G. O., served several years as secretary, and in 1916–19 was warden. He has published many anthems, songs and part-songs, and these organ-compositions: 'A Pastorale Suite,' in four movements, Andante Religioso, Cantilena, Canzona, Cantabile, Festival Postlude, Festival Finale, Mélodie Pastorale, Aria in D, Prelude on the tune 'Amsterdam,' Evening Meditation, and a Fantasie for organ and piano. He has also two published cantatas, 'The Shepherds of Bethlehem' and 'The Cross Victorious.' His *Hints on Organ-Accompaniment* is useful and popular. [R.8]

DEMARQUE. See Register, 2.

DENNÉE, CHARLES FREDERICK (Sept. 1, 1863, Oswego, N. Y.), entered the New England Conservatory in Boston at sixteen, graduated in 1883, and ever since has been a teacher of piano there. His teachers were A. D. Turner and Mme. Schiller in piano, and Emery in composition; he also studied with Von Bülow. Until disabled by an accident to his right wrist in 1897, he was active as a recitalist, giving over 1100 recitals in the United States and Canada. He was one of the pioneers in the lecture-recital field. As a teacher he has exerted a wide influence. His lyric and comic operas are 'The Defender,' 'The Belle of Newport,' 'Little Red Riding-Hood,' 'The Merry-go-round,' 'The Royal Barber,' 'The Chorus Girl' and 'The Electric Spark.' An overture for orchestra, a violin-sonata and a suite for piano and 'cello are in manuscript. As a composer of teaching-material for piano he has been especially successful. His *Progressive Technique* has been widely used, as also his other technical works. There are four sonatinas, a number of études and a large group of characteristic pieces for piano, besides some songs and choruses. He was editor of the new edition of the *Century Library of Music* and of certain volumes of *Music and Musicians*. [R.7]

DENNY, MAUDE A. See STATE UNIVERSITIES (Nev.).

DESTINN, EMMY [Kittl] (b. 1878). See Register, 9.

DÉTHIER, ÉDOUARD (b. 1885). See Register, 9.

DÉTHIER, GASTON MARIE (Apr. 19, 1875, Liège, Belgium), having been trained by his father, at twelve won a scholarship in the Liège Conservatory over sixty competitors. He graduated at seventeen, winning the gold medal for piano- and organ-playing and the first prize for fugue. At eleven he had been organist at St. Jacques' in Liège, and at fourteen made his début as concert-organist at Malines. He came to New York in 1894 as organist at St. Francis Xavier's on the recommendation of Guilmant. Since 1907 he has forsaken church-playing for concert-work and for duties as organ-teacher at the Institute of Musical Art. He has written many popular organ-works (J. Fischer & Bro.), of which the caprice 'The Brook' is an especial favorite. [R.8]

DETROIT CONSERVATORY OF MUSIC, THE, was founded in 1874 by Jacob H. Hahn, who remained its director till his death in 1902, when he was succeeded by Francis L. York, who is now its head. The annual enrollment of students is about 1600 and it has over 400 graduates. The faculty numbers about 70. Its main building is at 1013 Woodward Avenue. The Conservatory has always been managed with notable energy and breadth, and is to be counted among the constructive forces for sound musicianship.

DETROIT INSTITUTE OF MUSICAL ART, THE, was founded in 1914 and has won a place as an earnest school of high aspirations. Guy Bevier Williams is president, and the faculty includes about 50 teachers. It is located at 1117–21 Woodward Avenue.

DETROIT SYMPHONY ORCHESTRA, THE, was founded in 1914 by Weston Gales and conducted by him till 1918, when he was succeeded by Ossip Gabrilovitch. On Oct. 23, 1919, the Orchestra dedicated the new Orchestra Hall, built for its use.

DETT, ROBERT NATHANIEL (Oct. 11, 1882, Drummondville, Que.), graduated from the Niagara Falls Collegiate Institute in 1903, attended the Halsted Conservatory at Lockport, N. Y., and thence went to the Oberlin Conservatory, where he won a Mus.B. in 1908 —

probably the first Negro to receive this degree for original composition. Later he also attended Columbia University in New York. His teachers in composition were G. W. Andrews and R. G. Cole; he also has had training in community-music with P. W. Dykema. He taught for three years at Lane College in Jackson, Miss., two years at Lincoln Institute in Jefferson City, Mo., and in 1913 became head of the vocal department at Hampton Institute in Hampton, Va., and director of the Hampton Choral Union. As pianist he has appeared in New York, Chicago, Boston, Buffalo, Philadelphia and other cities. As composer he has shown 'how the characteristic accents of Negro music may be developed into genuine art-forms, without resorting to imitations of the white man's music' (G. D. Gunn). His works include

Suite, 'The Magnolia,' for piano — 'Magnolias,' 'The Deserted Cabin,' 'My Lady-Love,' 'Mammy,' 'The Place where the Rainbow Ends' (Summy).
Suite, 'In the Bottoms,' for piano — 'Night' (Prelude), 'His Song,' 'Honey,' 'Morning' (Barcarolle), 'Juba' (characteristic dance) (Summy).
Cantata, 'The Chariot Jubilee,' for chorus and orchestra (Church).
Choruses a cappella: 'Listen to the Lambs,' 'O Holy Lord,' 'Music in the Mine' (all Schirmer), 'I'll never turn back no more,' 'Weeping Mary,' 'America the Beautiful' (all J. Fischer & Bro.). Several arrangements of 'spirituals' are published by Church and by Birchard.
Sonata in A-flat, for piano.
Concert-Waltz and Ballade, for piano.
'The Album of a Heart,' idyllic pieces for piano.
Andante in F, for string-quartet.
Pieces for violin and piano.
Cantata, 'The Death of Moses,' text by Frederic. H. Martens.
Song-Cycle, 'The Heart of a Poet,' for mezzo voice.

He has also in manuscript a work on *Negro Music* and a book of verse. [R.9]

D'HEMARD, MME. See Register, 2.

'DIAPASON, THE,' of Chicago, a monthly journal devoted to the interests of organmakers and organists, was founded in 1910 by Siegfried E. Gruenstein, who has remained its editor and publisher. It is the official organ of the National Association of Organists and of the Organ-Builders' Association of America.

DICKERSON, JOSEPH L. See TUNE-BOOKS, 1810.

DICKINSON, CLARENCE (May 7, 1873, La Fayette, Ind.), was educated first at Miami University and in 1890–94 at Northwestern University, by the latter of which he was made A.M. in 1909 and Mus.D. in 1917. Miami University also made him Litt.D. in 1920. His musical training came from William Cutler, Wild and Weidig in Chicago, Reimann and Singer in Berlin, and Guilmant, Vierne and Moszkowski in Paris. In Chicago he was for a time at the head of the Cosmopolitan School of Music, founded the Musical Art Society and led it for three years, conducted the Musical Club in Aurora, Ill., the Bach Choir in Dubuque, Ia., and the Chicago English Opera Company, and was organist of St. James' (Episcopal) Church. In 1909 he removed to New York, becoming organist at the Brick (Presbyterian) Church and the Temple Beth-El, and since 1912 professor at the Union Theological Seminary, besides being for a time conductor of the Mendelssohn Glee Club and of the Bach Choir of Montclair, N. J. He was a founder of the A. G. O., and has given many organ-recitals, not only in the United States and Canada, but in France, Germany and Spain. His published compositions include many vocal solos and choruses for men's, women's or mixed voices; a symphony for organ, and other organ-pieces; and works for organ and stringed instruments. He has edited a series of *Sacred Choruses, Ancient and Modern* (80 numbers thus far), the texts mostly translated by Mrs. Dickinson, a *Historical Recital Series for Organ* (27 numbers thus far), a *Book of Eighty Amens* and a *Book of Forty Antiphons* (in press). Among his unpublished compositions are two light operas, 'The Medicine-Man' (Chicago, 1895) and 'Priscilla.' With his wife, Helen A. Dickinson, he has published *Excursions in Musical History*, 1917. He also contributed to *The American Encyclopedia of Music*, 1910. [R.7]

DICKINSON, EDWARD (Oct. 10, 1853, West Springfield, Mass.), graduated from Amherst College in 1876 and was musically trained mostly at the New England Conservatory and by Eugene Thayer in Boston and by Klindworth and Langhans at Berlin. From 1872 he was organist at Springfield, Mass., and in 1879–85 at Elmira, N. Y., where in 1883–92 he was also music-director at Elmira College. Since 1893 he has been professor in Oberlin College and Conservatory, devoting himself to the development of a system of instruction in the history and philosophy of music which is singular, if not unique, for scope, thoroughness and efficiency. In connection with this work as teacher he has published *Music in the History of the Western Church*, 1902, *The Study of the History of Music*, 1905 (3rd ed., 1914), *The Education of the Music-Lover*, 1911, and *Music and the Higher Education*, 1915— all works of sterling thought, presented with much earnestness and vigor of expression. He has also written much for magazines and reviews. In 1911 Oberlin College made him Litt.D. [R.6]

DIECKMANN, CHRISTIAN WILLIAM (b. 1880). See COLLEGES, 2 (Agnes Scott C., Ga.).

DIGGLE, ROLAND (b. 1885). See Register, 9.

DIPPEL, JOHANN ANDREAS (Nov. 30, 1866, Kassel, Germany), was originally trained at Kassel in 1882–87 for a banking career, but also studied singing with Frau Zottmayr. He made his début as tenor at the Bremen Stadt-Theater in 1887 as the Steuermann in 'Der fliegende Holländer,' and pursued further studies with Hey in Berlin, Leoni in Milan and Ress in Vienna. Until 1892 he remained at Bremen, but in 1890–91 sang at the Metropolitan Opera House, making his début in 'Asrael' in 1890 under the direction of Seidl. He made a concert-tour in America in 1892, sang at the Breslau Stadt-Theater in 1892–93, and then spent five seasons at the Vienna Imperial Opera. In 1898–1908 he was at the Metropolitan Opera House again, singing also at Covent Garden, the Munich Royal Opera and the Bayreuth Festivals. Then came two years as administrative manager of the Metropolitan Opera House and three (1910–13) as general manager of the Chicago-Philadelphia Opera Company. Since 1913 he has given light opera with his own company. As a singer he has an unusual repertory, including about 150 German, French and Italian operas and 60 oratorios. He has sung some rôles, such as that of Raoul in 'Les Huguenots,' in German, French and Italian. He sings all the Wagnerian works, including 'Parsifal.' [R.8]

DIPPER, THOMAS (d. 1763). See Register, 1.

'DISAPPOINTMENT, THE.' A comic opera of the ballad type by Andrew Barton, which was rehearsed for performance in Philadelphia in April, 1767, but withdrawn because some allusions were considered too personal. The text was immediately published in New York and a second edition in 1796 (with additions). The songs required numbered eighteen, among them being 'Yankee Doodle' — apparently the first literary reference to this melody. Unless Ralph's 'Fashionable Lady' (1730, London) was by an American, this is the first American opera. But who Andrew Barton was is not known. By some the name is conjectured to be a pseudonym, perhaps used by John Leacock. See Sonneck, 'Early American Operas,' *I. M. G. Sammelbde.* 6. 433–50.

DITSON, OLIVER (Oct. 20, 1811, Boston : Dec. 21, 1888, Boston). See article in Vol. i. 707. Ditson's personal career is intimately interwoven with the famous business that he established. His family, of Scottish derivation, for two generations had been identified with eastern Massachusetts. After a common-school education he was from 1823 clerk in the book-store of Samuel H. Parker, who was one of the original trustees of the Handel and Haydn Society. In 1826 he set out to learn the printer's trade, first under Isaac R. Butts, who printed 'The North American Review,' and then with Alfred Mudge, the founder of a house later famous. He also became organist at the Bulfinch Street Church. In 1835 he set up for himself as music-seller and publisher, and in 1836 with his former employer formed the firm of Parker & Ditson, dealing in pianos and music, and soon located in what later was famous as 'The Old Corner Bookstore' on Washington Street. In 1842 Ditson became sole proprietor of the business, which now rapidly expanded, necessitating repeated removals to larger quarters. In 1845 John C. Haynes was employed as clerk, soon demonstrating such capacity that in 1857 he was taken into partnership. Probably from before 1850 the printing and engraving was put in charge of John H. H. Graupner, the son of Gottlieb Graupner (see Register, 2). In 1860 a branch business was established in Cincinnati under John Church (from 1871 known as the John Church Company). In 1867, through the purchase of the business of Firth, Son & Co. in New York (see Register, 3), another branch was there constituted under the name of Chas. H. Ditson & Co., its head being Ditson's eldest son. In 1875 the stock of Lee & Walker in Philadelphia was purchased and the house of J. E. Ditson & Co. established, led by another son (discontinued in 1910). In 1877 Ditson absorbed the business of G. D. Russell & Co. in Boston. Thus he steadily gained a commanding position in different parts of the country — the most conspicuous instance in its class of a house organized by native American enterprise. Besides publishing a vast amount of music, popular and artistic, in sheet-form and book-form, he was in 1858–78 publisher of 'Dwight's Journal of Music,' in 1878–1903 of 'The Monthly Musical Record' (name varied later), and in 1903–18 of 'The Musician.' One of the most significant single undertakings has been the building up of the series known as 'The Musicians' Library' (80 vols. thus far). A large number of instruction-books and books about music have also been put forth. In 1917 the business removed to its latest building at 178–9 Tremont Street. See Fisher, *Music in Old Boston*, 1918. [R.3]

DITSON COMPANY, THE OLIVER. From 1857, when Haynes joined Ditson, the firm-name was Oliver Ditson & Co., which, after Haynes' death in 1907, was changed to its present form, Charles H. Ditson becoming president. See preceding article.

'DIXIE.' A famous song, written by Daniel D. Emmett in 1859 for Bryant's 'minstrel' troupe in New York. In the Civil War it became the favorite war-song of the South.

DOANE, WILLIAM HOWARD (1832–1915). See Register, 4.

'DOCTOR OF ALCANTARA, THE.' A comic light opera by Julius Eichberg, first produced in Boston in 1862 and long popular. The text was by the English critic B. E. Woolf.

DODGE, AVA L. B. See COLLEGES, 3 (Elon C., N. C.).

DOENHOFF, ALBERT VON (b. 1880). See Register, 8.

DOENHOFF, HELEN VON (b. 1861). See Register, 6.

DOERNER, ARMIN W. (b. 1851). See Register, 6.

DOHN, ADOLPH W. See Register, 4.

DOLGE, ALFRED (b. 1848). See Register, 5.

DOLL, JACOB, & SONS. A piano-making firm established in New York in 1871 by Jacob Doll (d. 1911), which has developed into a large business, incorporated with a capital of $1,000,000. All parts of their pianos are made in their own factories, and they have distinctive features in their player-pianos.

DOLMETSCH, ARNOLD (b. 1858). See Register, 9.

DONALDA, PAULINE (b. 1884). See Register, 9.

DONLEY, WILLIAM HENRY (Apr. 20, 1863, New Haven, Conn.), had his early education at Waterloo, Ia. Beginning music there and in New York, at the New England Conservatory in Boston he studied piano with Maas, organ with Whiting, theory with Emery, and later singing with Tinney of London. He made his début as concert-organist at nineteen, and has held positions as organist at Waterloo, Ia., Cedar Rapids, Ia., Belleville, Ont., Owen Sound, Ont., and Indianapolis, where he gave a series of over 200 recitals. At present he is organist at the large First Presbyterian Church in Seattle. He had official engagements at the Pan-American Exposition at Buffalo in 1901 and the Louisiana Purchase Exposition at St. Louis in 1904 and has given recitals throughout the United States. He has long specialized on organ-planning, and has drawn schemes for over 300 organs. He was probably the first in America to give organ-recitals on Wagner's 'Ring,' illustrated with lantern-slides and preceded by a lecture on Norse legends and the Nibelungen Lied. These have been given in many cities. He is now director of the People's Chorus in Seattle. [R.7]

'DON MUNIO, THE LEGEND OF.' A cantata for chorus and orchestra by Dudley Buck, who also wrote the text. It was first published in 1874 and has been popular ever since.

DOOLITTLE, AMOS. See TUNE-BOOKS, 1782.

DOUGLAS, CHARLES WINFRED (Feb. 15, 1867, Oswego, N. Y.), was educated at the Oswego High School and Syracuse University, where he studied music with Goetschius and G. A. Parker, receiving his Mus.B. in 1891. He later studied piano with Everett Steele in Denver and plain-chant under Mocquereau at Solesmes. He was assistant-organist at St. Paul's Cathedral in Syracuse in 1889–91; organist at Zion and St. Timothy's Churches in New York in 1892–3; minor canon and assistant-organist at St. John's Cathedral in Denver in 1894–97; canon preceptor at St. Paul's Cathedral in Fond du Lac, Wis., in 1907–10; and instructor in plain-chant at the General Theological Seminary in New York in 1914–16. Since 1907 he has been director of music for the Sisterhood of St. Mary. He has composed 'Missa de Angelis,' 'Asperges me,' 'Cantica Eucharistica,' 'Compline,' 'Missa Marialis,' 'Missa Penitentialis,' 'Missa Paschalis,' the Canticles at Even-song, the St. Dunstan Psalter and Kyrial, and a Mass in G for women's voices and small orchestra. He has written and lectured on musical topics, conducted summer-schools of church-music, and adapted English texts to Russian church-music. He is author of *Plain-song*, 1909, *Some Recent Contributions to the Philosophy of Music*, 1911, and *The History and Work of the Schola Cantorum*, 1913. He assisted in editing the *Hymnal* (P. E.), 1919. [R.7]

DOUGLASS, DAVID (d. 1786). See Register, 1.

DOUGLASS, IDA. See STATE UNIVERSITIES (Ariz.).

DOUILLET, PIERRE (b. 1861). See Register, 7.

DOUTY, NICHOLAS (Apr. 14, 1870, Philadelphia), was taught piano and singing by his mother, and sang in various choirs as both soprano and alto. He studied organ with Pyne, harmony and counterpoint under Cresson, and was assistant-organist at St. Mark's and St. James' when only seventeen. Later he studied singing with Castle, Aline Osgood Dexter, Randegger and Sbriglia. He has appeared as tenor with almost every large choral body in the East and Middle West. On important occasions his reliable musicianship has made him indispensable, and as a Bach interpreter he has won the highest praise. He has been soloist at all the festivals of the Bach Choir at Bethlehem, Pa. He has composed organ-pieces, piano-pieces, part-songs and songs (Schirmer, Ditson and Presser). He has contributed articles to 'The New Musical Review,' 'The Etude' and 'The Musician,' and translated many songs from French, Italian and German. He is

president of the Manuscript Music Society of Philadelphia, the Pegasus Club, and a vice-president of the Musical Art Club. [R.7]

DOUVILLIER, M. and MME. See Register, 2.

DOW, MARTHA CORA. See Register, 10.

DOWNES, EDWIN OLIN (Jan. 27, 1886, Evanston, Ill.), was a pupil of Kelterborn in piano, music-history and analysis, of Baermann in piano, of Norris and Heilman in harmony, and of Marshall in harmony. He has been music-critic for the Boston 'Post' since 1907. He is author of *The Lure of Music*, 1918, a crisp and acute summary of biography, criticism and analysis of well-known compositions, adapted to illustrations by graphophone records. He has edited *The Songs of Russia* (Carl Fischer), a collection of sixty songs, with Russian text and translations by George Harris, Jr., and others. He has lectured on the opera in courses at Boston University and the Lowell Institute, and wrote the program-notes for the premières of 'The Pipe of Desire' and 'The Sacrifice' at Boston and New York. In 1913–14 he taught theory and appreciation at Chautauqua. [R.9]

DRAKE, EARL R. (1865–1916). See Register, 8.

DRAKE, FREDERICK. See COLLEGES, 3 (Kingfisher C., Okla.).

DRANGOSCH, ERNESTO (b. 1882). See Register, 9.

DRESEL, OTTO (1826, Andernach, Germany : July 26, 1890, Beverly, Mass.), having been a pupil of Hiller at Cologne and of Mendelssohn at Leipzig, came to New York in 1848, where in 1851 he gave chamber-concerts with Eisfeld, and from 1852 lived in Boston. Until 1868, when he withdrew from concert-work, he was the leading pianist there, and until his death exercised a strong influence, partly through articles in 'Dwight's Journal.' He was a close friend of Franz, and made a piano-score of the latter's reorchestration of 'The Messiah.' He also prepared an edition of 'The Well-Tempered Clavichord.' An exceptionally severe critic of his own work, he is represented by only a few piano-pieces and songs, but these have been highly praised. Still in manuscript, though sometimes performed, are 'In Memoriam,' a ballad for soprano and orchestra, the words from Longfellow's tribute to Agassiz (1857); an 'Army Hymn' for soli, chorus and orchestra (1863), the words by Holmes; a piano-trio, and a quartet for piano and strings. In his *Musicians and Music-Lovers* Apthorp, speaking of Franz and Dresel, said, 'In both of these men was found in the highest perfection what I might call, for lack of a better name, the sense of musical beauty, the keenest sense for beauty of expression, beauty of form, proportion and color. They were staunch, lifelong friends; their agreement on musical subjects was as complete as their friendship; they both worked together toward the same end; though they lived long apart, neither gave anything to the world without the ordeal of its passing through the other's criticism; they died within two years of each other. It is well to speak of them together.' [R.4]

DRESSLER, LOUIS RAPHAEL (b. 1861). See Register, 6.

DREXEL LIBRARY, THE, was a collection of books, manuscripts, etc. (6000 items), formed by Joseph W. Drexel of Philadelphia from 1858 and bequeathed by him to the Lenox Library in New York in 1888. It now forms part of the music-division of the New York Public Library. See note in Vol. ii. 718, and article by Edward Silsky in the *M. T. N. A. Proceedings*, 1914, p. 211.

DUBOIS. See Register, 2.

‡ DUBOIS, FRANÇOIS CLÉMENT THÉODORE (Aug. 24, 1837, Rosnay, France). See article in Vol. i. 734–5, and add that he retired from the directorship of the Conservatoire in 1905.

DUBOIS, WILLIAM. See Register, 3.

DUFAU, JENNY. See Register, 10.

DUFFIELD, ELSIE. See COLLEGES, 3 (Olivet C., Mich.).

DUFRANNE, HECTOR. See Register, 9.

‡ DUKAS, PAUL (Oct. 1, 1865, Paris). See article in Vol. i. 738. He was made Chevalier of the Légion d'Honneur in 1906, and since 1909 has been professor of the orchestral class and member of the Conseil de l'Enseignement Supérieur and at the Conservatory. Additional works are the three-act opera 'Ariane et Barbe-Bleu,' text by Maeterlinck (1907, Paris, Opéra-Comique, 1911, New York, Metropolitan Opera House); the ballet 'La Péri' (1910); 'Villanelle' for horn and piano (1906); a piano-sonata in E-flat minor; 'Variations, Interlude and Finale' on a theme by Rameau, and 'Prélude Élégiaque,' both for piano.

DULCKEN, FERDINAND QUENTIN (1837–1902). See Register, 6.

DUNHAM, HENRY MORTON (July 27, 1853, Brockton, Mass.), having studied with Whiting, Petersilea and Paine, graduated from the New England Conservatory in 1873, and from Boston University College of Music in 1876. After some European experiences he returned to the Conservatory in 1878 as teacher of organ, a position he still holds. For a time he also taught in Boston University. He is also music-director of Lasell Seminary in Auburndale. He has been organist of the Porter (Congregational) Church in Brockton in 1873–83, of the Ruggles Street (Baptist)

Church in Boston in 1883–96, of the Shawmut (Congregational) Church in 1896–1906, and of the Harvard (Congregational) Church in Brookline in 1906–11. As a concert-organist he has given many recitals, including an annual series at Music Hall in Boston and at the St. Louis Exposition in 1904. His 'Cortège' for organ and orchestra, and a 'Meditation' for strings, harp, organ and orchestra, have been played at Boston Symphony Orchestra popular concerts. He has also composed a concerto for organ and orchestra; a 'Phantasy' for harp, two violins, organ and orchestra; the symphonic poem 'Aurora' for full orchestra and organ; a 'Duo Concertante' for 'cello and piano; sonatas, fugues and smaller pieces for organ; and choir-music. He has published a book of piano-studies, *Legato Fingering and Phrasing*, and, for organ, *Manual and Pedal Technique*, an *Organ School* (four parts), editions of Bach's smaller organ-works, modern French organ-compositions, etc. [R.6]

DUNHAM, J. B. (1799–1873). See Register, 3.

‡ DUNHILL, THOMAS FREDERICK (Feb. 1, 1877, Hampstead, London). See article in Vol. v. 634. His professorship at the Royal College of Music dates from 1905. He has made a specialty of chamber-music, both in his own composition, in promoting series of concerts, and by his *Chamber-Music, a Treatise for Students*, 1913. His own works in this genre now include Variations in F, for flute and piano; a quintet in E-flat, for piano, clarinet, horn, violin and 'cello; a quintet for strings and horn; a piano-quartet in B minor (Leslie Alexander prize); a piano-quintet in C minor; a sonata for violin and piano; two 'Phantasie' trios, one for piano, violin and 'cello, the other for piano, violin and viola; Variations for 'cello and piano; pieces for violin and piano; besides the song-cycle 'Songs of the River.' He has toured Australia, New Zealand and Canada as Examiner for the Associated Board, and has given many lectures on behalf of chamber-music.

DUNKLEY, FERDINAND LUIS (July 16, 1869, London), received his musical education from G. A. Higgs, the Royal College of Music and Trinity College of Music in London. He studied composition with Parry and organ with Martin. In 1893 he came to Albany, N. Y., as music-director at St. Agnes' School. Removing to Asheville, N. C., in 1899, he became director at Asheville College and conductor of the annual festivals. The years 1901–09 were spent in New Orleans as organist of St. Paul's and Touro Synagogue, and conductor of vocal and orchestral societies. Then followed three years as organist at

Christ Church in Vancouver, B. C. From 1912 he was in Seattle as organist at St. Mark's, at the First Methodist Church, and (from 1916) at the First Church of Christ, Scientist. He was director of the Chehalis Choral Society, and the St. Cecilia Club of Tacoma, and leader of community-singing. He was also vocal instructor at the Annie Wright Seminary in Tacoma, and on the faculty of the Stapp School of Music in Seattle. In the fall of 1920 he removed to Birmingham, Ala., to be organist at the Church of the Advent. He is a fellow of the R. C. O. and the A. G. O., and gave recitals at the Buffalo and St. Louis Expositions in 1901 and 1904. His compositions include the ballad for chorus and orchestra 'The Wreck of the Hesperus' (1894, Novello); 'The Elected Knight,' ballad for men's chorus and piano (Church Co.); a Sabbath Eve Service for Jewish Worship, including 'Adon Olom' (Bloch Pub. Co., orchestration in MS.); and songs, piano-pieces and anthems. Among his works in manuscript are the orchestral suite 'Among Yon Mountain-Fastnesses' (prize at the London Promenade Concerts in 1889), a sonata for 'cello and piano, a Sabbath Morning Service for Jewish Worship, and several settings of Fiona Macleod poems for solo or chorus. [R.8]

DUNN, JAMES PHILIP (Jan. 10, 1884, New York), graduated from the College of the City of New York in 1903, not having given special attention to music. He then studied with MacDowell, McWhood and Rybner at Columbia University, specializing in theory and composition. He has been organist at Holy Innocents' in New York, and St. Patrick's in Jersey City. He has composed a piano-quintet in G minor (1910, N. Y. Manuscript Society); a sonata in G minor for violin and piano (1912); a piano-trio in B-flat(1913); the tone-poem 'Annabel Lee,' for voice and orchestra (1913, People's Symphony Orchestra, New York); two string-quartets, many songs, piano- and organ-pieces. Two 'Lyric Scenes' are based on the stage-episodes 'The Fountain,' by Charles McMillan, and 'A Kiss in the Dark,' after Maurice Lavelle. [R.9]

DURST, SIDNEY C. (b. 1870). See Register, 9.

DUTTON, DEODATUS, JR. See TUNE-Books, 1829.

DVOŘÁK, ANTONIN (Sept. 8, 1841, Mühlhausen [Nelahozeves], Bohemia : May 1, 1904, Prague). See article in Vol. i. 755-9. His work as artistic director and teacher of composition at the National Conservatory in New York in 1892-95 exercised considerable influence on certain features of American music. Among his pupils were Rubin Goldmark, W. A. Fisher, H. R. Shelley, H. W. Loomis and Henry Schoenefeld. His 'New

World' Symphony, op. 95, his string-quartet in F, op. 96, and his string-quintet in E-flat, op. 97, all have to do with his American sojourn. Regarding the use of native thematic material, his statement in 'The Century Magazine' for February, 1895, may be quoted :

'A while ago I suggested that inspiration for truly national music might be derived from the Negro melodies or Indian chants. I was led to take the view partly by the fact that the so-called plantation-songs are indeed the most striking and appealing melodies that have been found on this side of the water, but largely by observation that this seems to be recognized, though often unconsciously, by most Americans. All races have their distinctive national songs which they at once recognize as their own, even if they have never heard them before. It is a proper question to ask, What songs, then, belong to the American and appeal more strikingly to him than any others? What melody will stop him on the street, if he were in a strange land, and make the home-feeling well up within him, no matter how hardened he might be, or how wretchedly the tunes were played? Their number, to be sure, seems to be limited. The most potent, as well as the most beautiful among them, according to my estimation, are certain of the so-called plantation-melodies and slave-songs, all of which are distinguished by unusual and subtle harmonies, the thing which I have found in no other songs but those of Scotland and Ireland.'

To the list of compositions may be added op. 112, unpublished; op. 113, a 'Festgesang' for chorus with piano four-hands; a 'Waldesruhe' for 'cello and orchestra; two symphonies, in E-flat and D minor; a 'Tragic Overture'; a 'Rhapsodie' in A minor; and a Berceuse and Capriccio for piano. [R.8]

DVORSKY, ANN. See COLLEGES, 3 (Carthage C., Ill.).

DWIGHT, JOHN SULLIVAN (May 13, 1813, Boston : Sept. 5, 1893, Boston). See article in Vol. i. 759, and note in iii. 688. He was the first strong American music-critic and his 'Journal' was a powerful force, though decidedly conservative. Among the contributors were A. W. Thayer, Otto Dresel and W. S. B. Mathews. As the latter said in his *Famous Composers, New Series,*

'"Dwight's Journal" was meant as the organ of the new movements in music, and during its earlier years was almost exclusively devoted to promoting the claims of the music of Schubert, Schumann, Chopin and Mendelssohn, and it looked somewhat coldly upon the extreme advances of Berlioz, Wagner and Liszt. . . . The great value of the 'Journal' lay in its sympathy with the modern romantic movement in music, and in translating fragments from the European writings of Wagner and the other new-comers. . . . It was a source of both light and heat. . . . The Harvard Musical Association, which began as a society of amateur lovers of good music, and later carried on chamber-concerts and finally symphony-concerts in Boston, and secured the appointment of a professor of music in Harvard, was largely Mr. Dwight's work; and the existing Boston Symphony Orchestra is a living monument to the value of the ideals he helped to bring into prominence.' [R.4]

'DWIGHT'S JOURNAL OF MUSIC.' See note in Vol. iii. 688, and article on Dwight in Vol. i. 759. Its founding was promoted by the Harvard Musical Association. In 1858–78 it was published by Oliver Ditson & Co., and in 1879–81 by Houghton, Mifflin & Co.

DWORZAK, ZDENKO VON (b. 1875). See Register, 10.

DYER, SAMUEL (1785–1835). See TUNE-BOOKS, 1817.

DYER, SUSAN H. See COLLEGES, 3 (Rollins C., Fla.).

DYHRENFURTH, JULIUS. See Register, 3.

DYKEMA, PETER WILLIAM (Nov. 25, 1873, Grand Rapids, Mich.), has been directing vocal and instrumental music since boyhood. After gaining his master's degree at the University of Michigan in 1896 he was urged at once to begin college teaching. Instead, he chose to become a high-school teacher of English and German in Aurora, Ill. After two years, for further experience, he moved down to be principal of a graded school in Indianapolis. Three years later, in the Ethical Culture School in New York, he sought to deal with still younger children, as well as students beginning college studies.

Thus he prepared for university work by knowing thoroughly the preparatory stages below. Meanwhile he had kept up musical studies, first with Stanley at Ann Arbor, later with Kelley and Cooper in Berlin and with Goetschius in New York. That every one could and should sing — the germ of the community-singing movement — he had always believed. This he applied from about 1901 with audiences at lectures under Dr. Leipziger, of the New York Board of Education. In 1913 he went to the University of Wisconsin, dividing his time between the School of Music and University Extension. The latter work was naturally called 'community-music' — perhaps the first use of the term for certain social applications of music. The primary aim was to get the people of Wisconsin to sing. But he also tried having children do song-composition in regular school work and enlisted them in performing choral works. He headed the committee that prepared the *Fifty-five Songs and Choruses for Community-Singing* (Birchard), and is identified with other similar publications. As a specialist on music for home, school and community he has written much for various journals. He is now publishing a work on *Community-Music*. [R.8]

E

EAMES, EMMA HAYDEN (Aug. 13, 1865, Shanghai, China). See article in Vol. i. 761. Her father had been a sea-captain in the East India trade, but took up law and practiced in Shanghai. Her first serious music-study in 1882 was with Miss Munger of Boston, with encouragement from Paine and Perabo. She soon became a church- and concert-singer. Her début in 'Roméo et Juliette' in 1889 was in immediate succession to Patti, who opened the season. She at once became a favorite in Paris and London. Late in 1891 she made her American début at the Metropolitan Opera House as Juliette, scoring a brilliant success, particularly as she was then and later associated with the De Reszké brothers. In 1892 she sang for a time at Madrid, but in later years limited herself almost exclusively to London and America. In England she was shown notable favor by Queen Victoria, at whose Jubilee she sang in 1897. Her répertoire included 25-30 rôles and the impressiveness of her combined qualities of voice, artistic instinct, beauty and skill in acting continued till her final year on the stage in 1908-09. Having been divorced from her first husband in 1907, in 1911 she was married a second time to the baritone Gogorza in Paris. In 1911-12 they made a joint concert-tour. Since 1914 she has lived in retirement in Bath, Me., but in 1916 sang in Portland for charity. [R.7]

EAMES, HENRY PURMORT (Sept. 12, 1872, Chicago, Ill.), spent three years at Cornell College in Iowa, and graduated from the law-school of Northwestern University. He studied piano, harmony and theory with Mathews, piano with Sherwood, Mme. Schumann, Kwast and (1908-09) Paderewski. He toured in America with Reményi in 1894-95, has appeared often as pianist in recitals and with orchestras, and concertized in France and Great Britain in 1908-11. In 1898-1908 he taught piano and lectured on theory at the University School in Lincoln, Neb. In 1911 he founded the Omaha School of Music, and in 1912 moved to Chicago, where he is head of the piano, orchestral and ensemble departments in the Cosmopolitan School of Music. In 1913-19 he was also music-director at the Illinois Wesleyan University at Bloomington, besides work at Lake Forest College. In 1906 Cornell College made him Mus.D. He was president of the Society of American Musicians in 1916-17. His unpublished works are 'The Sacred Tree of the Omahas,' a pageant-play by H. B. Alexander, for orchestra, soli and chorus, and a suite for orchestra. Incidental music to several short plays has been issued by Birchard & Co.; and also songs and short piano-works. He has written upon folk-music and the relations of the arts. [R.8]

EARHART, WILL (Apr. 1, 1871, Franklin, O.), gained his reputation as director of school- and community-music largely from work in Richmond, Ind., in 1900-12, though he had previously been supervisor in Ohio. In 1912 he came to Pittsburgh as director of music in the public schools, carrying out his progressive ideas on a larger scale. Since 1913 he has been music-director in the School of Education of the University of Pittsburgh. He stresses not only vocal music in school-courses, but also instrumental music, ensemble-playing, theory and music-appreciation, often including extensive studies of many styles and periods. In theory he emphasizes ear-training, analysis and proficiency in the use of materials. His development of ensemble-playing has called forth much popular interest, besides its direct benefit for the pupils. He has strongly advocated school-credit for music-study done outside high schools, and his plans have been widely copied. He has written *Music in the Public Schools*, 1914 (Bureau of Education, Bulletin No. 33), and (with Osbourne McConathy) *Music in Secondary Schools*, 1917 (Bureau of Education, Bulletin No. 49). He has edited *Art-Songs for High Schools*, 1910, and (with C. H. Congdon) *The Congdon Music-Primer No. 1*, *The Congdon Music-Reader No. 4*, and (with others) *The School-Credit Piano-Course*, 1918, besides many articles. He is active in the National Educational Association, the Music Supervisors' National Conference (president, 1915-16) and other societies. In 1920 he was made Mus.D. by the University of Pittsburgh. [R.8]

EASTERN MUSIC SUPERVISORS' CONFERENCE, THE, was started in 1918 as a branch of the national organization, intended mainly for New England and the Middle States. Its first meeting was held in Boston, the second in Hartford and the third in New York. The president for 1919-20 was Howard C. Davis of Yonkers, N. Y.

EASTMAN, GEORGE (July 12, 1854, Waterville, N. Y.), from about 1880 the founder and energetic promoter of the extensive photographic manufacturing business in Rochester, in 1919 announced the gift of $3,500,000 for the establishment of the Eastman School of Music in that city, to be administered under the care of the University of Rochester. In 1920 he made a further gift of $1,000,000. The permanent endowment-fund will be over $3,000,000. In addition to all the usual forms of instruction in a music-school of the highest class, it is proposed to give special attention to the combination of music with motion-picture appliances as a means of popular education. Details of the organization of the institution have not yet (1920) been announced.

EATON, LEWIS HORTON (b. 1861). See COLLEGES, 3 (Leland Stanford U., Cal.).

EBANN, WILLIAM BENEDICT (b. 1873). See Register, 8.

EBERHARD, ERNST (1839–1910). See Register, 4.

EBERSOLE, AMOS S. See COLLEGES, 3 (Goshen C., Ind.).

ECKHARD, J. See TUNE-BOOKS, 1816.

EDDY, HIRAM CLARENCE (June 23, 1851, Greenfield, Mass.). See article in Vol. i. 768. He remained as organist at the First Presbyterian Church in Chicago until 1896. His répertoire as recitalist includes practically the whole literature for the instrument. He has given over 400 recitals in Chicago alone, has played at most of the great Expositions — Philadelphia in 1876, Paris in 1879, Chicago in 1893 (21 recitals), Buffalo in 1901, St. Louis in 1904, Jamestown in 1907 and San Francisco in 1915 (40 recitals) — and has probably 'opened' more organs than any other organist. He has edited *The Church and Concert Organist*, 3 vols., 1882– , *The Organ in Church*, 1887, *Concert-Pieces for the Organ*, *Standard Compositions for the Organ*, 2 vols., and an *Organ-Method*, 2 vols. He was a founder of the A. G. O. and is an honorary member of the Accademia S. Cecilia in Rome. [R.6]

EDDY, SARA, née Hershey (b. 1852). See Register, 6.

EDSON, LEWIS (1748–1820). See TUNE-BOOKS, 1801.

EDVINA, MARIE LOUISE LUCIENNE, née Martin. See Register, 9.

EDWARDS, JOHN HARRINGTON (1834–1918). See Register, 9.

EDWARDS, JULIAN (1855–1910). See Register, 7.

'EDWIN AND ANGELINA.' A ballad opera, the text by Elihu H. Smith, M.D. (1771–1798), compiled from Goldsmith and developed into a play in 1791–93, and the music by Victor Pelissier, a horn-player in the Old American Company. It was produced in New York on Dec. 19, 1796. In composition it antedates 'The Archers' of Carr, but the latter was performed some months earlier. See Sonneck, 'Early American Operas,' *I. M. G. Sammelbde.* 6. 474–7.

EGBERT, WILLIAM GRANT (b. 1869). See Register, 7.

EGG, ARTHUR HENRY (May 6, 1891, Montreal), beginning as choir-boy in Montreal, studied organ, piano and theory for five years

with Illsley. At eighteen he was organist for a year at the church of St. John the Evangelist, and then, on the Strathcona scholarship, went to London for three years at the Royal College of Music. Here he studied organ with Parratt and Alcock, harmony and counterpoint with J. F. Bridge and Charles Wood. He was also organist at Emmanuel Church in West Hampstead. In 1913 he became a fellow of the R. C. O., and returned to Montreal to succeed W. Lynnwood Farnam as organist at Christ Church Cathedral, where he still is. He has much extended the répertoire and given special attention to annual Lenten recitals of choir- and organ-music, the programs ranging from Bach to modern composers. He teaches organ and theory at the McGill University Conservatorium and is lecturer and administrator of the Knowlton Church Choir Assembly, which has held five annual conferences. [R.9]

EICHBERG, JULIUS (June 13, 1824, Düsseldorf, Germany : Jan. 18, 1893, Boston). See article in Vol. i. 770. Among his teachers were also Eichler at Mayence, Frölich at Würzburg, Meerts and de Bériot at Brussels. Rietz introduced him to Mendelssohn, who gave him strong commendation. At Boston he was for a time music-supervisor in the public schools. Besides his operettas he wrote some chamber-music, many studies and pieces for the violin, songs and the patriotic chorus 'To thee, O Country, great and free.' His four operettas were all produced in Boston—in 1862, '65, '70, and '74 (?). 'The Doctor of Alcantara' was long a favorite. [R.4]

EISFELD, THEODOR (Apr. 11, 1816, Wolfenbüttel, Germany : Sept. 2, 1882, Wiesbaden, Germany), having studied violin with Karl Müller at Brunswick and composition with Reissiger at Dresden, in 1839–43 was director of the court-theater at Wiesbaden and then of the Concerts Viviennes at Paris. In 1848 he came to New York, where he exerted a strong artistic influence. In 1849–64 he was conductor of the Philharmonic Society (alternating more or less with Bergmann) and from 1850 of the new Harmonic Society. In 1851 he started a notable series of chamber-concerts, the first program containing Haydn's Quartet in B-flat, Mendelssohn's Trio in D minor (Dresel as pianist) and Beethoven's Quartet in F. In 1857 he was the first conductor of the Brooklyn Philharmonic Society, and in 1864–66 alternated with Thomas there. In 1866 he retired to Wiesbaden. In these later years he suffered much from the effects of having been one of the few survivors at the burning of the 'Austria' in mid-ocean in 1858. As a youth he had singing-lessons with Rossini, and was later an honorary member of the Accademia S. Cecilia in Rome. [R.4]

‡ ELGAR, EDWARD (June 2 1857, Broadheath, England). See articles in Vols. i. 772–4, and v. 635. Yale University gave him the degree of Mus.D. in 1905. The list of works should be extended as follows:

op. 52 Part-Songs, 'A Christmas Greeting,' for mixed voices.
   53 Four Part-Songs.
   54 Part-Song, 'Reveille,' for men's voices.
   55 Symphony No. 1, in A-flat (1908, Manchester).
56–57 Part-Songs, 'Angelus' and 'Go, song of mine.'
   58 'Elegy,' for string-orchestra
59–60 Six Songs and Two Songs.
   61 Concerto in B minor, for violin (1910).
   62 Romance for bassoon and orchestra.
   63 Symphony No. 2, in E-flat (1911).
64–65 Coronation Offertorium and March (1911).
   66 Masque, 'The Crown of India' (1912).
   67 Psalm 48, 'Great is the Lord.'
   68 Symphonic Study, 'Falstaff' (1913).
   69 Ode, 'The Music-Makers,' for contralto, chorus, and orchestra (1912, Birmingham).
   70 Adagio, 'Sospiri,' for strings, harp and organ.
71–73 Choral Songs — 'The Shower,' 'The Fountain,' 'Death on the Hills,' 'Love's Tempest,' 'Serenade.'
   74 Anthem, 'Give unto the Lord.'
   75 'The Carillon,' recitation with orchestra (1914).
   76 Symphonic Poem, 'Polonia' (1915).
   77 'Une Voix dans le Désert,' recitation with music.
   78 Suite, 'The Starlight Express,' for piano (1915).
   79 'The Belgian Flag,' recitation with music.
   80 Choruses, 'The Spirit of England' — 'To Women,' 'For the Fallen' (1916).
   82 Sonata for violin and piano (1919).
   83 Quartet for strings (1919).
   84 Quintet in A minor, for piano and strings.

See critical studies by R. J. Buckley, 1904, Newman, 1906, and Streatfeild, 1912, and article by D. G. Mason in 'The Musical Quarterly,' April, 1917.

ELGAR CHOIR, THE, of Hamilton, Ont., was organized in 1904 and gave its first concert in 1905. Its conductor from the first has been Bruce A. Carey, whose ability has given the Choir an enviable reputation for perfection of choral style. The membership is selected afresh each season with reference to quality and balance, the numbers varying usually from 100 to 150 or occasionally more. In 1911 and 1918 the work of the Choir was suspended. As a rule there are two annual concerts, and performances have been given in Toronto, Brantford, Detroit and Buffalo, making a total to 1918 of 25 concerts. When the projected Memorial Hall is built the Choir will have a permanent headquarters, and will then undertake an annual festival on a large scale. The main purpose is to promote a

cappella singing, but oratorios and other concerted works are occasionally given. In larger performances the Choir has had the assistance of the Toronto and Pittsburgh Symphony Orchestras and the Buffalo Orchestral Club. Besides its fine record in general interpretation, the Choir has to its credit the first performance in Canada of Verdi's Requiem (1909), and the first in Canada of Verdi's 'Laudi alla Vergine Maria' (1913), Lucas' 'Battle Ode' and 'Mariners of England,' and Dett's 'O Holy Lord' and 'Weeping Mary' — the last three being dedicated to it.

ELMAN, MISCHA (Jan. 20, 1892, Talnoe, Russia). See article in Vol. v. 635. His first appearance in New York was with the Russian Symphony Orchestra on Dec. 10, 1908, playing the Tchaikovsky concerto, followed a week later by a recital. Since then he has made annual tours and has been heard in all the large cities. He has made transcriptions for violin and piano of many classic compositions. [R.9]

ELSENHEIMER, NICHOLAS J. (b. 1866). See Register, 8.

ELSHUCO TRIO, THE, formed in 1918, consisted of Samuel Gardner, violin, Willem Willeke, 'cello, and Richard Epstein, piano. It was broken up by the death of Epstein in 1919.

ELSON, ARTHUR B. (Nov. 18, 1873, Boston), is the son and pupil of Louis C. Elson (see below). In 1895 he graduated from Harvard and in 1897 from the Massachusetts Institute of Technology. He has taught technical subjects in school and college, composed a string-quartet and several songs, and written a notable series of books, including A Critical History of Opera, 1901, Orchestral Instruments and their Use, 1902, Woman's Work in Music, 1903, Modern Composers of Europe, 1904, Music-Club Programs from all Nations, 1906, The Musician's Guide (chief contributor and editor), 1912, The Book of Musical Knowledge, 1914, A Pioneer School-Music Course, 1916, and A History of Vocal Music, 1918. He has also written many periodical articles and criticisms. [R.8]

ELSON, LOUIS CHARLES (April 17, 1848, Boston: Feb. 14, 1920, Boston), was long prominent as lecturer, teacher and writer on musical subjects. His first studies were with his mother, Hamann (piano) and Kreissmann (voice). In Leipzig he studied composition with Carl Gloggner-Castelli. He composed in smaller forms, songs, operettas and piano-works, but his chief interests were literary. From 1882 he was head of the theory-department of the New England Conservatory. He lectured at many leading universities and colleges, including Harvard, Yale, Vassar, Tulane, Cornell, Pennsylvania, Brown (15 lectures), and at the Lowell Institute (18 lectures) and the Drexel Institute. For seven years he lectured on music for the city of Boston, giving some 240 lectures with orchestra and singers to interest the masses. In 1880 his literary work began with 'Vox Humana,' a journal devoted to organ-music, and he became also music-critic for the 'Courier,' and editor of 'The Musical Herald.' From 1888 he was critic for the 'Daily Advertiser.' He was also correspondent and contributor to the 'Transcript,' 'Music and Drama,' 'The Musical Courier,' the New York 'Tribune' and 'Evening Post,' 'The Atlantic Monthly,' 'The Quarterly Review,' 'The Etude,' 'The Musician,' 'La Revue Musicale,' 'Die Musik' (till 1914), 'Correo Musical' (Buenos Aires), 'The Musical Quarterly,' etc. He published *Curiosities of Music*, 1883, *German Songs and Song-Writers*, 1884, *History of German Song*, 1886, *The Theory of Music*, 1890, *The Realm of Music*, 1892, *National Music of America and its Sources*, 1899, *European Reminiscences*, 1893, *Great Composers*, 1897, *Shakespeare in Music*, 1900 (republished in London), *Folk-Songs of Many Nations*, 1905, *A History of American Music*, 1904 (revised edition, 1915), *Music Dictionary*, 1906, *Pocket Music Dictionary*, 1907, *Syllabus of Musical History Lectures*, 1896, *Mistakes and Disputed Points of Music*, 1910, *Woman in Music*, 1917 and *Children in Music*. He was editor-in-chief of the *University Encyclopedia of Music*, 10 vols., 1912, and of *Modern Music and Musicians*, 20 vols., and was also connected editorially with *Famous Composers and their Works*, besides contributing to the *Standard Encyclopedia* and the *Encyclopedia Americana*. The range of his interest, his geniality of spirit and a lucid and facile style combined to make him widely effective in upbuilding an intelligent knowledge of music. [R.6]

EMERICK, ALBERT G. (1817 – ?). See Register, 4.

EMERSON, LUTHER ORLANDO (1820–1915). See Register, 4, and TUNE-BOOKS, 1853.

EMERY, STEPHEN ALBERT (Oct. 4, 1841, Paris, Me. : Apr. 15, 1891, Boston), after early training under H. S. Edwards in Portland, went to Leipzig in 1862 and studied with Plaidy, Papperitz, Richter and Hauptmann, then at Dresden with Spindler. Returning in 1864, he first located in Portland, but soon went to Boston, becoming teacher of piano and harmony at the New England Conservatory at its opening in 1867. Later he was also professor of theory and composition at Boston University. He was for a time assistant-editor of 'The Musical Herald.' At the Conservatory he remained till his death. An excellent teacher, he

numbered among his pupils many who later became important in various parts of the country. His published compositions number about 150 — songs, piano-pieces, part-songs, etc. His *Foundation-Studies in Pianoforte-Playing* (written for his own children) and his *Elements of Harmony*, 1880, have been widely used. [R.5]

EMMETT, DANIEL DECATUR (1818, Mt. Vernon, O. : June 27, 1904, Mt. Vernon), after working in a printer's shop and serving for a time in the army, from 1835 was in a circus-troupe. In 1843, with Brown, Whitlock and Pelham, he formed the first 'negro minstrel' troupe, the Virginia Minstrels, which began its highly successful career in New York and started a series of such companies. In 1858–65 he was associated with Dan Bryant in New York, writing the famous song 'Dixie' in 1859. In 1865–78 he continued with his own company. Others of his songs were 'Old Dan Tucker,' 'The Road to Richmond,' 'Walk Along, John,' etc. [R.4]

ENDE, AMELIA VON (b. 1856). See Register, 6.

ENDE, HERWEGH VON (1877–1919). See Register, 8.

ENGWERSON, OTTO. See COLLEGES, 3 (Denison U., Ohio).

‡ ENNA, AUGUST (May 13, 1860, Nakskov, Denmark). See article in Vol. i. 783. To the list of works add the operas 'Die Feen' (1893, Berlin); 'Das Streichholzmädel' and 'Lamia' (1897, Berlin); 'Ung Elskov' (1902, Berlin); 'Nattergalen' (1912, Berlin); 'Gloria Arsena' (1913, Berlin); and 'Komödianten' (1916); the ballets 'The Shepherdess and the Chimney-Sweep' (1901, Copenhagen) and 'St. Cecilia's Golden Shoe' (1904, Copenhagen); two symphonies, in D minor and C minor; 'Mutterliebe,' for chorus and orchestra; 'Märchen,' symphonic tone-pictures; a 'Festival Overture'; piano-pieces and songs.

ENNA, EMIL (b. 1877). See Register, 8.

ENSTONE, EDWARD. See Register, 1.

EPSTEIN, ABRAHAM ISAAC (b. 1857) and MARCUS ISAAC (b. 1855). See Register, 7.

EPSTEIN, RICHARD (1869–1919). See Register, 10.

ERB, JOHN LAWRENCE (Feb. 5, 1877, Berks Co., Pa.), went to school in Pottstown, Pa., where he was organist in 1892–94. For five years he studied at the Metropolitan College of Music and the Virgil Clavier School in New York. After ten years' teaching in New York and serving as organist at the Broome Street Tabernacle and the Second Unitarian Church in Brooklyn, he went to Wooster, O., where he was music-director at Wooster University and organist of the Westminster Presbyterian Church. In 1913–14 he was organist at the Fourth Presbyterian Church in Chicago. In 1914 he became director of the School of Music and organist at the University of Illinois in Urbana. Since 1915 he has also been state inspector of music-schools for Illinois. He has written organ- and piano-music, many songs, choruses and anthems. He has also published *Johannes Brahms, A Biography*, 1904, *Hymns and Church Music*, 1910, *Elements of Harmony*, 1911, and *Elementary Theory*, 1911, besides many contributions to magazines. He has been prominently identified with musical and educational organizations, and is in demand as a speaker. For two years he was vice-president of the Ohio Music Teachers' Association, and in 1913–15 secretary and in 1915–17 president of the M. T. N. A. He is a fellow of the A. G. O. and in 1916–17 was president of the Illinois Council of the N. A. O. He is now president of the Illinois Federation of Music Clubs, and a member of many committees for the promotion of music throughout the country. His energetic and clear-headed activities in these directions are prompted by high ideals regarding music-education for the masses. [R.8]

ERBEN, PETER (1769–1861). See TUNE-BOOKS, 1806.

‡ ERLANGER, CAMILLE (May 25, 1863, Paris : Apr. 24, 1919, Paris). See article in Vol. i. 789. Recent works are the operas 'Aphrodite' (1906, Paris), 'Bacchus Triomphant' (1909, Bordeaux), 'L'Aube Rouge' (1911, Rouen), 'La Sorcière' (1912, Paris) and 'Le Barbier de Deauville' (1917) ; incidental music to André-Legrand's 'La Reine Wanda' (1918, Paris) ; the symphonic piece 'La Chasse Fantastique'; the symphonic poem 'Maître et Serviteur' (after Tolstoi) ; a Requiem for double chorus and orchestra; piano-pieces and songs.

‡ ERLANGER, FRÉDÉRIC D' (May 29, 1868, Paris). See article in Vol. i. 789. To the list of works add the operas 'Tess' (1906, Naples) and 'Noël' (1912, Paris, 1913, Chicago). His pen-name is 'Frédéric Regnal.'

ERRANI, ACHILLE (1823–1897). See Register, 5.

ESCHMANN, KARL HENRY (b. 1891). See COLLEGES, 3 (Denison U., Ohio).

ESTEY, JACOB (1814–1890). See Register, 5.

ESTEY ORGAN COMPANY, THE, of Brattleboro, Vt., was started in 1846 by Jacob Estey. The present heads of the business are J. Gray Estey and J. Harry Estey of the third generation. The firm suffered from fire in 1857 and 1864 and from flood in 1869, but its progress was not checked. In somewhat over thirty years its sales increased from $2700 annually to over a million.

'ETUDE, THE.' See note in Vol. iii. 688. The first editor was Theodore Presser, its founder, assisted after a time by Charles W. Landon, in 1888–93 Eugene E. Ayres, in 1893–96 Arthur L. Manchester, in 1897–1907 W. J. Baltzell, and since 1907 James Francis Cooke. It is published monthly and the average edition is 200,000 copies.

EUTERPEAN SOCIETY, THE, of New York, was an amateur orchestral club, probably started in 1800, which continued to give at least one annual concert until 1847, perhaps longer. It accumulated a small library and some valuable instruments. See note in Sonneck, *Concert-Life*, pp. 203–4.

'EUTERPEIAD, THE,' was a musical periodical started in Boston in 1820. Another journal of the same name was published in New York in 1830–31.

EVANS, EDWIN (b. 1876). See Register, 9.

EVANS, FREDERICK VANCE (b. 1883). See Register, 9, and COLLEGES, 3 (Lawrence C., Wis.).

EVANS, J. See TUNE-BOOKS, 1807.

EVERETT, ASA BROOKS (1828–1875) and EVERETT, L. C. (1818–1867). See Register, 4.

‡ EXPERT, HENRI (May 12, 1863, Bordeaux, France). See article in Vol. i. 797. To the list of his books add *Les maîtres du clavecin des XVIIe et XVIIIe siècles; Amusements des musiciens français du XVIIIe siècle; Répertoire de musique réligieuse et spirituelle.* In 1909 he became deputy-librarian of the Paris Conservatory. He wrote the chapter on 16th-century French music in Lavignac's *Encyclopédie de la Musique* (1913-).

EYER, J. F. See TUNE-BOOKS, 1818.

EZERMAN, D. HENDRIK (b. 1880). See Register, 9.

F

FABRI, LUDWIG SCHMITT (b. 1874).
See Register, 9.

FAELTEN, CARL (Dec. 21, 1846, Ilmenau,
Germany), had some early lessons from
Montag, a pupil of Hummel, in Weimar,
and for years supported himself by casual
playing of violin and clarinet in orchestras.
From 1868 he studied piano and theory with
Schoch at Frankfort, but in 1870-71 was
forced to serve in the Franco-Prussian War.
After 1874 he appeared successfully as pianist
in several cities. From 1877 he taught in
the Hoch Conservatory at Frankfort under
Raff, after the latter's death in 1882 migrating
to America. Three years were spent teaching
at the Peabody Conservatory in Baltimore,
followed by twelve at the New England
Conservatory in Boston, where in 1890-97
he was director. He then established his
own Pianoforte School, which he has developed
in conjunction with his brother, Reinhold
Faelten (b. 1856, Germany), with marked
success (see below). Besides often appearing
as recitalist, he has drafted a series of instruction-books for piano-students. In the
preparation of this 'Faelten System' the two
brothers have collaborated. [R.7]

FAELTEN PIANOFORTE SCHOOL,
THE, of Boston, was founded in 1897 by Carl
and Reinhold Faelten, the former being
director. Although emphasizing piano-study,
its policy has been to magnify general musicianship at all stages of progress. About four-
fifths of the students are in the preparatory
department, and only those of marked ability
are encouraged to take advanced work. A
large part of the instruction is in classes,
conducted along somewhat original lines.
The faculty numbers twelve, and the students
nearly 700. The total enrolment has been
about 6000, with about 200 graduates. The
School is located at 30 Huntington Avenue.

FAIRCHILD, BLAIR (June 23, 1877,
Belmont, Mass.), came of musical stock and
while studying at Harvard took courses with
Paine and Spalding, continuing later with
Buonamici at Florence. For a time he was
pressed to enter business and in 1901-03 was
in diplomatic service, as attaché first at
Constantinople and then at Teheran. Since
1903 he has lived in Paris as student under
Widor and Ganaye and abundant composer.
Throughout the World War he was active in
relief-work. His works, many of them embodying impressions or material derived
from his sojourn in the Orient, include the
following :

'East and West,' op. 17, a poem in one movement,
for orchestra — also for piano, 4-hands (Durdilly).

Symphonic Poem, 'Zàl,' op. 38, after a Persian
legend (1918, Paris).
Symphonic Poem, 'Shah Féridoun,' op. 39, after
a Persian legend (Augener).
'Legende,' op. 31, for violin and orchestra — also
with piano (Demets).
'Tamineh,' sketch for orchestra, after a Persian
legend (Augener).
'Étude Symphonique,' op. 45, for violin and
orchestra.
'Dame Libellule,' op. 44, ballet-pantomime in
one act.
Arrangement of Schumann's Adagio and Allegro
(op. 70), for 'cello and orchestra.
Two Novelettes, op. 10, for string-quartet — also
for piano-trio or 'cello and piano (Durdilly).
Three Pieces, op. 11, for 'cello and piano or or-
chestra (Thompson).
Three Pieces, op. 12, for clarinet and piano or
orchestra (Pitault).
Sonata, op. 16, for violin and piano (Durdilly).
Quintet, op. 20, for piano and strings (Durdilly).
Rhapsody, op. 21, for piano and strings (Durdilly).
Trio, op. 24, for piano, violin and 'cello (Augener).
Concerto, op. 26, for violin, piano and strings —
also for violin and piano (Augener).
Quartet, op. 27, for strings (Demets).
Two Duos, op. 32, for violin and 'cello (Augener).
Six 'Esquisses,' op. 36, for violin and piano
(Augener).
Sonata, op. 43, for violin and piano (Durand).
'Mélodie' for violin and piano (Sénart).
Two 'Garden Sketches,' op. 18, for piano
(Durdilly).
Two Fugues for organ (Sénart).
Six Psalms, op. 33, for soli and chorus a cappella
(Augener).
Two 'Bible Lyrics,' op. 29, for soprano, chorus
and orchestra (Gray).
'In Memoriam,' for chorus a cappella (Thompson).
Requiem, for tenor and men's chorus, with piano
or organ (Thompson).
Six series of 'Stornelli Toscani,' opp. 5, 14, 23, 28,
30 (the last not yet out), settings of Tuscan
folk-poems (Thompson).
Twelve Persian Folk-Songs (Novello).
'A Baghdad Lover,' op. 25, cycle of nine songs for
baritone (Gray).
Five 'Greek Sea-Prayers,' op. 35 (Augener).
'Les Amours de Hafiz,' op. 38, seven songs
(Augener).
'Les Quatrains d'Al-Ghazali,' op. 40, eight songs in
French (Augener).
Several separate songs, some with orchestra.

He was made Chevalier of the Légion d'Honneur in 1919. [R.9]

FAIRCLOUGH, GEORGE HERBERT
(b. 1869). See Register, 7.

FAIRCLOUGH, WILLIAM ERVING (b.
1859). See Register, 7.

FAIRLAMB, JAMES REMINGTON (1838-
1908). See Register, 4.

'FAIRYLAND.' An opera, op. 77, by
Horatio Parker, the text by Brian Hooker.
In 1914 it won the prize of $10,000 offered by
the National Federation of Women's Clubs,
and was first produced at Los Angeles on
July 1, 1915.

FALK, LOUIS (b. 1848). See Register, 5.

200

FALLBERG, CARL (b. 1886). See COL-
LEGES, 2 (Sullins C., Va.).

'FALL OF UG, THE.' A 'masque of fear'
by Herman Perlet, to a text by Rufus Steele,
produced as No. 11 of the 'Grove-Plays' of
the Bohemian Club in California in 1913.
The scene is laid 'in a redwood forest in the
days when men fought with spears.'

FANCIULLI, FRANCESCO (1853–1915).
See Register, 6.

‡ FARJEON, HARRY (May 6, 1878, Ho-
hokus, N. J.). See article in Vol. v. 639.
His father was the English novelist B. L.
Farjeon, so that he has always been a British
subject, but his mother was the daughter of
Joseph Jefferson, the actor. The score of his
'Summer Vision' was lost when sent to
Germany for performance. Recent publi-
cations include Variations in A, for piano
(Augener), 'Peter Pan Sketches,' for piano
(Newman), 'Moorish Idylls,' for piano (Ashdown), an Air upon a Ground-Bass, and the
singing-game 'Proud Princesses'; besides the
following not actually out — Sonata in E, for
piano (Ashdown) and 'The Ballet of the
Trees' (1915) (Rogers). Unpublished are a
String-Quartet in B-flat, a 'Poem' for violins,
violas and orchestra, a Sonata in D, for 'cello,
'The Ballet of the Lake,' the ballet 'Terp-
sichore,' Variations on a Russian Air, for
piano, a Fugue for piano 4-hands, and the song-
cycle 'The Shepherds' Garland.'

FARNAM, W. LYNNWOOD (Jan. 13,
1885, Sutton, Que.), had early piano-lessons
from his mother, Miss M. L. Jackson and
G. W. Cornish, and in 1900–04 held the
Strathcona Scholarship at the Royal College
of Music in London, his teachers there being
Taylor and Sharpe for piano and Higgs,
Sewell and Hoyte for organ. In 1903 he
became A. R. C. M. and in 1904 A. R. C. O.
Returning to Montreal, in 1904–05 he was or-
ganist at St. James' (M. E.), in 1905–08 at St.
James the Apostle's, and in 1908–13 at Christ
Church Cathedral. In 1913–18 he was at
Emmanuel Church in Boston, and, after a
year in the Canadian army, in 1919–20 at the
Fifth Avenue Presbyterian Church in New
York, and is now at the Church of the Holy
Communion. [R.9]

FARNSWORTH, CHARLES HUBERT
(Nov. 29, 1859, Cesarea, Turkey), was the son
of missionary parents, had a general education
at Robert College in Constantinople, and
studied music in Boston and Worcester.
From 1876 he was organist and teacher at
Worcester. In 1888 he became the first
music-teacher in the University of Colorado
at Boulder, where he also taught in the public
schools and conducted choral and orchestral
societies. In 1900 he came to New York,
becoming in 1901 head of the department of

music and speech in Teachers College at
Columbia University, which he has strongly
developed. Popular education in music has
been his main object, and he has specialized
in the systematic treatment of public-school
music and in musical appreciation. He is
author of *Education through Music*, 1909, *How
to Produce and Listen to Music*, *The Teaching
of Elementary Music*, co-author of *Tonal
Phrase-Book*, editor of *Songs for Schools*,
1907, *Grammar-School Songs*, 1916, and co-
editor of *Folk-Songs*, 1916, *Chanteys and Singing-Games*, and *The Children's Hymnal*. He
has written articles on music-teaching in several
recent educational works in the *M. T. N. A.
Proceedings* and in various periodicals. In
1911–12 he was president of the New York
Clef Club and in 1913–14 of the M. T. N. A.
[R.6]

FARRAR, GERALDINE (Feb. 28, 1882,
Melrose, Mass.), began singing-lessons at
twelve with Mrs. J. H. Long of Boston, and
at thirteen sang in concert in Boston. She
studied in New York and Washington, in
Paris with Trabadello and in Berlin with
Graziani and Lilli Lehmann. In 1901 she
made her début as Marguerite in 'Faust'
at the Berlin Royal Opera House. Her success led to her being retained for three years,
with repeated renewals, and to engagements
at Stockholm, Warsaw, Munich, the Opéra-
Comique in Paris, and Monte Carlo. Her
American début was at the Metropolitan
Opera House in November, 1906, as Juliet in
'Roméo et Juliette.' Her repertory includes
the parts of Marguerite (in 'Faust,' 'Mefistofele,' and 'La Damnation de Faust'), Manon,
Micaëla, Carmen, Mignon, Elizabeth, Tosca,
Zerlina and Elvira, Juliet, Gilda, Violetta,
Thaïs, Angela (in 'Le Domino Noir'), Charlotte (in 'Werther'), Susanna and Cherubino (in 'Figaro'), Mimi, Madama Butterfly,
Desdemona, Elsa and Eva. She was the
first to sing the principal rôles in Mascagni's
'L'Amico Fritz' (1905), Camondo's 'The
Clown' (1905), Saint-Saëns' 'L'Ancêtre' (1906),
and Humperdinck's 'Königskinder' (1910). She
married the actor Lou Tellegen [Von Dom-
melen] in 1916. Highly gifted as an actress
as well as singer, she has also been successful
in film-productions, beginning with 'Carmen'
in 1915. Her autobiography was published
in 1916. [R.9]

FARWELL, ARTHUR (Apr. 23, 1872,
St. Paul), began his education at Baldwin
Seminary in St. Paul, and graduated from the
Massachusetts Institute of Technology in
1893, having specialized in electrical engineering. He turned to music and for six years
was a pupil of Norris in Boston, of Humperdinck in Berlin and of Guilmant in Paris.
He lectured on music at Cornell University in

1899–1901. He then established at Newton Center, Mass., the 'Wa-Wan Press' for the publication of music by Americans, and particularly those whose works 'were based on the melodies and folk-lore of the American Indians.' In 1903 he made investigations among the Indians in the Far West, and prepared a report on Indian Songs and Spanish-Californian Folk-songs for the American Institute of Archæology. In 1905 he founded the American Music Society, of which he is president. In 1909–15 he was on the editorial staff of 'Musical America,' in 1910–13 supervisor of municipal concerts in New York, in 1915–18 director of the Music School Settlement there, and in 1918–19 acting professor of music at the University of California. He has for years been deeply interested in community-music.

As composer he is best known by works based upon Indian themes, such as the 'Cornell' Overture, op. 9; *American Indian Melodies* for piano; the orchestral pieces 'Dawn,' 'Ichibuzzh' and 'The Domain of the Hurakan'; the Symbolistic Studies, for piano, opp. 16, 17, 18 and 24; 'Impressions of the Wa-Wan Ceremony,' op. 21; and the 'Navajo War-Dance,' op. 29. He wrote music for the Meriden, N. H., and Darien, Conn., pageants of 1913, for Mackaye's 'Caliban by the Yellow Sands,' a masque for the Shakespeare Tercentenary in New York in 1916, and for the community-masque 'The Evergreen Tree,' as well as incidental music for Parker's 'Joseph and his Brethren' and Sheldon's 'Garden of Paradise' (1913, New York). He has also a tone-poem, op. 34, for voice and orchestra, with words from Sterling's 'Duandon'; the song 'A Ruined Garden,' op. 14, with orchestra or piano; a setting of Whitman's 'Captain, my Captain' for chorus and orchestra; other choruses and many songs. He has written and lectured extensively and earnestly on behalf of American music. He edited *Music in America*, Vol. iv. of *The Art of Music*, 1915. [R.8]

‡ FAURÉ, GABRIEL URBAN (May 13, 1845, Pamiers, France). See article in Vol. ii. 15. In 1909 he was elected to the Académie and in 1910 was made commander of the Légion d'Honneur. In 1919 he retired as director of the Conservatory, Rabaud returning from America to take his place. Concerts of his music have been given in recent years at Paris and elsewhere, with growing appreciation of the scope and variety of his compositions. Among later works are the opera 'Pénélope' (1913, Paris), incidental music to Clemenceau's 'Le Voile du Bonheur,' and a piano-quintet in D minor. See biography by Vuillemin, 1914.

FAY, AMY (b. 1844). See Register, 6.

FAY, CHARLES NORMAN (b. 1848). See Register, 8.

FAY, MAUDE (b. 1883). See Register, 9.

'FEAST OF TABERNACLES, THE.' An oratorio or cantata by Charles Zeuner, published in 1832 and sung by the chorus of the Boston Academy in 1838.

FEDERLEIN, GOTTFRIED HEINRICH (b. 1883). See Register, 9.

FEDERLEIN, GOTTLIEB HEINRICH (b. 1835). See Register, 7.

FERRARI–FONTANA, EDOARDO (b. 1878). See Register, 10.

FERRATA, GIUSEPPE (Jan. 1, 1865, Gradioli, Italy), at fourteen won a scholarship at the Accademia S. Cecilia in Rome, studied under Sgambati, Terziani and Leonardi, and graduated in 1885, with a prize that secured him some instruction from Liszt. Until 1890 he gave piano-recitals in Italy. In 1892 he came to America and has been music-director in several schools and colleges. He is now head of the piano-department and professor of composition and instrumentation at Newcomb College in New Orleans. He was knighted by the King of Portugal in 1887 and twice later by the King of Italy, who in 1914 made him Commandatore in the Order of the Crown. His works include

Concerto, op. 5, for piano and orchestra.
Symphony in three movements, op. 40, for orchestra and chorus.
Quartet, op. 28, for strings (J. Fischer).
Two other string-quartets.
12 'Italian Spring Melodies,' op. 7, for violin and piano (Fischer).
'Méditation Religieuse,' op. 10, no. 1, for violin and piano (Fischer).
'Cortége Nuptial,' op. 20, no. 1, for violin and piano (Fischer).
Suite, op. 31, for violin and piano (Fischer).
Modern Suite for organ, and several other organ-works.
'Valse,' op. 24, for piano (Fischer).
'Romance sans Paroles' and 'Valse de Concert,' op. 25 (Schirmer).
'Toccata Chromatique,' op. 28, for piano (prize-composition, Art Publ. Soc.).
Messe Solenelle, op. 15, for soli, chorus and organ or orchestra (Fischer).
Missa in G, op. 18, for men's chorus and organ (Fischer).
Requiem Mass for mixed chorus.
'Tota pulchra est Maria,' op. 16, for mixed or women's chorus and organ (Fischer).
'Dies Irae,' op. 35, for chorus in eight real parts.
Cycle of 'Folk-Songs from the Spanish,' op. 8, for mixed quartet (Fischer).
Many piano-pieces (Fischer, Ricordi, Church), and several songs (Fischer, Schirmer, Ricordi).
Three dramatic operas in manuscript.

In 1908 four of the above works were awarded first prizes in a competition arranged by the Art Society of Pittsburgh. [R.8]

FESTIVALS, MUSICAL. Some notes are given in the Introduction (pp. 35–6) as to the genesis of the 'festival' idea. The first

experiments came before the Civil War — by
the Handel and Haydn Society of Boston in
1857 and at Worcester in 1858, though neither
of these series became established till the next
decade. Analogous undertakings in New England that have persisted are those held in
Maine (at Portland or Bangor) since 1897 and
at Springfield, Mass., since 1903. At numerous
points in other States where there are energetic
choral societies similar enterprises are in
operation. The May Festivals held biennially
at Cincinnati since 1873 long stood in a class
somewhat by themselves, though sporadically
imitated in other places. In Cincinnati and
also in Chicago operatic festivals were for a
time maintained. Since 1902 the Bohemian
Club of California has given a remarkable
series of 'Grove-Plays.' The Bethlehem Bach
Festivals in Pennsylvania were begun in 1900
(intermitted in 1905–11, when similar efforts
were made by Dr. Wolle at Berkeley, Cal.).
The Norfolk Festivals in Connecticut were
established on a broad scale in 1906. The
unique Peterboro Festivals in New Hampshire followed in 1910, the [Lockport (N. Y.)
Festivals in 1916, and the Berkshire Festivals
in Massachusetts in 1917. Several leading
educational institutions have become noted
for the significance of their annual musical
undertakings, especially the University of
Michigan since 1893, Northwestern University
in Illinois and Cornell University in New
York since 1909, with a host of others of less
importance in the South and West. Several
of the great Expositions have maintained
musical features that assumed a festival
quality, notably the Columbian at Chicago
in 1893 and the Panama-Pacific at San
Francisco in 1915. Various national groups
have held annual gatherings of a festival
character. The German singing-societies
started this custom in some form as early as
1850. Two of the comprehensive Sänger-
bunds have been continuously active since
1881 and 1892 respectively. Competitions
of Welsh societies have long been common.
Norwegian and Swedish festivals have occurred
since before 1910. All these latter tend to move
somewhat from place to place. The National
Federation of Musical Clubs has not only held
a national festival biennially since about 1900,
but is continually promoting smaller enterprises. The custom of holding local and
historical 'pageants' has spread widely since
about 1910, often leading to complex undertakings of decided significance.

FICHTHORN, CLAUDE L. See Colleges, 3 (Missouri Valley C.).

FIEDLER, AUGUST MAX (b. 1859).
See Register, 9.

FILLMORE, AUGUSTUS D. (1823– ?).
See Tune-Books, 1849.

FILLMORE, JOHN COMFORT (Feb. 4,
1843, Franklin, Conn. : Aug. 15, 1898,
Franklin), in 1862–65 studied at Oberlin
College, having some organ-lessons with G.
W. Steele. He then went to Leipzig, coming
under Papperitz, Richter and Hauptmann.
In 1867–68 he was director of the music-
department at Oberlin, in 1868–78 professor
of music at Ripon College in Wisconsin, and
in 1878–84 in a similar position at the Milwaukee College for Women. He founded the
Milwaukee School of Music in 1884, and was
its director until 1895, when he became
director at Pomona College in California.
A musical enthusiast, he influenced a wide
circle of pupils. He was one of the earliest
students of Indian music, and, with Miss
Fletcher and La Flesche, published *A Study
of Omaha Indian Music*, 1893, and many
magazine articles. His other books are *History of Pianoforte-Music*, 1883, *New Lessons
in Harmony*, 1887, *Lessons in Musical History*,
1888, *On the Value of Certain Modern Theories*
(von Oettingen's and Riemann's), and translations of Riemann's *Klavierschule* and *Natur
der Harmonik*, besides a long list of articles
and addresses. [R.5]

FINCK, HENRY THEOPHILUS (Sept.
22, 1854, Bethel, Mo.), spent his youth at
Aurora, Ore., whither his parents removed
to escape the turmoil of the Civil War. In
1876 he graduated from Harvard with highest
honors in philosophy and a fellowship. While
in college he took courses under Paine, though
specializing in psychology and æsthetics rather
than music. He attended the first festival
at Bayreuth in 1876 and spent the following
winter in Munich, devoting himself to Wagner-
ism. In 1878–81 he studied psychology at
Berlin, Heidelberg and Vienna, but also
wrote frequently for the New York 'Nation'
and 'World' and for the 'Atlantic Monthly'
on Darwinism, Schopenhauer and other subjects, including music. In 1881, when the
'Nation' and the 'Evening Post' were merged
under Schurz, Godkin and White, he became
a member of the staff (and has so continued
ever since), developing many critical views
about music and musicians that were then
novel. He has especially emphasized the
value of Wagner, Schumann, Chopin, Liszt,
Grieg, Tchaikovsky, Dvořák, MacDowell
and many others with enthusiastic acumen.
His literary skill has enabled him to present
facts and opinions so as to command the
interest of many readers and challenge re-
spectful attention. Since 1890 he has lectured
on music-history at the National Conservatory,
where he was associated with Dvořák and
Joseffy. In 1890 he married Abbie H. Cush-
man, a pupil of Joseffy, who has not only
shared his literary work, but herself written

on Paderewski and Rénaud in the 'Century Magazine' and is preparing a volume of musical and literary reminiscences.

His musical publications include *Chopin and Other Musical Essays*, 1889, *Wagner and his Works*, 2 vols., 1893 (in German, 1897), *Pictorial Wagner*, 1899, *Anton Seidl*, 1899, *Songs and Song-Writers*, 1900, *Grieg and his Music*, 1909 (1st ed. revised by Grieg and 2nd with letters from him to the author), *Success in Music*, 1909 (largely a record of personal relations with musicians), *Massenet and his Operas*, 1910 (partly based on matter supplied by the composer), *Richard Strauss*, 1917, and the following edited collections: *Fifty Master-Songs*, 1902, *Fifty Schubert Songs*, 1903, *Fifty Grieg Songs*, 1909, *One Hundred Songs by Ten Composers*, 1917. In the field of psychological æsthetics he has written *Romantic Love and Personal Beauty*, 1887, *Primitive Love and Love-Stories*, 1899, and *Food and Flavor*, 1913. Observations as a traveler are embodied in *The Pacific Coast Scenic Tour*, 1890, *Spain and Morocco*, 1891, and *Lotos-Time in Japan*, 1898. Aside from his championship of musicians and musical movements not at first appreciated, he considers his studies regarding the primitive love-impulse and the neglected sense of smell his most original work. [R.7]

FIQUÉ, KARL (b. 1867). See Register, 7.

FIRTH, JOHN (1789–1864). See Register, 3.

FISCHER, CARLO (b. 1872). See Register, 8.

FISCHER, EMIL (June 13, 1838, Brunswick, Germany : Aug. 11, 1914, Hamburg, Germany), was the son of parents who were good singers. He was first trained as player of the violin and horn. At eighteen he took up vocal study with his father, and in 1857 made his début at Graz as the Seneschal in Boieldieu's 'Jean de Paris.' He then sang in Pressburg, Stettin and Brunswick, directed the opera at Danzig in 1863–70, and sang at the Royal Opera in Rotterdam in 1875–80 and at the Dresden Court Opera in 1880–85. In 1885 he came to the Metropolitan Opera House in New York, singing during the first season directed by Seidl. Till 1891 and more or less till his retirement in 1898 he remained associated with the Metropolitan, extremely popular both as man and as artist. During his career he sang in 101 operas, and appeared 839 times in America. He continued in New York as teacher to the end of his life, spending the summers in Germany. His Sachs in 'Die Meistersinger' is often quoted as a model of both singing and acting; his Wotan, Hagen, King Mark, King (in 'Lohengrin') and Landgrave were almost equally distinguished. He was successful also in French and Italian

operas, though his Wagnerian interpretations were more famous. [R.7]

FISCHER, JOHN U. (1816– ?) and CHARLES S. (1818– ?). See Register, 4.

FISCHER, WILLIAM GUSTAVUS (1835–1912). See Register, 4.

FISHER, EDWARD (Jan. 11, 1848, Jamaica, Vt. : May 31, 1913, Toronto), had early training in Worcester, at the New England Conservatory in Boston and with Eugene Thayer. In Germany he studied piano with Loeschhorn and organ with Haupt. In 1875 he became music-director at the Ladies' College in Ottawa, and in 1879 organist at St. Andrew's in Toronto, where he continued for twenty years. During this time the St. Andrew's Choral Society expanded into the Toronto Choral Society. His most eminent accomplishment, however, was the foundation in 1887 of the Toronto Conservatory, of which he remained the head till his death and which he brought to a high degree of efficiency. He was also prominent in the establishment of the Canadian Society of Musicians, the Clef Club, the Canadian Guild of Organists and the Toronto Symphony Orchestra. [R.6]

FISHER, WILLIAM ARMS (Apr. 27, 1861, San Francisco), is descended from an old New England family. He first studied piano, organ and theory with J. P. Morgan in Oakland. In 1890 he came to New York, taking vocal lessons with several teachers there, and in 1892 went to London to work with Shakespeare. On his return he studied counterpoint, canon and fugue with Horatio Parker, composition and orchestration with Dvořák. He taught harmony at the National Conservatory of Music until 1895, when he removed to Boston. In 1897 he assumed his present position as editor and publishing-manager of the Ditson Company. As a song-composer he has had notable success. Of some 80 published songs the most popular are 'Under the Rose,' 'Gae to Sleep,' 'Sweet is Tipperary,' 'When Allah Spoke,' 'Oh, can night doubt its star.' He has also published an 'Elegy' for violin and piano, part-songs, anthems and carols, and edited a volume of 60 Irish songs, besides writing *Notes on Music in Old Boston*, 1918 — a brief, but striking historical sketch. [R.7]

FISK UNIVERSITY, Nashville, Tenn. (Congregational), one of the earliest institutions of higher education for negroes, has a peculiar musical interest. From its foundation in 1866 singing was taught by George L. White, the treasurer of the institution, who in 1871–74 conducted the famous tour of the 'Jubilee Singers' (q.v.). The present department of music offers systematic courses in piano, organ, violin, voice and public-school music, with credits in theory, history and pub-

lic-school methods towards an A.B. The Mozart Society, organized in 1880, serves as both
choir and oratorio-society. The department
has a good equipment, including a three-man-
ual organ. The principal is Jennie A. Robinson, with six other instructors.

FITZ, ASA. See TUNE-BOOKS, 1841.

FLAGG, JOSIAH (1738?–1794). See Register, 1, and TUNE-BOOKS, 1764.

FLAGLER, HARRY HARKNESS (b.
1870). See Register, 10.

FLAGLER, ISAAC VAN VLECK (1848–
1909). See Register, 6.

FLECK, HENRY THOMAS (b. 1863).
See COLLEGES, 2 (Hunter C., N. Y.).

FLETCHER, ALICE CUNNINGHAM
(1845, Boston), received her early education
in private schools in Boston. She has given
her life to investigations of the North American
Indians and efforts for their betterment.
Besides original work in the West, she has
repeatedly served as special representative
of the National Government. Since 1882
she has been assistant in ethnology at the
Peabody Museum in Cambridge, Mass., and
is prominent in various archæological and
folk-lore societies. She is author of A Study
of Omaha Music, 1893 (with La Flesche),
Indian Story and Song, 1900, and many
articles in the publications of the Bureau of
Ethnology and the Peabody Museum, 'The
American Anthropologist,' 'The Folk-Lore
Journal,' etc. [R.8]

FLETCHER, WILLIAM Z. See COL-
LEGES, 3 (Blue Ridge C., Md.).

FLINT, TIMOTHY (1780–1840). See
TUNE-BOOKS, 1816.

FLINT COMMUNITY MUSIC ASSOCI-
ATION, THE, of Flint, Mich., originated in
1913 in a choral society, which continued till
1915, being then interrupted by the war.
In 1917, however, it was revived in a new form,
'to create a common or general interest in
music.' George Oscar Bowen was secured as
director, and funds were appropriated by the
Board of Education, the Board of Commerce
and the Manufacturers' Association, amounting at first to about $8000 per year and now
increased to over $20,000. The foundational
activity is the maintenance of daily 'sings'
for various groups, especially in the large
factories. The public school buildings are used
for frequent neighborhood entertainments. A
chorus of limited size was formed for giving
works of some magnitude, and an orchestra
of 35. A Municipal Band of first-class order
is now projected, as well as other bands for
amateurs.

FLODIN, KARL (July 10, 1858, Wasa,
Finland, of German parents), though a
resident of Buenos Aires since 1907, is classed
as a strong influence in Finnish music. He
studied with Faltin in Helsingfors and at the
Leipzig Conservatory. For some years he
was music-critic in Helsingfors and in 1902–05
edited the 'Post' there. He has composed
a 'Cortége' for wind-instruments; incidental
music to Hauptmann's 'Hannele'; 'Helena,'
a scene from Goethe's Faust, for soprano and
orchestra; and much chorus-music. He is
the author of Finnish Music, 1900 (in Swedish), J. Sibelius (in 'Finnische Rundschau,'
1901), Die Entwicklung der Musik in Finnland
(in 'Die Musik,' 1903), Die Erweckung des
Nationalen Tones in der finnischen Musik
(in 'Die Musik,' 1904), and a biography of
Sibelius, which was ready for publication in
1916. [R.9]

FLOERSHEIM, OTTO (b. 1853). See Register, 6.

FLONZALEY QUARTET, THE, was
founded by Edward J. de Coppet of New
York. In the fall of 1902 he commissioned
Alfred Pochon to select the players, and in the
summer of 1903 rehearsals began at his summer
home, Flonzaley, near Lausanne in Switzerland. The original membership, which remained unbroken till 1917, included Adolfo
Betti, first violin, Alfred Pochon, second violin,
Ugo Ara, viola, and Ivan d'Archambeau, 'cello.
All but the last had been pupils of César
Thomson at Liège. At first Pochon and Betti
alternated positions. The members agreed to
devote themselves wholly to the Quartet, and
the original intention of the founder was that
it should not appear except more or less
privately or for charitable objects. In 1904,
however, a European tour was made, beginning
at Vienna, and at the end of December the
Quartet was heard in New York. The demand
was insistent on both sides of the water that
they should make regular and extensive tours.
Since then their superiority in every artistic
quality of interpretation and performance has
been everywhere acclaimed. In 1917 Ara felt
constrained to join the Italian army, and Louis
Bailly succeeded him. Since de Coppet's death
in 1916 the maintenance of the Quartet has
been assumed by his son André.

FLORIDIA, PIETRO, Barone NAPOLINO
(May 5, 1860, Modica, Sicily), at the Naples
Conservatory studied piano with Cesi, counterpoint and composition with Serrao and Rossi.
He began publishing piano-works while still
a student, and the comic opera 'Carlotta
Clepier' (later destroyed by the composer)
was given in Naples in 1882. In 1885–90
he toured as concert-pianist, locating at
Palermo in 1888 as first professor of piano
in the Conservatory. In 1889 he won the
first prize of the Società del Quartetto in
Naples for a symphony. The years 1892–1904
were devoted to composition in Milan. Coming to America in 1904, he taught at the

Cincinnati College of Music in 1906–08, and has since lived in New York, where from 1913 he has conducted the Italian Symphony Orchestra. In addition to the works named above, he has composed the operas 'Maruzza' (1894, Venice), 'La Colonia Libera' (1899, Rome), 'Paoletta' (1910, Cincinnati), and the grand opera 'The Scarlet Letter' (composed about 1902). Incidental music to Wilde's 'A Florentine Tragedy' was performed in New York in 1917. There is also a 'Fest-Ouvertüre' for orchestra. Among many songs may be cited 'Separation,' 'Why?' 'Nymph,' 'Night of Spring,' 'Nocturnal Landscape' (all Schirmer); 'Two Leaves,' 'When I am Dead,' 'The Apple' (all Carl Fischer); 'The Nun,' 'Pamphilo's Song,' adapted from Boccaccio by Bispham (both Ditson); and 'A Madrigal of the Italian Renaissance' (Breitkopf). He has also begun issuing a series of early Italian songs with revised or original accompaniments and critical notes (1st series of 40, Ditson). [R.9]

FLORIO, CARYL [William James Robjohn] (Nov. 3, 1843, Tavistock, England), was brought to America in 1857. In 1859–60 he sang at Trinity Church in New York — its first solo soprano-boy. In 1861–67 he was in a theatrical troupe, returning to New York in 1869 as teacher, organist, conductor and composer. In 1875–82 he conducted operas in New York, Havana and Philadelphia, and later concerts of his own works in New York. For a time he was music-director at the Baptist Female Institute in Indianapolis and in 1889–91 at Wells College in Aurora, N. Y. At different periods he has been organist at Trinity Church in Newport, R. I., Zion Church in New York, Mt. Calvary in Baltimore, and for many years at All Souls' in Biltmore, N. C., where in 1896–1901 he had charge of the music at the Vanderbilt estate. In 1886 he organized a Palestrina Choir in New York for the production of mediæval music, and has led other choral and orchestral societies. He has written the operettas 'Inferno' (1871), 'Les Tours de Mercure' (1872), 'Suzanne' (1876), and the opera 'Gulda' (1879), all to his own texts; also the opera 'Uncle Tom' (1882, Philadelphia), and the cantatas 'Songs of the Elements,' 'The Bridal of Triermain' and 'The Night at Bethlehem,' two symphonies, in G and C minor (the latter commended by Thomas), two overtures, a quintet for piano and saxophones (the first of its kind), two saxophone-quartets, a piano-concerto in F minor, four violin-sonatas, two piano-sonatas, much church-music, madrigals, part-songs and songs. [R.5]

FOBES, AZARIAH. See TUNE-BOOKS, 1809.

FOERSTER, ADOLPH MARTIN (Feb. 2, 1854, Pittsburgh), was first taught by his mother. In 1872–75 he studied at the Leipzig Conservatory, and in 1875–76 taught at the Fort Wayne (Ind.) Conservatory. Since 1876 he has lived in Pittsburgh, teaching and composing. For some years he conducted the Symphonic Society and the Musical Union (choral). His works include the following:

Orchestral —
'March-Fantasie,' op. 8 (1879, Pittsburgh, also Chicago under Scheel).
'Thusnelda,' op. 10 (1882, Baltimore, 1884, Pittsburgh, 1885, Boston, 1891, Brooklyn).
Suite No. 1, 'The Falconer,' op. 31 (1893, Scranton).
Festival March, op. 32 (1891, Pittsburgh, and often).
Dedication March, op. 43, for the opening of Carnegie Music Hall and Institute and founded on the tones A–C, Mr. Carnegie's initials (1895, and often).
Suite No. 2, op. 47 (in part 1898, Omaha Exposition, entire 1915, Pittsburgh).
Prelude to Goethe's 'Faust,' op. 48 (prize from Pittsburgh Art Society, 1898, and given then and later).
'American Ode,' op. 81 (1913, Pittsburgh Exposition, also New York).
'At Twilight,' op. 59 (Pittsburgh).
Lyric Suite, op. 82, for strings (1916, Pittsburgh).
'Love-Song,' op. 23, from Amelie Rives (1889, Pittsburgh and Detroit).
'Hero and Leander,' op. 44, from Tennyson (1897, Pittsburgh).
'Love-Visions' op. 80, words by composer (1913, Pittsburgh Exposition).
'Spring-Wanderings,' op. 82 (1918, Bangor).
'Verzweiflung,' op. 51, from Carl Hepp.
Festival Music, op. 9.
Symphonic Ode to Byron, op. 35.
Symphonic Poem, 'Sigrid,' op. 50.
Concerto in D minor, op. 52, for violin and orchestra.

Chamber —
Piano-Quartet No. 1, op. 21 (1887, Pittsburgh).
Piano-Trio, op. 29 (1890, Pittsburgh).
Quartet, op. 33, for strings (1891, Pittsburgh, and later).
Piano-Quartet No. 2, op. 40 (1896, Pittsburgh).
Serenade-Trio, op. 61 (1907, Pittsburgh).
Trio in D, op. 83 (1919, Lockport).
Fantasie, op. 15, for violin and piano.
Romanze and Melodie, op. 17, for violin and piano.
Novelette, op. 26, for violin and piano.
Suite No. 1, op. 36, for violin and piano.
Suite No. 2, op. 79, for violin and piano.
Albumblatt, op. 24, for 'cello and piano.
Cavatina, 'Devotion,' op. 39, for 'cello and piano.

Piano —
'Valse Caprice,' op. 5.
Nocturne, op. 7.
Sonett, op. 13.
'Eros,' op. 27.
'Exultation' and 'Lamentation,' op. 37.
12 Fantasy-Pieces, op. 38.
Suite, op. 46.

Organ —
Preludes in A-flat and D-flat.
Postlude in D minor.
Pastorale, op. 62.
Exaltation, Nocturne and Epigrams, op. 77.

Song-sets —
'Among Flowers,' op. 28.

ARTHUR FOOTE

Album of Lyrics, op. 53.
Five Songs, op. 57.
'Tristram and Iseult,' op. 60.
Greek Love-Songs, op. 63.
Garland of Songs, op. 64.
Four Love-Songs, op. 65.
Psalms 13 and 23, op. 66.
Child-Lyrics, op. 67, from Stevenson.
Second Album of Lyrics, op. 69.
Wreath of Songs, op. 70.
14 Selected Songs, op. 78.   [R.6]

FOLEY, ALLAN JAMES (1835–1899).
See Vol. ii. 70, and Register, 7.

FOLK-MUSIC. Of indigenous folk-music
the most unmistakable case in America is
that of the Indians. Somewhat less clear is
that of the Negroes, which doubtless embodies
elements derived from contact with white
races. To a different class belong numerous
forms that are in some measure transplantings
from Europe. It has recently been brilliantly
shown that in the highlands of Kentucky,
Tennessee and the Carolinas is a large amount
of English folk-music that was originally
introduced in the late 18th century or early
19th and has been preserved with modifications
and extensions. Somewhat parallel to this
is the Creole music of the lower Mississippi
region, which is distinctively French in derivation. This, however, has been much influenced by contact with artistic music in
various forms. Into the Northwest has much
more recently been brought a large amount
of imported folk-music from Scandinavian
sources. In every case where immigrants
of a particular nationality have settled in
considerable numbers it is likely that a certain
amount of folk-music will be found and will
continue in use for a long time. The essentially composite nature of the population of
the United States therefore favors the entry
and perpetuation of varied types of folk-music.
That same compositeness has more and more
rendered impossible any general type that is
distinctively 'American.' The nearest ap-
proach to such a type — and that entirely
one-sided and really untypical — are the
emotional religious songs of the 'Gospel
hymn' variety or the transient crops of war-
songs at one or two periods.

FOOTE, ARTHUR WILLIAM (Mar. 5,
1853, Salem, Mass.). See article in Vol. ii. 71.
He was organist of the First Unitarian Church
in Boston in 1878–1910, and president of the
A. G. O. in 1909–12. As a player he has
given many organ- and piano-recitals, and
appeared frequently in chamber-ensemble.
He is a member of the Institute of Arts and
Letters, and a Fellow of the American Academy
of Arts and Sciences. In 1919 Trinity College
gave him the degree of Mus.D.

Few American composers have won such
high esteem. The uniformly high quality
of his work in diverse forms has been coupled
with a surprising uniformity of success. His
orchestral works are played by leading orchestras, his chamber-music has become a
staple in American programs, his organ-music
is everywhere popular, and his songs are
prized alike by singers, accompanists and audiences. The Art of Music (Vol. iv. p. 340) says:

'Of his compositions as a whole it may be said
that they are astonishingly original in an age which
has found it all but impossible to escape imitation.
He is, like most of the great composers, largely self-
taught, and yet there is scarcely a trace of mannerisms, nor — what is even more remarkable — of
the mannerisms of others. His music is the pure
and perfectly formed expression of a nature at once
refined and imaginative. In these days of startling
innovations, the sincerity of which may not be
unhesitatingly trusted, it sounds none the less
spirited because it is unquestionably genuine and
relatively simple. It stands forth as a substantial
proof that delicate poetry and clear-cut workman-
ship have not yet failed to charm.'

On Thanksgiving Day in 1914, organists
throughout the country, by concerted arrangement, played his Festival March in F as an
expression of gratitude for his recovery from
a serious illness — a tribute seldom paid to
any musician.

The list of his most important works is as
follows:

For Orchestra —
   Overture, 'In the Mountains,' op. 14 (1887,
      Boston).
   Prologue, 'Francesca da Rimini,' op. 24 (1893,
      Boston).
   Serenade in E, op. 25, for strings (1886, Boston).
   Four Character Pieces after Omar Khayyám, op.
      48 (1912, Boston).
   Suite in D, op. 21, for strings (1886, Boston),
   Suite in D minor, op. 36 (1896, Boston).
   Suite in E, op. 63, for strings (1910, Boston).
   Concerto for 'cello and orchestra (1894, Chicago).
Chamber-Music —
   String-Quartet in G minor, op. 4 (1885).
   Piano-Trio in C minor, op. 5 (1884).
   Three Pieces for violin and piano, op. 9 — 'Mor-
      gengesang,' Menuet, Romance.
   Sonata in G minor, op. 20, for violin (1890, Kneisel).
   Piano-Quartet, op. 23 (1891, Kneisel Quartet).
   'Aubade Villageoise,' op. 31, for oboe and piano —
      Mélodie, Pastorale.
   String-Quartet in E, op. 32 (1894, Kneisel Quartet).
   Romanza for 'cello and piano, op. 33.
   Piano-Quintet, op. 38 (1898, Kneisel Quartet).
   Melody for violin and piano, op. 44.
   Piano-Trio in B-flat, op. 65 (1909, Kneisel Quartet).
   Ballade for violin and piano, op. 69.
   String-Quartet in D, op. 70.
   Canzonetta and 'A Song of Sleep,' op. 74, for
      violin and piano.
   'Légende,' op. 75, for violin and piano.
   Sonata for 'cello and piano, op. 76.
   Aubade for 'cello and piano.
Choral Works with Orchestra —
   'The Farewell of Hiawatha,' op. 11, for men's
      voices (1886, Boston).
   'The Wreck of the Hesperus,' op. 17 (1888, Boston).
   'The Skeleton in Armor,' op. 28 (1893, Boston).
   'Bedouin-Song,' for men's voices.

'In the Gateway of Ispahan,' for women's voices (1914, Boston).

Choral Works a cappella or with Piano —

For men's voices: 'If doughty deeds,' 'Into the silent land,' 'I love my love,' 'Bedouin-Songs,' 'Recessional,' 'The Munster Fusileers,' 'Bugle-Song,' 'Crossing the Bar,' 'A Song of April,' 'The Miller's Daughter,' 'Farewell to Summer.'

For women's voices: 'To Daffodils,' 'Lygeia' (cantata), Six Flower-Songs, op. 49, 'The Sky-lark' (duet), 'Where shall I find a white rose blooming?' (duet), 'The Green of Spring,' 'Gray Twilight,' 'Through the Rushes,' 'To-morrow,' 'The little creek goes winding,' 'Sigh no more, ladies.'

For mixed voices: 'The Wind and the Day,' 'Scythe-Song,' 'The Jumblies,' 'Vita nostra plena bellis,' op. 47 (motet.)

Songs —

'Go, lovely rose,' 'Elaine's Song,' 'I'm wearing awa',' 'Love me, if I live,' 'The Eden Rose,' 'On the Way to Kew,' 'Irish Folk-Song,' 'There sits a bird,' 'Roses in Winter,' 'I know a little garden-path,' 'Requiem,' 'A Song of Four Seasons,' 'Constancy,' 'Once at the Angelus,' 'In Picardie,' 'The roses are dead,' 'Bisesa's Song,' 'Ashes of Roses,' 'Persian Song,' from the 'Rubaiyat' (also with orchestra), 'Tranquillity,' 'Lilac-Time,' 'O swallow, flying south,' 'Memnon' — and about 100 others. Duets: 'A Song from the Persian' and 'The Voice of Spring,' for soprano and alto: 'Were all the world like you,' for soprano and tenor.

Church Music —

'Mount Carmel,' for women's voices.

'Hear my Prayer, O God,' for men's voices.

Various Te Deums and other canticles, and about 25 anthems, of which the best known are 'Still, still with Thee,' 'God is our Refuge,' 'And there were shepherds,' and 'Awake, thou that sleepest.'

For Organ —

Of about 20 works the best-known are a Festival March, Allegretto, Pastorale, Nocturne, Toccata and Suite in D, op. 54. (See article by H. V. Milligan in 'The Diapason,' April, 1919).

For Piano —

Suite in D minor, op. 15.

Suite in C minor, op. 30.

Three Pieces for left hand alone, op. 37.

Five Poems after Omar Khayyám, op. 41.

About 30 other works.

He has edited numerous educational works for the piano and published (with W. R. Spalding) *Modern Harmony*, 1905, and *Modulation and Related Harmonic Questions*, 1920. [R.6]

FORBUSH, ABIJAH. See TUNE-BOOKS, 1806.

FORMES, KARL JOHANN (Aug. 7, 1816, Mülheim-on-the-Rhine, Germany : Dec. 15, 1889, San Francisco). See article in Vol. ii. 88. His first American appearance was on Dec. 2, 1857, at the New York Academy of Music. He continued widely active for the next twenty years. In 1882 he married Pauline Greenwood, who had been his pupil in Philadelphia. His memoirs were published in 1888 as *Aus meinem Kunst- und Buhnenleben*, and he also wrote a *Method of Singing*, 3 vols. Shortly before his death he appeared in his favorite part of Don Basilio (in 'Il Barbiere

di Siviglia') at the Bijou Theatre in San Francisco. His vocal compass was from low C to F above the staff. See Upton, *Musical Memories*, pp. 132–3. [R.4]

FORNIA–LABEY, RITA, née Newman (July 17, 1878, San Francisco), began to sing at fifteen, studied with local teachers, and prepared for grand opera on the advice of Scalchi and Emil Fischer. After a year's study in Berlin with Nicklass-Kempner she was coloratura-soprano for the Hamburg Stadt-Theater for two years and then went to Paris for lessons with Jean de Reszké. She came to America in 1906 to join Savage's English-singing company, and since 1908 has been with the Metropolitan Opera House. She has also appeared at Covent Garden. Her repertory includes Elisabeth, Venus, Ortrud, Sieglinde, Gutrune, Amneris, Carmen, Rosina, Nedda, Leonora, Woglinde (in 'Das Rheingold' and 'Die Götterdämmerung'), and first Flower-Maiden in 'Parsifal.' In 1910 she married James P. Labey, of the Isle of Jersey. [R.9]

FORSYTH, CECIL (Nov. 30, 1870, Greenwich, England), was educated at Cranbrook and Edinburgh University (M. A., bursar and classical prizeman), and studied at the Royal College of Music in London with Stanford (composition) and Parry (musical history). For a time he played viola in the Royal Philharmonic and Queen's Hall Orchestras, and was also active as conductor. Since the end of 1914 he has lived in New York. He has composed the operas 'Westward Ho' and 'Cinderella'; two comic operas (with Alfred Scott-Gatty), produced at the Savoy and Aldwych Theatres, London; a viola-concerto in G minor and a 'Chant Celtique' for viola and orchestra, both performed by E. Férir under Wood's direction; four orchestral studies from *Les Misérables*, played by the Queen's Hall Orchestra; a setting of Keats' 'Ode to a Nightingale' for baritone and orchestra; two masses; chamber-music; songs and part-songs. He has also written *Music and Nationalism*, 1911, an extensive treatise on *Orchestration*, 1914, a readable *History of Music* (with Stanford), 1916, and *Choral Orchestration*, 1920. He wrote on 'The English Musical Renaissance' in Vol. iii. of *The Art of Music* (1915). [R.10]

FORSYTH, WESLEY OCTAVIUS (Jan. 26, 1863, near Toronto, Ont.), after preliminary training in Toronto, studied with Zwintscher, Krause and Jadassohn in Leipzig and with Epstein in Vienna. Since 1892 he has worked in Toronto as pianist and teacher, for a time as director of the Metropolitan School of Music, but recently as private teacher. His published compositions, about sixty altogether, are songs and piano-pieces.

A suite for orchestra, a string-quartet and many smaller works are still in manuscript. He has done much, by writing and teaching, for the development of piano-music in Canada. [R.8]

FOSTER, FAY, who was born in Leavenworth, Kan., began her public musical work early, being organist at twelve, accompanist for the Sherwood Concert Company at seventeen and head of a music-school in Onarga, Ill., at nineteen. At the Sherwood Music School in Chicago she studied singing with Mme. Dove-Boitte, piano with Sherwood and theory with Gleason. For twelve years she was in Europe, taking piano under Reisenauer in Leipzig, Menter and Schwartz in Munich, and Rosenthal in Vienna, singing at Cologne, Munich, Leipzig and Berlin, and composition under Jadassohn. Since 1911 she has lived in New York. Her waltz 'Die Woche' won a prize over many competitors in Berlin, and she holds prizes also for songs, women's choruses and piano-pieces. Of the songs 45 are published, with 9 part-songs. [R.8]

FOSTER, STEPHEN COLLINS (July 4, 1826, Pittsburgh : Jan. 13, 1864, New York). See article in Vol. ii. 90-1. Interest in his music and his unfortunate life does not diminish. It is possible that investigations now being made may shed light upon his story and dissipate some of the shadows across it. Noteworthy books are *Biography, Songs and Musical Compositions of Stephen C. Foster*, 1896, by Morrison Foster, his brother, and *Catalogue of First Editions of Stephen C. Foster*, 1915, by Walter R. Whittlesey and O. G. Sonneck, of the Library of Congress. A fresh biography, by Harold V. Milligan of New York, appeared in 1920. The following articles or references have value — article by Dr. Martin Darkow of Philadelphia in 'Die Musik,' 4te Jahrg., Heft 16; article by T. Carl Whitmer of Pittsburgh in 'The Musician,' Dec., 1913; article by César Saerchinger of New York in 'The International,' Feb., 1914; and summary in Elson's *History of American Music*, pp. 134-9.

Foster's father was a prominent business man who came to what is now Pittsburgh from Virginia, and his mother was of a well-known Maryland family. By descent and temperament he was a Southerner, and this explains his keen sympathy with the sentiment and form of the songs and music of the plantations. The entries in the Library of Congress *Catalogue* number about 200, including songs, duets, songs with chorus, a collection of instrumental pieces and arrangements called *The Social Orchestra*, 1854, and the many sacred tunes that Foster contributed to Horace Waters' *Athenæum Collection*, 1863. If the dates of publication be collated, it will

P

be seen that his early period (1844-55) was most productive in 1850-51, while the later period (1857-64) yields most in 1861-63. It is to the former that belong almost all the melodies by which he is now best known.

The house in Pittsburgh where Foster was born was bought by James H. Park and in 1914 presented to the city, which now maintains it as a Foster museum. Foster's daughter, Mrs. Marion Foster Welsh, lives in Pittsburgh. [R.4]

FOUCARD. See Register, 2.

FOUNDATION FOR NEEDY MUSICIANS OF THE UNITED STATES. See KNEISEL, FRANZ.

FOX, FÉLIX (May 25, 1876, Breslau, Germany), came to Boston when a child. He was trained there and in New York, from 1892 also at Leipzig, where he studied piano with Reinecke and composition with Jadassohn. Winning the Helbig prize, he continued under Philipp at Paris for two years. At Leipzig he made his début in 1896, and at Paris in 1897, bringing out some of MacDowell's music. Returning to Boston in 1897, he concertized for a year, playing with leading orchestras and giving many recitals. In 1898, with Carlo Buonamici, he established the Fox-Buonamici School in Boston, which they still conduct. He is an Officier d'Académie. [R.8]

FRADKIN, FREDRIC (April 2, 1892, Troy, N. Y., of Russian parents), began violin-study when only five, and at nine appeared as soloist with the American Symphony Orchestra. His teachers in New York were Jarrow, Schradieck, Bendix, Franko and Lichtenberg. In 1905 he went to Paris and studied first with G. Rémy and from 1907 in Lefort's class at the Conservatory. Here he won first prize in 1909. In 1909-10 he was concertmaster of the Bordeaux Opera Company, and in 1910-11 of the Louis Ganne Orchestra at Monte Carlo. After some study with Ysaÿe he returned to America, making his début in recital in New York on Jan. 10, 1911. He toured England in 1911-12 and 1913-14, spending the intervening year as concertmaster of the Vienna Konzertverein. In 1914-15 he was concertmaster of the Russian Symphony Orchestra in New York, in 1915-17 of the Diaghilev Ballet, and in 1918-19 of the Boston Symphony Orchestra — the first American to hold this post. [R.9]

FRAEMCKE, AUGUST (b. 1870). See Register, 9.

FRANCIS, WILLIAM (1763-1827). See Register, 2.

FRANKLIN, BENJAMIN (Jan. 17, 1706, Boston : Apr. 17, 1790, Philadelphia). See articles in Vol. ii. 103-4, 297-8. As Sonneck has brought out in his striking essay on 'Franklin's Musical Side' in his *Suum Cuique* (1916), Franklin had many contacts with music besides his organization of the musical glasses into a practical instrument. As a printer he probably had some connection with the early engraving of music in America. He was apprenticed to his brother James in Boston at the time when Walter's *Grounds and Rules of Musick* came out in 1721. At his own shop in Philadelphia he issued several reprints of Watts' *Psalms* (1729, '41), *Hymns* (1741, '42) and *Divine and Moral Songs for Children* (1737, '47), though none of these books contained music. Similarly, he printed Beissel's *Göttliche Liebes- und Lobestöne* in 1730 — the first German book in America — and his *Vorspiel der Neuen Welt* in 1732, both collections of poetry. But in 1730 he also published Daniel Warner's *The Singing-Master's Guide to his Scholars*, which involved some music-printing. He was still in Philadelphia, though deeply engaged in public affairs, when the issue of American collections of tunes began about 1760. There is reason to suppose, as Sonneck shows, that in 1759, while on a trip to England, he heard 'The Messiah' on Apr. 6, 1759, when Handel led for the last time. He was an expert guitar-player, fond of vocal and instrumental music generally, acquainted with considerable musical literature of the time, and wrote acutely and sympathetically to Lord Kames (1765) and others upon musical æsthetics. [R.1]

FRANKO, NAHAN (b. 1861). See Register, 6.

FRANKO, SAM (Jan. 20, 1857, New Orleans), was educated in Germany and France, studying violin with Joachim in Berlin, Vieuxtemps and Léonard in Paris, and composition with Alexis Hollaender in Berlin. He made his début at Breslau in 1867 and in New York in 1869. The years 1871–78 were spent in study and concertizing in Germany, and 1878–1880 in Paris, with many concerts at the Salle Pleyel. From 1880 he made New York his headquarters. He toured as soloist and first violin with the Mendelssohn Quintette Club of Boston; was member and later (1884–91) concertmaster of Thomas' Orchestra; was solo viola with the New York Philharmonic Society; and in 1881–1897 gave chamber-music concerts at Steinway Hall and the Aschenbroedel Club. In 1900–1909 he gave orchestral concerts of 'Old Music' in New York, providing the first hearings in America of many works from the 17th and 18th centuries. These programs he continued in 1910–14 in Berlin, where he also taught advanced violin-classes and led the orchestra-class at the Stern Conservatory. He returned to New York in 1915, resumed his concerts of 'Old Music,' and conducted

performances at the Park Theater by the Society of American Singers. For one season he was concertmaster at the Manhattan Opera House, and also for the Russian Ballet under Diaghilev. Prominent among his pupils are Emily Gresser, Fredric Fradkin, Jacques Gordon and Dora Becker. His published compositions for violin and piano are 'Meditation,' 'Lullaby,' 'Valse Gracieuse' and 'Mazurka de Concert' (Schuberth); and transcriptions for violin and piano, two violins, 'cello and piano, and string-orchestra, including many rare 18th-century works (Schirmer, Carl Fischer, Jungnickel, Ries and Erler). Unpublished are a Polonaise for violin alone, a 'Gypsy March' for orchestra, and piano-pieces. [R.5]

FRANOSCH, ADOLPH (1830–1880). See Register, 6.

FREDERIKSEN, FREDERIK CHRISTIAN (b. 1869). See Register, 10.

FREEMAN, EDWARD HENDEE (b. 1890). See COLLEGES, 3 (Muskingum C., Ohio).

FREER, ELEANOR, née Everest (May 14, 1864, Philadelphia), was the daughter of Cornelius Everest, who was a musical theorist. She studied singing with Marchesi and diction with Godard in Paris. After marrying Archibald E. Freer of Chicago in 1891 she pursued theory under Ziehn. She did not begin publishing until 1902, but was then already well-known as a song-composer. She has written some 140 songs, of which a large part are published. Her op. 22, a song-cycle for medium voice, comprises the entire *Sonnets from the Portuguese* of Mrs. Browning. Of these Ziehn said : 'It is a colossal work. It is marvelous enough that such sentiments could be poetically expressed forty-four times by one person, and more so that another could place these wonderful sonnets in a musical setting, and of the highest order.' She has also published a number of trios and quartets for men's, women's or mixed voices, and a group of piano-pieces. During the war she was a leader in charitable and relief organizations in Chicago, and was founder and treasurer of the Chicago Hospital Foundation at Paris. [R.8]

FREMSTAD, OLIVE NAYAN (1870?, Stockholm, Sweden), was the daughter of musical parents, living in Christiania, Norway, until she was twelve, when the family moved to Minnesota. She early began piano-study, appearing in public at ten, and at sixteen sang in church-choirs. In 1890 she came to New York, supported herself by accompanying, giving piano-lessons and singing in church, meanwhile studying voice with F. E. Bristol. In 1893 she went to Berlin, where she studied for a year and a half with Lilli Lehmann. Her début was made as Azucena in 'Il Trovatore' at Cologne in 1895. In 1896 she sang at Bayreuth, and engagements in Germany and Holland followed. In 1897–1900 she sang regularly at the Cologne opera, and filled guest-engagements at Covent Garden (first appearing as Venus in 'Tannhäuser'), Amsterdam, Antwerp and Vienna. She was at the Royal Opera in Munich in 1900–03, and made her American début at the Metropolitan Opera House in 1903 as Sieglinde in 'Die Walküre.' She sang for eleven seasons at the Metropolitan, and since 1914 has made concert- and opera-tours. Her successes have been made as Carmen and in all the leading Wagnerian rôles. She created the title-rôle in Strauss' 'Salome' at the Paris and New York performances, and in Gluck's 'Armide' in New York. She married Edson Sutphen of New York in 1906, was divorced in 1911, and married Harry Lewis Brainerd in 1916. [R.7]

FRENCH, JACOB (1754– ?). See TUNE-BOOKS, 1790.

FRENCH OPERA HOUSE, THE, in New Orleans, was opened in December, 1859, and was long famous as the oldest opera-house in the United States. It was destroyed by fire on Dec. 4, 1919.

FREUND, JOHN CHRISTIAN (Nov. 22, 1848, London), was educated at the London City School, Oxford and London Universities. While at Oxford he edited 'The Dark Blue Magazine,' and his play 'The Undergraduate' was produced at the Queen's Theatre, London. He came to New York in 1871. He became editor of 'The Musical and Dramatic Times,' and 'Music and Drama' in 1885, of the Dolgeville (N. Y.) 'Herald' in 1891–93, and since 1893 of 'The Music Trades,' 'Musical America,' and 'The Piano and Organ Purchaser's Guide.' In 1913 he began a propaganda for 'the musical independence of the United States,' based on the expenditure, at that time, of over $600,000,000 annually on music and musical industries, on the superior qualities of American musical instruments, and on the unreasonable notion that students must go to Europe for a complete musical education. He has made innumerable speeches on these topics throughout the country. In 1917 he established the Musical Alliance of the United States, which aims at the recognition of music as a vital factor in national, home and civic life, the extension of music-study in public schools, the promotion of American music, and the establishment of a National Conservatory of Music. [R.7]

FREY, ADOLF (b. 1865). See Register, 8.

FRICKER, HERBERT AUSTIN (b. 1868). See Register, 10.

FRIEDBERG, CARL RUDOLF HERMANN (b. 1872). See Register, 10.

FRIEDHEIM, ARTHUR (Oct. 26, 1859, Petrograd, Russia). See article in Vol. ii. 110. His first sojourn in America was in 1891–95, when he made tours under Steinway auspices. In 1900–01 he taught at the Chicago Musical College. Leaving London in 1908, he spent two years in Munich. In 1910 he gave recitals in the United States and Mexico, in 1911 took part in many Liszt centenary concerts in Germany, Hungary and America, and in 1912–13 made concert-tours in Canada. Since 1914 he has lived in New York. His overture to Lermontoff's 'A Hero of our Times' was performed in Petrograd in 1877. The opera 'The Last Days of Pompeii' has not been produced. In 1880 the piano-concerto in B was first performed at Weimar, Liszt playing the orchestral parts. In 1886 he orchestrated and conducted at a festival in Sondershausen the 'Vier ungarische Portrait-Skizzen' by Liszt, of which the score is lost. In 1890 his concerto in B-flat was performed under Mottl in Carlsruhe and hissed, but successfully given in New York, Leipzig and Munich. The American March 'E Pluribus Unum' was composed in 1894, but is not yet performed. In 1896 his arrangement of Liszt's 2nd Rhapsody for piano and orchestra was badly and unsuccessfully performed at Leipzig. In February, 1904, his opera 'Die Tänzerin' was successfully given at Cologne, Otto Lohse conducting; in 1906 it was twice badly performed at Leipzig. Unfinished operas are 'The Christians' (Nero) and 'Giulia Gonzaga.' The piano-score of 'Die Tänzerin' is printed at Leipzig. He has written much for periodicals, and is engaged on a commentary to the biographies of Liszt. [R.8]

FRIES, AUGUST (1822– ?). See Register, 4.

FRIES, WULF CHRISTIAN JULIUS (Jan. 10, 1825, Garbeck, Holstein : Apr. 19, 1902, Roxbury, Mass.), was largely self-taught. In youth he played a number of orchestral instruments, but finally devoted himself to the 'cello. From 1842 he played in the theater-orchestra at Bergen, and at Ole Bull's concerts. In 1847 he came to Boston with his brother August. When the Mendelssohn Quintette Club was organized in 1849 he was the 'cellist, continuing till 1870 and visiting nearly every considerable town in the country. He also belonged to the Musical Fund Society and the Harvard Musical Association. He played in chamber-music concerts with Rubinstein and von Bülow, but after 1875 confined himself to teaching and to concerts in New England. The impress of his gracious character and his sterling musicianship was wide and permanent. [R.4]

FRIML, CHARLES RUDOLF (Dec. 7, 1881, Prague, Bohemia), was educated in the Prague schools and Conservatory, studying piano with Jiránek and composition with Förster. For five years he was pianist for Kubelik, and visited the United States with him in 1901 and 1906. In 1906 he played his own piano-concerto in B with the New York Symphony Society. Since 1906 he has lived in New York, largely engaged on composition. His 'Christmas Carol' and 'Japanese Ballet' were produced at the Court Theater in Dresden; the comic operas first produced in this country are 'The Firefly' (1912, Syracuse), 'High Jinks' (1913, Syracuse), 'Katinka' (1915, Morristown, N. J.), and the musical comedy 'You're in Love' (1916, New Haven, Conn.). His compositions for piano, violin or 'cello and piano, and songs (Schirmer, Schmidt) number about 100, and find much acceptance. [R.9]

‡ FRISKIN, JAMES (Mar. 3, 1886, Glasgow, Scotland). See article in Vol. v. 640. On Feb. 15, 1916, he made his New York début as pianist, playing his own sonata and an unhackneyed program. To the list of works should be added a Sonata in G for violin and piano, and a Phantasy in F minor for piano and string-quartet.

FROST, RUFUS. See TUNE-BOOKS, 1805.

FRY, HENRY S. (Apr. 27, 1875, Pottstown, Pa.), is now organist at St. Clement's in Philadelphia, his previous positions having been at St. Paul's (Reformed Episcopal), the Princeton Presbyterian Church and Holy Trinity Memorial Chapel. He has given over 600 organ-recitals at conventions of the N. A. O., for the American Organ-Players' Club and at the Drexel Institute, etc. (including over 125 at the opening of new organs). He makes a specialty of teaching organ, and is an associate of the A. G. O. He writes for many musical publications, and is an officer in various associations (president of the N. A. O. in 1920). His compositions are 'Siciliano' and 'Variations on a Evening Hymn,' for organ; Magnificat and Nunc Dimittis in D; 'Voices of the Cross' (Lenten); two Christmas carols; 'The Souls of the Righteous,' and a song, 'Farewell.' [R.8]

FRY, WILLIAM HENRY (Aug. 10, 1813, Philadelphia : Sept. 21, 1864, Santa Cruz, West Indies), was the son of a publisher. Though largely self-taught in piano-playing, he had lessons in theory from L. Meignen, a graduate of the Paris Conservatory. At fourteen he composed an overture, and at twenty won a gold medal for another, which was played by the Philadelphia Philharmonic Society. In 1845 he composed 'Leonora,' which is often spoken of as the first American opera of importance. It was given in Philadelphia several times and revived (in Italian) at the Academy of Music in New York in March, 1858. In the interim he had joined the staff of the New York 'Tribune,' and in 1846 had gone abroad as European correspondent. He spent six years in London and Paris, and earned the friendship of Berlioz and other French musicians. On his return he became music-critic and editorial writer on the 'Tribune,' and gave lectures on musical history. The Jullien Orchestra played four of his overtures and a symphony. A second opera, 'Notre Dame de Paris,' on a libretto by his brother J. R. Fry, was brought out in Philadelphia in 1864 under the direction of Thomas. The list of his compositions includes the symphonies 'Santa Claus,' 'The Breaking Heart,' 'Childe Harold,' and 'A Day in the Country'; several overtures; a Stabat Mater, cantatas and songs. Although his music did not long survive, his influence as a writer and educator was marked and beneficial. [R.4]

FRYSINGER, J. FRANK (Apr. 7, 1878, Hanover, Pa.), from 1890 studied organ and harmony with F. W. Wolff in Baltimore, from 1898 piano with S. C. Engel and composition with Kelley, from 1900 piano with Burmeister, and from 1903 organ and composition with Kinder in Philadelphia and Wolstenholme in London. In 1909–11 he was organist at York, Pa., and music-director at Hood College in Frederick, Md. In 1911–18 he was chief organ-teacher at the University School of Music in Lincoln, Neb., and organist at the First Presbyterian Church, where he gave many recitals. Since 1918 he has been head of the organ and theory work at Augustana College in Rock Island, Ill. He is a fellow of the Guild of Church Organists in London, and member of the A. G. O and N. A. O. He has given many recitals throughout the country, and at the Jamestown and Panama Expositions. He has published about 100 works for organ, piano and voice. [R.9]

FUHR, HAYES McGUIRE. See COLLEGES, 3 (Hastings C., Neb.).

FULLERTON, CHARLES ALEXANDER (b. 1861). See Register, 8.

FULLERTON, ROBERT (b. 1867). See Register, 9.

FUNK, JOSEPH. See TUNE-BOOKS, 1848.

FURLONG, ATHERTON BERNARD (b. 1849). See Register, 6.

FURSCH–MADI, EMMY (1847–1894). See Register, 6.

G

GABERT, ABEL L. See COLLEGES, 1 (Catholic U., D.C.).

GABLER, ERNEST (d. 1883). See Register, 4.

GABRILOVITCH, OSSIP SALOMONO-VITCH (Jan. 26, 1878, Petrograd), studied piano at the Petrograd Conservatory under Rubinstein and in Vienna with Leschetizky, and composition with Navrátil, Liadov and Glazunov, making his début as a pianist in Berlin in 1896. He then toured in Germany, France, England, Russia, Holland and the United States, visiting the last in 1900, '01, '06, '09, '14, '15 and '16. In 1909 he married Clara Clemens, the daughter of 'Mark Twain.' In 1904–14 he lived in Munich, conducting orchestral concerts, and in 1907–18 he conducted series of orchestral concerts in New York. Since 1918 he has been conductor of the Detroit Symphony Orchestra. Both as player and as conductor he has established himself as an artist of the first rank.

In 1912–13 he gave a series of six recitals in Europe to illustrate the historical development of the piano-concerto, with these programs:

I.	Bach	Concerto in G minor
	Mozart	" in D minor
	Beethoven	" in C minor
II.	Beethoven	Concerto in G
		" in E-flat
		Fantasia with Chorus
III.	Mendelssohn	Capriccio Brillante
	Chopin	Concerto in E minor
	Schumann	" in A minor
	Weber	Concertstück
IV.	Rubinstein	Concerto in D minor
	Tchaikovsky	" in B-flat minor
	Liszt	" in E-flat
V.	Brahms	Concerto in D minor
		" in B-flat
VI.	Franck	Symphonic Variations
	Saint-Saëns	Concerto in C minor
	Strauss	Burlesque
	Rachmaninov	Concerto in C minor

In 1915–16 he gave another series of six historical recitals in New York, Boston and Chicago, with programs from these composers:

I.	Byrde	II.	Beethoven	Tchaikovsky
	Purcell	III.	Weber	Scriabin
	Couperin		Schubert	Rachmaninov
	Rameau		Mendelssohn	Leschetizky
	Daquin		Schumann	Paderewski
	Rossi	IV.	Chopin	Moszkowski
	Scarlatti	V.	Brahms	Debussy
	J. S. Bach		Liszt	Ravel
	P. E. Bach	VI.	Franck	Reger
	Handel		Grieg	Schönberg
	Haydn		MacDowell	Scott
	Mozart		Rubinstein	Grainger

His own published compositions include sets of two to five piano-pieces, opp. 1–3, 10 and 12, sets of two or three songs, opp. 5, 9 and 11, a 'Thème Varié' and a 'Mélodie' for piano, opp. 4 and 8, an 'Elegy' for 'cello and piano, op. 7, and an 'Ouverture-Rhapsodie' for orchestra, op. 6.   [R.9]

GADSKI, JOHANNA EMILIA AGNES (June 15, 1872, Anclam, Germany), was a pupil at Stettin of Mme. Schroeder-Chaloupka. She first appeared in Berlin in 1889 in 'Undine,' followed by engagements in Germany and Holland. From 1895 she sang almost continuously in the United States, at first with the Damrosch Opera Company and from 1898 at the Metropolitan Opera House, besides being heard often in England and Germany. In addition to her distinction as a great Wagnerian singer she has also been eminently successful in song-recitals. In 1892 she married Hans Tauscher. In 1917 she aroused much resentment by political intrigues and withdrew to Berlin.   [R.8]

GALE, CLEMENT ROWLAND (Mar. 12, 1862, Kew, England), was in 1878–80 an articled pupil at St. Peter's Church, Eaton Square, London, and then entered Exeter College at Oxford, where he graduated in arts in 1884 and in music in 1889. In 1884–85 he was music-master at Reading School. In 1885–89 he was in Edinburgh as sub-organist at St. Mary's Cathedral, and music-master at the Craigmount School and the John Watson Institute. Coming to New York in 1890, he was organist at Calvary Church for ten years, then at All Angels' in 1900–10, and since 1910 at Christ Church. He has been organist and instructor at the General Theological Seminary since 1901, and instructor in harmony, counterpoint and composition at the Guilmant Organ School since 1902. He has published many anthems, services, part-songs and organ-pieces. His unpublished compositions include Psalm 130 for solo voices, five-part chorus and orchestra; a Mass in G; a concert-overture; a 'Jubilate Deo' in cantata-form; many songs, part-songs, organ- and piano-pieces. He was a founder of the A. G. O., and has long been prominent in its affairs.   [R.8]

GALE, WALTER C. (Sept. 5, 1871, Cambridge, Mass.), graduated at the College of the City of New York in 1891. He was trained by Bassford and Sauret in piano, by Frank Damrosch in harmony and counterpoint, and by S. P. Warren in organ. After holding minor positions, in 1890 he became organist at the Brick (Presbyterian) Church, New York, going thence in 1893 to Holy Trinity for five years, part of this time being also assistant-organist at St. Thomas'.

In 1900–05 he was organist at All Souls', and since 1905 has been at the Broadway Tabernacle (Congregational). From 1901 he was private organist to Andrew Carnegie. He teaches at Miss Spence's School for Girls and directs the Orpheus Choral Society. His published works are mainly for church-use — anthems and solos. An organ-sonata in A minor is in MS. He was a founder of the A. G. O. and has been warden. [R.7]

GALES, WESTON (Nov. 5, 1877, Elizabeth, N. J.), as a boy was soprano-soloist in Elizabeth and New York. He early began piano-study and continued it with Sanford at Yale, where he graduated in 1898. He also studied theory with Parker and organ with Déthier. In 1899–1902 he was organist at Irvington-on-Hudson, in 1902–08 at Christ Church in New York, and in 1908–13 at Emmanuel Church in Boston. He is a recognized specialist in boy-choir training. He prepared the boys' choruses for the first New York performance of Wolf-Ferrari's 'Vita Nuova' and for various Bach works, and has executed similar tasks in Boston. During two summers he studied organ with Widor and Vierne in Paris. In the summer of 1913 he conducted orchestral concerts in Munich, Hamburg and Nuremberg. In 1914 he founded the Detroit Symphony Orchestra, and conducted it till 1918. [R.8]

GALESBURG MUSICAL UNION, THE, of Galesburg, Ill., is a choral society which about 1900 grew out of a smaller vocal club in the Conservatory connected with Knox College. Its conductor from the first has been William F. Bentley, the director of the Conservatory, and its membership averages about 150. Two concerts are given each year, assisted by the Conservatory orchestra or one from outside, such as the Chicago or Minneapolis Symphony Orchestras. Both oratorios and smaller works are given.

GALLI–CURCI, AMELITA (Nov. 18, 1889, Milan, Italy), had her general education at the Liceo Alessandro Manzoni and at International Institute of Languages at Milan. At the Milan Conservatory she studied piano under Appiani and graduated with a first prize in 1903. Self-taught as a singer, she made her début as Gilda in 'Rigoletto' at the Costanzi in Rome. During the next six years she sang at the principal theaters in Italy and Spain, besides touring in South America with Caruso and Titta Ruffo. In the United States she appeared with the Chicago Opera Company in Chicago in 1916, and in New York with the same company in 1918. Her success, both in opera and in concert, has been sensational, and she is universally placed in the first rank of coloratura-sopranos. Her répertoire includes Gilda, Lucia, Dinorah,

Rosina, Violetta, Amina, Lakmé, Leila, Elvira and Juliette. In 1908 she married the Italian painter Luis Curci, Marquis de Simeri (divorced in 1920). [R.10]

GALLICO, PAOLO (May 13, 1868, Trieste, Austria), appeared in recital as pianist as early as 1883. In 1886 he graduated from the Vienna Conservatory (class of Julius Epstein) with highest honors and two gold medals. He made concert-tours of Europe, and settled in New York in 1892, where he is an able concert-pianist and teacher. His compositions include the operetta 'Johannistraum,' the comic opera 'Harlekin' (Cranz), piano-pieces, songs and arias (Schirmer, Harms, Cranz). He has also edited some piano-music. [R.8]

GANDELL, SHIRLEY MARK KERR (b. 1866). See Register, 8.

GANNETT, ELMER K. See COLLEGES, 3 (Iowa Wesleyan C.).

GANTVOORT, ARNOLD JOHANN (b. 1857). See Register, 6.

GANZ, RUDOLPH (Feb. 24, 1877, Zurich, Switzerland), early began studying both 'cello and piano under Johannes Hegar for the one and Robert Freund for the other. In 1893–96 he continued the latter with his uncle, Carl Eschmann-Dumur, and composition with Blanchet, both in Lausanne. Then followed periods with Blumer (piano) in Strassburg and with Busoni (piano) and Urban (composition) in Berlin. At the end of 1899 he made his formal début as pianist with the Philharmonic Orchestra in Berlin, playing the Beethoven concerto in E-flat and the Chopin concerto in E minor. In 1900–05 he was head of the piano-department in the Chicago Musical College. He has since devoted himself to recital-tours in Europe and America with the greatest success. He is equally at home in the presentation of classical and modern music, and has an enormous répertoire. In Berlin alone he has played sixteen different concertos. His programs are comprehensive, including many works by modern composers. His most important compositions are a Symphony in E, op. 1, and a Concert-Piece for piano and orchestra, op. 4, both performed in Europe and America, but not yet published, with a set of piano-variations, op. 21, on a theme by Brahms. Published works include some 40 piano-pieces, about 200 songs and many men's choruses. [R.9]

GARCIA, MANUEL DEL POPOLO VICENTE (1775–1832). See Register, 3.

GARDEN, MARY (Feb. 20, 1877, Aberdeen, Scotland), was brought to America as a child, living in Chicopee, Mass., in Hartford, Conn., and from 1888 in Chicago. She began violin-study at six, piano at twelve and singing in 1893 with Mrs. S. R. Duff of Bangor, Me., who took her to Paris in 1895. Here she studied with Trabadello and Fugère. Her début as Louise was at the Opéra-Comique on Apr. 12, 1900, on a day's notice and without rehearsal, as a substitute for Mlle. Rioton. Even so she won success. She was well-known in Paris and London as singer and actress before she appeared in 'Thaïs' at the Manhattan Opera House in New York in 1907. She sang at the Manhattan until 1910, and has since been with the Chicago Opera Company. She has created the rôles of Mélisande in 'Pelléas et Mélisande' (1902, by request of the composer), Marie in 'La Marseillaise' (1900), Diane in 'La Fille du Tabarin' (1901) and Fiammette in 'La Reine Fiammette' (1903). Her rôles, many of which she has introduced in America, also include Salome (Strauss), Sapho, Griseldis, Marguerite (in 'Faust'), Carmen and Jean (in 'Le Jongleur de Notre-Dame'). [R.9]

'GARDEN OF ALLAH, THE.' An opera by Henry K. Hadley, produced by the Chicago Opera Company in 1918 in New York.

‡GARDINER, H. BALFOUR (Nov. 7, 1877, London, England). See article in Vol. v. 641. In 1912–13 he promoted a series of important choral and orchestral concerts in London, devoted largely to the production of unknown works by contemporary British composers, and these marked an epoch in recent musical progress in England. His own work was interrupted by the war, the only additions to his compositions being the 'Shepherd Fennel's Dance' for orchestra, 'News from Whydah,' for chorus and orchestra, and some unaccompanied choruses.

GARIEL, EDOARDO (Aug. 5, 1860, Monterey, Mexico), having studied with A. Daunic in Monterey and Marmontel in Paris, taught music, French and English at the State School in Saltillo in 1887–98, becoming director in 1899–1900. In 1900–08 he was supervisor of school-music in Mexico City, in 1908–15 professor of methodology for school-music at the Normal School for Girls, and in 1915–17 professor of harmony and music-pedagogy in the National Conservatory. In 1915 the government sent him to the United States to study teaching-methods, and on this trip he expounded original theories regarding harmony-teaching. He visited Spain, Italy, France and Switzerland on a similar mission in 1916. In 1917 he became director of the Escuela Nacional de Música y Arte Teatral in Mexico City. He is the author of *Chopin, Consideraciones sobre algunas de sus obras y la manera de interpretarlas*, 1895, *Solfeo Elemental*, 1905, 2 parts, *Solfeo y Canto Coral en notacion modal cifrada*, 1906, *Elementos de Solfeo y Canto Coral*, 1908, *Nuevo Sistema de Armonía basado en cuatro acordes fundamentales*, 1916, also in English (Schirmer)

as *A New System of Harmony based on four fundamental chords.* [R.7]

GARRISON, MABEL. See Register, 10.

GARTON, SAMUEL B. See COLLEGES, 3 (Earlham C., Ind.).

GASH, MRS. HENRY LEE. See COLLEGES, 3 (Hedding C., Ill.).

GATTI–CASAZZA, GIULIO (Feb. 3, 1869, Udine, Italy), was educated as a naval engineer at the Universities of Ferrara and Bologna, and graduated from the Naval Engineering College at Genoa in 1890. He succeeded his father as president of the theatrical committee at Ferrara in 1893, and for five years managed the Teatro Municipale. His marked success, aided by recommendations from Puccini, Mascagni and Franchetti, whose operas he produced at Ferrara, led to his becoming director of La Scala at Milan in 1898. There he worked for ten years, and, in conjunction with Toscanini as conductor, brought the performances to notable perfection. 'Rheingold' and 'Siegfried' were staged for the first time in Italy, 'Parsifal' was produced at concerts, Strauss' 'Salome,' Tchaikovsky's 'Eugene Onegin' and 'Pique Dame,' and many modern French as well as Italian operas were introduced. Since 1908 he has been General Director of the Metropolitan Opera House in New York, which has never been administered with greater sustained success. His policy in the selection of repertory and artists and the attention given to every detail of performance have earned him high renown. [R.9]

GAUL, HARVEY BARTLETT (Apr. 11, 1881, New York), at sixteen became a pupil of LeJeune and deputy-organist at St. John's Chapel. In 1900 he went to Emmanuel Church in Cleveland, remaining eight years. Here he was director of the Hough Choral Club and critic on the 'News,' besides going abroad for work with Armes at Durham and Gaul at Birmingham. After his marriage to Harriett Avery, the authoress, he removed to Paris to study under Decaux and d'Indy at the Schola Cantorum and with Widor and Guilmant, serving also as organist at St. Luke's Chapel. In 1910 he came to Calvary Church in Pittsburgh. He is also critic for the 'Post' and 'Sun,' and teaches at the Carnegie Institute of Technology and in private schools. His chief works are cantatas, organ-pieces, anthems, choruses and songs (Schirmer, Ditson, Gray, White-Smith, Birchard, etc.). [R.8]

GAY, MARIA (June 13, 1879, Barcelona, Spain), first studied sculpture, and her conversion to music came about curiously. At sixteen she was imprisoned for six months for singing a revolutionary song. She then took up the violin, made rapid progress, and also developed her voice, though without a teacher. Brought to Pugno's notice, she sang at some of his concerts, and thus was heard at Brussels by the director of the Théâtre de la Monnaie, where she made her début as Carmen in 1902 on five days' notice and with success. She then studied with Mme. Adiny in Paris for a year. She toured France, Belgium, Germany, Russia, Spain and England, appearing at Covent Garden in 1906 as Carmen. In 1908 she came to America, singing at the Metropolitan Opera House in 1908–09, with the Boston Opera Company in 1910–12, from 1913 with the Chicago Opera Company and later in Boston again. Her répertoire includes Carmen, Orfeo, Delilah, Azucena, Maddalena (in 'Rigoletto'), Santuzza, Suzuki, Charlotte (in 'Werther'), the Mother (in 'Louise'), Geneviève (in 'Pelléas et Mélisande), Carmela (in 'I Giojelli della Madonna'), Pilar (in 'La Habanera'), Lia (in 'L'Enfant Prodigue') and Brangäne. [R.9]

GAYNOR, JESSIE LOVEL, née Smith (Feb. 17, 1863, St. Louis), had no special musical training until after her graduation from Pritchett College in 1881. She then went to Boston, where she studied piano for two years with Maas. Later she had theory with Goodrich and Weidig in Chicago. Songs written for her own children led to her first book, *Songs of the Child-World*. She was then evolving simple methods for the beginnings of music-study and piano-playing. She has given much time to practical teaching and the development of teaching-methods. Her compositions include many for children, but those for older folk are equally popular. In her books of songs Mrs. Alice C. D. Riley has coöperated, writing many of the verses. The complete list includes about fifty songs published separately, of which 'The Slumber Boat' is perhaps the best-known; seven 'Songs to Little Folks'; an album of six 'Rose-Songs'; an album of seven songs; three operettas, 'The House that Jack Built,' 'The Toy-Shop'; 'Princess Bo-Peep'; choruses for mixed or women's voices; and several piano-pieces. Three volumes of 'Songs of the Child-World' are now published, and 'Sunday-school Songs for Little Children.' Educational works for the piano are *First Pedal-Studies*, *Miniature Melodies* (two books), *Melody-Pictures for Little Players*, and *Miniature Duets*. *Lilts and Lyrics* is a song-book for children's schools, and *Elements of Musical Expression* is for early use in dictation and ear-training. Several songs are unpublished, as is also a romantic operetta 'Pierre, the Dreamer.' She married Thomas W. Gaynor in 1886, and lives in St. Louis. [R.8]

GEBHARD, HEINRICH (July 25, 1878, Sobernheim, Germany), came to America when a boy. He attended the High School at Roxbury, Mass., and studied piano with Clayton Johns in Boston until 1895. After four years with Leschetizky in Vienna, he made his début with the Boston Symphony Orchestra in 1900. He has since held an enviable position in Boston as pianist and teacher. He is popular both as ensemble-player and recitalist, and has played in the first Boston performances of Franck's Quintet and 'Variations Symphoniques,' Fauré's G minor Quartet, and d'Indy's 'Mountain Symphony'; and in the first American performances of Strauss' 'Burleske,' Converse's 'Night and Day,' and Loeffler's 'A Pagan Poem.' He has composed a string-quartet, a sonata for violin and piano, waltzes for orchestra, and 12 piano-pieces (Boston Music Co.). [R.9]

GEDDES, PAUL R. See COLLEGES, 3 (Stetson U., Fla.).

GEER, E. HAROLD (Mar. 5, 1886, Tabor, Ia.), was the son of music-teachers and pioneers in musical education in Iowa, his father being for years director of Tabor College Conservatory. He began piano, violin and organ under his parents' direction. In 1906 he graduated from Doane College in Nebraska, and the next year at the Oberlin Conservatory. In 1907–09 he taught at Lake Erie College in Ohio, also pursuing graduate-studies in organ and composition under Andrews at Oberlin and playing in the Woodland Avenue Presbyterian Church in Cleveland. In 1909–11 he taught organ and theory at Albion College in Michigan, and then went to Paris for two years with Widor and Gédalge. In 1913–16 he was organist at the First Congregational Church in Fall River, Mass. Since 1916 he has been organist and assistant-professor at Vassar College. His compositions (unpublished) include a sonata for violin and piano, songs, short pieces for piano and organ, and arrangements for organ. He is a fellow of the A. G. O. [R.9]

GEERE, MARVIN DARWIN (b. 1883). See COLLEGES, 3 (Baker U., Kan.).

GEHOT, JEAN (1756?– ?). See Register, 2.

GEHRKENS, KARL WILSON (Apr. 19, 1882, Kelleys Island, O.), graduated from both Oberlin College and Oberlin Conservatory in 1905. For two years he taught algebra and German in the Oberlin High School, but in 1907 returned to the Conservatory to take charge of the department of school-music. His position there involves the training of teachers of public-school music and also the supervision of music in the Oberlin schools. He has been a leader in all school-music movements and is prominent in the Supervisors' National Conference. He is also active in the M. T. N. A., and since 1919 has been the efficient editor of its *Proceedings*. He has written *Music-Notation and Terminology*, 1916, *Essentials in Conducting*, 1919, an *Introduction to School Music-Teaching*, 1919, and many articles on various phases of music-education. [R.9]

GEIB, JOHN and ADAM. See Register, 3.

GEIBEL, ADAM (b. 1855). See Register, 7.

GEIGER, AUGUST (d. 1910). See COLLEGES, 2 (Brenau C., Ga.).

GEMÜNDER, AUGUST MARTIN LUDWIG (Mar. 22, 1814, Ingelfingen, Würtemberg : Sept. 7, 1895, New York), with his brother, was trained as a violin-maker by his father. In 1846 he came to Springfield, Mass., establishing a business which about 1852 became famous at New York. His instruments won first prizes at London in 1851, at Paris in 1867 and at Vienna in 1873, and have been used by the greatest players. The business was continued by four sons. [R.4]

GEMÜNDER, GEORG (1816–1899). See Register, 4.

GENSS, HERMANN (b. 1856). See Register, 8.

GERHART, I. See TUNE-BOOKS, 1818.

GERICKE, WILHELM (Apr. 18, 1845, Graz, Styria). See article in Vol. ii. 159. His second engagement as conductor of the Boston Symphony Orchestra was in 1898–1906, and he then returned to Vienna, retiring from musical activity. He showed an increased sympathy for modern music in his later years at Boston, without losing that 'passion for perfection' for which he was noted. To the list of his compositions are to be added a septet, a string-quartet, two sonatas for violin and piano and two for piano, a piano-quintet and trio, and a suite for orchestra. He has also orchestrated three sonata-movements of Bach and provided additional accompaniments for Handel's 'Judas Maccabæus.' [R.7]

GERMAN SINGING–SOCIETIES. Ritter, in his *Music in America*, lays just emphasis upon the zeal with which German immigrants early organized choral societies, originally for men's voices only. The New York Liederkranz was started in 1847, and from it diverged in 1854 the Arion. About the same time similar movements took place in many other cities. The Cincinnati Männerchöre united in a festival in 1849. The Milwaukee Musikverein was organized in 1849. Philadelphia, Baltimore, St. Louis and Chicago may be cited as other places where like activity was shown. At first all these societies were for men and cultivated only part-songs. All of them, also, were in a sense private — for members and their friends. But some of them expanded into

mixed choruses and undertook extensive performances of large choral works in a public way. Even in their more limited form they supplied within their own circle a useful stimulus, and when they gave concerted works and operas they became institutions of general culture. Their most fruitful influence was just before and just after the Civil War. Out of them in several cases grew more comprehensive enterprises that were permanent and powerful. In at least half a score of cities the enthusiasm over them supplied the basis for both choral and orchestral projects of much greater scope and public spirit.

GERMANIA ORCHESTRA, THE, was a coöperative troupe of German players, largely recruited from Gungl's band in Berlin, who came to New York in 1848. Originally they numbered twenty-four, all competent performers, led by Carl Lenschow. The latter was succeeded in 1850 by Carl Bergmann, and the number of members was at times increased. The first concert was on Oct. 5, 1848, in the Astor Place Opera House, followed by a series of sixteen, with four in Brooklyn. In December six concerts were given in Philadelphia, but with such ill-success that the troupe was temporarily disbanded. In March, 1849, they were reassembled at Washington to play at the inauguration of President Taylor. Thence they went to Baltimore, giving ten concerts and for the first time winning pecuniary success. On their way north they stopped at New Haven, Hartford, Springfield, Worcester and Providence. From April 14 they gave twenty concerts in Boston with such éclat that they were in much request elsewhere, not only in New England, but in the South and West. They played a remarkably long list of symphonies, overtures and lesser works, besides joining with choral societies in concerted works. Among the soloists assisting were Jenny Lind, Sontag, Camilla Urso and Ole Bull. In September, 1854, however, the laboriousness of travel led to the dissolution of the Orchestra. During six years they gave nearly nine hundred concerts. The influence of these was one of the most potent factors in the growth of American taste and knowledge. See article in 'Scribner's Magazine,' Nov., 1875, and the old print reproduced in Elson, *American Music*, p. 82.

GERVILLE–RÉACHE, JEANNE (1882–1915). See Register, 9.

GESNER, MAUDE EMMA. See COLLEGES, 3 (Western Maryland C.).

GIDEON, HENRY (Oct. 7, 1877, Louisville, Ky.), graduated from the Louisville Boys' High School in 1895. He studied music at Harvard, spent a year in Paris on a scholarship, and was made A.M. in 1906.

Since 1908 he has been organist at Temple Israel in Boston, and music-director at the Union Park Forum. With his wife, née Ramsay, he toured at intervals for three years. For a time he conducted the Cecilia Society. He edited the *Jewish Hymnal for Religious Schools*, 2nd ed., 1917. His compositions are part-songs for women's voices, 'As sing the thrushes' and 'A Jewish Lullaby,' four songs and a piano-arrangement of the Scherzo from Guilmant's Fifth Sonata (all Witmark). Unpublished are a Mass in F, a score of songs, and arrangements of Russian-Jewish folk-songs with English texts (version by Mrs. Gideon). He has led three musical pilgrimages through Europe, lectured for the Boston Opera Company, and written many articles for magazines. [R.9]

GILBERT, HENRY FRANKLIN BEL-KNAP (Sept. 26, 1868, Somerville, Mass.), had his school-education at Cambridge and Reading, Mass. He studied violin in Boston with Mollenhauer, harmony with Howard and Whiting at the New England Conservatory, and in 1889–93 composition with MacDowell — his first pupil after returning from Europe. While studying he played violin in small orchestras for support. In 1894, with Professor J. D. Whitney of Harvard, he gave concerts illustrating the Slavic tendencies in modern music. After some business experiences and varied further studies, he lived for a time in Paris — intent upon French literature. In 1901, being once more in America, he went again to Paris to hear Charpentier's 'Louise,' and then decided to devote himself to composition. Being intensely interested in folk-music generally, he threw in his lot with the circle represented by the Wa-Wan Press, though with more emphasis upon Negro than Indian sources. His list of works is as follows:

Orchestral —
   'Americanesque,' based on three minstrel-tunes (about 1903) (Gray).
   'Comedy-Overture on Negro Themes' (1911, New York, Pittsburgh, Boston and often since) (Gray).
   Three 'American Dances' (1911) (4-hand piano-arrangement, Boston Music Co.).
   'Negro Rhapsody' (1913, Norfolk Festival) (Gray).
   Two 'Episodes,' 'Legend,' 'Negro Episode' (Gray).
   Symphonic Prologue, 'Riders to the Sea,' after the tragedy of Synge, utilizing studies in Celtic folk-music (1915, Peterboro Festival) (Schirmer).
   'Salammbô's Invocation to Tanith,' after Flaubert, for soprano and orchestra (piano-score, Gray).
   Six 'Indian Sketches,' for chorus and orchestra.
   Hymn, 'To America' (piano-score, Birchard).
   Symphonic Ballet, 'The Dance in Place Congo,' based on four Creole themes quoted by Cable (1918, Metropolitan Opera House, thrice repeated and once in Boston).

Piano —
   'The Island of the Fay,' after Poe (Gray).
   'Indian Scenes,' 'Negro Dances' (Gray).

Songs —
   'Pirate Song,' text from Stevenson (often sung by Bispham).
   About 15 published by Gray, with others by Presser, Birchard, Ditson and Boston Music Co.
   (Edited) 'One Hundred Folk-Songs' (Birchard).

Of these the most ambitious is the 'Dance in Place Congo,' which called out both high praise and question for its depiction of rude vigor. To *The Art of Music* he contributed a chapter on 'Primitive Music,' and to E. S. Curtis' *North American Indian* one on 'Indian Music.' He has written thoughtful articles for 'Music,' 'The New Music Review' and 'The Musical Quarterly.' He has lectured on 'Humor in Music' at Harvard and Columbia in 1917–18, with piano-illustration by George Copeland. See article by Olin Downes in 'The Musical Quarterly,' January, 1918. [R.8]

GILBERT, TIMOTHY and LEMANUEL. See Register, 3.

GILBERT, WALTER BOND (Apr. 21, 1829, Exeter, England : Mar. 2, 1910, Oxford, England), after study with Alfred Angel, Wesley and Bishop, from about 1845 was organist at various places in England and took his first degree at Oxford in 1854. He was a founder of the R. C. O. and in later years one of its vice-presidents. From 1869 for thirty years he was organist at Trinity Chapel in New York, highly respected as player, composer and editor of church-music. In 1899 he retired on a pension and later went back to England. He was made Mus.D. by Toronto University in 1886 and by Oxford University in 1888. He composed the oratorios 'St. John' (1857) and 'The Restoration of Israel' (1859), services in C, E and A-flat (one written when only 17, but in standard use), anthems, hymn-tunes and organ-pieces. He wrote or edited *The Parish Church Manual*, 1854, *The Canticles*, 1856, *The Church Chorister*, 1872, *The Hymnal* (with A. B. Goodrich), 1872, *Organ-Preludes and Fugues*, 1880, *The Psalter*, 1882, and also *Memorials of All Saints' Church, Maidstone*, 1864, and *The Antiquities of Maidstone*, 1865. [R.5]

GILCHRIST, WILLIAM WALLACE (Jan. 8, 1846, Jersey City, N. J. : Dec. 20, 1916, Easton, Pa.), was for his whole life identified with Philadelphia (except for teaching at Cincinnati in 1872–73). His only teacher (from 1865) in organ, voice and theory was Dr. Clarke at the University of Pennsylvania. In 1874 he organized and for forty years conducted the Mendelssohn Club. He was conductor of the Philadelphia Symphony Orchestra, from which the present Philadelphia Orchestra developed, from 1892 the moving spirit in the Manuscript Music Society and president of the Musical Art Club. He was a leading vocal teacher, choirmaster at the Church of the New Jerusalem (Swedenborgian) and from 1882 voice-teacher at the Philadelphia Musical Academy. He was made Mus.D. by the University of Pennsylvania in 1896. In 1882 he won the Cincinnati Festival prize of $1000 for his setting of Psalm 46, Reinecke, Saint-Saëns and Thomas being the judges; he also won two prizes offered by the Abt Singing Society of Philadelphia and three offered by the Mendelssohn Glee Club of New York. He conducted his Symphony in C at the Philadelphia Orchestra concerts in 1910. He also composed a Christmas oratorio; Psalm 90; 'Song of Thanksgiving,' for chorus and orchestra; 'Easter Idyl'; the cantata 'The Rose' (1887); a 2nd Symphony, in D; a nonet for piano, strings, flute, clarinet and horn; a quintet for piano and strings; a string-quartet; a pianotrio; many songs; and a long list of anthems and church-music. His writing combined great technical dexterity with much imaginative power. [R.6]

GILES, THOMAS (b. 1883). See State Universities (Utah).

GILFERT, GEORGE. See Register, 2.

GILIBERT, CHARLES (1866–1910). See Register, 9.

GILLES, FRANK WOOD. See Colleges, 3 (Heidelberg U., Ohio).

GILLES, P. See Register, 3.

GILLETTE, JAMES ROBERT (b. 1886). See Register, 10.

GILLINGHAM, GEORGE (d. 1823?). See Register, 2.

GILMAN, BENJAMIN IVES (b. 1852). See Register, 8.

GILMAN, LAWRENCE (July 5, 1878, Flushing, N. Y.), one of the most active writers on the music of to-day, was educated at the Collins Street Classical School in Hartford, Conn., but was self-trained in music. In 1901–13 he was music-critic for 'Harper's Weekly,' and in 1911–13 also managing-editor. Since 1913 he has been musical and dramatic critic of 'The North American Review,' and recently also literary critic and member of the editorial staff. He is author of *Phases of Modern Music*, 1904, *Edward MacDowell*, 1904, *The Music of To-morrow*, 1906, *Guide to Strauss' Salome*, 1907, *Stories of Symphonic Music*, 1907, *Guide to Debussy's 'Pelléas et Mélisande,'* 1907, *Aspects of Modern Music*, 1908, *Life of Edward MacDowell*, 1909, and *Nature in Music*, 1914. He has composed 'A Dream of Death' and 'The Curlew,' recitations with music after Yeats (Schirmer). [R.9]

GILMORE, PATRICK SARSFIELD (1829–1892). See Vol. ii. 169, and Register, 4.

‡ GILSON, PAUL (June 15, 1865, Brussels,

Belgium). See article in Vol. ii. 169–70. To the list of works add the opera 'Gens de Mer' (1902), later known as 'Zeevolk' (1904); incidental music to 'Liefdebloem' and 'Rooversliefde'; two cantatas for soli, chorus and orchestra, 'David' and 'Les Suppliantes'; the symphonic poems 'Halia' and 'La Destinée'; 'Scotch Dances' and 'Suite Pastorale' for orchestra; and a 'Norwegian Suite' for wind-instruments. He has also written *Le Tutti Orchestral*, 1913, a treatise on dynamics.

GILSON COMPANY, THE F. H., of Boston, was founded in 1878 as a music-printing establishment. Besides attaining a position of leadership in this business, for many years it also did general book-publishing. Since 1889 it has been located at 54–60 Stanhope St.

GIORNI, AURELIO (b. 1895). See Register, 10.

GIORZA, PAOLO (1838–1914). See Register, 8.

'GIOVANNA DI NAPOLI.' An opera by Maurice Strakosch, produced in New York in 1860 (?).

GITTELSON, FRANK (June 12, 1896, Philadelphia), came of musical parents and early showed talent. He began violin with Paul Meyer in Philadelphia and Daniel Visanska in New York, and then studied with Auer and Flesch in Berlin. His début was in Berlin in 1913, Gabrilovitch conducting. A tour in Germany, Austria and Holland followed, and at this time Nikisch prophesied for him a brilliant career. In London he gave a joint-recital with Melba at Albert Hall. In America he appeared first in 1914, with the Philadelphia Orchestra. He has since played with leading orchestras and given many recitals. During the war he was assigned to the Radio Service. In 1919 he became professor of violin at the Peabody Conservatory of Music in Baltimore. He has practically introduced and repeatedly played the first violin-concerto of Alfredo d'Ambrosio, and expects soon to introduce a second concerto. [R.10]

GLASSON, T. BATH. See Register, 8.

‡ GLAZUNOV, ALEXANDER CONSTANTINOVITCH (Aug. 10, 1865, Petrograd, Russia). See article in Vol. ii. 175–177. In 1909–12 he was director of the Petrograd Conservatory, and then returned to his class in instrumentation and score-reading. To the list of works add

op. 73 'Ouverture Solennelle.'
    76 'Marche sur un thème russe,' for orchestra.
    78 Ballade, for orchestra.
    81 'Scène dansante,' for orchestra.
    82 Concerto in A minor, for violin (1904).
    83 Symphony No. 8, in E-flat.
    84 Dramatic Overture, 'Le Chant du Destin.'

op. 85 Two Préludes.
  87 'Prologue Symphonique, à Gogol' (1909).
  88 'Fantaisie Finnoise' (1910, Helsingfors).
  89 'Esquisses Finnoises' or 'Kalevala Suite'
       (1909).
  90 'Introduction et la Danse de Salomé.'
  91 'Cortége Solennel.'
  92 Concerto in F minor, for piano.
  93 Prelude and Fugue, for organ.
Without opus-number: Incidental music to
  Wilde's 'Salome' and to Grand Duke Constan-
  tine Alexander's passion-play, 'The King of
  the Jews.'

See biography by Ossowsky, 1907, and also
Montagu-Nathan, *Contemporary Russian Composers*, 1917.

GLEASON, FREDERIC GRANT (Dec.
17, 1848, Middletown, Conn. : Dec. 6, 1903,
Chicago). See article in Vol. ii. 177. Add
to list of works the piano-concerto in G
minor, op. 18. 'Edris' was played by the
Chicago Orchestra under Thomas on April
17–18, 1896, and also the 'Song of Life' on
Nov. 30, 1900, besides at other times the
prelude to 'Otho Visconti' and 'The Procession of the Holy Grail.' The opera 'Otho
Visconti' was given at the College Theatre,
Chicago, on June 4, 1907, under the direction
of Walter Keller. He was a member of the
New York Manuscript Society, the first
president of the Manuscript Society of Chicago
(1896–98), in 1884–89 music-critic of the
Chicago 'Tribune'; and in 1900–03 director
of the Auditorium Conservatory. [R.6]

GLEN, IRVING MACKEY (b. 1871).
See Register, 8, and STATE UNIVERSITIES
(Wash., Ore.).

‡GLIÈRE, REINHOLD MORITZOVITCH
(Dec. 30, 1874, O.S. or Jan. 11, 1875, N.S.,
Kiev, Russia). See note in Vol. ii. 179. In
1914 he became director of the conservatory
at Kiev. His larger works are the Symphonies
in E-flat, op. 8, and C minor, op. 25; the
symphonic poem 'Les Sirènes'; 'Ilia Muro-
metz,' op. 42, entitled a symphony, but really
a symphonic poem; the opera 'Awakened';
two string-quartets, op. 2 in A and op. 20 in
G; three string-sextets and a string-octet;
pieces for two pianos, opp. 41 and 61, and many
songs and smaller instrumental pieces.

GLOVER, WILLIAM HOWARD (1819–
1875). See Register, 5.

GLUCK, ALMA (May 11, 1886, Bucharest,
Rumania), was brought to New York as a
child (Reba Fierson) and was educated in
the public schools and the Normal College.
She began a business career as confidential
secretary before discovering that her voice
was worth cultivation. After studying in
1906–09 with Buzzi-Peccia, she sang for
Toscanini and Gatti-Casazza and was at once
engaged for the Metropolitan Opera House.
She made her début as Sophie in Massenet's
'Werther' in 1909, and later appeared in

'Orfeo,' 'I Pagliacci,' 'Armide,' 'Stradella'
and 'La Bohème.' In her first year at the
Metropolitan she sang eleven rôles and twenty
in all. In 1912 she gave up the stage for
concert-work, in which she had been and is
notably successful. The winter of 1912–13
was spent in study with Sembrich in Berlin.
She married the violinist Efrem Zimbalist in
1914. [R.9]

GODOWSKY, LEOPOLD (Feb. 13, 1870,
Wilna, Russian Poland), first appeared as
pianist at nine, and began American tours in
1884 with Clara Louise Kellogg and Emma
Thursby and later with the violinist Musin.
His studies prior to this date had been in
Wilna, with a few months at the Hochschule
in Berlin under Rudorff. In 1886 he returned
to Europe, expecting to study with Liszt, but
the latter's death prevented. In 1887–90 he
was a pupil of Saint-Saëns in Paris. His
second American tour began in 1890, and led
to a long sojourn, at first as instructor of
piano-teachers at the Broad Street Conservatory in Philadelphia, and in 1894 as
director of the piano-department of the
Chicago Conservatory. In 1900 he went to
Germany, and made his Berlin début in
December. For nine seasons his home was
there, the routine of teaching being varied by
many concert-trips. In 1909 he was made
director of the Master-School of Piano-Playing
at Vienna, with the title of Imperial Royal
Professor. In 1912 and 1913 he made tours
in America, and in 1914 again located in the
United States. Since 1918 he has held mas-
ter-classes for piano-playing on the Pacific
Coast and in the West. His concert-tours
have been almost continual, but he has found
time also to prepare and edit many educational works. He is editor-in-chief of *The
Progressive Series of Piano-Lessons*, 1912
(Art Publication Society, St. Louis). Huneker
calls his playing 'transcendental . . it is
the fine equilibrium of intellect and emotion
that compels admiration.' His compositions
for piano are as follows:

Sonata in E minor.
24 'Walzermasken.'
24 'Renaissance Pieces.'
53 Studies on Chopin's Études.
Concert-Paraphrases on Weber's 'Momento Ca-
  priccioso,' 'Perpetuum Mobile' and 'Invita-
  tion to the Dance.'
Cadenza to Beethoven's 4th Concerto in G.
  (The above published by Schlesinger.)
Symphonic Metamorphoses on Joh. Strauss'
  waltzes 'Kunstlerleben,' 'Fledermaus' and 'Wein,
  Weib und Gesang' (Cranz).
Concert-arrangement of Henselt's 'Si oiseau
  j'étais,' op. 2, no. 6 (Hofmeister).
Concert-Studies in C and E-flat.
Sarabande in C-sharp minor.
Menuet in A-flat.
Courante in E minor.
'Ein Dämmerungsbild' in E-flat.

'Valse-Idylle' in E.
Scherzino in C-sharp minor.
  (The above published by Schirmer.)
Toccata ('Perpetuum Mobile') in G-flat.
'Mélodie Méditative' in E-flat.
Capriccio in C minor.
' Arabesque ' in F.
' Barcarolle-Valse ' in F-A.
Concert-Paraphrase of Chopin's Waltz, op. 18.
Concert-Arrangement of Chopin's Rondo in E-flat,
  op. 16.
  (The above published by Schmidt.)
Nocturne, 'A Night in Spring' (Art Publ. Soc.).
12 'Impressions,' for violin and piano.
4 'Impressions,' for 'cello and piano.
34 'Miniatures,' for piano, 4-hands — developed
  from five-tone combinations.
  (The above published by Carl Fischer.)   [R.7]

GOEPFART, CHRISTIAN HEINRICH
(1835–1890). See Register, 6.

GOEPP, PHILIP HENRY (June 23, 1864,
New York), in 1872–77 attended school in
southern Germany and began to study the
piano, followed by further training in organ
and theory under P. B. Sparks in New York.
In 1884 he graduated from Harvard and took
the full course in composition under Paine.
He then became a law-student, was admitted
to the bar in Philadelphia and wrote articles
on legal subjects. Since 1891, however, music
has been his profession, starting with supple-
mental studies with W. M. Warner (piano),
Wood (organ) and Clarke (orchestration).
In 1892 he was a founder of the Manuscript
Music Society and long an officer in it. Since
1900 he has prepared the program-notes for
the Philadelphia Orchestra. He is organist
at the First Unitarian Church and theory-
professor at the Temple University, besides
much general teaching. He has published
a fairy-opera, 'The Lost Prince,' part-songs,
madrigals, anthems, children's songs and a
'Lullaby' for violin. He has besides several
orchestral marches (such as the 'Heroic'
and the 'Wedding'), a sonata for violin and
piano, variations for organ, many pieces for
piano or violin, a Christmas cantata and
many songs. He is most widely known for
his *Symphonies and their Meaning*, 3 vols.,
1898, 1902, 1913. He edited Madeira's *Annals
of Music in Philadelphia*, 1896, and has written
numerous magazine articles.   [R.8]

GOETSCHIUS, PERCY (Aug. 30, 1853,
Paterson, N. J.), until twenty assisted his
father as civil engineer, though eagerly using
means for self-discipline in music. In 1873
he entered the Stuttgart Conservatory,
studying piano with Lebert and Pruckner,
composition with Faiszt and instrumentation
with Doppler. In 1876 he began to teach
the theory-classes and in 1885 was made
Royal Professor in theory and history and
became critic for two journals. In 1890–92
he taught at Syracuse University, receiving a
Mus.D. in 1892. In 1892–96 he was at the

New England Conservatory, and in 1896–1905
taught privately in Boston. Since 1905 he
has been head of the work in theory and
composition at the Institute of Musical Art
in New York. In 1897–1905 he was organist
at the First Parish Church in Brookline.

His development of a rational and comprehensive system of theory-teaching was
partially suggested by the work of Faiszt,
but is chiefly due to his own persistent efforts
to organize tone-materials and show reasons
for the instinctive impulses of genius in using
and applying them, to lead students forward
by careful stages of information and experiment, and to keep their work vital by constant
analysis of good music. In pursuance of his
ambition he has produced a monumental
series of text-books, admirably arranged and
abounding in original definitions and directions.
These include *The Material Used in Musical
Composition*, Stuttgart, 1882 (2nd ed., rewritten,
New York, 1889, 14th ed., rewritten, 1913),
The Theory and Practice of Tone-Relations,
1892 (11th ed., revised, 1900, 15th ed., rewritten, 1916), *Models of the Principal Music-
Forms*, 1894, *History-Syllabus*, 1894, *The Homo-
phonic Forms of Musical Composition*, 1898,
Exercises in Melody-Writing, 1900 (rewritten,
1918), *Applied Counterpoint* — Invention, Cho-
rale-Elaboration, Fugue, Canon, 1902, *Lessons
in Music-Form*, analysis only, 1904, *Elementary
Counterpoint*, 1910, *The Larger Forms of Musical Composition*, 1915, and (with Thomas Tapper) *Essentials in Music-History*, 1914.

Unpublished compositions include a symphony, the overtures 'Samson' and Christmas,'
an orchestral suite, three concert-fugues for
piano, and many smaller pieces, instrumental
and vocal. He has published a piano-sonata
in B, two concert-fugues, seven Characteristic
Pieces in waltz-rhythm, a Minuet, a Wedding-
March (also organ), two Mazurkas, a Revery,
six anthems and the song 'The Lord is my
Shepherd.' He has edited the complete
piano-works of Mendelssohn (Cotta Edition),
Thirty Compositions of Mendelssohn (Ditson),
an analytic edition of 'The Songs without
Words' (Ditson), etc. He is one of the editors
of *The School-Credit Piano-Course* (Ditson).
He has also written many essays and articles
for musical journals.   [R.6]

GOFF, ANNA CHANDLER. See COL-
LEGES, 3 (Kentucky Wesleyan C.).

GOGORZA, EMILIO EDOARDO DE (b.
1874). See Register, 8.

'GOLD,' a 'forest-play,' was No. 14 of the
'Grove-Plays' of the Bohemian Club of
California. The music is by Humphrey J.
Stewart and the text by Frederick S. Myrtle.
It was given in August, 1916. The scene
is laid in a California forest, at first in pre-
historic time and then in 1776.

GOLDBECK, ROBERT (Apr. 19, 1839, Potsdam, Germany : May 16, 1908, St. Louis), was first trained in piano and harmony by his uncle, Louis Köhler, and later studied with Litolff. After sojourns in Paris and London, he came to New York in 1857 as teacher and composer. In 1867 he assisted Tourjée in establishing the New England Conservatory in Boston, but in 1868 moved to Chicago and started another there. In 1873–78 he was in St. Louis as conductor of the Harmonic Society and one of the directors of the Beethoven Conservatory. He then moved from place to place — New York in 1880–85, Germany in 1886–91, St. Louis in 1891–94, Chicago in 1894–99, London in 1899–1903, St. Louis in 1903–08. He composed two operas, 'Saratoga' and 'Newport' (1888); the operetta 'The Soldier's Return'; the cantata 'The Song of the Brave Man'; a symphony, 'Victoria'; other works for orchestra; two piano-concertos; a string-sextet; a piano-quintet; songs, choruses, and many piano-pieces. He compiled *Three Graduating Courses*, 6 vols. (piano, voice and 'cello), a *Harmony*, 1890, and an *Encyclopædia of Musical Education*, 3 vols., 1903. [R.4]

GOLDBLATT, MAURICE HENRY (b. 1883). See Register, 9.

'GOLDEN LEGEND, THE.' A cantata by Dudley Buck on a text taken from Longfellow. It won the $1000 prize of the Cincinnati Festival Association and was first given there in 1880.

GOLDMARK, RUBIN (Aug. 15, 1872, New York), is a nephew of Karl Goldmark, the Austrian composer. His general education was at the College of the City of New York and the University of Vienna. He studied piano as a boy with Alfred von Livonius in New York, and in 1889–91 attended the Vienna Conservatory, under Door (piano) and the Fuchs brothers (theory). Returning to New York, he studied with Joseffy and Dvořák at the National Conservatory, becoming teacher of piano and theory there. In 1894 he went to Colorado Springs for his health, and was director of the Colorado College Conservatory. Since 1902 he has been instructor in theory and lecturer in New York, with about 500 lecture-recitals in the United States and Canada. He was one of the founders of 'The Bohemians' and its president in 1907–10. His compositions for orchestra are the overture 'Hiawatha' (1900, Boston Symphony Orchestra), the tone-poem 'Samson' (1914, Boston), and the tone-poem 'Requiem for Orchestra,' suggested by Lincoln's Gettysburg address (1919, New York Philharmonic Society). He has also a piano-trio in D minor, a violin-sonata in B minor, and a string-quartet in A, besides

piano-pieces ('Twilight Fantasies,' 'In the Forest,' 'Prairie Idylls'), four pieces for violin and piano, a Romanza for 'cello, songs and choruses. [R.8]

GOMES, ANTONIO CARLOS (1839–1896). See Vol. ii. 200, and Register, 5.

GOMES DE ARANJO, JOÃO (b. 1849). See Register, 7.

GOODALE, EZEKIEL (1780– ?). See TUNE-BOOKS, 1817.

GOODRICH, ALFRED JOHN (May 8, 1847, Chilo, O. : April 25, 1920, Paris), was self-taught in music. His general education was in the public schools of Sacramento and San Francisco. For a time he taught theory at the Grand Conservatory in New York, but in 1876 went to the Fort Wayne (Ind.) Conservatory. For two years he was music-director at Martha Washington College, Abingdon, Va. He also taught in Chicago, was director of the vocal department of the Beethoven Conservatory in St. Louis, and lived in Paris in 1909–15. His books are *Music as a Language*, 1880, *The Art of Song*, 1888, *Complete Musical Analysis*, 1889, *Analytical Harmony*, 1894, *The Theory of Interpretation*, 1898, and *A Guide to Memorizing Music*, 1904 (revised, 1906). A treatise on *Synthetic Counterpoint* is still unpublished. On hearing Tchaikovsky's 5th Symphony he destroyed his early compositions, with the exception of a suite for piano. The list as it now stands includes a cantata, an overture, several orchestral works, chamber-music' piano-pieces and songs. [R.6]

GOODRICH, FREDERICK WILLIAM (b. 1867). See Register, 9.

GOODRICH, JOHN WALLACE (May 27, 1871, Newton, Mass.), began piano-study while in school, continuing later with Petersilea. He was already an organist at fifteen and had three years' training with Dunham in organ and with Chadwick in composition. He became organist at the Eliot Church in Newton and gave frequent recitals. In 1894 he went to Munich for work under Rheinberger and Abel, and in 1895 won a medal and gave a choral work with orchestra. In 1895–96 he was in Paris with Widor, and in 1896–97 was coach and ballet-conductor at the Leipzig Stadt-Theater. Since 1897 he has taught organ at the New England Conservatory in Boston, where in 1905–06 he was acting-director and since 1907 dean. In 1900–02 he was organist at the Church of the Messiah, and in 1902–09 at Trinity Church. In 1897–1909 he was organist for the Boston Symphony Orchestra, several times appearing as soloist. He still gives occasional recitals. He has been equally active as conductor, organizing the Choral Art Society in 1902 and leading it till 1908, directing the choral work of the Worcester Festivals in 1902–07, having charge of the Cecilia Society in 1907–10, and in 1907 conducting the orchestral concerts at Jordan Hall. From the inception of the Boston Opera Company in 1909 he was one of the regular conductors, continuing till the Company disbanded in 1912. He has published an 'Ave Maria,' after Scheffel, for chorus and orchestra, and 'Choral Music for a Requiem Celebration of the Holy Eucharist' (1918). He has translated Pirro's *J. S. Bach and his Works for the Organ*, 1902, and Niedermeyer and d'Ortigue's *Gregorian Accompaniment*, 1905, and has written *The Organ in France*, 1917, and has some essays on organ-building, Gregorian music, etc.

Besides his sympathy with the French school of organ-playing he is interested in all problems of church-music. In 1918–19 he was on the commission for revising the Episcopal Hymnal. He is chairman of the Music Committee of the City of Boston. During the war he was greatly interested in everything relating to band-music and held more than one supervisory office. In 1918 he had just outlined an extensive plan to train band-players throughout the country when the signing of the armistice cut short all vocational training. [R.7]

GOODRICH, WILLIAM M. (1777–1833?). See Register, 3.

‡ GOOSSENS, EUGÈNE (May 26, 1893, London), the son of a former opera-conductor of the same name, first studied at the Bruges Conservatory and the Liverpool College of Music. In 1907–11 he held a scholarship at the Royal College of Music in London, taking composition with Wood and Stanford and violin with Rivarde, and winning the Worshipful Company of Musicians' silver medal. In 1911–15 he played violin in the Queen's Hall Orchestra, resigning to become one of Beecham's assistant-conductors. His orchestral works began to be heard in 1912–13, when his op. 1 was given. The list of his works is as follows:

op. 1 'Variations on a Chinese Theme,' for orchestra (1911).
  2 'Miniature Phantasy,' for string-orchestra (1911) (Goodwin & Tabb).
  3 Octet for flute, clarinet, horn, harp and strings (1911).
  4a 'Chinese Folk-Song,' for violin and piano (1912) (Goodwin & Tabb).
  4b Serenade for flute.
  5 'Five Sketches' for flute, violin and piano (1912).
  6 Suite — Impromptu, Serenade, Divertissement — for flute, violin and harp (1913, Chester).
  7 'Five Impressions of a Holiday' — 'In the Hills,' 'By the Rivers,' 'The Water-Wheel,' 'The Village Church,' 'At the Fair' (1914, Chester).
  8 Symphonic Poem, 'Perseus,' for orchestra (1914).

op. 9 Songs, 'Chanson de Fortunio,' 'Chanson de Barberine,' from Alfred de Musset (1914, Chester).
  10 Concert-Study for piano (1915, Chester).
  11 Symphonic Prelude to a poem of Ossian, for orchestra (1915).
  12 Fantasy for string-quartet (1916, Chester).
  13 Rhapsody for 'cello and piano (1916, Chester).
  14 String-Quartet in C (1916, Chester).
  15 'Two Sketches' — 'By the Tarn,' 'Jack o' Lantern' — for string-quartet (1916, Chester).
  16 'Deux Proses Lyriques' — 'Hier dans le jardin ensoleillé,' 'Mon chemin s'était assombri' — from Edwin Evans (1916, Chester).
  17a Scherzo, 'Tam o' Shanter,' for orchestra (1916).
  17b 'Persian Idylls' — 'Breath of Ney,' 'Heart of Kalyan' — from Evans (1916, Chester).
  18 'Kaleidoscope,' 12 short piano-pieces (1917–18, Chester).
  19 Songs: 'Afternoon' by Jean-Aubry, 'Epigram' by Evans, 'Tea-Time' by Jean-Aubry (1917, Chester).
  20 'Four Conceits' for piano — 'The Gargoyle,' 'Dance-Memories,' 'A Walking-Tune,' 'The Marionette-Show' (1918, Chester).
  21 Sonata for violin and piano (1918, Chester).
  23 Overture and Incidental Music for Verhaeren's 'Philip II' (1918).
  24 Quintet in one movement for piano and strings (1919).

See sketch by Edwin Evans in 'The Musical Times,' July, 1919.

GORDON, HAMILTON S., of New York, is the name of a music-publishing business founded in 1846 by Stephen T. Gordon, previously an organist and teacher in Hartford, Conn. In 1854–55 the firm-name was Berry & Gordon (S. T. Gordon, T. S. Berry, Oliver Ditson and J. E. Gould), and they sold pianos and organs as well as music. This business was conducted under Gordon's name again in 1855–73, in 1873, Hamilton S. Gordon coming in, as S. T. Gordon & Son, and since 1891 as at present. S. T. Gordon died in 1891 and H. S. Gordon in 1914. The present partners are the latter's four sons. From 1894 the scope of the business was enlarged to include musical instruments generally and Edison phonographs. In 1905 the piano-making was transferred to the Gordon Piano Co., and soon the firm concentrated its attention upon publishing alone. In 1913 it moved to its present location at 141–145 West 36th St. At various times they have issued a large amount of useful literature, especially for the organ and for piano-teaching.

GORITZ, OTTO (b. 1873). See Register, 9.

GORNO, ALBINO (Casalmorano, Italy), was taught piano, organ and harmony by his father, entered the Milan Conservatory and at graduation received three gold medals. He came to America in 1881 as pianist and accompanist for Patti, and remained as teacher at the Cincinnati College of Music, where for years he has been head of the piano-department. His compositions include a 'Cantata to Garibaldi' (1882, New York); 'La Festa dei Montanari,' cantata for voices, piano and orchestra; an operetta, 'Cuore e Patria' (1881?, Milan); a 'Marinaresca' for piano and orchestra; many piano-pieces, songs and choruses. His *Material for the Study of the Pianoforte-Pedals*, 3 parts, 1894–1900, is an exhaustive treatise, with numerous classical and original examples. [R.7]

'GOSPEL HYMNS.' The title of a series of evangelistic hymn-books with tunes published in 1875–91.[1] Their remarkable vogue caused the name to be popularly applied to all hymns and tunes of a similar type. Neither title nor type was new.[2] Both words and music of this order had been in use in America — as also in England — from early in the 19th century, especially on occasions that were then novel, such as prayer-meetings, Sunday-schools and revivals. The issue of books with such music gradually increased till about 1860 and then, under several magnetic leaders, rapidly came to astonishing proportions.[3] The movement constituted a historic phenomenon that justifies remark.

The type of tune was essentially that of the folk-song, though not based upon actual songs of that kind. Salient features are an obvious melody upon a simple harmonic basis (usually without modulation), with the metric pattern often varied by divided pulses and other devices, a tendency to unify couplets more than lines, and a decided rhythmic swing and flow. In these regards the type was in grateful contrast with the traditional 'psalmody.' There was nothing to compete with it in arresting popular attention. Even down to the end of the century it circulated widely among thousands to whom more sophisticated music was wholly unknown. Such tunes, with their lilting, ballad-like verses, were seized upon because in a way they met the craving for folk-music. Here and there in the vast literature are songs of homely naïveté and even beauty. But as early as 1850 and much more after the success of Phillips, Bliss and Sankey about 1870,

[1] No. 1, by Bliss and Sankey; No. 2, 1876; No. 3, by Sankey, McGranahan and Stebbins, 1878; No. 4, 1881; No. 5, 1887; No. 6, 1891; with several issues in combination.

[2] For example, 'Gospel Melodies' (hymns) was issued in 1821, 'Gospel Hymns' in 1864 and 'Gospel Songs,' by Bliss, in 1874.

[3] The total number of distinct books of this class published during the century was probably not far from 1500. Of those by a single compiler (Sankey) more than 50,000,000 copies were sold !

the commercial element tended to vitiate the type. Both hymns and tunes were mechanically produced in large quantities, and promoters arranged 'conventions' and the like to sell their books. So 'catchy' was the style — like that of the war-songs in the '60s and recently — that it tended to prevent attention to better styles. Hence the frequent view that the whole movement is to be condemned. Yet it presents some analogies to much more dignified movements in England, where, however, conditions favored the development of the highly lyrical hymn and the artistic part-song tune. Nothing similar was possible in America till long after the modern forms were well established in England. Instead of the part-songs, the harmonized rhythmic air was inevitably pushed to the front, and the desire for immediate success with the thoughtless multitude kept down efforts to give the style distinction.

Regarding the 'Gospel Hymns' proper Sankey wrote in *My Life and the Story of the Gospel Hymns*, 1906. Of much broader scope and higher value is J. H. Hall, *Biography of Gospel Song and Hymn Writers*, 1914. The list of tune-writers and compilers in this latter includes about 65 persons at work before 1890, of whom the most notable are

William B. Bradbury	(1816–1868)
George F. Root	(1820–1895)
Luther O. Emerson	(1820–1915)
Tullius C. O'Kane	(1830–1912)
Theodore E. Perkins	(1831–)
William H. Doane	(1832–1915)
Horatio R. Palmer	(1834–1907)
Philip Phillips	(1834–1895)
Robert Lowry	(1826–1899)
Henry S. Perkins	(1838–1914)
Rigdon M. McIntosh	(1836–1899)
Hubert P. Main	(1839–)
William J. Kirkpatrick	(1838–)
T. Martin Towne	(1835–)
Elisha A. Hoffmann	(1839–)
William G. Fischer	(1835–1912)
Theodore F. Seward	(1835–1902)
John R. Sweney	(1837–1899)
Philip P. Bliss	(1838–1876)
Ira D. Sankey	(1840–1908)
Isaiah Baltzell	(1832–1893)
William A. Ogden	(1842–1897)
George C. Hugg	(1848–1907)
James McGranahan	(1840–1897)
Charles C. Case	(1843–)
James R. Murray	(1841–1905)
John H. Tenney	(1840–)
Benjamin C. Unseld	(1843–)
Daniel B. Towner	(1850–1919)
George C. Stebbins	(1846–)

GOSS, EDWIN L. See COLLEGES, 3 (Bates C., Me.).

GOTTSCHALK, L. GASTON (1847–?). See Register, 5.

GOTTSCHALK, LOUIS MOREAU (May 8, 1829, New Orleans : Dec. 18, 1869, Rio de Janeiro, Brazil). See article in Vol. ii. 205. His first studies were on the violin when only six; piano-study came later. Zimmerman, then head of the piano-department of the Paris Conservatory, refused even to hear the boy as a candidate; ten years later Gottschalk was himself judge at a Conservatory *concours*. His first appearance in Paris was at the Salle Pleyel in April, 1844, and Chopin then said to him, 'I predict you will become a king of pianists.' A few years later Berlioz wrote that 'he possessed all the different elements of a consummate pianist.' His first New York concert was at Niblo's on Feb. 10, 1853. He refused Barnum's offer of $20,000 and all expenses for a year's engagement. In the winter of 1855–56 he gave eighty concerts in New York. The years 1856–62 were 'squandered,' to use his own words, in the West Indies. He reappeared in New York at Irving Hall in 1862, and in the next three years gave concerts constantly in the North and Canada. In 1865 he visited California, going thence to Panama, Peru, Chili and finally Rio de Janeiro, where he arrived in May, 1869. His last concert was Nov. 24, 1869. His body was brought to New York, where services were held at St. Stephen's Church on Oct. 30, 1870. See Hensel, *Life and Letters of Louis Moreau Gottschalk*, 1870, Fors, *Gottschalk*, 1880, and Petersen, *Notes of a Pianist*, 1881. [R.4]

GOULD, JOHN EDGAR (1822– ?). See TUNE-BOOKS, 1846.

GOULD, NATHANIEL DUREN (1781–1864). See Register, 3, and TUNE-BOOKS, 1822.

GOW, GEORGE COLEMAN (Nov. 27, 1860, Ayer Junction, Mass.), graduated from Brown University in 1884 and from Newton Theological Seminary in 1889. His chief musical training was under B. C. Blodgett in Pittsfield and E. B. Story in Worcester, and from 1889 he was associated with them as teacher of piano and harmony at Smith College. In 1892–93 he studied with Bussler in Berlin. Since 1895 he has been professor at Vassar College, where he has developed a highly-organized department of music. His first book of songs appeared in 1884, with several others later, besides duets and part-songs. He is the author of a striking treatise on harmony, *The Structure of Music*, 1895, and wrote the articles on Harmony and Theory in the *American History and Encyclopedia of Music*, 1910, besides many essays in periodicals. Brown University made him Mus.D. in 1903. [R.7]

GOWEN, EDWIN A. See COLLEGES, 3 (Asbury C., Ky.).

GRABILL, E. W. See STATE UNIVERSITIES (S.D.).

GRABILL, GLENN G. See COLLEGES, 3 (Otterbein C., Ohio).

GRAINGER, PERCY ALDRIDGE (July

8, 1882, Melbourne, Australia). See article in Vol. v. 643. Though a composer from childhood, his first appearance as such was at a Balfour Gardiner concert in London in 1912, when he conducted his 'Mock Morris.' His American début in recital was at New York on Feb. 11, 1915; on Mar. 13 he played the Grieg concerto with the New York Philharmonic Society. In June, 1917, he enlisted as a bandsman in the Army, playing oboe and saxophone; a year later he became instructor at the Army Music-School and became a naturalized citizen. His extraordinary success as virtuoso is equaled by that of his compositions. Of him Cyril Scott has written ('Musical Quarterly' July, 1916) :

'Contemplating Grainger's entire musical personality (for, I would repeat, this is essential) I see in him all those elements which make the 'immortal artist.' For he exists as something quite new in musical expressibility; he has invented new forms or considerably enlarged and transformed old ones; he is a great harmonic inventor, yet, unlike Schönberg, he does not lead us into the excruciating. Furthermore, although at times he is a little too unafraid of the obvious, he is entirely consistent therein and one sees at once how little such a thing is the outcome of weakness. In addition to all these characteristics, he can equally show forth a poetry and pathos which speak in sublime dulcitude to the soul, and a rollicking liveliness which awakens energy almost in the limbs of the decrepit. Can one demand a more all-encompassing plane of emotions in one individuality than this? Truly it were difficult to find.'

Of his extensive total composition only about one-third is as yet published. The present list is as follows :

Suite, 'In a Nutshell' — 'Arrival, Platform Humlet,' 'Gay, but Wistful,' 'Pastoral,' 'The Gumsuckers' March' — for orchestra, piano and Deagan percussion-instruments, also for piano solo, two pianos and (in part) theater-orchestra (Schirmer).

'Molly on the Shore,' for orchestra, also for theater-orchestra, various smaller combinations and piano solo (Schott).

'Shepherd's Hey,' morris-dance for orchestra (Schott), also for 12 instruments (Schott), military band (Carl Fischer), piano solo (Schirmer).

'Colonial Song,' for violin, viola, 'cello, harp and orchestra, also for various other combinations (Schott).

'Mock Morris,' for 7-part string-orchestra, also for other combinations (Schott) and string-sextet (Schirmer).

'Irish Tune from County Derry,' for string-orchestra or a cappella chorus (Schott), also for military band (Fischer) and piano solo (Schirmer).

Clog-Dance, 'Handel in the Strand,' for one or more pianos and string-orchestra, also for other combinations (Schott).

Octet, 'My Robin is to the Greenwood Gone,' for flute, English horn and strings, also as piano-trio and for piano solo (Schott).

Wind-Quintet, 'Walking-Tune,' for flute, oboe, clarinet, horn and bassoon, also for piano solo (Schott).

Q

'La Scandinavie,' a group of melodies freely arranged for 'cello and piano, also (in part) for violin and piano (Schott).

'The Sussex Mummers' Christmas Carol,' for piano (Schott), also for violin or 'cello and piano (Schirmer).

Paraphrase of the 'Flower-Waltz' from Tchaikovsky's 'Nutcracker' Suite, for piano (Schott).

Arrangement of Stanford's 'Four Irish Dances,' for piano (Stainer & Bell).

'Knight and Shepherd's Daughter,' for piano (Schott).

'Children's March,' for piano (Schott).

'One more day, my John,' sea-chanty in the form of a 'preliminary canter,' for piano (Schirmer).

Lullaby from 'Tribute to Foster,' for piano (Schirmer).

'The Bride's Tragedy,' for double chorus and orchestra (Schott).

'Father and Daughter,' dance-song from the Faroe Islands, for five male soli, double chorus and orchestra (Schott).

'Sir Eglamore,' for double chorus, and orchestra (Schott).

'The Camp' and 'March of the Men of Harlech,' two Welsh fighting-songs, for double chorus and orchestra (Schott).

'The Hunter in his Career,' for double men's chorus and orchestra (Schott).

'Marching-Song of Democracy,' for chorus, orchestra and organ (Schirmer).

'The Merry Wedding,' bridal dance for soli, chorus and orchestra, organ *ad lib.* (Ditson).

'We have fed our seas for a thousand years,' from Kipling, for chorus and orchestra or brass (Schott).

'Marching-Tune,' Lincolnshire folk-song, for chorus and brass (Schott).

'I'm seventeen come Sunday,' for chorus and brass (Schirmer).

'Brigg Fair,' Lincolnshire folk-song, for tenor and a cappella chorus (Schott).

'At Twilight,' for tenor and a cappella chorus (Schott).

'Morning-Song in the Jungle' and 'The Innuit,' from Kipling, for a cappella chorus (Schott).

'A Song of Vermland,' for a cappella chorus (Schott).

'Tiger, Tiger,' from Kipling, for a cappella men's chorus, tenor *ad lib.* (Schott).

'There was a pig went out to dig,' for a cappella women's chorus.

'Willow, Willow,' old English song, with guitar or harp and strings (Schott) or piano (Schirmer).

'Died for Love,' Lincolnshire folk-song, with three strings or wood-winds or piano (Schott).

'Dedication,' from Kipling, song with piano (Schott).

'A Reiver's Neck-Verse,' from Swinburne, song with piano (Schott).

'Six dukes went a-fishin',' Lincolnshire folk-song, with piano (Schott).

See Parker, *Percy Aldridge Grainger, a Study,* 1918, and the article in 'The Musical Quarterly' quoted above. [R.10]

GRAM, HANS. See Tune-Books, 1793.

‡ GRANADOS Y CAMPINA, ENRIQUE (July 27, 1867, Lérida, Spain : Mar. 24, 1916, at sea[1]), in 1884–87 studied under Pujol at Barcelona and Pedrell at Madrid

[1] While escaping from the 'Sussex,' torpedoed by a German submarine.

and then went to Paris, where he attended de Bériot's class at the Conservatory intermittently because of ill-health. His zarzuela 'Maria del Carmen' was performed at the Royal Theater in Madrid in 1898. Part of 'Folleto' was given at Barcelona in 1903. 'Goyescas' dates from 1899. Not satisfied with its original form, he made from it a piano-suite (played in America by Schelling), and later rewrote the opera to a new libretto by Fernando Periquet. This was accepted at the Paris Grand-Opéra for 1914–15, but given up because of the war. Its première was at the Metropolitan Opera House in New York on Jan. 28, 1916 — the first Spanish opera, sung in Spanish, given in the United States. Both composer and librettist were present. It had five performances, with fair success. On Feb. 22 the composer and Miss Fitziu, the soprano, gave a recital of his music at Æolian Hall. His other works are the opera 'Miel de la Alcarria' (1893) ; two symphonic poems, 'La Nit del Mort' and 'Dante' (the latter played by the Chicago Symphony Orchestra in 1915, with Miss Braslau as contralto) ; 'Elisenda,' a poem for voice and small orchestra ; a quartet for strings and piano ; a trio ; songs ; and a number of piano-pieces, of which the two books of 'Goyescas' are most significant. See articles by Jean-Aubry in 'The Musical Times,' December, 1916, and by Newman, *ibid.*, August, 1917.

GRAND CONSERVATORY, THE, of New York, was founded in 1874 by Ernst Eberhard, who directed it for about forty years. Its plan was ambitious and for many years it had much success.

GRANT–SCHAEFER, GEORGE ALFRED (b. 1872). See Register, 8.

GRASSE, EDWIN (Aug. 13, 1884, New York), despite the handicap of blindness from infancy, has made an enviable record as violinist, pianist and composer. As a child he studied violin and harmony with Carl Hauser. In 1898 he went to study with Thomson in Brussels, and became a pupil of the Royal Conservatory, where in 1900 he won a first prize and in 1901 was awarded the 'Prix de Capacité,' 'with the very highest distinction.' On Joachim's advice he made his Berlin début in 1902 with the Philharmonic Orchestra, playing the Sinding concerto. His début in New York was with the Brahms concerto in 1903. He has toured with success in both Europe and America. His published compositions for violin and piano are a Sonata in C (Schirmer) ; a Scherzo Capriccioso and 'Waves at Play' (Schirmer) ; a Song without Words, no. 2, in G, 'In a Rowboat' and Polonaise, no. 1, in C (Carl Fischer) ; and an Arioso and Scherzo in A minor (Boston Music

Co.). In manuscript are a Symphony in G minor; an orchestral Suite in C; two trios (C and A) for piano, violin and 'cello; a Concerto in G for violin and orchestra; a String-Quartet in D minor; sonatas for piano and violin (A, E and A minor) and a sonata for organ and violin in D; a duet for two unaccompanied violins; many other pieces for violin and piano and piano solo; a 'Sonata-Fantasie' in G-sharp minor for organ; and a number of transcriptions for organ (including symphonic movements by Beethoven, Brahms and Tchaikovsky). [R.9]

GRASSI, ANTONIO DE' (b. 1880). See Register, 10.

GRAU, MAURICE (1849, Brünn, Austria : Mar. 14, 1907, Paris), was brought to America in 1854 and graduated from the College of the City of New York in 1867 and from the Columbia Law School. His connection with music dates from 1872, when with C. A. Chizzola he managed the tours of Rubinstein and Wieniawski. In 1874 they managed a season of opéra bouffe (in English) by Emma Soldene and company, and in 1875 Mme. Aimée and her French company. Later he promoted the Kellogg Opera Company and managed tours for Sarah Bernhardt, Salvini, Offenbach and others. In 1883–84 the firm of Abbey, Schoeffel and Grau leased the Metropolitan Opera House, and gave performances there and in other cities from Oct. 22 to Apr. 12, with such disastrous financial results that they did not make another attempt until 1891–92. They continued until 1897, when the whole burden was assumed by Grau. In 1903 ill-health led to his retirement. [R.6]

GRAUPNER, JOHANN CHRISTIAN GOTTLIEB (Oct. 6, 1767, Verden, Germany : Apr. 16, 1836, Boston), who had been an oboe-player in a Hanoverian regiment and honorably discharged, in 1788 went to London and in 1791–92 played there under Haydn. He came to Prince Edward's Island, and by 1795 was in Charleston, where he played in the City Theatre orchestra. Early in 1797 he settled in Boston, and besides playing oboe in and leading the Federal Street Theatre orchestra, played the double-bass and announced himself as teacher of oboe, German flute and violin (see Sonneck, Early Concert-Life, p. 306). He is credited with being 'the father of Negro song,' from the fact that on Dec. 30, 1799, at the end of the second act of 'Oroonoko' (Federal Street Theatre, Boston) he sang in character 'The Gay Negro Boy,' accompanying himself with the banjo. About 1800 he opened a music-store; he also engraved and published music. Soon after coming to Boston he began to assemble players for an orchestra, and this group may have been the

nucleus of the Philharmonic Orchestra, which gave its last concert in 1824 after a known existence of some fifteen years. He was an enthusiast for Haydn's music, was active and influential in musical affairs, and undoubtedly deserves Elson's title, 'the father of American orchestral music.' At Charleston in 1796 he married Mrs. Catherine Hillier, who had made her début at Boston as a singer in 1794 (as 'Mrs. Heelyer'). She was one of the most prominent and successful singers of the day. She died at Boston on May 28, 1821. For these dates and the Graupner family-record, see the Boston Symphony Orchestra Program-Book, 1909–10, pp. 920–23. [R.2]

GRAY, HERBERT WILLARD (b. 1868). See Register, 8.

GRAY COMPANY, THE H. W., of New York, was organized in 1906 by H. Willard Gray to take over the business of the American branch of Novello & Co., the great London publishers. This branch had been established in 1883, eight years before the change of laws which for the first time gave foreigners copyright-protection in America. At first only a few American works were taken into the catalogue, such as Parker's 'Hora Novissima' and Shelley's 'Vexilla Regis' (both 1893), but in 1894–1906 about 100 choral works were published, together with books like the Novello Music-Course for Public Schools, Parker's (P. E.) Hymnal, the Hymnal for Schools and The Institute Hymnal by Ives and Woodman, Stubbs' Manual of Intoning and The Choir-Service, Hulbert's Voice-Production, J. W. Goodrich's Gregorian Accompaniment and Hall's Choir-Boy Training. Since 1906 at least 3000 American compositions have been issued, including works by all the foremost composers. Converse's 'The Pipe of Desire,' the first American opera to be given at the Metropolitan Opera House, came out in 1907. Gilbert's works were taken over in 1912. Among important orchestral works are Converse's 'Endymion's Narrative' and 'Ormazd,' Gilbert's 'Comedy Overture' and 'Negro Rhapsody,' etc. The Company was the first to reduce the size of folio sheet-music to 9×12 in., an innovation now adopted by most music-publishers. In 1901 the issue began of 'The Church Music Review,' which, altered and enlarged, became 'The New Music Review' in 1904. This monthly, edited by H. W. Gray, has always maintained a high rank for keen editorials, able articles and trustworthy reports of musical happenings.

GREATOREX, HENRY WELLINGTON (1811–1858). See TUNE-BOOKS, 1851.

‡GRECHANINOV, ALEXANDER TIKHONOVITCH (Oct. 26, 1864, Moscow, Russia). See article in Vol. ii. 222. To the list of works add the 2nd symphony, op. 27;

the opera 'Sœur Béatrice' (withdrawn after
fourth performance because representing
the Virgin on the stage); a third string-
quartet, op. 70; two complete Liturgies, opp.
13 and 29; a 'Laudate Dominum,' op. 65,
a cantata for chorus and orchestra; a piano-
trio, op. 38; much church-music and many
songs. See chapter in Montagu-Nathan,
Contemporary Russian Composers, 1917.

'GREEN KNIGHT, THE,' was No. 9
of the plays of the Bohemian Club of California, produced in 1911. The music is by
Edward G. Stricklen and the text by Porter
Garnett. The scene is laid 'in a forest in
the other-world of dreams on a mid-summer-
night in the present.'

‡ GREENE, HARRY PLUNKET (June
24, 1865, near Dublin). See article in Vol.
ii. 232. He is professor of singing at the Royal
Academy and Royal College of Music in London. He has published *Interpretation in Song*.

GREENE, HERBERT WILBER (b. 1851).
See Register, 7.

‡ GRIEG, EDVARD HAGERUP (June 15,
1843, Bergen, Norway : Sept. 4, 1907, Bergen). See article in Vol. ii. 241-2. Complete
the list of works by adding

op. 68 Six 'Lyrische Stücke' for piano.
   69-70 Ten 'Lieder.'
   71 Seven 'Lyrische Stücke' for piano.
   72 'Norwegische Bauerntänze,' for piano.
   73 'Stimmungen,' seven piano-pieces.
   74 'Vier Psalmen,' a cappella.
(without opus-no.) Three piano-pieces and eleven
   songs.

GRIFFES, CHARLES TOMLINSON
(Sept. 17, 1884, Elmira, N. Y. : Apr. 8,
1920, New York), graduated at Elmira
Academy and began piano with Mary S.
Broughton. In Berlin he studied piano for
four years with Jedliczka and Galston, theory
with Klatte and Loewengard, and composition with Rüfer and Humperdinck. For
a time he taught in Berlin, but in 1907 returned to America and till 1920 taught at
the Hackley School for Boys in Tarrytown,
N. Y., and in New York. His first appearance
in Berlin was in June, 1904, at the Beethoven-
Saal, playing an unpublished piano-sonata
in F minor. His compositions (Schirmer)
include six German songs (1909-10), without
opus-number; three 'Tone-Images' for voice
and piano, op. 3 (1912); two Rondels for
voice and piano, op. 4 (1913); three 'Tone-
Pictures' for piano, op. 5 (1910-12) — 'The
Lake at Evening,' 'The Vale of Dreams,'
'The Night Winds'); three 'Fantasy-Pieces'
for piano, op. 6 (1912-14) — Barcarolle,
Notturno and Scherzo; four 'Roman Sketches'
for piano, after poems by William Sharp, op.
7 (1915-16) — 'The White Peacock,' 'Night-
fall,' 'The Fountain of the Acqua Paola,'

'Clouds' — first given by the composer at
the MacDowell Club in New York, 1918;
five poems of ancient China and Japan,
written for voice and piano on five-tone and
six-tone scales, op. 9 (1916-17) ; three songs,
op. 10 (1916) ; three poems of Fiona MacLeod
for soprano and orchestra or piano, op. 11
(piano-version, 1918) — first given by the
Philadelphia Orchestra with Marcia van
Dresser, 1918-19; 'These Things shall Be,'
for unison chorus (1916). His unpublished
works are 'The Pleasure-Dome of Kubla
Khan,' after Coleridge, a symphonic poem
for full orchestra; 'The Kairn of Koridwen,'
a dance-drama in two scenes, for flute, clarinets,
horns, harp, celesta and piano (1916) — given
at the Neighborhood Playhouse in New York,
1916-17; 'Schojo,' a Japanese mime-play for
four wind-instruments, four muted strings,
harp, tam-tam, Chinese drum and tympani —
first given by Michio Itow at Bohn's 'Ballet
Intime' in 1917 ; two pieces for string-quartet
— given by the Flonzaley Quartet, 1918-19;
a sonata for piano — first given by ¦the composer at the MacDowell Club, 1918; an
arrangement of two 'Tone-Pictures' from op.
5 for wind-instruments and harp — first
given by the Barrère Ensemble in New York,
1916; and a 'Poem' for flute and orchestra
(1918). [R.9]

GRIFFITH, CHARLES LEONARD (b.
1887). See COLLEGES, 3 (Penn. C., Iowa).

GRIMM, CARL HUGO (Oct. 31, 1890,
Zanesville, O.), studied with his father (see
below). Since 1905 he has taught piano,
organ and theory in Cincinnati. Since 1911
he has also been organist at the Reading Road
Temple, and since 1912 also at the Mt. Auburn
Baptist Church. His compositions include
'The Coming of the Anointed,' a cantata for
Christmas; 'The Great Miracle,' an Easter
cantata; a Sabbath Morning Service for the
Synagogue; many vocal solos, choruses and
anthems; an 'Invocation' for violin and piano
(or other combinations) ; and organ-music,
including a tone-painting, 'The Spirit of God
moved upon the face of the waters,' a 'Delphic
Song,' and a 'Festival Postlude.' [R.9]

GRIMM, CARL WILLIAM (June 8, 1863,
Dayton, O.), studied with Julius Fuchs in
Chicago and Homeyer at the Leipzig Conservatory. Since 1893 he has been continuously active in Cincinnati as teacher of
piano, organ and theory and as lecturer. He
has published a long list of instruction-books,
especially for piano and in harmony. His
piano-method is in its 17th edition and his
Modern Harmony in its 4th. [R.8]

GRINNELL MUSIC FESTIVAL AS-
SOCIATION, THE, of Grinnell, Ia., was
started in 1901 by Rossetter G. Cole, then
professor in Grinnell College. Its present

name and scope date from 1912. The conductors, after Mr. Cole, have been H. W. Matlack, W. B. Olds, D. L. Smith, E. B. Scheve and George L. Pierce (since 1907). The chorus numbers about 150, besides a local orchestra of 35. Two to six concerts are given annually, usually including one by a visiting orchestra. The enterprise is maintained by a body of guarantors. First performances are noted of Scheve's 'Requiem' (1909) and piano-concerto (1913).

GRISWOLD, ELIJAH. See Tune-Books, 1800.

GRISWOLD, GERTRUDE (1861–1912). See Register, 7.

GRISWOLD, PUTNAM (Dec. 23, 1875, Minneapolis : Feb. 26, 1914, New York), though his career was sadly brief, had remarkable success as a dramatic basso. He began study in 1897 at Oakland, Cal. In 1900 he went to Randegger in London, and in 1902 to Bouhy in Paris, Stockhausen in Frankfort and Emerich in Berlin successively. His début at Covent Garden was in 1901 and at Berlin and with the H. W. Savage 'Parsifal' company in America in 1904. In 1906–11 he sang at the Royal Opera in Berlin, where he was highly esteemed, and from 1911 he was with the Metropolitan Opera House in New York, specializing in Wagnerian rôles. [R.9]

GROLLE, JOHAN HENDRIK. See Register, 7.

GROSS, JACOB (1819– ?). See Register, 4, under Stieff.

GROUT, CHARLES HENRY (b. 1854). See Register, 6.

GRUENBERG, EUGENE (b. 1854). See Register, 8.

GUALDO, GIOVANNI (d. 1771?). See Register, 1.

GUELICH, HENRY D. See Colleges, 2 (Winthrop C., S. C.).

GUILBEAU, F. T. See State Universities (La.).

‡ GUILMANT, FÉLIX ALEXANDRE (Mar. 12, 1837, Boulogne, France : Mar. 30, 1911, Meudon, near Paris). See article in Vol. ii. 345. In 1894 he was one of the founders of the Schola Cantorum, where he became teacher of organ, as also in 1896 at the Paris Conservatory. He resigned his position at Ste.-Trinité in 1901. In 1893 and 1897–8 he made concert-tours in America. For list of works, see Baker, Dict. of Musicians, pp. 345–6.

GUILMANT ORGAN SCHOOL, THE, of New York, was founded in 1899 by William C. Carl, who has remained its head from the first. It aims to give a thorough training for both church and concert work. Besides instruction in organ-playing, there are courses in harmony, counterpoint and composition, in hymnology, in organ-construction and in tuning. The faculty numbers seven. The total number of graduates is about 115. The School began under the honorary presidency of Guilmant. At present Dubois and Bonnet are honorary president and vice-president, and there is an advisory board that includes four French and four English organists.

GUIRAUD, ERNEST (June 23, 1837, New Orleans : May 6, 1892, Paris). See article in Vol. ii. 259. His father, Jean Baptiste Guiraud, won the Prix de Rome at the Paris Conservatory in 1827. The son's teachers there were Marmontel (piano), Barbereau (harmony) and Halévy (composition). Philip Hale (in the Boston Symphony Orchestra Program-Book, 1910–11, p. 485) tells of his advising Debussy, if he wanted to take the Prix de Rome, to 'reserve for a later day' his score of 'Diane au Bois.' [R.4]

GULBRANSEN–DICKINSON COMPANY, THE, of Chicago, established in 1906, has become one of the leading makers of player-pianos and player-actions. It controls special devices and patterns that insure easy running and perfect adaptability to both upright and grand pianos.

GULLI, LUIGI (b. 1859). See Register, 10.

GUNN, GLENN DILLARD (Oct. 2, 1874, Topeka, Kan.), had his first piano-lessons in Topeka. In 1893–96 he was in Leipzig, studying piano with Zwintscher, Reinecke and Teichmüller and theory with Schreck, and making his début as pianist in 1896. In 1896–99 he assisted Teichmüller and toured in Germany. In 1900–01 he taught at the American Conservatory in Chicago and in 1901–06 at the Chicago Musical College. Since 1905 he has been extension-lecturer on music for the University of Chicago. In 1901–14 he was musical editor for the 'Journal,' the 'Inter-Ocean' and the 'Tribune' in succession. He has appeared as soloist with many leading orchestras and given recitals throughout the country. In 1915 he established the American Symphony Orchestra, for the performance of American works exclusively, with American soloists. He has published History and Sketches of Music, 1913, and is one of the editors of The Progressive Series (Art Publication Society, St. Louis). [R.8]

GUTTMAN–RICE, MELANIE (b. 1873). See Register, 9.

H

‡ HABERL, FRANZ XAVER (Apr. 12, 1840, Oberellenbach, Bavaria : Sept. 5, 1910, Ratisbon, Bavaria). See article in Vol. ii. 269. In 1907 he resigned as editor of the 'Kirchenmusikalisches Jahrbuch' and was succeeded by Karl Weinmann. A large part of his work in the field of Gregorian music has been invalidated by later research, so that his service-books no longer have papal sanction.

HACKETT, KARLETON SPALDING (Oct. 8, 1867, Brookline, Mass.), after graduating from the Roxbury (Mass.) Latin School and spending two years at Harvard, in 1889 went to Italy for four years of vocal study. Since 1893 he has lived in Chicago, at first singing much in concert and oratorio, but since 1898 mainly as teacher. In 1896–1911 he was head of the vocal department at Northwestern University in Evanston and also since 1896 at the American Conservatory. He has since been lecturer at the former and in 1906 became vice-president of the latter. In 1906 he began writing for the 'Evening Post' and since 1909 has been its musical critic. He has contributed articles to many periodicals and other publications, and has written a *History of Opera in Chicago in 'the Fifties.'* [R.8]

HACKH, OTTO CHRISTOPH (1852–1917). See Register, 7.

HADLEY, HENRY KIMBALL (Dec. 20, 1871, Somerville, Mass.), had lessons in piano and violin as a boy from his father and showed facility in composing before he was twelve. At the New England Conservatory he studied with Emery and Chadwick. In 1893–94 he toured with the Schirmer-Mapleson Opera Company as conductor. In 1894–95 he took counterpoint with Mandyczewski at Vienna. In 1895–1902 he was music-director at St. Paul's School in Garden City, N. Y. In 1904–09 he was conducting and composing in Europe, the last year at the Stadt-Theater in Mayence. In 1909 he became conductor of the Seattle Symphony Orchestra and in 1911–15 of the San Francisco Symphony Orchestra. Since 1915 he has been mostly occupied with composition, often serving as guest-conductor. In 1920 he was made associate-conductor of the New York Philharmonic Society. His works include

Symphony No. 1, 'Youth and Life' (1897, New York).
Symphony No. 2, 'The Four Seasons' (1901, taking the Paderewski prize and one from the New England Conservatory, given in 1901 by the New York Philharmonic Society and in 1902 by the Chicago Orchestra).
Symphony No. 3, in B minor (1906, given in 1907 by the Berlin Philharmonic Orchestra, the composer conducting, and in 1908 by the Boston Symphony Orchestra).

Symphony No. 4, 'North, East, South, West,' in D minor (1911, Norfolk Festival, Boston Symphony Orchestra and at Queen's Hall, London).
Overture, 'Hector and Andromache' (1894, given in 1895 by New York Symphony Society).
Overture, 'In Bohemia' (1902, Pittsburgh Orchestra).
Overture, 'Herod,' for tragedy by Stephen Phillips.
'Symphonic Fantasia,' op. 46 (1905).
'Oriental Suite' (1903, New York).
Tone-Poem, 'Salome' (1907, Boston Symphony Orchestra).
Tone-Poem, 'Lucifer' (1915, Norfolk Festival).
Rhapsody, 'The Culprit Fay' (1909, taking prize of National Federation of Musical Clubs, given by the Chicago Orchestra).
Three Ballet-Suites for orchestra.
Concert-Piece for 'cello and orchestra (1907).
Quintet for piano and strings.
Quartet for strings.
Sonata for violin.
Comic Opera, 'Nancy Brown' (1904).
Opera, 'Safie,' in one act (1909, Mayence).
Grove-Play, 'The Atonement of Pan' (1912, Bohemian Club, Cal.).
Opera, 'Azora, Daughter of Montezuma,' in three acts (1917, Chicago).
Opera, 'Bianca,' in one act (1918, taking the Hinshaw prize, given by the Society of American Singers, New York).
Opera, 'The Garden of Allah' (1918, New York).
Opera, 'Cleopatra's Night,' in two acts (1920, New York).
Incidental Music to 'The Daughter of Hamilcar' and 'Audrey.'
Lyric Drama, 'Merlin and Vivien,' op. 52, for voices and orchestra.
Cantata, 'In Music's Praise' (1899, taking the Ditson prize, given New York at People's Choral Union concert).
Cantatas, 'A Legend of Granada,' op. 45, 'The Nightingale and the Rose,' op. 54, 'The Fate of Princess Kiyo,' op. 58, and 'The Golden Prince,' op. 69, for women's voices and orchestra.
Lyric Drama, 'Ode to Music,' op. 75, from Henry van Dyke, for soli, chorus and orchestra (1917, Worcester Festival).
Seven Ballads for chorus and orchestra.
A Church Service.
About 150 Songs.

Regarding his music *The Art of Music* (1915) happily said, 'Everywhere in it is energy, fancy, the spirit of youth. It bubbles and glints, running an inexhaustible gamut of varying tints and ingenious and poetic tonal designs. It is the music of immense enjoyment of objective life, of actions, sights, emotions — too eager and full of action to be deeply reflective, too happy to be philosophic.' His 'Cleopatra's Night' is thought by many to be on the whole the most brilliant opera yet produced by an American composer. [R.8]

HAESCHE, WILLIAM EDWIN (Apr. 11, 1867, New Haven, Conn.), studied violin with Bernhard Listemann, piano with Perabo and composition with Horatio Parker, graduating

HENRY HADLEY

from the Yale Music School in 1897. Since 1902 he has conducted the New Haven Choral Union and other choral organizations. Since 1903 he has taught instrumentation in the Yale Music School. In 1907 he was one of the founders of the New Haven Symphony Orchestra, in which he has since been first violinist. His works include a Symphony in A-flat; a Sinfonietta in four movements; a tone-poem, 'The South'; the two overtures 'Fridjof and Ingeborg' and 'Spring-Time'; a 'Forest-Idylle' for orchestra (Schirmer); the suite 'Eyes of the Night,' for violin and piano (Witmark); a 'Characteristic Suite' for violin and piano (Harms); a 'Legend' for violin, 'cello and piano (Witmark); trios for violins and piano (Ditson); 'The Haunted Oak,' for soli, chorus and orchestra (Schirmer); 'Young Lovel's Bride', for women's voices and orchestra (Schirmer); two piano-suites (Presser); besides songs and pieces for violin and piano. [R.8]

HAGAN, HELEN EUGENIA (b. 1893). See Register, 10.

HAGEMANN, RICHARD (b. 1882). See Register, 9.

HAGEN, THEODORE (1823-1871). See Register, 4.

HAHN, CARL (b. 1874). See Register, 8.

HAHN, JACOB H. (1847-1902). See Register, 5.

HAHN, REYNALDO (b. 1874). See Vol. ii. 271, and Register, 7.

'HAIL, COLUMBIA.' See Vol. ii. 271-2, and articles by O. G. Sonneck in *I. M. G. Sammelbde.* 3. 139, and *Report on 'The Star-Spangled Banner' 'Hail, Columbia'*, etc., 1909.

HAILE, EUGEN (b. 1873). See Register, 9.

HAINES, FRANCIS W. (1822-1887) and NAPOLEON J. (1824-1900). See Register, 4.

HAINES BROTHERS. A well-known and successful firm of piano-makers, founded in 1851 by Napoleon J. Haines, with his brother Francis W. Haines, at first under the name of N. J. Haines & Co. They derived their skill in the line of tradition beginning with Nunns and traced through the New York Pianoforte Manufacturing Co. and (from 1840) A. H. Fale & Co. The Haines brothers were among the earliest makers of the modern 'overstrung' scales. They were the first to give up making 'square' pianos. The firm is now a part of the American Piano Co. Their factory is at East Rochester, N. Y.

HALE, EDWARD DANFORTH (b. 1859). See Register, 7.

HALE, PHILIP (Mar. 5, 1854, Norwich, Vt.), began piano-lessons while a boy at Northampton, Mass., where he was early also an organist. His general education was at Phillips (Exeter) Academy and Yale College, graduating in 1876. In 1880 he became a lawyer at Albany, where he also studied piano and theory with John Kautz and in 1879-82 was organist at St. Peter's. Giving up the law, in 1882 he went abroad for work with Haupt, Raif, Urban and Bargiel at Berlin, with Rheinberger at Munich and Faiszt at Stuttgart, and with Guilmant at Paris. In 1887-89 he was organist at St. John's in Troy and conducted the Schubert Club in Albany. Since 1889 he has worked in Boston, speedily becoming recognized as a critic of the first rank. In 1890-91 he was with the 'Post,' in 1891-1903 with the 'Journal,' and since 1903 with the 'Herald.' In 1898-1901 he also edited the 'Musical Record' for the Ditson Company, and in 1901-03 the 'Musical World.' Previously he had been correspondent for the 'Musical Courier,' New York, and lately has written editorials for the 'New Music Review' there. In 1889-1905 he was organist at the First (Unitarian) Church in Roxbury. His most continuous and substantial work has gone into the program-books of the Boston Symphony Orchestra, which he has prepared since 1901. His writing is always marked by accurate learning, brilliancy of expression and not a little satire and humor. He has also lectured in the Lowell Lectures in Boston and at many other places. He has edited *Modern French Songs*, 2 vols., and collaborated with L. C. Elson on *Great Composers and their Works*, 1900. His wife, née Irene Baumgras (b. Syracuse), whom he married in 1884 in Berlin, is an accomplished pianist and composer. [R.6]

HALL, JAY ROLLIN (b. 1860). See Register, 7.

HALL, LELAND (b. 1883). See Register, 10.

HALL, WALTER HENRY (Apr. 25, 1862, London, England), was prepared by Robert Thurnam, organist at Reigate, for the Royal Academy of Music, where for four years he studied piano under Harold Thomas, organ under Steggall and theory under Banister. He then became organist of Holy Trinity Church in Twickenham, and decided to specialize in choir-boy training and choral conducting. In 1883 he came to New York, and spent one year as assistant to Le Jeune at St. John's Chapel. From 1884 he was organist at St. Luke's in Germantown, Pa., from 1890 at St. Peter's in Albany, and in 1896-1913 at St. James' in New York. In 1893 he founded the Brooklyn Oratorio Society, of which he has been the only conductor. With it he has given a long list of oratorios and cantatas, with first performances in America of several important works. He has conducted various smaller societies, including the Musurgia Society (men's voices), the Mozart Society (women's voices) and the Yonkers Choral Society. In 1913 he was appointed to the new chair of Choral and

Church Music at Columbia University. A large chorus, not limited to students, was organized and regular concerts given in Carnegie Hall — recently transferred to the Gymnasium of the University and combined in a festival of three or more concerts, choral and orchestral. His duties include, besides lectures on choral music, afternoon services at the University Chapel, where a selected choir of forty sings representative church-music. He was one of the Committee on the Episcopal *Hymnal* in 1919. He has composed a Communion Service in G, a Magnificat and Nunc Dimittis in B-flat; a Festal Te Deum and other anthems, canticles and hymn-tunes. He is the author of *Essentials of Choir-Boy Training*, 1907, and many articles and reviews. [R.7]

HALL, WILLIAM JOHN (Feb. 2, 1867, London, England), was a solo choir-boy at eight, and later assistant-organist and treble soloist at Christ and Trinity Churches in London. He studied with Scotson Clark, Trego, Tuddenham and C. Thomas in London, Hauptmann in Berlin and Boncetti in Milan. Coming to Boston, he was a tenor in the Lyric Opera Company, then in succession music-director at Augustana College in Rock Island, Ill., at the College of Music in Cedar Rapids, Ia., conductor of the Mendelssohn Chorus in St. Paul, and organist at the cathedral in Davenport, Ia. For some years he has been located in St. Louis, where he is organist of the First Church of Christ, Scientist, and teaches theory at the Soldau High School. He is an associate of the A. G. O. and dean of the Missouri Chapter, and active in the Missouri Music Teachers' Association. He holds the degree of Mus.D. from Griswold College (England) and the Royal Academy of Arts and Sciences. He has composed the opera 'Tactics' (1890, Hinshaw Opera Co.) and the extravaganza 'Louisiana' (1904, St. Louis Exposition), the tone-poems 'Ecstasy' and 'Victory,' four light operas, many songs and instrumental pieces, many of which are published. [R.8]

HALLAM, LEWIS (d. 1755) and LEWIS, Jr. (1741–1808). See Register, 1.

HALLET & DAVIS PIANO COMPANY, THE, of Boston, is derived from the firm of Brown & Hallet, founded in 1835, in which Edwin Brown was the expert inventor and mechanician and Russell Hallet the supplier of capital. In 1840 they won a first prize from the Franklin Institute for refinement of tone. In 1843 Brown became one of the Chickering foremen and George H. Davis took his place. The firm then underwent several readjustments. About 1850, as Hallet & Davis, it became one of the best in the country, as attested, for example, by a gold medal from the Mechanics Institute in 1853. Mechanically and tonally their pianos have received numerous similar

awards in recent years. Their type of player-piano is called the 'Virtuolo.'

HAM, ALBERT (1858, Bath, England), after being a choir-boy in 1867–73, studied piano and organ with J. Hewitt and organ with Pyne. From 1880 he was organist at Ilminster and in 1893–97 organist at Taunton and conductor of two choral societies. He became F. R. C. O. in 1883 and was made Mus.D. by Dublin University in 1894. Since 1897 he has been organist at St. James' Cathedral in Toronto, where he also conducts the National Chorus and is examiner for Toronto University and several conservatories. He was one of the founders of the Canadian Guild of Organists and has been its only president. In 1906 Toronto University made him Mus.D. once more. His compositions include an Advent Cantata for solo, 8-part chorus and orchestra, the cantata 'The Solitudes of the Passion,' about a dozen strong anthems (Novello or Gray), services, offertory-sentences, etc. (Frowde), part-songs, a military march for piano and many marches played by bands in the British army. He has also written several hand-books for Novello — on the boy's voice, ornaments and graces, etc. [R.8]

'HAMADRYADS, THE,' was No. 3 of the 'Grove-Plays' of the Bohemian Club of California, described as 'a masque of Apollo.' The music is by William J. McCoy and the text by Will Irwin. It was produced in 1904.

HAMBOURG, BORIS (Dec. 27, 1884, Voronezh, Russia), the youngest of the three brilliant sons of Michael Hambourg, who was an able piano-teacher in Moscow, London and (from 1911) in Toronto. Brought up in London, he was first taught piano by his father, but soon turned to the 'cello and, on advice of Hugo Becker, studied under Walenn. In 1898–1903 he was at the Hoch Conservatory in Frankfort under Becker and Knorr (composition). In 1903 he made his début at the Tchaikovsky festival at Pyrmont, and then went with his brother Mark on a tour in Australia and New Zealand. He was first heard in London in 1904 and in Berlin in 1906, in the latter city giving a series of historical recitals that has been often repeated since. During the next four years he toured in Germany, France and the Low Countries, and also in South Africa. In 1910 he came to America, appearing first in Pittsburgh, and in 1911, with his father and his brother Jan, opened the Hambourg Conservatory in Toronto. Since 1916 he has lived in New York. He has composed and edited pieces for the 'cello, and written some songs. [R.10]

HAMBOURG, JAN (b. 1882). See above and Register, 10.

HAMBOURG, MARK (b. 1879). See above and Register, 8.

HAMBOURG, MICHAEL (1856–1916). See above and Register, 10.

HAMERIK, ASGER (Apr. 8, 1843, Copenhagen, Denmark). See article in Vol. ii. 277–8. In 1890 he was knighted by the King of Denmark. Since 1898 he has lived in Copenhagen. His 7th symphony, 'Chorale,' op. 40, utilizes a mezzo-soprano and chorus. Among his chamber-works are a concert-romance for 'cello and orchestra, a fantasia for 'cello and piano, and a piano-quartet, op. 61. [R.6]

HAMILTON, CLARENCE GRANT (June 9, 1865, Providence), had his general education in the Providence schools and Brown University, graduating in 1888. His piano-study was with Edward Hoffman, Foote, Dannreuther and Matthay, organ and theory with Macdougall and Chadwick. In 1889–1904 he was teacher and organist in Providence, and since 1904 has been professor at Wellesley College and organist in the Congregational Church. Since 1913 he has directed a summer music-school at Boothbay Harbor, Me., and in 1918 lectured at Boston University. He has composed choruses for Sophocles' 'Electra' (1912, Wellesley College) and for Euripides' 'Medea' (1914, ib.), both for women's voices, several songs and part-songs (Ditson, Hatch). He wrote nine chapters of Baltzell's *History of Music*, 1905, *Outlines of Music-History*, 1908 (revised, 1913), *Piano-Teaching, its Principles and Practice*, 1910, *Sound and its Relation to Music*, 1912, and is editor of Ditson's *School-Credit Piano-Course*, 1918. He has also written often for 'The Musician' and 'The Etude.' [R.7]

HAMILTON, EDWARD. See TUNE-BOOKS, 1845.

HAMLIN, EMMONS (d. 1881). See Register, 4.

HAMLIN, GEORGE JOHN (Sept. 20, 1868, Elgin, Ill.), after attending the Chicago schools and Phillips (Andover) Academy, studied singing with various American and European teachers. He was first heard as concert-tenor with the St. Louis Choral Society, and in 1898 won notice in Chicago for the first entire program of Strauss songs given in America. In 1904–06 he sang in England, France and Germany, and in 1911 made his operatic début in 'Natoma' with the Chicago Opera Company, in which he was a leading tenor till 1915. He has been successful in 'Carmen,' 'I Giojelli della Madonna,' 'Tosca,' 'Madama Butterfly,' 'The Cricket on the Hearth' and 'Madeleine.' His répertoire of oratorio rôles and songs is notably large. [R.8]

HAMMER, HEINRICH ALBERT EDUARD (b. 1862). See Register, 9.

HAMMERSTEIN, OSCAR (1847, Berlin, Germany : Aug. 1, 1919, New York), came to New York in 1863 a penniless and tradeless youth and found employment as cigar-maker.

Five years later he invented a cigar-making machine, for which he received $6000. All together he took out over a hundred patents in this business, in which he never lost interest and which brought him large wealth. In 1868 he wrote and produced three one-act comedies, one of them set to music by himself. His activity as theatrical manager began in 1870, with the leasing of the Stadt Theatre. In 1888 he built the Harlem Opera House, and followed it with the Columbus Theatre, the Harlem Music Hall, the Murray Hill Theatre, the (first) Manhattan Opera House (1892), the Olympia, the Victoria, the Republic, and the Harris, most of which he managed for a longer or shorter period. In 1906 he built the second and better-known Manhattan Opera House, which was opened with 'I Puritani' on Dec. 3. With such artists as Melba, Nordica, Tetrazzini, Garden, Bonci, Dalmorès, Bressler-Gianoli, Renaud, and Cleofonte Campanini as conductor, the Manhattan at once became a serious rival of the Metropolitan. In 1908 he built the Philadelphia Opera House, running it in conjunction with his New York venture. In April, 1910, the Metropolitan management bought the Hammerstein interests, with the stipulation that he should not produce opera in the United States for ten years. In 1910 he transferred his activities to England, building the London Opera House, opened on Nov. 13, 1911. After an unsuccessful season he sold this and in 1913 built the American Opera House in New York. His plans for opera here were blocked by injunction and the house (now known as the Lexington Opera House) has been used for grand opera only during visits by the Chicago Opera Company. In 1919 he announced his intention of resuming grand opera in New York in 1920. Despite a series of failures, he is to be remembered for the introduction of many great artists, of numerous modern French operas (especially 'Pelléas et Mélisande' and 'Louise') Strauss' 'Elektra,' etc., and for a thorough awakening of his competitors. See Krehbiel, *Chapters of Opera* and *More Chapters of Opera*. [R.7]

HAMMOND, WILLIAM CHURCHILL (Nov. 25, 1860, Rockville, Conn.), was a pupil in organ of Allen in Hartford and S. P. Warren in New York. Since 1885 he has been organist at the Second Congregational Church in Holyoke, Mass., where he has given a remarkable series of over a thousand recitals. In 1919, however, fire destroyed the church and with it his fine library. From 1890 he was instructor in organ at Smith College, and since 1900 has been head of the music-department at Mount Holyoke College, which he has brought to much efficiency. [R.7]

HANCHETT, HENRY GRANGER (Aug. 29, 1853, Syracuse, N. Y. : Aug. 19, 1918,

Siasconset, Mass.), studied medicine at Syracuse University and in 1884 graduated from the New York Homœopathic College, but soon devoted himself to music. His music-studies were begun with Ernest Held in Syracuse and continued with Sherwood, Kullak, A. K. Virgil, William Mason, and A. J. Goodrich. He taught at the Metropolitan College of Music in New York and many other schools, and for many years toured extensively in lecture-recitals. He lectured at the Brooklyn Institute in 1893–1903 and gave over 300 lectures and recitals in New York, about half of them in popular courses under the Board of Education. He was organist in New York churches in 1884–98, and was one of the founders of the A. G. O. in 1897. He was the inventor of the 'sostenuto' pedal for grand pianos in 1873. From 1907 he taught in Washington and in 1913–18 at Brenau College in Georgia. In addition to several books on medical topics, he wrote *Teaching as a Science*, 1882, *The Art of the Musician*, 1905, and *An Introduction to the Theory of Music*, 1916. His compositions, a₂Te Deum, a Benedictus, and an Easter anthem, are published by Schmidt. [R.6]

HANDEL AND HAYDN SOCIETY, THE, of Boston. See Vol. i. 367–8. In 1915 the Society celebrated its centenary by a four days' festival.

HANSON, HOWARD HAROLD (b. 1896). See Register, 10.

‡ HARCOURT, EUGÈNE D' (1855, Paris, France : Mar. 8, 1918, Paris), in 1882–86 studied at the Paris Conservatory with Massenet, Savard and Durand, and then spent four years in Berlin with Schulze and Bargiel. In 1892 he organized the Concerts Éclectiques Populaires in Paris (for which he built the Salle d'Harcourt), which were discontinued in 1895, but resumed in 1900 as Grands Oratorios à l'Église St.-Eustache. As commissioner of the French Government he studied music and music-educational conditions in Italy, Germany, Austria and the United States (1915, Panama-Pacific Exposition). He revisited America in 1917 and conducted works by French composers. His compositions are a Mass (1876, Brussels), the opera 'Tasso' (1903, Monte Carlo) ; three symphonies, two string-quartets, two ballets, cantatas and motets. He published *Quelques remarques sur l'exécution de Tannhäuser à l'Opéra*, 1895, *Aperçu analytique de la 1ʳᵉ à la 9ᵐᵉ symphonie de Beethoven*, 1898, *La musique actuelle en Italie*, 1907, *La musique actuelle en Allemagne et en Autriche-Hongrie*, 1908, *La musique actuelle aux États Scandinaves*, 1910. He also made French translations of Schumann's 'Genoveva' and Weber's 'Der Freischütz.'

HARDMAN, PECK & COMPANY, of New York, piano-makers, were incorporated in 1905 with a capital of $800,000. They have gained a high standing for excellence of tone and construction. Their type of player-piano is known as the 'Autotone.'

HARKER, F. FLAXINGTON (Sept. 4, 1876, Aberdeen, Scotland), was first taught by G. C. Dawson and A. W. Marchant and, after becoming sub-organist at York Minster, by Noble. Since 1900 he has been A. R. C. O. In 1901 he came to America to be organist at All Souls' in Biltmore, N. C., returning there in 1907–14 after three years at St. Martin le Grand's in New York. Since 1914 he has been organist at St. Paul's in Richmond, where he also conducts two choral societies. His compositions include the cantatas 'The Star of Bethlehem,' op. 42, and 'The Cross,' op. 50, with many services, anthems, choruses, sacred and secular songs and organ-pieces (all Schirmer). He has also edited Stainer's *The Organ* and several collections for Schirmer. [R.9]

HARMAN, CATHARINE MARIA (d. 1773). See Register, 1.

HARMATI, SANDOR (b. 1892). See Register, 10.

HARMON, JOEL (1773–1833). See TUNE-BOOKS, 1809.

HARMONIC SOCIETY, THE, of New York. An instrumental group by this name existed in 1773–74 (see Sonneck, *Concert-Life*, pp. 170–1, 174, 201), supplying players for several concerts. In 1849 a choral society thus entitled was formed in the hope of consolidating the interests of the Sacred Music Society and other organizations, and continued amid some ups and downs till 1869. In 1863 the Mendelssohn Society was set up by certain seceding members. During most of its history the conductor was Theodor Eisfeld.

HARMONICA. See article in Vol. ii. 297–8, and also under FRANKLIN.

HARMONICAL SOCIETY, THE, of New York, was established in 1797 to promote both vocal and instrumental music. Nothing is known of its activities in detail. At the end of 1799 it was merged with the St. Cecilia Society into the (first) Philharmonic.

HARMONIUM. See article in Vol. ii. 302–5, with reference to its relation to the American reed-organ.

HARPER, HARRY CLYDE (b. 1867). See Register, 7, COLLEGES, 2 (Irving C., Pa.), and STATE UNIVERSITIES (S. D.).

HARRINGTON, ADA. See COLLEGES, 3 (Kansas City U., Kan.).

HARRIS, CHARLES L. M. (b. 1863). See Register, 7.

HARRIS, GEORGE, JR. (b. 1884). See Register, 9.

HARRIS, WILLIAM VICTOR (Apr. 27, 1869, New York), studied singing with Courtney, composition with Schilling and conducting with Seidl. In 1889-95 he was organist in or near New York, in 1892-95 coached at the Metropolitan Opera House and in 1893-94 conducted the Utica Choral Union. In 1895-98 he was Seidl's assistant-conductor in summer-concerts. Since 1902 he has directed the St. Cecilia Club, a high-class women's chorus, for which special music has been written by Liza Lehmann, Stanford, Elgar, Henschel and others. Besides being a popular teacher, he has published over 100 choruses and songs, and has orchestral works in manuscript. [R.7]

HARRISON, THOMAS. See Register, 1.

HARRISS, CHARLES ALBERT EDWIN (Dec. 15, 1862, London, England), at eight was a choir-boy at St. Mark's in Wrexham, where his father, the organist, gave him his first organ-lessons. From 1875 he became Ouseley scholar at St. Michael's College at Tenbury, from 1880 assistant-organist at St. Giles' in Reading, and in 1881 organist at Welshpool and to the Earl of Powis. In 1882 he came to St. Alban's in Ottawa, and in 1883 moved to Montreal, where he was first at Christ Church Cathedral and later at St. James'. He founded a glee and madrigal society, and conducted the Montreal Philharmonic Society. In 1905 he promoted a series of choral festivals throughout the principal cities of Canada, with Sir Alexander Mackenzie as conductor. The next year he organized a concert of British music, conducted by the composers, at Queen's Hall in London, and in 1919 arranged an enormous choral 'Victory Celebration.' He has composed the cantata 'David before the King' (1890, Montreal), the opera 'Torquil' (1896, Montreal), the choral idyl 'Pan' (1906, London), songs, anthems, part-songs and organ-pieces. [R.7]

HARTFORD PHILHARMONIC ORCHESTRA, THE, of Hartford, Conn., was founded in 1900, largely through the efforts of Mrs. Charles Dudley Warner, and incorporated in 1914. Its conductors have been Richmond P. Paine in 1900-02, John S. Camp in 1902-11 and Robert H. Prutting since 1911. It numbers about 65 players and usually gives three or four concerts annually — about 75 to 1920. Its programs include most of the standard symphonies and overtures, with a large number of modern works.

HARTMANN, ARTHUR MARTINUS (July 23, 1881, Maté Szalka, Hungary), was brought to Philadelphia in early childhood and had violin-lessons from his father and later from Van Gelder and Loeffler. In composition he is mostly self-taught. He was but six when first heard in Philadelphia. Since 1893 he has played with almost all the great orchestras — in America 250 appearances before 1916. In Paris he gave recitals with Debussy. He holds

decorations from Rumania and Servia. Among his pupils are Visanski, Marcosson, Garagusi and Colton. He has published about 25 transcriptions for violin from Paganini, Kjerulf, Nordraak, Debussy and MacDowell, four 'Pieces' (Church), 'Bogdan' (Schirmer), a 'Suite in the Ancient Style,' 'Souvenir,' 'Cradle-Song,' 'Seven o'clock,' 'Autumn in Hungary' (all Carl Fischer) — all for violin; three 'Moods' (Church), six Preludes (Ditson), four 'Miniatures' (Carl Fischer), 51 old Hungarian Melodies (Presser) — all for piano; a 'Prière à Notre Dame,' for organ (Breitkopf); and several songs and part-songs (Gamble, Boston Music Co., Ditson). Unpublished are some orchestral works, 'At the Mid-Hour of Night,' for chorus and orchestra, part of a string-quartet, pieces for violin, viola d'amour and czimbalom, about 20 songs and two melodramas. [R.7]

HARTWELL, EDWARD. See TUNE-BOOKS, 1815.

‡HARTY, HAMILTON (Dec. 4, 1879, Hillsborough, Ireland). See article in Vol. v. 644. Recent works are the symphonic poems 'With the Wild Geese' (1910, Cardiff Festival) and 'A Tinker's Wedding,' 'Variations on an Irish Theme,' for violin and orchestra (1913, London), and the cantata 'The Mystic Trumpeter,' for baritone, chorus and orchestra (1913, Leeds Festival, 1914, Columbia University Chorus, New York). During the war he was Lieutenant R. N. V. R., and his musical activity ceased. Now he is conductor of leading orchestras in London, Manchester and Leeds.

HARVARD MUSICAL ASSOCIATION, THE, of Cambridge, Mass. See article in Vol. i. 368-9.

HARVARD UNIVERSITY, Cambridge, Mass., through its Division of Music offers courses in harmony, counterpoint, canon and fugue, vocal composition, instrumentation, history, appreciation, the evolution of orchestral style, Beethoven, Brahms and certain French composers, and advanced composition. There are no praxis-courses. One or more courses may be taken with credit toward an A.B.; but an A.B. 'with distinction' or 'with honors' in music requires either five or a majority of them, ability to use French, German, and Italian, and original composition. An A.M. or a Ph.D. in music is granted under appropriate conditions. Special students of maturity and ability may be enrolled. The Boott prize of $100 and the Knight prize of $30 are given annually for excellence in composition. The Naumburg fellowship for graduate-study is awarded biennially and a fellowship for work in Boston Music School Settlement annually. The Division — with the Pierian Sodality and several student-clubs in music — occupies a special building, largely the gift of James Loeb of New York. The first instructor in music was John K. Paine, appointed in 1862 and made professor in 1875. Among his assistants from 1895 was Walter R. Spalding, who as assistant- or associate-professor has been head of the Division since Paine's death in 1906. There are also three assistant-professors and one instructor. Besides the powerful stimulus to scholarship and creative activity exerted by the music-division since its establishment, the much earlier influence of the Pierian Sodality (from 1808) and its more serious descendant, the Harvard Musical Association (from 1837), is to be noted.

‡ HARWOOD, BASIL (Apr. 11, 1859, Olveston, England). See article in Vol. ii. 337. He was examiner for degrees at Oxford in 1900–01, '04–05, '08–09 and '14–15. In 1909 he retired from his posts there as organist and choragus. He was the musical editor of *The Oxford Hymn-Book*, 1908. To his compositions add

Capriccio, op. 16, for organ.
Psalm 137, 'As by the streams of Babylon,' op. 20, for soprano, chorus and organ (1907, Oxford).
Motet, 'Jesus, Thy boundless love to me,' op. 22, for soli, or semi-chorus, chorus, orchestra and organ (1909, London Festival of the Sons of the Clergy).
Three Cathedral Preludes, op. 25, for organ.
Sonata No. 2, in F-sharp minor, op. 26, for organ.
Concerto in D, op. 26, organ and orchestra (1910, Gloucester Festival).
Cantata, 'Song on May Morning,' op. 27, for soli or semi-chorus, chorus and orchestra (1913, Leeds Festival).
Morning, Evening and Communion Services in E minor, op. 28.

HARWOOD, FREDERICK. See Colleges, 3 (Henderson-Brown C., Ark.).

HASSARD, JOHN ROSE GREEN (1836–1888). See Register, 5.

HASTINGS, THOMAS (1787–1872). See Register, 3, and Tune-Books, 1816.

HASTINGS, THOMAS SAMUEL (1827–1911). See Tune-Books, with preceding.

HASTREITER, HÉLÈNE (Nov. 14, 1858, Louisville, Ky.). See article in Vol. ii. 341, with correction in v. 644. Her first appearance was in 1867 at a concert of the Milwaukee Musikverein. At twelve she sang in a Chicago choir. At sixteen she really made her début in 'Masaniello,' given by the Chicago Liederkranz. In Italy she studied from about 1880 under both the Lampertis, father and son, appearing on Italian stages from about 1883. She then returned to Chicago. Early in 1886 she was the leading contralto in the first season of the American Opera Company under Thomas, being specially successful in 'Orfeo.' She then returned to Europe, singing in oratorio and concert in England, and in opera in Italy. [R.6]

HATHAWAY, LEWIS J. See Colleges, 3 (Middlebury C., Vt.).

HATTSTAEDT, JOHN JAMES (b. 1851). See Register, 6.

HAUK, MINNIE (b. Nov. 16, 1852, New York). See article in Vol. ii. 341–2. From time to time curious reports have been given of her death, but in 1919–20 a fund was sought in New York by various friends to deliver her from financial troubles. [R.5]

HAVANA ITALIAN OPERA COMPANY, THE, was a troupe organized by Francesco Marty, primarily for performances in Havana, but in 1847–50 coming also to New York in the summer. The conductor was Arditi, and the singers were as a rule decidedly good. Besides standard Italian works, in 1850, 'Les Huguenots' was given for the first time in America.

HAWKINS, JOHN ISAAC.¶ See Register, 3.

HAWLEY, CHARLES BEACH (1858–1915). See Register, 6.

HAYDEN, PHILIP CADY (b. 1854). See Register, 7.

HAYNES, JOHN C. (1830–1907). See Register, 4.

HAYS, WILLIAM SHAKESPEARE (1837–1907). See Register, 4.

HAYTER, A. U. (1799–1873). See Register, 3.

HAZELTON, HENRY (1816– ?). See Register, 4.

HAZELTON BROTHERS, of New York, is a firm of piano-makers that has been prominent since 1850, when Frederick and Henry Hazelton became partners, later joined by John Hazelton, a third brother. They derived traditions of first-class work from Dubois & Stodart, and immediately gained recognition and success, as attested by a high award at the London Exposition of 1853 and often since. They were among the first to adopt the full iron frames and have introduced many refinements in scale. They have a comprehensive type of player-piano.

HEALY, PATRICK JOSEPH (1840–1905). See Register, 4.

HEATH, WILBUR F. (1843–1914). See Register, 6.

HECKSCHER, CÉLESTE DE LONGPRÉ, née Massey (1860, Philadelphia), studied piano with Zerdahal, composition with H. A. Lang and orchestration with Vassily Leps. She began to publish when but ten — songs like 'Serenade,' 'Gypsy Lullaby,' 'Pourquoi je t'aime,' 'L'Ange Gardien' and 'Music of Hungary.' Later came the Suite 'To the Forest,' for violin and piano, a Romance for 'cello and the piano-pieces 'Impromptu' and 'Valse Bohème.' 'Dances of the Pyrenees,' a pantomime or ballet d'action for orchestra, was first given in 1911 by the Philadelphia Orchestra and has since been played often elsewhere. Other works are a Pastorale for 'cello and piano, 'Passecaille' and other piano-works, and the anthem 'Out of the Deep.' An opera, 'The Rose of Destiny' is in manuscript. [R.6]

HEDDEN, WARREN ROSECRANS (Dec. 25, 1861, New York), studied with Messiter, Archer, Buck, Richard Hoffman and C. C. Müller, took his Mus.B. at Toronto University in 1896 and became F. A. G. O. in 1902. He is known as pianist, concert-organist, teacher, conductor and composer. In 1908–09 he was warden of the A. G. O., and during his term organized chapters in Cleveland, Rochester, Los Angeles, Toronto and Montreal. Since 1913 he has been director of the examinations that the Guild holds in some twenty cities. His best-known compositions are a Te Deum in D (Schirmer) and several Benedicites (Gray, Luckhardt). [R.7]

HEIFETZ, JASCHA (Feb. 2, 1901, Vilna, Lithuania), was extremely precocious musically, taking short violin-lessons from his father at three and playing by ear various studies and pieces with notable ease and purity of intonation. At four he entered the Vilna music-school and soon played in public with success. On Auer's advice he went to the Conservatory in Petrograd, where his entrance-test (Glazunov being one of the judges) won the highest mark yet given. At nine he played in the largest concert-hall in Petrograd, at ten with symphony orchestras at Odessa and Kiev, and at eleven in Pavlovsk and later in Berlin, where he made a sensation. Within a year he was heard with the Berlin Philharmonic under Nikisch, the Gewandhaus Orchestra at Leipzig and in Vienna under Safonov. His studies with Auer were carefully continued, and his general education under tutors. His last European tour was in Sweden, Norway and Denmark. When the Russian revolution broke out the Heifetz family came to the United States. His American début was in New York in 1917. Since then he has been extensively heard, always with the highest admiration. [R.10]

HEIN, CARL (b. 1864). See Register, 8.

HEINECKE, PAUL (b. 1885). See Register, 10.

HEINRICH, ANTON PHILIPP (1781–1861). See Register, 3.

HEINRICH, MAX (June 14, 1853, Chemnitz, Germany : Aug. 9, 1916, New York), having studied with Klitzsch in Zwickau and at the Dresden Conservatory, in 1873 came to Philadelphia as teacher, removing in 1876–82 to Judson College in Alabama. In 1882 he began his notable career as concert- and oratorio-baritone by singing in 'Elijah' under Leopold Damrosch in New York. He was remarkably successful in song-recitals (playing his own accompaniments) and specialized in works by Schubert, Schumann and Brahms. He sang also with leading orchestras and for a

time in opera. He taught singing at the Royal Academy of Music in London in 1888–93, lived in Chicago in 1894–1903, in Boston in 1903–10 and then in New York. His 'farewell' recital was given in Chicago in 1903, but his final public appearance was in New York in 1915. He wrote songs and melodramatic settings of Poe's 'Raven' and Waller's 'Magdalena,' edited classical German songs, translated song-texts, and wrote *Correct Principles of Classical Singing*. His daughter, Julia Heinrich (d. 1919), from 1915 sang at the Metropolitan Opera House. [R.6]

HEINROTH, CHARLES (Jan. 2, 1874, New York), studied piano with Friedheim and Spicker, organ with John White and composition with Herbert. In Munich he was a pupil of Hieber and Rheinberger. In 1893 he became organist at St. Paul's in Brooklyn, and in 1897–1907 was at the Church of the Ascension and Temple Beth-El in New York. He taught organ, harmony and counterpoint at the National Conservatory for some years. Since 1907 he has been organist and director of music at the Carnegie Institute in Pittsburgh — the first American to be thus chosen, his predecessors being Archer and Lemare. Each season he gives over seventy free organ-recitals (Saturday evenings and Sunday afternoons). These recitals cover the entire range of organ-music, so that the annual volumes of annotated programs constitute a handbook of organ-literature. During Lent the Saturday evenings are taken for lectures on pertinent musical topics, and in these he has been eminently effective. He is also organist at the Third Presbyterian Church and patron of the music-department of the Carnegie Institute of Technology. The total number of his recitals throughout the country now approximates 2000, including five at the Panama-Pacific Exposition in 1915, a series at the opening of the municipal organ in Springfield, Mass., and special programs before the A. G. O. and the N. A. O., besides many on important occasions. A recent critic says that 'the term virtuoso, which can be applied to comparatively few of our organists, belongs rightfully to him.' [R.8]

HEINTZMANN, THEODORE A. (1817–1899). See Register, 4.

HELD, ERNST CARL EBERHARDT (1823–1913 ?). See Register, 4.

HEMPEL, FRIEDA (June 26, 1885, Leipzig, Germany), having been trained at the Leipzig Conservatory, the Stern Conservatory in Berlin (with Selma Nicklass-Kempner), made her début at the Royal Opera House in Berlin in 'The Merry Wives of Windsor' in 1905. In 1905–07 she sang at the Court Opera in Schwerin, and in 1907–12 at the Royal Opera in Berlin. Her début at the Metropolitan

Opera House in New York was late in 1912. She has taken principal soprano-rôles in 'Die Entführung aus dem Serail,' 'Cosi fan tutti,' 'Le Nozze di Figaro,' 'Rigoletto,' 'Il Barbiere di Siviglia,' 'La Traviata,' 'Marta,' 'Lucia,' 'Un Ballo in Maschera,' 'Les Huguenots,' 'Die Zauberflöte,' 'Die Meistersinger,' 'Euryanthe,' 'La Bohème,'•etc. In 1911 she created the rôle of the Marschallin in Strauss' 'Der Rosenkavalier' at the Royal Opera in Berlin. In 1918 she married William B. Kahn, a New York banker of American birth. [R.10]

HENDERSON, WILLIAM JAMES (Dec. 4, 1855, Newark, N. J.), has been in various phases of newspaper-work since he was fifteen. He graduated from Princeton in 1886. He studied singing under Angelo Torriano and piano under Carl Langlotz (composer of the college-song 'Old Nassau'). In theory he is mostly self-taught. In 1883–1902 he was on the staff of the New York 'Times,' first as reporter, then as music-critic. Since 1902 he has been critic for the 'Sun.' In 1889–95 he lectured on music-history at the New York College of Music, and since 1904 has lectured on the development of vocal art at the Institute of Musical Art. His books are thoroughly interesting and valuable. They include *The Story of Music*, 1889 (12th ed., 1912), *Preludes and Studies*, 1891, *What is Good Music?*, 1898, *How Music Developed*, 1898, *The Orchestra and Orchestral Music*, 1899, *Richard Wagner, his Life and his Dramas*, 1901, *Modern Musical Drift*, 1904, *The Art of the Singer*, 1906, and *Some Forerunners of Italian Opera*, 1911 — the latter embodying much original research, besides *The Soul of a Tenor*, 1912, a psychological study more than a novel. He has written the libretti of several light operas and also of Damrosch's opera 'Cyrano de Bergerac' (1913), and published a volume of poems, *Pipes and Timbrels* (1905). In 1892–94 he was one of the associate-editors of *The Standard Dictionary*. He has always been an expert yachtsman and student of naval subjects, as witnessed by his *Sea-Yarns for Boys*, 1894, *Afloat with the Flag*, 1895, *The Last Cruise of the Mohawk*, 1897, and — his most widely-circulated book — *The Elements of Navigation*, 1895 (many editions, rewritten in 1918). For twelve years he was an officer in the Naval Militia, was commissioned lieutenant in the Spanish War, and in 1917–18 was instructor in navigation for the Naval Militia of New York. He has written stories, poems and essays for a large number of American and English magazines. He is a member of the Institutes of Arts and Letters and of Social Sciences. [R.7]

HENNIG, RUDOLPH (1845–1904). See Register, 6.

HENRY, BERTRAM CURTIS. See COLLEGES, 3 (Georgetown C., Ky.).

HENRY, HAROLD (b. 1884). See Register, 9.

HENRY, HUGH THOMAS (b. 1862). See Register, 7.

HENRY, JOHN (d. 1795). See Register, 1, under Storer.

HENSCHEL, ISIDOR GEORG (Feb. 18, 1850, Breslau, Germany). See article in Vol. ii. 381–2. In 1905–08 he taught at the Institute of Musical Art in New York. In 1914 he retired from public activity with a farewell recital in London, opening the program with the same aria from 'Rinaldo' that he sang at his first recital in 1877. In 1914 he was knighted by King George. A mass for eight voices a cappella was first given in 1916. He has published *Personal Recollections of Brahms*, 1907, and *Musings and Memories of a Musician*, 1919. [R.7]

HENSCHEL, LILLIAN JUNE, née Bailey (1860–1901). See Vol. ii. 382, and Register, 6.

HENSEL, OCTAVIA (1837–1897). See Register, 6.

HERBERT, THERESE, née Förster. See Register, 7.

HERBERT, VICTOR (Feb. 1, 1859, Dublin, Ireland). See article in Vol. ii. 384. Since 1904 he has devoted himself almost entirely to composition, conducting only upon occasion. His grand operas are 'Natoma' (1911, Philadelphia) and 'Madeleine' (1914, Metropolitan Opera House, New York). His comic operas are

'Prince Ananias,' 1894.
'The Wizard of the Mill,' 1895.
'The Gold Bug,' 1896.
'The Serenade,' 1897.
'The Idol's Eye,' 1897.
'The Fortune-Teller,' 1898.
'Cyrano de Bergerac,' 1899.
'The Singing-Girl,' 1899.
'The Ameer,' 1899.
'The Viceroy,' 1900.
'Babes in Toyland,' 1903.
'Babette,' 1903.
'It Happened in Nordland,' 1904.
'Miss Dolly Dollars,' 1905.
'Wonderland,' or 'Alice and the Eight Princesses,' 1905.
'Mlle. Modiste,' 1905.
'The Red Mill,' 1906.
'Dream-City,' 1906.
'The Magic Knight,' 1906.
'The Tatooed Man,' 1907.
'The Rose of Algeria,' 1908.
'Little Nemo,' 1908.
'The Prima Donna,' 1908.
'Old Dutch,' 1909.
'Naughty Marietta,' 1910.
'When Sweet Sixteen,' 1910.
'Mlle. Rosita,' 1911.
'The Lady of the Slippers,' 1912.
'The Madcap Duchess,' 1913.
'Sweethearts,' 1913.
'The Débutante,' 1914.
'The Only Girl,' 1914.
'Princess Pat,' 1915.

'Eileen,' 1917.
'Her Regiment,' 1917.
Also music for the ' The Fall of a Nation ' (photo-play), 1916.

HERBST, GOTTFRIED (b. 1887). See Register, 10.

HERING, JOHN NORRIS (June 3, 1886, Baltimore), was trained first as a choir-boy at St. Peter's and later at the Peabody Conservatory, where he graduated in 1906, his teachers being Randolph in piano, Barkworth in organ and Boise in composition. While studying he began memory-playing on the organ. For a year he taught at Hood College in Frederick, Md., substituted for Boise and Brockway at the Conservatory, and from 1913 taught in its preparatory department. As an organist he has been constantly employed since 1901, altogether in Baltimore except in 1909–10, when he was in New Orleans. Since 1911 he has been at Christ Church in Baltimore. Since 1903 he has given many recitals in Baltimore and elsewhere (as at the Jamestown Exposition in 1907), invariably from memory. He became F. A. G. O. in 1914, and has been prominent in the Maryland Chapter, becoming dean in 1919. Since 1910 he has been also engaged in newspaper-work with the Baltimore 'Star,' beginning as a reporter, but soon becoming music-critic and editorial writer. In 1919 he was authorized by the Maryland Academy of Sciences to organize a section for the study of music in its relations to science, and was made chairman thereof. He has composed two movements of a piano-trio in G, an organ-sonata in E minor, a concert-piece for organ, a rhapsody on a chromatic theme in B-flat for organ and other organ-pieces, service-music for both the Episcopal and Jewish services, and some other vocal music. [R.9]

HERITAGE, RICHARD ABRAHAM (b. 1853). See Register, 6, and COLLEGES, 3 (Valparaiso U., Ind.).

HERMAN, REINHOLD LUDWIG (b. 1849). See Register, 6.

HERRMANN, EDUARD (b. 1850). See Register, 7.

HERSHEY SCHOOL OF MUSICAL ART, THE, in Chicago, was established in 1875 by Sara Hershey and W. S. B. Mathews, attaining special success in its departments of organ, voice and composition. Clarence Eddy was general director almost from the first, and it was here that in 1877–79 he gave a series of 100 organ-recitals without repeating any work. In 1879 Miss Hershey became Mrs. Eddy, and in 1885 they discontinued the School.

HERTZ, ALFRED (July 15, 1872, Frankfort-am-Main, Germany), while a student at the Hoch Conservatory attracted the interest of Von Bülow. His teachers were Schwarz for piano, Urspruch for composition and Fleisch

for conducting. In 1891–92 he was conductor at the Stadt-Theater in Halle, followed by three seasons as Hofkapellmeister at Altenburg (Saxony), and four at the Stadt-Theater in Elberfeld-Barmen. After conducting concerts in London in 1899, in 1899–1902 he was Kapell-meister of the Breslau Stadt-Theater. In 1902 he came to New York as conductor of German opera at the Metropolitan Opera House, remaining until 1915. He conducted the first performances of Converse's 'Pipe of Desire,' Parker's 'Mona' and 'Fairyland,' and Damrosch's 'Cyrano'; also the first American performances of 'Parsifal' (1913), Strauss' 'Salome' and 'Rosenkavalier,' Thuille's 'Lobetanz' and Humperdinck's 'Königskinder.' Since 1915 he has been conductor of the San Francisco Symphony Orchestra. [R.9]

HERZOG, SIGMUND (b. 1868). See Register, 8.

HESS, WILLY (July 14, 1859, Mannheim, Germany). See article in Vol. ii. 390. It was in 1904 that he succeeded Kneisel as concertmaster of the Boston Symphony Orchestra, and, except for leave of absence in 1907–08, he continued till 1910, when he followed Halir at the Hochschule in Berlin. In 1904–07 he led the Boston Symphony Quartet and in 1908–10 the Hess-Schroeder Quartet, including Theodorowicz as second and Férir as viola. [R.5]

HESSELBERG, ÉDOUARD GREGORY (b. 1870). See Register, 8.

HESSELIUS, GUSTAVUS. See Register, 1.

HETLEY, JOYCE HAZEL (b. 1889). See COLLEGES, 3 (Vincennes U., Ind.).

HEWITT, JAMES (1770, England : 1827, New York), who had been violinist at the 'Professional Concerts' at Hanover Square in London, came to New York in 1792 with other musicians. He was at once recognized as both player and composer, had charge of many good concerts and became orchestra-leader for the Old American Company. In 1796 or '97 he bought out the New York branch of Carr's Musical Repository, and was in the publishing business even earlier. The music attributed to him includes a 'Battle' Overture in nine movements (1792), a 'Storm' Overture (1795), a setting of Collins' ode on 'The Passions' (1795, apparently the first melodrama written in America), the opera 'Tammany' (1794) and various music for 'The Patriot' (1794), 'Columbus' (1797), 'The Mysterious Marriage' (1799) and 'Pizarro' (1800). See Sonneck, Concert-Life, Early Opera and 'Early American Operas' in I. M. G. Sammelbde. 6. 459–64, 488–9. [R.2]

HEWITT, JAMES. See TUNE-BOOKS, 1812.

HEWITT, MISS S. See Register, 3.

HEWS, GEORGE (1806–1873). See Register, 3.

HEYDLER, CHARLES (b. 1861). See Register, 7.

HEYMAN, HENRY (Jan. 13, 1855, Oakland, Cal.), was educated at Oakland College (now the University of California). In 1870 he went to Leipzig, studying with David, Roentgen, Hermann, Reinecke and Jadassohn, and for five years was a violinist in the Gewandhaus Orchestra. Returning to San Francisco in 1877, he at once began a series of orchestral and chamber-music concerts, at which many important works were performed for the first time in San Francisco. In 1880 he made a concert-tour of Pacific Coast cities, visiting also Victoria and Vancouver. The next year he became concertmaster of the Philharmonic Orchestra, directed by Hinrichs, and also brought out a string-quartet by Kelley. In 1884 he made a concert-trip to Honolulu, and was appointed violinist to King Kalakaua and was knighted. By means of his many concerts, including those of the Heyman String-Quartet, he has continually introduced classic and modern compositions to California audiences. He has also worked to raise the social standing of local musicians. For over forty years he has been a member of the famous Bohemian Club and was made an honorary life-member in 1918. The dean of violinists and teachers on the Pacific Coast, he has an international reputation for hospitality extended to musicians and artists who visit San Francisco, and numbers among his friends an extraordinary number of celebrities. In the great fire of 1906 he lost not only his library and collection of instruments, with many valuable souvenirs, but all his manuscript works, including many revised violin-études. Compositions that have been dedicated to him are Saint-Saëns' 'Élégie' for violin and piano, Jadassohn's Romanza, op. 87, and Musin's Berceuse and Waltz. [R.6]

HEYMAN, KATHERINE RUTH WILLOUGHBY, born in Sacramento, had a variety of teachers in America and abroad. In 1899 she made her début as pianist with the Boston Symphony Orchestra and then toured extensively, in 1905-15 in Europe. Since 1916 she has traveled again in the United States. She has been active in presenting unfamiliar works — introducing American composers in Germany and Russia, and Russian composers in America. Thus in 1899 she gave the first American rendering of Arensky's concerto and in 1919 the first American recital of Scriabin alone (4th and 8th Sonatas, etc.). She has also lectured on the contrast between Oriental and Occidental music. Various songs have been published (Schirmer, Schmidt, etc.). [R.8]

HICKOK, J. H. See TUNE-BOOKS, 1840.

HIGGINSON, HENRY LEE (Nov. 18, 1834, New York : Nov. 15, 1919, Boston), after a partial course at Harvard was trained as a banker, but also in 1856-60 studied singing, piano and composition at Vienna. In the Civil War he became major and lieutenant-colonel by brevet in the 1st Mass. Cavalry, and in 1863 was badly wounded. From 1868 he was a member of the banking firm of Lee, Higginson & Co. He was always active in educational undertakings — on the corporation of Harvard from 1893, trustee of the Carnegie Institution, of the New England Conservatory, etc. In 1881 he established the Boston Symphony Orchestra, provided an endowment of about $1,000,000 for its maintenance, and for over thirty-five years directed its policy with conspicuous wisdom. In 1918 he relinquished control to a Board of Directors. [R.7]

HILL, EDWARD BURLINGAME (Sept. 9, 1872, Cambridge, Mass.), was born into Harvard traditions, being the son of a professor and grandson of a president. In 1894 he graduated there with highest honors in music, having taken all of the courses under Paine. He continued study with Lang, Bullard, Arthur Whiting, and Howard Parkhurst in Boston and New York, and with Breitner and Widor in Paris. Later he also took orchestration under Chadwick. For some years he taught piano and harmony in Boston, was critic for the 'Transcript' and wrote on music for magazines. Since 1908 he has been connected with the Division of Music at Harvard, at first as instructor and from 1918 as assistant-professor. Until the war he was head of the Boston group of the I. M. S., and is now president of the Composers' Club of Boston and secretary of the American Friends of Musicians in France. Besides developing unusual courses in the critical analysis of musical style for his Harvard classes, he has done fine original work. His compositions include

Six Songs, op. 6 (Breitkopf).
Four 'Sketches,' op. 7, for piano (Breitkopf).
Three 'Poetical Sketches,' op. 8, for piano (Breitkopf).
'Country Idyls,' op. 10, for piano (Schirmer).
Six Songs, op. 13, 14 (Boston Music Co.).
'Nuns of the Perpetual Adoration,' on text by Dowson, op. 15, for women's voices and orchestra (1909, Boston, and often since).
Symphonic Pantomime, 'Jack Frost in Midsummer,' on text by J. L. Smith, op. 16, for orchestra (1908, Chicago Orchestra, also in Boston and New York).
Symphonic Pantomime, 'Pan and the Star,' op. 19 (1914, MacDowell Festival and at Boston and Cincinnati).
Symphonic Poem, 'The Parting of Lancelot and Guinevere,' on text by Phillips, op. 22 (1915, St. Louis Orchestra, 1916, Boston Orchestra).
'Poem,' op. 23, violin and orchestra.
'Stevensoniana,' op. 24, four orchestral pieces after poems from Stevenson's 'Garden of Verses' (1918, New York Symphony Society and New England Conservatory Orchestra, 1919, Boston and Cincinnati Orchestras).
Anthem for chorus and band (1915, Centenary of Allegheny College, Meadville, Pa.).
'Autumn Twilight,' song for soprano and orchestra.   [R.8]

HILL, JUNIUS WELCH (Nov. 18, 1840 Hingham, Mass.), after studying with J. C. D. Parker in Boston, in 1860–63 was in Leipzig under Moscheles, Hauptmann, Reinecke, Plaidy and Richter. He was then organist at Tremont Temple, Shawmut Church, Tremont Street (M. E.) Church in Boston and at Harvard Church in Brookline. In 1884–97 he was professor at Wellesley College and then taught in Boston until, retiring from active musical life, he removed to Los Angeles. An excellent musician and teacher, he was particularly successful in establishing high standards for the music-department at Wellesley. Mrs. Beach was his pupil in 1881–82. He has composed many choruses for women's voices and edited collections of piano-music. [R.5]

HILL, URELI CORELLI (1802?–1875). See Register, 3, and TUNE-BOOKS, 1831.

HILL, URI K. See TUNE-BOOKS, 1806.

HILLE, GUSTAV (b. 1851). See Register, 6.

HINCKLEY, ALLEN CARTER (b. 1877). See Register, 8.

HINRICHS, GUSTAV (b. 1850). See Register, 6.

HINSHAW, WILLIAM WADE (Nov. 3, 1867, Union, Ia.), played the cornet at nine and led the village-band at thirteen. He graduated from Valparaiso (Ind.) University in 1888, studying voice and harmony there with R. A. Heritage, and later continued vocal study with L. G. Gottschalk and L. A. Phelps in Chicago, where he began to teach singing in 1891. In 1895–99 he was dean of the music-department at Valparaiso University, meanwhile being also choir-director in Chicago churches. In 1899 he made his début in opera at St. Louis, singing Mephisto in 'Faust' with the Savage Grand Opera Company, with which he sang for four years. In 1903 he opened the Hinshaw School of Opera in Chicago (later merged with the Chicago Conservatory), of which he was president till 1907. Since 1909 he has engaged in operatic work, first as founder and director of the International Grand Opera Company in Chicago, in 1910–13 as baritone at the Metropolitan Opera House in New York, and since 1917 as business-manager and president of the Society of American Singers in New York. His offer of a $1000 prize for a one-act opera by an American composer was awarded in 1917 to H. K. Hadley for 'Bianca.' His repertory includes over fifty rôles, from Wagner operas (he sang at the Wagner festival in Graz, 1912, and the 'Ring' festival in Berlin, 1914) to comic opera and baritone-parts in many oratorios. He has also given many song-recitals. [R.8]

‡ HINTON, ARTHUR (Nov. 20, 1869, Beckenham, England). See article in Vol. ii. 407. For some years he has been on the ex-

amining-staff of the Associated Board of the R. A. M. and R. C. M., and in consequence has made several visits to Australia, New Zealand, Canada, Ceylon and Jamaica. The list of his works may be revised as follows:

For orchestra —
  Suite, 'Endymion,' three 'scenes after Keats (Fischer)
  Fantasia, 'The Triumph of Cæsar.'
  Symphony No. 1, in B-flat.
  Symphony No. 2, in C minor.
For piano and orchestra —
  Concerto in D minor (London Philharmonic Society, Boston Symphony Orchestra, Worcester Festival, etc.).
For voice and orchestra —
  Scena, 'Semele,' text by Litchfield, for mezzo-soprano.
  Opera, 'Tamara,' in two acts.
Chamber-music —
  Quintet in G minor (Kneisel and Olive Mead Quartets).
  Bolero, 'Ave Maria,' 'Valse de Joie,' Berceuse and Meditation, for violin and piano.
For piano —
  'A Summer Pilgrimage,' six pieces (Fischer).
  Four Bagatelles.
  Valse Caprice, 'Carnival.'
  'Serenatella.'
  Three Characteristic Pieces.
  Rhapsody in B-flat minor.
  'Chant des Vagues.'
  'Étude Arabesque.'
  'Oriental Serenade.'
  Romance in A-flat.
Songs —
  'Butterflies,' two books, each of ten.
  'White Roses,' cycle of six.
  Eight Songs from Wm. Blake, two books.
  Three Lyrics from Browning's 'In a Gondola.'
  Five Songs from Litchfield.

HIRSCHLER, DANIEL A. (b. 1883). See COLLEGES, 3 (C. of Emporia, Kan.).

HISKEY. See Register, 3.

HISSEM-DE MOSS, MARY (b. 1871). See Register, 8.

HOCKETT, HOWARD L. See COLLEGES, 3 (Whittier C., Cal.).

HODGES, EDWARD (July 20, 1796, Bristol, England : Sept. 1, 1867, Clifton, England). See article in Vol. ii. 414. When he began at Trinity Church in 1846 there was much objection to the severity of English cathedral music. His Service in D, written to overcome this, he called his 'New York Service.' His total work included 25 anthems, 7 services, Psalms 91 and 122, etc. See Messiter, *History of the Choir and Music of Trinity Church*, 1906. [R.3]

HODGES, FAUSTINA HASSE (? , Bristol, England : Feb. 4, 1896, Philadelphia). See Vol. ii. 414, and Register, 5.

HODGES, JOHN SEBASTIAN BACH (1830, Bristol, England : May 1, 1915, Baltimore). See Vol. ii. 414. With his sister Faustina he was brought to New York in 1845. He graduated from Columbia in 1850 and from

B

the General Theological Seminary in 1854. In 1854–56 he was assistant at Trinity Church in Pittsburgh, in 1856–59 taught at Nashotah Theological Seminary in Wisconsin, in 1860 was rector at Grace Church in Newark, and from 1870 at St. Paul's in Baltimore, becoming emeritus in 1906. He was an excellent organist and composed many services, anthems, tunes and chants. He compiled *The Book of Common Praise*, 1868, and had much to do with the successive revisions of the Episcopal *Hymnal*. He founded in Baltimore the earliest choir-school in the United States. [R.5]

HODGKINSON, JOHN [real name Meadowcraft] (1767, England : 1805, Washington), and his wife, née Arabella Brett, were popular stage-singers who in 1792 were brought to New York by John Henry as leading members of the Old American Company, appearing chiefly in New York, Philadelphia and Boston, but also in Hartford and Providence, for about ten years. In 1794–96 Hallam and Hodgkinson replaced Henry in the direction of the Company and in 1796–98 Hodgkinson and Dunlap were similarly associated. From 1797 Hodgkinson managed the Haymarket Theatre in Boston at intervals. Both he and his wife often sang in concerts, but his ambition was for dramatic parts and the managing of companies. He had unusual memory, readiness and effectiveness as an actor. In 1796 he took the leading rôle in the production of Carr's 'The Archers.' In 1795–99 he was president of the Columbian Anacreontic Society in New York, which he probably founded. He died of yellow fever and his wife of consumption. See Sonneck, *Concert-Life* and *Early Opera*. [R.2]

HOERRNER, WILLIAM HENRY (b. 1865). See COLLEGES, 1 (Colgate U., N. Y.).

HOFFMAN, RICHARD (May 24, 1831, Manchester, England : Aug. 17, 1909, Mount Kisco, N. Y.). See article in Vol. ii. 414. On Dec. 1, 1897, he was given a testimonial concert to celebrate the fiftieth anniversary of his first appearance in New York. On this occasion, besides a Chopin Nocturne and Ballade, he played in Hummel's Septet (on the program in 1847), Mozart's Piano-Quartet in G minor and a Bach concerto. After this he gradually gave up playing in public, though teaching till his last days. He joined Gottschalk in two-piano pieces in the '60s at his New York concerts and played with Von Bülow in 1875 (Bach's Triple concerto in D minor). See his *Musical Recollections of Fifty Years*, with biographical sketch by his wife, 1910. [R.4]

HOFFMAN, RUDOLF. See COLLEGES, 3 (Baylor U., Tex.).

HOFMANN, JOSEF CASIMIR (Jan. 20, 1876, Podgorze, near Cracow, Galicia). See article in Vol. ii. 417. In 1888–94 he studied composition and orchestration with Urban at Berlin. In 1896 he made the first of many tours in Russia. Since 1898 he has spent most of his time in America, where he has played with all the leading orchestras and given innumerable recitals. In 1905 he married the daughter of J. B. Eustis, former ambassador to France. His compositions include five concertos (from 1898), two sonatas, a symphony in E and many shorter pieces. Some early works were put forth under the name 'Dvorsky.' He has published books on piano-playing (1898, 1900, 1914). [R.7]

HOHNSTOCK, ADELAIDE (? –1856) and KARL (1828–1889). See Register, 4.

HOLBROOK, JOSIAH. See TUNE-BOOKS, 1813.

‡ HOLBROOKE, JOSEF CHARLES (July 5, 1878, Croydon, England). See articles in Vol. ii. 418, and v. 645. In 1914–18 he was active in giving concerts in provincial cities for soldiers' charities. In the fall of 1919 he produced his chamber-works in recital in London. In 1920 he projects a world-tour. To the list of works the following may be added :

Scena, 'Marino Faliero' (1905, Bristol Festival).
Symphony, 'Les Hommages' (1906).
Dramatic Choral Symphony, in memory of Poe (1908).
Fantasie-Concerto, 'Gwyn-ap-Nudd,' for piano (1911).
Quartet, 'Impressions,' op. 51, for strings (Novello).
Quartet, 'Belgium-Russia, 1915,' for strings (Novello).
Quartet in two parts, 'Pickwick Club,' op. 68, for strings (Novello).
Three Suites, opp. 71, 73, 74 (Novello).
Four Ballets, 'The Moth and the Flame,' 'The Red Masque,' 'Coromanthe' and 'The Wizard.'
Operatic Trilogy, 'The Children of Don' (1912), 'Dylan' and 'Bronwen, Daughter of Llyr,' op. 79 (Novello).
Comic Opera, 'The Snob,' op. 82 (Novello).
Sextet, four dances for piano and strings (arr. as piano-duet, Ricordi).
Concerto for violin (Ricordi, also in piano-score).
Eight 'Mezzotints,' op. 56, for clarinet and piano (Ricordi).
Three Dramatic Songs, op. 69, with piano and strings (Enoch).
Six Piano Fantasies, 'The Orient': 'Java,' 'Burma,' 'Sumatra,' 'Siam,' 'Annam,' 'China' (Enoch).
Ten Études for piano, op. 53 (Ricordi).
'Taliessen's Song,' for tenor or baritone (Novello).

HOLDEN, ALBERT JAMES (1841–1916). See Register, 6.

HOLDEN, OLIVER (1765–1834?). See Register, 2, and TUNE-BOOKS, 1792.

‡ HOLLINS, ALFRED (Sept. 11, 1865, Hull, England). See article in Vol. ii. 420–1. On his second visit to America (1888) he came alone, and played concertos with the New York Philharmonic Society, the Boston Symphony Orchestra and other leading organizations. In 1907, '09 and '16 he made recital-tours in

South Africa — on the last opening the organ in the Town Hall at Johannesburg, for which he drew the specification. His great hobby is organ-mechanism. Among his numerous organ-works are Concert-Overtures in C and C minor, a Concert-Rondo, Grands Chœurs in G minor and C, Triumphal and Coronation Marches, several pieces of bridal-music, many preludes, etc.

HOLMAN–BLACK, CHARLES. See Register, 7.

HOLMBERG, GUSTAF FREDRIK (Aug. 17, 1872, Fridened Parish, Sweden), came to America in 1891, having had a good general education, including some violin-lessons. At Bethany College in Kansas, where he graduated from the music-school in 1899, he was concert-master and assistant-conductor in the orchestra at the annual festivals, and continued as teacher of violin and harmony. Since 1903 he has been music-director at the University of Oklahoma at Norman, where from small beginnings a notable department was rapidly developed, now forming part of the School of Fine Arts, of which he has been dean since 1909. Not only are choral and orchestral concerts prominent, but interscholastic contests in music, art and expression have since 1912 become keen and absorbing. He has also lectured widely on musical and artistic subjects. [R.8]

HOLMES, EDWARD (1797–1859). See Register, 4.

HOLMES, HENRY (1839–1905). See Vol. ii. 421, and v. 645, and Register, 8.

HOLSINGER, GEORGE B. See Colleges, 3 (Bridgewater C., Va.).

HOLST, EDVARD (1843–1899). See Register, 6.

‡ HOLST, GUSTAV VON (Sept. 21, 1874, Cheltenham, England). See article in Vol. v. 645. For a time, after leaving the Royal College, he was répétiteur and trombone-player with the Carl Rosa Opera Company, and later was connected with the Scottish Orchestra. He is still musical director at Morley College, and also principal music-teacher at St. Paul's Girls' School. In 1918, under the educational scheme of the Y. M. C. A., he went to Saloniki, Constantinople and Asia Minor as musical organizer in army-camps. The complete list of his works is as follows:

Opera, 'The Revoke,' op. 1, in one act (1895).
'Fantasiestücke,' op. 2, for oboe and strings (1896).
Quintet, op. 3, for piano and wind (1896).
Four Songs, op. 4 (1896) (Laudy).
'Clear and Cool,' op. 5, for five-part chorus and orchestra (1897).
Scena, 'Ornult's Drapa,' op. 6, for baritone and orchestra (1898).
Overture, 'Walt Whitman,' op. 7 (1899).
Symphony, 'Cotswolds,' op. 8 (1900, given at Bournemouth, 1902).
'Ave Maria,' for women's voices in eight parts (1900) (Laudy).

'Ballet-Suite' in E-flat, op. 10 (1900) (Novello).
Opera, 'The Youth's Choice,' op. 11 (1902).
Part-Songs, op. 12 (1902).
Symphonic Poem, 'Indra,' op. 13 (1903).
Quintet for wind, op. 14.
Six Songs for baritone, op. 15 (1902).
Six Songs for soprano, op. 16.
Ballad, 'King Estmere,' op. 17, for chorus and orchestra (1903) (Novello).
'The Mystic Trumpeter,' op. 18, for soprano and orchestra (1904).
'Song of the Night,' op. 19, no. 1, for violin and orchestra (1905).
'Invocation,' op. 19, no. 2, for 'cello and orchestra (1911, Queen's Hall).
Songs from 'The Princess,' op. 20, for women's voices (Novello).
Four Carols (Bayley & Ferguson).
Songs without Words, 'Marching-Song,' 'Country-Song,' op. 22, for small orchestra (1906) (Novello).
Opera, 'Sita,' op. 23, in three acts.
'Hymns from the Rig-Veda,' op. 24, for solo voice — 'Dawn,' 'Varuna,' 'Creation,' 'Indra,' 'Maruts,' 'Frogs,' 'Faith,' 'Vac' (Chester).
Song, 'The Heart Worships,' for soprano (Stainer & Bell).
'Songs of the West,' op. 21a, a selection from the West Country, for orchestra.
'A Somerset Rhapsody,' op. 21b, for orchestra (given by Edward Mason).
Opera di camera, 'Savitri,' op. 25 (1908, produced 1916).
'Choral Hymns from the Rig-Veda,' op. 26, four groups, for chorus or semichorus with orchestra or harp (1908–12, given by Mason) (Stainer).
Incidental Music to 'A Vision of Dame Christian,' op. 27a, a masque at St. Paul's School (1909).
Incidental Music to the Stepney Pageant, op. 27b, for children.
Two Suites for military band, op. 28 (1911).
Oriental Suite in E minor, 'Beni Mora,' op. 29, no. 1, for orchestra (1910, given at Gardiner concerts).
Fantastic Suite, 'Phantastes,' op. 29, no. 2, for orchestra (1911, given at Paton's Fund concerts).
Ode, 'The Cloud-Messenger,' op. 30, for chorus and orchestra (1910, given at Gardiner concerts) (Stainer).
'Christmas-Day,' for chorus and orchestra (Novello).
Four 'Part-Songs for Children,' from Whittier (Novello).
Two 'Eastern Pictures,' for women's voices and harp (1911) (Stainer).
'Hecuba's Lament,' from 'The Trojan Women,' op. 31, no. 1, for alto, women's voices and orchestra.
'Hymn to Dionysus,' op. 31, no. 2, for chorus and orchestra (given at Gardiner concerts) (Stainer).
Two Psalms for chorus, strings and organ (1912) (Augener).
Suite in C, for string-orchestra (1913).
Part-Songs, 'A Dirge for Two Veterans,' for men's voices and brass (1914) (Curwen).
Suite, 'The Planets' — 'Mars,' 'Venus,' 'Mercury,' 'Jupiter,' 'Saturn,' 'Uranus,' 'Neptune,' op. 32, for orchestra (1915, given in part by Philharmonic Orchestra, 1919).
Japanese Suite, op. 33, for orchestra (1916, given then and 1919).
Part-Songs, op. 34 (1916) (Augener).
Four Songs with violin, op. 35 (Chester).
Choruses from 'Alcestis,' for women's voices, harp and flutes.

Three **Hymns** for chorus and orchestra, op. 36
(Stainer).
Six Choral Folk-Songs, op. 36 (Curwen).
'The Hymn of Jesus,' op. 37, for two choruses
and semichorus, orchestra, piano and organ
(1917) (Stainer).
Part-Songs for Children, op. 38.
Ballet to the opera 'The Perfect Fool,' for or-
chestra (1918).
'Ode to Death,' words by Whitman, for chorus
and orchestra (1919).
See articles by Edwin Evans in 'The Musical
Times,' Oct., Nov., Dec., 1919.

HOLT, BENJAMIN (1774–1861). See
Register, 3, and TUNE-BOOKS, 1803.

HOLY, ALFRED (Aug. 5, 1866, Oporto,
Portugal), although the son of the director of
the Oporto Conservatory, had most of his training in violin and harp at the Prague Conservatory, where he graduated in 1885 and till
1896 played at the opera-house. In 1896–1903
he was harpist at the Berlin Royal Opera and
in 1903–13 at the Vienna Imperial Opera and
Philharmonic, besides playing at the Bayreuth
festivals. Since 1913 he has been solo harpist
in the Boston Symphony Orchestra. His
published works include some 35 solos, pieces
for harp and other instruments, transcriptions
and studies. A comedy-opera, 'Das Märchen
vom Glück,' was given in Hamburg in 1909.
[R.10]

HOLYOKE, SAMUEL ADAMS (1762–
1820). See Register, 2, and TUNE-BOOKS,
1791.

HOMER, LOUISE DILWORTH, neé Beatty
(1872?, Pittsburgh), the daughter of William
P. Beatty, who in 1869 founded the Pennsylvania College for Women, was educated in
Minneapolis and at West Chester, Pa. She
had some singing-lessons in Philadelphia and
then studied in Boston with W. L. Whitney and
Sidney Homer, marrying the latter in 1895 and
going with him to Paris, where she had further
instruction from Fidèle Koenig and Lhérie.
She first appeared as concert-contralto in Paris
under d'Indy and in 1898 made her stage-début
in 'La Favorita' at Vichy. In 1899–1900 she
was at Covent Garden in London, singing both
Italian and Wagnerian rôles, besides appearing
eighty times at La Monnaie in Brussels. From
1900 to 1919 she was continuously engaged at
the Metropolitan Opera House in New York.
She has also sung with all the leading orchestras,
at the Worcester, Springfield and Cincinnati
festivals and in recital. Her favorite rôles are
Amneris, Orfeo, Dalila and Fides (in 'Le Prophète'), but she has won success in many others, such as Madame de la Haltière (in 'Cendrillon'), Ortrud, Erda, Fricka (in 'Die Walküre'),
Waltraute, Brangäne, Magdalena (in 'Die Meistersinger'), the Witch (in 'Hänsel und Gretel'
and 'Die Königskinder'), Azucena, Laura (in
'La Gioconda'), Dame Quickly (in 'Falstaff'),
Hedwig (in 'Manru'), etc. [R.8.]

HOMER, SIDNEY (Dec. 9, 1864, Boston),
after training at the Boston Latin School and
Phillips (Andover) Academy, studied with
Chadwick in Boston, with two years at Leipzig
and three under Rheinberger, Abel and Hieber
at Munich. In 1888–95 he taught harmony
and counterpoint in Boston, lecturing also on
symphonies and the Wagnerian dramas. In
1895 he married Louise D. Beatty, who had
been his pupil in harmony. Since 1900 he has
lived in New York, almost wholly engaged with
song-composition. About 80 of his songs are
published by Schirmer, including 'Sweet and
Low,' 'Thy Voice is Heard,' 'A Woman's Last
Word,' 'Prospice,' 'The Poor Man's Song,'
'The Last Leaf,' 'Sing me a song of a lad that
is gone,' 'Requiem,' 'The Stormy Evening,'
songs from Stevenson's *A Child's Garden of
Verses*, 'The Pauper's Drive,' 'The Bandanna
Ballads' (including the popular 'Banjo Song'),
'Dearest,' 'The Song of the Shirt,' 'How's my
Boy,' 'Boats Sail on the Rivers,' 'Ferry me
across the water,' 'Six Songs of the Old
South,' 'Three Scotch Poems' and 'Home
they brought her warrior dead.' In addition
there are 'Mother Goose,' 35 songs (Macmillan)
and 'Homeland' (Flammer). See pamphlet
in Schirmer's *Course in Contemporary Musical
Biography*, 1919. [R.8]

HOOD, HELEN (June 28, 1863, Chelsea,
Mass.), was a pupil in Boston of Lang in piano
and of Chadwick in composition, and for a year
was under Moszkowski in piano in Berlin.
Most of her published works are songs, opp.
1, 2, 7 (six 'Song-Etchings'), 9, 13, 14, 18 (sacred), with three part-songs (including 'The
Robin,' op. 3), a Te Deum in E-flat, op. 15,
three piano-pieces, op. 8, eight for violin, and
piano, opp. 6, 10, two for two violins and piano,
op. 12, a piano-trio, op. 11, and a string-quartet in D, op. 16. [R.7]

HOOK, ELIAS (1805–1881) and GEORGE
G. (1807–1880). See Register, 3.

HOOK, E. & G. G., was an organ-making
business started in 1827 at Salem, Mass., by
Elias and George G. Hook, the former having
been an apprentice of William M. Goodrich.
In 1832 they moved to Boston, where they became for many years leading manufacturers.
Up to 1855 they built 170 organs. At that
time Frank H. Hastings (1836–1916) joined
them, becoming a partner in 1865, when the
firm became Hook & Hastings. In 1887 a fine
new factory was built at Kendal Green, Mass.,
and in 1893 the business was incorporated as
the Hook & Hastings Co. The total output
of the firm since the beginning is about 2500
instruments, including many that have been
famous. See Jones, *Handbook of American
Music and Musicians*, p. 76.

HOPE–JONES, ROBERT (Feb. 9, 1859,
Hooton Grange, England : Sept. 13, 1914,

by suicide, Rochester, N. Y.), at fifteen was organist of the Birkenhead School Chapel, at seventeen was apprenticed to Laird Bros., an electrical and shipbuilding firm at Birkenhead, and later became chief engineer of the National Telephone Co.   His interest in the organ persisted, and despite his progress as an electrical inventor, he turned to organ-building in 1889. He came to the United States in 1903, and for two years was with the Austin Organ Co. and for two more with the Skinner Co.   In 1907 the Hope-Jones Organ Co. was formed and located at Elmira, N. Y.; but in 1910 this was taken over by the Wurlitzer Co., and the plant moved to North Tonawanda, N. Y.   He held decidedly radical views about organ-making, introducing a long series of ingenious inventions and advocating them with zeal, but many of them have not been widely approved, despite their cleverness. See Vol. iii. 551–2, and Miller, *The Recent Revolution in Organ-Building*. [R.9]

HOPEKIRK, HELEN (May 20, 1856, Edinburgh, Scotland), had her early training in Edinburgh under Lichtenstein and Mackenzie, and continued at the Leipzig Conservatory, in Vienna under Leschetizky and Navrátil, and in Paris under Mandl (orchestration). Her début as pianist was at the Gewandhaus in Leipzig in 1879. She also played at the Crystal Palace in London, introducing the Grieg and Saint-Saëns (G minor) concertos, with the Scottish Orchestra under Manns and Henschel, with the Vienna Philharmonic under Richter, at the Richter concerts, in London, with Hallé's Manchester Orchestra, with the Boston Symphony under Henschel, Nikisch and Gericke, with orchestras directed by Thomas and Van der Stucken, and with the Kneisel Quartet and other chamber-music organizations, besides giving many recitals. Since 1883 she has lived in America, from 1897 becoming a favorite teacher in Boston. From 1919 she returned to Edinburgh for part of each year. She introduced in America many works by modern French composers, including pieces by Debussy, the d'Indy quartet (Boston, 1901), and the Faure quintet in D minor (New York, 1907). Her compositions include about 100 songs (about half of them published), such as 'Under the Still, White Stars' (violin-obbligato), 'My Heart's in the Highlands' (for chorus), eleven on poems of Fiona Macleod, 'Voice of the Mountains,' 'A Song of Glen Dun,' 'Blows the Wind To-day,' 'Reconciliation' (from Whitman), and three to Biblical words; a piano-concerto and a 'Concertstück' (both played with the Boston Symphony Orchestra), two piano-suites and several piano-pieces; sonatas for violin and piano, in E minor and D, and other violin-pieces; and some works for orchestra. [R.7]

HOPKINS, EDWARD JEROME (Apr. 4,

1836, Burlington, Vt.   :   Nov. 4, 1898, Athenia, N. J.), began organ-playing at ten, attended the University of Vermont and the New York Medical College, but from 1856, though self-taught in music, undertook teaching, lecturing and composing.   In 1856 he founded the American Music Association to promote works by American composers, in 1865 the Orpheon Free Schools in New York, which in twenty years enrolled over 30,000 pupils, and in 1868 'The New York Philharmonic Journal,' which he conducted till 1885. He gave 'lecture-concerts' throughout the country, and for some years was church-organist. He composed over 700 works — the operas 'Samuel' (1877, New York) and 'Dumb Love'; a symphony; 'Easter Festival Vespers' for three choirs, two organs, orchestra, harp and cantor; a fantasia for five pianos; etc.   Two collections of church-music, an Orpheon *Class-Book* and other works were published. [R.4]

HOPKINS, HARRY PATTERSON (b. 1873). See Register, 8.

HOPKINSON, FRANCIS (Sept. 21, 1737, Philadelphia : May 9, 1791, Philadelphia), seems likely to stand, as Sonneck calls him, 'the first native poet-composer of the United States.'   He was the first student matriculated at what is now the University of Pennsylvania, where he graduated in 1757 and was made A.M. in 1760 and LL. D. in 1790.   In 1761 he was admitted to the bar, in 1766–67 was in England, and became active in politics from 1768.   In 1774 he became a member of the Provincial Council of New Jersey and in 1776, representing that state, was a signer of the Declaration of Independence.   In 1787 he participated in the convention that framed the Constitution of the new United States.   In 1779 he was made Admiralty Judge for Pennsylvania and in 1790 Judge of the United States District Court.   Besides more serious writing, he exerted much influence through poems and satires.   His essays and miscellaneous writings were published in three volumes in 1792 (see Allibone, *Dictionary of Authors*).

He evidently took up the harpsichord when about seventeen and attained considerable proficiency.   At the College Commencement of 1760 he was represented as composer and he may have then played on the new organ. In 1764 the vestry of Christ and St. Peter's United Churches thanked him for teaching the children to sing, and in the same year the consistory of the Reformed Dutch Church in New York employed him to make an English version of their Psalter.   He invented an improved method of quilling harpsichords, which attracted attention in Europe, and he followed Franklin in experimenting with the harmonica.

A collection of songs composed by Hopkinson was begun in 1759, and his 'My days have been so wondrous free,' from that year, is doubtless the earliest extant secular piece of American origin. In 1788 a set of *Seven Songs for the Harpsichord or Forte-Piano* — 'the Words and Music by Francis Hopkinson' was published in Philadelphia. It is dedicated to Washington, and in so doing Hopkinson claims the credit 'of being the first Native of the United States who has produced a Musical Composition.' See O. G. Sonneck, article in *I. M. G. Sammelbde.* 5. 119–54, and *Francis Hopkinson and James Lyon*, 1905. Six of Hopkinson's songs, edited by H. V. Milligan, are published by Schmidt (1919). [R.1]

'HORA NOVISSIMA.' An oratorio by Horatio Parker, op. 30, finished in 1893 and first given by the New York Church Choral Society at Holy Trinity Church. The text, effectively translated by the composer's mother, is taken from the famous poem of Bernard of Cluny. It immediately took rank as the strongest oratorio by an American composer, and has been extensively performed both in America and in England.

HORN, CHARLES EDWARD (1786–1849). See Register, 3.

HORNER, RALPH JOSEPH (Apr. 28, 1848, Newport, England), after study at Leipzig under Moscheles, Reinecke, Richter and Papperitz, in 1868 settled in London as teacher of piano, singing and harmony. He conducted the Peckham Choral Society and in 1873–75 was choirmaster at St. Mary's, Peckham, In 1879–90 he conducted Sullivan's operas on tour, and also led operas at the Strand Theatre and the Alexandra Palace in London. In 1888 he moved to Nottingham, conducting musical societies and in 1895–1905 lecturing at University College. Durham University made him Mus.B. in 1893 and Mus.D. in 1898. Coming to New York, in 1906–09 he toured as operatic conductor, and then located in Winnipeg, Manitoba, as director of the Imperial Academy of Music and Arts. He has conducted musical societies, from 1916 was bandmaster in the Canadian Army, and is on the Council of the Canadian Guild of Organists. He has published the dramatic cantata 'Confucius,' many songs, choruses and piano-pieces. Unpublished are the grand opera 'Amy Robsart,' the comic operas 'The Belles of Barcelona' (1911, Winnipeg) and 'Mesmerania'; two oratorios, 'St. Peter' and 'David's First Victory'; four sacred cantatas; a symphony and other orchestral works; six operettas, of which 'Four by Honors' was played for over a year by D'Oyly Carte's Opera Company; a string-quartet; etc. [R.9]

HORSLEY, CHARLES EDWARD (1822–76). See Register, 6.

HORVATH, CECILE, née Ayres (b. 1889) and ZOLTAN DE (b. 1886). See Register, 10.

HOUGH, GEORGE. See TUNE-BOOKS, 1808.

HOUSELEY, HENRY (Sept. 20, 1851, Sutton-in-Ashfield, England), had his first engagements as organist at St. Luke's in Derby and St. James' in Nottingham. In 1888 he came to Denver, succeeding Dr. Gower as organist at St. John's Cathedral, where he has been held in honor ever since. He has also achieved success in promoting both choral and orchestral work in Denver. He is F. R. C. O. and a founder of the A. G. O. His compositions include a string-quartet; six orchestral pieces (Minneapolis, St. Louis and Denver Symphony Orchestras); three one-act operas, 'Pygmalion,' 'Narcissus and Echo,' and 'The Philippino' (all given in Denver); two comic operas, 'Native Silver' and 'The Juggler' (also in Denver); 12 organ-pieces (being published); the dramatic cantata, 'Omar Khayyám' (Gray); 12 anthems (Schmidt); and many songs. Five cantatas for chorus and orchestra, composed for the Cathedral and often performed, are 'The Nativity,' 'Calvary,' 'Easter-Morn,' 'The Resurrection-Morn'; and 'Awake and Sing.' [R.7]

HOWARD, GEORGE HENRY (1843–1917). See Register, 5.

HOWARD, KATHLEEN, born at Clifton, Ont., studied with Saenger in New York and Bouhy and Jean de Reszké in Paris. In 1907 she made her début as contralto in 'Il Trovatore' at Metz, continuing there for two seasons. In 1909–12 she sang at the Grand-Ducal Opera at Darmstadt, and then toured extensively on the Continent and in England, singing with leading orchestras and as 'guest' at opera-houses. In 1913 she took a prominent part at the Wagner Festival under Nikisch, and was the first to sing in England the Witch in 'Die Königskinder.' In 1913–15 she was with the Century Opera Company in New York and appeared also in concert. Since 1916 she has been at the Metropolitan Opera House. Her répertoire includes about eighty operas in four languages. In 1915 she sang in the première of Parker's 'Fairyland' and in 1917 at the first American performance of Rabaud's 'Mârouf.' She has published *Confessions of an Opera-Singer*, 1918. In 1916 she married Edward K. Baird, a New York lawyer who was president of the Century Opera Company. [R.9]

HOWE, ELIAS (1820–95). See Register, 5.

HOWE, JAMES HAMILTON (b. 1856). See COLLEGES, 3 (DePauw U., Ind.).

HOWE, SOLOMON. See TUNE-BOOKS, 1799.

HOWLAND, WILLIAM (b. 1871). See Register, 7.

‡ HUBAY, JENÖ (Sept. 14, 1858, Budapest, Hungary). See article in Vol. ii. 437. Add to

list of works the operas 'Moosröschen' (1903, Pest), 'Lavothas Liebe' (1906, Pest) and 'Anna Karenina' (1915, Pest), two symphonies and four violin-concertos.

HUBBARD, JOHN (1750–1810). See TUNE-BOOKS, 1789.

HUBBARD, JOHN. See TUNE-BOOKS, 1814.

HUBBARD, W. S. See TUNE-BOOKS, 1842.

‡ HUBER, HANS (June 28, 1852, Schöne-werd, Switzerland). See article in Vol. ii. 437–8. Recent works in large form are the operas 'Der Simplicius' (1912, Basle), 'Frutta di Mare' (1914, Basle) and 'Die schöne Belinde' (1916, Berne), six symphonies (making seven) and the oratorio 'Weissagung und Erfüllung,' be-sides a long list of lesser works, including much chamber-music. For complete list, see Baker, *Dict. of Musicians*, p. 418.

HUBERDEAU, GUSTAVE (b. 1878?). See Register, 9.

HUGHES, EDWIN (Aug. 15, 1884, Wash-ington), after study with local teachers, in1905–06 was under Joseffy in New York and in 1907–10 with Leschetizky in Vienna, becoming the latter's assistant in 1909. In 1910–12 he con-certized in America, and then for four years re-sided in Munich, appearing with much success with leading orchestras and in recital in the music-centers of Germany. Returning to America in 1916, he settled in New York, and has given many concerts there and elsewhere. In 1918 he succeeded Friedberg in the piano-faculty of the Institute of Musical Art. He is also on the editorial staff of Schirmer, the pub-lisher. He has composed songs and a concert-paraphrase for piano of the 'Wiener Blut' Waltz of Johann Strauss. He has written many articles on musical subjects for American, English and German publications. [R.9]

HUGHES, ROYAL D. See COLLEGES, 3 (Findlay C., Ohio).

HUGHES, RUPERT (Jan. 31, 1872, Lan-caster, Mo.), graduated from Adelbert College in Cleveland in 1892, and had some lessons in theory from W. G. Smith and from Kelley, as well as later from C. W. Pearce in London, but is largely self-educated in music. His first published songs date from 1892 — 'Tears, Idle Tears' and 'In a Gondola.' In 1900 appeared 'Midnight in Venice' and a group of ten on words by Riley. One of the most ambitious is 'Cain,' a dramatic monologue with original words, presenting some fruits of investigation in the realm of dissonances. Many songs and piano-pieces are as yet unpublished. His lat-est composition is a 'Funeral March for the American Dead in France.' Writing about music has occupied a large amount of his time and energy, and he has become known both for his acute discrimination and his picturesque style. He was music-critic for the New York 'Criterion' in 1898–90, and since then has been

a frequent contributor to various papers and periodicals. His *Contemporary American Com-posers*, 1900 (enlarged by Arthur Elson, 1915), was a pioneer work, based on the study of large quantities of manuscripts and printed music. His *Love-Affairs of Great Musicians*, 2 vols., 1903, was also a work of painstaking research. The more prosaic, but comprehensive *Musical Guide*, 2 vols., 1903, was later recast in one volume as *The Music-Lover's Cyclopedia*, 1912. He also compiled *Songs by Thirty Americans*, 1904, made up of original contributions. His novel '*Zal*,' 1905, is a study of the psychology of the concert-pianist. He has been also an industrious writer of stories (from 1899) and plays (from 1902), of which a list is given in *Who's Who in America*, besides contributing to magazines and cyclopedias. He began military service as a private in the N. Y. N. G. in 1897, becoming captain in 1908, and in 1916 was on active duty on the Mexican border. In 1917 he was assistant to the Adjutant-General in New York, and in 1918 was commissioned major in the United States Army. [R.8]

HUGO, JOHN ADAM (b. 1873). See Register, 8.

HULL, ALEXANDER. See COLLEGES, 3 (Pacific C., Ore.).

‡ HULL, ARTHUR EAGLEFIELD (1876, Market Harborough, England), was a pupil of J. H. Wood, Matthay and C. W. Pearce in London and holds the degree of Mus.D. from Oxford University. He is organist at Hudders-field Parish Church, principal of the Hudders-field College of Music and editor of 'The Monthly Musical Record.' He has composed the oratorio 'The Resurrection-Morning'; the cantata 'Hail, Festal Day,' op. 1; a para-phrase for organ on melodies by Grieg, op. 2; 'Variations Poétiques' for organ, op. 3; a toccatina on 'Corde Natus' for organ, op. 5; a fantasia on an old English carol and 'Prelude, Berceuse and Reverie,' for organ, op. 6; and 'Russian Country-Scenes' for piano, op. 7. He is author of *Organ-Playing, its Technique and Expression*, 1911, *Modern Harmony*, 1914, *Harmony for Students*, 1918, volumes on Scri-abin, Bach, Cyril Scott, and others, a *Short History of Music*, and *Modern Music-Styles*, all for 'The Music-Lover's Library,' of which he is general editor, and *The Sonata in Music*. He has also edited and annotated the complete organ-works of Bach and Mendelssohn (Au-gener). He is honorary director and acting-secretary of the British Music Society.

HÜLSKAMP, HENRY [Gustav Heinrich]. See Register, 4.

HUMISTON, WILLIAM HENRY [family-name originally Humberstone] (Apr. 27, 1869, Marietta, O.), graduated from the Chicago High School in 1886 and from Lake Forest College in 1891. Meanwhile he studied piano with Mathews and organ with Eddy. In 1889–91 and 1893–94 he was organist at Lake Forest and in 1891–93 in Chicago. From 1894 he continued study of the piano with W. B. Keeler in New York, of organ with Woodman and in 1897–1900 of composition with MacDowell, meanwhile holding positions as organist, teaching composition and lecturing on Wagner and MacDowell. In 1902–12 he was conductor for various traveling opera-companies. Since 1912 he has been connected with the New York Philharmonic Society as editor of the program-notes and since 1916 as assistant-conductor. In 1914 he directed at the MacDowell Club probably the first performance in America of Mozart's 'Bastien und Bastienne'; in 1916 a program on 'the lighter side of Bach,' which included the 'Peasant Cantata' with scenery and costume; and in 1918 a Bach program with orchestra which included the triple concerto in D minor and many solos from cantatas. He has specialized in the music of Bach, Wagner and MacDowell and has a notable library of their works. Of his own works he has conducted the Suite in F-sharp minor (1911), the 'Southern Fantasie' (1913), and 'Iphigenia' (1913, People's Choral Union, Boston Symphony Orchestra). The Suite is published in an arrangement for violin and piano, and some of his songs are in print. [R.7]

HUNEKER, JAMES GIBBONS (Jan. 31, 1860, Philadelphia), had his training as pianist under Cross in Philadelphia, Mathias in Paris and Joseffy in New York, becoming in 1881–91 the latter's assistant at the National Conservatory. In 1891–95 he was critic for the New York 'Recorder,' in 1895–97 for the 'Advertiser,' in 1900–12 for the 'Sun,' in 1917 contributor to the Philadelphia 'Press' and since 1918 to the New York 'Times.' He has been a prolific author, the list including *Mezzotints in Modern Music*, 1899, *Chopin, the Man and his Music*, 1900, *Melomaniacs*, 1902, *Overtones — Music and Literature*, 1904, *Iconoclasts, a Book of Dramatists*, 1905, *Visionaries*, 1905, *Egoists, a Book of Supermen*, 1909, *Promenades of an Impressionist*, 1910, *Franz Liszt*, 1911, *The Pathos of Distance*, 1912, *Old Fogy*, 1913, *New Cosmopolis*, 1915, *Ivory Apes and Peacocks*, 1915, *Unicorns*, 1917, and *Bedouins*, 1920. These have given him a high place among American essayists, and several of them have been translated into other languages. His extraordinary range of knowledge in music, literature and art, combined with his brilliant and witty style, holds the interest, however one may feel about his judgments. [R.7]

'HUNOLD DER SPIELMANN.' An opera by Hermann Genss, produced in San Francisco in 1914.

HUNTINGTON, JONATHAN (1771–1838). See Tune-Books, 1807.

HUPFELD, CHARLES P. See Register, 3.

‡ HURLSTONE, WILLIAM YEATES (Jan. 7, 1876, London : May 30, 1906, London). See article in Vol. ii. 447. Publication of his music has continued, and the following compositions may be added : Quartet in E minor, for piano and strings; piano-trio in G; sonata in F, for violin and piano; four 'English Sketches,' for violin and piano; sonatas in F and D, for 'cello and piano; four 'Characteristic Pieces,' for viola or clarinet and piano; Capriccio in B minor, for piano; five 'Miniatures,' for piano; the ballad 'Alfred the Great,' for chorus and orchestra; and many songs.

HUTCHINGS, GEORGE S. (1835–1913). See Register, 5.

HUSBAND, JOHN (1753?–1809?). See Tune-Books, 1807.

HUSS, GEORGE JOHN (1828–1904). See Register, 4.

HUSS, HENRY HOLDEN (June 21, 1862, Newark, N. J.), through his father is descended from the brother of the Bohemian patriot and martyr, John Huss. His first study was under his father, later continued with Boise and for three years with Rheinberger and Giehrl at the Munich Conservatory, where he graduated in 1885. At his graduation he played his Rhapsody for piano and orchestra — later also played with the Boston Symphony Orchestra in 1887 and in New York with Van der Stucken. His piano-concerto in B he has played with the Boston Symphony, New York Philharmonic, Pittsburgh, Cincinnati and St. Paul Orchestras. He has also given his violin-sonata with Hartmann, Kneisel, Spiering, Lichtenberg and others, and his 'cello-sonata with Schroeder, Hambourg, May Mukle and others. The Kneisel Quartet introduced his string-quartet, and an early piano-trio was given by the composer, Kneisel and Hekking in Boston. In 1904 he married Hildegard Hoffmann, the concert-soprano, and they have given many joint recitals in the United States and in Europe. His compositions include the following

'Wald-Idylle,' op. 2, for small orchestra (1884, Munich).

'Rhapsodie,' op. 3, for piano and orchestra (1886, Boston, 1887, New York).

Concerto in B, op. 10, for piano and orchestra (Schirmer).

Concerto in C minor, op. 12, for violin and orchestra, dedicated to Maud Powell.

Trio in D minor, op. 8, for piano, violin and 'cello (Larghetto published for piano and reed-organ).

Romanza and Polonaise, op. 11, for violin and orchestra.

Sonata in G minor, op. 19, for violin and piano, dedicated to Kneisel (Schirmer, 2d movement also as 'A Northern Melody').

Sonata, op. 24, for 'cello and piano, dedicated to Schroeder.

Quartet in G minor, op. 26, for strings.

Quartet in E minor, for strings, written at Ysaÿe's request and dedicated to him.

'Berceuse Slave,' for violin and piano, dedicated to Zimbalist (Ditson).

Romanza in E, for violin (or 'cello), dedicated to Maud Powell (Schirmer).

Ballade in F, op. 1, for piano (Schirmer).

Three Pieces, op. 5, for piano (Schmidt).

'Prelude Appassionata,' and 'The Rivulet' (étude), op. 7, for piano (Schmidt).

'Summer Sketch-Book,' op. 13, six pieces for piano (Schirmer).

'Quatre Préludes en forme d'études,' op. 17, for piano (Schirmer).

'Menuet et Gavotte Capricieuse,' op. 13, for piano (Schirmer).

Valse, Nocturne and Gavotte, op. 20, for piano (Schirmer).

'La Nuit,' op. 21, for piano (Schirmer).

Six Pieces, op. 23, for piano (Schirmer).

'Pastorale,' 'Album-Leaf' and 'Etude Mélodique,' for piano (Schmidt).

'Menuet Mignonne,' op. 27, for piano.

'Valse Intime,' for piano, dedicated to Bauer (Ditson).

Three Bagatelles, op. 30, and Three Pieces for Children, for piano (Art Publication Soc.).

'Ave Maria,' op. 4, for soli, women's chorus, strings, organ and harp (1888, New York) (Novello).

Festival Sanctus, op. 9, for chorus, orchestra and organ (Schuberth).

'Adeste Fideles,' op. 14, and 'Pater Noster,' op. 15, for six-part chorus a cappella (Schirmer).

Nocturne, 'How sweet the moonlight sleeps,' op. 27, for soprano, women's chorus and orchestra.

'The Recessional,' for chorus and piano (Silver, Burdett & Co.).

'O Captain, my Captain,' for men's chorus, piano and organ (Schirmer).

'The Fool's Prayer,' for men's chorus and piano (Schirmer).

'The Flag,' for men's chorus and piano (Schirmer).

'Mankind's Own Song,' for three-part women's chorus and piano (Schirmer).

'The Seven Ages of Man,' op. 16, for baritone and orchestra.

About 30 songs (many published by Schirmer or Schmidt).   [R.7]

HUTCHESON, ERNEST (July 20, 1871, Melbourne, Australia), when between five and seven, trained by Vogrich and Torrance, toured Australia as a child-pianist. At fourteen he went to Leipzig to study piano under Reinecke and Zwintscher and composition under Jadassohn. At nineteen he made a second tour in Australia. He then continued study under Stavenhagen at Weimar, where he was keeping alive the Liszt traditions. From 1898 he was highly successful in Berlin as pianist, conductor and composer. In 1900 he became chief piano-teacher at the Peabody Conservatory in Baltimore, but resigned in 1912 to have time for more concert-work. After two years in Europe, principally Germany, in 1914 he settled in New York. In 1911 he succeeded Sherwood as head of the piano-department of the Chautauqua Institution. The best-known of his many prominent piano-pupils is Olga Samaroff (Mrs. Stokowski). He has composed a symphonic poem, an orchestral suite, a piano-concerto, a concerto for two pianos and a violin-concerto.

Some piano-pieces have been published. He has also written the excellent text-book, *The Elements of Piano-Technique*, a guide to Strauss' 'Elektra,' and many musical articles.   [R.9]

HYDE, ARTHUR SEWALL (1875–1920). See Register, 8.

HYLLESTED, AUGUST (June 17, 1858, Stockholm, Sweden), played in public when but eight, for three years was trained by Holger Dahl and then went to the Copenhagen Conservatory to study piano with Neupert, composition and orchestration with Gade, counterpoint with Hartmann, violin with Tofte and organ with Attrup. He made his second tour of Scandinavia in 1875, and became conductor and organist at the Cathedral in Copenhagen. In 1879 he worked with Kullak and Kiel at Berlin and in 1880 won approval from Liszt. In 1883–84 he toured in Great Britain and in 1885 made his début in New York, followed by concerts in the United States and Canada. In 1886–91 he was assistant-director of the Chicago Musical College and in 1891–94 head of the piano-department in the Gottschalk Lyric School. After three years of concertizing in England, France, Germany and Scandinavia he returned to Chicago as player and teacher. He has received distinguished honors from more than one European court. His published works include 'Elizabeth,' a symphonic poem with double chorus (produced under his direction in 1897, London); incidental music to 'Die Rheinnixe'; a 'Marche Triomphale' for orchestra; 'Scandinavian Dances,' fantasias, two suites and smaller pieces for piano. In manuscript are two piano-trios, a piano-sonata, 'Variations Sérieuses,' a suite for piano and songs.   [R.7]

HYMN–BOOKS WITH TUNES. Except for a limited number of Psalters in the 17th century, American churches did not have service-books for congregational song that contained both words and music in conjunction until about 1850. During what may be called the first period of development of hymn-singing (1720–1820) such tunes as were imported, adapted or composed were accumulated in separate Tune-Books (see article), which, besides supplying material for the 'singing-schools,' tended more and more to build up choir-singing rather than to be used by congregations as such. In the early decades of the 19th century, however, when two or three types of religious assembly that were novel became common, a demand arose for books with words and music printed together. At first books of this kind were not meant for the more formal services, but for Sunday-schools, informal 'social' meetings and evangelistic gatherings. Thus was started a movement of publication that soon attained large dimensions. During the century since 1820 hundreds of small books have been put forth, representing various grades of ability, taste and sincerity. Taken together, these lesser books have contained a huge amount of original music, but usually of so trivial and ephemeral a character that no summary of them is here attempted.

But meanwhile, from the appearance in 1831 of Leavitt's 'Christian Lyre' and Hastings and Mason's 'Spiritual Songs' (its immediate rival), the new movement pointed toward a type of service-book for dignified church use, and such books began to be made after about 1850. The music was taken from existing tune-books or followed in their style. The bulk of it was American in origin. After 1860, however, the usage of Episcopal churches began to be affected by the transition in England that was embodied in 'Hymns Ancient and Modern' (1861 and later). This epoch-making book was at once imported, reprinted (from 1866), adopted by many Episcopal churches, and increasingly considered by editors of other denominations. The influence of the several types of tune in Anglican usage, combined probably with other tendencies in American music, produced a progressive alteration of standard in the demands of congregations and the practice of editors. Especially after 1880, the larger church hymnals, whether issued by denominational authority or by independent editors and publishers, have generally sought to combine tunes of many styles — the old American type, the juvenile or evangelistic type, the chorale-types of England and Germany, the English part-song type, etc. — and often also to stimulate fresh composition. The proportion of these elements varies greatly, and the scholarship and judgment of individual editors also vary. But, on the whole, there has been notable advance.[1]

On the whole, then, the series of books that has been compiled from various sources offers curious and interesting evidence of the growth of one side of popular musical culture — a side which undoubtedly affects the appreciation of a vast number of users and which has attracted effort in original composition that is by no means insignificant. The list is doubtless far from complete, but it is sufficient to indicate the extent of the literature. The editor's name is added in most cases, and an abbreviation that indicates the denomination for which the book is intended.

1831   *Christian Lyre*, Leavitt . . . . Pres. Cong.
      Spiritual Songs, Hastings, Mason Pres. Cong.
1839   *Hymns of Zion*, Thomas . . . . Univ.
1850   *Christian Psalmist*

[1] Copyright considerations have played no small part in the process. In many books commercial reasons have kept down the number of tunes protected by American copyright and increased that of tunes taken from English sources. Often what was artistically better was at the same time cheaper.

1851   *Christian Melodies*, Cheever, Sweetzer
       (numeral notation) . . . . .Cong.
       Temple Melodies, Jones . . . . .Cong.
1854   *Congregational Church Music*, Bacon . . . .Cong.
1855   *Plymouth Collection*, Beecher . . . . .Cong.
1857   *Hymns for the Use of the M. E. Church* . .Meth.
1858   *Church Melodies*, Hastings . . . . .Pres.
       Songs of the Church, Davies . . . . .Epis.
1859   *Baptist Chorals*, Manly, Everett . . . . . . .Bapt.
       Choralist, Day, Tappan, Curtis, Cheney
                                  Free-W. Bapt.
       Collection of Sacred Song, Hopkins . . . . . .Epis.
       Evangelical Psalmist, Seiss, McCron,
         Passavant . . . . .Luth.
       New Congregational Hymn & Tune Book,
         Nason. . . . . .Cong.
       Pastor's Selection, Burt . . . . .Pres.
       Puritan Hymn & Tune Book . . . . .Cong.
       Sabbath Hymn & Tune Book, Park,
         Phelps, Mason. .Cong.
1860   *American Hymn & Tune Book*,
       Stevens, McDonald
       Book of Hymns & Tunes, Longfellow . . . .Unit.
       Church Choral-Book, Baker, Tufts . . . . . .Cong.
       Psalmist, Edmands . . . . .Bapt.
       Psalms of David, Jones (tunes apart)
       Wesleyan Hymn & Tune Book, Everett
                                      Meth. So.
1861   *Gospel Psalmist*, Adams . . . . .Univ.
1862   *Songs for Social & Public Worship*, Mason
                                      Cong.
       Songs of the Church, Robinson . . . . .Pres.
1863   *Psalms of David*, Keys . . . . .Pres.
1864   *Church Pastorals*, Adams . . . . .Cong.
       Devotional Hymn & Tune Book,
         Rowland, Bradbury . . . . .Bapt.
1865   *Songs for the Sanctuary*, Robinson, Pres. Cong.
1866   *Book of Worship*, Bacon . . . . .Pres.
       Collection of Hymns . . . . .Meth. So.
       Common Praise, Waterbury . . . . .Epis.
       New Hymn & Tune Book, Phillips . . . . . .Meth.
       Presbyterian Hymnal . . . . .O. S. Pres.
1867   *Christian Hymnal*, Sewall . . . . .Swedbg.
       Church Hymn Book, Salter (tunes apart) Cong.
       Jubilee Harp . . . . .Advt.
1868   *Book of Praise* . . . . .Cong.
       Hymn & Tune Book, Livermore . . . . .Unit.
       Book of Common Praise, Hodges . . . . .Epis.
       Spiritual Harp . . . . .Spirit.
       Vestry Harmonies, Adams . . . . .Univ.
1869   *Hymns of the Church*, Thompson,
         Vermilye, Thompson . . . . .Ref. Dutch
       Hymns of the New Life . . . . .Pres. Cong.
1870   *Christian Hymn & Tune Book*, Hayden
       Christian Praise . . . . .Ref. Dutch
       Hymnal, Hutchins .Epis.
       Parish Hymnal, Tucker . . . . .Epis.
1871   *Baptist Praise Book*, Holbrook . . . . .Bapt.
       Christian Hymnal . . . . .Disciples
       Collection of Hymns, Shuey, etc. . . .Unit. Breth.
       Tribute of Praise, Tourjée . . . . .Cong.
1872   *Brethren's Hymn & Tune Book* . . . . .Dunkers
       Church Hymn Book, Hatfield . . . . .Pres.
       Hymnal, Goodrich, Gilbert . . . . .Epis.
       Hymnal, Tucker . . . . .Epis.
       Hymns of the Morning, Barker . . . . .Advt.
       Sacrifice of Praise, Murray, Gilman . . . . . .Pres.
       Church Book, Schmucker, Bird . . . . .Luth.
1873   *Baptist Hymn & Tune Book*, Evans . . . .Bapt.
       Church Harmonies, Bolles, Washburn . . . .Univ.
1874   *Hymns & Songs of Praise*, Hitchcock,
         Eddy, Schaff . . . . .Pres.
       Hymns for the Sanctuary . . . . . . .Unit. Breth.
1874   *Presbyterian Hymnal*, Duryea . . . . .Pres.
1875   *Hymns for Christian Devotion* . . . . .Univ.

1875	Psalms & Hymns & Spiritual Songs, Robinson ....Pres.
	Service of Praise ....Cong.
1876	Bible Songs.....................Cumb. Pres.
	Book of Worship (chants, not tunes) . .Swedbg.
	Christian Hymn Book..............Christ.
	Hymns & Tunes...............7th-D. Advt.
1877	Christian Hymnal, Burton, Parker, Twichell...........................Cong.
	Hymn & Tune Book..................Unit.
1878	Methodist Hymnal.................Meth.
	Reformed Church Hymnal ....Ger. Ref.
	Selection of Spiritual Songs, Robinson Pres. Cong.
1880	Book of Worship....................Luth.
	Christian Praise, Thompson......Ref. Dutch.
	Evangelical Hymnal, Hall, Lasar........Pres.
	Manual of Praise, Mead, Rice........Cong.
	Songs of Christian Praise, Richards....Cong.
	Worship in Song, Holbrook
1881	Choice Collection of Spiritual Hymns, Mennonite
	Church Praise Book, Stryker, Main......Pres.
	Hymns of the Advent..................Adv.
1882	Evangelical Hymn & Tune Book...Ev. Assoc.
	New Christian Hymn & Tune Book, Fillmore ....Disciples
	New Hymn Book.................Meth. So.
1883	Baptist Hymnal, Johnson, Doane.......Bapt.
	Church Book, Bacon..................Cong.
	Sacred Songs for Public Worship, Savage, Dow......................Unit.
	Duplex Hymn & Tune Book, Shotwell....Pres.
	Wesleyan Hymnal ....Wesl. Meth.
1884	Baptist Hymn Book, Thompson....Prim. Bapt.
	Brethren Hymnody.................Dunkers
	English & Latin Hymns (later, Catholic Hymnal).........................R. C.
	Laudes Domini, Robinson........Pres. Cong.
1885	Carmina Sanctorum, Hitchcock, Eddy, Mudge ....Pres.
1886	Book of Common Praise, Moore, Gilchrist..................Ref. Epis.
	Hymn & Tune Book, Durand, Lester Prim. Bapt.
	Hymnal Companion ....Ref. Epis.
	Songs of Pilgrimage, Hastings
1887	Christian Hymnal, Wilson ......7th-D. Advt.
	Church of God Selection
	Hymns of the Faith, Harris, Tucker, Glezen ....Cong.
	New Hymn & Tune Book ....Afr. Meth. Zion
	Psalter, with Music..............Unit. Pres.
	Seventh-Day Adventist Hymn & Tune Book ....7th-D. Advt.
1888	Hymns for the Sanctuary.......Unit. Breth.
1889	Church Song, Stryker.................Pres.

1889	Evangelical Lutheran Hymn Book......Luth.
	Hymn & Tune Book..............Meth. So.
1890	Church Hymnary, Bedell.........Ref. Epis.
	Hymnal — Amore Dei, Williams........Unit.
	Hymnal........................Ger. Ref.
	Hymns & Tunes................Mennonite
	Hymns of the Church Universal, Foote...Unit.
	Otterbein Hymnal, Lorenz........Unit. Breth.
	Primitive Hymns, Spiritual Songs & Sacred Poems, Lloyd.......Prim. Bapt.
1891	Hymns of the Ages, Kerr...........So. Pres.
1892	Christian Science Hymnal ....Chr. Sci.
	New Laudes Domini, Robinson....Pres. Cong.
1893	Church Book, Krauth.................Luth.
	Hymnal, Messiter....................Epis.
	Hymnal........................Afr. Meth.
	Magnificat......................Swedbg.
	Plymouth Hymnal, Abbott............Cong.
1894	Hymnal, Hutchins...................Epis.
	Hymnal, Tucker, Rousseau............Epis.
1895	Church Harmonies, Tenney, Lewis......Univ.
	Hymnal, Benson.....................Pres.
	Sacred Hymns & Tunes.........Wesl. Meth.
1897	Hymnal, Darlington.................Epis.
	In Excelsis.....................Pres. Cong.
1898	African M. E. Hymnal ....Afr. Meth.
	Sursum Corda, Johnson, Ayres......Bapt. (contains nearly 1350 tunes)
1899	Hymnal........................Luth.
1901	Brethren Hymnal.................Dunkers
	Gloria Deo
	Methodist Prot. Church Hymnal ..Meth. Prot.
	New Manual of Praise, Rice, Wright, Dickinson........................Cong.
	New Psalms & Hymns..............So. Pres.
1903	Hymnal, Parker ....Epis.
1904	Pilgrim Hymnal, Noyes, Ziegler........Cong.
1905	Hymns of Worship & Service.......Pres. Cong.
	Methodist Hymnal ....Meth.
1906	Church Hymns & Tunes, Turner, Biddle Pres. Cong.
	Friends' Hymnal ....Quaker
1910	Free Methodist (Wesleyan Methodist) Hymnal..........Free Meth., Wesl. Meth.
	Hymns of the Kingdom of God, Coffin, Vernon....................Pres. Cong.
	Hymns of the Living Church, Ives, Woodman....................Pres. Cong.
	Hymns of the Centuries, Shepard
	Hymnal, Benson.....................Pres.
1912	Hymns of the Church, Davis, Calkins....Cong.
	Riverdale Hymn Book, Dood, Longacre
	Songs of the Christian Life, Richards....Cong.
1913	American Hymnal, Dawson.......Pres. Cong.
	Hymnal of Praise, Eaton, Sallmon......Cong.
1914	New Hymn & Tune Book ....Unit.
1915	Church Hymnal.................Pres. Cong.
1918	Hymnal ....Epis.

I

IDE, CHESTER EDWARD (June 13, 1878, Springfield, Ill.), after having been a pupil of Prout, Corder and Davenport at the Royal Academy of Music in London, taught piano and harmony in Springfield till 1916. He has since taught harmony at the Music School Settlement in New York and piano privately. He has composed the orchestral suite 'Idyllic Dances'; the symphonic poem 'Pan's Dream of Syrinx'; an orchestral suite in four movements — 'Thoughts of Winter,' 'Frolic,' 'Fireside-Dreams,' 'Æolus'; songs with orchestra, 'Queen of Bubbles' and 'Autumn Songs' (texts by the composer); incidental music for Mackaye's masque 'Caliban'; songs and pianopieces. He has also edited a collection of 50 folk-songs for primary study (1917, Schirmer).
[R.9]

INDIAN MUSIC. Within the past half-century there has been a significant and growing interest in the music of the North American Indians. The motive behind this developing attention has been partly ethnological and partly artistic, and in the case of many investigators the two purposes have been happily blended. The one aim is to collect, analyze and codify the facts as part of the total body of knowledge regarding a vanishing race, so as to facilitate the comparison of them with similar facts in other fields. The other aim is to penetrate into sympathy with the instinct and impulse behind the facts, to interpret the artistic spirit which they embody, to set forth actual songs, themes or figures for general appreciation or for use in new production, or so to absorb the essence of the style as to incorporate its spirit in characteristic composition without direct imitation. What has been accomplished by critical research would have been of slight general value if it had not been for the zeal and sympathy of the searchers after meaning and beauty. These latter have lifted the whole subject into distinction.

Though it is popularly customary to class all the aborigines of North America under one name, they were far from being a unified race. Not less than sixty distinct tribes are counted, or even more, differing in language and customs and so widely separated that between them was no interchange. There is therefore no such thing as a general type or system of Indian music, except as all examples are alike primitive or unsophisticated, with an essential amalgamation of verse and song and a minimum use of instruments save in conjunction with vocal delivery. It is all folk-music of the most typical kind, shaped by a diffused tribal use and preserved by oral tradition as a precious tribal possession. As in many other cases, song is intimately interwoven with dancing, pantomime and other dramatic expression and all these artistic efforts often have a profound religious aspect.

There is dispute as to the scale-forms used, especially as there is so much variety in the phenomena. It is likely that the subconscious basis is usually pentatonic or hexatonic — as among other primitive peoples — but the practical treatment of melody is sometimes so overladen with curious intonations or shadings as to suggest to some a complicated scheme of quarter-tones, quite alien to traditional European music. Occasionally, however, melodies conform closely to lines that seem to us normal. Tonality seems to exist, though not that belonging with a developed harmonic system, but rather such as underlies ancient and mediæval schemes. Scales are probably conceived downward rather than upward.

There is an abundance of downright rhythm, but it often shifts from one type to another with amazing readiness, and, especially when drumming and singing are combined, often presents startling contradictions between voice and instrument. While the result seems chaotic to the cultivated hearer, it is usually held to with great persistence and repeated with fidelity, implying much positiveness of rhythmic conviction.

There is little trace of harmony. As a rule, songs are strictly in unison. The only instrument of importance is the drum — variously made — which is used without regard to its pitch-relation with the voices.

Although some scattered notes had been made previously, the first serious researches were in 1880 by Theodore Baker of New York, then studying at Leipzig University, in his thesis for a Ph.D.[1] These were made on the Seneca Reservation in western New York, with added points derived from western students at the Indian School at Carlisle, Pa. Next came Alice C. Fletcher's studies, first among the Omahas, and later among the Pawnees and other tribes of the plains west of the Mississippi.[2] To these followed investigations by Frederick R. Burton among the Ojibways in Ontario near Lake Huron,[3] and the extensive collection of material under the Hemenway Southwestern

[1] Ueber die Musik der nordamerikanischen Wilden, 1882.
[2] A Study of Omaha Indian Music, 1893, and Indian Story and Song from North America, 1900, with many articles besides.
[3] Songs of the Ojibway Indians, 1903, later embodied in the posthumous volume American Primitive Music, 1909.

252

Expedition, which was worked up particularly by Natalie Curtis,[1] and by Benjamin Ives Gilman, the latter of whom had first entered the field earlier.[2] These deal with the pueblo tribes of the southern Rocky Mountains. From time to time the literature has been augmented by monographs published by the Bureau of Ethnology, the United States Museum, the Carnegie Institution, etc., and by articles in magazines by detached observers. It is to be hoped that undeveloped sides of the subject will be further investigated and that the total data may be better correlated than has thus far been possible. It is unfortunate that scientific study did not begin earlier, when more tribes than now were still in existence and when their life was even more free and untouched.

In its artistic aspect what has been collected of Indian music is sufficient to arouse no little wonder and often positive admiration. It is true that the average listener finds its effects abnormal, so that he is often baffled in noting them down or reducing them to habitual forms of analysis. They are to him decidedly alien or 'barbarous.' Yet the best observers agree that the Indian himself finds in his singing a very real self-expression, affording outlet for imagination and emotion otherwise unembodied, so that song is his one particular fine art, absorbing the deepest interest of both performer and listener and often standing out as the climacteric embodiment of his social and tribal life. To one who appreciates this and becomes wonted to the unfamiliar idioms, many Indian melodies come to have a beauty of a singularly affecting kind. This beauty is of course enhanced by associations of thought arising from the topics of the songs, their actual texts and their habitual usage, and from whatever romance has collected about the history of this dignified and freedom-loving race. The imagination is also stirred by whatever can be understood of the dramatic, ceremonial and religious implications connected with verse and melody.

Without attempting an exhaustive catalogue, it may be well to make reference to some composers and works that illustrate how the impress of Indian themes, topics and sentiments has affected musical creation. Among these are Henry Schoenefeld's 'Suite Caractéristique,' op. 15, 'Indian Legends,' pantomime-ballet 'Machicanta' and an opera; Edward MacDowell's 'Indian' Suite, op. 48 (1896); Frederick R. Burton's cantata 'Hiawatha' (1898); Carl Busch's symphonic poem 'Minnehaha's Vision,' cantata 'The Four Winds,' 'Indian Legend' for violin, many songs, etc.; Ernest R. Kroeger's overtures 'Hiawatha' and 'Atala,' besides several piano-pieces; Henry F. Gilbert's

[1] *Songs of Ancient America*, 1905, and *The Indian's Book*, 1907.

[2] *Zuñi Melodies*, 1891, and *Hopi Melodies*, 1908.

'Indian Sketches' for piano (1914); Charles S. Skilton's 'Indian Dances' for orchestra; Arthur F. Nevin's opera 'Poia' (1910); Arthur Farwell's piano-works 'American Indian-Melodies,' 'Impressions of the Wa-Wan Ceremony,' op. 21, 'Navajo War-Dance,' op. 29, 'Dawn,' 'Ichibuzzh' and 'The Domain of the Hurakan'; Horace A. Miller's Theme and Variations, other piano-pieces and songs; Frederic Ayres' overture 'From the Plains'; Harold A. Loring's piano-pieces and songs (based on several years spent on reservations); Charles W. Cadman's opera 'The Land of Misty Water' and several striking songs; Victor Herbert's opera 'Natoma' (1911); varied works by Carlos Troyer (d. 1920), Thorvald Otterström and Mrs. Stella Prince Stocker; and large numbers of detached pieces by other hands. The foregoing examples illustrate varied treatments, from faithful transcriptions harmonized to purely fanciful imitations or suggestions. But together they testify to the strong impression that the study of Indian sources has made upon American composition. See article by Cadman in 'The Musical Quarterly,' July, 1915.

One of the objects of the Wa-Wan Press, founded in 1901 by Arthur Farwell, was to promote this movement by publishing both musical and literary material regarding it. Specially useful summaries are given in *The Art of Music*, Vol. i., and at various points in Vol. iv.

INDIANAPOLIS CONSERVATORY OF MUSIC, THE, was founded in 1897 by Edgar M. Cawley, who has since been at its head.

‡**INDY, PAUL MARIE THÉODORE VINCENT D'** (Mar. 27, 1851, Paris). See article in Vol. ii. 465–6. Since 1911 he has been sole director of the Schola Cantorum, and since 1912 professor of the orchestra-class in the Conservatory. In 1912 he was made an officer of the Légion d'Honneur. In 1905 he visited the United States, conducting several performances of his works in New York and Boston. Additional works to be noted are 'Petite Chanson Grégorienne,' op. 60, for piano, four hands; 'Jour d'Été à la Montagne,' op. 61, for orchestra — 'Aurore,' 'Jour,' 'Soir'; 'Souvenirs,' op. 62, poem for orchestra; 'Menuet sur le nom de Haydn,' op. 65, for piano; 'Pièce' in B-flat, op. 66, for organ; oratorio, 'Le Mystère de St.-Christophe' (1916, given in Paris, 1917); and 3rd Symphony, 'Sinfonia Brevis de Bello Gallico' (given by Boston Symphony Orchestra, 1919). Vol. ii. of his *Composition Musicale* came out in 1909, and he has also written *César Franck*, 1906, and *Beethoven, Biographie Critique*, 1911 (translated by Baker, 1913). See biographies by Deniau, 1903, Borgex, 1913, Sérieux, 1914, and in works on French Music generally, with Starczewski, *La Schola Cantorum*, 1905; also article by Hill in 'The Musical Quarterly,' April, 1915.

INGALLS, JEREMIAH (1764–1828). See TUNE-BOOKS, 1805.

INGRAM, FRANCES (b. 1888). See Register, 10.

INSTITUTE OF MUSIC PEDAGOGY, THE, of Northampton, Mass., is a summer-school for training public-school supervisors. It originated in an enterprise started in 1900 by Sterrie A. Weaver at Westfield, Mass. At his death in 1904 this was continued by Ralph L. Baldwin until 1907, when the School, now fully organized, was moved to Northampton and George O. Bowen and Lyman L. Wellman (d. 1908) became partners. Since then it has been conducted by Messrs. Baldwin and Bowen, with several other instructors. The number of students is 125–150 each year, and about 250 have graduated. The sessions continue three weeks, and are held in the Northampton High School, with exceptional advantages for demonstration and practice.

INSTITUTE OF MUSICAL ART, THE, of New York, came into being in 1904 under the hand of Frank Damrosch upon the basis of an initial endowment of $500,000 given by James Loeb, Esq., in memory of his mother, Betty Loeb. To this original endowment considerable additions were later made by gifts or subscription. Receiving its charter from the Board of Regents of the University of the State of New York, the Institute was opened in 1905, at first occupying a building remodeled from the fine old Lenox residences at Fifth Avenue and 12th Street. In 1910 it removed to a new and perfectly appointed building of its own at 120 Claremont Avenue, near Columbia University. Dr. Damrosch has continued as director from the beginning, and has consistently applied the progressive policy originally outlined.

With its liberal resources, the Institute has been able from the first to command the services of exceptional teachers in every branch, to sift its students rigorously with reference to ability and promise, to insist that every student, except the more advanced, shall pursue such studies as are prescribed for his special needs, to provide without extra charge many striking general recitals and lectures, and thus to maintain an educational standard that is at least unusual. In addition to the branches universally taught, attention is given to dramatic singing, choral work, chamber, orchestral and band music, general and special pedagogy, the training of supervisors for public schools, and lectures on historical and critical subjects. The faculty numbers over 70, about half of whom have served since the first years. The number of students was originally fixed at about 600, and this figure has been regularly maintained or exceeded. The total number enrolled up to 1920 has been about 8500, and the

graduates number about 600. The average size of the school chorus is 60, and of the orchestra 75. The equipment includes a reference library of over 2500 volumes, and a large circulating library of music.

The eminence of the Institute is attested by the large proportion of its graduates or recipients of artist-diplomas who now occupy positions of leadership throughout the country.

INTEN, FERDINAND VON (1848–1918). See Register, 5.

INTERNATIONAL MUSICAL SOCIETY, THE, founded at Leipzig in 1899 to promote advanced musical scholarship by maintaining a monthly *Zeitschrift* and quarterly *Sammelbände* and by fostering local and national associations of its members, with general Congresses at intervals, promptly secured 30–40 members in the United States. A National Section was organized in 1907, which held annual meetings until the outbreak of the European War in 1914 led to the dissolution of the central Society. The presidents of the Section were Albert A. Stanley (1907–1911) and Waldo S. Pratt. The total number of members rose to about 120, besides many libraries. The Section was officially represented at the Congresses of Vienna (1909), London (1911) and Paris (1914). Local groups of its members occasionally held special meetings. Although the apparent results of the Section in actual research and publication were slight, it drew attention to scholarly effort in a way that may lead to something more substantial in the future.

The meetings of the Section were regularly held in connection with those of the Music Teachers' National Association, and the following papers of the International Society were printed in the *Proceedings* of the M. T. N. A.:

Philip G. Clapp, 'The Symphonies of Gustav Mahler' (1914), C. Winfred Douglas, 'History and Work of the Schola Cantorum' (1913), George C. Gow, '16th-Century and 19th-Century Tendencies' (1908), Edward B. Hill, 'The Modern Interpretive Ballet' (1913), Bruno Hirzel, 'Operatic Italy in 1770, by an Eye-Witness' (1910), Otto Kinkeldey, 'Influence of the Folk-Song upon Artistic Progress' (1915), Fritz Krull, 'On the Causes for Fixing the Intervals of the Major Scale' (1912), Leo R. Lewis, 'Possibilities of Thematic Indexing' (1912), Charles H. Mills, 'History of Musical Degrees' (1912), 'Relation of the Drama of Adam de la Hale and Hans Sachs' (1915), Waldo S. Pratt, 'Need of a Progressive Policy' (1911), Edward Silsky, 'Music Division of the New York Public Library' (1914), O. G. Sonneck, 'Was Richard Wagner a Jew?' (1911), Theodore Zbinden, 'Value of Music to the Physician' (1915), Jaroslaw de Zielinski, 'North American Folk-Songs' (1908). In addition, more or less elaborate reports were made by Albert A. Stanley on the Vienna and London Congresses (1909, 1911), and by J. Lawrence Erb on the Paris Congress (1914).

Articles by members of the Section are as follows: Richard Aldrich, *Z*. xv. 78; Franz X. Arens, *Z*. iii. 321; Bruno Hirzel, *S*. x. 151, xiii. 348, *Z*. xii. 154;

Otto Kinkeldey, *S.* ix. 538; O. G. Sonneck, *S.* i. 630, iii. 139, v. 119, 329, vi. 428, viii. 112, xi. 312, xii. 297, 525, xiii. 392, xiv. 226, xv. 102, *Z.* i. 121, 388, ii. 158, 264, vii. 273, ix. 1, xiv. 170; Albert A. Stanley, *Z.* ii. 394.

Records of the Section meetings are printed in the *Proceedings* of the M. T. N. A., 1907–1916 inclusive. The Constitution is given in the report for 1907, and a list of members in that for 1910.

‡IPPOLITOV–IVANOV, MICHAEL MICHAILOVITCH (Nov. 19, 1859, Gatchina, Russia). See article in Vol. ii. 507, and note in v. 647. He succeeded Safonov as director of the Moscow Conservatory in 1906. To the list of works add an orchestral suite, op. 20; 'The Legend of the White Swan at Novgorod,' op. 24; the symphonic poem 'Iveria,' op. 42; an 'Armenian Rhapsody,' op. 48, for orchestra; and the operas 'Treachery' (1911) and 'Ole from Nordland' (1917).

‡IRELAND, JOHN (Aug. 13, 1879, Bowdon, England), the son of the editor of the Manchester 'Examiner,' studied under Stanford at the Royal College of Music until 1901 and graduated as Mus.B. at Durham University. He has since devoted himself to composition. The list of his works is as follows:

Overture, 'Midsummer.'
Symphonic Prelude, 'Tritons.'
Prelude, 'The Forgotten Rite' (Augener).
Orchestral Poem in A minor.
Overture, 'Pelléas et Mélisande.'
Sextet for strings, clarinet and horn.
Quartets in D minor and C minor, for strings.
Trio in E minor, for piano, violin and 'cello.
Trio, No. 2, in one movement, for piano, violin and 'cello (Augener).
Phantasie in A minor, for violin, 'cello and piano (Augener).
Trio in D minor, for piano, 'cello and clarinet.
Sonatas for violin and piano — No. 1, in D minor ♭, (Augener), No. 2, in A minor (Rogers), in C minor, and in G minor, in one movement.
Sonata in C minor, for piano.
'A Sea-Idyll' in three movements, for piano.

Two Rhapsodies, one in C-sharp minor, for piano (Rogers, one).
'Decorations' — 'The Island-Spell,' 'Moonglade,' 'The Scarlet Ceremonies' — for piano (Augener).
Preludes — 'The Undertone,' 'Obsession,' 'The Holy Boy,' 'The Fire of Spring' — for piano (Rogers).
'London Pieces' — 'Chelsea Reach,' 'Ragamuffin' — for piano (Augener).
'The Towing-Path,' for piano (Augener).
'Leaves from a Child's Sketch-Book,' for piano (Rogers).
About 20 songs (Augener, Boosey, Rogers, ⌈Curwen).
6 two-part songs (Novello, Curwen, Arnold).
Morning, Evening and Communion Services (Novello).
Anthem, ' Greater love hath no man than this' (Stainer).
'Elegiac Romance,' 'Sursum Corda' and 'Alla Marcia,' for organ (Novello).

See articles by Hull in 'Musical Opinion,' Feb., Mar., 1919, by Evans in 'The Musical Quarterly,' Apr. 1919, and in 'The Musical Times,' Aug., Sept., 1919.

ITALIAN SYMPHONY ORCHESTRA, THE, of New York, was founded in 1913 by Pietro Floridia and has been conducted by him since that time.

ITHACA CONSERVATORY OF MUSIC, THE, of Ithaca, N. Y., was founded in 1892 by W. Grant Egbert, who remained at its head till 1903 and returned in 1917, the director in 1903–05 being George C. Williams and in 1905–17 Eric Dudley. It now maintains a faculty of about thirty instructors, with courses in public-school music, dramatic art, physical training, etc., besides all the regular topics. The enrolment of students is about 600, the total since the beginning being about 11,000, with about 400 graduates. The Conservatory has four buildings at Dewitt Park.

IVES, ELAM, Jr. (1802–1864). See Tune-Books, 1829.

JACCHIA, AGIDE (Jan. 5, 1875, Lugo, Italy), attended the conservatory at Pessaro (a favorite pupil of Mascagni), graduating with honors in 1898. He began conducting at the Brescia Opera at twenty-three and continued for some years in Milan and Rome. He visited the United States in 1902 as assistant-conductor in Mascagni's company. In Italy he covered a large répertoire, including the newer works of Mascagni, Leoncavallo, Giordano, Catalani, Orefice, Filiasi, Fiocca and Romani. In 1907–09 he came with the Milano Opera Company to tour the Pacific Coast, Central America and Canada. In 1909 he conducted a brilliant season at the Academy of Music in New York, and in 1910 was general music-director of the Montreal Opera Company and of the National Opera Company of Canada successively. In 1914–15 he was chief conductor at the Century Theater in New York. The next season he conducted for the Boston National Opera Company, and since 1916 has led the Boston Symphony 'Pop' concerts in Symphony Hall. He has composed a 'Inno a Rossini,' a cantata for soprano, baritone, chorus and orchestra (1898, first prize in Bodiora contest at Pesaro), the National Hymn of Central America (1908, dedicated to the President of Guatemala), a Tarantelle, Gavotte, many songs and arrangements. [R.9]

JACKSON, GEORGE K. (1745–1823). See Register, 2, and TUNE-BOOKS, 1816.

JACKSON, HARRY DYER. See COLLEGES, 3 (Jamestown C., N. D.).

JACKSON, LEONORA (b. 1879). See Register, 8.

JACKSON, SAMUEL P. (1818–1885). See Register, 3.

JACOBI, JOHN OWEN. See Register, 1.

JACOBSOHN, SIMON E. (1839–1902). See Register, 6.

JACOBUS, CHARLES M. (1867–1918). See COLLEGES, 3 (Ohio Wesleyan U.).

JAEGER, JOHN AUGUST (b. 1879). See COLLEGES, 3 (Hamline U., Minn.).

JAMES, PHILIP (May 17, 1890, New York), had his general education in New York, where from 1904 he studied organ with J. W. Andrews and held several positions as organist. In 1908 he gave recitals at Albert Hall in London and for the Bach and Handel Society in Paris, followed by further study of composition with Norris and of orchestration with Elliott Schenck. In 1910 he became a fellow of the A. G. O. He has conducted various choral societies in and about New York. In 1917 he entered the Army, became lieutenant, was in active service in many of the severest battles, after the armistice was in 'Pershing's own band' at Chaumont,

in 1919 toured with this for the Victory Loan, and became its band-master. He has now resumed composition. His works include

Concert-overture for orchestra.
Symphonic Poem, 'Aucassin and Nicolette.'
Sonatas in A minor and D minor, for violin and piano.
Incidental Music to 'The House of Rimmon.'
Concert-Variations in A-flat, for piano.
Passacaglia in F, for piano.
'Méditation à Ste.-Clothilde,' for organ.
Cantatas, 'The Triumph of Israel,' 'The Nightingale of Bethlehem' and 'Spring in Mentone' (women's voices).
Te Deum in C, op. 3 ; Jubilate in C, op. 15 ; Magnificat and Nunc Dimittis in D.
Anthems : 'Child Jesus came to earth' and 'Christ is born,' op. 1 ; 'As now the sun's declining rays,' op. 2 ; 'The day is gently sinking,' op. 6 ; 'We pray Thee, gracious Lord' and 'Hail, dear Conqueror,' op. 10 ; 'I am the Vine,' op. 17 ; 'I have considered the days of old,' op. 14 ; Ps. 17, op. 20.
Choruses : (mixed voices) 'The Pride of May,' op. 5 ; 'I know a maiden,' op. 7 ; (men's voices) 'The Victors,' op. 12 ; (women's voices) 'Lullaby' and 'Phyllis,' op. 4 ; 'A Spring Song,' op. 18, 'My little pretty one,' op. 19.
Songs : 'Transit,' 'A Hush Song,' 'Dearie,' op. 8 ; 'The Secret,' op. 9, for baritone ; and others.
(Works with opus-number are published.) [R.9]

JANES, WALTER (1779–1827). See TUNE-BOOKS, 1807.

JANUSCHOWSKY, GEORGINE VON (1859?–1914). See Register, 7.

JARDINE, GEORGE (1801– ?) and JOHN. See Register, 3.

JARDINE & SON, of New York, an organ-making firm organized in 1860 to carry on the business established by George Jardine in 1834, which till 1899 was one of the most able and prominent in the country.

JARVIS, CHARLES. See Register, 3.

JARVIS, CHARLES H. (Dec. 20, 1837, Philadelphia : Feb. 25, 1895, Philadelphia), son of the foregoing, began study when only four and at seven made his first appearance as pianist. While in the public schools he studied theory with Leopold Meignen. As soloist he appeared with the New York Philharmonic Society, the Thomas Orchestra and other leading organizations. In 1862 he instituted in Philadelphia chamber-music and historical piano-recitals, in which during 30 years were presented over 800 compositions. He was an excellent teacher, maintaining always a high artistic standard. His few compositions are unpublished, except a Nocturne in D-flat issued by the Philadelphia Manuscript Music Society after his death. His fine library of music is in the Drexel Institute in Philadelphia. See article by T. Carl Whitmer in 'Music,' May, 1900. [R.4]

JEHIN-PRUME, FRANÇOIS (1839–1899). See Register, 5.

JENKS, STEPHEN (1772–1856). See TUNE-BOOKS, 1800.

JEPSON, HARRY BENJAMIN (Aug. 16, 1870, New Haven, Conn.), the son of Benjamin Jepson, long prominent in public-school music, graduated as A.B. from Yale in 1893 and became Mus.B. in 1894. He studied piano, organ and composition with Stoeckel, and continued the latter with Parker and organ and composition with Widor in Paris. From 1895 he was director of the University Choir and instructor in organ, in 1899 becoming assistant-professor in theory, and in 1906 professor and University organist. His recitals on the great organ in Woolsey Hall have won him much renown. In 1918–19 he had charge of the Yale Bureau at the University Union in Paris. His compositions include a 'Rhapsodie' for orchestra, a 'Fantasie' for organ and orchestra, two organ-sonatas (No. 1, in G minor, Novello), 'Veni, Creator Spiritus,' for men's voices (Novello), and these organ-works (all Schirmer) — 'Wedding-Song,' 'Rhapsodie,' Processional, 'Tempo di Minuetto,' Ballade, Caprice, 'Légende,' 'Sortie Nuptiale,' 'Pantomime,' 'Pastel,' 'L'Heure Exquise' and Toccata. He edited University Hymns, for men's voices, and has written on topics relating to the organ. [R.8]

‡ JOACHIM, JOSEPH (June 28, 1831, near Pressburg, Germany : Aug. 15, 1907, Berlin). See article in Vol. ii. 533–4, and list of biographies given in Baker, Dict. of Musicians, p. 441.

'JOB.' A dramatic poem, op. 24, by Frederick S. Converse, for soli, chorus and orchestra, first produced at the Worcester Festival of 1907 and at Hamburg in 1908. An oratorio of the same name was written by Benjamin C. Blodgett in 1889 and produced at Smith College.

JOCELYN, SIMEON (1746–1823). See TUNE-BOOKS, 1780.

'JOHN BROWN'S BODY.' See article in Vol. ii. 536–7. The reference in Elson, History of American Music, revised edition, 1915, is pp. 156–61.

JOHNS, CLAYTON (Nov. 24, 1857, Newcastle, Del.), after over three years spent in studying architecture in Philadelphia, in 1879 went to Boston to pursue music with Paine and Sherwood. In 1882–84 he was in Berlin, taking piano with Grabow, Raif and Rummel and composition with Kiel. Since 1884 he has been teaching, giving recitals and composing in Boston, from 1912 on the staff of the New England Conservatory. He has published a Melody, Berceuse, Intermezzo, Romance and Scherzino for violin and piano, an Introduction and Fugue for piano (played by Hofmann) and over 100 songs, many of which are widely used. Music for a 14th-century Mystery-Play

was written for a private performance. He is now publishing recent pieces for the piano. He has also written The Essentials of Pianoforte-Playing, 1909, and From Bach to Chopin, 1911. [R.7]

JOHNSON, ARTEMAS N. (1825?– ?). See TUNE-BOOKS, 1849.

JOHNSON & SON, of Westfield, Mass., was a firm of organ-makers that for many years exerted a useful influence by thorough and refined work. The business was established by William A. Johnson about 1860, and the firm constituted later by the admission of his son, William H. Johnson (b. 1837). In 1883 the business was taken over by Emmons Howard. The firm built over 700 instruments.

JOHNSTON, THOMAS (d. 1768?). See Register, 1.

JOHNSTONE, ARTHUR EDWARD (May 13, 1860, London, England), was educated in the public schools and the College of the City of New York, and studied piano with William Mason and Scharfenberg, organ and harmony with S. P. Warren and composition with Leopold Damrosch. For some years he taught privately, and was harmony-teacher at the summer-school of Cornell University. He was also musical editor for the American Book Company, resigning in 1919 to become executive editor of the Art Publication Society in St. Louis. He has composed a concert-overture for orchestra and organ (1915, Chicago Symphony Orchestra), about 1000 school-songs and piano-pieces. With H. W. Loomis he is author of The Lyric Music Series, 4 vols., for public schools. He has edited lessons for use with the player-piano and a system for teaching music by the phonograph. He is author of Instruments of the Modern Symphony Orchestra, a hand-book for students. [R.7]

JOHNSTONE-BISHOP, GENEVRA (b. 1864). See Register, 7.

JOLLS, JOHN M. See COLLEGES, 3 (Ursinus C., Pa.).

JONÁS, ALBERTO (June 8, 1868, Madrid, Spain), was trained in Madrid by Mendizabal, in Brussels by De Greef (winning all the first prizes at the Conservatory) and in Petrograd by Rubinstein. After his début as pianist in 1880 at Brussels he made extensive tours throughout Europe and America, giving over two thousand concerts. In 1894–98 he was chief piano-teacher at the School of Music in Michigan University, and in 1898–1904 director of the Michigan Conservatory in Detroit. In 1905–14 he taught in Berlin, attracting pupils from all over the world, including many now known as virtuosi. Since 1914 he has taught in New York. He has composed many piano-pieces that have won popularity (Schott, Lemoine, Schirmer, Carl Fischer, Ditson). He translated Gevaert's treatise on instrumenta-

8

tion into Spanish in 1903. His *Pianoscript Book* is highly regarded by master-teachers, and he is now publishing *The Master-School of Modern Piano-Virtuosity*, the latter being a monumental work in English, German, French and Spanish, prepared with the collaboration of Busoni, Sauer, Lamond, Rosenthal, Godowsky, Gabrilovitch, Ganz and others. He has also written for musical journals. [R.8]

JONES, ABNER. See TUNE-BOOKS, 1832.

JONES, F. O. See Register, 7.

JONES, MARGED EDITH. See COLLEGES 3 (Indiana Central U.).

JORDAN, EBEN DYER (1857–1916). See Register, 9.

JORDAN, JULES (Nov. 10, 1850, Willimantic, Conn.), since 1870 has been identified with Providence, where he began as tenor at Grace Church. After study with Osgood in Boston and Sbriglia in Paris, he was for thirteen years choir-master at Grace Church and became one of the best-known concert-tenors in New England. He sang in 'La Damnation de Faust' at its first American production in New York in 1880 under Leopold Damrosch. He has been the only conductor of the famous Arion Club of Providence since its organization in 1881, and has not missed one of its performances. In 1895 Brown University made him Mus.D. He has published the romantic opera 'Rip van Winkle,' in three acts (1898), the operettas 'The Buccaneers' and 'As Once of Old' (both to original texts), the cantatas 'The Wind-Swept Wheat,' for tenor, chorus and orchestra, and 'The Night-Service,' for soli, chorus and orchestra, the ballad 'Barbara Frietchie,' for soprano, chorus and orchestra, about 300 songs, anthems, etc., many of which have become noted. He has also written the opera 'Nisida,' in three acts (original text), the operettas 'Thistle-Down,' 'A Leap-Year Furlough' and 'The Rivals,' and some short works. [R.6]

JORDAN, MARY (b. 1879). See Register, 8.

JÖRN, KARL (b. 1876). See Register, 9.

JOSEFFY, RAFAEL (July 3, 1852, Hunfalu, Hungary : June 25, 1915, New York). See article in Vol. ii. 545–6. He was professor of piano at the National Conservatory in New York in 1888–1906. His *School of Advanced Piano-Playing*, 1902, was translated into German. He also published *First Studies for the Piano*, 1913, edited a monumental edition of Chopin's complete works (15 vols.) and studies by Czerny, Henselt, Moscheles, Schumann and Schlözer. See article by Edwin Hughes on his 'Contribution to Piano-Technic' in 'The Musical Quarterly,' July, 1916. [R.6]

JOURNALISM, MUSICAL. This term covers two forms of effort — the editing of musical periodicals and the provision of musical reports

and criticisms in non-musical periodicals, especially newspapers. An adequate account of these in America is not here attempted. But certain salient points may be stated.

Periodicals devoted to music began before there was a public to sustain them, so that many were short-lived. Apparently the first was the 'American Musical Magazine' of New York, begun in 1786 and succeeded in 1790 by 'Gilfert's Musical Magazine,' issued by George Gilfert, dealer in instruments.[1] These, like many later, were little more than serial issues of music-pieces. Ritter refers to a 'Euter-peiad' in 1821 as 'the first established musical journal in Boston,'[2] and another of the same name appeared in New York in 1830–31. H. T. Hach edited the 'Musical Magazine' in Boston in 1839–42. J. W. Moore twice started (1840, '43) 'The World of Music' at Bellows Falls, Vt., and as late as 1863 issued 'Moore's Musical Record' at Manchester, N. H.[3] One of L. A. Godey's early enterprises in Philadelphia from 1842 was 'The Lady's Musical Library,' edited by Charles Jarvis. In 1846 A. N. and J. Johnston set up in Boston 'The Musical Gazette' (fortnightly). In New York from 1850 I. B. Woodbury put forth an 'American Monthly Musical Review,' which in 1852 under Mason's more powerful lead became the 'Musical Review' and then the 'New York Musical Review,' Woodbury turning to the 'Musical Pioneer,' which he managed in 1855–68. These latter were connected with the promotion of 'psalmody' and its sequels. Another line in New York started with H. C. Watson's 'Musical Chronicle' of 1843, changed presently into the 'American Musical Times' and the 'Philharmonic Journal' and leading on to the 'American Art Journal,' begun by Watson in 1863, but developed from 1875 by W. M. Thoms till beyond 1900.[4] These magnified the relation between professional progress and trades like instrument-making and music-publishing, as have done the many journals fathered by J. C. Freund, from his 'Music-Trade Review' of 1875 to the present 'Music-Trades,' and others.

Meanwhile in Boston in 1852 began 'Dwight's Journal of Music,' which till 1881 continued to be the only really dignified and influential organ of musical report and criticism. From this branched off in 1878 Ditson's 'Musical Record,' edited at first by Dexter Smith, in 1897–1900 by Philip Hale and then by Thomas Tapper, and in 1903 succeeded by 'The Musician.' In New York the 'Dramatic and Musical Courier' began in 1880, being later trans-

---

[1] Spillane, *American Pianoforte*, pp. 99–101.

[2] *Music in America*, chap. vi.

[3] Jones, *American Music and Musicians*, p. 103.

[4] In 1870–71 Thoms issued a musical *daily*, 'The Journal of the Day.'

RAFAEL JOSEFFY

formed under Otto Floersheim and M. A. Blumenberg into the large and powerful 'Musical Courier.' In 1883 Theodore Presser founded 'The Etude,' which since 1884 in Philadelphia has been a prominent organ of private music-teaching. In 1880 O. L. Fox started 'The Indicator' in Chicago — the first of a long line of similar journals in the Middle West. After 1880 the number of enterprises becomes too large to be followed in detail. It is enough to identify as leaders in the field, of those that have been mentioned, 'The Musician', now published in New York, the 'Musical Courier' and 'The Etude,' besides 'The Musical Leader,' founded in 1896 at Chicago by Charles F. French, 'Musical America,' begun by Freund in 1898, the 'New Music Review,' issued by H. W. Gray since 1901, 'The Pacific Coast Musical Review' (weekly), begun in 1901 and now edited by Alfred Metzger, 'Music News,' started by C. E. Watt in Chicago in 1908, 'The Musical Observer,' issued since 1910 and now edited by Gustav Saenger, and several of later date.

Genuine 'magazines' have been few. 'Dwight's Journal' belonged partly to this class, especially in its earlier days. But the first serious enterprise of this kind was W. S. B. Mathews' 'Music,' issued in Chicago from 1891 till 1902, a monthly of real distinction, though carried forward very unequally. With this may be mentioned the 'Music Review,' also of Chicago, edited in 1892–94 by C. B. Cady. In 1915 came the 'Musical Quarterly', projected on the broadest lines and brilliantly edited by O. G. Sonneck. This not only has overtopped anything attempted in America, but takes rank as one of the great musical periodicals of the world.

Details regarding the rise of musical journalism in connection with newspapers and magazines of a general character are difficult to secure and classify. The New York 'Tribune' employed W. H. Fry as critic in 1852–63, followed in 1863–66 by H. C. Watson, in 1866–84 by J. R. G. Hassard and since then by H. E. Krehbiel. This pattern was presently imitated by other New York papers, so that now every leading paper has its musical editor, the significant circle including H. E. Krehbiel, H. T. Finck, W. J. Henderson, Richard Aldrich, J. G. Huneker, Lawrence Gilman and many others. Similarly in Boston prominent names stand out, like W. F. Apthorp, L. C. Elson, Philip Hale, H. T. Parker, and Olin Downes; while in Chicago are Felix Borowski, Maurice Rosenfeld and G. D. Gunn. These are but distinguished examples of a large and influential fraternity the country over. Under their hands what had been simply a gathering of musical items and the publication of matter more or less of the advertising variety has become dignified by a large amount of sane, illuminating and stimulating criticism.

JUBILEE SINGERS, THE, were a group of ten or twelve students in Fisk University (Tenn.), trained in singing Negro songs and organized to tour in the interest of the University. The first expedition in 1871 was so successful, both in raising money and in arousing interest in Negro music, that it was extended and repeated till 1874, covering not only many parts of the United States, but England as well. On the second trip to England Theodore F. Seward was musical director. The proceeds of the tours (about $150,000) were used in erecting Jubilee Hall, the first of the University buildings. Seward edited over 100 songs under the title *Jubilee Songs*. See J. B. T. Marsh, *The Story of the Jubilee Singers*, 1895.

JUCH, EMMA ANTONIA JOANNA (July 4, 1865, Vienna, Austria), was the daughter of American parents. She was educated in New York and studied singing there with Mme. Murio-Celli. Her concert-début as soprano was in 1882, and in 1883 she appeared in opera in 'Mignon' at Her Majesty's Theatre in London. For three seasons, under Mapleson, she sang Violetta, Queen of Night (in 'The Magic Flute'), Martha, Marguerite (in 'Faust'), The Queen (in 'Les Huguenots') and Isabella (in 'Robert le Diable'). In 1886–87 she was one of the principal sopranos in the American Opera Company under Thomas. In 1889 she organized the Emma Juch Grand Opera Company, which gave performances in the United States and Mexico for two seasons. She has since sung in concerts and festivals, including appearances with the leading orchestras and choral societies. In addition to the rôles named she has appeared as Aida, Valentine, Elsa, Elizabeth, Sieglinde and Senta, and created the part of Chrysa at the first American performance of Rubinstein's 'Nero.' [R.7]

'JUDITH'. An opera by George W. Chadwick, produced at the Worcester Festival in 1901 in concert-form. Though called a 'lyric opera,' it is virtually an oratorio.

JUHAN[JOAN], ALEXANDER. See Register, 2.

JUHAN [JOAN], JAMES. See Register, 1.

JUNG, J. B. (b. 1848?). See Register, 6.

‡ JUON, PAUL (Mar. 9, 1872, Moscow, Russia). See article in Vol. ii. 553–4. He settled in Berlin in 1897, and since 1906 has been professor of composition at the Hochschule. Among his later works are 'Wächterweise,' op. 31, for orchestra, two string-quintets, opp. 33, 44, the orchestral suite 'Aus einem Tagebuche,' op. 35, a 'Rhapsodie,' op. 37, for string-trio and piano, an orchestral Serenade, op. 40, two concertos for violin and orchestra, opp. 42, 49, and a piano-quartet, op. 50. He has published *Praktische Harmonielehre*, 1901, and a translation of M. Tchaikovsky's biography of his brother, 1900–04.

K

KAEUPER, HERMANN H. See Colleges, 3 (Millikin U., Ill.).

KAHN, OTTO HERMANN (Feb. 21, 1867, Mannheim, Germany), came to London in 1888 as employé of the Deutsche Bank and in 1893 a visit to New York led to permanent residence and citizenship. From 1897, as a member of Kuhn, Loeb & Co., he has participated in many financial operations of magnitude and has become trustee and director in numerous great corporations. Being himself a musician of talent and training, he has been increasingly identified with musical undertakings. He has been head of the Metropolitan Opera Company, of the Théâtre du Vieux Columbier, of the French-American Association for Musical Art and (till 1915) of the Century Opera Company, and in the directorate of the Boston Opera Company (1908–15), the Chicago Opera Association and the Royal Opera, Covent Garden, London. He has also been active in countless other enterprises. His services to the cause of the Allies in the World War were recognized by high honors from France, Italy and Spain. He is also LL.D. of the University of Michigan. [R.9]

KANSAS CITY SYMPHONY ORCHESTRA, THE, was founded in 1910 and from 1911 supported by an Orchestra Association, formed through the efforts of the Musical Club. Since 1912 a high standard has been maintained under the leadership of Carl Busch. Seven regular and six popular concerts are given annually. The usual force is 65 players, with Heinrich Rittmeister as concertmaster. The scope and quality of the programs is indicated by the list of larger works, which includes

Symphonies — three of Mozart, the first five of Beethoven, two each of Mendelssohn and Schumann, Raff's 'Lenore,' Franck's D minor, Goldmark's 'Country Wedding,' Brahms' 3rd, Saint-Saëns' 3rd, three of Tchaikovsky, two of Svendsen, Dvořák's 'New World,' Stanford's 'Irish,' Sibelius' 1st, two of Glazunov, Mrs. Beach's 'Gaelic' and Hadley's 4th.
Symphonic Poems — Liszt's 'Les Préludes' and 'Tasso,' Smetana's 'Moldau,' Saint-Saëns' 'Danse Macabre,' Olsen's 'Asgaardsreien,' Foote's 'Francesca da Rimini,' Bruneau's 'La Belle au Bois Dormant,' Busch's 'Minnehaha's Vision' and Sibelius' 'Finlandia.'
Concertos — Liszt's 2nd, Rubinstein's 4th, Saint-Saëns' 3rd for violin and 1st for 'cello, Bruch's 1st for violin, Tchaikovsky's 1st, Grieg's in A minor, and MacDowell's 2nd.

‡ KARG–ELERT, SIGFRID (Nov. 21, 1878, Oberndorf, Würtemberg), when a choirboy studied clarinet, viola and oboe without a teacher. Through Reznicek he obtained a three-year scholarship at the Leipzig Conservatory, where his teachers were Jadassohn,

Wendling and Homeyer, and later he entered Reisenauer's 'master-class' for pianists. He also devoted much time to the organ and the 'Kunstharmonium,' for which he has written extensively. His larger compositions are a Passacaglia in E-flat minor, op. 25, for organ; a Sonata in F-sharp minor, op. 50, for piano; 66 Choral-Improvisationen, op. 65, for organ; three organ-pieces, op. 72 — 'Harmonies du Soir,' 'Clair de Lune' and 'La Nuit'; a Chaconne and Fugue Trilogy with choral, op. 73, for organ; a Sonatina, op. 74, for organ; 'Benedictus' and 'Vom Himmel hoch,' op. 82, for soli, choir, violin, harp and organ; three Symphonic Chorales, op. 87, for organ; and three 'Pastelle,' op. 92, for organ. There are besides numerous songs, piano- and organ-pieces, much chamber-music and many educational works. See Baker, *Dict. of Musicians*, p. 451.

KARL, TOM (1846–1916). See Register, 6.

‡ KASTALSKY, ALEXANDER DIMITRIEVITCH (Nov. 28, 1856, Moscow, Russia), graduated at the Moscow Conservatory in 1882, having studied with Tchaikovsky, Hubert and Tanieiev. In 1887 he began to teach in the new Moscow Synodal School, and in 1901 became conductor of the Synodal Choir, which he gave an international reputation. He has worked vigorously to revitalize Russian church-music and has written much for service-use. He has also composed the a cappella oratorio 'The Furnace of Nabucho,' for soli and chorus (1909); the opera 'Clara Militche' (1916, Moscow); a Requiem for the soldiers of the Allies (1916); the cantata 'Le Chant d'Église'; the piano-suite 'En Géorgie'; a manual for self-instruction in church-music; and 'De Temps Passés,' 4 vols. of restorations of ancient music.

KAUFMANN, MAURICE (b. 1876). See Register, 8.

KAUN, HUGO (Mar. 21, 1863, Berlin, Germany), was a precocious composer, having written 160 pieces before he was sixteen. After a year at the Hochschule, he studied piano with the Raifs and composition with Kiel. His connection with American music arises from his having lived as teacher in Milwaukee in 1887–1902. During this time he left an impress on many talented pupils and his works were often given by Thomas. He has since worked in Berlin, where in 1912 he became member of the Royal Academy of Arts. For list of works, many of large dimensions, see Baker, *Dict. of Musicians*, p. 455. [R.7]

KEATING, HENRY S. See Tune-Books, 1808.

KÉFER, PAUL (b. 1875). See Register, 9.

KELBE, THEODORE (b. 1862). See Register, 9.

260

EDGAR STILLMAN KELLEY

KELLER, MATTHIAS (1813–1875). See Register, 4.

KELLER, WALTER (Feb. 23, 1873, Chicago), attended Baldwin-Wallace College in Ohio and in 1894 graduated from the American Conservatory in Chicago, also studying with Gleason in 1892–93 and '96–99. In 1894–96 he was at Leipzig, studying at the Conservatory and with Piutti. In 1899–1904 he taught at Northwestern University, and in 1906 joined the staff of the Sherwood Music School in Chicago, of which since 1911 he has been director. In 1903–18 he was organist at St. Vincent de Paul's, and since 1912 has also been dean of music at De Paul University, where he was made Mus.D. in 1916. He became a fellow of the A. G. O. in 1916, having been dean of the Illinois Chapter in 1914–15. In 1907 he conducted the première of Gleason's 'Otho Visconti,' and he now directs a choral club at Danville, Ill. He has written a comic opera, the melodrama 'Alaric's Death,' much Catholic and Anglican church-music, including organ-pieces, two canons for piano, and a synchronous Prelude and Fugue, op. 10, for two pianos (Gilbert), which is notable for ingenuity of structure. [R.8]

KELLEY, EDGAR STILLMAN (Apr. 14, 1857, Sparta, Wis.). See article in Vol. ii. 562–3. His San Francisco residences were in 1880–86 and 1892–96, and in 1886–92 and 1896–1900 he was in New York. In 1901–02 he was acting-professor at the Yale School of Music and conductor of its orchestral concerts. In 1902–10 he lived in Berlin and was active as a teacher of composition. Since 1910 he has been head of the composition-department in the Cincinnati Conservatory, and has also held a fellowship from the Western College for Women in Oxford, O. Besides his work as teacher and composer he has written many critical articles and published Chopin the Composer, 1913, an extremely able analysis of structure and method. In 1916 Miami University gave him the degree of Litt.D. and in 1917 the University of Cincinnati that of LL.D.

His music for 'Ben Hur' was first performed in 1899 and has since been given about 5000 times in English-speaking countries. Orchestral suites have been made from both this and his 'Macbeth' music. His piano-quintet, op. 20, and a string-quartet, op. 25, have been much played in America and Europe (both published 1907, Berlin). His larger works include incidental music for Lathrop's version of 'Prometheus Bound'; Symphony No. 1, 'Gulliver — his Voyage to Lilliput,' op. 15, with much fantastic humor, Symphony No. 2, 'New England,' op. 33, the movements of which bear mottoes from Bradford's diary on the 'Mayflower' (the third is based on the old tune 'China'), which was first given at the Nor-

folk Festival of 1913, the composer conducting, in Altenburg, Germany, at the Liszt Festival in 1914, and over twenty times since; the pantomimic suite for orchestra 'Alice in Wonderland,' first given at the Norfolk Festival of 1919; and a setting of 'Pilgrim's Progress' in the form of a miracle-play, which was first produced at the Cincinnati Festival of 1918 and recently repeated in New York. Among his smaller works are the songs 'Eldorado' and 'Israfel,' op. 8 (1901), choral settings of Whitman's 'My Captain,' op. 19, and Poe's 'The Sleeper,' op. 21, no. 7; and various piano-pieces. He has shown a marked tendency to emphasize the spirit and sentiment of American life, not only in his characteristic 'New England' symphony, but in many lesser works. Regarding such composition he has said: 'The American composer should apply the universal principles of his art to the local and special elements of the subject-matter as they appeal to him, and then, consciously or unconsciously, manifest his individuality, which will involve the expression of mental traits and moral tendencies peculiar to his European ancestry, as we find them modified by the new American environment.' See note upon his work in The Art of Music, iv. 368–73. [R.7]

KELLOGG, CLARA LOUISE (July, 1842, Sumterville, S. C. : May 13, 1916, New Hartford, Conn.). See article in Vol. ii. 563, and her autobiography, Memoirs of an American Prima Donna, 1913.

KELLY, THOMAS JAMES (b. 1870). See Register, 7.

KELSO, HUGH ALEXANDER, JR. (Aug. 26, 1862, Charleston, Ill.), before graduating from the Rice Collegiate Institute in 1881 studied under Albert Beuter of Bloomington, Ill., and spent three seasons with Mathews in Chicago. In 1883 he went to Sherwood in Boston, and remained his pupil or assistant-teacher for eleven years in Boston, New York and Chicago. In 1889–93 he taught at Chautauqua. In 1893, with his wife, née May Donally, a dramatic coach, he established the Kelso School of Musical and Dramatic Art in Chicago, of which he is still director. He has given piano-recitals in many cities and has lectured on piano-playing. He is the author of The Psychology of Movements as Applied to Artistic Piano-Playing, 1892, Interpretative Technic, Books 1, 2, 3, 4 and 9, 1898 and later, fifteen pamphlets on The Analysis of Musical Form, and has in manuscript a work on Embellishments. He has edited some works for the piano and written piano-pieces and songs, as yet unpublished. [R.7]

KEMP, ROBERT (1820–1897). See Register, 4.

'KENILWORTH.' An opera by Bruno Oscar Klein, produced in 1895 at Hamburg.

KENNA, J. See Register, 2.

KENT, EMANUEL. See TUNE-BOOKS, 1812.

KERNOCHAN, MARSHALL RUTGERS (b. 1880). See Register, 10.

KESSLER, LOUWILLIE. See COLLEGES, 3 (Greenville C., Ill.).

KIHL, VIGGO RICHARD (b. 1882). See Register, 10.

KILENYI, EDWARD (Jan. 25, 1884, Békésszentràndrás, Hungary), had his general education mainly at Budapest and Szarvas. Musically he was trained at the Scuola Musicale Nationale in Rome, at the Cologne Conservatory, where he had theory with Klauwell, and at Columbia University, where in 1913 he was Mosenthal Fellow and in 1914 took his A.M. with a thesis on 'Violin-Music before Corelli.' At Columbia he was a pupil of Rybner and Mason. He has composed a string-quartet (1912), an overture to a play by Kleist (1913), a one-act American opera, 'The Cry of the Wolf' (1916, with C. E. Parker), 'Modern Variations on an Old English Tune,' for violin and piano (1915), other violin-pieces and some humorous songs. He has written upon modern music for leading periodicals, with Eleanor Hague edited Spanish-American Folk-Songs, 1914, and contributed to The Art of Music, vols. iii. and vii. 1915–16. [R.10]

KILGEN, GEORGE, & SON, of St. Louis, is an organ-making business founded in 1851 by George Kilgen, and till 1873 located in New York. In 1885 he was joined by his son, Charles C. Kilgen, the management in recent years passing to the latter's sons. The firm has built about 1350 organs, of which about 135 have three manuals or more.

KILLEEN, EARLE G. See COLLEGES, 3 (Coe C., Iowa).

KILLEEN, FREDERIC THOMAS (b. 1880). See COLLEGES, 3 (Ohio Northern U.).

KIMBALL, JACOB (1761–1826). See TUNE-BOOKS, 1793.

KIMBALL, WILLARD (b. 1854). See Register, 6, and COLLEGES 3 (Grinnell C., Iowa).

KIMBALL, WILLIAM WALLACE (1828–1904). See Register, 4.

KIMBALL COMPANY, THE W. W., of Chicago, was founded in 1857 and has developed into one of the largest makers of pianos, reed-organs, pipe-organs and accessories in the country. Its output is over 30,000 instruments per year. It holds high awards from numerous expositions. It owns an extensive building, 300–310 South Wabash Avenue.

KIMBROUGH, HERBERT (b. 1876). See STATE UNIVERSITIES (Washington State C.).

KINDER, RALPH (b. 1876). See Register, 8.

KINDLER, HANS (b. 1892). See Register, 10.

KINGSLEY, GEORGE (1811–1884). See TUNE-BOOKS, 1839.

KINKELDEY, OTTO (Nov. 27, 1878, New York), graduated at the College of the City of New York in 1898 and took his A.M. in 1900 at New York University, in 1909 also winning a Ph.D. from the University of Berlin. His first music-study in New York was with Gustav Viehl and in 1900–02 with MacDowell. In 1902–07 he was in Berlin under Radecke, Egidi and Thiel at the Institute for Church Music and Kretzschmar, Wolf, Friedländer and Fleischer at the University. In 1898–1902 he was organist at the Chapel of the Ascension in New York and in 1903–05 at the American Church in Berlin. In 1909–14 he was connected with the University of Breslau, at first as instructor in organ and theory, lecturer on musicology and music-director and from 1910 full professor. During this time he published Orgel und Klavier in der Musik des 16. Jahrhunderts, 1910, and edited Erlebach's Harmonische Freude musikalischer Freunde for vols. 46–47 of the Denkmäler deutscher Tonkunst, 1914. Since 1915 he has been head of the music-division of the New York Public Library. In 1917–19 he served as captain of infantry at Camp Meade, Madison, Wis., and Grove City, Pa., assigned to training-duty. [R.8]

KLAUSER, JULIUS (1854–1907). See Register, 6.

KLAUSER, KARL (1823–1905). See Register, 4.

KLEE, EUGEN (b. 1869). See Register, 8.

KLEIN, BRUNO OSCAR (June 6, 1858, Osnabrück, Germany : June 22, 1911, New York), the son of the organist of the Cathedral at Osnabrück, was first trained by his father, and then spent two years at the Munich Conservatory, studying counterpoint with Rheinberger, piano with Baermann and score-reading with Wüllner. In 1878 he came to America and for five years traveled as concert-pianist. In 1884–94 he was organist at St. Francis Xavier's in New York and in 1884–1911 head of the piano-department at the Convent of the Sacred Heart. On the recommendation of Joseffy and William Mason, in 1887–92 he also taught counterpoint and composition at the National Conservatory. In 1904–11 he was organist at St. Ignatius'. His grand opera 'Kenilworth' was produced at Hamburg on Feb. 13, 1895, with Klafsky as Amy Robsart. An overture and detached pieces for orchestra; concert-pieces for violin, piano or voice, with orchestra; six masses; many piano-pieces; three volumes of songs, besides about 80 published separately — these make up the bulk of the list. The Sonata in G, op. 10, for violin and piano, and the quintet for soprano, violin, 'cello, horn and piano are regarded as representative works. [R.6]

KLEIN, HERMANN (b. 1856). See Register, 9.

KLEIN, KARL (b. 1884). See Register, 9.

KLEMM, JOHANN GOTTLOB (1690–1762). See Register, 1.

KLENGEL, PAUL K. (b. 1854). See Register, 8.

‡ KLINDWORTH, KARL (Sept. 25, 1830, Hanover, Germany : July or Aug., 1916, Stolpe, Germany). See article in Vol. ii. 587.

KNABE, WILHELM (1803–1864). See Register, 3.

KNABE & CO. See article in Vol. ii. 588. In 1908 the business was merged in the American Piano Company of New York. Charles Keidel, Jr., was president from 1912, succeeded in 1915 by William B. Armstrong. The factory remains in Baltimore. The form of player-piano used is known as the 'Knabe-Ampico.'

KNEISEL, FRANZ (Jan. 26, 1865, Bucharest, Rumania). See article in Vol. ii. 589. While in the Boston Symphony Orchestra (1891) he introduced in America the concertos of Brahms and Goldmark. In 1907 he was asked to serve on the jury at the violin-concours of the Paris Conservatory. The Kneisel Quartet was disbanded in 1917 to enable him to devote himself to teaching. He is still head of the violin-department of the Institute of Musical Art in New York. In 1912, while president of the Bohemians, he effected the organization of the Foundation for Needy Musicians, a chartered society which has accumulated a fund amounting to over $55,000 from gifts and concerts. In 1911 he was made Mus. D. by Yale University and in 1915 also by Princeton University. In 1918 he became an honorary member of the Harvard Musical Association in Boston. He has published the *Kneisel Collection of Violin-Pieces* (Church), *Advanced Exercises for the Violin* (Schirmer) and a Concert-Étude (Schirmer), and, with Bauer, is editing the Brahms sonatas. [R.7]

KNEISEL QUARTET, THE. See articles in Vol. i. 369 and iii. 369. In 1917, owing to Kneisel's obligations as teacher, it was disbanded, the farewell concerts being on March 13 in Boston and April 3 in New York. It had played for thirty-two seasons in the former city and for twenty-five in the latter, besides touring regularly in all parts of the country. During the last five years its members had been Franz Kneisel, Hans Letz, Louis Svečenski and Willem Willeke. The last three gave concerts in New York in 1917–18 with Kreisler as leader.

KNOCH, ERNST, (b. 1876). See Register, 10.

KNOETSCHEL [two names]. See Register, 1.

KOBBÉ, GUSTAV (Mar. 4, 1857, New York : July 27, 1918, Bay Shore, N. Y.), was educated in Wiesbaden and at Columbia University, graduating in 1877 and from the Law School in 1879. His study of piano and composition was with Hagen at Wiesbaden and Mosenthal in New York. Devoting himself to literary work, he was in 1879–80 editor of 'The Musical Review' and from 1880 music-critic in succession for the 'Sun,' 'World,' 'Mail and Express' and 'Herald.' In 1883 the 'World' sent him as correspondent to Bayreuth for the first performance of 'Parsifal.' He published *Wagner's Life and Works*, 2 vols., 1890 (2nd ed., 1896 and *Ring of the Nibelung* separately, 1889), *Opera-Singers*, 1901 (6th ed., 1913), *Loves of the Great Composers*, 1905, *How to Appreciate Music*, 1906, *Wagner and his Isolde*, 1906, *Famous American Songs*, 1906, and the novels *Signora, a Child of the Opera-House*, 1902, etc. [R.7]

KOELLING, ADOLPH (b. 1840). See Register, 6.

KOEMMENICH, LOUIS (Oct. 4, 1866, Elberfeld, Germany), had Krause and other musicians in Barmen for his first teachers of violin, piano, singing and theory. Later he studied with Kullak, Pfeiffer, Holländer and Tappert at Kullak's Academy in Berlin. In 1890 he came to Brooklyn to conduct the Sängerbund and other singing-societies, including in time the Junger Männerchor of Philadelphia in 1902–10, the New York Oratorio Society in 1912–17, the Mendelssohn Glee Club in 1913–19, the Beethoven Society in 1916, and since 1917 the New Choral Society. In 1910 he also conducted at the German Theater. He directed the first New York performances of Hegar's 'Manasse,' Taubmann's 'Eine deutsche Messe,' Georg Schumann's 'Ruth,' Bossi's 'Jeanne d' Arc,' and the first New York open-air performances of 'Caliban' and Verdi's Requiem. His compositions include music to 'New Yorker Kinder' (1894) ; 'Franz Schubert' (1918, MS.), and the men's choruses with orchestra, 'Der Schmied und das Grafenkind' (1892), 'The Magic Minstrel' (1897), 'Morning-Hymn' (1908) and 'To Madelon' (1918). Of his numerous a cappella men's choruses, 'Wer weiss wo' took first prize at the Brooklyn Sängerfest of 1900 and 'Lockung' the second prize at the New York Sängerfest of 1894. He has also written a number of songs (Schirmer, Leuckardt, Hug, Huntzinger). [R.8]

KOFLER, LEO (1837–1908). See Register, 6.

KOHLER, FRANZ (1877–1918). See Register, 8.

KOLAR, VICTOR (Feb. 12, 1888, Budapest, Hungary), was Bohemian by descent. He was a protégé of Kubelik at Prague for six years, during two of which he had lessons from Dvořák in composition, and graduated at the Conservatory in 1904. Coming to America, he was at first soloist with the Chicago Or-

chestra on a western tour under Rosenbecker.
From 1905 he played in the Pittsburgh Orchestra under Paur, in 1907–19 in the New York
Symphony Society, becoming assistant-conductor in 1915, and then became assistant-conductor of the Detroit Symphony Orchestra. In 1916 he conducted Casals' first New
York concert, and in 1917 directed the Red
Cross Pageant at Huntington, L. I., and its
New York repetitions. He has published
songs, violin-pieces and the symphonic suite
'Americana,' which won the prize offered by
the Illinois Music Teachers' Association (1914,
New York Symphony Society). He has also
written two symphonic poems, 'Hiawatha'
(1908, Pittsburgh Orchestra) and 'A Fairy-Tale' (1913, N. Y. Symphony Society); a
'Lyric' Suite ('Pastorale,' 'Cortège,' 'Divertissement') ; a Symphony No. 1, in D (1916, N. Y.
Symphony Society) ; and a string-quartet in
E minor (1917, Flonzaley Quartet).   [R.9]

‡ KONIUS, GEORGE EDWARDOVITCH
(Sept. 30, 1862, Moscow, Russia). See article
in Vol. ii. 595. He was one of Scriabin's earlier
teachers. Add to list of works the symphonic
poem 'La Forêt Bruisse,' op. 30 (1896, Moscow).

KORBAY, FRANCIS ALEXANDER
(May 8, 1846, Budapest, Hungary : Mar.
9, 1913, London). See article in Vol. ii. 595.
His song-recitals in America in 1871–94 did
much to stimulate interest. Among his pupils
were Susan Strong and Lillian Bailey (Mrs.
Henschel). His 'Hungarian' Overture was
played in 1912 at a Queen's Hall concert in
London.   [R.6]

KORN, CLARA ANNA, née Gerlach (Jan.
30, 1866, Berlin, Germany), German-American
in parentage, was brought to America in infancy, graduated at the Jersey City High
School in 1881 and was at first a school-teacher.
In 1891, gaining a scholarship at the National
Conservatory at Tchaikovsky's recommendation, she studied with Dvořák, Parker and
Klein, and in 1893–98 taught theory there.
She has published a piano-sonata, an arrangement for two pianos of Tchaikovsky's 'Overture Solennelle, 1812' (Jurgenson), piano- and
violin-pieces and songs, and has in manuscript
an opera, 'Our Last War,' a symphony in C
minor, a piano-concerto, some chamber-music
and songs with orchestra. She has written
articles for musical periodicals.   [R.8]

KORTSCHAK QUARTET, THE. See
BERKSHIRE QUARTET.

KOTZSCHMAR, HERMANN (July 4,
1829, Finsterwalde, Germany : Apr. 12,
1909, Portland, Me.), having been taught piano
and other instruments by his father and by
Hayne and Otto (composition) at Dresden,
became a member of a band and the opera-orchestra there. In 1848 he came to America
with the Saxonia Band and from 1849 was

organist at the First Church in Portland for
forty-seven years and then at the State Street
Church, beside conducting choral societies.
He wrote some church-music and piano-pieces.
At the dedication of the municipal organ in
Portland, which is his memorial. Mr. C. H. K.
Curtis of Philadelphia, the donor, spoke of him
as 'preëminent as organist, composer and
teacher, loved by all classes for his kindly spirit,
high ideals and devotion to music.'   [R.4]

KRAFT, EDWIN ARTHUR (Jan. 8, 1883,
New Haven, Conn.), had early lessons from his
brother, W. J. Kraft (see below), became organist at fifteen and studied at the Yale School
of Music under Parker and Jepson. In 1901–04
he was organist at St. Thomas' in Brooklyn, and
then studied further in Berlin with Grunicke
and Kelley and at Paris with Guilmant and
Widor. In 1905–07 he was organist at St.
Matthew's in Wheeling, W. Va., and founder
of an oratorio-society, in 1907–14 organist at
Trinity Cathedral in Cleveland, in 1914–16
city-organist at Atlanta, and since 1916 at the
Cathedral in Cleveland again. In 1909 he
became fellow of the A. G. O., and has been
in request as recitalist throughout the United
States and Canada. Many organ-works have
been dedicated to him.   [R.8]

KRAFT, FREDERICK WILLIAM. See
COLLEGES, 3 (Southwestern U., Tex.).

KRAFT, WILLIAM JACOB (Sept. 29,
1872, New Haven, Conn.), graduated in 1902
at the Yale School of Music and was Mosenthal Fellow at Columbia University in 1904,
besides becoming a fellow of the A. G. O. in
1903. He has been continuously organist at
various churches, in 1905–15 was organist at
the summer-school of Columbia University,
for a time taught in the New York public schools
and since 1912 has been associate-professor at
Teachers College. In 1919 he composed and
arranged the music for the pageant 'The Wayfarer,' given at the Methodist Centenary at
Columbus and repeated in New York. He has
published songs and anthems and has an orchestral scherzo, songs and other pieces in manuscript. With C. H. Farnsworth he has published
The Tonal Phrase-Book, 1915.   [R.8]

KRAMER, ARTHUR WALTER (Sept. 23,
1890, New York), was educated in the New
York public schools and at the College of the
City of New York, graduating in 1910. Music
he began under his father, Maximilian Kramer,
studying first the violin, which he continued
under Hauser and Arnold. In composition he
is largely self-taught. Since 1910 he has been
on the staff of 'Musical America.' He wrote
on 'The Modern Italians' for The Art of Music,
1916. His compositions have found favor with
soloists, choral societies and orchestras.
Among those not yet published are two 'Symphonic Sketches,' op. 16, a 'Symphonic Rhap-

HENRY E. KREHBIEL

sody' in F minor, op. 35, for violin and orchestra, two 'Sketches' for orchestra, op. 37a, a string-suite, op. 12, a string-quartet, op. 23, and the choral scene 'The Hour of Prayer,' op.36, no. 4, for baritone, chorus and orchestra. His published works include the following:

Songs — 'Allah,' 'I dreamed and wept a-dreaming,' 'A Sigh,' 'Come to Me,' 'Two Sappho Fragments,' 'Dark and Wondrous Night,' 'Tears,' 'O Perfect Love' (Ditson).
'For a Dream's Sake,' 'There is a garden in her face,' 'A Christmas-Carol,' 'Of the Robin and the Master,' 'Joy,' 'Eternal May' (J. Fischer).
'That Perfect Hour,' 'The Indian Serenade,' 'The Stirrup-Cup' (Huntzinger).
'A Nocturne,' 'The Return of Spring,' 'The Last Hour' (Church).
'The Relief,' 'Bes' ob All' (Schirmer).
'Swans' (Ricordi).
'Mother o' Mine,' 'We Two,' 'I shall Awake' (Carl Fischer).
'Green' (Boston Music Co.).
'A Lover's Litany' (White-Smith).
'At Sunset,' 'A Death-Song' (Thompson).
'The shadows gain upon the light' (Presser).
'A Phantasy,' 'In Explanation' (Bryant).
'A Christmas-Carol,' for chorus (J. Fischer).
'The Holy City of my Saviour's Grace,' for chorus (Church).
'The Passing Hours,' for chorus a cappella (Ditson).
'Mirage' (Ditson), 'When I Dwelt in Aready' and 'At Morning' (Church), 'There is a garden in her face' (J. Fischer), all for women's chorus.
'Old English Song' (White-Smith), 'Of all the dreams men dream' (Boston Music Co.), for men's chorus.
'Pastorale Réligieuse' in D-flat, for organ (White-Smith).
'Night-Song'(Gray) and 'Morning-Song' (Ditson), for organ.
Concert-Prelude in D minor, for organ (Church).
'In Elizabethan Days,' for violin (Carl Fischer).
'Chant Nègre,' for violin (Schirmer).
'Intermède Arabe,' for violin (Ditson).
Elegy in G minor, for violin (Boston Music Co.).
'Danse Espagnole,' for violin (Hauser).
'Eklog,' for violin (Schmidt).
Two Gavottes for violin (Carl Fischer, Witmark).
Elegy for string-quartet (Boston Music Co.).
Intermezzo for piano (J. Fischer).
Three Preludes for piano (Ditson).
'Rhapsody' and 'Valse Triste,' for piano (Church).
Romance in A-flat for piano (Carl Fischer).
(Several of the above are also adapted to other instruments.) [R.10]

KRAUS, ADRIENNE, née Osborne [Eisbein] (b. 1873). See Register, 9.

KRAUSS, ARNOLD (b. 1866). See Register, 8.

KREHBIEL, HENRY EDWARD (Mar. 10, 1854, Ann Arbor, Mich.). See article in Vol. ii. 599. He was associate-editor, for American topics, of the second edition of this Dictionary. He is still musical editor of the New York 'Tribune,' and has added the following books to his list: *Chapters of Opera*, 1908 (2nd ed., 1911), *A Book of Operas*, 1911, *The Pianoforte and its Music*, 1911, *A Second Book of Operas*, 1917, *Afro-American Folk-Songs*, 1914, *More Chapters of Opera*, 1919,

and an English version of 'Parsifal,' 1920. His position as Nestor among music-critics, his wide culture and experience, and his geniality of spirit and literary style, have given him more or less unique authority and influence. His long-awaited edition of Thayer's *Life of Beethoven* was finished in 1914, but publication has been delayed by war-conditions. This is based on the German editions and Thayer's original text, revised, annotated and with added concluding chapters. See his article on Thayer and his work in 'The Musical Quarterly,' October, 1917. [R.6]

KREINER, EDWARD (b. 1890). See Register, 10.

KREISLER, FRITZ (Feb. 2, 1875, Vienna, Austria). See article in Vol. ii. 599–600. At the outbreak of the war he reëntered the Austrian army and was wounded in the Galician campaign of 1914. In 1915 he came again to America and has since been active in concert. His compositions for violin and piano are 'Romance,' 'Caprice Viennois,' 'Tambourin Chinois,' 'Recitativo and Scherzo Caprice' (violin alone), 'Berceuse Romantique,' 'Rondino' (on a theme by Beethoven); 'Polichinelle,' 'La Gitana' (18th-century Arab-Spanish Gipsy-Song), 'Aucassin and Nicolette,' and 'Toy Soldier's March' (all Carl Fischer). A string-quartet (1919, Letz Quartet, in New York) is announced for publication, and a comic opera 'The Marriage-Knot' was brought out in 1919. Many of his transcriptions of classic and modern works are published by Carl Fischer. [R.7]

KREISSMANN, AUGUST (1823–1879). See Register, 4.

KRELL, ALBERT (1833–1900). See Register, 4.

KRIENS, CHRISTIAAN PIETER WILLEM (Apr. 29, 1881, Amsterdam, Holland), was the son of an orchestral conductor and early took up violin, piano and theory. He studied at the Hague Conservatory and won a gold medal there in 1895. The same year he made his début with his father's orchestra in Amsterdam, conducting his own 2nd symphony and playing the Beethoven violin-concerto and piano-concerto in E-flat. He then toured France, Holland and Belgium as violinist, and came to America in 1906 as conductor of the French Opera Company in New Orleans. Since 1907 he has been teacher and conductor in New York. In 1911 he started a Quartet and in 1912 a Symphony Club, mainly to afford training for young players, which has become large and effective. About eighty of his works are published here (Schirmer, Carl Fischer, Presser) and abroad. The list includes two symphonies, in C and F; the orchestral suite 'In Holland' (Concertgebouw, Lamoureux and Metropolitan Opera House Orchestras) ; a string-quartet in B-flat minor; two sonatas for violin and piano; the symphonic poem 'Les Rois en Exile'; many pieces for piano and violin and piano; and songs. [R.9]

KRITCH, WILLIAM E. See COLLEGES, 3 (Illinois C.).

KROEGER, ERNEST RICHARD (Aug. 10, 1862, St. Louis), began music with his father, Adolph E. Kroeger, and later studied piano with Egmont Froelich, Waldemar Malmene and Charles Kunkel, theory with W. Golder and P. G. Anton, violin with Spiering and instrumentation with L. Mayer — all of St. Louis. He has been organist at various churches, at present at the Church of the Messiah (Unitarian), and was a founder of the A. G. O. Since 1887 he has been music-director at Forest Park University, and since 1904 also head of the Kroeger School of Music. In 1893–1903 he conducted the Morning Choral Club and in 1910–12 the Amphion Club. In 1904 he had charge of the music-programs at the Louisiana Purchase Exposition. In 1896 he was president of the M. T. N. A. and in 1897–99 of the Missouri Association. In 1915 he played organ-recitals at the Panama-Pacific Exposition and gave instrumental courses at the University of California. He has also had similar courses at Cornell University. Since 1904 he has been a member of the French Academy and since 1915 of the National Institute of Arts and Letters. For many years he has given series of piano-recitals in St. Louis, as well as many in all parts of the United States. He has been peculiarly successful with lecture-recitals. His répertoire includes over 700 works. Among his compositions are the following:

Overtures — 'Endymion' (Ithaca), 'Thanatopsis' (St. Louis), 'Hiawatha' (Omaha), 'Sardanapalus' (New York), 'Atala' and 'Pittoresque.'
Scherzo in D minor and 'March of the Pioneers' (both St. Louis Symphony Orchestra).
'March of the Indian Phantoms' and the Suite 'Lalla Rookh' (both Louisiana Exposition).
Quartet in D minor, for piano and strings (1889, Philadelphia).
Quintet in F minor, for piano and strings (1890, Detroit).
Trio in E minor, for piano, violin and 'cello (1891, Cleveland).
Quartet in D minor, for strings (1914, St. Louis).
Sonata in F-sharp minor, for violin and piano (1908, St. Louis).
Romanza in B-flat, for 'cello and piano.
Rêverie in D minor, for violin and piano.
'A Masque of Dead Florentines,' for recitation or action (1911, St. Louis).
About 175 works for piano, including 'Fantasie-Polonaise' in E-flat, op. 26, 12 Concert-Études, op. 30, Suite, op. 33, Sonata in D-flat, op. 40, Scherzo in E-flat minor, op. 45, '16 Variations on an Elegiac Theme' in B minor, op. 54, etc.
For the organ — 3 Introduction and Fugues, opp. 27, 56, 77, 'Oriental Scenes,' op. 37, 'Marche Pittoresque' in D-flat, and 'Scène Persane' (with piano).

Over 80 separate songs and the cycle 'Memory,' op. 66, besides many other vocal works, secular and sacred.

KRONOLD, HANS (July 3, 1872, Cracow, Poland), had his general education in Leipzig, where he took up 'cello with Kiesling. During three years in Berlin he studied 'cello with Vollrath, piano and harmony with Hans Rasch. In 1886 he came to New York and continued 'cello-study with Hekking. For five seasons he played in the New York Symphony Society, but since 1900 has devoted himself to solo-playing and teaching. He has toured with leading singers, and with Maud Powell and other instrumentalists. For many years he has played at Sunday evening services at All Angels' Church. He has published pieces for 'cello and piano and for violin and piano, and songs (Ditson, Carl Fischer, Witmark). [R.7]

KUNITS, LUIGI VON (July 30, 1870, Vienna, Austria), graduated from the University of Vienna in law and classical philology. He studied violin with Kral, Gruen and Sevčik, music-history with Hanslick and composition with Jacksch and Bruckner. For a time he led the string-quartet of the Tonkünstlerverein. In 1893 he came to America as assistant-conductor and concert-master of the Austrian Orchestra at the Columbian Exposition in Chicago, where later he taught violin and composition and organized a string-quartet. In 1896–1910 he was concertmaster of the Pittsburgh Orchestra. Many solo appearances added to his reputation as a player, and he also conducted series of string-quartet concerts and taught at the Pittsburgh Conservatory and later in his own school. In 1910–12 he was again in Vienna as professor in the Patonay Conservatory and as soloist and conductor. Since 1912 he has been professor in the Canadian Academy of Music at Toronto and leader of the Academy String-Quartet. In 1915 he founded 'The Canadian Journal of Music' and became conductor of the Toronto Symphony Band. His compositions include two violin-concertos, a string-quartet in D minor, violin-pieces and études (Schirmer, Carl Fischer), songs and choruses. He has written The Hero as Musician — Beethoven, 1913, and many articles in musical journals. [R.8]

KUNKEL, CHARLES (b. 1840) and JACOB (1846–1882). See Register, 5.

KUNWALD, ERNST (b. 1868). See Register, 10.

KÜRSTEINER, JEAN PAUL (b. 1864). See Register, 8.

KÜRT, MELANIE (b. 1880). See Register, 10.

KUZDÖ, VICTOR (b. 1869). See Register, 7.

L

LACHMUND, CARL VALENTINE (Mar. 27, 1857, Booneville, Mo.), studied with Hiller, Jensen, Seiss and Gernsheim at the Cologne Conservatory, then with Moszkowski, Kiel and the brothers Scharwenka at Berlin, and in 1881–84 with Liszt at Weimar. He taught for a time in the Scharwenka Conservatory, Berlin, in Minneapolis, and since 1891 in New York. He made tours in 1880 with Wilhelmj and in 1887 with Marianne Brandt. In 1896 he founded the Women's String Orchestra Society of New York and conducted it for twelve consecutive seasons. He has composed two overtures for orchestra (the 'Japanese' played by Thomas, Seidl and Neuendorff), an 'Italian Suite' for orchestra, a trio for harp, violin and 'cello, and other instrumental works. Recent pieces for piano are a 'Valse-Impromptu' (Schuberth) and a 'Woodland Lullaby' (Church), and two airs de ballet for orchestra, 'La Capricieuse' and 'Coquetterie.' A comic operetta, 'Narrowly Averted,' is nearing completion. [R.7]

LA FLESCHE, FRANCIS (b. 1860?). See Register, 8.

LA FORGE, FRANK (Oct. 22, 1879, Rockford, Ill.), early evinced talent for composition. His first studies were with his sister Ruth LaForge Hall, a gifted pianist, who guided him until he was seventeen. Following this came four years of study with Wild in Chicago and four with Leschetizky in Vienna and with Labor and Navrátil (composition). He gained prominence at first by accompanying singers without notes, which has been his constant practice. After several seasons with Mme. Gadski he became pianist for Mme. Sembrich, and for six years they toured the musical world, giving concerts in all the great cities. Further tours were made with Mmes. Alda, Matzenauer and Schumann-Heink. His principal songs are 'Retreat,' 'To a Messenger,' 'I came with a Song,' 'When your dear hands,' 'Before the Crucifix,' 'Expectancy,' 'By the Lake,' 'Supplication,' 'A Song of the Open' and 'Longing.' His piano-compositions include a Valse de Concert, Gavotte, Gavotte and Musette, and Improvisation. He lives in New York, devoting himself to teaching when not on tour. [R.9]

LAHEE, HENRY CHARLES (b. 1856). See Register, 7.

LAHSER, CONRAD (b. 1872). See Colleges, 2 (Greensboro C., N. C.).

L'ALLEMAND, PAULINE (1862?– ?). See Register, 7.

LAMBERT, ALEXANDER (Nov. 1, 1862, Warsaw, Poland), having begun piano-study with his father at nine, was sent at twelve to the Vienna Conservatory, with letters from Rubinstein and Leschetizky. He graduated there in 1879 with high honors, having pursued piano with Epstein and composition with Bruckner. He continued alone for three years and then went to Liszt at Weimar. From 1883, besides teaching at the Berlin Neue Akademie, he concertized in Germany with Joachim, appeared in Berlin with the Philharmonic and Symphony Orchestras, gave many recitals and made a tour of Russia with Sarasate. He had visited America in 1880; in 1884 he returned, and appeared with much success with orchestras in Boston, New York and other cities, and gave recitals extensively. In 1887 he became director of the New York College of Music, which position he held till 1905, resigning to teach privately. Among his published compositions for piano are an Étude-Bourrée, Tarantelle, Valse Impromptu and Mazurka. His educational works, which are much used, are a *Piano-Method for Beginners* (Schirmer) and *A Systematic Course of Studies*, 3 vols., 1907. [R.7]

LAMBORD, BENJAMIN (June 10, 1879, Portland, Me. : June 6, 1915, Lake Hopatcong, N. J.), studied first with Arthur Whiting in Boston, from 1897 with MacDowell at Columbia University and from 1902 took up composition and orchestration with Rybner. In 1904–14 was organist at Kingsbridge, but in 1905–06 went abroad on a Mosenthal scholarship and in 1910 had work in orchestration under Vidal at Paris. At his death he was just entering upon work at the West End Presbyterian Church. In 1912 he founded the Lambord Choral Society, to give new works, especially by Americans, which in 1914 became the Modern Music Society and undertook orchestral works as well. His works include 15 songs, opp. 1, 3, 4, 7, 10 (the last with orchestra); part-songs, op. 2; a piano-trio, op. 5; 'Valse Fantastique,' op. 6, for piano; Introduction and Variations on an English dance-theme, op. 8, for orchestra; and 'Verses from Omar,' op. 11, for chorus and orchestra. The song 'Clytie,' op. 10, no. 2, is an example of his best work. He had completed two acts of the opera 'Woodstock,' published 'Ten Lyric Studies' for piano, and edited 'The Orchestra and Orchestral Music' in *The Art of Music*, Vol. viii. [R.9]

LAMONT, FORREST (b. 1889). See Register, 10.

LAMPERT, CARL ALBERT. See State Universities (Ky.).

'LAND OF HAPPINESS, THE.' A music-drama, No. 15 of the 'Grove-Plays' of the San

Francisco Bohemian Club, produced in 1917. The text is by Charles Templeton Crocker and the music by Joseph D. Redding. The action is laid in China in legendary times.

LANDSBURY, JOHN J. See STATE UNIVERSITIES (Ore.).

LANG, BENJAMIN JOHNSON (Dec. 28, 1837, Salem, Mass. : Apr. 3, 1909, Boston). See article in Vol. ii. 631–2. The last concert of the Cecilia Society which he conducted was on Apr. 16, 1907, when Pierné's 'The Children's Crusade' was given. He was organist of King's Chapel from 1885 until his death. His last appearance as conductor was on Feb. 12, 1909, when he led the Boston Symphony Orchestra and a chorus at a Lincoln Memorial service in Symphony Hall. At the Boston Symphony Orchestra concerts of Apr. 8 and 10, 1909, Mozart's Masonic funeral-music was played in his memory. Among his pupils were his daughter (see below), Arthur Foote, W. F. Apthorp and Ethelbert Nevin. [R.4]

LANG, HENRY ALBERT (Oct. 9, 1854, New Orleans), graduated from the Stuttgart Conservatory in 1875, having studied piano with Lebert and Pruckner and composition with Faiszt. He then continued composition with Lachner in Karlsruhe, taught there and at Riga and Königsberg, and till 1890 gave some concerts. For a year he lived in Galveston, Tex., but since 1891 has made his home in Philadelphia. Since 1913 he has been head of the theory-department of the Philadelphia Conservatory, which gave him the degree of Mus.D. in 1911. His compositions include Symphony No. 1, 'Fantasies of a Poet' (1914, Philadelphia Orchestra), Symphony No. 2, in C minor (1915. first prize, Illinois Music Teachers' Association), the orchestral suite 'Fantastic Dances,' a piano-trio in E major (1911, first prize for chamber-music, National Federation of Music Clubs), a piano-trio in C minor, a concerto for violin and orchestra, a sonata for 'cello, a piano-quintet in B-flat (1894, first prize, Utopian Club, Philadelphia), two string-quartets (1898, prizes, New York Music Teachers' Association, and 1913, Sinfonia), songs and piano-pieces. [R.8]

LANG, MARGARET RUTHVEN (Nov. 27, 1867, Boston). See article in Vol. ii. 632. Among recent compositions are a Te Deum in E-flat, a 'Christmas Cycle' for quartet, and the double a cappella chorus 'Wind.' The carol 'In Præsepio,' for mixed chorus, has been much sung, and 'The Heavenly Noël,' op. 57 (Schmidt), for mezzo-soprano, women's chorus, strings, harp, piano and organ, is one of the most valuable recent works for women's voices. She has been fortunate in her choice of texts for songs and choral works, and her settings show strong individuality, with a welcome absence of haste. [R.8]

LANGDON, CHAUNCEY (1764–1830). See TUNE-BOOKS, 1786.

LANGDON, WILLIAM CHAUNCY (b. 1871). See Register, 10.

LANGE, DANIEL DE (1841–1918). See Vol. ii. 633, and Register, 10.

LANGENUS, GUSTAVE (b. 1883). See Register, 9.

LANHAM, McCALL (b. 1877). See Register, 9.

LANIER, SIDNEY (Feb. 3, 1842, Macon, Ga. : Sept. 7, 1881, Lynn, N. C.), famous as one of the most spontaneous and mystically gifted of American poets, touched music in three ways. From childhood he showed a phenomenal instinct in appreciation and expression, developing such technical skill as to serve with distinction as first flutist (from 1873) in the Peabody Symphony Orchestra of Baltimore, and becoming recognized there for his sympathetic critical acumen. For years, also, at length as lecturer at Johns Hopkins University, he made careful studies in the musical aspects of poetic technique, publishing a lucid and able *Science of English Verse*, 1881, which remains a stimulating contribution to a neglected subject. And, finally, his poems contain numerous passages about music or couched in musical imagery — among whole poems being 'To Wagner', (1877) and 'To Beethoven' (1876–77), and the most sustained and characteristic use of musical analogies occurring in 'Life and Song' (1868) and especially 'The Symphony' (1875). He was invited to write the text for the opening cantata at the Centennial Exposition (Philadelphia, 1876), the music being composed by Dudley Buck. All his permanent work was done while in a losing fight with consumption. See his *Letters*, 1881, the Memorial prefixed to his *Poems*, 1884, and the biography by Mims, 1905, especially the remarkable chapter 'A Musician in Baltimore.' [R.6]

LANKOW, ANNA (1850–1908). See Register, 7.

LA ROSS, EARLE DOUGLASS (b. 1887). See Register, 9.

LAUCELLA, NICOLA (b. 1882). See Register, 9.

LAVALLÉE, CALIXA (Dec. 28, 1842, Verchères, Que. : Jan. 21, 1891, Boston), had piano-lessons from his father and appeared in public at ten. At fifteen he entered the Paris Conservatory, studying piano with Marmontel and instrumentation with Bazin and Boieldieu. In 1881 he made a concert-tour of the United States with Mme. Gerster. He attempted to start a conservatory in Quebec, and then located in Boston, where at the time of his death he was teaching in

the Petersilea Academy. He was active in
the promotion of music by Americans and
was president of the M.T.N.A. in 1887.
Of his compositions two are still popular,
the piano-étude 'The Butterfly,' op. 10, and
the Canadian national song 'O Canada.'
He also composed two operas, an oratorio,
a cantata, a symphony, two suites for orchestra, two string-quartets, a piano-trio,
a suite for 'cello and piano, a sonata for violin
and piano, many piano-pieces and some church-
music. [R.5]

‡ LAVIGNAC, ALEXANDRE JEAN AL-
BERT (Jan. 22, 1846, Paris : April, 1916,
Paris). See article in Vol. ii. 654. To the list
of works add Les Gaîtés du Conservatoire, 1900,
L'Éducation Musicale, 1902 (English trans. by
Esther Singleton, 1903) and Notions Scolaires
de Musique, 1905. He was editor-in-chief of
the great Encyclopédie de la Musique et Dic-
tionnaire du Conservatoire.

LAW, ANDREW (1748-1821). See Register, 2, and TUNE-BOOKS, 1778.

LAWRENCE, FREDERICK. See STATE
UNIVERSITIES (Ill.)

LAWRENCE, ROBERT. See STATE UNI-
VERSITIES (Ala.).

LAYTON, JOSEPH E. See COLLEGES, 3
(Missouri Wesleyan C.).

LEAVITT, JOSHUA (1794-1873). See
TUNE-BOOKS, 1831.

LEAVITT, W. J. D. (1841- ?). See Register, 5.

LE BARON, HARRISON D. See COL-
LEGES, 3 (Adrian C., Mich.).

LECKNER, MAX (b. 1842). See Register, 5.

LEE, THOMAS, JR. See TUNE-BOOKS,
1790.

LEE & WALKER, Philadelphia, was a
publishing-firm established in 1848 by Julius
Lee (d. 1875) and William Walker (d. 1857),
both of whom had been in the employ of George
Willig, whose business began as far back as
1794. For many years they issued much popular music and some books of importance. In
1876 the stock and good-will were purchased
by Oliver Ditson and became the nucleus for
J. E. Ditson & Co. Meanwhile the firm-name
was continued by Julius Lee, Jr., and J. F.
Morrison.

LEEFSON, MAURITZ (b. 1861). See Register, 7.

LEHMANN, FRIEDRICH J. (b. 1866).
See Register, 8.

LEHMANN, GEORGE (July 31, 1865,
New York), in 1880-83 was at the Leipzig
Conservatory, taking violin with Schradieck
and Hermann, harmony with Lammers and
counterpoint and fugue with Jadassohn. He
also studied one season with Joachim in
Berlin. In 1883 at Leipzig he won the Helbig

prize for violin-playing by a performance of
Joachim's Hungarian concerto at the Gewand-
haus. He toured as soloist and leader of the
Lehmann Quartet, in 1886-89 conducted the
Cleveland Symphony Orchestra and in 1889-
92 lived in Europe. In 1893 he settled in
New York as teacher and writer, but removed
to Berlin in 1907. Since 1916 he has been
director of the Lehmann Violin-School in
New York. He has written True Principles
of the Art of Violin-Playing, 1899, translated
De Bériot's Violin-Method (Schirmer) and
edited The Violinist's Lexicon, 1917, and 25
Pieces in the First Position. [R.7]

LEHMANN, GUSTAV ADOLF. See
COLLEGES, 3 (Bluffton C., Ohio).

LEHMANN, LILLI (Nov. 24, 1848, Würzburg, Germany). See article in Vol. ii. 667.
[R.7]

'LEIF ERIKSON.' A three-act opera by
Gerard Tonning, produced in 1910 at Seattle.

LEMARE, EDWIN HENRY (Sept. 9, 1865,
Ventnor, Isle of Wight). See article in Vol.
ii. 673. He was organist at the Carnegie
Institute in Pittsburgh in 1902-05, during
which time he gave 170 recitals. For some
years he held no official position, but toured
the world as concert-organist, making two
trips to Australia and New Zealand, besides
many in Europe and America. In 1915 he
gave over 100 recitals at the Panama Exposition. In 1917 he became city-organist at
San Francisco. His works (largely Novello)
include a long list of organ-pieces (two symphonies, overtures and smaller works), an
Easter cantata, church-music and many fine
organ-transcriptions. [R.9]

LEMONT, CEDRIC WILMOT (b. 1879).
See Register, 9.

‡ LENEPVEU, CHARLES FERDINAND
(Oct. 4, 1840, Rouen, France : Aug. 16,
1910, Paris). See article in Vol. ii. 674-5.
To list of works add 'Iphigénie,' scene for soli,
chorus and orchestra, a 'Messe de Mariage,'
a string-quartet, motets and piano-pieces.

‡ LEONCAVALLO, RUGGIERO (Mar.
8, 1858, Naples, Italy : Aug. 9, 1919, Naples). See article in Vol. ii. 678-80. He
toured the United States and Canada in 1906,
conducting 'I Pagliacci' and 'La Jeunesse
de Figaro.' In 1910 'Maia' and 'Malbruk'
were produced within four days (Rome), in
1912 'Reginetta delle Rose' (Rome and
Naples) and 'Gli Zingari' (London), and in
1916 'Ave Maria' and 'Gioffredo Mameli'
(Genoa). The operetta 'Are you there?'
was produced at London in 1913. He also
wrote the symphonic poem 'Serafita' and a
'Hymne France-Italie' (1916, Paris).

'LEONORA.' An opera by William H.
Fry, originally produced in Philadelphia by
the Seguin troupe in 1845 and repeated in

Italian in New York in 1858 at the Academy of Music under the direction of Anschütz. See Elson, *Hist. of American Music*, pp. 109–10.

LERNER, TINA (June 5, 1890, Odessa, Russia), studied piano with Rudolph Helm in Odessa when but six to nine, and then entered the Moscow Conservatory, where she was a pupil of Pabst until 1904. She made her début in Moscow in 1905, when she played Beethoven's 'Emperor' concerto with the Philharmonic Society. She made successful tours of Europe, and came to America in 1908, making her first appearance in New York in Rachmaninov's second concerto with the Russian Symphony Orchestra. She concertized in 1909–10, then spent two years in Europe and since 1912 has made her home in America. She married the pianist Louis Bachner in 1909, but was divorced in 1915 and married the violinist Vladimir Shavitch the same year. [R.9]

‡ LEROUX, XAVIER HENRI NAPOLÉON (Oct. 11, 1863, Velletri, Italy : Feb. 20, 1919, Paris). See article in Vol. ii. 681. To the list of operas add 'William Ratcliff' (1906, Nice), 'Théodora' (1906, Monte Carlo), 'Le Chemineau' (1907, Paris, also 1911, New Orleans), 'Le Carillonneur' (1912, Paris), 'La Fille de Figaro' (1914, Paris), 'Les Cadeaux de Noël' (1916, Paris) and '1814' (1918, Monte Carlo).

‡ LESCHETIZKY, THEODOR (June 22, 1830, Lancut, Austrian Poland : Nov. 17, 1915, Dresden, Germany). See article in Vol. ii. 681. From about 1890 till the end of his life he was exceedingly active as a teacher and was sought by pupils from all parts of the world. Among these were Fannie Bloomfield Zeisler, Mark Hambourg, Ossip Gabrilovitch, Artur Schnabel, Ethel Newcomb, Katherine Goodson, Frank LaForge and Ethel Leginska. He was four times married — to the concert-singer Anna Friedbourg in Petrograd, in 1880–91 to Annette Essipov, in 1894–1908 to Dominirska Benislavska, and in 1908 to Marie Pozborska (all pupils except the first) — being separated from the first three by divorce. See biographies by Countess Potocka, 1903, and A. Hullah, 1906, besides on his method, Marie Prentner, *The Modern Pianist*, 1903, and Malwine Brée, *The Leschetizky Method* (Eng. trans. by Arthur Elson, 1913.)

LESLIE, BENJAMIN. See TUNE-BOOKS, 1811.

LESTER, THOMAS WILLIAM (b. 1889). See Register, 10.

LE SUEUR, PETER (b. 1871). See Register, 8.

LETZ, HANS (b. 1887). See Register, 9.

LETZ QUARTET, THE, was formed in 1917 after the dissolution of the Kneisel Quartet. It consists of Hans Letz, Sandor Harmati, Edward Kreiner and Gerald Maas, and at once stepped into high estimation for superior musicianship.

LEVETT, DAVID MAURICE (1844–1914). See Register, 6.

LEVEY, STANLEY. See COLLEGES, 2 (Tennessee C.)

LEVITZKI, MISCHA (b. 1898). See Register, 10.

LÉVY, HENIOT (July 19, 1879, Warsaw, Poland), graduated from the Hochschule in Berlin in 1897, his teachers being Raif and Barth, and he also studied composition with Bruch. His début in 1898 was with the Berlin Philharmonic Orchestra and he then toured in Germany and Scandinavia. Since 1905 he has been active as teacher and pianist in Chicago, being in the faculty of the American Conservatory. He has given recitals and appeared with the Chicago and other orchestras. Among his publications are a piano-concerto, op. 1, a sonata for piano and violin, op. 6, a piano-trio, op. 10, variations and smaller pieces for piano. Unpublished are an overture, a piano-concerto, a string-quartet, a Passacaglia for violin and piano, a musical setting of Tennyson's 'Guinevere,' 16 songs (by Dunbar), other songs and piano-pieces. [R.9]

LEVY, JULES (1840?– ?). See Register, 5.

LEWING, ADELE (Aug. 6, 1866, Hanover, Germany), appeared as pianist at fourteen and had then already essayed composition. She graduated with honors at the Leipzig Conservatory in 1885, having studied under Reinecke and Jadassohn. She then became known as recitalist and concert-player in Europe and in America, where she also taught in Chicago and Boston, appearing with leading orchestras and quartets. In 1893–96 she studied piano with Leschetizky in Vienna and composition with Fuchs. Since 1897 she has worked in New York as teacher, player and composer. In 1899 she married Dr. B. W. Stiefel of New York. She has won many prizes for songs and piano-pieces (Columbian Exposition, 1893, Baltimore, 1910, etc.). [R.7]

LEWIS, FREEMAN (1780–1859). See TUNE-BOOKS, 1813.

LEWIS, LEO RICH (Feb. 11, 1865, South Woodstock, Vt.), had his general training in the Boston schools, graduated at Tufts College in 1887 and took post-graduate work at Harvard, with highest honors in music. In 1889–92 he was in Munich as pupil of Rheinberger in composition and as student of languages, and won a diploma in composition from the Akademie der Tonkunst. Since 1892 he has been in the faculty of Tufts College, at first as instructor in French and from 1895 as professor of music. Besides marked success in arousing enthusiasm among his students, he has been active in promoting attention to music in high schools and colleges generally. For many years he has been on the staff of the College Entrance Examination Board and since 1910 chief examiner in music. Early works were the cantata 'The Consolation of Music' (1895) and a sonata for violin and piano (1895). For the revivals at Tufts of Milton's 'Comus' and Dekker's 'Fortunatus' (1901, '06) he arranged the music from old scores. His music for 'Comus' has been repeated at other institutions. With S. W. Cole he has published *Harmonia* and *Melodia* (both 1905) and several other collections of school-music. Of his war-songs 'We Stand — a Song of Devotion to the United States' was specially popular. He has in manuscript a symphonic prelude for Browning's 'A Blot on the 'Scutcheon.' He is the originator of a system of card-indexing for music. He has written considerably in fields outside of music. [R.8]

‡ LIADOV, ANATOL CONSTANTINO-VITCH (May 11, 1855, Petrograd, Russia : August, 1914, Petrograd). See article in Vol. ii. 689. As professor in the Petrograd Conservatory from 1878 he was the teacher of many prominent Russian composers of the present generation. From 1894 he conducted the concerts of the Imperial Musical Society. Among later works were the symphonic poems 'Baba Yaga,' op. 56, 'Le Lac Enchanté,' op. 62, and 'Kikimora,' op. 63, choruses with orchestra to Maeterlinck's 'Sœur Béatrice,' op. 60, and the ballet 'Leila and Adelai' (unfinished).

‡ LIAPUNOV, SERGIUS MICHAILO-VITCH (Nov. 30, 1859, Yaroslav, Russia). See article in Vol. ii. 690. In 1902–10 he was music-inspector at St. Helen's Institute, and since 1910 has been professor at the Petrograd Conservatory. In recent years he has also appeared in European capitals as conductor or pianist. To the list of works add the 2nd piano-concerto, op. 38, a 'Rapsodie' on Ukrainian themes, op. 28, for piano and orchestra, and the symphonic poem 'Yelasova Vola,' op. 37. He edited letters between Tchaikovsky and Balakirev, 1912.

LIBRARIES, MUSICAL. See notes in Vol. ii. 717–20. The leadership of the Library of Congress, the Boston Public Library, the New York Public Library and the Newberry Library in Chicago, as there stated, has been maintained. But the public library of almost every large city, and even of many cities of moderate size, is now giving careful attention to the accumulation of books about music, collections and often well-selected sets of piano-scores, vocal music and even orchestral music. The purpose is naturally to encourage popular intelligence and appreciation rather than to collect material for scholarly research. Besides Harvard and Yale Universities, many others are now important, especially several of the great State Universities, like Michigan, California and Wisconsin. A few of the State Libraries, also, like those of New York, Kansas and California, are building up musical collections of importance. Some of the leading conservatories, like the New England Conservatory in Boston, the Institute of Musical Art in New York, the Oberlin Conservatory and the School of Music in Northwestern University, have valuable libraries, either of their own or in the institutions of which they are a part. Regarding the four leading libraries mentioned in Vol. ii. see articles in the *M.T.N.A. Proceedings*, 1908, pp. 269, 289; 1910, p. 188; 1914, p. 211; and 1909, p. 198, as well as papers relating to the subject in general in 1916, p. 47; 1917, p. 52; and 1918, p. 190. In the volume for 1917 is given the questionnaire issued by a committee working in conjunction with the Bureau of Education and a tentative summary of some of the statistics secured. The report of this committee has been drafted in detail, but has not yet been published. It is soon to appear as a Bulletin of the Bureau of Education.

The total number of books, pamphlets and pieces in the Library of Congress (Music-Division) is about 825,000. Of this number about 35,000 are books upon music, old and new. There are over 5000 scores of instrumental works, like symphonies, concertos, suites, etc., over 7000 vocal scores of operas, over 3000 orchestral operatic scores, and over 20,000 opera-librettos. There are also more than 5000 player-piano rolls.

The New York Public Library has over 125,000 books upon music, 7200 bound volumes of music and more than 1000 orchestral scores. It has an extensive collection of opera-librettos. In 1914 it received by gift the opera-collection of the late Julian Edwards, containing about 250 full scores of operas, oratorios, etc., 300 operatic vocal scores and 325 books on music.

The Boston Public Library contains more than 15,000 books on music, over 26,000 bound volumes of music, over 4000 orchestral scores and about 1000 scores of chamber-music works. It has a remarkable collection of programs of musical events in Boston for the past fifty years. It also has many autograph scores of important works by American composers.

The Newberry Library in Chicago has more than 13,000 books upon music or bound volumes of music.

LICHTENBERG, LEOPOLD (Nov. 22, 1861, San Francisco), began violin-study with Beaujardin and at eight appeared in concert. In 1873 Wieniawski, visiting San Francisco, heard him play and became his teacher at Brussels for three years, where he won first prize at the Conservatory in 1876. After a tour in Holland, made in Wieniawski's place, he returned to America and for a year traveled as soloist with the Thomas Orchestra. For a time he played in the Boston Symphony

Orchestra and then moved to New York, where in 1890 he became violinist in the first Margulies Trio, continuing in 1904 in the later Trio, and from 1899 became chief violin-teacher at the National Conservatory. [R.6]

LICHTENSTEIN, VICTOR (b. 1872). See Register, 8.

LIEBLING, EMIL (Apr. 12, 1851, Pless, Germany : Jan. 20, 1914, Chicago), first came to America when a youth, but had his musical training abroad. At Berlin he studied piano with Ehrlich and Kullak, at Vienna with Dachs and at Weimar with Liszt, while Dorn taught him composition. In 1874–76 he was teacher in the Kullak Conservatory. Meanwhile, in 1872, he had located in Chicago, where he became eminent as player, teacher and writer. His works for piano include a 'Gavotte Moderne,' op. 11; a 'Florence Valse,' op. 12; 'Feu Follet,' op. 17; Albumblatt, op. 18; Cradle-Song, op. 23; and 'Minuetto Scherzoso,' op. 28. He contributed brilliant articles to several periodicals and was one of the editors of *The American History and Encyclopedia of Music*, 1908. [R.5]

LIEBLING, LEONARD (Feb. 7, 1874, New York), is a nephew of the foregoing. He graduated from the College of the City of New York in 1897 and then went abroad to study piano at Berlin under Godowsky, Kullak and Barth and composition under Urban. After teaching and appearing as pianist there and in America, since 1899 he has been mostly engaged in literary work. He has written a number of comic operalibrettos, including 'Vera Violetta,' 'The Girl and the Kaiser,' 'The American Maid' (music by Sousa), etc. In 1902 he joined the staff of 'The Musical Courier' and since 1911 has been editor-in-chief. [R.8]

LIEBLING, MAX (b. 1845). See Register, 5.

LIEDERKRANZ, DER DEUTSCHE, of New York. See Vol. iii. 368–9, and Ritter, *Music in America*, chap. xix. Similar societies were early established in many cities where German singers were numerous, such as Cincinnati, Milwaukee, Chicago and St. Louis, and often aspired to elaborate choral concerts and even operatic performances in addition to the part-song singing of a social kind that was their original purpose.

'LIFE.' No. 17 of the 'Grove-Plays' of the San Francisco Bohemian Club, produced in 1919. The text is by Harry Leon Wilson and the music by Domenico Brescia.

'LIGHT OF ASIA, THE.' An oratorio by Dudley Buck, published in 1885 (Novello) and first performed in London in 1889. The text is taken from Edwin Arnold's well-known poem. It is the most elaborate of Buck's choral works.

LILIENTHAL, ABRAHAM WOLF (b. 1859). See Register, 7.

LIMBERT, FRANK L. (b. 1866). See Register, 8.

LINDEMAN, WILLIAM (1795–1875). See Register, 3.

LINDQUEST, ALBERT CHARLES (b. 1892). See Register, 10.

LISSER, LOUIS (b. 1850). See Register, 6, and COLLEGES, 2 (Mills C., Cal.).

LISTEMANN, BERNHARD (Aug. 28, 1841, Schlotheim, Germany : Feb. 11, 1917, Chicago), was trained as violinist at Sondershausen by Ullrich and at Leipzig by David (1856–57) and also, while in 1859–67 concertmaster of the court-orchestra at Rudolstadt, by Vieuxtemps (1861) and Joachim (1862). With his brother Fritz he came to America in 1867, toured with Leopold de Meyer and spent two years in Boston. In 1871–74 he was concertmaster of the Thomas Orchestra and in 1881–85 of the Boston Symphony Orchestra. In 1875–79 he was leader of the Philharmonic Club of Boston, in 1879–81 of the Philharmonic Orchestra which succeeded it, and in 1881–85 of the Listemann String Quartet, of all of which he was founder and moving spirit. In 1885–93 he taught in Boston, but also kept up tours with the Listemann Concert Company. From 1893 he worked in Chicago, at first as head of the violin-department of the Chicago College of Music. Before his retirement in 1911 he lived once more for two years in Boston. He published a Violin-Method, and composed violin-pieces and also a symphony. [R.5]

LISTEMANN, FRANZ (b. 1873). See Register, 8.

LISTEMANN, FRITZ [Ferdinand] (1839–1909). See Register, 5.

LISTEMANN, PAUL (b. 1871). See Register, 7.

LITCHFIELD COUNTY CHORAL UNION, THE. This enterprise, founded in 1899, is a memorial of Robbins Battell (1819–95), planned and munificently supported by his daughter and her husband, Carl Stoeckel, of Norfolk, Conn. Almost a century ago there was a Litchfield County Musical Association of which Battell was promoter and conductor. Its last concert in 1851 at Litchfield he directed. In 1875 he led a glee-club at Winsted, where in 1878 a choral society was formed, with R. S. Frary as conductor. From 1882 he arranged superior open-air concerts at Norfolk, which were repeated at Lakeville. In 1885 the Winsted chorus was reorganized, Richmond P. Paine, then of New Britain, being conductor. In 1897 Mrs. Stoeckel started the Norfolk Glee Club, led in 1899 by N. H. Allen. Its success led to the formation in that year of the present County

CHARLES M. LOEFFLER

Union, which links together the musical interests of a chain of five or six towns and villages in the northwestern corner of Connecticut. Of this organization five local choruses (Norfolk, Winsted, Salisbury, Canaan and Torrington) have been members since 1906. The chief conductors have been R. P. Paine (1899–1915) and Arthur Mees of New York. The total forces in recent years have included about 700 singers (not over 425 at any one concert) and a picked orchestra of 75–100 from New York, with a variety of distinguished soloists, vocal and instrumental. At present three concerts are given each year at Norfolk in the first week of June, and from time to time local concerts in other places. The June Festivals have acquired an extraordinary prestige for dignity and perfection, attracting visitors from all over the country. For these Festivals in 1904 Mr. Stoeckel erected an experimental building and this was later replaced by a more permanent structure, known as the 'Music Shed,' seating about 1450 auditors amid ideal acoustical conditions. Since the fifth year there has been no admission-fee charged, and no advertising of any sort is permitted. The heavy expenses for conductors, orchestras, soloists and invited composers are defrayed by Mr. and Mrs. Stoeckel as patrons. They have been strikingly successful not only in setting up a unique artistic center, but in making it a nucleus for community-enthusiasm.

The programs of the concerts include such standard choral works as 'Elijah,' 'Hymn of Praise,' 'Messiah,' 'The Redemption,' the Requiems of Verdi and of Brahms, the Stabat Maters of Rossini and of Dvořák, 'The Damnation of Faust,' 'Samson and Delilah,' 'Scenes from Hiawatha,' and a long list of great orchestral works and famous vocal solos. The following works have also been specially written for Norfolk and first performed there:

Parker — 'King Gorm the Grim' (1908), 'Collegiate' Overture (1911), 'The Dream of Mary' (1918).
Chadwick — 'Noël' (1909), 'Aphrodite' (1912), 'Tam O'Shanter' (1915), 'Land of our Hearts' (1918).
Coleridge-Taylor — 'Bamboula Rhapsodic Dance' (1910), 'Tale of Old Japan' (1912), Violin Concerto (1912), 'Negro Air' for violin and orchestra (1912), 'From the Prairie' (1914).
Hadley — Symphony No. 4, 'North, East, South, West' (1911), 'Lucifer' (1914).
Bruch — Konzertstück, op. 85, for violin and orchestra (1911).
Kelley — Symphony No. 2, 'New England' (1913), Alice in Wonderland ' (1919).
Gilbert — ' Negro Rhapsody ' (1913).
Sibelius — 'Aalottaret' (1914).
Stanford — Piano Concerto (1915), ' Irish Rhapsody,' No. 5 (1917), 'Verdun' (1918).
Stock — Violin Concerto (1915).

T

Loeffler — Symphony, 'Hora Mystica' (1916).
Grainger — Suite, 'In a Nutshell' (1916), 'The Warriors' (1917).
Carpenter — Symphony (1917).
Laucella — Symphonic Impressions, 'Whitehouse' (1917).
Smith, David Stanley — Symphony No. 2 (1918).
(In most cases these works were conducted by the composers in person.)

Considering all that this list implies as to the encouragement of original composition, with the employment of distinguished singers and players and the development through Mr. Paine's genius of a permanent chorus of extraordinary competence and sympathy, it is not strange that these Festivals stand out as peculiarly significant. See *Litchfield County Choral Union, 1900–1912*, 2 vols., 1912, edited by J. H. Vaill (privately printed).

LITTLE, HENRY. See TUNE-BOOKS, 1820.

LITTLE, WILLIAM. See TUNE-BOOKS, 1798.

LOCKE, ARTHUR WARE (b. 1883). See Register, 9.

LOCKE, FLORA ELBERTINE, née Huie (b. 1866). See Register, 7.

LOCKPORT FESTIVALS. See NORTH AMERICAN MUSIC FESTIVAL.

LOCKWOOD, ALBERT LEWIS (b. 1871). See Register, 8.

LOCKWOOD, SAMUEL PIERSON (b. 1879). See Register, 9.

LOEB, JAMES (b. 1867). See Register, 9.

LOEFFLER, CHARLES MARTIN TORNOV (Jan. 30, 1861, Mulhouse, Alsace). See article in Vol. ii. 763. To the list of works add a 'Divertimento Espagnole' for saxophone and orchestra (1901); Psalm 137, for women's chorus (1902); 'For One who Fell in Battle,' for double chorus (1906); the symphonic 'Pagan Poem,' after Virgil, for orchestra, piano and trumpets (Schirmer); the symphony in one movement 'Hora Mystica,' for orchestra and men's chorus (1916, Norfolk Festival); and 'Music to the Memory of Victor Chapman,' three movements for string-quartet (1917). He is working upon a one-act opera. [R.7]

LOMBARDI OPERA COMPANY, THE, was a South American troupe under the lead of Mario Lombardi which came to San Francisco in 1908 with success. In 1912 this was transformed into the Pacific Coast Grand Opera Company and produced, among other works, Strauss' 'Salome' and Zandonai's 'Conchita' (first time in America).

LONGY, GUSTAVE GEORGES LÉOPOLD (Aug. 29, 1868, Abbeville, France), was trained at the Paris Conservatory, studying oboe with Gillet and taking a second prize in 1885 and a first in 1886. He played in the Lamoureux, Châtelet, Folies-Bergère and

Opéra-Comique Orchestras. In 1898 he came to America as first oboist in the Boston Symphony Orchestra, a position still held with distinction. In 1900 he founded the Longy Club, made up of wind-instruments and piano (Heinrich Gebhard), which has given many notable chamber-music performances. The Boston Orchestral Club, which he conducted in 1899–1913, introduced many novelties, chiefly by French composers. In 1915 he was appointed conductor of the MacDowell Orchestra in Boston and in 1916 founded the Longy School of Music. He has been an Officier d'Académie since 1895 and Officier de l'Instruction Publique since 1911. [R.8]

LONGY CLUB, THE, of Boston. See preceding article.

LOOMIS, HARVEY WORTHINGTON (Feb. 5, 1865, Brooklyn), after a general education at the Brooklyn Polytechnic Institute, studied composition with Dvořák at the National Conservatory and piano with Mme. Schiller in New York. He has devoted himself mainly to composition, with success along several lines. Among his works is the opera 'The Traitor Mandolin' (1900) ; four comic operas — 'The Maid of Athens,' 'The Burglar's Bride,' 'Going Up?' and 'The Bey of Baba'; and many musical pantomimes — 'Put to the Test,' 'Her Revenge,' 'In Old New Amsterdam,' 'The Enchanted Fountain,' 'Love and Witchcraft' and 'Blanc et Noir.' His music for children is much appreciated — the cantata 'Fairy Hill,' 24 miniature piano-duets, 'Toy-Tunes' (text and music), 'Song-Flowers,' 2 vols., and many school-choruses. He also has written a sonata for piano, a sonata for violin and piano, and many pieces for piano, including 'Lyrics of the Red Man,' 2 books. He has added incidental music to the plays 'The Tragedy of Death' (René Peter) and 'The Coming of the Prince' (William Sharp), and prepared the musical recitations 'Sandalphon' and 'The Story of the Faithful Soul.' Besides writing for periodicals he has lectured on Indian music. [R.8]

LORENZ, EDMUND SIMON (b. 1854). See Register, 6.

LORENZ, JULIUS (b. 1862). See Register, 7.

LORENZ PUBLISHING COMPANY, THE, of Dayton, O., was founded in 1890 by Edmund S. Lorenz and incorporated in 1901. It has devoted itself to publishing church-music, especially for the use of the United Brethren and related denominations. Its publications number over 2500, including about 450 collections of hymns, anthems, and some organ-music, aggregating over 11,000,000 copies. It has also made a specialty of popular monthly periodicals relating to church-music, including 'The Choir-Leader' (from 1894), 'The Choir Herald' (from 1898), 'The Volunteer Choir' (from 1913), 'Der Kirchenchor' (from 1898) and 'The Organist' (from 1898), all except the last edited by E. S. Lorenz. It has also published the comprehensive manual by the latter on *Practical Church Music*, 1909. In 1901 Karl K. Lorenz, the founder's son, a graduate of Columbia University and a pupil of MacDowell, entered the business, and in 1905 Ira B. Wilson was added to the editorial force. In 1902 a branch was opened in New York and in 1914 one in Chicago.

LORENZO, LEONARDO DE (b. 1875). See Register, 10.

LORING, HAROLD AMASA (b. 1879). See Register, 9.

LORING CLUB, THE, of San Francisco, is a men's chorus, organized in 1876, which has maintained a high standard of excellence. Its present director is Wallace A. Sabin.

LOS ANGELES SYMPHONY ORCHESTRA, THE, was organized in 1897. Its conductor for many years has been Adolf Tandler. In 1915 it gave the first performance west of the Mississippi of Beethoven's 9th Symphony and in 1917 brought out Cadman's 'Thunderbird' Suite. The players number about 75.

LOTH, LOUIS LESLIE (b. 1888). See Register, 9.

LOUD, JOHN HERMANN (b. 1873). See Register, 8.

LOUD, THOMAS (d. 1834). See Register, 3, and TUNE-BOOKS, 1824.

LOUD, THOMAS C. (1812– ?). See Register, 3.

'LOUIS XIV.' An opera by Homer Moore, produced in 1917 at St. Louis.

'LOVE'S SACRIFICE.' A pastoral opera in one act by George W. Chadwick, first produced in 1915.

LOVETTE, T. S. See COLLEGES, 2 (Baylor C., Tex.).

LOVEWELL, SAMUEL HARRISON (Mar. 9, 1865, Wellesley, Mass.), graduated from the Boston schools and in 1891 from the New England Conservatory. From that time he has been organist at a succession of churches in Easton, Pa., Georgetown, Ky., Columbia, S. C., Walla Walla, Wash., Quincy, Ill., Jenkintown, Pa., and (from 1917) Taunton, Mass. In all these positions he has given frequent recitals on piano or organ, often with lectures. In 1893–96 he was music-director at the College for Women in Columbia, S. C., in 1898–1906 at Whitman College in Walla Walla, in 1906–11 of the Quincy (Ill.) Conservatory, and from 1919 at the Tome School, Port Deposit, Md., besides for some years being editor for C. W. Thompson & Co., Boston. He has specialized in theory, music-history and the training of boy-choirs. His compositions include a sonata in F minor, a Credo for soprano and chorus, a Romanza, etc. He has translated Riemann's *Single and Double Counterpoint, History of Notation* and *History of Music,* 5 vols. (only the first published). [R.8]

LUCAS, CLARENCE (Oct. 19, 1866, Niagara, Ont.). See article in Vol. ii. 776. By invitation of Richard Mansfield he came to America to conduct Grieg's music for the productions of 'Peer Gynt.' In 1903 he became London correspondent of the New York 'Musical Courier' and later associate-editor, with headquarters in New York. In 1919 he returned to London again as special correspondent. To the list of works add six operas (not given), and many songs, and pieces for piano or violin and piano. The Fantasy and Fugue, op. 22, is often played by Hambourg and other artists. [R.7]

LUCAS, GEORGE W. (1800– ?). See Register, 3.

'LUCILLE.' See 'ANTONIO.'

LUCKSTONE, ISIDORE (b. 1861). See Register, 7.

LUDDEN, WILLIAM (1823– ?). See Register, 4.

LUKKEN, ALBERT. See STATE UNIVERSITIES (Wyo.).

LUND, JOHN REINHOLD (Oct. 20, 1859, Hamburg, Germany), after general education at the Johanneum in Hamburg, studied piano with Conrad Dinkler there and in 1880 graduated at the Leipzig Conservatory, where his teachers were Reinecke, Paul, Richter and Wenzel. In 1880–83 he was chorus-master at the Bremen Opera House and for a year assistant-conductor at the Stettin Stadt-Theater. In 1884 he came to the Metropolitan Opera House in New York as assistant to Leopold Damrosch. In 1887 he went to Buffalo as conductor of the Buffalo Symphony Orchestra and the Orpheus Society. In 1903 he directed Victor Herbert operas and toured with various companies until 1914, when he returned to the Buffalo Orpheus and the municipal orchestra-concerts. He has composed 'Der Germanenzug,' 'Ein Griechisches Kriegslied,' 'Kaiser Karl' and 'Spring-Morning,' all for soli, chorus and orchestra; an Intermezzo, 'Liebeslied' and 'Im Garten' for string-orchestra; a suite, sonata and many pieces for piano; songs and choruses. [R.7]

LUSSAN, ZÉLIE DE (b. 1863). See Register, 7.

LUTKIN, PETER CHRISTIAN (Mar. 27, 1858, Thompsonville, Wis.), of Danish stock, was brought up in Chicago, where from 1868 he was solo alto in the pioneer boy-choir of the Interior at the (P. E.) Cathe-

dral, went to the choir-school and at fourteen became organist, though still not technically trained. Then he studied with Mrs. Watson, Gleason and Eddy, and in 1879–81 taught piano at Northwestern University in Evanston. In 1881–84 he was in Berlin, taking piano with Raif, theory with Bargiel and organ with Haupt (mostly at the Hochschule) and winning a scholarship at the Royal Academy, in 1883 studying piano with Stepanov at Vienna and in 1884 piano and composition with Moszkowski at Paris. In 1884–91 he was organist at St. Clement's in Chicago and in 1891–97 at St. James'. In 1888–92 he also taught theory at the American Conservatory, and in 1891 entered upon what has been his life-work — the development of the School of Music in Northwestern University, of which he has been dean since 1895. Besides bringing this School to great efficiency, he has steadily built up public interests, since 1893 conducting the Evanston Musical Club and in 1894–1901 another in Ravenswood. These choral societies, with the noted A Cappella Choir of the School and its orchestral forces, supplied the means for the establishment in 1908 of the Chicago North Shore Festivals, which are recognized as among the best of their kind. He was a founder of the A. G. O. in 1896, received a Mus.D. from Syracuse University in 1900, has been always active in the M. T. N. A. (president in 1911 and 1920) and vice-president of the American branch of the I. M. S. Besides papers and articles on various subjects, in 1908 he lectured at the Western Theological Seminary in Chicago, his lectures coming out as *Music in the Church,* 1910. He has been one of the editors of both the Methodist and the Episcopal Hymnals (1905, '18). His compositions include

Communion Service in C (Gray).
Festival Te Deum in A (Gray).
Te Deum in C (Novello).
Te Deum in B-flat (Summy).
Te Deum, 'Peace' (1919), first given at the North Shore Festival (Gray).
Magnificat and Nunc Dimittis in G, eight parts a cappella (Gray).
Magnificat and Nunc Dimittis in C (Gray).
Festival Magnificat and Nunc Dimittis in B-flat (Summy).
Magnificat in E minor, a cappella.
Jubilate in C (Novello).
Psalm 51, for soli, chorus and organ.
Psalm 137, a cappella (Gray).
Many anthems — 'Kingdom of Light,' 'What Jesus Said,' a cappella, 'I will sing of Thy power,' a cappella (all Gray); 'The day is past and over' (Novello); 'The Lord shall comfort Zion,' 'Like as a father,' a cappella, 'O Paradise,' a cappella, 'O little town of Bethlehem' (all Summy); besides carols, etc.
Two sacred trios for children (Silver, Burdett & Co.).
Many part-songs and songs (part Summy).
'Romance,' for 'cello (Summy), or string-quartet for violin and orchestra.

Nine Organ-Preludes based on hymn-tunes (Gray). Processional March, for organ.　　　[R.6]

LYMAN, RALPH HAINE (b. 1883). See STATE UNIVERSITIES (Ore.) and COLLEGES, 3 (Pomona C., Cal.).

LYNES, FRANK (1858–1913). See Register, 7.

LYON, JAMES (1735–1794). See Register, 1, and TUNE-BOOKS, 1759.

LYON & HEALY, of Chicago, was established in 1864 by Oliver Ditson, the Boston music-publisher, as a western branch, the two partners being George W. Lyon and Patrick J. Healy (d. 1905), both previously in the Boston store. They soon began to deal extensively in instruments, including those for bands, and entered the field of piano-making with the Lyon & Healy and Washburn pianos, building up a varied business of immense proportions. They also became a headquarters for rare and remarkable instruments, and one of the finest makers of harps in the world. The capital is now $3,000,000 and the president Robert B. Gregory. The offices and salesrooms are at Wabash Avenue and Jackson Boulevard and the piano-works on Fullerton Avenue.

M

MAAS, GERALD CHRISTOPHER (b. 1888). See Register, 10.

MAAS, LOUIS PHILIPP OTTO (June 21, 1852, Wiesbaden, Germany : Sept. 18, 1889, Boston), the son of a music-teacher, began piano-playing early. The family moved to England and he graduated at King's College in London. In 1867 he entered the Leipzig Conservatory, where he had four years with Reinecke and Papperitz. An overture was performed at the Gewandhaus in 1868 and a symphony in 1872. He taught in the Kullak Academy in 1873–74, studying with Liszt in the summer, and in 1875–80 was piano-teacher at the Leipzig Conservatory. After 1880 he lived in Boston, teaching at the New England Conservatory and in 1881–82 conducting the Philharmonic Orchestra. He was an excellent pianist, often heard in recitals, and a teacher of exceptional ability. He composed 'On the Prairies,' an American Symphony (1883), overtures and other orchestral music, a string-quartet, a piano-concerto, three sonatas and other piano-pieces and songs. [R.7]

MAAS, MARGUERITE WILSON (b. 1888). See Register, 10.

MACBETH, FLORENCE (b. 1891). See Register, 10.

MacCOLLIN, PAUL. See COLLEGES, 3 (Morningside C., Iowa).

‡ MacCUNN, HAMISH (Mar. 22, 1868, Greenock, Scotland : Aug. 2, 1916, London). See article in Vol. iii. 3. He was Beecham's assistant from 1910 at Covent Garden and His Majesty's and from 1915 at the Shaftesbury. In 1912 he succeeded Coleridge-Taylor as professor of composition and director of the opera-class at the Guildhall School of Music. In his later years he was not much engaged upon composition.

MACDOUGALL, HAMILTON CRAWFORD (Oct. 15, 1858, Warwick, R. I.), was trained by Bonner, Sherwood, S. B. Whitney and Lang. From 1874 he was organist in Providence and in 1895–1900 at Harvard Church in Brookline, Mass. He was the second American to become an associate of the R. C. O. (1883) and in 1896 was a founder of the A. G. O. — in 1908–11 dean of the New England Chapter. He has been active, also, in the M. T. N. A. and other educational bodies, has repeatedly given series of lectures at Brown University, at the Brooklyn Institute of Arts and Sciences, and at the Summer School of Church Music at Cambridge. Brown University made him Mus.D. in 1901. Since 1900 he has been professor at Wellesley College, where he has brought the music-department to a high pitch of organization and efficiency, besides exercising his notable ability as organist and choirmaster. His compositions include publications like a festival setting of 'Onward, Christian soldiers' for bass, chorus and orchestra (Presser), many anthems for mixed or men's chorus, several songs and part-songs, and 'The Red Cross Knight,' for men's chorus. He has also written a piano-trio in F minor, a Scherzo in A, Psalm 95 for tenor, bass, chorus and organ, much music for the Masonic ritual, etc. He has published Studies in Melody-Playing, 2 vols. (Presser), The National Graded Course for Pianists, 7 vols. (Hatch) and Studies for the Left Hand (Ditson). He has also contributed often to musical periodicals, especially upon organ- and piano-playing and church-music. [R.6]

MacDOWELL, EDWARD ALEXANDER (Dec. 18, 1861, New York : Jan. 23, 1908, New York). See article in Vol. iii. 4–6. He first appeared in America as pianist with the Kneisel Quartet in Boston on Nov. 19, 1888, playing three movements of his 1st Suite and Goldmark's Quintet in B-flat. On Mar. 5, 1889, he played his 2nd Concerto with the Thomas Orchestra in New York, and also in April with Gericke and the Boston Symphony Orchestra and in July with Van der Stucken at an American concert in Paris. His 'Indian' Suite was first given on Jan. 23, 1896, by the Boston Symphony Orchestra at the Metropolitan Opera House in New York. To the list of works add the 'Prologue' and 'Epilogue' to op. 38 (as in revised edition), 'In October' as the third movement of op. 42, and the following early works, published under the pen-name 'Edgar Thorn':

op. 1 'Amourette,' for piano.
2 'In Lilting Rhythm,' for piano.
3 'Love and Time' and 'The Rose and the Gardener,' for men's chorus a cappella.
4 'Forgotten Fairy-Tales,' for piano — 'Sung outside the Prince's Door,' 'Of a Tailor and a Bear,' 'Beauty in the Rose-Garden,' 'From Dwarfland.'
5 'The Witch,' for men's chorus a cappella.
6 'War-Song,' for men's chorus a cappella.
7 Six Fancies for piano — 'A Tin Soldier's Love,' 'To a Humming-Bird,' 'Summer-Song,' 'Across Fields,' 'Bluette,' 'An Elfin Round.'
8 Waltz for piano (announced in 1895 by Breitkopf, but did not appear).

His lectures at Columbia have been edited by W. J. Baltzell as Critical and Historical Essays, 1911. Additional biographies and monographs are E. F. Page, Edward MacDowell, His Works and Ideals, 1910, T. P. Currier, 'MacDowell as I Knew Him' in 'The Musical

Quarterly,' January, 1915, O. G. Sonneck, 'MacDowell versus MacDowell' in *M.T.N.A. Proceedings*, 1911, and also in *Suum Cuique*, 1916, and Sonneck, *Catalogue of First Editions of Edward MacDowell*, 1917, besides numerous chapters and passages in historical and critical books. Regarding his 'Indian' Suite Cadman has the following passage in an article on Indian music in 'The Musical Quarterly,' July, 1915:

'I regard the 'Indian' Suite an ideal guide for those who would build upon Indian themes. MacDowell has first of all given us charming music, fascinating and well-conceived music, aside from any color or atmosphere one may discover in its measures. It is not a mere ethnological report set to music. It is a distinct art-work and every movement conveys a definite picture of Indian life. The method of idealization is not abstruse. One can quickly discern the source of the themes — they are borrowed deftly from an ethnological paper by Dr. Theodore Baker, together with some other material. In the next place, MacDowell did not over-idealize or under-idealize (if these terms may be permitted) since there is a happy balance of musical values — of atmosphere obtained, of triumph, of dignity, even of melancholy, wedded to finely conceived contrasts and dynamics. Whether Mr. MacDowell ever seriously studied the subject of Indian folk-lore or folk-music I do not know. But I do know that he has had the genius to produce a work based on good thematic material, soundly worked out and withal pleasing to every musician and music-lover. And it rings *true!* It is the best orchestral illustration extant, I think, of what may and what may not be done with Indian folk-tunes. It serves to show, too, that it is possible to write music which reflects the oddities, the characteristics of Indian rhythm and melody, and at the same time to create something that may be analyzed freely *as music.*'

Enthusiasm for MacDowell's music and reverence for his memory have expressed themselves in various ways, as in the formation of MacDowell Clubs in several places, in the MacDowell Chorus in New York (1909) and especially in the MacDowell Memorial Association, with its artistic headquarters at the MacDowell summer-home at Peterboro, N. H., and the annual festivals held there since 1910. [R.7]

MacDOWELL MEMORIAL ASSOCIATION, THE, was formed soon after Mac-Dowell's death, largely to carry out his own idea concerning his summer-home at Peterboro, N. H. To the Association Mrs. Mac-Dowell transferred the property that it should be 'a center of interest to artists working in varied fields, who, being there brought into contact, may learn to appreciate fully the fundamental unity of the separate arts.' Besides becoming a summer-colony of distinctive character, this headquarters has since 1910 been the scene of an annual festival, chiefly musical, at which a variety of works, vocal and instrumental, by different composers have been given in a forest-setting. In 1910 and '19 there was an elaborate pageant, the music by Chalmers Clifton.

MACFARLANE, WILLIAM CHARLES (Oct. 2, 1870, London, England), was the son of Duncan Macfarlane (1836–1916), who became a naturalized American citizen in 1858. He had his whole education in New York. Besides early lessons from his father, he studied organ and theory with S. P. Warren in 1886–90. He was a choir-boy at Christ Church and in 1886 appeared as concert-organist at Chickering Hall. From 1885 he held various positions as organist, notably in 1889–1900 at All Souls', in 1898–1912 at Temple Emanu-El and in 1900–12 at St. Thomas'. In 1912–19 he was municipal organist at Portland, Me., where he annually gave about 40 recitals of high quality and conducted various other musical undertakings. In 1896 he was one of the founders of the A. G. O. and in 1897 won its Clemson medal for an anthem. In 1911, '14 and '17 he also took the Kimball prize of the Chicago Madrigal Club for a cappella works. In 1918 Bates College made him Mus.D. His organ-works include a Meditation, Reverie, Spring-Song, Cradle-Song, Scotch Fantasia and Scherzo, and he has written the cantata 'The Message of the Cross' (1907), the operettas 'Little Almond-Eyes' and 'Swords and Scissors,' anthems, songs and part-songs. [R.7]

MACKAY, JOHN (d. 1841). See Register, 3.

‡ MACKENZIE, ALEXANDER CAMP-BELL (Aug. 22, 1847, Edinburgh, Scotland). See article in Vol. iii. 9–11. His work for the Royal Academy of Music, of which he has been principal since 1888, was crowned in 1912 by the erection of a magnificent building at York Gate, Marylebone Road. He was president of the International Musical Society in 1908–12, including the congresses at Vienna (1909) and London (1911), and president of the R. C. O. in 1914–16. He is an honorary member of the Accademia di S. Cecilia in Rome. To the list of works should be added

op. 68 Suite for violin and orchestra (also piano).
 69 Cantata, 'The Sun-God's Return' (1910, Cardiff, 1911, Sing-Akademie, Vienna).
 70 Fantasie for pianoforte.
 71 Four Part-Songs.
 72 Air de Ballet, 'La Savannah,' for orchestra (also piano).
 73 Three Trios for women's voices.
 74 Scottish Rhapsody No. 3, 'Tam o' Shanter' for orchestra.
 75 'An English Joy-Peal' for orchestra.
 76 'Invocation' for orchestra.
 77 'Perfection,' part-song.
 78 'The Walker of the Snow,' song for baritone.
 79 Four Songs from Tennyson.

op. 80 Four Dance-Measures for violin and piano.
    81 An English Air with variations, for piano.
    82 Ancient Scots Tunes, for strings.
    83 'Odds and Ends,' for piano.
    84 'Jottings,' 2 books, for piano.
    85 Three School Part-Songs.
    86 Six Easy Impromptus for violin.
    87 Opera, 'St. John's Eve,' in one act (1919).
— Oratorio, 'The Temptation' (1915).

MACLEAN, JOSEPH. See COLLEGES, 2 (Agnes Scott C., Ga.).

MACLENNAN, FLORENCE GER-TRUDE, née Easton (Oct. 25, 1884, Middles-brough, England), was brought to Toronto in childhood, had her general education there and at ten appeared as child-pianist. She was trained as stage-soprano at the Royal Academy in London and by Haslam in Paris, made her début in 'Madama Butterfly' in 1903 in London, in 1904–07 was touring in America with the Savage Opera Company, in 1907–15 was a leading singer at the Berlin and Hamburg Opera Houses, as well as in London, in 1915–17 was with the Chicago Opera Company and since then at the Metro-politan Opera House in New York. Rôles that she 'created' include Beatrice in Naylor's 'The Angelus' (1909), Natoya in Nevin's 'Poia' (1910), Elektra in Strauss' 'Elektra' (English première, 1910), Elisabeth in Liszt's oratorio (American première as opera, 1918), etc. Her favorite rôles are Aida, Carmen, Elsa, Sieglinde, Cio-Cio-San, Elektra and Sa-lome. In 1904 she married the tenor Fran-cis Maclennan, and they have regularly sung together. [R.9]

MACLENNAN, FRANCIS (Jan. 7, 1879, Bay City, Mich.), was developed into an em-inent operatic tenor by Dufft and Tamaro in New York, Henschel in London and Eme-rich in Berlin. In 1902 he made his début in London as Faust, in 1904–07 sang in 'Par-sifal' and 'Madama Butterfly' in the United States with the Savage Opera Company, in 1907–15 was at the Royal Opera in Berlin (the first American to sing Tristan in Germany) and the Stadt-Theater in Hamburg, in 1915–17 with the Chicago Opera Company (mostly Wagnerian rôles) and from 1917 at the Metro-politan Opera House in New York. He has a large repertory and excels in Wagner and Verdi works. In 1904 he married the soprano Florence Easton, and since then they have been constantly associated in both opera and song-recitals. [R.9]

MACMILLEN, FRANCIS (Oct. 14, 1885, Marietta, O.), was trained as violinist from childhood, having lessons from Bernhard Listemann in Chicago, in 1895–99 from Markees and Joachim in Berlin, in 1900–02 from Thomson in Brussels, where he took two prizes, and then from Flesch and Auer in Petrograd. In 1903 he made appearances in Brussels and London and in 1906 with the New York Symphony Society. Since then he has made five notable tours in the United States, but in 1911–14 was in Europe. Every-where he has played with the leading orches-tras and has given many recitals. For the violin he has written a Barcarolle, a 'Sérénade Nègre,' 'Causerie,' 'Liebeslied,' 'Nijinsky' and other pieces, besides arrangements (all Carl Fischer). [R.9]

‡ MACPHERSON, CHARLES (May 10, 1870, Edinburgh, Scotland). See article in Vol. iii. 11–2. In 1916, after Martin's death, he was advanced to be organist at St. Paul's. In 1914 he was conductor of the London Church Choir Association. He is a fellow of the R. A. M. and the R. C. O. Among recent works are an 'Overture on Jacobite Airs,' a 'Fantasy on Scotch Tunes,' some organ-pieces, much church-music and part-songs.

MADEIRA, LOUIS CEPHAS. See Regis-ter, 4.

'MADELEINE.' An opera in one act by Victor Herbert on a text adapted from the French by Grant Stewart. It was first pro-duced at the Metropolitan Opera House in New York on Jan. 24, 1914, and three times repeated.

MADISON CHORAL UNION, THE, of Madison, Wis., was founded in 1893, largely through the efforts of President Charles K. Adams of the University of Wisconsin, with a desire to unite musical interests in the Univer-sity and the city. The conductors have been Fletcher A. Parker in 1893–1907, Rossetter G. Cole in 1907–09, Elias A. Bredin in 1909–10, Louis A. Coerne in 1910–15, Peter W. Dykema in 1915–18, and Irving W. Jones since 1918. The membership has ranged from 75 to 300, with an average of perhaps 150. Two concerts are usually given each year, with additional ones in years when a festival has been held. The University provides the conductor and place of rehearsal. The Union has lately made a feature of Yule-tide Festivals with emphasis upon the 'community' spirit.

MAERZ, JOSEPH (b. 1883). See COL-LEGES, 2 (Wesleyan Female C., Ga.).

‡ MAGNARD, LUCIEN DENIS GABRI-EL ALBÉRIC (June 9, 1865, Paris, France : Sept. 3, 1914, Baron, France). See article in Vol. iii. 23. To the list of works add the opera 'Bérénice' (1911, Opera-Comique, libretto by the composer) and a sonata for 'cello and piano (1910). According to Ernest Daudet (Chron-icles of 1915 and 1916), he was killed while de-fending his home from the depredations of a troop of German soldiers. A number of manu-scripts including the opera 'Guercœur,' are said to have been carried away by the latter.

MAGNUSSON, OSCAR MAGNUS. See COLLEGES, 3 (Upsala C., N. J.).

MAGUENAT, ALFRED. See Register, 10.

MAGUIRE, J. FRANCIS. See COLLEGES, 3 (Northwestern C., Ill.).

MAHLER, GUSTAV (July 7, 1860, Kalischt, Bohemia : May 11, 1911, Vienna). See articles in Vols. iii. 27–8, and v. 652. In New York he first conducted at the Metropolitan Opera House on Jan. 1, 1908, the opera being 'Tristan,' and in November and December he led the Symphony Society three times, producing at the second his 2nd Symphony. The operas given under him were various Wagnerian works, 'Don Giovanni,' 'Le Nozze di Figaro,' 'Fidelio,' 'The Bartered Bride' and 'Pique Dame' (the last two being American premières). His reorganization of the Philharmonic Society in 1909–11 was thorough and effective, but interrupted at the end by ill-health. His sudden death was from heart-trouble, complicated by pneumonia.

His 8th Symphony (first given in 1910 at the Munich Exposition under the composer) was produced in 1916 in Philadelphia under Stokowski, who conducted from memory, with an orchestra of 110, eight soloists, a divided chorus of 800 and a children's chorus of 150. It was thrice repeated there and also at the Metropolitan Opera House in New York. In 1917 it was given in Chicago under Stock with still larger forces. The 9th Symphony was first performed in 1912 at the Vienna Festival under Bruno Walter, and also given in 1913 by the Berlin Philharmonie under Oskar Fried. It was not fully completed or at least revised by the composer. In his will he is said to have directed that all material for the 10th Symphony should be destroyed. The list of his works is as follows:

For orchestra and chorus —
'Das klagende Lied,' for soprano, alto and tenor, chorus and orchestra.
Symphony No. 1, in D (1891).
Symphony No. 2, in C minor — with alto and chorus (1895).
Symphony No. 3, in D minor — with alto, women's and boys' choruses (1896).
Symphony No. 4, in G — with soprano (1901).
Symphony No. 5, in C-sharp minor (1904).
Symphony No. 6, in A minor (1906).
Symphony No. 7, in E minor (1908).
Symphony No. 8, in E-flat — with seven soloists, two choruses and boys' chorus (1910).
'Das Lied von der Erde,' for tenor and alto (or baritone) and orchestra.
Symphony No. 9, in D (1912).
For voice and orchestra —
'Des Knaben Wunderhorn' — 'Der Schildwache Nachtlied,' 'Verlorne Müh',' 'Trost im Ungluck,' 'Wer hat dies Liedlein erdacht,' 'Das irdische Leben,' 'Des Antonius von Padua Fischpredigt,' 'Rheinlegendchen,' 'Lied des Verfolgten im Turme,' 'Wo die schönen Trompeten blasen,' 'Lob des hohen Verstandes,' 'Es sungen drei Engel einen süssen Gesang,' 'Urlicht' (alto solo from 2nd Symphony); also 'Revelge,' 'Der Tambourg'sell.'

'Lieder eines fahrenden Gesellen' (words by composer) — 'Wenn mein Schatz Hochzeit macht,' 'Ging heut' Morgen über's Feld,' 'Ich hab' ein glühend Messer,' 'Die zwei blauen Augen von meinem Schatz.'
'Kindertotenlieder' (Rückert) — 'Nun will die Sonn' so hell aufgeh'n,' 'Nun seh' ich wohl, warum so dunkle Flammen,' 'Wenn dein Mütterlein,' 'Oft denk' ich, sie sind nur ausgegangen,' 'In diesem Wetter.'
'Five Lyrics' (Rückert) — 'Blicke mir nicht in die Lieder,' 'Ich atmet' einen linden Duft.' 'Ich bin der Welt abhanden gekommen,' 'Liebst du um Schönheit,' 'Um Mitternacht.'
For voice and piano — (all Schott)
'Frühlingsmorgen' and 'Erinnerung,' from R. Leander.
'Hans und Grete,' folk-song.
Serenade and Phantasie from Tirso de Molina's 'Don Juan.'
'Des Knaben Wunderhorn' — 'Um schlimme Kinder artig zu machen,' 'Ich ging mit Lust durch einen grünen Wald,' 'Aus! Aus!,' 'Starke Einbildungskraft,' 'Zu Strassburg auf der Schanz,' 'Ablösung im Sommer,' 'Scheiden und Meiden,' 'Nicht wiedersehen!' 'Selbstgefühl.'
Arrangements —
Weber's 'Die drei Pintos' (Kahnt).
Mozart's 'Die Hochzeit des Figaro' (Peters).
Suite from Bach's orchestral works, with continuo filled out (Schirmer).

Biographies have appeared by Schiedermair, 1900, Specht, 1905 (small), Stefan, 1908 and 1910–12 (in English, 1913), and Specht, 1913, besides numerous articles, etc. [R.9]

MAHR, EMIL (1851–1914). See Register, 7.

MAIN, HUBERT PLATT (b. 1839). See Register, 5.

MAITLAND, ROBERT GILLIES (b. 1875). See Register, 10.

MAITLAND, ROLLO FRANCIS (b. 1884). See Register, 9.

MALCHEREK, KARL AUGUST (b. 1873). See Register, 8.

MALLET, FRANCIS. See Register, 2.

'MAN IN THE FOREST, THE.' The first of the 'Grove-Plays' of the San Francisco Bohemian Club, produced in 1902. The text is by Charles K. Field and the music by Joseph D. Redding.

MANCHESTER, ARTHUR LIVINGSTON (Feb. 9, 1862, Bass River, N. J.), had his training in piano, organ and theory with Zeckwer and in voice with Gilchrist, Bussmann and Tubbs. Beginning as organist at thirteen, after 1882 he has held a series of positions as head of music-schools — in 1882–86 at the Beaver (Pa.) Musical Institute, in 1886–93 first at the State Normal School at Clarion, Pa., and then at Martha Washington College in Virginia, in 1904–13 at Converse College in Spartanburg, S. C., in 1913–18 at Southwestern University in Georgetown, Tex., and since 1918 at Hardin College in Mexico, Mo. In 1893–96 he was associate-editor of 'The Etude' in Philadelphia and in 1896–1902 editor of 'The Musician' in Boston. In

1900–02 he was president of the M. T. N. A. and active in extending its range and influence, in 1900–04 also editing 'The Messenger' as its official organ. While at Spartanburg he was conductor of the choral society and of the annual festivals. At intervals he has appeared in song- and lecture-recitals, often with emphasis upon the work of Franz. He has always been interested in whatever pertains to community-music, and prominent in discussions of music-education in schools and colleges. He published *Twelve Lessons on the Fundamentals of Voice-Production* (Ditson), and edited for the Bureau of Education a bulletin on *Music-Education in the United States*, 1908. [R.7]

MANHATTAN OPERA HOUSE, THE, was built by Oscar Hammerstein in 1906 on West 34th Street, New York, as a rival of the Metropolitan Opera House, and was managed by him for four seasons, 1906–10.[1]

The venture was audacious and picturesque, differing from its competitor in that it lacked the organized support of society leaders, that it eschewed German and that it devoted itself either to well-known popular favorites or to novelties of the French school. Musically, the marked feature for the first three seasons was the enthusiasm and genius of Cleofonte Campanini, who was both musical manager and conductor, being followed in 1909 by Enriquez de la Fuente. From the start Hammerstein was fortunate in securing many important artists, like the tenor Bonci, the bass Renaud, the soprano Bressler-Gianoli, and for a time both Melba and Calvé. In the second season he introduced Mary Garden and Tetrazzini, besides a long list of others. The smaller size of the auditorium as compared with the Metropolitan, and the exceptional perfection of the ensemble, made many of the performances extremely effective.

The novelties introduced were 'Thais' (Nov. 24, 1907), 'Louise' (Jan. 3, 1908), 'Siberia' (Feb. 6, 1908) 'Pelléas et Mélisande' (Feb. 19, 1908), 'Le Jongleur de Notre-Dame' (Nov. 27, 1908), 'La Princesse d'Auberge' (Mar. 10, 1909), 'Hérodiade' (Nov. 8, 1909), 'Sapho' (Nov. 17, 1909), 'Grisélidis' (Jan. 19, 1910) and 'Elektra' (Feb. 1, 1910), besides several interesting revivals of works not recently given.

In 1908 Hammerstein broadened his field by erecting the fine Philadelphia Opera House, but in 1910 he sold out to a syndicate friendly to the Metropolitan interest, agreeing not to undertake grand opera in New York for ten years.

[1] In 1893 Hammerstein used the same name for another house, also on 34th Street and built for the same purpose, which he sold precipitately after but a fortnight's experiment.

The record of the Manhattan, as given by Krehbiel (*Chapters of Opera*, pp. 426–7), is as follows:

	'06-07	'07-08	'08-09	'09-10
Auber — Fra Diavolo	4			
Audran — Mascotte				1
Bellini — Sonnambula	3		3	
Puritani	2		2	
Berlioz — Damnation of Faust		3		
Bizet — Carmen	19	11	2	6
Blockx — Princesse d'Auberge			3	
Charpentier — Louise		11	5	2
Debussy — Pelléas et Mélisande		7	4	3
Delibes — Lakmé				1
Donizetti — Elisir d'Amore	3			
Lucia	6	8	7	7
Fille du Régiment				2
Flotow — Martha	4			
Giordano — Andrea Chénier		1		
Siberia		3		
Gounod — Faust	7	4		3
Lecocq — Fille de Mme. Angot				2
Leoncavallo — Pagliacci	10	9	5	8
Maillart — Dragons des Villars				2
Mascagni — Cavalleria	8	4	3	4
Massenet — Hérodiade				6
Thaïs		7	7	6
Navarraise	2	5	1	2
Sapho				3
Grisélidis				4
Jongleur de Notre-Dame			7	5
Meyerbeer — Huguenots	5		2	
Dinorah	1	1		
Mozart — Don Giovanni	4	3		
Offenbach — Contes d'Hoffmann		11	7	8
Planquette — Cloches de Corneville				3
Ponchielli — Gioconda		4		
Puccini — Bohème	4		5	5
Tosca			5	3
Ricci brothers — Crispino e la Comare		3	3	
Rossini — Barbiere	2		3	
Saint-Saëns — Samson et Dalila			6	2
Strauss — Salome			10	4
Elektra				7
Thomas — Mignon	3			
Verdi — Ernani			1	4
Rigoletto	11	5	5	
Trovatore	6	5	1	4
Traviata	3	5	5	2
Ballo in Maschera	2	4		
Aida	12	9	2	3
Otello			6	
Wagner — Tannhäuser				3

MANN, ELIAS (1750–1825). See TUNE-BOOKS, 1778.

MANNES, CLARA, née Damrosch (b. 1869). See Register, 7, and following article.

MANNES, DAVID (Feb. 16, 1866, New York), after early education in the public schools, studied violin with Carl Richter, John Douglas and others, with summers in Europe, in 1891 with De Ahna in Berlin, in 1892–3 with Halir in Berlin and in 1903 with Ysaÿe in Brussels. From 1891 he was a first violinist in the Symphony Society and in 1898–1912 its concertmaster. In 1904 he founded the Symphony Club of New York, which he still conducts. From 1902 he was head of the violin-department in the Music Settlement School and its director in 1910–15. In 1912 he founded, on similar lines, the Music School Settlement for Colored People. Since 1916 he and his wife, née Clara Damrosch, have conducted the David Mannes Music School. With her he has since 1900 given many striking sonata-recitals, not only in New York, but in other large cities and (in 1913) in London. In recent years he has been director of the concerts at the Metropolitan Museum of Art. [R.7]

MANNEY, CHARLES FONTEYN (Feb. 8, 1872, Brooklyn), had his general education at the Brooklyn Polytechnic Institute and studied music in New York and Boston with W. A. Fisher, Wallace Goodrich and Goetschius. Since 1898 he has been associate-editor for the Ditson Company in Boston and conductor of the Footlight Orchestra. He has made a name as composer of over 50 graceful and individual songs (Ditson, Schirmer, Schmidt), the song-cycle 'A Shropshire Lad' (Ditson), the cantatas 'The Manger-Throne' and 'The Resurrection' (both Ditson), about 15 anthems, several carols, secular chorus (Ditson), piano-pieces (Ditson), etc. He has also edited *Folk-Songs and Other Songs for Children*, and made translations from French and German. [R.8]

MANNING, EDWARD BETTS (b. 1874). See Register, 8.

MANOLY, LUDWIG EMANUEL (b. 1855). See Register, 6.

'MANRU'. An opera by Ignace Jan Paderewski on a libretto made by Dr. Nossig from a Polish romance. It was first produced at Dresden in 1901 and repeated in other European cities. Its American première was on Feb. 14, 1902, at the Metropolitan Opera House, under the direction of Walter Damrosch, and it was twice repeated.

MANSFIELD, BELLE A. See COLLEGES, 3 (DePauw U., Ind.).

MANSFIELD, DANIEL H. (1810– ?). See TUNE-BOOKS, 1849.

MANSFIELD, ORLANDO AUGUSTINE (Nov. 28, 1863, Horningsham, England), graduated from Trinity College in London in 1885 and from the London College of Music in 1890. He was organist in Torquay at Holy Trinity in 1885–95 and at Belgrave Church in 1900–12. In 1892–1912 he was examiner at the London College of Music. Since 1912 he has been in America, till 1918 at Wilson College, Chambersburg, Pa., and in 1918–20 at Brenau College, Gainesville, Ga. He is a fellow of the R. C. O. and the A. G. O. and has given many organ-recitals in England and America. He has been twice made Mus.D. in Toronto, in 1890 by Trinity University, and in 1905 by Toronto University. He has published about 400 compositions and arrangements (including

30 prize-works) for piano, organ, choir or chorus. Among the latest are a set of Concert-Variations for organ and a part-song and anthems for women's voices. Unpublished are two cantatas, many organ-arrangements and a text-book on the rudiments. He has edited over 50 collections of piano- and church-music, and compiled *The Student's Harmony*, 4 vols., 1896 (10th edition, 1912). He has long been an effective writer of magazine-articles — over 500 — for musical periodicals on both sides of the ocean. [R.10]

MANUSCRIPT MUSIC SOCIETY, THE, of Philadelphia, was founded in 1892, W. W. Gilchrist being president and P. H. Goepp secretary. It has gathered into close fellowship the composers of the city, has maintained monthly meetings with performances of original works, has arranged public concerts in conjunction with the Philadelphia Orchestra and the principal choral societies, and from time to time has stimulated composition by offering prizes for choral and chamber-works. Nicholas Douty is now president.

MANUSCRIPT SOCIETY, THE, of New York. See Vol. iii. 372. This and the foregoing are examples of a class of associations existing in one form or another in several cities, often effective in many ways. That in Chicago was founded in 1896, F. G. Gleason being its first president.

MAPLESON, JAMES HENRY (1829?–1901). See Vol. iii. 44, and Register, 6.

MARCEL, LUCILLE (b. 1887?). See Register, 9.

MARCOSSON, SOL (b. 1869). See Register, 7.

MARCOUX, VANNI (b. 1879). See Register, 10.

MARETZEK, MAX (1821–1897). See Register, 4.

MARGULIES, ADELE (Mar. 7, 1863, Vienna, Austria), began piano-study at ten, continued under Door and Grädener at the Vienna Conservatory, taking first prize three years in succession, and made her début in 1879. In 1881 she came to New York, appearing at once in recital and early in 1883 with the Thomas Orchestra. Since then she has played with the Boston Symphony Orchestra and other orchestras and often in recital. In 1885 at a 'Novelty Concert' under Van der Stucken she introduced the second and third movements of MacDowell's 1st Concerto. In 1890–92 she formed the Margulies Trio with Lichtenberg and Herbert, and in 1904 this was revived in more permanent form with Lichtenberg and Schulz (Schroeder after 1915). This organization has introduced in America many chamber-works by Korngold, Juon, Reger, Georg Schumann and others, and is counted one of the best. Since 1887 she has also been chief piano-teacher at the National Conservatory. [R.7]

MARINE BAND, THE. The military band belonging to the U. S. Marine Corps, with headquarters at Washington and for that reason more or less associated with the National Government and traditionally regarded as its official musical organization.

The Marine Corps was established in 1798 and from the start had a fife-and-drum corps of 32 players. In 1802 this was transformed into a brass-band, which is known to have officiated on occasion outside the regular military routine, though the records were destroyed in the War of 1812. Beginning with 1854 the giving of open-air concerts at the Capitol or the White House became an established custom, and congressional action followed, increasing the Band's compensation and finally, in 1861, designating it as the chief band in the service. Up to this time the number of players had been 30. In 1898 it was officially increased to 60 (now 65). The leader was then given the pay of first lieutenant in the Corps, which in 1916 was changed to that of captain. A full list of the leaders is not available, especially as in earlier years different members alternated in the duty. In 1824–30 the leader was John Lewis Clubb, in 1830 Entius Friquet, in 1830–41 Francis Schenig, in 1841–42 Joseph Curveltier, in 1842–43 and again in 1848–54 Antonio Pons, in 1843–48 and again in 1854–71 Francis Scala, in 1871–73 Henry Fries, in 1873–80 Louis Schneider, in 1880–92 John Philip Sousa, in 1892–97 Francesco Fanciulli, and since 1898 William H. Santelmann. For at least fifty years, probably more, the Band has ranked as one of the best, if not the best, in the country. It has regularly officiated at functions of national importance at Washington and occasionally has appeared elsewhere, especially at the great Expositions, and has made concert-tours.

MARKS, JAMES CHRISTOPHER, Jr. (b. 1863). See Register, 9.

MARQUETTE UNIVERSITY, Milwaukee, Wis. (Roman Catholic), since 1911 has maintained a Conservatory of Music as one of its constituent schools. Its work is arranged under four heads: Preparatory Department (for children), Grade-school Course, in eight grades (as in a public school), Academic Course, usually requiring two years after completing the Grade-School Course, leading either to a Teacher's Certificate or to a Diploma, and Collegiate Course of two years, leading to a Mus.B. or to an Artist's Diploma. Unusually full opportunities are provided for mastery of band and orchestral instruments and for operatic experience (two works given annually in complete detail). The faculty numbers about 35. Liborius Semmann has been its only director.

MARSH, CHARLES HOWARD. See Colleges, 3 (U. of Redlands, Cal.).

MARSHALL, Mr. and Mrs. See Register, 2.

MARSHALL, CHARLES. See Colleges, 1 (U. of Notre Dame, Ind.).

MARSHALL, ELVIS COLLETT (b. 1865). See Colleges, 3 (Southwestern C., Kan.).

MARSHALL, JOHN PATTON (Jan. 9, 1877, Rockport, Mass.), from 1895 studied in Boston with Lang, Chadwick, MacDowell, Norris and Goodrich. In 1896–1905 he was organist at St. John's and since 1909 has been at the First (Unitarian) Church. In 1902–12 he taught at the Middlesex School in Concord, Mass., and since 1902 has been head of the music-department in Boston University. Since 1909 he has also been organist of the Boston Symphony Orchestra. In 1908–11 he lectured at the Harvard Summer School and since 1911 has been on the staff of the Massachusetts University Extension. He is also on the advisory board of the Boston public schools. He has published a *Syllabus of the History of Music*, 1906, and a *Syllabus of Music-Appreciation*, 1911, and has written piano-pieces and songs. During the war he was much engaged in promoting music in training-camps. [R.8]

MARSHALL, LEONARD. See Tune-Books, 1849.

MARSTON, GEORGE W. (1840–1901). See Register, 5.

‡ MARTEAU, HENRI (Mar. 31, 1874, Rheims, France). See article in Vol. iii. 65. His American tours were in 1892, '93, '94, '98 and 1906. In 1908 he resigned at the Geneva Conservatory to succeed Joachim at the Berlin Hochschule. As reserve-officer of the French army he was interned at the outbreak of the war. After his connection with the Hochschule was terminated on Oct. 1, 1915, he was allowed to leave the detention-camp, but compelled to remain in Germany. After the war he returned to Geneva. To the list of works add a concerto for violin (in suite-form), op. 15; a concerto for 'cello, op. 7; string-quartets in D-flat, op. 5, and D, op. 9; a string-trio in F, op. 12; a quintet for clarinet and strings, op. 13; 8 songs with string-quartet, op. 10; and smaller instrumental pieces.

MARTENS, FREDERICK HERMAN (July 6, 1874, New York), is a grandnephew of Karl P. Grädener, the Hamburg composer. He was trained under private tutors, especially in history and languages, and studied theory with Spicker, piano with H. C. Timm and William Barber in New York. Since 1907 he has been constantly active in literary work, contributing articles to leading musical journals, including the London 'Musical Record,' writing texts for operettas and cantatas and verses for songs, and translating texts in various languages. He is librettist of Page's 'The Contest of the Nations' and 'Old Plantation-Days,' Macfarlane's 'Little Almond-Eyes,' 'Swords and Scissors' and 'America, First,' Lester's 'The Frog-Prince,' 'Ballad of the Golden Sun,' 'Thyre the Fair,' etc., Dunn's 'The Phantom-Drum,' Bornschein's 'Zorah,' 'Onowa' and 'The Maypole of Merrymount,' James' 'Spring in Vienna,' etc. His verses have been set as songs by Cadman, Spross, Kramer, Speaks, Ornstein, Yamada and others. In 1914–17 he was one of the contributing editors of The Art of Music. He has also published Leo Ornstein: the Man, his Ideas, his Work, 1917, and Violin-Mastery, 1918. [R.9]

MARTIN, AUBREY WILLIS (b. 1879). See STATE UNIVERSITIES (Miami U., Ohio).

‡ MARTIN, GEORGE CLEMENT (Sept. 11, 1844, Lambourn, England : Feb. 23, 1916, London.) See article in Vol. iii. 65. He remained organist at St. Paul's till his death. A tablet commemorating his forty-two years' distinguished service was unveiled in the crypt on Oct. 31, 1917. In 1912 Oxford University conferred an honorary Mus.D. upon him. A full list of his works is given in 'The Musical Times,' April, 1916. It includes 20 services (complete or partial), 22 anthems (both services and anthems often with orchestra), 21 hymn-tunes, 5 carols, a collection of 84 tunes and carols, some secular songs and part-songs, editions of church-music by other composers, and the manual The Art of Training Choir-Boys.

MARTIN, RICCARDO [Christian name originally Hugh Whitfield] (Nov. 18, 1881, Hopkinsville, Ky.), encountered strong family opposition to musical aspirations, but began violin in Nashville, harmony with Irrgang in Berlin and singing with Carelli in Naples, and in 1896–1900 was under MacDowell in composition in New York. From this period date several songs (Ditson, Schirmer, Hamelle), men's choruses (Schirmer) and some choral and orchestral works. In 1901 he was enabled by H. H. Flagler to study for the opera-stage in Paris under Sbriglia, M. and Mme. Escalaïs and Jean de Reszké, developing into an effective tenor. His début as Faust was in 1904 at Nantes (the manager then affixing a stage-name that he has felt obliged to retain). He also sang in Verona and Milan in 1905–06, and in 1906 appeared in New Orleans and toured with the Henry Russell company. In 1907–15 he was regularly engaged at the Metropolitan Opera House, appearing first in 'Mefistofele' and later creating (for that stage) the tenor rôles in 'La Wally,' 'The Pipe of Desire,' 'Mona' and 'Cyrano de Bergerac,' and in Philadelphia with the Chicago Opera Company in 'The Cricket on the Hearth.' In 1910–11 he also sang at Covent Garden in London, appearing

first in 'Madama Butterfly,' and in 1910 was at the Teatro Arbeu in Mexico City. In 1916–17 he toured with the Boston Grand Opera Company. His favorite rôles are Enzo (in 'La Gioconda'), Manrico, Rodolfo, Avito (in 'L'Amore dei Tre Rè'), Cavaradossi and Pinkerton. He was the first American to sing the latter at the Metropolitan and at Covent Garden. [R.9]

MARTINELLI, GIOVANNI (b. 1885). See Register, 10.

MARTUCCI, PAOLO (b. 1885). See Register, 10.

MARYOTT, HAROLD BURNHAM (b. 1878). See Register, 9.

MARZO, EDUARDO (Nov. 29, 1852, Naples, Italy), came to America in 1867 as a boy-pianist, having then studied with Nacciarone and Miceli, but went back for composition-lessons under Pappalardo. From 1869 he traveled widely as musical director for troupes and accompanist for soloists, being associated with Carlotta Patti, Mario, Miss Cary, Ilma de Murska, Sauret, Tietjens, Sarasate and many others. Since 1878 he has worked in New York as vocal teacher, organist and composer. At present he is organist at the Church of the Holy Name and teaches in colleges at Mount St. Vincent and in New Rochelle. Since 1884 he has received distinguished decorations, royal and ecclesiastical, from Italy. In 1896 he was a founder of the A. G. O. His published works include 9 masses, 4 vespers, 40 songs and anthems for the Roman Catholic service; 3 Te Deums, 40 anthems and 35 solos for the Protestant service; a sacred cantata for chorus and orchestra; 6 operettas and cantatas for women's voices; about 40 part-songs for women's voices and about 40 secular songs. He has also edited many masses and motets (Schirmer, Ditson), several collections of Italian folk-songs, and The Art of Vocalization, 24 vols. In manuscript he has a setting of the Penitential Psalms, an orchestral prelude, preludes and fugues for string-quartet, etc. On Nov. 17, 1917, his friends gave him a banquet at the Waldorf-Astoria in celebration of his fiftieth year of activity in America. [R.5]

‡ MASCAGNI, PIETRO (Dec. 7, 1863, Leghorn, Italy). See article in Vol. iii. 71–2. In 1902 he made a brief and singularly ill-advised visit to the United States, conducting two or three of his works (including 'Iris') in New York, Boston, etc. In 1911 he made a trip to South America, which was more fortunate. To the list of operas add 'Isabeau' (1911, Buenos Aires, 1917, Chicago), 'Parisina' (1913, Milan), 'Lodoletta' (1917, Rome, 1918, New York), and one or two lesser works. He has written a 'Rapsodia Satanica' to accompany a cinema-film (1917, the Augusteo, Rome). See

biographies by Monaldi, 1899, Marvin, 1904, Bastianelli, 1910, and Pompei, 1912.

MASON, DANIEL GREGORY (1820–1869). See Register, 4.

MASON, DANIEL GREGORY (Nov. 20, 1873, Brookline, Mass.), is a son of Henry Mason (see below) and grandson of Lowell Mason. He graduated from Harvard in 1895. His teachers in music at various times were Johns, Ethelbert Nevin, Paine, Arthur Whiting, Chadwick and Goetschius in Boston or New York and d'Indy in Paris. Since about 1900 he has been increasingly prominent in New York as a skillful teacher, lecturer, critic and author, besides much notable composition. After lecturing at the Normal College in New York, for the American University Extension Society and at Teachers College, since 1910 he has been on the staff of Columbia University as assistant- or associate-professor. His activity as lecturer has extended to many other institutions, like the Brooklyn Academy of Arts and Sciences, the Institute of Musical Art, the American Institute of Applied Music, Smith College in Massachusetts, etc. For the Board of Education he has given over 250 popular lectures. His compositions are as follows:

'Birthday Waltzes,' op. 1, for piano.
'Elegy,' op. 2, for piano (Metzler).
Romance and Impromptu, op. 3, for piano (Church).
Four Songs, op. 4, for soprano, texts by Mary L. Mason (Church).
Sonata in G minor, op. 5, for violin and piano (Schirmer).
Variations on 'Yankee Doodle,' in the styles of various composers (Breitkopf).
Quartet in A, op. 7, for piano and strings (Schirmer).
Pastorale, op. 8, for piano, violin and clarinet (Mathot).
'Country-Pictures,' op. 9, for piano (Breitkopf).
Passacaglia and Fugue, op. 10, for organ (Gray).
Symphony in C minor, op. 11 (1916, Philadelphia Orchestra).
Music for 'The Pageant of Cape Cod,' op. 12 (1914, Bourne, Mass.).
Two Pieces for violin and piano, op. 13.
Sonata, op. 14, for clarinet and piano.
'Love-Songs,' op. 15, a cycle for soprano, texts by Mary L. Mason (Schirmer).
Impromptu and Ballade, op. 16, for piano (Impromptu, Ditson).
Intermezzo, op. 17, for string-quartet (1918, Flonzaley Quartet).
'Russians,' op. 18, song-cycle for baritone and orchestra, texts by Witter Bynner.
Quartet on Negro themes, op. 19, for strings.

He has also been a prolific and forceful author, his books including From Grieg to Brahms, 1902, Beethoven and his Forerunners, 1904, The Romantic Composers, 1906, The Appreciation of Music (with T. W. Surette) 1907, The Orchestral Instruments and What They Do, 1908, A Guide to Music, 1909 (two editions), A Neglected Sense in Piano-Playing, 1912, Great Modern Composers (with Mary L. Mason), 1916,

Short Studies of Great Masterpieces, 1918, and Contemporary Composers, 1918. His most conspicuous editorial work was The Art of Music, 14 vols. 1914–17, of which he was editor-in-chief. [R.9]

MASON, EDITH BARNES (b. 1892). See Register, 10.

MASON, EDWARD YOUNG (b. 1871). See COLLEGES, 3 (Illinois Wesleyan U. and Ohio Wesleyan U.).

MASON, HENRY (1831–1890). See Register, 4.

MASON, HENRY LOWELL (b. 1864). See Register, 7.

MASON, LOWELL (Jan. 8, 1792, Medfield, Mass. : Aug. 11, 1872, Orange, N. J.). See article in Vol. iii. 74. During his life in Savannah he was active first in the Independent Presbyterian Church and in 1827 a founder of the First Presbyterian Church.[1] In 1818 he and F. L. Abel, who taught him harmony, began making a collection of choral music, which he took to Boston in search of a publisher. It was partly due to the interest of G. K. Jackson that the work was finally taken up by the Handel and Haydn Society. Their failure to give Mason credit as compiler is surprising. The net proceeds of the venture were about $12,000 for the Society and the same for Mason — a fortunate wind-fall for both parties. The book's prestige and the fame of his choir in Savannah led to his being called in 1827 to be choir-master for three Boston churches. Of these the chief was that in Bowdoin Street, where Dr. Lyman Beecher was pastor, and here Mason soon concentrated his efforts as organist. In 1827–32 he was president and conductor of the Handel and Haydn Society, which he brought to a new standard of efficiency, though without undertaking any new work of signal importance.

His interest in Pestalozzi was aroused by books brought in 1829 from Europe by W. C. Woodbridge, who joined him in the effort to prove by classes the value of the system for the public schools. The Academy of Music, organized in 1833 (under the chairmanship of Samuel Eliot, mayor of the city, father of President Eliot of Harvard), was an immediate success (1500 pupils the first year), so that G. J. Webb was soon called in as assistant. The issue of Mason's Manual for Instruction, 1834, with its emphasis upon 'the thing before the sign,' led at once to the formation of normal classes and these, under the leadership of Mason and Webb, in turn started the movement for musical 'conventions' which soon spread beyond New England into New York, Ohio

[1] At that time the distinction between 'Congregational' and 'Presbyterian' in the naming of churches was only just establishing itself. The Independent Church was originally the former rather than the latter.

and further west. It was not till 1837 that
the authorities yielded to the pressure to introduce music into the public schools, and even
then made no appropriation for it, so that the
first year Mason not only served without salary,
but supplied all books and materials. He
remained in charge till 1841, being succeeded
by B. F. Baker. During his trip abroad in
1837 he heard the first English performance
of Mendelssohn's 'St. Paul' at Birmingham,
a rendering of 'Fidelio' in English (with Schroe-
der-Devrient) and innumerable concerts. At
Zurich he visited Pestalozzi, Nägeli and others.
On his second European trip, in 1853–54, he
remained about eighteen months. He was
now recognized as an authority and lectured
frequently on congregational singing and music-
education. His *Letters*, 1853, belong to this
trip. See also ACADEMY OF MUSIC (Boston),
CONVENTIONS, and PUBLIC SCHOOLS.

After 1854 he lived at Orange, N. J., where
his third son, William Mason, was then teaching. He had accumulated a considerable library, increased in 1852 by the purchase of the
collection of the famous organist Rinck. After
his death the library was given by the family
to Yale University. His degree of Mus.D.
was not absolutely the first in America (see
DEGREES), but certainly the first of distinction.

His remarkable power as leader and organizer
was due to a variety of characteristics. He
had keenness of intellect, patience of investigation and ability to marshal and impart information. His enthusiasm was ardent in
everything pertaining to the application of
music as an art to popular education and to the
exercises of social religion. He was eminently
magnetic as a leader or teacher of classes and
choirs, but strict in discipline and always serious
in purpose. His instinct was that of a true
educator, whose object lies outside himself,
rather than of the self-conscious artist. He
deliberately confined himself to those forms
of effort that he believed most important and
promising for the conditions of the period.
Even so, he was somewhat ahead of the age.
Yet so pervasive was his influence that he lived
to the verge of a new period, when much that
he did was lightly esteemed because rudimentary. See the more or less senseless treatment
of the subject in Ritter, *Music in America*.

There is no adequate biography as yet, but
one is being completed by his grandson, Henry
L. Mason, of Boston, who has kindly supplied
many details for this notice.

He was a fertile composer of hymn-tunes
and arranged many from various sources.
Those that continued popular longest are
usually known by the following names:

'Anvern'	'Boylston'	'Dort'
'Azmon'	'Cowper'	'Downs'
'Bethany'	'Danvers'	'Ernan'

'Fountain'	'Malvern'	'Sabbath'
'Haddam'	'Meribah'	'To-Day'
'Hamburg'	'Migdol'	'Uxbridge'
'Harwell'	'Missionary	'Ward'
'Hebron'	Hymn'	'Watchman'
'Henley'	'Naomi'	'Wesley'
'Hermon'	'Olivet'	'Work-Song'
'Inverness'	'Olmutz'	'Zebulon'
'Laban'	'Olney'	'Zerah'
'Litchfield'	'Rockingham'

It is not always realized that the technical
form of these, especially in their original rhythmic disposition, presents some historic interest apart from their deliberate simplicity.
For titles of his books in this field see TUNE-
BOOKS and HYMN-BOOKS.

He was the pioneer in song-books for juvenile
use, both sacred and secular, including many
devised specially for public schools. The full
list of these should be on record:

The Juvenile Psalmist, 1829 — believed by him
the first book with music for Sunday-Schools, *The
Juvenile Lyre*, 1830 — the first American school
song-book, *The Juvenile Singing-School*, 1835, *Sabbath-
School Songs*, 1836, *The Sabbath-School Harp*, 1837, *The
Juvenile Songster*, 1837 (London), *Juvenile Music
for Sunday-Schools*, 1839, *The Boston School Song-
Book*, 1840, *Little Songs for Little Singers*, 1840, *The
American Sabbath-School Singing-Book*, 1843, *Song-
Book of the School-Room*, 1845, *The Primary School
Song-Book*, 1846, *The Normal Singer*, 1856, *The
Song-Garden*, 3 parts, 1864–65 — with the *Manual
for Instruction of the Boston Academy in the Elements
of Vocal Music*, 1834.

To these may be added the part-song collections,
The Odeon, 1837, *The Boston Glee-Book*, 1838, *The
Lyrist*, 1838, *The Gentlemen's Glee-Book*, 1841, *21
Madrigals, Glees and Part-Songs*, 1843, *The Vocalist*,
1844, *The Glee-Hive*, 1851. At one point material
was incorporated in the periodical 'The Musical
Library,' 1834–35 (with Webb). [R.3]

MASON, LOWELL, JR. (1823–1885). See
Register, 4.

MASON, LUTHER WHITING (Apr. 3,
1828, Turner, Me. : July 14, 1896, Buckfield, Me.), was not related to the Lowell Mason
family. Though mainly self-taught in music,
he got his school-education by teaching it. He
was all his life engaged in public-school music,
from 1853 in Louisville, then in Cincinnati,
where he first perfected his system, from 1864
in Boston, at first devoting himself to supplying
the lack of instruction in the primary grades,
in 1879–82 in Japan as governmental supervisor,[1] and then in Boston again. With George
A. Veazie, Jr., he published a series of manuals
as *The National Music-Course*, making a trip
to Germany in connection with it and securing
such approval from the Leipzig Conservatory
that a German translation was issued. [R.4]

MASON, TIMOTHY B. See TUNE-BOOKS,
1834.

[1] It is said that his system was speedily introduced
into 30,000 Japanese schools. This unfamiliar style
of music led to the term 'Mason-song' for Western
music generally.

DR. WILLIAM MASON

MASON, WILLIAM (Jan. 24, 1829, Boston : July 14, 1908, New York). See article in Vol. iii. 74. His early studies were with Henry Schmidt in Boston. By 1846 he played at Harvard Musical Association concerts in piano-trios by Beethoven, Reissiger and Mayseder. After being at Leipzig he spent a year with Dreyschock at Prague. In 1853 he played Weber's 'Concertstück' in London with the Harmonic Union under Benedict. In 1854–55 he toured the United States as pianist and then settled in New York. His desire to introduce Brahms' Trio, op. 8, led to the Mason-Thomas Soirées. His piano-works numbered about 40, including 'Amitié pour Moi,' op. 4, 'Silver Spring,' op. 6, Ballade in B, op. 12, 'Monody,' op. 13, the mazurka-caprice 'Spring-Dawn,' op. 20, 'Rêverie Poétique,' op. 24, Berceuse, op. 34, Serenata, op. 39, Scherzo, op. 41, and 'Capriccio Fantastico,' op. 50. He published (with E. S. Hadley) a *Method for the Piano*, 1867, a *System for Beginners*, 1871, *Pianoforte-Technics*, 1878, and, most important of all, *Touch and Technic*, op. 44. For many years he was counted the foremost teacher in the country. [R.4]

MASON & HAMLIN COMPANY, THE, of Boston, was founded in 1854 by Henry Mason (son of Lowell Mason) and Emmons Hamlin, the latter having been in the employ of Prince & Co. of Buffalo. The business at first was the making of the form of reed-organ known as the melodeon, and the output began with about 450 instruments a year. But Hamlin brought with him his method of improving tone by twisting the reeds, and other improvements were rapidly made, so that the capacity of the factory was greatly increased and the quality improved. In 1861 what was called the 'cabinet organ' was first put on the market, often with several sets of reeds or 'stops.' This has been developed to a high pitch of perfection and has received numerous awards for excellence. In 1882 the Company began also to make pianos and since 1900 have introduced notable features, especially in the method of stringing and tuning. In 1869 Lowell Mason, Jr., became president, continuing till his death in 1885. The present president is Henry Lowell Mason, son of the founder.

MASON BROTHERS, of Boston, was a publishing firm formed in 1855 by Daniel Gregory Mason and Lowell Mason, Jr. (sons of Lowell Mason), largely to take over the issue of their father's books. They continued until 1869, when D. G. Mason died and Lowell Mason joined his brother Henry in the Mason & Hamlin Co.

MASON-THOMAS SOIRÉES, THE, in New York, were chamber-music recitals begun in 1855 and continued till 1868. The original

players were William Mason, piano, Theodore Thomas, first violin, Joseph Mosenthal, second violin, George Matzka, viola, and Carl Bergmann, 'cello. The latter was succeeded after a year by Brannes and he in turn by Frederic Bergner. Otherwise the quintet remained intact. These recitals were notable for the number of chamber-works introduced to America, as well as for the high standard of interpretation and performance.

‡MASSENET, JULES ÉMILE FRÉDÉRIC (May 12, 1842, Montaud, France : Aug. 13, 1912, Paris). See article in Vol. iii. 87–8. 'Ariane' was produced in 1906 (Paris), 'Thérèse' in 1907 (Monte Carlo), 'Bacchus' in 1909 (Paris), 'Don Quichotte' in 1910 (Monte Carlo), 'Roma' in 1912 (Monte Carlo), ' Panurge' in 1913 (Paris) and 'Cléopâtre' in 1914 (Monte Carlo), the last two posthumously. Still another work, 'Amadis,' remains unperformed. His *Souvenirs d'un Musicien*, 1912, were completed by Leroux. For bibliography see Baker, *Dict. of Musicians*, p. 588.

MATHEWS, WILLIAM SMITH BABCOCK (May 8, 1837, New London, N. H. : Apr. 1, 1912, Denver, Colo.), began music-study at ten, was organist at thirteen and teacher at Appleton Academy, Mt. Vernon, N. H., at fifteen. After study at Lowell and Boston, in 1860–63 he taught at the Wesleyan Female College in Macon, Ga., and then at Greensboro, S. C., Marion, Ala., Aurora, Ill., finally locating in Chicago in 1867. Here until 1893 he was organist at the Centenary (M. E.) Church, then and later a very active teacher and writer, and was influential in advancing musical standards in the Middle West. In 1910 he moved to Denver, hoping to profit by the change of climate, and spent his last years in literary and editorial work. He contributed to 'Dwight's Journal of Music' in 1866–72, edited 'The Musical Independent' in 1868–72 and in 1878–86 was music-critic for the Chicago 'Herald.' 'Record' and 'Tribune' successively. He established the monthly magazine 'Music' in 1891 and continued editor until 1902, when it was merged with 'The Philharmonic' and passed out of his hands. His books were *Outlines of Music-Form*, 1867, *The Emerson Organ-Method*, 1870 (with L. O. Emerson), *How to Understand Music*, 2 vols., 1880, 1888, *One Hundred Years of Music in America*, 1889, *Primer of Musical Forms*, 1890, *Popular History of Music*, 1891, *Dictionary of Musical Terms*, 1896 (with Emil Liebling), *Music, its Ideals and Methods*, 1897, *The Masters and their Music*, 1898, and *The Great in Music*, 3 vols., 1900–03. He collaborated with William Mason in his *Touch and Technic* and *Fundamental Piano-Technics*. He edited collections of Schumann, Chopin, etc., and was concerned with many pedagogical publications, the last

of which was *The Progressive Series*. His mind
was ready and fertile, acute and often fresh in
point of view, but much of his literary work
was over-hasty. [R.5]

MATHUSHEK, FREDERICK (1814–
1891). See Register, 4.

MATLACK, HENRY WILLIAM (b. 1875).
See Register, 8.

MATSON, CLYDE E. See COLLEGES, 3
(Sterling C., Kan.).

MATTFELD, MARIE. See Register, 8.

MATTHEWS, HARRY ALEXANDER
(Mar. 26, 1879, Cheltenham, England), was
trained by his father (see next article) and
came to Philadelphia in 1899. He has been
organist at the Second Presbyterian, St. Luke's
and Epiphany Churches. His works number
about 200, including the cantatas 'Life Everlasting,' 'The Conversion,' 'The Story of Christmas,' 'The Triumph of the Cross,' 'The City
of God' (1917, Luther Quadricentennial), 'The
Slave's Dream,' 'The Lake of the Dismal
Swamp' and 'The Song of the Silent Land,'
and many popular anthems, songs, duets,
piano- and organ-pieces. [R.8]

MATTHEWS, JOHN SEBASTIAN (Dec.
11, 1870, Cheltenham, England), was the son
of John Alexander Matthews, for over 45
years conductor of the Cheltenham Festivals.
Like his brother (see above), he was first
trained by his father and also by G. B. Arnold
at Winchester, assisting the latter as organist
at the Cathedral for three years. He has been
organist in America since 1891 — at St. Martin's in the Fields in Philadelphia, at St.
Mary's in Burlington, N. J., at St. Stephen's
in Boston, from 1901 at St. Peter's in Morristown, N. J., and since 1916 at Grace Church
in Providence. He has written the cantatas
'The Paschal Victor' (1913), 'The Eve of
Grace' (1914) and 'The Way of Life' (1919),
many effective anthems, like 'There's a Wide-
ness in God's Mercy,' 'Shepherd, with Thy
Tenderest Love,' 'I Sought the Lord,' 'When
wilt Thou save the people' and 'The Twilight-
Carol,' about 20 Christmas-carols, songs, part-
songs and organ-pieces. He has also in manuscript the comic opera 'Narragansett Pier.'
[R.8]

MATTIOLI, LINO (b. 1853). See Register, 7.

MATZENAUER, MARGARETE (b. 1881).
See Register, 10.

MATZKA, GEORGE (1825– ?). See
Register, 4.

MAUBOURG [–GOFFAUX] JEANNE
(b. 1875). See Register, 9.

MAUREL, VICTOR (b. 1848). See Register, 6.

MAXIM, ABRAHAM (1773–1829). See
TUNE-BOOKS, 1808.

MAXSON, FREDERICK (June 13, 1862,

Beverly, N. J.), was first a pupil of D. D.
Wood, the blind organist in Philadelphia, and
later of Guilmant. From 1884 he was organist
at the Central Congregational Church in
Philadelphia and since 1902 at the First Baptist Church. Besides being a successful organ-
teacher, privately and at the Leefson-Hille
Conservatory, he has been much in request as
recitalist in Philadelphia and throughout the
East. He is an associate of the R. C. O., fellow of the A. G. O., and head of the examiners
of the American Organ-Players' Club. His
works include organ-pieces like the Romance
in C (Gray), Festive March in E-flat (Gray),
Madrigal in G and 'A Spring-Time Fantasy'
(White-Smith), Grand Chorus in D (Weekes)
and Finale in B-flat (Church), various piano-
pieces (Presser, Schirmer, North, White-Smith),
a choral service, anthems and sacred solos
(Boner, Ditson, Gray, White-Smith). He has
also unpublished a 'Liberty Fantasia' and a
Festive March for organ. [R.7]

MAXWELL, LEON RYDER (Sept. 15,
1883, Medford, Mass.), graduated at Tufts
College in 1904, studying music there and in
Boston. In 1905–08 he was music-supervisor
in various towns near Boston, and then went
to study composition with Beer-Walbrunn
and voice with Hess in Munich, continuing
the latter with Braggiotti in Florence and
Dubulle in Paris. Since 1909 he has taught in
Newcomb College in New Orleans, becoming
head of its music-school in 1910. He has given
many song-recitals as baritone, lectured more
or less, written magazine-articles and prepared
the program-notes for the New Orleans Philharmonic Society and Symphony Orchestra.
Since 1912 he has conducted the University
Chorus, in 1913–15 was president of the Louisiana Music Teachers' Association, in 1917–19
was vice-president of the M. T. N. A., etc. His
compositions for voice, piano and organ, and for
string-quartet and orchestra, are as yet unpublished. He was co-editor with Leo R. Lewis
of *The Assembly Praise Book*, 1910. [R.9]

MAY, HIRAM. See TUNE-BOOKS, 1840.

MAYLATH, HEINRICH (1827–1883).
See Register, 5.

McCLELLAN, JOHN JASPER (b. 1874).
See Register, 8.

McCONATHY, OSBOURNE (b. 1875).
See Register, 8.

McCORMACK, JOHN (June 14, 1884,
Athlone, Ireland). See article in Vol. v. 652.
His American début was at the Manhattan
Opera House in New York, on Nov. 10, 1909,
in 'La Traviata.' In 1910–11 he sang with
the Boston Opera Company and in 1912–13
with the Chicago Opera Company. Since
then he has devoted himself mainly to concert-
work, in which he has had phenomenal success.
His operatic répertoire includes the tenor rôles

in 'Madama Butterfly,' 'La Bohème,' 'Faust,' 'Cavalleria Rusticana,' 'Don Giovanni,' 'La Traviata,' 'Rigoletto,' 'Lakmé,' 'La Fille du Régiment' and 'Tosca.' He became an American citizen in 1917. Holy Cross College made him Litt.D. in 1917. [R.9]

McCOY, WILLIAM J. (Mar. 15, 1848, Crestline, O.), was a pupil of William Mason, Reinecke and Hauptmann. For years he has been identified with the musical life of San Francisco. For the Bohemian Club there he has written the music for the 'Grove-Plays' 'The Hamadryads' (1904) and 'The Cave-Man' (1910), besides the unpublished opera 'Egypt' (1914). From the first of these the Prelude, Dance and 'The Naiads' Idyl' have often been given separately by various orchestras, and from the second 'The Song of the Flint' and 'The Dance of the Fireflies' are issued in piano-arrangement (Sherman, Clay & Co.). He has published many orchestral pieces and the overture 'Yosemite' (Bellman & Thümer), and has also a Symphony in F (1872, Leipzig). Among his chamber-works are an uncompleted violin-concerto, an Introduction and Valse Concertante for flute and orchestra, a sonata for violin and piano, and a Romance for saxophone and piano (Carl Fischer). He has a Mass in D minor for chorus and orchestra, an Ave Verum for men's chorus, solo and organ, 'Kol Nidrei' for cantor, contralto, chorus, orchestra and organ, and considerable other church-music. His published songs are also numerous (Ditson, Schirmer, Schuberth, Church, etc.). He is the author of *Cumulative Harmony*. [R.6]

McCUTCHAN, ROBERT GUY (Sept. 13, 1877, Mountayr, Ia.), graduated from Park College in 1898 and took a Mus.B. at Simpson College in 1904. In 1899–1901 he was teaching and concertizing, and in 1904 organized the music-department of Baker University in Kansas, remaining till 1910. After a year of study in France and Germany (while in Berlin directing the choir of the American Church), in 1911 he became dean of the School of Music at DePauw University in Greencastle, Ind. Since 1916 he has been president of the Indiana Music Teachers' Association and in 1920 became secretary of the M. T. N. A. Since 1917, under the State Council for Defense, he has been active in promoting community-singing (in the summer of 1918 he made about 165 speeches), with encouraging results. In view of this work and his interest in music in colleges he is preparing a work on *Music as a Social Force.* [R.8]

‡ M‘EWEN, JOHN BLACKWOOD (Apr. 13, 1868, Hawick, Scotland). See article in Vol. iii. 6–7. His works to 1919 include the following:

Symphony in F minor.
Symphony in A minor.

'Solway' Symphony in C-sharp minor.
'Three Border-Ballads' — 'Coronach,' 'The Demon Lover,' 'Grey Galloway' — for orchestra (Anglo-French Music Co.).
Two Overtures — 'Comedy,' 'Tragedy.'
Suite in E for orchestra.
Ballet-Suite for orchestra.
Highland Dances for string-orchestra.
Concerto for viola and orchestra.
String-quartets — No. 1, in G, No. 2, in C minor, No. 3, in G minor, No. 4, in A, No. 5, in F minor, No. 6, in F, No. 7, in E-flat, No. 8, in A minor (Novello), No. 11, in C minor (Ricordi), No. 13, 'Biscay,' in A (Anglo-French Co.), No. 14 'Threnody,' in E-flat (Anglo-French Co.).
Two Studies for string-quartet.
'Nugæ,' seven Bagatelles for string-quartet (Hawkes).
Phantasie-Quintet in E minor, for two violins, viola and two 'cellos.
Sonatas for violin and piano — No. 1, in E-flat, No. 2, in F minor (Anglo-French Co.), No. 3, in G, No. 4, in A (Anglo-French Co.).
Six Highland Dances for violin and piano (Novello).
Sonata in E minor, for piano (Novello).
Four Sketches for piano (Ricordi).
Suite, 'Vignettes from La Côte d'Argent,' for piano (Anglo-French Co.).
Sonatina in G, for piano (Anglo-French Co.).
'A Scene from Hellas,' for soprano and women's chorus.
'The Last Chantey,' for chorus.
'Hymn on the Nativity,' for soprano and chorus.
Opera Comique, 'The Royal Rebel.'
Recitation-music for the melodrama 'The Game-keeper.'
Accompaniment for 'Graih my Mree', for string-quartet, piano and drums.
Music for 'Romney's Remorse.'
Various songs and part-songs (Novello, Augener, Stainer, Anglo-French Co.).

His published books are *A Text-Book of Harmony and Counterpoint, The Elements of Music, A Primer of Harmony, Exercises on Phrasing in Pianoforte-Playing, The Thought in Music* (an enquiry into the principles of musical rhythm, phrasing and expression), *The Principles of Phrasing and Articulation in Music* and *The Foundations of Musical Æsthetics.*

McGILL UNIVERSITY, Montreal, has maintained since 1904 a Conservatorium of Music which in 1908 was fully incorporated into the University system under Harry C. Perrin as director and first University professor. The teaching-staff numbers about 25. Local examinations for certificates are held in about fifty places in the Dominion.

McKNIGHT, GEORGE MORGAN (b. 1866). See COLLEGES, 2 (Elmira C., N. Y.).

McPHAIL, A. M. (d. 1902). See Register, 3.

McPHEETERS, CLAUDIA. See COLLEGES, 2 (Milwaukee-Downer C., Wis.).

McWHOOD, LEONARD BEECHER (Dec. 5, 1870, Brooklyn), had his early education in Newark, graduated from Columbia University in 1893 and continued till 1898 as graduate-student and fellow in psychology, studying under MacDowell. From 1897 he assisted the latter and in 1904–10 was adjunct-professor. He also taught in 1902–07 at Vassar College, in 1907–16 at Drew Theological Seminary in Madison, N. J., in 1910–13 at the National Park Seminary in Washington, in 1913–18 at the Newark High School, and since 1918 has been professor at Dartmouth College. He has been active in furthering music as a collegiate study, and has lectured and written often on the subject. He has conducted choruses, orchestras and operatic performances. His works include three cantatas (one with orchestra), a light opera, many songs and instrumental pieces.   [R.8]

MEAD, OLIVE (Nov. 22, 1874, Cambridge, Mass.), began violin-study at seven, her teachers being Eichberg and Kneisel. She appeared as soloist in 1898 with the Boston Symphony Orchestra, and has since played with all the leading orchestras. In 1904 she organized the Olive Mead Quartet, including Elizabeth Houghton, Gladys North and Lillian Littlehales — this personnel continuing except that Vera Fonaroff has taken Miss Houghton's place. The Quartet has had great success throughout the East, and Miss Mead is also popular as a soloist.   [R.8]

MEES, ARTHUR (Feb. 13, 1850, Columbus), when but a lad was organist in his father's church and, after taking up instrumental study, began anthem-writing. In 1870 he graduated from Concordia College in Indiana and went to Cincinnati as teacher of piano and theory in the Wesleyan Female College, organist in a succession of churches and conductor of singing-societies. In 1873 Thomas was impressed with his work as accompanist at choral rehearsals, so that he was made organist at the first May Festival. In 1873–76 he was in Berlin, on Rubinstein's advice taking piano with Kullak, theory with Weitzmann and score-reading and conducting with Dorn. On his return to Cincinnati in 1880 he was trainer of the Festival Chorus, teacher of harmony at the new College of Music and organist for the Festivals. In 1886 he went to New York as assistant-conductor under Thomas of the National Opera Company. When this disbanded he directed the Orpheus Club in New York, the Albany Festivals and other choral organizations. In 1896–98 he moved to Chicago to assist in the direction of the Thomas Orchestra there and the chorus associated with it. Returning to New York, he then added the conducting of the Mendelssohn Glee Club (1898–1904), the Worcester Festivals, the Cecilia Society of Boston, the Bridgeport Oratorio Society and (from 1900) was associated with Paine in the Norfolk Festivals, in 1916 becoming his successor. During this extremely varied and significant career he has directed many first performances for America, as of Bantock's 'Omar Khayyám,' Pierné's 'St. Francis,'

Grainger's 'Marching-Song of Democracy,' Parker's 'The Dream of Mary,' Chadwick's 'Land of our Hearts,' Coleridge-Taylor's posthumous 'Orchestral Rhapsody,' Reger's 'The Nuns' (Worcester), Stanford's Piano-Concerto and Grainger's Suite 'In a Nutshell' (Norfolk). He has published Daily Studies for the Piano, Choirs and Choral Music, 1901, and edited important program-books for the New York Philharmonic Society (1887–96), the Chicago Symphony Orchestra (1896–98) and the Worcester Festivals. In 1901 Alfred University made him Mus.D.   [R.6]

MEGERLIN, ALFRED (b. 1880). See Register, 10.

‡ MELBA, MME. (May 19, 1861, near Melbourne, Australia). See article in Vol. iii. 104–5. In 1897–98 she was with the Damrosch Opera Company, in 1907 sang a few times at the Manhattan Opera House, in 1910 at the Metropolitan Opera House and in 1917 with the Chicago Opera Company. Since 1918 she has taught in Melbourne. See biography by Murphy, 1909.

MELIS, CARMEN (b. 1885). See Register, 9.

'MELODEON.' The name usually used at first for the American form of reed-organ.

MELTZER, CHARLES HENRY (1852, London, England), was musically trained in London and Paris, and became foreign correspondent for the Chicago 'Tribune' and the New York 'Herald.' He came to New York in 1888 and was dramatic critic for the 'Herald,' 'World,' 'American,' and 'Cosmopolitan Magazine.' In 1903–07 he was assistant to Grau and Conried at the Metropolitan Opera House. Besides many plays which have been successful on the stage, he has written several opera-librettos, such as 'The Garden of Allah,' 'The Sunken Bell' and 'Cophetua,' and prepared many singing-versions from the French, German and Italian, as of Monteverde's 'Orfeo,' 'Les Contes d'Hoffmann,' 'Les Dragons de Villars,' 'Die Walküre,' 'Das Rheingold' and 'Die Königskinder.' He has been a strong advocate of opera in English, of a National Conservatory and of a National Opera House.   [R.7]

MENDELSSOHN CHOIR, THE, of Toronto, was founded in 1894 by Augustus S. Vogt, who developed it to an extraordinary pitch of proficiency and remained conductor till 1917. He was succeeded by Herbert A. Fricker. Its singers are chosen by rigid tests year after year and its rehearsals carried out with the precision of an orchestra, and the result is a perfection of tone-quality, of accuracy, of elasticity, shading and artistic expressiveness unsurpassed in America — perhaps anywhere. In Toronto the Choir gives usually an annual festival of five performances, and it has repeatedly made tours in the United States, notably in 1912. Its répertoire includes almost everything of importance in choral music — a cappella or with orchestra.

MENDELSSOHN CLUB, THE CHICAGO, was organized in 1894 with Frederick W. Root as first conductor. Since 1895 its director has been Harrison M. Wild. The usual number of singers is about 70. Three regular concerts are given annually and three for charitable objects, making a total since organization of over 150. The repertory includes more than 500 works, with emphasis upon the finest part-songs, but including some works with orchestra, like Mendelssohn's music for 'Antigone,' David's 'Le Désert,' Reinecke's Festival Overture, op. 218, Wagner's 'Das Liebesmahl,' Brahms' Rhapsodie, Bruch's 'Frithjof,' Buck's 'Voyage of Columbus,' Zöllner's 'Young Siegfried' and Harling's 'Before the Dawn.' Many shorter works have been written especially for the Club. Some of the larger American compositions are Buck's 'Paul Revere's Ride' and 'Chorus of Spirits and Hours,' Foote's 'Farewell of Hiawatha,' Parker's Ode for Commencement-Day, 'The Leap of Roushan Beg' and 'Spirit of Beauty,' Cadman's 'The Vision of Sir Launfal,' and Harling's 'The Two Angels' and 'Death of Minnehaha.'

MENDELSSOHN CLUB, THE, of Philadelphia, was formed in 1874 by William W. Gilchrist out of his choir at St. Clement's and properly organized in 1876 as a glee-club of 16 voices. In 1879 the chorus was made mixed and the size increased to 30 singers. At times the membership has been as high as 150, and at present is about 100. Gilchrist continued as conductor till 1915, when ill-health forced a leave of absence. After his death at the end of 1916 N. Lindsay Norden became conductor. For a few years from 1889 the Club maintained its own orchestra, and it has repeatedly sung with the Philadelphia Symphony Orchestra. Thus in 1904, '07 and '14 it assisted in giving Beethoven's 9th Symphony and in 1916 in several performances of Mahler's 8th Symphony. In 1909, with other clubs, it celebrated the Mendelssohn Centenary. One of its most striking concerts was the giving of Henschel's Requiem in 1906. Mr. Norden has introduced many a cappella Russian works, hitherto unknown outside of Russia.

MENDELSSOHN GLEE CLUB, THE, of New York. See article in Vol. iii. 370. Frank Damrosch continued as conductor till 1909, being succeeded in 1909-13 by Clarence Dickinson, in 1913-19 by Louis Koemmenich and since 1919 by Nelson P. Coffin.

MENDELSSOHN QUINTETTE CLUB, THE, of Boston, was the first artistic chamber-music group in America. It was organized in

1849, with August Fries as leader, Gerloff (second violin), Thomas Ryan (viola or clarinet), Edward Lehmann (flute or viola) and Wulf Fries ('cello). Francis Riha soon replaced Gerloff. In 1858-77 William Schultze was leader, with Carl Meisel as second and Edward M. Heindl as flute. Ryan and Wulf Fries continued in the Club till its dissolution about 1895. The organization became well known throughout the country and for nearly fifty years exerted an invaluable influence, preparing the way for several later groups.

MENDELSSOHN SOCIETY, THE, of Chicago, was an early choral society, maintained in 1858-65 under the leadership of Adolph W. Dohn.

MENEELY, ANDREW (1801-1851). See Register, 3.

MENEELY & CO., of West Troy (now Watervliet), N. Y., for nearly a century have conducted a bell-founding business of national importance. The business was started in 1826 by Andrew Meneely, who in 1851 was succeeded by his sons Edwin A. Meneely (1829-1887) and George R. Meneely (1831-1915). In 1874 the present firm-name was adopted and in 1880 the present president, Andrew H. Meneely (b. 1853), came in. This famous factory has supplied a large number of the finest chimes in the country, as well as sets of bells for organs. They, with other manufacturers who have followed them, have introduced refinements and additions to European practice that have made American bells artistically notable.

MERRILL, ABRAHAM DOW (1796-1878). See TUNE-BOOKS, 1834.

MERRILL, WINFRED B. See STATE UNIVERSITIES (Ind.).

MERRY, HERBERT ORAL. See COLLEGES, 3 (Lincoln C., Ill.).

MERZ, KARL (Sept. 19, 1836, Bensheim, Germany : Jan. 30, 1890, Wooster, O.), early learned the violin and organ from his father, becoming organist at eleven. In 1854 he came to Philadelphia, through Bonawitz got employment in theater-orchestras, for a year was organist in the Sixth Presbyterian Church and tried critical writing. In 1856-59 he taught at a school near Lancaster, was then two years in the South, and on the outbreak of the Civil War in 1861 became music-director at Oxford Female College in Ohio, where he remained till 1882. From 1868 he contributed to 'Brainard's Musical World' and from 1873 was its editor, making a decided impression by his thoughtful articles. From 1882 he was head of the music-department of Wooster University at Wooster, O. He wrote a piano-trio, a piano-sonata in C minor, many piano-pieces and songs, the operettas 'The Last Will and Testament' (1877, Oxford), 'Katie Dean'

(1882, Oxford) and 'The Runaway Flirt' (published in 1868), and various choruses, quartets and organ-pieces. He published Methods for the reed-organ and piano, and *Elements of Harmony and Composition*, 1881. His collected essays appeared as *Music and Culture*, 1890. His fine library became the basis of the musical collection in the Carnegie Institute of Pittsburgh. [R.4]

‡ MESSAGER, ANDRÉ CHARLES PROSPER (Dec. 30, 1853, Montluçon, France). See article in Vol. iii. 183. He left Covent Garden in 1907. In 1908-14 he was director and chef d'orchestre at the Grand-Opéra in Paris, in 1908 succeeded Marty as conductor of the Concerts du Conservatoire and in 1918 brought this orchestra for 50 concerts in the United States and Canada under the auspices of the French government. On his return he retired from active conducting. To the list of works add the operas 'Fortunio' (1907, Paris, Opéra-Comique), and 'Beatrice' (1914, Monte Carlo).

MESSITER, ARTHUR HENRY (1834-1916). See Register, 5.

METCALFE, SAMUEL L. (1798-1856). See Tune-Books, 1817.

METROPOLITAN CONSERVATORY OF MUSIC, THE, of New York, was established in 1886 by Charles B. Hawley and Herbert W. Greene. Its scope was at first chiefly as a school of singing. Its scope was soon broadened, and in 1891 it was incorporated under the Board of Regents as the Metropolitan College of Music. Its faculty included S. P. Warren, H. R. Shelley, A. R. Parsons and others of high standing. In 1900 it was reorganized as the American Institute of Applied Music.

METROPOLITAN OPERA HOUSE, THE, in New York. See Vol. iii. 469-71. Conried's administration continued till February, 1908, when, after months of ill-health, he resigned. He was succeeded by Giulio Gatti-Casazza, who for ten years had been manager of La Scala in Milan, and his efficient, intelligent and on the whole sufficiently enterprising administration has continued ever since — the longest and most successful in the history of the institution. With him for two years was associated Andreas Dippel, who in 1910 joined the Philadelphia-Chicago Company.

In 1906-10 occurred the exciting competition between the Metropolitan and the Manhattan Opera Houses, which served to arouse much public attention and to stimulate managerial ambition on both sides. The directors of the Metropolitan finally bought off Hammerstein's interest and bound him not to produce grand opera in New York for ten years. In 1910 they fostered the formation of the Boston Opera Company and from that time extended their activities to Philadelphia and Baltimore. But in 1910 was also formed the Philadelphia-Chicago Grand Opera Company, which in the end came to be a strong rival, though not at once active in the New York field. Meanwhile in New York the Metropolitan promoted a new enterprise in 1909-11 at the New Theater for the production of works better suited to a smaller house. A similar secondary effort was made in 1913-15 in the Century Opera Company.

The outbreak of the World War in 1914 affected the Metropolitan in two ways. Large numbers of artists became available through temporary or permanent migration from Europe. And ultimately the entry of the United States into the contest led to the ejection of many German singers from the personnel and the removal of German works from the repertory. The general consequence was to alter the balance of performances in favor of French, Italian and other works. But the war did not interfere seriously with the continuity or significance of the successive seasons.

The catalogue of new works in the repertory is as follows :

1908-09 — D'Albert, 'Tiefland' (Nov. 23), Puccini, 'Le Villi' (Dec. 17), Catalani, 'La Wally' (Jan. 6), Smetana, 'The Bartered Bride' (Feb. 19).

1909-10 — Franchetti, 'Germania' (Jan. 22), Bruneau, 'L'Attaque du Moulin' (Feb. 8), Tchaikovsky, 'Pique Dame' (Mar. 5), Converse, 'The Pipe of Desire' (Mar. 18).

1910-11 — Gluck, 'Armide' (Nov. 14), Puccini, 'La Fanciulla del West' (Dec. 10), Humperdinck, 'Die Königskinder' (Dec. 28), Dukas, 'Ariane et Barbe-Bleue' (Mar. 29).

1911-12 — Thuille, 'Lobetanz' (Nov. 17), Wolf-Ferrari, 'Le Donne Curiose' (Jan. 3), Blech, 'Versiegelt' (Jan. 20), Parker, 'Mona' (Mar. 4).

1912-13 — Damrosch, 'Cyrano de Bergerac' (Feb. 27), Mussorgsky, 'Boris Godunov' (Mar. 19).

1913-14 — Strauss, 'Der Rosenkavalier' (Dec. 9), Montemezzi, 'L'Amore dei Tre Rè' (Jan. 14), Herbert, 'Madeleine' (Jan. 24), Charpentier, 'Julien' (Jan. 27), Wolf-Ferrari, 'L'Amore Medico' (Mar. 25).

914-15 — Giordano, 'Madame Sans-Gêne' (Jan. 25), Leoni, 'L'Oracolo' (Feb. 4), Mascagni, 'Iris' (Apr. 1).

1915-16 — Borodin, 'Prince Igor' (Dec. 30), Granados, 'Goyescas' (Jan. 28), Goetz, 'The Taming of the Shrew' (Mar. 15).

1916-17 — Bizet, 'Les Pêcheurs de Perles' (Nov. 13), Gluck, 'Iphigénie en Tauride' (Nov. 25), Polacco, 'Francesca da Rimini' (Dec. 22), De Koven, 'The Canterbury Pilgrims' (Mar. 8).

1917-18 — Rabaud, 'Mârouf' (Dec. 19), Liszt, 'St. Elizabeth' (Jan. 3), Mascagni, 'Lodoletta' (Jan. 12), Rimsky-Korsakov, 'Le Coq d'Or' (Mar. 6), Cadman, 'Shanewis' (Mar. 23), Gilbert, 'Dance in Place Congo' (Mar. 23).

1918-19 — Verdi, 'La Forza del Destino' (Nov. 15), Puccini, 'Il Tabarro,' 'Suor Angelica,' 'Gianni Schicchi' (Dec. 14), Weber, 'Oberon' in English (Dec. 28), Ricci, 'Crispino e la Comare' (Jan. 18), Leroux, 'La Reine Fiammette' (Jan. 24), Gounod, 'Mireille' (Feb. 28), Breil, 'The Legend,' Hugo, 'The Temple Dancer' (Mar. 12).

1919-20 — Rossini, 'L'Italiana in Algeri' (Dec. 5), Wolff, 'L'Oiseau Bleu' (Dec. 27), Leoncavallo, 'Zaza' (Jan. 16), Hadley, 'Cleopatra's Night' (Jan. 31), Tchaikovsky, 'Eugene Onegin' (Mar. 24).

The conspicuous conductors have been Alfred Hertz in 1902-15, Arturo Toscanini in 1908-15, Giorgio Polacco since 1912 and Artur Bodansky since 1915. For details about the many singers see Krehbiel, *More Chapters of Opera,* 1919, and the excellent articles on 'Music' in *The New International Year-Book,* 1907 ff. Krehbiel's book also supplies a wealth of historical and critical comment. Upon this and its predecessor, *Chapters of Opera,* 1908, this article is largely based.

Below is a tabular résumé of the performances (in the regular seasons) at the Metropolitan since its foundation:

	ABBEY	STANTON							ABBEY-GRAU	GRAU								
	'83-84	'84-85	'85-86	'86-87	'87-88	'88-89	'89-90	'90-91	'91-92	'93-94	'94-95	'95-96	'96-97	'98-99	'99-00	'00-01	'01-02	'02-03
Beethoven — Fidelio	.	3	.	3	4	2	.	3	2	.	1	.	.	.	1	1	.	.
Bizet — Carmen	5	.	2	.	.	.	.	3	1	12	7	11	7	2	11	.	7	2
Pêcheurs	.	.	.	.	.	.	.	.	.	.	.	1	.	.	.	.	.	.
Boito — Mefistofele	2	.	.	.	.	.	.	.	.	.	.	2	4	.	2	.	.	.
Donizetti — Lucia	3	.	.	.	.	.	.	.	.	2	3	3	2	1	2	2	.	.
Fille du Régiment	.	.	.	.	.	.	.	.	.	.	.	.	.	.	.	.	.	.
Favorita	.	.	.	.	.	.	.	.	.	.	.	2	2	.	.	.	3	6
Don Pasquale	.	.	.	.	.	.	.	.	.	.	.	.	.	.	3	.	1	1
Flotow — Martha	3	.	.	.	.	.	.	.	1	.	.	.	2	1	.	.	.	.
Gluck — Orfeo	.	.	.	.	.	.	.	.	4	1	.	1	.	.	.	.	.	.
Gounod — Faust	6	.	5	3	4	4	.	.	8	8	7	8	10	7	9	5	5	7
Philémon et Baucis	.	.	.	.	.	.	.	.	.	4	.	2	1	.	.	.	.	.
Roméo et Juliette	.	.	.	.	.	.	.	.	3	5	4	4	5	6	5	4	3	2
Meyerbeer — Robert le Diable	3	.	.	.	.	.	.	.	.	.	.	.	.	.	.	.	.	.
Huguenots	2	5	.	.	.	5	.	3	4	2	6	5	2	4	2	3	3	3
Prophète	1	9	3	5	2	3	.	1	2	.	.	.	.	2	2	.	.	1
L'Africaine	.	.	.	.	.	5	.	3	4	.	1	.	1	1	1	1	.	.
Dinorah	.	.	.	.	.	.	.	.	1	.	.	.	.	.	.	.	.	.
Mozart — Figaro	.	.	.	.	.	.	.	.	.	3	.	.	.	3	4	.	2	1
Don Giovanni	5	2	.	.	.	.	2	.	3	1	3	.	3	4	1	1	.	1
Magic Flute	.	.	.	.	.	.	.	.	.	.	.	.	.	5	.	3	2	.
Rossini — Barbiere	3	.	.	.	.	.	.	.	.	.	.	.	.	4	4	.	.	3
Semiramide	.	.	.	.	.	.	.	.	.	3	1	.	.	.	.	.	.	.
Guillaume Tell	.	3	.	.	.	3	2	.	.	2	.	.	.	.	.	.	.	.
Thomas — Mignon	4	.	.	.	.	.	.	.	2	.	1	.	.	1	.	.	.	.
Hamlet	1	.	.	.	.	.	.	.	2	1	.	2	1	.	.	.	.	.
Verdi — Ernani	.	.	.	.	.	.	.	.	.	.	.	.	.	.	.	.	.	3
Rigoletto	2	1	.	.	.	.	.	.	2	2	4	1	1	1	1	1	.	1
Trovatore	3	.	.	.	.	5	3	.	2	.	3	2	2	.	3	.	.	1
Traviata	4	.	.	.	.	.	.	.	.	1	1	2	3	2	2	.	1	4
Ballo in Maschera	.	.	.	.	.	.	4	.	.	.	.	.	.	.	.	.	.	1
Aida	.	.	.	.	4	.	3	3	2	.	3	4	3	3	5	3	5	7
Otello	.	.	.	.	.	.	.	.	1	.	4	.	.	.	.	.	3	3
Falstaff	.	.	.	.	.	.	.	.	.	3	3	.	.	.	.	.	3	3
Wagner — Rienzi	.	.	7	5	.	.	1	.	.	.	.	.	.	.	.	.	.	.
Hollander	.	.	.	.	.	.	5	4	.	.	.	.	.	.	3	1	.	.
Tannhäuser	.	9	4	6	4	5	5	7	.	2	.	3	3	6	5	4	2	4
Lohengrin	6	9	4	4	6	2	5	7	3	5	5	6	6	7	7	6	4	7
Rheingold	.	.	.	.	.	9	3	.	.	.	.	.	.	1	2	1	1	2
Walküre	.	7	4	3	4	4	3	4	.	.	.	2	.	4	6	3	3	3
Siegfried	.	.	.	.	11	6	2	4	.	.	.	.	6	1	2	1	1	3
Götterdämmerung	.	.	.	.	7	4	5	4	.	.	.	.	.	1	2	2	2	2
Tristan	.	.	.	8	3	.	5	3	.	.	.	6	2	5	3	4	3	4
Meistersinger	.	.	8	5	1	5	3	6	3	3	.	1	3	4	2	1	2	.
Auber — Masaniello	.	3	.	2	.	.	.	.	.	.	.	.	.	.	.	.	.	.
Bellini — Sonnambula	2	.	.	.	.	.	.	.	2	.	.	.	.	.	.	.	.	.
Norma	.	.	.	.	.	.	.	.	2	.	.	.	.	.	.	.	.	.
Puritani	1	.	.	.	.	.	.	.	.	.	.	.	.	.	.	.	.	.
Brüll — Goldene Kreuz	.	.	4	.	.	.	.	.	.	.	.	.	.	.	.	.	.	.
Cornelius — Barbier von Bagdad	.	.	.	.	.	5	4	.	.	.	.	.	.	.	.	.	.	.
Delibes — Lakmé	.	.	.	.	.	.	.	.	2	.	.	.	.	.	.	.	.	.
Ernst II. — Diana von Solange	.	.	.	.	.	.	.	2	.	.	.	.	.	.	.	.	.	.
Franchetti — Asrael	.	.	.	.	.	.	.	5	.	.	.	.	.	.	.	.	.	.

	ABBEY	STANTON							ABBEY-GRAU	GRAU								
	'83-84	'84-85	'85-86	'86-87	'87-88	'88-89	'89-90	'90-91	'91-92	'93-94	'94-95	'95-96	'96-97	'98-99	'99-00	'00-01	'01-02	'02-03
Goldmark — Queen of Sheba			15	4		5												
Merlin			5															
Halévy — Juive	5		3	3	2													
Nessler — Trompeter					7	4												
Ponchielli — Gioconda	4																	
Smareglia — Vasall von Szigeth								4										
Spontini — Cortez					4													
Weber — Freischütz		1																
Euryanthe					4													
Bemberg — Elaine											2						3	
Lara — Messalina																		
Leoncavallo — Pagliacci											3	2	2		1		1	6
Mancinelli — Ero e Leandro														2				2
Mascagni — Cavalleria									4	7	3	7	4		6	3	4	1
L'Amico Fritz										2							3	2
Massenet — Le Cid															2			
Werther																1		
Manon															4			
Navarraise																4		
Nicolai — Merry Wives																1	3	
Paderewski — Manru																	5	2
Puccini — Bohème																3		4
Tosca																2		
Reyer — Salammbô																		
Saint-Saëns — Samson et Dalila											1							
Smyth — Der Wald																		2

	CONRIED					GATTI-CASAZZA											
	'03-04	'04-05	'05-06	'06-07	'07-08	'08-09	'09-10	'10-11	'11-12	'12-13	'13-14	'14-15	'15-16	'16-17	'17-18	'18-19	'19-20
Beethoven — Fidelio	1	1			3	1							5		3		
Bellini — Sonnambula			2											3		4	
Puritani	4	4	2	1		6						9	5	3	7	5	7
Bizet — Carmen													3	3	3		
Pêcheurs														3			
Delibes — Lakmé			3											5	5	5	5
Donizetti — Elisir d'Amore		4	1	2		2	2										
Lucrezia Borgia		1															
Lucia	3	3	5	4	1	2			3		1		4	2		1	4
Fille du Régiment																	
Favorita		4															
Don Pasquale		2	2	1		1	2			2	2						
Flotow — Martha			4	3	3								4	3	5	5	4
Stradella				4	3	3											
Giordano — Fedora													6	2	3	3	
Mme. Sans-Gêne																	
Gounod — Faust	4	4	5	4	6	7	6	4	3	4	1				6	6	6
Roméo et Juliette	2	4		5				3									4
Mireille																	
Humperdinck — Hansel u. Gretel			11	8	5		4	6	7	4	6	4	4	1			
Königskinder								11	7	6	6						
Leoncavallo — Pagliacci	5	3	3	4	4	4	7	8	9	9	9	7	4	5	5	6	6
Zaza																	7
Mascagni — Cavalleria	8	3		1		7	7	7	6	5	3	3	4	3	6	6	5
Iris					5											5	3
Lodoletta																	

Meyerbeer — Huguenots . . . . 4 . . . . . . 5 . 3 . . . . .
    Prophète 5 6 5
    L'Africaine . . . . 2 . . . .
Mozart — Figaro . . . . . 1 2 . . . 6 . . . . . . 3 2 . . .
    Don Giovanni . . . . 2 . 4 . . . .
    Magic Flute . . . 4 . . . . . 9 6 6 4 3 . . .
Ponchielli — Gioconda . . . . 4 4 . . . 6 6 6 5 5 2 . . .
Puccini — Villi . . . . 5 . . . .
    Manon Lescaut . . . . . . 3 5 . . . 5 4 3 3 4 4 4 4
    Bohème 3 3 5 7 7 7 7 6 8 6 8 7 5 5 5 6 4
    Tosca . . . . 4 4 3 6 7 6 6 6 . . 5 7 6 3 5 6 6 5
Puccini — Butterfly 5 6 8 6 8 7 8 8 8 4 5 6 8 8
    Fanciulla del West . . . . 9 . 4 4 . . . .
    Il Tabarro, etc. 6 4
Rossini — Barbiere . . . 4 2 2 . 6 2 3 . . 3 . . 4 3 4 5 4
    Italiana in Algeri 3
Strauss, Richard — Salome . . . . . . 1 . . . .
    Rosenkavalier . . . . 9 5 5 3 . .
Verdi — Rigoletto . . . . 5 2 5 2 4 4 2 4 5 1 . . 5 5 5 3 5
    Trovatore . . . . . 4 . 6 5 6 6 4 4 . 6 4 5 3 2 2
    Traviata . . . . 3 4 2 3 6 5 3 3 2 3 5 5 2 2 3 3 .
    Ballo in Maschera . . . . 2 . . . . . 5 2 3 . .
    Aida 6 5 4 6 5 8 7 8 7 5 7 8 7 7 8 8 5
    Otello . . . . 6 5 4 3 . . . . .
    Falstaff . . . . 3 2 . . . .
    Forza del Destino 6 5
Wagner — Holländer . . . . . . 4 . . . .
    Tannhäuser . . . . 5 9 4 5 4 7 4 6 4 6 3 5 . .
    Lohengrin . . . . 5 6 5 5 2 . 6 6 6 3 6 5 5 5 .
    Rheingold . . . . 1 2 2 1 . 1 2 1 1 1 1 1 3 2 . .
    Walküre . . . . 4 4 3 2 3 5 4 5 5 6 7 7 5 4 . .
    Siegfried . . . . 2 2 3 4 3 2 3 2 3 2 4 3 3 5 . .
    Götterdämmerung . . . . 1 2 3 1 . 5 2 1 3 4 3 2 3 1 . .
    Tristan . . . . 4 2 3 4 6 4 5 4 5 5 5 4 5 5 . .
    Meistersinger . . . . . 7 4 . 4 5 2 5 3 5 4 3 5 5 . .
    Parsifal . . . . 11 8 4 2 . 5 3 4 3 3 3 4 3 3 . . 6

Berlioz — Damnation of Faust . . . 5 . .
Boieldieu — Dame Blanche . . 1 . . .
Boito — Mefistofele 7
Cilèa — Adriana Lecouvreur . . . 2
Goldmark — Queen of Sheba . . 5 .
Strauss, Johann — Fledermaus . . 4 1 .
    Zigeunerbaron . . . 1 5
Thomas — Mignon . . . .

    d'Albert — Tiefland 4
    Auber — Fra Diavolo . . . 3
    Blech — Versiegelt 4
    Borodin — Prince Igor 5 2 2
    Breil — The Legend 3
    Cadman — Shanewis . . . 5 3
    Catalani — Wally . . . 5
    Charpentier — Julien . . . 5
    Converse — Pipe of Desire . . 2
    Damrosch — Cyrano de Bergerac . . 5
    De Koven — Canterbury Pilgrims . . 6
    Dukas — Ariane . . 4 3
    Franchetti — Germania . . 5 2
    Gluck — Orfeo . . 5 5 5 2 3
    Armide . . 3 4
    Iphigénie en Tauride . . 5
    Goetz — Taming of the Shrew . . 2
    Francesca da Rimini . . 5 4
    Granados — Goyescas . . 4
    Hadley — Cleopatra's Night . . 4
    Halévy — Juive . . 7
    Herbert — Madeleine . . 4
    Hugo — Temple Dancer . . 3
    Leoni — Oracolo . . 6 . 2 6 3 5
    Leroux — Reine Fiamette . . 4
    Liszt — St. Elizabeth . . 5
    Massenet — Werther . . 2
    Manon . . 6 4 . 3 5 4 3 1 . . 4
    Thais . . 5 6 5
    Montemezzi — Amore dei Tre Rè . . 5 5 . 5 3 3

	GATTI-CASAZZA											
	'08–09	'09–10	'10–11	'11–12	'12–13	'13–14	'14–15	'15–16	'16–17	'17–18	'18–19	'19–20
Mussorgsky — Boris Godunov					4	6	6	6	4	6	4	3
Offenbach — Contes d'Hoffmann					7	2						
Parker — Mona				4								
Rabaud — Mârouf										6	3	2
Ricci — Crispino											3	
Rimsky-Korsakov — Coq d'Or										6	5	7
Saint-Saëns — Samson et Dalila								5	5	4	5	5
Smetana — Bartered Bride	6	1	4	2								
Tchaikovsky — Pique-Dame	4											
Eugene Onegin												4
Thuille — Lobetanz					5							
Weber — Freischütz	1											
Euryanthe									5			
Oberon											6	5
Wolf-Ferrari — Donne Curiose						5	3					
Amore Medico								4				
Segreto di Susanna						4	3					
Wolff — Oiseau Bleu												8

METS, ISABEL. See COLLEGES, 2 (Hamilton C., Ky.).

MEYER, CONRAD (d. 1881). See Register, 3.

MEYER, HENRY EDWIN. See COLLEGES, 3 (Howard Payne C., Tex.).

MEYER, JULIUS EDUARD (1822–1899). See Register, 4.

MEYER, MAX FRIEDRICH (b. 1873). See Register, 9.

MEYER, RUDOLPH J. See COLLEGES, 3 (Susquehanna U., Pa.).

MICHALEK, BOHUMIL (b. 1885). See Register, 9.

MICKWITZ, PAUL HAROLD VON (b. 1859). See COLLEGES, 3 (Southern Methodist U., Tex.).

MIDDELSCHULTE, WILHELM (Apr. 3, 1863, Werne, Germany), was trained at the Institute for Church Music in Berlin under Haupt, Loeschhorn, Alsleben, Commer and Schröder, and in 1888–91 was organist at the Lukas-Kirche. In 1891 he came to Chicago as organist at the Cathedral of the Holy Name, remaining four years. At this time he studied theory with Ziehn. In 1894–1918 he was organist of the Thomas (Chicago) Orchestra. In 1899–1919 he was organist at St. James' (R. C.), and also teacher of organ and theory in the Wisconsin Conservatory in Milwaukee. With the Chicago Orchestra under Thomas or Stock he has played works like the Handel Concertos in G and F, the Rheinberger Concertos in F and G minor, the Guilmant Concerto in D minor, Klose's Fantasia and Double Fugue, and Borowski's 'Allegro de Concert,' besides, for the first time in America, the Liszt-Kaun Fantasia and Fugue on 'Ad nos ad salutarem undam,' Oldberg's Concerto in F, Widor's Symphonia Sacra and 'Salvam fac populum tuum,' the Bach-Busoni 'Fantasia Contrappuntistica' (dedicated to him and arranged by him and Stock), his own Concerto in A minor and arrangement of Bach's Chaconne. These performances, with numerous recitals in America and Europe, give him high rank among living organists. He has published a Passacaglia in D minor, Canons and Fugue on 'Vater unser,' Toccata on 'Ein feste Burg,' Concerto in A minor, Meditation on 'Alle Menschen müssen sterben,' Canonical Fantasia on B–A–C–H and a cadenza to Handel's 4th Concerto, besides transcriptions of the Bach Chaconne, the Bach-Busoni Fantasia and parts of Wolf-Ferrari's 'I Giojelli della Madonna.' Unpublished are a Chaconne in E minor, arrangements of Bach's Chromatic Fantasia and Fugue and of the 'Musikalisches Opfer,' etc. [R.8]

MIDDLETON, ARTHUR D. (b. 1880). See Register, 9.

MIERSCH, KARL ALEXANDER JOHANNES (1865–1916). See Register, 8.

MIERSCH, PAUL FRIEDRICH THEODOR (b. 1868). See Register, 8.

MIESSNER, W. OTTO (May 26, 1880, Huntingburg, Ind.), after a high-school education, in 1900 gained a certificate from the College of Music in Cincinnati. In 1900–04 he was music-supervisor at Booneville, Ind., in 1904–09 at Connersville, Ind., and in 1910–14 at Oak Park, Ill. In 1909–10 he studied with Kelley. Since 1914 he has been music-director at the State Normal School in Milwaukee. He has written the cantatas 'The Queen of May,' op. 1 (Willis), and 'Christus,' op. 3; a Festival Overture, op. 5, for orchestra; a 'Liberty March,' op. 6, for orchestra; inci-

dental orchestral music for 'As You Like It'
and 'The Tempest,' opp. 7, 8; ' Miniature Operettas,' op. 9 (Am. Music Co.) ; Sonata in
E minor, op. 10, for piano (Am. Music Co.);
besides songs and piano-pieces. He has also
published *The Motif-Method of Music-Read-
ing* and *The Place of Music in Education*,
and collaborated in *The Progressive Music
Series*. [R.9]

MILLARD, CLEMENT. See TUNE-BOOKS,
1810.

MILLARD, HARRISON (1830–1895). See
Register, 4.

MILLER, DAYTON CLARENCE (b.
1866). See Register, 7.

MILLER, FRANK E. (Apr. 12, 1859,
Hartford, Conn.), graduated from Trinity College in 1881 and from the College of Physicians
and Surgeons in New York, settling there as
laryngologist. He has been a diligent investigator, practitioner and writer in this field,
not only inventing many novel instruments
pertaining to the throat and the ear and treat-
ing numerous famous singers, but evolving an
original general theory of vocal art-science
under the term 'kinæsthesia' (rhythmic vibra-
tion and its perception and coördination). He
has published *The Voice*, 1910, *Vocal Art-
Science*, 1917, and a great number of articles
in scientific periodicals. [R.7]

MILLER, GEORGE HAROLD. See COL-
LEGES, 3 (Dakota Wesleyan U., S. D.).

MILLER, HENRY F. (1825–1884). See
Register, 4.

MILLER & SONS PIANO COMPANY,
THE HENRY F., of Boston, was founded in
1863 by Henry F. Miller and since 1884 has
been conducted by his five sons, Edwin C.
Miller being now president. Their pianos
have always maintained a high technical excellence. They have recently introduced a
remarkably small grand. Their type of player-
piano is known as the 'Playerforte.'

MILLER, HORACE ALDEN (July 4, 1872,
Rockford, Ill.), after studying in Cornell College in Iowa, went to the Oberlin Conservatory,
gaining a Mus.B. in 1904. He then returned
to Cornell College to teach organ and theory,
continuing till now save for a year of study in
Munich and Berlin. His interest in Indian
music is shown by the works, 'Melodic Views
of Indian Life' (Summy), 'From the Forest'
(Ojibway songs) ; 'Arapaho Ghost-Dance,' a
Romance in A-flat (Musicians' Pub. Co., Los
Angeles) ; 'In the Linden Cradle' and 'For
the Golden Harvest' (Willis) ; 'Indian Legend'
and 'Indian Idyl,' for organ (Novello) ; and
four Indian Themes, for piano, and 'The Moon
Cycle,' six songs for high voice (Breitkopf). Unpublished are several songs, piano- and organ-
pieces and the orchestral 'From the Wickiup'
and 'The Indian Flute.' The latter have been

played by the Chicago Symphony Orchestra and
the Russian Symphony Orchestra. [R.9]

MILLER, RUSSELL KING (May 10, 1871,
Philadelphia), studied piano with Von Sternberg in Philadelphia, organ with S. P. Warren
and composition with Klein in New York.
After short engagements in different churches,
since 1901 he has been organist at Temple
Keneseth Israel, and since 1909 also music-
director at the Pennsylvania School for the
Blind. He appeared in recital at the Buffalo
and St. Louis Expositions. His organ-works
(all J. Fischer) include a 'Scherzo Symphonique' (1895), Nocturne and Epilogue (1897),
Festival March (1903, A. G. O. prize), Concert-Overture (1909), Festival Postlude, Impromptu and Cortège (1904), Elegy (1905),
'Chanson Pastorale' (1907) and Berceuse and
Serenade (1908), besides anthems, songs and
piano-pieces. [R.8]

MILLIGAN, HAROLD VINCENT (Oct.
31, 1888, Astoria, Ore.), from 1908 was in New
York studying organ with Carl, theory and
composition with C. R. Gale, Johnstone and
Noble. He was then organist for five years at
the Rutgers Presbyterian Church, two years
at Plymouth Church in Brooklyn, and now at
both the Fifth Avenue Baptist Church and the
West End Synagogue. He is a fellow of the
A. G. O. and in 1914–16 was its general secretary. He has thrice been across the continent
on recital-tours. He has written many songs,
organ-pieces, choral works, sacred and secular,
and two operettas (Schirmer, Schmidt), besides incidental music to plays. He is editor
of *The First American Composer* and *Colonial
Love-Lyrics* (both Schmidt), author of a biography of Stephen C. Foster, 1920, staff-writer
for 'The Diapason,' 'The New Music Review'
and 'The Woman's Home Companion,' and
otherwise active as a writer. [R.10]

MILLS, CHARLES HENRY (Jan. 29,
1873, Nottingham, England), was trained at
the Guildhall School of Music in London, took
lessons from Prout, Niecks and Peace and in
1904 won a Mus.B. from the University of
Edinburgh. In 1892–93 he visited America
as a pianist. From 1894 he was organist at
various places in Great Britain — in 1898–1900
conducting the Aberdeen Operatic Society,
in 1900 becoming city-organist at Aberdeen
and in 1906–07 being borough-organist at Sal-
ford. In 1907–08 he taught theory at Syracuse University, in 1908–14 was head of the
music-department at the University of Illinois,
and since 1914 has held a similar position at
the University of Wisconsin. He is a fellow
of the R. C. O. and the A. G. O., an associate
of the R. C. M. and in 1911 was made Mus.D.
by McGill University. He has written a Concert-Overture (Minneapolis Orchestra), incidental music to a Shakespearean masque and

to Aristophanes' 'Clouds' (both given at Madison, Wis.), the cantatas with orchestra 'Ode to St. Cecilia' (Schirmer) and 'The Wreck of the Hesperus' (Birchard), and various other vocal works, sacred and secular. [R.8]

MILLS, SEBASTIAN BACH (Mar. 13, 1838, Cirencester, England : Dec. 21, 1898, Wiesbaden, Germany). See article in Vol. iii. 210. For many years he was foremost in introducing works not previously heard in New York — Moscheles' G minor Concerto and Chopin's Fantasia in 1860, Chopin's F minor Concerto in 1861, Hiller's F-sharp minor Concerto in 1863, the Weber-Liszt Polonaise in 1864, Mozart's posthumous Concerto in C in 1865, Liszt's E-flat Concerto in 1867, Reinecke's F-sharp minor Concerto in 1872 (first time in America), von Bronsart's Concerto and Raff's Suite, op. 200, for piano and orchestra, in 1877. His own most popular works were 'Recollections of Home,' 1st Tarantelle, 'Fairy Fingers,' 2nd Barcarolle and 'The Murmuring Fountain.' [R.4]

MIMBERLEY, FRED W. See COLLEGES, 3 (Buena Vista C., Iowa).

MINNEAPOLIS SYMPHONY ORCHESTRA, THE, dates from 1903, when the Philharmonic Club (choral) felt the need of a permanent orchestra. Emil Oberhoffer, the leader of the Club, became the conductor of the new organization and has remained its efficient head ever since. The financial affairs have been ably managed, stability being secured by a guarantee-fund, now of $75,000 annually, pledged in five-year periods. In 1904 a beautiful Auditorium was provided by the Northwestern National Life Insurance Co. At first the number of players was about 50, but is now usually 80. The concertmasters have been Franz Danz (1903–08), F. A. Korb (1908–09), Richard Czerwonky (1909–18) and Guy H. Woodard (from 1918). Carlo Fischer, leading 'cellist in 1906–11, since 1911 has been program-editor. For three years 20 concerts were given annually, for the next eight 150 and since then about 175, making a total of over 2300. In Minneapolis the regular series includes 40, with 12 in St. Paul; the remainder are extras or on tour. In its home-concerts the Orchestra has built up a fine répertoire. Out of perhaps 300 important works by 75 composers from Haydn to Stravinsky the following may be mentioned :

Beethoven, Triple Concerto for piano, violin and 'cello; Brahms, Double Concerto for violin and 'cello; Borodin, 2nd Symphony; Guilmant, Symphony for organ and orchestra; Chausson, Symphony and Symphonic Poem, 'Viviane'; Ropartz, 4th Symphony; Glazunov, 6th Symphony; Aulin, 3rd Violin Concerto; Kalinnikov, 1st Symphony; Georg Schumann, Overture, 'Liebesfrühling'; MacCunn, Overture, 'Land of Mountain and Flood'; Hinton, Piano Concerto; Rabaud, 2nd Symphony;

Rachmaninov, 'Die Toteninsel'; Ravel, Suite, 'La Mère l'Oye'; Scheinpflug, Overture to a Shakespeare Comedy; Enesco, Rumanian Rhapsodies, Nos. 1 and 2. In addition, about 35 American composers have been represented, including the following works: Avery, Scherzo, 'A Joyous Prelude'; Mrs. Beach, 'Gaelic' Symphony, Piano Concerto; Bonvin, 'Festival Procession'; Busch, 'The Passing of King Arthur,' 'Minnehaha's Vision,' 'A Chippewa Vision,' 'Sequentahre,' etc.; Carpenter, Suite, 'Adventures in a Perambulator'; Chadwick, Suite Symphonique, 'Tam O'Shanter,' Symphonic Sketches, 'Lochinvar,' etc.; Cole, Symphonic Prelude, 'Cello Ballade; Converse, 'Endymion's Narrative'; Damrosch, Prelude to Act II of 'Cyrano'; Foote, String Suite in E, Character Pieces after the 'Rubáiyát'; Hadley, 'The Culprit Fay,' 3rd and 4th Symphonies, Overture, 'In Bohemia'; Herbert, Suite Romantique, 'Woodland Fancies,' Prelude to Act III of 'Natoma,' etc.; Kelley, 2nd Symphony, 'Aladdin'; Kolar, Suite, 'Americana'; Kroeger, 'Lalla Rookh'; MacDowell, 'Lancelot and Elaine,' 1st and 'Indian' Suites, etc.; Oldberg, Overture, 'Paolo and Francesca'; Saar, 'Gondoliere,' 'Chanson d'Amour'; Smith, Overture, 'Prince Hal'; Stock, Symphonic Waltz; Strube, Comedy Overture, 'Puck'; Weidig, Symphonic Suite, Three Episodes, etc.

First performances in America or absolutely (marked *) include these: Alfven, 3rd Symphony, 'Drapa,' Polonaise, 'Festspiel'; Aulin, Swedish Dances; Bleyle, 'Flagellantenzug'; Delius, 'Dance Rhapsody'; Dohnanyi, Suite, op. 19; Hinton, 2nd Symphony; Oberhoffer, *Overture Romantique, *March, 'Americana'; Pauly, Piano Concerto; Pitt, Serenade for small orchestra; Sibelius, Suite, 'Scènes Historiques,' 1st Violin Serenade; Skilton, *Two Indian Dances; Stenhammar, 'Midvinter'; Strauss, Festival Prelude; Smith, Suite, 'Impressions.'

MIRANDA, MAX. See COLLEGES, 3 (Beloit C., Wis.).

MISCHKA, JOSEPH (b. 1846). See Register, 5.

MITCHELL, LIVINGSTON HARVEY. See COLLEGES, 3 (Ouachita C., Ark.).

MITCHELL, NAHUM (1769–1853). See Register, 3, and TUNE-BOOKS, 1810.

MODERWELL, HIRAM KELLY (b. 1888). See Register, 10.

MODERN MUSIC SOCIETY, THE, of New York, was formed in 1913–14 to give both choral and orchestral works by recent composers, especially Americans. Its nucleus was the Lambord Choral Society, founded in 1912 by Benjamin Lambord.

MOHR, HERMANN (1830–1896). See Register, 7.

MOLLENHAUER, EDUARD (1827–1914). See Register, 4.

MOLLENHAUER, EMIL (Aug. 4, 1855, Brooklyn), the son of Friedrich Mollenhauer, the violinist, early evinced ability on his father's instrument. At nine he made his début at Niblo's Garden, at fourteen played in the orchestra at Booth's Theatre and at seventeen joined the Thomas Orchestra. Until 1884 he was also a member of the New York and Brooklyn Philharmonic Societies and for a time of the Symphony Society. He then removed to

Boston and in 1885–88 was in the Boston Symphony Orchestra, which he left to conduct the Germania (later the Boston Festival) Orchestra and also (till 1903) the Municipal Concerts. With the Festival Orchestra he not only toured extensively with a long list of soloists, vocal and instrumental, of the first order, but also participated in numerous choral festivals in different places. In 1899 he succeeded Lang as conductor of the Handel and Haydn Society, which he thoroughly reorganized. Since 1900 he has also led the Apollo Club and a number of choral societies besides, as in Brookline, Lynn, Salem and Newburyport. He conducted the Boston Symphony Orchestra at the St. Louis and San Francisco Expositions in 1904 and '15. His varied experience, technical skill and fine musicianship have given him great influence. [R.5]

MOLLENHAUER, FRIEDRICH (1818–1885). See Register, 4.

MOLLENHAUER, HEINRICH (1825–1889). See Register, 4.

MOLLENHAUER, LOUIS (b. 1863). See Register, 7.

MÖLLER, JOHN CHRISTOPHER. See Register, 2.

'MONA.' An opera in three acts by Horatio Parker, awarded the prize of $10,000 offered in 1909 by the Metropolitan Opera Company, produced on Mar. 4, 1912, and thrice repeated. The text is by Brian Hooker and develops a story in the time of the conquest of Britain by the Romans. See Krehbiel, *More Chapters of Opera*, pp. 255–65.

MONESTEL, ALEXANDER (b. 1865). See Register, 7.

MONTANI, NICOLA ALOYSIUS (b. 1880). See Register, 9.

MONTEUX, PIERRE (Apr. 4, 1875, Paris, France), was trained at the Paris Conservatory, studying solfeggio and harmony with Lavignac, counterpoint and fugue with Lenepveu and violin with Berthélier. From 1894 he conducted concerts in Paris, founding a series at the Casino de Paris to bring out examples of ultra-modern French music. He has conducted at the Théâtre des Champs-Élysées, the Châtalet and the Odéon in Paris, at Covent Garden and Drury Lane in London, and in Berlin, Vienna and Budapest. In 1916 he came to New York as conductor of the Russian Ballet and also led the concerts of the Civic Orchestral Society during the summer of 1917. In 1917–19 he conducted at the Metropolitan Opera House. In the fall of 1918 he took charge of the first concerts of the Boston Symphony Orchestra, pending the arrival of Rabaud, and in 1919 was elected to follow him as permanent conductor. He has directed first performances of Stravinsky's 'Le Rossignol' (opera), 'Petrouchka' and 'Le Sacre du

Printemps' (ballets), Debussy's 'Jeux' (ballet), Ravel's 'Daphnis et Chloé' (ballet) and Roger-Ducasse' 'Le Joli Jeu du Furet' (orchestral scherzo). [R.10]

'MONTEZUMA.' An opera in three acts by Frederick G. Gleason (text and music), of which only extracts have been performed.

'MONTEZUMA.' No. 2 of the 'Grove-Plays' of the San Francisco Bohemian Club, produced in 1903. The music is by Humphrey J. Stewart and the text by Louis A. Robertson. The scene is laid in Mexico in 1520.

MONTRESSOR. See Register, 3.

MOOG, WILSON TOWNSEND (b. 1881). See Register, 9.

MOORE, HENRY EATON (1803–1841). See TUNE-BOOKS, 1832.

MOORE, HOMER. See Register, 7.

MOORE, JOHN WEEKS (1807–1887). See Register, 4, and TUNE-BOOKS, 1849.

MOORE, MARY, née Carr. See Register, 9.

MOORE, W. H. A. See COLLEGES 3 (Cumberland U., Tenn.).

MOORS, HEZEKIAH. See TUNE-BOOKS, 1809.

MOOS, JEAN CARRODI. See COLLEGES, 3 (Bethany C., W. Va.).

MORGAN, GEORGE WASHBOURNE (Apr. 9, 1822, Gloucester, England : July, 1892, Tacoma, Wash.), was an articled pupil of Amott (organist of Gloucester Cathedral) and began playing regularly at twelve, first in Gloucester and then in London, where he also appeared in concert. About 1845 he became leader of the Philharmonic Society in Gloucester, in which he had sung as a boy, and was a competitor for the post of organist at Worcester Cathedral. Coming to New York in 1853, he was organist at St. Thomas' in 1854–55, Grace Church in 1855–68, St. Ann's (R. C.) in 1868–69, St. Stephen's (R. C.) in 1869–70, Brooklyn Tabernacle (Talmadge's) in 1870–82 and the Madison Avenue Collegiate (Ref. Dutch) Church in 1886–88. He gave a recital in Boston in 1859 and was the first player on the organ in Music Hall in 1863. He also played at the Centennial Exposition in Philadelphia in 1876. His brilliance as a performer made him popular, so that he did much to arouse enthusiasm for organ-music. He wrote a Morning Service, anthems (some with orchestra), organ-pieces, songs, etc. [R.4]

MORGAN, JOHN PAUL (1841–1879). See Register, 5.

MORGAN, MAUD (b. 1864). See Register, 6.

MORGAN, TALI ESEN (b. 1858). See Register, 7.

MORRIS, EDMON. See COLLEGES, 2 (Converse C., S. C.).

MORRIS, OWEN (1719–1809). See Register, 1.

MORRISON, CHARLES WALTHALL (b. 1856). See Register, 7.

MORSE, CHARLES FREDERIC (b. 1881). See Register, 9.

MORSE, CHARLES HENRY (Jan. 5, 1853, Bradford Mass.), graduated in 1870 from the Haverhill (Mass.) High School and in 1873 from the New England Conservatory in Boston, studying piano with J. C. D. Parker, Perabo and Baermann, organ with Whiting and Paine, theory with Emery and conducting with Zerrahn. He at once began teaching piano and organ in the Conservatory, but continued study at Boston University, where in 1876 he won probably the first Mus.B. given in the United States. Meanwhile he was organist at Tremont Temple, the Union and the Central Congregational Churches. In 1875–84 he was the first music-director at Wellesley College. In 1885–91 he was founder and director of the Northwestern Conservatory at Minneapolis, following the lines of the New England Conservatory and gaining immediate success, and was also organist in St. Paul and Minneapolis. In 1891–99 he was organist at Plymouth Church in Brooklyn and active in the Brooklyn Institute of Arts and Sciences. From 1901 he was the first professor of music at Dartmouth College, becoming emeritus in 1918. He has been a trustee of the New England Conservatory, in 1894–96 was president of the New York Music Teachers' Association, in 1896 a founder of the A. G. O. and member of its council, etc. He was one of the first to play Guilmant's works and to produce choral works of Gounod in the United States. He has edited *The Contemporary Organist* (Schirmer), two volumes of *The Church-Organist* and *The Junior Church-Organist* (White-Smith), *March-Album for Organ* (Schirmer), *Short and Easy Anthems* (Ditson), *The Plymouth Hymnal*, 1893 (with Lyman Abbott), *Songs for the Chapel* (men's voices), *The Wellesley Collection* (women's voices) and many separate vocal and organ-arrangements, besides publishing anthems and organ-pieces of his own (Schirmer, Schmidt). [R.6]

MORSE, FRANK EUGENE (b. 1856). See Register, 6.

MORSE, GEORGE FRANCIS. See Register, 7.

MORSELL, HERNDON (b. 1858). See Register, 7.

MOSENTHAL, JOSEPH (Nov. 30, 1834, Kassel, Germany : Jan. 6, 1896, New York), was trained by his father, Spohr, Bott, Kraushaar and others, and for four years played second violin under Spohr. In 1853 he migrated to New York, where in 1855–68 he was a member of the Mason-Thomas Quintet and in 1860–87 organist of Calvary Church, besides being forty years among the first violins of the

Philharmonic Society. From 1867 he was also leader of the Mendelssohn Glee Club, his life closing nearly thirty years later at a rehearsal. He wrote anthems, sacred songs, many fine part-songs for men's voices, such as 'Thanatopsis,' 'Blest Pair of Sirens,' 'The Music of the Sea,' and numerous secular songs. [R.4]

MOSS, THOMAS. See COLLEGES, 3 (Whitworth C., Wash.).

‡ MOTTL, FELIX (Aug. 24, 1856, Vienna, Austria : July 2, 1911, Munich, Germany). See article in Vol. iii. 277–8. While at Karlsruhe he gave the first complete rendering of Berlioz' 'Les Troyens' (1890), and the dates of the production of 'Fürst und Sänger,' the string-quartet in F-sharp minor and 'Pan im Busch' are 1893, '98 and 1900 respectively. While in New York in 1903–04 he conducted various Wagnerian operas and an orchestral concert, but did not actually conduct 'Parsifal' (though he directed rehearsals) because of the opposition of the Wagner family. Besides his extraordinary power as conductor he was extremely able as editor. His second revised version of Cornelius' 'Der Barbier von Bagdad' has become standard. He edited all the early overtures of Wagner and published a complete edition of his stage-works (1914). He was twice married, both times to operasingers.

MOUNTAIN, CHARLES WESLEY. See COLLEGES, 3 (Parsons C., Iowa).

MOZART CLUB, THE, of Pittsburgh, was organized in 1878 and incorporated in 1886. Its only conductor for forty years was James P. McCollum. Gradually expanding from a small circle of singers to a large chorus, and from 1886 giving programs only with orchestra or a cappella, the Club covered a large répertoire, including the larger sacred and secular works and a variety of lesser cantatas, etc., the orchestras assisting including those of Pittsburgh, Boston, Chicago and St. Paul. Almost all the leading soloists of the country appeared with it. The Club also pursued the policy of developing soloists within its own ranks or from Pittsburgh. Its work was greatly aided by the financial support of many public-spirited citizens.

MUCK, KARL (Oct. 22, 1859, Darmstadt, Germany). See article in Vol. iii. 314–5. His first term as conductor of the Boston Symphony Orchestra in 1906–08 was on leave of absence from Berlin, and on his return thither he was made General-Musikdirector. In 1912 he resigned to conduct the Boston Orchestra permanently, made a profound impression for several years, but in March, 1918, was arrested as an enemy alien, interned for more than a year and excluded from the country in August, 1919. [R.9]

MUENSCHER, JOSEPH. See Tune-Books, 1839.

MUKLE, MAY HENRIETTA (May 14, 1880, London, England), made her first appearance as 'cellist at nine and at seventeen gave a recital in London. She studied there with Hambleton and later with Pezze at the Royal Academy of Music. As soloist or in chamber-music groups she has toured Europe, America (several times), Australia (1903), South Africa (1905), Canada (twice), and in 1918 played in the first chamber-music recitals in Honolulu. In 1908 she traveled with the Maud Powell Trio, in which her sister, Anne Mukle, was pianist. She has also appeared often with symphony orchestras in Europe and America. 'The Hamadryad' and 'The Light Wind,' two fancies for 'cello and piano, are her only published works, but she has songs and small pieces for different instruments in manuscript. [R.9]

MÜLLER, CARL CHRISTIAN (July 3, 1831, Saxe-Meiningen, Germany : June 4, 1914, New York), having been taught piano by F. W. and Heinrich Pfeifer, harmony by Zöllner and organ by Butzert, came to New York in 1854. For a time he worked in a piano-factory, then entered the orchestra at Barnum's Museum and presently became its leader. In 1879–95 he taught harmony at the New York College of Music, and later was associated with the Grand Conservatory, the New York Conservatory and other schools. He published three organ-sonatas, a string-quartet, a sonata for violin and piano, choruses, and many pieces for piano and organ, and left also a symphony, an orchestral suite, an overture, an 'Idyl' for orchestra, a setting of Schiller's 'Die Kraniche des Ibicus' for soli, chorus and orchestra, and a 'Romanza' for horn, harp and orchestra. He translated Sechter's *Grundsätze der musikalischen Composition* as *Fundamental Harmony*, 1871 (9 later eds.), and added tables for primary instruction, modulation, chord-succession and harmonization. [R.4]

MÜLLER, FREDERICK WILLIAM (b. 1863). See Register, 8.

MURATORE, LUCIEN (1878, Marseilles, France), graduated in 1897 with a first prize from the Marseilles Conservatory, having studied bassoon as well as singing. He first appeared as an actor with Réjane and also Bernhardt. After three years in the army he prepared for lyric opera at the Paris Conservatory and made his début at the Opéra-Comique in 1902, creating the tenor-rôle in Hahn's 'La Carmélite' and also in 1903 that in Missa's 'La Muguette.' In 1905 he appeared at the Grand–Opéra as Rinaldo in 'Armide.' At the Opéra he created rôles in Massenet's 'Ariane' (1906), 'Bacchus' (1909) and 'Roma' (1912), Fevrier's 'Monna Vanna' (1909) and Hüe's 'Le Miracle' (1910) ; also at the first giving in that place of Strauss' 'Salome' (1910), Giordano's 'Siberia' (1911) and Saint-Saëns' 'Déjanire' (1911). In 1913 he came to America to join the Chicago Opera Company, with which he is still connected, though he returned to France for military duty in 1915. He married the soprano Lina Cavalieri in 1913. During the summer of 1917 he was engaged at the Teatro Colon in Buenos Aires. [R.10]

'MUSIC.' A monthly magazine founded by W. S. B. Mathews in 1891 at Chicago. He continued editor till December, 1902, after which the magazine was merged in 'The Philharmonic.' Although put together somewhat hastily and varying considerably in quality, this was the only journal devoted wholly or mainly to contributed articles until the appearance of 'The Musical Quarterly' in 1915. Many of its essays and studies were decidedly able. And it served to call attention to the dignity of the literary and scholarly treatment of musical subjects. See note in Vol. iii. 688.

MUSIC HALL. A building erected in Boston in 1852 to provide a suitable place for large choral and orchestral concerts. With a seating capacity of about 3000 and its central location (off Tremont and Winter Streets), it immediately became a notable headquarters for good music. In 1863, after vexatious delays and unexpected expenses, a concert-organ, made by Walcker of Ludwigsburg, Würtemberg, was introduced, being the first really large instrument in the United States. The organ was dedicated on Nov. 2, 1863, the performers being Lang, G. W. Morgan, Paine, Thayer, Tuckerman and Willcox — an extraordinary list for the time. For twenty years recitals were steadily given both by permanent organists and by visitors. In 1884 the organ was bought for the New England Conservatory, but proved unwieldy there and was finally broken up in 1897. Its advent was of great importance for American organ-building, since its tone-qualities were excellent and varied, though its action was sluggish and its construction in many respects clumsy. For a cut of the organ, see Elson, *History of American Music*, p. 262.

'MUSIC NEWS.' A weekly periodical founded in 1908 by Charles E. Watt in Chicago and since edited and published by him.

MUSIC SCHOOL SETTLEMENTS are music-schools planted in the poorer neighborhoods of many cities for the purpose of providing opportunity for artistic culture, especially among the foreign population. They have been notably successful in New York, Boston, Philadelphia and several cities in the West, becoming centers of culture and often developing singers and players of ability. The New York School was started in 1894 and owes its conspicuous expansion mainly to its later directors — Thomas Tapper in 1907–09, David Mannes in 1910–15 and Arthur Farwell since 1915. The number of pupils is about 1000 annually, and there are about 80 instructors. A notable feature is the maintenance of four orchestras, aggregating about 200 players. Besides owning many instruments, this school has an extensive library.

MUSIC SUPERVISORS' NATIONAL CONFERENCE, THE, was organized in 1907 to promote discussion and coöperation among those engaged in progressive musical work in public schools, especially supervisors. Its growth was rapid and it has become one of the notable influences in raising the standard of equipment among public-school teachers of music, in securing proper recognition for their work in general, in defining methods of credit for music-study both within and without the school-curriculum, in improving the connection between school and college work in music, in advancing the study of instruments and the formation of orchestras as well as singing and in promoting interest in community-music. The present number of members is about 1500. The annual meeting is held in the spring, and the proceedings are published. The president for 1920 is Hollis E. Dann, of Cornell University, and the secretary, Elizabeth Pratt, St. Louis, Mo.

MUSIC TEACHERS' NATIONAL ASSOCIATION, THE, was organized in 1876 at Delaware, O., by Theodore Presser and a small circle of earnest teachers in Ohio and neighboring states. With rare exceptions it has held annual meetings, with three days' sessions, that of 1919 being counted the forty-first.[1] Its original purpose was 'mutual improvement by interchange of ideas, to broaden the culture of music, and to cultivate fraternal feeling.' At present this is defined as 'the advancement of musical knowledge and education.' The founders, most of whom were connected with 'Normal Institutes' (teachers' summer-schools), had specially in mind the needs of scattered private teachers, and emphasized social contact, discussion of practical problems and the elevation of popular conceptions regarding musical work. The size of the Association and its geographical range have varied greatly. Altogether, its membership has probably included over 10,000 per-

sons, the average per year being now about 400. It has regularly aimed to publish each year an Annual Report in some form. These volumes, though varying much in character, are invaluable records of the progress of ideas.[1] The presidents have been Eben Tourjée (1876), James A. Butterfield (1878), Rudolf de Roode (1879), Fenelon B. Rice (1880–81), Arthur Mees (1882), Edward M. Bowman (1883–84, 1893–94, 1905), Smith N. Penfield (1885), Albert A. Stanley (1886), Calixa Lavallée (1887), Max Leckner (1888), Wilbur F. Heath (1889), Albert R. Parsons (1890), Jacob H. Hahn (1891), N. Coe Stewart (1895), Ernest R. Kroeger (1896), Herbert W. Greene (1897–98), Arnold J. Gantvoort (1899–1900), Arthur L. Manchester (1901–02), Rossetter G. Cole (1903, 1909–10), Waldo S. Pratt (1906–08), Peter C. Lutkin (1911, 1920), George C. Gow (1912), Charles H. Farnsworth (1913–14), J. Lawrence Erb (1915–17), Charles N. Boyd (1918–19). Of the many secretaries, H. S. Perkins was longest in office (1888–98), and notably efficient. Besides other general officers, for long periods there have been extensive lists of State vice-presidents. The Association was incorporated in 1887 under the laws of Indiana. Its constitution has been remodeled at intervals, the present form being that adopted in 1906.

The emphasis of the Association's discussions and effort has always been upon the problems and details of practical music-teaching, including raising the level of teachers and suggesting improved methods of teaching. Much attention has been given to questions about music in the public schools, in colleges and universities, and in community welfare. Every aspect of genuine musicianship in its practical applications has been somewhat considered. For many years, also, special effort was made to improve the recognition of American composition, including many recitals of American works and even the offering of prizes for such works. Through permanent committees on various subjects considerable general influence has been exerted.

The Association early advocated international copyright for music, and also the adoption of 'international' pitch. It fostered the formation of a large number of State Associations, and has been cordial in relation to many other associations, even when they tended to deplete its own ranks. In 1883 it was directly

[1] Delaware, O., 1876; Chautauqua, N. Y., 1878; Cincinnati, O., 1879, 1899, 1913; Buffalo, N. Y., 1880, 1915; Albany, N. Y., 1881; Chicago, Ill., 1882, 1888 (1893), 1920; Providence, R. I., 1883; Cleveland, O., 1884, 1892; New York City, 1885, 1897, 1898, 1905, 1907, 1916; Boston, Mass., 1886, 1910; Indianapolis, Ind., 1887; Philadelphia, Pa., 1889, 1919; Detroit, Mich., 1890; Saratoga Springs, N. Y., 1894; St. Louis, Mo., 1895, 1904, 1918; Denver, Colo., 1896; Des Moines, Ia., 1900; Put-in-Bay, O., 1901, 1902; Asheville, N. C., 1903; Oberlin, O., 1906; Washington, D. C., 1908; Evanston, Ill., 1909; Ann Arbor, Mich., 1911; Poughkeepsie, N. Y., 1912; Pittsburgh, Pa., 1914; New Orleans, La., 1917.

[1] No *Reports* apparently in 1877, 1879, 1891, 1893 (see 1894), 1898, 1905 (see 1906). From 1900 to 1905 the Association issued a periodical, *The Messenger* (quarterly, then bimonthly), ably edited by Arthur L. Manchester, which contained much more than the records of meetings. Since 1906 the Proceedings, under the title of *Studies in Musical Education, History and Æsthetics*, have been issued in handsome bound form (index to first ten volumes in 1915). It is unfortunate that complete files of the publications before 1900 are extremely rare.

concerned in the setting up of the American College of Musicians — the forerunner of several later efforts at 'standardization' — which, in spite of an excellent purpose and plan, did not have permanence. Various other enterprises might be named which expressed the practical energy that has usually characterized the Association's policy.[1]

MUSICAL ALLIANCE OF AMERICA, THE, was started in 1917 by John C. Freund of New York. Its special purposes are to advance the recognition of music as vital to national, civic and domestic life, to extend the study of music in the public schools, to magnify the importance of music by American composers and especially to urge the establishment of a National Conservatory. The movement has secured the interest of a large number of musicians of every class.

'MUSICAL AMERICA,' of New York. A weekly periodical established by John C. Freund in 1898 and since edited by him. After a break in publication, since 1905 it has been conducted on an enlarged scale as a record of manifold professional activities.

MUSICAL ART SOCIETY, THE, of New York. See article in Vol. iii. 335. The striking record of achievement of this society continues without break under the enterprising leadership of Frank Damrosch.

MUSICAL ASSOCIATION OF SAN FRANCISCO, THE. See SAN FRANCISCO SYMPHONY ORCHESTRA.

'MUSICAL COURIER, THE,' of New York. See note in Vol. iii. 689.

MUSICAL FUND HALL. A music-hall erected in 1824 for the Musical Fund Society of Philadelphia (see below) and used for its concerts and many others for more than thirty years. Its original plan was made by William Strickland and acoustically it was very successful. It was also so arranged as to be self-supporting from the rental of offices and studios. In 1847 it was elongated and re-arranged, so as to accommodate 1500. See cut and notes in Madeira, *Annals of Music in Philadelphia*.

MUSICAL FUND SOCIETY, THE, of Boston, was formed in 1847 by Thomas Comer on the lines of the Philadelphia Society, but only for orchestral concerts. It never reached a high plane of excellence in programs or performance, though improved in later years under G. J. Webb as conductor, and was discontinued in 1855.

MUSICAL FUND SOCIETY, THE, of New York, was, like the Boston Society, in-

tended to provide orchestral concerts. It was formed about 1828 and continued till after 1840, forming a bridge between the old and the new Philharmonic Societies.

MUSICAL FUND SOCIETY, THE, of Philadelphia, was founded in 1820 by a group of professional and amateur musicians who had met informally for several years to practice chamber-music. Leading spirits in the enterprise were Taylor, Carr, Hupfeld, Gilles, Cross and Schetky. The name arose from the fact that one of the objects was to establish a fund for the relief of needy musicians. The other was to give concerts of a high class, choral and orchestral. The first concert was given on Apr. 24, 1821. In 1824 Musical Fund Hall was built (see above). In 1825 an Academy of Fine Arts was projected, somewhat in connection with the University of Pennsylvania, but this educational effort ceased in 1832. The Society continued for almost forty years, serving as a center for the best musical interests of the city. In 1858 it was given up. Besides a goodly list of oratorios, symphonies and overtures, it introduced many eminent soloists, either in its regular concerts or under its patronage, such as Malibran, Ole Bull, Vieuxtemps, Herz, Jenny Lind and Sontag. See Madeira, *Annals of Music in Philadelphia and History of the Musical Fund Society*, 1896 (edited by P. H. Goepp). On May 4, 1920, a musical masque representing a 'Jenny Lind Concert in 1850' was given to commemorate the centenary of the Society.

MUSICAL GLASSES. See HARMONICA.

MUSICAL INSTRUMENTS, COLLECTIONS OF. See article in Vol. iii. 336–8, and articles in this volume on the BROWN COLLECTION in New York and the STEARNS COLLECTION in Ann Arbor.

'MUSICAL LEADER, THE.' See note in Vol. iii. 689.

'MUSICAL MONITOR, THE.' A monthly periodical issued since 1912 as the official organ of the National Federation of Musical Clubs. The editor is Mrs. David Allen Campbell.

'MUSICAL OBSERVER, THE.' A monthly periodical published since 1904 by Carl Fischer, New York. Its editor from the beginning has been Gustav Saenger.

'MUSICAL QUARTERLY, THE,' issued since 1915 by G. Schirmer, New York City, was the fruit of a long-standing desire on the part of Rudolph E. Schirmer to establish a musical periodical in English of the highest quality and of cosmopolitan scope. Its notable success from the start was insured by securing O. G. Sonneck (then of the Library of Congress) as editor. His energy, knowledge, tact and skill, with the disinterested liberality of the publishers, have combined to make the magazine uniquely significant. The dominant

---

[1] The detailed history of the Association is to be followed in its annual *Reports* or *Proceedings*. In 1893 H. S. Perkins issued a *Historical Handbook*, which is at least singular in style, and similar retrospects are found in the *Reports* for 1888 and 1893 and in the *Proceedings* for 1908, 1909, 1911 and 1914.

MUSICAL SOCIETY

purpose has been to stimulate the literary treatment of musical topics, historical, critical and practical. The original plan was to draw from foreign writers as freely as from American. The outbreak of the World War just before issues began naturally interfered with this somewhat, although the 150 articles in the first four volumes were about equally divided between Europe and America. All articles are in English, and some are accompanied by excellent illustrations.

The English contributors have been (to 1919) Herbert Antcliffe (3), Rutland Boughton (2), Ananda Coomaraswamy, Frederick Corder (4), A. Redgrave Cripps, Edward J. Dent (3), Edward R. Dibdin, Edwin Evans, W. H. Grattan Flood (2), J. A. Fuller-Maitland (4), Reginald Gatty (2), Percy Grainger, W. H. Hadow, Clement A. Harris (2), Ernest Hart, Arthur Hinton, A. Eaglefield Hull, Frank Kidson (3), W. J. Lawrence (4), M. Montagu-Nathan, John Palmer, D. C. Parker (4), C. Hubert H. Parry, John F. Runciman (2), Percy A. Scholes, Cyril Scott (3), Edward Speyer (2), W. Barclay Squire (4), C. Villiers Stanford (2), R. A. Streatfeild, Francis Toye (2), C. Stanley Wise. The French and Italians include Michel Brenet, R. D. Chennevière, Henri de Curzon (2), Guido A. Fano, Amédée Gastoué, Gabriel Grovlez, Jean Huré, G. Jean-Aubry (2), L. de La Laurencie, J. G. Prod'homme (7), Charles Quef, Camille Saint-Saëns, Julien Tiersot (3), Fausto Torrefranca. The Germans, Austrians and others are Oscar Bie, Elizabeth Foerster-Nietzsche, Viktor von Herzfeld, Edgar Istel (3), Hans Kleemann, Hugo Leichtentritt (2), Wilhelm Peterson-Berger, Egon Wellesz.

The articles by Americans are as follows: George W. Andrews, 'Music as an Expression of Religious Feeling'; Winton J. Baltzell, 'The American College Man in Music'; Phillips Barry, 'Greek Music'; Ludwig Bonvin, 'On Syrian Liturgical Chant'; Ernest Bruncken, 'The Philosophy of Copyright'; Charles L. Buchanan, 'Ornstein and Modern Music,' 'The Unvanquishable Tchaikovsky'; J. N. Burk, 'The Fetish of Virtuosity,' 'The Democratic Ideal in Music'; Natalie C. Burlin, 'The Classic Dance of Japan,' 'Black Singers and Players,' 'Negro Music at Birth'; Charles W. Cadman, 'The Idealization of Indian Music'; Sheldon Cheney, 'The Book-Plates of Musicians and Music-Lovers'; Philip G. Clapp, 'Sebastian Bach, Modernist'; D. A. Clippinger, 'Scientific Voice-Training'; T. P. Currier, 'Edward MacDowell as I Knew Him'; J. C. Deagan, 'A-440 Pitch Adopted'; Frances Densmore, 'The Study of Indian Music'; Olin Downes, 'An American Composer' (Henry F. Gilbert); Arthur Elson, 'Literary Errors about Music,' 'Sound and its Uses'; Louis C. Elson, 'Acoustics'; Carl Engel, 'De Gustibus,' 'Music we shall Never Hear,' 'The Miraculous Appeal of Mediocrity'; J. Lawrence Erb, 'Music in the American University,' 'Music in the Education of the Common Man'; Charles H. Farnsworth, 'The Judgment of Paris'; Harold Flammer, 'Advertising as a Fine Art'; Harvey B. Gaul, 'Bonnet-Bossi-Karg-Elert'; Sophie P. Gibling, 'Problems of Musical Criticism'; 'Types of Musical Listening'; Henry F. Gilbert, 'The American Composer,' 'The Survival of Music,' 'Folk-Music in Art Music,' 'Originality'; Lawrence Gilman, 'Taste in Music'; Philip Gordon, 'Franz Grillparzer'; George C. Gow, 'Rhythm, the Life of Music'; John C. Griggs, 'The Influence of Comedy upon Operatic Forms'; Eugene Gruenberg, 'Stage-Fright'; Henry J. Harris, 'The

Occupation of Musician in the United States'; Arthur Hartmann, 'The Czimbalom'; W. J. Henderson, 'The Function of Musical Criticism,' 'A Note on Floridity'; H. T. Henry, 'Music Reform in the Catholic Church,' 'Choir-Boys in Catholic Churches,' 'Wanted, a Historico-Musical Clearing-House'; Edward B. Hill, 'Vincent d'Indy'; Edwin Hughes, 'Musical Memory in Piano Playing,' 'Joseffy's Contribution to Piano Technic,' 'Liszt as a Lieder Composer'; James Huneker, 'The Classic Chopin'; Lewis M. Isaacs, 'A Friend of Dr. Johnson'; Edward Kilenyi, 'The Theory of Hungarian Music'; Henry E. Krehbiel, 'Alexander Thayer and his Life of Beethoven'; Ernst C. Krohn, 'The Bibliography of Music'; Frank Lester, 'Kluckhorn's Chord'; Arthur W. Locke, 'Note on Hoffmann's Kreisleriana'; Orlando A. Mansfield, 'Anomalies in Orchestral Accompaniments to Church Music,' 'Characteristics and Peculiarities of Mendelssohn's Organ Sonatas,' 'W. T. Best,' 'The Minuet in Handel's Messiah,' 'Musical Discrepancies'; Frederick H. Martens, 'The Attitude of the Dancer toward Music,' 'The Modern Russian Pianoforte Sonata'; Daniel G. Mason, 'A Study of Strauss,' 'Edward J. de Coppet,' 'A Study of Elgar,' 'Folk-Song and American-Music'; W. S. B. Mathews, 'Strength, Beauty and Satisfaction in Music'; Brander Matthews, 'The Convention of the Music-Drama'; Josephine McGill, 'Following Music in a Mountain Land,' 'Old Ballad Burthens'; E. W. Morphy, 'Violin Teaching and the Organization of Civic Orchestras'; Arthur Nevin, 'Two Summers with the Blackfeet Indians'; N. Lindsay Norden, 'The Boy-Choir Fad,' 'A Plea for Pure Church Music,' 'The Russian Liturgy and its Music'; Clara T. Nichols, 'Music in our Public Schools'; Katherine S. Oliver, 'On Friendship'; Waldo S. Pratt, 'On Behalf of Musicology'; William G. Rice, 'Tower Music of Belgium and Holland'; Francis Rogers, 'America's First Grand Opera Season,' 'Memories of Ethelbert Nevin,' 'The Male Soprano'; James F. Rogers, 'A Song of Rags,' 'Music as Medicine'; Frederick W. Root, 'Imagination and Fact in Voice Culture'; Cornelius Rübner, 'Niels W. Gade'; Algernon St. John-Brenon, 'Giuseppe Verdi'; Herbert Sanders, 'Counterpoint Revolutionized'; E. Sapir, 'Representative Music'; Carl E. Seashore, 'The Measurement of Musical Talent,' 'The Sense of Rhythm as a Musical Talent'; Herbert F. Small, 'On Opera'; C. Alphonso Smith, 'Ballads Surviving in the United States'; O. G. Sonneck, 'Liszt's Huldigungs Marsch and Weimar's Volkslied,' 'Guillaume Lekeu,' 'Rudolph E. Schirmer'; Sigmund Spaeth, 'Translating to Music'; Walter R. Spalding, 'The War in its Relation to American Music'; Constantin von Sternberg, 'Singing or Music,' 'On Plagiarism'; G.Edward Stubbs, 'Secularization of Sacred Music,' 'Why we have Male Choirs in Churches'; David C. Taylor, 'Voice Culture, Past and Present'; Carl Van Vechten, 'Shall we Realize Wagner's Ideals?' 'Notes on Gluck's Armide,' 'De Senectute Cantorum,' 'The Relative Difficulties of Depicting Heaven and Hell in Music'; Eva A. Vescelius, 'Music and Health'; Helen Ware, 'The American-Hungarian Folk-Song'; Wesley Weyman, 'The Science of Pianoforte Technique'; T. Carl Whitmer, 'A Post-Impressionistic View of Beethoven,' 'The Energy of American Crowd Music'; Herbert J. Wrightson, 'The Secret of Technique'; Jaroslaw de Zielinski, 'Russian Hunting Music.'

MUSICAL SOCIETY, THE, of Boston, apparently founded in 1785 and continuing till 1789, is important because probably directed by William Selby and because it carried through a performance of extracts from Handel's works in January, 1786, which seems to have stimulated similar efforts elsewhere. See Sonneck, *Concert-Life*, pp. 275–82.

'MUSICIAN, THE.' See article in Vol. iii. 688–9. Mr. Tapper ceased to be editor in 1907 and was succeeded by W. J. Baltzell, who continued till 1918, when the magazine passed from the Ditson Company to the Henderson Publications, Inc., New York.

MUSIKVEREIN, DER, of Milwaukee, was founded in 1847, giving its first concert in May, 1850. Its conductor till 1860 was Hans Balatka. Combining choral and orchestral efforts and being supported by a large German constituency, it stands out as one of the leading early factors in the development of musical interest in the Interior. For list of works performed up to 1880, see Ritter, *Music in America*, chap. xxi. The present conductor is Hermann A. Zeitz.

MUSIN, OVIDE (Sept. 22, 1854, Nandrin, Belgium). See article in Vol. iii. 342. His first American appearance was in 1883 with the New York Symphony Society under Leopold Damrosch. With the Philharmonic Society under Thomas he played the Godard concerto for the first time in America. Forming his own concert-troupe, he made many tours in the United States, in 1892 journeyed to Australia, New Zealand and Mexico, and in 1896 visited Japan, China and Manila. In 1908 he established a violin-school in New York. His decorations are many — Officier de l'Ordre de Léopold in Belgium, Commandeur de l'Ordre du Nisham Iftikar and Officier de l'Académie in France, member of the Ordre du Mérite in Holland, Officier de l'Ordre de Bolivar in Venezuela, etc. His violin-works (with or-

chestra or piano) include two Caprices, Valse de Concert, Mazurka de Concert, 'Extase,' Valse Lente, Berceuse, 'Mazurka Élégante' and 'Lullaby and Prayer.' He has made numerous transcriptions, as of Bach's Chaconne, Viotti's 22nd Concerto, Handel's Sonata in A, Tartini's 'Trillo del Diavolo' and Variations on a Corelli Gavotte (all Carl Fischer); a Prelude by Campagnoli, Pergolese's 'Canzonet Napolitaine,' Paganini's Romance in B minor, Radoux' 'Words from the Heart,' and many others in his own *Répertoire du Virtuose*. He has combined his own studies with those of Léonard in *The Belgian School of the Violin*, 4 vols., 1916, besides issuing many separate exercises and studies. His wife, née Annie Louise Hodges (b. 1856, Oshkosh, Wis.), is an accomplished soprano and has joined him in his many concert-tours. [R.7]

MUZIO, CLAUDIA (b. 1892). See Register, 10.

MYER, EDMUND JOHN (Jan. 21, 1846, York Springs, Pa.), after general education in Wyoming Seminary and Dickinson College in Pennsylvania, studied music in Philadelphia and New York. In 1878 he settled in the latter city, where he has since been active as a singer and teacher of singing. He founded the National Summer School of Music at Lake Chautauqua and Round Lake, N. Y., and has also taught summer-classes in Seattle, Wash. He is author of *Truths of Importance to Vocalists*, 1883, *The Voice from a Practical Standpoint*, 1886, *Voice-Training Exercises*, 1888, *Vocal Reinforcement*, 1891, *Position and Action in Singing*, 1897, *The Renaissance of the Vocal Art*, 1902, *The Vocal Instructor*, 1913, and *A Revelation to the Vocal World*, 1917. [R.6]

N

NACHEZ, TIVADAR (b. 1859). See Register, 10.

NAGEL, FRANK (b. 1870). See COLLEGES, 3 (Highland Park C., Iowa).

NAPOLEÃO, ARTHUR (b. 1843). See Register, 5.

‡ NÁPRAVNIK, EDUARD FRANTS-OVITCH (Aug. 24, 1839, near Königgrätz, Bohemia : Nov. 10, 1916, Petrograd, Russia). See article in Vol. iii. 352-3. There are Russian biographies by Weymarn, 1888, and Findeisen, 1898.

NARODNY, IVAN (b. 1874) and MARIA, née Mieler (b. 1888). See Register, 9.

NASH, W. See TUNE-BOOKS, 1836.

NATIONAL CONSERVATORY OF MUSIC OF AMERICA, THE, of New York and Washington, was founded in 1885 by Mrs. Jeannette M. Thurber and holds charters both from New York State (1885) and from Congress (1891), as to this latter being unique. Until about 1915 tuition was free, being provided by funds supplied by Mrs. Thurber and other supporters. The average number of pupils per year has been about 600. It has been specially successful in helping students of foreign birth and certain special classes, like the blind and those of Negro blood. At first vocal music was emphasized, with much attention to solfeggio, after the model of the Paris Conservatory, but all instrumental and theoretical branches were soon added. The list of distinguished teachers who have served for a longer or shorter time is long and imposing. Among the general directors have been Jacques Bouhy in 1885-89, Antonin Dvořák in 1892-95, Emil Paur in 1899-1902 and Wassily Safonov in 1906-09, and on the staff have been names like Mme. Fursch-Madi (1885-94), B. O. Klein (1887-92), Adele Margulies (since 1887), Joseffy (1888-96), Huneker (1888-98), Finck (since 1888), S. P. Warren, Victor Herbert, Anton Seidl, Frank Van der Stucken, Leo Schulz (since 1890), Leopold Lichtenberg (since 1899), Max Spicker (1895-1912) and many others. Humperdinck was invited to become director in 1913 and accepted, but was not released at Berlin. From time to time the Conservatory has offered prizes for composition — among the winners being Henry Schoenefeld with his 'Rural Symphony' (1892), Joshua Phippen of Boston with a piano-concerto, F. F. Bullard with a suite for strings, Horatio Parker with his cantata 'The Dream-King and his Love,' and G. W. Chadwick with a symphony. Marguerite Merington also took a prize for the opera-libretto 'Daphne.'

Special attention has been given to the development of the Conservatory orchestra and its operatic classes. It was while director that Dvořák wrote his 'New World' Symphony, the title being suggested by Mrs. Thurber.

NATIONAL ASSOCIATION OF ORGANISTS, THE, was organized in 1908 by Tali Esen Morgan as an outgrowth of gatherings promoted by him at Ocean Grove, N. J. Its first seven conventions (till 1914) were held at Ocean Grove. In 1915-17 they were at Springfield, Mass., in 1918 at Portland, Me., in 1919 at Pittsburgh and in 1920 at New York. The presidents have been Will C. Macfarlane in 1908-09, Mark Andrews in 1909-10, Homer N. Bartlett in 1910-11, Clarence Eddy in 1911-12, J. Christopher Marks in 1912-14, Arthur S. Brook in 1914-17, Frederick Schlieder in 1917-20 and now Henry S. Fry. The object of the Association is fraternal rather than academic. In a variety of ways it has served to arouse enthusiasm among its members and to advance the interests of organ-music as a specialty. The present membership is over 1000. Its official organ was at first 'The Musical World,' in 1915-19 'The Console,' which was wholly devoted to its affairs and well edited by M. M. Hansford, and now 'The Diapason.' Since 1912 the secretary has been Walter N. Waters, 24 W. 60th St., New York.

NATIONAL EDUCATIONAL ASSOCIATION, THE, since about 1880 has regularly given attention to questions relating to music, especially in the public schools, and has long maintained a Music Section for this purpose. Its Annual Proceedings have therefore included a large number of important papers on the subject. The president of the Section for 1920 is W. Otto Miessner of the Milwaukee State Normal School and the secretary Sarah B. Callinan, William Penn High School, Philadelphia.

NATIONAL FEDERATION OF MUSICAL CLUBS, THE, was founded in 1898 by Mrs. Theodore Sutro of New York. It has now grown to vast proportions, knitting together musicians and music-lovers throughout the country, and instigating activity of various sorts, from the development of the small local circle to the holding of great biennial assemblages in different places. Eleven such conventions have been held, the latest in 1919 at Peterboro, N. H., in connection with the MacDowell Memorial Colony there. The Federation publishes 'The Musical Monitor' as its official organ, the editor being Mrs. David A. Campbell. The president is Mrs. F. A. Seiberling, of Akron, O., and the secretary Mrs. John F. Lyons, Fort Worth, Tex. The entire country is divided into districts, each with its own officers, so that a large amount of local enthusiasm is stimulated. In connection with its biennial gatherings, as well as on a smaller scale in other ways, the Association aims to foster musical production by offering various prizes, often of large amount.

NATIONAL OPERA COMPANY, THE, was the name adopted by the American Opera Company for the season of 1886–87. Theodore Thomas continued as conductor, assisted by Gustav Hinrichs and Arthur Mees. The most notable event was the first American rendering of Rubinstein's 'Nero' (in English) on Mar. 14, 1887, at the Metropolitan Opera House. Massé's 'Galatea' was also given in Brooklyn on Dec. 30, 1886, and Delibes' ballet 'Coppelia' at the Metropolitan in March. The company spent most of its time on tour, winding up disastrously at San Francisco, though with two or three performances on the way back to New York.

'NATOMA.' A three-act opera by Victor Herbert on a text by Joseph D. Redding. It was foreshadowed in an announcement by Hammerstein as early as 1907, was submitted to Gatti-Casazza at the Metropolitan Opera House and partially tested in rehearsal, and was finally produced by the Chicago-Philadelphia Company at Philadelphia on Feb. 25, 1911, and repeated by the same Company at the Metropolitan on Feb. 28. The story is laid in Southern California during the Spanish domination and involves some Indian elements.

'NEC–NATOMA.' No. 12 of the 'Grove-Plays' of the San Francisco Bohemian Club, produced in 1914. The music is by Uda Waldrop and the text by J. Wilson Shields, the scene being long ago in the redwood forest.

NEFF, CHARLES DANIEL (b. 1867). See COLLEGES, 3 (Upper Iowa U.).

NEGRO MUSIC. See article in Vol. iii. 359–62. The bibliography is open to considerable extension, certainly so as to include Krehbiel, *Afro-American Folk-Songs*, 1914, Mrs. Curtis-Burlin, *Negro Songs*, 2 vols., 1918, with her articles in 'The Musical Quarterly,' January and October, 1919, and the summaries in *The Art of Music*, iv. pp. 284–311, and in *The American History and Encyclopedia of Music*, volume on 'American Music,' pp. 47–70. A striking article on 'Musical Culture in Negro Schools and Colleges,' by Mrs. Lydia H. Hamlin, is in the *M. T. N. A. Proceedings*, 1916, pp. 144–55. This latter calls attention to the way in which the Negro's innate capacity for song is being turned to practical account in present-day education. Interesting instances of strong artistic development among colored students in music-schools in many parts of the country might be cited. R. Nathaniel Dett, music-director at Hampton Institute, has notable distinction as composer and Harry T. Burleigh has made a mark as singer and songwriter. These are but conspicuous examples. In 1912 David Mannes started in New York a Music School Settlement for Colored People. In 1919 began the issue of a monthly periodical in Philadelphia, 'The Master-Musician,' devoted to the interests of Negro musicians.

Analogous to what was noted under INDIAN MUSIC is the increasing tendency among American composers to utilize Negro themes or at least the spirit and topics of Negro music. Chadwick in his 2nd Symphony (1885) was perhaps the first significant example. Dvořák's 'New World' Symphony (1893) doubtless exerted more influence, especially because expressing a strong conviction on the composer's part as to the value of this neglected source. Gilbert early began the series of works that includes the 'Negro Episode,' the 'Americanesque' (1903), the 'Comedy-Overture' (1911), the 'Negro Rhapsody' (1913) and 'The Dance in Place Congo' (1918). Humiston's 'Southern Fantasie' came out in 1906, and Powell's 'Sonata Virginianesque,' his suite 'In the South' and various lesser works were not much later. Innumerable cases might be cited of the use of Negro material in songs, as by Farwell, Ayres, Burleigh, Cook and others, besides the composers already named.

With reference to the extension of music-education it is not impossible that in the future the various colleges for Negroes will become able to magnify technical training so as to produce decided results. At present only two or three of these colleges emphasize music, notably Fisk University at Nashville, Hampton Institute in Virginia and Tuskegee Institute in Alabama.

NEIDLINGER, WILLIAM HAROLD (b. 1863). See Register, 8.

NEPOMUCENO, ALBERTO (b. 1864). See Register, 8.

NEUENDORFF, ADOLF (June 13, 1843, Hamburg, Germany : Dec. 4, 1897, New York), came to New York when a boy of twelve, studied violin with Weinlich and Matzka and piano with Schilling, at sixteen began playing the violin at the Stadt Theatre and at seventeen appeared as pianist. In 1861 he toured Brazil as violinist, on his return took up theory with Anschütz and in 1864 succeeded him as conductor of German opera in Milwaukee. In 1867–71 he was music-director of the new Stadt Theatre in New York, where he gave 40 light operas, and in the last season, with a troupe specially brought from Europe, a long list of German works, including the first American production of 'Lohengrin' (Apr. 15, 1871). In 1872 he joined Carl Rosa and Wachtel in giving a notable season of Italian opera at the Academy of Music, and for two years managed the Germania Theatre. In 1875 he gave German opera at the Academy, with Wachtel again and Mme. Pappenheim. At this time he was also leading a choral society and serving as church-organist. In 1876 he conducted Beethoven concerts and attended the opening of Wagner's opera-house at Bayreuth as correspondent of the 'Staats-Zeitung.' In 1877 he led the Wagner Festival at the Academy, including the first American presentation of 'Die Walküre' (Apr. 3). In 1878 he was conductor of the Philharmonic Society. The failure of the Germania Theatre in 1883 ruined him financially and he moved to Boston, but served as conductor in various connections, such as in 1887–88 with Josef Hofmann, in 1889–91 with the Emma Juch Company and in 1892 giving English opera in New York. In 1893–95 he was in Vienna, where his wife, Mme. Januschowsky, was prima donna at the Opera. From 1896 he was music-director at Temple Emanu-El in New York and in 1897 followed Seidl as conductor of the Metropolitan Orchestra. He composed two symphonies (1878, '80), the comic operas 'The Rat-Charmer of Hamelin' (1880), 'Don Quixote' (1882), 'Prince Woodruff' (1887) and 'The Minstrel' (1892), several overtures, cantatas, choruses and songs. [R.4]

NEUPERT, EDMUND (Apr. 1, 1842, Christiania, Norway : June 22, 1888, New York), had his first training from his father. From 1858 he studied in Berlin with Kullak and Kiel, becoming teacher in the former's Academy and associate of the latter in the Stern Conservatory. From 1868 he was leading piano-teacher at the Copenhagen Conservatory and in 1880–81 was assistant and for a short time successor of Nicholas Rubinstein at the Moscow Conservatory. After 1882 he was in New York, where his concert-playing made a deep impression — 'a sweep, power and breadth truly gorgeous and overwhelming,' said one critic. His compositions were almost wholly salon-pieces, études and exercises, including a Piano-School (1880), Concert-Études, op. 17, Octave-Studies, op. 18, Studies in Style, opp. 19–20, Poetical Études, opp. 25, 51, etc. [R.7]

NEVADA, EMMA [name originally Wixom] (1862, Alpha, Cal.). See article in Vol. iii. 365–6. In 1884–85 she was a member of Mapleson's troupe and as such sang not only in New York and San Francisco, but at the Grand Opera Festival in Chicago in May, 1885, and again in 1889. Since then she has been heard only in Europe. [R.7]

NEVIN, ARTHUR FINLEY (Apr. 27, 1871, Edgeworth, Pa.), after a partial course at the University of Pittsburgh, in 1891–93 studied in Boston at the New England Conservatory, taking piano with Otto Bendix, voice with Nobbs and theory with Goetschius, followed by four years in Berlin, studying piano with Klindworth and Jedliczka and composition with Boise and Humperdinck. In 1897–1910 he lived at Edgeworth engaged with teaching and composition, except that in 1903–04, having become deeply interested in Indian music, he lived among the Blackfeet Indians of Montana, noting their music and legends. This gave the basis for his opera 'Poia,' later composed at Edgeworth, and for many lectures, beginning with one in 1907 in the White House in Washington at President Roosevelt's invitation. On Apr. 23, 1910, 'Poia' was given at the Royal Opera in Berlin under Muck — the first American opera to be accepted by such a house — after preparation under the composer's direction. In 1911–14 he lived at Charlottesville, Va., busy with composition, and in 1914–15 was engaged in conducting in connection with the MacDowell Association's work at Peterboro, N. H. Since 1915 he has been head of the choral and extension-work of the University of Kansas, involving the oversight of 35 community-choruses. In 1917–18 he had leave of absence to direct music at Camp Grant in Illinois, where he drilled 41,000 soldiers in singing, led a massed band of 240 and occasionally had a chorus of 35,000 at one time. His works include, besides 'Poia' (published by Fürstner), the one-act opera 'A Daughter of the Forest' (1918, Chicago, published by Church), the masque 'A Night in Yaddo-Land,' the cantatas 'The Djinns,' with accompaniment for two pianos (divided prize from the Mendelssohn Club of Cleveland), and 'Roland,' a 'Miniature Suite' in five movements for orchestra, two other orchestral suites — 'Lorna Doone' and 'Love-Dreams,' a string-quartet in D minor, 'At the Spring' for string-orchestra, a piano-trio in C, 'Bakawali Dances' for orchestra (written for Ruth St. Denis), three piano-suites and other piano-pieces, about 25 songs and several choral works. See his article on his Indian experiences in 'The Musical Quarterly,' April, 1916. [R.8]

NEVIN, ETHELBERT WOODBRIDGE (Nov. 25, 1862, Edgeworth, Pa. : Feb. 17, 1901, New Haven, Conn.). See article in Vol. iii. 366. Interest in his music does not diminish, and Elson's calling 'The Rosary' 'the most famous American song' appears justified. It was first sung by Francis Rogers, accompanied by the composer, at a concert in Madison Square Garden Concert Hall in New York on Feb. 15, 1898. The pantomime 'Lady Floriane's Dream' was produced in New York the same year. To the list of works add the song-cycle 'Captive Memories,' (1900, New York) and his only choral work, 'The Quest.' After his death the orchestration of the latter was completed by Horatio Parker. See Thompson, *The Life of Ethelbert Nevin*, 1913, and article by Francis Rogers in 'The Musical Quarterly,' July, 1917. [R.7]

NEVIN, GEORGE BALCH (b. 1859). See Register, 7.

NEVIUS, J. W. See TUNE-BOOKS, 1817.

NEW ENGLAND CONSERVATORY OF MUSIC, THE, of Boston, was established in 1867 by Eben Tourjée, then in charge of a successful school in Providence. With him for a time was associated Robert Goldbeck, and the original faculty included Lang, Perabo, Emery, Zerrahn, Tuckerman and George E. Whiting. The conservatory was first located in rooms in the Music Hall Building, with easy access to the best concerts and to the great organ. In 1870 the first class of thirteen was graduated, and the Conservatory was incorporated with the provision that all profits from operation should be devoted exclusively to the interests of the institution. The director's activity in the Peace Jubilees of 1868 and 1872 undoubtedly helped progress. The faculty was steadily enlarged and strengthened, by 1875 including every important Boston musician, and the student-body increased rapidly, up to 1878 totaling over 14,000, coming from all parts of the United States and Canada. An early emphasis was given to public-school music, for which in 1874 a summer-school was opened at East Greenwich, R. I. When Luther W. Mason went to Japan in 1879–82 to introduce American methods, it was as a member of the Conservatory staff.

In 1882 the large St. James Hotel on Franklin Square was bought to provide better teaching facilities and a suitable dormitory for women-students. Here the Tourjées, husband and wife, created a genuine home for the pupils. In May of that year the thousandth Conservatory concert was given. But the financing of the big enterprise was difficult. Devices like providing some non-musical instruction were tried, and aid was sought, unsuccessfully, from the State. This burden hastened the director's death in 1891. He was followed in 1891 by Carl Faelten, who was in turn succeeded in 1897 by George W. Chadwick, the present director. The latter at once proceeded to organize the institution upon strictly musical lines, to strengthen the faculty by adding younger teachers who had had modern intensive training, and to lift the standard generally to that of the best European schools. Among the strong accessions were Helen Hopekirk, Carl Baermann, and Wallace Goodrich, who in 1907 became dean of the faculty. Plans were also developed for a new building, largely on the initiative and with the help of Eben D. Jordan, later president and munificent benefactor.

In 1902 the Conservatory removed to its present building on Huntington Avenue, close to the new Symphony Hall and various literary and educational centers. This building, designed by Wheelwright and Haven, is a model of convenience and taste — with ample offices and public rooms, a large auditorium (called Jordan Hall after the donor), a second auditorium, seating about 400, over fifty class-rooms, a library and museum, a music-store and printing-offices, etc. The business-manager is Ralph L. Flanders, whose efficient policy for over fifteen years has led to the practical extinction of the debt of over half a million inherited from earlier years.

The average number of students annually is above 3000 and the total registration since foundation over 100,000. The faculty of over seventy-five members includes teachers and soloists of national reputation. The regular courses, leading to a diploma in any one of the principal branches, are designed to prepare for a professional career as artist or teacher. Special students are also admitted, with full privileges as to lectures and recitals. Emphasis is placed upon the organ-department, the dramatic department, public-school music, the orchestra and the various ensemble-classes. The orchestra, numbering about seventy-five, is a complete symphonic organization, has rehearsals twice a week under the director or dean, gives several concerts with classical and modern programs, and assists in sundry Conservatory functions, including accompaniment of advanced students. It has supplied players for many of the leading orchestras of the country. Since 1905 the Conservatory has had relations with Harvard University whereby students of either can pursue certain studies with credit in the other. The library of almost 5000 volumes is strong in complete editions, cathedral music, choral, orchestral and chamber-works, and in books of general reference. The museum of instruments contains interesting specimens from Oriental and Asiatic countries. Women-students are provided for in a series of residences near by, under Conservatory management, with accommodation for about 200.

The Conservatory is supported by receipts from tuition and from invested funds, the latter largely coming by bequest from Eben D. Jordan and Mrs. Robert Dawson Evans.

Reference is made on pp. 33–4 to the unique eminence of the Conservatory in the history of American musical education. It was the first large music-school, and has always occupied a position of noble leadership and beneficent influence.

NEW HAVEN SYMPHONY ORCHESTRA, THE, was organized in 1896 more or less as an adjunct to the Yale School of Music. Until 1919 the conductor was Horatio Parker. In 1907 Isidore Troostwyk, the concertmaster, started the New Haven String Orchestra, which he has since conducted. Among first performances by this latter are Kriens' 'In Holland' Suite (1912) and a suite by Troostwyk (1914).

'NEW MUSIC REVIEW, THE.' See note in Vol. iii. 689. The first number of 'The Church Music Review' appeared in December, 1901. The 'Review' has occupied a place by itself for acute editorials, able contributed articles, useful summaries of leading events, the management of church music and for many years official records of the A. G. O.

NEW ORLEANS FRENCH OPERA TROUPE, THE, is the name most often used for various companies playing in New Orleans at intervals from about 1800 and often making considerable tours in the North. Most of these were troupes brought from Paris.

NEW ORLEANS OPERA HOUSE, THE, or The New French Opera House, was built by Boudousquié in 1859 and remained the home of brilliant productions until 1919, when it was destroyed by fire. Among works given here for the first time in America are Gounod's 'La Reine de Saba' and 'Le Tribut de Zamora,' Bizet's 'L'Arlésienne,' Massenet's 'Hérodiade,' 'Esclarmonde,' 'Werther,' 'Cendrillon' and 'Don Quichotte,' Salvayre's 'Richard III,' Saint-Saëns' 'Samson et Dalila,' Lalo's 'Le Roi d'Ys,' Reyer's 'Salammbô,' Cilèa's 'Adrienne Lecouvreur,' Giordano's 'Siberia' and Leroux' 'Le Chemineau.' The influence of the traditions of this House has been especially felt in Chicago and New York. See The Art of Music, iv. pp. 162–5.

NEW THEATRE, THE, in New York, was erected in 1909 primarily to provide a place for spoken drama. In 1909–10, however, it was the scene of a supplementary season of 40 performances by the forces of the Metropolitan Opera House, the works being lighter than those there given. In 1913–15 it was again used for opera under the name of The Century Theater (see CENTURY OPERA COMPANY).

NEW YORK CHAMBER MUSIC SOCIETY, THE, was formed in 1914 by Carolyn Beebe and Gustave Langenus. At first they shared the direction, but soon Miss Beebe became sole conductor. The aim has been to assemble a strong body of expert players of both string- and wood-instruments, to develop an ensemble like that of a string-quartet, and to build up a large and significant répertoire. The Society has had much success. In 1919 it was incorporated, and now controls the exclusive services of its players. The members are Miss Beebe, pianist and director, Pierre Henrotte and Scipione Guidi, violins, Samuel Lifschey, viola, Paul Kéfer, 'cello, Emil Mix, double-bass, Gustave Langenus, clarinet, William Kincaid, flute, Henri de Busscher, oboe, Ugo Savolini, bassoon, and Joseph Franzl, horn. All the members are American-born or naturalized citizens. The Society has introduced the following works:

(1917) Dubois' 'Deux Pièces en forme canonique'; d'Indy's Trio in B-flat, op. 29; Goepfart's Quartet in F, op. 98; Huss' Four Intermezzi; Sekles' Serenade in B-flat, op. 6; Mason's Scherzo-Caprice, op. 14a; Tovey's Variations on a theme of Gluck, op. 28; Holbrooke's Nocturne, 'Fairyland,' op. 57, no. 1; Huré's Quintet in D; (1918) Dubois' Quintet in F and Dixtuor in D; Juon's Divertimento in F, op. 51; Taylor's Suite, 'Through the Looking-Glass,' op. 12; Goossens' Suite in C, op. 6; (1919) Ries' Octet in A-flat, op. 128; Pirani's 'Gavotte Rococo' and 'Whirlwind' Scherzo; Tovey's Trio in D minor, op. 14; Goossens' Suite, 'Impressions of a Holiday,' op. 7; (1920) Lefebvre's Quintet in A; Griffes' Suite, op. 5; Sowerby's Quintet in D minor; Jungen's Trio in F-sharp, op. 30.

Several of these were written for the Society, and other special works are in prospect.

NEW YORK COLLEGE OF MUSIC, THE, was founded in 1878. In 1887–1905 the director was Alexander Lambert, who was succeeded by Carl Hein and August Fraemcke.

NEW YORK SACRED MUSIC SOCIETY, THE, was a choral society formed in 1823 on the basis of the choir of Zion Church. In 1831 it gave 'The Messiah' — the first complete performance in New York — and in 1838 the first American rendering of 'St. Paul,' both conducted by U. C. Hill. In 1849 it was replaced by the Harmonic Society.

NEW YORK TRIO CLUB, THE, was founded about 1867 by Bernardus Boekelman and directed by him as pianist till 1888. The other members were R. Richter, violinist, and Emil Schenck, 'cellist. In 1919 a New York Trio was formed with Clarence Adler, pianist, Scipione Guidi, violinist, and Cornelius Van Vliet, 'cellist.

NEWCOMB, ETHEL (b. 1879). See Register, 9.

NEWHALL, JAMES. See TUNE-BOOKS, 1802.

‡ NEWMAN, ERNEST (Nov. 30, 1868, Liverpool, England), was originally meant to enter Civil Service work in India, but was diverted by ill-health into business in Liver-

pool, taking up writing as an avocation. In 1903–05, however, he taught music in the Midland Institute at Birmingham, and since 1905 has been music-critic, in 1905–06 for the Manchester 'Guardian,' in 1906–19 for the Birmingham 'Post' and since 1919 for the London 'Observer.' His extensive knowledge and incisive style have made him eminent as a writer. He has published *Gluck and the Opera*, 1895, *A Study of Wagner*, 1899, *Wagner*, 1904, *Musical Studies*, 1905, *Elgar*, 1906, *Hugo Wolf*, 1907, *Richard Strauss*, 1908, *Wagner as Man and Artist*, 1914, and *A Musical Motley*, 1919, besides translating Weingartner's *Ueber das Dirigieren*, Schweitzer's *J. S. Bach*, and most of the Wagner opera-texts in the Breitkopf & Härtel edition. He has also edited *The New Library of Music* and *Fifty Songs of Hugo Wolf*, and was a contributor to *The Art of Music*, 1914–17.

NICHOLAS, CHARLES K. See Colleges, 3 (Midland C., Neb.).

NICHOLL, HORACE WADHAM (Mar. 17, 1848, Tipton, England). See article in Vol. iii. 372. From 1883 he was long a reader for Schirmer. In 1888–95 he taught harmony and ensemble-playing with Boekelman at Farmington, Conn. He has published 12 Grand Preludes and Fugues for piano (extraordinary for contrapuntal dexterity), an organ-sonata in A minor, op. 42, a piano-concerto in D minor, op. 10, a 'cello-sonata, op. 13, a violin-sonata, op. 21, etc. He has also issued a *Text-Book on Harmony*. [R.6]

NIELSEN, ALICE (b. 1876). See Register, 8.

NIELSEN, PER. See Colleges, 3 (Westminster C., Pa.).

NIKISCH, ARTUR (Oct. 12, 1855, Szent-Miklós, Hungary). See article in Vol. iii. 379–80. In 1912 he made a tour of the United States with the London Symphony Orchestra (85 players), giving 27 concerts during April, beginning in New York and including Chicago, Kansas City, St. Louis, Buffalo, Toronto, Ottawa, Montreal and New York again, all with notable success. See biographies by Pfohl, 1900, and Lipaiev, 1904. [R.7]

NIKITA [Louise Margaret Nicholson] (b. 1872). See Register, 7.

NILSSON, CHRISTINE (Aug. 20, 1843, near Wexiö, Sweden). See article in Vol. iii. 380–1. In August, 1916, a national tribute was given her by testimonial performances in the opera-houses and theaters, a public reception and the presentation of a medal on her birthday. [R.6]

NINISS, J. R. See Colleges, 2 (Queen's C., N. C.).

NOACK, SYLVAIN (Aug. 21, 1881, Rotterdam, Holland), at first aimed to be a

pianist, but took up the violin with Spoor and continued with Elderling at the Amsterdam Conservatory in 1898–1900, winning first prize at graduation. In 1900–03 he played in the Concertgebouw Orchestra and in 1903–05 taught in the Conservatory and was second in the Conservatory Quartet. In 1905–06 he was in Rotterdam and in 1906–08 concertmaster of the City Orchestra in Aix-la-Chapelle and leader of a quartet. From 1908 he was second concertmaster of the Boston Symphony Orchestra, appearing in 1909 as soloist in Saint-Saens' B minor Concerto and repeatedly later. In 1915, with Roth, Férir and Schroeder, he formed the Boston String Quartet. In 1919 he removed to Los Angeles to become concertmaster of the Philharmonic Orchestra. [R.9]

NOBLE, THOMAS TERTIUS (May 5, 1867, Bath, England). See article in Vol. v. 655. After fifteen years at York Minster, in 1913 he resigned to become organist at St. Thomas' in New York. Besides his duties there he has been often heard in recital elsewhere, making an extended tour in 1913 and playing at the Panama-Pacific Exposition in 1915. Columbia University made him an honorary A.M. in 1918. His list of works includes, besides those mentioned :

Anthems a cappella —
 'But now thus saith the Lord,' 'Go to dark Gethsemane,' 'A Christmas Pastorale,' 'Come, O Creator Spirit blest,' 'Come, O Thou Traveler unknown,' 'Fierce was the wild billow,' 'Grieve not the Holy Spirit of God,' 'Hail, gladdening light,' 'I will lay me down in peace,' 'Jesu, the very thought of Thee,' 'Let all the world,' 'O hearken thou unto the voice,' 'O Thou to whom all creatures bow' (8-part), 'O Wisdom, Spirit of the living God,' 'Rejoice to-day with one accord,' 'The Saints of God,' 'The Soul Triumphant,' 'The souls of the righteous.'
Anthems with accompaniment —
 'Glory to God in the highest,' 'Go not far from me' (from Zingarelli), 'Lord, we pray Thee' (from Haydn), 'A Prayer of Thanksgiving' (from Kremser), 'The Risen Christ,' 'When I consider Thy heavens,' 'Zadok the Priest' (from Handel).
 3 Processionals, 12 Christmas Carols, 2 Vesper Hymns.
Organ-Works —
 'An Elizabethan Idyll,' 'Intermezzo in A-flat,' 'Mélancolique,' 'Nachspiel,' 3 Short Pieces (Reverie, Elegy, Finale), Toccata and Fugue in F minor, Triumphal March, Solemn March in E minor, Theme and Variations in D-flat, and arrangements of Pleyel's Adagio in B-flat, Camidge's Concerto in G minor, Corelli's Suite in F, and of two Hebrew melodies.
Orchestral and Chamber-Works —
 Morris-Dance for orchestra.
 Suite for violin and orchestra.
 Several pieces for violin and piano.
 Several sacred and secular songs and part-songs.
                                                    [R.10]

NORDEN, N. LINDSAY (Apr. 24, 1887, Philadelphia), studied in New York with

Spicker, Weld and F. W. Robinson, graduated from Columbia University in 1909 and studied further with Rybner, gaining a Mus.B. in 1911. In 1904–05 he was organist at St. Bartholomew's Chapel and while in the University was assistant at the Chapel there. In 1906–15 he served at St. Mary's and in 1915–17 at All Saints', both in Brooklyn, and developed from 1912 the Æolian Choir there for the study and presentation of Russian music, giving about thirty recitals and bringing out over 80 works, some of them unperformed outside of Russia. Since 1916 he has been conductor of the Mendelssohn Club in Philadelphia, succeeding Gilchrist, and since 1917 organist at the Second Presbyterian Church there and at St. Paul's in Ogontz, besides teaching at the Episcopal Academy. In addition to his extensive editing of Russian works, he has published anthems and other service-music, and has written the overture 'King Melville,' a setting of 'Thanatopsis' for soli, chorus and orchestra, etc. He has contributed many articles on church-music to periodicals. [R.9]

NORDICA [Norton], LILLIAN (May 12, 1859, Farmington, Me. : May 10, 1914, Batavia, Java). See article in Vol. iii. 389–90, and note in Vol. v. 655. She first appeared in opera in America in 1883 at New York under Mapleson as Marguerite. She was at the Metropolitan Opera House in 1888–90 and 1891–92, and first appeared there as Isolde in 1895. She took the same rôle at the Grand-Opéra in Paris in 1910. In 1910–11 she sang with the Boston Opera Company and in 1911 made a concert-tour as well. Her last concert-trip was to Australia, beginning a world-tour, and her last concert was at Melbourne in December, 1913. [R.6]

NORFOLK (CONN.) FESTIVALS. See LITCHFIELD COUNTY CHORAL UNION.

NORMAL INSTITUTES. The name applied to summer-schools for teachers, such as began to be common just before the Civil War. The first example is said to have been that held by Root, Hastings and Bradbury in 1852 in New York. Emphasis was usually laid on vocal music and on elementary theory, with more or less instrumental demonstration through recitals. Though loosely conceived and dependent on the ability of particular leaders, these Institutes doubtless served a useful purpose. They foreshadowed such well-organized and established enterprises as the Chautauqua Institution, the summer-schools of various universities and certain detached schools for teachers that are now in operation. See CONVENTIONS.

NORMAL SCHOOLS. See STATE NORMAL SCHOOLS.

NORRIS, HOMER ALBERT (Oct. 4, 1860, Wayne, Me. : Aug. 14, 1920, New York), was first taught by Marston in Portland, studied with Turner, Emery and Chadwick at the New England Conservatory in Boston, and then spent four years in Paris with Guilmant, Dubois, Godard and Gigout. His early positions as organist were in Lewiston and Portland, Me., and in 1892–1904 he was at the Ruggles Street Church in Boston and in 1904–13 at St. George's in New York. He devoted himself largely to promulgating French ideas in composition and was one of the first to emphasize these in America, publishing *Practical Harmony on a French Basis*, 1896, and *The Art of Counterpoint*, 1899, besides numerous articles in leading periodicals. His compositions include the oratorio 'St. John the Baptist,' the cantata 'Nain,' a setting of Whitman's 'The Flight of the Eagle,' for soprano, tenor and baritone (1905), about 60 songs, including 'Twilight,' 'Peace' and the popular 'Rock-a-bye, Baby,' and pieces for organ and piano. [R.7]

NORTH AMERICAN MUSIC FESTIVALS, THE, are gatherings organized in 1916 by A. A. Van de Mark and held annually in Lockport, N. Y. The programs include papers and discussions upon varied topics of practical interest, with extended performances of music, vocal and instrumental, by American composers and interpreters. Several prizes are offered for works specially written in competition.

NORTHWESTERN CONSERVATORY OF MUSIC, THE, of Minneapolis, was founded in 1885 by Charles H. Morse and directed by him till 1891 after the model of the New England Conservatory.

NORTHWESTERN UNIVERSITY, Evanston, Ill. (Methodist), has had a School of Music since 1873, though at first not organically related to its total system. Since 1891, however, under the care of Peter C. Lutkin (dean from 1897) it has been not only in full standing among the constituent schools of the University, but more and more notable for the breadth of its instruction and the influence of its work. The faculty numbers about 35, and the students about 900 (including preparatory courses and summer-school). Special attention is given to ensemble-work, vocal and instrumental, and to public-school methods. The A Cappella Choir is a noted institution, as also the Musical Club and the Symphony Orchestra. See under CHICAGO NORTH SHORE FESTIVALS.

NORTON, SETH (d. 1818). See TUNE-BOOKS, 1816.

NORTON, WILLIAM WELLINGTON (b. 1881). See STATE UNIVERSITIES (N.D.).

'NOTRE DAME DE PARIS.' An opera by William H. Fry, produced in April, 1864, at Philadelphia.

NOVÁČEK, OTTOKAR EUGEN (May 13, 1866, Fehértemplom, Hungary : Feb.

MME. LILLIAN NORDICA

Copyright by Aimé Dupont

3, 1900, New York). See article in Vol. iii.
410. After 1893 he lived for a time in Berlin,
but returned to New York to play in the
Metropolitan Opera House orchestra. Brodsky played his violin-suite in Leipzig as early
as 1894. Busoni's performance of the piano-
concerto was with the Berlin Philharmonic
Orchestra in 1896. [R.8]

NOVAËS, GUIOMAR (Feb. 28, 1895,
São João da Boã Vista, Brazil), began study
at seven in São Paulo and appeared there as
pianist at nine. Her promise was such that
the Brazilian government assigned her a
subsidy and in 1909 she entered the Paris
Conservatory as first among nearly 400
applicants. After two years with Philipp in
1911 she graduated with a first prize, made
her formal début and entered upon a long
tour on the Continent, in England, and in
South America. In November, 1915, she
first played in New York and has since been
repeatedly heard there and elsewhere with
enthusiasm. Finck said of her in the 'Evening Post' at one time, 'More inspired playing
has never been heard in Æolian Hall, and
Æolian Hall audiences have heard all the foremost pianists of the time.' [R.10]

NOYES, EDITH ROWENA (Mar. 26,
1875, Cambridge, Mass.), in 1891–96 was a
pupil of MacDowell in Boston and of Chadwick, and has since worked there as pianist,
teacher, and composer. Her more important
works are the operetta 'Last Summer' (1898,
Lowell), a violin-sonata in F-sharp minor,
op. 70, on Indian themes, a piano-trio, op. 73,
and the pageant-opera 'Waushakum' (1917,
Framingham, Mass.), besides many piano-
pieces, songs, and anthems. In 1909 she
married Roy G. Greene. [R.8]

NOYES, EDWARD HIBBARD (Mar. 23,
1867, London, Ont.), first studied with Mr.
and Mrs. W. H. Sherwood in Boston and in
1885–87 was organist there. Between 1887
and 1895 he studied with Barth in Berlin, was
for a year court-pianist to Prince de Levin in

Russia, studied further with Mme. Essipov-
Leschetizky in Vienna and made a tour in
Norway and Sweden with the violinist Fred-
eriksen. Since 1895 he has taught in Boston
and also at the Hartford (Conn.) School of
Music, becoming noted through many able
pupils. In 1899–1901 he played in several
series of trio-recitals with Troostwyk, with
Leo Schulz, the 'cellist, with the Kneisel
Quartet, etc. He has published a few songs
(Thompson). [R.7]

NUNNS, ROBERT and WILLIAM. See
Register, 3.

NUNO, JAMES (Sept. 8, 1824, San Juan
de las Abadesas, Spain: July 17, 1908, Buffalo), was a choir-boy at the Barcelona Cathedral, studied composition with Merca-
dante in Italy and led small orchestras in
Barcelona for some years. In 1851 he became
band-master in the army and was sent to Cuba
to establish band-music there. About 1853
Santa Anna made him general band-inspector
in Mexico and he soon became one of the two
directors of the new National Conservatory
in Mexico City, besides composing the present
Mexican national hymn. In 1856 he managed
tours in the United States for singers from the
Italian opera, served as conductor with Thalberg and presently led both Italian and French
opera at Havana, being also associated with
Gottschalk. In 1863–69 he led opera-troupes
not only in Cuba, but in the United States,
Mexico and Central America, with singers
like Sontag, Grisi, Mario, Malibran, Kellogg
and Patti, and in 1864 assisted as conductor
at the welcome to Maximilian. After 1870
he lived at Buffalo, teaching singing and
conducting various societies, serving as
organist at different churches there and in
Rochester, and composing about 50 church-
works. In 1904, on invitation from President
Diaz, he was the guest of honor at the fiftieth
anniversary of the writing of his National
Hymn (first given on Sept. 15–16, 1854) and
received a remarkable ovation. [R.4]

O

OBER, MARGARETE (Apr. 15, 1885, Berlin, Germany), studied singing with Stolzenberg in Berlin in 1903-05 and later with Arthur Arndt, whom she married in 1910. Her début as stage-soprano was in 1906 at Frankfort in the rôle of Azucena. In 1906-07 her success at the Stettin Stadt-Theater was so pronounced that she was called to the Berlin Royal Opera. She created the title-rôle there in Massenet's 'Thérèse' in 1908 and that of Nenahu in Nevin's 'Poia' in 1910. In 1913 she was engaged for the Metropolitan Opera House, appearing on Nov. 21 as Ortrud. She has since remained there, until 1916 returning to Germany for the summers. Her répertoire includes the rôles of Brangäne, Ortrud, Fricka, Waltraute, Erda, Klytemnestra (in 'Iphigenia en Aulide'), Eglantine (in 'Euryanthe'), Fides, Dalila, Azucena, Amneris, Laura (in 'La Gioconda'), Marina (in 'Boris Godunov'), the Witch (in 'Hänsel und Gretel'), Octavian (in 'Der Rosenkavalier') and Katharina (in 'Der Widerspenstigen Zähmung'). [R.10]

OBERHOFFER, EMIL (Aug. 10, 1867, Munich, Germany), as a boy took up violin and organ with his father, in youth had advice from Kistler in piano and composition, and later studied piano with Philipp in Paris. Coming to America, after a brief stay in New York, in 1897 he located in St. Paul as conductor of the Apollo Club and from 1901 of the Minneapolis Philharmonic Club. This latter work led in 1903 to the organization of the Minneapolis Symphony Orchestra, which he has since directed with such ability that it has become one of the leading orchestras of the country. He has also been for a time organist at the Church of the Redeemer in Minneapolis and is on the music-staff of the University of Minnesota. [R.8]

OBERLIN COLLEGE, Oberlin, O. (Congregational), began to provide music-teaching as early as 1837, when George N. Allen, then a student, was designated as instructor in sacred music. He continued as such after graduating in 1839 and in 1841 was made professor, remaining in service till 1864. Two of his pupils, John P. Morgan and George W. Steele, in 1865 organized a Conservatory, which at first was only affiliated with the College in a general way. In 1867 Morgan withdrew and from 1869 the administration was taken up by Fenelon B. Rice, who remained in charge till his death in 1901, steadily building up the efficiency of the department in every direction. In 1884, by the gift of Lucien C. Warner and wife of New York,

the superior Warner Hall was built, which was later much extended by the addition of a fine concert-hall and further facilities. This hall seats about 1000, and there are two large lecture-rooms, 25 studios, an ample library and about 120 practice-rooms. The organ-equipment is unusually elaborate, including a large concert-organ, 2 for teaching and 21 for practice. In 1910 the Rice Memorial Hall was added to the plant, with almost as much opportunity for practice as in Warner Hall. Since 1901 the director has been Charles W. Morrison, who has effectively continued the energetic policy of earlier years. The faculty now numbers about 35 and the work of the Conservatory is so interlocked with that of the College that practically the whole student-body of 1500 comes under its influence. Music counts as a regular elective in the course for A. B. and post-graduate work may be taken leading to a Mus.B. (over 300 such degrees conferred). The usual number of pupils annually enrolled is over 600. Among the notable features of the curriculum are the emphasis upon organ, theory and history and the stimulus to choral music through the Oberlin Musical Union.

OBERLIN MUSICAL UNION, THE, is a choral society antedating the Oberlin Conservatory, though vitally related to it. Started in 1860, its first ten years were largely given to the performance of miscellaneous programs under various leaders, including C. H. Churchill, G. W. Steele, J. P. Morgan and J. C. Fillmore of Oberlin and some visiting conductors on certain occasions, such as E. M. Foote, B. F. Baker, and J. G. Barnett. In 1871-1900 Fenelon B. Rice was permanent conductor and since 1900 George W. Andrews. Since 1871 not much besides complete works has been given. The chorus usually numbers about 200 and three concerts are now given annually (nearly 200 since organization). A few performances have also been given in Cleveland with the Pittsburgh or Chicago Orchestras. 'The Messiah' was early taken up and in 1880-1903 was sung twice each year. 'Elijah' has been given about 15 times, 'St. Paul,' 5; Bach's Christmas Oratorio, 1; Beethoven's 9th Symphony, 2; his Missa Solemnis, 1; Brahms' Requiem, 2; Verdi's Requiem, 4; Bruch's 'Odysseus,' 4; Franck's 'Les Béatitudes,' 5; G. Schumann's 'Ruth,' 2; Saint-Saëns' 'Samson et Dalila,' 8; Elgar's 'Dream of Gerontius,' 3; Wolf-Ferrari's 'La Vita Nuova,' 2; Pierné's 'The Children's Crusade,' 2; concert performances of Wagner's 'Tannhäuser,' 'Lohengrin,' and 'Parsifal,'

etc. Several of these were the first renderings
in the Middle West.

O'BRION, MARY ELIZA (b. 1859). See
Register, 7.

ODELL & CO., J. H. & C. S., a well-known
firm of organ-builders in New York, was
founded in 1859 by John H. Odell (1830–99)
and Caleb S. Odell (1827–93), two brothers who
had been in the employ of Ferris & Stewart.
Their first modest factory was at 165 Seventh
Ave., and the first organ of importance made
was in 1863 for the South Baptist Church
(opening recital by G. W. Morgan and Mme.
Parepa-Rosa). In 1866 they patented a
system of pneumatic piston-knobs for controlling combinations which proved so succcessful
that increased business compelled them to
seek larger facilities at 407–9 West 42nd St.
The plant here was more than doubled in
1873, and is now finely equipped. In 1898
the firm patented its 'Vacuo-Exhaust' system,
a simple and efficient type of tubular action.
In 1914 was introduced a valuable electro-
magnetic action that was a decided improvement over the electro-pneumatic system
previously used. Altogether the firm has
built about 620 instruments, of which 6 are
4-manual and 60 3-manual. Among the
former are those in Temple Emanu-El, New
York City (1903) and St. Joseph's, Albany,
N. Y. (1913). The direction of the business
has remained with the Odell family, sons of
both founders succeeding in 1893, and two
grandsons of C. S. Odell following in 1911.

'ŒDIPUS TYRANNUS.' A setting of
Sophocles' play by John K. Paine, written
for performance at Harvard University in
1881. This was the first of its kind in America
and is counted one of Paine's strongest works.

OESTERLE, OTTO (1861–1894). See Register, 7.

OETTING, WILLIAM H. (Oct. 14, 1875,
Pittsburgh), studied with his father, who for
25 years was organist at the First German
Evangelical Church in Pittsburgh, and other
local teachers, followed by two years in Berlin,
continuing organ under Reimann and Egidi,
piano under Hutcheson and composition
under Boise. At the same time he taught the
English class in harmony at the Klindworth-
Scharwenka Conservatory. Since 1901 he
has been organist and teacher in Pittsburgh,
accompanist of the Apollo Club, in 1905–07
organ-recitalist at the Carnegie Institute, and
since 1915 one of the directors of the Pittsburgh
Musical Institute. At present he is organist at
the Sixth United Presbyterian Church. He has
written an overture, an orchestral Romanza
(Pittsburgh Festival Orchestra), an organ-
sonata, a Prelude and Fugue in E minor for
organ (Gray), piano-pieces, several anthems
(Church, Kranz), songs, etc. [R.8]

'OLD FOLKS' CONCERTS' was the name
given in 1854 to entertainments conducted
in Boston by Robert Kemp (1820–97), a
dealer in shoes, who sought to keep alive the
old-fashioned 'psalmody' for its homely
quaintness. Since then the term has been
indiscriminately applied to any rendering of
similar music, often presented grotesquely
and even in caricature. 'Father' Kemp
published an *Autobiography* in 1868.

OLDBERG, ARNE (July 12, 1874, Youngstown, O.), was the son of a noted authority
on pharmacy and from 1884 was educated
in Chicago, where he had his early training
in music, supplemented by study of the piano
with Leschetizky in Vienna and of composition
with Rheinberger in Munich. Since 1899 he
has been head of the piano-department at
Northwestern University in Evanston, Ill.
He has won distinction especially as composer of orchestral works, which have been
brought out not only at the North Shore
Festivals, but by the Chicago, Philadelphia,
Minneapolis and other orchestras. His
chamber-works, also, have secured a wide
hearing. His compositions include Symphonies in F minor, op. 23, and C minor, op.
34 (both taking prizes in national competitions), the overtures 'Paolo and Francesca,' op. 21 (1908, Chicago Orchestra), and
'Festival' (1909, North Shore Festival, 1910,
Chicago Orchestra), the orchestral fantasy
'At Night,' op. 38 (1916, Chicago Orchestra),
12 Variations, op. 19, for orchestra and organ
(1912, Chicago Orchestra, 1913, North Shore
Festival), a Rhapsody, op. 36 (1915, Chicago
Orchestra, etc.), a concerto for horn, op. 20,
an organ-concerto, op. 35 (1914, Chicago
Orchestra), a piano-concerto, op. 17, a string-
quartet in C minor, op. 15, two quintets, opp.
16, 24, for piano and strings and one in E-flat,
op. 18, for piano and wood-wind, a piano-
suite, op. 8, a piano-sonata, op. 28, Thematic
Variations for piano, op. 25, a 'Legend,' op. 26,
three 'Miniatures,' an 'Arabesque,' op. 31, an
'Improvisation,' op, 32, a ' Russian Prelude,'
op. 33, and many smaller works. [R.8]

OLDMIXON, Mrs., née George (1768– ?).
See Register, 2.

OLIVER, HENRY KEMBLE (1800–1885).
See Register, 3, and Tune-Books, 1848.

OLMSTED, TIMOTHY. See Tune-
Books, 1805.

'OMANO.' An opera by L. H. Southard,
based on Beckwith's 'Vathek,' twice given in
concert-form in Boston in 1858.

‡ O'NEILL, NORMAN (Mar. 14, 1875,
London, England). See article in Vol. v.
656. Recent works include the following:

'Overture Humoresque,' for orchestra.
'Hornpipe' for orchestra.
String-Quartet (Schott).

Incidental music for 'Freedom' (1918, New York), Dunsany's 'The Gods of the Mountain' (2 dances also for piano separately) and 'The Golden Doom,' Malleson's 'Paddy Pools,' 'Maurice's Own Idea' and 'Michael' (these three for string-quartet), the school-play 'Hiawatha' (Routledge), and Russian Songs for Tolstoi's 'Reparation' (piano, Ascherberg).
'The Swinburne Ballet,' for chorus and orchestra. The choruses 'Noël' (Stainer) and 'Lullaby' (Arnold).
Songs — 'The Eagles of England' (Elkin), 'The Warrior-Lover' (Schott), 'All for Me' and 'I Love you Dearly' (Boosey).
'Carillon,' for piano (Ascherberg).
Three Old English Pieces, for piano (Schott).
Four Songs without Words, for piano (Anglo-French Co.).
' In the Branches,' for piano (Anglo-French Co.)

'ONTI–ORA.' An opera in three acts by Gustav Hinrichs, produced in June, 1891, in Philadelphia.

OPERA IN THE UNITED STATES. See article in Vol. iii. 466–72. Many additional details are given under METROPOLITAN OPERA HOUSE, MANHATTAN OPERA HOUSE, CHICAGO-PHILADELPHIA OPERA COMPANY, BOSTON OPERA COMPANY, etc. See Krehbiel, *Chapters of Opera*, 3rd ed., 1911, and *More Chapters of Opera*, 1919, *The Art of Music*, iv. chap. vii. and *The International Year-Book*, 1907– .

OPPERMAN, ELLA SCOBLE. See COLLEGES, 2 (Florida State C. for Women).

ORATORIO SOCIETY OF BALTIMORE, THE, was founded in 1882 by Otto Sutro. Its first conductor was Fritz Finke (1882–94), followed by Joseph Pache, who is still in office. The chorus numbers 300–350 singers, and two or three concerts are given each year, partly supported by a body of patrons. The Society devotes itself to oratorio music of the highest class, including at least thirty works of large dimensions and representing all periods from Bach and Handel down to the present. Notable initial performances have been those of Hamerik's 'Symphonie Chorale' and 'Christian Trilogy,' Bruch's 'Moses' and Nowowiejski's ' Quo Vadis.'

ORATORIO SOCIETY, THE, of Newark, N. J. (formerly called the Schubert Vocal Society), was organized in 1878 by Louis Arthur Russell, who has been its conductor ever since. Originally formed to cultivate part-songs and cantatas, after a few years it added the larger field of oratorio left vacant by the disbanding of the Harmonic Society. Membership is limited to 125 singers. The regular series includes three performances, often with 'popular' concerts besides, and the Society has repeatedly coöperated efficiently in charitable undertakings, so that the total number of concerts has been towards 150. In 1894 Mr. Russell organized the Newark Symphony Orchestra, primarily to assist at the concerts of the Oratorio Society, but

also to give occasional instrumental performances. Besides a large variety of cantatas and lighter works, the Society has given the standard oratorios, sacred and secular, and many operas or parts of operas in concert-form. American works include Buck's 'Hymn to Music' and 'Light of Asia,' Chadwick's 'Lovely Rosabel,' Russell's 'Pastoral Rhapsody,' Parker's 'King Trojan,' 'Harold Harfagar' and 'A Star-Song,' and Hadley's 'In Music's Praise.'

ORATORIO SOCIETY, THE, of New York. See article in Vol. iii. 370–1. Frank Damrosch continued as conductor till 1912 and in 1912–17 was succeeded by Louis Koemmenich and in 1917 by Walter Damrosch. Among the more striking accomplishments of the Society in recent years were performances in 1907 of Wolf-Ferrari's 'La Vita Nuova,' in 1911 of Franck's 'Les Béatitudes,' Saint-Saëns' 150th Psalm and Grell's Missa Solemnis, in 1913 of Taubmann's 'Eine deutsche Messe' and Georg Schumann's 'Ruth,' in 1914 of Beethoven's Missa Solemnis, in 1915 of Bossi's 'Giovanna d'Arco,' etc. In April, 1920, the Society united in a festival with the Symphony Society (as previously in 1881) at which, among other works, Kelley's 'Pilgrim's Progress' was sung.

ORATORIO SOCIETY, THE, of Toronto, was founded in 1912. Its conductor is Edward Broome. The chorus numbers 200 or more. There are at least two concerts annually, often with the assistance of visiting orchestras, such as the Russian Symphony, the New York Philharmonic or the Cincinnati Symphony. The Society has given the only performance in Canada of Gardiner's 'News from Whydah' and Broome's 'Hymn of Trust.'

ORCHESTRAS. Aggregations of instruments were common in the various musical undertakings of the 18th century, as Sonneck's records abundantly show (see especially his *Concert-Life*), supplying overtures, symphonies and the accompaniments for operas and choral works of some magnitude. But these were not permanent in membership or under any steady rehearsal. The first important steps toward permanent orchestras were taken by the Musical Fund Society of Philadelphia from 1820 and the Philharmonic Society of New York from 1842. Stimulus to orchestral interest came notably from the tours of the Germania Orchestra in 1848–54, as from the visits of Gungl in 1849 and Jullien in 1853. During the whole decade before the Civil War the popular taste for instrumental ensembles was also much advanced in certain places by chamber-concerts. Every attempt to give opera on a large scale served to indicate orchestral possibilities. The establishing of 'symphony soirées' in New York by Theodore

Thomas in 1864 led soon to his epoch-making concert-tours (1869–78). After 1870 genuine symphony orchestras began gradually to multiply. Specially significant was the starting of the Cincinnati Festivals in 1873, of the New York Symphony Society in 1878, and of the Boston Symphony Orchestra in 1881. In almost all the larger cities — and in not a few smaller ones as well —there are now orchestral societies of importance. It has recently been said that twelve or fifteen of these are so far highly organized as to hold daily rehearsals. Besides giving series of concerts annually in their home-cities, most of the larger orchestras extend their influence by prolonged tours.

OREM, PRESTON WARE, born in Philadelphia, was educated at the Eastburn Academy and the University of Pennsylvania, and studied organ and theory with Clarke and piano with Jarvis and others. In 1889–95 he was organist at St. Paul's Pro-Cathedral in Los Angeles. He then returned to Philadelphia, taught one year at the Philadelphia Conservatory, and in 1896–1905 was on the staff of the Combs Conservatory. Since 1900 he has been editor and critic for the Presser Company and also conductor of the Presser Choral Society. In 1901–10 he was organist at the Walnut Street Presbyterian Church. His published works include a Romance for violin and orchestra, an 'American Indian Rhapsody' for piano (also for orchestra), many songs, piano-pieces, etc., besides arrangements and transcriptions. Unpublished works are a piano-quartet and quintet and a Ballet Suite for orchestra. He is author of a *Harmony-Book for Beginners*, which has had an enormous circulation. [R.8]

ORGAN. See general article in Vol. iii. 513–62, with some references to American facts. During the past thirty or forty years there has been an extraordinary growth in the United States and Canada in everything pertaining to organ-making, organ-playing and the popularization of organ-music. No adequate summary of all this can here be made. But certain remarks may be set down.

The same mechanical ingenuity and business enterprise that have made American piano-making eminent have been applied in the making of pipe-organs, though the two industries are so different that the facts in the latter field are not as obvious. Probably the improvements in organ-making are actually more varied and at least equally striking. The installation of the German organ in the Boston Music Hall in 1863 stimulated advance in a general way. About 1870 the experiments of Hilbourne L. Roosevelt in both voicing and mechanism were speedily followed by others. Competition soon became keen to offer effective solutions of problems in

pneumatic and electric action, in augmented, stabilized and graded wind-supply, in progressive and refined stop-specification, voicing and pipe-disposition, in the planning and internal adjustments of consoles, leading to unprecedented facilities for registration, etc. Along with these essential improvements, which have come into general use since about 1900, have gone others less tangible, especially in shop-efficiency, expertness in erecting and enterprise in developing a market. The extraordinary extension of the industry in the United States is also partly due to circumstances that are peculiar, such as the rapid building up of new communities, their geographical dispersion (encouraging the founding of organ-factories at many separate points), and the multiplicity of religious denominations and the number of churches relative to the population. There are perhaps 100 establishments, employing 2500–3000 workers. The annual output is probably over 2000 instruments, among which the proportion of those with three or four manuals has lately increased decidedly.

Within the last three decades organ-playing as a specialty has made remarkable advances. Every large conservatory and music-school provides elaborately for its study. The American and Canadian Guilds of Organists have done much to foster a high grade of technical skill and a serious professional purpose, while the National Association of Organists has stimulated zeal and ambition. Many periodicals devote much space to organ-interests, and several organ-journals have been started. Series of free organ-recitals are now extremely common, and many large cities provide municipal concerts. Recitalists make tours like pianists and violinists. Special recent developments are the frequent installation of large instruments in hotels, in fraternal lodges, and in theaters and places where photoplays are given. Organ-music, then, has become in many places one of the commonest and most popular forms of concert-music. The reaction of this upon organ-composition has already become noticeable. Leading journals are 'The Diapason,' published in Chicago, and 'The American Organist,' published in New York.

In the 'New Music Review,' February, 1910, is a valuable summary by Charles A. Radzinsky of the history of organ-making in New York City during the 19th century. Special tribute is paid to the genius of Henry Erben (d. 1884), who started in 1820 with Thomas Hall (d. 1877), but from 1824 proceeded alone, becoming one of the best-known makers in the country. He made nearly 150 organs for New York alone, the most famous being that in Trinity Church (1846). His business passed to his leading workman, Louis C. Harrison, later of Bloomfield, N. J. Meanwhile Hall in 1824 formed the firm of Hall & Lebagh, which about 1865 became Hall, Lebagh & Kemp. In their shop H. L. Roosevelt had his first training. Another series was founded about 1840 by Richard M. Ferris and the brothers Levi U. and William Stewart, in whose employ were the Odells and Midmer. Morgan Davis, who had been a piano-maker from about 1800, and his son, William H. Davis (d. 1888), also began in 1840, followed by two later generations. Thomas and Wiliam Robjohn became notable after 1850. Among their organs was that in the South (Reformed) Church, said to have been the first in America with an independent pedal-division (7 stops), the first pneumatic action and the first Vox Humana (imported from France by U. C. Burnap). The Robjohns became voicers for the Odells. In 1853–75 many instruments were made upon German lines by Francis Xavier Engelfried, whose two sons became voicers for Roosevelt. Reuben Midmer (d. 1895), who was trained both under Hall & Lebagh and under the Stewarts, set up for himself in 1860 and in 1888 was succeeded by his son. This firm now has its factory at Merrick, L. I., and its office in Brooklyn. It is noteworthy that many of the above pioneers in the industry were English by birth (except Engelfried).

The work of the Jardines, the Odells and the Roosevelts is referred to in separate articles.

ORNSTEIN, LEO (Dec. 11, 1895, Kremenchug, Russia), began studies at the Petrograd Conservatory which from 1906 were continued at the Institute of Musical Art in New York, Mrs. Thomas Tapper being his piano-teacher. His début as pianist was made in New York early in 1911, and he has since toured the country as soloist and recitalist. He has also played with distinction in London, Paris and Christiania. His compositions have aroused much discussion. He has been reported as saying:

'What are discords? I cannot tell. Somewhere there is a law of harmony. Where it is, what it is, I cannot tell, only I know that under certain conditions and at certain times I hear it, I get color-impressions, if you wish. If some of the tones are gray, somber, violent, is that my fault? Does this prove that because the human ear has been trained to certain combinations of sound only those sounds are true harmony? It is not so to me nor do I care whether the usage of musical form so considers it or not. In a word, I am not concerned with form or with standards of any nature.'

His publications to date include piano-pieces, songs and a sonata for violin and piano (Carl Fischer, Schott). See biography by F. H. Martens, 1917, and article by Charles L. Buchanan in 'The Musical Quarterly,' April, 1918. [R.10]

ORPHEUS CLUB, THE, of Springfield, Mass., was founded by Amos Whiting in 1873 for the cultivation of music for men's voices. Its conductors have been Louis Coenen (1874–79), George W. Sumner (1879–90), E. Cutter, Jr. (1890–94), Horatio W. Parker (1894–95) and John J. Bishop (since 1895). Until 1908 the average number of singers was about 40, but since then has risen to about 150. Till 1890 there were four concerts annually, till 1900 three, till 1905

two, and lately but one. The total number has been about 135. Among the longer works given are Grieg's 'Landerkennung,' Buck's 'King Olaf's Christmas' and 'Paul Revere's Ride,' Paine's 'Phœbus, arise!' Whiting's 'March of the Monks of Bangor,' Foote's 'Farewell of Hiawatha' and Baldwin's 'Hymn before Action.'

ORTH, JOHN (Dec. 2, 1850, near Annweiler, Bavaria), was brought to Taunton, Mass., when an infant and there gained a public-school education. He became a church-organist at twelve and in 1866–70 studied and taught in Boston. Five years in Germany followed, under Kullak, Lebert, Pruckner, Deppe and Liszt for piano, and Faiszt, Weitzmann, Kiel and Ph. Scharwenka for theory and composition. Since 1875 he has been located in Boston as pianist and teacher. His lecture-recitals on 'With Liszt in Weimar' have made him well known as a Liszt authority. He has published a number of piano-pieces and done much editorial work. He has also devoted time and attention to humanitarian and reform projects. In 1883 he married his pupil Lizette E. Blood (d. Sept. 14, 1913, Boston), who composed many teaching-pieces for piano, songs and operettas under the name L. E. Orth. [R.5]

OSBORN, A. STANLEY. See COLLEGES, 2 (Skidmore Sch., N. Y.).

OSBORN, JOHN (d. 1835). See Register, 3.

OSBORN-HANNAH, JANE (b. 1880?). See Register, 9.

OSGOOD, EMMA ALINE (1849, Boston : Nov. 8, 1911, Philadelphia), came of old New England stock. In her youth she sang at the Old South Church in Boston and was early successful in oratorio with singers like Miss Cary, Whitney, Fessenden and Babcock and under conductors like Zerrahn and Thomas. In 1873 she toured with the Mendelssohn Quintette Club. In 1875, after study with Randegger in London, she appeared at the Crystal Palace under Manns, so brilliantly that she at once entered on an English popularity that lasted for fifteen years, including engagements under all the leading conductors and at first performances of works like Liszt's 'St. Elizabeth' and Sullivan's 'The Light of the World,' besides being twice called to sing before Queen Victoria. Her early visits to America were in 1878, '80 and from '81, singing repeatedly at the Cincinnati and other Festivals, and establishing herself as a favorite. Her voice was high, but rich in quality, her enunciation finished, and her interpretation peculiarly sympathetic and effective. After giving up stage-work she married E. Milton Dexter of Philadelphia and became a noted teacher there. Nicholas Douty is one of her pupils. [R.6]

OSGOOD, GEORGE LAURIE (Apr. 4,
1844, Chelsea, Mass.), as a child was gifted
with an acute sense of pitch and had musical
advantages from the start. In 1866 he
graduated with honors from Harvard University, having taken organ and composition
under Paine and had three years' service as
leader of the college orchestra and glee-club.
Going then to Berlin, he spent three years
studying composition under Haupt and singing
under Sieber, besides forming an intimacy
with Franz at Halle. Then followed two
more years developing his tenor voice under
Francesco Lamperti in Milan. In 1871,
beginning at Vienna, he made a concert-tour
of Germany, interpreting German lieder and
old Italian songs, and in 1872 Thomas engaged
him for a season's tour in America with his
orchestra. In 1872 he settled in Boston and
for thirty years took a leading part in all its
musical affairs. He taught many successful
singers, gave annual series of chamber-concerts
and directed many choral societies. When
made director of the Boylston Club in 1875
he reorganized the society completely and
changed it from a men's to a mixed chorus.
Later it was known as the Boston Singers'
Society and was famous for excellent programs
and brilliant performances. For it he edited
The Boylston Collection (Ditson), which is
still widely used, and also translated the
texts of many choral works and songs. Since
1903 he has lived abroad, lately at Godalming,
England. His compositions are songs, anthems
and unaccompanied choral pieces. His *Guide
in the Art of Singing* has had several editions,
and a new work, *Mind and Melody*, is nearly
ready for the press. [R.6]

O'SHEA, JOHN AUGUSTINE (Oct. 15,
1864, Milford, Mass.), after public-school
training in 1885 graduated from the New
England Conservatory in Boston and in 1887
from the music-department of Boston University. He is now music-director in the
Boston public schools and organist at St.
Cecilia's. He is a member of the A. G. O.
and the N. A. O., and has given many inaugural organ-recitals throughout the country.
He played at the Buffalo Exposition in 1901
and the St. Louis Exposition in 1904, at the
latter being on the international jury of
awards in the music-section. His compositions include a string-quartet (medal at
Boston University), trios for piano, violin

and 'cello; a Mass in F and a Mass in honor
of St. Cecilia; a Barcarolle, 'Venetian Nights,'
for piano; the operetta 'Mother Goose';
the comic opera 'The Mirrors of Thule'; and
many songs. [R.7]

'OSTROLENKA.' An opera by Johann
H. Bonawitz, produced in 1875 in Philadelphia.

O'SULLIVAN, DENIS (1868–1908). See
Vol. iii. 571–2, and Register, 8.

'OTHO VISCONTI.' A romantic opera in
three acts by Frederick G. Gleason, who also
wrote the libretto. The overture was played
at the Gewandhaus in Leipzig in 1892 and by
Thomas in Chicago. The work as a whole was
given in the College Theatre in Chicago on
June 4, 1907.

OTIS, PHILO ADAMS (b. 1846). See Register, 6.

OTTAWA CHORAL SOCIETY, THE, of
Ottawa, Ont., was founded in 1897 by J.
Edgar Birch, who has been its only conductor.
Besides several of the standard oratorios,
it has given many shorter works, including
the first performance in America of Coleridge-
Taylor's 'Hiawatha's Wedding-Feast,' Mackenzie's 'The Dream of Jubal' (conducted by
the composer), etc.

OTTERSTRÖM, THORVALD (July 17,
1868, Copenhagen, Denmark), studied first
in Copenhagen and then with Sophie Menter
at Petrograd. In 1892 he came to Chicago,
where he has since been diligent as teacher
and composer. His piano-works have had
frequent performances in America and abroad,
many of them introduced by Mrs. Zeisler
and by Ganz, and the Chicago Orchestra has
given several of his orchestral works. He
has published a quintet for piano and strings,
24 preludes and fugues for piano, 7 concert-
studies for piano, 'The Spinning-Wheel' for
piano, and about 30 songs. He has also
written an orchestral 'Canon, Choral and
Fugue,' an 'American Negro' Suite, a violin-
sonata in G minor, a 'cello-sonata in C minor,
11 canons and a fugue on a theme by Grieg
for piano, 11 symmetric double crab-canons
for piano, the collection of piano-pieces
'Shifting Moods,' 43 Negro slave-songs
harmonized for chorus, 'Musical Pictures
of Chippewa Indian Life,' and a series of 27
tribal songs arranged for piano with scenario
by Alice Gerstenberg. [R.8]

OWST, WILBERFOSS GEORGE (b. 1861).
See Register, 8.

P

PACHE, JOSEPH (June 1, 1861, Friedland-bei-Waldenburg, Germany), studied at the Munich Conservatory in 1879–83, pursued piano with Klindworth in Berlin in 1883–85 and composition with Bruch in Breslau in 1885–86, besides having lessons from Barth (piano) and Hey (singing). Coming to New York in 1891, he taught for a year at the New York College of Music, and conducted choruses in New York, Newark and Trenton, N. J. In 1894 he went to Baltimore as conductor of the Baltimore Oratorio Society, a post which he still holds. He founded the Women's Philharmonic chorus in Baltimore, and for seven years conducted the York (Pa.) Oratorio Society. He has composed songs and choruses. [R.8]

PACHELBEL, CHARLES THEODORE. See Register, 1.

PACKARD, J. B. See TUNE-BOOKS, 1842.

PADELFORD, FREDERICK MORGAN (b. 1875). See Register, 8.

PADEREWSKI, IGNACE JAN (Nov. 6, 1860, Kurilovka, Russian Poland). See article in Vol. iii. 587–8. His first appearance in America was at Carnegie Hall in New York on Nov. 17, 1891, and during the six months following he played in 117 concerts. On his second American tour (1892–93) he gave 67 concerts in 26 cities. These visits were followed by others in 1895–96, 1900–01, 1901–02, 1907–08, 1913–14, and a final series of 30 recitals beginning in 1915–16. In August, 1915, he played at the San Francisco Exposition for the Polish Victims' Relief Fund, his first professional appearance as pianist after the war began. He presently gave up music for notable efforts in behalf of Poland. In addition to raising large sums of money, in 1917 he offered the United States an army of 100,000 Poles and 50 trained officers. As soon as conditions permitted he went to Poland, accompanied by his friend Ernest Schelling, the pianist. He was there elected premier on Jan. 26, 1919, and a month later the Allied Council at Paris recognized the Polish Republic under his leadership. He relinquished his office in 1920, but has continued politically influential.

His opera 'Manru,' produced at Dresden in 1901, was given at the Metropolitan Opera House in New York on Feb. 14, 1902. His symphony in B minor, op. 24, composed in 1904–08, was brought out by the Boston Symphony Orchestra on Feb. 13, 1909, Max Fiedler conducting. The three movements are in commemoration of Poland, and the third movement refers to the Polish uprising of 1863–64. It is said that he has deferred completing a fourth movement until his country is free. Other works are a Sonata in E-flat minor, op. 21, and Variations and Fugue, op. 23, both for piano. His second opera, 'Sakuntala,' text by Catulle Mendés, has not yet been produced. See biographies by Finck, 1895, Mossig (Leipzig) and Baughan, 1907, besides numerous accounts in magazines and general treatises. In addition to his estate at Morges, Switzerland, he owns two others near Paso Robles, Cal. [R.8]

PAGE, NATHANIEL CLIFFORD (Oct. 26, 1866, San Francisco), inherited musical aptitude from his mother, a poetess of some note and an amateur musician. At fourteen the cornet attracted his attention, later giving way to the French horn. But even earlier he had essayed composition and the writing of libretti. The study of harmony was taken up under local teachers, but in orchestration he has been entirely self-taught, gaining experience by playing in and directing orchestras. His light opera, 'The First Lieutenant,' was successfully produced at the old Tivoli Opera House in San Francisco in May, 1889. Seeking a wider field, he came to New York in 1895, and in 1896 directed his Petite Suite, 'Village Scenes,' for the Manuscript Society in Chickering Hall. In 1899 he was called to London to conduct his incidental music to 'The Moonlight Blossom' at the Prince of Wales Theatre. This and incidental music to 'A Japanese Nightingale' (produced in 1903 at Daly's Theatre, New York) were based on real Japanese themes. He has studied and worked in various branches of Oriental music — Japanese, Chinese, Arabian, etc. After composing and directing musical comedies, in 1905 he joined the editorial staff of the Ditson Company in Boston, but in 1910 returned to New York to devote his time to composition. His later works include the operas and cantatas 'The Contest of the Nations' (1913), 'Alice in Wonderland,' 'Old Plantation-Days' and 'Lord Howe's Masquerade,' 'A Mood of Spring' for piano, and numerous songs. He has revised and edited Home-Songs, Irish Songs, Stephen C. Foster Songs, Panseron's A B C of Music, and several hundred pieces in sheet-form. Unpublished are 'The First Lieutenant,' 'Carlotta,' 'Villiers,' 'Zorahda,' 'The President' and several musical comedies; incidental music to 'The Cat and the Cherub,' 'The Ghetto,' 'The Moonlight Blossom,' 'A Japanese Nightingale,' 'Joan of the Sword-Hand'; the orchestral 'Dream Suite,' 'Village Scenes,' 'Fantasie Symphonique on a Short Theme,' 'Romance' and 'Chop Suey' (Chinese Humoresque); and many songs. [R.7]

PAGEANTS, HISTORICAL. The development of symbolic celebrations in England from 1905 under the lead of Gilbert Parker inspired numerous efforts of a somewhat similar kind in America. The most active worker has been William Langdon, seconded by Arthur Farwell. Since 1908 hardly a year has been without some significant undertaking in which local history is commemorated through a dramatic spectacle with the aid of poetry and music. (For a list of Langdon's productions, see Register, 10.) All the great Expositions have included features of this general sort, and many civic functions have been elaborate. There has been a tendency, especially in Langdon's work, to emphasize the merely spectacular elements less and to mold the poetic and musical into better unity. This has been specially notable in some celebrations held at large educational institutions. See *The Art of Music*, iv. pp. 226–9.

PAILLARD, M. J. (d. 1868). See Register, 4.

PAILLARD COMPANY, THE M. J., of New York, was the American representative of the noted makers of music-boxes in Ste.-Croix, Switzerland (founded in 1814). The New York house was established in 1850 by M. J. Paillard, a grandson of the original founder, at first as Paillard & Martin. Its business was greatly developed by his nephew and son. See Jones, *Handbook of American Music*, p. 126.

PAINE, DAVID. See Tune-Books, 1839.

PAINE, JOHN KNOWLES (Jan. 9, 1839, Portland, Me. : Apr. 25, 1906, Cambridge, Mass.). See Vol. iii. 596–7. Add to list of works the string-quartet, op. 5 ; the piano-trio, op. 22 ; the sonata for violin and piano, op. 24 ; the Larghetto and Scherzo, op. 32, for 'cello and piano ; and the 'Duo Concertante' in A, op. 33, for violin, 'cello and orchestra ; besides many piano-pieces, variations and fantasias for organ, and vocal works. His lectures were posthumously edited by Albert A. Howard as *The History of Music to the Death of Schubert*, 1907. [R.5]

PAINE, RICHMOND PECK (Mar. 24, 1858, New Bedford, Mass.), began as a choir-boy and by 1872 was a regular organist. He had thorough training in technique and composition from N. H. Allen, then organist in New Bedford, and began recital-playing about 1876. In 1878 he succeeded Henry Wilson as organist at Christ Church in Hartford, Conn., from 1880 occupied the leading position at Meriden, and from 1885 a similar post at New Britain, where he remained twenty years. Thus was satisfied his original ambition of winning eminence as a church- and concert-organist. From 1883 he was associated with

W. S. Pratt at Hartford in developing an oratorio society, succeeding to the leadership there in 1892 and continuing ten years with great success. As early as 1885, however, he had begun similar work elsewhere, which gradually extended until he had led superior choral performances in many places in Connecticut, such as Winsted, Middletown, New Britain, Southington, Wallingford and Willimantic, and in Pittsfield, Mass., often managing festivals with combined choirs. In 1905 he was called to conduct the extensive choral enterprise of Carl Stoeckel at Norfolk, Conn. (see Litchfield County Choral Union), where he continued with increasing renown until 1915. Since his retirement he has lived at Norfolk. He is highly gifted as an executive musician, with a notable genius for choral leadership. His long experience, infallible taste and high ideals have given him an enviable influence and reputation. It is unfortunate that he has not chosen to express himself in composition. [R.6]

PALFREY, WARWICK. See Tune-Books, 1802.

PALLISER, ESTHER (b. 1872). See Register, 8.

PALMER, HORATIO RICHMOND (Apr. 26, 1834, Sherburne, N. Y. : Nov. 15, 1907, Yonkers, N. Y.), was brought up in a musical family and became organist at seventeen. He studied at the Rushford Academy of Music in New York, becoming director in 1857, and also in Berlin and Florence. In 1861 he settled in Chicago, where he established the magazine 'Concordia' in 1866, and published *The Song-Queen*, 1867 (over 200,000 sold) and *The Song-King*, 1871 (also an enormous sale). In 1874 he removed to New York, and in 1881 took charge of the Church Choral Union. This organization, for the improvement of church-music, grew to over 4000 singers in its third season. In 1887 he became Dean of the School of Music at Chautauqua, N. Y., continuing until 1891. He was made Mus.D. by the (old) University of Chicago in 1880 and by Alfred University in 1881. Of his many choral collections, besides those named above, *The Song-Herald* and *Concert-Choruses* were specially successful. He wrote a *Theory of Music*, 1876, a *Manual for Teachers* (public-school music), etc. [R.4]

PALMER, JAMES W. See Tune-Books, 1832.

PANIZZA, ETTORE (b. 1875). See Register, 8.

PARKER, FLETCHER ANDREW (b. 1842). See Register, 5, and State Universities (Wis.).

PARKER, GEORGE ALBERT (b. 1856). See Register, 7, and Colleges, 3 (Syracuse U., N. Y.).

PARKER, HENRY TAYLOR (b. 1867). See Register, 9.

PARKER, HORATIO WILLIAM (Sept. 15, 1863, Auburndale, Mass. : Dec. 18, 1919, Cedarhurst, N. Y.). See article in Vol. iii. 622–3. He remained at the head of the Yale School of Music till his death, but gave up conducting the New Haven Symphony Orchestra in 1919. In both positions he was succeeded by David Stanley Smith. For some time his health had not been good, but his death was due to a sudden illness while on the way to the South. The list of works should be extended to include

op. 62   'Crépuscule,' for mezzo-soprano and orchestra.
63   'The Shepherd's Vision.'
64   Ballad, 'King Gorm the Grim,' for chorus and orchestra.
65   Sonata in E-flat, for organ.
66   Songs for high schools.
67–8   Nine Organ-Pieces.
69   'The Norsemen's Raid,' for men's chorus and orchestra.
70   Seven Songs.
71   Opera, 'Mona,' libretto by Brian Hooker (prize of $10,000 from the Metropolitan Opera House, given there Mar. 14, 1912).
72   'Collegiate' Overture.
73   Cantata, 'A Song of the Times.'
74   Seven 'Greek Pastoral Scenes,' for soprano, alto, women's chorus, oboe, harp and strings.
75   Ballad, 'The Leap of Roushan Beg,' for tenor, men's chorus and orchestra.
76   Songs (not published).
77   Opera, 'Fairyland,' libretto by Brian Hooker (prize of $10,000 from the National Federation of Women's Clubs, given at Los Angeles, July 1, 1915).
78   Books of public-school music.
79   Oratorio, 'Morven and the Grail.'
80   Masque, 'Cupid and Psyche,' for 50th anniversary of the Yale Art School, June, 1916.
81   Music for the Yale Pageant, October, 1916.
82   Cantata, 'The Dream of Mary,' for soli, chorus and orchestra (1918, Norfolk Festival).
83   'Red Cross Hymn,' for contralto and orchestra.
84   'A. D. 1919,' for soprano and chorus.

He also published *Music and Public Entertainment*, 1911. [R.7]

PARKER, JAMES CUTLER DUNN (June 2, 1828, Boston : Nov. 27, 1916, Brookline, Mass.), studied law in Boston for three years after graduating from Harvard in 1848. Then his preference for music led him to go in 1851 to Leipzig, where he spent three years, studying piano with Moscheles and Plaidy, harmony with Richter and Rietz. Returning in 1854, he was active in Boston for over half a century, retiring in 1912. In 1864–91 he was organist at Trinity Church, organist of the Handel and Haydn Society, in 1871–97 teacher of piano, organ and harmony at the New England Conservatory, and

for a time at Boston University. As Elson remarks, 'the pupils graduated during his long era of activity would form a good-sized regiment.' Among them are Arthur Whiting, A. D. Turner, H. M. Dunham, C. H. Morse and H. C. Macdougall. His works included the 'Redemption Hymn' (1877), for soli, chorus and orchestra; a secular cantata, 'The Blind King'; the cantata 'St. John'; the oratorio 'The Life of Man'; church-music; and piano-pieces. [R.4]

PARKHURST, HOWARD ELMORE (1848–1916). See Register, 7.

PARKINSON, ELIZABETH ['Parkina'] (b. 1882). See Register, 9.

PARLOW, KATHLEEN (Sept. 20, 1890, Calgary, Alberta), was taken as a child to San Francisco, where she had violin-lessons with her cousin, Mr. Conrad, and later with Henry Holmes. Her first public performance there was at the age of six. On March 23, 1905, she gave her first recital at Bechstein Hall in London, later appeared with the London Symphony Orchestra, and was also bidden to play before the Queen. She studied with Auer in Petrograd in 1906–07, and subsequently played in Russia, Scandinavia, Germany, Holland and Belgium. Her first appearance on her return to America was late in 1910, when she played the Tchaikovsky concerto with the Russian Symphony Orchestra. She has since made several tours, appearing with the principal orchestras. [R.10]

‡PARRY, CHARLES HUBERT HASTINGS (Feb. 27, 1848, Bournemouth, England : Oct. 7, 1918, Rustington, near Littlehampton, England). See articles in Vol. iii. 624–7 and v. 657. Mention should be made of his late works, 'A Hymn to the Nativity' (1912, Hereford), the English 'Te Deum' (1913, Gloucester), and a 5th Symphony, in B minor. He published *Style in Musical Art*, 1911, and wrote the introduction to *The Art of Music*, 1914. During the war much of his time and energy was devoted to the Council for the Relief of the Professional Classes, and other charities. His funeral was at St. Paul's on Oct. 16, 1918. In the language of Hadow, 'There was no side of musical life in England which was not the better and nobler because he had lived.'

PARSONS, ALBERT ROSS (Sept. 16, 1847, Sandusky, O.), was musically precocious, playing the organ in public at nine and about 1860 being a regular organist in Indianapolis. From 1863 he began serious study with Ritter in New York, and in 1867–69 was under Moscheles, Wenzel, Reinecke, Papperitz and Richter at Leipzig, and in 1870–72 with Tausig, Kullak and Weitzmann at Berlin. Since 1872 he has been one of the best-known piano-teachers in New York.

For four years he was organist at Holy Trinity and for nine at the Fifth Avenue Presbyterian Church. In 1890 he was president of the M. T. N. A. and in 1893–1903 of the American College of Musicians. From 1885 he was head of the piano-department in the Metropolitan College of Music, continuing later with the American Institute of Applied Music. He was an early advocate of Wagner in America, translating his *Beethoven* (1870) and writing *Parsifal, or the Finding of Christ through Art*, 1893. He has also translated Lessmann's *Liszt*, published *The Science of Piano-Practice*, 1893, edited in English the Kullak edition of Chopin and the Holländer edition of Schumann, and written much on archæology and genealogy as well as music. He has composed songs and piano-pieces. [R.6]

PASMORE, HENRY BICKFORD (June 27, 1857, Jackson, Wis.), after studying organ and theory in San Francisco with J. P. Morgan and singing with S. J. Morgan, went abroad in 1882. In Leipzig he took composition with Jadassohn and Reinecke, singing with Frau Unger-Haupt, and in London singing with Shakespeare and Cummings. Returning to San Francisco, he became organist at St. John's and teacher of voice and composition at the University of the Pacific in San José. He has composed an overture, 'Miles Standish,' a 'Conclave March,' and the tone-poem 'Gloria California,' two operas, a Mass in B-flat, smaller choral works with orchestra, numerous songs and part-songs. He assisted in translating Jadassohn's *Harmonielehre*. His three daughters, Mary, Suzanne and Dorothy, constitute the Pasmore Trio, which has given many recitals in the West. [R.7]

PASTERNACK, JOSEF ALEXANDER (b. 1881). See Register, 8.

‡ PATTI, ADELINA (Feb. 10, 1843, Madrid, Spain : Sept. 27, 1919, Craig-y-Nos, Wales). See article in Vol. iii. 654–5.

PATTISON, JOHN NELSON (1845–1905). See Register, 5.

PATTON, WILLARD (May 26, 1853, Milford, Me.), early studied with his father and other local teachers, and with Buck, Bassini, Errani and Kohlmann, appearing as tenor from 1871 and leading a choral society in Bangor from 1875. His first operetta, 'The Gallant Garroter,' was produced in 1882. Since 1883 he has taught in Minneapolis, where for some years he had charge of the music-department of Hamline University, founded and led the Philharmonic Club for four years, and was president of the local teachers' association and its examiner. His oratorio, 'Isaiah' (Ditson), was brought out in 1895 and often given since. He has also published the cantatas 'The Call of Spring' (Lloyd), 'Summer' (Fischer), both

for women's voices, and the festival 'Usona' (Lloyd), anthems and sacred quartets (Molineaux, Dyer), male quartets (Gordon), and several series of songs (Lloyd, Nonpareil Ed.). He has also produced the light opera 'La Fianza' (1888), the opera 'Pocahontas,' the musical epic 'The Star of Empire,' the concert-ode 'Foot-stones of a Nation,' the symphonic fantasia 'The Spirit of '61,' the cantata 'The Atonement,' a Festival Te Deum in D-flat, a 'Tennyson Cycle' (eight songs from 'The Princess'), etc. [R.6]

PAULI, H. L. See COLLEGES, 2 (Hollins C., Va.).

PAULIN, NOAH E. See COLLEGES, 3 (Pacific Union C., Cal.).

PAUR, EMIL (Aug. 29, 1855, Czernowitz, Bukovina). See article in Vol. iii. 658. In 1899 and 1900 he conducted Wagner operas at the Metropolitan Opera House. His connection with the National Conservatory ran till 1902. In 1904–10 he was conductor of the Pittsburgh Symphony Orchestra, then returning again to Europe. In 1912–13 he was head of the Opera at Berlin, where he has since lived. His symphony 'In der Natur' (Leuckart) was first given by the Pittsburgh Orchestra in 1909, and at the same concert he played Brahms' piano-concerto in B-flat. He has also composed a string-quartet, a violin-concerto, a sonata for violin and piano, and piano-pieces. [R.8]

PEABODY CONCERTS. See Vol. iii. 660, and next article.

PEABODY CONSERVATORY, THE, of Baltimore, is a constituent part of the Peabody Institute, founded by George Peabody in 1857, which also includes a great Library and a fine Art Museum. The enterprise did not become actual till after the Civil War, and the Conservatory was not opened till 1868. Its directors have been Lucien H. Southard in 1868–71, Asger Hamerik in 1871–98, and Harold Randolph since 1898. Part of the Conservatory system is the maintenance of the Peabody Orchestra, of which its director is conductor. Hamerik raised these concerts into artistic importance, and Randolph has been signally successful in developing the efficiency of the Conservatory proper. The faculty numbers over 75. The number of pupils is more than 1700 annually, and about 11,500 since the beginning. Instruction is given in every branch of musical art, with some language-courses besides. Since about 1900 a distinct preparatory department has been in operation, of which May G. Evans has been superintendent. There are three student-orchestras, with over 100 members, and choruses with over 200 members. The opera-class presents several operas each year. The Conservatory has an arrangement with the

Johns Hopkins University whereby candidates for the B.S. degree in the latter may pursue certain courses in the former. It also offers courses which are counted for credit in the Baltimore public schools. Students in the Conservatory have the chance of attending over 250 recitals and concerts each year, including 20 artist-recitals and about 15 organ-recitals. The library contains nearly 2500 volumes, and the institution owns many instruments, including 5 organs and a full set of orchestral instruments. It occupies a large part of the Institute Building on Monument Square and also three annex-houses.

PEACE JUBILEES, THE, were large popular festivals planned and directed by the band-master P. S. Gilmore and held in Boston. The first, in 1869, was meant to celebrate the return of peace after the Civil War. There was an orchestra of 1000 and a chorus of 10,000, with many other sensational features. The second, in 1872, based on the idea of 'world peace,' was still more unwieldy and spectacular in design. The first was effective in arousing genuine popular enthusiasm, but the second was much less significant, though more pretentious. In 1873 Gilmore held another Jubilee at Chicago in celebration of its rebuilding after the fire of 1871. See Gilmore, *History of the National Peace Jubilee and Great Musical Festival*, 1877, Upton, *Musical Memories*, pp. 194–205, etc.

PEARCE, STEPHEN AUSTEN (Nov. 7, 1836, London, England : Apr. 9, 1900, Jersey City, N. J.), after study with J. L. Hopkins, graduated Mus.B. at Oxford in 1859 and Mus.D. in 1864. He held organ-appointments at London churches, visited the United States and Canada in 1864, and returned to London to give recitals at the Hanover Square Rooms and elsewhere. In 1872 he came to New York, where he was long active as organist, lecturer and writer. His organ-positions were at St. Andrews', St. George's, St. Stephen's (R.C.), Zion, Ascension, Fifth Avenue Collegiate (Ref. Dutch), and at the First Presbyterian Church in Jersey City. He taught vocal music at Columbia College, harmony and composition at the New York College of Music, lectured at the General Theological Seminary in New York, at the Peabody Institute and Johns Hopkins University in Baltimore, and gave lectures and recitals in many other cities. From 1874 he was musical editor of the New York 'Evening Post,' and contributed to 'The Musical Courier,' the *Encyclopædia Americana* and various periodicals. He edited a *Dictionary of Musical Terms in 21 Languages*, piano-music, and much church-music. He composed the three-act children's opera 'La Belle Américaine,' the oratorio 'Celestial

Visions,' the cantata 'The Psalm of Praise,' an overture, an 'Allegro Agitato' (Thomas Orchestra), songs and pieces for piano and organ. [R.5]

PEARSON, HENRY WARD (b. 1878). See COLLEGES, 2 (Hood C., Md.).

PEASE, ALFRED HUMPHRIES (1838–1882). See Register, 5.

PECK, DANIEL L. See TUNE-BOOKS, 1810.

PEDRELL, CARLOS (Oct. 16, 1878, Minas, Uruguay), a nephew of the Spanish composer and musicologist Felipe Pedrell, began studies in Montevideo, continuing with his uncle in 1898–1900, and then entering the Schola Cantorum in Paris, where his masters were Pierre de Bréville and d'Indy. Since 1906 he has been located in Buenos Aires, where he is inspector of music in the schools, lecturer at the University of Tucuman, and advisor for the Consejo Nacional de Educación on the national hymn, folk-songs, and musical policies generally. In 1915 he founded the Sociedad Nacional de Música, including a group of composers. His opera 'Ardid de Amor' was given six times in Buenos Aires in 1917. A second opera is 'Cuento de Abril.' Symphonic works are 'Une Nuit de Schéhérazade' (1908), 'Danza y Canción de Aixa' (1910), 'En el Estrado de Beatriz' (1910), 'Fantasia Argentina' (1910) and 'Ouverture Catalane' (1912). These have been repeatedly performed, especially in the series at the Colon under André Messager in 1916. He has also composed about 60 songs (26 published), many with orchestral accompaniment, four choruses with orchestra, and three a cappella, besides publishing over 50 transcriptions and adaptations for school-use. His wife, Suzanne S. de Pedrell (b. Sept. 15, 1892, Meing-sur-Loire, France), a pupil of Madame Giraudin in Paris, has won distinction in song-recitals. [R.9]

‡PEDRELL, FELIPE (Feb. 19, 1841, Tortosa, Spain). See article in Vol. iii. 668–9. In 1911 his seventieth birthday was celebrated by the publication of a series of 'Escritos heortásticos' by musical scholars of different countries. For many details about his compositions and his remarkable historical studies, see Baker, *Dict. of Musicians*, p. 690.

PELHAM, PETER, JR. (1721– ?). See Register, 1.

PELISSIER, VICTOR. See Register, 2.

PENFIELD, SMITH NEWELL (Apr. 4, 1837, Oberlin, O. : Jan. 7, 1920, New York), after graduating from Oberlin College in 1858, studied in New York with James Flint, in Leipzig with Moscheles, Papperitz, Reinecke, Plaidy, Richter and Hauptmann, graduating from the Conservatory in 1869, and in Paris with Delioux. He first taught in Rochester, and then went to Savannah, where he established the Conservatory and the Mozart Club. From 1882 he was in New York, where for many years he was organist at the Broadway Tabernacle, gave many organ-recitals, conducted choral societies and started the Arion Conservatory in Brooklyn. In 1885 he was president of the M. T. N. A. and in 1888–90 of the New York State Association. In 1885 New York University made him Mus.D. His works included Psalm 18, for soli, chorus and orchestra, an overture, a string-quintet, pieces for piano and organ, choruses and songs. [R.5]

PENNY, GEORGE BARLOW (b. 1861). See Register, 8, and STATE UNIVERSITIES (Kan.).

PEOPLE'S CHORAL UNION, THE, of New York. See Vol. iii. 371.

PEOPLE'S SYMPHONY ORCHESTRA, THE, of New York. See Vol. iv. 805.

PERABO, JOHANN ERNST (Nov. 14, 1845, Wiesbaden, Germany), began music with his father at five. In 1852 the family came to America and he had violin- and piano-lessons from several teachers. He entered the Leipzig Conservatory in 1862, studying piano with Moscheles and Richter, theory and composition with Hauptmann, Papperitz and Reinecke, and took the Helbig prize in 1865. After a year of teaching in New York and some recital-giving, since 1866 he has lived in Boston, becoming noted for his excellent playing of Beethoven. He has made a specialty of concert-transcriptions, including the first movement of Rubinstein's 'Ocean' and Schubert's 'Unfinished' Symphonies, of parts of 'Fidelio' and of some Loewe ballads. Mrs. Beach is one of his many pupils. Among his compositions for piano are 'Moment Musical,' op. 1; Scherzo, op. 2; Prelude, op. 3; Waltz, op. 4; Three Studies, op. 9; 'Pensées,' op. 11; and Prelude, Romance and Toccatina, op. 19. [R.5]

PERINI, FLORA (b. 1887). See Register, 10.

PERIODICALS, MUSICAL. See Vol. iii. 687–9, and JOURNALISM.

PERKINS, CHARLES CALLAHAN (1823–1886). See Register, 4.

PERKINS, DAVID WALTON (b. 1847). See Register, 8.

PERKINS, HENRY SOUTHWICK (1833–1914). See Register, 5.

PERKINS, JULIUS EDSON (1845–1875). See Register, 5.

PERKINS, ORSON (1802–1882). See Register, 3.

PERKINS, WILLIAM OSCAR (1831–1902). See Register, 5, and TUNE-BOOKS, 1859.

‡ PEROSI, LORENZO (Dec. 23, 1872, Tortona, Italy). See article in Vol. v. 658. His recent oratorios are 'Transitus Animæ' (1907), 'In Patris Memoriam' (1910) and 'Giorni di Tribulazione' (1916). He has also composed two symphonic poems, 'Dovrei non Piangere' and 'La Festa del Villaggio;' concertos for piano and violin; a sonata for violin; a suite for piano-trio; and many smaller vocal and instrumental works.

PERRIN, HARRY CRANE (Aug. 19, 1865, Wellingborough, England), was educated at Trinity College in Dublin, receiving Mus.B. in 1890, F.R.C.O. in 1892, Mus.D. in 1901, his teachers having been Stewart, Pearce and Bates. From 1886 he was in succession organist at St. Columba's College, at St. John's Church in Lowestoft, and at St. Michael's in Coventry, where he also conducted the Musical Society. In 1898 he became organist at Canterbury Cathedral and conductor of the Canterbury Musical Society. Since 1908 he has been professor and director at the McGill University Conservatorium in Montreal, which owes its fine organization and influence to his leadership. He has composed orchestral music, cantatas, songs and church-music. [R.9]

PERRIN, HENRY FOOTE. See STATE UNIVERSITIES (N. M.).

PERRY, EDWARD BAXTER (Feb. 14, 1855, Haverhill, Mass.), has been sightless since infancy, but has nevertheless achieved remarkable success as student, artist and teacher. After having graduated from the public schools of Medford in 1871, he studied piano with J. W. Hill in Boston, besides specializing in English literature. In 1875 he went abroad for further general and musical education at Berlin and Stuttgart. His piano-study was with Kullak, Pruckner and Clara Schumann, and in 1878 he was with Liszt at Weimar in the summer. Besides playing somewhat in public, he kept up diligent literary, historical and philosophical studies. In 1881–83 he taught at Oberlin College, and in 1883–85 he was again in Europe. Since 1885 he has been chiefly occupied with numerous and varied lecture-recitals in all parts of the country. Up to 1917 he had thus appeared more than 3300 times. In 1897–98 he engaged in concertizing in Europe. Since 1917 he has been director of music and dean of fine arts at the Woman's College in Montgomery, Ala. He has written *Descriptive Analysis of Piano-Works* and *Stories of Standard Teaching-Pieces*, with perhaps 300 articles for magazines. Best known among his piano-pieces are a Reverie, a Nocturne, an Impromptu, a 'Mazurka Caprice' and 'Why?' (Schmidt), 'Autumn Reverie,' 'The Portent,' 'Æolienne' and 'The Ballade of Last Island' (Presser), with several studies. His most important unpublished work is the 'Melusine' Suite, founded on a legend in the family of Prince Lusignan. This led the latter to confer on him the title of 'Chevalier de Melusine' (1898). In his works, as in his explanatory lectures, he exalts poetic significance more than technical structure. [R.7]

PERRY, EMORY (1799 - ?). See Register, 3.

PERSINGER, LOUIS (Feb. 11, 1887, Rochester, Ill.), spent his early years in Oklahoma and Colorado, where he had some lessons on violin and piano. In 1900, aided by the late W. S. Stratton, he began serious study in Leipzig, having violin under Becker, and piano, theory and conducting under Nikisch, and graduated from the Conservatory with the highest honors in 1904. Nikisch called him 'one of the most talented pupils' they had ever had. After a year of concert-work in America, he had two years at Brussels under Ysaÿe. In 1907 he was concertmaster of the Opera Orchestra there at its Vauxhall concerts, and in 1908 of the Blüthner Orchestra in Berlin. Returning then to America, he taught for a few months in Winnipeg, but in 1909–11 concertized in Germany, Austria and Denmark with such success that in 1912–13 he made a brilliant tour in the United States, appearing with all the leading orchestras from New York to San Francisco. Another season of concerts in Europe was followed in 1914–15 by service as concertmaster for the Philharmonic Orchestra in Berlin. Since 1915 he has been concertmaster and assistant-conductor of the San Francisco Orchestra, director of the Chamber Music Society and leader of the Community Music School Orchestra. In 1913 he married the pianist Angela Gianelli. [R.9]

PETERBORO (N.H.) FESTIVALS. See MacDowell Memorial Association.

PETERS, ABSALOM (1793–1869). See Tune-Books, 1823.

PETERS, RICHARD HARRY (b. 1867). See Register, 8.

PETERSILEA, CARLYLE (1844–1903). See Register, 5.

PETIT. See Register, 2.

PFEFFERKORN, OTTO W. G. See Colleges, 2 (Brenau C., Ga.).

‡ PFITZNER, HANS ERICH (May 5, 1869, Moscow, Russia). See article in Vol. iii. 696–7. He taught at the Stern Conservatory until 1907, and was conductor at the Theater des Westens in 1903–07. In 1907–08 he was conductor of the Kaim Orchestra in Munich, and then went to Strassburg as director of the conservatory and of municipal music, becoming in 1910 also conductor at the Opera. His latest opera is 'Palestrina'

(1919, Berlin). Other works are incidental music to Kleist's 'Käthchen von Heilbronn,' op. 17, and to Von Stach's 'Christelflein, op. 20; the eight-part a cappella chorus 'Columbus,' op. 16; a piano-trio in F, op. 8; a string-quartet in D, op. 13; and a piano-quintet in C, op. 23. His essays *Vom musikalischen Drama* were published in 1915.

PFITZNER, WALTHER (b. 1882). See Register, 10.

PHELPS, ELLSWORTH C. (1827– ?). See Register, 4.

PHILADELPHIA MUSICAL ACADEMY, THE, was founded in 1870 by John F. Himmelbach, who remained its director till 1876, when he was succeeded by Richard Zeckwer. In 1915 the latter was joined in the management by his son, Camille Zeckwer, and since 1917 the latter has been director with Frederick E. Hahn and Charlton L. Murphy. The Academy has had notable success. The faculty includes over 50 teachers, and the student-enrolment is about 800 in the main school, besides three branches in different parts of the city. The total number enrolled since the beginning is over 26,000. In 1917 the Academy was combined with the Hahn Conservatory. It has arrangements with other schools for special advantages in language-study and in dramatic art.

PHILADELPHIA SYMPHONY ORCHESTRA, THE. See article in Vol. iv. 805–6. Karl Pohlig continued as conductor until 1912, when he was succeeded by Leopold Stokowski, previously of Cincinnati. Under the latter the Orchestra has added laurels to its fine reputation. Since 1908 the number of players has been 80 or more. Popular concerts were added to the regular series in 1915, and in 1916 a movement started for a large permanent fund. Since 1914 the Orchestra has regularly played in New York, now giving five concerts there each year. Among the new works brought out have been Pohlig's Symphonic Poem, 'Per Aspera ad Astra' (1908), Volbach's Symphony in B minor (1910), Rabaud's 2nd Symphony (1913), Schönberg's 'Kammersymphonie' (1915), Sandby's Concerto in D, for 'cello (1916), Zeckwer's Symphonic Poem, 'Sohrab and Rustum' (1916), Mahler's 8th Symphony, with large choral forces (1916, three times and in New York), Elgar's music to Cammaerts' 'Le Drapeau Belge' (1918), Gardner's Symphonic Poem, 'New Russia' (1919), and Hadley's Concert-Overture, 'Othello' (1919).

PHILHARMONIC SOCIETY, THE, of Boston, is the name of more than one organization. One is mentioned as early as 1799. Another is said to have been started by Graupner in 1910, continuing till 1824. This may have been in some way connected with the first. In 1879 an orchestra was established by Bernhard Listemann, which in 1881 was continued under a society of guarantors. Listemann was succeeded by Maas and in 1881 by Zerrahn.

PHILHARMONIC SOCIETY, THE, of Brooklyn. See article in Vol. iv. 801.

PHILHARMONIC SOCIETY, THE, of Chicago, was formed in 1860 and did useful pioneer work under Hans Balatka until 1867, introducing eight of the Beethoven symphonies, two each of Mozart's and Gade's, one of Mendelssohn's, etc.

PHILHARMONIC SOCIETY, THE, of New York. See article in Vol. iv. 803–5. Safonov continued as conductor till 1909, succeeded by Gustav Mahler in 1909–11, who wrought a thorough change in discipline, bringing the orchestra to the highest state of finish. His illness and death led to the employment of Theodore Spiering as substitute in 1911. Since 1911 the regular leader has been Josef Stransky, who has greatly commended himself. The size of the band under Safonov was 125, but was reduced to 100 under Mahler. In 1912 the Society received a bequest of $1,000,000 from the late Joseph Pulitzer. In 1917 it celebrated its 75th anniversary with extended festival performances, and $110,000 was contributed toward a building-fund. Leopold Kramer was concertmaster in 1913–17 and Alfred Megerlin since 1917. Out of many new works produced may be mentioned Mahler's 1st and 5th Symphonies (1909, '11), Bizet's 'Roma' Suite (1911), Weingartner's 3rd Symphony and 'Merry Overture' (1911, '12), Korngold's 'Overture to a Play' (1912), Ritter's 'Olaf's Wedding-Dance' (1912), Reger's 'Romantic' and 'Ballet' Suites (1913), Ropartz' 4th Symphony and 'La Chasse du Prince Arthur' (1914), Bloch's 1st Symphony (1918), Wilson's Suite 'From my Youth' (1918), Rogers' 'To the Fallen,' Dvořák's 3rd Symphony, and Schmitt's 'Rhapsodie Viennoise' (all 1919).

An early society of this name was formed in 1800 by the union of the St. Cecilia and Harmonical Societies. How long it continued is not clear.

PHILE, PHILIP. See Register, 2.

‡ PHILIPP, ISIDOR (Sept. 2, 1863, Budapest, Hungary). See article in Vol. iii. 705. His educational works for piano are highly esteemed and widely used. They include *Exercises Journaliers*, *Problèmes Techniques*, *École d'Octaves*, *La Gamme Chromatique*, *Études Techniques*, etc. He has also composed many piano-pieces and some orchestral music, and has continued his valued arrangements and editions of the classics. He is Chevalier of the Légion d'Honneur and Officier d'Instruction Publique.

PHILLIPPS, ADELAIDE (1833–1882). See Vol. iii. 709–10, and Register, 4.

PHILLIPS, HAROLD DOCKRAY, born at Oxford, England, had early training at Peterborough Cathedral, and at sixteen was organist at St. Andrew's (Kensington) in London. Later he was musical scholar and organist at Caius College in Cambridge, where he became Mus.B. and A.M. He then played at the Duchess of Albany's church at Esher in Surrey and at St. Andrews (Holborn) in London, becoming also fellow of the R. C. O. In 1903 he came to Toronto as organist at St. Paul's, and thence went in 1906 to Baltimore to be head of the organ-department and lecturer on music-history at the Peabody Conservatory, where he gave annual series of recitals. From 1914 he was organist at the First Church (Scientist) and critic on the 'News.' In 1914 he was chosen to represent the German school of organ-music at a recital in New York arranged by the A. G. O. In 1920 he removed to New York. He has written an organ-sonata in D minor (Stainer & Bell), a symphony in C minor, two cantatas, a string-quartet in A-flat, and two piano-trios, in E and D-flat. [R.9]

PHILLIPS, HARRY (b. 1864). See Colleges, 3 (Macalester C., Minn.).

PHILLIPS, PHILIP (1834–1895). See Register, 4.

PHILLIPS, THOMAS (1774–1841). See Register, 3.

PHILLIPS, T. MORGAN. See Colleges, 3 (Hiram C., Ohio).

PHONOGRAPH. Edison's invention by this name (1876) was the first to both record and reproduce complex sounds mechanically. Its primary purpose was to transmit speech-sounds. But it was speedily extended by Edison and others to every sort of musical effect. Especially since 1900 and through the persistent ingenuity of American inventors, this general type of mechanical reproducer has become artistically significant. The process differs from that of the player-piano in that no actual musical instrument is employed in reproduction and that the user has little expressional control.

The 'records' employed are ordinarily disks of hard rubber, on the face of which indentations corresponding to the vibrations of the original effect are made by a stylus connected with a sensitive receiver. These records, mounted on a revolving spindle propelled by a motor, are traversed by a 'needle' of some special material (wood, fibre or a jewel) that is connected with a delicate 'diaphragm' like that of the telephone, which is thus thrown into vibrations like those of the original receiver. These vibrations, conducted through a 'tone-arm,' are made sonorous by passing out through a resonant projector of some form. Intensity is controlled by shutters or doors, and some modification of tone-quality is usually possible. But changes of speed affect the total pitch.

Although much employed for coarse effects, instruments of this class have also been applied with extraordinary success to recording superior vocal and instrumental performances, both solo and in ensemble. The best of these achievements are invaluable as historic records and for demonstrative purposes.

Some of the trade-names used are these :

'Æolian-Vocalion,' Æolian Co., New York.
'Bush & Lane,' Bush & Lane Piano Co., Holland, Mich.
'Cremona,' Cremona Phonograph Co., New York.
'Dulcitone,' Dulcitone Phonograph Co., South Haven, Mich.
'Edison,' Thos. A. Edison, Inc., Orange, N. J.
'Grafonola,' Columbia Graphophone Mfg. Co., New York.
'Kreiterphone,' Kreiter Mfg. Co., Milwaukee.
'Lauzon,' Michigan Phonograph Co., Grand Rapids, Mich.
'Magnola,' Magnola Talking Machine Co., Chicago.
'Mandel,' Mandel Mfg. Co., Chicago.
'Manophone,' Manophone Corp., Adrian, Mich.
'Natural Voice,' Natural Voice Phonograph Co., Oneida, N. Y.
'Paramount,' Paramount Talking Machine Co., Port Washington, Wis.
'Pathé,' Pathé Frères Phonograph Co., Brooklyn.
'Starr,' Starr Piano Co., Richmond, Ind.
'True-Tone,' Cameron Phonograph Co., New York.
'Victrola,' Victor Talking Machine Co., Camden, N. J.
'Violaphone,' Gretsch Mfg. Co., Brooklyn.

'PHYLLIS.' A romantic opera by Richard Henry Warren, produced in New York in 1900.

PIANOFORTE. See article in Vol. iii. 716-32, especially notes regarding American contributions to the instrument on pp. 726-30. Spillane (History of the American Pianoforte, 1890) seems to have shown that in many small details American makers were even earlier or more ingenious than is there indicated. The intimate relation between England and America led to a prompt interchange of mechanical ideas as well as of actual workmen, so that the two countries cannot be regarded apart. In the earlier sections of the REGISTER notes are given as to Behrent, Hesselius, Albrecht, Crehore, Taws, Van Hagen, the Babcocks, Bacon, Bourne, Chickering, Clark, Dubois, Dunham, Firth, the Geibs, the Gilberts, Hawkins, Hiskey, Knabe, Lindeman, the Louds, Mackay, Meyer, the Nunnses, Osborn, Schomacker, Stewart, Stodart, Wise, etc. — all of whom worked at least as early as 1840. The attention given to piano-making in America before 1850 is both a symptom and a cause of musical interest. After 1850 American pianos began to acquire something of the international prominence that they now have,

one of the striking factors being the enterprise of Steinway after 1853.

The enormous expansion of the industry of piano-making is shown by the fact that over 300 establishments are now in operation (not counting those merely occupied in making parts and fittings), employing towards 30,000 workmen. The census of 1910 placed the annual output at that time at about 375,000 instruments, of which nearly 9000 were grands. The value of this annual output was put at about $60,000,000. It is not likely that the number of separate concerns has much increased, but the amount of production is certainly greater. See Am. History and Encyclopedia of Music, 'American Music,' pp. 314-26.

Since 1900 the whole field of piano-making has been greatly modified by the multiplication of automatic devices for playing, chiefly those contained within the instrument (see PLAYER-PIANO). These have now been adopted by practically all makers, with numerous special points of interest in each case. This innovation has greatly extended the range of the market for pianos. Whether or not it has affected the character of their artistic use remains an open question. The mechanical difficulties of introducing 'playing' attachments have been so well overcome that they no longer need take away from an instrument's essentially artistic quality.

Details regarding many leading piano-makers are given in separate articles.

PIERCE, GEORGE LEAVITT (b. 1874). See COLLEGES, 3 (Grinnell C., Iowa).

PILCHER'S SONS, HENRY, of Louisville, Ky., is an organ-making business that has had a long history. Henry Pilcher, Sr. (d. 1880), began making organs in London in 1820. In 1832 he came to New York and for many years was associated with Henry Erben. His son, Henry Pilcher, Jr. (1828-91), after training in New York, about 1850 established himself in St. Louis, in 1861 moved to Chicago, and, after the great fire of 1871, went to Louisville, making a fine record for conscientious work in each city. Since 1884 the firm, now carried on by Robert E. and William E. Pilcher, has developed a large, fully-equipped factory. One of its largest four-manual organs is in the First Presbyterian Church of Atlanta.

'PILGRIM'S PROGRESS.' A 'musical mystery' for soli, chorus, organ and orchestra, by Edgar Stillman Kelley, on a text by Mrs. Elizabeth Hodgkinson. It was first produced at the Cincinnati May Festival in 1918, and repeated in New York in 1920 at the festival of the Oratorio and Symphony Societies.

PILLSBURY, AMOS. See TUNE-BOOKS, 1799.

PILZER, MAXIMILIAN (b. 1890). See Register, 9.

PINNEY, CLAUDE CHARLES. See COLLEGES, 3 (Tarkio C., Mo.).

'PIPE OF DESIRE, THE.' An opera in one act by Frederick S. Converse, first produced in Boston in 1906 and at the Metropolitan Opera House in New York in 1910.

PIRANI, EUGENIO DI (Sept. 8, 1852, Ferrara, Italy), was the son of a teacher of languages in Berlin. His general education was in Venice and much of his musical training at the Rossini Conservatory in Bologna. He also studied piano with Kullak at Berlin and composition with Kiel. In 1873–83 he taught in the Kullak Academy and toured as pianist on the Continent and in England. He had an important part in the Cristofori Commemoration in Florence, became a member of several Academies and received numerous decorations. In 1888 he was head of the German committee for the International Music Exhibition at Bologna. In 1898–1901 he was critic for the 'Kleines Journal' in Berlin. In 1901–06 he toured in both Europe and America with the soprano Alma Webster Powell, with whom in 1904 he founded a Musical Institute in Brooklyn which they still direct. He became an American citizen in 1916. He has written the operas 'Das Hexenlied' (1902, Prague) and 'Black Blood' (1904) ; a 'Scène Vénéziane,' op. 44, for piano and orchestra (1892) ; the symphonic poems 'Fête au Château,' op. 43 (1901), 'Woodland' and 'Belshazzar' ; 'Airs Bohémiens,' op. 35, for orchestra ; and many lesser instrumental and vocal works. His *High-School of Piano-Playing*, 1908 (4th ed., 1918), includes études that have been highly praised. [R.9]

‡PITT, PERCY (Jan. 4, 1870, London, England). See article in Vol. iii. 759. In 1906 he became an assistant-conductor at Covent Garden, and in 1907 principal conductor and general artistic adviser, following Messager. His symphony in G minor was played at the Birmingham Festival of 1906. Other recent compositions are an 'English Rhapsody' for orchestra, based on folk-songs, the ballet-pantomime 'Sakura,' a Serenade for orchestra, and 'Anactoria,' a symphonic poem for viola and orchestra.

PITTS, F. E. See TUNE-BOOKS, 1859.

PITTSBURGH MUSICAL INSTITUTE, THE, was organized in 1915 under the joint direction of Frank Milton Hunter, William H. Oetting, Dallmeyer Russell and Charles N. Boyd, Mr. Hunter retiring in 1919. Starting with an enrolment of about 400, it has now nearly trebled that number. There are about 25 teachers. The Institute has an arrangement for exchanging credits with the University of Pittsburgh.

PITTSBURGH SYMPHONY ORCHESTRA, THE. See article in Vol. iv. 806–7.

Emil Paur continued as conductor until 1910. In 1907 the Orchestra made an extensive tour in conjunction with the Mendelssohn Choir of Toronto. In 1908 the number of players was increased to 80, and Edward Tak secured as concertmaster. In 1910 difficulties arose about the guarantee-fund, resulting in the disbanding of the organization. In 1909 Paur brought out his 'In der Natur' Symphony.

PIUTTI, MAX (1852–1885). See Register, 6.

PLAYER–PIANO. See article on Automatic Appliances in Vol. i. 133–8. American inventors have been remarkably energetic and successful in perfecting devices to operate pianos mechanically, so that these are now in use throughout the world. The earlier effort was to make 'piano-players' — instruments apart from the piano itself. These were soon steadily replaced by mechanisms enclosed within the piano-case — whence the name 'player-piano.' The essential principles of the two types are similar. The motive power is pneumatic, secured through an exhaust-bellows operated either by the feet or by an electric motor. This propels the 'music-roll' (a paper-strip perforated with slots for the notes of a particular piece and often for variations in tempo or force) and actuates the mechanical units affecting the action of the hammers. The number of units was at first 44, then 65 or 72, and is now usually 88, corresponding to the full compass of the keyboard. Each unit connects by a tube with an opening in the 'tracker-bar,' over which the music-roll passes, and is put in action only when a slot in the roll matches with the opening. The tempo is set or varied by controlling the movement of the roll, but the force of the hammer-blow is governed by special arrangements associated with the operative units. These 'expression-devices' are directed either by levers controlled by the player's hands or automatically through the roll.

The tendency is for each piano-maker to develop his own type of 'player,' all aiming to secure extreme rapidity, certainty, delicacy and noiselessness of action. The eager competition between inventors has lifted the whole enterprise into artistic importance. Many companies have been organized to make 'player-actions' that can be installed in various makes of pianos. Such actions are also being widely applied to pipe-organs, even of the largest class, as well as to orchestrions. Below is a list of some of the trade-names by which 'player-mechanisms' are known, with the firms using them :

'Air-o-Player,' National Piano Co., Boston.
'Amphion,' Amphion Piano-Player Co., Syracuse.
'Ampico,' American Piano Co., New York.
'Angelus,' Wilcox & White Co., Meriden, Conn.

'Apollo,' Melville Clark Piano Co., Chicago.
'Artistano,' A. B. Chase Co., Norwalk, O.
'Artone,' Ahlstrom Piano Co., Jamestown, N. Y.
'Autola,' Horace Waters & Co., New York.
'Autopiano,' Autopiano Co., New York.
'Autopneumatic,' Autopneumatic Action Co., New York.
'Autotone,' Hardman, Peck & Co., New York.
'Carola Inner-Player,' Cable Co., Chicago.
'Cecilian,' Farrand Co., Detroit.
'Claviola,' Claviola Co., New York.
'Combinola,' Geo. P. Bent Co., Chicago.
'Concertone,' Mansfield Piano Co., New York.
'Electrelle,' American Piano Co., New York.
'Euphona,' Cable Co., Chicago.
'Exceltone,' Chase-Hackley Piano Co., Muskegon, Mich.
'Harmonola,' Price & Teeple, Chicago.
'Humana,' Lauter Co., Newark, N. J.
'Manualo,' Baldwin Co., Cincinnati.
'Master,' Winter & Co., New York.
'Melodigrand,' Melodigrand Co., New York.
'Modello,' Baldwin Co., Cincinnati.
'Musicale,' Mansfield Piano Co., New York.
'Oktavec,' Laffargue Co., New York.
'Pianino,' Wurlitzer Co., New York.
'Pianista,' Autopiano Co., New York.
'Pianola,' Æolian Co., New York.
'Playotone,' Autopiano Co., New York.
'Primatone,' Foster-Armstrong Co., East Rochester, N. Y.
'Simplex,' Simplex Player-Action Co., Worcester, Mass.
'Sterlitone,' Sterling Co., Derby, Conn.
'Symphonola,' Price & Teeple, Chicago.
'Tel-Electric,' 'Telektra,' Tel-Electric Co., Pittsfield, Mass.
'Troubadour,' Haddorff Piano Co., Rockford, Ill.
'Virtuolo,' Hallet & Davis Co., Boston.
'Wondertone,' Lindenberg & Co., Columbus, O.
In addition, there are numerous types that are known simply by the name of the firms using them.

For details of construction, see William Braid White, *The Player-Piano Up to Date*, 1914, and Harrison Louis Van Atta, *The Piano and Player-Piano*, 1914.

POCHON, ALFRED (b. 1878). See Register, 9.

POEHLMANN, HERMANN. See COLLEGES, 3 (Grove City C., Pa.).

POLACCO, GIORGIO (Apr. 12, 1875, Venice, Italy), as a boy studied in Petrograd, continuing under Coccon at the Liceo Marcello in Milan, where he later graduated from the Verdi Conservatory. He at once began a career as operatic conductor, first in London, for a few years in Milan and Rome and for several more at Buenos Aires and Rio de Janeiro. He also was guest-conductor at Lisbon, Warsaw, Petrograd and Mexico City. In 1906 he appeared at San Francisco, and in 1911–12, at Puccini's request, he had charge of Savage's productions of his 'Girl of the Golden West.' From 1912 he was one of the valued leaders at the Metropolitan Opera House in New York. In 1915 he replaced Toscanini at the latter's breakdown in health, and then succeeded as chief conductor. Since

1918 he has been with the Chicago Opera Company. His répertoire includes more than 150 operas — Italian, French, Russian and Wagnerian. He has often been chosen to bring out new Italian works, as, for example, Mascagni's 'L'Amico Fritz' in 1891. [R.9]

POMMER, WILLIAM HENRY (b. 1851). See STATE UNIVERSITIES (Mo.).

POND, SYLVANUS BILLINGS (1792–1871). See Register, 3, and TUNE-BOOKS, 1841.

POND, WILLIAM A., & COMPANY, is the firm-name assumed in 1867 for the business of piano-making and dealing in music and instruments originally established in 1821 by John Firth and William Hall. In 1832 they were joined by S. B. Pond, previously of Albany, who continued till 1850, when his son, William A. Pond (d. 1885), came in, ultimately succeeded by William A. Pond, Jr. The making of pianos early ceased to be a feature of the business, but publishing and dealing in musical merchandise of all sorts have been conspicuous.

POOL, DAVID. See TUNE-BOOKS, 1813.

POOLE, HENRY WARD (1825– ?). See Register, 4.

PORTER, ALICE A. See COLLEGES, 2 (Western College, Ohio).

PORTER, FRANK ADDISON (b. 1859). See Register, 7.

PORTER, WILLIAM S. See Register, 3.

POTTER, CARRIE CASLER. See COLLEGES, 3 (McMinnville C., Ore.).

POWELL, ALMA WEBSTER, née Hall (Nov. 20, 1874, Chicago), after early experience as soprano, from 1901 studied with Pirani in Berlin, making her début there in 'Il Barbiere di Siviglia' and taking the part of Renata at the first performance of Pirani's 'Hexenlied' in 1902 at Prague. She toured with him in Europe and America till 1906, but also in 1904 joined him in establishing a Musical Institute in Brooklyn which they still continue. Meanwhile she took courses with Rybner at Columbia University, where she gained a Mus. B. in 1910, M.A. in 1911, and Ph.D. in 1914 (the last in political science). Since 1914 she has given her chief attention to lecture-recitals, especially in colleges and universities. She is author of an *Advanced School of Vocal Art*, 1911. [R.9]

POWELL, JOHN (Sept. 6, 1882, Richmond, Va.), having graduated from the University of Virginia in 1901, first studied the piano with his sister, Mrs. Brockenbrough, and F. C. Hahr. In 1902–07 he continued with Leschetizky in Vienna and in 1904–07 took composition under Navrátil. He first appeared as pianist with the Tonkünstler Orchestra in November, 1907, and then for several years toured widely in Germany, France and England. In 1912 he appeared

MAUD POWELL

at Richmond and in 1913 in New York. Since then he has been heard throughout the country, often with the principal orchestras, always with notable success. His compositions bid fair to attract as much attention as his playing, especially as he has made striking and effective use of Negro themes and other folk-song material. The list includes

'Sonata Virginesque,' op. 7, for violin and piano — 'In the Quarters,' 'In the Woods,' 'At the Big House' (1908, Vienna).

Concerto in B minor, op. 13, for piano and orchestra.

'Sonate Psychologique,' op. 15, for piano (1912, London).

Suite, 'In the South,' op. 16, for piano — 'Humming-Birds,' 'Negro Elegy,' 'Pioneer Dance.'

Three Songs, op. 18.

String-Quartet, op. 19 (1910, Sevčik Quartet, London).

Variations and Double Fugue, op. 20, for piano (on a theme by Hahr).

'Sonate Noble,' op. 21, for piano.

Suite, 'At the Fair,' op. 22, for piano.

Concerto in E, op. 23, for violin and orchestra (1912, Zimbalist, New York).

'Sonata Teutonica,' op. 24, for piano (1914, Moiseivitch, London).

Sonata for violin and piano (1919, Zimbalist and the composer, New York).   [R.9]

POWELL, MAUD (Aug. 22, 1868, Peru, Ill. : Jan. 8, 1920, Uniontown, Pa.). See article in Vol. iii. 802. The works with orchestral accompaniment which she introduced in America include Saint-Saëns' Concerto No. 2, in C, Tchaikovsky's Concerto, Dvořák's Concerto, Huss' Concerto, Shelley's Concerto, Arensky's Concerto, Rimsky-Korsakov's 'Fantasie de Concert,' Lalo's Concerto in F minor and 'Concerto Russe,' Sibelius' Concerto in D minor, Coleridge-Taylor's Concerto and Bruch's Concert-Stück. She has also brought forward many works by Foote, Mrs. Beach, Herbert, Saar, Kramer, Bergh, Tirindelli, Burleigh, Grace White, Hartmann and Cadman. Violin-arrangements or transcriptions by her are published by Ditson, Schirmer, Breitkopf, Carl Fischer and Schuberth.

From 1905 she made annual concert-tours in America. A recent phase of her work was giving recitals in soldiers' camps throughout the country. This disclosed a gratifying preference on the part of the men for a better class of music than had at first been prescribed. Her death was extremely sudden, due to illness while on tour. [R.7]

POWER, FRANK A. See COLLEGES, 3 (Fairmount C., Kan.).

POWERS, EDWARD LEESON (b. 1872). See COLLEGES, 2 (Judson C., Ala.).

POWNALL, MRS. (d. 1796). See Register, 2.

POYNER, VIRGIA. See COLLEGES, 3 (Arkansas Cumberland C.).

PRATT, JOHN HARRADEN (Nov. 20, 1848, Freeport, Me.), was first trained in Portland, Me., by G. W. Marston in piano, organ and harmony. In 1873 he went to California, continuing in counterpoint and composition with J. P. Morgan. Still later, at Leipzig, after taking piano with Wenzel, Coccius and Zwintscher, and theory with Jadassohn, Alfred Richter and Paul, he graduated from the Conservatory in 1881. Returning then to the Pacific Coast, he taught theory at Mills College for a time and at the King Conservatory in San José, and has been organist at the Church of St. Mary the Virgin (P. E.) and the First Jewish Synagogue in San Francisco, besides serving many years at the Old People's Home and for Masonic bodies. He became a fellow of the A. G. O. in 1888, and in 1915 dean of the Northern California Chapter, as well as president of the Musicians' Club in San Francisco in 1902–03 and 1910–13. He has written a piano-trio in G, church-music and songs. [R.7]

PRATT, SILAS GAMALIEL (Aug. 4, 1846, Addison, Vt. : Oct. 30, 1916, Pittsburgh), was brought up in Chicago, where he was early a clerk in music-stores and began training himself in music. In 1868, going to Berlin, he took piano under Bendel and Kullak, and theory and composition under Wüerst and Kiel. Injury to his wrists checked his ambitions for a pianistic career and led him to emphasize composition. His orchestral 'Magdalene's Lament' (in one movement) and the lyric opera 'Antonio' date from this early time. In 1871 he became organist at the Church of the Messiah in Chicago, and in 1872 he was active in organizing the Apollo Club. In 1875–77 he was again in Germany, studying piano with Liszt and score-reading with Dorn. His 'Centennial' Overture was given on July 4, 1876, in Berlin under his direction and later at the Crystal Palace in London. In 1878 he gave symphony-concerts in Chicago, and in 1882 his opera 'Zenobia' was there brought out. In 1885 he produced his 'Prodigal Son' symphony and selections from 'Zenobia' at the Crystal Palace. In 1887 the opera 'Antonio' (revised as 'Lucille') was given in Chicago. In 1888–1902 he taught in New York, and in 1906 established an Institute in Pittsburgh. His other operas were 'The Triumph of Columbus,' in five acts (1892, New York) and 'Ollanta,' in six acts, the libretto by himself. He also wrote a 'Lincoln' Symphony, the symphonic poems 'Sandalphon' and 'A Tragedy of the Deep' (on the 'Titanic' disaster), two suites, a 'Reverie' and other orchestral works, the cantata 'The Last Inca,' many choruses, songs, etc. He was author of Lincoln in Story, 1901, and The Pianist's Mental Velocity, 1903. [R.6]

PRATT, WALDO SELDEN (b. 1857). See Register, 6.

PRESCOTT, ABRAHAM (1789– ?). See Register, 3.

PRESSER, THEODORE (July 3, 1848, Pittsburgh), was an early student at the New England Conservatory in Boston, studying there with Emery, Whiting, Parker, Hill and Lang, and later at the Leipzig Conservatory. He first taught at the Ohio Wesleyan University, at Xenia College in Ohio and at Hollins Institute in Virginia. In 1876 he was the leader in the group that founded the M.T.N.A. at Delaware, O. While in Virginia he started 'The Etude,' which in 1884 he moved to Philadelphia and which 'there speedily grew to an immense circulation. He also rapidly built up an extensive music-business, which is now one of the largest in the country. In 1906 he established the Presser Home for Retired Music-Teachers, which is now part of the extensive Presser Foundation (see following articles). He has written some piano-studies and other teaching-material, and has translated musical text-books. [R.5]

PRESSER FOUNDATION, THE, of Philadelphia, was created in 1916 by Theodore Presser to care for various philanthropic enterprises in which he had long been interested. Its field comprises at present the management of the Presser Home (see below), the giving of scholarships to needy musical students and the help of deserving musicians in special emergencies. Scholarships are now offered in over 75 institutions, scattered through 27 States, about one-eighth being in the Middle States, one-quarter in the South and the remainder in the Interior or the West. Most of the institutions are colleges, but a few are of university grade. Candidates are selected by the officers of the college in each case. The relief work is designed to aid those whose need and worthiness are fully established. The whole purpose of the Foundation, then, is to minister to the welfare of music-teachers as a class, both beginners and veterans. The present funds of the Foundation amount to more than $1,000,000. The president is James Francis Cooke.

PRESSER HOME FOR RETIRED MUSIC-TEACHERS, THE, of Philadelphia, is a unique enterprise in America, founded in 1906 by Theodore Presser. Its only parallel is the Verdi Casa di Riposa in Milan. Under certain conditions, including the payment of $200, musicians without regard to creed or nationality, men or women, who are sixty-five years old and have taught music in the United States for not less than twenty-five years, can be admitted. Up to 1919 there had been 53 admissions, 11 men and 42 women, representing 21 States and also Canada. Several have here come to the end of their days in peace.

The Home is now established in a superbly appointed building in Germantown. Its capacity is about 65.

PRÉVOST, EUGÈNE PROSPER (1809–1872). See Register, 3.

PREYER, CARL ADOLPH (July 28, 1863, Pforzheim, Germany), gave his first piano-recital at thirteen. He studied at the Stuttgart Conservatory, then with Navrátil in Vienna and with Urban and Barth in Berlin. In 1884 he came to America. In 1889–91 he was music-director at Baker University in Kansas, and since 1893 has been professor of piano and composition in the University of Kansas, becoming in 1915 associate-dean of Fine Arts. As pianist he has appeared with leading orchestras. His piano-works include a Theme with Variations, op. 32, a 'Norwegian Dance,' Canzonetta and 'Sérénade Espagnole,' op. 40, a Toccata and 'Dialogue without Words,' op. 36, a Sonata, op. 33, a Scherzo in B-flat minor, 'Brook-Nymphs,' the fantasie-pieces 'Consolation,' 'The Ballet-Dancer' and 'Combat,' and numerous and varied Études, opp. 30, 35, 43–45, besides a number of songs. Unpublished are two sonatas for piano and violin (A minor and F), a sonata in F minor for piano, a piano-quintet in A minor, and lesser works for piano. [R.7]

PRIEST, WILLIAM. See Register, 2.

PRINCE, GEORGE A., & COMPANY, of Buffalo, was formed about 1840 to make melodeons, soon becoming leaders in the trade. Prince made decided improvements, and in 1847 Hamlin, then one of his workmen, made the discovery that led to the later reed-organ. After having made about 75,000 instruments of both the old and new types, in 1875 the firm got into financial difficulties and was dissolved.

PROPERT, DAVID. See Register, 1.

PROTHEROE, DANIEL (Nov. 24, 1866, Ystradgyniais, Wales), attended the Normal College in Swansea, early became a competitor in eisteddfods, and organized his first choral society at sixteen. Coming to Scranton, Pa., in 1886, he there started the Cymrodorion Musical Society (250 voices). In 1894 he moved to Milwaukee, where in 1899 he became conductor of the Arion Male Chorus. Since 1904 he has been increasingly active also in Chicago, where he makes his home. He is music-director at the Central Church, at the Loring Institute and at the Chicago Training College, besides teaching at the Sherwood Music School and leading more than one choral society. His talent as chorus-conductor has led to his being several times one of the chief judges at the National Eisteddfod in Wales, as well as in competitions in America. In 1890 he became Mus.B. of Toronto University and in 1905 Mus.D. of the Grand Conservatory in New York. He has written the symphonic poem 'In the Cambrian Hills,' two string-quartets, the cantatas 'St. Peter,' 'A Song of Hope,' 'The Story of Bethlehem,' 'Lady Fair' (these for chorus and orchestra), 'Eastertide,' 'At the Cross,' and 'Children in Heaven' (allegorical, for children), a Mass in F, numerous choruses, such as 'The Nun of Nidaros' and 'Britons' (both for men's voices with orchestra), anthems and songs. He compiled the Hymnal for the Welsh Presbyterian Church and four books of ritual-music for the Scottish Rite, and has prepared courses on harmony and chorus-conducting. [R.7]

PSALMODY. See TUNE-BOOKS.

PUBLIC SCHOOLS, MUSIC IN THE. What is now known as 'the public school system' of the United States is only about a century old. Its establishment and the working out of its details were processes that occupied much time and engaged the efforts of many workers during the last decades of the 18th and the early part of the 19th centuries. From the earliest days, however, the colonists had been alive to the importance of general education, as is shown by the founding of 'colleges' and some 'academies,' as well as by less permanent undertakings on the part of single communities and of certain churches. As a rule, the instruction of young children was almost wholly left to parents and homes, just as it was in England at the same period. But somewhat before 1800, and much more just after it, a movement set in to arouse local communities to the need of elementary and secondary education of a more uniform and general character. This was analogous to movements in Europe, though perhaps not directly connected with them. A difficulty in American conditions was the strong instinct for local autonomy, which long prevented a desirable consolidation of effort over large areas, such as whole States. New England was on the whole ahead of other sections, but the Middle States soon joined in the movement.[1]

At intervals in the 18th century the importance of musical training for the young was recognized. Thomas Symmes urged it as early as 1720 in connection with his plea for singing by note. As fast as 'singing-schools' sprang up they appealed to boys and girls quite as much as to their elders — though they did not often include little children. In 1753 William Tuckey began classes for 'singing-scholars' in the rooms of Trinity Church in New York. Adgate's enterprises in Philadelphia from 1784 were in part directed toward the culture of children. These are samples of efforts put forth here and there by individuals. It was not until the idea of a general plan of popular education under civic control began to shape itself that the training of children in song was extensively undertaken.

It was William C. Woodbridge (1795–1845), from 1831 editor of a series of Annals of Education, who supplied the impetus for positive advance. He had personally investigated music-teaching in schools as it was developing in Europe, especially in Switzerland and Germany. He became convinced of the superiority of the Pestalozzian method, and brought back text-books and other material, some of which he translated. As Woodbridge was a teacher in Hartford, the first trials took place there as early as 1830 under Elam Ives, but of these no record is accessible. In that year Woodbridge lectured in Boston on 'Vocal Music as a Branch of Common Education,' illustrations being given by children trained by Lowell Mason. The latter was but slowly won to accept the principles enunciated by Pestalozzi, but finally adopted them in full. These principles were thus stated:

1. *To teach sounds before signs* — to make the child sing before he learns the written notes or their names.

2. *To lead him to observe*, by hearing and imitating sounds, their resemblances and differences, their agreeable and disagreeable effect, *instead of explaining* these things *to him* — in short, to make him *active* instead of *passive* in learning.

3. *In teaching but one thing at a time* — rhythm, melody, expression are taught and practiced separately before the child is called to the difficult task of attending to all at once.

4. *In making them practice each step of each* of these divisions, *until they are master of it, before passing to the next*.

5. The giving the principles and theory after practice, and as an induction from it.

6. The analyzing and practicing the elements of articulate sound in order to apply them to music.

7. Another peculiarity, which is not, however, essential to the system, is that the names of the notes correspond to those employed in instrumental music, and are derived from the letters, with variations for flats and sharps — a method whose utility is questioned by some, but which is deemed very important by others.[1]

In January, 1833, the Boston Academy of Music was started by Mason at Woodbridge's suggestion and with the help of George J. Webb. In 1834 Mason issued his famous *Manual*, explaining the principles and methods

---

[1] New York had a State Superintendent of Schools in 1812–21, and again after 1854. Massachusetts had a State Board of Education from 1837. These were the pioneers in consolidated administration. The Federal Government was favorable to systematic public education from soon after the Revolution, but its influence was confined to grants of public lands for school-use.

[1] In later years these principles were largely disregarded or forgotten, but it is interesting to note that the so-called modern 'observation' method rests upon the first, second and fifth of them.

to be used in the Academy's singing-classes
for children and youth. Samuel A. Eliot,
the president of the Academy, was then on
the city School-Committee (mayor in 1837–39)
and was heartily sympathetic with the movement to introduce music into the public
schools. In 1836, thanks to the efforts of
these advocates, a memorial to this effect
was laid before the committee, but without
result. A second attempt in 1837 secured
the committee's approval, but without their
providing funds for the arrangement. Mason
agreed to teach for a year without salary,
and in October, 1837, began work in the Hawes
School in South Boston. His success was so
obvious that in August, 1838, the committee
gave its official endorsement, putting Mason
in charge of music in all the schools, with
A. N. Johnson, G. F. Root, A. J. Drake and
J. A. Johnson as assistants. In 1841 Mason
resigned to devote himself to 'conventions'
and B. F. Baker succeeded him. A general
committee on music was first appointed in
1857. Music was not taught in the primary
grades at first, but was added in 1864 by
L. W. Mason. In 1868 H. E. Holt took charge
of the lower grammar grades, in 1869 Eichberg
became the first supervisor, and in 1872 music
was carried into all the high schools — thus
making the system complete.

In February, 1836, the trustees of the schools
in New York took up the question of music,
but decided to leave it to the boards of the
several schools, stipulating that it must not
involve expense or interfere with other studies.
In 1840, '43 and '47 motions to bring music
in were disapproved. In 1853 it was introduced, but without system. No definite
plan for it was issued till 1879, and, according
to Frank Damrosch, it was not really established till 1898.

In 1858 the Boston School Committee made
an inquiry as to the introduction of music
in other cities, the dates secured being these —
Boston, 1838; Buffalo, 1843; Pittsburgh,
1844; Cincinnati, 1846 (1844?); Chicago,
1848; Cleveland, 1851; San Francisco, 1851;
St. Louis, 1852. The first teacher in Buffalo
was Mr. Hazeltine; in Pittsburgh, L. P.
Lincoln; and in Cincinnati, Charles Aiken
(succeeded in 1879 by his son, W. H. Aiken,
who is still in service).[1] Among later examples
mention may be made of New Haven, Conn.,
where Benjamin Jepson began teaching in
seven schools in January, 1865, at first only
in the upper grades. Jepson published, at
his own expense, what appears to have been

the first *Music-Reader*.[1] He remained in
charge over forty-five years.

In 1884–85 the Bureau of Education reported that music was taught in the public
schools of 247 towns and cities, with some
90 special teachers. Twenty years later,
in a Bulletin of the Bureau (*Music-Education
in the United States*, 1908), the compiler,
Arthur L. Manchester, said:

'Teachers in public schools are steadily seeking to
improve both the matter and the method of their
phase of music-education, rectifying inaccuracies
of grading and bridging over the chasm between
elementary and advanced grades. The cultivation
of music in its foundational aspects and as part of
the life of the people is being given intelligent consideration. Pedagogic principles as a basis for
further development are being given attention, and
the trend is strongly toward efficiency, coördination
and coöperation'; adding, however, that 'among
the defects in our present scheme of music-education
there exists one of very serious character, namely,
a lack of systematic, wisely-planned, and thoroughly
carried-out foundational training.'

In 1914, in introducing another Bulletin
of the Bureau (*Music in the Public Schools*,
compiled by Will Earhart), Commissioner
Claxton said:

'That music plays an important part in the life of
a people and should therefore have an important place
in the system of education in any State or nation has
been understood by the foremost educators for three
thousand years. Among a practical, industrial
and commercial people, like ourselves, good music
is necessary not only for enjoyment and recreation,
but also for inspiration and for salvation from death
in the din and dust of trade; and this music should
be democratic in the truest and best sense. This
it can never be until it becomes an integral part of
the education given in the schools of all grades, as
it is in the schools of some other countries. It is
through an increasingly clear understanding of this
fact that music, not recognized in the course of study
of our earliest public schools, has, within the last
twenty-five or thirty years, been introduced to some
extent into the schools of most progressive cities
and of many towns, villages, and country communities, though by many it is still considered un-
essential and a fad. Sooner or later we shall not
only recognize the culture value of music, we shall
also begin to understand that, after the beginnings
of reading, writing, arithmetic and geometry, music
has greater practical value than any other subject
taught in the schools.'

From this report, presenting a detailed
account of conditions throughout the country,
some salient facts may be noted. In grades
below the high school 622 towns and cities
require music, and 59 do not — all but four
of the 622 having graded courses. St. Louis
has 700 pianos to 2194 school-rooms; Cincinnati, 250 pianos to 1000 rooms. In the vast
majority of schools the music-teaching is done
by grade-teachers under the guidance of a
supervisor, but, unfortunately, few schools

---

[1] See paper by Frances M. Dickey on 'The Early
History of Public School Music in the United States,'
M.T.N.A. Proceedings, 1913, where numerous details are given. The singing in Cincinnati early became famous, and since 1873 school-choruses have
often taken part in the biennial Festivals.

[1] In 1875 a choral society composed of 333 graduates
from these schools gave 'The Creation,' 'The Messiah'
and 'Elijah' under Jepson's direction.

require thorough preparation for this work. In 631 high schools 189 (30%) have no music except assembly-singing; 442 (70%) have some music other than assembly-singing. 238 high schools reported orchestras, with a total membership of 4181 players; in about one-third of the schools credit is given for orchestra-playing. Musical history or appreciation, or both, find place in 73 high schools, with a student-enrolment of 7587. Harmony is taught to 705 students in 39 systems; sight-singing and elementary theory in 58 schools, with 14,434 students. In 10 States music is required in the grades; in 37 States music is not required, but more or less adequate provision is made for music-teaching below high school grades. Five States require music in high schools (Arizona, Indiana, Iowa, Louisiana and Washington); 42 do not require it, but in these the development of high-school music is frequently equal to that in the others. 17 States require examinations for special teachers or supervisors; only 34 State institutions out of 87 make provision for training supervisors. The result is that supervisors are trained elsewhere privately as musicians, or if in normal schools, as teachers rather than musicians. While this report suffers from the usual failure of many persons to respond, fully or in part, to even an important questionnaire, it is of great value as showing average conditions, and the details of the report have been most carefully worked out.

In 1916 an elaborate and exhaustive thesis was prepared by Rose Yont of the University of Nebraska, and published as *Status and Value of Music in Education.*[1] This thesis deals with music in the public schools, normal schools, state universities and colleges, educational extension, and general education; it also contains a valuable bibliographical list. The author finds the number of music-supervisors to be 1343 (in 1913), of whom about 20% are men. The investigation, covering the entire country, 'showed great interest [among school authorities], emphatic approval of the subject as a school study, and a strong desire to learn the results of this investigation.' The Pacific States all present the feverish activity which characterizes most of the North Central States. Progressive school officers and educational leaders who favor broad culture have pushed the subject to the front very rapidly. California probably leads the States of the Union, in her uniform, deliberately planned and systematic presentation of the subject. The conditions in 1913 presented a remarkable and gratifying growth, except in the Southern States, as compared with similar data secured by Miss Yont in

[1] The Woodruff Press, Lincoln, Neb., 353 pp.

1907. There is a chapter on credit for private music-lessons outside of school, with interesting statistics and the conclusion that the people 'are more ready for the innovation than school authorities, who fear to take so radical a step.' A careful estimate places the sum paid in Nebraska for private music-lessons annually at about $1,000,000, while the State paid out only $36,182 for musical instruction. 'This would indicate that the schools are not supplying public demands in the teaching of this subject, while furthermore it shows enormous financial waste. The same amount judiciously spent in the schools would be more than adequate to supply all the children with proper musical training.'

Realizing the need of more uniformity of system and requirements, in music as in other subjects, the National Education Association in 1912 appointed a Commission on the Reorganization of Secondary Education. The committee on music under this included thirteen workers of national reputation, with Will Earhart as chairman and Osbourne McConathy as head of a subcommittee on course of study. In the preliminary statements issued in 1913 occur sentences like these:

'In common with the other arts and literature, and perhaps in a higher degree, music tends to develop finer subjective life in the individual.'

'A course in music that does not promise to adjust the learner in sympathetic response to the best music is lacking in its proper quality, whatever marks of efficiency it may show.'

'Failure to bring the graduates of public schools into sympathetic relation with the mature musical intelligence and interests of their various communities is due not so much to shortcomings in the work of the grades as to neglect or sad misdirection of the work in high schools.'

'If we would have an adult public interested in and appreciative of the great music of the masters, we must have general instruction in advanced phases of musical study.' 'To the high schools properly belongs the task of articulating the music in the grades with the enlightened musical understanding and interest of the community.'

The report of this committee, as published in a further Bulletin of the Bureau of Education in 1917, deals in detail with methods and results in ensemble-singing, chorus-practice, musical appreciation, harmony, counterpoint, orchestra-ensemble, credit for study under outside teachers, etc., with suggestions as to administration. To those not familiar with what is now being actually done in not a few high schools, or who suppose that all public school work in music has remained as it was fifty years ago, this report will be exceedingly interesting.

Until recently high-school graduates were not able to use music as a credit for college-entrance. In the *Proceedings* of the Music Supervisors' National Conference for 1919

is a report on this subject by Osbourne Mc-
Conathy, Edward B. Birge and Karl W.
Gehrkens, representing respectively the Supervisors' Conference, the N. E. A., and the M.
T. N. A. Through a questionnaire sent out
by the Bureau of Education they ascertained
that, out of 412 colleges replying, 191 allowed
some entrance-credit for music — 80 giving
one unit out of 15 or 16, and 111 two or more
units. Furthermore, out of the 412 colleges,
238 give credit toward the A.B. degree for
courses in music. The committee concludes
that entrance-credit will be granted more and
more. The rapidity and permanence of the
movement will depend upon the quality of
the work done in the secondary schools.

The marked improvement in public school
music since about 1900 has been due to the
combination of many causes, especially the
advance of public opinion as reflected by
school authorities and the zeal and wisdom
of many teachers in the school systems. As
a single index of the growth in interest it may
be noted that at the first meeting of the
Supervisors' Conference in 1911 the membership was 84, whereas in 1919 it was 700.
The number of institutions — normal schools,
colleges, universities and conservatories —
now offering more or less elaborate courses
of training for public-school teaching is impres-
sively large, implying both a demand and a
purpose. Hence large expectations for future
development seem to be justified.

Besides the literature referred to, especially
the *Bulletins* of the Bureau of Education and
Miss Yont's elaborate study, reference should
be made to the various volumes of the *Proceedings* of the M. T. N. A., the N. E. A., the
Supervisors' Conference (National and
Eastern), the successive volumes of 'School
Music,' 'The Journal of Education,' and
several musical periodicals, etc.

‡PUCCINI, GIACOMO (Dec. 28, 1858,
Lucca, Italy). See article in Vol. iii. 847–8,
and note in v. 660. Additional operas are
'La Fanciulla del West' (Dec. 10, 1910, New
York), 'La Rondine' (1917, Monte Carlo),
and the short 'Il Tabarro,' 'Suor Angelica'
and 'Gianni Schicchi' (Dec. 14, 1918, New
York). 'Madama Butterfly' was first sung
in New York on Nov. 12, 1906, by the Savage
Opera Company (in English) and at the
Metropolitan Opera House on Feb. 11, 1907.
On the latter occasion and at the première
of 'La Fanciulla del West' the composer was
present. All of his operas except 'Edgar'
and 'La Rondine' have been repeatedly given
in America with eminent success. For bibliography on Puccini, see Baker, *Dict. of Musicians*, p. 728.

PULITZER, JOSEPH (Apr. 10, 1847,
Budapest, Hungary : Oct. 29, 1911, on
board his yacht at Charleston, S. C.), arrived
in America in 1864, penniless and unable to
speak English. He served for a year in the
Civil War as a cavalry private. From 1865 he
was variously employed at St. Louis, where
from 1867 he was a reporter for the 'Westliche
Post,' becoming in 1871 managing-editor and
part-owner. In 1879 he combined two St.
Louis papers into the 'Post-Dispatch,' and in
1883 became owner of the New York 'World.'
In 1887, in the full tide of journalistic success,
his health failed and total blindness began to
come on. In 1903 he founded the School of
Journalism at Columbia University with an
initial gift of $1,000,000. At his death he
signalized his lifelong enthusiasm for music
by bequeathing $500,000 to the Philharmonic
Society of New York, with the stipulation
that his favorite composers, Beethoven,
Wagner and Liszt, should be frequently represented on its programs. [R.10]

PULLER, S. D. See TUNE-BOOKS, 1825.

'PURITANIA.' An opera by Edgar Stillman Kelley, to a text by C. M. S. McLellan,
written in New York and produced in Boston
on June 9, 1892.

PUTNAM, CLARENCE SIMEON. See
STATE UNIVERSITIES (N.D. Agric. C.).

PYCHOWSKI, JAN NEPOMUCENE
(1818–1900). See Register, 4.

Q

QUARLES, JAMES THOMAS (Nov. 7, 1877, St. Louis), was trained by Galloway (piano and organ), Vieh and Ehling (piano) and Kroeger (theory), and entered upon a career of great activity as organist. At sixteen he served the Cook Avenue Presbyterian Church, and in 1897, on graduating from the high school, went to the Central Congregational, in 1898 to the West Presbyterian, giving his first recitals, and in 1900 to the Lindell Avenue Methodist, where for thirteen years he gave monthly recitals. In 1903 he appeared at the Louisiana Purchase Exposition, and also became teacher at Lindenwood College, where he was later dean of Fine Arts. In 1905 he was made music-director at the Cathedral of the Scottish Rite, and in 1907 at Moolah Temple, organizing a band of singers which traveled widely to participate in conclaves. In 1906 he was studying in Paris under Widor. In 1907 he became organist of the St. Louis Symphony Orchestra, and also founded the Choral Art Society, which took up works like Brahms' Requiem, Dvořák's Stabat Mater, Schumann's 'Paradise and the Peri,' etc. In 1912 he made an extensive recital-tour in the East, and in 1913 became university-organist at Cornell University, being made assistant-professor in 1916. He has given there about 200 educational recitals, presenting almost all the masterpieces of organ-literature. He has played at the Panama-Pacific Exposition, at the first convention of the A. G. O., with the Boston and Chicago Orchestras, and in many other notable relations. He has written a considerable number of songs, anthems and short organ-works, most of which are unpublished. [R.8]

'QUEST OF THE GORGON, THE.' No. 4 of the 'Grove-Plays' of the California Bohemian Club, the text by Newton J. Tharp and the music by Theodore J. Vogt. It was produced in 1905.

R

‡ RABAUD, HENRI BENJAMIN (Oct. 10, 1873, Paris, France). He was a pupil of Massenet at the Paris Conservatory, where he won the Prix de Rome in 1894. He made his début as conductor at the Opéra in 1908, in 1914 was made principal conductor and in 1915 became leader of the Conservatory Orchestra. In 1918–19 he followed Muck as conductor of the Boston Symphony Orchestra, resigning to return to Paris as successor to Fauré in the directorship of the Conservatory. His operas include 'La Fille de Roland' (1904, Opéra-Comique), 'Mârouf, Savetier du Caire' (1914, Opéra-Comique), and music for French versions of 'The Merchant of Venice' and 'Antony and Cleopatra' (1916–17, Théâtre Antoine); two symphonies, in D minor and E minor (1895, '99); the symphonic poem 'La Procession Nocturne' (1899); 'Divertissement sur les Chansons Russes' (1901); 'Églogue' (1902); the prize-cantata 'Daphné' (1894); the oratorio 'Job' (1900), with a lyric poem on the same subject for baritone and orchestra (1905); Psalm 4 for soli, chorus and orchestra (1901); 'Hymne à la France Éternelle,' from Hugo (1916); a string-quartet, and an andante and scherzo for flute, violin and piano. His 'Mârouf' was introduced at the Metropolitan Opera House on Dec. 19, 1917.

RACHMANINOV, SERGEI VASSILIE-VITCH (Apr. 2, 1873, Onega, Russia). See article in Vol. iv. 11–2. His grandfather, an excellent pianist, was one of John Field's pupils. He had his first lessons from Anna Ornadtskaia, and at Petrograd studied under Demiansky and Cross, going thence to Moscow at the suggestion of Siloti, his cousin. His opera 'Aleko' was his final exercise there, winning a medal, 1893. For four years he was mainly busy with composition, as well as in 1899–1904. In 1897–98 he was private opera-conductor for Mamontov in Moscow. In 1904–06 he directed the Moscow Opera. In 1906–08 he lived in Dresden, composing and touring as pianist. In 1908–11 he was vice-president of the Russian Music Society, and in 1909–10 made his first American tour as pianist. In 1912–13 he led symphony concerts at Moscow. In 1917 he left Russia, and late in 1918 settled in New York. To the list of works should be added the one-act operas 'The Miser Knight' (1900, Moscow, 1910, Boston) and 'Francesca da Rimini' (1906, Moscow); Symphony No. 2, op. 27 (1906, '07); Symphony No. 3, 'The Bells,' op. 35 (1912); the symphonic poem 'The Island of Death,' after Böcklin, op. 29 (1907–08); the 3rd and 4th Piano-Concertos, opp. 30 and 40 (1909, '17); a piano-sonata in D

minor, op. 28; two sets of Preludes for piano, opp. 23 and 32; eight 'Études-Tableaux' (concert-studies) for piano, op. 39; three sets of songs, opp. 21, 26, 34; 12 anthems on early church themes; a setting of the Liturgy of St. Chrysostom (1910, Moscow Synodal Choir). See Montagu-Nathan, *Contemporary Russian Composers*, 1917, and 'The Etude,' October, 1919. [R.9]

'RAG-TIME.' See note in Vol. iv. 16. The term is now not at all confined to music of Negro origin or suggestion.

RAINS, LEON (b. 1870). See Register, 8.

RAISA, ROSA (b. 1893). See Register, 10.

RALSTON, FANNY MARION (b. 1875). See Register, 3, and COLLEGES, 2 (Rockford C., Ill.).

RANDOLPH, HAROLD (Oct. 31, 1861, Richmond, Va.), studied at the Peabody Conservatory in Baltimore, chiefly under Mme. Falk-Auerbach and Faelten for piano and Hamerik for composition. He first appeared as pianist with the Peabody Symphony Orchestra in 1885, being perhaps the first player both American-born and American-trained to receive general recognition. He has been soloist with all the leading orchestras and chamber-ensembles, and with Ernest Hutcheson has given many recitals for two pianos. In 1885–90 he was organist at the Baltimore (R.C.) Cathedral, and in 1890–96 at Emmanuel (P.E.) Church. He early began to teach at the Peabody Conservatory, and in 1898 succeeded Hamerik as director. His administration has been marked by remarkable energy and success. Among other undertakings, he has organized a Bach Choir, which has given Bach's St. Matthew Passion, Beethoven's Missa Solemnis and much a cappella music. [R.7]

RAPPOLD, MARIE (1880?, Brooklyn), was trained by Saenger and early sang in church and concert. A chance hearing by Conried led to her appearing at the Metropolitan Opera House as Sulamith in 'Die Königin von Saba' in 1905. Her success was immediate, and she has since sung at the Metropolitan almost every season, taking rôles like Aida, Desdemona, Marguerite (in 'Faust'), Eurydice, Venus, Elizabeth, Micaela, Inez, Elsa and the Princess (in 'Lobetanz'). In 1906 she separated from her husband so as to continue her stage-work, and in 1913 married the tenor Rudolf Berger. [R.9]

RATH, ERICH. See COLLEGES, 2 (Hollins C., Va.).

RAUSCH, FREDERICK. See Register, 2.

‡ RAVEL, MAURICE (Mar. 7, 1875, Ciboure, France). See article in Vol. v. 660–1

338

During the war he spent two years at the front. To the list of works add the ballets 'Daphnis et Chloë,' 'La Mère l'Oye' (after a piano-suite of five 'pièces enfantines') and 'Adelaïde' (after his 'Valses Nobles'); a 'Sérénade Grotesque,' a Menuet on the name of Haydn, 'Valses Nobles et Sentimentales,' a Prélude, and the Suite, 'Le Tombeau de Couperin' — all for piano; the songs 'Ballade de la Reine Morte d'Aimer,' 'Un Grand Sommeil Noir,' 'Si Morne,' 'Manteau de Fleurs,' 'Trois Poèmes' from Mallarmé, for voice, piano, flutes, clarinets and strings, and 'Vocalise en forme d'Habanera'; and piano-transcriptions of Debussy's Nocturnes and 'L'Après-midi d'un Faune.' See Jean-Aubry, *French Music of To-day*, 1919.

RAYMOND, GEORGE LANSING (b. 1839). See Register, 8.

READ, ANGELO McCALLUM (May 22, 1854, near St. Catherines, Ont.), had his general education at the Collegiate Institute in St. Catherines and early musical training in the United States. He spent five years at Leipzig under Reinecke, Richter, Jadassohn, Maas and Papperitz, with one year in Vienna for Leschetizky methods. He appeared as organist, composer and conductor at Leipzig in 1883. Making his home at Buffalo since 1894, he has conducted choral societies there, at St. Catherines and at Hornell, N. Y., besides acting as guest-conductor elsewhere. He is music-director at Ridley College in St. Catherines and at d'Youville College in Buffalo. He has written the dramatic cantata 'David's Lament,' op. 15, for soli, chorus, orchestra and organ (1903, St. Catherines Festival) (Schirmer); 'A Song of the Nativity,' op. 12, for tenor, women's quartet, chorus and organ (Schirmer); the Lenten cantata 'It is Finished,' op. 17 (Gray); 'O Salutaris Hostia,' for voice, violin and organ (1893, St. Ann's, Vienna); 'Ave Verum Corpus,' in canon-form a cappella (twice given at Leipzig); the 'Oriska Waltz,' op. 4, originally for piano, but also for orchestra; many piano-pieces, songs, choruses and anthems. He has unpublished an oratorio, a Mass in B-flat, several overtures, etc. He is an expert botanist, and has written articles on both musical and botanical subjects. [R.8]

READ, DANIEL (1757–1836). See Register, 2, and TUNE-BOOKS, 1785.

READ, JOEL (1753– ?). See TUNE-BOOKS, 1808.

REDMAN, HARRY NEWTON (b. 1869). See Register, 8.

REED, EPHRAIM. See TUNE-BOOKS, 1820.

REED, FRANK LeFEVRE (b. 1871). See Register, 8, and STATE UNIVERSITIES (Tex.).

REED, M. ELLERY. See COLLEGES, 3 (Beaver C., Pa.).

REED–ORGAN. American ingenuity has been peculiarly productive in developing the possibilities of the 'harmonium' or that form of organ which employs only small *free* reeds as tone-producers. The first experiments were made before 1820. At least as early as 1845 the French system of forcing the air out through the reeds was replaced by the distinctively American system of drawing it in by suction. The bellows, however, at first was single and the air-pressure fluctuating. The name 'melodeon' was early adopted (popularly corrupted into 'melodium'), and the form used resembled a small square piano. There were usually only one or two sets of reeds, and the tone-quality was monotonous. About 1850 Emmons Hamlin, then working for George A. Prince & Co., of Buffalo, discovered that twisting and bending the tongues of the reeds produced decided improvement in their tone, not only in power, but in variety of quality. In 1854 he joined Henry Mason in forming the Mason & Hamlin Co., of Boston, who speedily became the pioneers in developing instruments of unexampled breadth of effect. They put forth the 'organ-harmonium' in 1855 and the 'cabinet organ' in 1861 — the latter deriving its name from the fact that the case extended to the floor. The use of a double bellows greatly improved the air-supply, and variations in loudness were secured either by an 'automatic bellows' or a 'knee-swell' that controlled a lid on the box inclosing the reeds. From that time improvements were rapid, so that cabinet organs became artistically and commercially important. They were often made with many sets of reeds, differently voiced, with two keyboards, with a pedal-keyboard, etc. Other manufacturers took up the business on a large scale, and the use of reed-organs in homes, churches, lodges and similar assembly-places became widespread. See H. L. Mason, *History and Development of the American Cabinet Organ*.

A peculiar early variety was the 'lap-organ' or 'rocking-melodeon,' developed before 1850, especially in New Hampshire, in which the bellows rested on the player's knees and was worked by pressing with one or both arms, while the reeds were controlled by a keyboard more or less like that of an accordion. The 'vocalion,' introduced about 1890, uses pressure instead of suction and has large reeds with special air-chambers attached.

See articles in Vols. i. 77–8, ii. 302–5, and v. 360–1.

REINAGLE, ALEXANDER (1756, Portsmouth, England : Sept. 21, 1809, Baltimore). See note in Vol. iv. 57. He was a pupil of Raynor Taylor. He came to New

York in 1786, soon moved to Philadelphia, where he remained except for the year 1788–89 spent in New York. He promptly became a leader in all musical affairs, being an excellent pianist, singer, conductor, composer and operatic manager. With Thomas Wignell, in 1793 he formed a stock-company in Philadelphia, erected the New Theatre on Chestnut Street, which was opened early in 1794, and was pianist in the orchestra. Both plays and operas were given here for many years. Of the quality of his musicianship there is evidence in a few sonatas that are in the Library of Congress. He wrote new accompaniments and sometimes an overture for the musical plays that were brought from England. In 1795 for some reason he provided new music for 'The Sicilian Romance,' which had previously been given in England with music by William Reeves. In 1796 he furnished an overture, songs, choruses and recitatives for the pantomime 'The Witches of the Rock.' See Sonneck, *Early Concert-Life, Early Opera* (portrait on p. 118 and interior of the Chestnut Street Theatre at p. 113), and 'Early American Operas' in *I. M. G. Sammelbde*, 6. 465, 486–9. [R.2]

REMMERTZ, FRANZ (1845?– ?). See Register, 5.

REMY, ALFRED (Mar. 16, 1870, Elberfeld, Germany), was brought to New York in 1882, attended the public schools and graduated from the College of the City of New York in 1890. He pursued post-graduate studies in Germanic philology and literature at Columbia University, where he was made A.M. in 1905. In 1890–96 he studied piano and theory with Klein and part of this time violin with Charles Palm. In 1895–97 he was music-critic for 'Vogue' and 'The Looker-On,' and taught harmony at the International Conservatory, and in 1896–98 lectured on music-history at the College of Music. Since 1901 he has been on the staff of the *International Encyclopædia*, writing many articles on musical subjects and since 1907 preparing extremely valuable summaries of musical events for the *International Year-Book*. In 1906–15 he was extension-lecturer at Columbia, and since 1897 has also been instructor in languages in several institutions. In 1915 he undertook the editing of the 3rd edition of Baker's *Dictionary of Musicians*, 1919. In 1902 he married Egbertina Wilterdink, a fine pianist, with whom he has given lecture-recitals, chiefly on Wagner. His compositions, all written before 1896, include an opera, 'Hjördis,' based on Ibsen's 'Vikings of Helgeland,' an Intermezzo for orchestra, 'Elfenreigen' for strings, several vocal and some piano-pieces. [R.8]

RENWICK, LLEWELLYN LARAWAY (b. 1876). See Register, 8.

REUSS, EDUARD (1851–1911). See Register, 7.

REYNOLDS, WALTER GUERNSEY (b. 1873). See Register, 8.

RICE, FENELON B. (Jan. 2, 1841, Greensburg, O. : Oct. 6, 1901, Oberlin, O.), from about 1861 studied in Boston under Tufts, B. F. Baker and Edwin Bruce. In 1863–67 he was in charge of the music-department of Hillsdale College in Michigan, and then went to Leipzig for two years with Papperitz, Moscheles, Richter and Plaidy. From 1871 till his death he was director of the Oberlin Conservatory, creating the faculty and the ideals that raised it into national importance. He was gifted in organization and in pedagogical foresight, as well as in a fine idealism of mind and spirit. In 1880–81 he was president of the M.T.N.A. Hillsdale College made him Mus.D. in 1882. [R.6]

RICE, JOHN. See Register, 1.

RICE, WILLIAM GORHAM (b. 1856). See Register, 10.

RICH, THADDEUS (Mar. 21, 1885, Indianapolis), after training from his father and other local teachers in 1897–1900 studied at the Leipzig Conservatory under Hilf. In 1901–02 he played in the Gewandhaus Orchestra under Nikisch, and then worked under Joachim in Berlin for two years. In 1903–05 he was concertmaster at the Opera des Westens there, with some concertizing, and then returned to America. Since 1906 he has been concertmaster of the Philadelphia Orchestra. In addition to some appearances in concert, he has been active in presenting chamber-works, and is dean of the music-department of Temple University, which made him Mus.D. in 1913. [R.9]

RICHARDSON, ALFRED MADELEY (June 1, 1868, Southend-on-Sea, England), though the son of a Congregational minister, was educated at Keble College, Oxford, where he gained a scholarship in 1885 and became B.A. in 1889, M.A. in 1890, Mus.B. in 1888 and Mus.D. in 1897. He was also president of the University Musical Club and of Keble College Musical Society, and in 1889 took the Phillpotts Theological Prize. From 1889 he was organist in Worcester, in 1891–92 in London, in 1892–97 in Scarborough, and from 1897 at St. Saviour's in Southwark (London), which in 1905 became the cathedral of a new diocese. Here he developed choir-services of great beauty and dignity, including a unique treatment of the Psalms and a cappella Palestrina music. From 1905 he was in much request as lecturer before Church Congresses and elsewhere, and as judge at Eisteddfodau and other contests. He also gave organ-recitals and led various choral societies. In 1909 he was induced to come to America, first as organist at St. Paul's in Baltimore and since 1912 as instructor in theory at the Institute of Musical Art in New York. He has written many organ-pieces, anthems and part-songs, edited Communion Services by Tallis and Merbecke, and published *Choir-Training*, 1897, *Church Music for the Clergy*, 1902, *The Psalms, their Structure and Musical Rendering*, 1903, *The Southwark Psalter*, 1904, *Modern Organ-Accompaniment*, 1907, *Extempore-Playing*, *The Choir-Trainer's Art*, 1914 and *The Southwark Canticles*, 1918. [R.9]

RICHARDSON, NATHAN (1827–1859). See Register, 4.

RICHINGS, CAROLINE [Mrs. Bernard] (1827–1882). See Register, 4.

RIDER–KELSEY, CORINNE (b. 1879). See Register, 9.

‡ RIEMANN, KARL WILHELM JULIUS HUGO (July 18, 1849, Grossmehlra, Germany : July 11, 1919, Leipzig). See article in Vol. iv. 95–6. His original publications from 1900 include *Vademecum der Phrasierung*, 1900 (2nd ed., 1911), *Die Elemente der musikalischen Aesthetik*, 1900, *Epochen und Heroen der Musikgeschichte*, 1900, *Geschichte der Musik seit Beethoven*, 1901, *Handbuch der Musikgeschichte*, 5 parts, 1901, '05, '07, '11, '13 (musical examples, 1912), *Grosse Kompositionslehre*, 3 vols., 1902, '03, '13, *System der Musikalischen Rhythmik und Metrik*, 1903, *Grundriss der Musikwissenschaft*, 1908 (2nd ed., 1915), *Kleines Handbuch der Musikgeschichte*, 1908 (2nd ed., 1915), *Die byzantinische Notenschrift im 10.–15. Jahrhundert*, 2 vols., 1909, '15, and *Kompendium der Notenschriftkunde*, 1910, besides many introductions, analyses and detached articles. The 8th edition of his *Musiklexikon* was issued in 1916. Altogether, he stands out as the most commanding figure in the fields of research to which he devoted himself.

RIEMENSCHNEIDER, ALBERT (b. 1878). See Register, 8, and COLLEGES, 3 (Baldwin-Wallace C., Ohio).

RIGBY, RALPH. See COLLEGES, 3 (Berea C., Ky.).

RILEY, E. See TUNE-BOOKS, 1817.

RILEY, HERBERT (b. 1888). See Register, 10.

‡RIMSKY–KORSAKOV, NICHOLAI ANDREIEVITCH (Mar. 18, 1844, Tikhvin, Russia : June 21, 1908, Liubensk, near Petrograd). See article in Vol. iv. 102–5, and note in Vol. v. 661. In 1907 he conducted the Russian music-festival in Paris, and was made a corresponding member of the Académie. To the list of works add the opera 'Le Coq d'Or' (1910, Moscow, 1918, New York), a string-sextet and a quintet for piano, flute, clarinet, horn and bassoon. He published *The History of my Musical Life*, 1909, *Collected Musical Essays and Sketches*,

1911, and *The Foundations of Instrumentation*, 2 vols., 1913 (French translation by Calvocoressi, 1914). See biography by Montagu-Nathan, 1917, and his *History of Russian Music* and Newmarch's *The Russian Opera*, both 1915.

RING, EDYTHE M. See COLLEGES, 3 (Juniata C., Pa.).

RIO, ANITA (b. 1880). See Register, 9.

RIPPE, MABEL A. See COLLEGES, 3 (Wheaton C., Ill.).

'RIP VAN WINKLE.' Operas on this theme have been produced by George F. Bristow in 1855, by Jules Jordan in 1898 (published), and by Reginald De Koven in 1920. The last was his final work, produced in Chicago just before his death and in New York just afterward.

RITTER, FANNY, née Raymond (1840–1890). See Register, 6.

RITTER, FRÉDÉRIC LOUIS (June 22, 1834, Strassburg, Alsace : July 22, 1891, Antwerp, Belgium). See article in Vol. iv. 109. Although his *Music in America* (1883) was in many ways useful, especially in calling attention to a neglected subject, yet he was quite unfitted by sympathy to treat it adequately, so that many of his statements are open to dispute. To his publications should be added his appendix to *The Realm of Tones*, 1883, with biographies of American musicians, *Music in Relation to Intellectual Life*, 1891, and *Musical Dictation*. [R.4]

RITTMEISTER, HEINRICH (b. 1881). See Register, 9.

RIVAFINOLI. See Register, 3.

RIVARDE, SERGE ACHILLE (b. 1865). See Vol. iv. 110, and Register, 7.

RIVÉ, CAROLINE, née Staub (1822–1882). See Register, 4.

RIVÉ–KING, JULIE (Oct. 31, 1857, Cincinnati), began piano-lessons with her mother and played in public at eight. In 1866–72 she studied in New York with Mason and Mills, and in 1872 went to Reinecke in Leipzig. There she made her début in 1874, playing Beethoven's 3rd Concerto. After some study with Liszt, she appeared in 1875 with the New York Philharmonic Society. She has since given over 4000 concerts and recitals, more than 500 of them with orchestra. She traveled as soloist with both Thomas and Seidl. Her répertoire is very large and comprehensive, and she has introduced many works in America. Some of her piano-pieces have won much acceptance, such as 'Bubbling Spring,' 'Polonaise Héroique' and the Impromptu in A-flat. In 1876 she married Frank H. King of Milwaukee. For some years she has taught in the Bush Conservatory in Chicago. [R.6]

ROBBINS, CHARLES. See TUNE-BOOKS, 1805.

ROBERTS, ELI. See TUNE-BOOKS, 1812.

ROBESON, LILA P. (b. 1880). See Register, 9.

ROBINSON, CLARENCE CRAMER (b. 1879). See STATE UNIVERSITIES (Pa. State C.).

ROBINSON, FRANKLIN WHITMAN (June 27, 1875, New York), studied first at the National Conservatory under Joseffy (piano), Johnstone and Wetzler (organ), and Dvořák and Spicker (theory). In 1895 he graduated at the College of the City of New York, and in 1907 took an A.M. in music at Columbia under MacDowell and Rybner. In 1897–1908 he taught in the High School of Commerce, from 1897 was assistant-organist at St. Bartholomew's and in 1904–17 organist at St. Luke's in Philadelphia, and since 1908 has been instructor at the Institute of Musical Art in New York. Here he has developed an original course in teaching harmony through the ear, publishing *Aural Harmony*, 2 vols., 1918. [R.8]

ROBINSON, JENNIE ASENATH. See COLLEGES, 3 (Fisk U., Tenn.).

ROBYN, ALFRED GEORGE (b. 1860). See Register, 6.

ROCHESTER ORCHESTRA, THE, whose present name dates from 1912, was founded in 1900 by Hermann Dossenbach and at first called by his name. He has been its only conductor. The force consists of 60–65 players, a few of whom are regularly supplied from outside of Rochester. The concert-master is Arthur Hartmann. Behind the enterprise stands a group of guarantors, who meet a deficit of from $6000 to $10,000 per year. Six concerts are regularly given in each season, making about 100 since organization. A strong selection of standard works have been performed, including the following:

Three Symphonies by Mozart, eight by Beethoven, three by Schubert, four by Schumann, Raff's ' Im Walde,' Franck's D minor, Goldmark's 'Rustic Wedding,' three by Tchaikovsky, Stanford's 'Irish,' Borodin's 'Prince Igor,' four of Saint-Saëns' Symphonic Poems, Tchaikovsky's 3rd Suite, Massenet's music for 'Les Erinnyes,' Grieg's 'Sigurd Jorsalfar,' 'Peer Gynt' and 'Holberg' Suites, Rimsky-Korsakov's 'Scheherazade,' Charpentier's 'Impressions of Italy,' MacDowell's two Suites, Sibelius' 'Swan of Tuonela' and 'Finlandia'; besides most of the favorite overtures and numerous extracts from Wagner.

ROCHESTER SYMPHONY ORCHESTRA, THE, began in 1901 through the efforts of Dr. Justin H. Schopp and some members of the earlier Philharmonic Orchestra, an amateur organization led by Henri Appy. Like its predecessor, it is composed of amateurs. At its concerts a few professionals are added, bringing the number to about 70. Ludwig Schenck has been conductor from the first. Three concerts are given annually. In earlier years the

Orchestra appealed to the public in the usual way. But in 1907, by the aid of public-spirited friends and the coöperation first of the Board of Education and later of the city, it was enabled to make its concerts entirely free. For a time they were given in the East and West High Schools, but were soon transferred to the city Convention Hall. The success of this venture resulted in sundry other musical enterprises on the part of the city authorities for popular inspiration. Among the larger works undertaken are the following:

Four symphonies by Haydn, two by Mozart, Beethoven's 1st, 2nd, 5th and 8th, two by Schubert, Mendelssohn's 'Scotch,' Raff's 'Lenore,' Svendsen's 4th and Cowen's 'Welsh'; suites by Purcell, Bach, Saint-Saëns, Philipp Scharwenka, Grieg, Massenet, Tchaikovsky, Bizet and German; concertos by Bach, Handel, Mozart, Schumann, Chopin, Grieg and Lalo. In one of the early years there was a first performance of Hans Ebell's Concerto in F minor, the composer at the piano.

ROEDER, MARTIN (1851–1895). See Register, 8.

ROGERS, CLARA KATHLEEN, née Barnett (b. 1844). See Register, 6.

ROGERS, FRANCIS (b. 1870). See Register, 8.

ROGERS, JAMES HOTCHKISS (Feb. 7, 1857, Fair Haven, Conn.), began his education at Lake Forest Academy in Illinois. He took up music in Chicago with Towne and Eddy, and in 1875 went abroad for five years, studying in Berlin with Loeschhorn, Ehrlich, Rohde and Haupt, and in Paris with Fissot, Guilmant and Widor. After a year in Burlington, Ia., in 1883 he settled in Cleveland, where he is organist of the Euclid Avenue Temple and the First Unitarian Church, conductor of the Rubinstein Club and critic for the 'Plain-Dealer.' He has been notably successful in composition. Among his works are the following:

Songs: 'At Parting,' 'The Star,' 'Wind-Song,' 'Love's on the Highroad,' 'Autumn,' 'Wind and Lyre,' 'A Love-Note,' 'Invocation,' 'Sea-Fever,' 'Absence,' 'Wild Geese,' 'War,' 'Jewels,' 'Love has Wings,' 'Five Quatrains from the *Rubáiyát*,' 'Winter-Song,' 'Great Peace have They,' 'Ecstasy,' 'Rend your Hearts' and 'Julia's Garden.'

Part-Songs: (men's voices) 'The Name of France,' 'A Chant of Love for England,' 'Bedouin Love-Song,' 'It is She,' 'Red Rose, Red Rose'; (women's voices) 'The Snow-Storm,' 'The night has a thousand eyes,' 'A Song of the Gloaming,' 'My luve is like the red, red rose,' 'Three Fishers' and 'The Two Clocks.'

Anthems: 'The Earth is the Lord's,' 'Doth not Wisdom cry,' 'Show me Thy ways,' 'Seek Him that maketh the seven stars,' 'Awake up, my glory,' 'The Lord is my Strength,' 'Sing, O sing this blessed morn,' 'Beloved, if God so loved us,' 'Search me, O God' and 'The Lord is my Light.'

Cantatas: 'The Man of Nazareth' and 'The New Life.' Also Morning and Evening Services, and for New Year's Eve for the Synagogue.

For organ: Sonata in E minor, Suites in G minor and F minor, Concert-Overture in B minor, Grand Chœur, Christmas Pastorale, Arioso, Processional March, etc.

Many pieces and studies for piano.   [R.7]

ROLLER, CHARLES WILLIAM (b. 1877). See COLLEGES, 3 (Bridgewater C., Va.).

RONCONI, GIORGIO (1810–1890). See Register, 5.

RÖNTGEN, ENGELBERT (b. 1886). See Register, 10.

ROOSEVELT, HILBOURNE LEWIS (1848, New York : Dec. 29, 1885), very early developed an interest in acoustics, especially as related to organ-making. As a youth, against the wishes of his family, he became an apprentice in the shop of Hall, Labagh & Kemp, and made more than one trip to Europe to study organ-construction. In 1872 he opened his own factory on 18th Street, which in 1881 was moved to larger quarters on the same street. As early as 1868 he took out his first patent for an electric action, and about 1870 exhibited an organ equipped with it at an American Institute Fair in New York. In 1876 he built one of the great organs for the Centennial Exposition in Philadelphia (later sold to Mechanics Institute in Boston), and about 1878 installed the famous instrument at the Cathedral in Garden City, Long Island. After his untimely death the business was continued and extended by his brother, Frank H. Roosevelt. The firm had many specialties besides electric actions. They perfected a notable early form of tubular pneumatic action, paid great attention to orchestral voicing, strove to unite striking tonal features from different schools of organ-making, and were always eminent for painstaking and elaborate interior construction. In 1893, however, the business was given up and the stock and patents sold to the Farrand & Votey Co. of Detroit. Soon after the younger Roosevelt died, aged only thirty-two. [R.6]

ROOT, FREDERICK WOODMAN (June 13, 1846, Boston : Nov. 8, 1916, Chicago), was son and pupil of George F. Root. He studied piano with Blodgett, Mason and Goldbeck, organ with James Flint and voice with Bassini. He became organist of the Third Presbyterian Church in Chicago in 1863, and of the Swedenborgian Church there in 1865. In 1869–70 he studied with Vannuccini in Florence, and on his return to Chicago became distinguished as a voice-teacher. Among his pupils were Hope Glenn, Jessie Bartlett Davis, W. H. Clark, Charles W. Clark, Mackenzie Gordon, D. A. Clippinger and F. W. Wodell. He conducted the Mendelssohn Choral Club in 1879–85; wrote for or edited the ' Song Messenger' for many years,

and wrote much on topics connected with singing. He published The Technic and Art of Singing, Methodical Sight-Singing, Introductory Lessons in Voice-Culture, The Polychrome Lessons in Voice-Culture, and several collections of exercises and studies. He composed the cantata 'The Landing of the Pilgrims' (1875, Chicago), a burlesque operetta, songs, choruses and church-music. He was an examiner (1889) of the American College of Musicians, once president of the Chicago Literary Club, and a favorite lecturer. [R.5]

ROOT, GEORGE FREDERICK (Aug. 30, 1820, Sheffield, Mass. : Aug. 6, 1895, Bailey's Island, Me.). See article in Vol. iv. 138. In 1839 he became associated as teacher with A. N. Johnson in Boston, and was his assistant-organist at the Winter Street and Park Street Churches. He also began at this time to conduct choral classes. Two years later he joined Mason in teaching in the public schools. In 1844 he removed to New York, becoming teacher of voice at Abbott's School for Young Ladies, Rutgers Female Institute and Union Theological Seminary, and organist at the Mercer Street Presbyterian Church. He went to Paris in 1850, and studied voice for a year with Giulio Alary and Jacques Potharst. On his return he composed the cantata 'The Flower-Queen,' to a text by Fanny Crosby, and wrote some songs, under the name 'G. Friedrich Wurzel,' for the Christy Minstrels. Of these songs 'Hazel Dell' and 'Rosalie, the Prairie Flower' were most popular. The success of these led him to devote more time to composition, though he continued to hold 'conventions' in various cities. About 1858 he became a partner in the firm of Root & Cady (his brother, E. T. Root and C. M. Cady), music-dealers in Chicago, and in 1859 moved thither. When the Civil War opened he began composing songs which became extremely popular. The 'Battle-Cry of Freedom' (words and music) dates from 1861, and was followed by 'Just before the battle, mother,' 'Tramp, tramp, tramp, the boys are marching,' 'The Vacant Chair,' and many others. A full list is given in his autobiography, The Story of a Musical Life, 1891. The losses incident to the Chicago fire of 1871 led to the dissolution of the firm of Root & Cady, but Chicago remained his headquarters till the end of his life. The University of Chicago made him Mus.D. in 1881. His popular cantatas included 'Daniel' (1853), 'The Pilgrim Fathers' (1854), 'Belshazzar's Feast' (1860), and 'The Haymakers' (1857). He also wrote or edited some 70 collections, mainly for church, school or convention. See TUNE-BOOKS, 1849. [R.4]

ROSEN, MAX (b. 1900). See Register, 10.

ROSENBECKER, ADOLPH (1851–1919).
See Register, 6.

ROSENFELD, MAURICE BERNARD
(Dec. 31, 1867, Vienna, Austria), coming to
America when a child, had his general education at the College of the City of New York
and at Columbia University, studying piano
with Hyllested and Spanuth. In 1888 he
graduated from the Chicago Musical College,
and began teaching there at once, becoming
one of its directors in 1912. In 1911–12 he
directed the Sherwood Music School, in 1916
established his own school, and since 1917
has taught piano at the Hinshaw Conservatory.
He has often appeared as pianist in the West,
both in recital and with orchestra. In 1907–
1915 he was critic for the 'Examiner' and
since 1917 for the 'News,' besides acting in
1913–16 as correspondent for 'Musical
America.' He has given many lectures on
music-history and æsthetics before clubs
and is now lecturer at the Musical Association
Music School. He has written somewhat
for orchestra and chamber-ensemble. [R.7]

ROSEWALD, JULIE, née Eichberg (b.
1850). See Register, 5.

ROTHIER, LÉON (b. 1874). See Register,
10.

ROTHWELL, WALTER HENRY (Sept.
22, 1872, London, England), was brought up
in Vienna, entering the Imperial Academy
of Music at nine and graduating with high
honors in piano, composition and history.
His teachers there were Epstein, Bruckner
and Robert Fuchs, and at Munich Thuille
and Schillings. From 1888 he concertized
in Austria, Germany and Switzerland, and
in 1895 became Mahler's assistant at the
Hamburg Opera. After serving as opera-
conductor also at Mecklenburg, Breslau and
Vienna, in 1903 he was made director of the
Royal Opera at Amsterdam. In 1904–05,
at the invitation of H. W. Savage, he came
to direct the first English performances of
'Parsifal' in America, touring from coast to
coast. In 1905–07 he continued with Savage,
conducting 'Madama Butterfly' (first American performance in Washington). In 1908–15
he led the St. Paul Symphony Orchestra, and
in 1916 directed the Civic Orchestra in New
York in summer-concerts. In 1917–18 he
served as guest-conductor at Cincinnati and
Detroit, and in 1919 took charge of the Los
Angeles Philharmonic Orchestra, besides returning in 1920 to lead summer-concerts in
New York. He has written a piano-concerto,
two piano-sonatas, incidental music to Maeterlinck's 'Mort de Tintagiles,' a 'Bacchanale,'
to a poem by Untermeyer, for voice and
orchestra, and many songs. In 1908 he
married the singer Elizabeth Wolff, who came
to America to sing the title-rôle in 'Madama

Butterfly,' and has since appeared in recital
or with the St. Paul Orchestra. [R.9]

ROTOLI, AUGUSTO (1847–1904). See
Register, 7.

ROWE, NEILLE ODELL (b. 1886). See
COLLEGES, 3 (U. of Wooster, Ohio).

ROYER, CLARENCE DE VAUX (May
10, 1874, Lancaster, Pa. : Oct. 28, 1919,
Lancaster), was educated at the Franklin
and Marshall School in Lancaster and at the
New York College of Metaphysics, studying
also at the Philadelphia Musical Academy.
Here his teachers were Hill and Van Gelder
for violin, Mohr for piano and Zeckwer for
theory. Abroad he studied with Halir and
Moser in Berlin, Marsick in Paris and Ysaÿe
in Brussels. He made his début as violinist
at the Salle des Agricultures in Paris in May,
1897. He toured France, Germany, Switzerland, Belgium, Holland, Canada and the
United States, making in all over 1500 appearances. He also gave many lecture-recitals —
305 for the New York Board of Education
in fifteen years. In recent years he was
director of the violin-department in the New
York School of Music and Art. He contributed many articles to magazines, and
composed violin-studies and pieces, and songs.
He was a charter-member of the Musicians'
Club of New York and of the Chicago Guild
of Violinists. [R.8]

ROYER, CLIFFORD F. See COLLEGES,
3 (Alma C., Mich.).

RUDERSDORFF, HERMINE (1822–
1882). See Vol. iv. 189, and Register, 6.

RUDOLPHSEN, JOHN FREDERICK
(1827– ?). See Register, 4.

RUEGGER, CHARLOTTE (b. 1876). See
COLLEGES, 2 (Meredith C., N. C.).

RUIFROK, HENRI WILLEM JOHAN
(b. 1862). See Register, 7, and COLLEGES, 3
(Drake U., Iowa, Valparaiso U., Ind.).

RUSS, D. See TUNE-BOOKS, 1791.

RUSSELL, ELLA (Mar. 30, 1864, Cleveland), when about nine became a pupil at the
Cleveland Conservatory and a year later sang
in public. On the advice of Max Strakosch
she went to Paris and studied singing with
Mme. De la Grange and acting with Edouard
Pluque. Two years later she went to Italy
to be under Giovanni in Milan. Her début
was as Leonora in 'Il Trovatore' at Prato
in 1882, and her success led to engagements
at Florence, Turin and Milan. In 1883 she
made a tour of Spain with the tenor Tamberlik.
She then visited Vienna, Budapest, Berlin,
Warsaw, Petrograd and Moscow. Her first
appearance in England was at Covent Garden
in May, 1885, when she sang Gilda in 'Rigoletto,' and during four seasons there sang in 30
operas. Tours in the United Kingdom and Russia were followed by an engagement with the

Carl Rosa Opera Company. She has appeared at many important London concerts, and has sung, by command, at state and other concerts at Buckingham Palace. In private life she is the Countess di Rhigini. [R.7]

RUSSELL, FLORENCE. See COLLEGES, 3 (Cedarville C., Ohio).

RUSSELL, GEORGE ALEXANDER (b. 1880). See COLLEGES, 1 (Princeton U., N. J.).

RUSSELL, HENRY (1812–1900). See Vol. iv. 194–5, and Register, 3.

RUSSELL, LILLIAN (b. 1861). See Register, 7.

RUSSELL, LOUIS ARTHUR (b. 1854). See Register, 6.

RUSSIAN SYMPHONY ORCHESTRA, THE, of New York, was organized in 1904 to further the interests of Russian music. Modest Altschuler has been conductor from the beginning. Among the works introduced have been Rachmaninov's 2nd Symphony in 1909, Kajanus' 'Finnish Rhapsody' in 1911, Rimsky-Korsakov's Concerto in C-sharp minor and Ippolitov-Ivanov's 1st Symphony in 1914, Scriabin's 'Prometheus' in 1915, Liadov's 'The Enchanted Lake' in 1916 (the last two with the use of the 'color-keyboard' with the music), and Stravinsky's Symphony in E-flat in 1916. Several artists have made their American début with the Orchestra, such as Rachmaninov, Scriabin, Lhévinne and Elman. In 1918 Henri Verbrugghen, director of the Sydney Conservatory in Australia, appeared as guest-conductor in a program of Beethoven works. The Orchestra has often assisted in festivals in many places in the United States and Canada. In 1914 it gave a 'Wage-Earners' Carnival' of six days, presenting music of many countries.

RYAN, THOMAS (1827–1903). See Register, 4.

RYBNER, PETER MARTIN CORNELIUS (Oct. 26, 1855, Copenhagen, Den-

mark), studied violin and piano at the Copenhagen Conservatory under Gade and Hartmann, and at the Leipzig Conservatory (from 1873) under Reinecke and David, later going further with Von Bülow and Rubinstein. He made concert-tours as pianist through Germany, France, Italy, Norway and Sweden, and was for a time court-pianist to the Grand Duke of Baden. Located for some years in Karlsruhe, he directed the Conservatory there, was associate-conductor with Mottl at the Opera, and conducted the Philharmonic Society in 1892–1900. In 1904 he was called to Columbia University in New York to succeed MacDowell. This position he resigned in 1919 to devote himself to composition and private teaching. He has composed a Festival Cantata for soli, chorus and orchestra, op. 32; the symphonic poem 'Peace, War, and Victory,' op. 20; a Festival Overture, op. 27; a violin-concerto in G minor, op. 30; the three-act ballet 'Prince Ador,' op 35 (1903, Karlsruhe); a piano-trio, op. 9; pieces for piano, violin and piano, 'cello and piano, songs and choruses. He has also made concert-transcriptions of Wagner excerpts for piano, and written *Phases of Pianoforte-Study.* [R.9]

His daughter, Dagmar de Corval Rybner (Sept. 9, 1890, Baden), had her general education in Karlsruhe and Geneva, studying music at Karlsruhe, Neuchâtel and New York. She first appeared as pianist at the Metropolitan Opera House in New York in 1912, and has often been soloist with orchestras and in recital. She is now largely engaged upon composition. Several songs and a number of works for violin and piano have been published (Schirmer, Ditson, Breitkopf). [R.10]

RYDER, THOMAS PHILANDER (1836–1887). See Register, 4.

S

SAAR, LOUIS VICTOR FRANZ (Dec. 10, 1868, Rotterdam, Holland), came of a musical family, being connected with Moscheles and distantly with Schubert. His father was an opera-conductor at Covent Garden and the Metropolitan Opera House, and his mother was for a time a dramatic soprano. He himself graduated from the Strassburg Gymnasium in 1884 and pursued literature and history at the University there. In 1886–89 he was at the Munich Conservatory, studying with Rheinberger, Bussmeyer and Abel, and graduated with highest honors, taking also the Mendelssohn prize for composition in 1891 and the Wiener Tonkünstler prize in 1892. In 1894 he came to New York as accompanist at the Metropolitan Opera House. Later he taught theory at the National Conservatory, the College of Music and the Institute of Musical Art. In 1906–17 he was head of the theory and composition work at the College of Music in Cincinnati, and has since been in a similar position at the Chicago Musical College. His works have won many prizes — in Boston in 1899 for piano-music, in Baltimore in 1902 for a choral composition (Kaiser Prize, with 400 competitors), in 1911 and '12 from the Chicago Madrigal Club, and in 1912 (two) from the Art Publication Society for piano-pieces. His compositions number about 100, in many forms, the songs, violin-pieces and choral works being the best-known. They may be summarized as follows:

Chamber-music: String-Quartet in G, Piano-Quartet, op. 39 (Siegel), Quartet for clarinet, horn, 'cello and piano, Sonatas for violin and piano, op. 44 (Siegel), for 'cello and piano, and for horn and piano.
For violin: Canzonetta, op. 17 (Schuberth), 2 Pieces, op. 26 (Schuberth), 'Romance Mélodique,' op. 78 (Carl Fischer), 'En Berceau,' op. 86a, for violin and orchestra or two violins and piano (Church).
For piano: Suite, op. 6 (Ries & Erler), Suite, 4 hands, op. 27 (Schirmer, also as 'Rococo' Suite, for orchestra), many sets of pieces, some for 4 hands (Schmidt, Schirmer, Schuberth, Ditson, Leuckart, Church, Carl Fischer, Willis), 'The Proficient Pianist,' 2 Books (Willis).
For organ: 3 Recital-Pieces, op. 85 (Church).
For solo voice or duet: Many sets of songs, a few with violin or orchestra (Lewy, Breitkopf, Ries, Schuberth, Schirmer, Leuckart, Rieter-Biederman, Boston Music Co., Church, Ditson, Carl Fischer, Simrock).
For violin: 3 Quartets, op. 8 (Robitschek), 'Ritornelle,' op. 41, for 6 parts and orchestra (Rieter-Biederman), 2 for 6 parts a cappella, op. 57 (Schirmer), 'A Song of Consolation,' op. 71, with orchestra (Boston Music Co.), 2 4-part Hymns a cappella, op. 76 (Carl Fischer), Morning, Evening and Communion Services, 'The Lord's Prayer' in anthem-form (all Church).
For men's chorus: 'Battle Prayer,' op. 35, with orchestra (Hug), 'Forefathers' Tomb,' op. 36, with orchestra (Hug), 'Festival Hymn,' op. 48 (Forberg), 'Algerian Lullaby,' op. 63, with piano and bells (Bos-

ton Music Co.), 'Venetian Love-Song,' op. 68, with violin (Boston Music Co.), several sets, opp. 30, 42, 43 (Hug), 38 (Luckhardt & Belder), 46 (Forberg), 51 (Kahnt), 56 (Siegel).
For women's chorus: 'Nocturne,' op. 45, with tenor and violin (Siegel), 'Hallowing Night,' op. 55, with alto and orchestra (Schirmer), 3 Trios, op. 62 (Boston Music Co.), 2 Madrigals a cappella, op. 78 (Schirmer), 2 Madrigals with piano, op. 80 (Ditson).
Eight sets of Folk-Songs (English, Irish, Scotch, Negro, Swedish or Italian) for men's, women's or mixed chorus (Boston Music Co., Church).

He has also published a large number of orchestral and piano-arrangements. [R.8]

SABIN, WALLACE ARTHUR (Dec. 15, 1869, Culworth, England), began at thirteen to act as organist at various schools and churches in Oxford. His general education was at Charstock College and Magdalen College School, and his musical training under M. J. Monk at Banbury and T. W. Dodds at Oxford. In 1890 he became fellow of the R. C. O. Migrating to San Francisco in 1894–1906 he was organist at St. Luke's, and since 1906 has been at the First Church, Scientist. Since 1895 he has also been organist at Temple Emanu-El. He is a fellow of the A. G. O., and was recitalist at both the St. Louis and the San Francisco Expositions in 1904 and 1915. He has written two of the 'Grove-Plays' for the Bohemian Club — 'St. Patrick at Tara' in 1909 and 'The Twilight of the Kings' in 1918 — both for tenor, baritone, men's chorus and orchestra, besides much incidental music for the Club. He has made various settings for parts of the Jewish liturgy, published in Stark's *Service-Book*. He has published several part-songs for men's voices (Schirmer, Gray, Church), and has others in manuscript, together with much other music. He is director of the Loring Club, the Twentieth Century Musical Club and the Saturday Morning (Ladies') Orchestra. [R.8]

'SACRIFICE, THE.' An opera by Frederick S. Converse, produced by the Boston Opera Company on Mar. 3, 1911.

SAENGER, GUSTAV (May 31, 1865, New York), studied violin with C. Richter, Leopold Meyer and Leopold Damrosch and composition with C. C. Müller. For many years he was an active violinist and teacher, playing at the Metropolitan Opera House and with the Philharmonic and Symphony Societies. In 1893 he became assistant-conductor to Furst at the Empire Theater and later succeeded him. Thus he had charge of the music for all the productions of the Frohman companies, besides writing much original music for them. In 1897 Carl Fischer secured him as arranger, reviser and translator. This work increased so much that

346

in 1909 he withdrew from his theatrical position to become editor of the Fischer publications. He thus took up the care of 'The Metronome,' devoted to band and orchestra music, and in 1904 that of 'The Musical Observer,' a more general periodical. He has been specially successful in arranging music for the violin, and has also written a Concertino in G minor, op. 83, five 'Silhouettes,' op. 106, two Concert-Solos, op. 129, three 'Miniatures,'¦ op. 130, a *New School of Melody*, op. 96, besides other instrumental pieces and songs. [R.7]

SAENGER, OSCAR (Jan. 5, 1868, Brooklyn), sang in concert as a child and early studied the violin. In 1886 he secured a scholarship at the National Conservatory, where he took singing with Bouhy and dramatic art with Frederick Robinson, later being also under Klein. In 1889–97 he taught in the Conservatory. In 1891 he appeared as baritone with the Hinrichs American Opera Company, and in 1892 went with the Arion Society on its European tour. He has trained a long list of distinguished singers, like Leon Rains, Ellison Van Hoose, Sara Anderson, Allan Hinckley, Henri Scott, Marie Rappold, Paul Althouse, Lila Robeson, Mabel Garrison and Florence Hinkle. Rudolf Berger, previously baritone at the Berlin Opera, pronounced a tenor, and in 1909 he made a success as Lohengrin. [R.7]

SAERCHINGER, CÉSAR (Oct. 23, 1884, Aix-la-Chapelle, Germany), was educated in Halle, New York and Paris, giving special attention to linguistic studies. His mother taught him singing, and he took piano and theory with Lambord. With the latter in 1912 he founded the Modern Music Society in New York to give recent music, especially by American composers, and has been its secretary since 1912. He has become conspicuous for fine editorial work. He has contributed to the *National Cyclopedia of American Biography* and to Appleton's *Cyclopedia of American Biography*, 1906–12, was managing-editor of *The Art of Music*, 14 vols., 1914–17, musical editor of 'The International' in 1913–14 and of 'Current Opinion' since 1914, and brought out the very useful *International Who's Who in Music*, 1918. He has also contributed to Elson's ' Modern Music and Musicians,' 1918 (new ed.) and to journals like 'Musical America' and 'The Musical Quarterly.' [R.9]

SAFONOV, VASSILY ILYITCH (Feb. 6, 1852, Itsyoursky, Caucasus : Mar. 13, 1918, Kislovodsk, Caucasus). See article in Vol. v. 662–3. His first appearance as conductor of the New York Philharmonic Society was on Mar. 5, 1904. He served as conductor of this Society in 1905–09, and was also director of the National Conservatory. On his return to Russia he became conductor of the Imperial Musical Society at Petrograd. To the list of his piano pupils should be added Rachmaninov, Medtner and Grechaninov. He published *A New Formula for the Piano-Teacher and the Piano-Student*, 1916. [R.9]

ST. CECILIA SOCIETY, THE. Several societies of this name came into existence in the 18th century, the most important of them being that of Charleston, S. C., founded in 1762 (at first called 'St. Coecilia'¦), and long continuing as a center of interesting concert-activity (see Sonneck, *Concert-Life*, pp. 16–9, 22–4, 27–8, 40, with a rescript of the Society's rules). Another was at New York in 1791–99, then merged into the Philharmonic Society. There was a third at Newport, R. I., in 1793. Probably there were others.

ST. CECILIA SOCIETY OF AMERICA, THE, was organized in 1873 by John Singenberger as a branch of the Cäcilienverein of Franz Witt (1867) for the promotion of the Palestrina style in the Roman Catholic Church. The Society began holding annual meetings in 1874 and the issue of the periodical 'Cecilia.' See Mathews, *Hundred Years of Music in America*, pp. 277–82.

ST. LOUIS PAGEANT CHORAL SOCIETY, THE, was originally formed in 1914 under civic auspices to supply the choral parts of Converse's 'Masque of St. Louis,' given at the 150th anniversary of the founding of the city. Its success led to its continuance as a permanent choral society, the conductor being Frederick Fischer. Three or four concerts are given annually, besides more or less extension-work in furtherance of community-singing. Besides oratorios and similar works, the Society has presented several American cantatas, such as Converse's 'The Peace-Pipe' (1917), Farwell's 'The Evergreen-Tree' (1918), Paine's 'A Hymn of the West,' Skilton's 'The Witch's Daughter' and Busch's 'The American Flag' (all 1919).

ST. LOUIS SYMPHONY ORCHESTRA, THE, was founded in 1907, and has been led since then by Max Zach. Its present size is 80 players.

'ST. PATRICK AT TARA.' No. 7 of the 'Grove-Plays' of the San Francisco Bohemian Club, produced in 1909. The text is by H. Morse Stephens and the music by Wallace A. Sabin. The scene is laid 'on the Hill of Tara in Meath, Ireland, on Easter, 432.'

ST. PAUL SYMPHONY ORCHESTRA, THE, was formed in 1908 under the leadership of Walter H. Rothwell, who remained at its head till 1915, when conditions due to the war led to its discontinuance. Its place was taken by the St. Paul Philharmonic Orchestra, led by Josef Sainton, which gives 12 popular concerts annually.

'ST. PETER.' An oratorio by John K. Paine, first given at Portland, Me., in June, 1873, and by the Handel and Haydn Society in Boston on May 9, 1874.

‡ SAINT-SAËNS, CHARLES CAMILLE (Oct. 9, 1835, Paris, France). See article in Vol. iv. 207–9. In 1900 he was made Grand-Officer in the Légion d'Honneur and in 1913 received the Grand-Croix. He first visited the United States in October–December, 1906, and in 1915 returned as French representative at the Panama-Pacific Exposition. He there conducted some of his own works, including 'Hail, California.' In 1916 he visited South America. His list of works now includes the following :

op. 106   'Caprice Héroïque,' for two pianos.
   107   'Marche Réligieuse,' for organ.
   108   'Barcarolle,' for violin, 'cello, piano and organ.
   109   'Trois Préludes et Fugues,' for organ.
   110   'Valse Nonchalante,' for piano.
  1˙1   Six Études for piano.
   112   String-Quartet in E minor.
   113   'Chants d'Automne,' for men's chorus a cappella.
   114   'La Nuit,' for soprano, women's chorus and orchestra.
   115   Cantata, 'Le Feu Céleste,' for soprano, recitation, chorus, orchestra and organ.
   116   Dramatic Scene, 'Lola,' for two 'cellos and orchestra.
   117   'Marche de Couronnement,' for orchestra.
   118   'Romance du Soir,' for chorus a cappella.
   119   Concerto No. 2, in D minor, for 'cello.
   120   'Valse Langoureuse,' for piano.
   121   'À la France,' for men's chorus a cappella.
   122   'Caprice Andalouse,' for violin and orchestra.
   123   Sonata No. 2, in F, for 'cello.
   124   Fantaisie for violin and harp.
   125   March, 'Sur les Bords du Nil,' for military band.
   126   Cantata, 'La Gloire de Corneille,' for soli, chorus and orchestra.
   127   Psalm 150, for double chorus, organ and orchestra.
   128   Incidental Music to 'L'Assassinat du Duc de Guise.'
   129   "Le Matin,' for men's chorus a cappella.
   130   'Trois Tableaux Symphoniques' from music to 'La Foi.'
   131   'La Gloire,' for men's chorus a cappella.
   132   'La Muse et le Poëte,' for violin, 'cello and orchestra.
   133   'Ouverture de Fête.'
   135   Six Études for piano (left hand).
   136   Suite, 'Triptique,' for violin and piano.
   139   'Valse Gaie,' for piano.
   147   Motet, 'Tu es Petrus,' a cappella.
   148   Motet, 'Quam Dilecta,' a cappella.
   150   Seven Improvisations for organ.

Without opus-number :
  'Romance sans Paroles,' for piano.
  'Le Cygne,' for 'cello and piano.
  'Hymne Franco-Espagnole,' for band.
  'Lever de Soleil sur le Nil,' for alto and orchestra.
  'Sérénade d'Hiver,' for men's chorus a cappella.

Madrigal for tenor and men's chorus.
'Ode d'Horace,' for men's chorus a cappella.
À 'Deux,' two-part canon for children.
'Panis Angelicus,' for tenor, string-quintet and organ.
'Hail, California' (1915, Panama-Pacific Exposition).
'Honneur à l'Amérique,' for orchestra (1916).
Unpublished :
  'Le Carnaval des Animaux,' for orchestra.
  Overture, 'Spartacus.'
  Symphonies in F and D.
  Cantata, 'Ode à Ste.-Cécile,' for chorus and orchestra.
  Cantata for the centenary of the birth of Hoche (1868), for chorus and orchestra.

He has also published about 75 songs, many motets and numerous arrangements from composers old and new, and edited Charpentier's 'Le Malade Imaginaire' (1894), Gluck's 'Armide,' 'Orphée,' and 'Écho et Narcisse' for the Pelletan Edition (1875–1902), Rameau's works (1895–) and Mozart's piano-sonatas. He is author of Notice sur H. Reber, 1881, Matérialisme et Musique, 1882, Notes sur les Décors de Théâtre dans l'Antiquité Romaine, 1886, Gounod et le 'Don Juan' de Mozart, 1893, Problèmes et Mystères, 1894, École Buissonnière, 1913, Au courant de la Vie, 1914, and Germanophile, 1916, besides a volume of poems and three comedies. For further bibliography, see Baker, Dict. of Musicians, p. 804.

SAINTON, JOSEPH (b. 1878). See Register, 10.

SALEM ORATORIO SOCIETY, THE, of Salem, Mass., was founded in 1868. Its conductors have been Carl Zerrahn in 1868–98, W. S. Fenollosa in 1898–1900, Emil Mollenhauer in 1900–09, Alfred S. Denghausen in 1909–13 and Frederick Cate since 1913. The membership of the chorus is usually about 100. Two or three concerts are given annually. The Society has a small fund, received by legacy. Besides the more common oratorios, it has given Costa's 'Eli,' Handel's 'Joshua,' 'Judas Maccabæus' (5 times) and 'Samson' (3 times), and many modern works, like Bruch's 'The Cross of Fire,' Coleridge-Taylor's 'Hiawatha's Wedding-Feast,' Nováček's 'My Goddess,' Franck's Psalm 150, Verdi's Requiem, Dvořák's Stabat Mater, Dubois' 'Seven Last Words,' etc., besides a number of operas in concert-form.

SALIMENT, GEORGE EDWARD. See Register, 2.

SALMON, ALVAH GLOVER (1868–1917). See Register, 8.

SALTER, MARY ELIZABETH, née Turner (Mar. 15, 1856, Peoria, Ill.), had her early education in Burlington, Ia., where she studied singing under Alfred Arthur and Max Schilling, continuing later in Boston under O'Neill and Mme. Rudersdorff. For twenty years from about 1875 she was solo-soprano in churches in Boston, New York, New Haven, Syracuse, Buffalo, and Atlanta. She sang in concert with many noted artists and choral societies. In 1879–81 she taught at Wellesley College. Her song-writing developed unconsciously, without much influence from technical study. 'The Cry of Rachel' has become noted through its presentation by Mme. Schumann-Heink. In many cases she has written words as well as music. Out of a total list of nearly 150 the following sets may be named as in some way representative:

'Three Spring-Songs,' op. 4 (1904) (Schirmer).
'Five Songs,' op. 6 (1905) (Schirmer).
'Love's Epitome,' cycle of 5 (1905) (Schirmer).
'A Night in Naishapur,' cycle of 6 (1906) (Schirmer).
'Songs of the Four Winds,' op. 12 (1907) (Schirmer).
'Outdoor Sketches,' set of 6 (1908) (Schirmer).
'Lyrics from Sappho,' op. 18, set of 7 (1909) (Schirmer).
'From Old Japan,' op. 23, cycle of 6 (1911) (Summy).
'Eight Songs,' op. 24 (1912) (Schirmer).
'Four Songs,' op. 26 (1913) (Schmidt).
'Four Songs,' op. 33 (1916) (Ditson).
'Five Songs,' op. 34 (1916) (Schirmer).

She has also written a number of sacred songs and some hymn-anthems. In 1881 she married Sumner Salter (see below). [R.6]

SALTER, SUMNER (June 24, 1856, Burlington, Ia.), began as organist in 1875, while in Amherst College, where he graduated in 1877. He studied organ with B. D. Allen and Eugene Thayer, piano with J. C. D. Parker, singing with Osgood and theory with Paine. During his student-days in Boston he played in Lynn and Roxbury, taught in the Petersilea Academy, sang in the Boylston Club and led the Arion Club of Chelsea. In the summers of 1878 and '79 he taught with Sherwood at Lyons and Canandaigua, N. Y. In 1879–81 he was organist in Cleveland and taught at the Oberlin Conservatory. In 1881–86 he was organist at St. Paul's in Syracuse and conductor of the Cecilia Society. In 1886–89 he was at the First Methodist Church in Atlanta and director of the Musical Association (chorus and orchestra). In 1889–1900 he was in New York, first at the First Presbyterian and then at the West End Avenue Collegiate Church. In 1900–02 he was organist at Cornell University and teacher of voice in the Ithaca Conservatory. In 1902–05 he was organist of Broadway Tabernacle in New York, and since 1905 he has been organist at Williams College. While in New York he was a founder of the Manuscript Society in 1892, and of the A. G. O. in 1896, editor of 'The Pianist and Organist,' its first official organ, in 1895–98, and warden in 1899–1900. In 1897–98 he was president of the New York

Music Teachers' Association. He has given a large number of recitals, including two at the Buffalo Exposition in 1901, three at St. Louis in 1904, five at San Francisco in 1915 and about 175 at Williams College. He has written mostly for the voice, with special attention to part-songs and anthems for men's voices. The list of works includes about 25 songs (Phillips & Crew, Ditson, Church, Schirmer, etc.), and the following choral music:

For men's voices: 'Holy stars above me,' 'Twilight Revery,' 'Answered,' 'Daffodils,' 'The night-wind sleeps,' 'Tarry with me,' 'I will lift up mine eyes' (all Ditson); 'Let my voice ring out,' 'O mellow moonlight' (Rohlfing); 'The Sword' (Presser, prize-work); Benedictus in D, Jubilate in E-flat, Te Deum in C, 'The Lord is my Light,' 'Saviour, Source of every blessing' (all Schirmer); Deus Misereatur (Boosey).
For mixed voices: 'Homeward,' 'The day is gently sinking,' 'In the days of Herod the king,' 'Suffer little children,' 'Sun of my soul' (all Schirmer); 'Abide with me,' 'Alleluia' (Easter), 'O let your mingling voices rise,' 'Rock of Ages,' 'Harvest-Home' (all Ditson).
Also many responses and other service-music, and many arrangements.   [R.6]

SALTZMAN-STEVENS, MINNIE (1885?, Bloomington, Ill.), after studying with Chicago teachers went to Paris in 1905 for four years with Jean de Reszké. Her first appearance in opera was in 1909, when she sang Brünnhilde in 'Die Walküre' at Covent Garden in London, under Richter. Her success was such that she was invited to Bayreuth, where she sang Kundry in 1911. She sang Brünnhilde in the 'Ring' cycle at the Royal Opera in Lisbon in 1909, and many Wagnerian rôles at Covent Garden (four seasons), Berlin, Frankfort and Brussels. Engaged by the Philadelphia-Chicago Opera Company, she made her American début at Chicago in December, 1911, as Brünnhilde, and the next month sang Isolde in Philadelphia. Her engagement with the Chicago Company continued till 1914. In 1905 she married A. Newman Stevens of Bloomington. [R.9]

SALZÉDO, CARLOS (b. 1885). See Register, 10.

SAMAROFF, OLGA, née Hickenlooper (Aug. 8, 1882, San Antonio, Tex.), gained her musical education at the Paris Conservatory, being the first American woman admitted to piano-classes there, and with Jedliczka in Berlin. Her first appearance as pianist was with the New York Symphony Society under Walter Damrosch in 1905. Since then she has made extensive tours in the United States, Canada and Europe, both as soloist with leading orchestras and in recital. She has appeared jointly with Kreisler and Zimbalist and played often in ensemble, as with the Kneisel Quartet. In 1911 she married

Leopold Stokowski, the conductor of the Philadelphia Orchestra. In 1912–14 she was in retirement, owing to ill health. [R.9]

SAMPAIX, LÉON (b. 1878). See Register, 9.

SANDBY, HERMAN (Mar. 21, 1881, near Copenhagen, Denmark), began 'cello-study at seven with local teachers. In 1895 he went to the Frankfort Conservatory, spending five years under Hugo Becker. In 1896 he played before the Queen at Buckingham Palace in London. His formal début was made with the Copenhagen Orchestral Society in January, 1900. He toured in Scandinavia, Germany and Great Britain as soloist, playing in London with Carreño and Grainger. In 1914–16 he was first 'cellist of the Philadelphia Orchestra, his only orchestral engagement. Since 1916 he has devoted himself to solo-playing and composition. He has written a 'cello-concerto in D (1916, Philadelphia Orchestra); two string-quartets; incidental music to Mrs. Sandby's drama 'The Woman and the Fiddler' (1912, Philadelphia); and many transcriptions of Norwegian melodies for piano, violin and piano, 'cello and piano, and other combinations. His grand opera 'The Vikings of Helgeland' (Ibsen) is as yet unfinished, but the prelude to Act iv. was played by the Philadelphia Orchestra on Dec. 6, 1912. [R.10]

SANDERSON, LILLIAN (b. 1867). See Register, 8.

SANDERSON, SIBYL (Dec. 7, 1865, Sacramento, Cal. : May 16, 1903, Paris), was the daughter of a judge in the California Supreme Court. At nineteen she went to Paris for study at the Conservatory under Sbriglia and Mme. Marchesi. Her operatic début was in 1888 at the Hague. Making the acquaintance of Massenet, he became impressed with her compass of three octaves and wrote 'Esclarmonde' with her voice in mind. In this work she appeared at the Opéra-Comique in 1889. For two seasons she then sang at La Monnaie in Brussels. In 1894 she appeared at the Paris Grand-Opéra in 'Thaïs,' which Massenet wrote for her. In 1893, also, she sang in Saint-Saëns' 'Phryné,' which, too, was written for her. In 1897 she married the Chilean merchant Antonio Terry (d. 1900). She visited Petrograd, Moscow, London and New York (1895 and '98, Metropolitan Opera House), but her popularity was greatest in Paris. Massenet, in his *Souvenirs*, called her an 'ideal' Manon and an 'unforgettable' Thaïs. [R.7]

SANFORD, SAMUEL SIMONS (1849–1910). See Register, 6.

SAN FRANCISCO SYMPHONY ORCHESTRA, THE, is technically known as the Musical Association of San Francisco, which was formed in 1909 and supported by a circle of members who subscribe from $100 to $5000 annually. The first conductor was Henry K. Hadley, who in 1915 was succeeded by Alfred Hertz, formerly of the Metropolitan Opera House in New York. The average number of players is over 80. The number of concerts per year is now about 50. The répertoire includes almost all the standard symphonies, overtures and concertos, with a wide range of modern works of every kind. Premières are recorded for Frederic Jacobi's symphonic poem 'The Pied Piper' (1916) and 'A California Suite' (1917), first performances in America for Beethoven's newly-discovered Symphony (1912), and Dukas' danced-poem 'The Peri' (1916), and first in San Francisco for Moszkowski's Suite No. 1 (1912), Rachmaninov's 'Die Toteninsel' (1913), Reger's 'Romantique' Suite (1913), Pfitzner's Overture, 'Das Christ-Elflein' (1916), Grainger's British Folk-Song Settings and 'In a Nutshell' Suite (1916), Debussy's tone-picture 'Iberia' (1916), Schubert's Symphony No. 5 (1916), Georg Schumann's 'Variations and Double Fugue on a Merry Theme' (1917), Kelley's 'New England' Symphony (1917), and Schmitt's 'Rhapsodie Viennoise' (1918).

SANGER, ZEDEKIAH (1748–1820) See TUNE-BOOKS, 1808.

SÄNGERBUND, DER AMERIKANISCHE. German singing-societies early became notable in the Middle West, especially at Cincinnati, Chicago, Milwaukee and St. Louis. From about 1850 the custom of holding an annual Sängerfest became more or less established. In 1868 the scope of these festivals was enlarged so as to include mixed choral singing with orchestra. Thus, like the Liederkranz, the Sängerbund contributed to the advance of popular interest in choral and orchestral music on a large scale.

SANKEY, IRA DAVID (1840–1908). See Register, 6.

SANSONE, ERRICO (Aug. 13, 1859, Naples, Italy), studied violin with Pinto and composition with Serrao, making his début as violinist at Naples in 1877. He then taught at the Conservatory, led the Quartet Society, was concertmaster in the Symphony Orchestra and at the Teatro S. Carlo, and toured much as violinist and conductor. Coming to Chicago about 1895, he taught at the Chicago Conservatory and the Balatka Academy, played much in ensemble with Martucci, Godowsky, Ysaÿe and others, and became concertmaster of the St. Paul Symphony Orchestra. He has composed the five-act opera 'Abel,' the cantata 'The Legend of Wenonah,' a violin-concerto, two suites for string-quartet, violin-studies and songs. [R.8]

SANTELMANN, WILLIAM HENRY
(Sept. 24, 1863, Offensen, Germany), took up
violin-playing very young and at eighteen
began five years' study at Leipzig. In 1887
he came to Philadelphia with a visiting orchestra, and soon enlisted in the United States
Marine Band as violinist and baritone-player.
In 1895 he formed an orchestra of his own and
in 1896-98 was leader at the Columbia Theater,
but in 1898 returned to the Marine Band as
its director. This position he still holds,
having developed the Band into a significant
organization, not only in size, but in artistic
quality. In 1908 the George Washington
University made him Mus.D. His band-works
include the overture and suite 'Pocohontas,'
the concert-galop 'The Ride of the Hussars,'
several marches for band and orchestra, and
many arrangements and transcriptions. [R.7]

‡ SANTLEY, CHARLES (Feb. 28, 1834,
Liverpool, England). See article in Vol. iv.
222-3, and note in v. 664. He has published
The Singing-Master, 1900, The Art of Singing,
1908, and Reminiscences of My Life, 1909.

‡ SAPELNIKOV, VASSILY (Nov. 2, 1868,
Odessa, Russia). See article in Vol. v. 664.
His first teacher was Franz Kessler. In
1888 he made his début as pianist at Hamburg, playing Tchaikovsky's B-flat Concerto
under the composer's direction. He resigned
at Moscow in 1899, and has since lived not
only in Germany, but in Italy and England.
He is an honorary member of the London
Philharmonic Society. He has written some
fine short pieces for the piano.

SAPIO, ROMUALDO (b. 1858). See Register, 7.

SASLAVSKY, ALEXANDER (Feb. 9,
1876, Kharkov, Russia), studied violin with
Gorsky at Kharkov and with Gruen in Vienna.
In 1893 he toured in Canada and became one
of the first violins in the New York Symphony
Society. From 1903 he was concertmaster
and assistant-conductor under Walter Damrosch. In 1904 he was one of the founders of
the Russian Symphony Orchestra, its concertmaster till 1908 and one of its first soloists.
With these organizations he has toured
throughout the country. In 1907 he formed
a Quartet with Finkelstein, Weissmann and
Renard, since 1915 giving chamber-recitals
at Denver in the summers. In 1919 he became
concertmaster of the new Philharmonic Orchestra in Los Angeles, and is otherwise active as
soloist and teacher. [R.8]

‡ SAURET, ÉMILE (May 22, 1852, Dun-
le-Roi, France : Feb. 12, 1920, London). See
article in Vol. iv. 227-8. From 1908 he was
professor at Trinity College in London.

SAVAGE, HENRY WILSON, born in
Boston, graduated from Harvard in 1880
and went into real estate business in Boston.

One of his properties was the Castle Square
Theater. As it was a failure in other hands,
about 1895 he took hold of it himself, giving
both grand and light opera in English at
popular prices. Presently he sent out the
excellent Castle Square Company to other
cities. In 1900 he organized the English
Grand Opera Company, in the fall giving a
series of performances at the Metropolitan
Opera House in New York and then touring
the country. Among its achievements were
'Parsifal' in 1904-05 with Rothwell and
Moritz Grimm as conductors, 'Madama
Butterfly' in 1906-07 for the first time in
America, and 'The Girl of the Golden West,'
in 1911-12. Meanwhile other troupes under
his management were presenting light opera
and musical comedy in many places. As
president and director of Henry W. Savage,
Inc., and similar organizations, he has steadily
continued to purvey drama, musical comedy
and more or less opera to a large and diversified
public. [R.8]

'SCARLET LETTER, THE.' An opera,
based upon Hawthorne's romance, by Walter
Damrosch, produced in Boston on Feb. 10,
1896, and at the Metropolitan Opera House
in New York on Mar. 6. The libretto was
prepared by George Parsons Lathrop, Hawthorne's son-in-law. In 1855 L. H. Southard
completed an opera of the same name, and
parts of it were sung in Boston.

SCHAFFER [Scheffer], FRANCIS C. See
Register, 2, and TUNE-BOOKS, 1796.

SCHARFENBERG, WILLIAM (1819–
1895). See Register, 3.

SCHARWENKA, FRANZ XAVER (Jan.
6, 1850, Samter, Germany). See article in
Vol. iv. 249. He made concert-tours in America in 1910-11 and 1913-14. In 1914 he withdrew from the Klindworth-Scharwenka Conservatory, and established a school of his own
in Berlin. To the list of his compositions
add the 4th piano-concerto, in F minor, op.
82 (1908), two Ballades for piano, op. 85,
Variations for piano, op. 83, and also the
Methodik des Klavierspiels, 1908. [R.6]

SCHARWENKA, LUDWIG PHILIPP
(Feb. 16, 1847, Samter, Germany : 1918,
Charlottenburg, Germany). See article in
Vol. iv. 248-9. To the list of works add the
Symphony in D minor, op. 96 ; a 'Symphonia
Brevis,' in E-flat, op. 115 ; the symphonic poem
'Traum und Wirklichkeit,' op. 92 ; a violin-
concerto in G, op. 95 ; a piano-quintet in B
minor, op. 118 ; two string-quartets, in D minor
and D, opp. 117, 120 ; three piano-trios, in
C-sharp minor, G and E minor, opp. 100, 112,
121 ; a trio in A, op. 105, for violin, viola and
piano ; two violin-sonatas in B minor and E
minor, opp. 110, 114 ; a viola-sonata, op. 106 ;
and a 'cello sonata, op. 116. [R.8]

SCHEEL, FRITZ (Nov. 7, 1852, Lübeck, Germany : Mar. 13, 1907, Philadelphia), came of a line of orchestral conductors and began playing under his father at ten, in 1864–67 also studying under David at Leipzig. In 1869 he became concertmaster and conductor at Bremerhaven, in 1873 leader of summer-concerts in Schwerin, in 1884 followed Sitt as municipal conductor in Chemnitz, and in 1890 was orchestral conductor at Hamburg. In 1893 he came to New York, leading some orchestral concerts, in 1894 led the Trocadero concerts at the Columbian Exposition at Chicago, and in 1895–99 organized and conducted the San Francisco Symphony Orchestra. In the summer of 1899 his success at concerts at Woodside Park in Philadelphia led to the establishment in 1900 of the Philadelphia Symphony Orchestra, which under his leadership stepped into prominence. In 1905 he also undertook the direction of the Orpheus and the Euridice Clubs, but succumbed under the triple burden. [R.8]

SCHELLING, ERNEST HENRY (July 26, 1876, Belvidere, N.J.), was a pianistic prodigy in Philadelphia at four and a half. In 1882–85 he was under Mathias at the Paris Conservatory, and then with Moszkowski, Pruckner, Leschetizky, Huber, Barth and Paderewski (1898–1902, at Morges, Switzerland). He has given recitals in France, England, Germany, Spain, Russia and South America, besides many appearances in the United States. He has toured with the Boston Symphony, Chicago, Philadelphia and New York Philharmonic Orchestras, and played with leading orchestras in London, Paris, Petrograd and Amsterdam. He has composed a 'Fantastic Suite' for piano and orchestra (Rahter, Leipzig) ; a Symphony in C minor ; a 'Symphonic Legend' ; an orchestral suite ; a violin-concerto (1916, Boston, played by Kreisler) ; a sonata for violin and piano ; variations for piano on an original theme ; and other chamber-music and piano-pieces. The 'Fantastic Suite,' perhaps his best-known work, was written in 1905–06, orchestrated the next year, and first played by the composer with the Concertgebouw Orchestra in Amsterdam on Oct. 10, 1907, Mengelberg conducting. He played it with the Boston Symphony Orchestra and the New York Symphony Society in 1908, and in 1909 with the Thomas Orchestra in Chicago. It is in four movements, and the themes of the last are built on 'Dixie,' 'Old Folks at Home' and 'Yankee Doodle' (see thematic analysis by the composer in 'Die Musik,' vii. 17). He enlisted in the war and was made captain. He went to Poland with his intimate friend Paderewski in the fall of 1918. In the summer of 1919 he suffered severe injuries in an automobile accident in Switzerland. [R.9]

SCHENUIT, ALFONS WILLIAM (b. 1864). See Register, 8.

SCHETKY, J. GEORGE (d. [1831). See Register, 2.

SCHEVE, EDWARD BENJAMIN (Feb. 13, 1865, Herford, Germany), after attending the Cologne Gymnasium and the Geisenheim Institute, in 1885–88 studied at Kullak's Academy in Berlin under König (piano), Grunicke (organ) and Becker (composition). In 1886–88 he also taught in the Academy. In 1888 he came to Rochester as teacher and organist at the First Baptist Church, and in 1902 went to Chicago as director of the German-American Conservatory and organist at the First German Baptist Church. Since 1906 he has taught composition at Grinnell College in Iowa. In 1912 the College made him Mus.D. He has written a symphony in D minor, op. 38 (1917, Minneapolis Orchestra at Grinnell and Dubuque, Ia.) ; Festival March for orchestra, op. 12, with chorus and organ ad lib. (1909, Grinnell, 1911, Chicago Orchestra at Ravinia Park) ; a piano-concerto, op. 20 (1913, Chicago Orchestra) ; a violin-concerto, in E-flat, op. 35 ; a violin-sonata in C minor ; 'Four Sketches' for violin, 'cello and piano ; the oratorio 'The Death and Resurrection of Christ,' op. 11 (1906, Chicago, with the Chicago Orchestra) ; 'A Song of Penitence,' op. 17, for soli, chorus, orchestra and organ (1916, Grinnell) ; the piano-suite 'Twilight-Pictures,' op. 29 ; 'Meditations on Psalms,' op. 31, for piano with violin ad lib.; an organ-sonata in E-flat ; a 'Suite Religioso' for organ, op. 18 ; 24 Preludes and Postludes for organ, op. 9 ; and many songs, anthems and piano-pieces. [R.7]

SCHILLER, MADELINE (1850?–1911). See Register, 7.

SCHILLING, GUSTAV (1803–1881). See Register, 4.

‡SCHILLINGS, MAX VON (Apr. 19, 1868, Düren, Germany). See article in Vol. iv. 263. Since 1908 he has been general music-director at Stuttgart, and received the title ' von ' in 1912. To the list of works add the music-drama 'Mona Lisa,' op. 31 (1915), 'Dem Verklärten,' op. 21, for baritone, chorus and orchestra, 'Glockenlieder,' op. 22, for solo voice and orchestra, 'Hochzeitsglocken,' op. 26, for baritone, chorus and orchestra, the melodrama 'Jung Olaf,' op. 28, a violin-concerto in A minor, op. 25, and a string-quartet.

SCHINDLER, KURT (Feb. 17, 1882, Berlin, Germany), studied piano with Zieler, Gernsheim, L. C. Wolf and Ansorge, and composition with Bussler and Thuille. He also took courses in philosophy, psychology and literary and artistic history at the Universities of Berlin and Munich, especially with Friedländer, Woelfflin, Stumpff and

Erich Schmidt, meanwhile continuing with music. In 1902 he became conductor of the Stuttgart Opera, and in 1903 at the Municipal Theater in Würzburg, besides assisting Mottl and Zumpe at the Munich summer-festivals and Strauss in the winter at Berlin. In 1905 Conried brought him to the Metropolitan Opera House as assistant-conductor to Hertz and (1907–08) to Mahler. In 1907 he became reader and critic for G. Schirmer, except an interval in 1919–20. In 1909 he founded the MacDowell Chorus, which, with the House Music Society, in 1910 began concert-giving. In 1912 this became the Schola Cantorum, which he has made one of the significant institutions of New York. Since 1912 he has also been choir-director at Temple Emanu-El. In 1913 he was in charge of a gala-concert arranged by the Institute Français des États-Unis for the French ambassador, illustrative of the music of the various French provinces. He began publishing songs about 1900, about 25 before coming to America and the same number since. In recent years he has been much engaged with choral works, mostly based on the extensive folk-song material that he has collected. In his research-work he has the advantage of knowing many languages, including Russian and Spanish. He has edited five collections of Russian music, two of Spanish, one of Finnish student-songs, etc., besides reproducing many single illustrations from other national treasuries. He has made most of the translations, with Deems Taylor as collaborator. Among his many works are the following:

'Dance and Devotion,' op. 4, four songs from Gustav Falke.
Five Songs, op. 5, from Hartleben, Busse, Hölty and Brentano.
'Trois Mélodies de Paul Verlaine,' op. 7.
'Old Swiss Lays,' op. 9, from Gottfried Keller.
Three Songs from Keats, op. 11.
'Three Sonnets of Mediæval Italy,' op. 14, translated by Rossetti.
Three English Songs, op. 15, from Wilde, Swinburne and Meredith.
'Vasilissa the Fair' or 'The Prince and the Maiden,' for chorus.
'A Miracle of St. Raymond,' op. 18, after Movera, for 12-part chorus a cappella.
'A Miracle of the Virgin Mary,' op. 19, after a Spanish canticle, for 8-part chorus a cappella or 4-part with organ.
'The Virgin's Plaint,' op. 20, from the Mystery of Elx, after Pedrell, for solo, chorus and harp.

These, with many others from different sources, some of them variously arranged either for chorus or for solo, are mostly published by Schirmer (some Ditson or Gray). His collections include A Century of Russian Song from Glinka to Rachmaninoff, 1911, Masters of Russian Song, 2 vols., 1917, A Cappella Choruses from the Russian Liturgy, 1913–17, Sixty Russian Folk-Songs, 3 vols.,

1918–19, Songs of the Russian People, 1915, Ten Student-Songs of Finland, 1915, Six Old French Christmas Carols, 1908, The Development of Opera (illustrative selections from various periods), 1912, Old Spanish Sacred Motets, 1918, Modern Spanish Choral Works, 1918. He has also written articles on Mussorgsky and Schönberg, and numerous valuable introductions to his collections. [R.9]

SCHIRMER, GUSTAV (1829–1893). See Vol. iv. 265, and Register, 4 (also following articles).

SCHIRMER, GUSTAVE (1864–1907). See Register, 7 (also below).

SCHIRMER, RUDOLPH ERNEST (July 22, 1859, New York: Aug. 20, 1919, Santa Barbara, Cal.), the eldest son of Gustav Schirmer, was early educated in New York and Weimar, and graduated from Princeton University in 1880 and from Columbia Law School in 1884. At his father's death in 1893 he became president of the firm of G. Schirmer. Besides being more and more intimately concerned in the large business of this house, he was active in many other ways. He was a director in both the Oratorio and the Symphony Societies, a trustee of the Institute of Musical Art, and a donor of libraries to the latter, to Princeton University and to the city of Santa Barbara. With his younger brother, Gustave, he was not only instrumental in vastly extending the publishing-business in which they were both engaged, but in fostering whatever made for the extension of musical culture of the highest kind. [R.7]

SCHIRMER, G., INC., is the corporate name of the great publishing-firm in New York established, as told in Vol. iv. 265–6, by Gustav Schirmer and developed by his two sons. The total number of its publications is now about 30,000, of which perhaps 22,000 are piano-pieces, songs or part-songs. The Library of Musical Classics is approaching a total of 1500. A Scholastic Series (all originally published by the firm) was started in 1918. Two series of orchestral publications are also issued. The number of large piano-scores of operas and oratorios, and of full scores of chamber- and orchestral works, is constantly growing. In the Golden Treasury of Music are numerous collections, instrumental and vocal, many of which are unique in their way. American composers extensively represented include Mrs. Beach, Hadley, Goldmark, Campbell-Tipton, Burleigh, Herbert, De Koven, Coerne, Mason, John Powell, D. S. Smith, Rogers, Woodman, Schindler, Marzo, Sousa, Coombs, Vogrich, Friml, H. A. and J. S. Matthews, Strube, Speaks, and a host of others. Works by foreign composers are also numerous. Theoretical and historical treatises of importance have often been put forth, such as Goetschius' several text-books, Baker's *Dictionary of Musicians*, Sonneck's *Early Opera in America*, etc. Since 1915 'The Musical Quarterly,' a monthly of the highest class, has been added. The present headquarters is at 3 East 43rd Street, in a building specially erected in 1909. The engraving, printing and binding department is located in Long Island City — one of the finest music-making plants in the world, with a staff of 275 workers. Since 1891 the Boston Music Co. has been a branch of the business. A London branch was maintained in 1913–17, then becoming Winthrop Rogers, Ltd.

SCHLESINGER, DANIEL (1799–1838). See Register, 3.

SCHLESINGER, SEBASTIAN BENSON (1837–1917). See Register, 7.

SCHMIDT, ARTHUR P. (b. 1846). See Register, 5.

SCHMIDT, ARTHUR P., of Boston, is a music-publishing business established in 1876. It now has branches in New York and Leipzig. Besides an extensive general catalogue, the firm has made a specialty of the work of American composers, in both small and large forms. Among its notable publications for orchestra are Mrs. Beach's 'Gaelic' Symphony, Chadwick's 2nd and 3rd Symphonies, Foote's 'Francesca da Rimini' and Suites in D minor and E, Hadley's 'Four Seasons' Symphony, MacDowell's 'Lamia' and Suite in A, Paine's 2nd Symphony and 'Œdipus Tyrannus,' and Stojowski's Violin-Concerto; much chamber-music by these composers and others; and a notable list of cantatas and similar choral works of considerable dimensions. The catalogue of songs and piano-pieces is extensive and representative. In attention to this field Schmidt was one of the first and has always maintained prominence and importance. The Boston headquarters is at 120 Boylston St.

SCHMINKE, OSCAR EBERHARD (Dec. 12, 1881, New York), took a partial course at the College of the City of New York and graduated from the College of Dentistry in 1903. In 1910 he gave up his practice as dentist for composition. He had had training in piano and organ from Spielter and Déthier, with some lessons in theory from Spicker, but is largely self-taught. For the organ he has published an effective 'Marche Russe,' a 'March of the Toys,' an 'Elegy in the form of a March,' a Pastorale, Festal Postlude, etc., and several songs, among them 'A million little diamonds.' He also has settings of Tagore poems (one with orchestra), a Scherzo for piano, a 'Poëme Exotique,' a 'Fantasy on Oriental Themes' and other works for organ, and various choruses and songs. [R.10]

SCHMITZ, ADOLPH. See Register, 3.

SCHNABEL–TOLLEFSEN, AUGUSTA (b. 1885). See Register, 9.

SCHNECKER, PETER] AUGUST (1850–1903). See Register, 6.

SCHNEIDER, EDWARD FABER (b. 1872). See Register, 9.

SCHNEIDER, HANS (b. 1863). See Register, 7.

SCHOEBEL, OSCAR MELCHIOR (b. 1850). See COLLEGES, 3 (Campbell C., Kan.).

SCHOEN, ISAAC LEOPOLD (b. 1858). See Register, 7.

SCHOENEFELD, HENRY (Oct. 4, 1857, Milwaukee), first studied with his father, a 'cellist, and his brother, one of Joachim's pupils. From 1875 he had three years at Leipzig, with one at Weimar under Lassen. In 1879 he settled in Chicago as teacher and conductor, being connected with the Chicago Musical College and the Columbia School of Music, and leading the Germania Männerchor and other societies. Since 1904 he has been at Los Angeles, where he conducts the Germania Turnverein and the Woman's Symphony Orchestra. His compositions include an opera on an Indian subject; a dramatic scene, 'The Three Indians,' for bass, men's chorus and orchestra; the 'Rural' Symphony in G minor (National Conservatory prize, 1892); the 'Springtime' Symphony (Seidl Orchestra); the 'Festival' and 'In the Sunny South' Overtures; two 'American Rhapsodies' for orchestra; many works for small orchestra, such as two 'Indian Legends,' a 'Menuet Caractéristique,' the nocturne 'California,' a 'Suite Characteristic' (Summy), and many pieces for strings; a violin-concerto, a Sonata in G minor for violin and piano (Simrock), which won the Marteau prize in 1899; a 'cello-sonata, op. 70; a piano-concerto; an 'Air' for the G-string, with orchestra; several pieces for violin and for 'cello; and many piano-pieces, songs, choruses and various transcriptions. Many of these shorter works are published by Heffelfinger, Summy, Presser, Schmidt, Church, Luckhardt, etc. [R.6]

SCHOETTLE, GUSTAV (b. 1877). See Register, 8.

SCHOFIELD, ROBERT LE ROY (b. 1876). See Register, 8.

SCHOLA CANTORUM, THE, of New York, which began in 1909 as the MacDowell Chorus (fostered by the MacDowell Club) and had notable success as such, especially in conjunction with the Philharmonic Society under Mahler, in 1912 adopted its present name and has since steadily maintained its position as a foremost exponent of a cappella singing. Its only conductor has been Kurt Schindler, to whose indefatigable enthusiasm, with his striking ability in bringing to light works quite out of the line of ordinary rendering, its success has been mainly due. The chorus in recent years has averaged 150–200 singers, selected carefully for vocal skill and willingness to give time for thorough practice. Besides giving many more extended works that are rarely heard, the chorus has made a specialty of the folk-songs of many nations. Its concerts have always had high individuality, supplying an element in the season of the metropolis that is unique as well as charming. Among the works in its répertoire the following may be noted, most of them not before given in New York or America:

With orchestra —
Chabrier's 'Briséis' (1911), 'Ode to Music' (1911) and 'Epithalame de Gwendoline'; Liszt's 'St. Elizabeth' (1911) and Finale to the 'Dante' Symphony; Debussy's 'Le Martyre de St.-Sébastien' (1912) and 'Les Sirènes' (1910); a chorus from Busoni's 'Turandot'; Brahms' 'Gesang aus Fingal'; Rimsky-Korsakov's 'Christmas Eve'; Mussorgsky's 'Joshua' (1911); choruses from Borodin's 'Prince Igor'; Saint-Saëns' 'La Nuit'; Beethoven's 9th Symphony (1913); Verdi's Stabat Mater (1914); choruses from Purcell's 'King Arthur' and 'Dido and Æneas'; Zandonai's 'Padre Nostro'; Coleridge-Taylor's 'The Slave Singing at Midnight'; Gardiner's 'News from Whydah'; and Grainger's 'Father and Daughter.'

With piano —
Tiersot's 'Two Canadian Folk-Songs'; Mussorgsky's 'Cradle-Song'; Franck's 'La Vierge à la Crèche'; Wolf's 'Der Feuerreiter'; d'Indy's 'Sur la Mer'; Charpentier's 'Chant du Muletier' and 'Sérénade à Watteau'; Stojowski's 'Springtime' Cantata; Fairchild's 'A Bible Lyric'; and Suk's 'Seven Slavonic Folk-Songs.'

A cappella —
A great variety of old English Madrigals and Carols, Welsh Fighting-Songs, Russian Anthems and Folk-Songs, Finnish Student-Songs, French Folk-Songs and Madrigals of the Renaissance, Catalonian Folk-Songs and Christmas Songs, Negro Songs, etc.; also Strauss' 'Der Abend' (16-part); Bantock's Choral Ode from 'Atalanta in Calydon' (20-part); Bourgeault-Ducoudray's 'Ronde Brétonne'; etc.

‡ SCHOLES, PERCY A. (1877, Leeds, England), has given himself almost wholly to educational interests. In 1900–01 and '03 he was music-master at Kent College in Canterbury, in 1901–03 at Kingswood College in South Africa and from 1904 for a time teacher in the Leeds Municipal School of Music, and inspector for the Board of Education in London. He has long served as extension-lecturer for Oxford, London and Manchester Universities. He founded the Home Music-Study Union and since 1908 has been the energetic editor of its organ, 'The Music-Student,' which has included many articles of general importance, and also 'Youth and Music,' for children. He has published *Everyman and his Music*, 1917, *An Introduction to British Music*, 1918, and *A Listener's Guide to Music*, 1919, and has a

work on Purcell that is almost ready. He has also written extensively for periodicals. Besides holding a degree from Oxford, he is an associate of the R. C. M., on innumerable committees connected with musical enterprises, and president of the Union that regards music in the large 'public schools' like Eton, Harrow and the like. During the Great War he was extremely active as lecturer under the War Office and Y. M. C. A. and as organizer of musical activities in camps both in England and on the Continent. In 1915 he visited America at the invitation of the M. T. N. A. and inspected manifold musical enterprises, besides lecturing at many colleges.

SCHOMACKER [Schumacher], JOHANN HEINRICH (1800–1875). See Register, 3.

'SCHOOL MUSIC MONTHLY, THE.' See note in Vol. iii. 689. It is now known as 'School Music.' It has made its place not only by supplying general news and other material regarding public-school music, but by its faithful reports of the music-section of the National Education Association, the Supervisors' National Conference, the M. T. N. A., and other bodies dealing with this branch of musical education. There are now but five issues per year.

SCHOOL–MUSIC. See Public Schools.

SCHRADIECK, HENRY (Apr. 29, 1846, Hamburg, Germany : Mar. 25, 1918, Brooklyn). See article in Vol. iv. 274. He was head of the violin-department of the College of Music in Cincinnati in 1883–89. In 1894–98 he held a similar position in the National Conservatory in New York, going thence to the Broad Street Conservatory in Philadelphia. After 1912 he was also connected with the American Institute of Applied Music in New York. [R.7]

SCHREINER, FRANCIS C. See Colleges, 1 (Seton Hall C., N. J.).

SCHROEDER, ALWIN (June 15, 1855, Neuhaldensleben, Germany), was early a piano-pupil of his father and J. B. André, but later studied violin with De Ahna in Berlin and theory with Tappert. With his three brothers the Schroeder Quartet was formed in 1871–72, he taking the viola. Self-taught on the 'cello, he became first 'cellist in Liebig's Orchestra in 1875, and five years later joined the Gewandhaus Orchestra in Leipzig. Here he taught in the Conservatory and played in the Petri Quartet. In 1891 he came to Boston, becoming solo 'cellist in the Boston Symphony Orchestra and a member of the Kneisel Quartet. With the rest of the Quartet he resigned from the Orchestra in 1903 and removed to New York. He continued with the Quartet until the spring of 1907, when he returned to Germany. In Frankfort-am-Main he was for one year solo 'cellist of the Museum Orchestra and teacher in the Hoch Conservatory, but in 1908 he returned to Boston and joined the Hess-Schroeder Quartet. After two years this organization was disbanded, and he resumed (till 1912) his former place in the Symphony Orchestra. In 1915 he joined the Margulies Trio (New York) and the Boston String Quartet. As both soloist and ensemble-player he is held in the highest estimation. He has published *Études de Violoncelle, Technische Studien*, and *Neue Tonleiter-Studien*, and has edited *Kammermusikstudien*, 3 vols., and *Klassiches Album*, 2 vols. [R.8]

SCHUBERTH, JULIUS FERDINAND GEORG (1804–1875). See Register, 4.

SCHUBERTH, J., & CO. See article in Vol. iv. 335.

SCHUÉCKER, EDMUND (1860–1911). See Register, 8.

SCHUÉCKER, HEINRICH (1867–1913). See Register, 7.

SCHUÉCKER, JOSEPH E. (b. 1886). See Register, 9.

SCHULTZE, WILHELM HEINRICH (1828–1888). See Register, 6.

SCHULZ, LEO (Mar. 28, 1865, Posen, Germany), played in public on the 'cello when only five. He studied at the Berlin Hochschule and made his mature début in 1876. In 1885 he became principal 'cellist in the Philharmonic Orchestra, and in 1886–89 held the same position at the Gewandhaus in Leipzig. Coming then to America, he was for one year in the Boston Symphony Orchestra, but in 1890 began his long connection with the New York Philharmonic Society, unbroken save for the years 1906–08, when he played with the Symphony Society. For many years he taught at the National Conservatory and conducted its orchestra, and in 1904–15 he was a member of the Margulies Trio. For thirty years he has been much in request as soloist. He has written three string-quartets, a string-quintet, a piano-trio, a 'cello-concerto and other 'cello-pieces, a cantata and some songs. He has also edited several collections for his instrument. [R.7]

SCHUMANN-HEINK, ERNESTINE, née Rössler (June 15, 1861, Lieben, near Prague, Bohemia). See article in Vol. iv. 383–4. Her father was an army officer. From her Italian mother she learned many operatic airs as a child, and at eleven sang in the choir of the Ursuline convent at Prague. Her first real lessons were in 1874, from Marietta von Leclair of Graz, where in 1876 she was alto-soloist in Beethoven's 9th Symphony with the Academischer Gesangverein. At Dresden she studied with Aloysia Krebs-Michalesi and Franz Wüllner, and made her operatic début in 1878. Her first appearance at Berlin

was at Kroll's in 1887. In 1896–1906 (except 1904) she sang at all the performances of the 'Ring' at Bayreuth as Erda, First Norn or Waltraute. In 1898 she was engaged at the Berlin Opera, with leave to sing in the winters in New York. In America she was first heard as Ortrud on Nov. 7, 1898, in Chicago, and on Jan. 9, 1899, at the Metropolitan in New York. Her signal success led her to purchase release from her Berlin contract. In 1903–04 she made her first extended concert-tour in America, and the next year was everywhere heard in Edwards' 'Love's Lottery.' In 1908–09 she sang in opera and concert in the chief cities of Europe, in 1909 creating the rôle of Clytemnestra in Strauss' 'Elektra' at Dresden. She retired from the Metropolitan in 1904, but has occasionally sung there, at the Manhattan or with the Chicago Opera Company. Her activity has been mainly transferred to the concert-stage, with a hundred or more song-recitals annually and frequent engagements with leading orchestras. Her operatic répertoire includes about 150 rôles, from Wagnerian drama to light opera. She was the wife of Ernst Heink in 1882–92, of the actor Paul Schumann in 1893–1904, and of William Rapp, Jr., of Chicago in 1905–14. In 1905 she became an American citizen. [R.8]

SCHWAB, CHARLES M. (b. 1862). See Register, 9.

SCHWARTZ, GEORGE FOSS (b. 1872). See Register, 8.

‡ SCHWEITZER, ALBERT (Jan. 4, 1875, Kaysersberg, Alsace), is distinguished in theology, medicine and music. His university studies were at Strassburg, Paris and Berlin. In 1902 he began teaching at Strassburg, but turned aside to prepare for work as medical missionary in Equatorial Africa. There, nominally under the Mission Évangélique of France, he was stationed at Lambaréné on the Ogowé River. During the war he was interned as a German subject, but has lately returned to France. His chief theological books are *Die Religionsphilosophie Immanuel Kants*, 1899, and *Das Messianitäts- und Leidensgeheimniss — eine Skizze des Lebens Jesu*, 1901 (in English as *The Quest of the Historical Jesus*) — a specially significant work. Throughout his life he has been a musical student, beginning with organ-lessons in Mülhausen and Strassburg, and from 1893 with Widor in Paris. From 1896 he was organist for Bach concerts at Strassburg, from 1906 was organist for the Bach Society in Paris, and in 1909 was chairman of the organ-making conference at the I. M. G. Congress in Vienna. He has published *Jean-Sébastien Bach, le Musicien-Poëte*, 1905 (English translation, enlarged, by Ernest

Newman, 2 vols., 1911), which is an extraordinarily valuable work, *Deutsche und fran-
zösische Orgelbaukunst und Orgelkunst*, 1906,
and, as editor with Widor, of the complete
organ-works of Bach (Schirmer). See article
on 'Schweitzer as Missionary' in 'The Hibbert
Journal,' July, 1914.

SCIONTI, S. See COLLEGES, 2 (C. of St.
Catharine, Minn.).

SCOTT, CARLYLE (b. 1873). See STATE
UNIVERSITIES (Minn.).

‡ SCOTT, CYRIL MEIR (Sept. 27, 1879,
Oxton, England). See article in Vol. iv. 390.
After three years at Frankfort, he located
himself at Liverpool, chiefly occupied with
composition. He has also done much literary
work, and has lectured on occult philosophy.
His larger works are as follows:

Symphony No. 1 (given at Darmstadt, now
    destroyed).
Symphony No 2 (given by Wood), later rewritten
    as 'Three Orchestral Dances' (Birmingham,
    conducted by composer).
'Heroic' Suite, for orchestra (given by Richter at
    Manchester, later withdrawn).
Overture to 'Pelléas et Mélisande' (Frankfort).
Overture to 'Princess Maleine,' with chorus
    (Vienna), later revised.
'Christmas' Overture, with 'Nativity Hymn' for
    chorus (performance at Vienna stopped by the
    war).
'Ballad of Fair Helen of Kirkconnel,' for baritone
    and orchestra.
Two Passacaglias on Irish Themes, for orchestra
    (given by Beecham).
Piano-Concerto (given by Beecham at English
    Festival) (Augener).
Aubade for orchestra (Darmstadt, Dresden,
    Berlin), later revised.
Rhapsody for orchestra.
Opera, 'The Alchemist.'
'La Belle Dame sans Merci,' for soprano, baritone
    and orchestra.
Piano-Quartet, op. 16 (Boosey).
String-Quartets, opp. 28 and 31.
Piano-Quintet, op. 57.
Piano-Sextet, op. 26.
Piano-Trio — early work, now withdrawn.
'Tallahassee' Suite, for violin and piano (Schott).
'Handelian Rhapsody,' for piano (Elkin, edited
    by Grainger).
Piano-Sonata, op. 66 (Elkin).
'Pastoral Suite' for piano (Elkin).

He has also written a large number of piano-
pieces and songs, illustrating the versatility
of his mind and his peculiar power of imaginative expression. He has published seven
volumes of poems and *The Philosophy of
Modernism* (in connection with music), 1917.
See biography by Hull, 1918, besides many
articles in musical periodicals.

SCOTT, HENRI GUEST (Apr. 8, 1876,
Coatesville, Pa.), studied in Philadelphia and
under Saenger in New York. His first work
as bass was in church, concert and oratorio.
In 1909–10 he appeared at the Manhattan
Opera House, his first performance being as

Ramphis in 'Aida.' The next season he was
at the Teatro Adriano in Rome. In 1912–14
he was a leading artist for the Chicago Opera
Company, and since 1915 has been with the
Metropolitan Opera House in New York.
He is recognized as a basso of exceptional
gift. His favorite rôles are Mephisto,
Escamillo, Leporello, Basilio, the King (in
'Lohengrin' and 'Tristan'), Plunkett, Dr.
Miracle and Lothario. He is also noted as
an oarsman. [R.9]

SCOTTI, ANTONIO (Jan. 25, 1866, Naples, Italy). See article in Vol. v. 666.
His first American appearance was as Don
Giovanni on Dec. 27, 1899, at the Metropolitan Opera House in New York. He has
remained there ever since, but has also sung
often at Covent Garden in London. In 1919–
20 he toured extensively with his own company. To the list of rôles add Belcore, Falstaff, Germont, Ashton, Marcel, Escamillo,
Comte de Nevers and Valentin. [R.8]

‡ SCRIABIN, ALEXANDER NIKOLAI-
EVITCH (Jan. 10, 1872, Moscow, Russia
: Apr. 14, 1915, Moscow). See article in
Vol. iv. 402–3. He began extemporizing on
the piano at five, and early showed a remarkable musical memory. After leaving Moscow
he lived for a time in Switzerland and two years
in Brussels. He visited America in 1907, and
first went to London in 1914. His works
since 1903 are as follows:

Sonatas: No. 4, op. 30, in F-sharp; No. 5, op.
    53; No. 6, op. 62; No. 7, op. 64; No. 8, op. 66;
    No. 9, op. 68; No. 10, op. 70.
Preludes: opp. 31, 33, 35, 37, 39, 48, 67, 74.
'Poems': opp. 32, 34 ('Tragique'), 36 ('Satan-
    ique'), 41, 44, 54 ('de l'Extase'), 61 ('Noc-
    turne'), 63 ('Masque,' 'Étrangeté'), 69, 71, 72
    ('Vers la Flamme').
Waltzes: opp. 38, 47.
Mazurkas: op. 40.
Études: opp. 42, 65, and also in Pieces.
Symphony No. 3, 'The Divine Poem,' in C, op. 43.
'Prométhée' ('Poème de feu'), op. 60, first given,
    with color-keyboard, by Altschuler and the
    Russian Symphony Orchestra, Mar. 20, 1915,
    New York).
Pieces, etc.; opp. 45, 46, 49, 51, 52, 56, 57, 58, 59, 73.

See biography by Hull, 1916, and résumé
and bibliography in Baker, *Dict. of Musicians*,
p. 881.

SEALY, FRANK LINWOOD (b. 1858).
See Register, 7.

SEARCH, FREDERICK PRESTON (July
22, 1889, Pueblo, Colo.), from 1901 was trained
as a 'cellist in Jena, by Joseph Adamowski in
Boston, Mattioli and Rugovoy in Cincinnati
and Klengel in Leipzig, also taking theory
with Schreck and Reger and orchestration
with Hofmann and Sitt. In 1910–12 he was
in the Gewandhaus Orchestra under Nikisch.
In 1908–11 he was Leipzig correspondent for
'Music News' in Chicago. In 1912–15 he

gave concerts in America, appearing in New York in 1914. For a time he conducted summer-plays in California. In 1915–16 he led the 'cellos in the American Symphony Orchestra in Chicago, and in 1916–17 was in the orchestra of the Chicago Opera Company. In 1915–16 he was assistant-editor of 'The Violinist,' and in 1917 conducted at the performance of 'The Crisis.' Early in 1918 he enlisted as musician in the Navy and was appointed band-master. His works include four string-quartets, a string-sextet, two sonatas for 'cello and piano, a Festival Overture (1915, San Francisco Exposition, under Bendix), a 'Romantic Symphony' in D, and several shorter works, including 20 songs, besides incidental music for Heron's 'Montezuma,' Rice's 'Yolanda of Cyprus' and Hilliard and Heron's 'Tusitala,' and an 'Aztec Dance,' for string-quartet or orchestra. [R.10]

SEASHORE, CARL EMIL (Jan. 28, 1866, Mörlunda, Sweden), brought up in America, graduated at Gustavus Adolphus College in 1891 and took a Ph.D. at Yale in 1895, where he continued as teacher of psychology and philosophy till 1902. Since 1902 he has been at the State University of Iowa, becoming dean of the Graduate College in 1908. Early trained in music, he has given increasing attention to problems of musical psychology, conducting extensive experiments of various kinds, especially for ascertaining degrees of musical talent. He classifies the latter under these heads: Sensitivity, Action, Memory and Imagination, Intellect and Feeling. For each of these both quantitative and qualitative tests have been devised, leading to the making for a given case of a 'talent-chart.' Special apparatus employed includes inventions like the audiometer, the tonoscope, the spark-chronoscope, a serial-action apparatus and a chronograph. Some tests have been made into phonograph-form for school-use. The purpose throughout has been not only scientific, but also to give help in choosing a musical vocation and in overcoming technical difficulties. He has published The Psychology of Musical Talent, 1917, and a long series of articles in various periodicals, like 'The Musical Quarterly,' 'The Etude,' and the Proceedings of the M. T. N. A., 1913, '15, and as monographs in the University of Iowa Studies in Psychology. [R.8]

SEATTLE SYMPHONY ORCHESTRA, THE, was founded in 1907. Its conductor till 1909 was Michael Kegrize, followed by Henry K. Hadley in 1909–11. In 1911 its place was taken by the new Philharmonic Orchestra, led by John Spargur, which in 1919 secured a guaranty for three years that will enable it to resume concerts of the first order.

SEEBOECK, WILLIAM CHARLES ERNEST (Aug. 21, 1859, Vienna, Austria : 1907, Chicago), after early instruction from his mother, a pupil of Marchesi, began piano-study at ten with Graedener, going on later with Epstein and Grill, and taking theory with Nottebohm. Meanwhile he had collegiate education at the Theresianum. In 1875 he studied with Brahms, and in 1877–79 was in Petrograd, with Rubinstein for adviser. In 1881 he settled in Chicago as pianist, teacher and composer. For a time he taught harmony at the Chicago Musical College and was organist at the Jefferson Park Presbyterian Church. His published compositions are mostly songs and piano-pieces, but he left also two operas, 'The Gladiators' and 'The Missing Link,' a piano-quintet, two concertos and two sonatas for piano, variations for two pianos, 27 concert-études for piano, and over 200 songs. [R.7]

SEEGER, CHARLES LOUIS, Jr. (Dec. 14, 1886, Mexico City), graduated from Harvard in 1908, having specialized in music. In 1910–11 he volunteered as conductor at the Cologne Opera. Since 1912 he has been professor of music at the University of California. Recently he has made special studies in musicology and musicological methods. He has composed two masques for orchestra, 'Dedra' (1914) and 'The Queen's Masque' (1915), and an overture for full orchestra after Yeats' 'Shadowy Waters.' He has also composed chamber-music, a violin-sonata and about 25 songs (some Schirmer). With E. G. Stricklen he has published Outline of a Course in Harmonic Structure and Musical Invention, 1913, and Harmonic Structure and Elementary Composition, 1916. [R.10]

SEGUIN, ARTHUR EDWARD SHELDON (1809–1852) and ANN, née Childe (1814–1888). See Vol. iv. 408, and Register, 3.

SEIDL, ANTON (May 7, 1850, Pest, Hungary : Mar. 28, 1898, New York). See article in Vol. iv. 408. He was brought to America, after the death of Leopold Damrosch, to conduct German opera at the Metropolitan Opera House, and made his début with 'Lohengrin' on Nov. 23, 1885. During his career at the Metropolitan he conducted the first performance in America of 'Die Meistersinger' (Jan. 4, 1886), 'Tristan und Isolde' (Dec. 1, 1886), 'Siegfried' (Nov. 9, 1887), 'Die Gotterdämmerung' (Jan. 25, 1888), 'Das Rheingold' (Jan. 4, 1889), and the 'Ring,' complete (Mar. 4–11, 1889). Except in 1892–95, when German opera was temporarily eclipsed, he conducted at the Metropolitan till his death. In 1891, also, he succeeded Thomas as conductor of the New York Philharmonic Society, a position also retained to the end. He introduced many works by

modern composers, and conducted the première of Dvořák's 'New World' Symphony in
1893. See Krehbiel, *Anton Seidl*, 1898, and *Anton Seidl, Memorial by His Friends*, 1899. [R.7]

SEILER, EMMA (1821- ?). See Register, 5.

SEIPLE, STANLEY J. See COLLEGES, 3
(Thiel C., Pa.).

SELBY, WILLIAM (1738, England :
1798, Boston), came to Boston about 1771.
He had been an organist in England since
1767 and was also an excellent harpsichordist.
In 1774 he became organist at Trinity Church
in Newport, R. I., but by Easter, 1777, was
established at King's Chapel in Boston,
where he apparently remained till his death.
Besides conducting a shop for the sale of
groceries and liquor, he was much in evidence
as player, teacher and concert-manager, from
about 1782 also as composer. At some of
his concerts extracts from Handel's oratorios
were sung by the Musical Society, of which
he was promoter, if not conductor. His
programs show remarkable knowledge and
enterprise. His own works included songs,
anthems and instrumental pieces, among them
Voluntaries or Fugues for organ or harpsichord, a Concerto for organ or harpsichord
'with instrumental parts,' a Sonata for two
violins and 'cellos, etc. See Sonneck, *Concert-
Life in America*, with his remark that 'Boston's
musical history during the last thirty years of
the 18th century may be said to have centered
in the personality of this interesting and ambitious musician.' [R.1]

SEMBRICH, MARCELLA (Feb. 15, 1858,
Wisniewczyk, Galicia). See article in Vol.
iv. 409–10. Her first American appearance
was as Lucia at the Metropolitan Opera House
on Oct. 24, 1883. At Abbey's benefit at the
end of the season she played a violin-concerto
of De Bériot, with a Chopin nocturne and then
an aria from 'La Sonnambula' for encores,
besides taking the violin-obbligato in the
Bach-Gounod 'Ave Maria,' sung by Nilsson.
In 1897 she came again for a concert-tour,
and sang at the Metropolitan for the next
two seasons and, after another season of
concerts, from 1901 till her retirement in 1909.
At her farewell (Feb. 6, 1909) she appeared
in three of her famous rôles, Norina in 'Don
Pasquale,' Rosina in the 'Barbiere' and
Susanna in 'Figaro's Hochzeit' — the last
in German, Mahler conducting. Among the
many tributes were a string of pearls bought
by popular subscription and presented by
Mayor Low, and a punch-bowl from the
directors (who made her the first honorary
member of the Opera House Company), and
there was a ball at the Savoy and a dinner
from the musicians of the city. A day or
two later she left for London and a concert-

trip in Russia, returning from which in 1910
she bade farewell to the stage in Berlin, Frankfort and other German cities. In 1910–11
she was still active in concert and song-recitals
on both sides of the ocean, settling in Lausanne
and Nice. When the war broke out she was
in Switzerland. In October, 1914, she resumed song-recitals in New York, but her work
as head of the American Polish Relief so
exhausted her that at the opening of 1917
she permanently retired. She had just begun
a series of historical recitals that had been
planned to be her closing public act. Her
husband died in May, 1917. She makes her
home at present in New York. Of her eminence as a song-singer Henderson has said :
'The depth of expression attained by her in
her wonderful song-recitals is due to a combination of perfect tone with musical intelligence. Bigger tone, more brilliancy of
style, are demanded in opera, but in the
interpretation of the song complete revelation
of the poetic and musical content of the work
is the absolute requirement. This Mme.
Sembrich has been able to supply.' [R.7]

SEMMANN, LIBORIUS (b. 1873). See
Register, 8.

SENKRAH [Arma Leoretta Hoffmann,
née Harkness] (1864–1900). See Register, 7.

SEVERN, EDMUND (Dec. 10, 1862, Nottingham, England), had his training as violinist in America, studying with his father,
Franz Milcke and Bernhard Listemann, and
taking singing with George Sweet, piano with
T. Oelschleger and composition with Chadwick. In 1888–90 he was in Berlin under
Wirth for violin and Ph. Scharwenka for
composition. He began teaching at Hartford, Conn., and Springfield, Mass., and for
some years led chamber-groups and conducted
choral societies. He moved to New York in
1897, where in 1907–14 he gave lectures for
the Board of Education, but has lately confined himself to teaching and composition.
His published works include a concerto, four
suites and about 25 pieces for violin and piano,
a suite for two violins and piano, the concert-
waltz 'La Brunette' and a 'Gavotte Moderne'
for orchestra, about 20 songs, pieces for 'cello
and for piano, 36 teaching-pieces for violin
and *The Grün Modern Method for Violin*.
He has also two string-quartets, a violin-sonata,
a piano-trio, an 'Oriental' Suite for violin
and piano, the cantata 'Jephtha's Daughter,'
and, for orchestra, a Festival Overture, a
Polonaise in D, the symphonic poems 'Lancelot and Elaine' and 'Life, Death, Reunion'
and a fantasy on 'The Tempest.' Most of
these last have been publicly performed.
[R.8]

SEWALL, MAUD GILCHRIST (b. 1872).
See Register, 8.

SEWARD, THEODORE FRELING-HUYSEN (1835–1902). See Register, 5.

SEYDEL, IRMA (Sept. 27, 1896, Boston), the daughter of a violinist in the Boston Symphony Orchestra, was trained by him, Strube, Loeffler and Maquarre in Boston. When but nine she twice appeared with a group of players from the Orchestra, and at thirteen played as solo-violinist with the Gürzenich Orchestra in Cologne, once under Steinbach. Between 1912 and 1918 she appeared seven times with the Boston Symphony Orchestra, and also had engagements with many other leading symphony orchestras and in various German cities. [R.10]

SEYMOUR, LEWIS and THADDEUS. See TUNE-BOOKS, 1804.

‡SGAMBATI, GIOVANNI (May 18, 1843, Rome, Italy : Dec. 14, 1914, Rome). See article in Vol. iv. 431–3. For a bibliography, see Baker, *Dict. of Musicians*, p. 869.

SHACKLEY, FREDERICK NEWELL (b. 1868). See Register, 7.

‘SHANEWIS.’ An opera by Charles W. Cadman, produced at the Metropolitan Opera House on Mar. 23, 1918. The text is by Mrs. Nellie R. Eberhard.

SHAPLEIGH, BERTRAM (Jan. 15, 1871, Boston), early took up piano and ’cello along with other studies, and had lessons in composition from Whiting, Chadwick and MacDowell. At first he was engaged upon literature, but also took a medical degree and lectured on art-topics. His interest in the music of the Orient led to his concentrating upon musical work. In 1898 he built a house in Kent, England, and cultivated a considerable estate. In 1915, however, the house was burnt, including his large library and valuable scores, etc., and he returned to America. His published works include the orchestral suite ‘Rámáyana,’ op. 45, based upon five episodes in the Hindu epic (over 50 performances in the first two years); the orchestral suite ‘Gur Amir,’ op. 51, being four visions from the tomb of Tamerlane; the tone-poem ‘Mirage,’ op. 57, for chorus and orchestra; a setting of Poe’s ‘The Raven,’ op. 50, for chorus and orchestra (1908, Middlesbrough Festival); ‘The Dance of the Dervishes,’ op. 53 (Wolverhampton Festival); the 8-part choral works ‘The Fir-Tree and the Brook’ (a cappella), op. 54, ‘The Tale of the Dismal Swamp,’ op. 55, and ‘Vedic Hymn,’ op. 56 (all London Choral Society); the cycle for solo and small chorus, ‘Romance of the Year,’ op. 53; more than 100 songs, many of which are on Oriental themes; and many pieces for violin or ’cello and piano, or for piano alone. Unpublished are two symphonies, in B minor and A, opp. 62, 68; a Symphonic Prelude, op. 61; three ‘Con-

solations,’ op. 64, for orchestra; a ‘Poem,’ op. 65, for ’cello and orchestra; a string-quartet in G, op. 70; a piano-trio in E minor, op. 70; a Grand Mass in D, and various other settings for the Catholic service; a cantata based on the Song of Solomon; and five one-act operas and two grand operas. His wife, née Mabelle Carpenter, has supplied texts for many of his works. For some years he was musical adviser for Breitkopf & Härtel, and also edited ‘The Concert-Program Exchange.’ He has published two volumes of poetry and many articles on art-topics. [R.8]

SHARLAND, JOHN B. (1837–1909). See Register, 4.

‡ SHARP, CECIL JAMES (Nov. 22, 1859, London, England), after graduating from Cambridge in 1882, spent nine years in Adelaide, till 1889 as associate to the Chief Justice of South Australia, then as conductor of the Philharmonic Society and organist at the Cathedral. Since returning to England in 1892 he has been mainly occupied with music. In 1896–1905 he was principal of the Hampstead Conservatory in London, and since 1911 has been director of the English Folk-Dance Society and The Stratford-on-Avon School of Folk-Song and Dance. He has devoted himself to collecting and investigating folk-music, and in the pursuit of the subject has visited America. His *English Folk-Songs from the Southern Appalachians* (collected in part by Olive Dame Campbell), 1917, contains nearly 500 songs, ballads and tunes from this region. He is also author of *English Folk-Song — Some Conclusions*, 1907, *Folk-Dancing in Schools*, 1913, and *Folk-Singing in Schools*, 1914. He has edited a *Book of British Song*, 1902, *Folk-Songs from Somerset* (with C. L. Marson), 5 series, 1904–09, *English Folk-Songs for Schools* (with S. Baring-Gould, 1906, *Country-Dance Tunes* (with G. Butterworth), 8 parts, 1906–16 (including *The Country-Dance Book*, separately in 1906), *The Morris Book* (with George Butterworth and Herbert MacIlwaine), 5 parts, 1907–13 (including *A History of Morris Dancing*, 1907, rewritten, 1912), *English Folk-Carols*, 1911, *The Sword-Dances of Northern England*, 3 parts, 1911, *English Chanteys*, 1914, *A Midsummer-Night's Dream* (songs, dances and incidental music), 1914, 100 *English Folk-Songs*, 1916, *Folk-Songs, Chanteys and Singing-Games* (with C. H. Farnsworth), *A Collection of Selected Folk-Songs* (with R. V. Williams), 1918.

SHATTUCK, ARTHUR (Apr. 19, 1881, Neenah, Wis.), began piano-study with his mother and had seven years with Leschetizky before 1902. In 1901 he appeared as pianist with the Philharmonic Orchestra at Copenhagen. Until 1911 he lived in Paris, but made many concert-tours throughout Europe and even to Egypt in the East and to Iceland in the West. In 1911–12 he toured in America, appearing in New York with the Symphony Society. In 1912–15 he was again in Europe. Since then he has concertized in the United States, often with leading orchestras. In March, 1917, he was soloist with the San Francisco Orchestra under Hertz. [R.9]

SHAW, FRANK HOLCOMB. See COLLEGES, 3 (Cornell C., Iowa).

SHAW, OLIVER (1779–1848). See TUNE-BOOKS, 1808.

SHELDON, E. EDWIN. See COLLEGES, 3½ (Lebanon Valley C., Pa.).

SHELLEY, HARRY ROWE (June 2, 1858, New Haven, Conn.), began organ-playing at the Center Church in New Haven when but fourteen, and studied with Stoeckel at Yale College and later with Buck, Vogrich and Dvořák in New York. In 1878–81 and 1887–99 he was organist at the Church of the Pilgrims in Brooklyn, and in 1881–87 at Plymouth Church there. Since 1899 he has been at the Fifth Avenue Baptist Church in New York, and also on the teaching-staff of the Metropolitan College of Music and the American Institute of Applied Music. He has written two symphonies (No. 1, in E-flat, 1897, New York); a violin-concerto (1891); a 'Santa Claus' Overture; the orchestral suite 'Souvenir de Baden-Baden' (published for piano, 4 hands); the cantatas 'The Inheritance Divine,' 'Vexilla Regis' (1894, New York), 'Death and Life' and 'Lochinvar's Ride' (1915, New York); a Fantasia for piano and orchestra; many pieces for piano and for organ; and numerous songs and anthems, many of the latter extremely effective. He has made many organ-transcriptions, and issued the collections *The Modern Organist* and *Gems for the Organ*. [R.6]

SHEPARD, ANNIE AGNES, née Boll (b. 1859). See Register, 7.

SHEPARD, CLARENCE E. See COLLEGES, 3 (Carroll C., Wis.).

SHEPARD, FRANK HARTSON (1863–1913). See Register, 7.

SHEPARD, THOMAS GRIFFIN (1848–1905). See Register, 5.

SHEPHERD, ARTHUR (Feb. 19, 1880, Paris, Ida.), in 1892–94 studied at the New England Conservatory in Boston with Dennée and Faelten (piano) and Goetschius and Chadwick (composition). From 1897 he taught in Salt Lake City, led a theater-orchestra and also the Symphony Orchestra. Since 1908 he has taught harmony and counterpoint at the New England Conservatory. For three seasons he conducted the Musical Art Society, and in 1917 became conductor of the Cecilia Society, succeeding Clifton. His compositions include an 'Ouverture Joy-

euse,' op. 3 (Paderewski prize, 1902, given by the New York Symphony Society, 1905); two other overtures, 'The Festival of Youth' (1915, St. Louis Orchestra) and 'The Nuptials of Attila'; an orchestral suite, op. 5; a Humoreske for piano and orchestra; a Sonata in F minor, op. 4, for piano (Nat. Federation of Musical Clubs prize, 1909) (Boston Music Co.); 'Song of the Sea-Wind,' for women's voices and orchestra; 'The City of the Sea,' for baritone, chorus and orchestra, poem by Carman (1913, Chicago) (Schirmer); the motet 'The Lord has brought again Zion' (Ditson); the part-song for women's voices 'He came all so still' (Schmidt); and some piano-pieces and songs (Wa-Wan Press). [R.8]

SHERWOOD, WILLIAM HALL (Jan. 31, 1854, Lyons, N. Y. : Jan. 7, 1911, Chicago), was the son of Rev. L. H. Sherwood, the founder of the Lyons Musical Academy. He played frequently in public from his ninth year. In 1866–71 he taught in his father's school and secured a general education. After some lessons from William Mason in 1871 he went to Berlin, where he studied piano with Kullak and theory with Weitzmann. He later took composition with Doppler, piano with Deppe, counterpoint and composition with Richter, and finally piano with Liszt at Weimar. He gave successful concerts in Berlin and Hamburg, and returned to America in 1876. Concerts in New York, Boston, Philadelphia (including the Centennial Exhibition, with the Thomas Orchestra), Cincinnati and Chicago soon established his reputation as a virtuoso. He settled in Boston as a member of the New England Conservatory faculty, and numbered Arthur Whiting and Clayton Johns among his pupils. After a few years he forsook Boston for New York, and from 1889 made his home in Chicago. For eight years he was head of the piano-department of the Chicago Conservatory, but in 1897 withdrew to establish the Sherwood Piano School. A brilliant and popular pianist, he played with all the leading orchestras and gave recitals in every part of the United States and Canada. His services as a teacher were in great demand. Not strongly tempted by composition, he is represented only by a group of piano-pieces, a 'Scherzo Caprice,' op. 9, two suites, opp. 5 and 14, two sets of 'Gypsy Dances,' opp. 10 and 40, a 'Scherzo Symphonique,' an 'Allegro Patetico' and 'Medea.' [R.6]

SHIELDS, T. EDGAR. See COLLEGES, 2 (Moravian C., Pa.).

SHIRLEY, H. A. (b. 1865). See COLLEGES, 2 (Salem C., N. C.).

SHORT, LAURA GRANT. See COLLEGES, 2 (Rockford C., Ill.).

SHUMWAY, NEHEMIAH. See TUNE-BOOKS, 1793.

‡ SIBELIUS, JEAN (Dec. 8, 1865, Tavastehus, Finland). See article in Vol. iv. 447-8. His annual grant of 3000 marks from the Finnish Government ran from 1897 to 1907. In 1900 he toured in Scandinavia, Germany, France and Belgium with the Helsingfors Philharmonic Orchestra, conducting his own works. In 1914 he came to America to produce his symphonic poem 'Daughters of the Ocean' at the Norfolk Festival, and was then made Mus.D. by Yale University. To the list of works add the following:

op. 19 Melodrama, 'The Wood-Nymph.'
25 Suite in E-flat, for orchestra.
35, 50, 57, 60, 61 Songs.
42 Romanze in C, for strings.
58, 67, 68 Piano-Pieces.
48 Choral Ballad, 'Die gefangene Königin.'
52 Symphony No. 3, in C.
54 Suite for small orchestra, from music to 'Svanehvit.'
55 Symphonic Poem, 'Nächtlicher Ritt und Sonnenaufgang.'
56 String-Quartet in D minor, 'Voces Intimæ.'
59 Funeral March, 'In Memoriam,' for orchestra.
62 Canzonetta for strings, and 'Valse Romantique,' for small orchestra.
63 Symphony No. 4, in A minor.
64 Symphonic Poem, 'Der Barde.'
69 Two Serenades for violin and orchestra.
70 Symphonic Poem, 'Luonnotar,' with soprano solo.
71 Pantomime, 'Scaramouche,' in two acts.
72 Symphonic Poem, 'Daughters of the Ocean' (1914, Norfolk Festival).

Also, the first Finnish opera, 'The Maid in the Tower' (1896, Helsingfors); Symphony No. 5 (1916); 'The Old Man,' for baritone and men's chorus; Overtures in E and A minor; a string-quintet in G minor; two string-quartets, in A minor and B-flat; variations in E-flat minor for string-quartet; and a string-trio in A.

SILBER, SIDNEY (b. 1881). See Register, 9.

SILBY, REGINALD MILLS (b. 1884). See COLLEGES, 1 (Catholic U., D. C.).

SIMPSON, GEORGE ELLIOTT (b. 1876). See Register, 9.

SINFONIA FRATERNITY OF AMERICA, THE, was founded in 1898 by Ossian E. Mills to unite music-students in conservatories in a society of mutual benefit. It now has twelve chapters in various parts of the country, including several hundred members. The president since 1915 is F. Otis Drayton and the national headquarters is at the New England Conservatory in Boston.

SINGENBERGER, JOHN B. (b. 1848). See Register, 6.

SINGER, JACOB. See STATE UNIVERSITIES (Neb.).

SINGER, OTTO (July 26, 1833, Sora, Germany : Jan. 3, 1894, New York), after general education at the Kreuzschule in Dresden, in 1851-55 was at the Leipzig Conservatory with Richter, Moscheles and Hauptmann. He then taught in Leipzig for four years, and during this period a symphony and other of his works were played at the Gewandhaus. Next he went to Weimar (studying with Liszt), to Dresden, and in 1867 to New York. Here he taught in the Mason and Thomas Conservatory until its dissolution in 1873. At one of the Thomas concerts in 1869 he played his piano-concerto. In 1873 he went to Cincinnati as assistant-director to Thomas and continued there till 1893, teaching piano and theory from 1880 in the College of Music. For the Festival of 1876 he wrote the cantata 'The Landing of the Pilgrim Fathers,' and for the opening of Music Hall in 1878 the 'Festival Ode.' A successful chorus-leader, he trained the Festival chorus for some years, and directed several festivals of the North American Sängerbund. His 'Symphonic Fantasia' was performed by the Boston Symphony Orchestra under Gericke. Other works were an Andante and Variations for two pianos, a piano-sonata, a violin-sonata and piano-pieces. [R.5]

'SINGING-SCHOOLS.' Popular classes for teaching the rudiments of music and practicing hymn-tunes arose in New England before 1750 in consequence of the movement to introduce singing by note in the churches. They soon became common, not simply for the sake of the musical instruction, but as a form of social gathering. During the last half of the century they were much promoted by itinerant singing-masters who gradually produced a long list of tune-books for them (see TUNE-BOOKS). This general movement continued far into the 19th century and spread to the South and the West. In many cases it led to the holding of musical 'conventions,' and to a small degree influenced the establishment of music in the public schools and even of permanent music-schools. See Ritter, Music in America, chaps. ii-iv., Elson, Hist. of American Music, chaps. i-ii., Gould, Church Music in America, etc. The Musical Society of Stoughton, Mass., founded in 1786 and still existing, grew out of a local 'singing-school,' conducted from 1774 by Billings.

SINGLETON, ESTHER. See Register, 8.

SINSHEIMER, BERNARD (b. 1870). See Register, 7.

SITES, JOHN R. See COLLEGES, 3 (Willamette U., Ore.).

SKILTON, CHARLES SANFORD (Aug. 16, 1868, Northampton, Mass.), was educated at the Northampton High School and Yale, graduating in 1889. In that year he wrote music for the choral odes of 'Electra' for performance in Greek at Smith College.

After teaching languages in Newburgh, N. Y., in 1891 he went to Berlin for study with Bargiel, Boise and Heintz. In 1893–96 he was music-master at Salem Academy in North Carolina. He then studied further in New York with Buck and Shelley. In 1897 his violin-sonata in G minor was given a prize by the M. T. N. A. and performed by Dora Becker. In 1897–1903 he taught piano and theory at the State Normal School in Trenton, N. J., and then went to the University of Kansas at Lawrence, where he has been professor ever since. For twelve years he was also dean of Fine Arts, and he has been active as organizer and conductor. He is a fellow of the A. G. O. and has been dean of the Kansas Chapter, and is prominent in several teachers' associations, besides giving lectures and recitals. The fact that Haskell Institute, a government school for Indians, is near Lawrence led to his studying and collecting Indian music. In 1916 his 'Two Indian Dances,' originally written for a student-opera, were arranged for string-quartet and widely introduced by the Zoellner Quartet. As scored for orchestra they were also taken up by various orchestras, including the Queen's Hall Orchestra of London. In an organ-fantasy and sonata (1916) he has made some use of the whole-tone scale, and in his cantata 'The Witch's Daughter' (1917) he has given a serious musical treatment of the Salem Witchcraft, employing various modern devices. Besides the works named above he has a 'cello-sonata (1893), the cantata 'The Ballad of Carmilhan,' a Theme and Variations in E minor, for piano (1904), a Melody in B-flat, for organ (1913), besides other organ-pieces, 'Three Indian Scenes,' for string-quartet (1918), and 'Three Indian Sketches,' for piano (1919, Carl Fischer). He has also written a number of songs and choruses. His 'Witch's Daughter' was given in 1919 by the Pageant Choral Society and the Symphony Orchestra of St. Louis. [R.8]

SKINNER, ERNEST M., & COMPANY, of Boston, was organized in 1901 to employ the skill and genius of Ernest M. Skinner in organ-making. Under this or similar names it has continued to produce a highly significant series of instruments, many of the largest size, for important churches and institutions throughout the country, making a fine reputation for original and distinctive voicing, as well as for first-class construction. They have recently put forth an 'Orchestrator' which is adapted to the use of music-rolls with special success.

SKINNER, THOMAS. See TUNE-BOOKS, 1800.

SKINNER, T. STANLEY. See COLLEGES, 3 (Drury C., Mo.).

SKOVGAARD, AXEL (b. 1875). See Register, 9.

SLAVE–SONGS. See NEGRO MUSIC.

SLEEPER, HENRY DIKE (Oct. 9, 1865, Patten, Me.), had his general education at the Worcester Academy and Harvard College, and graduated from the Hartford Theological Seminary in 1891, with some post-graduate study. He took harmony and composition with B. D. Allen and Paine, organ with Hammond and Eddy, and singing with E. N. Anderson, F. W. Root and George Thorpe (London). After teaching at Beloit College in 1892–94, at Georgetown College in Kentucky in 1894–95, and at the University of Wisconsin in 1895–98, he went to Smith College in Massachusetts, where in 1904 he became head of the music-department, which under his hand has attained large proportions. He has also been church-organist in Worcester, Mass., Madison, Wis., and Hartford, Conn., and is a fellow of the A. G. O. He has always been efficient in promoting church-music, speaking and writing much on its behalf. In advancing the cause of academic credit for music-study he has also been increasingly active. He has written an orchestral Larghetto (given in popular concerts of the Boston Symphony Orchestra), an organ-suite in F minor, a choral 'Carmen Sæculare' (1904, Smith College), part-songs and songs, and has edited (in part) *The Common Order Choir-Book*, 1903, and the College Edition of *Hymns of Worship and Service*, 1909. While in college he edited *Songs of Harvard*, 1886, which was the first distinctively Harvard collection. [R.8]

'SLEEPY HOLLOW.' A three-act opera by Max Maretzek, produced in 1879 at the Academy of Music in New York.

SMITH, DAVID STANLEY (July 6, 1877, Toledo, O.), had academic training at the Toledo High School and Yale University, where he graduated in 1900, having had courses in composition with Parker. His first work in large form was an Overture in E-flat, op. 1, which was played at a students' concert in 1898. On graduating, his 'Ode for Commencement-Day,' op. 4, was given with baritone, men's chorus and orchestra. After a year at Yale as a post-graduate, he spent a year or more in London, Munich and Paris. In 1903 he received a Mus.B. from Yale, submitting as thesis a Prelude, Choral and Fugue for organ and orchestra, op. 10. In 1903 he began as instructor in the Yale School of Music, becoming assistant-professor in 1909, full professor in 1916, and in 1920 succeeding Parker as head of the School. In 1912 he had taken Parker's place as teacher and conductor of both the Symphony Orchestra and the Oratorio Society. In 1914 he gave lectures on music-history at the summer-session of the University of California. For many years he was also organist in New Haven churches, retiring in 1916, and since 1918 he has led the Choral Art Club. He is a fellow of the A. G. O., a member of the National Institute of Arts and Letters, and in 1918 Northwestern University made him Mus.D. The list of his more important compositions is as follows:

'Ouverture Joyeuse,' op. 11 (1904, Boston and New Haven).
Trio in G, op. 16 (Adamowski Trio, Boston and New Haven, and 1914, Berkeley, Cal.).
'Allegro Giocoso,' op. 17 (New Haven).
Quartet No. 1, in E minor, op. 19 (1912, Kneisel Quartet, Boston and elsewhere) (parts, Schirmer).
Symphonic Ballad, op. 24, for orchestra (St. Louis Orchestra and New Haven).
'The Fallen Star,' op. 26, for chorus and orchestra (Paderewski prize, 1909).
Symphony No. 1, in F minor, op. 28 (1912, Chicago Orchestra).
'The Djinns,' op. 30, for baritone, chorus and orchestra.
Overture, 'Prince Hal,' op. 31 (1912, New Haven, 1914, New York Symphony Society, and elsewhere).
An American opera in two acts, op. 36, text by Lee Wilson Dodd.
Quartet No. 2, in A, op. 37 (1915, Kneisel Quartet, 1918, Flonzaley Quartet), lately revised as op. 37b.
'Rhapsody of St. Bernard' ['Jesu, dulcis memoria'], op. 38, for soli, chorus, semichorus and orchestra (1918, Chicago North Shore Festival).
'Impressions,' op. 40, four pieces for orchestra.
Symphony No. 2, in D, op. 42 (1918, Norfolk Festival, and New York Philharmonic Society).
Other works are several groups of songs, such as opp. 15, 18 and 39; many anthems and part-songs, such as 'Pan,' op. 32, with oboe obbligato; a 'Tragic Prelude,' op. 41, for violin and piano; a Fantasy for piano and orchestra, op. 43; and a 'Sonata Pastorale,' op. 44, for oboe and piano.
[R.9]

SMITH, DE LOSS. See STATE UNIVERSITIES (Mont.).

SMITH, DEXTER (1839–1909). See Register, 5.

SMITH, ELLA MAY, née Dunning (b. 1860). See Register, 7.

SMITH, GERRIT (Dec. 11, 1859, Hagerstown, Md. : July 21, 1912, Darien, Conn.), studied at Hobart College, where he was for two years organist, going thence to Stuttgart to pursue music and architecture. From 1877 he studied organ with S. P. Warren and Eugene Thayer in New York, and piano with Sherwood, and, after a short term as organist in Buffalo, in 1880 was in Berlin under Haupt and Rohde. From 1885 till his death he was organist of the South (Reformed Dutch) Church in New York, where his choir and organ-recitals became noted. He also taught theory at the Master School in Brooklyn and for many years was music-director at Union Theological Seminary. He was a

founder of both the Manuscript Society and the A. G. O., first president of the one and first warden of the other, and active in music-teachers' associations. His chief work was the cantata 'King David,' but he also wrote various anthems, songs, piano-pieces, etc., and edited 25 *Song-Vignettes* for children. [R.6]

SMITH, IVY MAY. See COLLEGES, 3 (Atlantic Christian C., N. C.).

SMITH, LEO (b. 1881). See Register, 10.

SMITH, THOMAS MAX (b. 1874). See Register, 9.

SMITH, WILLIAM. See TUNE-BOOKS, 1798 and 1809.

SMITH, WILSON GEORGE (Aug. 19, 1855, Elyria, O.), from 1876 studied with Singer in Cincinnati and from 1880 with Moszkowski, Raif, the Scharwenkas, Kullak and Kiel in Berlin. Since 1882 he has been teacher and composer in Cleveland, from 1902 acting also as critic for the 'Press.' His compositions extend to op. 115, including some hundreds of pieces. He has been specially successful with technical works like 'Five-Minute Studies,' op. 53, 'Chromatic Studies,' op. 69, 'Thematic Octave-Studies,' op. 68, 'Transposition-Studies,' op. 70 (all Church), and 'Eight-Measure Studies,' 'Scale-Studies,' 'Preparatory Studies' (all Presser). Many of his songs have place in concert-programs, and he has been active in arranging and editing. Recent piano-works are 'Autumn Sketches,' op. 103, 'At the Bal Masque' (Fox), and 'Pictures of Child-Life' (Schirmer). [R.7]

SMITH COLLEGE, Northampton, Mass., though not belonging to the older group of women's colleges, has for some years been the largest of them. For that reason, and because emphasis upon music as an essential in general education was given from its foundation in 1875, it may be taken as an advanced type of its class. The development of its musical department has been almost wholly under the lead of two instructors, Benjamin C. Blodgett (1878–1903) and Henry Dike Sleeper (instructor from 1898, professor since 1904). The faculty numbers about 25. About 450 students take music-courses, those in praxis including piano, voice, organ, violin, harp, 'cello and one or two wind-instruments, while those in theory include all grades of composition, a variety of courses in appreciation and analysis, and extensive work in music-history. The students in theory-courses largely predominate. Since the College offers so large a public within itself, demonstrative music in the form of recitals and concerts has been developed to an extraordinary degree, including many symphonic and chamber-concerts, besides numerous solo reci-

O. G. SONNECK

tals. Work in music is credited for admission to the College, and towards graduation, just as other subjects. In praxis-courses two lessons per week with five hours of practice is counted for two hours' credit. In choosing her subjects of study a student may make music her 'major' or one of her 'minors.' Graduate-study in music is also encouraged. The choir of about 125 and the orchestra of 40 are important forms of ensemble-work. There is a considerable music-library, both of books about music and of musical literature, and the department owns many orchestral instruments, besides a harpsichord, a clavichord, a pianola, victrolas, etc. There are two buildings devoted to music-instruction. Besides 55 pianos, there are 4 organs, two of them of large size.

‡ SMYTH, ETHEL MAY (Apr. 23, 1858, London, England). See article in Vol. iv. 490-1. The four songs with orchestra were brought out at Queen's Hall in 1907 and often repeated in England, Paris and Germany, as also the chorus 'The Spirits of the Wood.' 'The Wreckers' was given in English in 1909, at the Afternoon Theater, in 1910 at Covent Garden, and in 1911 under Beecham. The two overtures to it are often given. In 1910 she was made Mus.D. by Durham University. Her latest opera, 'The Boatswain's Mate,' in two acts, on her own text (from Jacobs' story), and 'The Wreckers' were to have been given in Frankfort and Munich respectively in 1915, but were postponed by the war till 1920. She was a prominent suffrage agitator in 1911 and was imprisoned for two months in consequence. 'The March of the Women' and other suffrage-music date from this time. During the war she was in radio-work in France.

SNYDER, WILLIAM B. See TUNE-BOOKS, 1831.

SOCIETY FOR THE PUBLICATION OF AMERICAN MUSIC, THE, was organized in New York in 1919 for the issue of meritorious works and their distribution among its members and others. Its publishing-fund is derived from annual and life members. The selection of works is by a committee of eminent experts. At first attention will be given to chamber-music. The president is John Alden Carpenter and the secretary William B. Tuthill, 185 Madison Avenue.

SOHN, JOSEPH (b. 1867). See Register, 8.

SONNECK, OSCAR GEORGE THEODORE (Oct. 6, 1873, Jersey City, N. J.), was educated in Germany at the Frankfort Gymnasium and Heidelberg and Munich Universities (1893-97). He studied music-history with Sandberger, composition with M. E. Sachs, conducting at the Sondershausen Conservatory (1898), piano with Kwast and instrumentation with Knorr. In 1899 he was in Italy, then returning to America. In 1902-17 he was in charge of the Music-Division of the Library of Congress in Washington, where he transformed what had been a mere accumulation of copyright-material into one of the great music-libraries of the world, extending it in several special directions to extraordinary proportions. Since 1917 he has been with the house of G. Schirmer in New York, for whom since 1915 he has edited 'The Musical Quarterly.' His published compositions are several sets of highly original songs. But he is best known for his many and valuable books upon topics in musical history and criticism. These began as far back as 1897, when he issued a *Protest gegen den Symbolismus in der Musik*, but the main series is as follows: *Classification of Music and Literature of Music*, 1904 (revised, 1917), *Francis Hopkinson and James Lyon*, 1905, *Bibliography of Early Secular American Music*, 1905, *Early Concert-Life in America*, 1907, *Historical Report on 'The Star-Spangled Banner,' 'America,' 'Hail Columbia' and 'Yankee Doodle,'* 1909, *Critical History of 'The Star-Spangled Banner,'* 1914, *Catalogue of Opera-Librettos Printed before* 1800, 2 vols., 1914, *Early Opera in America*, 1915, *Catalogue of First Editions of Edward MacDowell*, 1917, *Catalogue of First Editions of Stephen C. Foster*, 1917, and *Suum Cuique* (essays), 1916. To the *I. M. G. Sammelbände* he contributed important studies, among them 'Francis Hopkinson, the First American Composer' (5. 119) and 'Early American Operas' (6. 428). He has also published two volumes of poetry, *Seufzer*, 1895, and *Eine Todtenmesse*, 1898. Besides his remarkable skill in investigation and the marshaling and presentation of historical data, he has shown notable enterprise and practical wisdom in promoting musical progress in numerous ways — as, for example, in the recent formation of the Society for the Publication of American Music and in furthering the issue of Krehbiel's long-delayed translation of Thayer's *Beethoven*. [R.8]

'SONS OF BALDUR, THE.' No. 6 of the 'Grove-Plays' of the San Francisco Bohemian Club, produced in 1908. The text is by Herman Scheffauer and the music by Arthur Weiss.

SORRENTINO, UMBERTO (b. 1889). See Register, 10.

SOULE, RALPH W. See COLLEGES, 3 (Tabor C., Iowa).

SOUSA, JOHN PHILIP (Nov. 6, 1854, Washington). See article in Vol. iv. 628. His father was Portuguese and his mother Bavarian, and both came to America in the early '40s, the former as a refugee because of revolutionary activity, the latter as a visitor.

They were married in Brooklyn, but soon moved to Washington. The son studied in 1864–67 with John Esputa, taking mostly violin, but also band-instruments, and from 1867, while playing in the Marine Band and in civilian orchestras, took up theory and composition with G. F. Benkert. From 1872 he led the orchestra at the Theatre Comique and played violin at Ford's Opera House. From 1874 he was leader or player in the Milton-Noble Comedy Company and in Morgan's Living Pictures Company. In 1876 he was under Offenbach in Philadelphia, writing for him the 'International Congress' fantasy (July 4, 1876). In 1876–79 he played at the Chestnut Street Theatre under Hassler and at the Arch Street Theatre under Zimmerman. He then became conductor of the Church Choir Company, writing for it his first comic opera, 'The Smugglers,' and of Mackey's Comedy Company, for which he wrote 'Our Flirtations.' After being in the Marine Band in 1880–92, he formed the Sousa Band, giving the first concert at Plainfield, N. J., on Sept. 26, 1892. With this he has made annual tours through the United States and Canada, besides four tours in Europe and one round the world. The Band has played at almost all the great Expositions, besides long engagements at various places. Its leader acquired the soubriquet of 'March King' in 1885 from a foreign journal. He has also been decorated by numerous crowned heads, academies and societies. In 1917 he became lieutenant in the Naval Reserve. His compositions make a long list, including 10 comic operas, 8 'suites,' the scenic 'Sheridan's Ride' and the symphonic 'Chariot-Race,' almost 100 marches, about 20 dances, about 50 songs, and several arrangements. [R.6]

SOUTHARD, LUCIEN H. (Feb. 4, 1827, Sharon, Vt. : Jan. 10, 1881, Augusta, Ga.), studied for a time at Trinity College in Hartford, whence, though expected to follow his father as physician, in 1846 he went to Boston in quest of music. In 1851–58 he was general supervisor there in the public schools. In 1858–60 he was in Norfolk, Va., leaving because of Northern sympathies. For a year he played an organ in Hartford, but enlisted in the Civil War and served in the Army of the Potomac as cavalry captain. He took part in many battles, was wounded early in 1865 and was then honorably discharged and returned to Boston. In 1868, when the Peabody Institute in Baltimore established its Conservatory, he was made its first director and the organizer of its orchestra, laying foundations on which from 1871 Hamerik built with more experience and brilliance. From 1871 he lived once more in Boston, moving in 1875 to Augusta. Between 1850

and 1870 he was steadily active in composition. He was notably successful with glees, churchmusic and organ-pieces. About 1855 he completed the opera 'The Scarlet Letter,' parts of which were sung at a 'convention' in that year. The score of this, loaned by his wife in New York, was lost. In January, 1858, another opera, 'Omano' (based on Beckford's 'Vathek,' Italian text by Manetta), was twice given in Boston in concert-form, with Lang as pianist and Adams as tenor. The score of this remained in his wife's hands. His publications included

Collection of Organ Voluntaries, 1849.
School Chimes, 1851; Union Glee Book, 1852; Haydn Collection of Church Music, 1851; Classical Chorus Book, 1853 — all edited with B. F. Baker — The Boquet, 1855, edited with G. W. Pratt; Vol. iii. of The Boston Melodeon, with E. H. Baker (first vols. by E. L. White, 1850); Lyra Catholica (masses, hymns and motets), 1866, with J. H. Willcox; The Offering, 1866.
A Course in Harmony, 320 pp., 1855.
Morning and Evening, 1865, for quartet-choirs.
Two masses (1867).
The Standard Singing School, 1868, a vocal method based on Garcia.
'Ave Maria' (1867?), Te Deum and Jubilate (1868), and the motets 'As the hart pants,' 'My heart doth find' and 'Praise waiteth for Thee' (1872).[1]   [R.4]

SOUTHGATE, CHARLES. See TUNE-BOOKS, 1800.

SOWERBY, LEO (May 1, 1895, Grand Rapids, Mich.), had all his formal training in Chicago under A. O. Anderson. He has taught theory at the American Conservatory, been organist at the South Congregational Church and served as critic for the 'Inter-Ocean.' In 1917 he enlisted in the Army and was made band-master of the Field Artillery, with rank of 2nd lieutenant. He first came into notice as composer through his violin-concerto in 1913 (all-American concert, Chicago Symphony Orchestra under Gunn). His works include the overture 'Comes Autumn-Time' (1918, New York Symphony Society) (Boston Music Co.); the orchestral suite 'Set of Four' (1918, Chicago Symphony Orchestra); the orchestral sketch 'The Sorrow of Mydath'; the orchestral 'Rhapsody on British Folk-Tunes'; a Serenade for strings (Berkshire Quartet); a piano-concerto and a 'cello concerto; sonatas for two violins and 'cello, for violin alone, for violin and piano, for piano and for organ; two suites for violin and piano; three chorale-preludes for organ; choruses a cappella; etc. [R.10]

SPAETH, SIGMUND (Apr. 10, 1885, Philadelphia), the son of parents both of whom had written or edited Lutheran church music, graduated from Haverford College in 1905

[1] Data for this notice were supplied by Mr. N. H. Allen, of Hartford.

and in 1910 took a Ph. D. at Princeton University, his thesis being on *Milton's Knowledge of Music* (published 1914). In Philadelphia he studied piano and violin, and at Princeton led the university choir, glee-club and orchestra. In 1910–12 he taught in Asheville, N. C., and has since lived in New York. In 1913 he was music-critic for 'Life,' in 1914–18 for the 'Mail,' and since 1919 for the 'Times,' besides writing for the Boston 'Transcript.' He has contributed many articles to magazines, prepared program-notes and made a specialty of translations of song-texts and opera-librettos. [R.10]

SPALDING, ALBERT (Aug. 15, 1888, Chicago), had early training on the violin in Italy, graduating from the Bologna Conservatory in 1902, besides later study of composition. In 1905, having continued violin under Lefort in Paris, he made his concert-début there, followed by many tours throughout Europe. He first appeared in America in 1908, with the New York Symphony Society. In 1917–19 he served in the Army as artillery observation-officer in France and Italy. Besides his eminence as a player, he has written two violin-concertos; a sonata for violin and piano; a suite for violin and piano (Carl Fischer) ; 'Etchings' (theme, variations and improvisation), for violin and piano; Theme and Variations for orchestra; four 'Serious Pieces' for piano; many violin-pieces (Schirmer, Hansen), including the popular 'Alabama'; and songs (Ditson). [R.9]

SPALDING, WALTER RAYMOND (May 22, 1865, Northampton, Mass.), the son of a clergyman, early became a choir-boy. At eleven he served more or less as organist, and soon took up study with S. B. Whitney and W. A. Locke (piano). From 1879 he was organist in his father's church. He graduated at Harvard in 1887, with honors in music, having taken various courses with Paine. A year of post-graduate study brought him an A.M. in music. As yet, however, he was equally interested in the classics and modern languages. In 1888–92 he taught languages at St. Mark's School in Southboro, Mass., but also had charge of the music there and in the village church. In 1892–95 he was in Paris with Guilmant and Widor and in Munich under Rheinberger and Thuille. In 1895 he became instructor in music at Harvard till 1900, also serving as organist at Christ Church in Cambridge and at Emmanuel Church in Boston. In 1903 he became assistant-professor at the University and in 1906 succeeded Paine as head of the music-division. Since 1895 he has also been music-instructor at Radcliffe College. He has been active in various committees for the promotion of music, including that on Army and Navy

Camp-Music during the war. He has published *Tonal Counterpoint*, 1904, and (with Arthur Foote) *Modern Harmony*, 1905, both widely used as text-books. To these is now added *Music, an Art and a Language*, 1920, a striking study in the field of appreciation. [R.7]

SPARGUR, JOHN MITCHELL (b. 1879). See Register, 8.

SPEAKS, OLEY (b. 1876). See Register, 8.

'SPECTRE BRIDEGROOM. THE.' An opera by William D. Armstrong, produced in St. Louis in 1899.

SPELMAN, TIMOTHY MATHER (b. 1891). See Register, 10.

SPENCER, ALLEN HERVEY (Oct. 30, 1870, Fairhaven, Vt.), studied piano in New York and Chicago with Sherwood and theory with Lutkin. Since 1892 he has been in the faculty of the American Conservatory in Chicago, and has given hundreds of piano-recitals in Chicago and elsewhere. His répertoire is comprehensive and his ability as interpreter unquestioned. He has published *Forty Lessons to a Teacher* and contributed many articles on piano-study to periodicals. [R.8]

SPENCER, ELEANOR (Nov. 30, 1890, Chicago), began public appearances as pianist at ten and then studied with Mason in New York, Bauer in Paris and Leschetizky in Vienna. In 1910 she gave her first recital in London. She has appeared with such orchestras as the Berlin Philharmonic, the Dresden Gewerbehaus, the Amsterdam Concertgebouw, the London Symphony, the Queen's Hall, the Brighton and the New York Philharmonic. Her first recital in America was in New York in 1913. Her tours have traversed Germany, Holland, England and the United States. [R.10]

SPENCER, S. P. See COLLEGES, 3 (Piedmont C., Ga.).

SPENCER, VERNON (b. 1875). See Register, 9.

SPICKER, MAX (Aug. 16, 1858, Königsberg, Germany : Oct. 15, 1912, New York), after training from Louis Köhler and Robert Schwalm, in 1877–79 studied at the Leipzig Conservatory with Reinecke, Wenzel, Paul and Richter, and then for three years conducted theater-orchestras in various German cities. In 1882 he came to New York as conductor of the Beethoven Männerchor. In 1888–95 he was director of the Brooklyn Conservatory, and in 1895 became teacher of harmony and counterpoint at the National Conservatory. In 1898–1910 he was also choir-master at Temple Emanu-El. For many years he was connected with the firm of G. Schirmer as reader, editing numerous works (among them 'The Messiah'). He composed

a suite for orchestra;] incidental music to
Schiller's 'Demetrius'; the cantata 'Der
Pilot,' for baritone, men's chorus and or-
chestra; choruses, church-music and songs.
He edited an *Anthology of Sacred Song*, 4
vols., an *Operatic Anthology*, 3 vols., *Aus aller
Herren Länder* (folk-songs arranged for men's
chorus); and *Synagogical Service*, 2 vols.
[R.7]

SPIELTER, HERMANN (b. 1860). See
Register, 8.

SPIERING, THEODORE (Sept. 5, 1871,
St. Louis), began violin-study with his father,
Ernst Spiering. In 1886–88 he was with
Schradieck in Cincinnati, followed by four
years with Joachim at the Berlin Hochschule.
On his return he became a member of the
Thomas Orchestra in Chicago, making his
début as soloist in February, 1893, with the
Schumann 'Phantasie.' He left the Orchestra in 1896, having three years previously
organized the Spiering Quartet. In twelve
seasons (1893–1905) this Quartet gave 400
concerts in the United States and Canada,
introducing many new works. His pedagogic
work in Chicago included association with
Godowsky at the Chicago Conservatory in
1898–99, the direction of the Spiering Violin
School in 1899–1902, and associate directorship of the Chicago Musical College in 1902–05.
Meanwhile he had been active as conductor,
with appearances in Chicago, the Spiering
Orchestra, and a May Festival tour in 1902.
In 1905 he removed to Berlin, making his
début in 1906 with the Philharmonic Orchestra and spending three years largely as
soloist, with tours in Germany, England
and Holland. For one season he was chief
violin-instructor at the Stern Conservatory.
In 1909 he returned to New York as concertmaster of the Philharmonic Society under
Mahler. In the spring of 1911 he substituted
during Mahler's illness, conducting 17 concerts.
In 1911–14 he again resided in Berlin, concertizing in Germany, Denmark and Switzerland, and conducting a series of symphony concerts (1912–14) with the Berlin Philharmonic and Blüthner Orchestras.
Novelties produced at these concerts were
symphonies by Dukas and Paul Gräner,
suites by Dohnanyi, Casella and Reger,
Kaun's overture 'Am Rhein,' Hadley's 'Culprit Fay,' and important works by Hausegger,
von Reznicek, Delius and others. He was
also musical adviser for the 'Neue Freie
Volksbühne.' Since 1914 he has lived in
New York, giving concerts, teaching, and
editing violin-works for Carl Fischer. His
published works are Five Songs, op. 1; six
Artist Studies for violin, op. 4, and five 'Impressions' for piano, op. 5. Violin-caprices,
a scherzo for string-quartet and songs are

still unpublished, as is also a treatise on
violin-study. [R.8]

SPRAGUE, ADELBERT WELLS (b.
1881). See STATE UNIVERSITIES (Me.).

SPRINGFIELD MUSIC FESTIVAL AS-
SOCIATION, THE, of Springfield, Mass.,
was started in 1889 as the Hampden County
Musical Association, the conductor till 1899
being George W. Chadwick. Another effort
under C. S. Cornell led to festival undertakings in 1901 and '02. In 1903 the present
Association was organized with John J.
Bishop as conductor, with increasingly successful festivals ever since. The chorus averages
about 350. Besides the standard oratorios,
there have been given works like Bruch's
'Arminius,' Chadwick's 'Phœnix Expirans,'
Franck's 'The Beatitudes,' Parker's 'Hora
Novissima,' Verdi's 'Aida' and Requiem,
and Wolf-Ferrari's 'La Vita Nuova.'

SPROSS, CHARLES GILBERT (Jan. 6,
1874, Poughkeepsie, N. Y.), as a youth
studied piano in Poughkeepsie with Adolph
Kuehn and composition with Helen J. Andrus,
continuing with Xaver Scharwenka and
Emil Gramm, and adding composition with
Lachmund. At seventeen he was organist
at St. Paul's in Poughkeepsie. Later he
played for eight years at the Second Presbyterian Church in Paterson, N. J., and five
years at the Rutgers Presbyterian Church
in New York. Since 1913 he has been organist of the First Presbyterian Church in
Poughkeepsie. As pianist and organist he
has appeared in concert throughout the
country. His services as accompanist have
been much in demand, and he has toured
with Mmes. Hempel, Garden, Destinn, Gadski,
Gluck, Case, Jomelli, Homer, Fremstad,
Melba, Schumann-Heink and Nielsen, also with
Ysaÿe, Gerardy and Amato. His published
works include three cantatas, 'The Word of
God,' 'The Glory of the Resurrection' and
'Christmas Dawn'; many anthems and
part-songs; a few piano- and violin-pieces;
and over 100 songs, many of them extensively
sung. [R.8]

SPRY, WALTER (Feb. 27, 1868, Chicago),
had early training in Chicago with Regina
Watson (piano) and Eddy (organ), and later
in Vienna with Leschetizky, in Berlin with
Rudorff and in Paris with Rousseau. In
1897–1900 he was director of the Quincy
(Ill.) Conservatory, in 1903–05 was Sherwood's
assistant, in 1900–03 also edited 'The Music
Review' for Summy, and in 1905–17 conducted
his own Piano School in Chicago. He is now
one of the leading piano-teachers at the
Columbia School of Music there. In 1918
he celebrated the twenty-fifth anniversary
of his first appearance in Chicago as pianist.
He has been soloist with the Chicago and

St. Louis Orchestras. He has written an overture, a string-quartet, piano-pieces, choruses
and songs. [R.8]

SQUIER, J. B. (1838–1912). See Register,
5.

‡ SQUIRE, WILLIAM BARCLAY (Oct.
16, 1855, London). See article in Vol. v. 667.
His *Catalogue of Old Printed Music [1487–1800]
in the British Museum*, 2 vols., 1912, is perhaps
his chief work, though his other books and
articles are all significant. He has repeatedly
contributed to 'The Musical Quarterly.'

STAHLBERG, FREDERICK (b. 1877).
See Register, 8.

STAIR, PATTY (Nov. 12, 1869, Cleveland),
was a pupil of Franklin Bassett. Since 1889
she has taught in the Cleveland Conservatory
and from 1892 also in the University School,
where and in various churches she has been
organist. In 1914 she was the first woman in
Ohio to become a fellow of the A. G. O. For
some years she has been active as conductor
of Women's Club choruses. She has become
known as the composer of many effective
songs, part-songs and choruses, and has also
written a three-act light opera, an operetta,
an Intermezzo for orchestra, some organ-
and piano-pieces, etc. [R.7]

STANBRIDGE, J. H. C. See TUNE-
BOOKS, 1844.

‡ STANFORD, CHARLES VILLIERS
(Sept. 30, 1852, Dublin, Ireland). See articles
in Vols. iv. 671–4, and v. 667. To the lists of
works may be added the 7th Symphony, op.
124; a piano-concerto in C minor, op. 126;
a string-quartet, op. 122; a piano-quartet,
op. 132; a clarinet-sonata, op. 129; an organ-
sonata; the operas 'The Critic' (from Sheridan) (1916) and 'The Traveling Companion';
incidental music to Parker's 'Drake' (1912);
and the cantatas 'Fairy Day' (1913) and
'Merlin and the Gleam' (1920). He has also
published *Studies and Manners*, 1908, *Musical
Composition*, 1911, *Pages from an Unwritten
Diary*, 1914, and (with Cecil Forsyth) a
History of Music, 1916.

STANLEY, ALBERT AUGUSTUS (May
25, 1851, Manville, R. I.), at sixteen was
already holding a responsible post as organist
in Providence. In 1871–75 he studied in
Leipzig under Papperitz, Reinecke, Richter
and Wenzel. During the last year he was
Richter's assistant and also occasional organist
at the Nikolai-Kirche. After a year of teaching at the Ohio Wesleyan College, in 1876–88
he was organist at Grace Church in Providence.
Since 1888 he has been professor at the University of Michigan and from 1893 conductor
of the May Festivals. In 1891–92 he was
secretary of the M. T. N. A. and in 1893
president; was a founder of the College of
Musicians, of the A. G. O. and of the Manu-

script Society; in 1899 was appointed American
representative of the I. M. G. and in 1906–12
president of its American Section, and is an
active member of the Musical Association of
Great Britain. In 1889 the University of
Michigan made him A. M. and in 1916 Northwestern University made him Mus.D. Besides his energetic development of the University School of Music, he has had charge of
the Stearns Collection of Musical Instruments,
given to the University in 1898, and of this he
has published an exhaustive and scholarly
Catalogue, 1918 (2nd edition in preparation).
His compositions include a Symphony in F,
an orchestral Scherzo in D, the symphonic
poem 'Attis,' a Suite in E for violin and piano,
a Canon and Fugue in E minor for piano,
the choral and orchestral works 'City of
Freedom,' 'A Psalm of Victory,' 'Chorus
Triumphalis,' 'Laus Deo' and 'Consecration
Hymn,' and incidental music to Mackaye's
'Sapho and Phaon,' to Euripides' 'Alcestis' and
'Menæchmi' — the last three employing Greek
motives and modes, and all with special
accompaniment simulating ancient instrumentation. All these have been given on
various civic or academic occasions. They are
now published as *Greek Themes in Modern
Musical Settings*, 1920, being Vols. xv. and xvi.
of the Humanistic Series of *University of Michigan Studies*. [R.5]

STANTON, EDMOND C. See Register, 7.

STARR, EDNA V. See COLLEGES, 3
(Rio Grande C., Ohio).

'STAR-SPANGLED BANNER, THE.'
See article in Vol. iv. 674–5, and also Sonneck,
Report on 'The Star-Spangled Banner,' etc.,
1909, and its enlarged reissue separately, 1914.

STASNY, KARL RICHARD (b. 1855).
See Register, 8.

STATE MUSIC TEACHERS' ASSO-
CIATIONS began to be formed in 1876, many
of them (after 1886) through the efforts of
the Music Teachers' National Association.
Some of them have been short-lived, but the
majority continue and are extremely serviceable
in bringing teachers into fellowship, in up-
holding professional standards and in advancing interest in American music and musicians.
At times the National and the State organizations have been knit together in some formal
way, but practical considerations prevent
close official union. In recent years the
State Associations have given increasing attention to problems of 'standardization' or
the fixing of rules and tests for professional
recognition. In several cases systems of
examination and certification have been set
up. The heads of all Teachers' Associations
are banded together in an Association of
Presidents and Past-Presidents.

In 1893 H. S. Perkins stated that the

2 B

earliest State Associations were those in Ohio (1876), Texas (1885), Illinois, Michigan, Kansas, Kentucky, Rhode Island, Alabama (1886), Indiana, Colorado (1887), New York (1889), Connecticut and New Hampshire (1890).[1]

The latest list of these Associations, with their presidents, is as follows:[2]

Arkansas, H. D. Tovey, Fayetteville; *California*, Mrs. Sofia N. Newstadt, 52 Hamilton Place, Oakland; *Connecticut*, Mariette N. Fitch, 48 Union St., Rockville; *Illinois*, C. E. Sindlinger, Streator; *Indiana*, Ralph Sloane, Richmond; *Iowa*, Henry Matlack, Grinnell; *Kansas*, Frank A. Beach, Normal School, Emporia; *Kentucky*, Anna C. Goff, Lexington; *Louisiana*, Florence Huberwald, 2024 Coliseum St., New Orleans; *Michigan*, Francis L. York, 1013 Woodward Ave., Detroit; *Minnesota*, George H. Fairclough, Pittsburgh Bldg., St. Paul; *Mississippi*, Mrs. E. H. Hart, Meridian; *Missouri*, Herbert Krumme, Moss Bldg., St. Joseph; *New York*, Frederick H. Haywood, Carnegie Hall, New York City; *Nebraska*, Henry C. Cox, 3320 Dewey Ave., Omaha; *North Carolina*, Mrs. Crosby Adams, Montreat; *North Dakota*, Mrs. Amy Simpson, Minot; *Ohio*, Katherine Bruot, 70 N. Prospect St., Akron; *Oklahoma*, Mrs. Mary E. Wharton-Hunt, Stillwater; *Oregon*, John C. Monteith, 525 Patten Rd., Portland; *Texas*, E. Clyde Whitlock, 1100 Hurley Ave., Fort Worth; *Vermont*, Lewis J. Hathaway, Middlebury; *Washington*, Herbert Kimbrough; Pullman; *Wisconsin*, Charles H. Mills, Madison.

STATE NORMAL SCHOOLS, MUSIC IN. In every State but one there are Normal Schools to train teachers for public-school work. The number in each State depends upon various considerations besides its size.[3] The total number in the whole country is about 180. In all these, with but trifling exceptions, some musical instruction is provided, but the amount and scope of it varies greatly. Many Schools are large (600–1000 students), while others are too small to have diversified curricula. On the whole, there is a difference between the East and the West. In New England, New York and the Southern States the number of music-instructors is rarely more than two or three, but in Indiana, Pa., there are 9, in Milwaukee 10, in Emporia, Kan., 13, in Mansfield, Pa., Valley City, N. D., and Greeley, Colo., 7, etc. Similarly, in the East and South the instruction is planned chiefly with reference to the training of the ordinary grade-teacher who teaches many other subjects than music, while in the West generally it provides also for the much more intensive training of supervisors. In many cases the western Schools are really music-schools, some of them open to other students besides those preparing for public-

[1] *Hist. of the M.T.N.A.*, pp. 87–8.

[2] *M.T.N.A. Proceedings*, 1919, p. 237.

[3] For example, Pennsylvania has 13, New York 10, Massachusetts, Wisconsin and Alabama 9 each, West Virginia and North Carolina 8 each, Virginia 7, Maine, Oklahoma and California 6 each, Illinois and Missouri 5 each, etc.

school teaching. Instruction in piano and violin (sometimes also organ) is rather common. Harmony is sometimes taught, and occasionally counterpoint and even orchestration. The number of pianos is sometimes notably large — Indiana, Pa., 38, Kutztown, Pa., 23, Mansfield, Pa., 20, Valley City, N. D., 20, Emporia, Kan., 19, Milwaukee, Bowling Green, Ky., Aberdeen, S. D., and Greeley, Colo., each 16, etc. Phonographs are nearly universal, some institutions having as many as ten. In a fair proportion of cases there is something of a musical library.

Besides the State Normal Schools there are other agencies for the special education of teachers. New York, Iowa and Colorado have State Teachers' Colleges, and many State Universities and other such complex institutions have Schools or Colleges of Education that aim at similar results. As a rule, however, music is not magnified in any of these, though students often have access to musical opportunities indirectly. Exceptional emphasis upon music is found in Teachers College in Columbia University, New York.

STATE UNIVERSITIES, MUSIC IN. The growth of the demand for 'public schools' in the early 19th century led naturally toward the development of 'state universities' as the culminating element in a system of free civic education. It is true that many 'colleges' founded before 1800 rested upon grants of public money and had been more or less governed by public authority. Some of them bore names as 'universities' of the States in which they were located. But the tendency of the 'college' system was to depend upon private or denominational endowment and to accent a single course of study, subject to fees for tuition. Beginning with the University of Michigan, founded in 1837, a new type rapidly became common, providing free tuition in many different lines and managed by boards of trustees responsible to the States as such. This new type naturally became characteristic of those sections of the country that were developed in the period of national expansion preceding the Civil War. Meanwhile, in the older sections, some of the 'colleges' were much enlarged in scope, so that several of them fulfilled for their respective States much of the function of a 'state university.'[1]

As public interest in music advanced, and the vocational opportunities connected with it became important, it was natural that gradually around or within the 'state universities' music-schools should spring up.

[1] Notable instances are Harvard (1636) in Massachusetts, Yale (1701) in Connecticut, Princeton (1746) in New Jersey, Columbia (1745) in New York, Brown (1764) in Rhode Island, Dartmouth (1769) in New Hampshire, Bowdoin (1794) in Maine, etc.

In many cases these were at first independent enterprises that were ultimately adopted into the university. In others they were started as departments like those in medicine, law, engineering, agriculture and the like. Recently such schools have often been combined with other departments into Schools or Colleges of Fine Arts. Although now generally reckoned as full members of the circle of departments, such Schools, owing to their use of individual rather than class methods in praxis-topics, have stood by themselves in requiring considerable tuition-fees, and there has been much hesitation about granting credit for work in praxis. Work in theory and history, however, has generally been credited, and often work of an ensemble-character, as in choruses or orchestras.

There are now nearly 100 institutions of higher education under State control. But about half of these are special in character, devoted to technology, industrial arts, mining, agriculture, etc. Some of the Agricultural Colleges have taken on a general and complex character, and a few of them have given special attention to music. These are therefore included in the present summary. But the State Teachers' Colleges are more naturally grouped with the State Normal Schools, as the State Women's Colleges are with Colleges for Women in general. In order to give some hint of the historical sequence, the institutions in the following condensed résumé are arranged more or less chronologically.

All the statements made in the article upon COLLEGES as to the general scope of instruction apply here, but with a few slight differences of emphasis. There is a somewhat greater prominence given to theoretical studies in several institutions, and some give no credit for praxis. In many of the institutions the aggregation of students is so large that choral and orchestral concerts command special attention, stimulating interest in organizations within the institution and making it possible to support visiting organizations. In many cases there is great attention given to military bands, notably at the University of Illinois. In most of the larger institutions the School of Music has separate buildings, often of importance, with large auditorium, organ, etc. Several of them have significant music-libraries.

The Universities of Michigan, Wisconsin, Illinois, Kansas, and Oklahoma stand out as those which have pushed music-departments into decided eminence. Several others, like Pennsylvania, Indiana, California and Colorado, have given prominence to thorough work in theory.

The total number of students in the State institutions where music is recognized is considerably over 100,000 each year, counting all departments. No doubt a fair proportion of this large number is affected in some way by the general activities of the School of Music, especially as these extend to public concerts. But in most cases the number of those actually taking serious courses in music is still extremely small. Two reasons for this are, first, that in the institutional system music is counted as belonging to the 'collegiate' or undergraduate division (hence not appealing to those in professional, technological or graduate divisions), and, second, that there are special fees required.[1] It is likely, however, that gradually the practical influence of music in university-life will decidedly increase. Thus far music has been emphasized chiefly for its use as an element of general culture or as a vocation. In a few cases steps have been taken to disclose its possibilities as a distinct object of scientific, historical and philosophical investigation.

In the following summary the same plan of statement is used as that in the article upon COLLEGES.

Founded before 1837

University of Pennsylvania, Philadelphia.
   Hugh A. Clarke (from 1875). No praxis.
Ohio University, Athens. See COLLEGES.
Miami University, Oxford, O.
   Aubrey W. Martin (from 1914) +2.
University of Alabama, University.
   Robert Lawrence (from 1917).
   [No music-courses at the Universities of Vermont, Maryland, Virginia, North Carolina, South Carolina and Georgia.]

Founded before 1861

University of Michigan, Ann Arbor.
   Albert A. Stanley (from 1888) +25. Calvin B. Cady, 1880–88.
Indiana University, Bloomington.
   Winfred B. Merrill (from 1919) +3. No credit for praxis. Charles D. Campbell, 1906–19.
University of Missouri, Columbia.
   William H. Pommer (from 1907) +1. No praxis.
State University of Iowa, Iowa City.
   Philip G. Clapp (from 1919) +8.
University of Wisconsin, Madison.
   Charles H. Mills (from 1914) +10. Fletcher A. Parker, 1880–1907, Rossetter G. Cole, 1907–09, Louis A. Coerne, 1910–14.
University of Minnesota, Minneapolis.
   Carlyle Scott (from 1904) +7. Emil Oberhoffer, 1902–04.
Louisiana State University, Baton Rouge.
   F. T. Guilbeau (from 1918).
University of California, Berkeley.
   Charles L. Seeger (from 1912) +4. No credit for praxis. J. Frederick Wolle, 1905–11.
University of Washington, Pullman.
   Irving M. Glen (from 1914) +7.
   [No music-courses at the University of Mississippi].

Founded before 1880

University of Nevada, Reno.
   Maude A. Denny (from 1913). No praxis.

[1] It is to be noted that recently the University of Illinois has inaugurated a plan whereby tuition in music shall be as free as that in any other subject.

University of Kentucky, Lexington.
  Carl A. Lampert. No praxis.
University of Wyoming, Laramie.
  Albert Lukken (from 1915) +6.
University of Illinois, Urbana.
  J. Lawrence Erb (from 1914) +10. Frederick
    Lawrence, 1901–08, Charles H. Mills, 1908–14.
West Virginia University, Morgantown.
  Louis Black +8. No credit for praxis.
University of Utah, Salt Lake City.
  Thomas Giles +6. No praxis.
University of Maine, Orono.
  Adelbert W. Sprague (from 1916).
University of Nebraska, Lincoln.
  Jacob Singer +1. No praxis, but courses credited
    under outside teachers.
Ohio State University, Columbus.
  No music-courses except in summer-school —
    William W. Campbell (from 1912).
University of Arkansas, Fayetteville.
  Henry D. Tovey (from 1908) +4.
University of Kansas, Lawrence.
  Harold L. Butler (from 1915) +4. George B.
    Penny, 1890–1903, Charles S. Skilton, 1903–15.
University of Oregon, Eugene.
  John J. Landsbury (from 1917) +11. Irving M.
    Glen, 1901–11, Ralph H. Lyman, 1913–17.
University of Colorado, Boulder.
  George M. Chadwick. No praxis. Charles H.
    Farnsworth, 1888–1900.

Founded before 1905

University of Texas, Austin.
  Frank L. Reed (from 1913) +4. No credit for praxis.
University of North Dakota, University.
  William W. Norton (from 1910) +3. No praxis,
    but courses credited under outside teachers.
University of South Dakota, Vermilion.
  Harry C. Harper (from 1918) +6. E. W. Gra-
    bill, 1900–17.
University of Arizona, Tucson.
  Ida W. Douglass. No credit for praxis.
University of Idaho, Moscow.
  Eugene E. Storer (from 1911) +3.
University of New Mexico, Albuquerque.
  Henry F. Perrin (from 1918).
University of Oklahoma, Norman.
  Fredrik Holmberg (from 1908) +12. Henry Gue-
    lich, 1903–08.
State University of Montana, Missoula.
  DeLoss Smith +5.
University of Florida, Gainesville.
  James W. Chapman.

State Colleges

Iowa State College, Ames.
  Archibold A. Bailey (from 1916) +2.
Pennsylvania State College, State College.
  Clarence C. Robinson +1.
Kansas State Agricultural College, Manhattan.
  Arthur E. Westbrook (from 1913) +8. Olof
    Valley, 1904–13.
North Dakota Agricultural College, Fargo.
  Clarence S. Putnam +1. No theory.
Montana State College, Bozeman.
  Aaron H. Currier (from 1915) +4.
Oklahoma Agricultural College, Stillwater.
  Bohumil Makovsky (from 1915) +6.

See various references in articles on COLLEGES
and PUBLIC SCHOOLS.

STEARNS, HENRY V. See COLLEGES, 2
(Illinois Woman's C.).

STEARNS COLLECTION OF MUSICAL

INSTRUMENTS, THE, at the University
of Michigan, Ann Arbor, was gathered by
Frederick Stearns (1831–1907), a chemist of
Detroit and the founder and for many years
head of an extensive pharmaceutical business there. The making of this collection
was a special enthusiasm with him from 1881
to 1897, though it was not the only line of
research to which he devoted effort and
generous expenditure. As with his other
collections, Mr. Stearns sought to make this
permanently useful by giving it to a public
institution. In 1898 it was offered to the
University and at once accepted. The donor
continued to add to it and provided funds
for its study and proper presentation.

The Collection contains over 1400 specimens, so selected as to give a fairly comprehensive view of the whole subject of
instrument-making, both in its intricate
ethnological variety and in its historical evolution as regards the implements of civilized
music. It has been minutely sifted, classified
and described by Albert A. Stanley, Director
of the University School of Music, and in 1918
he published under the University imprint
a monumental *Catalogue* of it, which not only
brings its contents within the easy ken of
intelligent students, but at the same time
sets up a standard of scientific classification
and nomenclature for the subject in general.
This volume of 260 pages has elaborate
indexes and frequent critical and historical
notes of unusual interest.

The arrangement adopted is analytic or
systematic rather than geographic or historical. Five classes are distinguished, according as sound-production arises (*a*) from
a solid body, like plates, bells, gongs, bars,
rods or tongues, (*b*) from a stretched mem-
brane, as in the various drums and tambour-
ines, (*c*) from a confined air-column, as in the
flutes, oboes, trumpets, etc., (*d*) from a
stretched string, as in harps, dulcimers, zithers,
lutes and viols, or (*e*) from either strings,
air-columns or reeds controlled or actuated
from a keyboard.

STEBBINS, GEORGE WARING (June
16, 1869, near Albion, N. Y.), was the son of
the singing evangelist, George C. Stebbins.
He studied in Brooklyn with H. E. Browne
and Woodman (organ), F. F. Powers (voice)
and Shelley (composition), with further work
in Paris under Sbriglia and Guilmant, and in
London under Henschel. Since 1893 he has
been organist in Brooklyn — at the Emmanuel
Baptist Church in 1894–99 and since 1902,
and at Plymouth Church in 1899–1902. He
was a founder of the A. G. O. and has appeared
often as recitalist. Since 1910 he has also
taught singing at the New York Teachers'
Training Institute, and from 1913 has con-

ducted the Singers' Club in New York and from 1916 the Long Island Musical Art Society. He has published many organ-pieces, anthems, choruses and songs. [R.8]

STECK, GEORGE (1829–1897). See Register, 4.

STECK, GEORGE, & CO., New York, is a piano-making business established in 1857 by George Steck. They secured high awards at the Vienna and Philadelphia Expositions of 1873 and 1876. The business is now a branch of the Æolian Company. Besides the New York factory there is another at Gotha, Germany.

STEERE, J. W., & SON ORGAN CO., THE, Springfield, Mass., was established in 1867, originally as Steere & Turner. In recent years, especially since Henry F. Van Wart came in 1911 as superintendent, they have produced many instruments of large size and notable excellence, among them those in Woolsey Hall at Yale University, in the Municipal Auditorium in Springfield, in the Piedmont Church in Worcester, and in the First Church, Scientist, in Kansas City.

STEFANO, SALVATORE DE (b. 1887). See Register, 10.

STEINBRECHER, FREDERIC W. (1818–?). See Register, 4.

STEINDEL, BRUNO (b. 1866). See Register, 8.

STEINER, LEWIS HENRY (1827– ?). See TUNE-BOOKS, 1859.

STEINERT, MORRIS (Mar. 9, 1831, Scheinfeld, Germany : Jan. 21, 1912, New Haven, Conn.), as a boy, while apprenticed to an optician, had lessons on the harpsichord from the village cantor and on the guitar from a chimney-sweep. Soon he began composing for orchestra, incidentally learning to play the 'cello. As vender of optical goods he traveled in Switzerland, Germany and Russia, and as dealer in hops visited France. About 1854 he came to America. In New York he joined Maretzek's opera-orchestra as 'cellist (Thomas being then one of the first violins), then traveled with a minstrel-troupe, and for a time worked in Savannah as clerk in a music-store and organist. The outbreak of the Civil War in 1861 led him to return to the North, where he finally settled in New Haven, at first on a salary of $100 per year. He taught, organized an orchestra, opened a music-store, and built up a prosperous business as dealer in pianos. He invented a form known as the 'Steinertone,' and more and more became interested in collecting rare and historic instruments. His collection of about 500 pieces he presented to Yale University in 1900, and endowed a prize in the School of Music in 1906, besides three scholarships. He was one of the founders in 1892 of the New

Haven Symphony Orchestra. In 1892 his collection was exhibited at the Vienna Exposition and in 1893 at the Columbian Exposition in Chicago. A handbook of it was published as *The M. Steinert Collection of Keyed and Stringed Instruments*, 1893. His name is also perpetuated in the piano-making firm M. Steinert's Sons & Co., of Boston. [R.4]

STEINWAY, HENRY ENGELHARDT (1797–1871). See Vol. iv. 691, and Register, 4.

STEINWAY & SONS, New York. See article in Vol. iv. 691–2, and references in Vol. iii. 729–32. Charles H. Steinway died in New York on Oct. 30, 1919.

STEPHENS, ALBERT JAMES (b. 1878). See COLLEGES, 3 (Fargo C., N. D.).

STERLING, ANTOINETTE (Jan. 23, 1850, Sterlingsville, N. Y. : Jan. 9, 1904, Hampstead, England). See article in Vol. iv. 693–4. During her residence in America in 1871–73 she was for a time soloist in Henry Ward Beecher's church in Brooklyn. Some songs written for and first sung by her became very popular, among them Sullivan's 'Lost Chord' (first sung at a Boosey Ballad concert, London, Jan. 31, 1877), Cowen's 'The Better Land,' Molloy's 'Darby and Joan' and Barnby's 'When the tide comes in.' [R.5]

STERLING, WINTHROP SMITH (Nov. 28, 1859, Cincinnati), graduated from the Cincinnati College of Music as gold medalist in 1883, and spent the next four years at the Leipzig Conservatory under Reinecke, Jadassohn and Zwintscher. He also studied there with R. Hoffman (composition) and Frau Unger-Haupt (voice), and in London with Turpin (organ), Shakespeare and Behnke (voice). In 1887–1903 he taught singing and composition at the Cincinnati College of Music, and was head of the organ-department. In 1903 he founded the Metropolitan College of Music, of which he is now dean. He has been organist in London and Cincinnati, gave organ-recitals at the Chicago, Buffalo and St. Louis World's Fairs and elsewhere, and has lectured on problems of singing and musical education. He has written a suite and an overture for orchestra, church-music, organ-and piano-pieces and songs. [R.7]

STERNBERG, CONSTANTIN IVANOVITCH, Edler von (July 9, 1852, Petrograd, Russia), when a boy, on Liszt's recommendation, became a pupil of Moscheles, Coccius and Richter at the Leipzig Conservatory. Later he studied with Kullak in Berlin, and made his début as pianist there in 1875, with encouragement from Rubinstein. He also served as chorus-master at the Stadt-Theater and as conductor at Brühl's, at Würzburg and Kissingen in the summers, and at the court-opera in Neu-Strelitz. In 1875–77 he was court-pianist at Schwerin and head of the Academy Music School. In 1875 and '77 he had lessons from Liszt. In 1877–78 he toured with the singer Mme. Désirée Artôt through Europe, Russia, Siberia, Asia Minor and Egypt. In 1880 he came to America on a concert-tour, and for six years after, at first alone, then with Wilhelmj and Minnie Hauk. In 1886 he became a citizen and settled first in Atlanta, removing in 1890 to Philadelphia, where he established the Sternberg School of Music, which he still directs. Most of his more than 100 works are for the piano. Many of them have been often played by Hofmann, Godowsky, Mme. Bloomfield-Zeisler and others. The 'Humoresque,' op. 26, the five Concert-Études, the 'Impromptu' and 'Caprice Hyppique' (Peters), the 'Nuit Arabe,' 'En Bohème' and the three ' Préludes,' op. 106, he regards as most characteristic. He has also written six piano-trios, and many choral works and songs. Besides frequent articles in magazines, he has published *The Ethics and Esthetics of Piano-Playing*, 1917. [R.7]

STEVENS, ROBERT W. See COLLEGES, 3 (U. of Chicago, Ill.).

STEVENSON, EDWARD IRENÆUS (b. 1868). See Register, 7.

STEVENSON, FREDERICK (Sept. 16, 1845, Newark, England), graduated at St. John's College in Sussex in 1866. In 1867–74 he was organist in Forest Hill and in 1874–82 in Blackheath, pursuing composition with Macfarren and J. F. Bridge and composing many works, including 'Cyrus,' besides conducting choral societies and teaching at the Blackheath Conservatory. In 1883 he became precentor at St. John's Cathedral in Denver, where, with Walter E. Hall, he developed choir-services of special excellence. Later he was at St. Mark's and the Synagogue, directed the Denver Conservatory and led the Concert Choir. From 1894 he was in Los Angeles as organist, conductor and composer. In 1905–18 he was specially engaged there and in Santa Barbara in developing his conception of modern harmony, and since 1918 has resumed teaching at Los Angeles. He has composed a large number of sacred solos with organ accompaniment (or other instruments), various anthems and part-songs, and the choral works 'Easter Eve and Morn,' 'Omnipotence,' 'Christmas Bells,' 'The Angel Gabriel,' etc. (Ditson, Church). He has also written somewhat for orchestra and chamber-instruments. [R.7]

STEWART, HUMPHREY JOHN (May 22, 1856, London, England), began at eleven as chorister and organist. He played in various London churches until 1886, when he came to San Francisco as organist of the Church of the Advent, going later to Trinity Church and the First Unitarian Church. In 1901, after giving recitals at the Buffalo Exposition, he went to Trinity Church in Boston, but after two years returned to San Francisco, this time at St. Dominic's. In 1915 he became official organist of the Exposition at San Diego, and still continues playing daily on the open-air organ at Balboa Park. It is interesting that the annual series of 250 to 300 recitals on this instrument, the first outdoor organ in the world, have been interrupted less than thirty times in five years by unfavorable weather. In 1919 the programs included 2270 selections from 385 composers. These recitals have established his reputation as a player of great ability and wide sympathy. As conductor he has been identified with various choral and orchestral organizations, notably the Handel and Haydn Choral Society of San Francisco. His oratorio 'The Nativity' (1888, Church) has had performances throughout the country. A romantic opera, 'Bluff King Hal' (1889), and two comic operas, 'His Majesty' (1890) and 'The Conspirators' (1900), have been performed, and he has also written the music for three of the 'Grove-Plays' of San Francisco Bohemian Club, 'Montezuma' (1903), 'The Cremation of Care' (1906), and 'Gold' (1916). He has composed the orchestral suites 'Montezuma' (1903) and 'Scenes in California' (1906), three masses, incidental music to several plays, songs, choruses, piano-, organ- and violin-music. The gold medal of the A. G. O. was awarded in 1899 for his anthem 'I beheld, and lo !'; and in 1907 he won prizes from the Chicago Madrigal Club and the Pittsburgh Male Chorus for other choral works. He is a founder of the A. G. O., an honorary life-member of the Bohemian Club, and has been or is president of several musical organizations. In 1898 the University of the Pacific made him Mus.D. [R.7]

STEWART, JAMES. See Register, 3.

STICKNEY, JOHN (1744–1827). See TUNE-BOOKS, 1774.

STIEFF, CHARLES M. (1805–1862). See Register, 4.

STIEFF, CHARLES M., is the firm-name of the piano-making business established in Baltimore by Charles M. Stieff in 1842 and steadily developed by his son, Frederick P. Stieff and two grandsons. Since before 1890 Herman Keuchen has been their chief designer, and his skill has done much to forward their reputation as leading makers.

STOCK, FREDERICK AUGUST [Friedrich Wilhelm August] (Nov. 11, 1872, Jülich, Germany), had early training from his father, a well-known band-master and composer of military music. In 1886–90 he studied at the

Cologne Conservatory under Wüllner, Japha, Humperdinck, Gustav Jensen and Gustav Holländer, becoming proficient in violin and composition. On his graduation with highest honors he was chosen from over fifty competitors as a first violinist in the famous Municipal Orchestra. In 1895, having met Thomas in Cologne, he came to the Chicago Orchestra. In 1901–05 he was assistant-conductor and in 1905 Thomas' successor. In 1918–19 he was temporarily withdrawn, awaiting completion of his American citizenship. In 1920 he added to his duties the care of the Civic Music Student Orchestra. His compositions include:

Symphony No. 1, in C minor (1910).
Symphony No. 2, in E-flat (1915, not yet given).
Symphonic Variations, in B minor (1904).
Symphonic Poem, 'Life,' in E-flat, in memory of Theodore Thomas (1905).
Overture, 'Life's Springtide,' in A (1912, given in 1913).
Overture, 'To a Romantic Comedy,' in D (1917, given in 1918).
Overture, 'Nature,' in D (not yet given).
Four Symphonic Sketches, 'The Seasons' (1911, given in 1912, Berlin).
Symphonic Waltz in D (1907, given at Winona Lake).
Improvisation and Wedding Music (1907, Pittsburgh).
Concerto in D minor, for violin (1915, Norfolk Festival, Zimbalist).
Festival March and 'Hymn to Liberty,' for 20th anniversary of the Chicago Orchestra (1910).
March and 'Hymn to Democracy,' in E-flat (1919).
Quartet in C minor, op. 6, for strings.
Quintet in B-flat minor, op. 8, for strings.
Sextet in F, op. 3, for strings.
Also songs, violin- and piano-pieces, and many orchestral arrangements.   [R.8]

STOCKER, STELLA, née Prince (Apr. 3, 1858, Jacksonville, Ill.), graduated at the University of Michigan, spent a year at Wellesley College and was later at the Sorbonne in Paris. She began music at the Jacksonville Conservatory, studied piano with Frau, Gliemann in Dresden and Xaver Scharwenka in Berlin, singing with Sbriglia in Paris (1910–13), and counterpoint and composition with Klein in New York. Being much attracted by the music of the Indians, she has lived among them, becoming a member of one of the Ojibway tribes, with the name 'O-mes-qua-wi-gi-shi-go-que' ('Red-Sky-Lady'). In her compositions Indian melodies appear without change, especially in the choruses of her plays. She has lectured on Indian music and legends in America and abroad. 'Sieur du Lhut,' a play in four acts, and 'The Marvels of Manabush,' an Indian pantomime in three acts, make liberal use of Indian themes. Earlier and more conventional works are the operettas 'Beulah, Queen of Hearts,' 'Ganymede' and 'Raoul,' besides pieces for piano. She is an active member of the New York and Chicago Manuscript Societies. [R.7]

STOCKHOFF, WALTER WILLIAM (Nov. 12, 1887, St. Louis), who is entirely self-taught in music, has been teaching in St. Louis since 1904. His published works include, for the piano, a Sonata, 'in contemplation of the Nations at War'; 'In the Mountains,' a set of seven impressions; a Lullaby; and twelve 'Quodlibets' (all Breitkopf); and also three piano-trios. He has in manuscript works for orchestra, piano and voice, and further chamber-music. His writing has been thus highly praised by Busoni: 'In the hands of an intelligent virtuoso, a sympathetic interpreter, the seven 'Impressions' will create a rich, brilliant and most fascinating effect.' [R.9]

STODART, ROBERT. See Register, 3.

STOECKEL, CARL (b. 1858). See Register, 8.

STOECKEL, GUSTAV JACOB (1819–1907). See Register, 4.

STOESSEL, ALBERT FREDERIC (Oct. 11, 1894, St. Louis), after preliminary education in St. Louis, became a pupil of Hess and Wirth at the Berlin Hochschule. His début as violinist was made there with the Blüthner Orchestra, and in America with the St. Louis Orchestra in 1915. In Berlin he was a member of the Willy Hess String-Quartet and was associated with leading artists in concert-work. After service in the U. S. Army he resumed concert-work in 1919. He has composed a string-quartet in D (1914, Berlin), a string-quintet in C minor (1915, Amsterdam), violin-pieces, and songs. [R.10]

STOEVING, CARL HEINRICH PAUL (May 7, 1861, Leipzig, Germany), after general training at the Gymnasium, had three years at the Leipzig Conservatory, with Schradieck as his chief teacher, followed by work with Léonard in Paris. In 1881–82 he taught violin at the Königsberg Conservatory, and in 1882–83 was concertmaster of a symphony-orchestra in Hamburg. After a concert-tour in Russia and Scandinavia, in 1884 he came to the United States and toured extensively, part of the time with the Mendelssohn Quintette Club. From 1896 he was in London, at first largely in concert-work, but from 1898 as teacher at the Guildhall School of Music and from 1907 at the Trinity School of Music. His *The Art of Violin-Bowing*, 1902, went to many editions in both English and German and made him known as an authority. He then added *The Story of the Violin*, 1905, an ingenious blending of history and romance that has become a classic, and, more recently, *Elements of Violin-Playing* and a *Key to Sevčik's Works*,

1914. He has also written stories and novelettes, with the violin as center of interest, for English and American magazines (also in book-form in German). In 1914 he returned to America, dividing his time as teacher between New York and the New Haven School of Music, of which he was director in 1914-18. He has published 'Lyric Pieces,' op. 1, 'Summer Idyls,' op. 2, 'At the Fountain,' op. 4, an Album-Leaf and Concert-Étude, op. 6, and a 'Danish Dance,' op. 8, all for violin and piano. He has also written a string-quartet, four pieces for string-orchestra, a violin-concerto in one movement, a Capriccio for four violins, a prize Romance for violin and orchestra, two song-cycles, etc. In manuscript he also has further literary works. [R.7]

STOJOWSKI, SIGISMOND DENIS ANTOINE (Apr. 8, 1870, Strzelce, Poland), the son of a Polish noble, had his early education in the Cracow Lyceum and under Zelenski at the Conservatory, graduating in 1887. As a child he played in the salon of Princess Czatoryska, once a pupil of Chopin, and in 1883 appeared with orchestra, playing Beethoven's C minor concerto with an original cadenza. In 1887-89 he studied at the Sorbonne in Paris and at the Conservatory under Diémer, Dubois and Delibes, graduating in 1889 with honors in piano and counterpoint, and then continuing under the guidance of Gorski and Paderewski. In 1891 he gave a concert in the Salle Érard with the Colonne Orchestra with an original program, including his piano-concerto in F-sharp minor and an orchestral Ballade. An orchestral suite from this period which attracted Tchaikovsky's interest was later given by Von Bülow in Hamburg and by Hallé in Manchester. After some years of life in Paris, with many concert-tours, in 1905-11 he was head of the piano-department of the Institute of Musical Art in New York and in 1911-17 at the Von Ende School, often returning to Europe for concerts — notably in 1913, when he gave his 2nd Concerto in London with Nikisch. He has played often with leading orchestras in America, and in 1912 gave a notable series of historical concerts in New York. During the war and since he has been specially active on behalf of Poland. As a teacher he is the authorized exponent of Paderewski's methods, and counts among his pupils players like Novaës, Levitzky, Arthur Loesser and Elenore Altman. In 1918 he married his former pupil, Luisa Morales-Machedo of Lima. His compositions include (all for piano except as noted)

Two 'Pensées Musicales,' op. 1 (Schott).
Deux Caprices, op. 2 (Augener).
Concerto in F-sharp minor, op. 3, for piano and orchestra (Augener).

Trois Intermèdes, op. 4 (Schott).
Quatre Morceaux, op. 5 (Schott).
Variations and Fugue, op. 6, for string-quartet.
Cantata, 'Le Printemps,' after Horace, op. 7, for chorus and orchestra (Novello, given at Buckingham Palace).
Three Piano-Pieces, op. 8 (Schott).
Suite in E-flat, op. 9, for orchestra (Schott).
'Deux Orientales,' op. 10 (Schott).
Five Songs, poems by Asnyk, op. 11 (Schott).
'Danses Humoresques,' op. 12 (Augener).
Sonata in G, op. 13, for violin and piano (Schott).
Three Piano-Pieces, op. 15 (Schott).
Deux Caprices, op. 16 (Schott).
Sonata in A, op. 18, for 'cello and piano (Schott).
'Cinq Miniatures,' op. 19 (Heugel).
Romanza, op. 20, for violin and orchestra (Peters).
Symphony in D minor, op. 21 (Peters, also for piano, four hands).
Concerto in G minor, op. 22, for violin and orchestra (Schmidt).
Symphonic Rhapsody, op. 23, for piano and orchestra (Peters).
Five 'Polish Idyls,' op. 24 (Peters).
Five 'Romantic Pieces,' op. 25 (Peters).
Four Piano-Pieces, op. 26 (Peters).
Fantaisie, op. 27, for trombone and piano (1905, for Paris Conservatory competition) (Evette).
Deux Mazurkas, op. 28 (Schmidt).
'Aus Sturm und Stille,' op. 29, six pieces (Peters).
'Trois Esquisses,' op. 30 (Schmidt).
Concerto in D, op. 31, for 'cello and orchestra (Heugel).
Concerto — Prologue, Scherzo, Variations, op. 32, for piano and orchestra (Heugel).
Six Songs, poems by Tetmajer, op. 33 (Heugel).
Trois Études de Concert, op. 35 (Heugel).
Four 'Poëmes d'Été,' op. 36 (Schirmer).
Sonata in E, op. 37, for violin and piano (Heugel).
Fantaisie, op. 38 (Heugel).
Five 'Aspirations,' op. 39 (Heugel).
'A Prayer for Poland,' op. 40, for chorus, organ and orchestra (Schirmer).
Other piano-pieces and songs, without opus-no. (Schott, Heugel).

Among unpublished works are an unfinished 2nd Symphony, a Ballade and Scherzo for orchestra, a Concerto in F minor for piano, a piano-quintet (unfinished), etc. [R.9]

STOKOWSKI, LEOPOLD ANTON STANISLAW (Apr. 18, 1882, London, England), was of Polish parentage. His early education was in England, France and Germany, and included violin, piano and organ. In 1905-08 he was organist at St. Bartholomew's in New York. After a year in Europe as guest-conductor, in 1909-12 he was conductor of the Cincinnati Orchestra, going thence in 1912 to be leader of the Philadelphia Orchestra. He holds a Mus.B. from Oxford and a Mus.D. from the University of Pennsylvania (1917). In 1911 he married the pianist Olga Samaroff. Among large works introduced by him in America are Mahler's 8th Symphony and his cycle 'Das Lied von der Erde,' Rabaud's 2nd Symphony and Schönberg's 'Chamber Symphony.' He has also been active in bringing out works by American composers (see PHILADELPHIA OR-

CHESTRA). His rise into prominence as an orchestral conductor of the first class has been extremely striking. [R.9]

STOLZ, PAUL G. See COLLEGES, 3 (Bucknell U., Pa.).

STONE, JOSEPH. See Register, 2, and TUNE-BOOKS, 1793.

STORER, EUGENE HAMILTON. See STATE UNIVERSITIES (Ida.).

STORER, MARIA (d. 1795). See Register, 1.

STOUGHTON MUSICAL SOCIETY, THE, of Stoughton, Mass., was organized in 1786 as a men's chorus. It grew out of a singing-school conducted by Billings. Though not the first musical organization in the United States, it occupies a unique place because of its unbroken history to the present as an active choral society. It is now a large mixed chorus. It issued the *Stoughton Collection*, 1828, and another compilation under similar name in 1878, the latter valuable because preserving old pieces of 'psalmody.'

STRAKOSCH, MAURICE (1825, Lemberg, Galicia : Oct. 9, 1887, Paris). See article in Vol. iv. 713. In January, 1857, he managed his first season of Italian opera in New York. In 1859 he took his company to Chicago for a series of performances. He wrote the operas 'Sardanapalus' and 'Giovanna di Napoli' (given in New York), some piano-pieces and the books *Souvenirs d'un Impresario*, 1887, and *Ten Commandments of Music for the Perfection of the Voice*, 1896. [R.4]

STRAKOSCH, MAX (1834–1892). See note in Vol. iv. 713, and Register, 4.

STRANSKY, JOSEF (Sept. 9, 1874, Hupoleč, Bohemia), was originally trained in medicine at the universities of Prague, Vienna and Leipzig, but also studied music under Lostak, Fibich and Dvořák in Prague and with Fuchs and Bruckner in Vienna. After his graduation in 1896 he turned to a musical career. In 1898–1900 he was conductor at the German National-Theater in Prague and in 1900–09 at the Hamburg Opera, with many engagements elsewhere in opera and concert. In 1909–10 he led the Blüthner Orchestra in Berlin and was chief conductor of the Wagner Concerts at the New Opera. In 1910–11 he was in charge of symphony-concerts in Dresden, besides further activity as guest-conductor. In 1911 he became Mahler's successor as conductor of the New York Philharmonic Society, where he introduced important reforms in the orchestra. He has written two operas ('Der General' often given in Hamburg), a Symphonic Suite (given in Dresden and Berlin), various songs (Schuberth, Simrock), and arrangements of Berlioz' 'Béatrice et Bénédict' and of Gluck's 'Paride ed Elena.' [R.10]

‡STRAUSS, RICHARD (June 11, 1864, Munich, Germany). See article in Vol. iv. 717–20, and note in v. 668. His further operas are 'Der Rosenkavalier' (1911, Dresden, 1913, New York), 'Ariadne auf Naxos' (1912, Stuttgart, and, revised, 1916, Berlin) and 'Die Frau ohne Schatten' (1919, Vienna), besides the ballet 'Josefs-Legende' (1914, Paris). He has also produced the elaborate 'Alpensymphonie' (1915, Berlin, 1916, Philadelphia, Cincinnati, New York). The latter is a fresh illustration of his technical mastery. See bibliography in Baker, *Dict. of Musicians*, pp. 921–2.

STRICKLAND, LILY TERESA (b. 1887). See Register, 9.

STRONG, EDWARD (b. 1870). See COLLEGES, 3 (Carleton C., Minn.).

STRONG, GEORGE TEMPLETON (May 26, 1856, New York). See article in Vol. iv. 728–9. His Symphony 'In the Mountains' was given in New York on Nov. 24, 1887, and the 'Sintram' Symphony on Apr. 12, 1892. The following works should be added:

'Märchen' — 'Gestrebt,' 'Gewonnen,' 'Geschei-tert,' op. 12, for violin and orchestra.
Tonstück for English horn and organ.
'Knights and Naiads,' for soli, chorus and orchestra.
Symphonic Idyl, 'An der Nixenquelle,' for two pianos.
Symphony No. 3, 'An der See.'
Four Pieces — 'At Sunset,' 'Peasants' Battle-March, 'In the Old Forest,' 'The Awakening of the Forest-Spirits,' for orchestra.

His humorous trio for violins and viola, 'A Village Music-Director,' was first given in America by the Flonzaley Quartet in 1917. [R.6]

STRONG, SUSAN (b. 1875?). See Register, 8.

STRUBE, GUSTAV (Mar. 3, 1867, Ballenstedt, Germany), had his first lessons from his father, and entered the Leipzig Conservatory in 1884, studying violin with Brodsky and Herrmann, piano with Reckendorf, and harmony and composition with Jadassohn and Reinecke. In 1890 he came as a first violinist to the Boston Symphony Orchestra, continuing till 1913. During this period he wrote three overtures, two symphonies, two violin-concertos, a string-quartet, two symphonic poems with viola obbligato, a 'cello-concerto, a Rhapsody for orchestra, a cantata for men's chorus and orchestra, a Rhapsody for chorus and orchestra, and many violin-pieces. For twelve years he was one of the conductors of the Popular Concerts, and for six years led the orchestral numbers at the Worcester Festivals. Since 1913 he has taught harmony, counterpoint and composition at the Peabody Conservatory in Baltimore, and since 1916 he has been conductor of the Baltimore Symphony Orchestra. Important pieces since 1913 are Variations for orchestra, the three-act American opera 'Ramona,' a sonata for violin and piano, a violin-concerto, a sonata for viola and piano, and two symphonic poems for orchestra. [R.8]

STUDEBAKER HALL, in Chicago, in the Fine Arts Building, was opened in 1895. It has always been a headquarters for concerts and from 1899 was long used for opera in English and other opera-performances. See Upton, *Musical Memories*, pp. 312–6.

STURANI, GIUSEPPE. See Register, 9.

SUCHER, F. J. See COLLEGES, 3(Eureka C., Ill.).

SULLY, MRS. See Register, 2.

SURETTE, THOMAS WHITNEY (Sept. 7, 1862, Concord, Mass.), graduated from Harvard in 1891, studying piano with Foote and theory with Paine. In 1883–93 he was organist at Concord, in 1893–94 music-master at the Hill School in Pottstown, Pa., and in 1895–96 organist at Christ Church in Baltimore. From 1895 he took up lecturing on music both under the American Society for the Extension of University Teaching and (since 1909) also on the extension-staff of Oxford University. His activity in this field has been extensive in America and England, and he has prepared useful syllabi of music-history. He has also published *The Appreciation of Music*, 1907, with D. G. Mason, *The Development of Symphonic Music*, 1915, *Music and Life*, 1917, and many articles. His compositions include the operetta 'Priscilla, or the Pilgrim's Proxy,' the dramatic ballad 'The Eve of St. Agnes,' for soli, chorus and orchestra (1898), the romantic opera 'Cascabel' (1899), anthems and instrumental pieces. [R.7]

SUTRO, FLORENCE EDITH, née Clinton (1865–1906). See Register, 7.

SUTRO, ROSE LAURA (b. 1870) and OTTILIE (b. 1872). See Register, 8.

SVEČENSKI, LOUIS (b. 1862). See Register, 7.

‡SVENDSEN, JOHAN SEVERIN (Sept. 30, 1840, Christiania, Sweden : June 14, 1911, Copenhagen, Denmark). See article in Vol. iv. 758–9. From 1896 he also conducted at the Royal Theater in Copenhagen. In 1908 he retired from active service.

SWAN, TIMOTHY (1758–1842). See Register, 2, and TUNE-BOOKS, 1785.

SWARTHOUT, MAX VAN LEWEN (b. 1880). See Register, 9.

SWEENEY, GEORGE C. See TUNE-BOOKS, 1810.

SWEETSER, JOSEPH EMERSON (1825–1873). See TUNE-BOOKS, 1849.

SWEETZER, BENJAMIN, JR. See TUNE-BOOKS, 1839.

SWIFT, SAMUEL (Jan. 19, 1873, Newark, N. J. : July 21, 1914, New York), graduated from the University of Pennsylvania in 1894, having also studied at the Philadelphia Musical Academy and been organist in 1891–93 at churches in Wilmington, Del. In 1894–1907 he was critic for the New York 'Evening Mail,' in 1900 going abroad as correspondent. In 1907–09 he was on the staff of the 'Tribune' and from 1909 on that of the 'Sun.' He was one of the founders of the New Music Society and a member of the MacDowell Club and other organizations. [R.8]

SYMPHONY HALL, in Boston, was built in 1899, especially to provide a headquarters for the Boston Symphony Orchestra. One of its leading founders was Maj. Henry L. Higginson, the patron of the orchestra. See cut in Vol. i. 368.

SYMPHONY SOCIETY OF NEW YORK, THE. See article in Vol. iv. 805. In 1914 Henry H. Flagler assumed responsibility for the financial support of the orchestra. In 1920 Mr. Damrosch took the orchestra to Europe for a tour of several weeks in France, Italy, the Low Countries and England. Among the novelties introduced have been Elgar's 2nd Symphony (1911), Sibelius' 4th Symphony, Fanelli's 'Tableaux Symphoniques' and Elgar's 'Falstaff' (1913), Kolar's Symphonic Suite and Ravel's 'Daphnis et Chloë' (1914), Delius' 'Summer Night on the River' and 'On Hearing the First Cuckoo,' and Damrosch's music for 'Iphigenia in Aulis,' 'Medea' and 'Electra' (1915, the last three repeated in 1918), and Griffes' 'Poem' for flute and orchestra (1919). In several seasons about 1910 series of Beethoven concerts were a feature. In 1908 a new-found Trio of his for harpsichord, flute and bassoon was brought out.

SZUMOWSKA, ANTOINETTE (Feb. 22, 1868, Lublin, Poland), had her general education in Warsaw and studied piano with Strobl and Michalowski there. In 1890–95 she was with Paderewski in Paris. In 1891 she appeared at the Salle Érard, in 1892 many times in England, and in 1893 toured again there and in Russia and Poland. In 1895 she came to America, playing with the Boston Symphony, New York Symphony and Thomas Orchestras. In 1896 she married the 'cellist Joseph Adamowski, and, with him and his brother, formed the Adamowski Trio. During the war she devoted herself largely to work as president of the Friends of Poland. [R.8]

T

TALBOT, HOWARD (b. 1865). See Register, 8.

TALBOT, THOMAS R. (b. 1884). See Register, 10.

TAMARO, JOSEF (1824–1902). See Register, 6.

‡ TANIEIEV, SERGEI IVANOVITCH (Nov. 25, 1856, Govt. of Vladimir, Russia : June 18, 1915, Moscow). See article in Vol. v. 17. In 1889–1906 he was professor of counterpoint and composition at the Moscow Conservatory, and his fine library was bequeathed to that institution. Among his famous pupils are Scriabin and Rachmaninov. To the list of works should be added a 'Suite de Concert,' op. 28, for violin and orchestra; two string-quintets, op. 14 in G and op. 16 in C; a string-quartet in B-flat, op. 19; a piano-quartet in E, op. 20; two string-trios, op. 21 in D and op. 31 in E-flat; a piano-trio in D, op. 22; a prelude and fugue in G-sharp minor, op. 29, for two pianos; about 40 songs and a number of choruses. See Montagu-Nathan, *Contemporary Russian Composers*, 1917.

TAPPER, BERTHA, née Feiring (1859–1915). See Register, 7.

TAPPER, THOMAS (Jan. 28, 1864, Canton, Mass.), gained his general education in history, literature and languages through private tutors. He studied music at the Petersilea Academy in Boston, continuing it with art-subjects in Europe. For some years he taught theory and composition in Boston. He edited 'The Musical Record and Review' in 1903–04 and 'The Musician' in 1904–07. Since 1905 he has been lecturer at the Institute of Musical Art in New York, in 1907–09 was director of the Music School Settlement, and since 1908 has been music-director at New York University. In 1911 he was made Litt.D. by Bates College. In 1895 he [married the able Norwegian pianist Bertha Feiring. He has been a frequent contributor to musical and literary magazines, and has published many books. Those directly relating to music include *Chats with Music-Students*, 1890, *The Music-Life*, 1892, *Music-Talks with Children*, 1896, *Pictures from the Lives of the Great Composers*, 1899, *The Child's Music-World*, 1896, *First Studies in Music-Biography*, 1900, *Education of the Music-Teacher*, *Essentials in Music-History*, 1914 (with Percy Goetschius), and many text-books for elementary and advanced music-study, such as *The Melodic Music-Course*, 28 vols., with charts (with F. H. Ripley), a series on *Music-Theory*, 6 vols., and *The Modern Graded Piano-Course*, 19 vols., besides a few

translations. He also has in preparation a number of further manuals on music-history, appreciation and theory. Besides specializing in musical education, he has recently given great attention to the subject of community-music, on which he has a book in view. Outside of music, he has published much in general literature and in the field of commercial efficiency. [R.7]

TAWS, CHARLES (d. 1833). See Register, 2.

TAYLOR, DAVID CLARK (Nov. 11, 1871, New York : Dec. 7, 1918, New York), graduated from the College of the City of New York in 1890, and studied music with O. W. Wilkinson, Alfred Remy and others. He was long connected with The Macmillan Company. He published *The Psychology of Singing*, 1908 (in German, 1910), *New Light upon the Old Italian Method*, 1916, *Self-Help for Singers*, 1914 (in German, 1914) and *The Melodic Method in School Music*, 1917. He had charge of the department of Vocal Music in *The Art of Music*, 1914–17, and wrote many articles upon topics related to singing. [R.9]

TAYLOR, JOSEPH DEEMS (Dec. 22, 1885, New York), was educated at the Ethical Culture School and graduated from New York University in 1906. He studied composition with Oscar Coon. Besides his work as composer, in 1916–17 he was war-correspondent for the (Sunday) 'Tribune' and since 1917 has been associate-editor of 'Collier's Weekly.' In 1919 he lectured in Denver on music-history and appreciation. His works include a symphonic poem, 'The Siren Song,' op. 2 (Nat. Federation of Musical Clubs prize, 1913), 'The Chambered Nautilus,' op. 7, for chorus and orchestra (1915, Schola Cantorum) (Ditson), the cantata 'The Highwayman,' op. 8, for chorus and orchestra (1914, Peterboro Festival) (Ditson), the song-cycle 'The City of Joy,' op. 9 (Ditson), the suite 'Through the Looking-Glass,' op. 12, for strings, wind and piano, 'Six Lyrics of James Stephens,' op. 13 (J. Fischer), Seven Transcriptions of Armenian Folk-Songs, op. 14 (J. Fischer). He has also edited the *Schumann Club Series*, arrangements for women's voices, 60 nos., 1919 (J. Fischer) and joined Schindler in translating many Russian and Alsatian folk-songs, beside other translations of Russian, French, German and Italian songs. [R.10]

TAYLOR, RAYNOR (1747, England : 1825, Philadelphia), like G. K. Jackson, who was nearly of the same age, had his first schooling as a boy in the Chapel Royal. In this capacity he is said to have assisted at Handel's funeral in 1759 — and to have lost his hat in the great man's grave. From about 1765 for some years he was organist at Chelmsford, not far from London. His success as a ballad-writer and his natural bent for the stage then led to his becoming music-director for one of the London theaters. Somewhere before 1785 he was the teacher of Reinagle, who was eleven years younger. In 1792 he came to Baltimore, gave some concerts there and at Annapolis, where for a time he was organist at St. Anne's, but in 1793 betook himself to Philadelphia. Here for thirty years he was the Nestor of the fine circle to which Reinagle, Carr and Schetky belonged. For most of this period he was organist at St. Peter's. In 1820 he was one of the founders of the Musical Fund Society and honored in its councils. As a player he was famous for improvisation. He was also a clever stage-singer, with a gift for the comic and burlesque. He composed both vocal and instrumental works, but nothing remains except some unimportant songs. In 1796 he gave a program, half of which was made up of his own compositions. In 1799 he and Reinagle prepared a 'Monody' over the death of Washington which made a deep impression. The titles of several plays by him or for which he wrote accompaniments are given by Sonneck (*Concert-Life*, pp. 42, 47, 140, 144–5, and in 'Early American Operas,' *I. M. G. Sammelbde.* 6. 458, 486, 488). See also Madeira, *passim*. [R.2]

TAYLOR, SAMUEL PRIESTLEY (1779–1875?). See Register, 3.

TAYLOR, VIRGIL CORYDON (1817– ?). See TUNE-BOOKS, 1846.

TECHNICON, THE. See note in Vol. ii. 266. The inventor, J. Brotherhood, was a Canadian. For some time he was in New York, seeking to promote the use of his apparatus, which he patented in many countries in 1885. His ideas as to the importance of training the extensor muscles as well as the flexors were sound, and the apparatus was well designed. For a time it was manufactured at Brattleboro, Vt.

'TEMPLE OF MINERVA, THE.' An 'oratorio' or, rather, an allegorical operetta in two scenes by Francis Hopkinson, given in Philadelphia in 1781 at an entertainment tendered by the French Minister to Gen. Washington. Only the libretto is extant. See Sonneck, *Francis Hopkinson*, and *I.M. G. Sammelbde.* 5. 148–51.

'TEMPLE–DANCER, THE.' A one-act opera by John Adam Hugo, produced at the Metropolitan Opera House on Mar. 12, 1919.

TERRIL, ISRAEL. See TUNE-BOOKS, 1806.

‡ TERRY, RICHARD RUNCIMAN (1865, Ellington, England). See article in Vol. v. 668. Besides going forward with his work in recovering early Catholic music in England, in 1911 he was extension-lecturer for Oxford University, in 1911–12 head of the Union of Music-Directors of Secondary Schools, in 1913 lecturer at Birmingham University and in 1915–17 examiner for Dublin and Birmingham Universities. He has written five masses, a Requiem and many motets, and has edited several collections of old English motets and *The Official Catholic Hymnal for England*, with a book on *Catholic Church-Music*. See article in 'Musical Opinion,' January, 1920.

‡ TETRAZZINI, LUISA (1874, Florence, Italy). See article in Vol. v. 668. In 1904 she sang as Gilda in 'Rigoletto' in San Francisco, and then went to Mexico and South America. Though announced at the Metropolitan Opera House for 1905–06 and at the Manhattan for 1906–07, she failed to appear in either case. But after her London début in 1907 she came to New York, appearing at the Manhattan as Violetta in 'La Traviata' on Jan. 15, 1908, continuing there till its closing in 1910. She then made concert-tours, sang at times with the Chicago and Boston Opera Companies and revisited England. In 1913–14 she was with the Chicago Opera Company, and made a tour in 1919–20.

TEYTE, MAGGIE (Apr. 17, 1889, Wolverhampton, England), after general education at St. Joseph's Convent in Wolverhampton, studied at the Royal College of Music in London, and in 1903–07 with Jean de Reszké in Paris. Her début was at Monte Carlo in 1907, as Zerlina. During the next two seasons she sang at the Opéra-Comique in Paris, appearing first as Mélisande in 'Pelléas et Mélisande.' In 1910–11 she sang in London, and from 1911–14 was with the Chicago Opera Company, making her American debut as Cherubino in 'Le Nozze di Figaro' on Nov. 4, 1911, in Philadelphia. Her first appearance in New York was in a song-recital on Nov. 16, when she was praised for her rendering of French songs. In 1915–17 she was with the Boston National Grand Opera Company. She has made concert-tours in America and England, singing with leading orchestras and in recital. Her favorite rôles are Mélisande and Mimi. [R.10]

THALBERG, MARCIAN (b. 1877). See Register, 10.

THATCHER, HOWARD RUTLEDGE (b. 1878). See Register, 9.

THAYER, ALEXANDER WHEELOCK (Oct. 23, 1817, South Natick, Mass. : July 15, 1897, Trieste, Austria). See article in Vol. v. 79–80. The story of Thayer and his *Life of Beethoven* is told by H. E. Krehbiel in 'The Musical Quarterly' for October, 1917. The manuscript for the English edition by Krehbiel has been ready since 1914, but publication has been deferred because of war conditions. Volumes ii. and iii. of the original, as revised by Riemann, were published in 1910–11. With the German edition complete, Krehbiel began the English version, and by the omission of unnecessary material expects to bring it within three volumes of about 500 pages each. Several plans are being made] (1920) to facilitate the issue of the long-awaited book. [R.4]

THAYER, ARTHUR WILDER (b. 1857). See Register, 6.

THAYER, WHITNEY EUGENE (Dec. 11, 1838, Mendon, Mass. : June 27, 1889, Burlington, Vt.), although beginning music-study rather early, did not pursue it seriously till he came under John K. Paine's influence and with him was chosen to play at the opening of the organ in Boston Music Hall on Nov. 2, 1863. Two years later he went to Berlin, taking organ and counterpoint with Haupt and composition with Wieprecht. On his return to Boston he was organist successively at the Arlington Street, Hollis Street, Old First Unitarian and New England Churches, and at Harvard Church in Brookline. In 1881–86 he was organist at the Fifth Avenue Presbyterian Church, in New York. After a year at Holy Trinity in Harlem, he gave up church-playing and devoted himself to teaching and composition. He gave many organ-recitals in America and abroad, beginning a long series in Boston in 1868. An enthusiast for the improvement of church-music, he gave many lectures, edited 'The Organist's Journal and Review' and 'The Choir Journal and Review,' and conducted the Boston Choral Union and the New England Church-Music Association. Among his pupils were Edward Fisher, Chadwick, J. W. Andrews, Sumner Salter, Gerrit Smith and W. C. Gale. He received the degree of Mus.D. from Oxford University. Among his compositions are a Festival Cantata for soli, eight-part chorus and orchestra, a Mass in E-flat, a fugue for organ, five organ-sonatas, organ-variations (two performers) on the Russian National Hymn; many detached organ-pieces; songs and part-songs; and a School of Organ-Playing, 5 parts. His private organ-studio in Boston, opened in 1875, was one of the first of its kind in the country. [R.5]

THAYER, WILLIAM ARMOUR (b. 1874). See Colleges, 3 (Adelphi C., N. Y.).

THEODORINI, HELENA (b. 1862). See Register, 8.

THIBAUD, JACQUES (Sept. 27, 1880, Bordeaux, France). See article in Vol. v. 83. His first visit to America was in 1903, and he has repeatedly come again, appearing with leading orchestras and in ensemble, especially in conjunction with Harold Bauer. [R.9]

THOMAS, ISAIAH (1749–1831). See Register, 2, and Tune-Books, 1786.

THOMAS, JOHN ROGERS (1829–1896). See Register, 4.

THOMAS, THEODORE (Oct. 11, 1835, Esens, Germany : Jan. 4, 1905, Chicago). See article in Vol. v. 88, with many additional data in iv. 801–3. Upton, Theodore Thomas, a Musical Autobiography, 2 vols., 1905, is a notable memorial. The second volume gives concert-programs from 1855 (the Mason-Thomas Soirées) to 1905 (the Chicago Orchestra series). There is also a long list of the works which he introduced in America. Rose Fay Thomas, Memories of Theodore Thomas, 1911, also sheds much light upon his character and career. The original title of the Chicago Orchestra was resumed in 1913. [R.4]

THOMAS ORCHESTRA, THE. See Vol. iv. 801–3, and references in preceding article.

THOMPSON, ALEXANDER STEWART (b. 1859). See Colleges, 3 (Ohio U.).

THOMPSON, JOHN WINTER (b. 1867). See Register, 8.

THOMS, WILLIAM M. (1852–1913). See Register, 5.

‡ THOMSON, CÉSAR (Mar. 18, 1857, Liège, Belgium). See article in Vol. v. 89. He visited America in 1894–95. Since 1914 he has been teacher of violin at the Paris Conservatory. He has edited collections of early Italian violin-music, has composed a Fantaisie on Hungarian themes for violin and is author of a violin-method (1913).

THOMSON, SAMUEL. See Tune-Books, 1810.

THUNDER, HENRY GORDON b. (1865). See Register, 7.

THURBER, JEANNETTE, née Meyer. See Register, 7.

THURSBY, EMMA CECELIA (Feb. 21, 1854, Brooklyn, N. Y.). See article in Vol. v. 99. Her first public appearance was at Bedford Church in Brooklyn, with Gilmore's Band. After a successful tour she then became soloist at the Broadway Tabernacle in New York at a salary of $3000. Later tours and her trip to Europe in 1878 were under the management of Maurice Strakosch. In 1896 she began her career in New York as teacher of singing. She is at work upon an autobiography, which is to include a study of her method of voice-development. [R.6]

‡ TIERSOT, JEAN BAPTISTE ÉLISÉE JULIEN (July 5, 1857, Bourg-en-Bresse, France). See article in Vol. v. 103–4. Since 1909 he has been chief librarian of the Paris Conservatory, succeeding Weckerlin. To the list of works add J. J. Rousseau, 1912 (in Maîtres de la Musique).

TIMM, HENRY CHRISTIAN (1811–1892). See Register, 3.

‡ TINEL, EDGAR (Mar. 27, 1854, Sinay, Belgium : Oct. 28, 1912, Brussels). See article in Vol. v. 112. From 1909 he was director of the Brussels Conservatory. His sacred opera 'Katharina' was produced in 1909 at Brussels.

TIRINDELLI, PIER ADOLFO (b. 1858). See Register, 7.

TOEDT, THEODORE J. (b. 1853). See Register, 6.

TOLLEFSEN, CARL HENRY (Aug. 15, 1882, Hull, England), after early education in the Brooklyn public schools, studied violin in New York with Lichtenberg, Kneisel and Schradieck and theory and composition with Goetschius and Goldmark, graduating from the Institute of Musical Art in 1908. For two years he was a first violin in the Symphony Society. He has taught in the National Conservatory, and is now head of the violin-department of both the Berkeley Institute and St. Francis Xavier Academy in Brooklyn. His wife, née Augusta Schnabel, was trained as pianist by Katha Widmann in Frankfort, and by Gallico and Godowsky in New York, making her début in 1906 with the Symphony Society, and later appearing with the Philharmonic Society, the Scandinavian Symphony Orchestra (of which her husband is leader) and the Kneisel Quartet. In 1909 the Tollefsen Trio was formed, in which Michael Penha is 'cellist, with Mr. and Mrs. Tollefsen as violinist and pianist respectively. The Trio has toured in almost all parts of the United States. [R.9]

TOLMAN, CARL JEAN (b. 1875). See COLLEGES, 2 (Coker C., S. C.).

TOMLINS, J. See TUNE-BOOKS, 1810.

TOMLINS, WILLIAM LAWRENCE (Feb. 4, 1844, London, England), as a choir-boy was a pupil of Macfarren and Silas. He became one of the managers of the London Tonic Sol-fa College in 1864. In 1870 he came to America, in 1875 located in Chicago and became director of the Apollo Club, then a men's chorus of sixty voices. He was instrumental in the change of the Club into a mixed chorus of ultimately 400 voices, and under his direction many excellent performances were given. His connection with the Club ceased in 1898. In 1883 he began organizing classes of school-children for chorus singing, and made a specialty of this work and of training teachers of school-music. In 1903 he established at Chicago the National Training School for School Music Teachers, and was engaged by the Chicago Board of Education as musical instructor for teachers in the grade schools. He returned to London in 1910. He is author of Children's Songs and How to Sing Them, 1885. [R.6]

TONNING, GERARD (b. 1860). See Register, 7.

TORONTO CONSERVATORY OF MUSIC, THE, was founded by Edward Fisher in 1886 and opened in 1887, being the first of its class in Canada. Dr. Fisher remained its efficient head until his death in 1913, and was then succeeded by Augustus S. Vogt. The institution was successful from the start, and has gone on expanding till it now is the largest music-school in the British Empire. Including its preparatory department, its faculty numbers 150 members. Since 1916 its enrollment has run considerably over 3000, not counting a still larger number who take examinations under its auspices elsewhere in Canada. In 1897 it bought a large tract of land near Queen's Park, where a series of buildings have been erected, including a recital-hall and a dormitory for women. From 1896 till 1918 it was so related to the University of Toronto that the degrees of Mus. B. and Mus. D. were accessible under the latter's strict system. The departments of instruction comprise the voice and all standard instruments, elocution, artistic dancing, kindergarten methods, tuning, and four foreign languages. The work in piano, organ and theory has always been notably strong. Special attention is given to the teaching of young children, and to training teachers for them. But facilities are ample for attaining advanced musicianship and virtuoso experience. Various forms of certificate and diploma, in both teachers' and artists' courses, with many scholarships and prizes, are provided. The equipment includes 110 pianos, 3 organs (that in the hall having three manuals and 41 stops), some orchestral instruments and a library of 650 volumes. The student orchestra numbers 50. The Conservatory maintains twelve branches in Toronto. Since 1898 it has also provided standardized local examinations in several subjects at an increasing number of other places outside. This system has lately been extended so as to apply to students in schools and colleges who cannot work so intensively as others. In 1919 over 100 centers for such examinations were listed, besides 25 schools, mostly in Ontario, but as far as Quebec on the east and Vancouver on the west. Nearly 4000 pupils apply for these examinations annually.

'TORQUIL.' An opera by Charles A. E. Harriss, produced in Montreal in 1896.

TORRINGTON, FREDERICK HERBERT (Oct. 20, 1837, Dudley, England : Nov. 20, 1917, Toronto, Ont.), was an articled pupil of James Fitzgerald at Kidderminster, studying piano, organ and theory. His first appointment as organist was at St. Anne's in Bewdley. In 1856 he came to Canada, and in 1857-69 was organist of St. James Street (M. E.) Church in Montreal, where he built up a reputation as organ-recitalist, violinist and conductor. At the Boston Peace Jubilee in 1869 he was leader of the Canadian Orchestra. For four years he remained in Boston as organist at King's Chapel, teacher in the New England Conservatory, violinist and conductor of choral societies. In 1873 he went to Toronto as organist at the Metropolitan Methodist Church (a position he held for 34 years) and conductor of the Toronto Philharmonic Society. In 1886 he arranged the first local festival, presenting 'Israel in Egypt,' 'Mors et Vita' and other large works. In 1888 he founded the Toronto College of Music, now affiliated with the University of Toronto. As principal of this school, and in many other ways, he aided in the introduction and popularization of good music in Canada. In 1892 he became president of the Canadian Society of Musicians. In 1903 he was associated with A. C. Mackenzie as conductor of a notable festival. The University of Toronto conferred upon him the honorary degree of Mus.D. His compositions included organ-pieces, services, songs and choruses. [R.4]

TOSCANINI, ARTURO (Mar. 25, 1867, Parma, Italy), was educated in the Musical Academy of Parma (now Conservatory), studying 'cello with Carini and theory with Ferrari and Dacci. Obtaining the first prize for 'cello at graduation, he played in orchestras, and in 1886 finally drifted to Rio de Janeiro. The incompetence of a conductor led to his unexpected début in this capacity on the second night of his engagement. On his return to Italy he again played in orchestras, but was soon engaged as conductor at the Teatro Regio in Turin. He then conducted successively at Treviso, Bologna, Genoa and La Scala in Milan in 1898. In 1898 he came to the Metropolitan Opera House in New York, as chief conductor. Resigning in April, 1915, he returned to Italy, and during the war lent his energies to the musical encouragement of patriotism and the relief of distressed musicians. In 1916-18 he gave series of operatic and open-air performances at the Dal Verne Theater, the Arena and the Verdi Conservatory in Milan, which yielded large sums for worthy causes. For his leadership of an army-band at Monte Santo he was awarded a silver medal. In the summer of 1919 he conducted festival performances, including several of Beethoven's 9th Symphony, at Turin and Milan. During his years at the Metropolitan he conducted Italian, German, French and Russian operas, all with impressive success. He introduced in America Puccini's 'Le Villi' (1908), Catalani's 'La Wally' (1909), Franchetti's 'Ger-

mania' (1910), Gluck's 'Armide' (1910), Dukas' 'Ariane et Barbe-bleu' (1911), Wolf-Ferrari's 'Le Donne Curiose' (1912), Mussorgsky's 'Boris Godunov' (1913), Wolf-Ferrari's 'L'Amore Medico' (1914) and Montemezzi's 'L'Amore dei Tre Rè' (1914). He also conducted there the premières of Puccini's 'La Fanciulla del West' (Dec. 10, 1910) and Giordano's 'Madame Sans-Gêne' (Jan. 25, 1915). He conducted nothing but opera in New York with the exception of two notable concerts in April, 1913, when he twice gave Wagner's 'Faust' Overture, Strauss' 'Till Eulenspiegel' and the 9th Symphony. In Italy he has been equally prominent as symphonic and operatic conductor. His nearsightedness has led to reliance upon a marvelous musical memory, and he conducts the most complicated scores without book. [R.9]

‡ TOSTI, FRANCESCO PAOLO (Apr. 9, 1846, Ortona, Italy : Dec. 3, 1916, Rome). See article in Vol. v, 131-2. After 1913 he lived in Rome.

TOURJÉE, EBEN (June 1, 1834, Warwick, R. I. : Apr. 12, 1891, Boston). See article in Vol. v. 134. Without being highly trained as a musician, his ability and enthusiasm as organizer made him influential and valuable, especially in establishing the New England Conservatory. In 1879 he recommended L. W. Mason as head of music-work in the schools of Japan and helped form the plans. In 1876 he was the first president of the M. T. N. A. He was one of the musical editors of the *Methodist Hymnal* of 1878. For a time he was managing-editor of 'The Musical Herald.' His degree of Mus.D. was from Wesleyan University. [R.4]

TOURRET, ANDRÉ (b. 1882). See Register, 10.

‡ TOVEY, DONALD FRANCIS (July 17, 1875, Eton, England). See article in Vol. v. 137. He studied for several years with Parry, and gratefully acknowledges his indebtedness for his advice and assistance. In 1914 he succeeded Niecks at the University of Edinburgh, and in 1916 organized the Reid Orchestra, giving university-students the chance to play with professionals. The result is the now well-established series of orchestral concerts. To the list of works add the following :

Symphony in D, op. 32 (1913, Aix-la-Chapelle, 1915, London).
'Sonata Eroica,' in C, for violin alone (Schott).
Sonata in D, for 'cello alone (Schott).
Sonata in G, for two 'cellos.
Trio in D, for piano, violin and 'cello (Schott).
Variations on a theme from Gluck, for flute and string-quartet (Schott).
Opera, 'The Bride of Dionysus,' in three acts, text by R. C. Trevelyan (Longmans, 1913).

He contributed over forty articles on musical subjects to the 11th edition of the *Encyclopædia Britannica.*

TOVEY, HENRY D. See STATE UNIVERSITIES (Ark.).

TOWERS, JOHN (b. 1836). See Register, 8.

TOWNER, CLEM A. (b. 1883). See COLLEGES, 2 (Oxford C., Ohio).

TRACY, JAMES MADISON (b. 1839). See Register, 5.

TRAETTA, FILIPPO (Jan. 8, 1777, Venice, Italy : Jan. 9, 1854, Philadelphia), was the son of the composer Tommaso Traetta (see Vol. v. 139–40). He studied with Fenaroli and Perillo at Venice and with Piccinni at Naples. Imprisoned for political reasons, he escaped from Italy and settled in Boston in 1799. After sojourns in New York and Virginia, in 1822 he located at Philadelphia as singing-teacher, and a year later established the American Conservatorio. He composed the oratorios 'Jerusalem in Affliction' (1828) and 'Daughter of Zion' (1829) ; the opera 'The Venetian Maskers'; the cantatas 'The Christian's Joy,' 'Prophecy,' 'The Nativity' and 'The Day of Rest'; a 'Washington's Dead-March'; and published *Vocal Exercises, Rudiments of the Art of Singing* and *An Introduction to the Art and Science of Music.* [R.3]

TRAMONTI, ENRICO (b. 1876). See Register, 9.

'TREASURED TOKENS.' An opera in two acts by J. Remington Fairlamb, given at the Chestnut Street Theatre in Philadelphia before 1870.

TREHARNE, BRYCESON (May 30, 1879, Merthyr Tydvil, Wales), held the Érard scholarship at the Royal College of Music in London, where he was a pupil of Stanford, Parry, Walford Davies, Dannreuther, Pauer and Franklin Taylor. In 1900–01 he taught at the University of Wales in Aberystwyth, and then spent ten years at the University of Adelaide, South Australia. In 1908–11 he was director of the Repertory Theatre at Adelaide, where he not only managed many modern plays but also composed much incidental music. In 1911 he came to Paris, and later lived in Milan, Berlin and Munich. Interned at Ruhleben when the war broke out, he found opportunity to write many songs, some orchestral music and part of an opera. When released in 1916 he came from England to America, since 1917 making his home in New York. Of his 200 songs or more some 40 are now published, including 'The Night,' 'The Huguenot,' 'Jeannette,' 'The Fair Circassian,' 'Invocation,' 'A Farewell,' 'The Aftermath,' 'Dreams,' 'Love's Tribute,' 'The Song of France,' 'Renunciation' and 'A Lover's Prayer.' He has besides the two cantatas for women's voices 'A Song of

Spring' and 'England, my Mother,' orchestral music and two operas. [R.10]

TREMAINE, WILLIAM B. (1840–1907). See Register, 5.

TRIO DE LUTÈCE, THE, of New York, was formed in 1913, consisting of Georges Barrère, flute, Paul Kéfer, 'cello, Carlos Salzédo, harp.

'TRIUMPH OF BOHEMIA, THE.' No. 5 of the 'Grove-Plays' of the San Francisco Bohemian Club, produced in 1907. The text is by George Sterling and the music by Edward F. Schneider. The scene is laid in the redwood forest on a midsummer-night.

'TRIUMPH OF COLUMBUS, THE.' An opera in five acts by Silas G. Pratt, produced in concert-form at the Quadricentennial Columbus Celebration in New York in 1892.

TROOSTWYK, ISIDORE (July 3, 1862, Zwolle, Holland), was a pupil of Joachim at the Berlin Hochschule, where he graduated in 1881. After tours in Holland in 1881 and in Germany with Anton Schott the next year, from 1883 he taught violin at the Musiek-School van Toonkunst in Amsterdam and was concertmaster of the Orkest-Vereeniging, changing in 1888 to a similar post in the Concertgebouw. In 1890 he came to America, in 1895 becoming head of the violin-department of the Yale Music School and in 1902 assistant-professor there. He is concertmaster of the New Haven Symphony Orchestra and the founder and conductor of the New Haven String Orchestra. [R.8]

TROWBRIDGE, JOHN ELIOT (1845–1912). See Register, 6.

TRUETTE, EVERETT ELLSWORTH (Mar. 14, 1861, Rockland, Mass.), had his general education at Phillips (Andover) Academy and the Massachusetts Institute of Technology. In 1881 he graduated from the New England Conservatory and was given a Mus.B. by Boston University in 1883. He then had two years of organ-study with Haupt in Berlin, Guilmant in Paris and Best in London and Liverpool. Since 1885 he has been organist and teacher in Boston, from 1897 at the Eliot Church in Newton, where he has given more than 110 cantatas with soloists and chorus. He was a founder of the A. G. O. and is now dean of the New England Chapter. He has given over 400 recitals throughout the country and has trained many players of prominence. He has edited several collections, including *Schmidt's Standard Organ Collection*, 2 vols., and *Bach Pedal-Études*, and has composed an organ-suite, op. 29, 'Five Organ-Pieces for the Church Service,' op. 31, and many anthems and organ-pieces. He is also author of *Organ Registration*, 1919. [R.7]

TRUNK, RICHARD (b. 1879). See Register, 10.

TUBBS, FRANK HERBERT (b. 1853). See Register, 6.

TUCKER, HIRAM G. (b. 1851). See Register, 6.

TUCKERMAN, SAMUEL PARKMAN (1819–1890). See Register, 4, and TUNE-BOOKS, 1840.

TUCKEY, WILLIAM (1708, Somersetshire, England : Sept. 14, 1781, Philadelphia), apparently came to New York before 1753. In March, 1754, he announced himself as a 'singing-master,' claiming to have been a vicar-choral at Bristol Cathedral and parish-clerk there, and offering to 'amend the singing in publick congregations' and to 'set to musick any piece on any subject.' He taught charity-scholars at Trinity Church and in the '60s arranged special church-music with orchestra. Probably he has the credit of the first performance in America of the overture and sixteen numbers from 'The Messiah,' which took place on Jan. 16, 1770 at Mr. Burns' New Room. In 1771 he solicited subscriptions for the publication of various works. It is not clear how he was later occupied. He was buried in the grounds of Christ Church in Philadelphia. See Sonneck, *Concert-Life*, pp. 176–81. [R.1]

TUFTS, JOHN (1689–1750). See TUNE-BOOKS, 1721?.

TUFTS, JOHN WHEELER (1825–1908). See Register, 4.

TUNE-BOOKS. Throughout the 17th century, and in many places till long after 1800, the words of congregational song in the churches of the Colonies were exclusively metrical versions of the Psalms. What we now call 'hymns' — verses not aiming to metricize the prose of the Scripture, but freely and originally composed — were first made popular in England from 1706 by Isaac Watts and still more abundantly from 1740 by the Wesleys. Watts' hymns began to be reprinted in America about 1740, though doubtless imported earlier. After 1750 hymns were gradually adopted by many churches, though without displacing the Psalms.

The music required for both Psalms and hymns was in general form the same — melodies in distinct phrases adapted to the rhythm and meter of the few customary verse-types. Until nearly the end of the 18th century the only rhythm used in the American churches was iambic, except for a slight infusion of anapæsts in a few cases. Trochaic rhythm seems to have been unrealized, as it was in England until Charles Wesley revealed its stirring possibilities. The prevailing stanza was of four lines, though sometimes six or eight.[1]

Melodies thus formed were known as 'Psalm-Tunes,' because originally used for the Psalms. Out of this came the general term 'Psalmody' for the total body of tunes, for the practice or custom of singing and also in time for the books that served as manuals.[1]

Until after 1750 the tunes used were entirely derived from English sources, and most of them were of English origin. Yet it is to be noted that the music brought to Plymouth and Salem was that contained in Ainsworth's Psalter (1612), which was compiled in Amsterdam and included much that differed from the less varied and vigorous forms later brought to Boston and presumably to all other places outside of New England, which was derived from the musical editions of Sternhold and Hopkins' Psalter of 1562 or later.[2]

Though these books provided a considerable body of good melodies, the actual practice of singing everywhere degenerated or became almost obsolete during the 17th century, owing to the scarcity of books with music and the growing inability to use musical notation. When the so-called 'Bay Psalm Book,' originally compiled in 1640, came to have tunes added in 1690, their number was small and their variety slight.

About 1720, perhaps earlier, a few ministers began to agitate for the restoration of singing on a systematic basis. The ensuing controversy between 'singing by rote' and 'singing by note' lasted more than a decade, but was finally settled in favor of the latter. This led soon to the setting up of 'singing-schools,' the appearance of itinerant 'singing-teachers,' and finally to a demand for tune-books (manuals of instruction, combined with a selection of actual tunes).[3]

The extensive movement thus inaugurated centered first in New England, especially Massachusetts and Connecticut, but spread to New York and Pennsylvania, and ultimately to the West and South. The churches most affected were those called Congregational or Presbyterian, but in most cases the movement had a general community influence. At the time of the Revolution and the rise of national feeling it was linked up with secular

Variants were 8-8-8-8 or 'Long Meter,' 6-6-8-6 or 'Short Meter,' and, rarely, 6-6-6-6-4-4-4-4 or 'Hallelujah Meter.' In certain usages, too, 10-10-10-10 or 'Tens' was not infrequent.

[1] This term has persisted long after Psalmody proper was in some degree displaced by Hymnody. With reference to the music that accompanied both one might wish that there were warrant for some fresh term like 'Tunody.'

[2] It is unfortunate that the musical richness of Ainsworth has not been more generally recognized. It contained 39 tunes, many of which have decided value, as they certainly have surprising vivacity.

[3] An excellent summary of this period is given in Curwen, *Worship-Music*, 1st series, under 'New England Psalmody.'

[1] By far the most frequent formula of syllables for the lines was 8-6-8-6 — the old 'ballad-meter' — which hence came to be called 'Common Meter.'

2 c

singing of the patriotic type. It did not confine itself to 'tunes,' but expanded to 'anthems' and 'odes.' Though the technical art displayed by editors and presently composers was often crude and faulty, the movement did much to spread skill in singing, to awaken popular interest in music and to prepare the way for more artistic enterprises. In many communities the old 'Psalmody' occupied somewhat the place of folk-song. Tunes were at first printed from engraved plates. The first use of music-type was in 1767, and soon became common, though not very satisfactory till after 1800.

The subjoined bibliography indicates something of the enormous extent of the early tunebook literature. It is largely condensed and rearranged from Metcalf, *American Psalmody*, 1917, which in turn was an extension of James Warrington, *Short Titles of Books . . of Psalmody*, 1898, but includes matter from other sources. Some lesser titles and many details about editions, etc., are omitted. The chronological sequence is suggested by arranging the compilers according to the date when they entered the field.[1]

The reform in singing was set on foot by two books:

John Tufts (1689–1750), minister at Newburyport, *Introduction to the Art of Singing*, 1721 (also '26–'44), with a peculiar letter-notation, M, F, S, L (for *mi, fa, sol, la*), on the staff instead of notes.

Thomas Walter (1696–1725), minister at Roxbury, *Grounds and Rules of Music*, 1721 (also '23–'64).

Both of these derived their tunes from Playford.

From 1760 —

James Lyon (1735–94), Presbyterian minister in Philadelphia in 1764 and then in Nova Scotia and Maine: *Urania*, Phila. 1762 (also '67, '73). See Sonneck, *Hopkinson and Lyon*, 1905.

Tunes in Three Parts, Phila. 1763, printed by Anthony Armbruster (d. 1796).

Psalm Tunes for Christ and St. Peter's Churches, Phila. 1763.

Josiah Flagg (?1738–94), pioneer in Boston in sacred and secular music: *Collection of Best Psalm Tunes*, 1764 (engraved by Paul Revere); *Collection of Tansur's and Other Anthems*, 1766 — both Boston. See Sonneck, *Concert-Life*, p. 261.

Psalms of David for the Dutch Reformed Church, New York, 1767.

William Billings (1746–1800), an eccentric and illiterate tanner, with a contagious zeal for promoting social song through popular instruction and his own energetic, but unschooled, efforts at composition: *New England Psalm Singer*, 1770; *Singing Master's Assistant*, 1778 (also '79, '81); *Music in Miniature*, 1779; *Psalm Singer's Amusement*, 1781; *Suffolk Harmony*, 1786; *Continental Harmony*, 1794 — all Boston. All but 11 tunes were original.

Andrew Law (1748–1821), self-taught singing-teacher of Cheshire, Conn., who traveled widely

[1] No attempt is made to include the German hymnody of Pennsylvania, which was wholly unconnected with that of the English Colonies.

(as far as Baltimore): *Select Number of Plain Tunes*, Boston, 1767 (and to '75); *Select Harmony*, 1778 (also to '92); *Collection of Best Tunes and Anthems*, 1779 (and to '82); *Musical Primer*, New Haven, 1780 (and to 1812), and Supplement, 1811; *Collection of Hymn Tunes*, 1782 (and to '92); *Rudiments of Music*, 1783 (and to '93); *Christian Harmony*, 2 vols., 1794 (and to 1805); *Musical Magazine*, 6 nos. 1792–1801 (combined, 1805); *Art of Singing*, 2 vols. 1794–96 (and to 1810); *Harmonic Companion*, Phila. 1807 (and to '19); *Art of Playing the Organ*, 1809 (also '19) — all first at Cheshire except as noted. Besides his great activity as author and compiler, Law was noted for advocating setting the melody in the soprano instead of tenor, and for experiments with 'character-notes' (notes with heads varying according to their scale-relation), at first (about 1800) with but four varieties, later with seven, and at first posited as if upon a staff, but without staff-lines — a curious device to emphasize scale-relations while avoiding typographical difficulties.

Essex Harmony, Newburyport, 1770, printed or compiled by Bailey, Part I, Salem, 1802.

John Stickney (1744–1827): *Gentleman's and Lady's Musical Companion*, Newburyport, 1774 (and to '83).

Elias Mann (1750–1825), singing-teacher at Northampton, Mass.: *Northampton Collection*, 1778 (and to 1802); *Massachusetts Collection*, Boston, 1807. See also Albee below.

From 1780 —

Simeon Jocelyn (1746–1823): *Collection of Favorite Psalm Tunes*, 1780 (also '87); *Chorister's Companion*, New Haven, 1782, with Amos Doolittle (and to '92), and Parts II–III, 1790+; *Federal Harmony*, Boston, 1793.

Oliver Brownson: *Select Harmony*, New Haven, 1783 (also '91); *New Collection of Sacred Harmony*, Simsbury, 1797.

Daniel Read (1757–1836), comb-maker and singing-teacher at New Haven: *American Singing Book*, New Haven, 1785 (and to '93) and Supplement, 1787; *Musical Magazine, Vol. I*, New Haven, 1786–7; *Introduction to Psalmody*, New Haven, 1790; *Columbian Harmonist, Nos. 1–4*, New Haven, 1793–1810 (No. 1 also to 1810) and Supplement; *American Musical Miscellany*, Northampton, 1798; *New Haven Collection*, Dedham, 1818.

Timothy Swan (1758–1842), singing-teacher in Massachusetts and Vermont: *Federal Harmony*, 1785 (and to '92); *Songster's Assistant*, Suffield, 1800; *New England Harmony*, Northampton, 1801; *Songster's Museum*, Northampton, 1803.

Worcester Collection, Worcester, 1786, printed by Isaiah Thomas (1749–1831), the author of a notable *History of Printing*, 1810 (reprinted 1874).

Tunes Suited to Psalms and Hymns of the Book of Common Prayer, Phila. 1786.

Andrew Adgate (d. 1793), an enterprising promoter of popular music in Philadelphia through classes and concerts under the name of 'The Uranian Society' or 'Academy' (from 1784); *Lessons for the Uranian Society and Uranian Instructions*, 1785–7; *Select Psalms and Hymns*, 1787; *Rudiments of Music*, 1788 (and to 1803); *Selection of Sacred Harmony*, 1788 (and to 1803 or later, edited by Husband). See Sonneck, *Concert-Life*, p. 103 ff.

Chauncey Langdon (1764–1830): *Beauties of Psalmody*, New Haven, 1786.

John Aitken: *Litanies and Vesper Hymns and Anthems*, Phila. 1787 (also '91).

Gamut or Scale of Music, Hartford, 1788 (and to 1818).

John Hubbard (1750–1810): *Harmonia Selecta,* Worcester, 1789.

Jacob French (b. 1754): *New American Melody,* 1789; *Psalmodist's Companion,* 1793; *Harmony of Harmony,* Northampton, 1802.

From 1790 —

Asahel Benham: *Federal Harmony,* New Haven, 1790 (and to '95); *Social Harmony,* Wallingford, 1798 (also '99).

Thomas Lee, Jr.: *Sacred Harmony,* Boston, 1790.

William Young: *Selection of Sacred Harmony,* Phila. 1790 (also '94).

D. Russ: *Uranian Harmony,* Phila. 1791.

Samuel A. Holyoke (1762–1820), singing-teacher in eastern Massachusetts and New Hampshire: *Harmonia Americana,* Boston, 1791; *Massachusetts Compiler,* Boston, 1795, with Holden below and Hans Gram; *Columbian Repository,* Exeter, 1800 or '02; *Occasional Music,* Exeter, 1802; *Christian Harmonist,* Salem, 1804; *Instrumental Assistant,* 2 vols. ?1800–7; *Vocal Companion,* Exeter, 1807; etc. See also Kimball below.

Oliver Holden (1765–1834?), carpenter, bookseller and singing-teacher at Charlestown, Mass.: *American Harmony,* 1792; *Union Harmony,* 2 vols. 1793; *Charlestown Collection,* 1803; *Plain Psalmody,* 1800 — all Boston. See also Holyoke above.

Baltimore Collection of Sacred Music, Balto. 1792.

Nehemiah Shumway: *American Harmony,* Phila. 1793 (also 1801).

Jacob Kimball (1761–1826), lawyer and then singing-teacher in Massachusetts: *Rural Harmony,* Exeter, 1793; *Essex Harmony,* Exeter, 1800, with Holyoke.

Joseph Stone and Abraham Wood (1752–1804): *Columbian Harmony,* 1793.

John Asplund (d. 1807): *New Collection,* Balto. 1793.

Supply Belcher (1751–1836): *Harmony of Maine,* Boston, 1794.

Thomas H. Atwell: *New York (and Vermont) Collection of Sacred Harmony,* 1794 (and to 1805).

S. Babcock: *Middlesex Harmony,* Watertown, 1795 (also 1803).

B. Dearborn: *Vocal Instructor,* 1796.

Daniel Belknap (1771–1815): *Harmonist's Companion,* Boston, 1797; *Evangelical Harmony,* 1800; *Middlesex Collection,* 1802 (also '08); *Village Compilation,* Boston, 1806; *Middlesex Songster,* 1809?.

D. Wright: *American Musical Miscellany,* 1798.

Truman S. Wetmore (1774–1861) of Winchester, Conn.: *Republican Harmony,* 1798 (MS).

Village Harmony, Exeter, 1798 (and often to 1821).

William Little and William Smith: *Easy Instructor,* Albany, 1798 (and often to 1831).

Amos Pillsbury: *United States Sacred Harmony,* Boston, 1799.

Jonathan Benjamin: *Harmonia Cœlestis,* Northampton, 1799.

Solomon Howe: *Worshipper's Assistant,* Northampton, 1799; *Farmer's Evening Entertainment,* Northampton, 1804; *Divine Hymns,* Greenwich, 1805.

From 1800 —

Andrews: *Plain Psalmody,* 1800.

Charles Southgate: *Harmonia Sacra,* 1800 (also '18?).

Merit N. Woodruff: *Devotional Harmony,* 1800 (engraved).

Modern Collection of Sacred Music, Boston, 1800.

Elijah Griswold: *Connecticut Harmony,* 1800, with

Thomas Skinner; *Hartford Collection,* Hartford, 1807, with Stephen Jenks below.

Stephen Jenks (1772–1856), of Connecticut and Ohio: *New England Harmonist,* New Haven, 1800 (also '03); *American Compiler,* No. 1, Northampton, 1803, with Griswold above; *Delights of Harmony,* New Haven, 1804 = *Norfolk Compiler,* Dedham, 1805; *Royal Harmony of Zion,* Dedham, 1810 = *Union Compiler,* 1818; *Zion's Harp,* New York, 1824.

John Cole (1774–1855): *Episcopalian Harmony,* 1800 (also '11); *Collection of Anthems,* n. d.; *Collection of Psalm Tunes,* Boston, 1803; *Beauties of Psalmody,* 1805 (also '27); *Divine Harmonist,* 1808; *Ecclesiastical Harmony,* 1810; *Ministrel Songs,* 1812; *Devotional Harmony,* 1814; *Songs of Zion,* 1818; *Seraph,* 1821 (and to '27); *Sacred Melodies,* Nos. 1–3, 1828; *Union Harmony,* 1829 (character-notes); *Laudate Dominum,* 1842 (also '47) — all but one at Baltimore.

Uri K. Hill: *Vermont Harmony,* Northampton, 1801; *Sacred Minstrel,* Boston, 1806; *Handelian Repository,* NewYork, 1814; *Solfeggio Americano,* New York, 1820.

Warwick Palfrey (1787–1838): *Evangelical Psalmodist,* Salem, 1802.

Elisha West: *Musical Concert,* Northampton, 1802.

Bartholomew Brown, teacher in Boston, in 1832–38 conductor of the Handel and Haydn Society: *Bridgewater Collection,* Boston, 1802 (and often to 1839, after 1810 = *Templi Carmina?),* with Holt and Mitchell below; *Columbian and European Harmony,* 1802–4.

Abraham Maxim (1773–1829): *Oriental Harmony,* Exeter, 1802; *Northern Harmony,* Hallowell?, 1804? (and to '16).

Abijah Forbush: *Psalmodist's Assistant,* Boston, 1803 (also '06).

James Newhall: *Vocal Harmony,* Northampton, 1803.

Benjamin Holt (1774–1861): *New England Sacred Harmony,* Boston, 1803. See also Brown above.

Walter Janes (1779–1827): *Massachusetts Harmony,* Boston, 1803; *Harmonic Minstrelsy,* Dedham, 1807.

Lewis and Thaddeus Seymour: *Musical Instructor,* 1803?; *New York Selection of Sacred Music,* New York, 1809 (and to '16), with Lewis Edson (1748–1820).

William Cooper: *Original Sacred Music,* Boston, 1803?; *Beauties of Church Music,* Boston, 1804. See also Sweeney below.

Ebenezer Child: *Sacred Musician,* Boston, 1804.

Jeremiah Ingalls (1764–1828): *Christian Harmony,* Exeter, 1805.

Charles Robbins: *Columbian Harmony* or *Maine Collection,* Exeter, 1805.

Rufus Frost: *Medford Harmony,* Boston, 1805.

Samuel Capen: *Norfolk Harmony,* Boston, 1805.

Salem Collection of Classical Sacred Music, Salem, 1805.

Timothy Olmsted: *Musical Olio,* Northampton, 1805 (also '11).

Israel Terril: *Vocal Harmony, No. 1,* New Haven, 1805?.

Amos Albee (b. 1772): *Norfolk Collection,* Dedham, 1805; *Columbian Sacred Harmonist,* Dedham, 1808, with Mann above and Shaw below.

Benjamin Carr (1769–1831), a versatile singer and organist in Philadelphia: *Masses, Vespers and Litanies,* 1805; *Lessons in Vocal Music,* Balto. 1811?; *Collection of Chants,* Phila. 1816; *Chorister,* Phila. 1820.

First Church Collection of Sacred Music, Boston, 1806 (also '15).

Peter Erban (1769–1861): *Selection of Psalm and Hymn Tunes*, New York, 1806.

Suffolk Collection of Church Music, Boston, 1807.

J. Bushnell: *Musical Synopsis*, Northampton, 1807.

Middlesex Collection, Boston, 1807 (also to '11).

John Husband (?1753–1809?): *Collection of Hymns and Psalms*, Lancaster, Pa. 1807. See also Adgate above.

J. Evans: *David's Companion*, New York, 1807 (and to '10).

Amos Blanchard: *Newburyport Collection*, Exeter, 1807; *American Musical Primer*, Exeter, 1808.

Jonathan Huntington (1771–1838): *Apollo Harmony*, Northampton, 1807; *Classical Music*, Boston, 1812.

Charles Woodward: *Ecclesiæ Harmonia*, Phila. 1807? (also '09); *Sacred Music in Miniature*, Phila. 1812.

Stephen Addington: *Sacred Music*, Phila. 1807?; *Valuable Selection of Psalm and Hymn Tunes*, Phila. 1808.

Zedekiah Sanger (1748–1820), minister from 1776 at Duxbury, Mass., from 1788 at South Bridgewater: *Meridian Harmony*, Dedham, 1808.

George Hough: *Modern Harmony*, 1808.

Trinity Church Hymns, Boston, 1808.

Joel Read (b. 1753): *New England Selection*, Boston, 1808 (also '12).

Henry S. Keating: *Key to Harmony*, Balto. 1808.

Samuel Willard (1776–1859), minister at Deerfield, Mass., from 1807, and author of several hymnbooks: *Deerfield Collection*, Northampton, 1808? (also '18); *Regular Hymns with Musical Directions*, 1823?.

Daniel L. Peck: *Musical Medley*, Dedham, 1808: *Selection of Sacred Music*, Phila. 1810.

Oliver Shaw (1779–1848), a blind singer and singing-teacher: *Columbian Sacred Harmonist*, Dedham, 1808, with Albee and Mann; *Providence Selection*, Dedham, 1815 = *Melodia Sacra*, Providence, 1819; *Social and Sacred Melodist*, Providence, 1845.

Hezekiah Moors: *Province Harmony*, Boston, 1809.

Azariah Fobes: *Delaware Harmony*, Phila. 1809.

Maryland Selection, Balto. 1809, published by Gillet, Wheeler & Co.

Joel Harmon (1773–1833): *Columbian Sacred Minstrel*, Northampton, 1809; *Musical Primer*, Harrisburg, 1814?.

William Smith: *Churchman's Choral Companion*, New York, 1809; *Chants for Public Worship*, 1814. Perhaps also see Little above.

From 1810—

Collection of Sacred Music for West Church, Boston, 1810.

J. Tomlins: *Sacred Music, No. 1*, Boston, 1810.

George C. Sweeney: *Sacred Music*, Boston, 1810, with Cooper above.

Samuel Thomson: *Columbian Harmony*, Dedham, 1810.

Nathan Chapin and Joseph L. Dickerson: *Musical Instructor*, Phila. 1810.

George E. Blake (1775–1871): *Vocal Harmony*, Phila. 1810.

John Wyeth (1770–1858): *Repository of Sacred Music*, Harrisburg, 1810 (and to '34) and Part II, 1813 (also '20).

Clement Millard: *United States Harmony*, 1810?.

Nahum Mitchell (1769–1853), at one time member of Congress and also Circuit Judge in Massachusetts: *LXXX Psalm and Hymn Tunes* or *Brattle Street Collection*, Boston, 1810. See also Brown and Holt above.

Benjamin Leslie: *Concert Harmony*, Salem, 1811.

Hollis Street Collection of Psalm and Hymn Tunes, Boston, 1811.

Francis C. Schaffer: *Hymns Set to Music*, Boston, 1811.

James Hewitt: *Harmonia Sacra*, Boston, 1812.

'An American': *Columbian Harp*, Northampton, 1812.

Eli Roberts: *Hartford Collection*, New London, 1812.

Evangelical Songster, Newburyport, 1812.

Selection of Psalm Tunes for . . . the Protestant Episcopal Church in the State of New York, 1812?.

Emanuel Kent: *David's Harp*, Balto. 1812 (and later).

Josiah Holbrook: *American and European Harmony*, 1813, with David Pool.

Solomon Warriner (1778–1860): *Springfield Collection*, Springfield, 1813. See also Hastings below.

Japhet C. Washburn: *Parish Harmony* or *Fairfax Collection*, 1813?; *Temple Harmony*, 1818? (also '21?).

Freeman Lewis (1780–1859): *Beauties of Harmony*, 1813? (also '16).

William Bull (1762–1842): *Music Adapted to Language*, 1813?.

Portsmouth Collection of Sacred Music, Exeter, 1814.

John Hubbard: *Volume of Sacred Music*, Newburyport, 1814.

Select Harmony, Boston, 1815 (also '17), being Part IV of Samuel Worcester's *Christian Psalmody* (collection of psalms and hymns).

Edward Hartwell: *Chorister's Companion*, Exeter, 1815.

Isaac P. Cole: *Third Presbyterian Church Collection*, Phila. 1815; *Pocket Edition of Psalm and Hymn Tunes*, New York, 1834 (and to '39).

John Armstrong: *Pittsburg Selection of Psalm Tunes*, Pittsburg, 1816.

Timothy Flint (1780–1840), minister at Lunenburg, Mass., till 1815 and then missionary in the West: *Columbian Harmonist*, Cincinnati, 1816 (character-notes).

T. D. Baird: *Science of Praise*, Zanesville, O., 1816.

George K. Jackson (1745–1823), an organist from England who was active in several Boston churches: *Choice Collection of Chants*, Boston, 1816; *Choral Companion*, Boston, 1817. Earlier works in England. It was Jackson's approval that secured the publication of Lowell Mason's first collection under the auspices of the Handel and Haydn Society.

J. Eckhard: *Choral Book*, Boston, 1816.

Thomas Hastings (1787–1872), the chief pioneer in developing choral singing and instruction in New York State, first at Utica and from 1832 in New York City: *Musica Sacra* or *Springfield and Utica Collections Combined*, Utica, 1816 (and often to '38), with Warriner above and Seth Norton (d. 1818); *Musical Reader*, Utica, 1817 (also '19); *Spiritual Songs for Social Worship*, Utica, 1831, with Mason below; *Union Minstrel*, Phila. 1834 *Musical Miscellany*, 2 vols. (from his 'Musical Magazine'), New York, 1836; *Manhattan Collection*, New York, 1836; *Sacred Lyre*, New York, 1840; *Psalmodist*, New York, 1844, with Bradbury below (also the next three); *Choralist*, New York, 1847; *Mendelssohn Collection*, New York, 1849; *Psalmista*, New York, 1851; *Selah*, New York, 1856, with his son Thomas S. Hastings (1827–1911); *Church Melodies*, New York, 1859, with the same. Hastings was besides an industrious and fairly able writer of hymns (see Julian, *Dict. of Hymnology* and Benson, *The English Hymn*), which appeared first in *Spiritual Songs*,

1831, in *The Mother's Hymn Book*, 1834, in *The Christian Psalmist*, 1836, in *Devotional Hymns and Religious Poems*, 1850, etc. He also published a *Dissertation on Musical Taste*, 1822 (also '53); *History of Forty Choirs*, 1854; *Sacred Praise*, New York, 1856. He was Mason's special coadjutor in the movement for improving church music, sharing in the latter's high ideals, though with less technical equipment.

Ezekiel Goodale (b. 1780): *Hallowell Collection*, Hallowell, Me. 1817 (also '19).

Collection of Sacred Music for Churches which Sing without a Choir, New York, 1817?.

J. W. Nevius: *New Brunswick Collection*, New Brunswick, N. J., 1817 (and to '40), with Cornelius Vanderventer and John Frazee.

Samuel L. Metcalfe (1798–1856), professor of Chemistry in Transylvania University, Lexington, Ky.: *Kentucky Harmonist*, 1817? (and to '26).

E. Riley: *Sacred Melodies*, 1817?.

Samuel Dyer (1785–1835): *New Selection of Sacred Music*, Balto. 1817 (and to '28 or later); *Selection of Anthems*, Balto. 1817 (and to '51, then edited by his son, Samuel O. Dyer); *Philadelphia Selection of Sacred Music*, New York, 1828.

I. Gerhart and J. F. Eyer: *Choral Harmonie*, 1818 (also '22).

New Haven Collection, Dedham, 1818.

Francis D. Allen: *New York Selection of Sacred Music*, 1818 (and to '33): *Selection of Sacred Music for the Dutch Reformed Church*, New York, 1818?.

Old Colony Collection, 2 vols., Boston, 1818–19? (also '23).

Valuable Collection of Sacred Music, Exeter, 1818.

Jonathan Mayhew Wainwright (1792–1854), Episcopal minister of English birth, but graduated at Harvard, from 1819 settled in New York: *Set of Chants*, Boston,1819; *Music of the Church*, New York, 1828 (also '50); *Psalmodia Evangelica*, 1838.

Arthur Clifton: *Original Psalm Tunes*, Balto. 1819.

James M. Winchell (1791–1820), Baptist minister in Boston from 1814, and compiler of an edition of Watts' hymns: *Sacred Harmony*, Boston, 1819.

From 1820 —

James P. Carroll: *Songs of Zion*, 1820?.

Henry Little: *Wesleyan Harmony*, Hallowell, Me. 1820 (also '21).

Ephraim Reed: *Musical Monitor*, Ithaca, N. Y. 1820 (and to '27).

Wesleyan Selection of the John Street Church, New York, 1820.

Methodist Harmonist, New York, 1821 (also '28).

C. C. Abbott: *Young Convert's Pocket Companion*, Boston, 1822.

Lowell Mason (1792–1872): *Boston Handel and Haydn Society Collection of Church Music*, 2 vols., Boston, 1822 (and often later); *Lyra Sacra*, 1832; *Choir* or *Union Collection*, 1833; *Boston Academy's Collection*, 3rd ed., 1835; *Occasional Psalmody*, 1837; *Songs of Asaph*, 1838; *Seraph*, 1838; *Boston Anthem Book*, 1839; *Modern Psalmist*, 1839; *Carmina Sacra*, 1841; *Boston Academy Collection of Choruses*, 1844; *Psaltery*, 1845; *National Psalmist*, 1848; *Cantica Laudis*, 1850; *Boston Chorus Book*, 1851; *New Carmina Sacra*, 1852 — his most successful book; *Home Book of Psalmody*, 1852; *Hallelujah*, 1854; besides about 15 books for children and perhaps half as many collections of secular glees and part-songs. Several of the above were edited jointly with George J. Webb below; see also Hastings above. As to the significance of Mason and his colleagues, see statement at the close of this article, HYMN-BOOKS, and individual article.

Nathaniel D. Gould (1781–1864), singing-teacher in Massachusetts and New Hampshire, teacher of penmanship, and author of an interesting, but slender *History of Church Music in America*, Boston, 1853: *Social Harmony*, Boston, 1822; *National Church Harmony*, Boston, 1832; *Sacred Minstrel*, 1840.

Absalom Peters (1793–1869): *Sacred Music*, 1823.

Alling Brown: *Gamut*, New Haven, 1823; *Musical Cabinet* or *New Haven Collection*, New Haven, 1824 (also '30).

Massachusetts Collection, Greenfield, 1823.

Thomas Loud [Jr.]: *Psalmist*, Phila. 1824.

S. D. Puller: *Small Collection of Sacred Music*, Harrisburg, 1825.

Allen D. Carden: *Missouri Harmony*, 1827 (character-notes).

Stoughton Collection, 1828, issued by the Musical Society of Stoughton, Mass.

Elam Ives, Jr. (1802–64): *American Psalmody*, Hartford, 1829 (also '30), with Deodatus Dutton.

From 1830 —

Samuel F. Bradford: *Music of the Church*, Phila. 3rd ed. 1830.

Psalmist or *Chorister's Companion*, Boston, 1831.

Joshua Leavitt (1794–1873), lawyer in New York and later editor of 'The Evangelist' and 'The Independent': *Christian Lyre*, New York, 1831, and Supplement, which introduced the practice of printing the hymns in full in conjunction with the tunes. See HYMN-BOOKS.

William B. Snyder and W. L. Chappell: *Western Lyre*, 1831 (character-notes).

Henry E. Moore (1803–41): *New Hampshire Collection*, Concord, 1832 (and later) and Supplement, 1834; *Choir*; *Collection of Anthems, Choruses and Set Pieces*; *Northern Harp*.

Christian Psalmody, printed by Barrett & Coleman, N. H. 1832.

Abner Jones: *Melodies of the Church*, New York, 1832; *Temple Melodies*, New York, 1840.

Charles Zeuner (1795–1857), a Saxon who came to Boston in 1824, was organist of the Handel and Haydn Society in 1830–37 and of Park Street Church, and from 1854 organist in Philadelphia: *American Harp*, Boston, 1832; *Ancient Lyre*, Boston, 1842?.

James W. Palmer: *Western Harmonia Companion*, 1832 (character-notes).

Abraham Dow Merrill (1796–1878): *Wesleyan Harp*, Boston, 1834, with W. C. Brown; *Vestry Harp*, 1845.

Robert Willis: *Lexington Cabinet*, Lexington, Ky. 1834 (character-notes).

Timothy B. Mason: *Ohio Sacred Harp*, 1834 (at first in character-notes); *Sacred Harp* or *Eclectic Harmony*, Vol. i, 18th ed. Boston, 1836.

Thomas Whittemore (1800–61), from 1820 Universalist minister at Milford, Mass., and Cambridge, later prominent in business and political life and author of many religious books: *Songs of Zion*, 1836; *Gospel Harmonist*, 1841; as well as juvenile collections.

W. Nash: *Sacred Harmony*, 1836.

Occasional Psalm and Hymn Tunes, Boston, 1838.

Joseph Muenscher: *Church Choir*, Columbus O. 1839.

Benjamin Sweetzer, Jr.: *Cumberland Collection of Church Music*, 1839.

David Paine: *Portland Sacred Music Society's Collection of Church Music*, Portland, Me. 1839.

George Kingsley (1811–84): *Harp of David*, New York, 183–?; *Sacred Choir*, 1839; *Sacred Harmonist; Templi Carmina*, Northampton, 1853; besides several juvenile books.

From 1840 —

George J. Webb (1803–87), an Englishman who became organist of the Old South Church in Boston in 1830 and coworker with Mason in various enterprises, including the foundation of the Boston Academy in 1833 and the editing of 'The Musical Library' in 1835–36, was conductor of the Handel and Haydn Society in 1840–43 and an influential teacher till 1870, when he removed to Orange, N. J. and taught in New York for some years: *Massachusetts Collection of Psalmody*, Boston, 1840; *Cantica Ecclesiastica*, Boston, 1859; besides several juvenile text-books and collections. See also Lowell Mason above.

Ancient Harmony Revived, Boston, 1840 (and to '56).

Hiram May: *Harp*, Perry, Me., 1840?.

J. H. Hickok: *Social Lyrist*, Harrisburg, 1840.

Thomas Comer, who founded the Musical Fund Society in Boston in 1847: *Boston Musical Institute's Collection of Church Music*, 1841.

Sylvanus Billings Pond (1792–1871), at first an instrument-maker at Albany, from 1832 in New York, entering the business later known as Wm. A. Pond & Co.: *United States Psalmody*, New York, 1841.

Asa Fitz and E. R. Dearborn: *Vestry Singing Book*, Boston and New York, 1841. Fitz issued many other books for school-use.

J. B. Packard and W. S. Hubbard: *Songs of Canaan*, Boston, 1842.

Benjamin F. Baker (1811–89), early prominent as a church singer and leader in Salem, Portland and Boston, in 1841 Mason's successor in the Boston public schools: *Boston Musical Education Society's Collection*, Boston, 1842, with Woodbury below; *Choral*, Boston, 1845, also with Woodbury; *Haydn Collection of Church Music*, 1850, with L. H. Southard; *Melodia Sacra*, 1852, with Johnson and Osgood below.

Isaac B. Woodbury (1819–58), from 1839 member of a traveling glee-club in New England and later, after some study abroad in 1851, teacher and editor in New York of 'The Musical Review' (from 1850) and 'The Musical Pioneer' (see Baker above): *Anthem Dulcimer*, New York, 1850; *Liber Musicus*, 1851; *Cythera; New Lute of Zion*; besides many secular collections.

H. W. Day: *David's Harp*, 1842; *Numeral Harmony*, 1846; *One-Line Psalmist*, 1849 — these two in a numeral notation.

Chants and Anthems for the Church of the Messiah, New York, 1843.

Ureli C. Hill (?1802–75), a New York violinist (pupil of Spohr) and founder of the Philharmonic Society in 1842: *New York Sacred Music Society's Collection of Church Music*, 1843.

William B. Bradbury (1816–68), an organist in Boston from 1834 and from 1840 teaching, composing and editing in New York (see Hastings above and Hamilton below): *Shawm*, 1853, with Root below; *Jubilee*, 1858; etc.

Edward Hamilton: *Songs of Sacred Praise* or *American Collection*, Boston, 1845, with Bradbury above.

J. H. C. Stanbridge and W. H. W. Darley: *Cantus Ecclesiæ*, Phila. 1844.

Edward L. White: *Modern Harp*, Boston, 1846, with John E. Gould (1822–75); *Harmonia Sacra*, Boston, 1851, also with Gould. He also edited two vols. of 'The Boston Melodeon,' 1850, a third being added by L. H. Southard and E. H. Baker.

T. Bissell: *Boston Sacred Harmony*, 1846.

Virgil C. Taylor (b. 1817): *Sacred Minstrel* or *American Church Music Book*, New York, 1846; *Choral Anthems*, Boston, 1850.

J. B. Aikin: *Church Minstrel*, Phila. 1847 (character-notes).

Henry K. Oliver (1800–85), a writer upon the making and use of mathematical instruments and a musical amateur in Boston and Salem: *National Lyre*, with Tuckerman below and S. A. Bancroft; *Collection of Church Music*, 1860; *Original Hymn Tunes*, 1875.

Samuel P. Tuckerman (1819–90), organist in Boston from 1840 (studying in England in 1849–53) to 1856, after which he lived abroad for many years: *Episcopal Harp*, 184–?; *Cathedral Chants*, 1858; *Trinity Collection of Church Music*, New York, 1864. See also Oliver above.

George F. Root (1820–95), in 1839–44 A. N. Johnson's partner in Boston and closely associated with Mason and Webb, removing in 1845 to New York and to Chicago in 1860: *Collection of Church Music*, New York, 1849, with Joseph E. Sweetser (1825–73); *Diapason*, 1860; besides a large number of secular cantatas, instruction-books, songs and cantatas. See also Bradbury above.

Daniel H. Mansfield (b. 1810): *American Vocalist*, Boston, 1849.

Artemas N. Johnson (b. 1817), a music-dealer in Boston, choir-leader and organist, editor of 'The Musical Gazette' and 'The Musical Journal': *Bay State Collection*, Boston, 1849, with Josiah Osgood and S. Hill; *Handel Collection of Church Music*, 1854; besides books on Harmony (1844, '54) and juvenile collections.

Leonard Marshall: *Antiquarian*, 1849; *Harpsichord* or *Union Collection*, 1852, with E. N. Stone.

Augustus D. Fillmore (b. 1823), Christian minister in Ohio: *Universal Musician; Christian Psalmist* — both probably before 1850.

John W. Moore (1807–87), editor in Vermont and New Hampshire, and author of an *Encyclopædia of Music* (1854): *Sacred Minstrel*, before 1850.

From 1850 —

Richard S. Willis (1819–1900), brother of the poet N. P. Willis, editor and author in New York: *Church Chorals*, New York, 1850. In 1855 he published *Our Church Music*, a discussion for pastors and people.

Joseph Funk, a music-publisher at Dayton, Va.: *Genuine Church Music*, 1848? (as *Harmonia Sacra*, '50).

Henry W. Greatorex (1811–58), an English organist at Hartford, later in New York: *Collection of Psalm and Hymn Tunes, Chants, Anthems and Sentences*, Boston, 1851.

William Bullock: *Songs of the Church*, Halifax, N. S., 1854.

John Zundel (1815–82), a German organist, at Plymouth Church in Brooklyn in 1850–78: *Psalmody*, New York, 1855.

William H. Walter (b. 1825), organist at Newark, New York and Washington: *Selection of Psalms*, 1857; *Manual of Church Music*, 1860.

F. E. Pitts, minister at Nashville, Tenn.: *Zion's Harp*, Louisville, before 1859.

Lewis H. Steiner (b. 1827), physician in Baltimore: *Cantate Domino*, Boston, 1859, with Henry Schiving.

C. Warren: *Missouri Harmony*, Cincinnati, probably before 1860.

A. Aldrich: *Sacred Lyre*, Boston, 1859.

Among those whose works began before 1860, but continued much later, are especially:

Luther O. Emerson (1820–1915): *Romberg Collection*, Boston, 1853; etc.

William O. Perkins (1831–1902): *Choral Harmony*, 1859; etc.

The total amount of original music in these books is considerable and includes 'anthems' as well as 'tunes' in many cases. Most of it has the interest of being indigenous, since practically all the compilers and contributors were native Americans and had no ambition except to serve an actual musical situation as they knew it.

Detailed discussion of the styles exemplified cannot be attempted here. They are perhaps more varied than is usually realized, with some interesting analogies to similar work elsewhere. As to harmony, they keep mainly to a small selection of chords, without much inversion or modification. Modulation is wanting or extremely limited. A curious impulse toward 'fuguing' or a kind of counterpoint, which Billings and a few others indulged, did not long continue. As to melody, some good specimens of diatonic procedure occur, the interest lying in the solidity of the chord-succession. But the prevailing tendency is toward the free skips and arpeggiations of secular song. The rather numerous rhythmic and metric patterns imply the same relationship. As compared with the complexity and studied art of the English part-song or glee tunes that were plentifully introduced after the Civil War, these old tunes certainly lack richness. But they are almost always singable, and some of them have no small individuality.

As illustrating the persistence of the type, and also suggesting an easy means of reference to it, it may be noted that in Hatfield's *Church Hymn Book* (1872)— a large and carefully edited book — out of about 450 tunes at least 175 are taken from this older Psalmody. Among the specimens thus preserved are Billings' 'Jordan' (1781) — though not his better-known 'Chester' — Edson's 'Bridgewater' and 'Lenox' (1782), Holyoke's 'Arnheim' (1785), Daniel Read's 'Lisbon' and 'Windham' (1785), Holden's 'Coronation' (1793), Swan's 'China' (1800), Ingalls' 'Northfield' (1805), John Cole's 'Geneva' (1805), Mitchell's 'Pilesgrove' (1802), Norton's 'Devonshire' (1818), more than 20 by Hastings, including 'Retreat' (1822), 'Rock of Ages' and 'Zion' (1830), 'New Haven' (1833), 'Rhine' (1836), 'Arcadia' (1839), and 'Peniel' (1850), nearly 45 of Lowell Mason's original tunes, including 'Missionary Hymn' (1824), 'Hebron,' 'Laban,' 'Litchfield,' 'Rockingham,' 'Uxbridge' and 'Wesley' (1830), 'Olivet' (1831), 'Boylston' (1832), 'Sabbath' (1834), 'Admah' (1835), 'Ariel' and 'Naomi' (1836), 'Zerah' (1837), 'Gerar' and 'Meribah' (1839), 'Harwell' and 'Migdol' (1840), 'Ernan' (1850), 'Henley' (1854) and 'Bethany' (1859), besides many of his arrangements, Gardiner's 'Dedham' (1830), N. D. Gould's 'Woodland' (1832), Oliver's 'Federal Street' (1832) and 'Merton' (1843), Zeuner's 'Missionary Chant' and 'Telemann' (1832) and 'Oaksville' (1839), Pond's 'Armenia' (1835), Webb's 'Webb' (1837), Kingsley's 'Heber,' 'Tappan' and 'Ware' (1838) and 'Southport' (1853), nearly 20 by Bradbury, including 'Brown' (1840), 'Braden,' 'Rest' and 'Zephyr' (1844), 'Woodworth' (1849), 'Aletta' (1856) and 'Even Me' (1862), Ives' 'Beulah' (1846), Woodbury's 'Edmeston' (1848) and 'Siloam' (1850), Taylor's 'Louvan' and 'Solitude' (1849), J. E. Gould's 'Bera' (1849), Greatorex's 'Bemerton' and 'Leighton' (1849), Sweetser's 'Octavius' and 'Rose Hill' (1849), Zundel's 'Lebanon' (1855). Root's 'Shining Shore' (1859), etc. In addition, there are many tunes by composers who did not edit books, such as 'Kentucky' and 'Rockbridge' (1822) by Aaron Chapin, 'Expostulation' (1830) by Josiah Hopkins (1786–1862), 'Holley' (1835) by George Hews (1806–73), 'Martyn' by Simeon B. Marsh (1836), 'State Street' (1844) by Jonathan C. Woodman (1813–94), 'Wimborne' by Whittaker (1849), 'Maitland' (1850) by George N. Allen (1812–77), 'Rathbun' (1851) by Ithamar Conkey (1815–67), 'Solitude' by L. T. Downes (1851), 'Stockwell' (1851) by Darius E. Jones (1815–81), etc.

The list of books might be much prolonged, since the issue of tune-books continued plentifully beyond the time of the Civil War. The latter part of it, as here extended to about 1860, is doubtless incomplete, especially after about 1825, and perhaps somewhat inaccurate, since the data are not as well brought together as for the earlier time. What is here set down, however, makes an impressive showing of a persistent line of musical effort for more than a century. The total number of books included is nearly 375, by about 200 compilers whose names are known. The editions of the earlier books were relatively small, so that as business ventures they could hardly have been remunerative, while their influence was local and temporary. But of Mason's various works it is said that over a million copies were sold, which implies wide distribution and a settled demand.[1]

With the advent of Mason and Hastings, or at least from about 1830, the old Psalmody plainly entered upon a second stage. The original instinctive efforts toward popular training in the rudiments of singing, toward what is now called 'community music,' and toward the discipline and enrichment of church-services — these all remained in force. But now the leading spirits were men of better technical training, of more independent station and of broader outlook. From Mason onward many of them had considerable study in Europe. Many of them, too, secured honorable place as private teachers and certainly were in contact with other phases of musical progress besides that represented in their tune-books.

Mason came just when the public school was first establishing itself as an institution. He was so much interested that in 1832 he gave up the leadership of the Handel and Haydn Society to become what would now be called 'music-supervisor' for the public schools of

[1] See 'Jour. of Education,' Sept. 1857, and Allibone, *Dict. of Authors*,

Boston. Before 1840, besides attracting inquirers and students to Boston, he began to
exert influence elsewhere, either by conducting
classes himself or by encouraging the holding
of 'musical conventions' to stir up popular
interest and help in training teachers — thus
starting a movement that continued for many
decades and is to-day represented by the
Chautauqua Institution and numerous
'summer schools.' His own direct impress
was felt as far west as Cincinnati and as far
south as Philadelphia and Baltimore. That
Mason was the pioneer in the present immense
expansion of public-school music throughout
the country is obvious. In some sense he
was also an instigator for the growth of
systematic musical instruction in other ways.
From the itinerant 'singing-teacher' of the
time of Billings to the modern 'music-school'
seems like passing between things essentially
discrete. Yet in the work of Mason and his
colleagues they were historically connected.

Mason's great enthusiasm was for choral
singing. He himself organized and led large
choirs in Boston and elsewhere. It is clear
that he proposed thus to lift and direct popular
standards. But it proved that this emphasis
actually led very soon to a separation of
interest between choir and congregation,
especially as about 1850 musical leaders began
to be more and more those of foreign birth,
with no sympathy with the traditions of the
old Psalmody. In time the distinction thus
fostered between the 'artistic' and the
'popular' was greatly accentuated by the
replacement of the chorus-choir by the quartet
or similar small force of trained singers. In
time, also, the distinction worked itself out
in the development of a new type of church-
hymnal, with words and music combined.
The movement in this direction, which began
soon after 1830 (see HYMN-BOOKS), came to
have two diverse branches. One of these
grew into the dignified and artistic hymnals
of the present day — in which surely Mason
would have rejoiced. The other veered off
into the music of the choirless assembly — the
Sunday-school, the camp-meeting and the
revivalist's campaign — whence arose the

so-called 'Gospel hymns,' in countless myriads
and of uncertain essential quality. It is
curious that two branches from the same
original stalk of primitive Psalmody should
bear such dissimilar fruits in the half-century
since the Civil War and be arrayed in so much
hostility to each other as they are. And it
is unfortunate that after 1860 the types of
'popular' sacred song which most obviously
were derived from the traditional Psalmody
should not have been more affected by the
general advance in musical culture and taste
in other fields. The consequence has been
that musicians who have reacted against the
vapid and merely noisy forms of this later type
have been led to underestimate the historic
significance of the earlier Psalmody, much of
which was at least sincere and dignified.

TURNER, ALFRED DUDLEY (1854–
1888). See Register, 6.

TURNER, ARTHUR HENRY (b. 1873).
See Register, 8.

TWADDELL, WILLIAM POWELL (b.
1879). See COLLEGES, 2 (Tifft C., Ga.).

'TWILIGHT OF THE KINGS, THE.'
A 'masque of democracy,' No. 16 of the
'Grove-Plays' of the San Francisco Bohemian
Club, produced in 1918. The text is by
Richard M. Hotaling and the music by
Wallace A. Sabin.

TYLER. See Register, 2.

TYLER, ABRAM RAY (Dec. 24, 1868,
Brooklyn), was trained as pianist and organist
in Brooklyn and New York by Buck, Mason,
Bowman and Rybner, and for several years
was organist in New York. In 1902–11 he
was music-director at Beloit College in Wisconsin, continuing afterward as lecturer, and
since 1916 has been organist at Temple
Beth-El in Detroit. He has given many
organ-recitals in different places, as at the
Pan-American Exposition in Buffalo in 1901.
For a time he was secretary of the A. G. O.,
and has been dean of the Michigan Chapter.
He has published a violin-sonata, a piano-
trio, music for Protestant and Jewish services,
and settings of Greek plays. [R.8]

TYRWHITT, GERALD HUGH. See
BERNERS.

U

UHE, ARTHUR EMIL (b. 1892). See Register, 10.

'UNCLE TOM.' An opera by Caryl Florio, produced in Philadelphia in 1882.

UNIVERSITIES, MUSIC IN. See COLLEGES and STATE UNIVERSITIES.

UNIVERSITY MUSICAL SOCIETY, THE, of the University of Michigan, at Ann Arbor, was first organized in 1879 under the lead of Calvin B. Cady, then acting-professor. Membership was limited to the trustees, faculty and graduates of the University, and the general purpose was to promote music as a part of its educational system. In 1888 it was incorporated, with power to establish and maintain a School of Music, an orchestra, a chorus and an annual series of high-class concerts. All these purposes have been brilliantly realized.

The University School of Music was founded in 1889, when Albert A. Stanley became professor. Reorganized in 1891 on its present basis, its relation to the whole life of the institution has been remarkably intimate. There are now about 30 in the faculty, and the annual enrolment runs over 500, coming from the whole United States and several foreign countries. The number of pupils since the first is nearly 8000. The School has a commodious building, erected in 1892 and much enlarged and completely modernized in 1917. The equipment is ample and excellent.

The University Symphony Orchestra, with an average membership of 50 or more, gives several concerts each season before large audiences. The programs include a wide range of standard instrumental literature.

The University Choral Union began in 1879 and since 1893 has had an average membership of about 300. Its répertoire includes all the leading sacred and secular works, some not previously given in America. Since 1893 a May Festival has been held, consisting usually of six concerts, with the most eminent soloists and a large orchestra, such as the Chicago Orchestra. Five 'pre-festival' concerts are also given with visiting artists. In the Festival series about 2000 works have been given, including about 75 important choral works. Ten of the best orchestras and over 300 famous soloists have assisted. In addition, about 1200 concerts or recitals of significance have been given under the auspices of the School of Music, covering most of the range of ensemble and solo music. All concerts, except those of the Choral Union and at the Festival, are free. It is estimated that about 40,000 persons have sung in the chorus for periods of a year to three years.

UNSCHULD, MARIE VON (May 17, 1881, Olmütz, Austria), studied piano at the Vienna Conservatory and later with Leschetizky and Stavenhagen, violin with Dont, and counterpoint and composition with Grädener. After appearing in Vienna as pianist and in various cities in Europe and America, in 1904 she established the Von Unschuld University of Music in Washington. She has lectured at several institutions, and is author of The Hand of the Pianist, 1901, and Supplement, 1906, The Scale-Practice, 3 vols., 1910, The Von Unschuld Method of Pianoforte-Playing and Teaching, 1911, The Graded Course, 1912, Art of and Means for Pianoforte-Instruction, 1915, and Handbook of General Musical Knowledge, 1915. In 1907 she married Henry Lazard of Newport, R. I. [R.9]

UPTON, GEORGE PUTNAM (Oct. 25, 1835, Roxbury, Mass. : May 20, 1919, Chicago), was educated at the Roxbury Latin School and Brown University, graduating in 1854. From 1855 for more than sixty years he lived in Chicago as an active journalist. At first he was on the staff of the 'Native Citizen,' then of the 'Evening Journal,' and from 1860 of the 'Tribune.' During the Civil War he was an active war-correspondent. He early established himself as musical critic. He heard the earliest important operatic and orchestral performances in Chicago, and wrote the first newspaper criticisms that appeared there. In 1872 he was one of the founders of the Apollo Club and its first president. He was a zealous supporter of Theodore Thomas in all his enterprises, both before and after his going to Chicago. He was a member of numerous writers' associations. His numerous books were marked by great pains as to accuracy, a genial and broad-minded spirit and much felicity of expression. They include Letters of Peregrine Pickle (musical and literary), 1869, Woman in Music, 1880, Standard Operas, 1886 (many editions, enlarged), Standard Oratorios, 1887, Standard Cantatas, 1888, Standard Symphonies, 1889, Musical Pastels, 1902, Standard Light Operas, 1902, Theodore Thomas, an Autobiography, 2 vols., 1905, Life of Reményi, 1906, Standard Concert-Guide, 1908 (revised, 1918), Standard Concert-Repertory, 1909, Standard Musical Biographies, 1910, In Music-Land, 1913, The Song, 1914. He also translated Nohl's biographies of Haydn, Beethoven, Wagner and Liszt, Max Müller's Memories and Theodor Storm's Immensee. His autobiographic Musical Memories, 1908, contains much valuable information, presented with much charm. [R.5]

URANIAN SOCIETY, THE, of Philadelphia, was the formal outgrowth of an effort
in 1784 by Andrew Adgate to establish classes
for instruction in psalmody. The Society
took shape in 1785 as a body of subscribers
'to establish a Free School for the spreading of
the knowledge of vocal music.' From the
outset occasional concerts were given in the
hall of the University of Pennsylvania. In
1787 the name Uranian Academy was adopted
and Adgate was called president. At that
time the number of pupils to be received was
set at 300, with three places of instruction.
Among the trustees and patrons were Dr.
Benjamin Rush and Francis Hopkinson.
Data about the Academy after 1790 are wanting. Adgate died in 1793, but traces of the
name 'Uranian' are found until after 1800.
In 1793–97, perhaps longer, a Uranian Musical
Society existed in New York. See Sonneck,
Concert-Life, pp. 103–18, 203.

URSO, CAMILLA (June 13, 1842, Nantes,
France : Jan. 20, 1902, New York), was
the daughter of an orchestral player. She
began to study the violin in her sixth year, and
at nine became a pupil of Massart at the Paris
Conservatory. In 1852 she came to America
as a child-performer, playing in concerts
with Sontag and Alboni. After three years
her parents settled in Nashville, Tenn., and
for seven years she devoted herself to violin-
practice. In 1862 she took up concert-work
again, appearing first in New York at a Philharmonic concert. Thereafter for thirty years
she made constant tours in America and
Europe with great success. She visited Australia in 1879 and 1894, and South Africa in
1895. The last years of her life were spent in
New York. See an interesting reference to her
in Upton, *Musical Memories*, pp. 70–1. [R.4]

UTT, PAUL RALPH (b. 1882). See
COLLEGES, 3 (Ottawa U., Kan.).

V

'VALERIE.' A four-act opera by J. Remington Fairlamb, produced by an amateur troupe in Washington about 1870.

VALLERIA, ALWINA (b. 1848). See Register, 6.

VALLE-RIESTRA, JOSÉ (b. 1859). See Register, 8.

VALLEY, OLOF. See STATE UNIVERSITIES (Kansas State C.).

VALTON, PETER. See Register, 1.

VAN BROEKHOVEN, JOHN A. (b. 1856). See Register, 7.

VAN CLEVE, JOHN SMITH (Oct. 30, 1851, Maysville, Ky.), lost his sight in early childhood and had his schooling at the Ohio Institute for the Blind, where he had piano-lessons from H. J. Nothnagel. He went to the Woodward High School in Cincinnati, Ohio Wesleyan University and Boston University. In Cincinnati he studied with W. Steinbrecher, and in Boston with Lang and Apthorp. He taught at the Ohio Institute for the Blind in 1872–75, at Janesville, Wis., in 1875–79, and then moved to Cincinnati, where he taught piano and theory, lectured on music and literature at the College of Music and Conservatory of Music, and was music-critic, first for the 'Commercial' and after 1883 for the 'News-Journal.' He gave many lecture-recitals, and was much in demand as teacher. In 1897 he removed to Chicago, later to Troy, N. Y., and in 1913 to New York. He received the degree and Ph.D. from Twin Valley College in 1892. He has published a 'Gavotte Humoresque' for piano, lectures, poems and many miscellaneous articles. As a writer, he has decided gifts of presentation and diction. [R.6]

VAN DER STUCKEN, FRANK VALENTIN (Oct. 15, 1858, Fredericksburg, Tex.). See article in Vol. v. 217. He studied theory and composition with Benoît and violin with Émile Wambach in Brussels in 1866–76. From this period date a Gloria for chorus and orchestra, a Te Deum for soli, chorus and orchestra, and a 'Festmarsch' for orchestra. He spent the years 1876–78 at Leipzig, receiving aid from Reinecke, Grieg and Langer. His first concert in America was on Apr. 4, 1884, at Steinway Hall in New York. Besides his work with the Arion Society he became active as an orchestral conductor, and was the first to present orchestral programs entirely by American composers. On July 12, 1889, he gave such a program at the Paris Exposition. In 1892 he conducted the concerts on the European tour of the Arion Society. He was in demand as festival-conductor, and officiated thus at Indianapolis in 1887, New-

ark in 1891 and New York in 1894. In 1895–1907 he was conductor of the Cincinnati Symphony Orchestra, and till 1903 also director of the College of Music. He conducted the Cincinnati May Festivals in 1906–12, the Wagner Festival at Antwerp in 1913, the Festival of Dramatic Music there in 1914, and has given many orchestral programs of his own music in America and abroad. For the last ten years he has made his home in Europe, coming to America only upon occasion. In 1919 he conducted orchestral works in Copenhagen. Additional orchestral works are a suite, 'Festzug,' 'Pagina d'Amore,' 'Idylle,' 'Rigaudon,' the festival-march 'Louisiana,' a waltz for strings, a 'Festival Hymn' for men's chorus and orchestra, etc. His 'Tempest' music was first given at Breslau in 1862, the 'William Ratcliff' prologue at Weimar in 1883, and the 'Pax Triumphans' at the Brooklyn Festival of 1900. [R.7]

VAN DRESSER, MARCIA (b. 1880). See Register, 8.

‡ VAN DYCK, ERNEST MARIE HUBERT (Apr. 2, 1861, Antwerp, Belgium). See article in Vol. v. 217. Since 1906 he has been professor of singing at the Antwerp and Brussels Conservatories. His American début was as Tannhäuser in 1898 at the Metropolitan Opera House, where he continued to sing regularly till 1902.

VAN GORDON, CYRENA [name originally Pocock] (b. 1893). See Register, 10.

VAN HAGEN, PETER ALBRECHT (d. 1800?, New York), in 1774 appeared in Charleston as teacher of organ, piano, stringed instruments and composition. In 1789 he was located as teacher and player in New York, assisted in concerts by his wife and son. In 1796 the family moved to Boston, where father and son played in theater-orchestras, were church-organists and managed a music-store. The father is probably the son of Peter Albrecht Van Hagen, who was a pupil of Geminiani, violinist and organist at Rotterdam. If so, he was himself a pupil of Honauer in Paris. See Sonneck, *Concert-Life*, especially p. 23, and *I. M. G. Sammelbde.* 6. 478.

VAN HOOSE, ELLISON (Aug. 18, 1869, Murfreesboro, Tenn.), after first lessons from his mother, studied in New York for five years with Perry Averill and Isadore Luckstone, then with Fidèle Koenig and Jean de Reszké in Paris, Sir Henry Wood and Franco Navora in London and Antonio Cotogni in Rome. He sang tenor in New York church-choirs until 1897, when he was engaged by the Damrosch-Ellis Opera Co., and made his début in Philadelphia as Tannhäuser. During the two following seasons he continued with the same company, and appeared in orchestral concerts in London and elsewhere in England· In 1899-1900 he was at the Mayence Opera, and for the next ten years sang variously in concert, opera and oratorio. In 1903-05 he made two American tours with Mme. Melba, and in 1906-07 with Mme. Sembrich. In 1911-12 he sang with the Chicago Opera Company, and has since specialized in oratorio and concert-work. With the New York Oratorio Society he participated in the American première of Elgar's 'Dream of Gerontius' on Dec. 6, 1903. [R.8]

VAN VECHTEN, CARL (June 17, 1880, Cedar Rapids, Ia.), graduating from the University of Chicago in 1903, and has devoted himself to writing on musical and allied subjects. His books are *Music after the Great War*, 1915, *Music and Bad Manners*, 1916, *Interpreters and Interpretations*, 1917, *The Merry-Go-Round*, 1918 and *The Music of Spain*, 1919. He has championed the cause of the moderns in music. He was one of the first in America to write of Stravinsky, Ornstein and Satie. He has devoted several essays to modern stage-decoration, with particular emphasis on the work of Adolphe Appia. His *Music of Spain* is the only book on the subject in English. He was assistant musical editor of the New York 'Times' for four years, edited the program-notes for the Symphony Society in 1910-11, contributed the musical biographical notes to the revised edition of the *Century Dictionary*, and was Paris correspondent for the 'Times' in 1908-09 and dramatic critic for the 'Press' in 1913-14. [R.9]

VAN VLECK, JACOB. See Register, 2.

VAN VLIET, CORNELIUS (Sept. 1, 1886, Rotterdam, Holland), began violin and piano at six, but at nine changed to the 'cello and at twelve was heard in concert. He studied with Eberle in Rotterdam and Mossel in Amsterdam, and joined the Concertgebouw Orchestra under Mengelberg. Thence in 1903 he went as leading 'cellist to the Leipzig Philharmonic and the Prague Philharmonic, followed by solo-engagements in Helsingfors, Munich (1905) and Vienna (1908) under Weingartner. In Helsingfors he also taught chamber-music in the Conservatory. In 1911-12 he concertized in America and then joined the Minneapolis Symphony Orchestra and the Minneapolis Trio. Since 1919 he has been located in New York, chiefly occupied with concert-work. He is 'cellist in the New York Trio. [R.10]

VAN ZANDT, MARIE (Oct. 8, 1861,[1] New York : Dec. 31, 1919, Cannes, France).

[1] '1858' in Who's *Who in America*, 1901-12, but '1860' in *International Year-Book*, 1919.

See article in Vol. v. 585-6. In 1898 she married Professor Tcherinov of the Moscow Imperial Academy and retired from the stage. Delibes wrote 'Lakmé' for her, but her greatest success was as Mignon. [R.6]

VEAZIE, GEORGE AUGUSTUS (1835-1915). See Register, 5.

VECSEI, DESIDER JOSEF (b. 1882). See Register, 10.

VENTH, CARL (Feb. 16, 1860, Cologne, Germany), was a pupil of Hiller, Japha, Jensen and Klauwell at the Cologne Conservatory, and of Wieniawski and Dupont at the Brussels Conservatory, graduating from the latter in 1877 and making his début as violinist with the Utrecht Symphony Orchestra in 1878. He then became concertmaster of the Flemish Opera in Brussels, and the next year held a similar position at the Opéra-Comique in Paris. He came to America in 1880 and from 1884 was concertmaster at the Metropolitan Opera House. In 1888 he established the Venth College of Music in Brooklyn, where he also conducted the Brooklyn Symphony Orchestra and choral societies. Moving to Texas in 1908, he became head of the violin-department in the Kidd-Key College and conducted the Dallas Symphony Orchestra. At present he is dean of fine arts in the Texas Woman's College at Fort Worth, conductor of the Fort Worth Symphony Orchestra and divisional band-superintendent at Camp Bowie. He has published the comic opera 'Fair Betty'; the cantatas 'The Resurrection,' 'Myth-Voices,' 'From Olden Times' and 'The Quest of Beauty'; the piano-suite 'Frithjof and Ingeborg,' and many piano-pieces; about twenty-five pieces for violin; and a considerable group of songs. Two operas and a cantata are in manuscript, as also several orchestral works, two string-quartets, a piano-trio and sonata, two violin-concertos and three sonatas for piano and violin. [R.7]

VERE, CLÉMENTINE DUCHÊNE DE, was born at Paris. She studied there and with Mme. Albertini-Baucardé at Florence, where at sixteen she made her début as Marguerite de Valois in 'Les Huguenots.' She then sang in Italy, France, Spain, Mexico, Germany, England and Australia, meeting with equal success in opera and concert. She sang Marguerite in Berlioz' 'Damnation de Faust' in New York in 1896, and in 1897 joined the Metropolitan Opera House Company. Later she made several tours of England with the Moody-Manners Opera Company. Since 1914 she has lived in New York as singer and teacher. In 1892 she married Romualdo Sapio, the conductor. Her répertoire includes Violetta, Gilda, Micaela, Marguerite de Valois, the Infanta (in 'Le Cid'), Marguerite (in 'Faust') Ophelia, Aïda, Rachel, Elsa, Lucia and Dinorah. [R.7]

‡ VIARDOT–GARCIA, MICHELLE FERDINANDE PAULINE (July 18, 1821, Paris, France : May 18, 1910, Paris). See article in Vol. v. 267–8. There are biographies by La Mara, 1882, and Torrigi, 1901, and collections of letters by Kaminski, 1907, and in 'The Musical Quarterly,' July, 1915, January, 1916.

‡ VIDAL, PAUL ANTONIN (June 16, 1863, Toulouse, France). See article in Vol. v. 271. Since 1906 he has been chief conductor at the Opéra-Comique. To the list of works add the operas 'La Reine Fiammette' (1898) and 'Ramses' (1908), the operetta 'Le Mariage d'Yvette' (1893), the pantomimes 'Columbine Abandonnée' (1888), and 'La Révérance' (1890), the lyric fantasy 'Eros' (1892), incidental music to Haraucourt's 'Juan de Manara' and to Pigeon's 'Amour dans les Enfers,' and the orchestral suite 'Les Mystères d'Éleusis.'

'VIERJÄHRIGE POSTEN, DER.' An opera by Gustav Hinrichs, produced in San Francisco in 1877.

‡ VIERNE, LOUIS VICTOR JULES (Oct. 8, 1870, Poitiers, France), in 1888–94 was a pupil at the Paris Conservatory of Franck and Widor. At graduation he won the first organ-prize and became Widor's assistant at St.-Sulpice. Since 1900 he has been organist at Notre-Dame. He is professor at the Schola Cantorum and Officier de l'Instruction Publique. He has given recitals with great success in France, Holland, England, Switzerland and Spain, and a visit to America is in prospect. His works include the following:

'Ave Maria,' op. 1, for soprano and organ.
Prélude in F-sharp minor, op. 2, for organ.
Allegretto and 'Prélude Funèbre,' op. 3, for organ.
'Tantum ergo,' op. 4, for chorus and orchestra.
'Le Soir' and 'Légende,' op. 5, for viola or 'cello and piano.
Largo and Canzonetta, op. 6, for oboe and piano.
Communion, op. 7, for organ.
String-Quartet in D minor, op. 12.
Symphony No. 1, in D minor, op. 14, for organ (1899, Pèregally & Parvy).
'Ave verum,' op. 15, for contralto and organ.
Messe Solennelle in C-sharp minor, op. 16, for chorus and orchestra.
'Suite Bourgignonne,' op. 17, for piano (seven movements also for orchestra).
Trois Airs de Ballet, op. 18, for piano.
Symphony No. 2, in E minor, op. 20, for organ (Pèregally).
Legend, 'Praxinoë, Princesse d'Égypte,' op. 22, for soli, women's voices and orchestra.
Sonata in G minor, op. 23, for violin and piano.
Symphony in A minor, op. 24.
Rapsodie, op. 25, for harp.
Sonata in B minor, op. 27, for 'cello and piano.
Symphony No. 3, in F-sharp minor, op. 28, for organ (1912, Durand).
Messe Basse (1913, Library of Catholic Art).
'24 Pièces en style libre,' op. 31, for organ (1915, Durand).

Symphony No. 4, in G minor, op. 32, for organ (1918, Schirmer).
12 Préludes, op. 33, for piano.
2 Nocturnes, in A minor and E, op. 35, for piano.
Poem, 'Psyché,' op. 36, for voice and orchestra.
Poem, 'Les Djinns,' op. 37, for voice and orchestra.
Poem, 'Éros,' op. 38, for voice and orchestra.
'Les Cloches,' op. 41, for piano.
2 Nocturnes, in D-flat and C-sharp minor, op. 42, for piano.
Songs, opp. 8, 10, 11, 13, 26, 29 and 40.

VIGNA, ARTURO. See Register, 9.

VIGNETI, GEORGES (b. 1882). See Register, 10.

VILIM, JOSEPH ALOIS (Jan. 18, 1861, Chicago), studied violin in Chicago and in Prague, graduating at the Prague Conservatory in 1883. In 1884–87 he was teacher of violin at the Chicago Musical College, in 1887–99 director of the violin-department at the American Conservatory and in 1894–96 a first violin in the Thomas Orchestra. In 1899 he founded the Vilim American Violin School (which he directed till 1918), and organized the Dvořák Quintet, the Beethoven String Quartet and the Vilim Home Trio (with his sons Richard and Mark). He now has a violin-studio at Coronado, Cal. He is author of Violin-Technique Guide and Seven Days' Exercises for the Advanced Violinist. A book on How to Practice Paganini and Difficult Compositions is nearing completion. [R.7]

'VINTAGE, THE,' or 'Sterne's Maria.' An opera in two acts by Victor Pelissier, the text by William Dunlap, produced in New York, on Jan. 14, 1799. See Sonneck, article in I. M. G. Sammelbde. 6. 482.

'VIOLINIST, THE,' of Chicago, is a monthly periodical established in 1900. Its editor till 1906 was Ray G. Edwards and since 1908 has been Ada E. Taylor. A Violinist's Guide was first issued in 1916, giving useful information about violin-makers.

VIRGIL PRACTICE CLAVIER. See article in Vol. ii. 266.

VIX, GENEVIÈVE (b. 1887). See Register, 10.

VOCALION. See article in Vol. v. 360–1.

VOGRICH, MAX WILHELM KARL (Jan. 24, 1852, Szeben, Austria : June 10, 1916, New York), began piano-study at five and played in public at seven. In 1866–69 he was at the Leipzig Conservatory, taking piano with Moscheles, Wenzel and Reinecke, and theory and composition with Hauptmann, Richter and Reinecke. In 1870–78 he traveled as pianist throughout Europe and also in Mexico and South America. In 1878 he came to New York, gave recitals there and toured the country with Wilhelmj. In 1882–86 he lived in Australia, then in New York till 1902, in Weimar till 1908, in London till 1914 and again in New York. The latter part of his life was given to composition and to work as adviser to G. Schirmer. The list of his works includes the operas 'Vanda' (1875, Florence), 'King Arthur' (1893, Leipzig) and 'Der Buddha' (1904, Weimar), all to his own librettos; incidental music to Wildenbruch's 'Die Lieder des Euripides' (Weimar) ; the dramatic scene 'The Highland Widow' ; the oratorio 'The Captivity' (1891, Metropolitan Opera House) ; the cantatas 'The Diver' and 'The Young King and the Shepherdess' ; a Missa Solemnis ; two symphonies, in E minor and A minor ; an Andante and Intermezzo for violin and orchestra ; a concerto in E minor for piano ; 'Memento Mori' for violin and orchestra (1912, Berlin) ; a violin-concerto, 'E pur si muove' (dedicated to Elman and played by him, 1913, Berlin, and 1917, New York) ; many pieces for piano, violin and piano ; songs and choruses. [R.6]

VOGT, AUGUSTUS STEPHEN (Aug. 14, 1861, Washington, Ont.), in 1881–82 studied at the New England Conservatory in Boston with Emery, Buckingham and Dunham, and in 1885–88 at the Leipzig Conservatory under Reinecke, Rehberg, Ruthardt, Papperitz and Jadassohn. In 1888–92 he was teacher of piano at the Toronto College of Music, going in 1892 to the Toronto Conservatory, where since 1913 he has been director. Under his administration this has become the largest and best-equipped school of music in the Dominion and one of the foremost in America. In 1894 he founded the Mendelssohn Choir, continuing as conductor till 1917 and making it one of the finest choral bodies in the world. In 1907 the University of Toronto gave him the honorary degree of Mus.D. In 1888–1906 he was organist at the Jarvis Street Baptist Church. He has written several a cappella choruses and a book on *Modern Pianoforte-Technic*, 1900. [R.7]

VOLAVY, MARGUERITE (b. 1886). See Register, 10.

‡ VOLBACH, FRITZ (Dec. 17, 1861, Wipperfürth, near Cologne, Germany). See article in Vol. v. 376. He continued at Mayence until 1907, when he became music-director and professor at Tübingen. In 1899 he secured a Ph.D. with a thesis upon *Die Praxis der Händel-Aufführung*. In 1900 he was in charge of a musical celebration at Mayence of the quinquecentenary of Gutenberg's birth. He is equally celebrated as instrumentalist, conductor and composer. Additional works are a Symphony in B minor, op. 33, the comedy-opera 'Die Kunst zu lieben,' op. 34 (1910, Düsseldorf), 'König Laurins Rosengarten,' op. 38, for baritone, men's chorus and orchestra, and incidental music to the tragedy 'König Tulga.' For list of books, see Baker, *Dict. of Musicians*, p. 991.

VOLPE, ARNOLD (July 9, 1869, Kovno, Russia), in 1884–87 studied violin at the Warsaw Musical Institute with Isidor Lotto and in 1887–91 at the Petrograd Conservatory with Auer, followed by work in theory and composition in 1893–97 with Soloviev. In 1898 he came to New York, where in 1902 he founded the Young Men's Symphony Orchestra and in 1904 the Volpe Symphony Orchestra. In 1910 he also undertook the direction of the orchestra of the Brooklyn Institute, and in 1910–14 and 1919 conducted series of municipal concerts in New York. In 1916 he established his own music-school. [R.8]

W

WADDEL, FRANCES E. See COLLEGES, 3 (Geneva C., Pa.).

WADE, HENRY T. See COLLEGES, 2 (Lake Erie C., Ohio).

WAINWRIGHT, MISS. See Register, 1.

WAINWRIGHT, JONATHAN MAYHEW (1792–1854). See Register, 3, and TUNE-BOOKS, 1819.

WALKER, EDYTH (b. 1870). See Register, 8.

‡ WALLACE, WILLIAM (July 3, 1860, Greenock, Scotland). See article in Vol. v. 424–5. His 'The Passing of Beatrice' was the first symphonic poem by a British composer. In 1899 he became Bantock's assistant in conducting daily concerts at Brighton, and later, in the latter's absence, edited 'The New Quarterly Musical Review' for about half its existence. He prepared the analytical program for the concert in London on Dec. 15, 1896, which called attention to many new British composers. He has been active as secretary of the Society of British Composers and honorary secretary of the Philharmonic Society. In 1911 he was one of the composers chosen for orchestral representation at the Congress of the I. M. G., and also at the Festival of British Music in 1915. During the war he was in service as ophthalmologist. In the list of compositions note that the date of the cantata 'The Massacre of the Macpherson' is 1899 and that of the song-cycle 'Lords of the Sea' is 1901, and that a large number of works are published by Schott, Bayley & Ferguson, Stainer & Bell, Cramer, Ricordi, Boosey, etc. 'The Outlaw' was performed in 1913. He has made many translations of texts, as of Berlioz' 'The Damnation of Faust,' Missa's 'Muguette,' Strauss' 'Feuersnot,' Leroux' 'Le Chemineau' (Richepin's text), Delius' 'A Mass of Life,' cantatas by Weingartner and Krug-Waldsee, and many songs by Sibelius and Weingartner. He is author of a mystery-play, *The Divine Surrender*, 1895, *The Musical Faculty*, 1914, besides numerous articles.

WALLER, FRANK LAIRD. See Register, 9.

WALTER, GEORGE WILLIAM (1851–1911). See Register, 5.

WALTER, THOMAS (1696–1725). See TUNE-BOOKS, 1721.

WALTER, WILLIAM HENRY (1825– ?). See TUNE-BOOKS, 1848.

WARD, FRANK EDWIN (Oct. 7, 1872, Wysox, Pa.), in 1892–97 studied in New York with Spanuth (piano), J. P. Lawrence (organ and theory), Pearce (theory) and Macfarlane (organ), and in 1898–1903 was under MacDowell at Columbia University, winning the Mosenthal fellowship. In 1902–13 he was organist at the University, and also in 1900–05 at Rye, N. Y., since 1902 at Temple Israel and since 1906 at Holy Trinity. Since 1909 he has had charge of theory-classes at Columbia. His works include

Sonata No. 1, in E minor, op. 1, for violin and piano.
Magnificat and Nunc Dimittis in E-flat, op. 2.
Sonata No. 2, in G, op. 9, for violin and piano.
Rhapsodie in F minor, op. 10, for violin (or 'cello) and piano.
'Rhapsodie Bohème,' op. 12, for two pianos.
Scherzo, 'Peter Pan,' op. 13, for orchestra.
Magnificat and Nunc Dimittis in F, op. 14.
Sonata No. 1, in F minor, op. 15, for organ.
Quartet in F minor, op. 18, for piano and strings.
Lenten Cantata, 'The Saviour of the World,' op. 20, for soli, chorus and orchestra.
Quartet in C minor, op. 22, for strings (Nat. Federation of Musical Clubs prize, 1917).
Christmas Cantata, 'The Divine Birth,' op. 23, for soli, chorus and organ.
Communion Service in A-flat, op. 24.
Symphony No. 1, 'Shakespearean Moods,' op. 25.
Solemn Mass in G minor, op. 29.
'An Ocean Rhapsody,' op. 31, for orchestra (also for violin, 'cello, harp and organ).
Quartet in G minor, for strings.
Trio for piano, violin and 'cello.
Sonata No. 2, in D minor, for organ.
Also about 30 anthems; many songs, opp. 4, 6, 7, 27, 30; part-songs, opp. 8, 11, 21; organ-pieces, opp. 16, 17, 19, 26, 33, 35; piano-pieces, opp. 3, 5, 28, 34; etc. [R.8]

WARE, HARRIET (Aug. 26, 1877, Waupun, Wis.), after graduating from Pillsbury Academy in Minnesota, studied piano with William Mason in New York. Vocal work with Mme. La Grange in Paris followed, and composition with Sigismond Stojowski there, and with Kaun in Berlin. Her published compositions are the cantata 'Sir Oluf,' for women's voices, soprano and baritone solos and orchestra; 'Undine,' a lyric tone-poem (words by Edwin Markham); 'The Cross,' for voice and piano or orchestra (words by Markham); 'A Day in Arcady,' song-cycle for two voices; many songs and piano-pieces. The most important work in manuscript is a piano-concerto. She has made many appearances as composer-pianist. [R.9]

WARE, HELEN (Sept. 9, 1887, Woodbury, N. J.), began the violin with Frederic Hahn in Philadelphia, and at the University there studied harmony and counterpoint with Clarke. She then spent two years under Sevčik at Pisek and Vienna, and two with Hubay at Budapest. Making her début in recital at Budapest in 1912, she was the first American violinist to tour in Hungary. The bent of her interest is shown by the booklet

Poetry and Power of Hungarian and Slav Music, and by many articles on this subject in musical journals. Besides much European experience, she has twice toured throughout America. Lately she has given more time to composition than to concerts. Her works for violin and piano include 'Hungarian Camp-Songs' (Presser), a 'Hungarian Love-Song' (Presser), the Hungarian phantasy 'Cinka Panna' (Carl Fischer), the cradle-song 'Gentle Shadows' (Witmark), a 'Caprice Genett' and other transcriptions (C. Fischer, Schirmer), besides many songs. [R.10]

WARNER, JAMES F. See Register, 4.

WARNERY, EDMOND (b. 1876). See Register, 10.

WARNKE, HEINRICH (b. 1871). See Register, 9.

WARREN, C. See TUNE-BOOKS, 1855.

WARREN, GEORGE WILLIAM (Aug. 17, 1828, Albany, N. Y. : Mar. 17, 1902, New York), had his general education at Racine University, but was self-taught in music. In 1846–58 he was organist at St. Peter's in Albany, and for two years at St. Paul's. In 1860 he came to Brooklyn and for ten years was at Holy Trinity. From 1870 until his death he was organist at St. Thomas's in New York. He composed much church-music and some piano-pieces, and edited *Warren's Hymns and Tunes, as sung at St. Thomas's Church,* 1888. [R.4]

WARREN, RICHARD HENRY (Sept. 17, 1859, Albany, N. Y.), the son and pupil of the preceding, in 1880–86 was organist at All Souls' in New York, in 1886–1905 at St. Bartholomew's and since 1907 at the Church of the Ascension. In 1886–95 he was conductor of the Church Choral Society, which he founded, and brought out with it many important choral works, including some not before heard in America (Parker's 'Hora Novissima' was written for it). In 1905 he gave summer-concerts of orchestral music at St. Nicholas Garden. His works include several operettas (1880–1899), the romantic opera 'Phyllis' (1900, New York), some works for orchestra, a string-quartet, much church-music and songs. [R.7]

WARREN, SAMUEL PROWSE (Feb. 18, 1841, Montreal, Que. : Oct. 7, 1915, New York), the son of the organ-maker S. R. Warren (see below), began organ-study at eleven, and early played at St. Stephen's Chapel in Montreal and at the American Church. In 1861–64 he was in Berlin, taking piano with Gustav Schumann, organ and theory with Haupt and instrumentation with Wieprecht. After two years again in Montreal, in 1866–68 he was organist at All Souls' in New York, whence in 1868 he moved to Grace Church, continuing, save for two years

at Trinity (1874–76), till 1894 and becoming one of the foremost church-musicians in the country. In 1880–88 he also conducted the New York Vocal Union. As a concert-player he was held in universal esteem, giving hundreds of recitals in New York alone. He was a founder of the A. G. O., and the teacher of many notable organists. His standards were of the highest and he was able to transmit them to his pupils. He composed much church-music, vocal and instrumental, part-songs and piano-pieces, and made a long series of fine organ-transcriptions of orchestral works. He had a remarkable musical library. [R.5]

WARREN, SAMUEL RUSSEL (d. 1882). See Register, 3.

WARRINER, SOLOMON (1778–1860). See TUNE-BOOKS, 1813.

WASHBURN, JAPHET COOMBS. See TUNE-BOOKS, 1813.

WASS, EDWARD HAMES (b. 1874). See COLLEGES, 1 (Bowdoin C., Me.).

WATSON, HENRY C. (1818–1875). See Register, 4.

WATT, CHARLES E. See Register, 8.

WA-WAN PRESS, THE, was a publishing enterprise set on foot by Arthur Farwell in 1901 at Newton Center, Mass. Its stated object was ' primarily to publish the most progressive and significant compositions by American composers, wholly upon considerations of artistic merit ; and secondarily to give due attention to the development of the various forms of primitive folk-songs in America.' For a series of years it energetically fulfilled both of these objects, issuing a variety of works, some of them of large dimensions, by about forty American composers, including a striking number of settings or idealizations of Indian and Negro materials. It was one of the most influential factors in stimulating interest in types of work that had previously not received proper attention. The good-will of the enterprise has recently been transferred to G. Schirmer, Inc., in New York.

WEAD, CHARLES KASSON (b. 1848). See Register, 9.

WEAVER, JOHN KNOWLES (b. 1868). See COLLEGES, 3 (Kendall C., Okla.).

WEAVER, MIRIAM H. See COLLEGES, 3 (Wittenberg C., Ohio).

WEBB, FRANK RUSH (b. 1851). See Register, 6.

WEBB, GEORGE JAMES (June 24, 1803, near Salisbury, England : Oct. 7, 1887, Orange, N. J.), after study with Alexander Lucas in Salisbury, became organist at Falmouth, but in 1830 resigned to come to Boston. There he was organist at the Old South Church and soon became an intimate associate of Lowell Mason in various musical projects.

He was his assistant in teaching children's classes and they together founded the Boston Academy of Music in 1833. He was not only an excellent singing-teacher, but a good conductor. He was influential in furthering choral music of a high class and before 1855 was efficient in directing the Musical Fund Society's orchestra. In 1870 he removed to Orange, N. J., but continued to teach in New York till his retirement in 1885. For his publications, see TUNE-BOOKS (partly under Mason). He composed some anthems, part-songs and songs.[1]

WEBB, THOMAS SMITH (d. 1819). See Register, 3.

WEBER, ALBERT (1828–1879). See Register, 4.

WEBER PIANO COMPANY, THE, of New York, is the present name of the business established in 1852 by Albert Weber and from 1879 carried forward by Albert Weber, Jr. From about 1870 its instruments became generally recognized as having a special beauty of tone, as well as mechanical finish, so that they received many awards in competitions. Since 1903 the Company has formed part of the Æolian, Weber Piano & Pianola Co. The annual output of this division is about 5000 instruments.

WEIDIG, ADOLF (Nov. 28, 1867, Hamburg, Germany), was the son of an orchestral player and was educated in the Hamburg schools, studying music also in the Conservatory under Riemann, Von Bernuth and Bargheer. Later he graduated at the Munich Conservatory in 1891, having worked with Rheinberger and Abel. In 1888 he won the Mozart prize at Frankfort with a string-quartet. In 1892 he came to Chicago, becoming one of the first violins in the Thomas Orchestra and playing viola in the Spiering Quartet. Since 1893 he has been connected with the American Conservatory, teaching violin and theory, and from 1898 one of its directors. He has exerted a wide and wholesome influence as teacher, and has often appeared as orchestral conductor both in America and in Europe, often of his own compositions. He has written a symphony in C minor, a symphonic suite in three movements, the tone-poem 'Semiramis,' three overtures, a suite for string-orchestra, three string-quartets (D minor, A and C minor), a string-quintet, and published a Capriccio and 'Three Episodes' for orchestra (Schott), a string-quartet in C (Schott), a piano-trio (Augener), a suite for violin and piano (Schott), three 'Morceaux de Salon' for violin and piano (Schott), a Serenade for strings (Summy), an

[1] The well-known tune bearing his name, however, is adapted from the secular song ' 'Tis dawn, the lark is singing.'

2 D

'Italian' suite for violin and piano, the song-cycle 'The Buccaneer,' 10 a cappella choruses, and a large number of lesser pieces for violin and piano or for piano, besides about 25 songs. (Ditson, Carl Fischer, Silver, Burdett & Co., etc.). [R.8]

WEIL, HERMANN (b. 1878). See Register, 10.

WEIL, OSCAR (b. 1839). See Register, 5.

‡ WEINGARTNER, PAUL FELIX, Edler von Münzberg (June 2, 1863, Zara, Dalmatia). See article in Vol. v. 488. He resigned as conductor at the Vienna Opera in 1910, but continued as symphony-conductor. In 1912–14 he was capellmeister at the Hamburg Stadt-Theater, and from 1914 was court-director at Darmstadt. Besides extensive tours as conductor in the whole of Europe except Russia, he has visited the United States several times, in 1905 leading four concerts for the New York Philharmonic Society, in 1906 making a tour with the Symphony Society, and in 1912 and '13 appearing as conductor of opera with the Boston Opera Company. His first wife was Marie Juillerat, the second the Baroness Feodora von Dreifus, and the third, from 1913, the operatic soprano Lucille Marcel. To the list of works add the operas 'Kain und Abel' (1914, Darmstadt) and 'Die Dame Kobold' (1916, Darmstadt), incidental music to Voss' 'Frühlingsmärchenspiel' and Weiser's version of 'Faust' (both 1908, Weimar), Symphony No. 3, in E, op. 49, a quintet for clarinet, strings and piano, op. 50, and various songs and men's choruses. For a full list of his books and of critical writing about him, see Baker, Dict. of Musicians, p. 1022.

WEISBACH, HARRY (b. 1886). See Register, 8.

WEISS, CARL THOMAS (b. 1844). See Register, 6.

WELD, ARTHUR CYRIL GORDON (Mar. 4, 1862, Jamaica Plain, Mass. : Oct. 11, 1914, near West Point, N. Y.), after early piano-lessons, in 1879–87 studied composition and orchestration at Dresden with Becker, Foerster and Von Comiar-Fiedlitz, at Berlin with Neumann and at Munich with Rheinberger, Abel and Levi, graduating from the Munich Conservatory with honors. While at Munich he wrote several large works that were there performed, including a string-quartet in C (1885, one movement given by the Kneisel Quartet, 1890), a Romanza for small orchestra (1886, also Boston, 1887), an Andante and Scherzo for septet (1886) and the orchestral suite 'Italia' (1887, also at Worcester Festival, 1888, and by the Boston Symphony Orchestra, 1890). Other works of this period are a 'Benedictus Dominus Israel' for soli, double quartet, chorus and orchestra, an 'Ode in Time of Peace' for double quartet and organ (1890, Boston), four Madrigals (1890) and many songs of which several are published (Schmidt). After a time he went to Milwaukee, where he was dramatic critic and conductor of an orchestra. Later he came to New York, where he conducted the first productions of the comedy 'Florodora' and became general director for the H. W. Savage Company. In 1913 he went to London to conduct performances of 'Adele.' He was intimate with the actor James K. Hackett, and in 1914 took charge of the musical features in his plays. He wrote several light operas, incidental music for various plays and many songs. He died suddenly while driving his automobile. [R.7]

WELLS, HOWARD, who was born at Rockford, Ill., after four years of piano-study in Chicago with Godowsky and two with Mrs. Zeisler, appeared six times as soloist with the Thomas Orchestra, besides being heard frequently in recitals. In 1907 he went to Vienna for study with Leschetizky, with whom he was associated seven years. In 1908 he became one of his assistants and after moving to Berlin continued to take pupils from Berlin to Vienna. He lived in Berlin five years, concertizing in various musical centers and appearing with prominent orchestras. At the outbreak of the war he returned to Chicago and established himself as teacher. He has published *Ears, Brain and Fingers*, a text-book for pianists and teachers, 1914. [R.9]

WELS, CHARLES (1825–1906). See Register, 4.

WELTE, EMIL (b. 1841). See Register, 5.

WERRENRATH, GEORGE (1838–1898). See Register, 6.

WERRENRATH, REINALD (Aug. 7, 1883, Brooklyn), the son of the tenor George Werrenrath (see above), besides early violin-training, had vocal lessons from his father. His general education was in the Brooklyn public schools and at New York University, where he graduated in 1905. His later studies were with Dufft, Mees, Stephens and Maurel, the last preparing him for operatic work. His first important engagement was at the Worcester Festival of 1907. He has since sung throughout the country, appearing with all the leading orchestras and at various festivals. His operatic début as baritone was at the Metropolitan Opera House in 1919 in 'I Pagliacci' and as Valentine in 'Faust.' In 1912–16 he organized and conducted the University Heights Choral Society. He has written the men's choruses 'The Cavalier's Song' and 'Siesta' (Schirmer) and edited *The New Arion*, for men's voices, and two volumes of Scandinavian songs (both Ditson). [R.9]

WERTIME, RUDOLPH. See COLLEGES, 2 (Wilson C., Pa.).

WEST, ELISHA. See TUNE-BOOKS, 1802.

WEST, J. See Register, 2.

WESTBROOK, ARTHUR E. See STATE UNIVERSITIES (Kansas State C.).

WESTLAKE, A. VERNE. See COLLEGES, 3 (Taylor U., Ind.).

WESTRAY, the MISSES. See Register, 2.

WETMORE, TRUMAN S. (1774–1861). See TUNE-BOOKS, 1798.

WETZLER, HERMANN HANS (Sept. 8, 1870, Frankfort-am-Main, Germany), in 1885–92 studied at the Hoch Conservatory in Frankfort, his teachers being Frau Schumann (piano), Heermann (violin), Scholz (composition), Knorr (counterpoint) and Humperdinck (score-reading). He then came to New York and in 1897–1901 was organist at Trinity Church. In 1902 he gave orchestral concerts at Carnegie Hall, leading to the Wetzler Symphony series in 1903 (Richard Strauss directed four programs of his own works in February and March, 1904). Returning to Germany, he has since been conductor at the city-theaters of Hamburg in 1905–08, Elberfeld in 1905–09, Riga in 1909–13, Halle in 1913–15, Lübeck in 1915–19, and Cologne since 1919. He has also led symphony-concerts in Petrograd, Berlin and other cities. He has written the symphonic poem 'Engelskonzert,' a concert-overture, Easter music for wind-instruments and organ, etc. [R.8]

WEYMAN, WESLEY (July 6, 1877, Boston), is of old Colonial ancestry. His early education was directed toward languages and literature, and he graduated from Harvard in 1898, having taken theory-courses under Paine. In 1898–1901 he was one of the latest pupils of William Mason in New York, where he began giving recitals in 1901. In 1905–08 he taught at the Institute of Musical Art, and in 1909–13 he had further studies with Leschetizky and Godowsky in Vienna, with Moszkowski in Paris, with Mathay and Bowen in London, and with Safonov at various places. From 1912 he appeared as recitalist in London and made tours in Germany and Scandinavia. In 1914 he returned to New York and Boston, occupied largely with teaching and literary work. He is an expert in New England genealogy, and has published histories of the Standish and Ramsdell families. [R.9]

WHARTON, MARY. See COLLEGES, 2 (Belhaven C., Miss.).

WHEELDON, HERBERT ARTHUR (June 6, 1864, Derby, England), was trained as organist by Crow in Ripon, Turpin and Pearce in London. He became a fellow of the R. C. O. in 1889 and took his Mus.B. at Canterbury in 1890. In 1882–85 he played at Ripon, in 1889–90 at Eastbourne, in 1891–93 at Ipswich and in 1897–1907 in London, from 1896 at St. Saviour's in Upper Chelsea. In 1907–13 he was organist at the Metropolitan Church in Toronto and in 1908–15 examiner in music for Toronto University. In 1911–13 he gave over 500 daily recitals, covering a large répertoire of classic and modern organ-music. Through his efforts, after his resignation the position of organist in this church was endowed and the organist must hold a degree from one of the leading English universities and engage to give 25 recitals annually. He has published Evening Services in A and B-flat (Novello) and many organ-pieces (Novello, Rogers, Gray, White-Smith). [R.9]

WHEELER, LYMAN WARREN (1837–1900). See Register, 5.

WHELPLEY, BENJAMIN LINCOLN (b. 1864). See Register, 7.

WHITE, ALICE H. See COLLEGES, 3 (Colby C., Me.).

WHITE, CAROLINA [Carolyn] (Dec. 23, 1883, Dorchester, Mass.), was trained as concert-soprano by Weldon Hunt in Boston, where she began appearances in 1905. In 1907 she studied in Naples with Sebastian and Paolo Longone, assistant-director at San Carlo (whom she married in 1910). Her début in opera was at San Carlo as Gutrune in 'Die Götterdämmerung' in 1908. During the next two years she sang in 'Aida,' 'Mefistofele,' 'Tosca,' 'Manon Lescaut,' 'Madama Butterfly,' 'La Gioconda' and 'Iris' at Venice, Rome, Milan and Lucerne. In 1910–14 she was with the Chicago Opera Company, appearing first as Santuzza. In 1911 she sang the rôle of Countess in the first American performance of 'Il Segreto di Susanna' and that of Maliella in that of 'I Giojelli della Madonna' in 1912. In 1915–17 she was heard in concert and has since sung in light opera. [R.9]

WHITE, EDWARD L. See Register, 4, and TUNE-BOOKS, 1846.

WHITE, HENRY KIRK (d. 1907). See Register, 4.

WHITE, JOHN (1785–1865). See Register, 3.

WHITE, JOHN (Mar. 12, 1855, West Springfield, Mass. : July 18, 1902, Bad-Nauheim, Germany), in 1861–63 studied organ with Buck and then went to Berlin for organ and counterpoint with Haupt. In 1880–83 he was organist at St. Francis Xavier's in New York, and again went to Germany, this time to study composition with Rheinberger in Munich. In 1887–96 he was organist at the Church of the Ascension in New York. The rest of his life was spent in Munich. He was an accomplished player, gave many recitals both in America and in Germany,

and some of the best American organists were among his pupils. He composed the oratorio 'Alpha and Omega,' a Missa Solemnis, a Requiem, a Te Deum, and other church-music. He also edited many organ-pieces. [R.7]

WHITE, JOSEPHINE, née Sumption (b. 1879). See COLLEGES, 2 (Colorado Woman's C.).

WHITEHILL, CLARENCE EUGENE (Nov. 5, 1871, Marengo, Ia.), originally was in business in Chicago, but incidentally studied voice with L. A. Phelps and sang in church-choirs. Mme. Melba and Campanari induced him to prepare for the stage. He went to Paris, studied with Sbriglia and Giraudet, and made his début as Friar Lawrence in 'Roméo et Juliette' at La Monnaie in Brussels in 1899. In 1900 he sang at the Opéra-Comique in Paris, and also appeared as leading baritone with the H. W. Savage English Opera Company at the Metropolitan Opera House in New York, singing seventeen rôles in a short season. Returning to Germany, he studied with Stockhausen at Frankfort and had the advice of Frau Wagner at Bayreuth for Wagnerian parts. He filled engagements at Lübeck, Elberfeld and Cologne (1903–08). In 1909–11 he was at the Metropolitan Opera House in New York, first appearing as Amfortas. In 1911–15 he was with the Chicago Opera Company and in 1916 returned to the Metropolitan. He has sung at Bayreuth three seasons, at Covent Garden five and at Munich two. His greatest success has been made in Wagnerian rôles. [R.9]

WHITEHOUSE, HORACE. See COLLEGES, 3 (Ohio Wesleyan U.).

WHITHORNE [Whittern], EMERSON (b. 1884). See Register, 9.

WHITING, ARTHUR BATTELLE (June 20, 1861, Cambridge, Mass.), is a nephew of George E. Whiting, the Boston organist. He studied piano with Sherwood at the New England Conservatory, and harmony, counterpoint and composition with Maas and Chadwick. At the Munich Conservatory in 1883–85 he was in the classes of Rheinberger, Bussmayer and Abel. During 1885–95 he lived in Boston, where he composed a concert-overture (1885, Boston Symphony Orchestra), a suite for strings and horns, a Concerto in D minor and a Fantasy in B-flat minor for piano and orchestra. These latter he has played with various large orchestras. Since 1895 he has lived in New York, composing many anthems, other vocal works and piano-pieces (Schirmer), making transcriptions of the toccatas and suites of Bach and Handel for piano, and preparing Damper-Pedal Studies, 2 vols. Since 1907 he has been largely occupied with giving concerts of chamber-music at Harvard, Yale and Princeton Universities, designed with a definite educational purpose. He has also become an authoritative exponent of music for obsolete instruments, and from 1911 has given illustrative programs upon the harpsichord, often with other artists in ensemble. [R.7]

WHITING, GEORGE ELBRIDGE (Sept. 14, 1842, Holliston, Mass.). See article in Vol. v. 517-8. He gave up his work at the New England Conservatory in 1897 and at the Church of the Immaculate Conception in 1910, having been organist at the latter for about thirty years. To the list of works should be added the choral march 'Our Country,' for chorus and orchestra (1909, inauguration of President Taft), four concert-études for organ (Presser), many other organ-pieces (Novello, Ditson), various collections of organ-studies, etc., a Grand Sonata in A minor for organ, 20 Preludes and Postludes for advanced performers, 2 vols., the cantata 'The Tale of the Viking,' from Longfellow (Schirmer), three masses on plain-chant melodies, in B-flat and F, two sets of vespers and offertories for the Catholic service, and many other ritual settings, services for the Episcopal Church, anthems, part-songs and songs, besides new organ-accompaniments for several works, including Rossini's Stabat Mater. [R.4]

WHITMER, THOMAS CARL (June 24, 1873, Altoona, Pa.), after graduating from Franklin and Marshall College, studied in Philadelphia and New York with Gilchrist, Jarvis and S. P. Warren. In 1899-1909 he was music-director at Stephens College in Missouri, in 1909-16 at the Pennsylvania College for Women in Pittsburgh, and in 1916-19 taught at the Pittsburgh Musical Institute. Since 1916 he has been organist at the Sixth Presbyterian Church in Pittsburgh. His work as composer has but gradually come to be known (see appreciation in The Art of Music, iv. 428-30). It includes six music-dramas or 'Mysteries' — 'The Creation,' 'The Covenant,' 'The Nativity,' 'The Temptation,' 'Mary Magdalene,' 'The Passion' — for full orchestra (text by composer), with an explanatory essay 'Concerning a National Spiritual Drama'; a 'Syrian Ballet' in four movements, for orchestra, (1918, Pittsburgh and Philadelphia); an 'Elegiac Rhapsody' for low voice, chorus and orchestra; Psalm 84, for alto, chorus, violin, harp and organ (Pittsburgh); an 'Athenian' sonata in D minor, for violin and piano (given many times); three 'Character-Moods' and a 'Meditation' for piano and strings; music for the Pittsburgh Centennial Pageant in 1916, including a notable 'Hymn to America';

the men.'s choruses 'The Keepers' (a cappella) and 'The Song of a City' (Willis, given in Pittsburgh and New York); a setting of Tennyson's 'Strong Son of God,' for baritone, unison chorus and organ, and other anthems; a long list of songs, many with orchestral accompaniment; a 'Poem of Youth' in two movements, for piano and orchestra (1914, M. T. N. A. meeting); and a number of organ-pieces. He has written Considerations on Music, The Way of My Mind, 1918, and the texts for his 'Mysteries' and for 'Symbolisms,' the latter a series of six dramas that he has set for reader and piano, besides words for other works. He has also contributed noteworthy articles to various journals. [R.8]

WHITNEY, FLOSSIE EMELINE. See COLLEGES, 3 (Defiance C., Ohio).

WHITNEY, MYRON WILLIAM (Sept. 5, 1836, Ashby, Mass. : Sept. 19, 1910, Sandwich, Mass.), came to Boston in 1852, and soon began to study singing with E. H. Frost. His first appearance as an oratorio-bass was in a Christmas performance of 'The Messiah' at Tremont Temple in 1858. He sang in concerts and oratorios for the next ten years, and then studied in Florence under Vannucini and in London under Randegger. After his return to Boston he was recalled to England for a season of concerts and festivals, but from 1876 his activities were confined to America. He was the only soloist at the opening of the Centennial Exposition in Philadelphia in 1876. He made two tours with the Thomas Orchestra, and he was one of the bassos in the American Opera Company in 1886-87. He sang with the Handel and Haydn Society of Boston, the New York Oratorio Society, at the Cincinnati Festivals of 1873, '75, '78 and '80, and at a long list of other festivals and oratorio-performances throughout the country. With the Boston Ideal Opera Company from 1879 he was the leading basso, and for many years was successfully identified with light opera. In 1890 he retired from the concert-stage. [R.4]

WHITNEY, SAMUEL BRENTON (June 4, 1842, Woodstock, Vt. : Aug. 3, 1914, Brattleboro, Vt.), was trained as organist by local teachers, by Charles Wels in New York, and chiefly by Paine in Boston. In 1871 he became organist at the Church of the Advent in Boston, where he established a choral service of rare excellence and wide renown. He was a leader in the establishment of the Massachusetts Diocesan Choir Guild in 1876, and was its choir-master for many years. His Communion Service in G was composed for his 25th anniversary at the Church of the Advent (1896) and the Magnificat and Nunc Dimittis in E-flat for the 35th (1906). In 1908 he resigned, but

continued as director emeritus. An excellent
organist, he gave many recitals in his earlier
years, and was noted for his Bach playing
and for improvisations. He was professor of
organ-playing and lecturer at the Boston
University and the New England Conservatory, and at the latter taught classes
in church-music. He directed many choir and
choral festivals throughout New England.
His compositions included a piano-trio, music
for piano and organ, church-services, anthems
and hymn-tunes. He was a founder of the
A. G. O., and an examiner in the American
College of Musicians. [R.5]

WHITTEMORE, THOMAS (1800-1861).
See TUNE-BOOKS, 1836.

WHITTLESEY, WALTER R. (b. 1861).
See Register, 8.

WICKHAM, FLORENCE PAULINE
(1882, Beaver, Pa.), was trained as an operatic
contralto by Alice Groff in Philadelphia and
then in Berlin by Emmerich and Frau
Mallinger. In 1902 she made her début at
Wiesbaden in 'Le Prophète.' In 1904-05
she toured in America with the H. W. Savage
Company, singing Kundry in 'Parsifal.'
After a year, when she was guest at the Theater
des Westens in Berlin, in 1906-09 she was
engaged at the Opera at Schwerin, also singing
in 1907 at Covent Garden and in 1908 in
Berlin. In 1909-12 she was with the Metropolitan Opera House in New York. Her
répertoire of 45 operas includes the rôles of
Amneris, Kundry, Ortrud, Fricke, Wal-
traute, Brangäne, Magdalena, Laura (in 'La
Gioconda'), Emilia (in 'Otello'), Orfeo and
Adriano (in 'Rienzi'). In 1911 she married
Eberhard L. Lueder of New York. [R.9]

‡ WIDOR, CHARLES MARIE (Feb. 22,
1845, Lyons, France). See article in Vol.
v. 518-9. In 1910 he succeeded Lenepveu
as member of the Institut and in 1913 became
secretary. He is also Chevalier in the Légion
d'Honneur. Add to the list of works, besides
the eight organ-'symphonies' in opp. 13 and
42, the 'Symphonie Romane' and the 'Symphonie Gothique,' a string-quartet in A minor,
op. 66, a 2nd violin-sonata, op. 79, a Choral
and Variations for harp and orchestra, and
a 3rd orchestral Symphony, in F minor,
with organ. He is author of *Technique de
l'Orchestre Moderne*, 1904 (2nd ed., 1906,
and in German and English), and of an essay
on Greek Music in relation to Gregorian (1895),
and has edited *L'Orgue Moderne* and (with
Schweitzer) a monumental edition of Bach's
works (Schirmer). Biographies have appeared
by Reynaud, 1900, and Rupp, 1912.

WIGNELL, THOMAS (d. 1803). See Register, 2.

WILCOX & WHITE COMPANY, THE,
of Meriden, Conn., is the successor of the

Wilcox & White Organ Co., which was formed
in 1876 to compete with the Estey Organ Co.
in making reed-organs, the original founders
being H. C. Wilcox and J. H. and H. K.
White. Prior to 1908 they made about 50,000
organs. The present company was formed in
1897. They have made a specialty of the
'Angelus,' a player-attachment brought out
in 1895, and have developed a large business
in player-pianos and in music-rolls. Their
'orchestral' piano has a set of reeds included.

WILD, HARRISON MAJOR (Mar. 6,
1861, Hoboken, N. J.), had most of his musical
education in Chicago under Liebling, Cres-
wold and Eddy, but in 1878-79 also studied
in Leipzig with Zwintscher, Rust and Richter.
Since 1876 he has been almost continuously
an organist in Chicago, playing at the Church
of the Ascension five years, at Unity Church
thirteen and since 1895 at Grace Church,
where he has made the services specially
notable. He has also won a fine reputation
as choral conductor, since 1898 leading the
Apollo Musical Club, since 1902 the Mendelssohn Club (men's voices), and since 1905 the
Mendelssohn Club of Rockford. With the
first two of these he has introduced a long
list of important works, performed with great
perfection. He is also active as an organ-
recitalist, and has been dean of the Western
Chapter of the A. G. O. [R.6]

WILD, WALTER. See COLLEGES, 2 (Pennsylvania C. for Women).

WILDE, EDWIN ERNEST (b. 1887).
See COLLEGES, 3 (Brown U., R. I.).

WILKINS, HERVE D. (1848-1913). See
Register, 5.

WILLARD, BENJAMIN W. See Register, 3.

WILLARD, SAMUEL (1776-1859). See
TUNE-BOOKS, 1813.

WILLCOX, JOHN HENRY (1827-1875).
See Register, 4.

WILLEKE, WILLEM (b. 1878). See Register, 9.

WILLIAMS, ALBERTO (Nov. 23, 1862,
Buenos Aires, Argentina), while at the Buenos
Aires Conservatory secured governmental assistance for study in Paris, where his teachers
were Mathias and De Bériot in piano, Durand
in harmony, and Guiraud, Godard and Franck
in composition. After his return in 1899 he
conducted symphony-concerts, and in 1903
founded the Conservatorio de Música de
Buenos Aires, which has grown to a school
of over 1200 pupils, with branches in the
principal cities of the Argentine Republic.
In 1900 he gave a concert of his works with
the Philharmonic Orchestra in Berlin. He
has composed three symphonies, three suites,
two overtures and a march for orchestra;
three sonatas for violin and piano; a sonata

for 'cello and piano; a piano-trio; many songs and piano-pieces. He has published works on theory and also five volumes of poems. [R.7]

WILLIAMS, HARRY EVAN (Sept. 7, 1867, Mineral Ridge, O. : May 24, 1918, Akron, O.), was a mine- and steel-mill worker in his early years, and he sang in an octet-club which attained considerable local reputation. For four years he studied with Mme. Louise von Feilitsch in Cleveland, and made his first appearance as tenor in 1891 at Galion, O., though his real début was at the Worcester Festival of 1896. In New York he then became a pupil of Ffrançon Davies, Ben Davies, Mrs. Topping-Brown, John Dennis Mehan and James Sauvage. Dissatisfied with his work, he retired for a period in 1904, but reappeared with great success in the later years of his life. He was soloist at nearly all the principal festivals of the country, including about 15 appearances at Worcester. He gave perhaps 1000 song-recitals, after 1900 exclusively in English; and was equally successful in song and oratorio. [R.8]

WILLIAMS, VICTOR (1816– ?). See Register, 4.

WILLIS, RICHARD STORRS (1819–1900). See Register, 4, and TUNE-BOOKS, 1850.

WILLIS, ROBERT. See TUNE-BOOKS, 1834.

WILSON, GEORGE H. See Register, 7.

WILSON, HENRY (Dec. 2, 1828, Greenfield, Mass. : Jan. 8, 1878, Hartford, Conn.), was musically inclined from childhood, but was forced to learn the printer's trade for support. Diligence in this latter enabled him to study music in Boston from about 1848, though double labor undermined his health. About 1850 he became teacher and organist at St. James' in Greenfield, removing in 1854 for a few months to Springfield. A chance meeting with Alexander W. Thayer led to their going to Europe together and a lifelong friendship. A year's study in Leipzig followed, during which he wrote entertaining letters for the Springfield 'Republican.' From 1855 for twenty-two years he was organist at Christ Church in Hartford, going for a short time afterward to Park Church. The peculiar impress of his personality and gifts was shown by the tributes after his death, including addresses by Charles Dudley Warner, Bishop Williams and Rev. N. J. Burton, and many letters, among them those of J. G. Holland and Dudley Buck. These appreciations were gathered into a small memorial in 1878. He was preëminently a church-musician, throwing a notable emotion into whatever he wrote or rendered. His compositions were almost wholly for church

use. They lacked solidity and balance, but for a time were extremely popular and effective. [R.4]

WILSON, MORTIMER (Aug. 6, 1876, Chariton, Ia.), in 1894–1900 studied in Chicago with Jacobsohn, Gleason and Middelschulte. In 1901–07 he taught theory in the University School of Music at Lincoln, Neb., and then had three years in Leipzig, at first studying with Sitt and Reger and then teaching. From 1911 he was at the Atlanta Conservatory and conductor of the Symphony Orchestra, and in 1916–18 taught at Brenau College in Gainesville, Ga. He is now consulting-editor for the National Academy of Music in New York. He has written The Rhetoric of Music, 1907. His published works include 'From My Youth,' op. 5, 8 miniatures for violin, 'cello and piano; sonatas in D and E, opp. 14, 16, for violin and piano; 7 organ-preludes, op. 7; the piano-suites 'In Georgia,' op. 25, 'Suite Rustica,' op. 44a and 'By the Wayside,' op. 44b; 'Suwannee Sketches,' op. 39, for violin and piano; nursery-songs and piano-pieces. Unpublished are five symphonies, a 'Country-Wedding' orchestral suite, violin-quartets, a suite, trio and sonata for violin and piano, an organ-sonata, the piano-suite 'In Imagery,' and a book of songs. Some of his works have been given by symphony-orchestras in Chicago, Atlanta, Leipzig and Prague, by the Sittig Trio in New York, etc. [R.9]

WINCHELL, JAMES MANNING (1791–1820). See TUNE-BOOKS, 1819.

WINCHESTER, AMASA. See Register, 3.

WINGATE, RAY W. See COLLEGES, 3 (Alfred U., N.Y.).

WINKLER, EMIL KARL (b. 1860). See COLLEGES, 2 (Wells C., N. Y.).

WINKLER, J. A. E. See COLLEGES, 2 (Hollins C., Va.).

WISE, JOHN J. See Register, 3.

WISKE, C. MORTIMER (b. 1853). See Register, 7.

WITEK, ANTON (Jan. 7, 1872, Saaz, Austria), in 1883–89 was a pupil of Bennewitz at the Prague Conservatory. In 1894 he became concertmaster of the Philharmonic Orchestra in Berlin, and also began tours with the Danish pianist Vita Gerhardt (whom he later married). In 1903, with her and Joseph Malkin, he formed the Philharmonic Trio. In 1905 he made a sensation by playing in one evening concertos by Beethoven, Paganini and Brahms, in 1907 brought out in Berlin the newly-discovered concerto in A by Mozart, and in 1909 also the long-lost concerto in C by Haydn. In 1910 he became concertmaster of the Boston Symphony Orchestra, making his first appearance as soloist on Oct. 29 with the Beethoven concerto.

In 1914, when Malkin also joined the orchestra, the former trio-group was revived as the Witek-Malkin Trio. In 1918 he resigned from the Orchestra. [R.10]

WITHERSPOON, HERBERT (b. 1873). See Register, 8.

WODELL, FREDERICK WILLIAM (Dec. 17, 1859, London, England), gained his general education in public schools in England and the United States, studying piano with E. T. Manning, Ferdinand Dewey and Ada P. Emery, voice chiefly with F. W. Root and Shakespeare, and composition with Manning and Norris. He has had wide experience as singer, and for many years conducted the People's Choral Union in Boston (400 voices), giving two oratorio-concerts annually. He has made a specialty of teaching singing to classes of both adults and children, and has often lectured upon the methods used. He has published *Choir and Chorus Conducting*, 1908 (new ed., 1919), and *How to Sing by Note*, 1915. He has also written a two-act light opera, 'The Court of Love' (1912, Boston); the cantata 'The Gift of Love,' from 'Endymion,' for soprano and women's chorus (1919, Brookline); the cantata 'The American Flag,' for tenor, baritone, men's chorus and piano or orchestra (1915, Boston) (Thompson); and many anthems, part-songs and songs (various publishers). [R.7]

‡ WOLF-FERRARI, ERMANNO (Jan. 12, 1876, Venice, Italy). See article in Vol. v. 558. The list of works should be extended as follows:

Operas: 'I Quattro Rusteghi' (1906, Munich, in German).
'I Giojelli della Madonna' (1911, Berlin, in German, 1912, Chicago, in Italian).
'L'Amore Medico' (1913, Dresden, in German, 1914, New York, in Italian).
Mystery, 'Talitta Cumi,' or 'Die Tochter des Jairus,' op. 3, for soli, chorus and orchestra.
Sonata in G minor, op. 1, for violin.
Piano-Trio in D, op. 5.
Piano-Quintet in D-flat, op. 6.
Piano-Trio in F-sharp, op. 7.
'Kammersymphonie' in B-flat, op. 8.
Sonata in A minor, op. 10, for violin.
'Rispetti,' opp. 11-12.
Impromptus for piano, op. 13.
Three Piano-Pieces, op. 14.

His dramatic works have been brought out in Germany because of his inability to agree with the Italian house that controls publication in Italy. When he came to America in 1912 to superintend the production of 'I Giojelli della Madonna' he had never heard any of his works given in Italian. His name unites those of his German father, the distinguished painter August Wolf, and of his Italian mother.

WOLFF, A. See Register, 2.

WOLFSOHN, CARL (Dec. 14, 1834, Alzey, Germany : 1907, N. J.), was a pupil of Aloys Schmitt at Frankfort, where he made his début as pianist in 1848. He then studied with Lachner, made concert-tours and lived for two years in London before coming to America in 1854. He located in Philadelphia as pianist, orchestral conductor and teacher, and for about twenty years gave series of chamber-music concerts. In 1863 he undertook recitals embodying the entire series of Beethoven sonatas, which were given twice in Philadelphia and twice in New York with notable success. Later he presented the complete piano-works of Schumann and of Chopin in similar series of recitals. In 1873 he moved to Chicago, and to his other activities added the direction of the Beethoven Society, a choral organization. He was widely known as a teacher of piano, was one of the early champions of Wagner in America, and did much to raise the standards of chamber-music both in Philadelphia and in Chicago. Among his many pupils Mme. Bloomfield-Zeisler is perhaps the most widely known. [R.4]

WOLLE, JOHN FREDERICK (Apr. 4, 1863, Bethlehem, Pa.), comes of a long line of musical ancestors and had his first lessons from a sister and a cousin. In 1879 he graduated at the Moravian Parochial School, having specialized in music, and began teaching in Bethlehem. In 1881-84 he was organist at Trinity Church there and had organ-lessons from Wood in Philadelphia. In 1884-85 he studied with Rheinberger in Munich, returning to be organist for twenty years at the Moravian Church. Before going to Germany he had organized choral societies in Bethlehem and Easton, and the former, after giving standard oratorios, he led to concentrate upon Bach's music. With it in 1888 he gave the first complete rendering in America of the St. John Passion, and in 1892 he gave also the St. Matthew Passion. After a period of inactivity, in 1898 work was resumed, and in 1900 the B minor Mass was given. In 1887-1905 he was organist at the Packer Memorial Church at Lehigh University. In 1904 the Moravian College made him Mus. D. (also the University of Pennsylvania in 1919). In 1905-11 he was professor at the University of California, where he organized a chorus of 300, conducted symphony-concerts and directed performances of Greek dramas. Besides being in 1907-09 organist at the First Congregational Church in Berkeley, he assembled a Bach Choir of 125, which gave the St. Matthew Passion and the Mass in 1909-10. Returning to Bethlehem in 1911, he resumed the notable administration of the Bach Choir (see article), was organist at the Salem Lutheran Church and conducted choral societies in Harrisburg, York and

Lancaster. He was a founder of the A. G. O., and has appeared as soloist not only at the Chicago and the St. Louis Expositions, but often elsewhere. He has made organ-transcriptions from Bach and Wagner and composed for chorus and orchestra, but of his original works none are published. See Walters, *Bethlehem Bach Choir*, 1918. [R.7]

WOLLENHAUPT, HERMANN ADOLF (1827–1863). See Register, 4.

WOOD, ABRAHAM (1752–1804). See Tune-Books, 1793.

WOOD, CARL PAIGE (b. 1885). See Register, 9.

WOOD, DAVID DUFFIELD (Mar. 2, 1838, near Pittsburgh : Mar. 27, 1910, Philadelphia), lost his sight by accident in childhood and at five went to the Philadelphia School for the Blind, where he was an apt pupil in music and mathematics. In 1853 he became assistant-teacher in music and in 1887 director. He there conducted remarkably successful performances of standard oratorios and of Bach cantatas. In 1864 he became organist at St. Stephen's, remaining exactly 46 years (last service two days before his death). For about 25 years he also played at the evening services at the Baptist Temple, where he often brought out oratorios. He was a superior player and one of the first to specialize in Bach in America. Many of his pupils became prominent. His compositions were mostly for the church and were sung at St. Stephen's from manuscript. In 1911 the H. W. Gray Co. began publishing a series of his anthems. [R.4]

‡ WOOD, HENRY JOSEPH (Mar. 3, 1870, London, England). See article in Vol. v. 560–1. He visited America in 1904. In 1911 he was knighted. In 1918 the conductorship of the Boston Symphony Orchestra, in succession to Muck, was offered him, but was declined.

WOOD, MARY, née Knight (b. 1859). See Register, 7.

WOOD, MARY ANNE, née Paton (1802–1864). See Vol. iii. 653–4, and Register, 3.

WOOD, WILLIAM L. See Colleges, 3 (Hobart C., N. Y.).

WOODBURY, ISAAC BAKER (1819–1858). See Tune-Books, 1839.

WOODMAN, JONATHAN CALL (1813–1894). See Register, 4.

WOODMAN, RAYMOND HUNTINGTON (Jan. 18, 1861, Brooklyn), was the son and pupil of J. C. Woodman. In 1881–85 he also studied composition and orchestration under Buck and later organ under Franck in Paris. In 1880, after a year with a church in Norwich, Conn., he became organist at the

First Presbyterian Church in Brooklyn, where he has recently celebrated his fortieth anniversary. He has also taught at Packer Institute and the Master School of Music. In 1894–97 he edited a church-music department for the New York 'Evangelist.' He is a founder and fellow of the A. G. O., and has done much brilliant recital-work. He is also fellow of the Brooklyn Institute of Arts and Sciences, and head of its music-section. His published songs, anthems, cantatas and pieces for organ or piano number about 125. Of unpublished works the more important are an 'Ode to Music,' for baritone, chorus and orchestra, a 'Reverie' for string-orchestra, harp and organ, and a four-movement organ-suite. [R.6]

WOODRUFF, MERIT N. See Tune-Books, 1800.

WOODWARD, CHARLES. See Tune-Books, 1800.

WOOLF, BENJAMIN EDWARD (1836–1901). See Register, 5.

WOOLLS, STEPHEN (d. 1799). See Register, 1.

WORCESTER, SAMUEL (1770–1821). See Tune-Books, 1815.

WORCESTER MUSICAL FESTIVALS. See article in Vol. v. 562–3. The series has continued without break except in 1918, when the festival was canceled on account of the influenza epidemic. The chief conductor until 1919 was Mees, assisted in 1909–1915 by Gustav Strube. The new conductor is Nelson P. Coffin. The major works to be added to the list are Liszt's Missa Solemnis (1909), Bantock's 'Omar Khayyám' (1910), Reger's 'The Nuns' (1911), Georg Schumann's 'Ruth' (1912), Pierné's 'St. Francis of Assisi' (1913), Wolf-Ferrari's 'La Vita Nuova' (1914), Beethoven's Choral Fantasia (1915), Parker's 'Red Cross Hymn,' Grainger's 'Marching-Song of Democracy' and Hadley's 'Ode to Music' (all 1917). In 1919 a program of works by a variety of American composers was presented.

WORK, HENRY CLAY (1832–1884). See Register, 4.

WORLEY, CHANDLER. See State Universities (Miss.).

WRANGELL, LUDWIG HEINRICH (b. 1872). See Register, 9.

WRIGHT, D. See Tune-Books, 1798.

WRIGHT, WILLIAM LYNDON. See Colleges, 3 (New York U.)

WRIGHTSON, HERBERT JAMES (b. 1869). See Register, 8.

WRIGHTSON, SYDNEY LLOYD (b. 1869). See Register, 7.

WYETH, JOHN (1770–1858). See Tune-Books, 1810.

Y

'YANKEE DOODLE.' See article in Vol. v. 574–7, and the exhaustive study in Sonneck, *Report on 'The Star-Spangled Banner,' 'Hail, Columbia,' 'America' and 'Yankee Doodle,'* 1909.

YARNOLD, BENJAMIN. See Register, 1.

YON, PIETRO ALESSANDRO (Aug. 8, 1886, Settimo Vittone, Italy), after study as a child with Burbatti, the cathedral-organist at Ivrea, entered the Milan Conservatory as pupil of Fumagalli. He won a scholarship for pianists at the Turin Conservatory in 1901, and spent three years there under Venezia (piano), Remondi (organ) and Bolzoni (composition). In 1904 he went to the Academy of St. Cecilia in Rome, where his teachers were Renzi (organ), Bustini and Sgambati (piano), and De Sanctis (theory). He graduated in 1905 with honors in each department, the first prize-medal of the Academy and a special medal from the Italian Minister of Public Instruction. For two years he was substitute-organist at the Vatican and the Royal Church of Rome. In 1907 he became organist at St. Francis Xavier's in New York. There and through extensive tours as virtuoso he has earned a great and well-deserved reputation. Among his many works (Ricordi, J. Fischer, Schirmer) are the following:

Sonata No. 1, for organ.
'Sonata Cromatica,' for organ.
Toccata for organ.
Two Concert-Studies for organ.
'Christmas in Sicily,' 'Pastorale Sorrentina,' 'Elegia,' 'Gesù Bambino,' all for organ.
Ten Divertimenti for organ.
Six Masses and about ten Motets.
Several piano-pieces and songs.   [R.9]

YORK, FRANCIS LODOWICK (Mar. 9, 1861, Ontonagon, Mich.), had his general education in the Ann Arbor High School and the University of Michigan, graduating in 1882. While there he studied with Cady,

and later continued in Detroit with Batchelder and in Paris with Guilmant (1892, '98). From 1888 he has been advocate of school-credits for music, first at Ann Arbor and lately in Detroit. In 1892–96 he taught at the University School of Music in Ann Arbor, and in 1896–1902 at the State Normal School in Ypsilanti. Since 1902 he has been the exceedingly efficient head of the Detroit Conservatory and organist at the Central Methodist Church. He has always been a strong supporter of American music, especially interested in the works of MacDowell. He was organ-recitalist at the Buffalo and St. Louis Expositions of 1901 and 1904, and has played often elsewhere. His 'Spring-Song' for organ, several transcriptions and some church-music have been published (Schirmer). A comic opera, 'The Inca' and further organ-pieces are in manuscript. He has also written *Harmony Simplified*, 5th ed., 1900, and *Counterpoint Simplified*, 1907. In 1905 he prepared for the French government a report upon American music-schools. He is one of the editors of the Schirmer Library, and has written many articles for periodicals. He has always been prominent in the M. T. N. A. and in the Michigan Association. [R.8]

YOUNG, HELEN F. See COLLEGES, 2 (Sweet Briar C., Va.).

YOUNG, WILLIAM. See Register, 2, and TUNE-BOOKS, 1790.

YOUNG PEOPLE'S SYMPHONY CONCERTS. See Vol. iv. 805.

YSAŸE, EUGÈNE (July 16, 1858, Liège, Belgium). See article in Vol. v. 580–2. In 1898 he declined an invitation to succeed Seidl as conductor of the New York Philharmonic Society. In 1918, as guest-conductor, he directed the Cincinnati Festival and other concerts, and was later appointed permanent conductor of the Symphony Orchestra. [R.10]

Z

ZACH, MAX WILHELM (b. 1864). See Register, 7.

ZAHM, JOHN AUGUSTINE (b. 1851). See Register, 8.

ZAY, WILLIAM HENRI (b. 1869). See Register, 8.

ZBINDEN, THEODORE (b. 1877). See Register, 10.

ZECH, FREDERICK (May 10, 1858, Philadelphia), began piano-study in San Francisco with Heckmanns and Schumacher, continuing in 1877–82 in Leipzig with Kullak, Breslaur and Neumann (composition). He also taught for two years in Kullak's Academy. Since 1882 he has been teacher of advanced piano-pupils in San Francisco, at intervals also conducting symphony-concerts. He has written the operas 'La Paloma' and 'Wakin-yon'; symphonies in B minor, C minor, F minor and C; the symphonic poems 'The Eve of St. Agnes' (1898), 'Lamia' (1902), 'The Raven' (1902) and 'The Wreck of the Hesperus' (1909); four piano-concertos; a violin-concerto; a 'cello-concerto; a piano-quintet; two string-quartets; a piano-trio; three violin-sonatas; a flute-sonata; and two clarinet-sonatas. All those for orchestra have been given in San Francisco, and the first two symphonic poems also in Germany. [R.7]

ZECKWER, CAMILLE (June 26, 1875, Philadelphia), the son of Richard Zeckwer (see below), was trained in the Philadelphia Musical Academy, graduating in 1893. He further studied composition with Dvořák in New York in 1893–95 and with Ph. Scharwenka in Berlin, where he also took violin with Zajic. He soon engaged in teaching in the Philadelphia Academy, of which he is now director with Frederick E. Hahn. Besides being a pianist of fine ability, he has given much attention to composition. His works include the symphonic poem 'Sohrab and Rustum,' op. 30 (1915, Philadelphia Orchestra); a piano-concerto in E minor, op. 8 (1899, Philadelphia Orchestra, also 1904, '14); the cantata 'The New Day,' op. 24 (Cleveland Mendelssohn Club prize, 1914); the three-act opera 'Jane and Janetta,' op. 20; a suite for violin and piano, op. 1; a 'Swedish Fantasy,' op. 6, for violin and orchestra; a piano-trio, op. 3; a string-quartet, op. 4; a piano-quartet, op. 9; a piano-quintet in E minor, op. 5; two violin-sonatas, opp. 2, 7; a 'Sérénade Mélancolique,' op. 27, for violin, 'cello and piano; and various piano-pieces, songs and choruses [R.8]

ZECKWER, RICHARD (Apr. 30, 1850, Stendal, Germany), was educated at the Stendal Gymnasium, Leipzig University and Leipzig Conservatory, his music-masters being Papperitz, Richter, Reinecke, Paul and Hauptmann. In 1869 he came to Philadelphia, making his first appearance as pianist at the Academy of Music on Dec. 1. A few months later he began to teach at the Philadelphia Musical Academy, recently opened. In 1876 he became its director and continued over forty years in fruitful service, resigning in 1917, when the Academy was merged with the Hahn Conservatory. In 1870–77 he was organist at St. Vincent de Paul (R. C.) Church in Germantown, and of the Philadelphia Cathedral in 1877–80. He has lectured on acoustics at the Franklin Institute and the Academy of Natural Science, and has published the pamphlet *A Scientific Investigation of Legato-Touch*, 1902, the result of original investigations. He has written two overtures, 'The Bride of Messina' and 'Festival,' a string-quartet, a violin-sonata, four piano-sonatas, many songs and piano-pieces (Ditson, Presser). [R.6]

ZEISLER, FANNIE, née Bloomfield (July 16, 1863, Bielitz, Austria). See article in Vol. i. 341. The birth-year is correct as here given. She is a cousin of the pianist Moritz Rosenthal and a sister of Maurice Bloomfield, professor of Sanscrit at Johns Hopkins University. In recent years she has been kept back from great activity by ill-health, but is now resuming concert-work as of old. [R.6]

'ZENOBIA.' An opera in four acts by Silas G. Pratt, produced in concert-form in Chicago in 1882 and on the stage in March, 1883. The libretto, by the composer, is based upon a romance of William Ware.

Another opera on the same subject, in three acts, is by Louis Adolphe Coerne. It was several times given in Bremen in 1905–06, and instrumental numbers have been played in America.

ZERRAHN, CARL (July 28, 1826, Malchow, Germany : Dec. 29, 1909, Milton, Mass.). See article in Vol. v. 595. His first lessons, at twelve, were with Friedrich Weber in Rostock, and later he studied in Hanover and Berlin. In the Germania Orchestra he played first flute, thus having part in the important influence of that organization. In 1855–63 he conducted one of the several orchestras in Boston known by the name Philharmonic, and was practically the only leader of the concerts of the Harvard Musical Association in 1865–82. Besides his work as conductor of the Handel and Haydn Society and of the Worcester Festivals, he was for many years in charge of the Salem Oratorio Society and other smaller organiza-

BERNHARD ZIEHN

tions. At the second Peace Jubilee (1872) he led the chorus of 20,000. He was also a teacher of singing, harmony and composition at the New England Conservatory. In all these ways he left a significant impress upon the development of American choral music. [R.4]

ZEUCH, WILLIAM EDWARD (b. 1878). See Register, 9.

ZEUNER, CHARLES [Heinrich Christoph] (1795–1857). See Register, 3, and TUNE-BOOKS, 1832.

ZIEGFELD, FLORENZ (b. 1841). See Register, 5.

ZIEGLER, ANNA ELIZABETH, née Koelling (b. 1867). See Register, 7.

ZIEHN, BERNHARD (Jan. 20, 1845, Erfurt, Germany : Sept. 8, 1912, Chicago), was not at first specially trained in music. He studied at the teachers' seminary in Erfurt and taught three years at Mühlhausen. In 1868–70 he taught higher mathematics, German and music-theory at the German Lutheran School in Chicago. After 1871 he concentrated wholly upon the investigation of the theory of music and the teaching of it. This led to a series of monumental books, including *System der Uebungen für Klavierspieler*, 1881, *Lehrgang für den ersten Klavierunterricht*, 1881, developing the idea of 'symmetrical inversion' of material, *Harmonie- und Modulationslehre*, 1888 (2nd ed., 1909, in English, 1907), which was his chief work, *Five- and Six-Part Harmonies, How to Use Them*, 1911, and *Canonical Studies, a New Technic of Composition*, 1912 (English and German). He also wrote a treatise on the execution of ornaments in classical works (Hamburg, 1883), contributed an elaborate discussion of the ecclesiastical modes to 'Die Musik,' and wrote many other articles for German periodicals. An article on poison-ivy in the vicinity of Chicago was commended by the U. S. Department of Agriculture. Two comments on his *Harmonielehre* may be quoted :

(Hugo Kaun) In this book 'one finds thousands of illustrations embracing the entire literature of music. His knowledge in this respect was unique. But aside from these it is above all his own harmonic combinations that make this work so valuable. He did not write his book by utilizing existing material; he himself was a pathfinder. In all the modern works there is scarcely a harmonic combination that he did not point out as early as 1888.'

(Busoni) 'Over the beautiful lines of the Gothic fugue Ziehn paints in the colors of a great and new harmony, the harmony that arises from the application of a relentless logic to the problems of voice-leading, that achieves absolute independence for each voice, yet at their meeting-points permits most original harmonies to develop. He is a theoretician who points to the possibilities of undiscovered lands — a prophet through logic. As a master of harmony he stands alone.'

He solved the uncompleted last work of Bach, a fugue of which Bach gave the first, second and part of the third out of four themes (see Schweitzer, *Bach*, i. 424). On Ziehn's basis Busoni wrote out the 'Fantasia Contrappuntistica' as a series of seven fugues, of which three are variations of others. This was for piano, and Middelschulte has arranged it for organ, and he and Stock also made an orchestral transcription.

Among his famous pupils may be named Mrs. Zeisler, Mrs. Middelschulte, Regina Watson, Grace Chadbourne and Eleanor Freer, with Kaun, Carpenter, Bradley, Deis, Arthur Dunham, Gunn, Otto Wulf and Middelschulte. [R.5]

ZIELINSKI, JAROSLAW DE (b. 1847). See Register, 5.

ZIMBALIST, EFREM (Apr. 9, 1889, Rostov-on-the-Don, Russia). See article in Vol. v. 596. His Berlin début was in 1907, when he played the Brahms concerto with extraordinary impression. His first English appearance the same year was followed by immediate engagements under Nikisch and Richter. Within a year he was equally recognized in France and Russia. He was the first after Joachim to appear at the Gewandhaus on New Year's Day, as the latter had done for fifty years. He first came to America in 1911, playing the Glazunov A minor concerto with the Boston Symphony Orchestra on Oct. 27. This visit led to permanent settlement and to numerous later appearances with orchestra and in recital. He has composed a set of 'Slavonic Dances' for violin and orchestra, a 'Suite in the Old Style' for violin and piano, and songs. In 1914 he married the soprano Alma Gluck. [R.10]

ZIMMERMANN, MATTHIAS. See Register, 1.

ZOELLNER, JOSEPH (b. 1862). See Register, 7.

ZUCCA, MANA (b. 1891). See Register, 9.

ZUNDEL, JOHN (1815–1882). See Register, 4, and TUNE-BOOKS, 1855.

The names in the foregoing pages that fall outside the American field are as follows:—

ARENSKY	FARJEON	LAVIGNAC	SANTLEY
BALAKIREV	FAURÉ	LENEPVEU	SAPELNIKOV
BANTOCK	FRISKIN	LEONCAVALLO	SAURET
BATH	GARDINER	LEROUX	SCHILLINGS
BAX	GILSON	LIADOV	SCHOLES
BEECHAM	GLAZUNOV	LIAPUNOV	SCHWEITZER
BELL	GLIÈRE	MACCUNN	SCOTT, CYRIL
BERNERS	GOOSSENS	MACKENZIE	SCRIABIN
BOITO	GRANADOS	MACPHERSON	SGAMBATI
BORDES	GRECHANINOV	MAGNARD	SHARP
BOSSI	GREENE	MARTEAU	SIBELIUS
BOUGHTON	GRIEG	MARTIN, G. C.	SMYTH
BOWEN	GUILMANT	MASCAGNI	SQUIRE
BRIDGE, J. F.	HABERL	MASSENET	STRAUSS
BRUCH	HARCOURT, D	M'EWEN	SVENDSEN
BUCK, P. C.	HARTY	MELBA	TANIEIEV
CARSE	HARWOOD	MESSAGER	TERRY
CILÈA	HINTON	MOTTL	TETRAZZINI
COLERIDGE-TAYLOR	HOLBROOKE	NÁPRAVNIK	THOMSON
COWEN	HOLLINS	NEWMAN	TIERSOT
CUI	HOLST, VON	O'NEILL	TINEL
DALE	HUBAY	PARRY	TOSTI
DAVEY	HUBER	PATTI	TOVEY
DAVIES	HULL	PEDRELL	VAN DYCK
DEBUSSY	HURLSTONE	PEROSI	VIARDOT-GARCIA
DELIUS	INDY, D'	PFITZNER	VIDAL
DUBOIS	IPPOLITOV-IVANOV	PHILIPP	VIERNE
DUKAS	IRELAND	PITT	VOLBACH
DUNHILL	JOACHIM	PUCCINI	WALLACE
ELGAR	JUON	RABAUD	WEINGARTNER
ENNA	KARG-ELERT	RAVEL	WIDOR
ERLANGER, C.	KASTALSKY	RIEMANN	WOLF-FERRARI
ERLANGER, F. d'	KLINDWORTH	RIMSKY-KORSAKOV	WOOD, H. J.
EXPERT	KONIUS	SAINT-SAËNS	

Printed in the United States of America.